Also by William J. Bennett

COUNTING BY RACE: Equality from the Founding Fathers to
Bakke (with Terry Eastland)
OUR CHILDREN AND OUR COUNTRY: Improving America's
Schools and Affirming the Common Culture
THE DE-VALUING OF AMERICA: The Fight for Our Culture
and Our Children
THE BOOK OF VIRTUES: A Treasury of Great Moral Stories

Edited, with Commentary, by

William J. Bennett

SIMON & SCHUSTER

New York London Toronto Sydney Tokyo Singapore

The
MORAL
COMPASS

•

Stories for a
Life's Journey

SIMON & SCHUSTER
Rockefeller Center
1230 Avenue of the Americas
New York, NY 10020

A leatherbound signed first edition of this
book has been published by Easton Press.

Designed by Karolina Harris
Picture Research by Natalie Goldstein

Manufactured in the United States of America

1   3   5   7   9   10   8   6   4   2

Library of Congress Cataloging-in-Publication Data
The moral compass : stories for a life's journey /
edited with commentary by William J. Bennett.
p.   cm.
Sequel to: Book of virtues.
1. Literature—Collections.   2. Conduct of life—
Literary collections.   I. Bennett, William John, 1943–   .
PN6014.M36   1995
808.8'038—dc20   95-4783
CIP
ISBN 0-684-80313-5

To America's teachers:

in homes, schools, and churches

Contents

Introduction

LIKE *The Book of Virtues,* this book aims to aid in the task of the moral education of the young. *The Book of Virtues* identified and examined ten traits of character—self-discipline, compassion, responsibility, friendship, work, courage, perseverance, honesty, loyalty, and faith. In this volume we find those same virtues, but this time we meet them in a different place: the stages of a life's journey.

Children learn most of their first character lessons in the home, which is where this book begins. Those early lessons stay with children as they make their way into the world, shaping the way they see life, and to a large degree determining whether they live it well. Later, as young people and then as adults, through various stages of life, they must make countless choices that call the virtues into play. As the chapters of this book unfold, we witness many of those choices and their implications. The stories and poems in these pages can serve as reference points on a moral compass, giving our children a clearer sense of direction in matters of right and wrong, helping to guide their actions in day-to-day living, as well as in those occasional, momentous decisions required of every individual.

The basic assumption underlying this volume is that much of life is a moral and spiritual journey, and that we undertake it, at least in large part, to find our way morally and spiritually. Thus it makes no sense to send young people forth on such an endeavor having offered them only some timid, vacillating opinions or options about conduct in the hope that in the course of their wanderings, they will stumble onto some more definite personal preferences which will become their "values." We must give our children better equipment than that. We must raise them *as moral and spiritual beings* by offering them unequivocal, reliable standards of right and wrong, noble and base, just and unjust. " 'Tis virtue . . . which is the hard and valuable part to be aimed at in education," the philosopher John Locke reminded us, "and not a forward pertness of any little arts of shifting. All other considerations and accomplishments should give way and be postponed to this." The stories in this book aim at clear concepts of good and bad without hesitation or apology. They treat life as a moral endeavor.

Of course, sound character education cannot come solely through hearing and reading stories, no matter how great they are. The training of the heart and the mind toward the good involves much more. (We would do well to remember that the Greek word *charakter* means "enduring marks," traits that can be formed in a person by an almost infinite number of influences.) Moral education must involve following rules of good behavior. It must involve developing good habits, which come only through repeated practice. And character training must provide example by placing children in the company of responsible adults who show an allegiance to good character, who demonstrate the clear difference between right and wrong in their own everyday habits.

Nevertheless, the books and stories we share with our children can be important moral influences. They can be invaluable allies for parents and teachers; as President Charles W. Eliot of Harvard observed, "In the campaign for character, no auxiliaries are to be refused." Literature can be a crucial part of a home, school, community, or culture's *ethos*—another ancient Greek term meaning the distinguishing character or guiding beliefs, the habits of the denizens. As every parent and teacher knows, children love stories. Even in an age of computer games and electronic toys, there is still resonant power in the phrase "Once upon a time . . ." And so *what* we choose to read to our children matters a great deal. Legends, folktales, sacred stories, biographies, and poems can introduce the youngest children to the virtues; they can clarify notions of right and wrong for young people; and they can serve as powerful reminders of mankind's best ideals all the way through adulthood. More than one great man or woman at a critical instant has recalled a simple fable, a familiar verse, a childhood hero.

Philosophers, theologians, and poets have long regarded wisdom as the sibling virtue of morality. If an individual is to do good, the tenets of the heart must be informed and directed by a well-ordered mind. In fact, the classical Greek thinkers regarded prudence as one of the fundamental virtues; to them, the word meant not circumspection, as it does to us today, but rather the ability to govern and discipline oneself by the use of reason. It meant being able to recognize the right choice in specific circumstances, and it was the intellectual virtue that made it possible to put the moral virtues into action. The reader will find stories involving such practical wisdom scattered throughout this book; knowing them may help us handle some of the tough situations that crop up in everyday life. Furthermore, there are many stories in this book that deal with a grander notion of wisdom, stories that help us try to gain even some ultimate knowledge of self, of our fellow human beings, and of God's will. These stories may aid in arriving at a guiding philosophy of life. They have been selected with this standard in mind.

Originally I had not intended to put together a second collection of moral stories, and agreed to do so only at the urging of readers who loved the material they found in *The Book of Virtues* and wrote to ask for more. I confess, however, that I began this project with a certain degree of doubt in my mind. Even though the quarry of wonderful literature is deep, and *The Book of Virtues* had barely scratched the surface, I still wondered how difficult it would be to assemble a second volume that would equal the first in terms of offering timeless stories that both instruct and entertain. As it turned out, my doubts proved to be groundless.

In order to dig a bit deeper into that mine of wonderful literature, I decided to take a close look at some of the books American children were reading in their homes and schools around the turn of the twentieth century. The wealth of material was astonishing, and it comprises a large part of this volume. Much of it, after a little updating for the modern ear (and abridging to meet restrictions of an anthology), is every bit as instructive *and* entertaining today as it was one hundred years ago.

I think that in some ways this is a more interesting collection than *The Book of Virtues.* Many of these stories seem to me more intriguing and more imaginative than those in the first volume. There are more stories of the spirit, more stories from the deeper recesses of the human heart. I think readers will find a greater number of unfamiliar stories in this volume; I hope this book will help today's public discover some old tales that were favorites in another era but have slipped out of the modern, popular canon. There are also many stories and characters here (the Gordian knot, the race from Marathon, the triumph of Florence Nightingale) that we adults already know—or should know—and want to pass on to our children. As Wordsworth put it, "What we have loved, others will love, and we will teach them how." In this respect, I hope this book is a contribution to our cultural as well as to our moral literacy.

Although this book is grounded solidly in the heritage of Western Civilization, there are many countries, many cultures, many traditions represented here. Like the American people, these stories come from all over the globe, and they serve a valuable purpose in our collective consciousness. Many of these stories have been handed down from generation to generation for hundreds of years. They have stood the test of time. They contain the wisdom of the ages.

Although the chapters in this book are arranged according to different stages of life, the reader should not conclude that the stories in any one section are meaningful only to certain ages or groups (that is, that Chapter One is only for youngsters still at home, or that Chapter Five is only for married people). On the contrary, I think there is something for every age in every chapter. For example, even young children need to hear stories about what it is like to be a spouse or a parent so they can begin to be aware of the joys and responsibilities that will come when they, too, begin their own families. And adults can profit by re-reading and reminding themselves of the first, basic lessons life offers, not only because it will help them teach their own young children but also because those first lessons are often the most important ones, the ones even we adults need to attend to again and again.

Some chapters address certain virtues more than others. Chapter Three, for example, which is meant to help in facing the tough times of life, concentrates largely on perseverance and courage. Chapter Four, which inspires us to help each other along life's journey, deals mostly with compassion. Clearly, these virtues are valuable at any age, and so are most of the stories in those sections. The book's seven chapters are not strictly chronological phases of life; on the contrary, much of life is a process of repeating our ventures, our plans, our aspirations, learning and growing with each new effort.

As in *The Book of Virtues,* I have tried to arrange each chapter so that the easier material comes first; when selections share certain themes and lessons, however, I have grouped those readings together. In short, this book, like its predecessor, is mainly for browsing, for finding favorite stories and passages, for reading out loud to each other, for memorizing snatches of verses. And I hope that most of these stories are ones both young and old can enjoy, especially together.

Although most of the ideas and themes in this book are as old and universal as human nature, it would be difficult to put together such a collection without keeping in mind some of the specific currents in today's culture. As Flannery O'Connor observed, "You have to push as hard as the age that pushes against you." I have therefore included, for example, many stories about families—and how to keep them strong—because of the current plight of that institution. The decline of the American family constitutes perhaps the greatest long-term threat to our children's well-being; we should not hesitate to place before young people examples that help instill a reverence for the blessings and duties of home and hearth. The reader will also find some stories dealing with gratitude and ingratitude. In today's public discourse, there seems to be little expression of the former, and much time given to the latter in the form of griping and complaining and pointing fingers. Sometimes we need to remind ourselves that thankfulness is indeed a virtue. Gratitude is something we very much need to show.

The most encouraging feedback I received about *The Book of Virtues* was that children—not just their parents—love those old stories and ask to hear them again and again. I hope this book delights and entertains just as much and that these stories help young people understand that virtues are not bothersome things that take all the fun out of life. Rather, I hope these wonderful stories and verses will help them understand that virtues can make life worthwhile, can help in the tasks of both meaning and contentment. Children should know that loving life and living well go hand in hand. "Through our great good fortune, in our youth our hearts were touched with fire," Justice Oliver Wendell Holmes wrote of his own childhood. "It was given to us to learn at the outset that life is a profound and passionate thing." I hope this book inspires readers to remember that life is a profound and passionate journey, and I hope it can be a compass of sorts to help guide the way.

I would like to thank Bob Asahina for his now customary scrutiny, wisdom, and fine editing; Sarah Pinckney, Bob's colleague at Simon and Schuster, for her patience, cooperation, and helpfulness; and Bob Barnett for sagacious counsel and clinical judgment on the vagaries of contracts and the ways of negotiation. I am once again indebted to John Cribb for his energy, imagination, good taste, and prodigious efforts at home, in libraries, and on countless plane rides. He is the keeper of the story vault. At that he has no equal.

Finally, to my family again I offer my thanks. John and Joseph were the audience in mind and sometimes actually in place as this book was put together. I hope they like it. Elayne's love and counsel were the most important mainstay for this as for so many of my other work projects. "Her candle goeth not out by night," and the readers of this book are the beneficiaries.

One

·

HOME
AND
HEARTH

ALL children need bread and shelter. But a true home, of course, is much more than that. Children also need love and order and, because they are not born knowing the difference between right and wrong, a place where they can begin to develop a moral sense. The transmission of virtues is one important reason for a home, and attention to the virtues is one of the important ties that bind a family together. "It is the peculiarity of man, in comparison with the rest of the animal world," Aristotle wrote, "that he alone possesses a perception of good and evil, of the just and the unjust, and of other similar qualities; and it is association in these things which makes a family."

And so home is the place where we receive our first instruction in the virtues. It is our first moral training ground, the place where we can come to know right from wrong through the nurturing and protective care of those who love us more than anyone else. Our character takes shape under the guidance of the *do*s and *don't*s, the instructions, the exhortations we encounter around the house. Equally important, our moral sense emerges under the influence of examples set by mother, father, sisters, and brothers. In the familiar world of home and hearth, we learn the habits of virtue that will fortify us when we venture into the world.

In this chapter we find some of these lessons of home and hearth. We find family members helping each other along, and looking toward each other for help. We find siblings showing what "brotherhood" and "sisterhood" really mean. We see children learning about chores and responsibilities and self-sacrifice, and learning to help parents out of love. We encounter young hearts giving loving obedience. We witness the growth of conscience, of a desire to live up to the expectations of those who love us. We witness how our loyalty and courage and perseverance see families through hard times with a love that can overcome any number of obstacles.

Of course, no home is perfect. Home can be the place where we get our first look at vices as well as virtues. And, unfortunately, some homes are simply not good places—not all homes are havens; not all hearths have a warm glow. But *all* homes teach lessons, even if they are the wrong kind of lessons. And so even though many homes do not resemble the best ones we find in these pages, the stories here are no less valuable because they give us all something at which to aim. They remind us of the kind of conditions families need and the attention children deserve. We set these examples before our eyes in order to keep raising our sights and our efforts.

These first lessons stay with us long after we leave home. In our affections and our memories, they remain forever a part of us, often the most cherished part of us. "Where shall a man find sweetness to surpass his own home and parents?" Odysseus asks in Homer's *Odyssey.* "In far lands he shall not, though he find a house of gold." The early experiences of home become a moral compass point, guiding and instructing us for the rest of life's journey.

And in one sense, the moral journey that begins with leaving home is the search for opportunities to offer others the same nurture and love we received in our own childhood. The memory of home becomes a past, an experience, an ideal we seek to re-create in our later lives, and in the new lives we shepherd into the world. We build our own homes, offer our own lessons, nurture our own children in the strength and knowledge once gained beside the first warm hearth of home.

HUSH, LITTLE BABY

The first notes we hear are those cradle songs that spring from a parent's heart. Lullabies abound in every age and every culture. By such promises of nurture and protection babies find trust to rest and grow.

> Hush, little baby, don't say a word,
> Papa's going to buy you a mockingbird.
> And if that mockingbird won't sing,
> Papa's going to buy you a diamond ring.
> If that diamond ring turns brass,
> Papa's going to buy you a looking glass.
> If that looking glass gets broke,
> Papa's going to buy you a billy goat.
> If that billy goat won't pull,
> Papa's going to buy you a cart and bull.
> If that cart and bull turns over,
> Papa's going to buy you a dog named Rover.
> If that dog named Rover won't bark,
> Papa's going to buy you a horse and cart.
> If that horse and cart fall down,
> You'll still be the sweetest baby in town!

•

CRADLE SONG

Johannes Brahms

> Lullaby and good night, with roses bedight,
> With lilies bedecked, is baby's wee bed.
> Lay thee down now and rest, may thy slumber be blest,
> Lay thee down now and rest, may thy slumber be blest.

•

SWEET AND LOW

Alfred Tennyson

Sweet and low, sweet and low,
    Wind of the western sea,
Low, low, breathe and blow,
    Wind of the western sea!
Over the rolling waters go,
Come from the dying moon, and blow,
    Blow him again to me;
While my little one, while my pretty one, sleeps.

Sleep and rest, sleep and rest,
    Father will come to thee soon;
Rest, rest, on mother's breast,
    Father will come to thee soon;
Father will come to his babe in the nest,
Silver sails all out of the west
    Under the silver moon:
Sleep, my little one, sleep, my pretty one, sleep.

•

WHAT BRADLEY OWED

Adapted from Hugh T. Kerr

Home is the place where first lessons are learned. And it is the place where much of what you do, you do for love.

There was once a boy named Bradley. When he was about eight years old, he fell into the habit of thinking of everything in terms of money. He wanted to know the price of everything he saw, and if it didn't cost a great deal, it did not seem to him to be worth anything at all.

But there are a great many things money cannot buy. And some of them are the best things in the world.

One morning when Bradley came down to breakfast, he put a little piece of paper, neatly folded, on his mother's plate. His mother opened it, and she could hardly believe it, but this is what her son had written:

Mother owes Bradley:	
For running errands	3 dollars
For taking out the trash	2 dollars
For sweeping the floor	2 dollars
Extras	1 dollar
Total that Mother owes Bradley	8 dollars

His mother smiled when she read that, but she did not say anything.

When lunchtime came she put the bill on Bradley's plate along with eight dollars. Bradley's eyes lit up when he saw the money. He stuffed it into his pocket as fast as he could and started dreaming about what he would buy with his reward.

All at once he saw there was another piece of paper besides his plate, neatly folded, just like the first one. When he opened it up, he found it was a bill from his mother. It read:

Bradley owes Mother:	
For being good to him	nothing
For nursing him through his chicken pox	nothing
For shirts and shoes and toys	nothing
For his meals and beautiful room	nothing
Total that Bradley owes Mother	nothing

Bradley sat looking at this new bill, without saying a word. After a few minutes he got up, pulled the eight dollars out of his pocket, and placed them in his mother's hand.

And after that, he helped his mother for love.

•

NAILS IN THE POST

M. F. Cowdery

**In this tough story from a Civil War-era school reader, we find
another kind of lesson that some homes offer. Here is a father
giving his son stern but loving moral instruction.**

There was once a farmer who had a son named John, a boy
very apt to be thoughtless, and careless about doing what he was
told to do.

One day his father said to him, "John, you are so careless and
forgetful, that every time you do wrong, I shall drive a nail into this
post, to remind you how often you are naughty. And every time you
do right I will draw one out." His father did as he said he would,
and every day he had one and sometimes a great many nails to
drive in, but very seldom one to draw out.

At last John saw that the post was quite covered with nails, and
he began to be ashamed of having so many faults. He resolved to
be a better boy, and the next day he was so good and industrious
that several nails came out. The day after it was the same thing, and
so on for a long time, till at length only one nail remained. His
father then called him, and said: "Look, John, here is the very last
nail, and now I'm going to draw it out. Are you not glad?"

John looked at the post, and then, instead of expressing his joy,
as his father expected, he burst into tears. "Why," said the father,
"what's the matter? I should think you would be delighted; the nails
are all gone."

"Yes," sobbed John, "the *nails* are gone, but the *scars* are there
yet."

So it is, dear children, with your faults and bad habits; you may
overcome them, you may by degrees cure them, but the scars remain. Now, take my advice, and whenever you find yourselves
doing a wrong thing, or getting into a bad habit, stop at once. For
every time you give in to it, you drive another nail, and that will
leave a *scar* on your soul, even if the nail should be afterwards
drawn out.

•

NORTHWEST PASSAGE

Robert Louis Stevenson

There is no better place to begin learning about bravery than in the safe confines of home. For many children, the first great adventure is that long, perilous journey up the stairs to bed. Making it can be a first exercise in courage.

1. GOOD NIGHT

When the bright lamp is carried in,
The sunless hours again begin;
O'er all without, in field and lane,
The haunted night returns again.

Now we behold the embers flee
About the firelit hearth; and see
Our faces painted as we pass,
Like pictures, on the window glass.

Must we to bed indeed? Well then,
Let us arise and go like men,
And face with an undaunted tread
The long black passage up to bed.

Farewell, O brother, sister, sire!
O pleasant party round the fire!
The songs you sing, the tales you tell,
Till far tomorrow, fare ye well!

2. SHADOW MARCH

All round the house is the jet-black night;
    It stares through the windowpane;
It crawls in the corners, hiding from the light,
    And it moves with the moving flame.

Now my little heart goes a-beating like a drum,
  With the breath of the bogy in my hair;
And all round the candle the crooked shadows come,
  And go marching along up the stair.

The shadow of the balusters, the shadow of the lamp,
  The shadow of the child that goes to bed—
All the wicked shadows coming, tramp, tramp, tramp,
  With the black night overhead.

3. IN PORT

Last, to the chamber where I lie
My fearful footsteps patter nigh,
And come from out the cold and gloom
Into my warm and cheerful room.

There, safe arrived, we turn about
To keep the coming shadows out,
And close the happy door at last
On all the perils that we past.

Then, when Mama goes by to bed,
She shall come in with tiptoe tread,
And see me lying warm and fast
And in the Land of Nod at last.

•

THE HILL

Laura E. Richards

**Brothers and sisters help each other along, first up backyard hills,
and later up life-long climbs.**

I cannot walk up this hill," said the little boy. "I cannot possibly
do it. What will become of me? I must stay here all my life, at the
foot of the hill. It is too terrible!"

"That is a pity!" said his sister. "But look, little boy! I have found such a pleasant game to play. Take a step, and see how clear a footprint you can make in the dust. Look at mine! Every single line in my foot is printed clear. Now, you try, and see if you can do as well!"

The little boy took a step.

"Mine is just as clear!" he said.

"Do you think so?" said his sister. "See mine, again here! I tread harder than you, because I am heavier, and so the print is deeper. Try again."

"*Now* mine is just as deep!" cried the little boy. "See! Here, and here, and here, they are just as deep as they can be."

"Yes, that is very well," said the sister, "but now it is my turn; let me try again, and we shall see."

They kept on, step by step, matching their footprints, and laughing to see the gray dust puff up between their bare toes.

By and by the little boy looked up.

"Why," he said, "we are at the top of the hill!"

"Dear me!" said his sister. "So we are!"

•

THE THREE BILLY GOATS GRUFF

This familiar Norse tale is about an age-old job for big brothers—looking out for little brothers.

Once upon a time there were three billy goats who lived in a meadow at the foot of a mountain. They were all three brothers, and their last name was Gruff.

One fine day they said to each other, "Let's go up on the hillside, and eat grass, and make ourselves fat."

The youngest of the three started out first. After a while, he came to a bridge. Now the little billy goat did not know it, but under this bridge lived a terrible Troll, with eyes as big as a saucer, and a nose as long as a poker. As the Smallest Billy Goat Gruff went trip-trap, trip-trap over the bridge, the Troll roared out, "WHO'S THAT tripping over my bridge?"

"It's I, the Smallest Billy Goat Gruff. I'm going up on the hillside to eat grass, and make myself fat."

"Well, I'm coming to gobble you up!" roared the Troll.

"Oh, don't do that! I'm so little, I'll make scarcely a mouthful. My brother the Middle-Sized Billy Goat Gruff will be along soon. He'll make a much better meal. You'd better wait for him."

"Very well, be off with you!" said the Troll.

So the little goat ran on, trip-trap, trip-trap, across the bridge and up on the mountain, where he was safe.

Pretty soon, along came the second Billy Goat Gruff.

He went *trip-trap, trip-trap,* over the bridge.

"WHO'S THAT tripping over my bridge?" roared the Troll.

"It's I, the Middle-Sized Billy Goat Gruff. I'm going up on the hillside to eat grass, and make myself fat."

"Well, I'm coming to gobble you up!" roared the Troll.

"Oh, don't do that! I'm not very big, and I won't make much of a meal. My brother the Big Billy Goat Gruff will be along soon. He'll make a much better dinner. You'd better wait for him."

"Very well, be off with you!" said the Troll.

So the Middle-Sized Billy Goat Gruff ran on, *trip-trap, trip-trap,* across the bridge and up on the mountain, where he was safe.

After a while, along came the Big Billy Goat Gruff. *TRIP-TRAP, TRIP-TRAP* he went over the bridge, and it creaked and groaned under his weight.

"WHO'S THAT tripping over my bridge?" roared the Troll.

"IT'S I, THE BIG BILLY GOAT GRUFF!" said the billy goat in a big voice of his own.

"Well, I'm coming to gobble you up!" roared the Troll.

"HO! HO!" laughed the Big Billy Goat Gruff. "You don't say so! Well, come along! I'll crush you to bits, body and bones!" That's what Big Billy Goat Gruff said in his big, rough voice.

Up came the Troll. He jumped on the bridge and put down his big, bushy head and ran at the billy goat. The Big Billy Goat Gruff put down his head and ran at the Troll, and they met in the middle of the bridge.

But the Big Billy Goat Gruff's head was harder than the Troll's, so he knocked him down, and thumped him about, and took him up on his horns, and threw him over the edge of the bridge, into the river below! The Troll sank out of sight, and no one ever saw him again.

Then the Big Billy Goat Gruff went up on the hillside with the other Billy Goat Gruffs, who knew all along their big brother would punish the terrible Troll. And they all ate grass, and ate grass, and ate grass, until they were so fat they could hardly walk home.

•

BEAUTIFUL HANDS

Adapted from Lawton B. Evans

Happy homes need helpful hands.

Some young girls were talking by the brook, boasting of their beautiful hands. One of them dipped her hands in the sparkling water and the drops looked like diamonds falling from her palms.

"See what beautiful hands I have! The water runs from them like precious jewels," said she, and held up her hands for the others to admire. They were very soft and white, for she had never done anything but wash them in clear, cold water.

Another one of them ran to get some strawberries and crushed them in her palms. The juice ran through her fingers like wine from a wine press until her fingers were as pink as the sunrise in the early morning.

"See what beautiful hands I have! The strawberry juice runs over them like wine," said she, and she held up her hands for the others to admire. They were very pink and soft, for she had never done anything but wash them in strawberry juice every morning.

Another one gathered some violets and crushed the flowers in her hands until they smelled like perfume.

"See what beautiful hands I have! They smell like violets in the deep woods in the spring time," said she, and she held up her hands for the others to admire. They were very soft and white, for she had never done anything but wash them in violets every morning.

The fourth girl did not show her hands but held them in her lap. An old woman came down the road and stopped before the girls. They all showed her their hands and asked her which were the most beautiful. She shook her head at each one and then asked to see the hands of the last girl, who held hers in her lap. The last girl raised her hands timidly for the old woman to see.

"Oh, these hands are clean, indeed," said the old woman, "but they are hard from toil. These hands have been helping Mother and Father dry the dishes, and sweep the floor, and wash the windows, and weed the garden. These hands have been taking care of the baby, and carrying hot tea to Grandma, and showing little brother how to build his blocks and fly his kite. Yes, these hands have been busy making the house a happy home, full of love and care."

Then the old woman fumbled in her pocket and brought out a ring set with diamonds, with rubies redder than strawberries, and turquoise bluer than violets.

"Here, wear this ring, my child. You deserve the prize for the most beautiful hands, for they have been the most helpful."

And the old woman vanished, leaving the four girls still sitting by the brook.

•

THE BROWNIES

Adapted from Juliana Horatia Ewing

In English folklore, brownies are good-natured fairies or elves who perform services at night, such as washing, mending, and sweeping. Juliana Horatia Ewing wrote this widely loved tale about the little people, in the mid-nineteenth century. The story helped inspire Robert and Agnes Baden-Powell to found the junior branch of the Girl Guides movement in England (now called the Brownie Girl Scouts in the United States).

"Children are a burden," said the tailor to himself as he sat at his bench, stitching away.

"Children are a blessing," said the kind old lady who sat knitting at the window. "It is the family motto. The Trouts have had large families and good luck for generations."

It was the tailor's mother who spoke. She knew the history of the whole family going back years and years, and which of the Trouts were buried under which old stones in the graveyard. And she had an endless supply of tales about ghosts and fairies and hobgoblins and such, much to her grandchildren's delight.

"Children are a blessing!" she declared again.

"But look at Tommy," the tailor argued. "That boy does nothing but whittle sticks from morning till night. I almost have to lug him out of bed in the mornings. If I send him on an errand, he loiters. If I give him a little chore to do, he does it unwillingly and with such poor grace that it would be far better for me to do it myself. He's not a bad one, mind you, I'm not saying that. But he's not much help, and I did hope he would be a blessing rather than a burden."

"Well, there's still Johnny," the old lady murmured.

"Johnny's too young to be much of a help right now," Mr. Trout replied. "And he won't turn out any different from Tommy if his older brother doesn't stop leading him by the nose."

Now, the thing the boys loved more than anything else in the world was to hear their grandmother tell them the old stories of times gone by. One evening as they sat beside the fire, she told them about a brownie who used to live in the Trout house and help them with the work.

"What was he like, Granny?" Tommy asked.

"Like a little man, they say, my dear."

"What did he do?"

"He came in before the family was up, and swept up the hearth, and lit the fire, and set out the breakfast, and tidied the room, and did all sorts of housework. Sometimes he weeded the garden or threshed the corn. He saved endless trouble. But he never would be seen, and was off before anyone could catch him. The family could hear him laughing and playing about the house sometimes, though."

"Did they give him any wages, Granny?"

"No, my dear. He did it for love. They left a glass of water for him overnight, and now and then a bowl of bread and milk or cream. He liked that, for he was very dainty."

"Oh, Granny! Where did he go?"

"I don't know, dear."

"I wish he'd come back!" both boys cried at once.

"He'd tidy the room," said Johnny.

"And sweep the floor," said Tommy.

"And wash the dishes," said Johnny.

"And pick up our toys," said Tommy.

"And do everything!" they both decided. "We wish he hadn't gone away."

"Well, there are plenty of brownies," the old lady said. "Perhaps the Trouts will have another someday."

"But how do we get one?" Tommy asked.

"Only the Old Owl knows that, my dear. You'd have to ask her."

That night, when they crawled into bed, little Johnny was soon in the land of dreams, but Tommy could not get the thought of the brownie out of his mind.

"There's an owl living in the old shed by the pond," he thought. "It may be the Old Owl herself, and she knows, Granny says. When Father's gone to bed and the moon rises, I'll go."

Soon the moon rose like gold, and went up into the heavens like silver, flooding the moors with a pale ghostly light and painting black shadows under the stone walls. Tommy crept softly out of bed, through the kitchen, and out onto the moor.

It was a glorious night, although everything but the wind and Tommy seemed asleep. The stones, the walls, and the gleaming lanes were intensely still. The church tower in the valley seemed awake and watching, but silent. The houses in the village all had their eyes shut, that is, their window blinds down, and it seemed to Tommy as if the very moors had drawn white sheets over themselves and lay sleeping too.

"Hoot! Hoot!" said a voice from the woods behind him. Somebody else was awake, then.

"It's the Old Owl," said Tommy—and there she came, swinging heavily across the moor with a flapping, stately flight, and sailed into the shed by the pond. Though Tommy ran hard, she was in the shed some time before him. When he got inside, there sat the Old Owl, blinking down at him with yellow eyes.

"Come up! Come up!" she said hoarsely.

She could speak then! Beyond all doubt it was *the* Old Owl, and none other. Tommy shuddered.

"Come up here! Come up here!" said the Old Owl.

The Old Owl sat on a beam that ran across the shed. Tommy had often climbed up for fun; he climbed up now, and sat face to face with her, and thought her eyes looked as if they were made of flame.

"Now, what do you want?" said the owl.

"Please," said Tommy, who felt rather reassured, "can you tell me where to find the brownies, and how to get one to come and live with us?"

"Oohoo!" said the owl, "that's it, is it? I know of two brownies."

"Hurrah!" said Tommy. "Where do they live?"

"In your house," said the owl.

Tommy was aghast.

"In our house!" he exclaimed. "Whereabouts? Let me rummage them out. Why do they do nothing?"

"One of them is too young," said the owl.

"But why doesn't the other work?" asked Tommy.

"He is idle, he is idle," said the Old Owl, and she gave herself such a shake as she said it, that her fluff went flying through the shed, and Tommy nearly tumbled off the beam in his fright.

"Then we don't want them," he said. "What is the use of having brownies if they do nothing to help us?"

"Perhaps they don't know, as no one has told them," said the owl.

"I wish you would tell me where to find them," said Tommy. "I could tell them."

"Could you?" said the owl. "Oohoo! Oohoo!" Tommy couldn't tell whether she was hooting or laughing.

"Of course I could," he said. "They might be up and light the fire, and spread the table, and that sort of thing, before Father comes down. Besides, they could *see* what was wanted. The brownies did all that in Granny's mother's young days. And then they could tidy the room, and sweep the floor, and wash the dishes, and pick up my toys. Oh! there's lots to do."

"So there is," said the owl. "Oohoo! Well, I can tell you where to find one of the brownies, and if you find him he will tell you where his brother is. But this depends upon whether you feel equal to undertaking it, and whether you will follow my directions."

"I am quite ready to go," said Tommy, "and I will do as you tell me. I feel sure I could persuade them. If they only knew how everyone would love them if they made themselves useful!"

"Oohoo! Oohoo!" said the owl. "Now pay attention. You must go to the north side of the pond when the moon is shining and turn yourself around three times, saying this charm:

> Twist me, and turn me, and show me the Elf!
> I looked in the water and saw . . .

Then you look in the pond, and if you see the brownie, you must think of a word that will finish the rhyme. If you do not see the brownie, or if you fail to think of the word, it will be of no use."

"Is the brownie a merman, that he lives underwater?" asked Tommy, wriggling himself along the beam.

"That depends on whether he has a fish's tail," said the owl, "and this you can discover for yourself."

"Well, the moon is shining, so I shall go," said Tommy. "Good-bye, and thank you, ma'am." And he jumped down and went, saying to himself as he ran, "I believe he is a merman all the same or else how could he live in the pond? I know more about brownies than Granny does, and I shall tell her so." For Tommy was somewhat opinionated, like other young people.

The moon shone very brightly on the center of the pond. Tommy knew the place well, for there was a fine echo there. Around the edge grew rushes and water plants, which cast a border of shadow. Tommy went to the north side and turning himself three times, as the Old Owl had told him, he repeated the charm:

> Twist me, and turn me, and show me the Elf!
> I looked in the water and saw . . .

Now for it! He looked in and saw . . . the reflection of his own face.

"Why, there's no one but myself!" said Tommy. "And what can the word be? I must have done it wrong."

"Wrong!" said the echo.

Tommy was most surprised to find the echo awake at this time of night.

"Hold your tongue!" he said. "Matters are provoking enough by themselves. Belf! Celf! Delf! Felf! Gelf! Helf! Jelf! What rubbish! There can't be a word to fit. And then to look for a brownie and see nothing but myself!"

"Myself!" said the echo.

"Will you be quiet?" said Tommy. "If you told me the word, there would be some sense to your interference. But to roar 'Myself!' at me, which neither rhymes nor fits—it does rhyme, though, as it happens. How very odd! And it fits, too:

> Twist me, and turn me, and show me the Elf!
> I looked in the water and saw myself!

What can it mean? The Old Owl knows, as Granny would say. I shall go back and ask her."

"Ask her!" said the echo.

And so he did. He went back to the shed, and there sat the Old Owl as before.

"Oohoo!" said she, as Tommy climbed up. "What did you see in the pond?"

"I saw nothing but myself," Tommy said indignantly.

"And what did you expect to see?" asked the owl.

"I expected to see a brownie," said Tommy. "You told me so."

"And what are brownies like, pray?" inquired the owl.

"The one Granny knew was a useful little fellow, something like a little man," said Tommy.

"Ah," said the owl, "but at present this one is an idle little fellow, something like a little man. Oohoo! Oohoo! Are you quite sure you didn't see him?"

"Quite," answered Tommy sharply. "I saw no one but myself."

"Hoot! Hoot! How touchy we are! And who are you, pray?"

"I'm not a brownie," said Tommy.

"Don't be too sure," said the owl. "Did you find the rhyme?"

"No," said Tommy. "I could find no word with any meaning that would rhyme but 'myself.' "

"Well, that rhymes," said the owl. "What else do you want?"

"I don't understand," said Tommy humbly. "You know I'm not a brownie, am I?"

"Yes, you are," said the owl, "and a very idle one too. All children are brownies."

"But I couldn't do work like a brownie," said Tommy.

"Why not?" inquired the owl. "Couldn't you sweep the floor, light the fire, spread the table, tidy the room, wash the dishes, and pick up your own toys? As you said, there's lots to do."

"Please," said Tommy, "I should like to go home now, and tell Johnny. It's getting cold, and I am so tired!"

"Very well," said the Old Owl. "I think I had better take you."

"I know the way, thank you," said Tommy.

"Just lean against me," insisted the owl. "Lean with your full weight, and shut your eyes."

Tommy lay his head against the Old Owl's feathers. He had a vague idea that she smelled of heather and thought it must be from living on the moor. He shut his eyes and leaned with his full weight, expecting that he and the owl would certainly fall off the beam together. Down . . . feathers . . . fluff . . . he sank and sank. He could feel nothing solid. He jumped up with a start to save himself, opened his eyes, and found that he was sitting in bed, with Johnny sleeping at his side! But even odder was that it was no longer moonlight but early dawn.

"Get up, Johnny," he cried. "I've got a story to tell you!" And
while Johnny sat up and rubbed his eyes open, Tommy told him
everything.

And from that day forward, the Trout household had two of
the most useful brownies in the whole land.

●

MR. NOBODY

Does this man live at your house? This is a great poem to help
teach responsibility. It's fun to read out loud too.

> I know a funny little man,
>   As quiet as a mouse,
> Who does the mischief that is done
>   In everybody's house!
> There's no one ever sees his face,
>   And yet we all agree
> That every plate we break was cracked
>   By Mr. Nobody.
>
> 'Tis he who always tears our books,
>   Who leaves the door ajar,
> He pulls the buttons from our shirts,
>   And scatters pins afar;
> That squeaking door will always squeak
>   For, prithee, don't you see,
> We leave the oiling to be done
>   By Mr. Nobody.
>
> He puts damp wood upon the fire,
>   That kettles cannot boil;
> His are the feet that bring in mud,
>   And all the carpets soil.
> The papers always are mislaid,
>   Who had them last but he?
> There's no one tosses them about
>   But Mr. Nobody.

The finger-marks upon the door
   By none of us are made;
We never leave the blinds unclosed,
   To let the curtains fade.
The ink we never spill, the boots
   That lying round you see
Are not our boots; they all belong
   To Mr. Nobody.

•

THE TREE THAT WAS LONESOME

Home is shelter from storms—all sorts of storms.

There was once an old oak tree that had stood for a long time in the forest.

Many years before, a great storm had swept through the forest. This storm had left the oak only a crooked, ugly tree. It was no longer straight and beautiful like the others. Each spring it covered its ugliness with new green leaves. In the fall the leaves turned to a pretty crimson cloak. But the winds of the forest always swept by. They carried the leaf cloak of the old oak tree away with them. Then it was left with nothing to cover its ugliness.

After years and years, the old oak tree began to feel hollow. It felt as if its heart as well as its body were hurt. The wind sighed through its bare branches one fall when it was very, very old indeed. It made the old oak speak. "No one wants me. I am of no more use in the world," the oak said.

Tap, tap, rap-a-tap-tap! That was Mr. Red-headed Woodpecker. He was hammering at the trunk of the old oak tree. Tap, tap! He hammered and drilled. He worked until he had made a little round front door. It led into his winter house in the trunk of the tree. He had found a ready-made pantry there. It was full of grubs for himself and his family to eat when the cold days came. The walls of his house were warm. It was snug and cozy.

"How grateful I am for this hollow tree," sang Mr. Red-headed Woodpecker.

Whisk, whirr! That was Bobby Squirrel. He ran up the trunk of the old oak tree until he came to the round hole that was his little front window. Bobby Squirrel peeped inside. Oh, how comfortable and snug was the little house that he saw! He lined it with moss. Where the bark stuck out and made shelves, Bobby Squirrel laid piles and piles of nuts. They were ready to feast upon when the cold days came. He would be able to live there, warm in his fur overcoat and well fed. He would be safely sheltered until spring came.

"How grateful I am for this hollow tree," chattered Bobby Squirrel.

Then a strange thing happened to the tree. The beating of the wings of the bird and the happy heart of the little squirrel inside it warmed it. They made the heart of the old oak tree full of joy.

Instead of sighing in the wind, the old oak tree's boughs sang with happiness. The fall rains had left tears on the ends of its twig fingers. Now they turned to diamonds until its twig hands sparkled with them. The snow covered its ugly body with a cloak of white. The starlight at night and the sun in the day time set a crown upon its head.

In all the forest there was no tree more glad, or more beautiful, than the old oak tree.

•

THE PRINCE'S HAPPY HEART

A close-knit and loving home is worth more than a kingdom, as the little prince discovers in this story.

I

Once upon a time there was a little Prince in a country far away from here. He was one of the happiest little Princes who ever lived. All day long he laughed and sang and played. His voice was as sweet as music. His footsteps brought joy wherever he went. Every one thought that this was due to magic. Hung about the Prince's neck on a gold chain was a wonderful heart. It was made of gold and set with precious stones.

The godmother of the little Prince had given the heart to him when he was very small. She had said as she slipped it over his curly head: "To wear this happy heart will keep the Prince happy always. Be careful that he does not lose it."

All the people who took care of the little Prince were very careful to see that the chain of the happy heart was clasped. But one day they found the little Prince in his garden, very sad and sorrowful. His face was wrinkled into an ugly frown.

"Look!" he said, and he pointed to his neck. Then they saw what had happened.

The happy heart was gone. No one could find it, and each day the little Prince grew more sorrowful. At last they missed him. He had gone, himself, to look for the lost happy heart that he needed so much.

II

The little Prince searched all day. He looked in the city streets and along the country roads. He looked in the shops and in the doors of the houses where rich people lived. Nowhere could he find the heart that he had lost. At last it was almost night. He was very tired and hungry. He had never before walked so far, or felt so unhappy.

Just as the sun was setting the little Prince came to a tiny house. It was very poor and weather stained. It stood on the edge of the forest. But a bright light streamed from the window. So he lifted the latch, as a Prince may, and went inside.

There was a mother rocking a baby to sleep. The father was reading a story out loud. The little daughter was setting the table for supper. A boy of the Prince's own age was tending the fire. The mother's dress was old. There were to be only porridge and potatoes for supper. The fire was very small. But all the family were as happy as the little Prince wanted to be. Such smiling faces and light feet the children had. How sweet the mother's voice was!

"Won't you have supper with us?" they begged. They did not seem to notice the Prince's ugly frown.

"Where are your happy hearts?" he asked them.

"We don't know what you mean," the boy and the girl said.

"Why," the Prince said, "to laugh and be as happy as you are, one has to wear a gold chain about one's neck. Where are yours?"

Oh, how the children laughed! "We don't need to wear gold hearts," they said. "We all love each other so much, and we play that this house is a castle and that we have turkey and ice cream for supper. After supper mother will tell us stories. That is all we need to make us happy."

"I will stay with you for supper," said the little Prince.

So he had supper in the tiny house that was a castle. And he played that the porridge and potato were turkey and ice cream. He helped to wash the dishes, and then they all sat about the fire. They played that the small fire was a great one, and listened to fairy stories that the mother told. All at once the little Prince began to smile. His laugh was just as merry as it used to be. His voice was again as sweet as music.

He had a very pleasant time, and then the boy walked part of the way home with him. When they were almost to the palace gates, the Prince said:

"It's very strange, but I feel just exactly as if I had found my happy heart."

The boy laughed. "Why, you have," he said. "Only now you are wearing it inside."

•

WE THANK THEE

Blessings of the home often last longer when we remember to be grateful for them. Gratefulness is too often a forgotten virtue in our day.

> For mother-love and father-care,
> For brothers strong and sisters fair,
> For love at home and here each day,
> For guidance lest we go astray,
>   Father in Heaven, we thank Thee.
>
> For this new morning with its light,
> For rest and shelter of the night,
> For health and food, for love and friends,
> For ev'rything His goodness sends,
>   Father in Heaven, we thank Thee.

•

THE GOLDEN WINDOWS

Retold by Laura E. Richards

We often dream of the splendors of faraway places, but on inspection those attractions are seldom as precious as home.

All day long the little boy worked hard, in field and barn and shed, for his people were poor farmers, and could not pay a workman; but at sunset there came an hour that was all his own, for his father had given it to him. Then the boy would go up to the top of a hill and look across at another hill that rose some miles away. On this far hill stood a house with windows of clear gold and diamonds. They shone and blazed so that it made the boy wink to look at them. But after a while the people in the house put up shutters, as it seemed, and then it looked like any common farmhouse. The boy supposed they did this because it was supper-time; and then he would go into the house and have his supper of bread and milk, and so to bed.

One day the boy's father called him and said: "You have been a good boy, and have earned a holiday. Take this day for your own; but remember that God gave it, and try to learn some good thing."

The boy thanked his father and kissed his mother. Then he put a piece of bread in his pocket, and started off to find the house with the golden windows.

It was pleasant walking. His bare feet made marks in the white dust, and when he looked back, the footprints seemed to be following him, and making company for him. His shadow, too, kept beside him, and would dance or run with him as he pleased; so it was very cheerful.

By and by he felt hungry, and he sat down by a brown brook that ran through the alder hedge by the roadside, and ate his bread, and drank the clear water. Then he scattered the crumbs for the birds, as his mother had taught him to do, and went on his way.

After a long time he came to a high green hill; and when he had climbed the hill, there was the house on the top. But it seemed that the shutters were up, for he could not see the golden windows. He came up to the house, and then he could well have wept, for the windows were of clear glass, like any others, and there was no gold anywhere about them.

A woman came to the door, and looked kindly at the boy, and asked him what he wanted.

"I saw the golden windows from our hilltop," he said, "and I came to see them, but now they are only glass."

The woman shook her head and laughed.

"We are poor farming people," she said, "and are not likely to have gold about our windows. But glass is better to see through."

She bade the boy sit down on the broad stone step at the door, and brought him a cup of milk and a cake, and bade him rest. Then she called her daughter, a child of his own age, and nodded kindly at the two, and went back to her work.

The little girl was barefooted like himself, and wore a brown cotton gown, but her hair was golden like the windows he had seen, and her eyes were blue like the sky at noon. She led the boy about the farm, and showed him her black calf with the white star on its forehead, and he told her about his own at home, which was red like a chestnut, with four white feet. Then when they had eaten an apple together, and so had become friends, the boy asked her about the golden windows. The little girl nodded, and said she knew all about them, only he had mistaken the house.

"You have come quite the wrong way!" she said. "Come with me, and I will show you the house with the golden windows, and then you will see for yourself."

They went to a knoll that rose behind the farmhouse, and as they went the little girl told him that the golden windows could only be seen at a certain hour, about sunset.

"Yes, I know that!" said the boy.

When they reached the top of the knoll, the girl turned and pointed; and there on a hill far away stood a house with windows of clear gold and diamonds, just as he had seen them. And when they looked again, the boy saw that it was his own home.

Then he told the little girl that he must go. He gave her his best pebble, the white one with the red band, that he had carried for a year in his pocket; and she gave him three horse-chestnuts, one red like satin, one spotted, and one white like milk. He kissed her, and promised to come again, but he did not tell her what he had learned. He went back down the hill, and the little girl stood in the sunset light and watched him.

The way home was long, and it was dark before the boy reached his father's house; but the lamplight and firelight shone through the windows, making them almost as bright as he had seen them from the hilltop. When he opened the door, his mother came to kiss him, and his little sister ran to throw her arms about his neck, and his father looked up and smiled from his seat by the fire.

"Have you had a good day?" asked his mother.

Yes, the boy had had a very good day.

"And have you learned anything?" asked his father.

"Yes!" said the boy. "I have learned that our house has windows of gold and diamonds."

•

THE LEGEND OF THE CHRIST CHILD

Adapted from a retelling
by Elizabeth Harrison

This beautiful old story reminds us that in homes where love is, God is.

Once upon a time, long, long ago, on the night before Christmas, a little child was wandering all alone through the streets of a great city. There were many people in the street, fathers and mothers, sisters and brothers, uncles and aunts, and even gray-haired grandfathers and grandmothers, all of whom were hurrying home with bundles of presents for each other and for their little ones. Fine carriages rolled by, express wagons rattled past, even old carts were pressed into service. All things seemed in a hurry and glad with expectation of the coming Christmas morning.

From some of the windows bright lights were already beginning to stream, until it was almost as bright as day. But the little child seemed to have no home, and wandered about listlessly from street to street. No one took any notice of him, except perhaps Jack Frost, who bit his bare toes and made the ends of his fingers tingle. The north wind, too, seemed to notice the child, for it blew against him and pierced his ragged garments through and through, causing him to shiver with cold. Home after home he passed, looking with longing eyes through the windows in upon the glad, happy children, most of whom were helping to trim the Christmas trees for the coming morrow.

"Surely," said the child to himself, "where there is so much gladness and happiness, some of it may be for me." So with timid steps he approached a large and handsome house. Through the windows he could see a beautiful Christmas tree already lighted. Many presents hung upon it. Its green boughs were trimmed with gold and silver ornaments. Slowly he climbed up the broad steps and gently rapped at the door.

It was opened by a tall and stately footman. He had a kindly face, although his voice was deep and gruff. He looked at the little child for a moment, then sadly shook his head and said, "Go down off the steps. There is no room here for such as you." He looked sorry as he spoke. Through the open door a bright light shone, and the warm air, filled with the fragrance of the Christmas pine, rushed out from the inner room and greeted the little wanderer like a kiss. As the child turned back into the cold and darkness, he wondered why the footman had spoken thus, for surely, thought he, those little children would love to have another companion join them in their joyous Christmas festival. But the little children inside did not even know that he had knocked at the door.

The street grew colder and darker as the child passed on. He went sadly forward, saying to himself, "Is there no one in all this great city who will share the Christmas with me?" Farther and farther down the street he wandered, to where the homes were not so large and beautiful. There seemed to be little children inside of nearly all the houses. They were dancing and frolicking about. Christmas trees could be seen in every window, with beautiful dolls and trumpets and picture-books and balls and tops and other wonderful toys hung upon them.

In one window the child noticed a little lamb made of soft, white wool. Around its neck was tied a red ribbon. It had evidently been hung on the tree for one of the younger children. The little wanderer stopped before this window and looked long and earnestly at the beautiful things inside, but most of all was he drawn toward the white lamb.

At last, creeping up to the windowpane, he gently tapped upon it. A little girl came to the window and looked out into the dark street where the snow had now begun to fall. She saw the child, but she only frowned and shook her head, and said, "Go away and come some other time. We are too busy to take care of you now." Back into the dark, cold street he turned again. The wind was whirling past him and seemed to say, "Hurry on, hurry on, we have no time to stop. 'Tis Christmas Eve and everybody is in a hurry tonight."

Again and again the child rapped softly at door or window-pane. At each place he was refused admission. One mother feared he might have some ugly disease which her darlings would catch; another father said he had only enough for his own children, and none to spare for beggar brats. Still another told him to go home where he belonged, and not to trouble other folks.

The hours passed; the night grew later, and the wind colder, and the street darker. Farther and farther the little one wandered. There was scarcely anyone left on the streets by this time, and the few who remained did not notice the child. Suddenly ahead of him there appeared a bright, single ray of light. It shone through the darkness into the child's eyes. He looked up, smiling, and said, "I will go where the little light beckons. Perhaps they will share their Christmas with me."

Hurrying past all the other houses he soon reached the end of the street and went straight up to the window from which the light was streaming. The house was old and small, but the child cared not for that. The light seemed still to call him in. From what do you suppose the light came? Nothing but a candle which had been placed in an old cup with a broken handle, in the window, as a glad token of Christmas Eve. There was neither curtain nor shade at the small, square window, and as the little child looked in he saw standing upon a neat, wooden table a small Christmas tree. The room was plainly furnished, but it was very clean. Near the fireplace sat a sweet-faced mother with a little two-year-old on her knee and an older child beside her. The two children were looking into their mother's face and listening to a story. She must have been telling them a Christmas story, I think. A few bright coals were burning in the fireplace, and all seemed light and warm within.

The little wanderer crept closer to the windowpane. So sweet was the mother's face, so loving seemed the little children, that he took courage and tapped gently, very gently, on the door. The mother stopped talking, the little children looked up. "What was that, Mother?" asked the little girl at her side.

"I think it was some one tapping on the door," replied the mother. "Run quickly and open it, dear, for it is a bitter cold night to keep anyone waiting in this storm."

"Oh, Mother, I think it was the bough of the tree tapping against the windowpane," said the little girl. "Do please go on with our story."

Again the little wanderer tapped upon the door.

"My child! My child!" exclaimed the mother, rising. "That cer-

tainly was a rap on the door. Run quickly and open it. No one must
be left out in the cold on Christmas Eve."

The child ran to the door and threw it wide open. The mother
saw the ragged stranger standing without, cold and shivering, with
bare head and almost bare feet. She held out both hands and drew
him into the warm, bright room. "You poor dear child," was all she
said, and, putting her arms around him, she drew him close to her
breast. "He is very cold, my children," she exclaimed. "We must
warm him."

"And," added the little girl, "we must love him and give him
some of our Christmas, too."

"Yes," said the mother, "but first let us warm him."

The mother sat down beside the fire with the child on her lap,
and her own two little ones warmed his half-frozen hands in theirs.
The mother smoothed his tangled curls, and, bending low over his
head, kissed the child's forehead. She gathered the three little ones
close to her and the candle and the firelight shone over them. For
a moment the room was very still. I think she must have been
praying. Then she whispered to the little girl, who ran into the
other room and returned with a bowl of bread and milk for the
little stranger.

By and by the little girl said, softly, to her mother, "May we not
light the Christmas tree, and let him see how beautiful it looks?"

"Yes," replied the mother. With that she seated the child on a
low stool beside the fire, and went herself to fetch the few simple
ornaments which from year to year she had saved for her children's
Christmas tree.

And as they busied themselves about the tree, they began to
notice that the room had filled with a strange and wonderful light.

Brighter and brighter it grew, until it shone like the sun; from floor to ceiling all was light as day. And when they turned and looked at the spot where the little wanderer had sat, it was empty. There was nothing to be seen. The child was gone, but the light was still in the room.

"Children," the mother said quietly, "I believe we have had the Christ Child with us tonight."

And she drew her dear ones to her and kissed them, and there was great joy in the little house.

•

MY TWO HOMES

Henry Hallam Tweedy

Many children feel at home in their house because they know it is part of God's house.

> Of all the houses in the world
>   The one that I love best
> Is that in which I wake and play
>   And lay me down to rest.
>
> My father built it by his toil;
>   My mother makes it home;
> You cannot find a lovelier place
>   No matter where you roam.
>
> The rooms are clean and bright and fair
>   With pictures, books, and toys,
> And food, and clothes, and beds, and chairs
>   For all the girls and boys.
>
> We children work and care for it,
>   And help to keep it clean,
> Our palace of true happiness,
>   Where mother reigns as queen,

And father guards us with his strength,
    A wise and gracious king,
To whom we pay the honor due,
    And glad obedience bring.

So full of love and joy it is,
    So safe and bright and warm,
I would not go too far from it
    Lest I should come to harm.

And yet when I go out of doors
    And look up at the sky,
I know I'm in my Father's house,
    And that His love is nigh.

For God is Father—Mother, too!
    The world is my big home;
The green grass is the carpet,
    And the blue sky is the dome.

On every side are pictures;
    The fields are full of food;
And all the things that God has made
    Are beautiful and good.

He keeps me by His mighty power,
    He loves me as His child;
His paths are bright with happiness,
    His laws are just and mild.

And all His children in this house,
    So wonderful and fair,
Should love each other, learn His truth,
    And trust His love and care.

I thank thee, Father, for these homes,
    Where we may dwell with Thee,
And cast out fear, and share the joys
    Thou givest full and free.

●

THE MATSUYAMA MIRROR

This charming Japanese tale was popular with American children around the turn of the twentieth century. It was handed down from parent to child in Japan over many generations, and dates to a time when people living outside of cities knew nothing of mirrors or their uses. It reminds us that in many ways, we grow up in our parents' image. We hope their virtues become our virtues.

I

Long ago there lived, in a quiet spot in far away Japan, a young man and his wife. They had one child, a little daughter, whom they loved dearly. I cannot tell you their names, for they have been long since forgotten; but the name of the place where they lived was Matsuyama.

It happened once, while the little girl was still a baby, that the father had to go to the great city, the capital of Japan, upon some business. It was too far for the mother and her little baby to go, so he set out alone, after bidding them good-by and promising to bring them home some pretty present.

The mother had never been farther from home than the next village, and she could not help being a little frightened at the thought of her husband taking such a long journey; and yet she was a little proud, too, for he was the first man in all that countryside who had been to the big town where the King and his great lords lived, and where there were so many beautiful and curious things to be seen.

At last the time came when she might expect her husband back, so she dressed the baby in her best clothes, and herself put on a pretty blue dress which she knew her husband liked.

You may fancy how glad this good wife was to see him come home safe and sound, and how the little girl clapped her hands, and laughed with delight, when she saw the pretty toys her father had brought for her. He had much to tell of all the wonderful things he had seen upon the journey, and in the town itself.

"I have brought you a very pretty thing," said he to his wife. "It is called a mirror. Look and tell me what you see inside." He gave to her a plain, white, wooden box, in which, when she opened it, she found a round piece of metal. One side was white like frosted silver, and ornamented with raised figures of birds and flowers; the other was bright as the clearest crystal. Into it the young mother looked with delight and astonishment, for from its depths was looking at her a smiling, happy face.

"What do you see?" again asked the husband, pleased at her astonishment, and glad to show that he had learned something while he had been away.

"I see a pretty woman looking at me, and she moves her lips as if she were speaking, and—dear me, how odd, she has on a blue dress just like mine!"

"Why, it is your own face that you see," said the husband, proud of knowing something that his wife didn't know. "That round piece of metal is called a mirror. In the town everybody has one, although we have not seen them in this country place before."

The wife was charmed with her present, and for a few days could not look into the mirror often enough, for you must remember that this was the first time she had seen a mirror, so of course it was the first time she had ever seen the reflection of her own pretty face. But she considered such a wonderful thing far too precious for everyday use, and soon shut it up in its box again, and put it away carefully among her most valued treasures.

II

Years passed, and the husband and wife still lived happily. The joy of their life was their little daughter, who grew up the very image of her mother, and who was so dutiful and affectionate that everybody loved her. Mindful of her own little passing vanity on finding herself so lovely, the mother kept the mirror carefully hidden away, fearing that the use of it might breed a spirit of pride in her little girl.

She never spoke of it; and as for the father, he had forgotten all about it. So the daughter grew up as simple as the mother had been, and knew nothing of her own good looks, or of the mirror which would have reflected them.

But by and by a sad misfortune came to this happy little family. The kind mother fell sick; and, although her daughter waited upon her day and night, with loving care, she got worse and worse, until at last there was no hope but that she must die.

When she found that she must so soon leave her husband and

child, the poor woman felt very sorrowful, grieving for those she was going to leave behind, and most of all for her little daughter.

She called the girl to her and said, "My darling child, you know that I am very sick; soon I must die, and leave your dear father and you alone. When I am gone, promise me that you will look into this mirror every night and every morning. There you will see me, and know that I am still watching over you." With these words she took the mirror from its hiding place and gave it to her daughter. The child promised, with many tears, and so the mother, seeming now calm and resigned, died a short time after.

Now this obedient and dutiful daughter never forgot her mother's last request, but each morning and evening took the mirror from its hiding place, and looked in it long and earnestly. There she saw the bright and smiling vision of her lost mother; not pale and sickly as in her last days, but the beautiful young mother of long ago. To her, at night, she told the story of the trials and difficulties of the day; to her, in the morning, she looked for sympathy and encouragement in whatever might be in store for her.

So day by day she lived as in her mother's sight, striving still to please her as she had done in her lifetime, and careful always to avoid whatever might pain or grieve her.

Her greatest joy was to be able to look in the mirror and say, "Mother, I have been today what you would have me be."

Seeing her every night and morning, without fail, look into the mirror, and seem to hold converse with it, her father at length asked her the reason for her strange behavior.

"Father," she said, "I look in the mirror every day to see my dear mother and to talk with her." Then she told him of her mother's dying wish, and how she had never failed to fulfill it. Touched by so much simplicity, and such faithful, loving obedience, the father shed tears of pity and affection. Nor could he find it in his heart to tell the child that the image she saw in the mirror was but the reflection of her own sweet face, becoming more and more like her dear mother's, day by day.

•

THE APRON STRING

Laura E. Richards

The much-derided apron string can come in handy, especially
when its fibers are the virtues we've learned at home. Those
bonds stay with us.

Once upon a time a boy played about the house, running by
his mother's side; and as he was very little, his mother tied him to
the string of her apron.

"Now," she said, "when you stumble, you can pull yourself up
by the apron-string, and so you will not fall."

The boy did that, and all went well, and the mother sang at her
work.

By and by the boy grew so tall that his head came above the
window-sill; and looking through the window, he saw far away
green trees waving, and a flowing river that flashed in the sun, and
rising above all, blue peaks of mountains.

"Oh, Mother," he said, "untie the apron-string and let me go!"

But the mother said, "Not yet, my child! Only yesterday you
stumbled, and would have fallen but for the apron-string. Wait yet
a little, till you are stronger."

So the boy waited, and all went as before; and the mother sang
at her work.

But one day the boy found the door of the house standing
open, for it was spring weather. He stood on the threshold and
looked across the valley, and saw the green trees waving, and the
swift-flowing river with the sun flashing on it, and the blue mountains rising beyond. And this time he heard the voice of the river
calling, and it said "Come!"

Then the boy started forward, and as he started, the string of
the apron broke.

"Oh! how weak my mother's apron-string is!" cried the boy;
and he ran out into the world, with the broken string hanging
beside him.

The mother gathered up the other end of the string and put it
in her bosom, and went about her work again; but she sang no
more.

The boy ran on and on, rejoicing in his freedom, and in the fresh air and the morning sun. He crossed the valley, and began to climb the foothills among which the river flowed swiftly, among rocks and cliffs. Now it was easy climbing, and again it was steep and craggy, but always he looked upward at the blue peaks beyond, and always the voice of the river was in his ears, saying "Come!"

By and by he came to the brink of a precipice, over which the river dashed in a cataract, foaming and flashing, and sending up clouds of silver spray. The spray filled his eyes, so that he did not see his footing clearly; he grew dizzy, stumbled, and fell. But as he fell, something about him caught on a point of rock at the precipice-edge, and held him, so that he hung dangling over the abyss; and when he put up his hand to see what held him, he found that it was the broken string of the apron, which still hung by his side.

"Oh! how strong my mother's apron-string is!" said the boy. And he drew himself up by it, and stood firm on his feet, and went on climbing toward the blue peaks of the mountains.

•

FOUR DAUGHTERS

This story from South America reminds us that the habits we learn in the home are the habits we carry with us into the world.

There once lived a mother who had four daughters, named Margarita, Emilia, Carmen, and Maria. The three eldest children were lazy and rude and rarely obeyed their mother. Only the youngest, Maria, did what she could to be a loving daughter.

The time came when the mother called her children together.

"You are growing older now, and so am I," she told them. "I will not be able to take care of you forever. You must learn to work so you can make your own ways in the world someday. So I have chores for each of you to do. Margarita, you must dust away the cobwebs. Emilia, you must sweep the floor. Carmen, you must rake the yard. And Maria, you must weed in the garden."

But Margarita, the eldest daughter, scowled.

"Dust? I can't be expected to dust!" she hooted. "I need my

beauty sleep." She packed her bag and left the house to find some quiet place to lay down her head.

Emilia, the next daughter, threw up her arms and paced the room in circles.

"I don't know how to sweep," she grunted. "I'm sure I can't learn how. I'm going for a stroll in the countryside. It's much more pleasant there."

She packed her bags and left the house.

Carmen, the next daughter, banged her fist on the table.

"I don't know how to work either!" she shrieked. "I've got better things to do, you know. I'm moving to town. People there know how to have fun."

She too packed her bags and left the house with a frown.

Only Maria, the youngest daughter, put on a smile.

"Don't worry, Mother," she said. "I'll work in the garden and plant as many flowers as it will hold, and sell them in town at market. That way I can stay with you and take care of you as you grow old."

Time passed, and Maria kept her word. Her garden flourished, as did her trade at the marketplace, and she made enough money to give some comfort to her mother.

But at last the day came when the old woman sensed her time had come. She sent Maria to find her sisters so she might tell them good-bye.

Marie found Margarita asleep in the shady forest.

"Mother is ill and asks you to come home," she told her.

"I'm sleeping right now," Margarita yawned. "It's much too early. Tell her I'll come later."

Maria found Emilia wandering the countryside, searching the fields for scraps of food left from the harvest.

"I don't have time to come home," she said. "I'm hoping to pick up some dinner."

Maria found Carmen walking the town lanes and alleys, knocking on door after door, looking for handouts.

"I can't come home just now," she muttered. "No one feels generous today. I must keep knocking if I am to eat." She turned her back to rap on another door.

Maria returned to her mother, who grieved at her daughters' fates.

"My Margarita will live in the darkness of the forest for the rest of her life, sleeping the days away," she cried. "My Emilia will spend her life wandering aimlessly, content to live on what lies on the ground. My Carmen will knock and knock for the rest of her days, grubbing for morsels. Only you, Maria, will be welcomed and beloved by all."

The old woman closed her eyes and drew her last breath.

And her prophecy came true.

After her death, Margarita became an owl, and to this day she dwells in the darkest parts of the forest, sleeping the days away.

Emilia turned into a ugly vulture, and now circles the country skies, hoping to dine on whatever she finds lying on the ground.

Carmen changed into a woodpecker, and you can still hear her knocking and knocking all day long, grubbing for morsels.

As for little Maria, she is still hard at work in her garden, tending her flowers, sipping the nectar from their silky cups. And everywhere she goes, she is welcomed and beloved, for Maria turned into a hummingbird.

●

THE NEW LEAVES

Adapted from Laura E. Richards

Here's a great story for the New Year that will help children understand what "turning over a new leaf" means. Better to learn good habits in the home than out in the world, where turning the leaves may be much tougher.

"Wake up!" said a clear little voice. Tommy woke, and sat up. At the foot of the bed stood a boy about his own age, all dressed in white, like fresh snow. He had very bright eyes, and he looked straight at Tommy.

"Who are you?" asked Tommy.

"I am the New Year!" said the boy. "This is my day, and I have brought you your leaves."

"What leaves?" asked Tommy.

"The new ones, to be sure!" said the New Year. "I hear bad accounts of you from my Daddy—"

"Who is your Daddy?" asked Tommy.

"The Old Year, of course!" said the boy. "He said you asked too many questions, and I see he was right. He says you are greedy, too, and that you sometimes pinch your little sister, and that one day you threw your reader into the fire. Now, all this must stop."

"Oh, must it?" said Tommy. He felt frightened, and did not know just what to say.

The boy nodded. "If it does not stop," he said, "you will grow worse and worse every year, till you grow up into a Horrid Man. Do you want to be a Horrid Man?"

"N-no!" said Tommy.

"Then you must stop being a horrid boy!" said the New Year. "Take your leaves!" And he held out a packet of what looked like notebook paper, all sparkling white, like his own clothes.

"Turn over one of these every day," he said, "and soon you will be a good boy instead of a horrid one."

Tommy took the leaves of paper and looked at them. On each leaf a few words were written. On one it said, "Help your mother and father!" On another, "Pick up your toys!" On another, "Stop tracking mud across the floor!" On another, "Be nice to your little sister!" And on still another, "Don't fight Billy Jenkins!"

"Oh!" cried Tommy. "I *have* to fight Billy Jenkins!" He said—"

"Good-by!" said the New Year. "I shall come again when I am old to see whether you have been a good boy or a horrid one. Remember,

> "Horrid boy makes horrid man.
> You alone can change the plan."

He turned away and opened the window. A cold wind blew in and swept the leaves out of Tommy's hand. "Stop! stop!" he cried. "Tell me—" But the New Year was gone, and Tommy, staring after him, saw only his mother coming into the room. "Dear child!" she said. "Why, the wind is blowing everything about."

"My leaves! My leaves!" cried Tommy. Jumping out of bed, he looked all over the room, but he could not find one.

"Never mind," said Tommy. "I can turn them just the same, and I mean to. I will not grow into a Horrid Man." And he didn't.

THE NIGHT WIND
Eugene Field

At home that guardian of virtue we call conscience takes root. It
talks to us often, even when we don't ask it to.

Have you ever heard the wind go "Yooooo"'?
　'Tis a pitiful sound to hear.
It seems to chill you through and through
　With a strange and speechless fear.
It's the voice of the night that broods outside
　When folks should be asleep;
And many and many's the time I've cried
To the darkness that brooded far and wide
　Over the land and the deep:
"Whom do you want, O lonely night,
That you wail the long hours through?"
And the night would say in its ghostly way:
　　"Yoo—oo—oo—oo! Yoo—oo—oo—oo!
　　Yoo—oo—oo—oo!"

My mother told me long ago
　(When I was a little lad),
That when the night went wailing so,
　Somebody had been bad.
And then, when I was snug in bed,
　Whither I had been sent,
With the blankets drawn up around my head,
I'd think of what my mother'd said,
　And wonder what boy she meant.
"And who's been bad today?" I'd ask
Of the wind that hoarsely blew.
And that voice would say in its awful way:
　　"Yoo—oo—oo—oo! Yoo—oo—oo—oo!
　　Yoo—oo—oo—oo!"

That this was true I must allow—
    You'll not believe it though!—
Yes, though I'm quite a model now,
    I was not always so.
And if you doubt what things I say,
    Suppose you make the test;
Suppose when you've been bad some day,
And up to bed you're sent away
    From mother and the rest—
Suppose you ask, "Who has been bad?"
    And then you'll hear what's true.
For the wind will moan in its ruefullest tone:
    "Yoo—oo—oo—oo! Yoo—oo—oo—oo!
    Yoo—oo—oo—oo!"

•

THE GARDEN OF THE FROST FLOWERS
Retold by Frances Jenkins Olcott

Home is a place of protection from very real dangers beyond the doorstep—dangers from nature and dangers from man. This sad story in which a child dies, retold from a poem by William Cullen Bryant, reminds children that when they are young, they must not stray too far alone, and they must take seriously their parents' warnings.

THE PROMISE MADE

In the olden time, long, long ago, there dwelt on a mountain side a cottager, his wife, and his little girl named Eva. A lovely spot was their home, for near it was a glen through which dashed a brook fringed with many sweet-smelling Spring flowers.

But then Winter came, the little brook was fringed with other blossoms. Strange white ones with crystal leaves and stems grew there in the clear November nights. For when the Winter Winds blew hard, down from the mountain top came a troop of Little People of the Snow. A beautiful Fairy race they were, with bright locks, and voices like the sounds of steps on crisp Snow. With trailing robes they came, some flying through the air, others tripping lightly across the icy fields.

They threw spangles of silvery Frost upon the grass and edged the brook with glistening parapets. They built crystal bridges over the stream, and, touching the water, turned its face to glass. Then they shook, from their full laps, so many Snowflakes that they covered the whole world with a soft blanket.

Now Eva had often heard about these Little People, but she had never seen them. One Mid-Winter day, when she was twelve years old, she dressed herself warmly to play in the Snow.

"Do not stay too long," said her mother, as she wrapped her furry coat around the child and put on her fur boots. "Do not stay too long, for sharp is the Winter Wind. And go no farther than the great Linden Tree on the edge of our field."

All this Eva promised, and went skipping from the house. Now she climbed the rounded snow swells that felt firm with Frost beneath her feet, and now she slid down them into the deep hollows. So she played alone and was happy.

But as she was clambering up a very high drift, she saw a tiny maiden sitting on the Snow. Lily-cheeked she was, with flowing flaxen hair and blue eyes that gleamed like Ice, while her robe seemed of a more shadowy whiteness than her cheeks.

When she saw Eva, this tiny creature bounded to her feet, and cried: "Oh, come with me, pretty Friend. I have watched you often, and know how well you love the Snow, and how you carve huge-limbed Snowmen, Lions, and Griffins. Come, let us ramble over these bright fields. You shall see what you have never seen before."

So Eva followed her new friend. Together they slid down drifts and climbed white mounds, until they reached the spot where the great Linden Tree stood.

"Here I must stop," said Eva, "for I promised my mother I would go no farther."

But the little Snow Maiden laughed.

"What!" cried she. "Are you afraid of the Snow? of the pure Snow? of the innocent Snow? It has never hurt any living thing. Surely your mother made you promise that because she thought you had no one to guide you. I will show you the way and bring you safely home."

By such smooth words Eva was won to break her promise, and she followed her new playmate. Over glistening fields they ran, and down a steep bank to the foot of a huge Snowdrift or Hill of Snow.

There the Winds had carved a shelf of driven snow, that curtained a wide opening in the hill.

"Look! Look! Let us enter here!" cried the little creature merrily. "Come, Eva, follow me."

IN THE GARDEN OF FROST FLOWERS

Straight under the shelflike curtain Eva and the little Snow Maiden crept, and walked along a passage with white walls. Above them in the vaulted roof were set Snow Stars that cast a wintry twilight over all.

Eva moved with awe and could not speak for wonder; but the little Snow Maiden, laughing gayly, tripped lightly on before. Deeper and deeper they went into the heart of the Hill of Snow. And now the walls began to widen; and the vaulted roof rose higher and higher, until it expanded into a great white dome above their heads.

Eva looked about her. She stood in a large white garden, where everything seemed to be spun out of delicate silent Frost.

At her feet grew snow-white plants with lacelike leaves and spangled flowers. At her side Palm Trees reared their stately white columns tufted with frosted plumes. Huge Oaks, with icelike trunks, waved their transparent branches in the silent air, while their gnarled roots seemed anchored deep in glistening banks. Light sprays of Myrtle, and snowy Roses in bud and bloom, drooped by the winding walks.

All these things—flowers, leaves, and trees—seemed delicately wrought from stainless alabaster. Up the trees ran Jasmine vines with stalks and leaves as colorless as their blossoms. All this Eva saw with wonder and delight.

"Walk, softly, dear Friend," said the little Snow Maiden. "Do not touch the frail creation round you, nor sweep it with your skirt.

"Now, look up, and behold how beautifully this Garden of Frost Flowers is lighted. See those shifting gleams that seem to come and go so gently. They are the Northern Lights that make beautiful our Winter Palace.

"Here on long cold nights I and my comrades, the Little People of the Snow, make this garden lovely. We guide to this place the wandering Snowflakes and, piling them up into many quaint shapes, bid them grow into stately columns, glittering arches, white trees, and lovely flowers of Frost.

"But come now, dear Eva, and I will show you a far more wonderful sight."

The Dance of the Little People of the Snow

As she spoke, the little Snow Maiden led her to a windowpane of transparent ice set in the Snow wall.

"Look," said she, "but you may not enter in."

Eva looked.

Lo! she saw a glorious, glistening palace hall from whose lofty roof fell stripes of shimmering light, rose-colored, and delicate green, and tender blue.

This light flowed downward to the floor, enveloping in its rainbow hues a joyous multitude of tiny folk, whirling in a merry dance. Silvery music sounded from cymbals of transparent Ice skillfully touched by tiny hands.

Round and round they flew beneath the dome of colored lights, now wheeling and now turning. Their bright eyes shone under their lily brows. Their gauzy scarfs, sparkling like snow wreaths in the Sun, floated in the dizzy whirl.

Eva stood entranced in wonder, as all these Little People of the Snow, dancing and whirling in the colored lights, swept past the icy windowpane.

Long she gazed, and long she listened to the sweet sounds that thrilled the frosty air. Then the intense cold around her numbed her limbs, and she remembered the promise to her mother.

The Promise Broken

"Alas!" she cried, "too long, too long am I lingering here! Oh, how wickedly I have done to break my promise! What must they think, the dear ones at home?"

With hurried step she found the snowy passage again, and followed it upward to the light, while the little Snow Maiden ran by her side, guiding her feet.

When she reached the open air once more, a bitter blast came rushing from the clear North, chilling her blood, and she shrank in terror before it. But the little Snow Maiden, when she felt the cutting blast, bounded along, uttering shouts of joy, and skipping from drift to drift. And she danced around Eva, as the poor child wearily climbed the slippery mounds of frozen snow.

"Ah me!" sighed Eva at last, "Ah me! My eyes grow heavy. They swim with sleep."

As she spoke, her lids closed, and she sank upon the ground and slept.

Then near her side sat the little Snow Maiden, watching her slumber. She saw the rosy color fade from Eva's rounded cheeks, and the child's brow grow white as marble, while her breath slowly ceased to come and go. All motionless lay her form; and the little Snow Maiden strove to waken her, plucking her dress, and shouting in her ears, but all in vain.

Then suddenly was heard the sound of steps grating on the Snow. It was Eva's parents searching for their lost child. When they found her, lying like a fair marble image in her deathlike sleep, and when they heard from the little Snow Maiden how she had led Eva into the Garden of Frost Flowers, their hearts were wrung with anguish.

They lifted the dear child up and bore her home. And though they chafed her limbs and bathed her brow, she never woke again. The little maid was dead.

Now came the funeral day. In a grave dug in the glen's white side they buried Eva, while from the rocks and hills around a thousand slender voices rose, and sighed, and mourned, until the echoes, taking up the strains, flung them far and wide across the icy fields.

From that day the Little People of the Snow were never seen again. But all during the long, cold Winter nights, invisible tiny hands wove around Eva's grave frost wreaths, and tufts of silvery rime shaped like flowers one scatters on a bier.

•

JOSEPH AND HIS BROTHERS

Retold by J. Berg Essenwein
and Marietta Stockard

Joseph embodies the true spirit of brotherhood: his love was so
great, he not only forgave but saved those who betrayed him, and
made for them a new home. The story is from the book of Genesis
in the Bible.

Long ago, in the land of Canaan, there lived a rich shepherd
and farmer called Jacob. He had great flocks and many servants. He
had also twelve sons, and the best loved of his sons was Joseph.
Perhaps it was because Joseph himself was always gentle and obedient; perhaps it was because of his beautiful mother, Rachel, who
had died when the little brother, Benjamin, was born; but at any
rate, Jacob loved Joseph deeply and tenderly.

His brothers grew angry and jealous because of this great love.
"Our father will give him all of his riches, and make him ruler over
us," they said.

When Joseph was seventeen years old, his father gave him a
beautiful coat of many colors. He walked among his brothers
dressed in the coat, and they grew more jealous and angry still.
Sometimes he talked to them of strange dreams he had, which
seemed to mean that some day he would be more rich and powerful than they. This made them hate him bitterly.

At last, one day when they had driven their flocks to pastures
which were far away from home, Jacob called Joseph to him and
said: "Go see whether it be well with thy brethren and with the
flocks; and bring me word again."

Joseph was always glad to serve his father, so he set out toward
Shechem to find his brothers. But they had driven their flocks still
farther away, and Joseph wandered in the fields for a long time
before he came to them.

When they saw him far off, the jealousy which had been making their hearts more wicked each day grew into hatred so black
that they began to plan to murder their own brother. But Reuben,
the oldest of the brothers, determined to save Joseph if he could.

He seemed to agree with them, and said: "Let us cast him into this pit here in the wilderness and leave him." He meant to return, however, and send Joseph away home to their old father.

As Joseph drew near to them, his brothers began to mock him. "Behold the dreamer!" they scoffed. "Let us now see what will become of his dreams!" They caught him and with rough hands stripped off his beautiful coat, and threw him into the deep pit. Then they sat near and ate their food, laughing at Joseph's cries and pleadings.

While they sat there, a caravan of merchants came along the highway. Their camels were loaded with spices and myrrh which they were carrying down into Egypt.

"Come," said Judah, "let us sell Joseph to these Ishmaelites. They will carry him down into Egypt, and we shall never see him again. We shall be rid of him, and still we shall not have his blood upon our hands."

The brothers agreed, and lifted Joseph from the pit. He begged most piteously to be allowed to go back home, but they hardened their hearts, and sold him for twenty pieces of silver. Then the Ishmaelites set him upon a camel, and carried him away into the strange land of Egypt.

Reuben came back to the pit and found Joseph gone. He rent his clothes in his great grief, but the other brothers said: "We are well rid of him. Now he will never rule over us."

They took Joseph's coat and tore it, then dipped it in the blood of a kid so that their father would think some wild beast had slain his son. When Jacob saw the coat, he mourned most piteously.

Meantime, the Ishmaelites continued their journey down into Egypt, carrying the lonely lad. But God comforted him in his dreams. He remembered too the teaching of his father, and faith and courage stayed in his heart.

When they arrived in Egypt, Joseph was sold to Potiphar, who was an officer of the king, called Pharaoh. Soon Joseph's gentle ways and comely looks caused him to be loved and trusted by all. Whatever he did prospered, so the Egyptian captain saw that God was with him, and he made him the overseer of his house. There Joseph learned the customs of the land, he learned to command men, and learned the needs of the country.

But the happy, prosperous days soon came to an end. The wife of Potiphar filled her husband's mind with wicked lies concerning Joseph, and caused him to be thrown into prison. Some servants of

Pharaoh who had angered him were in the prison at this time, and Joseph talked with them so wisely that they knew that his knowledge came from God.

Two long years went by, and at last Pharaoh was troubled by strange dreams and needed counsel. The chief butler, who had been in the prison with Joseph, remembered his great wisdom. "Send for that young Hebrew prisoner," he said to King Pharaoh; "he will interpret your dream."

Then Pharaoh sent and called Joseph. He was brought from his dungeon and placed before the king. He listened to the king's strange dream of seven lean cows coming from the river and devouring seven fat cows; of seven blasted ears of corn springing up and devouring seven ears that were full and good. And God gave Joseph the wisdom to know the meaning of the dream.

"O King," he said, "there are seven years of great plenty at hand, but these seven years will be followed by seven years of famine in the land. Let the king command that food be gathered and stored during the seven years of plenty."

Pharaoh believed Joseph's words and made him chief ruler in the land. Only the king himself was greater than he. He gave him riches and power, and the high-born maiden Asenath for his wife.

In the seven years that followed, Joseph caused great storehouses to be built and filled with grain, so when the years of famine came there was bread in Egypt, but in no other land. People came from all the neighboring countries into Egypt to buy bread.

Now the aged Jacob heard that there was bread in Egypt, so he sent his ten sons there. Benjamin, the youngest son, he sent not. He feared that evil might befall this other son of his beloved Rachel, the mother of Joseph.

The ten brothers journeyed down to Egypt, and stood before the governor of the land. They bowed down before him, not knowing that the rich and powerful governor was their own brother whom they had sold to the Ishmaelites long years before. But Joseph knew them, and he remembered the dreams of his boyhood. He felt glad for the strange, hard things which had come to him, because through them this day had become possible.

His heart yearned for his own people, but he wished to test his brothers, so he spoke to them roughly and accused them of being spies. "You say you have a younger brother at home. Go fetch him so that I may know you are true men."

When they would not promise to fetch Benjamin, he threw them into prison for three days. Then they stood before him again, and at first talked among themselves in deep distress. At last they told Joseph about their brother whose anguish they had not heeded when they sold him into slavery long years before. "It is because of our guilt that this sorrow has come upon us," they said.

Joseph went out from them and wept at their words, but he felt that the time had not yet come for him to make himself known to them. So he caused Simeon to be bound and kept as a hostage, then he filled their sacks with corn and sent them back to Canaan. But every man's money was secretly placed in the mouth of his sack.

The brethren were filled with wonder and fear when they found it there. They returned to Jacob, their father, and told him all that had befallen them; and his heart was troubled for his children.

At last the food was all gone, and unless they would starve they must return to Egypt, so Jacob at last consented to send Benjamin with them as the strange man had demanded. He sent rich presents, too, and double the money for the grain he wanted to buy, hoping thus to please the powerful governor.

When at last the brothers stood before Joseph, and he saw Benjamin with them, he ordered the ruler of his house to make ready a great feast for them. They bowed themselves to the ground before him, and told him of the money in their sacks.

"Fear not," he said, "the God of your father hath given you treasure."

He brought out to them Simeon, whom he had kept as a hostage, and treated them with great kindness. At last he sent them on their way again, and as before, every man's money was placed in his sack. But in the sack of Benjamin, Joseph's own drinking cup was placed.

When they had gone out of the city, Joseph sent his steward after them, and he said: "Why have you rewarded evil for good? You have taken away the cup from which my lord drinks."

He compelled them to open their sacks, and when the cup was found in the sack of Benjamin, they cried out in great distress, and hastened back to the city. They threw themselves at Joseph's feet and begged for the liberty of their young brother.

Judah said: "His brother is dead, and he alone is left of his mother, and his father loves him." Judah begged that he be made a servant in the lad's place.

Then Joseph knew that their hearts were no more filled with jealousy and selfishness, and he cried out to them: "I am Joseph, your brother. Grieve no more that you sold me, for God did send me before you to preserve life."

Then he kissed his brothers and showed great love for them. "Go," he said, "fetch our father and all your households down from Canaan. The best part of the land of Egypt shall be yours."

Joseph's brothers did as he commanded. They journeyed down into Egypt, and made their homes there. Then at last Jacob held Joseph's children in his arms and blessed them, and there was great happiness between them throughout all their days.

•

THE PLACE OF BROTHERHOOD

This beautiful Jewish story reminds us that home should be the place where we learn about selflessness and how to practice it with those closest to us. King Solomon built the Temple of Israel to house the Ark of the Covenant in the tenth century B.C.

In the days of King Solomon there lived two brothers who reaped wheat in the fields of Zion. One night, in the dark of the moon, the elder brother gathered several sheaves of his harvest and left it in his brother's field, saying to himself: "My brother has seven children. With so many mouths to feed, he could use some of my bounty." And he went home.

A short time later, the younger brother slipped out of his house, gathered several sheaves of *his* wheat, and carried it into his brother's field, saying to himself: "My brother is all alone, with no one to help him harvest. So I'll share some of my wheat with him."

When the sun rose, each brother was amazed to find he had just as much wheat as before!

The next night they paid each other the same kindness, and still woke to find their stores undiminished.

But on the third night, they met each other as they carried their gifts into each other's fields. Each threw his arms around the other and shed tears of joy for his goodness.

And when Solomon heard of their love, he built the Temple of Israel there on the place of brotherhood.

THREE THINGS

Here are three important levers, the ones that raise children, raise efforts, and raise hearts and minds.

> I know three things must always be
> To keep a nation strong and free.
> One is a hearthstone bright and dear,
> With busy, happy loved ones near.
> One is a ready heart and hand
> To love and serve and keep the land.
> One is a worn and beaten way
> To where the people go to pray.
> So long as these are kept alive,
> Nation and people will survive.
> God keep them always everywhere—
> The home, the heart, the place of prayer.

•

CORNELIA'S JEWELS
Adapted from retellings by James Baldwin and William J. Sly

Cornelia was the daughter of Scipio Africanus, a famous Roman general who defeated Hannibal and the Carthaginians. She married Tiberious Sempronius Gracchus, a powerful consul, and lived amid the lavish trappings of the Roman nobility. After her husband died, however, she had to sell most of her property and learn to live simply. This Roman legend about Cornelia's real wealth takes place in the second century B.C.

It was a bright morning in the old city of Rome many hundred years ago. Two brothers were playing in a garden when their mother, Cornelia, called them into the house.

"A friend is coming to dine today," she told them. "She is very rich, and she will show us her jewels."

Soon the woman arrived. Her fingers sparkled with rings. Her arms glittered with bracelets. Chains of gold hung about her neck, and strands of pearls gleamed in her hair.

"Did you ever see anyone so pretty?" the younger boy whispered to his brother. "She looks like a queen!"

They gazed at their own mother, who was dressed only in a white robe. Her hands and arms were bare, and for a crown she had only long braids of soft brown hair coiled about her head. But her kind smile seemed to light her face more than any bright stone could.

"Would you like to see some more of my treasures?" the rich woman asked. A servant brought a box and set it on a table. When the lady opened it, there were heaps of blood red rubies, sapphires as blue as the sky, emeralds as green as the sea, diamonds that flashed like sunlight.

The brothers looked long at the gems.

"Ah!" whispered the younger. "If only our mother could have such beautiful things!"

At last, however, the box was closed and carried away.

"Tell me, Cornelia," the rich woman said with a pitying smile, "is it true you have no jewels? Is it true you are too poor?"

Cornelia smiled. "Not at all," she said. "I have jewels far more valuable than yours."

"Then let me see them," the lady laughed. "Where are they?"

Cornelia drew her boys to her side.

"These are my jewels," she smiled. "Are they not far more precious than your gems?"

The two boys, Tiberius and Caius Gracchus, never forgot their mother's pride and love and care. Years later, when they had become great statesmen of Rome, they liked to think of this scene in the garden. And when the Roman people erected statues to honor the brothers, they did not forget to pay tribute to the woman who showed them how to be wise and good. The Romans inscribed her tomb this way: "Cornelia, Mother of the Gracchi."

•

THE STORY OF THE FIRST DIAMONDS
Retold by Florence Holbrook

In all times and places, the dearest thing is the tear of mother love.

The chief of an Indian tribe had two sons, whom he loved very dearly. This chief was at war with another tribe, and one dark night two of his enemies crept softly through the trees till they came to where the two boys lay sound asleep. The warriors caught the younger boy up gently, and carried him far away from his home and his friends.

When the chief woke, he cried, "Where is my son? My enemies have been here and have stolen him."

All the Indians in the tribe started out in search of the boy. They roamed the forest through and through, but the stolen child could not be found.

The chief mourned for his son, and when the time of his death drew near, he said to his wife, "Moneta, my tribe shall have no chief until my boy is found and taken from our enemies. Let our oldest son go forth in search of his brother, and until he has brought back the little one, do you rule my people."

Moneta ruled the people wisely and kindly. When the older son was a man, she said to him, "My son, go forth and search for your brother, whom I have mourned these many years. Every day I shall watch for you, and every night I shall build a fire on the mountain top."

"Do not mourn, Mother," said the young man. "You will not build the fire many nights on the mountain top, for I shall soon find my brother and bring him back to you."

He went forth bravely, but he did not come back. His mother went every night to the mountain top, and when she was so old that she could no longer walk, the young men of the tribe bore her up the mountain side in their strong arms, so that with her own trembling hand she could light the fire.

One night there was a great storm. Even the brave warriors were afraid, but Moneta had no fear, for out of the storm a gentle voice had come to her that said, "Moneta, your sons are coming home to you."

"Once more I must build the fire on the mountain top," she cried. The young men trembled with fear, but they bore her to the top of the mountain.

"Leave me here alone," she said, "I hear a voice. It is the voice of my son, and he is calling, 'Mother, Mother.' Come to me, come, my boys."

Coming slowly up the mountain in the storm was the older son. The younger had died on the road home, and he lay dead in the arms of his brother.

In the morning the men of the tribe went to the mountain top in search of Moneta and her sons. They were nowhere to be seen, but where the tears of the lonely mother had fallen, there was a brightness that had never been seen before. The tears were shining in the sunlight as if each one of them was itself a little sun. Indeed, they were no longer tears, but diamonds.

The dearest thing in all the world is the tear of mother-love, and that is why the tears were made into diamonds, the stones that are brightest and clearest of all the stones on the earth.

•

THE BOY WHO KISSED HIS MOTHER

Eben E. Rexford

As many a philosopher, biographer, and poet has considered, there seems to be an age-old, life-long link between the virtues of men and their love for their mothers.

> She sat on the porch in the sunshine,
>   As I went down the street—
> A woman whose hair was silver,
>   But whose face was blossom sweet,
> Making me think of a garden,
>   Where, in spite of the frost and snow
> Of bleak November weather,
>   Late, fragrant lilies grow.
>
> I heard a footstep behind me,
>   And the sound of a merry laugh,
> And I knew the heart it came from
>   Would be like a comforting staff
> In the time and the hour of trouble,
>   Hopeful and brave and strong;
> One of the hearts to lean on
>   When we think that things go wrong.
>
> I turned at the click of the gate-latch
>   And met his manly look;
> A face like his gives me pleasure,
>   Like the page of a pleasant book;
> It told of a steadfast purpose,
>   Of a brave and daring will—
> A face with a promise in it
>   That God grant the years fulfill.
>
> He went up the pathway singing.
>   I saw the woman's eyes
> Grow bright with a wordless welcome,
>   As sunshine warms the skies.

"Back again, sweetheart mother,"
    He cried, and bent to kiss
The loving face that was lifted
    For what some mothers miss.

That boy will do to depend on,
    I hold that this is true—
From lads in love with their mothers
    Our bravest heroes grew.
Earth's grandest hearts have been loving hearts,
    Since time and earth began.
And the boy who kissed his mother
    Is every inch a man.

•

ABOUT ANGELS

Laura E. Richards

Here is a story about a true guardian angel, the kind who watches
over us from the moment we come into the world.

"Mother," said the child, "are there really angels?"

"The Good Book says so," said the mother.

"Yes," said the child. "I have seen the picture. But did you ever
see one, Mother?"

"I think I have," said the mother, "but she was not dressed like
the picture."

"I am going to find one!" said the child. "I am going to run
along the road, miles, and miles, and miles, until I find an angel."

"That will be a good plan!" said the mother. "And I will go
with you, for you are too little to run far alone."

"I am not little any more!" said the child. "I have trousers; I am
big."

"So you are!" said the mother. "I forgot. But it is a fine day,
and I should like the walk."

"But you walk so slowly, with your lame foot."

"I can walk faster than you think!" said the mother.

So they started, the child leaping and running, and the mother stepping out so bravely with her lame foot that the child soon forgot about it.

The child danced on ahead, and presently he saw a chariot coming towards him, drawn by prancing white horses. In the chariot sat a splendid lady in velvet and furs, with white plumes waving above her dark hair. As she moved in her seat, she flashed with jewels and gold, but her eyes were brighter than her diamonds.

"Are you an angel?" asked the child, running up beside the chariot.

The lady made no reply, but stared coldly at the child. Then she spoke a word to her coachman, and he flicked his whip, and the chariot rolled away swiftly in a cloud of dust, and disappeared.

The dust filled the child's eyes and mouth, and made him choke and sneeze. He gasped for breath, and rubbed his eyes; but presently his mother came up, and wiped away the dust with her blue gingham apron.

"That was not an angel!" said the child.

"No, indeed!" said the mother. "Nothing like one!"

The child danced on again, leaping and running from side to side of the road, and the mother followed as best she might.

By and by the child met a most beautiful maiden, clad in a white dress. Her eyes were like blue stars, and the blushes came and went in her face like roses looking through snow.

"I am sure you must be an angel!" cried the child.

The maiden blushed more sweetly than before. "You dear little child!" she cried. "Some one else said that, only last evening. Do I really look like an angel?"

"You *are* an angel!" said the child.

The maiden took him up in her arms and kissed him, and held him tenderly.

"You are the dearest little thing I ever saw!" she said. "Tell me what makes you think so!" But suddenly her face changed.

"Oh!" she cried. "There he is, coming to meet me! And you have soiled my white dress with your dusty shoes, and pulled my hair all awry. Run away, child, and go home to your mother!"

She set the child down, not unkindly, but so hastily that he stumbled and fell; but she did not see that, for she was hastening forward to meet her lover, who was coming along the road. (Now if the maiden had only known, he thought her twice as lovely with the child in her arms; but she did not know.)

The child lay in the dusty road and sobbed, till his mother

came along and picked him up, and wiped away the tears with her blue gingham apron.

"I don't believe that was an angel, after all," he said.

"No!" said the mother. "But she may be one some day. She is young yet."

"I am tired!" said the child. "Will you carry me home, Mother?"

"Why, yes!" said the mother. "That is what I came for."

The child put his arms round his mother's neck, and she held him tight and trudged along the road, singing the song he liked best.

Suddenly he looked up in her face.

"Mother," he said, "I don't suppose *you* could be an angel, could you?"

"Oh, what a foolish child!" said the mother. "Who ever heard of an angel in a blue gingham apron?" And she went on singing, and stepped out so bravely on her lame foot that no one would ever have known she was lame.

•

APPIUS

Retold by H. Twitchell

This Roman legend reminds us that life provides opportunities for children to return the love and nurture given to them by their parents. The story echoes an even earlier incident that has become one of the immortal images of classical literature—that of Aeneas, the founder of Rome, bearing his aged father, Anchises, out of the burning ruins of Troy at the close of the Trojan War.

At the time when the Roman Republic was nearing its ruin and the Empire was about to be born, many innocent persons fell victims to the general misrule. They were proscribed and banished for the slightest offense, and their property was confiscated by the state.

Among the proscribed ones was an old man who had always been held in great respect by all. He had twice served as consul, and had grown old and infirm in the service of the state. When the

Triumvirs who ruled Rome decreed that he should leave the city forever, he could scarcely believe that men could be so ungrateful.

He had not the strength to undertake a long journey, so he decided to remain in his house, although he knew that his disobedience would be punished by death.

His son, young Appius, who was absent from the city, heard of the danger threatening his venerable parent. He hastened home at once to try to save his father, who at first refused to listen to his plea.

"Why should I seek death in a foreign land, when I can find it here?" he said. "With my infirmities, I could not get beyond the walls, even if I wished to do so. I should be killed in the streets, and I would rather die in my bed."

The evening of the last day that he was to be permitted to remain came. The son again urged his father to save himself.

"I know you cannot walk," said the boy, "but I can carry you. Trust yourself to me, and strength will be given me to bear you out of the city."

The father at last yielded to his son's entreaties. Taking his precious burden on his back, Appius walked through the streets of Rome, applauded by the multitude. Moved by the sight of this filial devotion, those in power did not interfere with the passage of the pair.

The hour was fast approaching when the old man was to meet death if found within the city walls, and the two were yet a long way from the gates. The boy bent under his load, and his strength was nearly exhausted. Still he pressed on, cheered by the cries of the populace, and a few seconds before the expiration of the allotted time, he passed out of the city.

Still the old consul was not safe, as he was not to remain in Roman territory. Under cover of night, Appius carried him to the seashore, where they embarked for Sicily.

This devoted act was inscribed in the annals of the Republic, so that it might not be forgotten. When Appius became a man, he was recalled to Rome, where he held many important positions.

•

THE LITTLE GIRL WHO DARED

Henry W. Lanier

This story reminds us that home is where your loved ones are, even in a prairie schooner crossing the desert. And it reminds us that love of family is the engine of much courage in the world. The scene is one in a chain of incidents that led to the most famous disaster of the overland pioneer crossings. Virginia Reed's act of love and bravery had enormous consequences for the Donner Party. Later, in the winter of 1846–1847, when snows trapped the group in the Sierra Mountains, Virginia's father led relief efforts to save his family and former comrades. Forty of the eighty-seven emigrants survived the cold and hunger, little Virginia among them.

Three years before the gold discovery at Sutter's Mill drew thousands across the continent, a prairie caravan was laboring over the desolate Nevada sandhills, west of the Humboldt River.

It was composed of a party of more than eighty men, women, and children, who had split off from a large caravan at Fort Bridger, lured by reports of a much shorter route. Among them was James T. Reed, with his wife and daughter, and two families named Donner.

Reed's oxen, crazed with thirst, had dashed off into the wastes of Salt Lake Desert, and disappeared forever. Indians had just stolen more oxen at the Humboldt sink. The travelling was exhausting. Men's nerves had become frazzled.

Another of the endless succession of sand dunes appeared ahead.

The cattle were so weary that it had become customary to put a double team to each wagon in pulling up these sandy hills; and since this made twice the number of trips, it was very exasperating to the teamsters.

Wearily the drivers halted, and prepared to unhitch and double up. But one man, named Snyder, swore he wouldn't bother with it; he started his oxen up the incline with shouts and loud crackings of his whip. The straining beasts labored up the slope, the heavy wagon wheels sinking deep in the soft, binding sand. It was too much, even for their patient strength. They stopped, exhausted and blown. The driver's utmost urgings and savage lashings could not force them a foot farther.

Wild with sullen rage, Snyder began to belabor the poor beasts unmercifully. Reed, who had gone on over the brow of the hill to pick out a road ahead, came back to witness the man's brutal abuse of the meek creatures, who, with gasping breath and rolling eyes, tried to shrink away from the blows which he rained on their heads and shoulders with the butt end of his heavy whip handle.

The useless cruelty was too much for Reed. He tried to quiet the driver, who was working himself into a frenzy where it seemed probable he would kill one or more of the oxen outright.

This interference snapped Snyder's already quivering nerves. Leaping to the wagon tongue, he turned his fury on Reed. Three times he brought his hickory handle savagely down on the other man's head, till the blood streamed from the scalp wounds.

Instinctively, Reed's wife rushed forward. Snyder was blind with rage by this time; the next blow fell upon her head.

Seeing the maniac raise his bludgeon for still another blow, Reed drew his hunting knife, and tackled him as if he were the wild beast he was imitating. The quick thrust entered Snyder's side, killing him almost instantly.

The men of the party held an informal court. The dead body spoke more loudly to them than the provocation which had brought on the tragedy. With a cowardice that declared for the uttermost penalty, yet strove to dodge the direct responsibility, the majority came to a singular and frightful decision.

A committee announced to Reed that he was to go forth alone into the surrounding desert, with nothing but the clothes he wore.

This meant death by slow torture. Without food, water, gun, ammunition, or bedding, a solitary man in that encompassing infinity of sand had nothing to expect but to perish through starvation and the unspeakable, lingering agonies of thirst. But it enabled his judges to preserve a faint pretense of his having wandered off of his own volition.

Reed refused. Any man who had come across those hundreds of miles of desert would unhesitatingly have chosen to stand up before a firing squad in preference to this protracted suicide.

But his overwhelmed wife, catching desperately at any straw, begged him so piteously to take this forlorn chance, that he finally accepted the verdict.

Mrs. Reed's pleadings made his executioners relent to the extent of permitting him to take a horse, instead of going on foot.

So he fared forth under the blazing sun to meet what seemed like an inexorable sentence.

Wife and twelve-year-old daughter watched him disappear into the pitiless desert. Then they went back to their own wagon, where the sight of every article seemed to bring a fresh pang. The leaders of the party were human enough, and they tried to show a rough sympathy for the suffering pair, but it was only too evident that any open professions were a painful mockery. They presently withdrew and the mother and daughter were left as alone and isolated as if there were some contagious disease in their canvas-roofed home on wheels.

Automatically, habit drove them to preparations for supper. Trying to support each other by encouraging hopes that deceived neither, they choked down the rough food.

Presently, Virginia, who had disappeared for a short while before sundown, looked up at her mother's tearstained face.

"Mamma," said she resolutely, "I'm going out to find Father and take him something to eat as well as his gun and pistols."

"What do you mean, child?" exclaimed Mrs. Reed. "You can't find your father."

"Yes, I can," insisted the girl. "I'm not going alone; I've asked Milt, and he's going with me."

Mrs. Reed protested. It seemed like merely adding a last horror to this nightmare day.

But twelve-year-old Virginia had made up her mind. She knew the Vigilance Committee had stationed guards to see that no attempt was made to interfere with the punishment; she was full of childish tremors at the thought of the night-enfolded desert and the wild beasts that howled through the darkness; but her daddy was out there with nothing to eat—and she was going to do something to help him no matter what happened.

When the camp was quiet and all the children who might run in were asleep, she got together what their scanty stock offered—a piece of bacon, some crackers, coffee, and sugar. A tin cup, the gun and pistols, and some ammunition were collected. Next a lantern and a supply of matches.

Her mother lay helpless, watching these preparations in increasing doubt.

"How will you find him this dark night?" she whispered.

"I'll look for the horse's tracks and follow them."

The woman shook her head hopelessly.

But just then soft footsteps sounded outside. They listened, breathless. A gentle rap came against the wagon.

"That's Milt now," whispered Virginia.

Carefully she gathered up the weapons and handed them to a silent figure outside. In silence she hugged her mother, who murmured a few words of prayer. Descending cautiously, she and the friendly Milton set out on their difficult mission.

The flare of many fires lit up little circles in the encompassing blackness, amid which the canvas wagoncovers loomed with ghostly dimness. Taking advantage of the shadows, they crept toward the outer edge of the circle.

Ahead the flickering light of the fires showed the guard, tramping back and forth, the only moving sign of life in the whole encampment. To one side of him the shadow of the wagons stretched out into the solid black wall of the solitudes that surrounded all.

Lying flat, they wormed their way noiselessly forward to pass this danger point. A horse stamped restlessly behind. The sentry stopped short. Virginia and Milton froze to the ground like frightened partridge chicks. The man scanned the motionless camp; he turned for a long gaze outward into the void night; then he resumed his monotonous beat.

Hardly daring to draw a breath, the two again wriggled ahead, serpent-wise. The guard was left behind. They ventured to crawl on hands and knees. They were out into the open: rising to their feet, they hastened on across the sand, and were swallowed up in the sea of darkness.

When they had reached a safe distance Virginia touched her companion's arm.

"Let's light the lantern," she whispered.

Standing between it and the camp, Milton lit the candle in the lantern. The girl took it and, covering it with her skirt so that it shone only downward, began to walk to and fro, searching this tiny moving circle of illumination for the horse's footprints.

It was hard to find. Back and forth and farther out she looked in vain. The care necessary to prevent a flash of the lantern's light from reaching the guard and at the same time scrutinize every foot of the ground was confusing amid the obscurity. They had slowly worked their way completely around the camp when a low exclamation of delight came from Virginia.

There was a hoofprint in the loose sand. Kneeling down, she

made sure. A little farther on the marks were plain. Relieved and eager, they hastened in that direction.

It was a long journey, with no landmarks to show the progress, and the inevitable loss of time when they occasionally lost the trail. Mile after mile they followed these mute guides, which seemed to lead on into an endless nowhere. The mournful howls of marauding coyotes made the child shudder every time they moaned across the plain. The shrill, savage screech of a mountain lion seemed even more threatening, as it split the silence close beside them. She knew well that there were prowling wolves about, dangerous on their night roamings. Even Milton, who scorned these night prowlers like any stout frontier boy, stopped paralyzed with fear when, a little later, another sound came which was made by no wild beast, but a far more dangerous animal; they judged it to mean the presence, not far off, of one of the Indian bands who had been lurking about their advance to pick off straggling humans or cattle.

But even this most excruciating terror of childhood was not as compelling as the thought of her father, alone and hungry and unarmed among these dangers.

They stopped for a few moments, dreading to hear the war-whoop. All was silent. Virginia started on again.

For what seemed like hours they labored on.

At last the girl gave a cry, pointing ahead.

"There's Papa!" she exclaimed.

Milton scanned the blackness. "It's a fire, sure enough."

Neither gave vent to the thought which presently flashed upon them that the tiny point of light off there might be kindled by the Indians who loomed so large in their minds. Reassuring themselves by again studying the footprints that had led them so far, they hurried toward this beacon.

A disconsolate figure sat hunched over in front of the blaze, head between hands.

As the two drew near it suddenly sprang up, and Reed gazed wonderingly out from his circle of light, expecting some attack.

And then a slender little figure, dropping the lantern to the ground, sped out of the encircling blackness into her daddy's arms.

Sorely against her will, Virginia started back for the camp with her companion at the first break of dawn.

But she had the proud satisfaction of seeing her father, with the fresh courage and confidence she had brought him, ride off westward with better than a fighting chance of escape.

The Donner party which had cast him out was destined, after a ghastly struggle, to leave half its members dead among the cruel snows of the winter Sierras; but plucky little Virginia was one of the half which finally reached the pleasant valleys of California.

•

DR. JOHNSON AND HIS FATHER
James Baldwin

English poet, critic, essayist, and lexicographer Samuel Johnson (1709–1784) was regarded by many contemporaries as the leading man of letters of his time. His reputation for brilliant and witty conversation remains unsurpassed to this day. The man of great learning added this realization to his store of wisdom: An opportunity for love and duty brushed aside in childhood can live as a deep regret long into adulthood. As recounted in this moving story, Johnson's father was a respected but rather unsuccessful bookseller.

I

It is in a little bookshop in the city of Lichfield, England. The floor has just been swept and the shutter taken down from the one small window. The hour is early, and customers have not yet begun to drop in. Out of doors the rain is falling.

At a small table near the door, a feeble, white-haired old man is making up some packages of books. As he arranges them in a large basket, he stops now and then as though disturbed by pain. He puts his hand to his side, coughs in a most distressing way, then sits down and rests himself, leaning his elbows upon the table.

"Samuel!" he calls.

In the farther corner of the room there is a young man busily reading from a large book that is spread open before him. He is a very odd-looking fellow, perhaps eighteen years of age, but you would take him to be older. He is large and awkward, with a great round face, scarred and marked by a strange disease. His eyesight must be poor, for, as he reads, he bends down until his face is quite near the printed page.

"Samuel!" again the old man calls.

But Samuel makes no reply. He is so deeply interested in his book that he does not hear. The old man rests himself a little longer and then finishes tying his packages. He lifts the heavy basket and sets it on the table. The exertion brings on another fit of coughing; and when it is over he calls for the third time, "Samuel!"

"What is it, Father?" This time the call is heard.

"You know, Samuel," he says, "that tomorrow is market day at Uttoxeter, and our stall must be attended to. Some of our friends will be there to look at the new books which they expect me to bring. One of us must go down on the stage this morning and get everything in readiness. But I hardly feel able for the journey. My cough troubles me quite a little, and you see that it is raining very hard."

"Yes, Father; I am sorry," answers Samuel; and his face is again bent over the book.

"I thought perhaps you would go down to the market, and that I might stay here at the shop," says his father. But Samuel does not hear. He is deep in the study of some Latin classic.

The old man goes to the door and looks out. The rain is still falling. He shivers, and buttons his coat.

It is a twenty-mile ride to Uttoxeter. In five minutes the stage will pass the door.

"Samuel, will you not go down to the market for me this time?"

The old man is putting on his great coat.

He is reaching for his hat.

The basket is on his arm.

He casts a beseeching glance at his son, hoping that he will relent at the last moment.

"Here comes the coach, Samuel." And the old man is choked by another fit of coughing.

Whether Samuel hears or not, I do not know. He is still reading, and he makes no sign nor motion.

The stage comes rattling down the street.

The old man with his basket of books staggers out of the door. The stage halts for a moment while he climbs inside. Then the driver swings his whip, and all are away.

Samuel, in the shop, still bends over his book.

Out of doors the rain is falling.

II

Just fifty years have passed, and again it is market day at Uttox-eter.

The rain is falling in the streets. The people who have wares to sell huddle under the eaves and in the stalls and booths that have roofs above them.

A chaise from Lichfield pulls up at the entrance to the market square.

An old man alights. One would guess him to be seventy years of age. He is large and not well-shaped. His face is seamed and scarred, and he makes strange grimaces as he clambers out of the chaise. He wheezes and puffs as though afflicted with asthma. He walks with the aid of a heavy stick.

With slow but ponderous strides he enters the market place and looks around. He seems not to know that the rain is falling.

He looks at the little stalls ranged along the walls of the market place. Some have roofs over them and are the centers of noisy trade. Others have fallen into disuse and are empty.

The stranger halts before one of the latter. "Yes, this is it," he says. He has a strange habit of talking aloud to himself. "I remember it well. It was here that my father, on certain market days, sold books to the clergy of the county. The good men came from every parish to see his wares and to hear him describe their contents."

He turns abruptly around. "Yes, this is the place," he repeats.

He stands quite still and upright, directly in front of the little old stall. He takes off his hat and holds it beneath his arm. His great walking stick has fallen into the gutter. He bows his head and clasps his hands. He does not seem to know that the rain is falling.

The clock in the tower above the market strikes eleven. The passersby stop and gaze at the stranger. The market people peer at him from their booths and stalls. Some laugh as the rain runs in streams down his scarred old cheeks. Rain is it? Or can it be tears?

Boys hoot at him. Some of the ruder ones even hint at throwing mud; but a sense of shame withholds them from the act.

"He is a poor lunatic. Let him alone," say the more compassionate.

The rain falls upon his bare head and his broad shoulders. He is drenched and chilled. But he stands motionless and silent, looking neither to the right nor to the left.

"Who is that old fool?" asks a thoughtless young man who chances to be passing.

"Do you ask who he is?" answers a gentleman from London. "Why, he is Dr. Samuel Johnson, the most famous man in England. It was he who wrote *Rasselas* and the *Lives of the Poets* and *Irene* and many another work which all men are praising. It was he who made the great *English Dictionary,* the most wonderful book of our times. In London, the noblest lords and ladies take pleasure in doing him honor. He is the literary lion of England."

"Then why does he come to Uttoxeter and stand thus in the pouring rain?"

"I cannot tell you. But doubtless he has reasons for doing so." And the gentleman passes on.

At length there is a lull in the storm. The birds are chirping among the housetops. The people wonder if the rain is over, and venture out into the slippery street.

The clock in the tower above the market strikes twelve. The renowned stranger has stood a whole hour motionless in the market place. And again the rain is falling.

Slowly now he returns his hat to his head. He finds his walking stick where it had fallen. He lifts his eyes reverently for a moment, and then, with a lordly, lumbering motion, walks down the street to meet the chaise which is ready to return to Lichfield.

We follow him through the pattering rain to his native town.

"Why, Dr. Johnson!" exclaims his hostess, "we have missed you all day. And you are so wet and chilled! Where have you been?"

"Madam," says the great man, "fifty years ago, this very day, I tacitly refused to oblige or obey my father. The thought of the pain which I must have caused him has haunted me ever since. To do away the sin of that hour, I this morning went in a chaise to Uttoxeter and did do penance publicly before the stall which my father had formerly used."

The great man bows his head upon his hands and sobs.

Out of doors the rain is falling.

•

THE WOUNDED PINE TREE
Babrius

This fable is told by Babrius, a Greek poet who penned several
Aesop-like fables around the second century.

Deep in the forest, a woodcutter was cutting down a stout old
pine. With each blow of his ax, the giant tree shuddered and cursed
the cold, hard steel that splintered its side.

It was a tough old tree. After a while the woodsman inserted a
large, wooden wedge into the cut in order to pry the trunk apart.
He pounded away at the wedge; amid a great ripping and splinter-
ing, the noble pine toppled and hurtled toward the ground. As it
fell, it groaned:

"How can I blame the ax, which is no kin of mine, as much as
this wicked wedge, which is my own brother?"

*Pain inflicted by outsiders is never so terrible as suffering
caused by one's own kin.*

•

A FATHER'S RETURN

This wonderful story is told in many different versions in African
folklore. This one reminds us that the essence of home and hearth
is one soul reaching for another. And it reminds us that the need
of a son for his father ought to be one of the strongest ties that
bind a family.

There once was a man who considered himself the happiest
man alive because he had a loving wife and four healthy sons. The
oldest son was named Keen-Eyes because he could follow tracks
through field and jungle better than anyone else in the village. The
second son was known as Sharp-Ears because he knew best the call
of every creature in the wilderness. The third son was named
Strong-Arms because he never failed to win any contest of strength.

The fourth son was only a baby, but his father was sure the boy would grow up to be as skilled and devoted as his brothers.

One morning the family woke to discover the father had disappeared. By nightfall he had not returned, and the next morning brought no sign of his whereabouts.

They talked it over and wondered where he might have gone.

"Perhaps he decided to go visit our uncle," said Keen-Eyes, shrugging his shoulders.

"Or maybe he went to the festival in the next village," suggested Sharp-Ears.

"Or he may have gone into the hills, to enjoy the cool mountain breezes," said Strong-Arms.

Their mother remained quiet and shook her head uncertainly.

Another day passed, then a week, and still their father did not return. Sometimes his sons wondered out loud where he might have gone, but after a while they did not talk about it any longer. They feared he was dead.

But the youngest son had no such thoughts, and one morning, as he sat on his mother's lap, he opened his mouth and spoke his first words:

"Where is Father? I want to see my father."

His older brothers gazed at him.

"That's right," said Keen-Eyes. "Where is Father?"

"Some harm may have come to him," said Sharp-Ears.

"We really should go look for him," suggested Strong-Arms.

The three older brothers started out at once, following a path deep into the jungle.

"Look, he came this way," pointed Keen-Eyes. "I can see his tracks on the trail." He led his brothers over hills and into valleys, through fields and woods, farther and farther from home. But at last the tracks disappeared, and even Keen-Eyes lost the trail.

"We must give up," he declared.

"Wait!" urged Sharp-Ears. "I hear someone crying out."

He led his brothers even deeper into the wilderness, farther than they had ever ventured before, pausing every now and then to strain for the sound only he could hear.

At last they came upon a river, and beside it lay their father, holding a growling leopard at bay with his spear!

"We must save him!" yelled Strong-Arms, and without waiting for his brothers he threw himself onto the pouncing beast and crushed it in his mighty grasp.

"You came just in time," gasped their father. "I came into the jungle to hunt but fell and hurt my leg. I could not make it home. I've lived on what food I could find, but my strength was failing, and the leopard had moved in for the kill."

His sons dressed his wounded leg, brought food to build his strength, and carried him home to their village. Everyone listened to the story of how Keen-Eyes, Sharp-Ears, and Strong-Arms had saved their father, and everyone praised their skill and devotion.

But the fame went to the brothers' heads, and they began to argue among themselves about who was the most responsible for their father's rescue.

"If it were not for me, we would never have known which way to look," boasted Keen-Eyes. "I followed his trail deep into the jungle."

"Yes, but you lost it," reminded Sharp-Ears. "I heard him crying out and led us to the river."

"But what good would that have done if I had not been there?" asked Strong-Arms. "I was the one who killed the leopard and saved our father from certain death."

They debated among themselves, and at last asked their father himself to decide who was the most responsible for his return.

He listened to their arguing and then raised his hand for quiet.

"To all three of you I owe my life," he told them, "for you each played a part in my rescue. But if you ask which of my sons did the most to bring me home, I must tell you it is not you, Sharp-Eyes, nor you, Keen-Ears, not even you, Strong-Arms. The one who truly brought me home is here."

He took his youngest son into his arms.

Then everyone recalled that this was the son whose first words had been, "Where is Father?" It was the little boy's loving heart that had brought his father home.

•

SIMON'S FATHER

Guy de Maupassant

This nineteenth-century story of a boy without a father has truths
for all times, perhaps most poignantly for the late twentieth century, when fatherlessness is epidemic. Little boys want to be men,
but they need good men to show them how. The lucky boys have
such men as fathers.

Noon had just struck. The school door opened and the youngsters tumbled out, rolling over each other in their haste to get out
quickly. But instead of promptly dispersing and going home to
dinner as was their daily wont, they stopped a few paces off, broke
up into knots and set to whispering.

The fact was that that morning Simon, the son of La Blanchotte,
had, for the first time, attended school.

They had all of them in their families heard talk of La Blanchotte; and, although in public she was welcome enough, the mothers among themselves treated her with compassion of a somewhat
disdainful kind, which the children had caught without in the least
knowing why.

As for Simon himself, they did not know him, for he never
went abroad, and did not go galloping about with them through
the streets of the village or along the banks of the river. Therefore,
they loved him but little; and it was with a certain delight, mingled
with considerable astonishment, that they met and that they recited
to each other this phrase, set afoot by a lad of fourteen or fifteen
who appeared to know all, all about it, so sagaciously did he wink.
"You know . . . Simon . . . well, he has no father."

La Blanchotte's son appeared in his turn upon the threshold of
the school.

He was seven or eight years old. He was rather pale, very neat,
with a timid and almost awkward manner.

He was on the point of making his way back to his mother's
house when the groups of his schoolfellows perpetually whispering
and watching him with the mischievous and heartless eyes of children bent upon playing a nasty trick, gradually surrounded him and
ended by enclosing him altogether. There he stood fixed amidst

them, surprised and embarrassed, not understanding what they were going to do with him. But the lad who had brought the news, puffed up with the success he had met with already, demanded, "How do you name yourself, you?"

He answered, "Simon."

"Simon what?" retorted the other.

The child, altogether bewildered, repeated, "Simon."

The lad shouted at him, "One is named Simon something . . . that is not a name . . . Simon indeed."

And he, on the brink of tears, replied for the third time, "I am named Simon."

The urchins fell a-laughing. The lad triumphantly lifted up his voice. "You can see plainly that he has no father."

A deep silence ensued. The children were dumbfounded by this extraordinary, impossible monstrous thing—a boy who had not a father; they looked upon him as a phenomenon, an unnatural being, and they felt that contempt, until then inexplicable, of their mothers for La Blanchotte grow upon them. As for Simon, he had propped himself against a tree to avoid falling and he remained as though struck to the earth by an irreparable disaster. He sought to explain, but he could think of no answer for them, to deny this horrible charge that he had no father. At last he shouted at them quite recklessly, "Yes, I have one."

"Where is he?" demanded the boy.

Simon was silent. He did not know. The children roared, tremendously excited; and these sons of toil, most nearly related to animals, experienced that cruel craving which animates the fowls of a farmyard to destroy one among themselves as soon as it is wounded. Simon suddenly espied a little neighbor, the son of a widow, whom he had always seen, as he himself was to be seen, quite alone with his mother.

"And no more have you," he said, "no more have you a father."

"Yes," replied the other, "I have one."

"Where is he?" rejoined Simon.

"He is dead," declared the brat with superb dignity, "he is in the cemetery, is my father."

A murmur of approval rose amidst the scapegraces, as if this fact of possessing a father dead in a cemetery had caused their comrade to grow big enough to crush the other one who had no father at all. And these rogues, whose fathers were for the most part evil-doers, drunkards, thieves and ill-treaters of their wives, hustled each other as they pressed closer and closer, as though they, the legitimate ones, would stifle in their pressure one who was beyond the law.

He who chanced to be next to Simon suddenly put his tongue out at him with a waggish air and shouted at him, "No father! No father!"

Simon seized him by the hair with both hands and set to work to demolish his legs with kicks, while he bit his cheek ferociously. A tremendous struggle ensued between the two combatants, and Simon found himself beaten, torn, bruised, rolled on the ground in the middle of the ring of applauding vagabonds. As he arose, mechanically brushing his little shirt all covered with dust with his hand, someone shouted at him, "Go and tell your father."

He then felt a great sinking in his heart. They were stronger than he was, they had beaten him and he had no answer to give them, for he knew well that it was true that he had no father. Full of pride he attempted for some moments to struggle against the tears which were suffocating him. He had a choking fit, and then without cries he commenced to weep with great sobs which shook him incessantly. Then a ferocious joy broke out among his enemies, and, naturally, just as with savages in their fearful festivals, they took each other by the hand and set about dancing in a circle about him as they repeated as a refrain, "No father! No father!"

But Simon quite suddenly ceased sobbing. Frenzy overtook him. There were stones under his feet. He picked them up and with all his strength hurled them at his tormentors. Two or three were struck and rushed off yelling, and so formidable did he appear that the rest became panic stricken. Cowards, as a crowd always is in the presence of an exasperated man, they broke up and fled. Left alone, the little thing without a father set off running toward the fields, for a recollection had been awakened which brought his soul to a great determination. He made up his mind to drown himself in the river.

He remembered, in fact, that eight days before a poor devil who begged for his livelihood, had thrown himself into the water because he had no more money. Simon had been there when they had fished him out again; and the sight of the fellow, who usually seemed to him so miserable, and ugly, had then struck him—his pale cheeks, his long drenched beard and his open eyes being full of calm. The bystanders had said, "He is dead."

And someone had said, "He is quite happy now."

And Simon wished to drown himself also because he had no father, just like the wretched being who had no money.

He reached the neighborhood of the water and watched it flowing. Some fishes were sporting briskly in the clear stream and occasionally made a little bound and caught the flies flying on the surface. He stopped crying in order to watch them, for their housewifery interested him vastly. But, at intervals, as in the changes of a tempest, altering suddenly from tremendous gusts of wind, which snap off the trees and then lose themselves in the horizon, this thought would return to him with intense pain, "I am about to drown myself because I have no father."

It was very warm and fine weather. The pleasant sunshine warmed the grass. The water shone like a mirror. And Simon enjoyed some minutes the happiness of that languor which follows weeping, in which he felt very desirous of falling asleep there upon the grass in the warmth.

A little green frog leapt from under his feet. He endeavored to catch it. It escaped him. He followed it and lost it three times following. At last he caught it by one of its hind legs and began to laugh as he saw the efforts the creature made to escape. It gathered itself up on its large legs and then with a violent spring suddenly stretched them out as stiff as two bars; while, its eye wide open in its round, golden circle, it beat the air with its front limbs which worked as though they were hands. It reminded him of a toy made with straight slips of wood nailed zigzag one on the other, which by a similar movement regulated the exercise of the little soldiers stuck thereon. Then he thought of his home and next of his mother, and overcome by a great sorrow he again began to weep. His limbs trembled; and he placed himself on his knees and said his prayers as before going to bed. But he was unable to finish them, for such hurried and violent sobs overtook him that he was completely overwhelmed. He thought no more, he no longer saw anything around him and was wholly taken up in crying.

Suddenly a heavy hand was placed upon his shoulder, and a rough voice asked him, "What is it that causes you so much grief, my fine fellow?"

Simon turned round. A tall workman with a black beard and hair all curled, was staring at him good naturedly. He answered with his eyes and throat full of tears, "They have beaten me . . . because . . . I . . . have no . . . father . . . no father."

"What!" said the man smiling, "why, everybody has one."

The child answered painfully amidst his spasms of grief, "But I
... I ... I have none."

Then the workman became serious. He had recognized La
Blanchotte's son, and although but recently come to the neighborhood he had a vague idea of her history.

"Well," said he, "console yourself, my boy, and come with me
home to your mother. They will give you ... a father."

And so they started on the way, the big one holding the little
one by the hand, and the man smiled afresh, for he was not sorry
to see this Blanchotte, who was, it was said, one of the prettiest girls
of the countryside, and, perhaps, he said to himself, at the bottom
of his heart, that a lass who had erred might very well err again.

They arrived in front of a little and very neat white house.

"There it is," exclaimed the child, and he cried "Mamma."

A woman appeared and the workman instantly left off smiling,
for he at once perceived that there was no more fooling to be done
with the tall pale girl who stood austerely at her door as though to
defend from one man the threshold of that house where she had
already been betrayed by another. Intimidated, his cap in his hand,
he stammered out, "See, madam, I have brought back your little
boy, who had lost himself near the river."

But Simon flung his arms about his mother's neck and told
her, as he again began to cry, "No, Mamma, I wished to drown
myself, because the others had beaten me ... had beaten me ...
because I have no father."

A burning redness covered the young woman's cheeks, and,
hurt to the quick, she embraced her child passionately, while the
tears coursed down her face. The man, much moved, stood there,
not knowing how to get away. But Simon suddenly ran to him and
said, "Will you be my father?"

A deep silence ensued. La Blanchotte, dumb and tortured with shame, leaned herself against the wall, both her hands upon her heart. The child, seeing that no answer was made him, replied, "If you do not wish it, I shall return to drown myself."

The workman took the matter as a jest and answered laughing, "Why, yes, I wish it certainly."

"What is your name, then?" went on the child, "so that I may tell the others when they wish to know your name?"

"Phillip," answered the man.

Simon was silent a moment so that he might get the name well into his head; then he stretched out his arms quite consoled as he said; "Well, then, Phillip, you are my father."

The workman, lifting him from the ground, kissed him hastily on both cheeks, and then made off very quickly with great strides.

When the child returned to school next day he was received with a spiteful laugh, and at the end of school when the lads were on the point of recommencing, Simon threw these words at their heads as he would have done a stone, "He is named Phillip, my father."

Yells of delight burst out from all sides.

"Phillip who? . . . Phillip what? What on earth is Phillip? Where did you pick up your Phillip?"

Simon answered nothing; and immovable in faith he defied them with his eye, ready to be martyred rather than fly before them. The schoolmaster came to his rescue and he returned home to his mother.

During three months, the tall workman, Phillip, frequently passed by the Blanchotte's house, and sometimes he made bold to speak to her when he saw her sewing near the window. She answered him civilly, always sedately, never joking with him, nor permitting him to enter her house. Notwithstanding which, being, like all men, a bit of a coxcomb, he imagined that she was often rosier than usual when she chatted with him.

But a fallen reputation is so difficult to recover and always remains so fragile that, in spite of the shy reserve La Blanchotte maintained, they already gossiped in the neighborhood.

As for Simon, he loved his new father much, and walked with him nearly every evening when the day's work was done. He went regularly to school and mixed with great dignity with his schoolfellows without ever answering them back.

One day, however, the lad who had first attacked him said to him, "You have lied. You have not a father named Phillip."

"Why do you say that? demanded Simon, much disturbed.

The youth rubbed his hands. He replied, "Because if you had one he would be your mamma's husband."

Simon was confused by the truth of this reasoning, nevertheless he retorted, "He is my father all the same."

"That can very well be," exclaimed the urchin with a sneer, "but that is not being your father altogether."

La Blanchotte's little one bowed his head and went off dreaming in the direction of the forge belonging to old Loizon, where Phillip worked.

This forge was as though entombed in trees. It was very dark there, the red glare of a formidable furnace alone lit up with great flashes five blacksmiths, who hammered upon their anvils with a terrible din. They were standing enveloped in flame, like demons, their eyes fixed on the red-hot iron they were pounding; and their dull ideas rose and fell with their hammers.

Simon entered without being noticed and went quietly to pluck his friend by the sleeve. He turned himself round. All at once the work came to a standstill and all the men looked on very attentive. Then, in the midst of this unaccustomed silence, rose the little slender pipe of Simon; "Phillip, explain to me what the lad at La Michande has just told me, that you are not altogether my father."

"And why that?" asked the smith.

The child replied with all its innocence, "Because you are not my mamma's husband."

No one laughed. Philip remained standing, leaning his forehead upon the back of his great hands, which supported the handle of his hammer standing upright upon the anvil. He mused. His four companions watched him, and, quite a tiny mite among these giants, Simon anxiously waited. Suddenly, one of the smiths, answering to the sentiment of all, said to Phillip, "La Blanchotte is all the same a good and honest girl, and stalwart and steady in spite of her misfortune, and one who would make a worthy wife for an honest man."

"That is true," remarked the three others.

The smith continued, "Is it this girl's fault if she has fallen? She had been promised marriage and I know more than one who is much respected today, and who sinned every bit as much."

"That is true," responded the three men in chorus. He resumed, "How hard she has toiled, poor thing, to educate her lad all alone, and how much she has wept since she no longer goes out, save to go to church, God only knows."

"This also is true," said the others.

Then no more was heard than the bellows which fanned the fire of the furnace. Phillip hastily bent himself down to Simon. "Go and tell your mamma that I shall come to speak to her."

Then he pushed the child out by the shoulders. He returned to his work and with a single blow the five hammers again fell upon their anvils. Thus they wrought the iron until nightfall, strong, powerful, happy, like hammers satisfied. But just as the great bell of a cathedral resounds upon feast days above the jingling of the other bells, so Phillip's hammer, dominating the noise of the others, clanged second after second with a deafening uproar. And he, his eye on fire, plied his trade vigorously, erect amid the sparks.

The sky was full of stars as he knocked at La Blanchotte's door. He had his Sunday blouse on, a fresh shirt, and his beard was trimmed. The young woman showed herself upon the threshold and said in a grieved tone, "It is ill to come thus when night has fallen, Mr. Phillip."

He wished to answer, but stammered and stood confused before her.

She resumed, "And still you understand quite well that it will not do that I should be talked about any more."

Then he said all at once, "What does that matter to me, if you will be my wife!"

No voice replied to him, but he believed that he heard in the shadow of the room the sound of a body that sank down. He entered very quickly; and Simon, who had gone to his bed, distinguished the sound of a kiss and some words that his mother said very softly. Then he suddenly found himself lifted up by the hands of his friend, who, holding him at the length of his herculean arms, exclaimed to him, "You will tell them, your schoolfellows, that your father is Phillip Remy, the blacksmith, and that he will pull the ears of all who do you any harm."

On the morrow, when the school was full and lessons were about to begin, little Simon stood up quite pale with trembling lips. "My father," said he in a clear voice, "is Phillip Remy, the blacksmith, and he has promised to box the ears of all who do me any harm."

This time no one laughed any longer, for he was very well known, was Phillip Remy, the blacksmith, and was a father of whom anyone in the world would have been proud.

•

FATHER

Edgar Guest

**Often we do not fully recognize some of the important lessons of
home and hearth until those who have taught us are gone.**

Used to wonder just why father
   Never had much time for play,
Used to wonder why he'd rather
   Work each minute of the day.
Used to wonder why he never
   Loafed along the road an' shirked;
Can't recall a time whenever
   Father played while others worked.

Father didn't dress in fashion,
   Sort of hated clothing new;
Style with him was not a passion;
   He had other things in view.
Boys are blind to much that's going
   On about 'em day by day,
And I had no way of knowing
   What became of father's pay.

All I knew was when I needed
   Shoes I got 'em on the spot;
Everything for which I pleaded,
   Somehow, father always got.
Wondered, season after season,
   Why he never took a rest,
And that *I* might be the reason
   Then I never even guessed.

Father set a store on knowledge;
   If he'd lived to have his way
He'd have sent me off to college
   And the bills been glad to pay.

That, I know, was his ambition:
  Now and then he used to say
He'd have done his earthly mission
  On my graduation day.

Saw his cheeks were getting paler,
  Didn't understand just why;
Saw his body growing frailer,
  Then at last I saw him die.
Rest had come! His tasks were ended
  Calm was written on his brow;
Father's life was big and splendid,
  And I understand it now.

•

THE DROVER'S WIFE

Henry Lawson

In this story by Australian writer Henry Lawson (1867–1922), our hearts are touched by a lone mother's struggle to make a safe place for her children. And we are moved by her young son's final determination that he will be there for his family. This is a tale from another age and another side of the world that remains all too relevant to our time and culture.

The two-roomed house is built of round timber, slabs, and stringy-bark, and floored with split slabs. A big bark kitchen standing at one end is larger than the house itself, verandah included.

Bush all round—bush with no horizon, for the country is flat. No ranges in the distance. The bush consists of stunted, rotten native apple-trees. No undergrowth. Nothing to relieve the eye save the darker green of a few she-oaks which are sighing above the narrow, almost waterless creek. Nineteen miles to the nearest sign of civilization—a shanty on the main road.

The drover, an ex-squatter, is away with sheep. His wife and children are left here alone.

Four ragged, dried-up-looking children are playing about the house. Suddenly one of them yells: "Snake! Mother, here's a snake!"

The gaunt, sun-browned bushwoman dashes from the kitchen, snatches her baby from the ground, holds it on her left hip, and reaches for a stick.

"Where is it?"

"Here! gone into the wood-heap!" yells the eldest boy—a sharp-faced urchin of eleven. "Stop there, Mother! I'll have him. Stand back! I'll have the beggar!"

"Tommy, come here, or you'll be bit. Come here at once when I tell you, you little wretch!"

The youngster comes reluctantly, carrying a stick bigger than himself. Then he yells, triumphantly:

"There it goes—under the house!" and darts away with club uplifted. At the same time the big, black, yellow-eyed dog-of-all-breeds, who has shown the wildest interest in the proceedings, breaks his chain and rushes after that snake. He is a moment late, however, and his nose reaches the crack in the slabs just as the end of its tail disappears. Almost at the same moment the boy's club comes down and skins the aforesaid nose. Alligator takes small notice of this, and proceeds to undermine the building; but he is subdued after a struggle and chained up. They cannot afford to lose him.

The drover's wife makes the children stand together near the doghouse while she watches for the snake. She gets two small dishes of milk and sets them down near the wall to tempt it to come out; but an hour goes by and it does not show itself.

It is near sunset, and a thunderstorm is coming. The children must be brought inside. She will not take them into the house, for she knows the snake is there, and may at any moment come up through a crack in the rough slab floor; so she carries several armfuls of firewood into the kitchen, and then takes the children there. The kitchen has no floor—or, rather, an earthen one—called a "ground floor" in this part of the bush. There is a large, roughly-made table in the centre of the place. She brings the children in, and makes them get on this table. They are two boys and two girls —mere babies. She gives them some supper, and then, before it gets dark, she goes into the house, and snatches up some pillows and bedclothes—expecting to see or lay her hand on the snake any minute. She makes a bed on the kitchen table for the children, and sits down beside it to watch all night.

She has an eye on the corner, and a green sapling club laid in readiness on the dresser by her side; also her sewing basket and a copy of the *Young Ladies' Journal.* She has brought the dog into the room.

Tommy turns in, under protest, but says he'll lie awake all night and smash that blinded snake.

His mother asks him how many times she has told him not to swear.

He has his club with him under the bedclothes, and Jacky protests:

"Mummy! Tommy's skinnin' me alive wif his club. Make him take it out."

Tommy: "Shet up, you little—! D'yer want to be bit with the snake?"

Jacky shuts up.

"If yer bit," says Tommy, after a pause, "you'll swell up, an' smell, an' turn red an' green an' blue all over till yer bust. Won't he, Mother?"

"Now then, don't frighten the child. Go to sleep," she says.

The two younger children go to sleep, and now and then Jacky complains of being "skeezed." More room is made for him. Presently Tommy says: "Mother! listen to them (adjective) little possums. I'd like to screw their blanky necks."

And Jacky protests drowsily.

"But they don't hurt us, the little blanks!"

Mother: "There, I told you you'd teach Jacky to swear." But the remark makes her smile. Jacky goes to sleep.

Presently Tommy asks:

"Mother! Do you think they'll ever extricate the (adjective) kangaroo?"

"Lord! How am I to know, child? Go to sleep."

"Will you wake me if the snake comes out?"

"Yes. Go to sleep."

Near midnight. The children are all asleep and she sits there still, sewing and reading by turns. From time to time she glances round the floor and wallplate, and, whenever she hears a noise, she reaches for the stick. The thunderstorm comes on, and the wind, rushing through the cracks in the slab wall, threatens to blow out her candle. She places it on a sheltered part of the dresser and fixes up a newspaper to protect it. At every flash of lightning, the cracks between the slabs gleam like polished silver. The thunder rolls, and the rain comes down in torrents.

Alligator lies at full length on the floor, with his eyes turned towards the partition. She knows by this that the snake is there. There are large cracks in that wall opening under the floor of the dwelling-house.

She is not a coward, but recent events have shaken her nerves. A little son of her brother-in-law was lately bitten by a snake, and died. Besides, she has not heard from her husband for six months, and is anxious about him.

He was a drover, and started squatting here when they were married. The drought of 18— ruined him. He had to sacrifice the remnant of his flock and go droving again. He intends to move his family into the nearest town when he comes back, and, in the meantime, his brother, who keeps a shanty on the main road, comes over about once a month with provisions. The wife has still a couple of cows, one horse, and a few sheep. The brother-in-law kills one of the latter occasionally, gives her what she needs of it, and takes the rest in return for other provisions.

She is used to being left alone. She once lived like this for eighteen months. As a girl she built the usual castles in the air; but all her girlish hopes and aspirations have long been dead. She finds all the excitement and recreation she needs in the *Young Ladies' Journal,* and Heaven help her! takes a pleasure in the fashion-plates.

Her husband is an Australian, and so is she. He is careless, but a good enough husband. If he had the means he would take her to the city and keep her there like a princess. They are used to being apart, or at least she is. "No use fretting," she says. He may forget sometimes that he is married; but if he has a good cheque when he comes back he will give most of it to her. When he had money he took her to the city several times—hired a railway sleeping compartment, and put up at the best hotels. He also bought her a buggy, but they had to sacrifice that along with the rest.

The last two children were born in the bush—one while her husband was bringing a drunken doctor, by force, to attend to her. She was alone on this occasion, and very weak. She had been ill with a fever. She prayed to God to send her assistance. God sent Black Mary—the "whitest" gin in all the land. Or, at least, God sent King Jimmy first, and he sent Black Mary. He put his black face round the door post, took in the situation at a glance, and said cheerfully: "All right, missus—I bring my old woman, she down alonga creek."

One of the children died while she was here alone. She rode nineteen miles for assistance, carrying the dead child.

It must be near one or two o'clock. The fire is burning low. Alligator lies with his head resting on his paws, and watches the wall. He is not a very beautiful dog, and the light shows numerous old wounds where the hair will not grow. He is afraid of nothing on the face of the earth or under it. He will tackle a bullock as readily as he will tackle a flea. He hates all other dogs—except kangaroo-dogs—and has a marked dislike to friends or relations of the family. They seldom call, however. He sometimes makes friends with strangers. He hates snakes and has killed many, but he will be bitten some day and die; most snake-dogs end that way.

Now and then the bushwoman lays down her work and watches, and listens, and thinks. She thinks of things in her own life, for there is little else to think about.

The rain will make the grass grow, and this reminds her how she fought a bush fire once while her husband was away. The grass was long, and very dry, and the fire threatened to burn her out. She put on an old pair of her husband's trousers and beat out the flames with a green bough, till great drops of sooty perspiration stood out on her forehead and ran in streaks down her blackened arms. The sight of his mother in trousers greatly amused Tommy, who worked like a little hero by her side, but the terrified baby howled lustily for his "mummy." The fire would have mastered her but for four excited bushmen who arrived in the nick of time. It was a mixed-up affair all round; when she went to take up the baby he screamed and struggled convulsively, thinking it was a "blackman"; and Alligator, trusting more to the child's sense than his own instinct, charged furiously, and (being old and slightly deaf) did not in his excitement at first recognize his mistress's voice, but continued to hang on to the moleskins until choked off by Tommy with a saddle strap. The dog's sorrow for his blunder, and his anxiety to let it be known that it was all a mistake, was as evident as his ragged tail and a twelve-inch grin could make it. It was a glorious time for the boys; a day to look back to, and talk about, and laugh over for many years.

She thinks how she fought a flood during her husband's absence. She stood for hours in the drenching downpour, and dug an overflow gutter to save the dam across the creek. But she could not save it. There are things that a bushwoman cannot do. Next morning the dam was broken, and her heart was nearly broken too, for she thought how her husband would feel when he came home and saw the result of years of labour swept away. She cried then.

She also fought the pleuro-pneumonia—dosed and bled the few remaining cattle, and wept again when her two best cows died.

Again, she fought a mad bullock that besieged the house for a day. She made bullets and fired at him through cracks in the slabs with an old shotgun. He was dead in the morning. She skinned him and got seventeen-and-sixpence for the hide.

She also fights the crows and eagles that have designs on her chickens. Her plan of campaign is very original. The children cry "Crows, Mother!" and she rushes out and aims a broomstick at the birds as though it were a gun, and says "Bung!" The crows leave in a hurry; they are cunning, but a woman's cunning is greater.

Occasionally a bushman in the horrors, or a villainous-looking sundowner, comes and nearly scares the life out of her. She generally tells the suspicious-looking stranger that her husband and two sons are at work below the dam, or over at the yard, for he always cunningly inquires for the boss.

Only last week a gallows-faced swagman—having satisfied himself that there were no men on the place—threw his swag down on the verandah, and demanded tucker. She gave him something to eat; then he expressed his intention of staying for the night. It was sundown then. She got a batten from the sofa, loosened the dog, and confronted the stranger, holding the batten in one hand and the dog's collar with the other. "Now you go!" she said. He looked at her and at the dog, said "All right, mum," in a cringing tone, and left. She was a determined-looking woman, and Alligator's yellow eyes glared unpleasantly—besides, the dog's chawing-up apparatus greatly resembled that of the reptile he was named after.

She has few pleasures to think of as she sits here alone by the fire, on guard against a snake. All days are much the same to her; but on Sunday afternoon she dresses herself, tidies the children, smartens up baby, and goes for a lonely walk along the bush track, pushing an old perambulator in front of her. She does this every Sunday. She takes as much care to make herself and the children look smart as she would if she were going to do the block in the city. There is nothing to see, however, and not a soul to meet. You might walk for twenty miles along this track without being able to fix a point in your mind, unless you are a bushman. This is because of the everlasting, maddening sameness of the stunted trees—that monotony which makes a man long to break away and travel as far as trains can go, and sail as far as ship can sail—and further.

But this bushwoman is used to the loneliness of it. As a girl-wife she hated it, but now she would feel strange away from it.

She is glad when her husband returns, but she does not gush or make a fuss about it. She gets him something good to eat, and tidies up the children.

She seems contented with her lot. She loves her children, but has no time to show it. She seems harsh to them. Her surroundings are not favorable to the development of the "womanly" or sentimental side of nature.

It must be near morning now; but the clock is in the dwelling-house. Her candle is nearly done; she forgot that she was out of candles. Some more wood must be got to keep the fire up, and so she shuts the dog inside and hurries round to the wood-heap. The rain has cleared off. She seizes a stick, pulls it out, and—crash! the whole pile collapses.

Yesterday she bargained with a stray blackfellow to bring her some wood, and while he was at work she went in search of a missing cow. She was absent an hour or so, and the native black made good use of his time. On her return she was so astonished to see a good heap of wood by the chimney, that she gave him an extra fig of tobacco, and praised him for not being lazy. He thanked her, and left with head erect and chest well out. He was the last of his tribe and a King; but he had built that wood-heap hollow.

She is hurt now, and tears spring to her eyes as she sits down again by the table. She takes up a handkerchief to wipe the tears away, but pokes her eyes with her bare fingers instead. The handkerchief is full of holes, and she finds that she has put her thumb through one, and her forefinger through another.

This makes her laugh, to the surprise of the dog. She has a keen, very keen, sense of the ridiculous; and some time or other she will amuse bushmen with the story.

She had been amused before like that. One day she sat down "to have a good cry," as she said—and the old cat rubbed against her dress and "cried too." Then she had to laugh.

It must be near daylight now. The room is very close and hot because of the fire. Alligator still watches the wall from time to time. Suddenly he becomes greatly interested; he draws himself a few inches nearer the partition, and a thrill runs through his body. The hair on the back of his neck begins to bristle, and the battle-light is in his yellow eyes. She knows what this means, and lays her hand on the stick. The lower end of one of the partition slabs has a large crack on both sides. An evil pair of small, bright bead-like eyes glisten at one of these holes. The snake—a black one—comes slowly out, about a foot, and moves its head up and down. The dog lies still, and the woman sits as one fascinated. The snake comes out a foot farther. She lifts her stick, and the reptile, as though suddenly aware of danger, sticks his head in through the crack on the other side of the slab, and hurries to get his tail round after him. Alligator springs, and his jaws come together with a snap. He misses, for his nose is large, and the snake's body close down in the angle formed by the slabs and the floor. He snaps again as the tail comes round. He has the snake now, and tugs it out eighteen inches. Thud, thud comes the woman's club on the ground. Alligator pulls again. Thud, thud. Alligator gives another pull and he has the snake out—a black brute, five feet long. The head rises to dart about, but the dog has the enemy close to the neck. He is a big, heavy dog, but quick as a terrier. He shakes the snake as though he felt the original curse in common with mankind. The eldest boy wakes up, seizes his stick, and tries to get out of bed, but his mother forces him back with a grip of iron. Thud, thud—the snake's back is broken in several places. Thud, thud—its head is crushed, and Alligator's nose skinned again.

She lifts the mangled reptile on the point of her stick, carries it to the fire, and throws it in; then piles on the wood and watches the snake burn. The boy and dog watch too. She lays her hand on the dog's head, and all the fierce, angry light dies out of his yellow eyes. The younger children are quieted, and presently go to sleep. The dirty-legged boy stands for a moment in his shirt, watching the fire. Presently, he looks up at her, sees the tears in her eyes, and, throwing his arms round her neck exclaims:

"Mother, I won't never go drovin'; blarst me if I do!"

And she hugs him to her wornout breast and kisses him; and they sit thus together while the sickly daylight breaks over the bush.

•

A Worn Path

Eudora Welty

Often love of one's own summons the most miraculous human strengths. In this splendid story, an old woman's love for her grandson quietly knocks down all obstacles the world sets before her, including her own frailty and suffering.

It was December—a bright frozen day in the early morning. Far out in the country there was an old Negro woman with her head tied in a red rag, coming along a path through the pinewoods. Her name was Phoenix Jackson. She was very old and small and she walked slowly in the dark pine shadows, moving a little from side to side in her steps, with the balanced heaviness and lightness of a pendulum in a grandfather clock. She carried a thin, small cane made from an umbrella, and with this she kept tapping the frozen earth in front of her. This made a grave and persistent noise in the still air, that seemed meditative like the chirping of a solitary little bird.

She wore a dark striped dress reaching down to her shoe tops, and an equally long apron of bleached sugar sacks, with a full pocket: all neat and tidy, but every time she took a step she might have fallen over her shoelaces, which dragged from her unlaced shoes. She looked straight ahead. Her eyes were blue with age. Her skin had a pattern all its own of numberless branching wrinkles and as though a whole little tree stood in the middle of her forehead, but a golden color ran underneath, and the two knobs of her cheeks were illumined by a yellow burning under the dark. Under the red rag her hair came down on her neck in the frailest of ringlets, still black, and with an odor like copper.

Now and then there was a quivering in the thicket. Old Phoenix said, "Out of my way, all you foxes, owls, beetles, jack rabbits, coons and wild animals!... Keep out from under these feet, little bob-whites.... Keep the big wild hogs out of my path. Don't let none of those come running my direction. I got a long way." Under her small black-freckled hand her cane, limber as a buggy whip, would switch at the brush as if to rouse up any hiding things.

On she went. The woods were deep and still. The sun made the pine needles almost too bright to look at, up where the wind rocked. The cones dropped as light as feathers. Down in the hollow was the mourning dove—it was not too late for him.

The path ran up a hill. "Seem like there is chains about my feet, time I get this far," she said, in the voice of argument old people keep to use with themselves. "Something always take a hold of me on this hill—pleads I should stay."

After she got to the top she turned and gave a full, severe look behind her where she had come. "Up through pines," she said at length. "Now down through oaks."

Her eyes opened their widest, and she started down gently. But before she got to the bottom of the hill a bush caught her dress.

Her fingers were busy and intent, but her skirts were full and long, so that before she could pull them free in one place they were caught in another. It was not possible to allow the dress to tear. "I in the thorny bush," she said. "Thorns, you doing your appointed work. Never want to let folks pass, no sir. Old eyes thought you was a pretty little *green* bush."

Finally, trembling all over, she stood free, and after a moment dared to stoop for her cane.

"Sun so high!" she cried, leaning back and looking, while the thick tears went over her eyes. "The time getting all gone here."

At the foot of this hill was a place where a log was laid across the creek.

"Now comes the trial," said Phoenix.

Putting her right foot out, she mounted the log and shut her eyes. Lifting her skirt, leveling her cane fiercely before her, like a festival figure in some parade, she began to march across. Then she opened her eyes and she was safe on the other side.

"I wasn't as old as I thought," she said.

But she sat down to rest. She spread her skirts on the bank around her and folded her hands over her knees. Up above her was a tree in a pearly cloud of mistletoe. She did not dare to close her eyes, and when a little boy brought her a plate with a slice of marble-cake on it she spoke to him. "That would be acceptable," she said. But when she went to take it there was just her own hand in the air.

So she left that tree, and had to go through a barbed-wire fence. There she had to creep and crawl, spreading her knees and stretching her fingers like a baby trying to climb the steps. But she talked loudly to herself: she could not let her dress be torn now, so late in the day, and she could not pay for having her arm or her leg sawed off if she got caught fast where she was.

At last she was safe through the fence and risen up out in the clearing. Big dead trees, like black men with one arm, were standing in the purple stalks of the withered cotton field. There sat a buzzard.

"Who you watching?"

In the furrow she made her way along.

"Glad this not the season for the bulls," she said, looking sideways, "and the good Lord made his snakes to curl up and sleep in the winter. A pleasure I don't see no two-headed snake coming around that tree, where it come once. It took a while to get by him, back in the summer."

She passed through the old cotton and went into a field of dead corn. It whispered and shook and was taller than her head. "Through the maze now," she said, for there was no path.

Then were was something tall, black, and skinny there, moving before her.

At first she took it for a man. It could have been a man dancing in the field. But she stood still and listened, and it did not make a sound. It was as silent as a ghost.

"Ghost," she said sharply, "who be you the ghost of? For I have heard of nary death close by."

But there was no answer—only the ragged dancing in the wind.

She shut her eyes, reached out her hand, and touched a sleeve. She found a coat and inside that an emptiness, cold as ice.

"You scarecrow," she said. Her face lighted. "I ought to be shut up for good," she said with laughter. "My senses is gone. I too old. I the oldest people I ever know. Dance, old scarecrow," she said, "while I dancing with you."

She kicked her foot over the furrow, and with mouth drawn down, shook her head once or twice in a little strutting way. Some husks blew down and whirled in streamers about her skirts.

Then she went on, parting her way from side to side with the cane, through the whispering field. At last she came to the end, to a wagon track where the silver grass blew between the red ruts. The quail were walking around like pullets, seeming all dainty and unseen.

"Walk pretty," she said. "This the easy place. This the easy going."

She followed the track, swaying through the quiet bare fields, through the little strings of trees silver in their dead leaves, past cabins silver from weather, with the doors and windows boarded shut, all like old women under a spell sitting there. "I walking in their sleep," she said, nodding her head vigorously.

In a ravine she went where a spring was silently flowing through a hollow log. Old Phoenix bent and drank. "Sweet-gum makes the water sweet," she said, and drank more. "Nobody know who made this well, for it was here when I was born."

The track crossed a swampy part where the moss hung as white as lace from every limb. "Sleep on, alligators, and blow your bubbles." Then the track went into the road.

Deep, deep the road went down between the high green-colored banks. Overhead the live-oaks met, and it was as dark as a cave.

A black dog with a lolling tongue came up out of the weeds by the ditch. She was meditating, and not ready, and when he came at her she only hit him a little with her cane. Over she went in the ditch, like a little puff of milkweed.

Down there, her senses drifted away. A dream visited her, and she reached her hand up, but nothing reached down and gave her a pull. So she lay there and presently went to talking. "Old woman," she said to herself, "that black dog come up out of the weeds to stall you off, and now there he sitting on his fine tail, smiling at you."

A white man finally came along and found her—a hunter, a young man, with his dog on a chain.

"Well, Granny!" he laughed. "What are you doing there?"

"Lying on my back like a June-bug waiting to be turned over, mister," she said, reaching up her hand.

He lifted her up, gave her a swing in the air, and set her down. "Anything broken, Granny?"

"No sir, them old dead weeds is springy enough," said Phoenix, when she had got her breath. "I thank you for your trouble."

"Where do you live, Granny?" he asked, while the two dogs were growling at each other.

"Away back yonder, sir, behind the ridge. You can't even see it from here."

"On your way home?"

"No sir, I going to town."

"Why, that's too far! That's as far as I walk when I come out myself, and I get something for my trouble." He patted the stuffed bag he carried, and there hung down a little closed claw. It was one of the bob-whites, with its beak hooked bitterly to show it was dead. "Now you go on home, Granny!"

"I bound to go to town, mister," said Phoenix. "The time come around."

He gave another laugh, filling the whole landscape. "I know you old colored people! Wouldn't miss going to town to see Santa Claus!"

But something held old Phoenix very still. The deep lines in her face went into a fierce and different radiation. Without warning, she had seen with her own eyes a flashing nickel fall out of the man's pocket onto the ground.

"How old are you, Granny?" he was saying.

"There is no telling, mister," she said, "no telling."

Then she gave a little cry and clapped her hands and said, "Git on away from here, dog! Look! Look at that dog!" She laughed as if in admiration. "He ain't scared of nobody. He a big black dog." She whispered, "Sic him!"

"Watch me get rid of that cur," said the man. "Sic him, Pete! Sic him!"

Phoenix heard the dogs fighting, and heard the man running and throwing sticks. She even heard a gunshot. But she was slowly bending forward by that time, further and further forward, the lids stretched down over her eyes, as if she were doing this in her sleep. Her chin was lowered almost to her knees. The yellow palm of her hand came out from the fold of her apron. Her fingers slid down and along the ground under the piece of money with the grace and care they would have in lifting an egg from under a setting hen. Then she slowly straightened up, she stood erect, and the nickel was in her apron pocket. A bird flew by. Her lips moved. "God watching me the whole time. I come to stealing."

The man came back, and his own dog panted about them. "Well, I scared him off that time," he said, and then he laughed and lifted his gun and pointed it at Phoenix.

She stood straight and faced him.

"Doesn't the gun scare you?" he said, still pointing it.

"No, sir, I seen plenty go off closer by, in my day, and for less than what I done," she said, holding utterly still.

He smiled, and shouldered the gun. "Well, Granny," he said, "you must be a hundred years old, and scared of nothing. I'd give you a dime if I had any money with me. But you take my advice and stay home, and nothing will happen to you."

"I bound to go on my way, mister," said Phoenix. She inclined her head in the red rag. Then they went in different directions, but she could hear the gun shooting again and again over the hill.

She walked on. The shadows hung from the oak trees to the road like curtains. Then she smelled wood-smoke, and smelled the river, and she saw a steeple and the cabins on their steep steps. Dozens of little black children whirled around her. There ahead was Natchez shining. Bells were ringing. She walked on.

In the paved city it was Christmas time. There were red and green electric lights strung and crisscrossed everywhere, and all turned on in the daytime. Old Phoenix would have been lost if she had not distrusted her eyesight and depended on her feet to know where to take her.

She paused quietly on the sidewalk where people were passing by. A lady came along in the crowd, carrying an armful of red-, green- and silver-wrapped presents; she gave off perfume like the red roses in hot summer, and Phoenix stopped her.

"Please, missy, will you lace up my shoe?" She held up her foot.

"What do you want, Grandma?"

"See my shoe," said Phoenix. "Do all right for out in the country, but wouldn't look right to go in a big building."

"Stand still then, Grandma," said the lady. She put her packages down on the sidewalk beside her and laced and tied both shoes tightly.

"Can't lace 'em with a cane," said Phoenix. "Thank you, missy. I doesn't mind asking a nice lady to tie up my shoe, when I gets out on the street."

Moving slowly and from side to side, she went into the big building, and into a tower of steps, where she walked up and around and around until her feet knew to stop.

She entered a door, and there she saw nailed up on the wall the document that had been stamped with the gold seal and framed in the gold frame, which matched the dream that was hung up in her head.

"Here I be," she said. There was a fixed and ceremonial stiffness over her body.

"A charity case, I suppose," said an attendant who sat at the desk before her.

But Phoenix only looked above her head. There was sweat on her face, the wrinkles in her skin shone like a bright net.

"Speak up, Grandma," the woman said. "What's your name? We must have your history, you know. Have you been here before? What seems to be the trouble with you?"

Old Phoenix only gave a twitch to her face as if a fly were bothering her.

"Are you deaf?" cried the attendant.

But then the nurse came in.

"Oh, that's just old Aunt Phoenix," she said. "She doesn't come for herself—she has a little grandson. She makes these trips just as regular as clockwork. She lives away back off the Old Natchez Trace." She bent down. "Well, Aunt Phoenix, why don't you just take a seat? We won't keep you standing after your long trip." She pointed.

The old woman sat down, bolt upright in the chair.

"Now, how is the boy?" asked the nurse.

Old Phoenix did not speak.

"I said, how is the boy?"

But Phoenix only waited and stared straight ahead, her face very solemn and withdrawn into rigidity.

"Is his throat any better?" asked the nurse. "Aunt Phoenix, don't you hear me? Is your grandson's throat any better since the last time you came for the medicine?"

With her hands on her knees, the old woman waited, silent, erect and motionless, just as if she were in armor.

"You mustn't take up our time this way, Aunt Phoenix," the nurse said. "Tell us quickly about your grandson, and get it over. He isn't dead, is he?"

At last there came a flicker and then a flame of comprehension across her face, and she spoke.

"My grandson. It was my memory had left me. There I sat and forgot why I made my long trip."

"Forgot?" the nurse frowned. "After you came so far?"

Then Phoenix was like an old woman begging a dignified forgiveness for waking up frightened in the night. "I never did go to school, I was too old at the Surrender," she said in a soft voice. "I'm an old woman without an education. It was my memory fail me. My little grandson, he is just the same, and I forgot it in the coming."

"Throat never heals, does it?" said the nurse, speaking in a loud, sure voice to old Phoenix. By now she had a card with something written on it, a little list. "Yes. Swallowed lye. When was it?—January—two, three years ago—"

Phoenix spoke unasked now. "No, missy, he not dead, he just the same. Every little while his throat begin to close up again, and he not able to swallow. He not get his breath. He not able to help himself. So the time come around, and I go on another trip for the soothing medicine."

"All right. The doctor said as long as you came to get it, you could have it," said the nurse. "But it's an obstinate case."

"My little grandson, he sit up there in the house all wrapped up, waiting by himself," Phoenix went on. "We is the only two left in the world. He suffer and it don't seem to put him back at all. He got a sweet look. He going to last. He wear a little patch quilt and peep out holding his mouth open like a little bird. I remembers so plain now. I not going to forget him again, no, the whole enduring time. I could tell him from all the others in creation."

"All right." The nurse was trying to hush her now. She brought her a bottle of medicine. "Charity," she said, making a check mark in a book.

Old Phoenix held the bottle close to her eyes, and then carefully put it into her pocket.

"I thank you," she said.

"It's Christmas time, Grandma," said the attendant. "Could I give you a few pennies out of my purse?"

"Five pennies is a nickel," said Phoenix stiffly.

"Here's a nickel," said the attendant.

Phoenix rose carefully and held out her hand. She received the nickel and then fished the other nickel out of her pocket and laid it beside the new one. She stared at her palm closely, with her head on one side.

Then she gave a tap with her cane on the floor.

"This is what come to me to do," she said. "I going to the store and buy my child a little windmill they sells, made out of paper. He going to find it hard to believe there such a thing in the world. I'll march myself back where he waiting, holding it straight up in this hand."

She lifted her free hand, gave a little nod, turned around, and walked out of the doctor's office. Then her slow step began on the stairs, going down.

•

"ONE, TWO, THREE!"

Henry Cuyler Bunner

The play of kindred spirits across generations can be one of the great blessings of family. In our time, it is an irony that even though people live to record numbers of years, many children do not know the joy of playing with their grandparents.

It was an old, old, old, old lady,
  And a boy that was half past three;
And the way that they played together
  Was beautiful to see.

She couldn't go running and jumping,
  And the boy, no more could he;
For he was a thin little fellow,
  With a thin little twisted knee.

They sat in the yellow twilight,
  Out under the maple tree;
And the game that they played I'll tell you,
  Just as it was told to me.

It was Hide and Go Seek they were playing,
  Though you'd never have known it to be—
With an old, old, old, old lady,
  And a boy with a twisted knee.

The boy would bend his face down
  On his one little sound right knee,
And he'd guess where she was hiding,
  In guesses One, Two, Three!

"You are in the china closet!"
  He would cry, and laugh with glee—
It wasn't the china closet;
  But he still had Two and Three.

"You are up in Papa's big bedroom,
   In the chest with the queer old key!"
And she said: "You are *warm* and *warmer;*
   But you're not quite right," said she.

"It can't be the little cupboard
   Where Mamma's things used to be—
So it must be the clothespress, Gran'ma!"
   And he found her with his Three.

Then she covered her face with her fingers,
   That were wrinkled and white and wee,
And she guessed where the boy was hiding,
   With a One and a Two and a Three.

And they never had stirred from their places,
   Right under the maple tree—
This old, old, old, old lady,
   And the boy with the lame little knee—
This dear, dear, dear old lady,
   And the boy who was half past three.

•

THESEUS AND THE STONE

Adapted from retellings by Charles Kingsley and Nathaniel Hawthorne

Home is the place to build strength and resolve before going out
into the world. Plutarch and Appolodorus, among other ancient
writers, have left us accounts of how the Greek hero Theseus
journeyed toward manhood.

In the old city of Troezen, in Greece, there lived long ago a
princess named Aithra. She had one young son named Theseus, the
bravest lad in all the land. Aithra smiled whenever she looked at
him, but it was a sad kind of smile, for the boy had never seen his
father, who lived far across the sea.

One day she took her son into a grove which stood behind the temple. She led him to a tall oak, beneath whose shade grew arbutus and lentisk and purple heather bushes. There she sighed, and said, "Theseus, my son, go into that thicket, and at the base of the tree you will find a great flat stone. Lift it and bring me what lies underneath."

Theseus pushed his way through the thick bushes, seeing they had not been moved for many years. And searching among their roots he found a great flat stone, all overgrown with ivy and moss.

He tried to lift it, but he could not. He tried till the sweat ran down his brow from heat and the tears from his eyes for shame, but all was to no avail. At last he came back to his mother and said, "I have found the stone, but I cannot lift it. Nor do I think any man could in all Troezen."

His mother sighed and said, "The gods wait long, but they are just. Let it be for another year. The day may come when you will be a stronger man than lives in all Troezen."

And when a full year was past she led Theseus again up to the temple and bade him lift the stone, but he could not.

Then she sighed and said the same words again, and again they went home together. The next year they made the same pilgrimage, but Theseus could not lift the stone then, nor the year after. He longed to ask his mother the meaning of the stone and what might lie underneath it, but her face was so sad he had not the heart to ask.

Meanwhile the rock seemed to be sinking farther and farther into the ground. The moss grew over it thicker and thicker, until at last it looked almost like a soft green seat, with only a few gray knobs of granite peeping out. The overhanging trees, also, shed their brown leaves upon it, as often as the autumn came, and at its base grew ferns and wildflowers and vines, which crept over its surface. To all appearance the rock was as firmly fastened as any other portion of the earth's substance.

But as impossible as the task looked, Theseus was growing certain he would someday get the upper hand of the stone.

"Mother, it has moved!" he cried, after one of his attempts. "The earth around it is a little cracked!" And he showed her the place where he thought the stem of a flower had been partly uprooted by the movement of the rock. Aithra only sighed, for she knew the time was coming when she must send her son forth among the perils of the world.

So in order to grow strong Theseus spent all his days in wrestling and boxing and taming horses, and hunting the boar and the bull, and chasing goats and deer among the rocks, till upon all the mountains there was no hunter so swift as Theseus.

And when his eighteenth year was past, Aithra led him again to the temple, and said, "Theseus, lift the stone this day, or never know who you are."

And Theseus went into the thicket and stood over the stone and tugged at it—and it stirred! His spirits swelled within him, and he said, "If I break my heart in my body, it shall come up." He wrestled with the sluggish stone, straining every sinew, as if it were a living enemy. He heaved, he lifted. He resolved now to succeed, or else perish there and let the rock be his gravestone forever! Aithra stood gazing at him, and clasped her hands, partly with a mother's pride and partly with a mother's sorrow. And slowly the great rock rose from the bedded moss and earth, uprooting the shrubs and flowers along with it, and was turned on its side. Theseus had conquered!

And when he looked beneath the stone, on the ground lay a sword of bronze, with a hilt of glittering gold, and by it a pair of golden sandals. He caught them up and burst through the bushes like a wild boar, and leaped to his mother, holding them high above his head.

When she saw them she wept in long silence, hiding her face in her shawl, and Theseus stood by her wondering, and wept also, although he knew not why. And when she was tired of weeping she lifted her head and said, "Bring what you have found, and come with me where we can look down upon the sea."

They went outside the sacred wall and looked down over the bright blue sea. Aithra pointed across the water and said: "There is Attica, where the Athenian people dwell. It is a fair place, a land of olive oil and honey, the joy of gods and men. What would you do, son Theseus, if you were king of such a land?"

Then his heart grew great within him, and he said: "If I were king of such a land, I would rule it wisely and well in wisdom and in might, that when I died all would weep over my tomb and cry, 'Alas for the shepherd of his people.' "

Aithra smiled and said: "Your father is King Aegeus of Athens. When he went to be king, he bade me treat you as a child until you should prove yourself by lifting this heavy stone. That task accomplished, you are to put on his sandals. in order to follow in your father's footsteps, and to gird on his sword, so that you may fight giants and dragons, as King Aegeus did in his youth. And you are to go to him in Athens and say, 'The stone is lifted.' "

But Theseus wept. "Shall I leave you, O my mother?" he cried. She answered, "Weep not for me. That which is fate must be, and grief is easy to those who do naught but grieve."

Then she kissed Theseus and wept over him, and went into the temple, and Theseus saw her no more.

•

IN THE UTTERMOST PARTS OF THE SEA
Hans Christian Andersen

As we go out into the world, we find that lessons we've learned and loved at home stay with us and sustain us. Virtues travel well. The title of this beautiful Hans Christian Andersen story comes from Psalm 139: "If I take the wings of the morning, and dwell in the uttermost parts of the sea, even there shall Thy hand lead me, and Thy right hand shall hold me."

Some large ships were sent up toward the North Pole, for the purpose of discovering the boundaries of land and sea, and of trying how far men could make their way.

A year and a day had elapsed. Amid mist and ice had they, with great difficulty, steered farther and farther. The winter had now begun; the sun had set, one long night would continue during many, many weeks. One unbroken plain of ice spread around them; the ships were all fast moored to it. The snow lay about in heaps and had even shaped itself into cubiform houses, some as big as our barrows, some only just large enough for two or three men to find shelter within. Darkness they could not complain of, for the Northern Lights—Nature's fireworks—now red, now blue, flashed unceasingly, and the snow glistened so brightly.

At times when it was brightest came troops of the natives, strange-looking figures, clad in hairy skins, and with sledges made out of hard fragments of ice. They brought skins to exchange, which the sailors were only too glad to use as warm carpets inside their snow houses, and as beds whereon they could rest under their snowy tents, while outside prevailed an intensity of cold such as we never experience during our severest winters. But the sailors remembered that at home it was still autumn, and they thought of the warm sunbeams and the leaves still clinging to the trees in varied glories of crimson and gold. Their watches told them it was evening and time for rest, and in one of the snow houses two sailors had already lain down to sleep. The youngest of these two had with him his best home treasure, the Bible that his grandmother had given him at parting. Every night it lay under his pillow. He had known its contents from childhood, and every day he read a portion; and often as he lay on his couch, he recalled to mind those holy words of comfort, "If I should take the wings of the morning, and remain in the uttermost parts of the sea, even there should Thy hand lead me, and Thy right hand should hold me."

These sublime words of faith were on his lips as he closed his eyes, when sleep came to him, and dreams with sleep—busy, swift-winged dreams, proving that though the body may rest, the soul must ever be awake. First he seemed to hear the melodies of songs dear to him in his home. A mild summer breeze seemed to breathe upon him, and a light shone upon his couch, as though the snowy dome above him had become transparent. He lifted his head and behold! The dazzling white light was not the white of a snow wall; it came from the large wings of an angel stooping over him, an angel with eyes beaming with love. The angel's form seemed to spring from the pages of the Bible, as from the pitcher of a lily blossom. He extended his arms and lo! The narrow walls of the snow hut sank back like a mist melting before the daylight. Once again the green meadows and autumnal-tinted woods of the sailor's home lay around him, bathed in quiet sunshine. The stork's nest was empty, but the apples still clung to the wild apple tree. The blackbird whistled in the little green cage that hung in the lowly window of his childhood's home. The blackbird whistled the tune he had taught him, and the old grandmother wound chickweed about the bars of the cage, as her grandson had been wont to do. The smith's pretty young daughter stood drawing water from the well, and as she nodded to the grandmother, the latter beckoned to her, and held up a letter to show her, a letter that had come that morning from the cold northern lands, from the North Pole itself, where the old woman's grandson now was—safe under God's protecting hand. And the two women, old and young, laughed and wept by turns—and he the while, the young sailor whose body was sleeping amid ice and snow, his spirit roaming in the world of dreams, under the angel's wings, saw and heard it all, and laughed and wept with them. And from the letter these words were read aloud, "Even in the uttermost parts of the sea, His right hand shall hold me fast"; and a sweet, solemn music was wafted round him, and the angel drooped his wings. Like a soft protecting veil they fell closer over the sleeper.

The dream was ended; all was darkness in the little snow hut, but the Bible lay under the sailor's head, faith and hope abode in his heart. God was with him, and his home was with him, "even in the uttermost parts of the sea."

•

CHRISTMAS AT SEA

Robert Louis Stevenson

Often it is hard to leave, but we go knowing that home and hearth make a point on our compass for the rest of life's journey.

The sheets were frozen hard, and they cut the naked hand;
The decks were like a slide, where a seaman scarce could stand,
The wind was nor'-wester, blowing squally off the sea;
And cliffs and spouting breakers were the only things a-lee.

They heard the surf a-roaring before the break of day:
But 'twas only with the peep of light we saw how ill we lay.
We tumbled every hand on deck instanter, with a shout,
And we gave her the maintops'l, and stood by to go about.

All day we tacked and tacked between the South Head and the
   North;
All day we hauled the frozen sheets, and got no further forth;
All day as cold as charity, in bitter pain and dread,
For very life and nature we tacked from head to head.

We gave the South a wider berth, for there the tide-race roared;
But every tack we made we brought the North Head close aboard;
So 's we saw the cliffs and houses, and the breakers running high,
And the coastguard in his garden, with his glass against his eye.

The bells upon the church were rung with a mighty jovial cheer;
For it's just that I should tell you how (of all days in the year)
This day of our adversity was blessèd Christmas morn,
And the house above the coastguard's was the house where I was
    born.

O well I saw the pleasant room, the pleasant faces there,
My mother's silver spectacles, my father's silver hair;
And well I saw the firelight, like a flight of homely elves
Go dancing round the china-plates that stand upon the shelves!

And well I knew the talk they had, the talk that was of me,
Of the shadow on the household and the son that went to sea;
And O the wicked fool I seemed, in every kind of way,
To be here and hauling frozen ropes on blessèd Christmas Day.

They lit the high sea-light, and the dark began to fall.
"All hands to loose topgallant sails!" I heard the captain call.
"By the Lord, she'll never stand it," our first mate Jackson cried.
. . . "It's the one way or the other, Mr. Jackson," he replied.

She staggered to her bearings, but the sails were new and good,
And the ship smelt up to windward just as though she understood.
As the winter's day was ending, in the entry of the night,
We cleared the weary headland, and passed below the light.

And they heaved a mighty breath, every soul on board but me,
As they saw her nose again pointing handsome out to sea;
But all that I could think of, in the darkness and the cold,
Was just that I was leaving home and my folks were growing old.

•

THE HAMPSHIRE HILLS

Eugene Field

As this beautiful story reminds us we go into the world wisely, go
through the world bravely, and go out of the world peacefully
when we start with the great fortification that is home.

One afternoon many years ago two little brothers named Seth
and Abner were playing in the orchard. They were not troubled
with the heat of the August day, for a soft, cool wind came up from
the river in the valley over yonder and fanned their red cheeks and
played all kinds of pranks with their tangled curls. All about them
was the hum of bees, the song of birds, the smell of clover, and the
merry music of the crickets. Their little dog Fido chased them
through the high, waving grass, and rolled with them under the
trees, and barked himself hoarse in his attempt to keep pace with
their laughter. Wearied at length, they lay beneath the bellflower
tree and looked off at the Hampshire hills, and wondered if the
time ever would come when they should go out into the world
beyond those hills and be great, noisy men. Fido did not understand it at all. He lolled in the grass, cooling his tongue on the
clover bloom, and puzzling his brain to know why his little masters
were so quiet all at once.

"I wish I were a man," said Abner, ruefully. "I want to be
somebody and do something. It is very hard to be a little boy so
long and to have no companions but little boys and girls, to see
nothing but these same old trees and this same high grass, and to
hear nothing but the same bird songs from one day to another."

That is true," said Seth. "I, too, am very tired of being a little
boy, and I long to go out into the world and be a man like my
gran'pa or my father or my uncles. With nothing to look at but those
distant hills and the river in the valley, my eyes are wearied; and I
shall be very happy when I am big enough to leave this stupid
place."

Had Fido understood their words he would have chided them,
for the little dog loved his home and had no thought of any other
pleasure than romping through the orchard and playing with his
little masters all the day. But Fido did not understand them.

The clover bloom heard them with sadness. Had they but listened in turn they would have heard the clover saying softly: "Stay with me while you may, little boys; trample me with your merry feet; let me feel the imprint of your curly heads and kiss the sunburn on your little cheeks. Love me while you may, for when you go away you never will come back."

The bellflower tree heard them, too, and she waved her great, strong branches as if she would caress the impatient little lads, and she whispered: "Do not think of leaving me: you are children, and you know nothing of the world beyond those distant hills. It is full of trouble and care and sorrow; abide here in this quiet spot till you are prepared to meet the vexations of that outer world. We are for *you*—we trees and grass and birds and bees and flowers. Abide with us, and learn the wisdom we teach."

The cricket in the raspberry hedge heard them, and she chirped, oh! so sadly: "You will go out into the world and leave us and never think of us again till it is too late to return. Open your ears, little boys, and hear my song of contentment."

So spake the clover bloom and the bellflower tree and the cricket; and in like manner the robin that nested in the linden over yonder, and the big bumblebee that lived in the hole under the pasture gate, and the butterfly and the wild rose pleaded with them, each in his own way; but the little boys did not heed them, so eager were their desires to go into and mingle with the great world beyond those distant hills.

Many years went by; and at last Seth and Abner grew to manhood, and the time was come when they were to go into the world and be brave, strong men. Fido had been dead a long time. They had made him a grave under the bellflower tree—yes, just where

he had romped with the two little boys that August afternoon Fido lay sleeping amid the humming of the bees and the perfume of the clover. But Seth and Abner did not think of Fido now, nor did they give even a passing thought to any of their old friends—the bellflower tree, the clover, the cricket, and the robin. Their hearts beat with exultation. They were men, and they were going beyond the hills to know and try the world.

They were equipped for that struggle, not in a vain, frivolous way, but as good and brave young men should be. A gentle mother had counselled them, a prudent father had advised them, and they had gathered from the sweet things of Nature much of that wisdom before which all knowledge is as nothing. So they were fortified. They went beyond the hills and came into the West. How great and busy was the world—how great and busy it was here in the West! What a rush and noise and turmoil and seething and surging, and how keenly did the brothers have to watch and struggle for vantage ground. Withal, they prospered; the counsel of the mother, the advice of the father, the wisdom of the grass and flowers and trees, were much to them, and they prospered. Honor and riches came to them, and they were happy. But amid it all, how seldom they thought of the little home among the circling hills where they had learned the first sweet lessons of life!

And now they were old and gray. They lived in splendid mansions, and all people paid them honor.

One August day a grim messenger stood in Seth's presence and beckoned to him.

Who are you?" cried Seth. "What strange power have you over me that the very sight of you chills my blood and stays the beating of my heart?"

Then the messenger threw aside his mask, and Seth saw that he was Death. Seth made no outcry; he knew what the summons meant, and he was content. But he sent for Abner.

And when Abner came, Seth was stretched upon his bed, and there was a strange look in his eyes and a flush upon his cheeks, as though a fatal fever had laid hold on him.

"You shall not die!" cried Abner, and he threw himself about his brother's neck and wept.

But Seth bade Abner cease his outcry. "Sit here by my bedside and talk with me," said he, "and let us speak of the Hampshire hills."

A great wonder overcame Abner. With reverence he listened, and as he listened a sweet peace seemed to steal into his soul.

"I am prepared for Death," said Seth, "and I will go with Death this day. Let us talk of our childhood now, for, after all the battle with this great world, it is pleasant to think and speak of our boyhood among the Hampshire hills."

"Say on, dear brother," said Abner.

"I am thinking of an August day long ago," said Seth, solemnly and softly. "It was so *very* long ago, and yet it seems only yesterday. We were in the orchard together, under the bellflower tree, and our little dog—"

"Fido," said Abner, remembering it all, as the years came back.

"Fido and you and I, under the bellflower tree," said Seth. "How we had played, and how weary we were, and how cool the grass was, and how sweet was the fragrance of the flowers! Can you remember it, brother?"

"Oh, yes," replied Abner, "and I remember how we lay among the clover and looked off at the distant hills and wondered of the world beyond."

"And amid our wonderings and longings," said Seth, "how the old bellflower tree seemed to stretch her kind arms down to us as if she would hold us away from that world beyond the hills."

"And now I can remember that the clover whispered to us, and the cricket in the raspberry hedge sang to us of contentment," said Abner.

"The robin, too, carolled in the linden."

"It is very sweet to remember it now," said Seth. "How blue and hazy the hills looked; how cool the breeze blew up from the river; how like a silver lake the old pickerel pond sweltered under the summer sun over beyond the pasture and broom-corn, and how merry was the music of the birds and bees!"

So these old men, who had been little boys together, talked of the August afternoon when with Fido they had romped in the orchard and rested beneath the bellflower tree. And Seth's voice grew fainter, and his eyes were, oh! so dim; but to the very last he spoke of the dear old days and the orchard and the clover and the Hampshire hills. And when Seth fell asleep forever, Abner kissed his brother's lips and knelt at the bedside and said the prayer his mother had taught him.

In the street without there was the noise of passing carts, the cries of tradespeople, and all the bustle of a great and busy city; but, looking upon Seth's dear, dead face, Abner could hear only the music voices of birds and crickets and summer winds as he had heard them with Seth when they were little boys together, back among the Hampshire hills.

WE ARE SEVEN

William Wordsworth

This moving poem reminds us that families remain together even after death.

A simple child,
That lightly draws its breath,
And feels its life in every limb,
What should it know of death?

I met a little cottage girl:
She was eight years old, she said;
Her hair was thick with many a curl
That clustered round her head.

She had a rustic, woodland air,
And she was wildly clad;
Her eyes were fair, and very fair;
Her beauty made me glad.

"Sisters and brothers, little maid,
How many may you be?"
"How many? Seven in all," she said,
And wondering looked at me.

"And where are they? I pray you tell."
    She answered, "Seven are we;
And two of us at Conway dwell,
    And two are gone to sea;

"Two of us in the churchyard lie,
    My sister and my brother;
And, in the churchyard cottage, I
    Dwell near them with my mother."

"You say that two at Conway dwell,
    And two are gone to sea,
Yet ye are seven! I pray you tell,
    Sweet maid, how this may be."

Then did the little maid reply,
    "Seven boys and girls are we;
Two of us in the churchyard lie
    Beneath the churchyard tree."

"You run about, my little maid;
    Your limbs they are alive;
If two are in the churchyard laid,
    Then ye are only five."

"Their graves are green, they may be seen,"
    The little maid replied:
"Twelve steps or more from my mother's door,
    And they are side by side.

"My stockings there I often knit;
    My kerchief there I hem;
And there upon the ground I sit,
    And sing a song to them.

"And often after sunset, sir,
    When it is light and fair,
I take my little porringer,
    And eat my supper there.

"The first that died was Sister Jane;
    In bed she moaning lay,

Till God released her of her pain;
  And then she went away.

"So in the churchyard she was laid;
  And, when the grass was dry,
Together round her grave we played,
  My brother John and I.

"And when the ground was white with snow,
  And I could run and slide,
My brother John was forced to go,
  And he lies by her side."

"How many are you, then," said I,
  "If they two are in heaven?"
Quick was the little maid's reply:
  "O Master! we are seven."

"But they are dead; those two are dead!
  Their spirits are in heaven!"
'Twas throwing words away; for still
The little maid would have her will,
  And said, "Nay, we are seven!"

•

PRAYER FOR HOME AND FAMILY

Robert Louis Stevenson

This beautiful prayer sums up, I think, what family life should be.
I read it for the first time recently, and hope to make it familiar in
the Bennett home.

Lord, behold our family here assembled. We thank Thee for
this place in which we dwell; for the love that unites us; for the
peace accorded us this day; for the hope with which we expect the
morrow; for the health, the work, the food, and the bright skies,
that make our lives delightful; for our friends in all parts of the
earth.

Let peace abound in our small company. Purge out of every heart the lurking grudge. Give us grace and strength to forbear and to persevere. Offenders, give us the grace to accept and to forgive offenders. Forgetful ourselves, help us to bear cheerfully the forgetfulness of others.

Give us courage and gaiety and the quiet mind. Spare to us our friends, soften to us our enemies. Bless us, if it may be, in all our innocent endeavors. If it may not, give us the strength to encounter that which is to come, that we may be brave in peril, constant in tribulation, temperate in wrath, and in all changes of fortune, and down to the gates of death, loyal and loving one to another.

As the clay to the potter, as the windmill to the wind, as children of their sire, we beseech of Thee this help and mercy for Christ's sake.

Two

·

INTO
THE
WORLD

BEFORE long, the time comes when we leave the safety and security of home and venture into the world on our own. At first we go forth slowly, step by step, reaching new milestones without quite realizing they are leading us on toward independence—the first trip across the street without anyone to hold our hand, the first day at school, the first slumber party at a friend's house, the first summer job, a first rite of passage at church or temple, and on and on until suddenly we look back and discover we've left home far behind. It dawns on us that the world is wide and often unfamiliar, and our journey has only begun. George Eliot recorded how all young people surely feel when they reach that place of poignant recognition: "They had entered the thorny wilderness, and the golden gates of their childhood had forever closed behind them."

This chapter helps us get ready for that time. It helps us with those first faltering steps across home's threshold and into the world beyond. The lessons offered here can serve as guides to help us choose the right paths; they can be supports to make our footing a bit more sure in a world that does not always deal gently with missteps. Life can be a rough and tough journey; the ground can be hard, the air can get cold. So here we find a few lessons that will help us get into and keep the good habits we'll need for the long haul. We find stories, for example, about watching what we say, and about how good manners will take us further. We discover a few things about facing duty, getting on with a job, and doing good work. We see the value of controlling our appetites, our tempers, and our egos. We'll need these lessons in self-discipline and re-sponsibility if we're to last the whole journey.

Not all the lessons the world teaches are moral truths, and by

no means are all of the stories in this chapter lessons in moral
virtue. As we travel forward, we need to know some other rules of
the road too, ones having to do with how the world works. It can
be a complicated place, and it's not always enough simply to be
good; sometimes you need to act *smart* as well. As the gospel of
Matthew says, "wise as serpents, harmless as doves." And so here
we find a few stories that add to our store of practical, everyday
wisdom, stories illustrating intellectual virtues at work. We discover
the importance of knowing our own—and other people's—
strengths and weaknesses. We learn about using what we've earned
and what we've been given to good advantage, about recognizing
what's good for us and what will only bring trouble, about asking
when fights are worthwhile and when clearly they are not. We see
there are times to take advice and times to rely on our own good
judgment.

At times, the world can be a dangerous place. We encounter
all sorts of strangers. Sometimes they are kind but sometimes they
are not, and it pays to be ready. In this chapter, then, we find stories
reminding us that there are those waiting to lay traps for us. We
meet some people who want everything—including what's ours—
and will do anything to get it. We learn a few things about honesty
and dishonesty, and pick up a few pointers on choosing the right
kind of friends. These lessons in prudence are important, we discover, because the virtues are not always in abundant supply.

Our journey may be a bit smoother and safer if we go armed
with these examples. They may help us see more clearly and wisely,
and so keep out of harm's way. Of course, we *will* make a few
wrong turns and fall into a few traps. In fact, we learn wisdom and
virtue from our failures as much as from our successes. And as
someone once observed, anyone who never made a mistake never
made a discovery either. But since the world can be a stern taskmas-
ter, the examples we find in this chapter may at least help soften
the blows. And if nothing else, they'll help us learn that though we
make mistakes, we don't make them alone. And most of our mistakes aren't fatal. For most wrong paths taken, there is a way back
to the crossroads to try again, another day.

HOW FIVE LITTLE ANGELS
LOST THEIR WINGS

Mary Stewart

This is a story about going from one world into another, and the
attitudes and dispositions with which we face that new world. It's
about choosing smiles over tears, and effort over complaint and
regret.

Five little angels perched upon the golden bar of Paradise
peering down curiously at the world below.

"See it shine in the sunshine, like a ball of fire!" cried one.

"See it dance around, like this—" exclaimed another, springing off the bar and flying around in a circle.

"Look at the gay colors, like broken bits of rainbow!" cried the
third. "They must be the earth flowers. I like them better than the
flowers of Paradise, all gold and silver!"

"Do you see those tiny white spots?" asked the fourth. "St. Joan
of Arc told me those were flocks of sheep. They are so sweet, she
says. She took care of them when she was a shepherdess upon the
earth."

"Listen, listen!" cried the fifth. "That is a sound we never hear
in Paradise! What is it?"

They all listened, their bright angel faces growing puzzled and
troubled.

It was the sound of a child crying.

"Oh, let us fly right down to him and comfort him!" cried one.

"Yes, let us tell him that Heaven is near and angels are guarding him and let us take him a little star for a present!" suggested
another.

"We have no feet; we could not walk upon the earth and he
might not know how to play with us," objected the third.

"Look!" cried the fourth. "It is growing dark upon the earth;
there are clouds around it hiding the stars. There must be many
children who are afraid or lonely, for listen, now!"

The sobs and whimpers of many children rose to their ears.
Perhaps the happy children were all asleep, for there was no sound
of laughter or singing.

"Come, come!" cried the fifth little angel. "Let us fly to Gabriel, the guardian of the angels' nursery. He loves all small things, babies and angels, and he will give us feet so that we can run upon the earth and play with the lonely children."

Gabriel was bending over a great bed of silver lilies when the five little angels came flying toward him. They were all talking at once.

"Please, dear Gabriel, we want to fly down to earth!"

"Oh, give us some little legs and feet that we may play in the meadows with the earth children who are crying!"

"We want to tell the lonely children that Heaven is close to them always!"

"Ah, Gabriel, listen to the weeping children and send us right down to them that we may make them smile."

The little angels fluttered about the big beautiful one, who stood straight and shining as a great lily himself, his wings folded like closed petals.

"Little angels, listen," he said, and his voice was music. "It is a long, dangerous journey which you wish to take. It is hard to live on the earth and remain an angel. Every time you are cross or selfish a feather from your wings will fly back to Paradise. If you lose them all you will never be able to return. The children below need you, but those who need you the most do not live in green fields and tend the sheep; they live in ugly cities, in houses where the sun seldom finds his way. Can you keep your golden smiles and your angel wings there?"

"Yes, yes, dear Gabriel! Listen to these sad sounds, and help us to hurry away!"

Out of the golden box where gifts for newborn babies are kept Gabriel took five pairs of small legs and feet. The toes were all pink and dimpled and the five angels were filled with delight. They put them on and danced about, clapping their hands and fluttering their wings.

"All the children upon the earth will be dancing like this before we come home!" they cried. "Now, dear Gabriel, are we ready?"

Gabriel stooped over and kissed each one upon his forehead.

"Keep the blue of the skies in your eyes, the light of Heaven in your smiles and love in your hearts!" he said.

"Farewell, farewell!" they cried. "Here is a shining cloud to carry us down. Watch us and listen; you will hear no sounds of tears tomorrow night!"

But alas! The little angels were so excited over their journey and the strange sights of the world that they kept putting off the work they had come to do.

Reaching the earth just as the sun rose they fell into a meadow full of daisies and buttercups. Of course they had to try their new feet, dancing over the flowers; they had to answer the calls of the birds, and gaze at their own reflections in the pool. By that time they were tired—a feeling they had never known in Paradise—and they lay down in the long grass to sleep. When they woke the moon was shining and the only sound they heard was "Kerchonk! Kerchonk!" from the gay young frogs. Laughing with merriment they ran to the stream and waded down it, splashing their pink toes in the silver water and imitating the frogs.

So the days went by. Their wings were invisible to the people of the world and passersby thought them merely beautiful children, the most beautiful they had ever seen. For a time the angels were not hungry for our kind of food and when they were they walked boldly up to a palace and asked for part of the feast that was going on.

"What princely children!" exclaimed the guests. "Your family, of course?" they asked the old King.

Now the old King had had very ugly, disagreeable children who had grown up and had equally hideous and cross children of their own. He was delighted with the looks of the little angels in the starry clothes and was glad to receive them as part of the royal family. They were given all the sweets they could eat, crowns were placed upon their heads, and at first they had a splendid time. Then they were put in charge of teachers who tried to make them study out of dull books.

"We know more than any books; have we not come from Paradise?" they asked each other. They tore up the books and stamped upon them and, all unnoticed by them, a few feathers flew back to Heaven.

Then their star robes grew dingy and the old King, who spoiled them and let them have whatever they wished, ordered the finest clothes in the kingdom made for them.

Proudly the angels strutted around in purple and gold, eating the richest food, playing all the time and never contented. Every day feathers drifted back to Gabriel's garden, but the angels did not mind.

"Wings are of no use to us here," they said. "We can have whatever we want and when we wish to return to Paradise we will."

They had forgotten the lonely children they came to play with, the frightened, sick children they had longed to comfort.

One day, discontented with everything, they were playing in the royal garden at sunset.

"These roses have thorns on them!" cried one angel pulling an enormous crimson rose to bits.

"Those lilies don't stand straight!" scolded another, tearing down a splendid white lily.

"This butterfly won't stay still long enough to let me catch him!" complained the third.

"Look at this one; it is far bigger and I will catch it!" cried the fourth. He chased the gorgeous black and orange butterfly over the garden, trampling down whole beds of fragrant flowers as he ran.

"Ah see, I have it!" he cried. "It shall follow me wherever I go!"

He opened his clenched hand in which he had crushed the poor butterfly. Its wings were broken and its color rubbed. It crawled painfully over the angel's hand, and the child began to cry. They were the first tears an angel had ever shed, and the others looked bewildered and frightened. Suddenly they remembered when they had heard a child cry before. It was in Paradise when, leaning over the golden bar, they had heard the lonely earth children and had longed to comfort them.

"We had wings once too," cried an angel. "We have lost them, like this butterfly, and we are not of any use either!"

The littlest angel began to cry also.

"I want to fly back to Paradise!" he sobbed. "We are all too little to be left here alone!"

In a bed of lilies they all gathered, watering the crushed flowers with their tears. They were lonely and ashamed. "What must Gabriel think of us now?" they wailed.

Then the fifth angel sprang up.

"Tears don't help a bit!" he cried. "We are still angels and there are many children who need us. We cannot go back to Paradise, but listen to me. We can make the world so like Heaven that we won't be lonely here anymore!"

"Let us start right off!" cried the other angels, struggling to their feet.

"Brave little angels! What will they do next?" asked Gabriel, looking down upon them and smiling.

Out through the garden gates in the moonlight the five ran, and as they thought again their angel thoughts, tiny wings began to sprout from their shoulders. No one saw the wings, at least no grown-up person did. But perhaps you have seen them. I am sure you have heard them fluttering near you!

For from that moment the angels lived with the children of the earth. They sought them far and near. Whenever a child is ill, wherever a child is lonely or sorrowful, one of the five little angels is by his side in a flash, bringing smiles and laughter to his eyes instead of tears. We hear their angel voices in the songs of the happy children; we see the five little angels in eyes that dream, in smiles of love and of courage everywhere.

Their wings are quite grown out now; they could fly back to Paradise if they wished, but they are so blissful in bringing Heaven to the children of the earth that they never think of leaving.

"Dear little angels," said Gabriel watching and listening. "May the blessing of Heaven be with you day and night!"

•

GRANDFATHER STORK

Katharine Pyle

The next three poems are fanciful, but they carry a very real message. Disregard the advice and directions of those who love you, and the world may instruct you in a much harsher way.

A very naughty boy was John;
    He quarrelled with his food,
And would not eat his bread and milk,
    As all good children should.
It grieved his kind mamma to see
    How thin and thinner grew
Her little John, in spite of all
    That she could say or do.
Above the chimney Father Stork
    Heard all that Johnny said,
And how each day he pushed away
    The bowl of milk and bread.
And so it was, when kind mamma
    Had left the house one day,

In through the kitchen door he came
  And carried John away.
Upon the roof the little storks
  Live high up in the sky,
And far below them in the street
  They hear the folks go by.
The old stork brings them, in his beak,
  The eels and frogs for food;
But these he will not let them have
  Unless they're very good.
Such things poor Johnny could not eat;
  And as he sat and cried,
He thought of all the bread and milk
  He used to push aside.

"If I were only home again,
  I would be good," he said,
"And never, never turn away
  From wholesome milk and bread."
If little John was thin before,
  Now thinner every day
He grew, until you'd think the wind
  Would carry him away.
So, when at last he was so lean
  His bones seemed poking through,
There came a sudden gust of wind,
  And, puff! away he blew.
And when it blew him to the street,
  How fast he hurried home!
And, oh, how glad his mother was
  To see her Johnny come!
But gladder still she was to find
  That he had grown so good,
And never now would turn away
  From wholesome simple food.

•

OLD MOTHER WEBTOES

Katharine Pyle

"Oh please, mamma," said little Jane,
  "May I go out to play?"
"No, no," her mother answered her,
  "I fear 'twill rain today."
"With my umbrella green," said Jane,
  "I will not mind the wet."
But still mamma replied, "No, no;
  A cold I fear you'd get."
But oh, Jane was a naughty girl!
  On her own way intent;
Soon as mamma had turned away,
  Out in the street she went.

The streets were wet and lonely;
  No children there at play;
Only old Mother Webtoes
  The frog abroad that day.
Now little Jane she seizes,
  In spite of all her cries,
And green umbrella, Jane and all,
  Away with her she flies.
Far, far off in the river,
  Upon a moisty stone,
Old Webtoes and her children
  Live in a hut alone;
And Jane's big green umbrella
  Old Webtoes hides away.
She makes her sweep, she makes her scrub;
  Jane has no time to play.
She spreads a bed of rushes,
  Where Jane may sleep at night,
And wakes her in the morning
  As soon as it is light.
"Get up," cries Mother Webtoes;
  "The breakfast you must get."
"Oh let me stay in bed," says Jane;
  "The floor is cold and wet."
But Mother Webtoes stamps her foot,
  And makes the child arise;
But as Jane sobs, behind the door,
  Ah, what is this she spies?
It is her green umbrella;
  She sets it now afloat,

And down the river in it sails,
  As if it were a boat.
"Oh Mother Webtoes, only look,"
  She hears the young frogs scream;

"The little girl you brought to us
  Is sailing down the stream."
But Jane is quite too far away
  For them to catch her then,
And when at last she drifts ashore
  She sees her home again.

She rushes to her mother's arms
  With sobs and streaming eyes—
"Oh Mother, Mother dear, forgive
  Your naughty Jane," she cries.

•

THE LITTLE FISH THAT WOULD NOT DO AS IT WAS BID

Ann Taylor

"Dear mother," said a little fish,
"Pray is not that a fly?
I'm very hungry, and I wish
You'd let me go and try."

"Sweet innocent," the mother cried,
And started from her nook,
"That horrid fly is put to hide
The sharpness of the hook."

Now, as I've heard, this little trout
Was young and foolish, too,
And so he thought he'd venture out,
To see if it were true.

And round about the hook he played,
With many a longing look,
And—"Dear me," to himself he said,
"I'm sure that's not a hook.

"I can but give one little pluck;
Let's see, and so I will."
So on he went, and lo! it stuck
Quite through his little gill.

And as he faint and fainter grew,
With hollow voice he cried,
"Dear mother, had I minded you,
I need not now have died."

•

TWENTY FROGGIES

George Cooper

A great event in every young life is that long-awaited first day of
going to school. This little poem helps us get ready.

> Twenty froggies went to school,
> Down beside a rushy pool,
> Twenty little coats of green,
> Twenty vests all white and clean.
>
> "We must be in time," said they,
> "First we study, then we play;
> That is how we keep the rule,
> When we froggies go to school."
>
> Master Bullfrog, brave and stern,
> Called his classes in their turn,
> Taught them how to nobly strive,
> Also how to leap and dive.
>
> Taught them how to dodge a blow,
> From the sticks that bad boys throw.
> Twenty froggies grew up fast,
> Bullfrogs they became at last.
>
> Polished to a high degree,
> As each froggie ought to be.
> Now they sit on other logs,
> Teaching other little frogs.

•

GOING TO SCHOOL

John Martin

It makes all the difference when a young mind goes to school
with this thought: The opportunity to learn is one of the great
blessings of life.

> Dear God, a schoolday comes again,
>   With many things for me to do.
> Please bless my Heart and guide my Brain
>   And make me thoughtful, strong, and true.
> My lessons may seem dull to me,
>   And study hours long and dry,
> But if You help me, then I'll see
>   How fast those useful hours fly.
>
> O God, go forth with me today,
>   And help my Head and guide my Hand,
> For You are wise and know a way
>   To make me learn and understand.
> Open my Heart and Eyes to see
>   How kind is every study hour;
> For each one offers Gifts to me
>   Like Wisdom, Patience, Love, and Power.
>   Amen.

•

IN *ADAM'S* FALL . . .

From The New England Primer

Here are a few of the famous rhymes that introduced generations
of seventeenth- and eighteenth-century schoolchildren to the alphabet. These verses remind us that in times past, children encountered their first lessons within the framework of hard-nosed

realities. First, life is no easy road. Second, each human being ventures down that road possessing a morally responsible soul. These little rhymes may be outdated as a way of learning to read and write, but modern parents and teachers will find the old lessons of mortality and immortality still worth pondering.

In *Adam*'s fall,
We sinned all.

Heaven to find,
The *Bible* mind.

The *Cat* does play,
And after slay.

The *Dog* doth bite
A thief at night.

The Idle *Fool*
Is whipped at school.

As runs the *Glass,*
Man's life doth pass.

Job feels the rod
Yet blesses God.

Young pious *Ruth*
Left all for truth.

Young *Samuel* dear
The Lord did fear.

Time cuts down all,
Both great and small.

While *Youth* do cheer
Death may be near.

•

THE FOX AND THE CAT

It's not necessarily *how much* you know, but *what* you know, that counts.

It happened once that the cat met Mr. Fox in the wood, and because she thought he was clever and experienced in all the ways of the world, she addressed him in a friendly manner.

"Good morning, dear Mr. Fox! How are you, and how do you get along in these hard times?"

The fox, full of pride, looked at the cat from head to foot for some time, hardly knowing whether he would deign to answer or not. At last he said: "Oh, you poor whisker wiper, you silly piebald, you starveling mouse hunter! What has come into your head? How dare you ask me how I am getting on? What sort of education have you had? How many arts are you master of?"

"Only one," said the cat meekly.

"And what might that one be?" asked the fox.

"When the dogs run after me, I can jump into a tree and save myself."

"Is that all?' said the fox. "I am master of a hundred arts, and I have a sackful of cunning tricks in addition. But I pity you. Come with me, and I will teach you how to escape from the dogs."

Just then a huntsman came along with four hounds. The cat sprang trembling into a tree, and crept stealthily up to the topmost branch, where she was entirely hidden by twigs and leaves.

"Open your sack, Mr. Fox! Open your sack!" cried the cat, but the dogs had gripped him, and held him fast.

"Oh, Mr. Fox!" cried the cat, "you with your hundred arts, and your sackful of tricks, are held fast, while I, with my one, am safe. Had you been able to creep up here, you would not have lost your life."

Cat

•

THE TONGUE AND HOW TO USE IT

Retold by F. J. Gould

Discipline in what we say (especially what we say about others)
is one of the most important kinds of training. There are some
words that can't be recaptured once they've escaped.

Saint Philip Neri, a beloved priest of sixteenth-century Rome,
was sought out by the rich and poor, the noble and common
people alike, for his ability to look into hearts and minds.

A young lady once went to the good man, Saint Philip Neri, to
confess her sins. He knew one of her faults only too well. She was
not a bad-hearted girl, but she often talked of her neighbors, and
spoke idle tales about them. These tales were told again by others,
and much harm was done, and no good.

Saint Philip said: "My daughter, you do wrong to speak ill of
others, and I order you to perform penance. You must buy a fowl
in the market. Then walk out of the town, and as you go along the
road pull the feathers from the bird and scatter them. Do not stop
until you have plucked every feather. When you have done this,
come back and tell me."

She said to herself that this was a very singular punishment to
suffer. But she made no objection. She bought the fowl, walked out,
and plucked the feathers as she had been bidden. Then she went
to Saint Philip and reported what she had done.

"My daughter," said the Saint, "you have carried out the first
part of the penance. Now there is a second part."

"Yes, Father?"

"You must now go back the way you came and pick up all the
feathers."

"But, father, this cannot be done. By this time the wind has
blown them all ways. I might pick up some, but I could not possibly
gather up all."

"Quite true, my daughter. And is it not so with the unwise
words that you let fall? Have you not often dropped idle tales from
your lips, and have they not gone this way and that, carried from
mouth to mouth until they are quite beyond you? Could you possibly follow them, and recall them if you wanted to do so?"

"No, Father."

"Then, my daughter, when you are inclined to say unkind things about your neighbor, close your lips. Do not scatter these light and evil feathers by the wayside."

•

WORDS ARE WONDERFUL THINGS

Mrs. E. R. Miller

Keep a watch on your words, my darling,
    For words are wonderful things;
They are sweet like the bees' fresh honey,
    Like the bees they have terrible stings;
They can bless like the warm, glad sunshine,
    And brighten a lonely life;
They can cut, in the strife of anger,
    Like an open, two-edged knife.

•

THE TALKATIVE TORTOISE

*Adapted from a retelling
by Sara Cone Bryant*

This story comes from a collection of ancient fables from India known as *The Fables of Bidpai*. It underscores the importance of knowing when to keep your mouth shut.

Once upon a time, a Tortoise lived in a pond with two Ducks, who were her very good friends. She enjoyed the company of the Ducks, because she could talk with them to her heart's content. The Tortoise liked to talk. She always had something to say, and she liked to hear herself say it.

After many years of this pleasant living, the pond became very low, in a dry season, and finally it dried up. The two Ducks saw that they could no longer live there, so they decided to fly to another region, where there was more water. They went to the Tortoise to bid her goodbye.

"Oh, don't leave me behind!" begged the Tortoise. "Take me with you. I must die if I am left here."

"But you cannot fly!" said the Ducks. "How can we take you with us?"

"Take me with you! Take me with you!" said the Tortoise.

The Ducks felt so sorry for her that at last they thought of a way to take her. "We have thought of a way which will be possible," they said, "if only you can manage to keep still long enough. We will each take hold of one end of a stout stick, and you take the middle in your mouth. Then we will fly up in the air with you and carry you with us. But remember not to talk! If you open your mouth, you are lost."

The Tortoise said she would not say a word, she would not so much as move her mouth, and she was very grateful. So the Ducks brought a strong little stick and took hold of the ends, while the Tortoise bit firmly on the middle. Then the two Ducks rose slowly in the air and flew away with their burden.

When they were above the treetops, the Tortoise wanted to say, "How high we are!" But she remembered, and kept still.

When they passed the church steeple she wanted to say, "What is that which shines?" But she remembered, and held her peace.

Then they came over the village square, and the people looked up and saw them. "Look at the Ducks carrying a Tortoise!" they shouted. And everyone ran to look.

The Tortoise wanted to say, "What business is it of yours?" But she didn't.

She heard the people shout, "Isn't it funny! Isn't it strange! Look at it! Look!" And she began to grow angry. But she kept her mouth shut.

Then the people began to laugh. "Did you ever see such a funny sight in all your life?" they jeered.

And the Tortoise could stand it no longer.

She opened her mouth and yelled, "Be quiet, you stupid—"

But before she could say any more, she had fallen to the ground.

And that was the end of the Tortoise.

•

THE WISE OLD OWL

Someone once observed that we have two ears and one mouth
and should learn to use them in that proportion.

> A wise old owl sat in an oak,
> The more he heard the less he spoke;
> The less he spoke the more he heard.
> Why aren't we all like that wise old bird?

•

THE TWELVE MONTHS

Retold by James Baldwin

Politeness, etiquette, good manners, civility—the habits these
words represent are underrated and underused in our time. This
old story from eastern Europe illustrates how far those habits can
take you.

A very long time ago there were two little girls who lived in a
little house with a cross old woman.

One of the little girls was named Dobrunka. She was the
daughter of the cross woman, and she was as cross as her mother.

The other little girl was very pretty, and she was as good as she
was pretty. But Dobrunka and her mother were very unkind to her.
Her name was Katinka.

Now Dobrunka was idle and lazy, and she sat in the house and
did nothing all day long.

But Katinka was kept very busy. She did the sweeping and the
cooking and the spinning and the weaving and the milking and the
churning.

Every day the cross woman with whom she lived scolded her,
and sometimes she punished her. Dobrunka scolded her, too, and
set hard tasks for her to do.

One day in January Dobrunka said, "Here, Katinka! Go out into the woods and pick a bunch of violets for me. I want them to wear in my hair."

"A bunch of violets!" answered Katinka. "Why, it is winter, and violets do not grow in the snow."

"Hold your tongue and do as I tell you," said Dobrunka.

"Yes," said the cross woman, "go into the woods; and if you come back without the violets, you shall be punished."

Poor Katinka went into the woods. Her shoes were thin and worn. She had not so much as a shawl to throw over her shoulders.

The wind blew cold. The ground was covered with snow. There was not even a path among the trees.

Do you wonder that the child wept?

She lost her way. She was hungry and very cold. Night was coming on.

As she was climbing a little hill she saw a light among some big rocks in front of her. Could it be a fire? How she wished she could warm herself by it!

Yes, it was a fire—a great blazing fire, built in the mouth of a little cave.

Katinka went nearer.

Around the fire she saw twelve white stones, and on each stone a strange-looking person was sitting. Each person wore a long cloak that covered his shoulders and body and even his feet. Over his head a hood was drawn.

Katinka saw that three of the cloaks were white like snow, three were green like the leaves of the trees in summer, three were yellow like the wheat in harvest time, and three were purple like ripe grapes.

The child was not afraid.

"Please, good men," she said, "may I warm myself at your fire? I am almost dead with cold."

"Certainly, dear child," said one who wore a white cloak. "Come and sit with us. We are the Twelve Months."

"I thank you, Mr. Month," said Katinka; and she went forward and stood by the one who had spoken. Then to this one she said, "I think you must be January."

"You are right," he said. "But who are you, and why do you come here in the deep snow?"

"I am looking for violets," Katinka answered.

"For violets, indeed!" cried January. "This is not the time for them. They do not grow in the snow."

"I know it," said Katinka, "but the woman I live with said I must bring some or she would punish me. Can you tell me where I can find them?"

January did not answer. But he stood up and spoke to one of the green-cloaked fellows.

"Brother March," he said, "it is for you to help this poor child."

March arose, and oh, how the wind blew! Then he stirred the fire with his long staff.

As the flames curled up, warm and bright, the snow melted and the trees began to bud. Then green grass sprang up everywhere, and pretty flowers bloomed in sunny places.

"Now, dear child," said March, "gather your violets quickly."

Katinka ran joyfully here and there and picked as many as her hands could hold. She was now quite warm; she had forgotten the cold and the snow.

"Thank you, Mr. March," she said. "Thank you, Mr. January. Thank you all."

Then she ran quickly home through the snow.

Think of the surprise of Dobrunka and her mother!

"Where did you get those things?" asked the woman.

"I found them in the woods," said Katinka. "The ground under the bushes was covered with them."

Dobrunka took the violets, but she did not so much as thank the poor child.

The next morning the cross girl thought of something else. She wanted some strawberries. Nothing would do but she must have some strawberries.

"Katinka," she said, "go into the woods and get some ripe red strawberries for me."

"Why, it is winter," said Katinka, "and strawberries do not grow in the snow."

"Hold your tongue and do as I tell you," said Dobrunka.

"Yes," said the cross woman, "go out and gather some strawberries; and if you come back without them you shall be punished."

Then she pushed the child out into the snow and shut the door behind her.

Katinka went far into the woods, looking for the light she had seen the day before. She was very tired, when all at once she saw the mouth of the little cave right before her.

The fire was burning bright and warm, and the Twelve Months were sitting in their places, with their long cloaks over their shoulders.

"Please, good men," she said, "may I warm myself at your fire? I am almost dead with cold."

"Certainly, dear child," said January. "But why have you come back to us today?"

"I am looking for strawberries," answered Katinka.

"For strawberries, indeed!" cried January. "This is not the time for strawberries."

"I know it," said the child, "but the woman I live with said I must bring some or she would punish me. Can you tell me where I can find them?"

Then January said, "Brother June, it is for you to help the child."

June arose. His cloak was yellow as gold, and his hood was covered with roses.

He stirred the fire with his staff. The cheery blaze flamed up. The snow melted. The trees put on their leaves. The fields were green. The sun was warm. Summer had come.

"Now gather your strawberries quickly, my child," said June.

Katinka filled her apron with the ripe red fruit. She had forgotten that it was ever winter.

"Thank you, Mr. June. Thank you, Mr. January. Thank you all," she said.

Then she ran quickly home through the snow.

Think of the surprise of Dobrunka and her mother!

"Where did you get those things?" asked the woman.

"Out yonder in the woods," said Katinka. "There were so many that the ground was red with them."

Dobrunka and her mother took the strawberries and ate every one of them. But they never so much as thanked the poor child.

On the third morning the cross girl had another fancy. She

wanted some red apples. Nothing would do but she must have some red apples.

So Katinka was sent out into the snow-covered woods to get them.

She found the little cave without any trouble. The Twelve Months were still sitting around their fire.

"Welcome again, dear child," said January. "Come and warm yourself."

When she was quite warm and happy, he said, "Now tell us why you have come to us this third time."

Katinka told him about the red apples, and how she would be punished if she did not carry some home.

"Brother September," said January, "it is your turn to help this child."

September stood up. His beard was long and gray. His cloak was purple. On his head was a wreath of autumn leaves.

He stirred the fire with his staff. The flames leaped up. The snow melted. The ground was warm and dry. Crickets chirped in the tall grass. The trees were dressed in beautiful colors—red, brown, and gold. It was autumn.

"Now gather your apples quickly, dear child," said September.

Katinka looked up. An apple tree full of the finest fruit was before her.

She shook it. A red apple fell at her feet. She shook it again. Another red apple fell at her feet.

"Hurry home, Katinka," said September.

She picked up the two apples and turned to go.

"Thank you, Mr. September. Thank you, Mr. January. Thank you all," she said.

Think of the surprise of cross Dobrunka and her mother!

"Apples right off the tree in January!" they cried. "Where did you get them?"

"Out yonder in the woods. The tree is so full that it looks like a red cherry tree in summer."

"And you brought only two!" cried Dobrunka. "You ate all the rest on the way."

"Oh, no, Dobrunka. I was allowed to shake the tree only twice, and these two apples were all that fell."

"Begone! You do not tell the truth," said the cross girl, and she struck Katinka with her hand.

Then she and her mother ate the apples, but did not thank the one who brought them.

"The finest fruit I ever tasted," said the mother.

"Yes, and I wish I had more," said Dobrunka.

"What a pity to leave a tree full of them in the woods," said the mother. "Katinka must milk the cows now, or I would send her right back to gather the rest."

"Mother, give me my fur cloak," said Dobrunka. "I will go out and find the tree myself. I will shake it so hard that all the apples will fall into my lap."

The mother did not want her to go. Night was coming. It was cold. But Dobrunka would not listen.

She wrapped her fur cloak around her. She drew her hood over her head. She hurried out into the woods.

Dobrunka soon lost her way. The ground was all covered with snow. There was not so much as a footpath anywhere.

After a while she saw a light far up on the side of a hill.

She climbed and climbed. She climbed through the snow till she was very tired.

At last she came to the little cave and saw the Twelve Months sitting around their blazing fire.

Without so much as saying "Good evening," she pushed forward, in front of them, and began to warm herself.

"Why have you come here?" asked January. "What is it you are looking for?"

"That is none of your business, old gray-head," answered the unmannerly girl.

January's face grew dark. He lifted his staff. He spoke one word to his brothers.

All at once the fire went out. The cave was nowhere to be seen. The Twelve Months had vanished.

Dark clouds covered the sky. More snow began to fall. The wind roared in the trees.

What could cross Dobrunka do now? Where could she find shelter from the storm and the night?

She stumbled about among the trees and the rocks. She called for help, but no one heard her.

All night long the cross mother waited and watched for Dobrunka.

She stood at the window and looked out at the snow. She listened to the roar of the wind.

In the morning she put on her fur cloak and her hood. "I must go and find Dobrunka," she said.

She hurried out into the great woods. The snow was still falling. The wind was still blowing. There was not even a track to be seen.

"Dobrunka! Dobrunka!" she called. But Dobrunka did not hear. She would never answer her.

At home Katinka was busy with her spinning wheel. Now and then she went to the door and looked out and listened.

"I wish they would come," she said to herself.

At noon she cooked a fine dinner. She set the table. She waited and waited.

But no one came to eat with her.

The snow was still falling. The wind was still blowing.

In the evening she milked the cows and fed the chickens. She made a fresh fire. She brushed the hearth. She set the two chairs before it.

"I fear that something has happened to them," she said.

She went to the door again. The snow was still falling. The wind was still blowing. Another dark night had come.

Day after day Katinka waited, but no word did she ever hear of the cross woman or of cross Dobrunka.

As there was no one else to claim it, the house was now her own. So also were the cows and the chickens and the pretty garden, and the green fields on both sides of the house.

She was busy, busy, busy, all the time. But she was her own mistress, and no cross words were heard in her house.

The Twelve Months did not forget the child.

March brought violets to her door every year.

April watered the fields and made the grain sprout and grow.

May brought sunshine and nesting birds and soft balmy winds.

June remembered to bring plenty of red strawberries.

July ripened the wheat.

August brought loads of sweet hay to Katinka's barn.

September gave her ripe apples, and allowed her to shake the trees as much as she wished.

October brought many a basket of purple grapes into her kitchen.

November found everything housed and safe for the winter.

December filled the child's arms with Christmas presents.

January made the fire glow in the chimney and covered the roof of the house with a soft white blanket.

And even February brought good gifts to the gentle child. Can you guess what they were?

Thus kind Katinka lived a happy and contented life, and everybody loved her. As the old saying has it, she had spring in her heart, summer in her fields, autumn in her orchard, and winter at her door.

•

RULES OF BEHAVIOR

Hearts, like doors, will open with ease
To very, very little keys,
And don't forget that two of these
Are "I thank you" and "If you please."

•

HOW THE BRAZILIAN BEETLES
GOT THEIR COATS

Retold by Elsie Eells

Don't estimate other people's strengths and weaknesses too quickly, particularly by judging only appearances. Often you'll be surprised at how wrong you are, as we see in this tale from Brazil.

In Brazil the beetles have such beautifully colored, hard-shelled coats upon their backs that they are sometimes set in pins and necklaces like precious stones. Once upon a time, years and years ago, they had ordinary plain brown coats. This is how it happened that the Brazilian beetle earned a new coat.

One day a little brown beetle was crawling along a wall when a big gray rat ran out of a hole in the wall and looked down scornfully at the little beetle. "O ho!" he said to the beetle, "how slowly you crawl along. You'll never get anywhere in the world. Just look at me and see how fast I can run."

The big gray rat ran to the end of the wall, wheeled around,

and came back to the place where the little beetle was slowly crawling along at only a tiny distance from where the rat had left her.

"Don't you wish that you could run like that?" said the big gray
rat to the little brown beetle.

"You are surely a fast runner," replied the little brown beetle
politely. Her mother had taught her always to be polite and had
often said to her that a really polite beetle never boasts about her
own accomplishments. The little brown beetle never boasted a
single boast about the things she could do. She just went on slowly
crawling along the wall.

A bright green and gold parrot in the mango tree over the wall
had heard the conversation. "How would you like to race with the
beetle?" he asked the big gray rat. "I live next door to the tailor
bird," he added, "and just to make the race exciting I'll offer a
brightly colored coat as a prize to the one who wins the race.
You may chose for it any color you like and I'll have it made to
order."

"I'd like a yellow coat with stripes like the tiger's," said the big
gray rat, looking over his shoulder at his gaunt gray sides as if he
were already admiring his new coat.

"I'd like a beautiful, brightly colored new coat, too," said the
little brown beetle.

The big gray rat laughed long and loud until his gaunt gray
sides were shaking. "Why, you talk just as if you thought you had a
chance to win the race," he said, when he could speak.

The bright green and gold parrot set the royal palm tree at the
top of the cliff as the goal of the race. He gave the signal to start and
then he flew away to the royal palm tree to watch for the end of the
race.

The big gray rat ran as fast as he could. Then he thought how
very tired he was getting. "What's the use of hurrying?" he said to
himself. "The little brown beetle cannot possibly win. If I were
racing with somebody who could really run it would be very different." Then he started to run more slowly, but every time his heart
beat it said, "Hurry up! Hurry up!" The big gray rat decided that it
was best to obey the little voice in his heart so he hurried just as
fast as he could.

When he reached the royal palm tree at the top of the cliff he
could hardly believe his eyes. He thought he must be having a bad
dream. There was the little brown beetle sitting quietly beside the
bright green and gold parrot. The big gray rat had never been so

surprised in all his life. "How did you ever manage to run fast enough to get here so soon?" he asked the little brown beetle as soon as he could catch his breath.

The little brown beetle drew out the tiny wings from her sides. "Nobody said anything about having to run to win the race," she replied, "so I flew instead."

"I did not know that you could fly," said the big gray rat in a subdued little voice.

"After this," said the bright green and gold parrot, "never judge anyone by his looks alone. You never can tell how often or where you may find concealed wings. You have lost the prize."

Then the parrot turned to the little brown beetle who was waiting quietly at his side. "What color do you want your new coat to be?" he asked.

The little brown beetle looked up at the bright green and gold parrot, at the green and gold palm trees above their heads, at the green mangoes with golden flushes on their cheeks lying on the ground under the mango trees, at the golden sunshine upon the distant green hills. "I choose a coat of green and gold," she said.

From that day to this the Brazilian beetle has worn a coat of green with golden lights upon it.

And until this day, even in Brazil, where the flowers and birds and beasts and insects have such gorgeous coloring, the rat wears a dull gray coat.

•

THE PIG BROTHER
Laura E. Richards

Hearing the truth from friends or strangers may sometimes shame us. Like many medicines, shame may not feel good, but its bitter taste can help set us straight. This is a great story for those who can't remember to pick up their toys, clothes, or dirty dishes.

There was once a child who was untidy. He left his books on the floor, and his muddy shoes on the table. He put his fingers in the jam pots, and spilled ink on his best shirt. There was really no end to his untidiness.

One day the Tidy Angel came into his nursery.

"This will never do!" said the Angel. "This is really shocking. You must go out and stay with your brother while I set things right here."

"I have no brother!" said the child.

"Yes, you have!" said the Angel. "You may not know him, but he will know you. Go out in the garden and watch for him, and he will soon come."

"I don't know what you mean!" said the child, but he went out into the garden and waited.

Presently a squirrel came along, whisking his tail.

"Are you my brother?" asked the child.

The squirrel looked him over carefully.

"Well, I should hope not!" he said. "My fur is neat and smooth, my nest is handsomely made and in perfect order, and my young ones are properly brought up. Why do you insult me by asking such a question?"

He whisked off, and the child waited.

Presently a wren came hopping by.

"Are you my brother?" asked the child.

"No indeed!" said the wren. "What impertinence! You will find no tidier person than I in the whole garden. Not a feather is out of place, and my eggs are the wonder of all for smoothness and beauty. Brother, indeed!" He hopped off, ruffling his feathers, and the child waited.

By and by a large Tommy Cat came along.

"Are you my brother?" asked the child.

"Go and look at yourself in the glass," said the Tommy Cat haughtily, "and you will have your answer. I have been washing myself in the sun all the morning, while it is clear that no water has come near you for a long time. There are no such creatures as you in my family, I am humbly thankful to say."

He walked on, waving his tail, and the child waited.

Presently a pig came trotting along.

The child did not wish to ask the pig if he were his brother, but the pig did not wait to be asked.

"Hallo, brother!" he grunted.

"I am not your brother!" said the child.

"Oh, yes, you are!" said the pig. "I confess I am not proud of you, but there is no mistaking the members of our family. Come along, and have a good roll in the barnyard! There is some lovely black mud there."

"I don't like to roll in mud!" said the child.

"Tell that to the hens!" said the pig brother. "Look at your hands, and your shoes, and your shirt! Come along, I say! You may have some of the pig swill for supper, if there is more than I want."

"I don't want pig swill!" said the child, and he began to cry.

Just then the Tidy Angel came out.

"I have set everything right," she said, "and so it must stay. Now, will you go with the Pig Brother, or will you come back with me, and be a tidy child?"

"With you, with you!" cried the child, and he clung to the Angel's dress.

The Pig Brother grunted.

"Small loss!" he said. "There will be all the more swill for me!" And he trotted on.

●

THE CAT AND THE PARROT
Retold by Sara Cone Bryant

Some people want everything—what belongs to them, to you, to me, to everyone. Here is unbridled appetite, the kind that knows no self-discipline.

Once there was a cat and a parrot. And they had agreed to take turns asking each other to dinner. First the cat should ask the parrot, then the parrot should invite the cat, and so on. It was the cat's turn first.

Now the cat was very stingy. He provided nothing at all for dinner except a pint of milk, a little slice of fish, and a biscuit. The parrot was too polite to complain, but he did not have a very good time.

When it was his turn to invite the cat, he cooked a fine dinner. He had a roast of meat, a pot of tea, a basket of fruit, and, best of all, he baked a whole basketful of little cakes—little, brown, crispy, spicy cakes! Oh, I should say as many as five hundred. And he put four hundred and ninety-eight of the cakes before the cat, keeping only two for himself.

Well, the cat ate the roast, and drank the tea, and sucked the fruit, and then he began on the pile of cakes. He ate all the four hundred and ninety-eight cakes, and then he looked round and said: "I'm hungry; haven't you anything to eat?"

"Why," said the parrot, "here are my two cakes, if you want them."

The cat ate up the two cakes, and then he licked his chops and said, "I am beginning to get an appetite. Have you anything to eat?"

"Well, really," said the parrot, who was now rather angry, "I don't see anything more, unless you wish to eat me!" He thought the cat would be ashamed when he heard that, but the cat just looked at him and licked his chops again, and slip! slop! gobble! Down his throat went the parrot!

Then the cat started down the street. An old woman was standing by, and she had seen the whole thing, and she was shocked that the cat should eat his friend. "Why, cat!" she said, "how dreadful of you to eat your friend the parrot!"

"Parrot, indeed!" said the cat. "What's a parrot to me? I've a great mind to eat you, too." And before you could say "Jack Robinson," slip! slop! gobble! Down went the old woman!

Then the cat started down the road again, walking like this, because he felt so fine. Pretty soon he met a man driving a donkey. When he saw the cat he said, "Get out of my way, cat. I'm in a hurry and my donkey might tread on you."

"Donkey, indeed!" said the cat. "Much I care for a donkey! I have eaten five hundred cakes, I have eaten my friend the parrot, I have eaten an old woman—what's to hinder my eating a miserable man and a donkey?"

And slip! slop! gobble! Down went the old man and the donkey.

Then the cat walked on down the road, jauntily, like this. After

a little, he met a procession, coming that way. The king was at the head, walking proudly with his newly married bride, and behind him were his soldiers, marching, and behind them were ever and ever so many elephants, walking two by two. The king felt very kind to everybody, because he had just been married, and he said to the cat, "Get out of my way, pussycat, get out of my way—my elephants might hurt you."

"Hurt me!" said the cat, shaking his fat sides. "Ho, ho! I have eaten five hundred cakes, I have eaten my friend the parrot, I have eaten an old woman, I have eaten a man and a donkey; what's to hinder my eating a beggarly king?"

And slip! slop! gobble! Down went the king; down went the queen; down went the soldiers—and down went all the elephants!

Then the cat went on, more slowly. He had really had enough to eat now. But a little farther on he met two crabs, scuttling along in the sand. "Get out of our way, pussycat," they squeaked.

"Ho, ho ho!" cried the cat in a terrible voice. "I have eaten five hundred cakes, I have eaten my friend the parrot, I have eaten an old woman, a man with a donkey, a king, a queen, his men-at-arms, and all his elephants; and now I'll eat you too."

And slip! slop! gobble! Down went the two crabs.

When the crabs got down inside, they began to look around. It was very dark, but they could see the poor king sitting in a corner with his bride on his arm; she had fainted. Near them were the men-at-arms, treading on one another's toes, and the elephants, still trying to form in twos—but they couldn't, because there was not room. In the opposite corner sat the old woman, and near her stood the man and his donkey. But in the other corner was a great pile of cakes, and by them perched the parrot, his feathers all drooping.

"Let's get to work!" said the crabs. And, snip, snap, they began to make a little hole in the side, with their sharp claws. Snip, snap, snip, snap, till it was big enough to get through. Then out they scuttled.

Then out walked the king, carrying his bride; out marched the men-at-arms; out tramped the elephants, two by two; out came the old man, beating his donkey; out walked the old woman, scolding the cat; and last of all, out hopped the parrot, holding a cake in each claw. (Remember, two cakes were all he wanted.)

But the poor cat had to spend the whole day sewing up the hole in his coat!

•

GREEDY

Sydney Dayre

Often we are guilty of the same sins we see in others.

> A greedy fellow? I should say!
> They passed the apples round this way
> And then he snatched—he couldn't wait—
> The biggest one upon the plate.
>
> Such greediness I do despise!
> I had been keeping both my eyes
> Upon that apple, for, you see,
> The plate was coming, next, to me.
>
> 'Twas big and mellow, just the kind
> A greedy chap would like to find.
> He laughed as if he thought it fun—
> *I* meant to take that very one.

•

THE FRIEND OF A FRIEND OF A FRIEND

There are some people who seek any connection or pretext, no matter how tenuous, to get something for themselves. The reward for such behavior should be equally tenuous.

Djuha is a widely loved "wise fool" of Arab folklore.

One day a friend who loved to hunt came to visit Djuha. "I've brought you a rabbit I just caught," he said proudly as he stepped into the house. "It will make a fine dinner."

Djuha gladly cooked the rabbit into a stew, and they sat down to a fine feast.

The very next day a stranger knocked on Djuha's door. "Who are you?" inquired Djuha.

"I'm a neighbor of your friend the hunter, who brought you the rabbit yesterday," he said.

Djuha politely invited him inside and set a dinner before him. "These are the leftovers of our rabbit stew," Djuha said, and the visitor ate heartily.

The very next day another stranger knocked on Djuha's door.

"Who are you?" asked Djuha.

"I'm a cousin of the neighbor of your friend the hunter, who brought you the rabbit," he explained.

"Come in," said Djuha. He sat the man at the table, and set before him a bowl of hot water.

"What's this?" asked the stranger.

"That," said Djuha, "is water boiled in the very same pot as the rabbit of my friend who is the neighbor of your cousin."

•

SPIDER'S TWO FEASTS

Those who can't put their desires in order often get trapped between them. This folk tale comes from Africa.

Long ago, back in the days when animals could talk just as easily as you and I, Spider looked very different than he does now. Today, of course, he has a big, fat head and a big, fat body, with a little, bitty waist in between where his eight long legs stick out. In olden days, though, Spider did not have such a trim waistline. He was big and plump all over. This is the story of how his belly got so thin.

One day Spider was walking through the forest when he met Hare hopping down the path.

"Good morning," called Spider. "Why are you hopping so fast?"

"Don't you know?" asked Hare. "Upstream Town is giving a wedding feast. They'll be eating soon. Everyone is invited."

Spider was so happy, he danced a little dance on his eight long legs.

"How lucky for me," he thought, patting his plump belly. "There'll be yams and fish, and rice and beans. I can eat all I want!"

At once he started toward Upstream Town.

Just then he met Fox trotting the other way.

"Good morning," called Spider. "Why are you trotting so fast?"

"Haven't you heard?" asked Fox. "Downstream Town is giving a harvest feast. They'll be serving soon. Everyone is invited."

Now Spider was so happy, he jumped in the air and flipped a little flip with his eight long legs.

"Two feasts!" he thought, rubbing his fat belly. "I am very happy. I'll go to both! I'll hurry to Downstream Town and fill my stomach. Then I'll run to Upstream Town and fill it again!"

So he turned and started toward Downstream Town.

But before long, a new thought made him stop in his tracks.

"I wonder where the food will be served first?" he thought. "I must go to that town and eat as much as I can. Then I can hurry to the other town in time for my second feast. But how can I know which village will eat first?"

Spider sat down on a rock to ponder his problem. If he went the wrong way, he might miss a whole feast! The terrible thought made his plump belly growl and his eight long legs tremble all over.

Then suddenly he had an idea.

He ran home as fast as he could and found two long ropes. Then he called two of his children and took them to a place on the river halfway between Upstream Town and Downstream Town.

Spider tied one long rope around his waist and gave the other end to his son.

"Take this rope to Upstream Village," he said. "When the feast begins, pull hard, and I will know to come."

Then Spider tied the other long rope around his waist too, and gave the end to his daughter.

"Now, you take your rope to Downstream Village," he told her. "When the feast begins there, pull hard, and I will know to come."

So Spider's son went to Upstream Village with his long rope, and Spider's daughter went to Downstream Village with her long rope, and Spider sat down in between.

"Now I'll know who serves food first," he gloated, smacking his lips. "I can go there and eat my fill, and then go to the second village and have another feast!"

He was very pleased with himself.

An hour passed, but nothing happened. Another hour passed, and still Spider felt no tug on either rope. His plump belly began to growl again, and he started to grow angry.

But then Spider got a rude surprise, because Upstream Village and Downstream Village began their feasts at the same time! Spider's son tugged on his rope in Upstream Village, and Spider's daughter tugged on her rope in Downstream Village, and poor Spider was caught in between.

Now, Spider's children were young and strong, and when their father failed to come, each began pulling harder and harder. Spider just bobbed back and forth in one place, with the ropes around his waist getting tighter and tighter. His children kept pulling, harder and harder, and the ropes kept squeezing Spider, tighter and tighter. Spider waved his eight legs in the air for help, but no one saw him, because they were all at the feasts.

Finally the feasts were over. Spider's children stopped pulling and hurried back to where they had left their father. They found him lying on the ground, gasping for breath, for the ropes had squeezed his big, plump waist thinner than a stick!

And when they took the ropes off, Spider stayed that way. To this day, he has a skinny little waist between his big, fat head and his big, fat body.

And whenever people see him, they think of how he tried to have two feasts at once.

•

FORTUNE AND THE BEGGAR

Ivan Krylov

Philosophers have noted that human desires often increase with the means of their gratification. The next two tales show the principle in action. Many times we want to say, "Just a little more ... more ... more." Wisdom teaches us when to say, "Enough."

The first story comes from Russian fable writer Ivan Krylov (1768–1844).

One day a ragged beggar was creeping along from house to house. He carried an old wallet in his hand, and was asking at every door for a few cents to buy something to eat. As he was grumbling at his lot, he kept wondering why it was that folks who had so much money were never satisfied but were always wanting more.

"Here," said he, "is the master of this house—I know him

well. He was always a good businessman, and he made himself wondrously rich a long time ago. Had he been wise he would have stopped then. He would have turned over his business to someone else, and then he could have spent the rest of his life in ease. But what did he do instead? He took to building ships and sending them to sea to trade with foreign lands. He thought he would get mountains of gold.

"But there were great storms on the water. His ships were wrecked, and his riches were swallowed up by the waves. Now his hopes all lie at the bottom of the sea, and his great wealth has vanished like the dreams of a night.

"There are many such cases. Men seem to be never satisfied unless they can gain the whole world.

"As for me, if I had only enough to eat and to wear I would not want anything more."

Just at that moment Fortune came down the street. She saw the beggar and stopped. She said to him: "Listen! I have long wished to help you. Hold your wallet and I will pour this gold into it. But I will pour only on this condition: All that falls into the wallet shall be pure gold; but every piece that falls upon the ground shall become dust. Do you understand?"

"Oh, yes, I understand," said the beggar.

"Then have a care," said Fortune. "Your wallet is old, so do not load it too heavily."

The beggar was so glad that he could hardly wait. He quickly opened his wallet, and a stream of yellow coins was poured into it. The wallet soon began to grow heavy.

"Is that enough?" asked Fortune.

"Not yet."

"Isn't it cracking?"

"Never fear."

The beggar's hands began to tremble. Ah, if the golden stream would only pour forever!

"You are the richest man in the world now!"

"Just a little more," said the Beggar. "Add just a handful or two."

"There, it's full. The wallet will burst."

"But it will hold a little more, just a little more!"

Another piece was added, and the wallet split. The treasure fell upon the ground and was turned to dust. Fortune had vanished. The beggar had now nothing but his empty wallet, and it was torn from top to bottom. He was as poor as before.

•

THE STONE LION

*Adapted from a retelling
by W. P. O'Connor*

This tale is from Tibet.

Once there were two brothers who lived with their mother in a large house on a farm. Their father was dead. The older brother was clever and selfish, but the younger was kind and gentle. The older brother did not like the younger because he was honest and never would cheat to get the best of a bargain, so one day he said to him: "You must go away. I cannot support you any longer."

So the younger brother packed all his belongings and went to bid his mother goodbye. When she heard what the older brother had done, she said: "I will go with you, my son. I will not live here any longer with so hard-hearted a man as your brother."

The next morning the mother and the younger brother started out together. Toward night they came to a hut at the foot of a hill. It was empty except for an axe, which stood behind the door. But they managed to get their supper, and stayed in the hut all night.

In the morning they saw that on the side of the hill near the hut was a great forest. The son took the axe, and went up on the hillside and chopped enough wood for a load to carry to the town on the other side of the hill. He easily sold it, and with a happy heart brought back food and some clothing to make them both comfortable.

"Now, Mother," he said. "I can earn enough to keep us both, and we shall be happy here together."

Day after day he went out and cut the wood, and at night carried it to the village and sold it. And they always had plenty to eat and what they needed to make them happy and comfortable.

One day the boy went farther up the hill than he had ever gone before in search of better timber. As he climbed up the steep hillside, he suddenly came upon a lion carved from stone.

"Oh!" thought the boy, "this must be the guardian deity of this mountain. I will make him some offering tomorrow."

That night he bought two candles, and carried them to the lion.

He lighted them and put one on each side of the lion, praying that his own good fortune might continue.

As he stood there, suddenly the lion opened his great stone mouth, and said: "What are you doing here?"

The boy told him the story of his hard-hearted brother, and how he and his mother had left home, and were living in the hut at the foot of the hill.

When he had heard the story, the lion said: "If you will bring a bucket here tomorrow, and put it under my mouth, I will fill it with gold for you."

The next day the boy brought the bucket and put it under the lion's mouth.

"You must be very careful to tell me when it is nearly full," said the lion, "for if even one piece of gold should fall to the ground, great trouble would be in store for you."

The boy was very careful to do exactly as the lion told him, and soon he was on his way home to his mother with a bucketful of gold.

They were so rich now that they bought a large, beautiful farm, and went there to live. Everything the boy undertook seemed to prosper. He worked hard and grew strong; and before many years had passed he was old enough to marry and bring a bride to the home. But the mother still lived with them, and they were all very contented and happy.

At last the hard-hearted brother heard of their prosperity. He too had married and had a little son. So he took his wife and the little boy, and went to pay his younger brother a visit. It was not long before he had heard the whole story of their good fortune, and how the lion had given them all the gold.

"I will try that, too," he said.

So he took his wife and child and went to the very same hut his brother had lived in, and there they passed the night.

The very next morning he started out with a bucket to visit the Stone Lion.

When he had told the lion his errand, the lion said: "I will do that for you, but you must be very careful to tell me when the bucket is nearly full; for even if one little piece of gold touches the ground, great misery will surely fall upon you."

Now the older brother was so greedy that he kept shaking the bucket to get the gold pieces closer together. And when the bucket was nearly full he did not tell the lion, as the younger brother had done, for he wanted all he could get.

Suddenly one of the gold pieces fell upon the ground.

"Oh," cried the lion, "a big piece of gold is stuck in my throat. Put your hand in and get it out. It is the largest piece of all."

The greedy man thrust his hand at once into the lion's mouth —and the lion snapped his jaws together.

And there the man stayed, for the lion would not let him go. And the gold in the bucket turned into earth and stones.

When night came, and the husband did not come home, the wife became anxious, and went out to search for him. At last she found him, with his arm held fast in the lion's mouth. He was tired, cold, and hungry. She comforted him as best she could, and brought him some food.

Every day now the wife must go with food for her husband. But there came a day when all the money was gone, and the baby was sick, and the poor woman herself was too ill to work. She went to her husband and said: "There is no more food for you, nor for us. We shall all have to die. Oh! if we had only not tried to get the gold."

The lion was listening to all that was said, and he was so pleased at their misfortune that he began laughing at them. And as he laughed, he opened his mouth, and the greedy man quickly drew out his hand, before the lion had a chance to close his jaws again!

They were glad enough to get away from the place where they had had such ill luck, and so they went to the brother's house once more. The brother was sorry for them, and gave them enough money to buy a small place, and there the hard-hearted brother took his family and lived.

The younger brother and his wife and his mother lived very happily in their beautiful home, but they always remembered the Stone Lion on the hillside, who gave them their good fortune.

THE MAN WHO LOVED MONEY
BETTER THAN LIFE

Retold by Mary H. Davis and Cheow-Leung

Greed is a very powerful emotion. It can sting, it can wound, it can break—it can kill. This tale is from China.

In ancient times there was an old woodcutter who went to the mountain almost every day to cut wood.

It was said that this old man was a miser who hoarded his silver until it changed to gold, and that he cared more for gold than anything else in all the world.

One day a wilderness tiger sprang at him, and though he ran, he could not escape, and the tiger carried him off in its mouth.

The woodcutter's son saw his father's danger, and ran to save him if possible. He carried a long knife, and as he could run faster than the tiger, who had a man to carry, he soon overtook them.

His father was not much hurt, for the tiger held him by his clothes. When the old woodcutter saw his son about to stab the tiger he called out in great alarm: "Do not spoil the tiger's skin! Do not spoil the tiger's skin! If you can kill him without cutting holes in his skin we can get many pieces of silver for it. Kill him, but do not cut his body."

While the son was listening to his father's instructions the tiger suddenly dashed off into the forest, carrying the old man where the son could not reach him, and he was soon killed.

And the wise man who told this story said, "Ah, this old man's courage was foolishness. His love for money was stronger than his love for life itself."

•

The Little Loaf

Refusing to grab for all you can is a virtue. Sometimes it's a virtue that even brings a reward. This story comes from a Civil War–era school reader.

Many years ago, there was a great famine in Germany, and the poor people suffered from hunger. A rich man who loved children sent for twenty of them and said: "In this basket there is a loaf of bread for each of you. Take it and come back again every day till the famine is over. I will give you a loaf each day."

The children were very hungry. They seized the basket and struggled to get at the largest loaf. They even forgot to thank the man who had been kind to them. After a few minutes of quarreling and snatching for bread, everyone ran away with his loaf except one little girl named Gretchen. She stood there alone at a little distance from the gentleman. Then, smiling, she took up the last loaf, the smallest of all, and thanked him with all her heart.

Next day the children came again, and they behaved as badly as ever. Gretchen, who would not push with the rest, received only a tiny loaf scarcely half the size of the others. But when she came home and her mother began to cut the loaf, out dropped six shining coins of silver.

"Oh, Gretchen!" exclaimed her mother, "this must be a mistake. The money does not belong to us. Run as quickly as you can and take it back to the gentleman."

So Gretchen carried it back, but when she gave the gentleman her mother's message, he said: "No, no, it was not a mistake. I had the silver baked into the smallest loaf in order to reward you. Remember that the person who is contented to have a small loaf rather than quarrel for a larger one will find blessings that are better than money baked in bread."

•

THE MISER

Aesop

To a large degree, the value of our possessions depends on how we use them.

A miser had a lump of gold, which he buried in the ground, coming to the spot every day to look at it.

One day, finding that it was stolen, he began to tear his hair and lament loudly.

A neighbor, seeing him, said, "Pray do not grieve so. Bury a stone in the hole and fancy it is the gold. It will serve you just as well, for when the gold was there you made no use of it."

THE DOG IN THE MANGER

Aesop

This fable about selfishness is the origin of the phrase "dog in the manger."

A dog was lying in a manger full of hay.

A horse, a cow, a sheep, and a goat came one by one and wanted to eat some of the hay. But the dog sprang up growling and snarling, and would not let them have so much as a mouthful.

"What a selfish beast," said the cow to her companions. "He cannot eat the hay himself, and yet neither will he let those who can."

People often begrudge others what they themselves cannot enjoy.

•

THE TOWN MOUSE AND THE COUNTRY MOUSE
Retold by Sara Cone Bryant

We sometimes tell ourselves that other people's lives are easier than our own. The truth is that every life has its share of hard knocks; as Ishmael notes in *Moby Dick*, "The universal thump is passed around." Giving thanks for your own blessings is usually more productive than longing for someone else's life.

This tale is a widely loved fable from Aesop.

Once a little mouse who lived in the country invited a little mouse from town to visit him. When the little Town Mouse sat down to dinner he was surprised to find that the Country Mouse had nothing to eat except barley and grain.

"Really," he said, "you do not live well at all. You should see how I live! I have all sorts of fine things to eat every day. You must come to visit me and see how nice it is to live in the town."

The little Country Mouse was glad to do this, and after a while he went to town to visit his friend.

The very first place that the Town Mouse took the Country Mouse to see was the kitchen cupboard of the house where he lived. There, on the lowest shelf, behind some stone jars, stood a big paper bag of brown sugar. The little Town Mouse gnawed a hole in the bag and invited his friend to nibble for himself.

The two little mice nibbled and nibbled, and the Country Mouse thought he had never tasted anything so delicious in his life. He was just thinking how lucky the Town Mouse was, when suddenly the door opened with a bang, and in came the cook to get some flour.

"Run!" whispered the Town Mouse. And they ran as fast as they could to the little hole where they had come in. The little Country Mouse was shaking all over when they got safely away, but the little Town Mouse said, "That is nothing; she will soon go away and then we can go back."

After the cook had gone away and shut the door, they stole softly back, and this time the Town Mouse had something new to show. He took the little Country Mouse into a corner on the top shelf, where a big jar of dried prunes stood open. After much tugging and pulling they got a large dried prune out of the jar on to the shelf and began to nibble at it. This was even better than the brown sugar. The little Country Mouse liked the taste so much that he could hardly nibble fast enough. But all at once, in the midst of their eating, there came a scratching at the door and a sharp, loud *meow!*

"What is that?" said the Country Mouse. The Town Mouse just whispered, "Sh!" and ran as fast as he could to the hole. The Country Mouse ran after, you may be sure, as fast as *he* could. As soon as they were out of danger the Town Mouse said, "That was the old cat. She is the best mouser in town—if she once gets you, you are lost."

"This is very terrible," said the little Country Mouse. "Let us not go back to the cupboard again."

"No," said the Town Mouse, "I will take you to the cellar; there is something special there."

So the Town Mouse took his little friend down the cellar stairs and into a big cupboard where there were many shelves. On the shelves were jars of butter, and cheeses in bags and out of bags. Overhead hung bunches of sausages, and there were spicy apples in barrels standing about. It smelled so good that it went to the little Country Mouse's head. He ran along the shelf and nibbled at a cheese here, and a bit of butter there, until he saw an especially rich, very delicious-smelling piece of cheese on a queer little stand in a corner. He was just on the point of putting his teeth into the cheese when the Town Mouse saw him.

"Stop! stop!" cried the Town Mouse. "That is a trap!"

The little Country Mouse stopped and said, "What is a trap?"

"That thing is a trap," said the little Town Mouse. "The minute you touch the cheese with your teeth something comes down on your head hard, and you're dead."

The little Country Mouse looked at the trap, and he looked at the cheese, and he looked at the little Town Mouse. "If you'll excuse me," he said, "I think I will go home. I'd rather have barley and grain to eat in peace and comfort, than have brown sugar and dried prunes and cheese—and be frightened to death all the time!"

So the little Country Mouse went back to his home, and there he stayed all the rest of his life.

•

THE DISCONTENTED STONECUTTER

There is a big difference between healthy ambition and consuming envy. In this old Japanese tale we see the latter, always longing for something in the distance.

Once upon a time in Japan, there was a poor stonecutter, named Hofus, who used to go every day to the mountainside to cut great blocks of stone. He lived near the mountain in a little stone hut, and worked hard and was happy.

One day he took a load of stone to the house of a rich man. There he saw so many beautiful things that when he went back to his mountain he could think of nothing else. He began to wish that he too might sleep in a bed as soft as down, with curtains of silk and tassels of gold. And he sighed:

"Ah me! Ah me!
If Hofus only were rich as he!"

To his surprise, the voice of the Mountain Spirit answered:

"Have thou thy wish!"

When Hofus returned home that evening his little hut was gone, and in its place stood a great palace. It was filled with beautiful things, and the best of all was a bed of down, with curtains of silk and tassels of gold.

Hofus decided to work no more. But he was not used to being idle, and time passed slowly—the days seemed very long.

One day as he sat by the window he saw a carriage dash past. It was drawn by snow-white horses. In it sat a prince, while before and behind were servants in suits of blue and white. One was holding a golden umbrella over the prince.

When the stonecutter saw this, he began to feel unhappy, and he sighed:

"Ah me! Ah me!
If Hofus only a prince might be!"

And again the same voice that he had heard on the mountain answered:

"Be thou a prince!"

Straightway Hofus was a prince. He had servants dressed in crimson and gold, and he rode in a carriage with a golden umbrella over his head.

For a short time he was happy, but one day, as he walked in the garden, he saw that the flowers were drooping, and the grass was dry and brown. And when he rode out he felt the hot sun burn him in spite of his umbrella.

"The sun is mightier than I," thought he, and then he sighed:

"Ah me! Ah me!
If Hofus only the sun might be!"

And the voice answered:

"Be thou the sun!"

Straightway the great sun he became. He burned the grass and rice fields; he dried up the streams. Rich and poor alike suffered from the terrible heat.

One day a cloud came and rested in front of him and hid the earth from his sight. He was angry and cried:

"Ah me! Ah me!
If Hofus only a cloud might be!"

And the voice answered:

"Be thou a cloud!"

Straightway a cloud he became. He floated before the face of the sun and hid the earth from it.

Then day after day the cloud dropped rain. The rivers overflowed, and the rice fields were covered with water. Towns were swept away. Only the great rocks on the mountainside stood unmoved midst the flood.

The cloud looked at them in wonder, then he sighed:

"Ah me! Ah me!
If Hofus only a rock might be!"

And the voice answered:

"Be thou a rock!"

Straightway a rock he became. Proudly he stood. The sun could not burn him and the rain could not move him.

"Now, at last," he said, "no one is mightier than I."

But one day he was awakened from his dreams by a noise—tap! tap! tap!—down at his feet. He looked and there was a stonecutter driving his tool into the rock. Another blow and the great rock shivered; a block of stone broke away.

"That man is mightier than I!" cried Hofus, and he sighed:

"Ah me! Ah me!
If Hofus only the man might be!"

And the voice answered:

"Be thou thyself!"

And straightway Hofus was himself again—a poor stonecutter, working all day upon the mountainside and going home at night to his little hut. But he was content and happy, and never again did he wish to be other than Hofus the stonecutter.

•

How Hippo Was Humbled

Here is an African story about self-absorption. Being stuck on yourself is not a good place to be.

Once upon a time, long ago, Hippopotamus was the most beautiful creature of all the beasts in the bush. She had soft, shiny fur and fine, silky eyelashes. Her ears were long and slender, and her tail, which she loved to wave high in the air, was the thickest and bushiest tail anyone had ever seen.

In those days Hippo did not live in the dark river waters, as she does now. She lived on land so all the other animals could see what a handsome creature she was. She used to sit by the river's edge all day long, waving her thick, bushy tail and staring at her own reflection in the water.

"How beautiful I am!" she would sigh, turning this way and that so she could admire her own features. "What silky fur! What stunning ears! What a magnificent tail! I am by far the most admirable beast in the bush!"

Then one day an awful fire rose deep in the bush. The hot winds spread flames in every direction, and all the animals fled toward the river, where Hippo gazed happily at her own image.

The elephants thundered by, thrashing their trunks in despair.

The giraffes galloped past, craning their long necks to see the flames close behind.

The lions bounded by, roaring the alarm.

"Ah," Hippo said to herself, "they've all come to admire me."

She gazed happily at her reflection and never saw the flames raging closer and closer.

"I hope they all notice my fine, silky lashes," she remarked, leaning over the water.

But just then a spark caught her long, bushy tail, which she happened to be waving so proudly.

"Help!" she cried, hopping around and around, trying to blow out the flames. But it did no good.

"Help!" she yelled. "Help! My soft, shiny fur will catch on fire!" And it did.

So of course she did the only thing she could to save herself. She hopped right into the river, where she sank to the bottom and held her breath as long as she dared. When she finally came up for air, the bush fire had burned itself out.

Hippo dragged herself out of the water and sat down on the bank.

"That was awful," she moaned. "I'm soaked to my bones, and there's mud all over my shiny fur coat. I must look like a mess."

She leaned over the water to gaze at herself.

But who was this bald, wrinkled creature staring back at her? Hippo gasped.

Her shiny fur coat was burned away! Her fine, silky eyelashes were singed, baring two bulging, beady eyes. Her slender, long ears had shriveled into two ugly stubs. And worst of all, her thick, bushy tail was gone!

Poor Hippo was so ashamed, she jumped right back into the river to hide herself from the other animals. She stays in the water to this day, poking only her eyes and nose above the surface, and coming out only at night when no one can see her.

•

ARACHNE

Retold by Flora Cooke

It's important to do your best. But it's also important to remember
that there is almost always someone who can do the same thing
just as well, if not better. The ancients considered excessive pride,
or hubris, a fatal character flaw.

Arachne was a beautiful maiden who had wonderful skills in weaving and embroidery. The nymphs left their groves and fountains to gather round her loom. The naiads came from the rivers and the dryads from the trees, and never tired of watching her.

She took the wool as it came from the backs of the newly washed sheep and formed it into rolls. She separated it with her deft fingers, and carded it until it looked as light and soft as a cloud. She twirled the spindle in her skillful hands and wove the web. Often she embroidered it with her needle in beautiful, soft colors.

Arachne's father was famed throughout the land for his skill in coloring. He dyed her wool in all the hues of the rainbow.

Her work was so wonderful that people said, "Surely Athena must have taught this maiden." But Arachne proudly denied this. She could not bear to be thought a pupil even of the goddess of the loom.

"If Athena thinks she can weave better than I, let her try her skill with mine," said she boastfully. "If I fail, I will pay the penalty."

In vain her father told her that perhaps Athena, unseen, guided her hands. Arachne would not listen, and would thank no one for her gift, for vanity had turned her head. She said again, "Let Athena try her skill with mine if she dares."

One day as she was boasting to the nymphs of the beauty of

her work, an old woman appeared before her and advised her to accept her rare gift humbly. Arachne looked at the old woman angrily and said, "Keep your advice for others, old dame. I do not need it."

But the old woman said, "Listen to me. I have great age and much experience, and I have come to warn you. Until now, Athena has aided you, asking for no gratitude, but she can help you no more until you grow less selfish and vain. Above all, I advise you to ask forgiveness of Athena. Perhaps she may yet pardon your selfish pride. Challenge your fellow mortals, if you will, but do not, I beg of you, seek to compete with the goddess."

But Arachne said, "Begone. I fear not Athena, no, nor anyone else. Nothing would please me so much as to weave with Athena, but she is afraid to weave with me."

Then suddenly the old woman threw aside her cloak, and there before Arachne's very eyes stood a tall, majestic, gray-eyed goddess, crowned with a golden helmet.

"Athena is here," she said. Then the nymphs bent low in homage, but Arachne stood erect. She grew pale but gave no other sign of fear.

"Come, foolish girl, since you wish to try your skill with me," said Athena, "let the contest begin."

Both went quickly to work, and for hours their shuttles flew swiftly in and out. Athena used the sky for her loom, and in it she wove a picture too beautiful to describe. If you wish to know more about it, look at the western sky when the sun is setting.

She was still merciful, and at length she began a smaller web nearer to Arachne's loom. In this she wove a warning, showing how other boastful mortals had failed when they dared to compete with the gods. She hoped that the girl would even yet repent her rashness. But Arachne refused this last chance to save herself. She would not lift her eyes from her own work.

Her weaving was so fine and beautiful that even Athena was forced to admire it. The figures upon it seemed ready to speak and to live, but into her web she had woven many of the faults and failings of the gods, and her work was full of spite.

When the task was finished, Arachne lifted her eyes to Athena's work. Instantly she knew that she had failed. Ashamed and miserable, she tried to hang herself in her own web, but Athena cried, "Stay, wretched and perverse girl. You shall not die. You shall live to do the work for which you are best fitted. You and your children shall be among the greatest spinners and weavers upon the earth.

You shall be the mother of a great race, which shall be called spiders. Wherever men shall see your web, they shall destroy it even as I destroy yours." And as she spoke, the goddess with her shuttle tore the maiden's wonderful web from top to bottom.

Then Athena touched Arachne's forehead with her spindle thrice, and she became smaller and smaller, until she was scarcely larger than a fly.

And from that day to this Arachne and her family have been faithfully spinning and weaving, but they do their work so quietly and in such dark places that few people know what marvelous webs they weave. Some early morning, you may see their webs gleaming with dew, spread across the grass or hanging between the branches of a tree.

•

THE GOLD BREAD
Adapted from a retelling by Kate Douglas Wiggin and Nora Archibald Smith

Some people think they are better than everyone else, and therefore deserve better. But as this young bride learns to her regret, expecting too much can lead to too little.

In many places, bread symbolizes home and family (an ancient idea preserved in our custom of serving cake at wedding celebrations). In some eastern European countries, the bride is greeted in her new home with bread and salt.

Once upon a time there was a widow who had a beautiful daughter. The mother was modest and humble; the daughter, Marienka, was pride itself. She had suitors from all sides, but none satisfied her. The more they tried to please her, the more she disdained them.

One night, when the poor mother could not sleep, she took her beads and began to pray for her dear child, who gave her more than one care. Marienka was asleep by her side. As the mother gazed lovingly at her beautiful daughter, Marienka laughed in her sleep.

"What a beautiful dream she must have to laugh in this way!"

said the mother. Then she finished her prayer, hung her beads on the wall, laid her head on the same pillow with her daughter, and fell asleep.

"My dear child," said she in the morning, "what did you dream last night that you laughed so?"

"What did I dream, mama? I dreamed that a nobleman came here for me in a copper coach, and that he put a ring on my finger set with a stone that sparkled like the stars. And when I entered the church, the people had eyes for no one but the blessed Virgin and me."

"My daughter, my daughter, that was a proud dream!" said the mother, shaking her head. But Marienka went out singing.

The same day a wagon entered the yard. A handsome young farmer in good circumstances came to ask Marienka to share a peasant's bread with him. The mother was pleased with the suitor, but the proud Marienka refused him, saying, "Though you should come in a copper coach and put a ring on my finger set with a stone that sparkled like the stars, I would not have you for a husband." And the farmer went away storming at Marienka's pride.

The next night the mother awoke, took her beads, and prayed still more earnestly for her daughter, when behold! Marienka laughed again as she was sleeping.

"I wonder what she is dreaming," said the mother, who prayed, unable to sleep.

"My dear child," she said the next morning, "what did you dream last night that you laughed aloud?"

"What did I dream, mama? I dreamed that a nobleman came here for me in a silver coach, and that he offered me a golden diadem. And when I entered the church, the people looked at me more than they did at the blessed Virgin."

"Hush! you are blaspheming. Pray, my daughter, pray that you may not fall into temptation."

But Marienka ran away to escape her mother's sermon.

The same day a carriage entered the yard. A young lord came to entreat Marienka to share a nobleman's bread with him.

"It is a great honor," said the mother. But vanity is blind.

"Though you should come in a silver coach," said Marienka to the new suitor, "and should offer me a golden diadem, I would not have you for a husband."

"Take care, my child," said the poor mother. "Pride is a device of the Evil One."

"Mothers never know what they are saying," thought Marienka, and she went out shrugging her shoulders.

The third night the mother could not sleep for anxiety. As she lay awake, praying for her daughter, behold! Marienka burst into a loud fit of laughter.

"Oh!" said the mother, "what can the unhappy child be dreaming now?" And she continued to pray till daylight.

"My dear child," said she in the morning, "what did you dream last night?"

"You will be angry again if I tell you," answered Marienka.

"No, no," replied the mother. "Tell me."

"I dreamed that a noble lord, with a great train of attendants, came to ask me in marriage. He was in a golden coach, and he brought me a dress of gold lace. And when I entered the church, the people looked at nobody but me."

The mother clasped her hands. Marienka, half dressed, sprang from the bed and ran into the next room, to avoid a lecture that was tiresome to her.

The same day three coaches entered the yard, one of copper, one of silver, and one of gold, the first drawn by two horses, the second by four, and the third by eight, all caparisoned with gold and pearls. From the copper and silver coaches alighted pages dressed in scarlet breeches and green jackets and cloaks, while from the golden coach stepped a handsome nobleman all dressed in gold. He entered the house, and, bending one knee on the ground, asked the mother for her daughter's hand.

"What an honor!" thought the mother.

"My dream has come to pass," said Marienka. "You see, mother, that, as usual, I was right and you were wrong."

She ran to her chamber, tied the betrothal knot, and offered it smilingly as a pledge of her faith to the handsome lord, who, on his side, put a ring on her finger set with a stone that sparkled like the stars, and presented her with a golden diadem and a dress of gold lace.

The proud girl ran to her room to dress for the ceremony, while the mother, still anxious, said to the bridegroom, "My good sir, what bread do you offer my daughter?"

"Among us," said he, "the bread is of copper, silver, and gold. She can take her choice."

"What does this mean?" thought the mother. But Marienka had no anxiety. She returned as beautiful as the sun, took her lover's

arm, and set out for the church without asking her mother's blessing. The poor woman was left to pray alone on the threshold, and
when Marienka returned and entered the carriage, she did not even
turn around to look at her mother or to bid her a last farewell.

The eight horses set off at a gallop and did not stop till they
reached a huge rock, in which was a hole as large as the gate of a
city. The horses plunged into the darkness, the earth trembled, and
the rock cracked and crumbled. Marienka seized her husband's
hand.

"Don't be alarmed, my fair one. In a moment it will be light."

All at once a thousand lights waved in the air. The dwarfs of
the mountain, each with a torch in his hand, came to salute their
lord, the King of the Mines. Marienka learned for the first time her
husband's name. Whether he was a spirit of good or evil, at least he
was so rich that she did not regret her choice.

They emerged from the darkness, and advanced through
bleached forests and mountains that raised their pale and gloomy
summits to the skies. Firs, beeches, birches, oaks, rocks, all were of
lead. At the end of the forest stretched a vast meadow, the grass of
which was of silver; and at the bottom of the meadow was a castle
of gold, inlaid with diamonds and rubies. The carriage stopped
before the door, and the King of the Mines offered his hand to his
bride, saying, "My fair one, all that you see is yours."

Marienka was delighted. But it was impossible to make so long
a journey without being hungry. It was with pleasure, therefore,
that she saw the mountain dwarfs bring in a table, everything on
which glittered with gold, silver, and precious stones. The dishes
were marvelous—side dishes of emeralds, and roasts of gold on
silver trays. Everyone ate heartily except the bride, who begged her
husband for a little bread.

"Bring the copper bread," said the King of the Mines.

Marienka could not eat it.

"Bring the silver bread," said he.

Marienka could not eat it.

"Bring the gold bread," said he, at length.

Marienka could not eat it.

"My fair one," said the King of the Mines, "I am very sorry. But
what can I offer you? We have no other bread."

The bride burst into tears. Her husband laughed aloud. His
heart was of metal, like his kingdom.

"Weep, if you like," he cried, "it will do you no good. What
you wished for you possess. Eat the bread that you have chosen."

And so the rich Marienka lives in her underground castle, always hungry, and always hunting in vain for a few roots growing down into the earth, ones she might be able to eat.

But once a year, in the springtime, when the ground opens to receive the fruitful rain, Marienka returns to earth. Dressed in rags, pale and wrinkled, she begs from door to door, only too happy when anyone throws her a crust. And thus she receives from a few kind souls what she lacks in her palace of gold—a little bread and a little pity.

•

THE DISCONTENTED PIG

Retold by Katherine D. Cather

Almost every worthwhile job requires at least a little unpleasant or inconvenient work. But running away from it won't make things easier. Contentment is not synonymous with effortlessness.

This story comes from Thuringia, an ancient region of Germany.

Ever so long ago, in the time when there were fairies, and men and animals talked together, there was a curly-tailed pig. He lived by himself in a house at the edge of the village, and every day he worked in his garden. Whether the sun shone or the rain fell he hoed and dug and weeded, turning the earth around his tomato vines and loosening the soil of the carrot plot, until word of his fine vegetables traveled through seven counties, and each year he won the royal prize at the fair.

But after a time the little pig grew tired of the endless toil. "What matters it if I do have the finest vegetables in the kingdom," he thought, "since I must work myself to death getting them to grow? I mean to go out and see the world and find an easier way of making a living."

So he locked the door of his house and shut the gate of his garden and started down the road.

A good three miles he traveled, till he came to a cottage almost hidden in a grove of trees. Lovely music sounded around him and Little Pig smiled, for he had an ear for sweet sounds.

"I will go look for it," he said, following in the direction from which it seemed to come.

Now it happened that in that house dwelt Thomas, a cat, who made his living playing the violin. Little Pig saw him standing in the door pushing the bow up and down across the strings. It put a thought into his head. Surely this must be easier and far more pleasant than digging in a garden!

"Will you teach me to play the violin, friend cat?" he asked.

Thomas looked up from his bow and nodded his head.

"To be sure," he answered. "Just do as I am doing."

And he gave him the bow and fiddle.

Little Pig took them and began to saw, but squeak! quang! No sweet music fell upon his ear. The sounds he heard were like the squealing of his baby brother pigs when a wolf came near them.

"Oh!" he cried. "This isn't music!"

Thomas, the cat, nodded his head.

"Of course not," he said. "You haven't tried long enough. He who would play the violin must work."

"Then I think I'll look for something else," Piggywig answered, "because this is quite as hard as weeding my garden."

And he gave back the bow and fiddle and started down the road.

He walked on and on, until he came to a hut where lived a dog who made cheese. He was kneading and molding the curd into cakes, and Little Pig thought it looked quite easy.

"I think I'd like to go into the cheese business myself," he said to himself. So he asked the dog if he would teach him.

This the dog was quite willing to do, and a moment later Little Pig was working beside him.

Soon he grew hot and tired and stopped to rest and fan himself.

"No, no!" exclaimed the dog, "you will spoil the cheese. There can be no rest time until the work is done."

Little Pig opened his eyes in amazement.

"Indeed!" he replied. "Then this is just as hard as growing vegetables or learning to play a violin. I mean to look for something easier."

And he started down the road.

On the other side of the river, in a sweet green field, a man was taking honey out of beehives. Little Pig saw him as he crossed the bridge and thought that of all the trades he had seen, this suited him best. It must be lovely there in the meadow among the flowers. Honey was not heavy to lift, and once in a while he could have a mouthful of it. He ran as fast as he could go to ask the man if he would take him into his employ.

This plan pleased the bee man as much as it pleased the pig.

"I've been looking for a helper for a year and a day," he said. "Begin work at once."

He gave Little Pig a veil and a pair of gloves, telling him to fasten them on well. Then he told him to lift a honeycomb out of a hive.

Little Pig ran to do it, twisting his curly tail in the joy of having at last found a business that suited him. But buzz, buzz! The bees crept under his veil and inside his gloves. They stung him on his fingers, his mouth, his ears, and the end of his nose, and he squealed and dropped the honey and ran.

"Come back, come back!" the man called.

"No, no!" Little Pig answered with a big squeal. "No, no, the bees hurt me!"

The man nodded his head.

"Of course they do," he said. "They hurt me too! That is part of the work. You cannot be a beekeeper without getting stung."

Little Pig blinked his beady eyes and began to think hard.

"It seems that every kind of work has something unpleasant about it. To play the violin you must practice until your arm aches. When you make cheese you dare not stop a minute until the work is done, and in taking honey from a hive the bees sting you until your head is on fire. Work in my garden is not so bad after all, and I am going back to it."

So he said goodbye to the bee man and was soon back in his carrot patch. He hoed and raked and weeded, singing as he worked, and there was no more contented pig in all that kingdom. Every autumn he took his vegetables to the fair and brought home the royal prize, and sometimes, on holidays, the cat and the dog and the bee man came to call.

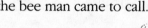

•

THE BLIND MEN AND THE ELEPHANT

*Learning how to work with others is one of the most important
lessons confronting us as we begin to make our way through life.
Cooperation moves us along faster and further.*

There lived in India six friends who were all blind.

Now India, of course, is a land of that greatest of land beasts,
the elephant. But, naturally, since these friends were all blind, they
did not know what an elephant looks like.

One day they were sitting together talking when they heard a
great roar.

"I believe that is an elephant in the street," one said.

"Now is our chance to find out what kind of creature the
elephant is," said another.

So they all went into the street.

The first blind man reached out and touched the elephant's
ear.

"Ah," he said to himself, "the elephant is a rough, wide thing.
It is like a rug."

The second blind man felt the elephant's trunk.

"Now I understand," he thought. "The elephant is a long,
round thing. It is like a giant snake."

The third blind man touched the elephant's leg.

"Well, I wouldn't have guessed it," he said. "The elephant is
tall and firm, just like a tree."

The fourth blind man felt the elephant's side.

"Now I know," he thought. "The elephant is wide and smooth,
like a wall."

The fifth blind man put his hands on the elephant's tusk.

"The elephant is a hard, sharp animal, like a spear," he
decided.

The sixth blind man touched the elephant's tail.

"Well, well," he said. "It gives a mighty roar, but the elephant
is just a thing like a long, thin rope."

Afterward the six blind friends sat down again to talk about the
elephant.

"It is rough and wide, like a rug," said the first.

"No, it is long and round, like a snake," said the second.

"Don't be silly," laughed the third. "It is tall and firm, like a tree."

"No, it is not," growled the fourth. "It is wide and smooth, like a wall."

"Hard and sharp, like a spear!" shouted the fifth.

"Long and thin, like a rope!" yelled the sixth.

And so a fight started. Each one insisted he was right. He had touched it with his own hands, hadn't he?

The owner of the elephant heard all the shouting and came to see what the fuss was about.

"Each of you is right, and each of you is wrong," he told them. "One man may not be able to find the whole truth by himself—just a small part of it. But if we work together, each adding our own piece to the whole, we can find wisdom."

●

ALL GOD'S CREATURES HAVE WORK TO DO

This clever tale from southeast Asia helps us learn the difference between first-rate work and second-rate effort. It is good reading before starting a job.

Two cousins grew up side by side from the day they both entered the world. They learned to crawl and toddle together, and later how to run and swim and play ball and all the other things boys do together. They were constant and devoted friends.

But eventually they began to drift apart, as sometimes happens as even good friends move through life. One cousin took to his books, found a certain delight in learning, studied hard, and passed his exams with flying colors. The other cousin decided books weren't such good companions. He skipped school a good bit so he could continue to swim and play ball, ignored his lessons, and ended up failing his exams.

As is usually the way of the world, fortune rewarded the first cousin, who ended up becoming an adviser to the king himself.

The second cousin soon found himself employed as an oarsman on his majesty's royal yacht.

One day the king and all his royal advisers embarked on a journey up the river. They sat under a wide canopy in the bow of the boat, where the breeze was best, and discussed affairs of state as the yacht moved along.

The sight of his cousin sitting at ease with royalty irked the oarsman no end.

"Look at that lazy fellow, lounging there in the shade, while I must break my back in the sun," he thought as he rowed. "What gives him the right to sit up there, any more than me? After all, aren't we both God's creatures?"

The more he thought about it, the angrier he grew.

"Look at those useless louts," he began grumbling to his fellow oarsmen. "They call themselves advisers, but all they do is sit and gab. Why should we sweat so hard to push their carcasses against the current? There's nothing fair about it. They ought to be back here rowing too. Aren't we all God's creatures?"

That evening, they tied to shore to make camp. Everyone ate and fell asleep quickly.

The oarsman woke in the middle of the night to find a firm hand shaking him by the shoulder. It was the king himself.

"There's a strange noise coming from over there," he said, pointing. "I can't get to sleep from wondering what it is. Please go find out."

The oarsman jumped off the boat and ran up a hill. He came back a few minutes later.

"It's nothing, Your Majesty," he said. "A cat has just given birth to a litter of noisy kittens."

"Ah, I see," said the king. "What kind of kittens?"

The oarsman had not looked to see. He ran up the hill again and came back.

"Siamese," he said.

"And how many kittens are there?" the king inquired.

Again, the oarsman had not noticed. He went back.

"Six kittens," he reported.

"How many males and how many females?" the king asked.

The oarsman ran back once again.

"Three males and three females," he cried, beginning to lose his breath.

"I see," said the king. "Come with me."

They tiptoed to the bow of the boat, where the king woke the oarsman's cousin.

"There's a strange noise up on that hill," he told him. "Go find out what it is."

The adviser disappeared into the darkness and returned in a moment.

"It is a newborn litter of kittens, Your Majesty," he said.

"What kind of kittens?" the king asked.

"Siamese," answered his adviser.

"How many?"

"Six."

"How many males and how many females?"

"Three males and three females. The mother gave birth in an overturned barrel just after we arrived. The cats belong to the mayor of the village. He hopes they have not disturbed you, and invites you to come take your pick if the court is in need of a royal pet."

The king looked at the oarsman.

"I overheard your grumbling earlier today," he said. "Yes, we are all God's creatures. But all God's creatures have work to do. I had to send you to shore four times for answers. My adviser went only once. That is why he is my adviser, and you must row the boat."

•

THE MAN AND HIS PIECE OF CLOTH

Retold by P. V. Ramaswami Raju

Rarely does lasting satisfaction come through escape. Living in the world means living with its responsibilities and cares, as this fable from India reminds us.

A man in the East, where they do not require as much clothing as in colder climates, gave up all worldly concerns and retired to a wood, where he built a hut and lived in it.

His only clothing was a piece of cloth which he wore round his waist. But, as ill-luck would have it, rats were plentiful in the wood, so he had to keep a cat. The cat required milk to keep it, so a cow had to be kept. The cow required tending, so a cow-boy was employed. The boy required a house to live in, so a house was built for him. To look after the house a maid had to be engaged. To provide company for the maid a few more houses had to be built and people invited to live in them. In this manner a little township sprang up.

The man said, "The further we seek to go from the world and its cares, the more they multiply!"

•

THE STORY OF THE TWO FRIENDS

Retold by Rosetta Baskerville

Am I wise, or am I a fool? That is the central question of this wonderful tale from Uganda. The question itself sets us on the road toward wisdom. The story is largely about work, and the instruction this young boy receives from the animals in the forest is not very different from the advice the young James Madison and his College of New Jersey classmates got from their teacher, Dr. Witherspoon: "Do not live useless and die contemptible."

Once upon a time there were a potter and his wife who had one child, a little boy, and as he grew older they were grieved to see that he was different from all other children.

He never played with them, or laughed, or sang. He just sat alone by himself. He hardly ever spoke to his parents, and he never learned the nice polite manners of the other children in the village. He sat and thought all day, and no one knew what he thought about, and his parents were very sad.

The other women tried to comfort the potter's wife. They said, "Perhaps you will have another baby, and it will be like other children." But she said, "I don't want another baby. I want this one to be nice." And the men of the village tried to cheer the potter. "Strange boys often become great men," they said. And one old man said, "Leave the boy alone. We shall see whether he is a wise man or a fool."

The potter went home and told his wife what the men had said, and the boy heard him, and it seemed to wake him up. He thought it over for a few days, and at last one morning at dawn he took his stick in his hand and went into the forest to think there.

All day he wandered about, and at last he came to a little clearing on the side of a hill from which he could look down over the country. The sun was setting over the distant blue hills, and everything was touched with a pink and golden light, and deep shadows lay on the banana gardens and forests in the distance. But the boy saw none of these things. He was footsore and weary and miserable, and he sat down on a fallen log, tired out with his long day. Suddenly a lion came out into the clearing.

"What are you doing here all alone?" he said severely.

"I am very miserable," said the boy, "and I have come into the forest to think, for I do not know whether I am a wise man or a fool."

"Is that all you think about?" said the lion.

"Yes," answered the boy, "I think about it night and day."

"Then you are a fool," said the lion decidedly. "Wise men think about things that benefit the country." And he walked away.

An antelope came bounding out into the clearing and stopped to stare at the boy.

"What are you doing here?" he asked.

"I am very miserable," answered the boy. "I don't know whether I am a wise man or a fool."

"Do you ever eat anything?" said the antelope.

"Yes," said the boy, "my mother cooks twice a day, and I eat."

"Do you ever thank her?" said the antelope.

"No, I have never thought of that," answered the boy.

"Then you are a fool," said the antelope. "Wise men are always grateful." And he bounded off into the forest again.

Then a leopard came up and looked suspiciously at him.

"What are you doing here?" he asked crossly.

"I am very miserable," answered the boy. "I don't know if I am a wise man or a fool."

"Do they love you in your village?" asked the leopard.

"No, I don't think they do," said the boy. "I am not like other boys. I don't know them very well."

"Then you are a fool," said the leopard. "All boys are nice; I often wish *I* were a boy. Wise men mix with their fellows and earn their respect." And he walked off sniffing.

Just then the big gray elephant came shuffling along the forest path, swinging his tail as he walked, and picking a twig here and a leaf there as he passed under the trees.

"What are you doing here all alone in the jungle when the sun is setting?" he asked. "You should be at home in your village."

"I am very miserable," said the boy. "I don't know if I am a wise man or a fool."

"What work do you do?" asked the elephant.

"I don't do any work," said the boy.

"Then you are a fool," said the elephant. "All wise men work." And he swung away down the path which leads to the pool in the forest where the animals go to drink, and the boy put his head down in his hands and cried bitterly, as if his heart would break, for he did not know what to do.

After a little while he heard a gentle voice by his side. "My little brother, do not cry so; tell me your trouble." The boy raised his tear-stained face and saw a little hare standing by his side.

"I am very miserable," he said. "I am not like other people, and nobody loves me. I came into the forest to find out whether I am a wise man or a fool, and all the animals tell me I am a fool." And he put his head in his hands again and cried more bitterly than ever.

The hare let him cry on for a little while, and then he said: "My little brother, do not cry anymore. What the animals have told you is true. They have told you to think great thoughts, to be grateful and kind to others, and, above all, to work. All these things are great and wise. The animals are never idle, and they marvel to see how men, with all their gifts, waste their lives. Think how surprised they are to see a boy like you, well and strong, doing nothing all day, for they know that the world is yours if you will make it so."

The sun had set behind the distant hills and the soft darkness was falling quickly over the forest, and the hare said: "Soon it will be chilly here. You are tired and hungry, and far from your village. Come and spend the night in my home and we will talk of all these things."

So they went into the forest again, and the hare brought the boy water in a gourd and wonderful nuts to eat, and made him a soft bed of dry leaves.

And they talked of many things till the boy said, "My father is a potter, and I think I should like to be a potter too."

"If you are, you must never be content with poor work," said the hare. "Your pottery must be the best in the country. Never rest until you can make really beautiful things; no man has any right to send imperfect work out into the world."

"Nobody will believe in me when I go home; they will think I am mad," said the boy.

And the little hare answered: "Man's life is like a river, which flows always on and on. What is past is gone forever, but there is clear water behind. No man can say it is too late, and you are only a boy with your life before you."

"They will laugh at me," said the boy.

"Wise men don't mind that," said the hare. "Only fools are discouraged by laughter; you must prove to them that you are not a fool. I will teach you a song to sing at your work. It will encourage you:

> "When the shadows have melted in silver dawn,
> Farewell to my dreams of play.
> The forest is full of a waking throng,
> And the treetops ring with the birds' new song,
> And the flowers awake from their slumber long,
> > And the world is mine today.

> "My feet are sure and my hands are strong.
> Let me labor and toil while I may.
> When the sun shall set in a sea of light,
> And the shadows lengthen far into the night,
> I shall take the rest which is mine by right,
> > For I'll win the world today."

In the early morning the hare went with the boy to the edge of the forest and they swore an oath of friendship, which is as sacred in the jungle as among men, and the hare said: "Come back sometimes and see me, and we will spend a long day together in the forest. Come to this place and sing my song, and the birds will tell me you are there if I am too far away to hear."

So the boy went back to his village, and found his mother digging in the garden; he knelt down and greeted her as all nice children do, and saw how pleased she was. Then he went to his father, and said: "I want to be a potter. Teach me your work and I will try to learn it." And the potter was very much pleased to think that he would have a son to take on his trade after him, and all the people in the village heard and they rejoiced with the potter and his wife.

The boy worked hard, and after years he became a famous potter, and people came from all parts of the country to buy his pottery, for everyone knew that he never sold anything that was not beautiful and well made.

He made beautiful black pottery, and sometimes he put a design in white on it, and everything he made was good.

But sometimes the old dark moods would return and he would feel sick of his work and all the people round him, and then he would go away at dawn to the edge of the forest and sing the hare's song, and the little hare would come running down the forest path, and the two friends would spend a long day together, while the man would shake out his heart and all its sorrows to the hare, and he never failed to get love and comfort and encouragement in return, and went back to his work full of hope.

This all happened many years ago. Nowadays men think they are much wiser than the animals, but sometimes you may see a strange look in the eyes of an animal, as if it would say, "That man thinks he is wise, but he is only a fool." And the animals in the forests and jungles and in our houses watch everything we do, and they marvel when they see how some men waste their lives.

•

THE UNFRUITFUL TREE

Friedrich A. Krummacher

Chronic, selfish suspicion rarely wins happy success. A generous, optimistic spirit makes it easier to take the risks that lead to real reward.

A farmer had a brother in town who was a gardener, and who possessed a magnificent orchard full of the finest fruit trees, so that his skill and his beautiful trees were famous everywhere.

One day the farmer went into town to visit his brother, and was astonished at the rows of trees that grew slender and smooth as wax tapers.

"Look, my brother," said the gardener, "I will give you an apple tree, the best from my garden, and you, and your children, and your children's children shall enjoy it."

Then the gardener called his workmen and ordered them to take up the tree and carry it to his brother's farm. They did so, and the next morning the farmer began to wonder where he should plant it.

"If I plant it on the hill," said he to himself, "the wind might catch it and shake down the delicious fruit before it is ripe; if I plant it close to the road, passersby will see it and rob me of its luscious apples; but if I plant it too near the door of my house, my servants or the children may pick the fruit."

So, after he had thought the matter over, he planted the tree behind his barn, saying to himself, "Prying thieves will not think to look for it here."

But behold, the tree bore neither fruit nor blossoms the first year nor the second. Then the farmer sent for his brother the gardener, and reproached him angrily, saying: "You have deceived me and given me a barren tree instead of a fruitful one. For, behold, this is the third year and still it brings forth nothing but leaves!"

The gardener, when he saw where the tree was planted, laughed and said: "You have planted the tree where it is exposed to cold winds, and has neither sun nor warmth. How, then, could you expect flowers and fruit? You have planted the tree with a greedy and suspicious heart. How, then, could you expect to reap a rich and generous harvest?"

•

YOUR MISSION
Ellen Gates

We can go into the world with this certainty: There is much worthwhile work waiting for every one of us. But we must go to it. And when we take it up, we should remember these words from Ecclesiastes: "Whatsoever thy hand findeth to do, do it with thy might."

If you cannot on the ocean,
   Sail among the swiftest fleet,
Rocking on the highest billows,
   Laughing at the storms you meet,
You can stand among the sailors,
   Anchored yet within the bay;
You can lend a hand to help them,
   As they launch their boats away.

If you are too weak to journey
   Up the mountain, steep and high,
You can stand within the valley,
   While the multitude go by.
You can chant in happy measure,
   As they slowly pass along;
Though they may forget the singer,
   They will not forget the song.

If you have not gold and silver
   Ever ready to command,
If you cannot toward the needy
   Reach an ever-open hand,
You can visit the afflicted,
   O'er the erring you can weep;
You can be a true disciple
   Sitting at the Saviour's feet.

If you cannot in a conflict
   Prove yourself a soldier true,
If where the fire and smoke are thickest
   There's no work for you to do,
When the battlefield is silent,
   You can go with careful tread;
You can bear away the wounded,
   You can cover up the dead.

Do not stand then idly waiting
For some greater work to do;
Fortune is a lazy goddess,
She will never come to you.
Go and toil in any vineyard,
Do not fear to do or dare;
If you want a field of labor,
You can find it anywhere.

•

FOR YOU AND ME

Laura E. Richards

There is no shortage of people who are filled with all sorts of
explanations about why they can't help doing what they do. They
act, as Shakespeare put it, as though they were "villains on necessity, fools by heavenly compulsion." The truth is that your best
guardian angels (whether they be parents, teachers, ministers, or
friends) are the ones who don't buy bad excuses.

"I have come to speak to you about your work," said the Angel-
who-attends-to-things. "It appears to be unsatisfactory."

"Indeed!" said the man. "I hardly see how that can be. Perhaps
you will explain."

"I will!" said the Angel. "To begin with, the work is slovenly."

"I was born heedless," said the man. "It is a family failing
which I have always regretted."

"It is ill put together, too," said the Angel. "The parts do not
fit."

"I never had any eye for proportion," said the man. "I admit it
is unfortunate."

"The whole thing is a botch," said the Angel. "You have put
neither brains nor heart into it, and the result is ridiculous failure.
What do you propose to do about it?"

"I credited you with more comprehension," said the man. "My
faults, such as they are, were born with me. I am sorry that you do
not approve of me, but this is the way I was made. Do you see?"

"I see!" said the Angel. He put out a strong white hand, and taking the man by the collar, tumbled him neck and crop into the ditch.

"What is the meaning of this?" cried the man, as he scrambled out breathless and dripping. "I never saw such behavior. Do you see what you have done? You have ruined my clothes, and nearly drowned me besides."

"Oh yes!" said the Angel. "This is the way *I* was made."

•

INDUSTRY AND SLOTH

Procrastination is not neutral between action and inaction. Procrastination *is* inaction.

A lazy young man, asked why he lay in bed so long, jocosely answered: "Every morning of my life I hear cases in court. Two fine damsels, named Industry and Sloth, are at my bedside, as soon as I awake, presenting their different cases. One entreats me to get up, the other persuades me to lie still; and then they alternately give me various reasons why I should rise and why I should not. As it is the duty of an impartial judge to hear all that can be said on both sides, I am detained so long that before the pleadings are over it is time to go to dinner."

•

RIP VAN WINKLE
Adapted from Washington Irving

Don't sleep your life away.

At the foot of the Catskill Mountains lies a little village of great antiquity, having been founded long ago by the Dutch. And in one of these houses, there lived many years since, while the country was yet a province of Great Britain, a simple, good-natured fellow by the name of Rip Van Winkle.

Now, the great error in Rip's composition was an aversion to all kinds of profitable labor. It could not be from want of perseverance, for he would sit on a wet rock, with a rod as long and heavy as a Tartar's lance, and fish all day without a murmur, even though he would not be encouraged by a single nibble. He would carry a fowling piece on his shoulder for hours together, trudging through woods and swamps, and up hill and down, to shoot a few squirrels or wild pigeons. Or he would assist the children of the village in their sports, make their playthings, fly their kites and shoot their marbles, and tell them long stories of ghosts and witches. Whenever he went dodging about the village, he was surrounded by a troop of them hanging onto his pants and clambering up his back.

He would never refuse to assist a neighbor even in the roughest toil, such as husking Indian corn, or building stone fences. The women of the village, too, used to employ him to run their errands, and to do such little odd jobs as their less obliging husbands would not do for them. In a word, Rip was ready to attend to anybody's business but his own. As to doing family duty, and keeping his farm in order, he found it impossible.

In fact, he declared it was of no use to work on his farm; it was the most pestilent little piece of ground in the whole country. Everything about it went wrong, and would go wrong, in spite of him. His fences were continually falling to pieces. His cow would go astray or get among the cabbages. Weeds were sure to grow quicker in his fields than anywhere else. The rain always made a point of setting in just as he had some outdoor work to do. And so his estate had dwindled away under his management, acre by acre, until there was little more left than a mere patch of potatoes. His children, too, were as ragged and wild as if they belonged to nobody, and promised to inherit the habits, with the old clothes, of their father.

Yes, Rip was one of those happy mortals who take the world easy, and would rather starve on a penny than work for a pound. If left to himself, he would have whistled his life away in perfect contentment. But his wife kept continually dinning in his ears about his idleness, his carelessness, and the ruin he was bringing on his family. Morning, noon, and night, her tongue was incessantly going. Rip had but one way of replying to lectures of that kind. He would shake his head, cast up his eyes, take his gun in hand, and stroll away into the woods with his old dog, Wolf, where he could enjoy some peace and quiet.

One day, on one such ramble with Wolf, he wandered far into the highest parts of the Catskills, shooting at squirrels and admiring the scenery. Before he knew it, the mountains began to throw their long blue shadows over the valleys. He saw it would be dark long before he could reach the village, and he heaved a heavy sigh when he thought of encountering the terrors of Dame Van Winkle.

He was about to descend when he heard a strange, unearthly voice calling his name: *Rip Van Winkle! Rip Van Winkle!*

Wolf bristled his back. Rip looked around but could see nothing but a crow winging its solitary flight across the mountain. He turned to descend again, when he heard the same cry ring through the still evening air: *Rip Van Winkle! Rip Van Winkle!*

And suddenly he saw a strange figure toiling slowly up the rocks, bending under the weight of something he carried on his back. He was a short, square-built old fellow, with thick, bushy hair and a grizzled beard. He was dressed in the antique Dutch fashion with a broad belt and buckles on his shoes and big, baggy britches gathered in at the knees. He bore on his shoulder a stout keg that seemed full of liquor, and made signs for Rip to approach and assist him with the load.

Rip complied with his usual alacrity and followed the old gnome, who spoke not a word but clambered farther up a narrow gully.

Deeper and deeper into the mountains they climbed, through a steep gorge. As they ascended, Rip every now and then heard long rolling peals, like distant thunder, although the sky was perfectly clear.

At last they came to a sort of amphitheater, surrounded by boulders and cliffs. And here new wonders presented themselves, for on a level spot in the center was a company of short, bearded men, all dressed in the same quaint Dutch fashion, with broad belts and high-crowned hats with feathers, red stockings, and wooden shoes. They were playing at ninepins, and whenever the balls rolled along the green turf, they echoed along the mountains like rumbling peals of thunder.

As Rip and his companion approached, they suddenly stopped their play, and stared at him with such statuelike gazes that his heart turned within him, and his knees knocked together. His companion now poured the keg's contents into cups, and made signs to Rip to wait among the company. As he did so the little men drank, wiped their beards, and in silence returned to their game.

By degrees Rip's awe subsided. He even ventured to taste the beverage, which he found to have excellent flavor. He was naturally a thirsty soul, and was soon tempted to try some more. One taste provoked another. He repeated his visits to the keg so often that at length his senses were overpowered, his eyes swam in his head, his head gradually declined, and he sank snoring upon the turf.

It was a bright, sunny morning when he woke. The birds were hopping and twittering among the bushes, and an eagle was wheeling aloft, breasting the pure mountain breeze. There was no sign of the strange little man with the keg of liquor, or the woebegone party at ninepins.

"Surely," thought Rip, "I have not slept here all night." He whistled for Wolf, but the dog had disappeared. He looked around for his gun, but in place of his well-oiled weapon, he found a rusty, worm-eaten old firelock, and he was vexed to think the little men of the mountain must have stolen his gun, and perhaps his dog too, and left him this sorry exchange.

As he rose to walk he found himself stiff in the joints. "These mountains do not agree with me," he thought.

With some difficulty he started down the mountainside, through the gorge he and his companion had ascended the previous evening. He was astonished to find that, whereas it had been dry as a bone before, a mountain stream now foamed through its bottom, leaping from rock to rock.

"I must have come up a different way," thought Rip. "This can't be right."

But at last he reached the village. As he approached he grew bewildered, for the place was greatly altered. There were houses and streets he had never seen before. Strange names were over the doors, and unfamiliar faces at the windows—everything was strange.

He met a number of people he did not know, which surprised him, for he thought himself acquainted with everyone in the country round. Their dress, too, was of a strange fashion. They all stared at him, and invariably stroked their chins when they saw him, which caused Rip to do the same—when, to his astonishment, he found his beard had grown a foot long!

A troop of children gathered at his heels, hooting after him, and pointing at his beard. He made his way to his own house and could not believe his eyes. It had gone to decay—the roof fallen in, the windows shattered, and the doors off the hinges. He called for his wife and children. The lonely chambers rang for a moment with his voice, and then all again was silence.

He hurried to his old resort, the village inn—but it too was changed. The sign of King George was still there, under which he had smoked many a peaceful pipe. But the king's coat had been changed from red to blue, the head was decorated with a cocked hat instead of a crown, and the legend underneath now read GENERAL WASHINGTON.

A crowd of people was there, as usual, but Rip knew none of them. And they were talking about things which meant nothing to his poor, addled brain—rights of citizens, elections, liberty, Bunker Hill.

They gazed with some curiosity at Rip and his long, grizzled beard, and at length crowded round him, and asked whom he was seeking.

"Where's Nicholas Vedder?" inquired Rip.

"Why, Nicholas Vedder, he is dead and gone these sixteen years!"

"Where's brother Brom Dutcher?"

"He went off to the army and never came back."

"Where's Van Brummel, the schoolmaster?"

"He went off to the wars too, was a great militia general, and is now in Congress."

Rip's heart died away at hearing these sad changes, and it dawned on him that he must have been asleep for years and years. But he cried out in despair, "Does nobody here know Rip Van Winkle?"

"Oh, Rip Van Winkle!" exclaimed two or three. "Oh, to be sure, that's Rip Van Winkle yonder, leaning against the tree."

And to his amazement he saw a precise counterpart of himself, just as he had been on the day he went up the mountain—apparently as lazy, and certainly as ragged. It was his own son! His daughter was there too; she had married a stout, cheery farmer, whom Rip recognized as one of the urchins who used to climb on his back. But his wife had long since passed away.

Rip's children gave him a home, and he became the most popular old man in the village. He took his place once more on the bench at the inn door, and people never grew tired of hearing him tell his strange story of how he slept his life away.

And who were the strange company of little gnomes who played at bowling that long-ago evening when Rip fell asleep? It is said they were spirits of the crew of old Henry Hudson, who first explored that region, and gave his name to its great river and valley. And even to this day, when the thunderstorm of a summer afternoon rolls across the Catskill Mountains, people say it is just old Henry and his fellows at their game of ninepins again.

•

THE INGRATITUDE AND INJUSTICE OF MEN TOWARDS FORTUNE

Jean de La Fontaine

It's easy to take credit for successes we meet as we journey into the world. The harder and nobler habit is accepting responsibility for failures as well.

A merchant, trading o'er the seas,
　　Became enriched by every trip.
No gulf nor rock destroyed his ease;
　　He lost no goods from any ship.

To others came misfortunes sad,
　　For Fate and Neptune had their will.
Fortune for him safe harbors had;
　　His servants served with zeal and skill.

He sold tobacco, sugar, spices,
　　Silks, porcelains, or what you please;
Made boundless wealth (this phrase suffices)
　　And "lived to clutch the golden keys."

'Twas luxury that gave him millions:
　　In gold men almost talked to him.
Dogs, horses, carriages, postillions,
　　To give this man seemed Fortune's whim.

A friend asked how came all this splendor.
  "I know the 'nick of time,' " he said,
"When to be borrower and lender:
  My care and talent all this made."

His profit seemed so very sweet,
  He risked once more his handsome gains.
But, this time, baffled was his fleet:
  Imprudent, he paid all the pains.

One rotten ship sank 'neath a storm,
  And one to watchful pirates fell;
A third, indeed, made port in form,
  But nothing wanted had to sell.

Fortune gives but one chance, we know;
  All was reversed, his servants thieves.
Fate came upon him with one blow,
  And made the mark that seldom leaves.

The friend perceived his painful case.
  "Fortune, alas!" the merchant cries.
"Be happy," says his friend, "and face
  The world, and be a little wise.

To counsel you is to give health:
  I know that all mankind impute
To Industry their peace and wealth,
  To Fortune all that does not suit."

Thus, if each time we errors make,
  That bring us up with sudden halt,
Nothing's more common than to take
  Our own for Fate or Fortune's fault.

Our good we always make by force,
  The evil fetters us so strong;
For we are always right, of course,
  And Destiny is always wrong.

•

THE DANCING HORSES OF SYBARIS

Retold by James Baldwin

From the ancient Greek city Sybaris we get the modern word
"sybarite," meaning someone devoted to luxury or pleasure. Singing and dancing and having fun are fine, but as we see here,
preparation for life must include readiness for sterner stuff as well.
This story takes place around 510 B.C.

In the south of Italy there was once a flourishing Greek colony
called Sybaris. The town was well situated for commerce, the surrounding country was very fertile, the climate was the finest in the
world, and for some centuries the Sybarites were industrious and
enterprising, carrying on a profitable trade with other countries
and heaping up immense wealth. But too much good fortune finally
proved their ruin. Little by little they lost their habits of labor and
thrift and, instead, gave themselves up to pleasure. Finally, leaving
all kinds of necessary work to their slaves, they laid aside the cares
of life, and spent their days in eating and drinking, in dancing and
in listening to fine music, or in attending the circus and watching
the feats of acrobats and performing animals.

It is said, indeed, that prizes were offered to any man who
would invent some new kind of amusement. A certain flute player
hit upon the idea of teaching the horses to dance, and since those
creatures were as fond as their masters of pleasure, he found it a
very easy thing to do. It was not long before the sound of a pipe
would set the heels of every warhorse in the country to beating
time with it. Imagine, if you please, a whole nation of dancing
people and dancing horses—what a free-from-care time of it they
must have had!

But the most pleasant summer must come to an end, even for
grasshoppers. The Sybarites had for neighbors a community of hard
workers, students, and tradesmen, called Crotoniates, who lived
temperately, drank water from the original Croton River, listened
to lectures by Pythagoras, and looked with longing eyes upon the
fair gardens and stately white palaces of Sybaris. The Crotoniates
several times came to blows with the Sybarites; but as their army
was much smaller, and they had no cavalry whatever, they were

beaten in every battle. Their foot soldiers were of no use at all
when opposed to the onsets of the Sybarite warhorses.

But true worth is sure to win in the end. When a spy reported
to the Crotoniates that he had seen all the horses in Sybaris dancing
to the music of a pipe, the Croton general saw his opportunity at
once. He sent into the Sybarite territories a large company of shepherds and fifers armed with nothing but flutes and shepherds'
pipes, while a little way behind them marched the rank and file of
the Crotoniate army. When the Sybarites heard that the enemy's
forces were coming, they marshaled their cavalry—the finest in the
world at that time—and sallied forth to meet them.

They thought it would be fine sport to send the Crotoniates
scampering back across the fields into their own country, and
half of Sybaris went out to see the fun. What an odd sight it must
have been—a thousand fancifully dressed horsemen, splendidly
mounted, riding out to meet an array of unarmed shepherds and a
handful of ragged foot soldiers!

The Sybarite ladies wave their handkerchiefs and cheer their
champions to the charge. The horsemen sit proudly in their saddles, ready at a word to make the grand dash—when, hark! a thousand pipes begin to play not "Yankee Doodle" or "Rule Britannia"
but the national air of Crotona, whatever that may be. The order is
given to charge; the Sybarites shout and drive their spurs into their
horses' flanks—what fine sport it is going to be! But the war steeds
hear nothing, care for nothing, but the music. They lift their slender
hoofs in unison with the inspiring strains.

And now the armed Crotoniates appear on the field, but the
pipers still pipe, and the horses still dance—they caper, curvet,
caracole, pirouette, waltz, trip the light fantastic hoof, forgetful of
everything but the delightful harmony. The Sybarite riders have
been so sure of the victory that they have taken more trouble to
ornament than to arm themselves. Some of them are pulled from
their dancing horses by the Crotoniate footmen; others slip to the
ground and run as fast as their nerveless legs will carry them back
to the shelter of the city walls. The shepherds and fifers retreat
slowly toward Crotona, still piping merrily, and the sprightly horses
follow them, keeping step with the music.

The dancing horses cross the boundary line between the two
countries; they waltz over the Crotoniate fields, they caracole gaily
through the Crotoniate gates, and when the fifers cease their playing the streets of Crotona are full of fine warhorses!

Thus it was that the Sybarites lost the fine cavalry of which they had been so proud. The complete overthrow of their power and the conquest of their city by the Crotoniates followed soon afterward —for how, in any contest between so idle and so industrious a community, could it have been otherwise?

•

THE MAN WHO LOVED WAR TOO MUCH

Adapted from a retelling by F. J. Gould

Courage and perseverance are great virtues to bring to a struggle, but only when the struggle has a worthy aim. From the restless fighting of Pyrrhus (319–272 B.C.) we get the expression "Pyrrhic victory," a win gained at too great a cost. This retelling is based on an account by the ancient historian Plutarch.

Once Pyrrhus, king of Epirus in ancient Greece, was listening to two flute players. One played a lively melody, the other a somber tune. When they were done, one of the musicians asked the king which air he liked best.

"Neither," answered Pyrrhus. "The song I like best is the song of sword clashing on sword, and the tune of an arrow leaving the bow."

Pyrrhus loved the joy of battle. He was too restless to stay in his own land and look after the comfort of his own people. His passion was to subdue foreign kingdoms, to add more and more territories to his own. He longed to conquer as Alexander the Great had conquered. As soon as one war was done, he began another, and though he was often beaten, he never shrank from fighting again.

Eventually he made up his mind to pit his strength against Rome. He readied his fleet and prepared to sail. Just before he went aboard, a friend said to him: "The Romans are fierce fighters. But even if the gods favor you, and you beat them, what will you do then?"

"I shall go up and down Italy, and every town will surrender to me."

"And what then?"

"Next, I'll make myself master of the fruitful isle of Sicily."

"Will that be the end?"

"No. Then I'll be ready to cross the sea to Africa and capture the great city of Carthage."

"And after that?"

"I'll march against Macedonia, a country I've long wished to add to my domain."

"And after that?"

"Why, after that, we shall take our ease, make merry, and give thanks for our great fortune."

"Then had we not better take our ease, make merry, and give thanks for our fortune now, instead of looking for so many fights? Why not rest now, instead of seeing so many lands ruined, so many lives lost?"

Pyrrhus turned away from his friend.

He landed on the shores of Italy with a vast army. The Romans marched forward to meet him. The fighting was furious. Battle after battle raged. After one great contest the day belonged to Pyrrhus, but the loss of life was dreadful. As he walked the field, surveying the heaps of dead, one of his officers congratulated him on the triumph.

Pyrrhus smiled grimly. "One more victory like this," he said, "and we are ruined." From that time, a battle won at too great a price has been called a Pyrrhic victory.

At last he was forced to leave Italy, and then to abandon Sicily, and so he took ship and carried his beaten army—what was left of it—back to Epirus. Still he could not rest. He went to war with

Macedonia and conquered the land of Alexandria, but the Macedonian king managed to regain his kingdom. Pyrrhus went to the Peloponnesus and fought against the Spartans, but they drove him from their territory. The fighting went on and on.

The last campaign was against the Greek city of Argos. The end was inglorious. The battle raged through the streets, and Pyrrhus was in the thick of it. An old woman threw a tile from the roof of her house, and it struck the warrior king on the head. He staggered, stunned and defenseless. The enemy closed in. Seconds later he was dead.

And so he was never able to "take his ease, make merry, and give thanks for his great fortune."

•

WOO SING AND THE MIRROR
Retold by Mary H. Davis and Cheow-Leung

This story from China illustrates an ancient proverb from that land: The fire you kindle against another often burns you more than it burns him. For some people, controlling temper is the hardest kind of self-discipline.

One day Woo Sing's father brought home a mirror from the great city.

Woo Sing had never seen a mirror before. It was hung in the room while he was out at play, so when he came in he did not understand what it was, and thought he saw another boy.

This made him very happy, for he thought the boy had come to play with him.

He spoke to the stranger in a very friendly way, but received no reply.

He laughed and waved his hand at the boy in the glass, who did the same thing, in exactly the same way.

Then Woo Sing thought, "I will go closer. It may be that he does not hear me." But when he began to walk, the other boy imitated him.

Woo Sing stopped to think about these strange actions, and he

said to himself, "This boy mocks me; he does everything that I do."
And the more he thought about it, the angrier he became, and soon
he noticed that the boy became angry too.

So Woo Sing grew very much enraged and struck the boy in
the glass, but he only hurt his hand and he went crying to his father.

The father said, "The boy you saw was your own image. This
should teach you an important lesson, my son. Try not to lose your
temper with other people. You struck the boy in the glass and hurt
only yourself.

"Now, remember that in real life when you strike without
cause you will hurt yourself most of all."

THE AMERICAN BOY

Theodore Roosevelt

**Many boys and young men want everyone to think they are tough.
Well, here is the right kind of toughness. This old-fashioned essay
with its old-fashioned language expresses sentiments much in
need today. It was written by one of our toughest presidents.**

Of course what we have a right to expect of the American boy
is that he shall turn out to be a good American man. Now, the
chances are strong that he won't be much of a man unless he is a
good deal of a boy. He must not be a coward or a weakling, a bully,
a shirk, or a prig. He must work hard and play hard. He must be
clean-minded and clean-lived, and able to hold his own under all
circumstances and against all comers. It is only on these conditions
that he will grow into the kind of American man of whom America
can be really proud. . . .

There is no need for a boy to preach about his own good
conduct and virtue. If he does he will make himself offensive and

ridiculous. But there is urgent need that he should practice decency; that he should be clean and straight, honest and truthful, gentle and tender, as well as brave. If he can once get to a proper understanding of things, he will have a far more hearty contempt for the boy who has begun a course of feeble dissipation, or who is untruthful, or mean, or dishonest, or cruel, than this boy and his fellows can possibly, in return, feel for him. The very fact that the boy should be manly and able to hold his own, that he should be ashamed to submit to bullying without instant retaliation, should, in return, make him abhor any form of bullying, cruelty, or brutality.

The boy can best become a good man by being a good boy— not a goody-goody boy, but just a plain good boy. I do not mean that he must love only the negative virtues; I mean he must love the positive virtues also. "Good," in the largest sense, should include whatever is fine, straightforward, clean, brave, and manly. The best boys I know—the best men I know—are good at their studies or their business, fearless and stalwart, hated and feared by all that is wicked and depraved, incapable of submitting to wrongdoing, and equally incapable of being aught but tender to the weak and helpless. A healthy-minded boy should feel hearty contempt for the coward, and even more hearty indignation for the boy who bullies girls or small boys, or tortures animals. One prime reason for abhorring cowards is because every good boy should have it in him to thrash the objectionable boy as the need arises.

Of course the effect that a thoroughly manly, thoroughly straight and upright boy can have upon the companions of his own age, and upon those who are younger, is incalculable. If he is not thoroughly manly, then they will not respect him, and his good qualities will count for but little; while, of course, if he is mean, cruel, or wicked, then his physical strength and force of mind merely make him so much the more objectionable a member of society. He cannot do good work if he is not strong and does not try with his whole heart and soul to count in any contest; and his strength will be a curse to himself and to everyone else if he does not have thorough command over himself and over his own evil passions, and if he does not use his strength on the side of decency, justice, and fair dealing.

In short, in life, as in a football game, the principle to follow is:

Hit the line hard; don't foul and don't shirk, but hit the line hard!

•

THE STAG AT THE POOL

Aesop

"Know thyself" was one of the most important dictates of the ancient Greek philosophers. Take the time to learn your true strengths and real weaknesses.

A thirsty Stag came to a spring to drink. As he drank, he looked into the pool of water and saw himself. He was very proud of his horns when he saw how big they were and what branches they had. But he looked at his feet, and took it hard that they should be so thin and weak.

Now, while he was thinking about these things, a Lion sprang out and began to chase him. The Stag turned and ran. As he was very fleet, he outran the Lion so long as they were on the open plain. But when they came to a wooded place, the Stag's horns became caught in the branches of the trees. He could not run, and the Lion caught up with him.

As the Lion fell upon him with his claws, the Stag cried out: "What a wretch am I! I was made safe by the very parts I scorned, and have come to my end by the parts I gloried in!"

•

THE ACHILLES HEEL

Adapted from a retelling by James Baldwin

This famous story from Greek mythology reminds us that every human being has a place where he can be hurt, and that even the strongest need to be aware of their own vulnerability. We should also remember that once we've seen someone else's soft spot, we usually do not want to hit it. In battle, taking advantage of a weakness is smart; in everyday living, it's often cruel.

Mightiest of all the Greeks who went to fight the Trojans was Achilles. He was the son of King Peleus and the sea nymph Thetis, and when he was born a soothsayer predicted that his life, though glorious, would be short.

His mother determined to prove the prophecy wrong, and that her son would never die. With the child in her arms she went down to the gloomy kingdom of Hades. There around the underworld flowed the dark river Styx, the sacred stream by which the gods swore unbreakable oaths. If a mortal were dipped into its black waters, no sword or arrow or other weapon could ever injure him.

Thetis held the boy by the heel, between her thumb and forefinger, and gently lowered him into the stream. The mysterious river enveloped the infant hero, and hardened his flesh against all harm. In her haste to get out of that sunless world, however, the loving mother forgot that the waters had not touched the child's skin where she gripped him. And so in that heel, and only there, lay a tiny spot where he could be harmed.

She carried the babe back, and showed her work proudly to Peleus. The father's gray locks and wrinkled visage scared the child, and Peleus turned away, saying, "He is, after all, only a little whiner!" And they thereafter called him Ligyron, which means whining.

But soon Peleus sent the young Ligyron to live with the wise centaur Chiron, a creature half-man and half-horse, who had a famous school for heroes on the wooded slopes of Mount Pelion. Chiron changed the lad's name to Achilles and fed him with the hearts of lions and the marrow of bears and wild boars. The boy learned how to use the bow and manage horses, and how to take care of his own body that he might always be strong and brave. He slept in the open air, and chased wild boars through the forest, and overthrew savage robbers in mountain passes. And when he was finished at Chiron's school, he went back to his home a tall, yellow-haired youth, strong-limbed, and as graceful as he was brave. His mother wept when she saw him, for she remembered the soothsayer's prophecy. But his old father was proud of him, and took him out to show him the treasures of his palace.

"Here," said the king, "is the matchless armor of bronze which the gods gave me on my wedding day. No man has ever worn it, but soon you will be big enough for it to fit you. See this fair, round shield with many an image of beauty engraved upon it, and this helmet with its nodding horsehair plume—was ever anything so delightful to a young warrior's eye? And here is the ashen spear which your arms will soon be able to hurl. And, lastly, here are Swift and Old Gold, the noblest steeds that any mortal ever owned. All these things are yours, my son!"

And so Achilles grew up to be one of the greatest heroes. He sailed with the Greeks in the long war against Troy, and there proved himself to be the champion of his people. But as strong as he was, and as brave as he was, he was not perfect—as no mortal is. He wanted to make sure everyone knew he was the strongest and bravest. He thought and talked too much of his own glory. He had a hot temper. When he did not get his way, he sat in his tent and pouted. And his doom, which the soothsayer had foretold, came soon enough.

One day, while hard fighting was going on beneath the walls of Troy, Achilles drove his chariot close up to the famous gate and stopped to taunt the unhappy Trojans who stood upon the battlements. Vainly did the faithful steed Old Gold champ upon his foaming bit and rear in his traces and strain hard against his reins; for he knew of the fate that threatened his master and wanted to carry him away from the danger. But Achilles, standing high in the chariot, boasted of his great deeds: how from the sea he had laid waste twelve cities, and from the land eleven; how he had vanquished the queen of the Amazons, and had slain Hector, the hope of the Trojans; how he had taken great spoils and countless treasures from many lands; and how, in all the world, there was no name so terrible as his, no, not even the name of the sun-bright Apollo.

But scarcely had the last rash boast passed his lips when a gleaming spear circled down upon him from above. His armor could not ward off the swift death it brought. Some say the fatal weapon was hurled from the battlements by Paris, the perfidious prince who had caused all that sad war. Others assert it came from the hands of no mortal man, but was cast from the sky by great Apollo himself, offended beyond measure by the hero's boasting. I do not know which of these stories is true, nor does it matter now. All I need say is that the missile found the one mark on the heel where it could tear the flesh. The destroyer of three and twenty cities fell headlong and helpless in the dust, as many another boaster has done since his day, and the great world went on as before. And his wonderful war steeds, no longer restrained by his voice and hand, sprang wildly away and galloped with the speed of wind across the plain.

•

THE MAN, THE BOY, AND THE DONKEY

Retold by James Baldwin

Trying to please is fine, but even the art of pleasing requires some common sense, self-discipline, and the courage to say no when necessary. This tale has been told for centuries in Africa, Asia, and Europe.

Once upon a time a man and his son were going to market, and they were leading their donkey behind them. They had not gone far when they met a farmer, who said, "You are very foolish to walk all the way to town with that lazy donkey following behind you. What is a donkey good for, if not to ride upon?"

"Well, I never thought of that," said the man, "and I am very willing to please you." So he put the boy on the donkey, and they started again on their journey.

Soon they passed some men by the roadside. "See that lazy boy," said one of them. "He rides on the donkey, and makes his poor old father walk behind."

When the man heard this, he called to the boy and said, "Stop a minute! Let us see if we cannot please these men." Then he told the boy to get off, and mounted the donkey himself.

Two women next met them, and one said to the other, "Did you ever see so lazy a man? He rides and takes his ease, while his son walks behind."

The man did not know what to do. "My son," he said, "I think we should try to please everybody, but how can we please the women and the men at the same time?" After a while he thought of a plan. He took the boy up behind him, and the donkey went jogging along with both of them on his back.

When, at last, they came into the town, a crowd of men began to jeer and point at them. The man stopped and said, "What is the matter, my good friends?"

"Matter enough!" said the men. "You ought to be ashamed of yourself for being so cruel to that donkey. It is too much for so small an animal to carry so heavy a load."

"I had not thought of that," said the man. "It does seem hard for the donkey, but then we were only trying to please some of our friends." So he and his son got off and tried to think what to do next.

They thought and thought till at last a happy idea came into their minds. They found a long pole, and tied the donkey's feet to it. Then after a great deal of hard work, they raised the pole on their shoulders. The donkey did not like this, but he could not help himself.

It was as much as the man and boy could do to carry him. But they stood up very straight, while all the people laughed at the funny sight. "I think that we are pleasing everybody now," said the man.

When they came to Market Bridge, the donkey got one of his feet loose, and kicked out. This made the boy drop his end of the pole. The donkey fell on the bridge and rolled over into the river and was drowned.

"I think, my son," said the Man, "that we may learn a lesson from all this."

"What kind of a lesson, Father?"

"Try to please everybody, and you will please nobody."

●

THE SPIDER AND THE FLY
Mary Howitt

Unfortunately, as long as there is dishonesty in the world, there will be people ready to lay traps for us. We must learn to recognize them and guard against their wiles. Not everyone who talks sweetly offers sweets.

"Will you walk into my parlor?" said the spider to the fly,
" 'Tis the prettiest little parlor that ever you did spy.
The way into my parlor is up a winding stair,
And I have many curious things to show when you are there."
"Oh, no, no," said the little fly, "to ask me is in vain,
For who goes up your winding stair, can ne'er come down again."

"I'm sure you must be weary, dear, with soaring up so high;
Will you rest upon my little bed?" said the spider to the fly.
"There are pretty curtains drawn around; the sheets are fine and
    thin,
And if you'd like to rest awhile, I'll snugly tuck you in!"
"Oh, no, no," said the little fly, "for I've often heard it said,
They never, never wake again who sleep upon your bed!"

Said the cunning spider to the fly: "Dear friend, what can I do
To prove the warm affection I've always felt for you?
I have within my pantry good store of all that's nice;
I'm sure you're very welcome—will you please to take a slice?"
"Oh, no, no," said the little fly, "kind sir, that cannot be;
I've heard what's in your pantry, and I do not wish to see."

"Sweet creature," said the spider, "you're witty and you're wise;
How handsome are your gauzy wings, how brilliant are your eyes!
I have a little looking-glass upon my parlor shelf;
If you'll step in one moment, dear, you shall behold yourself."
"I thank you, gentle sir," he said, "for what you're pleased to say,
And bidding you good morning now, I'll call another day."

The spider turned her round about, and went into her den,
For well she knew the silly fly would soon come back again;
So she wove a subtle web in a little corner sly,
And set her table ready to dine upon the fly.
Then she came out to her door again, and merrily she sings:
"Come hither, hither, pretty fly, with the pearl and silver wings;
Your robes are green and purple; there's a crest upon your head;
Your eyes are like the diamond bright, but mine are dull as lead!"

Alas! alas! how very soon this silly little fly,
Hearing her wily, flattering words, came slowly flitting by.
With buzzing wings he hung aloft, then near and nearer drew,
Thinking only of his brilliant eyes, and his green and purple hue—
Thinking only of his crested head—poor foolish thing! At last

Up jumped the cunning spider, and fiercely held him fast.
She dragged him up her winding stair, into her dismal den,
Within her little parlor—but he ne'er came out again!

And now, dear little children, who may this story read,
To idle, silly, flattering words, I pray you ne'er give heed.
Unto an evil counselor close heart and ear and eye,
And take a lesson from this tale of the spider and the fly.

•

THE WOLF AND THE LAMB

Aesop

Here is wolfish behavior, the kind that no evidence, no argument, no plea will stop. When we go into the world, we have to watch out for people like this.

A Wolf saw a Lamb drinking at a brook and set about finding some good reason for catching him. He went to a place a little higher up the stream, and called out:
"How dare you muddy the water that I am drinking!"
"How can I," said the Lamb, humbly, "when I drink with the tips of my lips only? And, besides, the water runs from you to me, not from me to you."
"Well, last night, while I was trying to sleep, you kept me awake forever with your bleating."
"But how could that be?" asked the Lamb. "I slept on the other side of the hill, inside my master's barn, with my nose nestled into my mother's side."
"Well, you called my father names a year ago," growled the Wolf, finding another reason.
"I was not born a year ago," said the poor Lamb.
"You can make all the excuses you want," said the Wolf, "but I am hungry, and shall eat you just the same." And without further ado, he gobbled up the little lamb.

Some people, having made up their minds to do wrong, will not be stopped by the best of reasons.

•

HOW THE OSTRICH GOT
HIS LONG NECK

This story from Africa reminds us that choosing the wrong friends
against good advice can mean big trouble.

Long ago Ostrich had a short neck, just like all the other birds.
In those days Ostrich wanted more than anything to be friends with
Crocodile. All the other birds warned Ostrich he was making a
mistake.

"You can't trust Crocodile," Monkey said. "He's mean, and has
no manners, and scares all the other animals away from the river."

"He's lazy, too," Wildebeest warned. "All he does is lie around
all day, basking in the sun and waiting for dinner."

"And he thinks only of himself," Elephant added. "He'll snap at
you as soon as you turn your back. No, Crocodile can't be trusted."

But Ostrich paid no attention at all and insisted on playing with
Crocodile.

One day Crocodile was quite hungry, for he had skipped
breakfast that very morning. So he said to Ostrich: "My good friend,
I have a terrible toothache today. Would you mind sticking your
head into my mouth and seeing what's wrong with me?"

He opened his jaws wide, very wide.

"Why, of course, dear Crocodile," Ostrich said.

And he stuck his head inside.

"But you have so many teeth!" Ostrich called. "Which is the
one that aches?"

"It's one in the back," Crocodile moaned. "Look in the back!"

So Ostrich stuck his head in further.

"It's awfully dark in here," he called out again. "And so many
teeth! I'm still not sure which one aches."

"It's in the very, very back," Crocodile assured him. "Go back
just a little more."

So Ostrich stuck his head in even further.

"Here?" he called.

"There!" Crocodile shouted. And he snapped his jaws shut on
poor Ostrich's head!

"Help!" Ostrich yelled, and he pulled as hard as he could to get his head out. But Crocodile pulled right back.

They both pulled, and they pulled. Ostrich pulled one way, and Crocodile pulled the other. And as they pulled, Ostrich's neck began to stretch.

And s–t–r–e–t–c–h.

And S—T—R—E—T—C—H!

They pulled all day long, and Ostrich's neck grew longer and longer. It must have hurt quite a bit, but Ostrich kept pulling all the same, because of course he did not want to lose his head.

At last Crocodile got tired of pulling and let go. Ostrich jumped back and ran away from the river as fast as he could. And to this day he has a long neck to remind him to stay away from the likes of Crocodile.

●

A SOUND FOR A SMELL

The world is full of people who will try to get something they don't deserve—often, money they haven't earned. Here is wisdom that recognizes the false claims of greed. Various versions of this tale are told throughout Africa, Asia, and other parts of the world.

A poor traveler stopped at midday to rest in the shade of a spreading tree. He had journeyed far and had only a single piece of bread left for his lunch. But across the road stood a stall where a baker sold rich pastries and cakes, and the traveler enjoyed inhaling the fragrances wafting across the way while he munched on his thin, stale morsel.

When he rose to continue his journey, the baker suddenly ran across the road and seized him by the collar.

"Just a minute!" the baker cried. "You must pay me for my cakes!"

"What do you mean?" the startled traveler protested. "I haven't touched your cakes."

"You thief!" the baker shouted. "It's perfectly obvious you've enjoyed your own stale biscuit only by sniffing the pleasant odors of my bakery. You won't leave until you've paid me for what you've taken. I don't work for nothing, my friend."

A crowd gathered and urged the two to take their dispute before the local judge, who was a wise old man. The judge listened to their arguments, thought a long time, then rendered his judgment.

"You are right," he told the baker. "This traveler has savored the fruits of your labor. I rule the smell of your cakes is worth three gold coins."

"That's absurd!" the traveler objected. "Besides, I've spent all my money on my journey. I don't have a penny to pay."

"Ah," said the judge, "in that case I will help you." He pulled three gold coins from his own pocket, which the baker quickly reached to take.

"Not yet," said the judge. "You say this traveler merely smelled your cakes?"

"That's right," replied the baker.

"But he never swallowed a bite?"

"I told you he did not."

"He never tasted a pastry?"

"No!"

"And never touched your pies?"

"No!"

"Then since he has consumed only vapors, you must be paid with sound. Open your ears and receive what you deserve."

The wise judge let the gold coins tumble from one hand to the other so that their tingling entered the baker's greedy ears.

"If you had been kind enough to help this poor man along his way," the judge said, "then truly you would have found golden reward in Heaven."

•

PROCRUSTES THE PITILESS

Retold by James Baldwin

When we last saw Theseus in Chapter One, he had left home and set out to find his father in Athens. The road was long and full of surprises, even terror. Like most of us, Theseus soon learned that the world can be a dangerous place. Sometimes we meet those who would do us harm. It takes good judgment to recognize

them, and courage and strength to overcome them. From the
villain Procrustes we get the expression "procrustean bed," meaning a situation into which we are violently or arbitrarily forced.

Athens was now not more than twenty miles away, but the road
led through the Parnes Mountains, and was only a narrow path
winding among the rocks and up and down many a lonely wooded
glen. Theseus had seen worse and far more dangerous roads than
this, and so he strode bravely onward, happy in the thought that he
was so near the end of his long journey. But it was very slow
traveling through the mountains, and he was not always sure that
he was following the right path. The sun was almost down when he
came to a broad green valley where the trees had been cleared
away. A little river flowed through the middle of this valley, and on
either side were grassy meadows where cattle were grazing; and on
a hillside close by, half hidden among the trees, there was a great
stone house with vines running over its walls and roof.

While Theseus was wondering who it could be that lived in
this pretty but lonely place, a man came out of the house and
hurried down to the road to meet him. He was a well-dressed man,
and his face was wreathed with smiles. He bowed low to Theseus
and kindly invited him to come up to the house and be his guest
that night.

"This is a lonely place," he said, "and it is not often that travelers pass this way. But there is nothing that gives me so much joy as
to find strangers and feast them at my table and hear them tell of
the things they have seen and heard. Come up, and sup with me,
and lodge under my roof; and you shall sleep on a wonderful bed
which I have—a bed which fits every guest and cures him of every
ill."

Theseus was pleased with the man's ways, and as he was both
hungry and tired, he went up with him and sat down under the
vines by the door. The man said: "Now I will go in and make the
bed ready for you, and you can lie down upon it and rest. And later,
when you feel refreshed, you shall sit at my table and sup with
me, and I will listen to the pleasant tales which I know you will
tell."

When he had gone into the house, Theseus looked around
him to see what sort of a place it was. He was filled with surprise at
the richness of it—at the gold and silver and beautiful things with

which every room seemed to be adorned—for it was indeed a place fit for a prince. While he was looking and wondering, the vines before him were parted and the fair face of a young girl peeped out.

"Noble stranger," she whispered, "do not lie down on my master's bed, for those who do so never rise again. Fly down the glen and hide yourself in the deep woods ere he returns, or else there will be no escape for you."

"Who is your master, fair maiden, that I should be afraid of him?" asked Theseus.

"Men call him Procrustes, or the Stretcher," said the girl—and she talked low and fast. "He is a robber. He brings here all the strangers that he finds traveling through the mountains. He puts them on his iron bed. He robs them of all they have. No one who comes into his house ever goes out again."

"Why do they call him the Stretcher? And what is that iron bed of his?" asked Theseus, in no way alarmed.

"Did he not tell you that it fits all guests?" said the girl. "Most truly it does fit them. For if a traveler is too long, Procrustes hews off his legs until he is of the right length; but if he is too short, as is the case with most guests, then he stretches his limbs and body with ropes until he is long enough. It is for this reason that men call him the Stretcher."

"Methinks that I have heard of this Stretcher before," said Theseus. Then he remembered that someone had warned him to beware of the wily robber Procrustes, who lurked in the glens of the Parnes peaks and lured travelers into his den.

"Hark! hark!" whispered the girl. "I hear him coming!" And the vine leaves closed over her hiding place.

The very next moment Procrustes stood in the door, bowing and smiling as though he had never done any harm to his fellow men.

"My dear young friend," he said, "the bed is ready, and I will show you the way. After you have taken a pleasant little nap, we will sit down at table, and you may tell me of the wonderful things which you have seen in the course of your travels."

Theseus arose and followed his host. When they had come into an inner chamber, there, surely enough, was the bedstead of iron, very curiously wrought, and upon it a soft mattress which seemed to invite him to lie down and rest. But Theseus, peering about, saw the ax and the ropes with cunning pulleys lying hidden behind the curtains; and he saw, too, that the floor was covered with stains of blood.

"Now, my dear young friend," said Procrustes, "I pray you to lie down and take your ease, for I know that you have traveled far and are faint from want of rest and sleep. Lie down, and while sweet slumber overtakes you, I will have a care that no unseemly noise, or buzzing fly, or vexing gnat disturbs your dreams."

"Is this your wonderful bed?" asked Theseus.

"It is," answered Procrustes, "and you need but lie down upon it, and it will fit you perfectly."

"But you must lie upon it first," said Theseus, "and let me see how it will fit itself to your stature."

"Ah, no," said Procrustes, "for then the spell would be broken," and as he spoke his cheeks grew ashy pale.

"But I tell you, you must lie upon it," said Theseus, and he seized the trembling man around the waist and threw him by force upon the bed. No sooner was he prone upon the couch than curious iron arms reached out and clasped his body in their embrace and held him down so that he could not move hand or foot. The wretched man shrieked and cried for mercy, but Theseus stood over him and looked him straight in the eye.

"Is this the kind of bed on which you have your guests lie down?" he asked.

But Procrustes answered not a word. Then Theseus brought out the ax and the ropes and the pulleys, and asked him what they were for, and why they were hidden in the chamber. Procrustes was still silent, and could do nothing now but tremble and weep.

"Is it true," said Theseus, "that you have lured hundreds of travelers into your den only to rob them? Is it true that it is your wont to fasten them in this bed, and then chop off their legs or stretch them out until they fit the iron frame? Tell me, is this true?"

"It is true! it is true!" sobbed Procrustes. "Now kindly touch the spring above my head and let me go, and you shall have everything that I possess."

But Theseus turned away. "You are caught," he said, "in the trap which you set for others and for me. There is no mercy for the man who shows no mercy." And he went out of the room and left the wretch to perish by his own cruel device.

Theseus looked through the house and found there great wealth of gold and silver and costly things which Procrustes had taken from the strangers who had fallen into his hands. He went into the dining hall, and there indeed was the table spread with a rich feast of meats and drinks and delicacies such as no king would scorn, but there was a seat and a plate for only the host and none at all for guests.

Then the girl whose fair face Theseus had seen among the vines came running into the house. She seized the young hero's hands and blessed and thanked him because he had rid the world of the cruel Procrustes.

"Only a month ago," she said, "my father, a rich merchant of Athens, was traveling toward Eleusis, and I was with him, happy and carefree as any bird in the green woods. This robber lured us into his den, for we had much gold with us. My father he stretched upon his iron bed, but me he made his slave."

Then Theseus called together all the inmates of the house, poor wretches whom Procrustes had forced to serve him. He divided the robber's spoils among them and told them they were free to go wheresoever they wished. And on the next day he went on, through the narrow crooked ways among the mountains and hills, and came at last to the plain of Athens, and saw the noble city and, in its midst, the rocky height where the great Temple of Athena stood. And, a little way from the temple, he saw the white walls of the palace of the king.

•

ONE WORD AGAINST ANOTHER

Here's a real bold-faced lie. Some people act on the theory that if they hold their heads high enough, no one will question their lies. This Arab tale echoes a remark by Ralph Waldo Emerson: "The louder he talked of his honor, the faster we counted our spoons."

One day a neighbor knocked on the town mayor's door and asked, "Will you lend me your donkey for a while?"

"My good friend," the mayor replied, "you know there is nothing in the world I wouldn't do for you. I'd love to lend you my donkey. But I'm afraid he's away today."

Just then the donkey gave a bray loud enough to wake the dead.

"Well, this is my lucky day," said the neighbor. "It seems your donkey is here after all."

"How dare you!" protested the mayor, puffing up with shocked indignation. "Are you going to believe my donkey and doubt me, a man of distinction and status?"

•

FISH OR CAT?

This Arab tale reminds us that honesty is the best policy, if for no other reason than truth has a way of coming out in the end.

A man went at sunrise to his favorite spot on the river, cast his line, and pulled in a fat, shining fish. It weighed exactly six pounds.

He took it home and proudly showed it to his wife.

"Prettiest fish I ever caught," he said. "Six pounds of pure pleasure. I'll cook a grand feast tonight." Then he left the house and went to work.

His wife could not take her eyes off the fish. It made them water, it looked so tempting. At last she couldn't stand it any longer. She cooked it and sent for her brother, and they gorged themselves until there wasn't a morsel left.

That evening the man came home to find no fish.

"I'm so sorry," his wife cried, "but while I was in the garden the cat got into the kitchen and ate the whole thing, from head to tail!"

The man seized the cat and plopped it on a scale. It weighed exactly six pounds.

"If this is my fish, then where is the cat?" he asked. "And if this is the cat, then I wonder just where my fish might be."

•

THE THREE RIOTERS
Adapted from Geoffrey Chaucer

Unfortunately, there are some people (often young men) who go
into the world looking for trouble, and it usually finds them. This
famous story, "The Pardoner's Tale" from Chaucer's *Canterbury
Tales*, may help us choose the kind of people we want to be with
both in friendship and at work.

In Flanders there once lived a company of young men who
gave themselves over to folly and wrongdoing. They lounged about
the taverns all day, drinking, swearing, singing, dancing, and gam-
bling. And their gluttony and idleness made them so wicked that
when they heard of any other wrong thing, they not only laughed
at it but went straightway and sought out the sin for themselves.

Three of these rioters, of whom I have spoken, were sitting at
the tavern drinking, early one morning, when they chanced to hear
a bell ring. It was being carried at the head of a funeral procession
—as was the custom in those days. One of the rioters thereupon
called the tavern boy to him and said: "Go out and ask the name
of the dead man who passes by. And look you, report it to me
speedily."

"Sir," quoth the lad, "I do not need to ask, as the name was
told me here not two hours agone. He was, in sooth, a mate of
yours, and was slain only last night, while he sat here drinking, by
that prowling thief called Death who lays low all the people in this
country. With his spear he smote his heart in two and went his way
in silence. This very pestilence has slain thousands; and, master, ere
you come into his sight it were well that you be prepared to meet
him. For so my mother teaches me."

"By holy Mary, the child speaks truth," said the innkeeper, "for
Death hath slain both man and woman, child and page, to be found
in a large village within a mile of here. I think he must live there,
so many have met their end."

"Odds boddikins!" cried one of the rioters, springing up, "is
it then so great a peril to meet him? *I'll* seek him out, by hedge
and highway—and to this I make my vow! Hearken ye, my mates,
for we three are one in this. Let each of us hold up his hand and

swear to become the other's brother; and we will seek out and slay this traitor Death, who by stealth has slain so many of our friends."

The others loudly cheered him in their drunken way, and took the oath to stand together and make an end of Death before nightfall. So they started up at once and directed their steps toward the village of which the host had spoken; and many an oath they swore, on the way, of what they should accomplish.

They had not gone more than half a mile when they came to a stile, where they met a poor old man, who greeted them civilly enough with: "God be with you, my lordings."

But the proudest of these three rioters made answer: "Why, how now, churl! Why is your bag of bones so wrapped up, clear to your face? And how do you manage to hang on to life so long?"

The old man gave him a straight look and said: "I live thus because I cannot find—either in city or in village, though I walked to India—anyone who will change his youth for my age. And so I must still keep my age as long as it is God's will, for Death, alas! will not come and take me. Thus I go up and down, a restless wanderer."

Here the old man drew himself up with dignity and added: "But, sirs, it shows no courtesy in you to speak to one of my years so rudely, since he has done you no harm in word or deed. In Holy Writ you may read for yourselves that ye should respect the gray hairs of the aged. I have no more to say, but must go on my way."

"Nay, old churl, *that* you shall not do," said another of the gamesters with an oath. "You have just spoken of that arch traitor Death who has been slaying all our friends in the country round about. Belike you are his spy, so tell us where he is or it shall go hard with you!"

"Nay, sirs," replied graybeard, "speak not so rashly for your souls' good. But if you are so set upon finding Death, I can tell you which way to go. Turn up this crooked bypath; for in yonder grove I saw him sitting beneath a tree, and there he will abide for all your boasts. See ye that oak? Close by it ye shall find him. God save you, sirs, who would benefit mankind, and mend you all!"

But before the old man had quite finished his speech the three rioters turned and ran toward the oak he had shown them. There they saw no one; but on the ground they discovered a heap of golden coins, bright and round—well-nigh seven bushels of them, they thought. So delighted were they to see this great heap of glittering gold that they speedily forgot all about Death, whom they had been seeking. But Death was nearby, for all that, and did not forget them, as you shall see.

Down they squatted by this precious hoard and dug their fingers deep into it, and let the coins trickle through their fingers hungrily. The worst of the three was the first to speak a word.

"Brothers," said he, "take heed to what I say. This treasure will make our fortune, so that we may spend all the rest of our lives in mirth and jollity. Lightly as it comes we'll lightly spend. By heaven, who would have thought we should tumble into such luck!"

Thereupon he counseled them with rare cunning that they should not try to carry the treasure off in the daytime, lest they should be arrested for thieves. Instead, he advised that they draw lots, and the one chosen should go back to town for meat and drink, while the other two should remain in the grove and hide the gold until nightfall.

The counsel seemed good to the others, and they drew, and the lot fell to the youngest to go back for food. He therefore started without loss of time.

No sooner was he out of sight than the first speaker said to the other: "You know well that you are my sworn brother, so I will tell you something to your profit. Here is bright gold heaped up plentifully which is to be divided among three of us. But one of us is away, and if I can shape it so that the gold need only be divided between *two,* have I not done you a friendly turn?"

The other listened greedily but answered: "I know not how it can be done. Our mate knows all about the gold, and we couldn't fool him."

"Well, I can tell you how, and that in a few words, if you'll keep it dark," said the first one.

"Tell away," said the other. "I shall not betray you."

The first one tapped him on the shoulder and said in a low voice: "Look you, there are two of us, and two are stronger than one. When the youngster comes back we will make a game of him. You can pretend to wrestle with him while he is sitting down, and I will watch my chance and stab him. Then draw your dagger and do the same. After that, my dear friend, there will be only two of us to share the gold."

The other ruffian nodded his head at this, and so they plotted to murder the third in cold blood.

Meanwhile the young man who had gone to town was not idle

in wickedness, for all the way there he could not get his mind off the beauty of those new bright coins of gold.

"Oh Lord!" said he to himself, "if I could only devise a plan so that I might have all this treasure for myself, I should be the merriest fellow under the canopy of heaven!"

At last the fiend, our common enemy, put it into his head that he should buy poison and thus make an end of both his fellows. The fiend knew he would do this wicked thing for the sake of all the gold, and that he never would repent.

So the young man lost no time in going to an apothecary's shop, in the town, and he asked, plausibly enough, for some rat poison. He said there was a polecat roaming in his yard, which had carried off his fat geese, and he wanted some poison strong enough to kill the beast.

The apothecary answered: "You shall have something so strong that no living creature in this world could withstand it—even if he took an amount no greater than a grain of wheat."

The wretched plotter was secretly glad to hear this and bought the poison without delay. Then in the next street he bought three large bottles of wine. Into two of them he put the poison, while he kept the third pure for his own use. For he purposed to toil all night at carrying and hiding the gold away, after he had brought his comrades to a violent end.

When he had prepared his three bottles, he bought some meat also and went back to the other two rioters laden as if to dine.

What need is there of telling the rest? For as the other two had already planned, they slew the young man without delay.

When the bloody deed was done, the first one said: "Ha! now

that the young fool is out of the way, let us sit and drink and make us merry, and afterward we can bury the body."

And with the word he picked up one of the bottles which contained the poison. He drank deeply and gave it to his companion. The apothecary had told true. Within a little while the poison took effect and they both died in fearful agony.

Thus ended the two murderers, slain by the man they had murdered. And thus came Death—whom they had forgot—to seek his own at the last.

•

THE CAMEL'S NOSE

Sometimes trouble comes looking for us. This tale gives us some advice about how to keep trouble at bay.

One cold night, as a sheik lay in his tent, a camel thrust the flap aside and looked in.

"I pray thee, master," he said, "let me put my nose within the tent, for it is cold outside."

"By all means," yawned the sheik, who was bored and listless from having reposed on his pillows all day. "Do so if you wish."

The camel poked his nose into the tent.

"If I might but warm my neck also," he said presently.

"It's all the same to me," answered the sheik. So the beast stuck his neck inside, and contented itself for a while by looking about.

Soon the camel, who had been turning his head from side to side, spoke up again.

"It will take but little more room if I put my forelegs within the tent. I would feel a great deal better."

The sheik simply shrugged and rolled to one side to make a little more room.

The camel had hardly planted his forefeet within the tent when he said: "Master, I'm keeping the flap open by standing here like this. I think I ought to come all the way inside."

"Whatever you like," the sheik nodded, moving over some more so the beast might enter.

So the camel came forward and crowded into the tent. No sooner was he inside than he looked hard at the sheik.

"I think," he said, "that there is not enough room for both of us here. It will be best for you to stand outside, as you are the smaller. Then there will be room enough for me."

And with that he pushed the sheik out into the cold and darkness.

It is a wise rule to resist the beginnings of evil.

•

THE TWO TRAVELERS AND THE OYSTER

I include this old tale because it seems especially fit for modern times. It reminds us, as the English essayist Samuel Butler said, that in law nothing is certain but the expense. In the end, it's less costly simply to act honestly and responsibly.

As two men were walking by the seaside at low water they saw an oyster, and they both stooped at the same time to pick it up. One pushed the other away, and a dispute ensued.

A traveler was coming along at the time, and they determined to ask him which of the two had the better right to the oyster.

While each was telling his story, the traveler gravely took out his knife, opened the shell, and loosened the oyster. When they had finished, and were listening for his decision, he just as gravely swallowed the oyster, and offered them each a shell.

"The Court," said he, "awards you each a shell. The oyster will cover the costs."

•

HABIT

William James

The writer Flannery O'Connor once observed: "Time is very dangerous without a rigid routine. . . . Routine is a condition of survival." One of America's greatest philosophers concurs here. William James (1842–1910) reminds us that habits are forged, not inherited. And he asserts that the right kinds of habits are essential not only for survival in the world but also for the ability to do some good in the world.

No matter how full a reservoir of *maxims* one may possess, and no matter how good one's *sentiments* may be, if one has not taken advantage of every concrete opportunity to *act,* one's character may remain entirely unaffected for the better. With mere good intentions, hell is proverbially paved. And this is an obvious consequence of the principles we have laid down. A "character," as J. S. Mill says, "is a completely fashioned will"; and a will, in the sense in which he means it, is an aggregate of tendencies to act in a firm and prompt and definite way upon all the principal emergencies of life. A tendency to act becomes effectively ingrained in us only in proportion to the uninterrupted frequency with which the actions actually occur, and the brain "grows" to their use. Every time a resolve or a fine glow of feeling evaporates without bearing practical fruit is worse than a chance lost; it works so as positively to hinder future resolutions and emotions from taking the normal path of discharge. There is no more contemptible type of human character than that of the nerveless sentimentalist and dreamer, who spends his life in a weltering sea of sensibility and emotion, but who never does a manly concrete deed. . . .

It is not simply *particular lines* of discharge, but also *general forms* of discharge, that seem to be grooved out by habit in the brain. Just as, if we let our emotions evaporate, they get into a way of evaporating; so there is reason to suppose that if we often flinch from making an effort, before we know it the effort-making capacity will be gone; and that, if we suffer the wandering of our attention, presently it will wander all the time. Attention and effort are . . . but two names for the same psychic fact. To what brain processes they

correspond we do not know. The strongest reason for believing
that they do depend on brain processes at all, and are not pure acts
of the spirit, is just this fact, that they seem in some degree subject
to the law of habit, which is a material law. As a final practical
maxim, relative to these habits of the will, we may, then, offer
something like this: *Keep the faculty of effort alive in you by a little
gratuitous exercise every day.* That is, be systematically ascetic or
heroic in little unnecessary points, do every day or two something
for no other reason than that you would rather not do it, so that
when the hour of dire need draws nigh, it may find you not un-
nerved and untrained to stand the test. Asceticism of this sort is like
the insurance which a man pays on his house and goods. The tax
does him no good at the time, and possibly may never bring him a
return. But if the fire *does* come, his having paid it will be his
salvation from ruin. So with the man who has daily inured himself
to habits of concentrated attention, energetic volition, and self-
denial in unnecessary things. He will stand like a tower when everything rocks around him, and when his softer fellow mortals are
winnowed like chaff in the blast.

•

Is There a Santa Claus?

Francis P. Church

As we head further into the world, and gain more experience, we
lose some of the fixtures of our childhood. But we also learn there
are more things in life than we can see. This famous editorial
appeared in *The New York Sun* on September 21, 1897. Many
newspapers continue to reprint it around Christmastime.

We take pleasure in answering at once and thus prominently
the communication below, expressing at the same time our great
gratification that its faithful author is numbered among the friends
of *The Sun:*

Dear Editor—I am 8 years old
Some of my little friends say there is no Santa Claus.
Papa says, "If you see it in *The Sun* it's so."
Please tell me the truth, is there a Santa Claus?
Virginia O'Hanlon
115 West 95th street.

Virginia, your little friends are wrong. They have been affected by the skepticism of a skeptical age. They do not believe except they see. They think that nothing can be which is not comprehensible by their little minds. All minds, Virginia, whether they be men's or children's, are little. In this great universe of ours man is a mere insect, an ant, in his intellect, as compared with the boundless world about him, as measured by the intelligence capable of grasping the whole of truth and knowledge.

Yes, Virginia, there is a Santa Claus. He exists as certainly as love and generosity and devotion exist, and you know that they abound and give to your life its highest beauty and joy. Alas! how dreary would be the world if there were no Santa Claus! It would be as dreary as if there were no Virginias. There would be no childlike faith then, no poetry, no romance to make tolerable this existence. We should have no enjoyment, except in sense and sight. The eternal light with which childhood fills the world would be extinguished.

Not believe in Santa Claus! You might as well not believe in fairies! You might get your papa to hire men to watch in all the chimneys on Christmas Eve to catch Santa Claus, but even if they did not see Santa Claus coming down, what would that prove? Nobody sees Santa Claus, but that is no sign there is no Santa Claus. The most real things in the world are those that neither children nor men can see. Did you ever see fairies dancing on the lawn? Of course not, but that's no proof that they are not there. Nobody can conceive or imagine all the wonders there are unseen and unseeable in the world.

You tear apart a baby's rattle and see what makes the noise inside, but there is a veil covering the unseen world which not the strongest man, nor even the united strength of all the strongest men that ever lived, could tear apart. Only faith, fancy, poetry, love, romance, can push aside that curtain and view and picture the supernal beauty and glory beyond. Is it all real? Ah, Virginia, in all this world there is nothing else real and abiding.

No Santa Claus! Thank God! he lives, and he lives forever. A thousand years from now, Virginia, nay, ten times ten thousand years from now, he will continue to make glad the heart of childhood.

Three

•

STANDING
FAST

''LOOK at a man in the midst of doubt and danger, and you will learn in his hour of adversity what he really is," wrote the Roman philosopher Lucretius. "It is then that true utterances are wrung from the recesses of his breast. The mask is torn off; the reality remains."

Some people's lives are filled with more hardship than others. But make no mistake—every life's journey has some tough stretches. Everyone is tested, everyone brought to the line. There will be occasional bumps in the road, unpleasant surprises, irritating delays, annoying mistakes and accidents. There will be days when everything seems to go wrong. ("When sorrows come, they come not single spies, but in battalions," Shakespeare observes in *Hamlet*.) And there will be those moments when our whole world seems to be falling apart. Adversity is a large part of life, and the sooner we learn to deal with it, the easier life will be for us.

This chapter helps us get ready for those times when the path suddenly gets steeper, the road rockier, when the wind and rain are at your face, and part of you wants more than anything else to turn back. At times like these, you may need almost every virtue in your arsenal to help you stand fast—perseverance, courage, self-discipline, responsibility, industry, integrity. And you may need the loyalty and friendship of one or two good companions, as well as faith in God to see you through the struggle.

We meet a few heroes in this chapter. Some are famous because of the way they stood fast in times of crisis. Others are ordinary people who stepped forward to take the tests of life we all must face. Here we find people standing firm at their posts and sticking to their assignments, even though temptation beckons them away. We witness people winning by small steps, tackling tasks piece by piece. We discover that sometimes the only way to get out of a tough spot is simply to buckle down and get to work. We see what it's like to blaze a rough trail where nobody has gone before. And we learn a few things about facing very bad situations, ones where certain pain and loss lie ahead.

Of course, virtues such as perseverance and courage must be informed by practical wisdom. You have to be able to recognize *when* the time is right to stand fast, and then you have to know *what* to do to hold your ground. The stories in this chapter, as in the last, help sharpen our intellectual virtues as well as our moral ones. We meet examples of reason giving direction to action. We learn the value of ingenuity in tough spots and fortitude under heavy fire. We see real concentration in action, a harnessing of thought and talent that brings the whole mind and whole heart to a task. And we witness the courage of imagination, the kind that dares to stick up for worthy ideas when everyone else shouts they're wrong.

If met correctly, of course, most of the troubles we encounter in life become opportunities to know and add to the strength of our virtues. The blows of adversity can be the best chances for improvement. "The gem cannot be polished without friction, nor man perfected without trials," a Chinese proverb says. Any real achievement, any worthwhile prize will probably come at the cost of a few failures. We set our sights and try and try again until we reach our goal.

The ultimate test, however, is not whether we finally reach that goal but how we conduct ourselves along the way. For sometimes the path is too steep to make it all the way to the top, and we must trust that the struggle itself was worth it and ready ourselves for new tests knowing, as the clergyman Henry Ward Beecher put it more than one hundred years ago, "We are always in the forge, or on the anvil; by trials God is shaping us for higher things."

•

THE HILL MOTHER

Adapted from a story by Katharine Pyle

When it's time to do a daring deed, take on a tough task, or face the unknown, there's no better ally than a loyal brother or sister.

Once upon a time, a very, very long time ago, in a poor hut at the edge of a forest, there lived a woodcutter and his wife and their two little children, Peter and Roselein. The father and mother worked hard, and Peter and Roselein helped them as best they could by being good, and the little family was happy in their cottage beside the woods.

One night while they were sitting in front of the fire, the father stretched his weary back and sighed, " 'Tis a pity we should be so poor for so long, when the gold of the Hill Mother lies somewhere out there—piles of it to be found for the seeking."

"Who is the Hill Mother?" the children asked together.

"Don't be filling their heads full of nonsense!" cried their mother. "The next thing you know, they'll be clambering all over the countryside like fools, looking for pots of fool's gold."

"Tell us! Tell us!" the children begged.

So their father told them all about the Hill Mother, how she was an old, old woman who lived under a hill, beyond the Desolate Rocks. There she hoarded a treasure greater than anyone had ever seen. All through the year she kept it hidden away under the hill, but every midsummer night, when the moon was at the full, she brought it out and counted it there by moonlight. Then, if anyone found her, he might ask of her anything he wished, and she would be obliged to grant it.

"But those who find her never come back," said their father.

"And why not?" cried the children.

"Well, first of all, because of her servants, the little hill men. They will dance around you and bewitch you, so you can never remember your way home again."

"Never?"

"Never. And on top of that, as soon as she grants your wish, she has you in her power, and you must go down with her under the hill."

"Forever?"

"Forever. Unless, of course, you trick her, and make her see the first morning light. Then she must let you go. But she's a crafty old hag, and no one's been able to trick her yet."

"Enough of your silly tales," scolded the mother. "Now off to bed with you two little ones, and no dreaming Hill Mothers and treasures, either."

But, of course, as soon as Peter and Roselein were in bed, they resolved to go in search of the Hill Mother's gold.

"This is midsummer, and the moon is full," whispered Peter. "We'll have to go tonight."

"But what about the little hill men?" asked Roselein. "What if they make us forget how to get home?"

"We must take something to mark the way," said Peter.

"Our pennies!" cried Roselein. She reached under the bed, and pulled out a little brown bag. It was their pennies they had saved for Christmas. "We'll take them and drop them as we go along. If we forget the way, we can follow them back."

So when the house was all dark, and their parents in bed, they opened a window and crawled out. They journeyed on and on through the forest, dropping pennies behind them, and Peter sang along the way:

> *Though forests be lonely,*
> *Though shadows be gray,*
> *A heart that is merry*
> *Will lighten the way.*

> *Though feet may be weary,*
> *And rough be the road,*
> *A heart that is merry*
> *Will lighten the load.*

And finally they came to a wide, gray country where there was nothing but rocks and twisted thorn bushes.

These were the Desolate Rocks.

And now the way grew so rough that they could hardly go on. One of Roselein's shoes was quite worn through, and great holes appeared in the sole. But she went on, singing to herself to keep up her spirits:

Past the Desolate Rocks,
Over brier and stone,
Through mist and through moonlight
We wander alone.

The moon's sinking low,
And the bats are all out,
But brave heart and true heart
Should never feel doubt.

Suddenly they saw before them the strangest-looking thorn-bush they had ever seen.

They stopped and looked at it. Soon it began to move, and they saw it was not thornbush after all, but an old woman, very gray and bent. It was the Hill Mother!

She sat in the moonlight, counting a great golden treasure that lay heaped all around her.

And in and out among the rocks shadowy figures were dancing and hopping. These were her servants, the little hill men.

As they danced, they were singing. Their voices were like the whistling of the wind through thorn branches.

The old Hill Mother paid no attention to them even when they brushed against her, but went on counting, counting her treasure.

Peter and Roselein, hidden among the rocks, lay watching and listening to the hill men's song:

As black as a thorn bush, and withered and old,
See the old Hill Mother counting her gold.
Old woman, old woman, is all of it thine?

The Hill Mother paid no heed to them, but counted on:

One hundred, twelve hundred, two thousand and nine—

Again the hill men sang:

> *Deep under the hills, with the rocks overhead,*
> *The hammers are beating, the fires burn red.*
> *Old Hill Mother, say, shall we never be free?*

Still the Hill Mother counted on:

A thousand, twelve thousand, a million and three—

The hill men sang and danced about:

> *See the old Hill Mother counting alone,*
> *As dry as a leaf and as cold as a stone!*
> *The moonlight is fading, the night has grown late.*

Two million, ten million, and thirty and eight!

counted the Hill Mother.

The hill men began calling to each other from among the rocks:

"Has a mist come over the moon, or is it sinking low?"

"It is sinking low."

"Has it yet touched the forest beyond the Desolate Rocks?"

"It still swings clear."

"Then there is time yet for the Old Hill Mother to count her treasure!" shouted all together.

But as they began dancing again, one of them spied Peter and Roselein, peering from behind their rock.

"Look, look, Long Nose," cried one to another, "there is something hiding behind a rock. Look and tell us what it is."

"I look through the moonlight," said Long Nose, "and I see what it is. It is two human beings, such as we used to be."

"How did they come here?"

"Even as we did, long ago."

"Why do they bend and stoop as they come?"

"They are looking for treasure, the Hill Mother's treasure, just as we once did!"

Shrilly the little men began singing again:

> *Who is it comes hither while dews are still cold?*
> *Two seeking the Hill Mother, seeking her gold.*
> *They have found her—have found her!*
> *Their journey is done.*

> *Ten billion, twelve billion, and twenty and one!*

counted the Hill Mother.

"Old Hill Mother, old Hill Mother, look up," shouted the hill men, "for someone is coming!"

Then the old Hill Mother raised her head and looked about her.

Her eyes were small and dim.

When she saw Peter and Roselein, she rose, and the gold pieces in her apron fell clinking among the rocks.

"Who are you, and what are you seeking here among the Desolate Rocks?" she croaked.

Peter told her they had come in search of the Hill Mother.

"Then you need look no further, for I am she. And now why have you come, and what would you have of me?"

"We would have you grant us a wish," answered Roselein.

"That I will," said the Hill Mother, "only you must make haste. For the moment yonder moon drops out of the sky, I must take my treasure and hide under the hill, ere the first morning light breaks overhead."

They had their wish ready, but there was one thing they wanted to know. If the Hill Mother granted it, would they have to go down under the hill with her and live there too?

"And what if you should?" cackled the Hill Mother. "Down under the hill it is wide and warm, and there you would find more treasure than you've seen in your dreams."

That might be true, but Peter and Roselein said they could not go down under the hill with her, for their parents would be waiting for them at home. If wishing a wish would make them go down under the hill, they would have to go home without it.

"Ask me your wish, ask me your wish!" cried the Hill Mother.

But they would not.

"Then come, my little hill men," cried the Hill Mother. "Weave about them in and out and round and round until they forget the way they came, for they shall never go home from the Desolate Rocks!"

And before they could escape, the little hill men had joined hands in a circle about them, and they began spinning round and round so fast that the children's heads spun, and they grew so dizzy they could hardly stand.

As they danced, the little men sang in their strange, windy voices:

> *Wing of bat and claw of beast,*
> *East be west and west be east.*

> *Eager hands and gaping mouth,*
> *South be north and north be south.*

> *Think not, children, to steal away.*
> *The Hill Mother speaks, and all obey.*

Then the hill men broke from the circle, each whirling away by himself.

Peter and Roselein stood with their hands to their heads. Think and think as they would, they could not remember the way home.

"Now you have forgotten the way you came," cried the Hill Mother, "so you had better ask me your wish, and then come down under the hill with me willingly, for come you must."

"Very well," said Roselein. "Then our wish is that you should fill my shoe with gold."

The old Hill Mother clapped her shadowy hands and laughed until the rocks echoed. The hill men, too, laughed shrilly and clapped.

"Hee-hee!" they cried. "They might have asked for half of her treasure, and now for as much as her shoe will hold, they'll go down and live with her under the hill forever!"

Roselein slipped off her worn-out shoe and held it out to the Hill Mother.

"There it is," she said. "Now fill it!"

Still chuckling, the Hill Mother picked up a double handful of gold and poured it into the shoe, thinking to fill it at once.

But the gold all ran through the hole in the sole, and left it as empty as ever.

"Look, look," cried the hill men, "the gold is running out!"

Then the Hill Mother knew she had been tricked.

"But I will fill it yet!" she shrieked.

With mad haste she poured more gold into the shoe, and more and more. But it was no use. The shoe was still empty.

Lower and lower sank the moon. More and more wildly the Hill Mother gathered her treasure and poured it into the shoe, crying as she poured:

> *A hole in the shoe! A hole in the shoe!*
> *Oh, what can the poor old Hill Mother do?*

Suddenly the moonlight was gone. The moon had sunk down behind the forest, and a cock crowed.

The Hill Mother gave a shrill cry—

> *The night has passed, and the cocks do crow.*
> *They have fooled the Hill Mother! Woe! Ah, woe!*

And just then the first morning light crept into the sky. Wailing and wringing her hands, the Hill Mother fled away into the hill, and it closed behind her with a boom.

But the little hill men jumped about among the rocks.

"Now Roselein, now Peter, the treasure is yours," they cried, "but what good will it do you? You have forgotten the way home, so you will have to stay here with us among the rocks forever."

But the children were not afraid. "We may have forgotten," they said, "but we can still find the way home. All we have to do is follow the pennies we dropped as we came."

When the hill men heard that, they gathered round, begging Peter and Roselein to take them home with them. They, too, had once lived in the world of boys and girls, but none of them knew the way back now. The Hill Mother had bewitched them and made them forget.

The children were willing, and in haste the hill men brought from among the rocks the bags they had brought with them when they came, long ago, in search of the Hill Mother's gold.

These they filled with treasure. Then, shouldering them as though they were packs, they followed Peter and Roselein as they traced their way among the rocks, following the pennies they had dropped, back toward the forest and home.

•

THE MOUSE WHO WAS AFRAID

Retold by Catherine T. Bryce

Sometimes the size and strength of a body mean less than the kind of heart it carries inside. All the muscle in the world can't make up for the heart that's not brave.

Once there was a little gray mouse. He lived in the same house as an old gray cat. The little mouse was afraid of the cat.

"How happy I would be but for that old cat," he said. "I am afraid of her all the time. I wish I were a cat."

A fairy heard the little mouse say this. She felt sorry for him. So she turned him into a big gray cat.

At first he was very happy. But one day a dog ran after him.

"Oh dear!" he said. "It is not much fun to be a cat. I am afraid of that dog all the time. I wish I were a big dog."

Again the fairy heard him. She felt sorry for the old gray cat. So she turned him into a big dog.

Once more he felt happy. Then one day he heard a lion roar.

"Oh, just hear that lion!" he cried. "I am afraid when I hear him. It is not so safe to be a dog after all. How I wish I were a lion. Then I would be afraid of no one."

Off he ran to the fairy.

"Dear fairy," he said, "please turn me into a big, strong lion."

Again the fairy was sorry for him. She made him into a big, strong lion.

One day a man tried to kill the lion. Once more he ran to the fairy.

"What now?" asked the fairy.

"Make me into a man, dear fairy," he cried. "Then no one can make me afraid."

"Make you into a man!" cried the fairy. "No, indeed, I will not. A man must have a brave heart. You have only the heart of a mouse. So a mouse you shall become again, and a mouse you shall stay."

So saying, she turned him back into a little gray mouse, and away he ran to his old home.

•

THE KNIGHTS OF THE SILVER SHIELD

Raymond M. Alden

Sometimes courage means resisting the call to action elsewhere
and standing fast at your post.

There was once a splendid castle in a forest, with great stone
walls and a high gateway and turrets that rose way above the tallest
trees. The forest was dark and dangerous, and many cruel giants
lived in it, but in the castle was a company of knights, who were
kept there by the king of the country to help travelers who might
be in the forest and fight with the giants whenever they could.

Each of these knights wore a beautiful suit of armor and carried a long spear, while over his helmet there floated a great red
plume that could be seen a long way off by any one in distress. But
the most wonderful things about the knights' armor were their
shields. They were not like those of other knights, but had been
made by a great magician who had lived in the castle many years
before. They were made of silver and sometimes shone in the
sunlight with dazzling brightness. But at other times the surface of
the shields would be clouded as though by a mist, and one could
not see his face reflected there as he could when they shone
brightly.

Now, when each knight received his spurs and his armor, a
new shield was also given him from among those that the magician
had made; and when the shield was new its surface was always
cloudy and dull. But as the knight began to do service against the
giants or went on expeditions to help poor travelers in the forest,
his shield grew brighter and brighter, so that he could see his face
clearly reflected in it. But if he proved to be a lazy or cowardly
knight and let the giants get the better of him or did not care what
became of the travelers, then the shield grew more and more
cloudy, until the knight became ashamed to carry it.

But this was not all. When any one of the knights fought a
particularly hard battle and won the victory, or when he went on
some hard errand for the lord of the castle and was successful, not
only did his silver shield grow brighter, but anyone looking into
the center of it could see something like a golden star shining in its

very heart. This was the greatest honor that a knight could achieve, and the other knights always spoke of such a one as having "won his star." It was usually not till he was pretty old and tried as a soldier that he could win it. At the time when this story begins, the lord of the castle himself was the only one of the knights whose shield bore the golden star.

There came a time when the worst of the giants in the forest gathered themselves together to have a battle against the knights. They made a camp in a dark hollow not far from the castle and gathered all their best warriors together. All the knights made ready to fight them. The windows of the castle were closed and barred, the air was full of the noise of armor being made ready for use, and the knights were so excited that they could scarcely rest or eat.

Now there was a young knight in the castle named Sir Roland, who was among those most eager for the battle. He was a splendid warrior, with eyes that shone like stars whenever there was anything to do in the way of knightly deeds. And though he was still quite young, his shield had begun to shine enough to show plainly that he had done bravely in some of his errands through the forest. This battle, he thought, would be the great opportunity of his life. And on the morning of the day when they were to go forth to it, and all the knights assembled in the great hall of the castle to receive the commands of their leaders, Sir Roland hoped that he would be put in the most dangerous place of all, so that he could show what knightly stuff he was made of.

But when the lord of the castle came to him, as he went about in full armor giving his commands, he said: "One brave knight must stay behind and guard the gateway of the castle, and it is you, Sir Roland, being one of the youngest, whom I have chosen for this."

At these words Sir Roland was so disappointed that he bit his lip and closed his helmet over his face so that the other knights might not see it. For a moment he felt as if he must reply angrily to the commander, and tell him that it was not right to leave so sturdy a knight behind, when he was eager to fight. But he struggled against this feeling and went quietly to look after his duties at the gate. The gateway was high and narrow, and was reached from outside by a high, narrow bridge that crossed the moat which surrounded the castle on every side. When an enemy approached, the knight on guard rang a great bell just inside the gate, and the bridge was drawn up against the castle wall, so that no one could come across the moat. So the giants had long ago given up trying to attack the castle itself.

Today the battle was to be in the dark hollow in the forest, and it was not likely that there would be anything to do at the castle gate, except to watch it like a common doorkeeper. It was not strange that Sir Roland thought someone else might have done this.

Presently all the other knights marched out in their flashing armor, their red plumes waving over their heads, and their spears in their hands. The lord of the castle stopped only to tell Sir Roland to keep guard over the gate until they all returned, and to let no one enter. Then they went into the shadows of the forest, and were soon lost to sight.

Sir Roland stood looking after them long after they had gone, thinking how happy he would be if he were on the way to battle like them. But after a little he put this out of his mind, and tried to think of pleasanter things. It was a long time before anything happened, or any word came from the battle.

At last Sir Roland saw one of the knights come limping down the path to the castle, and he went out on the bridge to meet him. Now this knight was not a brave one, and he had been frightened away as soon as he was wounded.

"I have been hurt," he said, "so that I cannot fight anymore. But I could watch the gate for you, if you would like to go back in my place."

At first Sir Roland's heart leaped with joy at this, but then he remembered what the commander had told him on going away, and he said:

"I should like to go, but a knight belongs where his commander has put him. My place is here at the gate, and I cannot open it even for you. Your place is at the battle."

The knight was ashamed when he heard this, and he presently turned about and went into the forest again.

So Sir Roland kept guard silently for another hour. Then there came an old beggar-woman down the path to the castle, and asked Sir Roland if she might come in and have some food. He told her that no one could enter the castle that day, but that he would send a servant out to her with food, and that she might sit and rest as long as she would.

"I have been past the hollow in the forest where the battle is going on," said the old woman, while she was waiting for her food.

"And how do you think it is going?" asked Sir Roland.

"Badly for the knights, I am afraid," said the old woman. "The giants are fighting as they have never fought before. I should think you had better go and help your friends."

"I should like to, indeed," said Sir Roland. "But I am set to guard the gateway of the castle, and cannot leave."

"One fresh knight would make a great difference when they are all weary with fighting," said the old woman. "I should think that, while there are no enemies about, you would be much more useful there."

"You may well think so," said Sir Roland, "and so may I; but it is neither you nor I that is commander here."

"I suppose," said the old woman then, "that you are one of the kind of knights who like to keep out of fighting. You are lucky to have so good an excuse for staying at home." And she laughed a thin and taunting laugh.

Then Sir Roland was very angry, and thought that if it were only a man instead of an old woman, he would show whether he liked fighting or no. But as it was an old woman, he shut his lips and set his teeth hard together, and as the servant came just then with the food he had sent for, he gave it to the old woman quickly, and shut the gate that she might not talk to him anymore.

It was not very long before he heard some one calling outside. Sir Roland opened the gate, and saw standing at the other end of the drawbridge a little old man in a long black cloak.

"Why are you knocking here?" he said. "The castle is closed today."

"Are you Sir Roland?" said the little old man.

"Yes," said Sir Roland.

"Then you ought not to be staying here when your commander and his knights are having so hard a struggle with the giants and when you have the chance to make of yourself the greatest knight in this kingdom. Listen to me! I have brought you a magic sword."

As he said this, the old man drew from under his coat a wonderful sword that flashed in the sunlight as if it were covered with diamonds. "This is the sword of all swords," he said, "and it is for you, if you will leave your idling here by the castle gate and carry it to the battle. Nothing can stand before it. When you lift it, the giants will fall back, your master will be saved, and you will be crowned the victorious knight—the one who will soon take his commander's place as lord of the castle."

Now Sir Roland believed that it was a magician who was speaking to him, for it certainly appeared to be a magic sword. It seemed so wonderful that the sword should be brought to him that he reached out his hand as though he would take it, and the little old man came forward as though he would cross the drawbridge into the castle. But as he did so, it came to Sir Roland's mind again that that bridge and the gateway had been entrusted to him, and he called out, "No!" to the old man, so that he stopped where he was standing. But he waved the shining sword in the air again, and said: "It is for you! Take it, and win the victory!"

Sir Roland was really afraid that if he looked any longer at the sword, or listened to any more words of the old man, he would not be able to keep himself within the castle. For this reason he struck the great bell at the gateway, which was the signal for the servants inside to pull in the chains of the drawbridge, and instantly they began to pull, and the drawbridge came up, so that the old man could not cross it to enter the castle nor Sir Roland to go out.

Then, as he looked across the moat, Sir Roland saw a wonderful thing. The little old man threw off his black cloak, and as he did so he began to grow bigger and bigger, until in a minute more he was a giant as tall as any in the forest. At first Sir Roland could scarcely believe his eyes. Then he realized that this must be one of their giant enemies, who had changed himself to a little old man through some magic power, that he might make his way into the castle while all the knights were away. Sir Roland shuddered to think what might have happened if he had taken the sword and left the gate unguarded. The giant shook his fist across the moat that lay between them, and then, knowing that he could do nothing more, he went angrily back into the forest.

Sir Roland now resolved not to open the gate again and to pay no attention to any other visitor. But it was not long before he heard a sound that made him spring forward in joy. It was the bugle of the lord of the castle, and there came sounding after it the bugles of many of the knights that were with him, pealing so joyfully that Sir Roland was sure they were safe and happy. As they came nearer, he could hear their shouts of victory. So he gave the signal to let down the drawbridge again, and went out to meet them. They were dusty and bloodstained and weary, but they had won the battle with the giants; and it had been such a great victory that there had never been a happier homecoming.

Sir Roland greeted them all as they passed in over the bridge, and then, when he had closed the gate and fastened it, he followed them into the great hall of the castle. The lord of the castle took his place on the highest seat, with the other knights about him, and Sir Roland came forward with the key of the gate, to give his account of what he had done in the place to which the commander had appointed him. The lord of the castle bowed to him as a sign for him to begin, but, just as he opened his mouth to speak, one of the knights cried out:

"The shield! The shield! Sir Roland's shield!"

Everyone turned and looked at the shield which Sir Roland carried on his left arm. He himself could see only the top of it, and did not know what they could mean. But what they saw was the golden star of knighthood shining brightly from the center of Sir Roland's shield. There had never been such amazement in the castle before.

Sir Roland knelt before the lord of the castle to receive his commands. He still did not know why everyone was looking at him so excitedly and wondered if he had in some way done wrong.

"Speak, Sir Knight," said the commander, as soon as he could find his voice after his surprise, "and tell us all that has happened today at the castle. Have you been attacked? Have any giants come hither? Did you fight them alone?"

"No, my lord," said Sir Roland. "Only one giant has been here, and he went away silently when he found he could not enter."

Then he told all that had happened through the day.

When he had finished, the knights all looked at one another, but no one spoke a word. Then they looked again at Sir Roland's shield, to make sure that their eyes had not deceived them, and there the golden star was still shining.

After a little silence the lord of the castle spoke.

"Men make mistakes," he said, "but our silver shields are never mistaken. Sir Roland has fought and won the hardest battle of all today."

Then the others all rose and saluted Sir Roland, who was the youngest knight that ever carried the golden star.

•

HANS THE SHEPHERD BOY
Retold by Ella Lyman Cabot

Hans was a little shepherd boy who lived in Germany. One day he was keeping his sheep near a great wood when a hunter rode up to him.

"How far is it to the nearest village, my boy?" asked the hunter.

"It is six miles, sir," said Hans. "But the road is only a sheep track. You might easily miss your way."

"My boy," said the hunter, "if you will show me the way, I will pay you well."

Hans shook his head. "I cannot leave the sheep, sir," he said. "They would stray into the wood and the wolves might kill them."

"But if one or two sheep are eaten by the wolves, I will pay you for them. I will give you more than you can earn in a year."

"Sir, I cannot go," said Hans. "These sheep are my master's. If they are lost, I should be to blame."

"If you cannot show me the way, will you get me a guide? I will take care of your sheep while you are gone."

"No," said Hans, "I cannot do that. The sheep do not know your voice, and—" Then he stopped.

"Can't you trust me?" asked the hunter.

"No," said Hans. "You have tried to make me break my word to my master. How do I know that you would keep your word?"

The hunter laughed. "You are right," said he. "I wish I could trust my servants as your master can trust you. Show me the path. I will try to get to the village alone."

Just then several men rode out of the wood. They shouted for joy.

"Oh, sir!" cried one. "We thought you were lost,"

Then Hans learned to his great surprise that the hunter was a prince. He was afraid that the great man would be angry with him. But the prince smiled and spoke in praise of him.

A few days later a servant came from the prince and took Hans to the palace.

"Hans," said the prince, "I want you to leave your sheep to come and serve me. I know you are a boy whom I can trust."

Hans was very happy over his good fortune. "If my master can find another shepherd to take my place, then I will come and serve you."

So Hans went back and tended the sheep until his master found another shepherd. After that he served the prince many years.

•

THE HONEST FARMER
Retold by Ella Lyman Cabot

The dictionary defines integrity as "an uncompromising adherence to a moral code" and says the word traces its origins to a
Latin term meaning "untouched." Here is integrity, untouched
and unshaken by altered circumstances.

There was a war in Germany long ago, and thousands of soldiers were scattered over the country. A captain of the cavalry, who
had a great many men and horses to feed, was told by his colonel
that he must get food from the farms nearby. The captain walked
for some time through the lonely valley, and at last knocked at the
door of a small cottage. The man who opened it looked old and
lame. He leaned on a stick.

"Good day, sir," said the captain. "Will you kindly show me a
field where my soldiers can cut the grain and carry it off for our
army?" The old man led the soldiers through the valley for about a
mile, and in the distance they saw a field of barley waving in the
breeze.

"This is just what we want. We'll stop here," exclaimed the
captain.

"No, not yet," said the old man. "You must follow me a little
farther."

After another mile or two, they came to a second field of
barley. The soldiers dismounted, cut down the grain, tied it in
sheaves, and rode away with it.

Then the captain said to the old farmer: "Why did you make us
walk so far? The first field of barley was better than this one."

"That is true, sir," answered the honest old man, "but it was
not mine."

•

WHY THE THUMB STANDS ALONE

Sometimes standing fast means standing alone, as we see in this folktale from Africa.

Once five fingers stood side by side on a hand. They were all friends. Where one went, the others went. They worked together. They played together. They ate and washed and wrote and did their chores together.

One day the five fingers were resting on a table together when they spied a gold ring lying nearby.

"What a shiny ring!" exclaimed the First Finger.

"It would look good on me," declared the Second Finger.

"Let's take it," suggested the Third Finger.

"Quick! While nobody's looking!" whispered the Fourth Finger.

They started to reach for the ring when the Fifth Finger, the one named Thumb, spoke up.

"Wait! We shouldn't do that!" it cried.

"Why not?" demanded the other four fingers.

"Because that ring does not belong to us," said the Thumb. "It's wrong to take something that doesn't belong to you."

"But who is going to know?" asked the other fingers. "No one will see us. Come on!"

"No," said the Thumb. "It's stealing."

Then the other four fingers began to laugh and make fun of the Thumb.

"You're afraid!" said the First Finger.

"What a goody-goody," sang the Second Finger.

"You're just mad because the ring won't fit you," muttered the Third Finger.

"We thought you were more fun than that," said the Fourth Finger. "We thought you were our friend."

But the Thumb shook its head.

"I don't care what you say," it answered. "I won't steal."

"Then you can't hang around with us," shouted the other four fingers. "You can't be our friend."

So they went off in a group by themselves, and left the Thumb alone. At first they thought Thumb would follow them and beg them to take it back. But Thumb knew they were wrong and stood fast.

That is why today the thumb stands apart from the other four fingers.

•

LINCOLN LICKS THE BULLIES

This fight is famous not because it is a fight, but because it gives a glimpse of the fighter's character. Abraham Lincoln disliked quarrels, but he liked unfairness and bullying even less. As we see here, he acted according to the advice Polonius gave to his son Laertes in *Hamlet:* "Beware of entrance to a quarrel but, being in, bear't that th' opposed may beware of thee."

In the passage to adulthood, many boys and girls reach a time when they must face a bully. This story may help.

When Abraham Lincoln was still a young man, he went to work for a fellow named Denton Offutt in New Salem, Illinois. Offutt was impressed with Lincoln's six-foot-four, 185-pound frame; but he was even more impressed with the youngster's brains and ambition, so he offered him a job as a clerk in his general store.

Offutt's store was a favorite loafing place for the New Salem boys and young men. Among these were some of the roughest fellows in the settlement. They were known as the "Clary Grove Boys," and they were always ready for a fight, in which they would sometimes prove themselves to be bullies and tormentors. So when Offutt began to brag about his new clerk, the Clary Grove Boys made fun of him, whereupon the storekeeper cried:

"What's that? You can throw him? Well, I reckon not. Abe Lincoln can outrun, outwalk, outwrassle, knock out, and throw down any man in Sangamon County."

This was too much for the Clary Grove Boys. They took up Offutt's challenge and set up against Abe as their champion one Jack Armstrong.

All this was done without Lincoln's knowledge. He had no

desire to get into a row with anyone—least of all with the bullies who made up the Clary Grove Boys.

"I won't do it," he said, when Offutt told him of the proposed wrestling match. "I never tussle and scuffle, and I will not. I don't like this wooling and pulling."

"Don't let them call you a coward, Abe," said Offutt.

Of course, you know what the end would be to such an affair. Nobody likes to be called a coward—especially when he knows he is not one. So, at last, Lincoln consented to "rassle" with Jack Armstrong. They met, with all the boys as spectators. They wrestled, and tugged, and clenched, but without result. Both young fellows were equally matched in strength.

"It's no use, Jack," Lincoln at last declared. "Let's quit. You can't throw me, and I can't throw you. That's enough."

With that, all Jack's backers began to cry "coward!" and urged on the champion to another tussle. Jack Armstrong was now determined to win, by fair means or foul. He tried the latter and, contrary to all rules of wrestling, began to kick and trip, while his supporters stood ready to help, if need be, by breaking in with a regular free fight. This foul play roused the lion in Lincoln. He hated unfairness and at once resented it. He suddenly put forth his Samson-like strength, grabbed the champion of the Clary Grove Boys by the throat, and, lifting him from the ground, held him at arm's length and shook him as a dog shakes a rat. Then he flung him to the ground, and, facing the amazed and yelling crowd, he cried: "You cowards! You know I don't want to fight. But if you try any such games, I'll tackle the whole lot of you. I've won the fight."

He had. From that day, no man in all that region dared to tackle young Lincoln, or to taunt him with cowardice. And Jack Armstrong was his devoted friend and admirer.

•

GOD WILL PROVIDE

This Mexican folktale is an adaptation of Aesop's "Hercules and the Wagoner." It teaches the age-old moral that God helps those who help themselves. Good, hard work is often the best way out of a tough spot.

One sunrise two neighboring farmers set out for market in town. Their wagons were piled high with tomatoes that would ripen quickly in the hot noonday sun, so they pushed their horses steadily all morning, not wanting their precious cargoes to spoil on the way.

But the poor beasts were tired by the time they reached the steepest hill outside town, and strain as they might, they could not get up the slope. The wagons sat at the bottom of the hill, with the climbing sun beating down mercilessly.

"There's nothing to do but let them rest," said the first farmer, shrugging. "And come to think of it, I could use a little siesta myself. We've been on the road since sunup. I think I'll lie under this tree for a while."

"But you can't!" his companion exclaimed. "By the time you wake up, your load will be ruined."

"Don't worry, my friend. God will provide. He always does. I'll just say a few prayers before I doze off." He rolled over on his side with a yawn.

The second farmer, meanwhile, strode to the back of his wagon and, putting his shoulder to the rear, began to shove as hard as he could. He yelled at his horse to pull forward, but to no avail. He pushed till the veins stood out on his neck, and he cursed at the top of his lungs, but his cart ascended the hill not one inch.

Just then the Lord and Saint Peter passed along the road as they sometimes did, for often they walk abroad in order to look into men's hearts. The Lord saw the frantic, swearing farmer struggling with his load. He smiled and laid a kind hand on the wheel, and at once the cart rose to the top of the hill.

The Lord passed on with Saint Peter at his side. The Gate-keeper's gaze bent downward, as if he were pondering their every step.

"I don't understand," he said at last. "Why did you help that man? Even as we came upon him, we heard him cursing most irreverently. And yet you did not help his friend, who offered his prayers for your help."

The Lord smiled.

"The man I helped cursed, it's true, but not with his heart. That is just the way he talks to his horse. In his heart, he was thinking fondly of his wife and children and aged parents, who depend on his labor and need him to return with some profit for his toil. He would have stayed there pushing all day. His friend, on the other hand, calls on me only when he believes he needs me. What he thinks of is sleep. So let him have his nap."

•

THE HEEDLESS MAN AT THE GATES OF PARADISE

Shakespeare wrote that "readiness is all." Ancient dervish teachers used this tale to teach that lesson.

There was once a man who, like most of us, knew in his heart and mind the way to Heaven. He knew he should love his neighbor as himself, honor his parents, and deal with all men honestly. He knew to help the needy and defend the innocent. He knew humility and patience and self-restraint were the way of the wise.

And this man surely tried to do all these things—but only once in a while. He would help a friend if he happened to remember the friend was in need, or say a prayer of thanksgiving if convenient, or give money to the poor if stricken with a guilty conscience. But most of the time he was too busy with his own affairs.

The habits he practiced impressed themselves upon his soul. He developed the shortcoming of heedlessness. Opportunities for exemplary behavior came and went; occasionally he seized them, but usually he did not even notice the chance to do good.

Then one day he died. As he climbed the path toward Paradise, he looked back at his life. He recalled the times he had loved and aided his fellow creatures and judged them sufficient.

When he reached the towering gates of Heaven, though, he discovered they were locked.

A voice sounded from the air.

"Watch carefully," it warned. "The gates open only once every ten thousand years."

He stood wide-eyed and trembling in expectation. He resolved to stay alert. But, unaccustomed to practicing the virtue of mindfulness, he soon found his attention drifting away. After watching for what seemed an eternity, his shoulders slumped and his head began to nod. His eyelids fluttered, sank, and closed for a second in sleep.

At that instant the mighty gates swung open—and before he could open his eyes, crashed shut again with a thunder that tumbled the heedless from Paradise.

●

OPPORTUNITY

Edward Rowland Sill

It's not the sword—it's the man.

This I beheld, or dreamed it in a dream:
There spread a cloud of dust along the plain;
And underneath the cloud, or in it, raged
A furious battle, and men yelled, and swords
Shocked upon swords and shields. A prince's banner
Wavered, then staggered backward, hemmed by foes.
A craven hung along the battle's edge,
And thought: "Had I a sword of keener steel—
That blue blade that the King's son bears—but this
Blunt thing—!" he snapt and flung it from his hand,
And lowering crept away and left the field.
Then came the King's son, wounded, sore bestead,
And weaponless, and saw the broken sword,
Hilt-buried in the dry and trodden sand,
And ran and snatched it, and with battle shout
Lifted afresh he hewed his enemy down,
And saved a great cause that heroic day.

●

THE MAGIC SWORD

There is an old, old story from the days of knights in shining armor, about a very ordinary youth who was afraid to test his skill at arms on the tournament field. At length some of his friends, thinking to have some fun with him, presented him with a sword which they said possessed an ancient, magical power: The man who wielded it could never meet defeat in battle.

To their amazement, the youth sprang to the field and quickly put the gift to use, winning game after game. Never had anyone witnessed such speed and daring at arms. With each tournament, the news of his artistry spread, and before long he was hailed as the foremost knight of the realm.

At last, thinking it would now do no harm, one of his friends revealed the jest and confided that the instrument contained no magic at all, but was just an ordinary sword.

At once terror seized the young knight. When he stood at the edge of the field of combat, his legs shook beneath him, his breath caught in his throat, and his fingers lost all grip. No longer able to believe in his sword, he could not believe in himself. He never fought again.

•

THE GORGON'S HEAD

Adapted from a retelling by James Baldwin

Here is a great Greek hero who perseveres to overcome a series of obstacles, any one of which would deter a feeble heart.

Long ago on a distant island kingdom lived a beautiful woman named Danaë and her son, a brave and tall youth named Perseus. The king of this island was a man called Polydectes, and he was so pleased by Danaë's beauty that he wanted her to become his wife. But he was an evil, cruel man, and she did not like him at all, so she refused all of his offers. Polydectes thought Perseus was to blame for this and that if he could find some excuse to send the young man on a far journey, he might force Danaë to have him whether she wished or not.

To this end he gave a great feast, and announced that every guest was expected to bring a rich present. For he knew that Perseus, being poor, could not afford such a gift.

When the great banquet began, Perseus stood at the door, sorrowfully watching all the wealthy nobles go in, and his face grew red as they pointed at him and sneered, "What has Perseus to give?"

At last the lad grew mad with shame and, hardly knowing what he said, cried out, "See if I do not bring a better present than all of yours together!"

"Hear the boaster!" laughed Polydectes. "And what are you to bring—the head of Medusa?"

"Yes! I will bring that," swore Perseus, and he went away in anger while everyone laughed at him because of his foolish words.

And what was this Medusa's head which he had so rashly promised to bring?

Far, far away, on the very edge of the world, there lived three strange monsters, sisters, called the Gorgons. They had the bodies and faces of women, but they had wings of gold, and terrible claws of brass, and live serpents growing out of their heads instead of hair. They were so awful to look upon that no one could bear the sight of them. Whoever saw their faces was turned to stone. Two of these monsters had charmed lives, and no weapon could ever do them harm. But the youngest, whose name was Medusa, might be killed if indeed anybody could deliver the fatal stroke.

Perseus strode away from the king's palace, feeling sorry that he had ever spoken so rashly. He did not even know how to find the awful Gorgons. He went down to the shore and stood looking out over the sea while the sun went down and the moon rose. Then, all at once, two persons stood before him. Both were tall and noble. They were Hermes, the messenger of the gods, and Athena, the goddess of wisdom. They told Perseus they would help him.

"You must go first to the three Gray Sisters, who live beyond the frozen sea, in the far, far north," said Athena. "They have a secret which nobody knows, and you must force them to tell you. Ask them where you shall find the three Maidens who guard the golden apples of the West. When they have told you, go straight there. The Maidens will give you three things you will need to obtain the terrible head, and they will tell you how to find the home of the Gorgons."

"But I have no ship. How shall I go?" asked Perseus.

"You shall take my winged sandals," said Hermes. He took off the wonderful shoes, and put them on the youth's feet; and before Perseus could thank them for their kindness, he found himself speeding into the sky, swifter than any eagle.

The winged sandals bore him over the sea, straight toward the north. On and on he went, and soon the sea was passed. He flew over cities and towns and a range of snowy mountains covered with mighty forests, and then a vast plain where many rivers wandered, seeking the sea. Then came frozen marshes and a wilderness of snow, and finally an ocean of ice. On and on he winged his way, among toppling icebergs and over frozen billows and through air the sun never warmed, and at last he came to the cavern where the three Gray Sisters dwelled.

These creatures were so old they had forgotten their own age. The long hair that covered their heads had been gray since they were born. They had among them only a single eye and a single tooth, which they passed back and forth from one to another. Perseus heard them mumbling and crooning in their dreary home, and he stood very still and listened.

"We know a secret we will never tell, don't we, sisters?" said one.

"Ha! ha! That we do! That we do!" chattered the others.

"Give me the tooth, sister, that I may feel young and handsome again," said one.

"And give me the eye that I may look out and see the world," said another.

"Ah yes, yes, yes," mumbled the third, as she took both the tooth and the eye and held them out blindly toward the others.

Quick as thought, Perseus leaped forward and snatched both of the precious things from her hand.

"Where is the tooth? Where is the eye?" screamed the two, reaching out their long arms and groping here and there. "Have you dropped them, sister? Have you lost them?"

"I have your tooth and your eye," said Perseus, "and you shall not touch them again until you tell me your secret. Where are the Maidens who keep the golden apples of the Western Land?"

Then the Gray Sisters wept and coaxed and threatened. They moaned and mumbled and shrieked, but their words did not move him.

"Sisters, we must tell him," at last one said.

"Ah yes, we must part with the secret to save our eye," said the others.

Then they told him what road he should follow to find the Maidens; and when they had made everything plain to Perseus, he gave them back their eye and tooth.

"Ha! ha!" they laughed. "Now the golden days of youth have come again!" Perseus leaped into the air again. And from that day to this, though the winds still whistle through their cheerless cave, and the cold waves murmur on the shore of the wintry sea, and the ice mountains topple and crash, no other man has ever seen the three Gray Sisters.

The winged sandals now bore Perseus southward. He left the frozen wilderness behind and soon came to a sunny land, where there were green forests and flowery meadows and hills and valleys, and at last a pleasant garden with all kinds of fruits and blossoms. And here he found the three Maidens of the West dancing and singing around a tree of golden apples.

Perseus told them of his quest, and said he had come to ask them to give him three things to help him fight the Gorgons. The Maidens answered they would give him not three things but four. One of them gave him a sharp sword, which she fastened to the belt at his waist. Another gave him a shield, which was brighter than any looking glass. The third gave him a magic pouch, which she hung by a long strap over his shoulder. Finally they all three gave him a magic helmet, the Helmet of Darkness; and when they had put it on his head, there was no creature on earth or in the sky that could see him.

Then they told him where he could find the Gorgons, and what he should do to obtain the terrible head and escape alive. Perseus donned the Helmet of Darkness, and sped away toward the farthest edge of the earth. And the three Maidens went back to their tree to sing and to dance and to guard the golden apples until the old world should become young again.

Perseus flew so swiftly it was not long until he had crossed the mighty ocean that encircles the earth and had come to the sunless land that lies beyond. He heard the sound of someone breathing heavily, and he looked around sharply to see where it came from. Among the foul weeds that grew close by the bank of a muddy river there was something glittering in the pale light.

He flew a little nearer, but he did not dare look straight forward, lest he should meet the gaze of a Gorgon, and be changed to stone. Instead, he turned around and held the shining shield before him in such a way that by looking into it he could see objects behind him as in a mirror.

Ah, what a dreadful sight it was! Half hidden among the weeds lay the three monsters, fast asleep, with their golden wings folded about them. Their brazen claws were stretched out as though ready to seize their prey, and their shoulders were covered with sleeping snakes. The two largest of the Gorgons lay with their heads tucked under their wings as birds hide their heads when they go to sleep. But the third, who lay between them, slept with her face turned up to the sky, and Perseus knew she was Medusa.

Very stealthily he went nearer and nearer, always with his back toward the monsters and always looking into his bright shield to see where to go. Then he drew his sharp sword and, dashing it quickly downward, struck a blow so sure, so swift, that the head of Medusa was severed from her shoulders and the black blood gushed like a river from her neck. Quick as thought he thrust the terrible head into his magic pouch, leaped into the air again, and flew away with the speed of wind.

Then the two older Gorgons awoke, and rose with dreadful screams, and spread their great wings to dash after him. They could not see him, for the Helmet of Darkness hid him from their eyes, but they scented the blood of their sister's head, and they followed him, sniffing the air. As he flew he could hear the clatter of their golden wings and the snapping of their horrible jaws. But the winged sandals were swift as the wind, and soon he had left the monsters far behind.

He flew on, toward home, until he passed over a country of sunshine and palm trees and a great river flowing from the south. Here, as he looked down, a strange sight met his eyes: He saw a beautiful girl chained to a rock by the seashore, and far away a huge beast swimming to devour her.

At once Perseus flew down, drew his sharp sword, and cut the chain which held her. By this time the monster was close at hand, lashing the water with its tale and opening its wide jaws so as to swallow both Perseus and the girl. But as it came roaring toward the shore, Perseus lifted the head of Medusa from its pouch and held it high. When the beast saw the dreadful face it stopped short and was turned into stone. And men say that the stone beast may be seen in that same spot today.

The girl told him her name was Andromeda, and that she was the princess of that land. She had been chained to the rock as an offering to the terrible beast, which was destroying the whole land. At once Perseus asked her to be his wife, and they were married with a great feast, and the two young people lived happily for some time in that sunny place.

But Perseus had not forgotten his mother, so one fine summer day he sailed home, taking Andromeda with him. He left his ship on the beach, and found his mother, and they wept over each other.

Then Perseus went up to the palace of Polydectes with the head of Medusa in his pouch. When he came to the great hall, the evil king sat at his table, with all his nobles on either side, feasting and drinking wine. Perseus stood upon the threshold and called Polydectes by name, but none of the guests knew the stranger, for he was changed by his long journey. He had gone out a boy, and he had come home a man and a great hero.

But Polydectes the Wicked knew him and scornfully called,

"Ah, foolish boaster! Have you found it easier to make a promise than to fulfill it?"

"When a promise is made to right a wrong, sometimes the gods help fulfill it," Perseus answered. And turning aside his own eyes, he drew open the pouch, held aloft the Gorgon's head, and cried, "Behold!"

Pale grew Polydectes and his guests as they looked upon the dreadful face. They tried to spring away, but they never rose from their seats. They stiffened, each man where he sat, into a ring of cold gray stones.

Then Perseus turned and left them, went down to his galley by the shore, and sailed away with his mother and his bride.

●

HEROES

William Canton

We all should have one or two heroes to help us stand fast and think right.

> For you who love heroic things
>   In summer dream or winter tale,
> I tell of warriors, saints, and kings,
>   In scarlet, sackcloth, glittering mail,
> And helmets peaked with iron wings.
>
> They beat down Wrong; they strove for Right.
>   In ringing fields, on grappled ships,
> Singing, they flung into the fight;
>   They fell with triumph on their lips,
> And in their eyes a glorious light.
>
> That light still gleams. From far away
>   Their brave song greets us like a cheer;
> We fight the same great fight as they,
>   Right against Wrong; we, now and here;
> They, in their fashion, yesterday.

•

PROTEUS

Adapted from a retelling
by Elizabeth Harrison

Here's a great story to remember when someone tells you to "Hold on!" The tale, from *The Odyssey,* takes place on the island of Pharos near Egypt. Menelaus was the king of Sparta and one of the leaders of the Greeks in the Trojan War.

After the long and cruel Trojan War was over, King Menelaus started in his good ship for his much loved home in Sparta. His crew hoisted the sails, and they began the long voyage across the dark, mysterious sea.

For a while the wind was favorable and helped them along their journey. Then one evening they stopped for the night in a sheltered bay on the coast of a little island. The next morning they woke to find the wind blowing steadily in the opposite way from the one they wished to sail. They waited all day, hoping the strong breeze would die down, or at least change its direction. The next day passed, and the next, and another, and still the wind blew steadily away from their beloved homes.

Although it was invisible, it had more strength than all of them, and they could make no headway against it. Day after day it blew a fierce, wild gale over their heads, scattering the clouds across the sky, dashing the waves against the shore, whirling the dust into their faces, and hurriedly uttering hoarse whispering sounds as it passed them. They knew it was warning them against daring to continue their homeward journey.

Twenty days had come and gone, and still the wind kept up its fierce, loud tone of command as it rushed from the faraway west, shook the waters of the vast ocean, swept over the small, rocky island, and sped on toward the east. The courage of the poor sailors was almost exhausted. Their provisions were giving out. They tried to catch fish to satisfy each day's hunger, but it was hard when the surf was so wild.

Menelaus, their chief, went wandering alone on the seashore. He was very unhappy, for he feared that all this trouble had come because he and his comrades had done something to displease the gods. So he was much distressed in mind as he walked along the sandy beach.

The sun was sinking to rest, the evening shadows were settling down between the rocky hills, the darkness of night was approaching, when suddenly there stood before him a beautiful being of so dazzling an appearance that he knew she could not be a woman, she must be an immortal. Her saffron robes gleamed with light as do the sunset clouds. Her face was as radiant as are the last rays of the departing sun. It was the beautiful goddess Idothea. Her face suddenly became stern as she looked at King Menelaus and asked him why he tarried idly upon the small, rocky island. He replied that he did not willingly remain, but that he must surely have sinned against the gods, as they had sent a strong, fierce wind to hinder his homeward voyage. Then he earnestly begged her to tell him what to do. The stern look left her face as she heard him confess that he had done wrong. She came nearer to him, and her glittering robes changed from saffron to pink, and blue, and even gray, and the lights played above, around, and about her in the most wonderful fashion, changing each moment as she spoke.

She told him that she was the daughter of Proteus, the Ancient of the Deep, who, living for thousands and thousands of years in the bottom of the great ocean, had gone wherever the restless waves of the sea had gone, and had learned the secrets of both land and water. He knew the song of the winds and could interpret every message they brought from the gods. Therefore he, and he alone, could tell Menelaus what it was that the strong, fierce wind had been crying out to him and his companions for the past twenty days.

This sea god, Proteus, was a most remarkable being. He had the power to change himself into whatever form he chose. The only way to get any secret from him was to catch him when he was asleep, and then to *hold on* to him, no matter what shape he might choose to take, until at last he returned to his original form of the old man of the sea.

Idothea told Menelaus that this strange father of hers would rise out of the sea at about noon the next day, and would walk over to a large cavern not far distant, where his sea calves took their daily sleep, and that when he had counted them to see if they were all there, he would lie down in the midst of them and go to sleep also. This, said she, would be the time for Menelaus and three of his trusted sailors to spring upon him and seize him firmly, and she added that they must *hold on to him, no matter what happened,* until he changed back into his own form, that of an old man. Then they could ask him any questions they wished and he would be compelled to answer them.

Having given Menelaus these instructions, the beautiful goddess suddenly plunged into the ocean and the green waves closed over her.

With bowed head and mind filled with anxious thought, Menelaus returned to his men. They gathered round their boats on the seashore and ate their scanty evening meal. Silently and solemnly the night settled down upon the landscape and made the trees look like dark, shadowy forms, and the outlines of the hills grew dim, and the ocean was covered by the hush of the darkness, and silence reigned over all.

The sailors threw themselves down upon the sand and were soon fast asleep. Menelaus lay beside them, but his mind was troubled. What would the next day bring forth? He was to meet the strange and terrible Ancient of the Deep, and was to struggle fiercely with him. Would he be able to cope with the monster? Would he have the courage to hold on to him? What awful and unknown shapes might not the creature take?

The night slowly wore away, and when the faint purplish light softened the eastern sky, he arose, and going apart from his sleeping comrades, he knelt down and prayed earnestly to the ever-living gods. Then, returning to his men, he awoke the three whom he could trust the most, and taking them with him, sought the spot where the goddess Idothea had promised to meet him. She, radiant as the dawn, was already there awaiting him.

Quickly digging four oblong holes in the wet sand, she commanded Menelaus and his three companions to lie down in them. This they did, and she skillfully spread over each of them a sealskin. Then the radiant goddess seated herself on a rock not far away, to await her father's coming.

After a while, the sea calves rose from the depths of the ocean and began crawling along the sand. They came in throngs and laid themselves down in rows upon the sandy shore beside the brave but anxious heroes. Soon the sunlit waves parted from right to left and slowly and solemnly Proteus, the Ancient of the Deep, appeared. His hair and beard and garments were covered with white foam. He walked over to where his sea calves lay basking in the sun and counted them. This was a trying time for Menelaus. His heart

beat loud and fast, so great was his fear that he and his companions might be discovered. But the goddess had done her work too well for that. Proteus did not notice any difference between them and the beasts which lay about them. Having finished his task, he stretched his body upon the sand beside his flock, ready for his afternoon nap.

Now was the critical moment! Menelaus and his men, throwing off the sealskins, sprang forward with loud shouts, and before the old sea god knew it, they had fast hold of his arms and legs.

Proteus, having the power to change his body into whatever shape he pleased, suddenly transformed himself into a roaring lion, so fierce and strong that it seemed as if he might crush anything that came in his way. Still Menelaus and his stouthearted men *held on.* Then, in an instant the lion became a fiery panther whose glaring eyes struck terror into their hearts, but still they *held on.* In a moment more a large snake was twisting and writhing in their hands, hissing and darting his forked tongue out as if he would gladly poison all of them, still they *held on.* Shape after shape the monster assumed, but still they *held on.* Now it was a clear, harmless stream of water flowing gently through their hands. Again it was a flame of fire darting here and there threatening to scorch their faces and even to burn out their eyes; still they *held on.* Then it became a beautiful tree, tall and stately, with broad spreading branches and shining green leaves, still they *held on.*

At last, finding that his enchantments were of no avail, he changed back into his real form and, turning to Menelaus, he said, "What wouldst thou have?" Menelaus begged him to tell why he and his faithful sailors were kept from crossing the dark waters of the sea to their distant homes. Then Proteus, the Ancient of the Deep, who knew all secrets of both gods and men, told him the cause of their troubles. In their impatience to get back to their homes, they had neglected to worship the gods and ask them for guidance to their journey's end. It was their own thoughtlessness that kept them prisoner.

Menelaus now understood what the wind had been trying to tell him. The very next day, he and his men paid due worship to the gods. Then right merrily the wind whistled and sang about their ears as it filled their white sails and helped them to speed across the blue water. In a few days they had reached their beloved homeland.

But never to the end of their lives did they forget the terrible struggle with the mighty Proteus, Ancient of the Deep, where by *holding on* they had won the silent battle. And oftentimes they told the story to their children and grandchildren, just as I am telling it to you today.

•

THE DOG OF MONTARGIS

Retold by James Baldwin

This unusual old story reminds us that loyalty is the virtue that helps us stand fast beside our friends—and our memories of our friends.

In the old castle of Montargis in France, there was once a stone mantelpiece of workmanship so rare that it was talked about by the whole country. And yet it was not altogether its beauty that caused people to speak of it and remember it. It was famous rather on account of the strange scene that was carved upon it. To those who asked about its meaning, the old custodian of the castle would sometimes tell the following story.

It happened more than five hundred years ago, when this castle was new and strong, and people lived and thought in very different ways than they do now. Among the young men of that time there was none more noble than Aubrey de Montdidier, the nephew of the Count of Montargis; and among all the knights who had favor at the royal court, there was none braver than the young Sieur de Narsac, captain of the king's men at arms.

Now these two men were devoted friends, and whenever their

other duties allowed them, they were sure to be in each other's company. Indeed, it was a rare thing to see either of them walking the streets of Paris alone.

"I will meet you at the tournament tomorrow," said Aubrey gaily, one evening, as he was parting from his friend.

"Yes, at the tournament tomorrow," said De Narsac, "and be sure that you come early."

The tournament was to be a grand affair. A gentleman from Provence was to run a tilt with a famous Burgundian knight. Both men were noted for their horsemanship and their skill with the lance. All Paris would be out to see them.

When the time came, De Narsac was at the place appointed. But Aubrey failed to appear. What could it mean? It was not at all like Aubrey to forget his promise; it was seldom that he allowed anything to keep him away from the tournament.

"Have you seen my friend Aubrey today?" De Narsac asked this question a hundred times. Everybody gave the same answer and wondered what had happened.

The day passed and another day came, and still there was no news from Aubrey. De Narsac had called at his friend's lodgings, but could learn nothing. The young man had not been seen since the morning before the tournament.

Three days passed, and still not a word. De Narsac was greatly troubled. He knew now that some accident must have happened to Aubrey. But what could it have been?

Early in the morning of the fourth day he was aroused by a strange noise at his door. He dressed himself in haste and opened it. A dog was crouching there. It was a greyhound, so thin that its ribs stuck out, so weak that it could hardly stand.

De Narsac knew the animal without looking at the collar on its neck. It was Dragon, his friend Aubrey's greyhound—the dog who went with him whenever he went out, the dog who was never seen save in its master's company.

The poor creature tried to stand. His legs trembled from weakness. He swayed from side to side. He wagged his tail feebly, and tried to put his nose in De Narsac's hand. De Narsac saw at once that he was half starved.

He led the dog into his room and fed him some warm milk. He bathed the poor fellow's nose and bloodshot eyes with cold water. "Tell me where your master is," he said. Then he set before him a full meal that would have tempted any dog.

The greyhound ate heartily, and seemed to be much stronger. He licked De Narsac's hands. Then he ran to the door and tried to make signs to his friend to follow him. He whined pitifully.

De Narsac understood. "You want to lead me to your master, I see." He put on his hat and went out with the dog.

Through the narrow lanes and crooked streets of the old city, Dragon led the way. At each corner he would stop and look back to make sure that De Narsac was following. He went over the long bridge—the only one that spanned the river in those days. Then he trotted out through the gate of St. Martin and into the open country beyond the walls.

In a little while the dog left the main road and took a bypath that led into the forest of Bondy. De Narsac kept his hand on his sword now, for they were on dangerous ground. The forest was a great hangout for robbers and lawless men, and more than one wild and wicked deed had been enacted there.

But Dragon did not go far into the woods. He stopped suddenly near a dense thicket of briers and tangled vines. He whined as though in great distress. Then he took hold of the sleeve of De Narsac's coat, and led him round to the other side of the thicket.

There under a low-spreading oak the grass had been trampled down. There were signs, too, of freshly turned-up earth. With moans of distress the dog stretched himself upon the ground, and with pleading eyes looked up into De Narsac's face.

"Ah, my poor fellow!" said De Narsac, "you have led me here to show me your master's grave." And with that he turned and hurried back to the city; but the dog would not stir from his place.

That afternoon a company of men, led by De Narsac, rode out to the forest. They found in the ground beneath the oak what they had expected—the murdered body of young Aubrey de Montdidier.

"Who could have done this foul deed?" they asked of one another. And then they wept, for they all loved Aubrey.

They made a litter of green branches, and laid the body upon it. Then, the dog following them, they carried it back to the city and buried it in the king's cemetery. And all Paris mourned the untimely end of the brave young knight.

After this, the greyhound went to live with the young Sieur de Narsac. He followed the knight wherever he went. He slept in his room and ate from his hand. He seemed to be as much devoted to his new master as he had been to the old.

One morning they went out for a stroll through the city. The streets were crowded, for it was a holiday and all the fine people of Paris were enjoying the sunlight and the fresh air. Dragon, as usual, kept close to the heels of his master.

De Narsac walked down one street and up another, meeting many of his friends, and now and then stopping to talk a little while. Suddenly, as they were passing a corner, the dog leaped forward and planted himself in front of his master. He growled fiercely and crouched as though ready for a spring. His eyes were fixed upon someone in the crowd.

Then, before De Narsac could speak, he leaped forward upon a young man whom he had singled out. The man threw up his arm to protect his throat, but the quickness of the attack and the weight of the dog caused him to fall to the ground. There is no telling what might have followed had not those who were with him beaten the dog with their canes, and driven him away.

De Narsac knew the man. His name was Richard Macaire, and he belonged to the king's bodyguard.

Never before had the greyhound been known to show anger toward any person. "What do you mean by such conduct?" asked his master as they walked homeward. Dragon's only answer was a low growl, but it was the best that he could give. The affair had put a thought into De Narsac's mind which he could not dismiss.

Within less than a week the thing happened again. This time Macaire was walking in the public garden. De Narsac and the dog were some distance away. But as soon as Dragon saw the man, he rushed at him. It was all that the bystanders could do to keep him from throttling Macaire. De Narsac hurried up and called him away; but the dog's anger was fearful to see.

It was well known in Paris that Macaire and young Aubrey had not been friends. It was remembered that they had had more than one quarrel. And now the people began to talk about the dog's strange actions, and some went so far as to put this and that together.

At last the matter reached the ears of the king. He sent for De Narsac and had a long talk with him. "Come back tomorrow and bring the dog with you," he said. "We must find out more about this strange affair."

The next day De Narsac, with Dragon at his heels, was admitted into the king's audience room. The king was seated in his great chair, and many knights and men at arms were standing around him. Hardly had De Narsac stepped inside when the dog leaped quickly forward. He had seen Macaire, and had singled him out from among all the rest. He sprang upon him. He would have torn him in pieces if no one had interfered.

There was now only one way to explain the matter.

"This greyhound," said De Narsac, "is here to denounce the Chevalier Macaire as the slayer of his master, young Aubrey de Montdidier. He demands that justice be done, and that the murderer be punished for his crime."

The Chevalier Macaire was pale and trembling. He stammered a denial of his guilt, and declared that the dog was a dangerous beast, and ought to be put out of the way. "Shall a soldier in the service of the king be accused by a dog?" he cried. "Shall he be condemned on such testimony as this? I, too, demand justice."

"Let the judgment of God decide!" cried the knights who were present.

And so the king declared that there should be a trial by the judgment of God. For in those rude times it was a very common thing to determine guilt or innocence in this way—that is, by a combat between the accuser and the accused. In such cases it was believed that God would always aid the cause of the innocent and bring about the defeat of the guilty.

The combat was to take place that very afternoon in the great common by the riverside. The king's herald made a public announcement of it, naming the dog as the accuser and the Chevalier Macaire as the accused. A great crowd of people assembled to see this strange trial by the judgment of God.

The king and his officers were there to make sure that no injustice was done to either the man or the dog. The man was allowed to defend himself with a short stick. The dog was given a barrel into which he might run if too closely pressed.

At a signal the combat began. Macaire stood on his guard while the dog darted swiftly around him, dodging the blows that were aimed at him, and trying to get at his enemy's throat. The man seemed to have lost all his courage. His breath came short and quick. He was trembling from head to foot.

Suddenly the dog leaped upon him and threw him to the ground. In great terror Macaire cried to the king for mercy, and acknowledged his guilt.

"It is the judgment of God!" cried the king.

The officers rushed in and dragged the dog away before he

could harm the guilty man. Macaire was hurried off to the punishment which his crimes deserved.

And this is the scene that was carved on the old mantelpiece in the castle of Montargis—this strange trial by the judgment of God. Is it not fitting that a dog so faithful, devoted, and brave should have his memory thus preserved in stone?

•

HERCULES KILLS THE HYDRA

The killing of the Hydra was the second of the famous twelve labors Hercules performed for his cousin Eurystheus, king of Mycenae. The myth reminds us that some battles require the help of good friends.

The second labor of Hercules was the killing of the Hydra, a terrible serpent that dwelled among the murky swamps. The murderous beast had nine heads on nine long necks, and the middle head was immortal. This gigantic water snake ravaged the herds and the flocks of the countryside; whenever any mortal came near its den, it rushed out, seized him, and tore him limb from limb with its nine dripping sets of fangs. And yet it was a confident Hercules who rode forth in a chariot with his friend Iolaus to face this demon of the bottomless swamps.

When the Hydra saw the hero approaching, it slunk away, and hid in its lair. It feared this man with arms as stout as limbs of oak, and a great lion's skin draped for a cloak over his shoulders. From the depths of its den, its eighteen slitted eyes peered out at the sword flashing like the fire of the sun and the huge, knotted club swinging at his side.

But Hercules soon devised a way to bring it out of hiding. He soaked an arrow in brimstone and pitch, set fire to it, and sent it winging its flaming way into the Hydra's den. Out came the serpent, wounded by the missile and choking from the smoke now pouring forth from the burning nest.

As soon as it crept out, Hercules attacked. His gleaming sword swept through the air and at once lopped off one of the heads. He told himself it was going to be an easy victory. But he was reckoning without knowing his enemy—for hardly had the head fallen than the startled hero saw two others spring up on the severed neck! He struck off one of these, and still two more living heads grew in its place!

This was indeed a problem, and at first Hercules did not know what to do. He fought the serpent valiantly, but what does valor count when, no matter how you wound your foe, it cannot be killed and never loses strength?

To make matters worse, a gigantic crab now crawled to the aid of the serpent. It was sent by Juno, the queen of the gods, who bore an ancient grudge against Hercules. This strange enemy tried to distract the hero so that the Hydra could deliver a fatal strike; it crawled about the ground while Hercules struggled with the snake, pinching and biting his feet. Hercules, however, soon put an end to the crab's attempts. He trod upon it and crushed it into the ground.

Now he turned all his strength to defeating the Hydra. It was no easy matter to fight a foe who had so many heads, every one with fangs that could inflict the death sting. Hercules knew he could not fight on to victory alone. So he called upon Iolaus to help him. His friend had really only come to watch the great fight, but he did not hesitate to take part when needed.

Battling fiercely, Hercules shouted out his instructions. Iolaus tore a limb from a tree, set the end on fire, and stood beside Hercules with the blazing torch. Then as soon as Hercules knocked off a head, Iolaus touched the fire to the severed neck, searing it closed and keeping new heads from springing up.

On and on the fighting went. Iolaus used up a whole forest of torches sealing the wounds of the dreaded snake. At last, however, the battle was won. The Hydra lay dead at the feet of the victors—all except the immortal middle head. But Hercules cut it off also, and buried it beneath a huge rock so it could never get free. Then, before leaving the scene, he dipped the tips of his arrows in the poisonous blood of his victim. Henceforth even the slightest scratch from these arrows would be fatal.

And so Hercules and Iolaus rode away to announce their victory. But the angry Juno raised the vanquished foes and placed them in the heavens. Even today, you can see them blazing overhead on a starry night—Hydra the Serpent, and Cancer the Crab.

•

FOR THE LOVE OF A MAN
Jack London

Friends pull each other through hard times. They bet on each
other. They do both—literally—in this excerpt from one of the
most popular American adventure stories, *The Call of the Wild.*
The book tells the story of a dog named Buck, who is adopted by
John Thornton, an Alaskan who is the first human being to show
him kindness.

For the most part, Buck's love was expressed in adoration.
While he went wild with happiness when Thornton touched him or
spoke to him, he did not seek these tokens. Buck was content to
adore at a distance. He would lie by the hour, eager, alert, at Thornton's feet, looking up into his face, dwelling upon it, studying it,
following with keenest interest each fleeting expression, every
movement or change of feature. Or, as chance might have it, he
would lie farther away, to the side or rear, watching the outlines of
the man and the occasional movements of his body. And often, such
was the communion in which they lived, the strength of Buck's gaze
would draw John Thornton's head around, and he would return
the gaze, without speech, his heart shining out of his eyes as Buck's
heart shone out.

But in spite of this great love he bore John Thornton, which
seemed to bespeak the soft civilizing influence, the strain of the
primitive, which the Northland had aroused in him, remained alive
and active. Faithfulness and devotion, things born of fire and roof,
were his; yet he retained his wildness and wiliness. He was a thing
of the wild, come in from the wild to sit by John Thornton's fire,
rather than a dog of the soft Southland stamped with the marks of
generations of civilization. Because of his very great love, he could
not steal from this man, but from any other man, in any other camp,
he did not hesitate an instant; while the cunning with which he
stole enabled him to escape detection.

He was older than the days he had seen and the breaths he
had drawn. He linked the past with the present, and the eternity
behind him throbbed through him in a mighty rhythm to which he
swayed as the tides and seasons swayed. He sat by John Thornton's

fire, a broad-breasted dog, white-fanged and long-furred; but behind him were the shades of all manner of dogs, half-wolves and wild wolves, urgent and prompting, tasting the savor of the meat he ate, thirsting for the water he drank, scenting the wind with him, listening with him and telling him the sounds made by the wild life in the forest; dictating his moods, directing his actions, lying down to sleep with him when he lay down, and dreaming with him and beyond him and becoming themselves the stuff of his dreams.

So peremptorily did these shades beckon him, that each day mankind and the claims of mankind slipped farther from him. Deep in the forest a call was sounding, and as often as he heard this call, mysteriously thrilling and luring, he felt compelled to turn his back upon the fire and the beaten earth around it, and to plunge into the forest, and on and on, he knew not where or why; nor did he wonder where or why, the call sounding imperiously, deep in the forest. But as often as he gained the soft unbroken earth and the green shade, the love for John Thornton drew him back to the fire again.

Thornton alone held him. The rest of mankind was as nothing. Chance travelers might praise or pet him; but he was cold under it all, and from a too demonstrative man he would get up and walk away. When Thornton's partners, Hans and Pete, arrived on the long-expected raft, Buck refused to notice them till he learned they were close to Thornton; after that he tolerated them in a passive sort of way, accepting favors from them as though he favored them by accepting. They were of the same large type as Thornton, living close to the earth, thinking simply and seeing clearly; and ere they swung the raft into the big eddy by the sawmill at Dawson, they understood Buck and his ways.

For Thornton, however, his love seemed to grow and grow. He, alone among men, could put a pack upon Buck's back in the summer traveling. Nothing was too great for Buck to do, when Thornton commanded. One day (they had grubstaked themselves from the proceeds of the raft and left Dawson for the headwaters of the Tanana) the men and dogs were sitting on the crest of a cliff which fell away, straight down, to naked bedrock three hundred feet below. John Thornton was sitting near the edge, Buck at his shoulder. A thoughtless whim seized Thornton, and he drew the attention of Hans and Pete to the experiment he had in mind. "Jump, Buck!" he commanded, sweeping his arm out and over the chasm. The next instant he was grappling with Buck on the extreme edge, while Hans and Pete were dragging them back into safety.

"It's uncanny," Pete said, after it was over and they had caught their speech.

Thornton shook his head. "No, it is splendid, and it is terrible, too. Do you know, it sometimes makes me afraid."

"I'm not hankering to be the man that lays hands on you while he's around," Pete announced conclusively, nodding his head toward Buck.

"Py Jingo!" was Hans's contribution. "Not mineself either."

Later on, in the fall of the year, Buck saved John Thornton's life. The three partners were lining a long and narrow poling-boat down a bad stretch of rapids on the Forty Mile Creek. Hans and Pete moved along the bank, snubbing with a thin Manila rope from tree to tree, while Thornton remained in the boat, helping its descent by means of a pole, and shouting directions to the shore. Buck, on the bank, worried and anxious, kept abreast of the boat, his eyes never off his master.

At a particularly bad spot, where a ledge of barely submerged rocks jutted out into the river, Hans cast off the rope, and, while Thornton poled the boat out into the stream, ran down the bank with the end in his hand to snub the boat when it had cleared the ledge. This it did, and was flying downstream in a current as swift as a millrace, when Hans checked it with the rope and checked too suddenly. The boat flirted over and snubbed in to the bank bottom up, while Thornton, flung sheer out of it, was carried downstream toward the worst part of the rapids, a stretch of wild water in which no swimmer could live.

Buck had sprung in on the instant, and at the end of three hundred yards, amid a mad swirl of water, he overhauled Thornton. When he felt him grasp his tail, Buck headed for the bank, swimming with all his splendid strength. But the progress shoreward was slow, the progress downstream amazingly rapid. From below came the fatal roaring where the wild current went wilder and was rent in shreds and spray by the rocks which thrust through like the teeth of an enormous comb. The suck of the water as it took the beginning of the last steep pitch was frightful, and Thornton knew that the shore was impossible. He scraped furiously over a rock, bruised across a second, and struck a third with crushing force. He clutched its slippery top with both hands, releasing Buck, and above the roar of the churning water shouted: "Go, Buck! Go!"

Buck could not hold his own, and swept on downstream, struggling desperately, but unable to win back. When he heard Thornton's command repeated, he partly reared out of the water, throwing his head high, as though for a last look, then turned obediently toward the bank. He swam powerfully and was dragged ashore by Pete and Hans at the very point where swimming ceased to be possible and destruction began.

They knew that the time a man could cling to a slippery rock in the face of that driving current was a matter of minutes, and they ran as fast as they could up the bank to a point far above where Thornton was hanging on. They attached the line with which they had been snubbing the boat to Buck's neck and shoulders, being careful that it should neither strangle him nor impede his swimming, and launched him into the stream. He struck out boldly, but not straight enough into the stream. He discovered the mistake too late, when Thornton was abreast of him and a bare half-dozen strokes away while he was being carried helplessly past.

Hans promptly snubbed with the rope, as though Buck were a boat. The rope thus tightening on him in the sweep of the current, he was jerked under the surface, and under the surface he remained till his body struck against the bank and he was hauled out. He was half-drowned, and Hans and Pete threw themselves upon him, pounding the breath into him and the water out of him. He staggered to his feet and fell down. The faint sound of Thornton's voice came to them, and though they could not make out the words of it, they knew that he was in his extremity. His master's voice acted on Buck like an electric shock. He sprang to his feet and ran up the bank ahead of the men to the point of his previous departure.

Again the rope was attached and he was launched, and again he struck out, but this time straight into the stream. He had miscalculated once, but he would not be guilty of it a second time. Hans paid out the rope, permitting no slack, while Pete kept it clear of coils. Buck held on till he was on a line straight above Thornton; then he turned, and with the speed of an express train headed down upon him. Thornton saw him coming, and, as Buck struck him like a battering ram, with the whole force of the current behind him, he reached up and closed with both arms around the shaggy neck. Hans snubbed the rope around the tree, and Buck and Thornton were jerked under the water. Strangling, suffocating, sometimes one uppermost and sometimes the other, dragging over the jagged bottom, smashing against rocks and snags, they veered in to the bank.

Thornton came to, belly downward and being violently propelled back and forth across a drift log by Hans and Pete. His first glance was for Buck. Thornton went carefully over Buck's body, when he had been brought around, finding three broken ribs.

"That settles it," he announced. "We camp right here." And camp they did, till Buck's ribs knitted and he was able to travel.

That winter, at Dawson, Buck performed another exploit, not so heroic, perhaps, but one that puts his name many notches higher on the totem pole of Alaskan fame. This exploit was particularly gratifying to the three men; for they stood in need of the outfit which it furnished, and were enabled to make a long-desired trip into the virgin East, where miners had not yet appeared. It was brought about by a conversation in the Eldorado Saloon, in which men waxed boastful of their favorite dogs. Buck, because of his record, was the target for these men, and Thornton was driven stoutly to defend him. At the end of half an hour one man stated that his dog could start a sled with five hundred pounds and walk off with it; a second bragged six hundred for his dog; and a third, seven hundred.

"Pooh! Pooh!" said John Thornton. "Buck can start a thousand pounds."

"And break it out, and walk off with it for a hundred yards?" demanded Matthewson, a Bonanza king, he of the seven hundred vaunt.

"And break it out, and walk off with it for a hundred yards," John Thornton said coolly.

"Well," Matthewson said, slowly and deliberately, so that all could hear, "I've got a thousand dollars that says he can't. And there it is." So saying, he slammed a sack of gold dust of the size of a bologna sausage down upon the bar.

Nobody spoke. Thornton's bluff, if bluff it was, had been called. He could feel a flush of warm blood creeping up his face. His tongue had tricked him. He did not know whether Buck could start a thousand pounds. Half a ton! The enormousness of it appalled him. He had great faith in Buck's strength and had often thought him capable of starting such a load; but never, as now, had he faced the possibility of it, the eyes of a dozen men fixed upon him, silent and waiting. Further, he had no thousand dollars; nor had Hans or Pete.

"I've got a sled standing outside now, with twenty fifty-pound sacks of flour on it," Matthewson went on with brutal directness, "so don't let that hinder you."

Thornton did not reply. He did not know what to say. He glanced from face to face in the absent way of a man who has lost the power of thought and is seeking somewhere to find the thing that will start it going again. The face of Jim O'Brien, a Mastodon king and old-time comrade, caught his eyes. It was as a cue to him, seeming to rouse him to do what he would never have dreamed of doing.

"Can you lend me a thousand?" he asked, almost in a whisper.

"Sure," answered O'Brien, thumping down a plethoric sack by the side of Matthewson's. "Though it's little faith I'm having, John, that the beast can do the trick."

The Eldorado emptied its occupants into the street to see the test. The tables were deserted, and the dealers and gamekeepers came forth to see the outcome of the wager and to lay odds. Several hundred men, furred and mittened, banked around the sled within easy distance. Matthewson's sled, loaded with a thousand pounds of flour, had been standing for a couple of hours, and in the intense cold (it was sixty below zero) the runners had frozen fast to the hard-packed snow. Men offered odds of two to one that Buck could not budge the sled. A quibble arose concerning the phrase "break out." O'Brien contended it was Thornton's privilege to knock the runners loose, leaving Buck to "break it out" from a dead standstill. Matthewson insisted that the phrase included breaking the runners from the frozen grip of the snow. A majority of the men who had witnessed the making of the bet decided in his favor, whereat the odds went up to three to one against Buck.

There were no takers. Not a man believed him capable of the feat. Thornton had been hurried into the wager, heavy with doubt; and now that he looked at the sled itself, the concrete fact, with the regular team of ten dogs curled up in the snow before it, the more impossible the task appeared. Matthewson waxed jubilant.

"Three to one!" he proclaimed. "I'll lay you another thousand at that figure, Thornton. What d'ye say?"

Thornton's doubt was strong in his face, but his fighting spirit was aroused—the fighting spirit that soars above odds, fails to recognize the impossible, and is deaf to all save the clamor for battle. He called Hans and Pete to him. Their sacks were slim, and with his own the three partners could rake together only two hundred dollars. In the ebb of their fortunes, this sum was their total capital; yet they laid it unhesitatingly against Matthewson's six hundred.

The team of ten dogs was unhitched, and Buck, with his own harness, was put into the sled. He had caught the contagion of the excitement, and he felt that in some way he must do a great thing for John Thornton. Murmurs of admiration at his splendid appearance went up. He was in perfect condition, without an ounce of superfluous flesh, and the one hundred and fifty pounds that he weighed were so many pounds of grit and virility. His furry coat shone with the sheen of silk. Down the neck and across the shoulders, his mane, in repose as it was, half bristled and seemed to lift with every movement, as though excess of vigor made each particular hair alive and active. The great breast and heavy forelegs were no more than in proportion with the rest of the body, where the muscles showed in tight rolls underneath the skin. Men felt these muscles and proclaimed them hard as iron, and the odds went down to two to one.

"Gad, sir! Gad, sir!" stuttered a member of the latest dynasty, a king of the Skookum Benches. "I offer you eight hundred for him, sir, before the test, sir, eight hundred just as he stands."

Thornton shook his head and stepped over to Buck's side.

"You must stand off from him," Matthewson protested. "Free play and plenty of room."

The crowd fell silent; only could be heard the voices of the gamblers vainly offering two to one. Everybody acknowledged Buck a magnificent animal, but twenty fifty-pound sacks of flour bulked too large in their eyes for them to loosen their pouch-strings.

Thornton knelt down by Buck's side. He took his head in his two hands and rested cheek on cheek. He did not playfully shake him, as was his wont, or murmur soft love curses, but he whispered in his ear. "As you love me, Buck. As you love me," was what he whispered. Buck whined with suppressed eagerness.

The crowd was watching curiously. The affair was growing mysterious. It seemed like a conjuration. As Thornton got to his feet, Buck seized his mittened hand between his jaws, pressing in with his teeth and releasing slowly, half reluctantly. It was the answer, in terms not of speech but of love. Thornton stepped well back.

"Now, Buck," he said.

Buck tightened the traces, then slacked them for a matter of several inches. It was the way he had learned.

"Gee!" Thornton's voice rang out, sharp in the tense silence.

Buck swung to the right, ending the movement in a plunge that took up the slack and with a sudden jerk arrested his one hundred and fifty pounds. The load quivered, and from under the runners arose a crisp crackling.

"Haw!" Thornton commanded.

Buck duplicated the maneuver, this time to the left. The crackling turned into a snapping, the sled pivoting and the runners slipping and grating several inches to the side. The sled was broken out. Men were holding their breaths, intensely unconscious of the fact.

"Now, MUSH!"

Thornton's command cracked out like a pistol-shot. Buck threw himself forward, tightening the traces with a jarring lunge. His whole body was gathered compactly together in the tremendous effort, the muscles writhing and knotting like live things under the silky fur. His great chest was low to the ground, his head forward and down, while his feet were flying like mad, the claws scarring the hard-packed snow in parallel grooves. The sled swayed and trembled, half-started forward. One of his feet slipped, and one man groaned aloud. Then the sled lurched ahead in what appeared a rapid succession of jerks, though it never really came to a dead stop again ... half an inch ... an inch ... two inches.... The jerks perceptibly diminished; as the sled gained momentum, he caught them up, till it was moving steadily along.

Men gasped and began to breathe again, unaware that for a moment they had ceased to breathe. Thornton was running behind, encouraging Buck with short, cheery words. The distance had been measured off, and as he neared the pile of firewood which marked the end of the hundred yards, a cheer began to grow and grow, which burst into a roar as he passed the firewood and halted at command. Every man was tearing himself loose, even Matthewson. Hats and mittens were flying in the air. Men were shaking hands, it did not matter with whom, and bubbling over in a general incoherent babel.

But Thornton fell on his knees beside Buck. Head was against head, and he was shaking him back and forth. Those who hurried up heard him cursing Buck, and he cursed him long and fervently, and softly and lovingly.

"Gad, sir! Gad, sir!" spluttered the Skookum Bench king. "I'll give you a thousand for him, sir, a thousand, sir—twelve hundred, sir."

Thornton rose to his feet. His eyes were wet. The tears were streaming frankly down his cheeks. "Sir," he said to the Skookum Bench king, "no, sir. You can go to hell, sir. It's the best I can do for you, sir."

Buck seized Thornton's hand in his teeth. Thornton shook him back and forth. As though animated by a common impulse, the onlookers drew back to a respectful distance, nor were they again indiscreet enough to interrupt.

•

THE MUTINY

Alphonse de Lamartine

This crossing will stand forever as a triumph of unyielding courage and perseverance over fear of the unknown. It's a great episode to remember whenever we encounter rough passages in our own lives. The year, of course, is 1492.

When Columbus left the Canaries to pass with his three small ships into the unknown seas, the eruptions of Teneriffe illuminated the heavens and were reflected in the sea. This cast terror into the minds of his seamen. They thought that it was the flaming sword of the angel who expelled the first man from Eden, and who now was trying to drive back in anger those presumptuous ones who were seeking entrance to the forbidden and unknown seas and lands. But the admiral passed from ship to ship explaining to his men, in a simple way, the action of volcanoes, so that the sailors were no longer afraid.

But as the peak of Teneriffe sank below the horizon, a great sadness fell upon the men. It was their last beacon, the farthest sea-mark of the Old World. They were seized with a nameless terror and loneliness.

Then the admiral called them around him in his own ship, and told them many stories of the things they might hope to find in the wonderful new world to which they were going—of the lands, the islands, the seas, the kingdoms, the riches, the vegetation, the sunshine, the mines of gold, the sands covered with pearls, the mountains shining with precious stones, the plains loaded with spices. These stories, tinged with the brilliant colors of their leader's rich imagination, filled the discouraged sailors with hope and good spirits.

But as they passed over the trackless ocean, and saw day by day the great billows rolling between them and the mysterious horizon, the sailors were again filled with dread. They lacked the courage to sail onward into the unknown distance. The compass began to vacillate, and no longer pointed toward the north; this confused both Columbus and his pilots. The men fell into a panic, but the resolute and patient admiral encouraged them once more. So buoyed up by his faith and hope, they continued to sail onward over the pathless waters.

The next day a heron and a tropical bird flew about the masts of the ships, and these seemed to the wondering sailors as two witnesses come to confirm the reasoning of Columbus.

At eve and morning the distant waning clouds, like those that gather round the mountaintops, took the form of cliffs and hills skirting the horizon. The cry of "land" was on the tip of every tongue. Columbus by his reckoning knew that they must still be far from any land. But fearing to discourage his men he kept his thoughts to himself, for he found no trustworthy friend among his companions whose heart was firm enough to bear his secret.

During the long passage Columbus conversed with his own thoughts, with the stars, and with God, who he felt was his protector. He occupied his days in making notes of what he observed. The nights he passed on deck with his pilots, studying the stars and watching the seas. He withdrew into himself, and his thoughtful gravity impressed his companions sometimes with respect and sometimes with mistrust and awe.

Each morning the bows of the vessels plunged through the fantastic horizon which the evening mist had made the sailors mistake for a shore. They kept rolling on through the boundless and bottomless abyss. Gradually terror and discontent once more took possession of the crews. They began to imagine that the steadfast east wind that drove them westward prevailed eternally in this region, and that when the time came to sail homeward, the same wind would prevent their return. For surely their provisions and water could not hold out long enough for them to beat their way eastward over those wide waters!

Then the sailors began to murmur against the admiral and his seeming fruitless obstinacy, and they blamed themselves for obeying him, when it might mean the sacrifice of the lives of one hundred and twenty sailors.

But each time the murmurs threatened to break out into mutiny, Providence seemed to send more encouraging signs of land. And these for the time being changed the complaints to hopes. At evening little birds of the most delicate species, that build their nests in the shrubs of the garden and orchard, hovered warbling about the masts. Their delicate wings and joyous notes bore no signs of weariness or fright, as of birds swept far away to sea by a storm. These signs again aroused hope.

The green weeds on the surface of the ocean looked like waving corn before the ears are ripe. The vegetation beneath the water delighted the eyes of the sailors tired of the endless expanse of blue. But the seaweed soon became so thick that they were afraid of entangling their rudders and keels, and of remaining prisoners forever in the forests of the ocean, as ships of the northern seas are shut in by ice. Thus each joy soon turned to fear, so terrible to man is the unknown.

The wind ceased, the calms of the tropics alarmed the sailors. An immense whale was seen sleeping on the waters. They fancied there were monsters in the deep which would devour their ships. The roll of the waves drove them upon currents which they could not stem for want of wind. They imagined they were approaching the cataracts of the ocean, and that they were being hurried toward the abysses into which the deluge had poured its world of waters.

Fierce and angry faces crowded round the mast. The murmurs rose louder and louder. They talked of compelling the pilots to put about and of throwing the admiral into the sea. Columbus, to whom their looks and threats revealed these plans, defied them by his bold bearing or disconcerted them by his coolness.

Again nature came to his assistance, by giving him fresh breezes from the east, and a calm sea under his bows. Before the close of the day came the first cry of "Land ho!" from the lofty poop. All the crews, repeating this cry of safety, life, and triumph, fell on their knees on the decks, and struck up the hymn, "Glory be to God in heaven and upon earth." When it was over, all climbed as high as they could up the masts, yards, and rigging to see with their own eyes the new land that had been sighted.

But the sunrise destroyed this new hope all too quickly. The imaginary land disappeared with the morning mist, and once more the ships seemed to be sailing over a never-ending wilderness of waters.

Despair took possession of the crews. Again the cry of "Land ho!" was heard. But the sailors found as before that their hopes were but a passing cloud. Nothing wearies the heart so much as false hopes and bitter disappointments.

Loud reproaches against the admiral were heard from every quarter. Bread and water were beginning to fail. Despair changed to fury. The men decided to turn the heads of the vessels toward Europe, and to beat back against the winds that had favored the admiral, whom they intended to chain to the mast of his own vessel and to give up to the vengeance of Spain should they ever reach the port of their own country.

These complaints now became clamorous. The admiral restrained them by the calmness of his countenance. He called upon Heaven to decide between himself and the sailors. He flinched not. He offered his life as a pledge, if they would but trust and wait for three days more. He swore that, if, in the course of the third day, land was not visible on the horizon, he would yield to their wishes and steer for Europe.

The mutinous men reluctantly consented and allowed him three days of grace.

At sunrise on the second day rushes recently torn up were seen floating near the vessels. A plank hewn by an axe, a carved stick, a bough of hawthorn in blossom, and lastly a bird's nest built on a branch which the wind had broken, and full of eggs on which the parent-bird was sitting, were seen swimming past on the waters. The sailors brought on board these living witnesses of their approach to land. They were like a message from the shore, confirming the promises of Columbus.

The overjoyed and repentant mutineers fell on their knees before the admiral whom they had insulted but the day before, and craved pardon for their mistrust.

As the day and night advanced, many other sights and sounds showed that land was very near. Toward day delicious and unknown perfumes borne on a soft land breeze reached the vessels, and there was heard the roar of the waves upon the reefs.

The dawn, as it spread over the sky, gradually raised the shores of an island from the waves. Its distant extremities were lost in the morning mist. As the sun rose it shone on the land ascending from a low yellow beach to the summit of hills whose dark-green covering contrasted strongly with the clear blue of the heavens. The foam of the waves broke on the yellow sand, and forests of tall and unknown trees stretched away, one above another, over successive terraces of the island. Green valleys, and bright clefts in the hollows afforded a half glimpse into these mysterious wilds. And thus the land of golden promises, the land of future greatness, first appeared to Christopher Columbus, the Admiral of the Ocean.

•

THE CRISIS

Thomas Paine

These famous words by Thomas Paine appeared during the winter of 1776–1777, a time that may have been the gloomiest hour for the American revolutionary cause. The patriot forces seemed unable to win a battle. George Washington's army had been routed out of New York, driven across New Jersey, and lay shivering on the Pennsylvania side of the Delaware River. More and more men deserted every day. Racked by hunger, cold, and disease, those who remained simply waited in misery for their enlistments to expire so they could go home. Washington himself confided in a letter to a relative: "I think the game is pretty near up." Amid this crisis of morale, Paine implored the colonists not to give up the fight.

These are the times that try men's souls. The summer soldier
and the sunshine patriot will, in this crisis, shrink from the service
of their country; but he that stands it *now,* deserves the love and
thanks of man and woman. Tyranny, like hell, is not easily conquered; yet we have this consolation with us, that the harder the
conflict, the more glorious the triumph. What we obtain too cheap,
we esteem too lightly: it is dearness only that gives every thing its
value. Heaven knows how to put a proper price upon its goods;
and it would be strange indeed if so celestial an article as FREEDOM
should not be highly rated. . . .

I call not upon a few, but upon all: not on *this* state or *that*
state, but on *every* state: up and help us; lay your shoulders to the
wheel; better have too much force than too little, when so great an
object is at stake. Let it be told to the future world, that in the depth
of winter, when nothing but hope and virtue could survive, that the
city and the country, alarmed at one common danger, came forth
to meet and to repulse it. Say not that thousands are gone, turn out
your tens of thousands; throw not the burden of the day upon
Providence, but *"show your faith by your works,"* that God may
bless you. It matters not where you live, or what rank of life you
hold, the evil or the blessing will reach you all. The far and the
near, the home counties and the back, the rich and the poor, will
suffer or rejoice alike. The heart that feels not now, is dead: the
blood of his children will curse his cowardice, who shrinks back at
a time when a little might have saved the whole, and made *them*
happy. I love the man that can smile in trouble, that can gather
strength from distress, and grow brave by reflection. 'Tis the business of little minds to shrink; but he whose heart is firm, and whose
conscience approves his conduct, will pursue his principles unto
death.

•

A PRAYER AT VALLEY FORGE

Valley Forge has become a place forever linked in the American
mind with the virtues of courage, perseverance, and loyalty to
cause. Some 9,000 of George Washington's troops went into camp
there in the late autumn of 1777. By the time the snows of winter

were gone, only 6,000 remained. Here is a story of heroic resolve
of ordinary men, as well as an example of how faith helped one
extraordinary man lead the rest through.

During the Revolutionary War the British army seized Philadelphia, the "rebel capital" where the Congress had been meeting.
They marched into the city with colors flying and bands playing,
and made themselves at home for the winter. George Washington
could do nothing to stop them. Once the British were in the city,
the only thing he could do was see that they did not get out into
the countryside to do any mischief. So he chose for his winter
quarters Valley Forge, a place only a few miles from Philadelphia.
There the American army could defend itself if attacked, and it
could keep close watch on the British.

It would have been easier to fight many battles than to spend
that winter in Valley Forge. It was December, and there was no
shelter of any kind. Men and officers bravely set to work constructing huts for themselves. They built some of heavy logs, with
roofs made of small trees wrapped with straw and laid side by side.
Clay was spread on top of that. The windows were simply holes cut
through the logs and covered with oiled paper.

Such a house was the height of luxury at Valley Forge. Most of
the huts were made of piled-up sod, or fence rails held together by
twisted twigs and daubed with clay. The snow sifted in at every
opening, the rain dripped through even the best of the roofs, and
the wind howled and roared and blew in at every crevice. There
were few blankets, and many brave defenders of their country lay
on the frozen ground because they had not even straw to put under
their heads. Sometimes they sat up all night, crowding up to the
fires to keep from freezing.

Their clothing was worse than their shelter. The whole army
was in rags. Many of the men had no shirts, even more were without
shoes. Wherever they walked, the snow was marked with blood.
Some cut strips from their precious blankets and wound them
about their feet to protect them from the freezing ground.

Food was scanty. Sometimes for several days the soldiers went
without meat, and some companies went without even bread. When
the word went around "no meat tonight," the soldiers groaned, but
they never yielded.

Here is an entry in the diary of one of the men:

"There comes a soldier—his bare feet peep through his worn-out shoes, his legs nearly naked from the tattered remains of an only pair of stockings... his shirt hanging in strings... his face meager—his whole appearance pictures a person forsaken and discouraged. He comes, and cries with an air of wretchedness and despair... I am sick, my feet lame, my legs are sore, my body covered with this tormenting itch. My clothes are worn out, my constitution is broken, my former activity is exhausted by fatigue. Hunger and cold. I fail fast. I shall soon be no more."

One cold day a Quaker farmer was walking along a creek at Valley Forge when he heard the murmur of a solemn voice. Creeping in its direction, he discovered a horse tied to a sapling, but no rider.

The farmer stole nearer, following the sound of the voice. There, through a thicket, he saw a lone man, on his knees in the snow.

It was General Washington. His cheeks were wet with tears as he prayed to the Almighty for help and guidance.

The farmer quietly slipped away. When he reached home, he said to his wife, "The Americans will win their independence! George Washington will succeed!"

"What makes thee think so, Isaac?" she asked.

"I have heard him pray, Hannah, out in the woods today," he said. "If there is anyone on this earth the Lord will listen to, it is this brave commander. He will listen, Hannah. Rest assured, He will."

●

MOLLY PITCHER

Here is an American "Horatius at the Bridge."

It was the twenty-eighth day of June, 1778. Two great armies, which were engaged in one of the world's most decisive struggles, were on the plains of Monmouth in New Jersey. Riding up and down the lines of the American forces was the great Washington, urging on the soldiers of freedom with words of encouragement and command.

The brilliant uniforms of the British glittered in the sunlight, and at their head rode the gallant General Clinton, whose military bravery had won for him the admiration of Europe.

The fighting was fierce and determined. Shell and shot mingled with the roar of cannon, and the beat of every instant left more wounded on the field.

The issue of the battle was doubtful. Neither side knew which was to be the victor, for triumph seemed within the grasp of either, at the instant.

In the midst of the conflict was a lad named William Hays. Not for an instant did he leave his post as artilleryman, even when it looked like the American forces might be thrown back.

"I'll not retreat," he muttered, "as long as there is another man on the field to fight."

By the side of this brave lad stood a young woman, scarcely out of her girlhood. It was Molly, his wife, and her face was set with determination.

"I will follow William through the army," she had said. "I can help the soldiers when they are in trouble, and I can stand it as well as he."

The laughing eyes and keen wit of Molly had brought cheer to many of the heartsick soldiers. Patiently she had ministered to their needs, and tenderly she had bound their bleeding wounds. The day was intensely hot; the temperature soared close to one hundred degrees. One by one, gasping soldiers began to drop from thirst and exhaustion, so Molly grabbed an artillery bucket and began carrying water from a cool spring to the troops. "Here comes Molly with her pitcher!" they would shout, and afterward she was known as Molly Pitcher.

But on one of her trips a deadly ball whizzed past her head— and William fell wounded. There was no one to take his place, and the cannon's crew prepared to abandon the field. But without a moment's hesitation, Molly grabbed the rammer staff from her fallen husband's hand and began swabbing and reloading the gun. Boom! Boom! It echoed across the battlefield, as she reloaded each time with the agility of a trained artilleryman.

"The enemy is almost upon us!" cried one of the soldiers.

"Stand fast," replied Molly.

The cheers of the soldiers rang down the line. The battle was turning, and there in the ranks stood Molly Pitcher—a cannoneer.

When the fighting was over, and the British were in retreat, the soldiers gathered about her to praise her courage, but she did not hear their words. She was bending over her husband, nursing his wounds.

The next day the story of Molly Pitcher passed through the camp. General Nathanael Greene heard it and strode straight to Molly's tent.

"Come, my brave girl," he said. "I want to take you to General Washington."

As they reached the tent of the great commander, he rose with his grave and stately manner, and with a courteous bow to the Irish girl, he extended his hand.

"You have made a brave stand," he said. "We will win our liberty, if we all stand fast like you."

It is said the young woman was awarded a warrant as a non-commissioned officer, and thereafter the admiring army called her "Sergeant Molly."

Such is the tale of Molly Pitcher, heroine of the American Revolution. The battlefield monuments tell of her courage, and an old rhyme recalls her deed:

> Moll Pitcher she stood by her gun
> And rammed the charges home, sir;
> And thus on Monmouth's bloody field
> A sergeant did become, sir.

•

THE STAR-SPANGLED BANNER

Adapted from Eva March Tappan

Many people sing the first verse of this song several times a year
without knowing the context of its birth or the story of how our
flag became the national symbol of perseverance through perilous
times.

The year 1814 found the people of Maryland in trouble. A
British fleet of some fifty ships had sailed into the Chesapeake Bay.
Their cannon soon would be aimed at some town, but nobody
knew which. The ships sailed up one river, came back down, and
sailed up another, as if they had not decided which port would fall
under their guns. All along the shores, people fired alarms and lit
signal fires to let their neighbors know danger was near. The ships
lingered, hesitated, then suddenly spread sails and ran to the north,
up the bay.

"They will surely destroy us," thought the people of Annapolis.
They crammed their household goods into wagons and carts, even
into wheelbarrows, and hurried inland as fast as they could. But the
ships sailed past Annapolis.

Suddenly there was no question which town they meant to
attack. It was Baltimore. With forty-five thousand inhabitants, the
port was the third-largest city in the country and a rich prize. To
take it, however, the British fleet would have to get past Fort
McHenry, which guarded Baltimore's harbor.

As the warships crept upstream toward the fort, the crews
could see a gigantic flag with fifteen white stars and fifteen red and
white stripes fluttering in the breeze above the ramparts. It was the
work of widow Mary Young Pickersgill, a seamstress who special-
ized in making flags for Baltimore's merchant ships. Her own house
wasn't large enough for the job of stitching the enormous banner
together, so she and her thirteen-year-old daughter Caroline had
worked on it in a Baltimore brewery. Now it flew as a proud, defiant
symbol of an upstart country that was about to take on the most
powerful nation in the world.

At 7 A.M. on the morning of September 13, the big British guns
took aim at the flag and let loose a horrifying fire. They shot huge,

200-pound bombshells designed to explode on impact, scattering wreckage far and wide. Often, however, the erratic bombs blew up in midair. The shelling lasted nearly twenty-four hours. When dark fell the fleet used signal rockets, which traced fiery arcs across the night sky. It was a spectacular sight.

"If Fort McHenry can stand, the city is safe," Francis Scott Key muttered to himself, and he gazed anxiously through the smoke to see if the flag was still flying.

The Maryland lawyer had a particularly agonizing view of the battle—he watched from a little American vessel tied fast to the side of the British flagship. A friend had been seized as a prisoner by the British, and Key had gone out under a flag of truce to ask for his release. The British commander finally agreed to the request, but he had no intention of letting Key go back to the city with any information he might have picked up. "Until the battle is over, you and your boat stay here," he ordered.

Key had no choice but to wait it out, pacing the deck and hoping the fort could hold out. The firing went on. As long as daylight lasted, he could catch glimpses of the Stars and Stripes whenever the wind swayed the clouds of smoke. When night came, he could still see the banner now and then by the blaze of the cannon.

Finally the firing stopped. Key strained his eyes to see if the flag was still flying. "Could the fort have held out?" he wondered.

At last the faint gray of dawn appeared. He could see that some flag was flying, but it was too dark to tell whose. More and more eagerly he gazed. It grew lighter. A sudden breath of wind caught the banner, and it floated out on the breeze. It was no English flag. It was Mary Pickersgill's Stars and Stripes, still waving through the smoke and mist! Fort McHenry had stood, and the city was safe.

Overcome with emotion, Key took from his pocket an old letter and began scribbling on its back a few lines and phrases.

The British departed, and the little American boat sailed back to the city. Key gave a copy of the poem he had just written to his uncle, who had been helping defend the fort. His uncle sent it to a printer and had it struck off on some handbills. Before the ink was dry the printer snatched one up and hurried to a tavern where many patriots were assembling.

"Listen to this!" he cried, waving the paper, and he read:

O say, can you see by the dawn's early light,
What so proudly we hailed at the twilight's last gleaming,
Whose broad stripes and bright stars, through the perilous fight
O'er the ramparts we watch'd were so gallantly streaming?
And the rockets' red glare, the bombs bursting in air,
Gave proof through the night that our flag was still there.
O say, does that star-spangled banner yet wave
O'er the land of the free and the home of the brave?

"Sing it! Sing it!" the whole company cried. Someone mounted a chair and sang the poem to an old tune. The song caught on at once. Halls, theaters, and houses soon rang with its strains as the British fleet disappeared over the horizon.

Frances Scott Key's words never lost their popularity, and more than a century later, in 1931, Congress designated "The Star-Spangled Banner" as our national anthem.

•

THE MARINES' HYMN

There is an entire organization devoted to the ideal of fidelity to task. Its motto is a great one to adopt when seeing your way through a tough job: Semper Fidelis—Always Faithful.

From the Halls of Montezuma
To the shores of Tripoli
We fight our country's battles
On the land as on the sea.
First to fight for right and freedom
And to keep our honor clean;
We are proud to claim the title
Of United States Marines.

Our flag's unfurled to every breeze
From dawn to setting sun;
We have fought in every clime and place
Where we could take a gun.

In the snow of far-off Northern lands
And in sunny tropic scenes;
You will find us always on the job—
The United States Marines.

Here's health to you and to our Corps
Which we are proud to serve;
In many a strife we've fought for life
And never lost our nerve.
If the Army and the Navy
Ever look on Heaven's scenes,
They will find the streets are guarded
By United States Marines.

•

THE RACE FROM MARATHON

Here is the classic story of endurance, the tale which lends its name to our popular modern contest. This original run, which took place in 490 B.C., covered about twenty-five miles, the distance from Marathon to Athens. The current distance for modern marathon races was established in 1908, when King Edward VII of England wished to watch the start of the Olympic event from his home at Windsor Castle. Thereafter, 26 miles 385 yards—the distance from the castle to London's Olympic stadium—became the official marathon distance.

Twenty-five hundred years ago, Darius I of Persia established an empire that stretched across Asia and into Africa. Darius himself was called "the Great King," or simply "the King," as if there were no other ruler on the face of the earth. And he intended that there should be no other if he should have his way. He made up his mind to make himself master of the Greeks, known far and wide for their skill in peace and courage in war.

Darius sent heralds to every state in Greece to demand tributes of earth and water as symbols that the land and sea belonged to him alone. Some of the states submitted, others proudly refused.

Athens was among the latter. The Athenians threw the Persian heralds into a muddy ditch. "There you will find both earth and water for your master," they cried.

When Darius heard of the rebuke he assembled his vast army, readied his fleet, and set sail over the Aegean Sea. The Athenians heard of his approach. Soon their city would be overrun. At once they thought of appealing to the famous Spartans, whose state lay 140 miles to the south, across the Isthmus of Corinth.

The rulers of Athens, seated in grave council on the Acropolis, sent for Pheidippides, their champion runner. They commanded him to hurry and urge Sparta to come to their aid.

Pheidippides ran. He scrambled up rocky paths, passed through shadowy gorges, crossed rivers that ran over slippery stones. For two days and two nights he ran, carrying the urgent plea. He reached Sparta hungry, dusty, and footsore.

But the Spartans, though fearless of Darius, were envious and mistrustful of Athens. They looked at Pheidippides in silence. They smiled darkly and murmured among themselves, while the messenger stood waiting.

"We must not act in haste," they said at last. "We must think it over. Besides, you know our custom; we never fight when the moon is at the half. Wait until the moon is full. Then perhaps we will come."

Pheidippides wanted to shout in anger and despair. But there was no time for bitterness—he had to let his countrymen know. He did not stop to trade insults with the Spartans. Back over the hills and plains he rushed, fording the streams, clambering over boulders, threading his way through forests. He arrived in Athens with the word: The Spartans will not help. The Athenians must depend on their own resources.

Now the Persians had landed on the Greek coast and gone into camp on the plain of Marathon, about twenty-five miles away. The Athenians resolved to oppose them at once. The weary but dauntless Pheidippides took his long spear and his heavy shield, and marched out with 10,000 men picked to meet the foe.

You can read in the history books how the outnumbered Greeks came down from the hills to meet the enemy. The Athenians charged courageously amid awful shouting and dreadful clash of arms. For a while the Persians stood fast, hurling their missiles, but at last the Greeks broke their line. When the day was over, Darius and his army were fleeing to their ships.

The Greek general called on Pheidippides. "Take the news to Athens as fast as you can. Tell them of our victory."

Already exhausted from battle, Pheidippides flung down his shield and began to run as he had never run before. He thought only of his home and his worried people, waiting to know if they were destined to live or die. His heart pounded, his temples throbbed, the muscles in his legs trembled, but not once did he stop. One mile, five miles, ten, twenty, twenty-five miles back to the city. The anxious citizens made way as he staggered to the center and gasped:

"Rejoice! We conquer!"

The Athenians shouted for joy, but Pheidippides sank to the ground. And when the people raised him in their arms, they saw he was dead.

•

HENRY BOX BROWN'S ESCAPE

Henry Box Brown

Of all the stories of breathtaking escapes from slavery, Henry Box Brown's 1848 trip from Richmond to Philadelphia remains one of the most celebrated journeys to freedom on the Underground Railroad. Here are courage and ingenuity born of desperate circumstances.

At length, after praying earnestly to Him, who seeth afar off, for assistance, in my difficulty, suddenly, as if from above, there darted into my mind these words, "Go and get a box, and put yourself in it." I pondered the words over in my mind. "Get a box?" thought I. "What can this mean?" But I was not "disobedient unto the heavenly vision," and I determined to put into practice this direction, as I considered it, from my heavenly Father. I went to the depot, and there noticed the size of the largest boxes, which commonly were sent by the cars, and returned with their dimensions. I then repaired to a carpenter, and induced him to make me a box of such a description as I wished, informing him of the use I intended to make of it. He assured me I could not live in it; but as it was dear liberty I was in pursuit of, I thought it best to make the trial.

When the box was finished, I carried it, and placed it before my friend, who had promised to assist me, who asked me if that was to "put my clothes in." I replied that it was not, but to *"put Henry Brown in!"* He was astonished at my temerity; but I insisted upon his placing me in it, and nailing me up, and he finally consented.

After corresponding with a friend in Philadelphia, arrangements were made for my departure, and I took my place in this narrow prison, with a mind full of uncertainty. . . .

I laid me down in my darkened home of three feet by two, and like one about to be guillotined, resigned myself to my fate. My friend was to accompany me, but he failed to do so; and contented himself with sending a telegraph message to his correspondent in Philadelphia, that such a box was on its way to his care.

I took with me a bladder filled with water to bathe my neck with, in case of too great heat; and with no access to the fresh air, excepting three small gimblet holes, I started on my perilous cruise. I was first carried to the express office, the box being placed on its end, so that I started with my head downwards, although the box was directed, "this side up with care." From the express office, I was carried to the depot, and from thence tumbled roughly into the baggage car, where I *happened* to fall "right side up," but no thanks to my transporters. But after a while the cars stopped, and I was put aboard a steamboat, *and placed on my head.* In this dreadful position, I remained the space of an hour and a half, it seemed to me, when I began to feel of my eyes and head, and found to my dismay, that my eyes were almost swollen out of their sockets, and the veins on my temple seemed ready to burst. I made no noise, however, determining to obtain *"victory or death,"* but endured the terrible pain, as well as I could, sustained under the whole by the thoughts of sweet liberty.

About half an hour afterwards, I attempted again to lift my hands to my face, but I found I was not able to move them. A cold sweat now covered me from head to foot. Death seemed my inevitable fate, and every moment I expected to feel the blood flowing over me, which had burst from my veins. One half hour longer and my sufferings would have ended in that fate, which I preferred to slavery; but I lifted up my heart to God in prayer, believing that he would yet deliver me, when to my joy, I overheard two men say, "We have been here *two* hours and have travelled twenty miles, now let us sit down, and rest ourselves." They suited the action to the word, and turned the box over, containing my soul and body, thus delivering me from the power of the grim messenger of death, who a few moments previously, had aimed his fatal shaft at my head, and had placed his icy hands on my throbbing heart. . . .

Soon after this fortunate event, we arrived at Washington, where I was thrown from the wagon and again as my luck would have it, fell on my head. I was then rolled down a declivity, until I reached the platform from which the cars were to start. During this short but rapid journey, my neck came very near being dislocated, as I felt it crack, as if it had snapped asunder. Pretty soon, I heard someone say, "There is no room for this box, it will have to remain behind." I then again applied to the Lord, my help in all my difficulties, and in a few minutes I heard a gentleman direct the hands to place it aboard, as "it came with the mail and must go on with it." I was then tumbled into the car, my head downwards again, as I seemed to be destined to escape on my head; a sign probably, of the opinion of American people respecting such bold adventurers as myself; that our heads should be held downwards, whenever we attempt to benefit ourselves. Not the only instance of this propensity, on the part of the American people, towards the colored race. We had not proceeded far, however, before more baggage was placed in the car, at a stopping place, and I was again turned to my proper position.

No further difficulty occurred until my arrival at Philadelphia. I reached this place at three o'clock in the morning, and remained in the depot until six o'clock, A.M., at which time, a wagon drove up, and a person inquired for a box directed to such a place, "right side up." I was soon placed on this wagon, and carried to the house of my friend's correspondent, where quite a number of persons were waiting to receive me. They appeared to be some afraid to open the box at first, but at length one of them rapped upon it, and with a trembling voice, asked, "Is all right within?" to which I replied, "All right." The joy of these friends was excessive, and like the ancient Jews, who repaired to the rebuilding of Jerusalem, each one seized hold of some tool, and commenced opening my grave. At length the cover was removed, and I arose, and shook myself from the lethargy into which I had fallen; but exhausted nature proved too much for my frame, and I swooned away.

•

JINKYSWOITMAYA

C. H. Claudy

This story is from *The Youth's Companion,* a Boston magazine
that from 1827 until 1929 provided instructive and entertaining
reading for American children. Here's a great tale about putting
yourself on the line.

A proverb has it that "one man's meat is another man's poison," and true enough it is that what one assimilates with pleasure
another can only take with pain. The "water" was a terror to Jinks
for reasons which will appear anon; but he had resources of courage in other matters, which, for all they called him a coward, proved
him a hero after all.

"It was in the spring of 1897," says Mr. C. H. Claudy, writing in
The Youth's Companion, "while I was employed on botanical and
geological work in Alaska, that I made the acquaintance of 'Jinkys-
woitmaya,' whom we called 'Jinks' for short. He was the son of a
Russian 'claim-jumper' and an Aleut Indian squaw, and he lived in
the little village of Nutchek, Hinchinbrook Island, Prince William
Sound.

"Jinks had had rather an unhappy life, for he was, in the estimation of his companions, a coward; he had an innate fear of water.
Jinks could not be induced to enter a canoe for any purpose whatever, and on that account he was the scorn of the island, for the
Aleuts sport and hunt on the sea as if it were their natural element.
But Jinks is no physical coward, and this is the story of how I found
it out.

"I had been in the village just two days, when we had one of
those terrific rainstorms that occasionally visit the Alaskan coast late
in the spring. For three days and nights it rained in sheets. During
my enforced idleness I made the acquaintance of Jinks, who could
speak a little English, and speedily became fond of me, because I
never snubbed him nor spoke his name with the obnoxious Aleutian adjective which means 'one who is afraid' at the end of it.

"Jinks was then about fifteen years old, but strong and wiry,
and more than ordinarily bright.

"It was on the third day of our acquaintance, I think, that Jinks
told me of the wonderful view from a plateau of a mountain on the

island. He said it could be reached by about five hours' climbing. This view, I thought, must be remarkable indeed, and so it happened that, when Jinks shyly proffered his services as guide, I made ready to go as soon as the rain should cease.

"After waiting a day for the streams to subside and the wet ground to dry, we started. We carried a knapsack of food, a canteen of cold tea, a rifle, a sheath-knife apiece, forty feet of three-eighths rope, a hatchet, and a binocular.

"Tramping for an hour steadily west, we came to the foot of Mount Kenia, a hill some four thousand feet high, halfway up which was the wondrous view. Then our difficulties began. The way lay through dense woods for awhile, the ground getting steeper and steeper.

"Now and then a stone would start from our feet and go bounding down the mountain, smashing into trees, rebounding, going on again, until finally stopped by a tangle of underbrush; or, escaping that, it would go on and on until only the echoes of its crashing descent told that it was still on its way. The heavy rain had made the ground easy to our feet, but occasionally the foothold would prove treacherous, and we would slip down on our faces. Several times we came to banks so steep and slippery it seemed as if we were stalled; but Jinks could climb like a monkey, and would crawl up ahead somehow, fasten the rope to a tree and let it down to me, that I might haul myself bodily up after him. We finally reached the end of our climb, at a point about twenty-five hundred feet above the sea level.

"Here we turned to the right, on a natural road of rock, traversing a sort of miniature cañon.

"At the end of half an hour's walk we found ourselves at a standstill, brought up against a blank rock wall thirty feet in height. Nothing disconcerted, Jinks tied the rope about his waist, kicked off his disreputable footwear, and began to climb the wall. How he did it I don't know, for I found it difficult even with the help of the rope he let down to me.

"Once arrived on top, I soon forgot all my tribulations in the wonderful sight. We were on a narrow plateau, perhaps fifty feet wide—a rift in the mountain, which rose in sheer rock walls on each side of us at a distance of a quarter of a mile. A thin line of trees was ahead of me, and beyond them the ocean. Going through the trees, I found myself on the edge of a precipice, with the Pacific Ocean spread out before me.

"Directly in front the rock sloped away steeply for about forty feet, then took an abrupt dive downward, going sheer to the sea in a perpendicular line, about three thousand feet.

"The Alaskan gulf below looked like a huge panorama. Away off on the horizon I could see, with the aid of my glass, the white sails of a hull-down ship. On each side of me stretched away in limitless perspective the Alaskan continuation of the Rocky Mountains—snow-capped always. I will not attempt to describe the vast and desolate scene over which brooded such a silence, accentuated by the occasional single sad call of a gull.

"For perhaps the half of an hour we looked and said nothing. Jinks appeared quite satisfied with my first involuntary expression of delight at the picture, and I did not insult his perceptions by attempting to explain to him how fine I thought it.

"Then we lunched, and after that I walked a rod or two along the brink of the incline and sat down on a little knoll of grass-covered earth, letting my feet hang over on the rock slope below, and prepared to enjoy the changing lights and shadows of the clouds on the sunlit sea, while Jinks went to sleep reclining against a tree directly behind me.

"Then it happened! As I was sitting there peacefully, my thoughts on anything but the recent rainstorm, the little knoll, its cohesive force loosened by the water it contained, gently detached itself from the rock and slid, with me on it, swiftly down the forty feet of rock slope toward the brink beyond.

"As I went down that terrible slide, my first thought was to jump to safety, my next to spread out and attempt to catch on some projection of rock, and my last a prayer for help. Jinks says I screamed and woke him, but I have no recollection of it. In three or four seconds I had arrived at the edge, convinced that another instant would see me hurtling through the air to the rocks three thousand feet below. On the very edge I stopped, caught on a small uprising bit of rock. I was flat on my back, my arms extended on either side of me and above my head. I was bent in the form of a bow; my body from my waist down was over the brink.

"I did not faint and I was not frightened, which sounds absurd, I know; but it is true. Scientists will tell you that in moments of great and sudden danger, the instinct of self-preservation overcomes mere fear. Be that as it may, I was cool, calm, and much alive to my very slim chance of escape. I could not move. I don't mean that I was held, or that I was paralyzed, but I knew that if I should try to move I must fall over the brink.

"My senses were abnormally keen. I heard the cry of a gull so clearly that I thought it very close, but just then the bird came into my range of vision and I saw it was a long distance away. Jinks's shouting from forty feet above seemed right at my ear—by straining my eyes upward I could see the top of his head—but as he was excited and talked Aleutian, I could not understand him. Turning my eyes the other way and looking toward where my feet should have been, I could see a little strip of sea, the horizon, and the sails of a ship. I remembered I had seen a ship before; I tried to think when, but could not. It bothered my sense of location to see only the sails of a ship when it was between me and the horizon, but then I reflected that its hull was in the zone I could not see.

"I did not think of ways to extricate myself, because in one mental flash I knew my only hope was in Jinks and the rope, and I knew he had left it tied to the tree where he had fastened it for me to climb over the rocky wall at the end of the cañon. A little bit of earth, loosened from above in some way, struck me gently in the face. What if a large amount should come down on me before Jinks could get back with the rope?

"*'But it won't—I'm quite sure it won't—Jinks will be here in a minute now—and then—and then—I'll get out of this mess— the rope——'* and then a horrible thought: *'Suppose the rope is not long enough to reach?'*

"Hope is, in a way, the father of fear, and fear came to me now —with the nearness of relief. I was cold. I didn't tremble; I suppose I was too much afraid that if I did I must fall over the brink. But I was very much frightened by my thought that perhaps the rope would not be long enough to reach me.

"Although it seemed to me that I had been hanging a long time on the edge of the precipice, I realized that I thought so simply from the swiftness and number of my impressions. I tried really to calculate the time, and finally decided I had been there nearly twenty minutes; but that estimate was excessive.

"As the fright in a measure subsided, my body ached in protest against the strained position of the muscles; and then suddenly I forgot pain.

"I heard Jinks. 'Comin' now, misser. Got rope, get up minute now——' finishing off with a long string of Aleutian, which, although incomprehensible, was very comforting. I could not see anything of him, except once in a while the top of his head. It occurred to me, however, that there was really nothing to prevent my turning my head on one side. This I did, very slowly and carefully; and at last, by dint of much straining of eyes, I was able to see Jinks away above me, and in a curiously inverted and distorted perspective, working madly to get the rope untangled.

"In a moment he had finished, and then I had the impatient pleasure of seeing the rope coming slowly down the rock face, twisting and turning, like a thin, long snake. It was curious to watch, because it was all seen out of the corner of my eye—seen as one sees in a dream—shapeless, vague, and yet painfully real.

"Now I heard nothing, felt nothing, neither pain nor fright—saw nothing but this travesty of a snake coming slowly towards me. Slowly crawling, sliding, stopping and coming on down, catching on bits of rock and dropping again, it gradually came nearer. Of course it really came down in a few seconds—just as fast as Jinks could pay it out—but impatience and the abnormally acute state of my nerves made it seem a long time. And then it stopped—just six inches above my hand!

"My arms were stretched to their fullest extent, but the rope did not reach my hands. It did not seem to me to matter much; it must have been that I supposed Jinks had not finished paying out all the rope. Then, after a moment, the rope receded some four or five feet, underwent sundry gyrations, and Jinks disappeared from view. Then the rope descended again, this time with about a foot to spare.

"I held my breath, got a good firm grip with one hand, then with the other; and then, putting my weight on it slowly and timorously, afraid it might give in some way, I began to haul myself up. At last I got my feet on the rock, and the rest was easy. Turning on my face, I could help my arms in their task of hauling by sticking my toes into cracks and on projections, as I had seen Jinks do. Halfway up I had a terrible moment; the rope seemed to give a little, and at the same time I heard a smothered cry from Jinks.

"Now I was but ten feet from the top—now eight—now six— four—three feet—another haul and I was almost there—one foot —safety!

"And then I understood why Jinks was not in sight. He lay at full length on his face, his arms locked round the tree he had used as a pillow earlier in the day, the rope knotted around one ankle. The rope had not been long enough, and Jinks had lengthened it with his own body!

"Anyone who has ever attempted to remain suspended by the arms for more than a few seconds will have some faint idea of what poor Jinks must have suffered on that rack. I weigh one hundred and eighty pounds. The pain he endured without a murmur can be indicated by results. One of his arms was out of joint; that accounted for the sudden give in the rope and the smothered cry. The flesh on the ankle where the rope had been tied was cruelly crushed and bruised.

"Except for seeing him lying there suffering that I might live, I must have fainted away in reaction from the nervous strain. What I did do was perhaps as weak, but I trust excusable. I fell on my face beside Jinks, with one arm round his neck, and burst into sobs. In a moment he was sitting up, his dark face shining with joy, in spite of his pain, that he had saved 'misser' from death.

"I bound up his poor, crushed foot, pulled his arm back into place, and with infinite difficulty helped him home. We arrived just before midnight. We were nursed back to health and strength, and so loud were my praises of Jinks, he soon became the hero of the town. Through the aid of the missionary, I was enabled to make them all understand what a really brave fellow he was, and what an heroic thing he had done in risking his life and enduring pain that another might live.

"Jinks carries a wonderful watch now—and inside the cover is the inscription, 'From a grateful man to a brave one.' "

•

SCYLLA AND CHARYBDIS
Adapted from a retelling
by Edmund Carpenter

From *The Odyssey,* here is the classic rough passage, the kind
where you know there may be losses, where you gather your
courage, lower your head, and push through as best you can.

For ancient mariners there were countless terrors, both real
and imagined, on the rolling seas. But none was more dreaded than
a certain narrow passage of water said to be off the coast of southern Italy. It was a very treacherous strait, for there were two hideous
points, one on either side, that all sailors strived to shun. These
were called Scylla and Charybdis.

The first was a lofty crag, reaching even to the heavens with its
sharp peak. Dark clouds always hovered about its top, and perpetual darkness rested upon its summit. So steep was its face, and so
smooth, that no mortal could clamber up or down, though he might
have twenty hands and feet. Midway up the face of this great cliff
was a cave so high above the water no bowman, however strong,
could reach it with his arrow from a passing ship.

In this cave dwelt Scylla, the hideous monster who gave her
name to the crag itself. She had six long, scaly necks, and upon each
neck was a frightful, barking head. Each of these six heads had three
rows of sharp, greedy teeth, all set closely together. The story was
that Scylla hid herself within the cave, but every so often would
lean far out of the opening. The glaring eyes in her six heads would
scan the waters below. No passing fish or dolphin could escape her
dreadful vigilance, for when she saw one she would reach out and
catch it in her claws, draw it into her cave, and devour it. Seamen
were careful to avoid this crag, for if they allowed their vessel to go
too near, Scylla would suddenly reach down and snatch some poor,
unfortunate sailor from the deck and disappear with him into her
den.

On the other side of the strait was another crag, called
Charybdis. This peak was not so lofty as the other, and on its top
grew a tall, fine fig tree, always covered with leaves and fruit. But at
the foot of the cliff was a great gulf in the rock, down which the

water was sucked with great violence, forming a tremendous whirl-pool. Then suddenly the water would come boiling back out, as powerfully as it had been sucked in, tossing onto the waves the planks of old ships and skeletons of hapless sailors. So fierce were these movements of the water that, if a passing vessel should chance to go too near, it would be either drawn into the vortex and sucked down out of sight, or else it would be tossed about, thrown against the rock, and crushed and all the crew drowned.

It was on the long voyage home, after the Trojan War, that Ulysses and his crew came to this horrible strait where they must pass between Scylla and Charybdis.

When the heroes came within sight and hearing of the place they were filled with fear. The oars fell from their hands, and the blood drained from their faces. The horrid murmur of the fiends cut into their very brains. The towering rocks seemed to threaten them with disaster; the boiling surf hid, they knew, treacherous spots.

Ulysses, seeing the state of his men, went up and down the deck encouraging them and reminding them that they had pulled through greater perils together. He begged that they give him the same trust they had offered before and assured them he would lead them through if only they would exert all the strength and wit they had. In particular he cheered up the pilot who sat at the helm, and told him he must now show more firmness than other men, as he had more responsibility committed to him. Ulysses ordered him to steer away from the whirlpool, as it would surely swallow them all, and set a course by the higher rock.

The crew heard him, and nerved again by their captain's gallant bearing, took to the oars. Ulysses, in his shining armor, stood on the prow of the vessel, two gleaming javelins in his hand, on guard, lest the six-mouthed Scylla should attack them as they swept by her rock.

The whirlpool of Charybdis swirled dark and cavernous before them as the ship entered the strait. The crew saw how horribly the black throat drew into her all the whirling deep, so that even the bone-strewn sands at the bottom of the sea lay bare. Then suddenly she disgorged the troubled waters again, in a great cloud of spray, so that all about her the ocean boiled as in a kettle.

The noise of the thundering waves, the roaring of Charybdis, the barking of the hideous Scylla, the howling of the wind, all these were deafening and terrifying. But, spurred on by Ulysses, the men toiled at the sweeps and as they gradually drew away from the whirlpool, it seemed that all might yet be well.

But it was not to be. From her black den, Scylla suddenly darted out her six long necks, and before Ulysses could strike, she seized half a dozen mariners! Ulysses heard their shrieks, coming from high in the air, and saw them with their heels turned up, and their hands thrown out to him for sweet life. He could do nothing. In all his sufferings he never had beheld a sight so full of miseries.

The remainder of the crew, terror-stricken at the fate of their companions, pulled frantically to get out of danger before the monster could make a second swoop. Angry at missing their prey, Charybdis boomed and Scylla barked. But the vessel shot through the roaring narrows and into the open sea. And the men, weary and heavy of heart, bent over their oars, and longed for rest.

•

THE SPHINX

Adapted from a retelling
by Elsie F. Buckley

Here is a famous Greek tale about that virtue we call fortitude, the firmness of mind that enables a person to face danger with courage and self-control. Here is someone who makes intelligence count in the nick of time.

It happened in times past that the gods, being angry with the inhabitants of Thebes, sent into their land a very troublesome beast called the Sphinx. This beast had the face and breast of a fair woman, but the claws of a lion and wings of an eagle. It lay crouched on top of a rock, halting all travelers who passed by and posing a riddle. Those who answered it could pass safely, but those who failed were killed. And no one had succeeded in solving the riddle.

One day a traveler named Oedipus came to the seven-gated Thebes, where he found all the people in deep distress and mourning because of the terrible monster. He stood in the marketplace and talked with the citizens.

"What is this famous riddle that none can solve?" he asked.

"No one can say," they answered. "For he who would solve the riddle must go up alone to the rock where the monster sits. There it chants the riddle, and if he cannot answer, it tears him from limb to limb. And if none go up to try the riddle, the monster swoops down on the city and carries off its victims. Our wisest and bravest have gone up, and our eyes have seen them no more. Now there is no one left courageous enough to face the terrible beast."

"I will go up and face this monster," Oedipus said. "It must be a tough riddle indeed if I cannot answer it."

"Oh, overbold and rash," they cried, "why do you think you can succeed, when so many have failed?"

"Better to try, and fail, than never to try at all."

"Yet, where failure is death, surely a man should think twice?"

"A man can die but once, and how better than in trying to save his fellows?"

They marveled at his answer, and seeing that nothing would turn him from his purpose, they showed him the path to the Sphinx's rock. All the people went with him to the edge of the city with their prayers and blessings. At the gate they left him, for he who goes up to face the Sphinx must go alone, and none can stand by to help him.

He crossed first a river and then a wide plain, where the mountain of the Sphinx stood dark and clear on the other side. Then he prayed to Pallas Athena, the gray-eyed goddess of wisdom, and she took all fear from his heart.

He went boldly up to the rock, where the monster sat waiting to spring on its prey, and for all his courage his heart beat fast as he looked upon it. For at first it appeared like a mighty bird, with great wings of bronze and gold. The glancing sunbeams played about them, casting a halo of light around, and in the midst of the halo the face shone out pale and beautiful as a star at dawn. But when it saw him coming near, a greedy fire lit up its eyes, and it put out its cruel claws and lashed its tail from side to side like an angry lion.

Nevertheless, Oedipus spoke steadily.

"I have come to hear your famous riddle, and answer it or die."

"Foolhardy manling, a dainty morsel the gods have sent this day, with your fair young face and fresh young limbs."

And it licked its cruel lips.

Then Oedipus felt his blood boil within him, and he wished to slay it then and there.

"Come, tell me your famous riddle, foul Fury that thou art, that I may answer it and rid the land of this curse."

And this is what the monster asked:

"At dawn it creeps on four legs. At noon it strides on two. At sunset and evening it totters on three. What is this thing, never the same, yet not many, but one?"

It chanted slowly, its eyes gleaming cruel and cold.

Oedipus thought within himself.

"Now or never must my learning and wit stand me in good stead, or in vain have I talked with the wisest men and learned the old secrets of Phoenicia and Greece."

The gods who had given him understanding sent light into his heart, and he boldly answered:

"What can this creature be but man, O Sphinx? For, a helpless babe at the dawn of life, he crawls on his hands and feet. At noontime he walks erect in the strength of his youth. And at evening he supports his tottering limbs with a staff, the prop and stay of old age. Have I not guessed the answer to your famous riddle?"

With a loud cry of despair, and answering him never a word, the great beast sprang up from its seat on the rock and hurled itself over the precipice into the yawning gulf below.

Far away across the plain the people heard its cry, and they saw the flash of the sun on its brazen wings like a gleam of lightning in the summer sky. They sent up a great shout of joy to heaven, and poured out from every gate onto the open plain. Some raised Oedipus on their shoulders, and with shouts and songs bore him into the city. Then and there they made him their monarch, for who better to lead them than the slayer of the Sphinx and the savior of the city?

So Oedipus became king of Thebes, and wisely and well did he rule, and for many a long year the land prospered.

A TRUTH SPEAKER

Retold by Grace H. Kupfer

In this tale about the ancient writer Philoxenus (436–380 B.C.), we witness two important intellectual virtues in action: honesty and steadfastness. And we see the kind of courage it sometimes takes to speak the truth to power. In the end, the story speaks well of both Philoxenus and Dionysius.

There ruled in the city of Syracuse, in Sicily, many hundreds of years ago, a tyrant by the name of Dionysius. Not only was he sometimes ruthless in his actions, but he was vain of his own talents. His court was made up of flatterers, who were afraid to speak anything but praise to his face, though they spoke ill of him when there was no danger of being overheard.

Dionysius, among other vanities, considered himself a great poet. On all occasions he wrote verses. And when he had composed them, he would assemble all his courtiers and read the lines aloud. Then they would all lift their hands and exchange glances, as though in admiration of his genius, and exclaim over the beauty of the poetry, until even Dionysius was satisfied.

The most learned man in Syracuse at that time was a philosopher by the name of Philoxenus. Dionysius became so conceited, because of the flattery of all his courtiers, that he made up his mind to summon Philoxenus, so that he, too, might hear the poems and praise the poet.

Philoxenus came. The poems were read to him, and Dionysius eagerly awaited the critic's words of praise and admiration. But none came; for, instead, to the amazement of all, the philosopher, in disdain, said the verses were so bad that they did not deserve the name of poetry, nor did their author deserve the name of poet. Dionysius, almost beside himself with rage at this unexpected frankness, called his guards and ordered Philoxenus to be removed, in chains, to a deep, underground dungeon, where only the worst criminals were sent.

When the news of this action reached the ears of the friends of Philoxenus, they were very angry. As weeks passed, and still their friend was kept a prisoner in that underground dungeon, they became much excited, and at last sent to Dionysius a letter begging for the philosopher's release.

Perhaps Dionysius was afraid of rousing the anger of so many of his subjects, or possibly he had an entirely different reason, as you will presently see. At all events, he agreed to release the philosopher, provided he would come once more to dine with him.

Philoxenus came. After a great feast, at which all the courtiers were present, the king arose and read some new verses he had written. He wanted the truth-speaking Philoxenus to hear them, because he himself thought them uncommonly good. So, too, judging from their gestures and praises, did the fawning courtiers. Philoxenus alone sat silent, saying nothing and betraying nothing by the expression of his face.

This did not in the least suit Dionysius. He controlled his impatience as long as he could; but when Philoxenus continued silent, the king at length turned to him, and thinking he would not again dare to rouse his monarch's anger, said, "Tell me, Philoxenus, your opinion of this latest poem of mine."

You may be sure neither he nor his court expected the answer that was given. For, turning his back on the feast and the feasters, Philoxenus approached the guards of the banquet hall, and exclaimed, in a tone of disgust, "Take me back to my dungeon!" Nothing could more plainly have shown his opinion of the king's bad verses. He knew that by expressing his view honestly he would incur certain punishment; so he chose the simpler method of going back to prison of his own free will.

The courtiers were very much startled at this plain speaking, and looked in terror to see what Dionysius would do. But even this king, vain as he was, seems to have had a sense of humor, and a respect for real moral courage. For, turning with a smile from his trembling courtiers to the calm and untroubled Philoxenus, he bade him depart in peace.

•

THE SCULPTOR AND THE SISTINE CHAPEL

The question is not whether you will suffer disappointment in life
—everyone does—but what it stirs inside you. As George Eliot
wrote, everything depends not on the mere fact of disappointment, but on the nature affected.

One winter morning in 1494, young Michelangelo Buonarroti
looked sadly out his window at a brilliant, white Florence. A heavy
snow had fallen all night on the town. It lay now on the streets and
plazas, churches and palaces, even the towers and spires—it had
turned the whole place into a marble city. But that beauty only
made Michelangelo forlorn. It reminded him that his friend and
patron, the great Duke Lorenzo de' Medici, was gone forever. It was
Lorenzo who had recognized the young sculptor's brilliance, who
had taken him into his palace, and given him block after block of
marble to carve.

But now the great Duke was dead, and in his place ruled his
son, Piero. Piero was proud and foolish, and had no use for artists
and their statues. Horses and games and feasts amused him; he
bestowed more honor on his stableboy, because he could outrun a
horse at full gallop, than he did on a mere sculptor. And so Michelangelo sat at his window, gazing down on the snow with his deep-
set eyes, thinking of how it, too, would melt away to nothing, like
his own talents and dreams.

He was shaken from his gloominess by a sudden knocking
below. He leaned out the window. One of Piero's impudent messengers was beating on his door.

The page, looking up, caught sight of the boy.

"Come down, Michelangelo! This is your day. Piero has summoned his famous young sculptor. He wants you to carve a statue
for him, at last!"

Michelangelo caught his breath. Had he heard right?

"What are you waiting for?" the messenger called. "Hurry up!
His Magnificence won't wait forever, you know."

"Do you mean it?" Michelangelo asked. "Piero has never called
me to the palace before."

"He is now, my young friend. He has much marble for you to work your magic with. Hurry!"

Michelangelo threw on a cloak and scurried down the stairs to the street. Silently he trudged at the messenger's side, but his heart leapt with every step.

"This is the day you've been waiting for, is it not?" his haughty companion laughed as they crossed the snow-covered plaza. "To sculpt again for the great Medici family—what could be more wonderful?"

A moment later they were in the palace. In an upper chamber they found Piero, surrounded by a crowd of his friends, standing at a long window that looked down on the gardens.

"He's here!" Piero shouted. "You probably thought we would never call upon you, young maestro. But today we have need for your talent. You do have great talent, do you not, my friend?"

Michelangelo clenched his fists. He met Piero's eyes.

"So your father used to think," he answered quietly.

Piero flushed, then turned to the window.

"You will go down to the gardens," he announced. "There you will find all the white marble your heart desires, lying heaped upon the ground. I am giving a dinner tonight, and I want my guests to be able to see one of your brilliant statues. Of course, tomorrow morning the sun will do away with all your hard labor. But nothing lasts forever, does it, young maestro?"

Michelangelo staggered back. He could not believe his ears. He, Michelangelo, the pride of Florence—must build a statue of snow!

A surge of anger welled up inside of him. It seemed to squeeze his chest, grip his breath, strangle his throat. He glared at the grinning expressions of Piero and his friends and wanted more than anything to strike out at them, to smash them, and make them feel his fury. But he knew he dared not. He felt a deep shame and longed to run and hide and never have to been seen by these arrogant fools again.

But something inside of him made him stand where he was. Michelangelo was young, and this was a cruel moment for a boy to face. But he was also confident. He knew he possessed a rare and wonderful talent, and that nothing could stand in its way. The waves of rage and humiliation passed over him, and he found an answer.

"I will do your bidding, O great Medici," he said quietly, and left them standing there.

A moment later he was in the gardens, relieved to be alone, his eyes fixed on the white, flawless blanket at his feet.

"I will show them what I can do," he muttered. "Even in snow, I will show them what I can do."

He began to work quickly. He stooped and gathered the snow, pushed it into a mound, packed it tight, and stooped for more. Hour after hour he gathered snow, building it into the kind of huge, hard block that always set his thoughts on fire.

Then he began to carve. He sculpted with all of his skill and power. A head emerged, then limbs, and hands and feet. The icy mass was coming to life. A huge figure was being born in the garden, full of vigor and strength. Every once in a while Michelangelo would stand back and look at his work. It needed more snow packed here, some scraped away there. The lips weren't quite right —they must be shaped again. Michelangelo labored in peace, mindless of everything except his art.

And at last the enormous man of snow was done.

It was finished, and it was good. It would be gone tomorrow. The sun would see to that. But for a few brief hours, it would make Florence a more beautiful and noble place.

A gasp brought Michelangelo back to the world of his troubles. He turned and found Piero standing behind him.

The Duke was gazing at the figure of snow. The proud sneer had melted away from the nobleman's mouth. A gleam of wonder showed in his eyes, and then a shadow of sorrow.

"Snow—not snow!" he murmured. "Something this beautiful should never pass away."

And so it was that Michelangelo proved his mettle. And with his chisel he proved his mastery over stone. The years passed. He won for himself all of Italy's praise. He was called to Rome, to carve statues for Pope Julius II. Full of excitement, he traveled to the famous marble quarries at Carrara to select gigantic blocks. He was overwhelmed by the sight of the great rocks; in every one he saw some figure waiting to be released from its slumber. He spent six happy months examining, choosing, buying, rejecting, his mind full of the images to come.

But when he finally got back to Rome with his marbles, he found the Pope had changed his mind. Julius led him into the Sistine Chapel, a huge, narrow box of a room with high walls and a huge, curved ceiling.

"I want it decorated," he said, pointing overhead. "I want you to paint it."

Michelangelo blanched.

"But I am a sculptor!" he protested. "I'm no painter."

"Did you not learn to mix colors in the studio of the master Ghirlandaio? You have only to remember the lessons he taught you."

"But I haven't painted in years! Get Raphael to do it. He is skillful with the brush."

"Nonsense. Raphael is busy. Besides, I have seen many of your drawings. No one can equal them."

Michelangelo looked up at the high ceiling. All of it—ten thousand square feet—would have to be filled with pictures. It would take months. He thought of his beautiful marbles and how they would lie useless while he wasted his time here. He shuddered.

This is not what I want to do! he thought. He choked back his rage and disappointment.

It is not easy to say no to a Pope, especially an insistent one. Michelangelo finally consented, but with a heavy heart.

Up the ladders, into the scaffolding went Michelangelo, to lie on his back and paint overhead. It was torturous work. The colors dripped onto his face and burned his eyes, and made him hate the job all the more.

"I'm a sculptor, not a painter!" he muttered.

It was many years since he had done any painting. He feared he could not do the work. He asked other artists to help him, but he found they were more a hindrance than a help. He sent them away and erased what they had done.

He worked alone, seeing nobody but his color-grinder and the Pope. If it had to be done, it would be done right, he told himself. In silence and solitude, he lay there painting.

Then, to his horror, the surfaces he had finished began to mold.

"I told your Holiness I was not painter!" he cried. "All I have done is destroyed." But it was soon found that he had made the plaster too wet, and no harm would result.

He kept going. He began his days at dawn. He did not stop until he could no longer see to paint. Many nights he did not leave the chapel at all. He lay on his back, and painted. He grew so used to his cramped position that whenever he received a letter during that period, he had to hold it over his head and bend backward to read it. He hardly took time for his meals, often contenting himself with a crust of bread. He became ill from exhaustion. But he kept going.

Sometimes the impatient Pope would climb the scaffolding and watch the work.

"When will you make an end?" was his constant cry.

"When I am done," answered the artist.

And gradually there emerged across the ceiling some of the most perfect and dignified scenes ever created by human hand: God the Father, separating light from dark; the creation of Adam and Eve; the fall of man; the great flood. They came one after another from the tips of Michelangelo's brushes, more than three hundred figures, every one sublime, every one possessing the same power and grandeur of the master's sculptures.

After four long years of enormous fatigue and sad isolation, the immense task was finished. The scaffolding was taken down, and the doors of the Sistine Chapel were thrown open. Great crowds came to look up and stand amazed. When Raphael came to see the work—the same Raphael that Michelangelo had begged the Pope to employ instead of himself—he thanked God that he had been born in the same century as Michelangelo.

The crowds still come to see the Sistine Chapel ceiling, to wonder at the physical performance of one man covering such a vast space alone, and the artistic achievement of bringing so many grand visions to life. They stand and gape at the power of a single man's determination and genius. If you go to Rome, you can join them and gaze up at one of the world's magnificent paintings, set forth by the hand of a sculptor.

•

THE MAN WHO MOVED THE EARTH

The Polish astronomer Nicolaus Copernicus (1473–1543) was not the first to assert that the earth moves, but he was the first to prove it. Here is the kind of courage willing to risk the scorn of public opinion for the sake of the truth, and the kind of perseverance willing to tackle a worthwhile job even if it takes a lifetime of lonely work.

It began with mathematics. At age twenty-one, Nicolaus Copernicus was dazzling the learned men of the university at Cracow with his extraordinary abilities. In fact, the college had grown a bit boastful of its star student, and whenever visiting dignitaries arrived, young Copernicus was given chalk and blackboard and put through the paces. He could work out problems involving a dozen figures and many fractions with a directness and precision that made him a wonder in that part of the world.

A college professor traveling through Poland invited the young genius to come to Italy with him and teach mathematics. Copernicus accepted and traveled to Bologna. There he heard a series of lectures on astronomy—lectures that changed not only his life but how men regarded their universe. For as Copernicus listened, his heart beat fast. At once he perceived how mathematics could be made valuable in calculating the movements of the stars.

For fourteen centuries, the best astronomers had based all of their science on the great book *The Almagest,* written by Ptolemy. It taught that the earth was the center of the universe, and that the sun and stars moved around it. To this theory, priests and astrologers gradually added their own explanations of the heavens. Most assumed that the earth was flat and had four corners. The stars were jewels hung in the sky and were moved about by angels. An angel looked after each star as well as all persons who were born under that star's influence, or else appointed some other angel for the purpose. Every person had a guardian angel to protect him from the evil spirits that occasionally broke out of Hell and came up to earth to tempt men.

In talking to astronomers, Copernicus perceived that very seldom did they know anything of mathematics. This ignorance on their part caused him to doubt them entirely. He sat up all night in the belfry of the cathedral and watched the stars. They moved steadily, surely, and without caprice. It was all natural, and could be reduced, Copernicus thought, to a mathematical system.

And so he began to study the matter. As he wondered and pondered, the truth began to dawn on him: The universe does not revolve around the earth. Indeed, the earth is a globe *revolving around the sun.* Like the other planets, it too is a heavenly body.

He began to teach what he was learning. In his lectures he made various references to Columbus's recent voyage, mentioning the obvious fact that in sailing westward he did not fall over the edge of the world into Hell itself, as it had been prophesied he would. He also explained that the red sky at sunset was not caused by reflections from Hell, nor was the sun moved behind a mountain by giant angels at night. He pointed out that to a man on a boat, the shores seemed to be moving past; could not the seeming movements of the stars likewise be caused by the moving of the earth?

Then, one day, a cardinal came from the Vatican to visit the young mathematician. In all kindness he cautioned him, and in love explained to him it was all right for a man to believe what he wished, but to teach others things that were not authorized was a mistake.

Copernicus was abashed. He was a deeply religious man. He only wanted to help men find the truth and understand the laws of God. He had thought his new ideas would add to the knowledge of Creation, and the beauty of the Church as well. It crushed him now to hear the rumors circulating—that he was trying to "dethrone God by a tape measure and a yardstick." Certain priests publicly denounced him. They declared he was guilty of heresy and accused him of stating things he could not prove. "You would have us believe the earth wobbles around the sun, like a moth around a lamp!" they sneered. "Outrageous!"

And so Copernicus packed his bags and went back to Poland. There he became a canon of the cathedral in the sleepy town of Frauenburg. And there he was a watched man. He lived in practical isolation and exile, for the Church had forbidden him to speak publicly on unauthorized themes. The universities and prominent churchmen were ordered to leave Copernicus and his theories alone.

Yet the humdrum duties of a country clergyman did not still his longing to know and understand the truth. He visited the sick, closed the eyes of the dying, kept his parish register. But his heart was in mathematics. In the back of the old church register he recorded long rows of figures as he worked at some astronomical problem. In the upper floor of the barn, in back of his old, dilapidated farmhouse, he cut holes in the roof to watch the stars. They came out for him nightly and moved in majesty across the sky. "They do me great honor," he said. "I am forbidden to converse with great men, but God has ordered for me a procession."

While the whole town slept, he watched the heavens and made minute records of his observations. He digested all that had been written on the subject of astronomy. Slowly and patiently he tested every hypothesis with his rude and improvised instruments. "Surely God will not damn me for wanting to know the truth about His glorious works," he used to say. "To look at the sky, and behold the wondrous works of God, must make a man bow his head and heart in silence. I have thought, and studied, and worked for years, and I know so little—all I can do is to adore when I behold this unfailing regularity, this miraculous balance and perfection of adaptation. The majesty of it all humbles me into the dust."

The exile in Frauenburg gave him leisure to pursue his theories in quiet. "God has set me apart," he wrote, "that I may study and make plain His works." But still that he could not make his discoveries known was a constant, bitter disappointment to him.

The simple, hard-working gardeners with whom he lived had a reverent awe for the great man. They guessed his worth, but still had suspicions of his sanity. They took his nightly vigils for a sort of religious ecstasy, and a wholesome fear made them quite unwilling to disturb him. So passed the days, and from a lighthearted, ambitious man, Copernicus had grown old and bowed, and nearly blind from continuously watching the stars at night.

But his work, *On the Revolutions,* was at last complete. For forty years he had worked at it, and for twenty-seven years, he himself said, not a day or night had passed without his having added something to it.

He felt that he had in this book told the truth. If men wanted to know the facts about the heavens they would find them here. He had built a science of astronomy he knew would stand secure.

But what should he do with all this mass of truth he had discovered? It was in his own brain, and it was in the hundreds and hundreds of pages of this book, which he had rewritten five times. In a few years at most his brain would be stilled in death. In five minutes, ignorance and malice might reduce the book to ashes and a lifetime of labor go for naught.

To send the book to Rome and ask for permission to publish it was out of the question. Too many people there would object. The request would be refused. The manuscript might even be destroyed.

To publish it at home without the consent of the Bishop would be equally dangerous. For in this volume, all that the priests taught of astronomy had been contradicted and refuted.

Copernicus waited, and worried, and pondered.

At last, at the urging of friends, he decided to send the manuscript to the city of Nuremberg to be printed. Hoping to free himself from accusations of heresy, he dedicated his work to Pope Paul III, who was a scholar and himself a lover of astronomy. "I am fully aware, Holy Father," he wrote, "that as soon as they hear that in these volumes of mine about the revolutions of the spheres of the universe I attribute some sort of motion to the Earth, some persons will immediately raise a cry of condemnation against me. . . . It will be a simple matter for you by your authority and your judgment to suppress attacks by slanderous tongues, although—as the proverb has it—there is no cure for the bite of a false accuser."

How would the world receive the book? Copernicus could only guess and wait.

The months went by, and fear, anxiety, and suspense had their sway. He was stricken with fever. In his delirium he called out, "The book—tell me—they surely have not burned it—you know I wrote no word but truth!"

On May 24, 1543, a messenger arrived from Nuremberg. He carried a copy of the printed book. He was admitted to the sick-room, where he placed the volume in the hands of the stricken man. It is said that a gleam of sanity came to Copernicus. He smiled and, taking the book, gazed upon it, stroked its cover as though caressing it, opened it, and turned the leaves. Then closing the volume and holding it to his heart, he closed his eyes, and sank to sleep, to wake no more.

•

GALILEO AND THE LEANING TOWER

Sometimes the most valuable kind of intellectual virtue is the courage to dispute "what everybody knows." It does not mean simply being disagreeable, or arguing just for the sake of being different. This kind of virtue is rooted in deep study, careful reflection, and a willingness to prove a claim, as we see in this famous story about the Italian astronomer, physicist, and mathematician Galileo (1564–1642).

In Italy some four hundred years ago there lived a young man named Galileo Galilei. He possessed an intensely inquiring spirit—that is to say, he was the kind of man who makes a point of seeing whatever he looks at, thinking about it afterward, and asking the question: "Why?" He started out as a student of medicine, but soon gave up that plan to spend time on what he really loved—physics and mathematics. He turned his whole mind to the pursuit, and by the time he was twenty-six years old, he became a professor of mathematics at the University of Pisa.

In those times, most people accepted without question the theories and statements inherited from the great thinkers of past ages. It did not enter their minds to test the truth of these statements for themselves. They regarded Aristotle, the ancient Greek philosopher, as the greatest of all authorities. "The master hath said it" was the motto in Galileo's day. Scholars committed Aristotle's doctrines to memory; doubting them was considered an act of blasphemy, if not a crime. Students were actually fined for disagreeing with the opinions of the ancients.

Now, one of the statements of Aristotle was this: The speed at which an object falls to earth depends upon its weight. A ten-pound weight, for example, will fall ten times faster than a one-pound weight.

But Galileo had noticed different objects falling to the ground, and he thought differently. He made a few experiments, and satisfied himself.

"Aristotle was wrong," he announced. "Weight has nothing to do with how fast objects fall. It is the resistance of air which affects the rate of the descent. As long as two objects can overcome the resistance of the air to the same extent, they will reach the ground at the same time, no matter how much they weigh. A heavy stone and a light stone will fall at exactly the same rate of speed."

The other professors at the university were shocked and angry. They declared that of course Aristotle had been right and that Galileo was making a fool of himself. He should be quiet and stop bothering them with his silly notions, if he wanted to keep his job.

"All right," said Galileo. "We'll have a little test—my theory against Aristotle's. If I'm wrong, I'll be quiet. Meet me at the tower."

The bell tower in Pisa is known the world over, of course, as the Leaning Tower, because it stands at an angle and looks as though it might topple to the ground at any time. Construction of the tower had begun in 1174; by the time the builders reached the third story, one side was sinking into the soft ground. They tried to compensate by making the remaining floors taller on the leaning side, but the settling continued. When it was finished, the 179-foot tower leaned so much that any object dropped from the top story on the lower side would land some fifteen or twenty feet from the building's base.

Up climbed Galileo. A crowd of scholars, students, and interested townspeople gathered on the lawn below. With every step, he could hear their snickers and jeers.

At the top, on the uppermost gallery, he placed two iron balls. One weighed ten pounds. The other weighed just one. And the question to be answered was this: When Galileo pushed them off, at exactly the same instant, would the heavier ball hit the ground first, as Aristotle had maintained, or . . . ?

Balancing the weights carefully on the balcony, Galileo rolled them over together.

From far below, the breathless crowd saw the two balls plunge over the edge. They came hurtling straight down. They fell at first side by side, then—side by side—and then finally—

There was a tremendous thud. One single thud. They had struck the ground together.

Galileo was right and Aristotle wrong.

Even then, some who had seen would not believe their own eyes. It is very difficult to let go of old ideas, especially ones that have persisted for centuries. Some of the professors made all sorts of excuses and continued to insist that Aristotle was correct. After all, if they were to admit that Galileo was right, how many more of the great Aristotle's principles might also be wrong? It was better, they thought, to silence this troublemaker. They booed and hissed Galileo at his lectures, and made his life as miserable as they could.

But Galileo was not one to be browbeaten. He said goodbye to Pisa, and took a job teaching at the University of Padua, where thoughts were given a bit more freedom. There he went on searching, questioning, and discovering, and showing the world what can be done when someone dares to think for himself.

•

On His Blindness

John Milton

In 1652, one of the world's greatest poets went blind. Yet during the next several years of his life, John Milton composed in his head and gradually dictated to his daughters, friends, and assistants his epic *Paradise Lost*, perhaps the most profound poem ever written in the English language. The sonnet below, one of Milton's most popular pieces, gives some hint of the patience and faith that turned years of affliction into a time of extraordinary creation.

When I consider how my light is spent,
　Ere half my days in this dark world and wide,
　And that one talent which is death to hide
　Lodged with me useless, though my soul more bent
To serve therewith my Maker, and present
　My true account, lest he returning chide,
　"Doth God exact day-labor, light denied?"
　I fondly ask. But Patience, to prevent
That murmur, soon replies, "God doth not need
　Either man's work or his own gifts; who best
　Bear his mild yoke, they serve him best. His state
Is kingly: thousands at his bidding speed,
　And post o'er land and ocean without rest;
　They also serve who only stand and wait."

•

Beethoven's Triumph

Ludwig van Beethoven (1770–1827) is one of the most beloved composers of all times, not just because of the glory of his music, but also because of the courage he brought to his life and his art.

As a child, Ludwig van Beethoven could play the piano better than most adults. He gave his first public concert when he was only seven years old; at age eleven, he worked as an organist at the Court of Cologne; at twelve he published his first significant composition. Four years later he visited Vienna and played for the great Mozart, who afterward left the room saying: "Watch that boy! Someday he will make the world talk about him."

Ludwig's father, who was a singer at Court, had visions of making piles of gold by charging people to hear his "wonder child." It seems he thought more about the money—and the drink it could buy—than he did about Ludwig's happiness. He used to reel into the house in the early hours of the morning, haul the sleepy boy from bed to piano, and conduct forced lessons until dawn, never sparing a few knocks and blows when the exhausted child missed a note.

It is a wonder that his father's harshness did not make Ludwig hate all music. Perhaps it was his gentle mother who helped him keep his courage through those troubling times. But when Ludwig was seventeen, his mother died. His father at once sold her clothes so he could buy more drink.

Ludwig felt the loss deeply. Now there was no one to take care of his two younger brothers. Taking matters into his own hands, he asked the prince to pay him half his father's salary so he could support his brothers. His request was granted, his father's career at the Court came to an end, and Ludwig became the head of the family. For the rest of his life he looked after his brothers, even though they often got into trouble and caused him more than enough anguish.

In 1792, when he was not quite twenty-two years old, Ludwig moved to Vienna to study under Joseph Haydn, the most famous living composer. Those years in Vienna were filled with hard work. He learned to play many instruments. He studied the horn, viola, violin, and clarinet, so he would better know how to write music for the orchestra. He labored over his scores, writing, correcting, revising, rejecting, and starting over again.

Gradually, the word of his genius spread. The citizens of Vienna were a music-loving people. Whenever they could, they flocked to hear Beethoven play. He gave a series of concerts in 1795, one of them for the benefit of Mozart's widow and children. From then on, his success seemed assured. For the next several years he wrote, and traveled, and performed, and made himself into a truly great musician.

Then, sometime before he was twenty-eight years old, he began to notice a humming in his ears. At first he tried to ignore it, but it only grew worse and worse. Finally, reluctantly, he consulted doctors. Their diagnosis was worse than a sentence of death: Beethoven was going deaf.

For a long time he could not bear to tell anyone. He shunned all company. "I confess I am living a wretched life," he wrote to a friend. "For two years I have avoided almost all social gatherings because it is impossible for me to say to people: 'I am deaf.' If I belonged to another profession, it would be easier. . . ."

He found refuge in the country, where he could take long walks alone through the woods. "My deafness troubles me less here than elsewhere," he wrote. "Every tree seems to speak to me of God."

Convinced he was going to die, Beethoven confessed his shame and despair in a testament he meant to leave behind for his brothers. "I could not bring myself to say to people, 'Speak louder, shout, for I am deaf,'" he wrote. "How should I bring myself to admit the weakness of a sense which ought to be more perfect in me than in others, a sense which I once possessed in the greatest perfection? . . . I must live like an exile. If I venture into company a burning dread falls on me, the dreadful risk of letting my condition be perceived. . . . What humiliation when someone stood by me and heard a flute in the distance, and *I* heard *nothing,* or when someone heard the herdboy singing, and I again heard nothing. Such occurrences brought me near to despair, a little more and I had put an end to my own life. . . ."

And yet Beethoven did something much more courageous than give up. He gave himself to his art. He went on writing music, even though what he wrote grew fainter and fainter in his own ears. As his hearing faded, his music began to take on a quality much different from the elegant compositions written by earlier composers. Many of Beethoven's works grew stormy and emotional and thrilling—much like his own courageous and turbulent life. Strange and wonderful to say, he wrote much of his best music, the music we remember him for, after he lost his ability to hear.

Eventually Beethoven went completely deaf. He was lonely and often unhappy, and yet he managed to compose uplifting music. His last symphony, the Ninth, concludes with the famous Ode to Joy. When the work was complete, Beethoven agreed to conduct an orchestra and choir in a concert in Vienna.

The hall was packed. Beethoven took his place in the center of the orchestra, with his back to the audience, and at a signal from him the music began. The magnificent strains entranced the audience. Yet Beethoven himself heard nothing. He followed the score only in his mind. The musicians had been directed to watch him, but to pay not a bit of attention to his beating of the time.

When it was over, the great master lowered his arms. He stood amid the silence, fumbling with his score. One of the singers tugged at his sleeve and motioned for him to look. Beethoven turned around.

He saw people on their feet, clapping their hands, waving their hats, throwing their arms into the air. The deaf musician bowed, and every eye in the audience held a tear.

The final years of this great soul's life were sad. During his last illness he found great comfort in reading music. A friend sent him some of Haydn's compositions, and he passed many pleasant hours gazing over the notes. He found much comfort, too, in Schubert's Songs. He died in 1827, and it is said that among his final words were these: "I shall hear in heaven."

•

THOMAS CARLYLE AND *THE FRENCH REVOLUTION*

Here is an extraordinary story of equanimity and determination in the midst of disaster. We all may not be able to maintain this kind of composure, but Carlyle's perseverance is a virtue we can all attain.

In the early part of 1835, Thomas Carlyle finally finished work on the first volume of his famous *French Revolution*. Writing it had been a terrific struggle. For almost two years he had read histories and made notes in preparation for the task, and then he had spent months painstakingly writing and revising his manuscript. It was a sleepless, exhilarating time for him. By the time the first volume was complete, his nerves were strained and his bank account almost empty. Yet he had confidence in his work—he thought it was going to be "a tolerable enough book."

He was delighted when his good friend the philosopher John

Stuart Mill offered to read the manuscript. Mill himself was a student of the Revolution and had long given his friend encouragement about the project. Carlyle tied the pages up in a neat bundle and handed it to him, hoping Mill could make some helpful suggestions.

One night, when Carlyle and his wife Jane were sitting before the fireplace, there came a knock at the door. Mill staggered in and collapsed in a chair. His hands trembled. His face was ashen.

"Why, Mill," gasped Carlyle, "what ails you, man? What is it?"

It was a moment before Mill could speak.

"It's about your manuscript," he stuttered. "An accident—it was wrapped in newspaper—the housekeeper—thought it was trash—put it into the fire. It's burned. All of it."

It was the only copy.

A deathly silence filled the room. Carlyle gaped at his friend, unable to comprehend the disastrous news. For what seemed an eternity, the three sat motionless, as if the tragedy had drained all life out of them.

Then Carlyle quietly put his hand on his friend's shoulder.

"Don't feel so bad, Mill," he said gently. "I'm sure it wasn't very good. Regardless, good or bad, it's gone now, and feeling guilty will not do a thing to bring it back. Accidents like this happen. Let's think no more about it."

Mrs. Carlyle turned her face away, unable to keep back the tears.

They talked a while longer. Carlyle steered the topic of conversation to other things. At length Mill left, still broken. As he closed the door behind his friend, Carlyle turned to his wife and said: "Well, Mill, poor fellow, is terribly cut up. We must endeavor to hide from him how very serious this business is to us."

And serious it was. Not only was the manuscript gone, so were the notes Carlyle had used to write it—he had thrown them away as he wrote. The book existed only in his memory. And he was down to the last penny of his savings. He did not know whether or not he should simply abandon the project. He went to bed that night full of utmost despair, feeling "something cutting or hard grasping me round the heart."

Yet the next morning he decided he would start over.

"I will not quit the game while the faculty is given me to try playing," he wrote in his journal. "Oh, that I had faith! Oh, that I had! Then were there nothing too hard or heavy for me. Cry silently to thy inmost heart to God for it. Surely He will give it thee. At all events, it is as if my invisible schoolmaster had torn my copybook when I showed it, and said, 'No, boy! Thou must write it better.' What can I, sorrowing, do but obey—obey and think it the best?"

And so he went back to his desk and began the daunting journey again. He wrote through the spring of that year, and into the hot summer, pushing "to be done with that burnt manuscript." By autumn he had succeeded in rewriting what was lost, and turned again to the work's second volume. He wrote on and on, feverishly, stubbornly. When volume two was complete, he plunged into volume three of the "wild, savage book" that "has come out of my own soul, born in blackness, whirl-wind and sorrow."

Almost two years after he had given his original manuscript to Mills, Thomas Carlyle finished his great *French Revolution,* "ready both to weep and pray." The work endures to this day as a classic of literature and a testament to one man's spirit of endurance.

•

THE TITANIC

From The Sun

The name *Titanic* has become synonymous with sea tragedy. It is worth knowing that even in the midst of such awful catastrophe, there were acts of heroism more moving than the disaster itself— such as the self-sacrifice of Mrs. Isador Straus, who sprang out of a lifeboat back onto the deck of the ship to stay behind with her husband. "We have been long together through a great many years," she told him. "We are old now. Where you go, I will go." They went down together. And there were acts of cowardice as well. These newspaper reports from the New York *Sun,* published just after the sinking, remind us that extreme conditions often bring out the best and the worst in the human character.

The 46-thousand-ton liner, the largest vessel that had ever put to sea, struck an iceberg late on the night of April 14–15, 1912. The supposedly unsinkable ship was on its maiden voyage from Southampton to New York. It went down with a loss of more than 1,500 lives.

The *Titanic* had been making good time and everyone aboard was happy in the hope of getting to New York in record time. The ship had worked beautifully. Sunday was calm and clear. There was no moon as the night fell, but it was perfectly clear. The sea was smooth. No icebergs had been sighted during the day or evening, at least none that were in a dangerous distance of the ship.

The *Titanic* was making twenty-two knots an hour as night fell upon the sea. The passengers promenaded the decks in the evening, gathered in the lounging rooms or smoking rooms. There was music in the music room and some singing. They had not begun to retire at 10 o'clock, except for a few women and children. The beautiful night kept many on deck.

There was a watch set forward and in the crow's nest. These men had powerful night glasses. They kept a careful watch on the sea ahead. So far as they could see there was no ice near the ship. But at 11:37 there loomed up directly in the path of the *Titanic* an enormous iceberg. It was of a color almost of the water itself. It could not be perceived one moment, but the next it was seen to be a mountain towering at least 100 feet above the sea and almost the area of a city block.

There was only time for the man in the crow's nest and the watch forward to shout "Ice ahead!" and for the quartermaster to bring his wheel down hard, when the *Titanic* smashed into a big berg. First came a smash on the port side forward, which split the berg and ran the *Titanic* into the berg itself, after which there was a heavy crash to the starboard. The *Titanic* had split off a part of the berg that was above water. Hundreds of tons of ice were in this way precipitated on the forward upper deck. The *Titanic,* it was afterward discovered, had literally climbed up on all of that part of the berg that was under water and below her keel.

Men came out of the smoking room asking: "What the devil was that? Did we hit something?" Women in the various lounging rooms, music room and grill room said: "Mercy! What could that have been?" There was no excitement. The electric lights did not even flicker at this time, and it was more in the perfunctory manner of people who were bored and wanted something to divert themselves that they arose in a leisurely way and walked out on the upper decks to see what it was. They could see stewards walking rapidly about and they stopped them and asked them what was the matter only to get the reply: "I don't know. We may have run into a little bit of ice, perhaps."

It was at 12:25 A.M. that Captain Smith, who had returned to the bridge, transmitted orders through Chief Officer Murdock that all persons should be assembled on the upper deck. Four hundred stewards and kitchen men immediately rushed through the ship, from lower to highest deck, summoning all persons on deck. There was yet no excitement. Women arose leisurely under orders to dress themselves in their warmest clothing. One woman who was rather indignant at being awakened was halfway to the deck when she remembered that she had not locked her trunk. She returned and performed this service and climbed leisurely to the upper deck.

Second Steward Dodd reported to Mr. Murdock, the first officer, fifteen minutes later that every person was on deck. Still there was no panic, no excitement or fear. The electric lights still burned and passengers all massed starboard and port on the upper deck. There was a little feeling of fear that ran through the crowd ten minutes later, however, when Chief Officer Murdock called sharply:

"Crews to the boats! Women and children first!"

At this time, although none yet believed that a tragedy was about to happen, little murmurs of dissent came, particularly from the women. Wives announced that they would not be separated from their husbands; mothers said they would not leave their sons; sisters their brothers. A few threw their arms around their menfolk and that sentiment showed itself among all classes of the ship.

"Come on," was the command from the officers, and there was a pause, no woman wishing to take the first step forward. Another moment's pause and the still more curt command: "Put them in."

The crew of the first boat simply grabbed the first woman they saw, hurled her up in the air, and dropped her into the boat. They turned again and grabbed another. Thereafter that was the general scene on both sides of the upper deck, members of the crew grabbing any woman who might have her arms around the neck of a man and passing her into the boat. In this the men were assisted by husbands, brothers, and sons.

Mrs. John Jacob Astor positively declined to leave her husband and he, with a steward, simply picked her up, carried her over and put her in boat No. 1. Every man, every crew seen that night remembered that during all this ordeal John Jacob Astor was not only cool but did valiant work in assisting the crew in getting the women into the boats.

It was then that the only display of cowardice was made. A

band of men from the steerage made for one of the boats. Murdock brought his revolver up to a level, with a curt declaration: "I'll kill the first man that rushes."

Three men rushed. There were two shots. Two men dropped, one shot through the head, the other with his jaw torn off. There was no use to shoot the third man. Quicker than a bullet could reach him a fist of the husky quartermaster landed on the point of the third man's jaw and he went down like a poleaxed ox. Then the work of filling the boats went on.

The boats swung from the davits after they were filled, one after another. Originally the rules called for six men of the crew and one person in command for each, but as the boats were filled, members of the crew in the boats obtained permission to get out.

"You can get along with four, sir," a steward would say. "I'll get out."

The order to lower the boats came from Captain Smith at 2 o'clock, and they all took the water. Members of the crew aboard each of the sixteen boats and the collapsibles got them away from the sides and rested on their oars fifty feet distant. "Go on!" was the command, and the crew obeying the orders began to pull their oars.

The eyes of all those in the little boats remained fixed on the *Titanic*. They could see that she had sunk about twenty-five feet at the head, raising her enormous stern high out of the water. But not a soul on those small boats thought even then that the great ship could sink. There was no moon, but still the night was clear. The light of the stars and the long rows of lights from the decks and portholes of the *Titanic* enabled them to see the men they had left moving along her deck further aft, but still showing no signs of excitement. Nobody in the small boats thought it possible that they were soon to see the greatest tragedy of the sea.

And then without warning, as the last boat got a mile away from the *Titanic,* the men and women in those small boats saw the bow of the *Titanic* dip down as if it had been pulled by a giant hand, while the last flicker of electric lights disclosed a great gap two-thirds aft. The big ship had split in two.

The forward part simply slipped into the water like a flash and as it swung down under the water there came a series of explosions. The forward boilers had blown up. That part of the boat carried with it hundreds of men in the engine room and stokehole.

The after part of the ship, upon which all the passengers and crew who were on deck had taken refuge, bobbed back from the spot, bent forward, and then a weak cheer came from the horror-stricken people in the boats as the hulk appeared to right itself, stood up on an even keel and floated. But prayers of thankfulness and cheer were changed almost in an instant.

There came from the front of the remaining hulk a great puff of steam as the roar of another great explosion came to them. The huge mass of steel was rent asunder. The fragment of ship suddenly choked up and the whole thing slid down under the water carrying with it the thousand or more men who had remained on it. As she went down her band was heard to play.

Not all of the last-minute actions aboard the Titanic *were heroic, as this further report from* The Sun *shows:*

A man in woman's clothes was among the survivors in lifeboat 10, according to Mrs. Mark Fortune of Winnipeg, who was rescued with her three daughters on that boat. Mrs. Fortune's husband, a Winnipeg real estate broker, and her son, Charles, were lost. Her daughters, Alice, Mabel, and Ethel, unite with her in saying that a man saved his life by his woman's dress, one of the daughters having the seat next to his in the lifeboat.

The lifeboat, said Mrs. Fortune, was greatly overcrowded. Four of the crew were in her and the rest were supposed to be women, with the exception of one stoker and a Chinese man. There was a figure dressed in a brown mackintosh with a shawl like that of a steerage passenger over its head. The face was completely hidden. Miss Alice Fortune sat directly beside the supposed woman.

Soon after the boat had left the ship the four sailors were transferred to another boat and at this time it was discovered that the figure was that of a man. When somebody asked who he was he refused to reply. The stoker and the Chinese man, who were the only men at the oars, demanded that the impostor bear a hand. He said that he did not know how to use an oar and the stoker struck him in the face.

The women then were put to the oars, rowing as best they could in the crowded condition of the boat. As sunrise came they saw the lights of the *Carpathia* in the west. They were the last boatload taken aboard that vessel. The women, in spite of their warm garments, were numb with cold. They were lifted aboard and heard and saw no more of the male impostor.

•

THE CONQUEST OF EVEREST
James Ramsey Ullman

To students of mountaineering such as myself, this story stands for the courage of explorers in all times. You may never have heard of George Herbert Leigh Mallory, but you have probably heard his famous answer when asked why he wanted to climb the world's highest mountain: "Because it is there." No one knows whether or not Mallory and Andrew Irvine became the first human beings to reach the top of Mount Everest in 1924. We only know they are heroes for trying to raise the human achievement to new heights. "Whether a man accepts from Fortune her spade and will look downward and dig," Justice Oliver Wendell Holmes wrote, "or from Aspiration her axe and cord, and will scale the ice, the one and only success which it is his to command is to bring to his work a mighty heart."

Bitterly chagrined at the failure of his first effort, Mallory was determined to have one last fling before the monsoon struck. Everest was *his* mountain, more than any other man's. He had pioneered the way to it and blazed the trail to its heights; his flaming spirit had been the principal driving force behind each assault; the conquest of the summit was the great dream of his life. His companions, watching him now, realized that he was preparing for his mightiest effort.

Mallory moved with characteristic speed. With young Andrew Irvine as partner he started upward from the col the day after Norton and Somervell descended. They spent the first night at Camp V and the second at Camp VI, at 26,800 feet. Unlike Norton and Somervell, they planned to use oxygen on the final dash and to follow the crest of the northeast ridge instead of traversing the north face to the couloir. The ridge appeared to present more formidable climbing difficulties than the lower route, particularly near the base of the summit pyramid where it buckled upward in two great rock towers which the Everesters called the First and Second Steps. Mallory, however, was all for the frontal attack and had frequently expressed the belief that the steps could be surmounted. The last Tigers descending that night from the highest camp to the col brought word that both climbers were in good condition and full of hope for success.

One man only was to have another glimpse of Mallory and Irvine.

On the morning of June eighth—the day set for the assault on the summit—Odell, the geologist, who had spent the night alone at Camp V, set out for VI with a rucksack of food. The day was as mild and windless as any the expedition had experienced, but a thin gray mist clung to the upper reaches of the mountain, and Odell could see little of what lay above him. Presently, however, he scaled the top of a small crag at about twenty-six thousand feet, and, standing there, he stopped and stared. For a moment the mist cleared. The whole summit ridge and final pyramid of Everest were unveiled, and high above him, on the very crest of the ridge, he saw two tiny figures outlined against the sky. They appeared to be at the base of one of the great steps, not more than seven or eight hundred feet below the final pinnacle. As Odell watched, the figures moved slowly upward. Then, as suddenly as it had parted, the mist closed in again, and they were gone.

The feats of endurance that Odell performed during the next forty-eight hours are unsurpassed by those of any mountaineer. That same day he went to Camp VI with his load of provisions, and then even higher, watching and waiting. But the mountaintop remained veiled in mist and there was no sign of the climbers returning. As night came on, he descended all the way to the col, only to start off again the following dawn. Camp V was empty. He spent a solitary night there in subzero cold and the next morning ascended again to Camp VI. It was empty too. With sinking heart he struggled upward for another thousand feet, searching and shouting, to the very limit of human endurance. The only answering sound was the deep moaning of the wind. The great peak above him loomed bleakly in the sky, wrapped in the loneliness and desolation of the ages. All hope was gone. Odell descended to the highest camp and signaled the tidings of tragedy to the watchers far below.

So ended the second attempt on Everest—and, with it, the lives of two brave men. The bodies of George Mallory and Andrew Irvine lie somewhere in the vast wilderness of rock and ice that guards the summit of the world. Where and how death overtook them no one knows. And whether victory came before the end no one knows either. Our last glimpse of them is through Odell's eyes —two tiny specks against the sky, fighting upward.

•

THE MAN WHO BROKE THE
COLOR BARRIER

Hal Butler

Jack Roosevelt Robinson (1919–1972) was playing baseball for
the Kansas City Monarchs in the Negro leagues in 1945 when
he learned that Branch Rickey, general manager of the Brooklyn
Dodgers, wanted to see him. Until that time, no black had ever
played major league baseball, and there seemed to be an unwrit-
ten rule among club owners to keep it that way. But Branch
Rickey was looking for a man to break the barrier.

The question he put to Jackie Robinson was this: "Do you
have the guts not to fight back?" Rickey knew the first black major
league player would suffer horrible abuse. But he also firmly believed that the only way to win public acceptance was for that
man to take every insult and threat and nasty name without showing anger—and play great baseball all the while. His plan was
for Robinson to spend one year with the Dodgers' farm team in
Montreal, then head for the majors. "You'll have to promise me
that for three years you will not answer back," he said. "You
cannot win this by a retaliation. You can't echo a curse with a
curse, a blow with a blow."

It was an incredibly daunting demand, but Jackie Robinson
stepped up to the plate without hesitation. Over the next several
years, he taught the nation that what mattered was not the color
of his skin, but his skill with the bat and ball—and the content of
his character. Here is an astounding story of self-control. Here is
the kind of courage and perseverance it takes to blaze a rough
trail so others can follow.

On October 23, 1945, Branch Rickey officially announced that
the Brooklyn Dodgers had signed Jackie Robinson to a contract and
assigned him to play with the Montreal Royals in the International
League. The unexpected announcement received a mixed reaction.
Some farsighted people were in favor of blacks playing in the
higher echelons of baseball; others were hostile and bitter. Even

those in favor, however, expressed doubt that it would work. The sports editor of the New York *Daily News* put it bluntly: "Robinson will not make the grade in the big league this year or next. He is a 1000-to-1 shot."

It didn't take long for the bigots to react to the appearance of Robinson on a baseball field occupied by white players. The Montreal team held spring training at Daytona Beach, Florida, but they allowed early comers to take drills at a nearby camp in Sanford. Jackie worked out for just two days in Sanford, and then the ax fell. Sanford's prejudiced civic leaders demanded that he get out of town.

The insolent demand infuriated Robinson, but he remembered Branch Rickey's words: *You will have to take everything they dish out and never strike back.* Without a word, he left town.

Two weeks later, another difficult situation arose. The Royals had an exhibition game scheduled with the Jacksonville team. When the team arrived at the Jacksonville park, they found the gate padlocked. The game had been called off because Robinson was on the team!

But it was when the Royals met Indianapolis in a spring training game at De Land, Florida, that Jackie suffered his most embarrassing moment. In the first inning Robinson tried to score from second base on a hit. He had to slide home to make it, stirring up a cloud of dust in the process. As the umpire called him safe, Jackie looked up through the dust to see a white policeman standing over him. The policeman had run onto the field and stood scowling down at him.

"Get off the field right now," he snarled, "or I'm putting you in jail!"

Clay Hopper, the Montreal manager, came bounding from the dugout.

"What's going on?" he demanded.

The policeman looked at him coldly. "We ain't havin' Nigras mix with white boys in this town," he said. "Now you tell that Nigra I said to git!"

Again, without a word, Robinson left.

Despite such unpleasant moments, Jackie Robinson established himself as Montreal's second baseman before spring training ended. Most of his teammates had by this time accepted him and recognized him as a talented ballplayer. But there were a few who would not. Robinson was aware of the resentment these few players had for him, and he knew he would simply have to overcome this dislike by his play on the field. He could do it by becoming the best second baseman Montreal had ever seen. That was his goal, his way of fighting back.

The Montreal Royals opened their season against Jersey City, and some 35,000 people were in the stands at Roosevelt Stadium. Jackie was understandably nervous in his first time at bat, and he grounded weakly to the infield. But on his second trip to the plate he hit a line drive into the left-field seats, and the crowd applauded him as he circled the bases.

His first hit for Montreal had been a home run, and the people in the stands had reacted warmly. Maybe, now that he had left the South, he would gain acceptance after all.

But acceptance did not come easily. Robinson found that rival players were violently hostile. As Branch Rickey had predicted, opposing pitchers threw at him continually, and time after time Jackie hit the dirt, got up, brushed himself off and said nothing. He was constantly insulted from the dugouts by opposing players who called him vile names that were unprintable—but he said nothing. One time in Syracuse a rival player held up a black cat and shouted, "Hey, Robinson! Here's one of your relatives!" Again, Jackie said nothing.

Once, during this trying season, Branch Rickey went to Montreal to talk to Robinson. "As long as you are in baseball," he told Jackie, "you will have to conduct yourself as you are doing now. That is the cross you must bear."

Robinson agreed. He was determined to take it all and fight back only on the diamond with base hits, stolen bases and great fielding plays.

He did this so well that he helped the Montreal Royals win the

International League pennant and the Little World Series in 1946. Jackie was the batting champion, with a .349 average, and was named Rookie of the Year. His performance made him a sure bet to be with the Brooklyn Dodgers the following year.

But when Branch Rickey announced that Robinson would play first base for Brooklyn (Eddie Stanky was a solid fixture at second base), the protests started. Some of the players took the news without complaint, but a dissident group signed a petition announcing that they would not play with a black player. Rickey called the protesting players into his office and told them bluntly that Robinson would play with the Dodgers whether they liked it or not. Some backed down and agreed to play. Others asked to be traded. Rickey obliged a few of them by shipping them to other clubs, but he was not able to rid himself of all of them.

If the 1946 season with Montreal was a bad dream, the 1947 season with the Dodgers turned out to be a nightmare for Robinson. Everything Branch Rickey had predicted would happen to him did—and more. Pitchers threw at him, making him hit the dirt in almost every game to escape injury. Efforts were made to spike him on the bases. Vicious insults flowed from the dugouts of opposing teams.

Even off the field, Robinson experienced troubles. In some cities where the Dodgers played, Robinson was not allowed to stay in the same hotel with the other players; there were restaurants he was forbidden to enter. But Robinson exhibited a courage few men have been called on to show. He took it all, never losing his temper, never striking back, even though many times he was tempted to hit back with his fists. Jackie Robinson was determined to follow to the letter the instructions of the man who had helped him break into the major leagues.

The hostility toward Jackie Robinson reached a high point on May 6, when the St. Louis Cardinals were scheduled to meet the Brooklyn Dodgers for the first time. A group of Cardinal players decided they would go on strike and refuse to play the game because of Robinson's presence. If that succeeded, they intended to mobilize players on other teams and call a general National League strike.

Fortunately, a sports writer on the New York *Herald Tribune* exposed the plot against Robinson before it happened, and Ford Frick, then president of the National League, took immediate and bold action. He sent a stinging ultimatum to the players planning to strike.

"If you do this," it warned, "you will be suspended from the league. You will find that the friends you think you have in the press box will not support you, that you will be the outcasts. I do not care if half the league strikes. All will be suspended. This is the United States of America, and one citizen has as much right to play as any other."

The Cardinal players had no recourse but to cancel the strike. But the insults and taunts continued with renewed vigor. One day, when they had reached new heights of viciousness, Pee Wee Reese, the Dodger shortstop who had been born in Ekron, Kentucky, jogged over from his position to talk to Robinson. He placed his hand gently on Jackie's shoulder as he talked, and a newspaper photographer shot the picture. The photograph appeared in newspapers across the country, and the fact became known that Reese, among all the Dodger players, was the most sympathetic toward Robinson's difficult problem. He saw in Robinson a superb ballplayer, and the color of his face mattered not.

By mid-season there were signs that most of the Dodgers were beginning to accept Robinson on an equal footing. The reason was obvious. Robinson, despite his troubles, was playing spectacular ball, and his play won him the respect that was due him. It required a superman to play good baseball under the tensions that gripped Robinson throughout this critical year, and Jackie proved himself to be a superman. In his first major-league season, he hit .297, batted in 18 runs, collected 12 home runs and stole 29 bases. In the World Series that followed against the New York Yankees, he contributed seven hits in 27 times up for a .259 batting average. And when the season ended, Jackie Robinson was named the National League Rookie of the Year.

•

THE PIONEER FAMILY

Alexis de Tocqueville

In 1831 the French government sent a young aristocrat named Alexis de Tocqueville to the United States to study its prison system. The observant Tocqueville saw much more than jailhouses during his journey; his study of the democratic experiment unfolding in the New World resulted in his classic *Democracy in America*. Less familiar to students of politics is Tocqueville's *A Fortnight In the Wilderness*, also based on his American notebooks, from which the selection below is excerpted. This wonderful portrait of a pioneer family tells us much about the legacy of our American heritage. Goethe once said that you must labor to possess what you have inherited. We must practice that labor today.

The little bell which the pioneer takes care to hang round the necks of his cattle, that he may find them in the dense forest, announces from a great distance the approach to the clearing. Soon you hear the stroke of the axe. As you proceed traces of destruction prove the presence of man. Lopped branches cover the road, trunks half calcined by fire, or maimed by steel, are still standing in the path. You go on, and reach a wood, which seems to have been struck with sudden death. Even in the middle of summer the withered branches look wintry. On nearer examination a deep gash is discovered round the bark of each tree, which, preventing the circulation of sap, quickly kills it. This is generally the planter's first measure. As he cannot in the first year cut down all the trees on his new property, he kills them to prevent their leaves overshadowing the Indian corn which he has sowed under their branches.

Next to this incomplete attempt at a field, the first step of civilization in the wilderness, you come suddenly upon the owner's dwelling. It stands in a plot more carefully cleared than the rest, but in which man still sustains an unequal struggle with nature. Here the trees have been cut down but not uprooted, and they still encumber with their stumps the ground that they formerly shaded. Round these withered remnants, corn, oak saplings, plants, and weeds of every kind spring pell-mell, and grow side by side in the stubborn and half-wild soil. In the centre of this strong and diversified vegetation, stands the planter's log-house. Like the field round it, this rustic dwelling is evidently a new and hasty work. Its length seldom exceeds thirty feet; its width twenty, and height fifteen. The walls as well as the roof are composed of half-hewn trees; the cracks are filled up with moss and mud. As the traveller advances the scene becomes more animated. At the sound of his steps a group of children who had been rolling in the dirt jump up hastily, and fly towards the paternal roof, frightened at the sight of man, while two great half-wild dogs, with ears erect, and lengthened noses, come out of the hut and, growling, cover the retreat of their young masters.

At this moment the pioneer himself appears at his door. He casts a scrutinizing glance on the newcomer, bids his dogs go in, and himself sets immediately the example without exhibiting either uneasiness or curiosity.

On entering the loghouse the European looks around with wonder. In general there is but one window, before which sometimes hangs a muslin curtain; for here, in the absence of necessaries, you often meet with superfluities. On the hearth, made of hardened earth, a fire of resinous wood lights up the interior better than the sun. Over the rustic chimney are hung trophies of war or of the chase; a long rifle, a doeskin and eagles' feathers. On the right hangs a map of the United States, perpetually shaken by the wind which blows through the cracks of the wall. On a rough shelf near it are placed a few odd volumes, among them a Bible, the leaves and binding of which have been spoilt by the devotion of two generations, a Prayer-book, and sometimes one of Milton's poems, or Shakespeare's plays. With their backs to the wall are placed some rude seats, the product of the owner's industry; chests instead of wardrobes, agricultural tools, and specimens of the crop. In the middle of the room is an unsteady table, the legs of which, still covered with leaves, seem to have grown where they stand. Round this table the family assemble for their meals. On it is left an English china teapot, spoons, generally of wood, a few cracked cups, and some newspapers.

The appearance of the master of this dwelling is as remarkable as his abode. His sharp muscles and slender limbs show him at the first glance to be a native of New England; his make indicates that he was not born in the desert. His first years were passed in the heart of an intellectual and cultivated society. Choice impelled him to the toilsome and savage life for which he did not seem intended. But if his physical strength seems unequal to his undertaking, on his features, furrowed by care, is seated an expression of practical intelligence, and of cold and persevering energy. His step is slow and measured, his speech deliberate, and his appearance austere. Habit, and still more, pride, have given to his countenance a stoical rigidity, which was belied by his conduct. The pioneer despises (it is true) all that most violently agitates the hearts of men. His fortune or his life will never hang on the turn of a die, or the smiles of a woman. But to obtain competence he has braved exile, solitude, and the numberless ills of savage life; he has slept on the bare earth, he has exposed himself to the fever of the woods, and the Indian's tomahawk. Many years ago he took the first step. He has never gone back; perhaps twenty years hence he will still be going on without desponding or complaining. Can a man capable of such sacrifices be cold and insensible? Is he not influenced by a passion, not of the heart but of the brain, ardent, persevering, and indomitable?

His whole energies concentrated in the desire to make his fortune, the emigrant at length succeeds in making for himself an entirely independent existence, into which even his domestic affections are absorbed. He may be said to look on his wife and children only as detached parts of himself. Deprived of habitual intercourse with his equals, he has learnt to take pleasure in solitude. When you appear at the door of his lonely dwelling, the pioneer steps forward to meet you. He holds out his hand in compliance with custom, but his countenance expresses neither kindness nor joy. He speaks only to question you, to gratify his intelligence, not his heart; and as soon as he has obtained from you the news that he wanted to hear he relapses into silence. One would take him for a man who, having been all day wearied by applicants and by the noise of the world, has retired home at night to rest. If you question him in turn, he will give you in a clear manner all the information you require. He will even provide for your wants, and will watch over your safety as long as you are under his roof. But, in all that he does there is so much constraint and dryness; you perceive in him such utter indifference as to the result of your undertakings, that your gratitude cools.

Still the settler is hospitable in his own way, but there is nothing genial in his hospitality, because, while he exercises it, he seems to submit to one of the painful necessities of the wilderness. It is to him a duty of his position, not a pleasure. This unknown person is the representative of the race to which belongs the future of the New World; a restless, speculating, adventurous race, that performs coldly feats which are usually the result of passionate enthusiasm; a nation of conquerors, who endure savage life without feeling its peculiar charms, value in civilized life only its material comforts and advantages, and bury themselves in the wilds of America, provided only with an axe and a file of newspapers!

In describing the settler, one cannot forget the partner of his sufferings and perils. Look at the young woman who is sitting on the other side of the fire with her youngest child in her lap, superintending the preparations for supper. Like the emigrant, this woman is in the prime of life; she also recollects an early youth of comfort. The remains of taste are still to be observed in her dress. But time has pressed hardly upon her: in her faded features and attenuated limbs it is easy to see that life has to her been a heavy burden. And, indeed, this fragile creature has already been exposed to incredible suffering. At the very threshold of life she had to tear herself from the tender care of her mother, from the sweet fraternal ties that a young girl can never leave without tears, even when she quits her home to share the luxurious dwelling of a young husband. The wife of the settler, torn at once and forever from the cradle of her childhood, had to exchange the charms of society and of the domestic circle for the solitude of the forest. Her marriage bed was placed on the bare ground of the desert. To devote herself to austere duties, to submit to unknown privations, to enter upon an existence for which she was not fitted; such has been the employment of her best years; such have been the delights of her married life. Destitution, suffering, and lassitude have weakened her delicate frame, but have not dismayed her courage. While deep sadness is painted on her chiselled features, it is easy to descry religious resignation, peace, and a simple, quiet fortitude, enabling her to meet all the ills of life without fearing or defying them.

Round this woman crowd the half-clothed children, glowing with health, careless of the morrow, true children of the wilderness. Their mother turns on them from time to time a mingled look of sadness and of joy. Judging from their strength and her weakness, it would seem as if she had exhausted herself in giving them life, and without regretting the cost. The loghouse consists of a single room, which shelters the whole family at night; it is a little world, an ark of civilization in the midst of a green ocean. A few steps off the everlasting forest extends its shades, and solitude again reigns.

•

THE DEATH OF BECKET
Arthur Penrhyn Stanley

Here is one of the most famous martyrs in history. When Henry II
of England made Thomas Becket the archbishop of Canterbury in
1162, the king fully expected his friend to help him gain strict
control over the English clergy. But Becket, feeling his first duty
was to the church, resolved to defend its rights and privileges,
even at the cost of angering Henry. Relations between the king
and archbishop steadily deteriorated until one day in 1170, when
a bitter Henry uttered some violent words about the archbishop
in front of his followers. Four of his leading knights took the king's
remarks literally. On December 29 they rode toward Canterbury
and tragedy.

For hundreds of years after his death, Becket's tomb was a
destination of religious pilgrimages. The travelers of Chaucer's
Canterbury Tales told their stories en route to the shrine of the
"blisful martir" who considered his cause more vital than his life.

The vespers had already begun, and the monks were singing
the service in the choir, when two boys rushed up the nave, announcing, more by their terrified gestures than by their words, that
the soldiers were bursting into the palace and monastery. Instantly
the service was thrown into the utmost confusion; part remained at
prayer, part fled into the numerous hiding places the vast fabric
affords, and part went down the steps of the choir into the transept
to meet the little band at the door.

The Archbishop continued to stand outside, and said: "Go and
finish the service. So long as you keep in the entrance, I shall not
come in." They fell back a few paces, and he stepped within the
door, but, finding the whole place thronged with people, he paused
on the threshold, and asked, "What is it that these people fear?"
One general answer broke forth, "The armed men in the cloister."
As he turned and said, "I shall go out to them," he heard the clash
of arms behind. The knights had just forced their way into the
cloister, and were now (as would appear from their being thus seen
through the open door) advancing along its southern side.

They were in mail, which covered their faces up to their eyes, and carried their swords drawn. Three had hatchets. Fitzurse, with the ax he had taken from the carpenters, was foremost, shouting as he came, "Here, here, king's men!" Immediately behind him followed Robert Fitzranulph, with three other knights; and a motley group—some their own followers, some from the town—with weapons, though not in armor, brought up the rear.

At this sight, so unwonted in the peaceful cloisters of Canterbury, not probably beheld since the time when the monastery had been sacked by the Danes, the monks within, regardless of all remonstrances, shut the door of the cathedral, and proceeded to barricade it with iron bars. A loud knocking was heard from the band without, who, having vainly endeavored to prevent the entrance of the knights into the cloister, now rushed before them to take refuge in the church. Becket, who had stepped some paces into the cathedral, but was resisting the solicitations of those immediately about him to move up into the choir for safety, darted back, calling aloud as he went, "Away, you cowards! By virtue of your obedience I command you not to shut the door—the church must not be turned into a castle." With his own hands he thrust them away from the door, opened it himself, and catching hold of the excluded monks, dragged them into the building, exclaiming, "Come in, come in—faster, faster!"

The knights, who had been checked for a moment by the sight of the closed door, on seeing it unexpectedly thrown open, rushed into the church. It was, we must remember, about five o'clock in a winter evening; the shades of night were gathering, and were deepened into a still darker gloom within the high and massive walls of the vast cathedral, which was only illuminated here and there by the solitary lamps burning before the altars. The twilight, lengthening from the shortest day a fortnight before, was but just sufficient to reveal the outline of objects.

In the dim twilight they could just discern a group of figures mounting the steps of the eastern staircase. One of the knights called out to them, "Stay." Another, "Where is Thomas Becket, traitor to the king?" No answer was returned. Fitzurse rushed forward, and, stumbling against one of the monks on the lower step, still not able to distinguish clearly in the darkness, exclaimed, "Where is the Archbishop?"

Instantly the answer came: "Reginald, here I am, no traitor, but the archbishop and priest of God. What do you wish?" And from the fourth step, which he had reached in his ascent, with a slight motion of his head—noticed apparently as his peculiar manner in moments of excitement—Becket descended to the transept. Attired, we are told, in his white rochet, with a cloak and hood thrown over his shoulders, he thus suddenly confronted his assailants.

Fitzurse sprang back two or three paces, and Becket, passing by him, took up his station between the central pillar and the massive wall which still forms the southwest corner of what was then the chapel of St. Benedict. Here they gathered around him, with the cry, "Absolve the bishops whom you have excommunicated."

"I cannot do other than I have done," he replied, and turning to Fitzurse, he added, "Reginald, you have received many favors at my hands. Why do you come into my church armed?"

Fitzurse planted the ax against his breast, and returned for answer, "You shall die—I will tear out your heart." Another, perhaps in kindness, struck him between the shoulders with the flat of his sword, exclaiming, "Fly—you are a dead man."

"I am ready to die," replied the primate, "for God and the Church; but I warn you, I curse you in the name of God Almighty, if you do not let my men escape."

The well-known horror which in that age was felt at an act of sacrilege, together with the sight of the crowds who were rushing in from the town through the nave, turned their efforts for the next few moments to carrying him out of the church. Fitzurse threw down the ax, and tried to drag him out by the collar of his long cloak, calling, "Come with us—you are our prisoner."

"I will not fly, you detestable fellow," was Becket's reply, roused to his usual vehemence and wrenching the cloak out of Fitzurse's grasp. The three knights struggled violently to put him on Tracy's shoulders. Becket set his back against the pillar, and resisted with all his might, while Grim, vehemently remonstrating, threw his arms around him to aid his efforts. In the scuffle, Becket fastened upon Tracy, shook him by his coat of mail, and exerting his great strength, flung him down on the pavement. It was hopeless to carry on the attempt to remove him. And in the final struggle which now began, Fitzurse, as before, took the lead. He approached with his drawn sword, and waving it over his head, cried, "Strike, strike!" but merely dashed off his cap. Tracy sprang forward and struck a more decided blow.

The blood from the first blow was trickling down his face in a thin streak; he wiped it with his arm, and when he saw the stain, he said, "Into thy hands, O Lord, I commend my spirit." At the third blow, he sank on his knees—his arms falling, but his hands still joined as if in prayer. With his face turned toward the altar of St. Benedict, he murmured in a low voice, "For the name of Jesus, and the defense of the Church, I am willing to die." Without moving hand or foot, he fell flat on his face as he spoke. In this posture he received a tremendous blow, aimed with such violence that the scalp or crown of the head was severed from the skull.

"Let us go—let us go," said Hugh of Horsea. "The traitor is dead; he will rise no more."

The Life Heroic

I like the man who faces what he must
    With step triumphant and a heart of cheer;
    Who fights the daily battle without fear;
Sees his hopes fail, yet keeps unfaltering trust
That God is God; that somehow, true and just,
    His plans work out for mortals. Not a tear
    Is shed when fortune, which the world holds dear,
Falls from his grasp. Better with love a crust
Than living in dishonor; envies not,
    Nor loses faith in man, but does his best,
Nor ever murmurs at his humbler lot,
    But with a smile and words of hope gives zest
To every toiler. He alone is great
Who by a life heroic conquers fate.

Four

•

EASING THE PATH

" "**A** man's true wealth hereafter, is the good he does in this world to his fellow man," Mohammed told us. "When he dies, people will say, 'What property has he left behind him?' but the angels will ask, 'What good deeds has he sent before him?' "

Virtues are not just about making our own journeys through life smoother and more successful. There is an abundance of literary, philosophical, and theological authority which reminds us that easing others' paths should be an equal—if not more important—concern. This chapter helps us examine the question: What do we owe to other people? These stories illustrate the meaning of words such as compassion, kindness, charity, generosity, beneficence, and sacrifice. We meet people who in one way or another seize opportunities to do good for their fellow travelers.

In Harper Lee's much-loved novel *To Kill a Mockingbird*, Atticus Finch offers his daughter some invaluable advice. "If you can learn a simple trick," he says, "you'll get along a lot better with all kinds of folks. You never really understand a person until you consider things from his point of view . . . until you climb into his skin and walk around in it." Trying to put yourself into another's place, to share for a moment his or her feelings, is often the starting point of compassion. But there's more to true compassion than just emotion. To help someone, you usually have to *do* something, not just *feel* something. Compassion takes the name of action. It means exerting yourself and bestowing some effort for someone else's sake.

Like anything else involving effort, compassion takes practice. We have to work at getting into the habit of standing with others in their distress. Sometimes offering help is a simple matter that does not take us far out of our way—remembering to speak a kind word to someone who is down, or spending an occasional Saturday morning volunteering for a favorite cause. At other times, helping involves some real sacrifice. "A bone to the dog is not charity," Jack London observed. "Charity is the bone shared with the dog, when you are just as hungry as the dog." If we practice taking the many small opportunities to help others, we'll be in shape to act when those times requiring real, hard sacrifice come along.

There is another reason for practicing helpfulness: We need to develop the ability to judge who truly needs aid and who doesn't. Not everyone who asks is really needy or deserving. Furthermore, we have to be able to discern what *kind* of help people need. Easing someone's path does not mean simply providing the path of least resistance. Sometimes the best way to help people is to hold them responsible; accepting no excuses can sometimes be the best kind of aid we can offer. And finally, the reality of life is that if we spend *all* of our time trying to help *everyone,* we will only end up neglecting our responsibilities to ourselves, our families, and to others who depend on us. So like all virtues, compassion must be tempered, and it must be informed by a good measure of reason.

Of all the virtues, when exercised properly with whole heart and discerning mind, compassion may bring the greatest degree of fulfillment. It enriches our lives with a sense of nobleness and purpose, makes us morally awake, and encourages us about life generally. Most people, thinking back over their lives, remember the times they spent giving and helping and loving as the very best moments. But feeling good in the future should not be the prime motivation for doing good. Sincerely helping others brings the real satisfaction. As Jeremy Bentham observed, the way to be comfortable is to make others comfortable; the way to make others comfortable is to appear to love them; the way to appear to love them—is to love them in reality.

THE PRINCESS WHO WANTED TO BE BEAUTIFUL

In the end, there are few things more beautiful than a kind heart.

Once upon a time there was a little Princess who was very unhappy because she was not as pretty to look at as she thought a little Princess should be.

She sat in the garden and was sorrowful and cried a great deal of the time, because she felt quite sure that no one would ever make her a queen.

One day she sat by the wall of the garden with her hands in her lap, and was looking very sad. An old woman, very bent and gray, and carrying a bundle, passed along the road outside and looked over the wall.

"Why do you cry, little Princess?" she asked.

"Because I am not beautiful," the little Princess replied, "and so I shall never be made a queen."

"Why do you not go out into the world and find someone who can make you beautiful?" asked the old woman as she started again on her way. And this seemed like such a new adventure that the little Princess went out through the garden gate and started down the road.

The old woman had disappeared as if the road had taken her into its gray dust, but before the little Princess had gone very far she overtook a boy. He was stumbling along the road as if it were hard for him to find his way. He put out his hand and touched the little Princess' silken sleeve.

"Where are you going?" he asked.

"I am going to find someone who will help to make me beautiful," the little Princess said. "I am not pretty enough to be a queen."

"Wait a while and help me," said the little boy. "I am blind, and I cannot find my way home."

So the little Princess took the blind boy's hand in hers and walked along with him, leading him very gently, until they came to the cottage by the side of the road where he lived.

Then the little Princess went on, hurrying, for she felt that she had lost a great deal of time. But before she had gone very far, she saw a little girl standing by the edge of the woods and crying. When the little girl saw the Princess, she looked up and asked, "Where are you going?"

"I am going to find someone who will help me to be beautiful," the little Princess said. "I am not pretty enough to be a queen."

"Wait awhile and help me," said the little girl. "My mother is ill, and I went to the dairy to fetch her some milk and eggs, but I have no money, and they say that I must pay."

The little Princess pulled from the silk bag at her side a bright gold piece. She had but two of them to buy herself food on her journey, but she gave one to the child. "This is to pay for the milk and eggs," she said. Then the little girl laughed with happiness. Her smile was as bright as the sunshine that came down through the trees and lighted them both.

"Now I must make great haste," thought the little Princess. "It is getting on in the day and I am no more beautiful than when I started." But she had gone only a little way when she came suddenly upon the same old woman, who had spoken to her in the morning.

"Did you do as I bade you?" asked the old woman.

"Yes," said the little Princess. "But I am still ugly to look at," she added, dropping her head.

"Oh no, you are not," said the old woman. "Look!" And she held a little mirror before the face of the Princess.

A strange thing had happened. The little Princess's eyes, in leading the little blind boy, had grown as bright as stars. Her hair was as shining as the gold piece which she had given away.

"Shall I ever be a queen!" asked the Princess.

The old woman took a small gold crown from the bundle she carried and set it upon the little Princess' head.

"You are a queen, my dear!" she said.

•

HOW THE ROBIN'S BREAST
BECAME RED

Retold by Flora Cooke

This Native American tale shows us how someone very small can
be a big help to others.

Long ago in the Far North, where it is very cold, there was only
one fire. A hunter and his little son took care of this fire and kept it
burning day and night. They knew that if the fire went out the
people would freeze and the white bear would have the Northland
all to himself.

One day the hunter became ill and his son had to do all the
work. For many days and nights he bravely took care of his father
and kept the fire burning.

The great white bear was always hiding near, watching the
fire. He longed to put it out, but he did not dare, for he feared
the hunter's arrows. When he saw how tired and sleepy the little
boy was, he came closer to the fire and laughed wickedly to himself.

One night the poor boy grew so tired that he could keep
awake no longer and fell fast asleep. Then the white bear ran as fast
as he could and jumped upon the fire with his wet feet, and rolled
upon it until he thought it was all out. Then he trotted happily away
to his cave among the icebergs.

But a little gray robin had been flying near, and had seen what
the white bear was doing.

She was greatly worried when she thought that the fire might
be out, but she was so little that she could do nothing but wait until
the bear was out of sight.

Then she darted down swiftly and searched with her sharp
little eyes until she found a tiny live coal. This she fanned patiently
with her wings for a long time.

Her little breast was scorched red, but she did not stop until a
fine red flame blazed up from the ashes.

Then she flew away to every hut in the Northland. Wherever
she touched the ground a fire began to burn.

Soon, instead of one little fire, the whole north country was lighted up, so that people far to the south wondered at the beautiful flames of red and yellow light in the northern sky.

But when the white bear saw the fires, he went farther back into his cave among the icebergs and growled terribly. He knew that now there was no hope that he would ever have the Northland all to himself.

This is the reason that the people in the north country love the robin, and never tire of telling their children how its breast became red.

THE STAR JEWELS
Adapted from the Brothers Grimm

This beautiful little story echoes the words we find in the gospel of Matthew in the Bible: "I was hungry and you gave me food. . . . I was naked and you clothed me."

A little girl once lived all alone with her old grandmother upon the borders of a forest. They were so poor that they were scarcely able to buy food to eat or clothes to cover them.

"Never mind, Granny," the little girl would say. "Some day I will be big enough to work, and then I will earn so much that I will be able to buy everything that we need, and to give something to other poor folk as well.

One day the child went off into the forest to gather sticks. These she hoped to sell for a few pennies in the town over beyond the hill. She was to be gone all day, so she took with her into the forest a bit of bread, which was all they had left to eat.

It was winter, and the air was bitterly cold. The child wrapped her little shawl about her, and ran on as fast as she could. She was hungry, but she intended to save her crust until after the sticks were gathered.

Just as she reached the edge of the forest she met a boy, even smaller than she herself, and he was crying bitterly.

The little girl had a tender heart. She stopped and asked the child why he was weeping.

"I am weeping," he answered, "because I am hungry."

"Have you had nothing to eat today?" she asked.

"I have had nothing, and I am starving, for I do not know where to go for food."

The little girl sighed. "You are probably hungrier than I am," she said, and she took the crust from her pocket and gave it to the boy. Then she again hurried on.

A little farther on, she met another child who was even more miserable-looking than the first, for this child seemed almost frozen with cold. Her clothing hung about her in rags, and her skin looked blue through the rents.

"Ah," cried she, "if I had but a warm little dress like yours! Help me, I pray you, or I will certainly die of cold."

The good little girl was filled with pity. "It is not right," thought she, "that I should have both a dress and a shawl. I will give one of them to this poor child."

She took off her dress and gave it to the child, and then wrapped the shawl closely about her shoulders. In spite of the shawl she felt very cold. Still she was near the place where the sticks were to be found, and as soon as she had gathered them she would run home again.

She hastened on, but when she reached the place where the sticks were she saw an old woman already there, gathering up the fallen wood. The old woman was so bent and poor and miserable-looking that the little girl's heart ached for her.

"Oh, oh!" groaned the old woman. "How my poor bones do ache. If I had but a shawl to wrap about my shoulders I would not suffer so."

The child thought of her own grandmother, and of how she sometimes suffered, and she had pity on the old woman.

"Here," said she, "take my shawl," and slipping it from her shoulders, she gave it to the old woman.

And now she stood there in the forest with her arms and shoulders bare, and with nothing on her but her little shift. The sharp wind blew about her, but she was not cold. She had eaten nothing, but she was not hungry. She was fed and warmed by her own kindness.

She gathered her sticks and started home again. It was growing dark and the stars shown through the bare branches of the trees. Suddenly an old man stood beside her. "Give me your sticks," said he, "for my hearth is cold, and I am too old to gather wood for myself."

The little girl sighed. If she gave him the sticks she would have to stop to gather more. Still she would not refuse him. "Take them," she said, "in heaven's name."

No sooner had she said this than she saw it was not an old man who stood before her, but a shining angel.

"You have fed the hungry," said the angel, "you have clothed the naked, and you have given help to those who asked it. You shall not go unrewarded. See!"

At once a light shone around the child, and it seemed to her that all the stars of heaven were falling through the bare branches of the trees, but these stars were diamonds and rubies and other precious stones. They lay thick upon the ground. "Gather them together," said the angel, "for they are yours."

Wondering, the child gathered them together—all that she could carry in the skirt of her little shift.

When she looked about her again the angel was gone, but the child hastened home with her treasure. It was enough to make her and her old grandmother rich. From then on they lacked for nothing. They were not only able to have all they wished for, but to give to many who were poor. So they were not only rich, but beloved by all who knew them.

●

MR. STRAW

It's interesting to compare this wonderful tale from Japan with the story of Mr. Vinegar (told in the Self-Discipline chapter of *The Book of Virtues*). Mr. Vinegar keeps trading down as he follows his foolish impulses. Mr. Straw, on the other hand, trades up; he quite unintentionally raises himself by lifting a hand to help others.

Once upon a time, long ago of course, for that's when most good stories take place, there lived a man named Mr. Straw. Mr. Straw had no home, he had no wife, he had no children, he had nothing but the shirt on his back, in fact. For Mr. Straw had no luck. He was always poor and had little to eat, so he was as thin as a piece of straw. That, you see, is why people called him Mr. Straw.

Every morning, Mr. Straw went to the temple to ask the Goddess of Fortune for better luck. One day he heard a voice.

"The first thing your hand touches when you leave the temple will bring you great fortune," it whispered.

Mr. Straw rubbed his eyes, pinched himself, and looked all around him. The temple was empty.

"Was I dreaming, or was that the Goddess of Fortune?" he wondered. He rushed out of the temple to find his new luck.

But poor Mr. Straw tripped on the temple steps and tumbled all the way down to the bottom, where he lay in the dirt. When he picked himself up, he found his hand was clutching a piece of straw.

"Well," he thought, "a piece of straw is a pretty worthless thing. But since the Goddess of Fortune meant me to pick it up, I'd better not throw it away."

So he walked along, holding the piece of straw.

Before long a dragonfly came and began to buzz around his head. Mr. Straw waved and shooed, but it wouldn't go away. It buzzed and whirred and flew circles around him.

"Very well," said Mr. Straw. "Since you won't go away, you must stay with me."

He caught the dragonfly and tied his straw to its tail, so it looked like a little kite on a tiny string. And he kept walking down the road.

Pretty soon he met the flower lady and her little boy coming the other way. They were going to the market to sell their flowers. They had been walking a long time, and the boy was hot and tired, and the dust brought tears to his eyes. But when he saw Mr. Straw's dragonfly buzzing on the end of the straw, his face lit up.

"Mother," he said, "can I have a dragonfly? Please?"

"Well," thought Mr. Straw, "the Goddess of Fortune told me this piece of straw would bring me luck. But this little boy is hot and tired, and it will make him happy."

So he gave the boy the dragonfly on the straw.

"You are very kind," the flower lady said. "I have nothing to give you in return except this rose. Will you take it?"

Mr. Straw thanked her and went on his way, holding his rose.

After a while he saw a young man sitting on a tree stump, holding his head in his hands. He looked so forlorn, Mr. Straw asked him what was the matter.

"This evening I'll ask my belle to marry me," the youth cried. "But I'm a poor man and have no gift to bring her."

"Well, I'm a poor man too," Mr. Straw said. "I have nothing valuable, but if you want to give her this rose, you are welcome to it."

The youth perked up when he saw the splendid rose.

"Please take these three oranges in return," he said. "It's all I have to offer."

So Mr. Straw set off again, carrying three plump, juicy oranges. Soon he met a peddler pulling a little cart.

"Can you help me?" the peddler panted. "I've been pulling this cart all day, and I'm so thirsty I'm going to faint! I need a drink of water."

"I'm afraid there are no wells nearby," Mr. Straw said, "but you can have these oranges and drink the juice."

The peddler was so grateful he reached into his cart and pulled out his finest roll of silk.

"You're very, very kind," he said. "Please take this cloth in return."

So Mr. Straw set off once again, this time with his silk under his arm.

Before long, he met a princess in a golden carriage. She wore a worried look, but her face lit up when she saw Mr. Straw.

"Where did you get that silk?" she cried. "It's just what I've been looking for. Today is my father's birthday, and I want to make him a new royal robe."

"Well, since it's his birthday, you're welcome to have this silk," Mr. Straw said.

The princess couldn't believe her luck.

"You're very thoughtful and kind," she said with a smile. "Please take this jewel in return."

She rode away, leaving Mr. Straw holding a jewel that gleamed like the fire of the sun.

"Well, well," he told himself. "I started with a worthless piece of straw, and suddenly I find I have a jewel. Something tells me this has gone far enough."

He took the jewel straight to a merchant and sold it. Then he took the money and bought a great rice field. He worked hard in his field, and every year it grew more and more rice, and before too long he was a rich man.

But his wealth did not change him one bit. He always shared his rice with the hungry, and built a school for the village children, and helped anyone who needed a hand. And everyone said it all came from one little piece of straw, but Mr. Straw knew his luck really came from his kindness.

•

THE LINE OF GOLDEN LIGHT
Elizabeth Harrison

In this story, a brave girl's journey to make the path easier for her sister smooths the way for others as well.

Once upon a time there lived a child whose name was Avilla. She was sweet and loving, and fair to look upon, and had everything in the world to make her happy, but she had a little blind sister, and Avilla could not be perfectly happy as long as her sister's eyes were closed so that she could not see God's beautiful world, nor enjoy His bright sunshine. Little Avilla kept wondering if there was not something that she could do which would open this blind sister's eyes.

At last, one day, she heard of an old, old woman, nobody knew how old, who had lived for hundreds of years in a dark cave, not many miles away. This queer old woman knew a secret enchantment, by means of which the blind could receive their sight. The child, Avilla, asked her parents' permission to make a journey to the cave, in order that she might try to persuade the old woman to tell her this secret. "Then," she exclaimed joyfully, "my dear sister need sit no longer in darkness." Her parents gave a somewhat unwilling consent, as they had heard many strange stories about the old woman. At last, however, one fine spring morning, Avilla started on her journey. She had a long distance to walk, but the happy thoughts in her heart made the time pass quickly, and the soft, cool breeze seemed to be whispering a song to her all the way.

When she came to the mouth of the cave, it looked so dark and forbidding that she almost feared to enter it, but the thought of her little blind sister gave her courage, and she walked in. At first she could see nothing, for all the sunshine was shut out by the frowning rocks that guarded the entrance. Soon, however, she discerned the old woman sitting on a stone chair, spinning a pile of flax into a fine, fine thread. She seemed bent nearly double with age, and her face wore a look of worry and care, which made her appear still older.

The child Avilla came close to her side and thought, She is so aged that she must be hard of hearing. The old woman did not turn her head or stop her spinning. Avilla waited a moment and then took fresh courage and said, "I have come to ask you if you will tell me how I can cure my blind sister."

The strange creature turned and stared at her as if she were very much surprised. She then spoke in a deep, hollow voice, so hollow that it sounded as if she had not spoken for a very long time. "Oh," said she with a sneer, "I can tell you well enough, but you'll not do it. People who can see trouble themselves very little about those who are blind!" This last was said with a sigh, and then she scowled at Avilla until the child's heart began to beat very fast.

But the thought of her little blind sister made her brave again, and she cried out, "Oh, *please* tell me. I will do anything to help my dear sister!"

The old woman looked long and earnestly at her this time. She then stooped down and searched in the heap of the fine-spun thread which lay at her side until she found the end of it. This she held out to the child, saying, "Take this and carry it all around the world, and when you have done that, come to me and I will show you how your blind sister may be cured." Little Avilla thanked her and eagerly seized the tiny thread, and wrapping it carefully around her hand that she might not lose it, turned and hastened out of the close, damp cave.

She had not traveled far before she looked back to be sure the thread had not broken, it was so thin. Imagine her surprise to see that instead of its being a gray thread of spun flax, it was a thread of golden light, that glittered and shone in the sunlight, as if it were made of the most precious stuff on earth. She felt sure now that it must be a magic thread, and that it somehow would help her to cure her blind sister. So she hastened on, glad and happy.

Soon, however, she approached a dark, dense forest. No ray of sunlight seemed ever to have fallen on the trunks of its trees. In the distance she thought she could hear the growl of bears and the roar of lions. Her heart almost stopped beating. "Oh, I can never go through that gloomy forest," said she to herself, and her eyes filled with tears. She turned to retrace her steps, when the soft breeze which still accompanied her whispered, "Look at the thread you have been carrying! Look at the golden thread!" She looked back, and the bright, tiny line of light seemed to be actually smiling at her, as it stretched across the soft green grass, far into the distance, and, strange to say, each tiny blade of grass which it had touched, had blossomed into a flower. So, as the little girl looked back, she saw a flowery path with a glittering line of golden light running through it. "How beautiful!" she exclaimed. "I did not notice the flowers as I came along, but the enchanted thread will make the next traveler see them."

This thought filled her with such joy that she pushed forward into the dark woods. Sometimes she knocked her head against a tree which stood in her way, sometimes she almost feared she was lost, but every now and then she would look back and the sight of the tiny thread of golden light always renewed her courage. Once in a while she felt quite sure that she could see the nose of some wild beast poking out in front of her, but when she came nearer it proved to be the joint in a tree trunk, or some strange fungus which had grown on a low branch. Then she would laugh at her own fear and go on. One of the wonderful things about the mysterious little thread which she carried in her hand was, that it seemed to open a path behind it, so that one could easily follow in her footsteps without stumbling over fallen trees, or bumping against living ones. Every now and then a gray squirrel would frisk by her in a friendly fashion, as if to assure her that she was not alone, even in the twilight of the dark woods. By and by she came to the part of the forest where the trees were less dense, and soon she was out in the glad sunshine again.

But now a new difficulty faced her. As far as she could see stretched a low, swampy marsh of wet land. The mud and slime did not look very inviting, but the thought of her little blind sister came to her again, and she bravely plunged into the mire. The dirty, dripping mud clung to her dress and made her feet so heavy that she grew weary lifting them out of it. Sometimes she seemed to be stuck fast, and it was only with a great effort that she could pull out, first one foot, and then the other. A lively green frog hopped along beside her and seemed to say, in his funny, croaking voice, "Never mind the mud, you'll soon be through it." When she had at last reached the end of the slippery, sticky marsh, and stood once more on firm ground, she looked back at the tiny thread of golden light which trailed along after her. *What* do you think had happened? Wherever the mysterious and beautiful thread had touched the mud, the water had dried up, and the earth had become firm and hard, so that any other person who might wish to cross the swampy place could walk on firm ground. This made the child Avilla so happy, that she began to sing softly to herself.

Soon, however, her singing ceased. As the day advanced, the air grew hotter and hotter. The trees had long ago disappeared, and now the grass became parched and dry, until at last she found herself in the midst of a dreary desert. For miles and miles the scorching sand stretched on every side. She could not even find a friendly rock in whose shadow she might rest for a time. The blazing sun hurt her eyes and made her head ache, and the hot sand burned her feet. Still she toiled on, cheered by a swarm of yellow butterflies that fluttered just ahead of her. At last the end of the desert was reached, just as the sun disappeared behind a crimson cloud. Dusty and weary, the child Avilla was about to throw herself down on the ground to rest. As she did so, her eyes turned to look once more at the golden thread which had trailed behind her all day on the hot sand. Lo, and behold! What did she see? Tall shade trees had sprung up along the path she had traveled, and each tiny grain of sand that the wonderful thread had touched was now changed into a diamond, or ruby, or emerald, or some other precious stone. On one side the pathway across the desert shone and glittered, while on the other the graceful trees cast a cool and refreshing shade.

Little Avilla stood amazed as she looked at the beautiful trees and the sparkling gems. All feeling of weariness was gone. The air now seemed mild and refreshing, and she thought that she could hear in the distance some birds singing their evening songs. One by one the bright stars came out in the quiet sky above her head, as if to keep guard while she slept through the night.

The next morning she started forward on her long journey round the world. She traveled quite pleasantly for a while, thinking of how cool and shady the desert path would now be for anyone who might have to travel it, and of the precious jewels she had left for someone else to gather up. She could not stop for them herself, for she was too anxious to press forward and finish her task, in order that her little blind sister might the sooner see.

After a time she came to some rough rocks tumbled about in great confusion, as if angry giants had hurled them at each other. Soon the path grew steeper and steeper, and the rocks sharper and sharper, until they cut her feet. Before her she could see nothing but more rocks until they piled themselves into a great mountain, which frowned down upon her, as much as to say, "How dare you attempt to climb to my summit?" The brave child hesitated. Just then two strong eagles with outspread wings rose from their nest of sticks on the side of a steep cliff nearby and soared majestically and slowly aloft. As they passed far above her head they uttered a loud cry which seemed to say, "Be brave and strong and you shall meet us at the mountaintop."

Sometimes the ragged edges of the rocks tore her dress, and sometimes they caught the tiny golden thread, and tangled it so that she had to turn back and loosen it from their hold. The road was very steep and she was compelled to sit down every few minutes and get her breath. Still she climbed on, keeping the soaring eagles always in sight. As she neared the top, she turned and looked back at the enchanted thread of golden light which she had carried through all the long, strange journey. Another marvelous thing had happened! The rugged path of sharp, broken rocks had changed into broad and beautiful white marble steps, over which trailed the shining thread of light. She knew that she had made a pathway up this difficult mountain and her heart rejoiced.

She turned again to proceed on her journey, when, only a short distance in front of her, she saw the dark cave in which lived the strange old woman who had bidden her carry the line of light around the world. She hastened forward, and on entering the cave, she saw the old creature, almost bent double, still spinning the mysterious thread. Avilla ran forward and cried out, "I have done all you told me to do, now give sight to my sister!"

The old woman sprang to her feet, seized the thread of golden light and exclaimed, "At last! At last! I am freed!"

Then came so strange and wonderful a change that Avilla could hardly believe her own eyes. Instead of the ugly, cross-looking old crone, there stood a beautiful princess, with long golden hair and tender blue eyes, her face radiant with joy. Her story was soon told. Hundreds of years ago she had been changed into the bent old woman and shut up in the dark cave on the mountainside, because she, a daughter of the King, had been selfish and idle, thinking only of herself, and her punishment had been that she must remain thus disguised and separated from all companions and friends until she could find someone who would be generous and brave enough to take the long, dangerous journey around the world for the sake of others. Her mother had been a fairy princess and had taught her many things which we mortals have yet to learn. She showed the child Avilla how, by dipping the golden thread into a spring of ordinary water, she could change the water into golden water, which glittered and sparkled like liquid sunshine. Filling a pitcher with this they hastened together to where the little blind sister sat in darkness waiting for someone to come and lead her home. The beautiful princess told Avilla to dip her hands into the bowl of enchanted water, and then press them upon the closed eyes of her sister. They opened! And the little blind girl could see!

After that the fairy princess came and lived with little Avilla and her sister, and taught them how to do many wonderful things, of which I have no time to tell you today.

THE LAME BOY

Mrs. Charles A. Lane

By cheering on others, we encourage ourselves too.

He was little. He was lame. He was only six years old. His mother was a poor washerwoman, and they lived in a tiny room on a narrow street of a great city.

All day long he sat in his high chair, looking down into the narrow street. He could see, by leaning forward, a bit of blue sky over the tall warehouse opposite. Sometimes a white cloud would drift across the blue. Sometimes it was all dull gray.

But the street was more interesting. There were people down there. In the early morning men and women were hurrying to their work. Later the children came out and played on the pavement and in the gutters. Sometimes they danced and sang, but often they were quarrelsome. In the spring the street-organ man came, and then everybody seemed happy.

The boy's sad little face looked out all day long. Only when he saw his mother coming did he smile and wave his hand.

"I wish I could help you, Mother," he said one night. "You work so hard, and I can't do anything for you."

"Oh, but you do!" she cried quickly. "It helps me to see your face smiling down at me from the window. It helps me when you wave your hand. It makes my work lighter all day to think you will be there waving to me when I go home."

"Then I'll wave harder," said the little fellow.

And the next night a tired workman, seeing the mother look up and answer the signal, looked up too. Such a little, pinched face as he saw at the high window. But how cheery the smile was! The man laughed to himself and waved his cap, and the boy, a little shyly, returned the greeting.

So it went. The next evening the workman nudged his comrade to look up at the "poor little chap sitting, so patient, at the window," and again the smile shone out as two caps waved in the air below him.

Days came and passed, and the boy had more friends. Men and women went out of their way to send a greeting to him. Life didn't seem quite so hard to them when they thought how dreary it must be for him. Sometimes a flower found its way to him, or an orange, or a colored picture. The children stopped quarreling when they saw him watching them, and played games to amuse him. It pleased them to see how eager he was to share in their good times.

"Tell the lad we couldn't get on without him," said one of the weary laborers to the mother one night. " 'Tis a great thing to have a brave heart. It makes us all brave, too. Tell him that."

And you may be sure she did.

•

WAUKEWA'S EAGLE

James Buckham

Offer kindness, and you may be repaid in kind.

One day, when the Indian boy Waukewa was hunting along the mountainside, he found a young eagle with a broken wing lying at the base of a cliff. The bird had fallen from an aerie on a ledge high above, and being too young to fly, had fluttered down the cliff and injured itself so severely that it was likely to die. When Waukewa saw it he was about to drive one of his sharp arrows through its body, for the passion of the hunter was strong in him and the eagle plunders many a fine fish from the Indian's drying-frame. But a gentler impulse came to him as he saw the young bird quivering with pain and fright at his feet, and he slowly unbent his bow, put the arrow in his quiver, and stooped over the panting eaglet. For fully a minute the wild eyes of the wounded bird and the eyes of the Indian boy, growing gentler and softer as he gazed, looked into one another. Then the struggling and panting of the young eagle ceased. The wild, frightened look passed out of its eyes, and it suffered Waukewa to pass his hand gently over its ruffled and draggled feathers. The fierce instinct to fight, to defend its threatened life, yielded to the charm of the tenderness and pity expressed in the boy's eyes; and from that moment Waukewa and the eagle were friends.

Waukewa went slowly home to his father's lodge, bearing the wounded eaglet in his arms. He carried it so gently that the broken wing gave no twinge of pain, and the bird lay perfectly still, never attempting to strike with its sharp beak the hands that clasped it.

Warming some water over the fire at the lodge, Waukewa bathed the broken wing of the eagle, and bound it up with soft strips of skin. Then he made a nest of ferns and grass inside the lodge, and laid the bird in it. The boy's mother looked on with shining eyes. Her heart was very tender. From girlhood she had loved all the creatures of the woods, and it pleased her to see some of her own gentle spirit waking in the boy.

When Waukewa's father returned from hunting, he would have caught up the young eagle and wrung its neck. But the boy pleaded with him so eagerly, stooping over the captive and defending it with his small hands, that the stern warrior laughed. "Keep it, then," he said, "and nurse it until it is well. But then you must let it go, for we will not raise up a thief in the lodges." So Waukewa promised that when the eagle's wing was healed and grown so that it could fly, he would carry it forth and give it its freedom.

It was a month—or, as the Indians say, a moon—before the young eagle's wing had fully mended and the bird was old enough and strong enough to fly. And in the meantime Waukewa cared for it and fed it daily, and the friendship between the boy and the bird grew very strong.

But at last the time came when the willing captive must be freed. So Waukewa carried it far away from the Indian lodges, where none of the young braves might see it hovering overhead and be tempted to shoot their arrows at it, and there he let it go. The young eagle rose toward the sky in great circles, rejoicing in its freedom and its strange, new power of flight. But when Waukewa began to move away from the spot, it came swooping down again; and all day long it followed him through the woods as he hunted. At dusk, when Waukewa shaped his course for the Indian lodges, the eagle would have accompanied him. But the boy suddenly slipped into a hollow tree and hid, and after a long time the eagle stopped sweeping about in search of him and flew slowly and sadly away.

Summer passed, and then winter; and spring came again, with its flowers and birds and swarming fish in the lakes and streams. Then it was that all the Indians, old and young, braves and squaws, pushed their light canoes out from shore and with spear and hook waged pleasant war against the salmon and the red-spotted trout. After winter's long imprisonment, it was such joy to toss in the sunshine and the warm wind and catch savory fish to take the place of dried meats and corn!

Above the great falls of the Apahoqui the salmon sported in the cool, swinging current, darting under the lee of the rocks and leaping full length in the clear spring air. Nowhere else were such salmon to be speared as those which lay among the riffles at the head of the Apahoqui rapids. But only the most daring braves ventured to seek them there, for the current was strong, and should a light canoe once pass the danger point and get caught in the rush of the rapids, nothing could save it from going over the roaring falls.

Very early in the morning of a clear April day, just as the sun was rising splendidly over the mountains, Waukewa launched his canoe a half-mile above the rapids of the Apahoqui, and floated downward, spear in hand, among the salmon riffles. He was the only one of the Indian lads who dared fish above the falls. But he had been there often, and never yet had his watchful eye and his strong paddle suffered the current to carry his canoe beyond the danger point. This morning he was alone on the river, having risen long before daylight to be first at the sport.

The riffles were full of salmon, big, lusty fellows, who glided about the canoe on every side in an endless silver stream. Waukewa plunged his spear right and left, and tossed one glittering victim after another into the bark canoe. So absorbed in the sport was he that for once he did not notice when the canoe began to glide more swiftly among the rocks. But suddenly he looked up, caught his paddle, and dipped it wildly in the swirling water. The canoe swung sidewise, shivered, held its own against the torrent, and then slowly, inch by inch, began to creep upstream toward the shore. But suddenly there was a loud, cruel snap, and the paddle parted in the boy's hands, broken just above the blade! Waukewa gave a cry of despairing agony. Then he bent to the gunwale of his canoe and with the shattered blade fought desperately against the current. But it was useless. The racing torrent swept him downward; the hungry falls roared tauntingly in his ears.

Then the Indian boy knelt calmly upright in the canoe, facing the mist of the falls, and folded his arms. His young face was stern and lofty. He had lived like a brave hitherto—now he would die like one.

Faster and faster sped the doomed canoe toward the great cataract. The black rocks glided away on either side like phantoms. The roar of the terrible waters became like thunder in the boy's ears. But still he gazed calmly and sternly ahead, facing his fate as a brave Indian should. At last he began to chant the death-song, which he had learned from the older braves. In a few moments all would be over. But he would come before the Great Spirit with a fearless hymn upon his lips.

Suddenly a shadow fell across the canoe. Waukewa lifted his eyes and saw a great eagle hovering over, with dangling legs, and a spread of wings that blotted out the sun. Once more the eyes of the Indian boy and the eagle met; and now it was the eagle who was master!

With a glad cry the Indian boy stood up in his canoe, and the eagle hovered lower. Now the canoe tossed up on that great swelling wave that climbs to the cataract's edge, and the boy lifted his hands and caught the legs of the eagle. The next moment he looked down into the awful gulf of waters from its very verge. The canoe was snatched from beneath him and plunged down the black wall of the cataract; but he and the struggling eagle were floating outward and downward through the cloud of mist. The cataract roared terribly, like a wild beast robbed of its prey. The spray beat and blinded, the air rushed upward as they fell. But the eagle struggled on with his burden. He fought his way out of the mist and the flying spray. His great wings threshed the air with a whistling sound. Down, down they sank, the boy and the eagle, but ever farther from the precipice of water and the boiling whirlpool below. At length, with a fluttering plunge, the eagle dropped on a sand bar below the whirlpool, and he and the Indian boy lay there a minute, breathless and exhausted. Then the eagle slowly lifted himself, took the air under his free wings, and soared away, while the Indian boy knelt on the sand, with shining eyes following the great bird till he faded into the gray of the cliffs.

•

WHY THE WATER IN RIVERS IS NEVER STILL

Adapted from a retelling by Florence Holbrook

Remember, really helping usually involves real work. If you take on the responsibility of helping others, stick to it—or you can end up doing more harm than good.

All kinds of strange things came to pass in the days of long ago, but perhaps the strangest of all was that brooks and rivers used to keep watch over little children. The children and brooks ran about together, through the fields and forests. Sometimes the brooks ran first and the children followed. Sometimes the children ran first and the brooks followed. Of course, if any animal came near that would hurt the children, a brook quickly flowed around them, so that they stood on an island and were safe from harm.

In those days lived a little boy and a little girl who were the son and daughter of the king. When the children were old enough to run about, the king called the rivers and brooks to come before him. They came gladly, for they felt sure that something pleasant would happen, and they waited so quietly that no one would have thought they were so full of frolic.

"I have called you," said the king, "to give you the care of my two little children. They like so well to run about, and of course it will be pleasant for them to have many playmates. So I felt that it would be better to ask every river and every brook to see that they are not hurt or lost."

"We shall have the king's own son and daughter for our playmates!" whispered the rivers. "Nothing so pleasant ever happened to us before."

But the king went on, "If you keep my children safe, and follow them so closely that they are not lost, then I will give you whatever gift you wish. But if I find that you have forgotten them one moment and they are lost or hurt, then you will be punished as no river was ever punished before."

The rivers and even the most frolicsome little brooks were again quiet for a moment. Then they all cried together, "O king, we will be good. There were never better friends than we will be to your children."

At first all went well, and the playmates had the merriest times that could be thought of. Then came a day when the sunshine was very warm, but the king's children ran faster and farther than boys and girls had ever run in the world before, and even the brooks could not keep up with them. The rivers had never been weary before, but when this warm day came, one river after another had some reason for being quiet.

One complained, "I have followed the children farther than any other river."

"Perhaps you have," said another, "but I have been up and down and round and round till I have forgotten how it seems to be quiet."

Another declared, "I have run about long enough, and I shall run no more."

A little brook said, "If I were a great river, perhaps I could run farther."

And a great river replied, "If I were a little brook, of course I could run farther."

So they talked, and the day passed. Night came before they knew it, and they could not find the king's little boy and girl.

"Where are my children?" cried the king.

"Indeed, we do not know," answered the brooks and rivers in great fear, and each one looked at the others.

"You have lost my children," said the king, "and if you do not find them, you shall be punished. Go and search for them."

"Please help us," the rivers begged of the trees and plants, and everything that had life began to search for the lost children.

"Perhaps they are underground," thought the trees, and they sent their roots down into the earth.

"Perhaps they are in the east," cried one animal, and he went to the east.

"They may be on the mountain," said one plant, and so it climbed to the very top of the mountain.

"They may be in the village," said another, and so that one crept up close to the homes of men.

Many years passed. The king was almost brokenhearted, but he knew it was of no use to search longer, so he called very sadly, "Search no longer. Let each plant and animal make its home where it is. The little plant that has crept up the mountain shall live on the mountaintop, and the roots of the trees shall stay underground. The rivers—" Then the king stopped, and the rivers trembled. They knew that they would be punished, but what would the punishment be?

The king looked at them. "As for you, rivers and brooks," he declared, "it was your work to watch my little boy and my little girl. The plants and trees shall find rest and live happily in their homes, but you shall ever search for my lost children, and you shall never have a home."

So from that day to this the rivers have gone on looking for the lost children. They never stop, and some of them are so troubled that they flow first one way and then the other.

•

WHY EVERGREEN TREES NEVER LOSE THEIR LEAVES

Retold by Florence Holbrook

It's always easy to find a reason not to help another. This is perhaps the hardest part about learning compassion—fighting to
overcome our own excuses when they are merely selfish ones.

Winter was coming, and the birds had flown far to the south,
where the air was warm and they could find berries to eat. One
little bird had broken its wing and could not fly with the others. It
was alone in the cold world of frost and snow. The forest looked
warm, and it made its way to the trees as well as it could, to ask for
help.

First it came to a birch tree. "Beautiful birch tree," it said, "my
wing is broken, and my friends have flown away. May I live among
your branches till they come back to me?"

"No, indeed," answered the birch tree, drawing her fair green
leaves away. "We of the great forest have our own birds to help. I
can do nothing for you."

"The birch is not very strong," said the little bird to itself, "and
it might be that she could not hold me easily. I will ask the oak." So
the bird said: "Great oak tree, you are so strong, will you not let me
live on your boughs till my friends come back in the springtime?"

"In the springtime!" cried the oak. "That is a long way off. How
do I know what you might do in all that time? Birds are always
looking for something to eat, and you might even eat up some of
my acorns."

"It may be that the willow will be kind to me," thought the
bird, and it said: "Gentle willow, my wing is broken, and I could
not fly to the south with the other birds. May I live on your branches
till the springtime?"

The willow did not look gentle then, for she drew herself up
proudly and said: "Indeed, I do not know you, and we willows
never talk to people whom we do not know. Very likely there
are trees somewhere that will take in strange birds. Leave me at
once."

The poor little bird did not know what to do. Its wing was not yet strong, but it began to fly away as well as it could. Before it had gone far a voice was heard. "Little bird," it said, "where are you going?"

"Indeed, I do not know," answered the bird sadly. "I am very cold."

"Come right here, then," said the friendly spruce tree, for it was her voice that had called. "You shall live on my warmest branch all winter if you choose."

"Will you really let me?" asked the little bird eagerly.

"Indeed, I will," answered the kindhearted spruce tree. "If your friends have flown away, it is time for the trees to help you. Here is the branch where my leaves are thickest and softest."

"My branches are not very thick," said the friendly pine tree, "but I am big and strong, and I can keep the North Wind from you and the spruce."

"I can help, too," said a little juniper tree. "I can give you berries all winter long, and every bird knows that juniper berries are good."

So the spruce gave the lonely little bird a home. The pine kept the cold North Wind away from it. The juniper gave it berries to eat. The other trees looked on and talked together wisely.

"I would not have strange birds on my boughs," said the birch.

"I shall not give my acorns away for anyone," said the oak.

"I never have anything to do with strangers," said the willow, and the three trees drew their leaves closely about them.

In the morning all those shining, green leaves lay on the ground, for a cold North Wind had come in the night, and every leaf that it touched fell from the tree.

"May I touch every leaf in the forest?" asked the wind in its frolic.

"No," said the Frost King. "The trees that have been kind to the little bird with the broken wing may keep their leaves."

This is why the leaves of the spruce, the pine, and the juniper are always green.

•

SHELTERING WINGS

Harriet Louise Jerome

Love brings warmth and life.

It was intensely cold. Heavy sleds creaked as they scraped over the jeweled sounding board of dry, unyielding snow. The signs above shop doors shrieked and groaned as they swung helplessly to and fro. The clear, keen air seemed frozen into sharp little crystalline needles that stabbed every living thing that must be out in it. The streets were almost forsaken in mid-afternoon. Businessmen hurried from shelter to shelter. Every dog remained at home. Not a bird was to be seen or heard. The sparrows had been forced to hide themselves in crevices and holes. The doves found protected corners and huddled together as best they could. Many birds were frozen to death.

A dozen or more doves were gathered close under the cornice of the piazza of a certain house, trying with little success to keep warm. Some small sparrows, disturbed and driven from the cozy place they had chosen, saw the doves and came flying across the piazza.

"Dear doves," chirped the sparrows, "won't you let us nestle near you? Your bodies look so large and warm."

"But your coats are frosted with cold. We cannot let you come near us, for we are almost frozen now," murmured the doves sadly.

"But we are perishing."

"So are we."

"It looks so warm near your broad wings, gentle doves. Oh, let us come! We are so little, and so very, very cold!"

"Come," cooed a dove at last, and a trembling little sparrow fluttered close and nestled under the broad white wing.

"Come," cooed another dove, and another little sparrow found comfort.

"Come! Come!" echoed another warm-hearted bird, and another, until at last more than half the doves were sheltering small, shivering sparrows beneath their own half-frozen wings.

"My sisters, you are very foolish," said the other doves. "You mean well, but why do you risk your own beautiful lives to give life to worthless sparrows?"

"Ah! they are so small, and so very, very cold," murmured the doves. "Many of us will perish this cruel night. While we have life let us share its meager warmth with those in bitter need."

Colder and colder grew the day. The sun went down behind the clouds suffused with soft and radiant beauty, but more fiercely and relentlessly swept the wind around the house where the doves and sparrows waited for death.

An hour after sunset a man came up to the house and strode across the piazza. As the door of the house closed heavily behind him, a little child watching from the window saw something jarred from the cornice fall heavily to the piazza floor.

"Oh, Papa," she cried in surprise, "a poor frozen dove has fallen on our porch!"

When he stepped out to pick up the fallen dove the father saw the others under the cornice. They were no longer able to move or to utter a cry, so he brought them in and placed them in a room where they might slowly revive. Soon more than half of the doves could coo gratefully, and raise their stiffened wings. Then out from beneath the wing of each revived dove fluttered a living sparrow.

"Look, Papa!" cried the child. "Each dove that has come to life was holding a poor little sparrow close to her heart."

They gently raised the wings of the doves that could not be revived. Not one had a sparrow beneath it.

Colder and fiercer swept the wind without, cutting and more piercing grew the frozen, crystalline needles of air, but each dove that had sheltered a frost-coated sparrow beneath her own shivering wings lived to rejoice in the glowing gladsome sunshine of the days to come.

•

HOW THE ANIMALS GOT SUNLIGHT

Here's the kind of perseverance that tries against the odds, even when others before have tried and failed. It's also the kind of intellectual persistence that would learn from others' mistakes. Different versions of this enchanting tale were widespread among Native American peoples.

Once the world was continually dark, and all the animals kept fumbling around and knocking into each other, and they never knew where they were in such blackness. Finally they called a great council to decide how to solve the problem.

"What we need is light," the Owl said. The Owl presided over the meeting because he could see better in the dark than the other animals.

"That's right! We need light," everyone cried. "But where do we get it?"

"It's not an easy thing," the Owl warned. "They say there is light on the other side of the world. But that's a long way away. The journey will be dangerous. Whoever goes may well never come back."

"Then who should go?" everyone cried at once. "Who will risk the journey?"

There was a long silence. All the birds and beasts shuddered in the blackness.

At last they heard a lowly voice.

"I'll try," the Possum offered. "I have a long, bushy tail. I can wrap some light inside its fur and carry it home behind me."

So the Possum set out alone, traveling to the east. He walked for days and days across the black earth, never knowing where he really was, until finally he began to see a little glow in the sky.

He hurried toward it, and it grew lighter and lighter. Soon it was so bright it hurt his eyes, and he had to squint to keep it from blinding him. And even today, when you see a possum, you'll see how he keeps his eyes closed in narrow slits, so you'd almost think he was sleeping.

Finally, when he'd gone all the way to the other side of the world, the Possum found the sun. He grabbed a piece as fast as he could and wrapped it up in his long, bushy tail, and turned for home.

But the journey home was just as long, of course, and the piece of sun was too hot and bright for poor Possum. It burned all the fur off his tail and it fell onto the ground. That's why, today, Possum's tail is long and bare.

"Possum tried and failed," all the animals cried when he came home in darkness. "Now we'll never have any light."

"I'll try now," offered the Vulture. "Maybe this journey calls for someone with wings."

So the Vulture flew east, and finally he came to the sun. He dived and snatched a piece of it in his claws.

"Possum tried to carry the sun with his tail and dropped it," he told himself. "I'll try carrying it on my head."

Vulture set the piece of sun on his head and turned for home, but the sun was so hot that before long it had burned away all the feathers on his crown. He grew dizzy and lost his way, and began wandering around and around until the piece of sun tumbled to the ground. That is why today a vulture's head is bald, and you'll still see him drifting in circles high overhead.

"Now we're truly finished," the animals cried when Vulture returned in darkness. "Possum and Vulture tried as best they could, but it wasn't enough."

"Maybe we need to try one more time," a tiny voice rose from the weeds. "I'll go this time."

"Who is that?" the animals asked. "Who said that?"

"It's me, Old Lady Spider. I know I'm small and slow, but perhaps I'm the one who can make it."

Before she started, she gathered a bit of wet clay, and with her eight tiny hands she made a little pot.

"Possum and Vulture had nothing to carry the sun in," she said. "I'll put it in this pot."

Then she spun a thread and fastened the end to a rock.

"Possum and Vulture were blinded and lost from the sun's light on the way back," she said. "But I'll follow this thread home."

So she set out, traveling east, spinning her thread behind her as she walked. When she reached the sun, she pinched off a small piece and put it in her clay pot. It was still so bright she could hardly see, but she turned and followed her thread home.

She came walking out of the east all aglow, looking like the sun itself. And even today, when Old Lady Spider spins her web, it looks like the rays of the rising sun.

She reached home at last. All the animals could see for the first time. They saw how tiny and old Spider was, and they wondered that she could make the journey alone. Then they saw how she had carried the sun in the little pot, and that was when the world learned to make pots out of clay and set them in the sun to dry.

But Old Lady Spider had had enough of being so close to the sun. That is why, today, she spins her web in the early morning hours, before the sun is too high and hot.

•

WHY THE CHIMES RANG

Adapted from Raymond M. Alden

Little acts of kindness do not go unnoticed above, even if they go unseen by the crowd below.

There was once in a faraway country a wonderful church with a gray stone tower, with ivy growing over it as far up as one could see. In the tower was a chime of Christmas bells.

Every Christmas eve all the people of the city brought to the church their offerings to the Christ Child. When the greatest and best offering was laid on the altar, there would come sounding through the music of the choir the voices of the Christmas Chimes far up in the tower. Some said the wind rang them, and others that they were so high that the angels could set them swinging.

But the fact was that no one had heard the chimes for years and years. There was an old man living not far from the church, who said that his mother had spoken of hearing them when she was a little girl. But now it was said the people had been growing less careful of their gifts for the Christ Child, and that no offering was brought great enough to deserve the music of the chimes.

A number of miles from the city, in a little country village, lived a boy named Pedro and his little brother.

The day before Christmas was bitterly cold, but the two boys started on their way to the Christmas celebration. Before nightfall they had trudged so far, hand in hand, that they saw the lights of the big city just ahead of them. Indeed, they were about to enter one of the great gates in the wall that surrounded it when they saw something dark on the snow near their path, and stepped aside to look at it. It was a poor woman who had fallen just outside the city, too sick and tired and cold to get in where she might have found shelter. Pedro, finding that he could not rouse her, said, "It's no use, little brother. You will have to go alone to the church."

"Alone?" cried little brother. "And you will not see the Christmas Festival?"

"No," said Pedro, and he could not help a little choking sound of disappointment in his throat. "See this poor woman, her face looks like the Madonna in the chapel window, and she will freeze to death if nobody cares for her. If you get a chance, little brother, to slip up to the altar without getting in anyone's way, take this little silver piece of mine and lay it down for my offering, when no one is looking."

The great church was truly a wonderful place that night. After the service, the people took their gifts to the altar for the Christ Child. Some brought wonderful jewels; some baskets of gold so heavy that they could scarcely carry them down the aisle. A great writer laid down a book that he had been making for years and years. And last of all walked the king of the country, hoping with all the rest to win for himself the chime of the Christmas bells.

There was a great murmur through the church as the people saw the king take from his head the royal crown, all set with diamonds and other precious stones, and lay it gleaming on the altar as his offering to the Holy Child. "Surely," they said, "we shall hear the bells now." But the chimes did not ring.

The procession was over. The gifts were all on the altar, and the choir had begun the closing hymn. Suddenly the organist stopped playing, and everyone looked at the old minister, who was standing in his place and holding up his hand for silence. As the people strained their ears to listen, there came softly but distinctly, swinging through the air, the sound of the bells in the tower! So far away and yet so clear seemed the music, so much sweeter were the notes than anything else that had been heard before, rising and falling away up there in the sky, that the people in the church sat for a moment very still. Then they all stood up together and stared at the altar, to see what great gift had awakened the long-silent bells.

But all that the nearest of them saw was the childish figure of Pedro's brother, who had crept softly down the aisle when no one was looking, and had laid Pedro's little piece of silver on the altar.

•

PRINCE HARWEDA AND THE MAGIC PRISON

Elizabeth Harrison

In this imaginative and magical story, we witness the moral education of a selfish brat. Sometimes those who care about us—
whether they be fairy godparents or real parents—have to teach
tough lessons in order to ease our paths for the long run, the run
of a life.

Little Harweda was born a Prince. His father was King over all
the land and his mother was the most beautiful Queen the world
had ever seen and Prince Harweda was their only child. From the
day of his birth everything that love or money could do for him had
been done. The very wind of heaven was made to fan over an
aeolian harp that it might enter his room, not as a strong fresh
breeze, but as a breath of music. Reflectors were so arranged in the
windows that twice as much moonlight fell on his crib as on that of
any ordinary child. The pillow on which his head rested was made
out of the down from hummingbirds' breasts and the water in
which his face and hands were washed was always steeped in rose
leaves before being brought to the nursery. Everything that could
be done was done, and nothing which could add to his ease or
comfort was left undone.

But his parents, although they were King and Queen, were not
very wise, for they never thought of making the young Prince think
of anybody but himself and he had never in all his life given up any
one of his comforts that somebody else might have a pleasure. So,
of course, he grew to be selfish and peevish, and by the time he
was five years old he was so disagreeable that nobody loved him.
"Dear, dear what shall we do?" said the poor Queen mother and
the King only sighed and answered, "Ah, what indeed!" They were
both very much grieved at heart for they well knew that little
Harweda, although he was a Prince, would never grow up to be a
really great King unless he could make his people love him.

At last they decided to send for his fairy godmother and see if
she could suggest anything which would cure Prince Harweda of

always thinking about himself. "Well, well, well!" exclaimed the godmother when they had laid the case before her. "This is a pretty state of affairs and I his godmother too! Why wasn't I called in sooner?" She then told them that she would have to think a day and a night and a day again before she could offer them any assistance. "But," she added, "if I take the child in charge you must promise not to interfere for a whole year."

The King and Queen gladly promised that they would not speak to or even see their son for the required time if the fairy godmother would only cure him of his selfishness. "We'll see about that," said the godmother. "Humph, expecting to be a King some day and not caring for anybody but himself—a fine King he'll make!" With that, off she flew, and the King and Queen saw nothing more of her for a day and a night and another day. Then back she came in a great hurry. "Give me the Prince," said she. "I have his house all ready for him. One month from today I'll bring him back to you. Perhaps he'll be cured and perhaps he won't. If he is not cured then we shall try two months next time. We'll see, we'll see." Without any more ado, she picked up the astonished young prince and flew away with him as lightly as if he were nothing but a feather or a straw. In vain the poor Queen wept and begged for a last kiss. Before she had wiped her eyes, the fairy godmother and Prince Harweda were out of sight.

They flew a long distance until they reached a great forest. When they had come to the middle of it, down flew the fairy, and in a minute more the young Prince was standing on the green grass beside a beautiful pink marble palace that looked something like a good-sized summer house.

"This is your home," said the godmother, "In it you will find everything you need and you can do just as you choose with your time." Little Harweda was delighted at this, for there was nothing in the world he liked better than to do as he pleased, so he tossed his cap up into the air and ran into the lovely little house without so much as saying "Thank you" to his godmother.

"Humph," said she as he disappeared, "you'll have enough of it before you are through with it, my fine Prince." With that off she flew.

Prince Harweda had no sooner set his foot inside the small rose-colored palace than the iron door shut with a bang and locked itself. For you must know by this time that it was an enchanted house, as of course, all houses are that are built by fairies.

Prince Harweda did not mind being locked in, as he cared very little for the great beautiful outside world, and the new home which was to be *all his own* was very fine, and he was eager and impatient to examine it. Then too he thought that when he was tired of it, all he would have to do would be to kick on the door and a servant from somewhere would come and open it. He had always had a servant ready to obey his slightest command.

His fairy godmother had told him that it was *his* house. Therefore he was interested in looking at everything in it.

The floor was made of a beautiful red copper that shone in the sunlight like burnished gold and seemed almost a dark red in the shadow. He had never seen anything half so fine before. The ceiling was of mother-of-pearl and showed a constant changing of tints of red and blue and yellow and green, all blending into the gleaming white, as only mother-of-pearl can. From the middle of this handsome ceiling hung a large gilded bird cage containing a beautiful bird, which just at this moment was singing a glad song of welcome to the Prince. Harweda, however, cared very little about birds, so he took no notice of the songster.

Around on every side were costly divans covered with richly embroidered spreads and piled up with many sizes of soft down pillows. "Ah," thought the Prince, "here I can lounge at my case with no one to call me to stupid lessons!" Wonderfully carved jars and vases of wrought gold and silver stood about on the floor and each was filled with a different kind of perfume. "This is delicious," said Prince Harweda. "Now I can have all the sweet odors I want without the trouble of going out into the garden for roses or lilies."

In the center of the room was a fountain of sparkling water which leaped up and fell back into its marble basin with a kind of rhythmical sound that made a faint, dreamy music very pleasant to listen to.

On a table near at hand were various baskets of the most tempting pears and grapes and peaches, and near them were dishes of all kinds of sweetmeats. "Good," said the greedy young Prince, "that is what I like best of all," and therewith he fell to eating the fruit and sweetmeats as fast as he could cram them into his mouth. He ate so much he had a pain in his stomach, but strange to say, the table was just as full as when he began, for no sooner did he reach his hand out and take a soft mellow pear or a rich, juicy peach than another pear or peach took its place in the basket. The same thing occurred when he helped himself to chocolate drops or marshmallows or any of the other confectionery upon the table.

For, of course, if the little palace was enchanted, everything in it was enchanted also.

When Prince Harweda had eaten until he could eat no more he threw himself down upon one of the couches and an invisible hand gently stroked his hair until he fell asleep. When he awoke he noticed for the first time the walls, which, by the way, were really the strangest part of his new home. They had in them twelve long, checkered windows which reached from the ceiling to the floor. The spaces between the windows were filled in with mirrors exactly the same size as the windows, so that the whole room was walled in with windows and looking glasses. Through the three windows that looked to the north could be seen the far distant mountains Beautiful, as they were called, towering high above the surrounding country; sometimes their snow-covered tops were pink or creamy yellow as they caught the rays of the sunrise; sometimes they were dark purple or blue as they reflected a storm cloud. From the three windows that faced the south could be seen the great ocean, tossing and moving, constantly catching a thousand gleams of silver from the moonlight. Again and again, each little wave would be capped with white from its romp with the wind. Yet, as the huge mountains seemed to reach higher than man could climb, so the vast ocean seemed to stretch out farther than any ship could possibly carry him. The eastern windows gave each morning a glorious vision of sky as the darkness of the night slowly melted into the still gray dawn, and that changed into a golden glow and that in turn became a tender pink. It was really the most beautiful as well as the most mysterious sight on earth if one watched it closely. The windows on the west looked out upon a great forest of tall fir trees and at the time of sunset the glorious colors of the sunset sky could be seen between the dark green branches.

But little Prince Harweda cared for none of these beautiful views. In fact, he scarcely glanced out of the windows at all, he was so taken up with the broad handsome mirrors, for in each of them he could see himself reflected and he was very fond of looking at himself in a looking glass. He was much pleased when he noticed that the mirrors were so arranged that each one not only reflected his whole body, head, arms, feet and all, but that it also reflected his image as seen in several of the other mirrors. He could thus see his front and back and each side, all at the same time. As he was a handsome boy, he enjoyed these many views of himself immensely, and would stand and sit and lie down just for the fun of seeing the many images of himself do the same thing.

He spent so much time looking at and admiring himself in the wonderful looking glasses that he had very little time for the books and games which had been provided for his amusement. Hours were spent each day, first before one mirror and then another, and he did not notice that the windows were growing narrower and the mirrors wider until the former had become so small that they hardly admitted light enough for him to see himself in the looking glass. Still, this did not alarm him very much, as he cared nothing whatever for the outside world. It only made him spend more time before the mirror, as it was now getting quite difficult for him to see himself at all. The windows at last became mere slits in the wall and the mirrors grew so large that they not only reflected little Harweda but all of the room besides in a dim, indistinct kind of a way.

Finally, however, Prince Harweda awoke one morning and found himself in total darkness. Not a ray of light came from the outside and of course, not an object in the room could be seen. He rubbed his eyes and sat up to make sure that he was not dreaming. Then he called loudly for someone to come and open a window for him, but no one came. He got up and groped his way to the iron door and tried to open it, but it was, as you know, locked. He kicked it and beat upon it, but he only bruised his fists and hurt his toes. He grew quite angry now. How dare anyone shut him, a Prince, up in a dark prison like this! He yelled for his fairy godmother, calling her all sorts of horrid names. Then he upbraided his father and mother, the King and Queen, for letting him go away with such a godmother. In fact, he blamed everybody and everything but himself for his present condition, but it was of no use. The sound of his own voice was his only answer. The whole of the outside world seemed to have forgotten him.

As he felt his way back to his couch he knocked over one of the golden jars which had held the liquid perfume, but the perfume was all gone now and only an empty jar rolled over the floor. He laid himself down on the divan but its soft pillows had been removed and a hard iron framework received him. He was dismayed and lay for a long time thinking of what he had best do with himself. All before him was blank darkness, as black as the darkest night you ever saw. He reached out his hand to get some fruit to eat, but only one or two withered apples remained on the table—was he to starve to death? Suddenly he noticed that the tinkling music of the fountain had ceased. He hastily groped his way over to it and he found in place of the dancing, running stream stood a silent pool of water. A hush had fallen upon everything about him. A dead silence was in the room. He threw himself down upon the floor and wished that he were dead also. He lay there for a long, long time.

At last he heard, or thought he heard, a faint sound. He listened eagerly. It seemed to be some tiny creature not far from him, trying to move about. For the first time for nearly a month he remembered the bird in its gilded cage. "Poor little thing," he cried as he sprang up, "you too are shut within this terrible prison. This thick darkness must be as hard for you to bear as it is for me." He went toward the cage and as he approached it the bird gave a sad little chirp.

"That's better than nothing," said the boy. "You must need some water to drink, poor thing," he continued as he filled its drinking cup. "This is all I have to give you."

Just then he heard a harsh, grating sound, as of rusty bolts sliding with difficulty out of their sockets, and then faint rays of light not wider than a hair began to shine between the heavy plate mirrors. Prince Harweda was filled with joy. "Perhaps, perhaps," said he softly, "I may yet see the light again. Ah, how beautiful the outside world would look to me now!"

The next day he was so hungry that he began to eat one of the old withered apples, and as he bit it he thought of the bird, his fellow-prisoner. "You must be hungry, too, poor little thing," said he as he divided his miserable food and put part of it into the bird's cage. Again came the harsh, grating sound, and the boy noticed that the cracks of light were growing larger. Still, they were only cracks, nothing of the outside world could be seen. Still, it was a comfort not to have to grope about in total darkness. Prince Harweda felt quite sure that the cracks of light were a little wider, and on going up to one and putting his eye close to it as he would to a pinhole in a paper, he was rejoiced to find that he could tell the greenness of the grass from the blue of the sky. "Ah, my pretty bird, my pretty bird!" he cried joyfully. "I have had a glimpse of the great beautiful outside world and you shall have it too."

With these words, he climbed up into a chair and, loosening the cage from the golden chain by which it hung, he carried it carefully to the nearest crack of light and placed it close to the narrow opening. Again was heard the harsh, grating sound and the walls moved a bit and the windows were now at least an inch wide.

At this the poor Prince clasped his hands with delight. He sat himself down near the bird cage and gazed out of the narrow opening. Never before had the trees looked so tall and stately, or the white clouds floating through the sky so lovely. The next day as he was carefully cleaning the bird's cage so that the little creature might be somewhat more comfortable, the walls again creaked and groaned and the mirrors grew narrower by just so many inches as the windows widened. But Prince Harweda saw only the flood of sunshine that poured in, and the added beauty of the larger landscape. He cared nothing whatever now for the stupid mirrors, which could only reflect what was placed before them. Each day he found something new and beautiful in the view from the narrow windows. Now it was a squirrel frisking about and running up some tall tree trunk so rapidly that Prince Harweda could not follow it with his eyes. Again it was a mother bird feeding her young. By this time the windows were a foot wide or more.

One day as two white doves suddenly soared aloft in the blue sky the poor little canary who had now become the tenderly cared for comrade of the young Prince, gave a pitiful little trill. "Dear little fellow," cried Prince Harweda, "do you also long for your freedom? You shall at least be as free as I am." So saying, he opened the cage door and the bird flew out.

The Prince laughed as he watched it flutter about from chair to table and back to chair again. He was so much occupied with the bird that he did not notice that the walls had again shaken and the windows were now their full size, until the added light caused him to look around. He turned and saw the room looking almost exactly as it did the day he entered it with so much pride because it was all his own. Now it seemed close and stuffy and he would gladly have exchanged it for the humblest home in his father's kingdom where he could meet people and hear them talk and see them smile at each other, even if they should take no notice of him.

One day soon after this the little bird fluttered up against the windowpane and beat his wings against it in a vain effort to get out. A new idea seized the young Prince and, taking up one of the golden jars, he went to the window and struck on one of its checkered panes of glass with all his force. "You shall be free, even if I can not," said he to the bird. Two or three strong blows shivered the small pane and the bird swept out into the free open air beyond. "Ah, my pretty one, how glad I am that you are free at last," exclaimed the Prince as he stood watching the flight of his fellow prisoner. His face was bright with the glad, unselfish joy over the bird's liberty. The small pink marble palace shook from top to bottom, the iron door flew open and the fresh wind from the sea rushed in and seemed to catch the boy in its invisible arms. Prince Harweda could hardly believe his eyes as he sprang to the door. There stood his fairy godmother, smiling and with her hand reached out toward him.

"Come, my godchild," said she gently, "we shall now go back to your father and mother, the King and Queen, and they will rejoice with us that you have been cured of your terrible disease of selfishness."

Great indeed was the rejoicing in the palace when Prince Harweda was returned to them a sweet, loving boy, kind and thoughtful to all about him. Many a struggle he had with himself and many a conquest over the old habit of selfishness, but as time passed by he grew to be a great and wise King, loving and tenderly caring for all his people and loved by them in return.

•

JOHN SMITH AT JAMESTOWN

Like all pioneers, the first English colonists in America quickly discovered that survival meant self-reliance. It is doubtful the settlers at Jamestown, Virginia, would have lasted long enough to learn the lesson without the stern voice of John Smith, who

THE MORAL COMPASS

bluntly warned that "idleness and sloth" would be the colonists'
ruin, and that they "must be more industrious, or starve." Drawing
from Saint Paul, Smith laid down his famous dictum: "He that will
not work shall not eat." The settlers' sudden change of heart and
habit provides us with one of the earliest lessons from American
history. Sometimes the best way to ease the path is to accept no
excuses, and to let it be known that people must pull their own
weight.

One day in May in the year 1607, three small ships came sailing
up a broad river. On the decks of the ships stood more than one
hundred Englishmen, anxiously peering at the shores. They had
spent many weeks crossing the ocean, and now they were looking
toward a new home. Finally, at a place where a large piece of land
jutted into the river, the ships stopped and the men stepped ashore.

The Indians called this river Powhatan, after their mighty chief.
The Englishmen, however, named it the James River, after their
own king.

Among the Englishmen was a sturdy young man with keen
blue eyes and red hair and a big red beard. His name was Captain
John Smith. He was a brave man and a good soldier, the kind of
leader a small group of adventurers far from home could depend
on.

Right away the Englishmen took out their sharp axes and began
to chop at the thick, tall trees. They built huts where they could
keep dry and sleep, a church where they could pray, and a fort
where they could stay in times of danger. They named their little
village Jamestown, and they called that part of the world Virginia.

When the excitement of reaching the New World wore off,
however, many of the settlers at Jamestown began to shirk their
duties. Some had been "gentlemen" in England and were not used
to working hard with their hands. They did not know how to obey
orders. They slipped away from their jobs, or slumped over their
tasks. They were much better at quarreling among themselves and
watching others do all the work.

Some of the settlers were quite willing to work, but only if it
was the kind of work they wanted to do. They longed to search for
treasure. They had heard the New World was full of silver and gold
and precious pearls. They thought treasure hunting would be much
easier work than clearing fields to grow food.

Others grew discouraged over the thought of being separated from home by the wide ocean. They were frightened by the Indians in the unknown forests. They feared the deadly diseases that seemed to strike so quickly in this new land. Brooding, they sat in their huts and complained about the heat in summer and the cold in winter.

But if some of the settlers were not good at working, they were very good at eating and drinking. When dinnertime came, they were just as hungry as those who labored, and expected to share in the fruits of that labor. The colonists at Jamestown put all the vegetables they grew and all the game they hunted into one collection called the common store. This common store supplied food for the whole village. And so those who were too lazy to do their duties could still eat as long as a few men worked to put food into the common store.

But before long supplies began to grow short. There were too many mouths wanting to be fed, and too few hands willing to do the work. Captain John Smith did his best to keep the colony from falling to pieces. He made many trips up the rivers and into the forests to trade with the Indians for food. He spoke to the men again and again about the need to grow crops. He warned them that disaster was near unless they changed their ways.

His arguments did little good. Too many settlers still spent their time arguing with each other and hiding from work. Some of them plotted to steal food from the rest. And still they dreamed of growing rich from treasure. One time, after a fire broke out and destroyed many of the cabins, Smith could barely get the colonists to rebuild the village. They were too busy digging yellow dirt which they thought held gold.

Finally Captain Smith gathered the settlers together and gave a stern speech. He told them the colony was on the verge of starvation because so many men refused to do any useful work. Up until then, about forty hard workers had been feeding one hundred and fifty idlers. But now things would have to change, or they would all die of hunger. No longer would the colony's common store be open to everyone, workers and idlers alike. In the future, there would be a new rule. "He that will not work shall not eat," Smith declared. Unless someone was sick, every man would have to pull his own weight.

Then Captain Smith began to give each one duties. To help everyone remember their tasks, he posted a chart in the fort for all to see. It listed the name of every man, his duties for the week, and those duties he had fulfilled. The chart made it plain who was working and, therefore, who would eat.

At once things changed. Men who had done nothing but argue and complain suddenly bent to their tasks. The colonists began planting more corn. They made fishnets out of vines. They caught crabs and gathered oysters. They picked wild berries, and hunted deer and wild turkeys in the forest.

Under Captain Smith's orders, they built more houses. They planted gardens, and went to work raising hogs and chickens. They put a sturdier roof on the church. They built up the wall around their fort to make it stronger, and dug a well inside so they would have plenty of water to drink in times of danger.

And so the Jamestown colony did not fall to pieces. Under Smith's firm hand, the settlers began to pull together.

One day in the autumn of 1609, Captain Smith and some of his men were sailing down the river when some gunpowder in their boat exploded, burning Smith terribly. He jumped into the water to put out the flames and nearly drowned before his men could pull him back into the boat. A short time later, Captain Smith returned to England to recover from his wounds. Jamestown had lost its best leader.

The colony faced many more years of hardship and hunger. Often the settlers were sick because the food they ate was spoiled, or because the water they drank was not pure. Sometimes they lived in peace with the Indians, but often there was bloodshed. The mosquitoes brought malaria, and always the sight of the empty, wide river brought loneliness. More than once the people of Jamestown thought of giving up and going back to England.

But most of them stayed, and labored, and against great odds made a home on the edge of the New World. John Smith had led them through the first hard months. He had shown them how to work for their own good. Now they struggled on, determined that their settlement would survive. And survive it did, for today we remember Jamestown as the first successful English colony in America.

•

Pocahontas

*Adapted from retellings by James Baldwin
and Grace Humphrey*

Historians have long debated the accuracy of Captain John Smith's
dramatic account of how Pocahontas saved his life. Whether the
incident was in fact a daring rescue or part of an orchestrated
ritual, the Indian princess's own life remains an example of courage, compassion, and friendship. She was no small player in the
destiny of the Jamestown colony in Virginia, the first successful
English settlement in America. As John Smith later wrote, 'She,
next under God, was still the instrument to preserve this colony
from death, famine, and utter destruction."

There was once a little Indian girl whose name was Pocahontas. Her father was a great chief, or Indian king, and his name was
Powhatan. Her home was not far from a broad river, in that part of
our country which is now called Virginia.

One summer when Pocahontas was about ten years old, some
white men came up the river and began to build a town on its
banks. They came in a great ship that was many times larger than
any canoe, and everything they did was so wonderful that the Indians were at first very much afraid of them.

At that time all this country was a wild land. There were no
pleasant farms or busy cities, but only woods and swamps and
lonely prairies. King Powhatan and his people had always lived in
the great forest. They spent their time in hunting and fishing. They
had never heard of any other way of living.

They watched the strange white men as they landed from the
ship. They watched them as they began to build queer houses of
logs on the shore. Then Powhatan grew bold, and asked them
where they came from, and what they were doing in his country.

The strangers pointed to the east, and said, "We came from
England, on the other side of the great sea. We are building homes
for ourselves here in this country, which does not belong to you,
but to our good King James."

"I do not see how that can be," said Powhatan. "My people

have always lived in this country, and it must be ours. Yet there is room here for you also."

Little by little the Indians made friends with their strange neighbors. On some days they brought them corn which they sold for beads and other trinkets; at other times they brought them game which they had killed in the woods.

Captain John Smith, the leader of the Englishmen, wanted to learn all about the country. So, one day, he started with two men to explore the rivers and the woods.

"The white men are looking at our lands," said the Indians. "Soon they will want to drive us away from them."

"We must not let them," said others. "We must drive them back to their own place."

One day some Indians lay in wait in the woods for Captain Smith and the two men. They killed the two men, and took Smith prisoner. They tied Smith's hands behind him, and led him from one Indian town to another. They did not know what to do with him. At last they took him to the great chief, King Powhatan.

Captain Smith was led into a long house built of the green boughs of trees. Two hundred Indians were there, and all wanted to see him put to death. King Powhatan stood at one end of the room. On his shoulders he wore a cape of raccoon skins, and around his neck hung chains of pearls.

The warriors stood in rows on each side, and they too were dressed in furs and feathers. Behind the warriors were the Indian women. Their necks were painted red; their heads were covered with the white down of birds; over their shoulders hung strings of beads.

All the Indians shouted when Smith was led into the room. The queen brought water for him to wash his hands. Another woman gave him a bundle of feathers to use as a towel. After this they brought him food. They gave him such a dinner as he had not had for many a day. And then the warriors and the king talked about what they should do with him.

At last it was agreed that Captain Smith should die. Two large stones were rolled into the room and placed in front of King Powhatan. Then Smith, with his arms tied behind him, was led to them. His head was laid on one of them.

All at once a cry was heard among the Indian women. The little maiden Pocahontas ran across the room, and threw herself at her father's feet. She asked him to spare the white man's life.

The king looked very cross, and did not seem to hear the child.

Two tall warriors stepped forward, each with a heavy club in his hand. Then Pocahontas threw herself down by the side of the prisoner. She took his head in her arms. "You cannot kill him without first killing me," she said.

The heart of the old king was touched, and he told his warriors to lay down their clubs. Smith was lifted from the ground, the cords were taken from his arms, and he was treated with great kindness. He was given some presents and sent back to his people.

After that, Pocahontas was always a good friend to the white people who made their homes in Virginia. Frequently she would go with her brothers or friends carrying corn or venison to the settlers, who were close to starving. Often at the risk of her own life she would let them know if there was danger. When her father wanted to make war upon them, she would say, "Let us live in peace with each other."

After she grew up, and Captain John Smith had gone back to England, Pocahontas fell in love with one of the settlers, a man named John Rolfe, and he fell in love with her. They were married in a log church, and a year later a son was born. The whole colony hoped the new little family would help bond the Indians and settlers in lasting friendship.

When they had been married two years, Pocahontas, John Rolfe, and their baby Thomas traveled to England. Everywhere she went there, Pocahontas was received with great honor as a foreign princess, and known as Lady Rebecca. She was entertained at banquets and receptions. She went to the theaters. Bishops and great lords and ladies drove in their coaches to call upon her.

She was presented to the king and the queen, who welcomed her with pomp and ceremony. She carried herself as the daughter of a king, and among all the ladies of the court, none was a greater favorite, for her beauty and gentle ways won all hearts.

John Smith had been away exploring again, but now, returning to England, he heard everyone talking of Pocahontas. Remembering old times and all he owed his little friend, he at once went to visit her. When Smith appeared she was greatly moved and for a long time could not speak. At last she said, "They told me you were dead!" Then the two good friends sat down for a long talk of the old days in Virginia, and all that had happened since their separation.

Though she was so admired in England, Pocahontas did not really belong there. More and more her thoughts turned toward home. She wearied of crowded London and longed for the forest again. Every day she would stand by the window, looking toward the west, where Virginia and her early life lay. She thought much of the old days, of the changes that had come to her and her people, and the appearance of the fair-haired stranger and his Englishmen.

John Rolfe worried about his wife's homesickness, and feared she would fall ill with longing. He wanted to get her back to Virginia, but first they must wait for their ship to be loaded with supplies. At last word came that all was ready, and sailors came to take them aboard.

But though she had set her face to the west, Pocahontas was not to return to her home. A sudden weakness overcame her, and she fell asleep. At age twenty-two, in a foreign land, she died and was buried in a little church.

The story of Pocahontas is full of romance, of adventure, of gentleness and daring courage. She did far more than save Smith's life, for it was through her friendship with the English that the colony was supplied with food. It was her marriage that made possible, at least for a brief time, peace between two peoples. It was she, said John Smith, who saved Virginia from famine, confusion, and death.

•

THE FIRE BEARER

Adapted from retellings by Fanny E. Coe and Flora Cooke

The ancient Greeks revered Prometheus as the earliest teacher and benefactor of mankind, a god who by a selfless act of compassion became the founder of human civilization. The tale recounted below contains an important, sobering lesson, however. Good acts are not always rewarded. Often those who make paths easier for others do so at the cost of making their own lives harder. This retelling of the myth is based on the account by the Greek playwright Aeschylus.

Ages ago, the Greeks believed that the world was ruled by many gods. Their chief god was named Zeus. Zeus lived on the top of a high mountain. Fleecy clouds hid his home from the sight of men.

There had once been giants in the world. These giants had fought with Zeus. They had piled the mountains one upon the other and had tried to climb to Zeus's palace. Zeus had fought them with fire. He had thrown thunderbolts into the faces of the giants. At last they were beaten and put into dark prisons underground.

There were only two sons of giants left on the earth. The name of one of these was Prometheus.

Prometheus had a kind heart. He longed to help those about him. Now, besides Prometheus and his brother, there were men dwelling upon the earth.

The men of those days were poor and unhappy. They lived in caves and holes in the earth. They were cold and often hungry. What food they had they ate raw. They had no dishes, no tools, no comforts.

Prometheus saw all this. "Poor man," he said, "how I pity him! If he only had fire! Then he would be happy."

Prometheus thought a long time. Then he said aloud, "I will do what I can."

He went to Zeus. "I have come to beg a gift for man. Give him fire. He needs it sorely."

Zeus frowned darkly. "Never," he cried. "Fire is not for man. If he had it he might grow wise; he might even grow to be as strong as the gods themselves. He must never have it."

Prometheus went away. He again saw little children freezing in the snows of winter. He saw hunger. He saw men living like beasts. Then he set his teeth together and clenched his fist. "Man shall have fire!" he cried. "Zeus may kill me, but man shall have fire."

He walked along the seashore searching for a certain reed. This reed was hollow. Then he set out on a long journey eastward.

One morning, he came to his journey's end. It was by the sea. As he stood there, a golden flush was in the sky. Then the great car of day, the golden sun itself, came slowly up out of the ocean.

Prometheus touched one of the blazing chariot-wheels with his reed. It caught fire. The fire was held in the hollow of the reed, and with this gift Prometheus went westward again.

It was midwinter. Snows were deep on the ground. Ice covered the rivers. Men were hiding in their holes in the earth.

Prometheus entered one of these caves. "See this wonder!" he said. He had two or three stones piled together. Then he had wood laid on this first hearth. Then a touch of the reed and lo! the first fire. Blue fingers were spread out to the wonderful warmth. Pinched faces smiled at each other in the lovely glow. "Summer is come again!" they cried.

Thus man came to know heat and light. The gift of fire turned the cave into a home.

Men from far and near came to wonder. Men from far and near wanted the gift of fire in their homes also. They gathered stones and wood, and Prometheus was glad to give them glowing coals. They called him the helper of mankind.

Prometheus was also the teacher of mankind. He showed men how to cook their food, how to make dishes, how to make tools, and how to dig metal from the earth.

Men learned quickly. In a very short time they grew busy and happy.

One day, Zeus happened to look down on the earth. It seemed strange to him. He saw towns and ships. He saw mines and forges. He saw a fire in every house.

"What!" he thundered. "Man has fire! Who has done this?"

Then someone said, "Prometheus!"

"He shall pay well for this," said Zeus.

He called to him two strong servants. "Seize Prometheus, and lead him to the top of yonder mountain. There Hephaestus will finish your work."

Hephaestus was Zeus's son. He was the blacksmith of the gods. Hephaestus was sorry for Prometheus, but he could not disobey Zeus.

Prometheus was forced to the top of the mountain by the strong servants. There Hephaestus loaded him with chains. These chains he fastened to a rock.

There Prometheus lay for ages. The suns of summer scorched him. The snows of winter fell upon his upturned face. Worst of all, Zeus sent a great vulture every day to tear his flesh and feed upon his liver, which then healed every night, so that the vulture preyed upon him again and again. Zeus said he must stay in this torment until he returned the fire to heaven.

So Prometheus stayed on the bleak mountaintop, bearing his pain in silence. Sometimes he grew so weary and faint-hearted that he was tempted to free himself and give back the fire to Zeus.

But when he looked down upon his people and saw smoke rising from their homes, he knew the fire was helping them, and how happy and contented they were. Always he grew strong and patient again to wait for the release which he knew would finally come to him.

And after many, many years a Greek hero who was coming over the mountains saw Prometheus. It was Hercules. He shot the vulture with a golden arrow, unbound the chains, and set the great-hearted giant free.

•

HOW THE INDIANS LEARNED TO HEAL

Retold by Mabel Powers

When we help each other, we often learn all sorts of things about our world and ourselves. Practicing compassion brings wisdom, this Iroquois tale reminds us.

A long, long time ago, some Indians were running along a trail that led to an Indian settlement. As they ran, a rabbit jumped from the bushes and sat before them.

The Indians stopped, for the rabbit still sat up before them and did not move from the trail. They shot their arrows at him, but the arrows came back unstained with blood.

A second time they drew their arrows. Now no rabbit was to be seen. Instead, an old man stood on the trail. He seemed to be weak and sick.

The old man asked them for food and a place to rest. They would not listen but went on to the settlement.

Slowly the old man followed them, down the trail to the wig-wam village. In front of each wigwam, he saw a skin placed on a pole. This he knew was the sign of the clan to which the dwellers in that wigwam belonged.

First he stopped at a wigwam where a wolf skin hung. He asked to enter, but they would not let him. They said, "We want no sick men here."

On he went toward another wigwam. Here a turtle's shell was hanging. But this family would not let him in.

He tried a wigwam where he saw a beaver skin. He was told to move on.

The Indians who lived in a wigwam where a deer skin was seen, were just as unkind. Nor was he permitted to enter wigwams where hung hawk, snipe, and heron skins.

At last he came to a wigwam where a bear skin hung.

"I will ask once more for a place to rest," he thought.

And here a kind old woman lived. She brought food for him to eat, and spread soft skins for him to lie upon.

The old man thanked her. He said that he was very sick. He told the woman what plants to gather in the wood, to make him well again.

This she did, and soon he was healed.

A few days later the old man was again taken sick. Again he told the woman what roots and leaves to gather. She did as she was told, and soon he was well.

Many times the old man fell sick. Each time he had a different sickness. Each time he told the woman what plants and herbs to find to cure him. Each time she remembered what she had been told.

Soon this woman of the Bear clan knew more about healing than all the other people.

One day, the old man told her that the Great Spirit had sent him to earth, to teach the Indian people the secrets of healing.

"I came, sick and hungry, to many a wigwam door. No blanket was drawn aside for me to pass in. You alone lifted the blanket from your wigwam door and bade me enter.

"You are of the Bear clan, therefore all other clans shall come to the Bear clan for help in sickness.

"You shall teach all the clans what plants, and roots, and leaves to gather, that the sick may be healed.

"And the Bear shall be the greatest and strongest of the clans."

The Indian woman lifted her face to the Great Spirit to thank him for this great gift and knowledge of healing. When she turned again to the man, he had disappeared.

No one was there, but a rabbit was running swiftly down the trail.

•

THE HAPPY PRINCE

Oscar Wilde

"There is no Mystery so great as Misery," the Happy Prince says in this tale. But the greatest mystery and miracle of the story is really his own charity.

High above the city, on a tall column, stood the statue of the Happy Prince. He was gilded all over with thin leaves of fine gold, for eyes he had two bright sapphires, and a large red ruby glowed on his sword hilt.

He was very much admired indeed. "He is as beautiful as a weathercock," remarked one of the Town Councillors who wished to gain a reputation for having artistic tastes, "only not quite so useful," he added, fearing lest people should think him unpractical, which he really was not.

"Why can't you be like the Happy Prince?" asked a sensible mother of her little boy who was crying for the moon. "The Happy Prince never dreams of crying for anything."

"I am glad there is someone in the world who is quite happy," muttered a disappointed man as he gazed at the wonderful statue.

"He looks just like an angel," said the Charity Children as they came out of the cathedral in their bright scarlet cloaks and their clean white pinafores.

"How do you know?" said the Mathematical Master. "You have never seen one."

"Ah! but we have, in our dreams," answered the children, and the Mathematical Master frowned and looked very severe, for he did not approve of children dreaming.

One night there flew over the city a little Swallow. His friends had gone away to Egypt six weeks before, but he had stayed behind, for he was in love with the most beautiful Reed. He had met her early in the spring as he was flying down the river after a big yellow moth, and had been so attracted by her slender waist that he had stopped to talk to her.

"Shall I love you?" said the Swallow, who liked to come to the point at once, and the Reed made him a low bow. So he flew round and round her, touching the water with his wings, and making

silver ripples. This was his courtship, and it lasted all through the summer.

"It is a ridiculous attachment," twittered the other Swallows, "she has no money, and far too many relations." And indeed the river was quite full of Reeds. Then, when the autumn came, they all flew away.

After they had gone he felt lonely and began to tire of his ladylove. "She has no conversation," he said, "and I am afraid that she is a coquette, for she is always flirting with the wind." And certainly, whenever the wind blew, the Reed made the most graceful curtsies. "I admit that she is domestic," he continued, "but I love traveling, and my wife, consequently, should love traveling also."

"Will you come away with me?" he said finally to her, but the Reed shook her head, she was so attached to her home.

"You have been trifling with me," he cried. "I am off to the Pyramids. Good-by!" and he flew away.

All day long he flew, and at nighttime he arrived at the city. "Where shall I put up?" he said; "I hope the town has made preparations."

Then he saw the statue on the tall column.

"I will put up there," he cried. "It is a fine position, with plenty of fresh air." So he alighted just between the feet of the Happy Prince.

"I have a golden bedroom," he said softly to himself as he looked round, and he prepared to go to sleep. But just as he was putting his head under his wing a large drop of water fell on him. "What a curious thing!" he cried. "There is not a single cloud in the sky, the stars are quite clear and bright, and yet it is raining. The climate in the north of Europe is really dreadful. The Reed used to like the rain, but that was merely her selfishness."

Then another drop fell.

"What is the use of a statue if it cannot keep the rain off?" he said. "I must look for a good chimney pot," and he determined to fly away.

But before he had opened his wings, a third drop fell, and he looked up, and saw—ah! what did he see?

The eyes of the Happy Prince were filled with tears, and tears were running down his golden cheeks. His face was so beautiful in the moonlight that the little Swallow was filled with pity.

"Who are you?" he said.

"I am the Happy Prince."

"Why are you weeping then?" asked the Swallow; "you have quite drenched me."

"When I was alive and had a human heart," answered the statue, "I did not know what tears were, for I lived in the Palace of Sans-Souci, where sorrow is not allowed to enter. In the daytime I played with my companions in the garden, and in the evening I led the dance in the Great Hall. Round the garden ran a very lofty wall, but I never cared to ask what lay beyond it, everything about me was so beautiful. My courtiers called me the Happy Prince, and happy indeed I was, if pleasure be happiness. So I lived, and so I died. And now that I am dead they have set me up here so high that I can see all the ugliness and all the misery of my city, and though my heart is made of lead yet I cannot choose but weep."

"What! Is he not solid gold?" said the Swallow to himself. He was too polite to make any personal remarks out loud.

"Far away," continued the statue in a low musical voice, "far away in a little street there is a poor house. One of the windows is open, and through it I can see a woman seated at a table. Her face is thin and worn, and she has coarse, red hands, all pricked by the needle, for she is a seamstress. She is embroidering passionflowers on a satin gown for the loveliest of the Queen's maids of honor to wear at the next Court ball. In a bed in the corner of the room her little boy is lying ill. He has a fever, and is asking for oranges. His mother has nothing to give him but river water, so he is crying. Swallow, Swallow, little Swallow, will you not bring her the ruby out of my sword hilt? My feet are fastened to this pedestal and I cannot move."

"I am waited for in Egypt," said the Swallow. "My friends are flying up and down the Nile, and talking to the large lotus flowers. Soon they will go to sleep in the tomb of the great King. The King is there himself in his painted coffin. He is wrapped in yellow linen, and embalmed with spices. Round his neck is a chain of pale green jade, and his hands are like withered leaves."

"Swallow, Swallow, little Swallow," said the Prince, "will you not stay with me for one night, and be my messenger? The boy is so thirsty, and the mother so sad."

"I don't think I like boys," answered the Swallow. "Last summer, when I was staying on the river, there were two rude boys, the miller's sons, who were always throwing stones at me. They never hit me, of course; we swallows fly far too well for that, and besides, I come of a family famous for its agility. But still, it was a mark of disrespect."

But the Happy Prince looked so sad that the little Swallow was sorry. "It is very cold here," he said, "but I will stay with you for one night, and be your messenger."

"Thank you, little Swallow," said the Prince.

So the Swallow picked out the great ruby from the Prince's sword, and flew away with it in his beak over the roofs of the town.

He passed by the cathedral tower, where the white marble angels were sculptured. He passed by the palace and heard the sound of dancing. A beautiful girl came out on the balcony with her lover. "How wonderful the stars are," he said to her, "and how wonderful is the power of love!"

"I hope my dress will be ready in time for the State ball," she answered. "I have ordered passionflowers to be embroidered on it: but the seamstresses are so lazy."

He passed over the river, and saw the lanterns hanging to the masts of the ships. At last he came to the poorhouse and looked in. The boy was tossing feverishly on his bed, and the mother had fallen asleep, she was so tired. In he hopped, and laid the great ruby on the table beside the woman's thimble. Then he flew gently round the bed, fanning the boy's forehead with his wings. "How cool I feel!" said the boy. "I must be getting better." And he sank into a delicious slumber.

Then the Swallow flew back to the Happy Prince, and told him what he had done. "It is curious," he remarked, "but I feel quite warm now, although it is so cold."

"That is because you have done a good action," said the Prince. And the little Swallow began to think, and then he fell asleep. Thinking always made him sleepy.

When day broke he flew down to the river and had a bath. "What a remarkable phenomenon!" said the Professor of Ornithology as he was passing over the bridge. "A swallow in winter!" And he wrote a long letter about it to the local newspaper. Everyone quoted it, it was full of so many words that they could not understand.

"Tonight I go to Egypt," said the Swallow, and he was in high spirits at the prospect. He visited all the public monuments, and sat a long time on top of the church steeple. Wherever he went the Sparrows chirruped, and said to each other, "What a distinguished stranger!" So he enjoyed himself very much.

When the moon rose he flew back to the Happy Prince. "Have you any commissions for Egypt?" he cried. "I am just starting."

"Swallow, Swallow, little Swallow," said the Prince, "will you not stay with me one night longer?"

"I am waited for in Egypt," answered the Swallow. "Tomorrow my friends will fly up to the Second Cataract. The river horse couches there among the bulrushes, and on a great granite throne sits the God Memnon. All night long he watches the stars, and when the morning star shines he utters one cry of joy, and then he is silent. At noon the yellow lions come down to the water's edge to drink. They have eyes like green beryls, and their roar is louder than the roar of the cataract."

"Swallow, Swallow, little Swallow," said the Prince, "far away across the city I see a young man in a garret. He is leaning over a desk covered with papers, and in a tumbler by his side there is a bunch of withered violets. His hair is brown and crisp, and his lips are red as a pomegranate, and he has large and dreamy eyes. He is trying to finish a play for the Director of the Theatre, but he is too cold to write anymore. There is no fire in the grate, and hunger has made him faint."

"I will wait with you one night longer," said the Swallow, who really had a good heart. "Shall I take him another ruby?"

"Alas! I have no ruby now," said the Prince. "My eyes are all that I have left. They are made of rare sapphires, which were brought out of India a thousand years ago. Pluck out one of them and take it to him. He will sell it to the jeweler, and buy firewood, and finish his play."

"Dear Prince," said the Swallow, "I cannot do that." And he began to weep.

"Swallow, Swallow, little Swallow," said the Prince, "do as I command you."

So the Swallow plucked out the Prince's eye, and flew away to the student's garret. It was easy enough to get in, as there was a hole in the roof. Through this he darted, and came into the room. The young man had his head buried in his hands, so he did not hear the flutter of the bird's wings, and when he looked up he found the beautiful sapphire lying on the withered violets.

"I am beginning to be appreciated," he cried. "This is from some great admirer. Now I can finish my play," and he looked quite happy.

The next day the Swallow flew down to the harbor. He sat on the mast of a large vessel and watched the sailors hauling big chests out of the hold with ropes. "Heave ahoy!" they shouted as each chest came up. "I am going to Egypt!" cried the Swallow, but nobody minded, and when the moon rose he flew back to the Happy Prince.

"I am come to bid you good-by," he cried.

"Swallow, Swallow, little Swallow," said the Prince, "will you not stay with me one night longer?"

"It is winter," answered the Swallow, "and the chill snow will soon be here. In Egypt the sun is warm on the green palm trees, and the crocodiles lie in the mud and look lazily about them. My companions are building a nest in the Temple of Baalbec, and the pink and white doves are watching them, and cooing to each other. Dear Prince, I must leave you, but I will never forget you, and next spring I will bring you back two beautiful jewels in place of those you have given away. The ruby shall be redder than a red rose, and the sapphire shall be as blue as the great sea."

"In the square below," said the Happy Prince, "there stands a little match girl. She has let her matches fall in the gutter, and they are all spoiled. Her father will beat her if she does not bring home some money, and she is crying. She has no shoes or stockings, and her little head is bare. Pluck out my other eye, and give it to her, and her father will not beat her."

"I will stay with you one night longer," said the Swallow, "but I cannot pluck out your eye. You would be quite blind then."

"Swallow, Swallow, little Swallow," said the Prince, "do as I command you."

So he plucked out the Prince's other eye, and darted down with it. He swooped past the match girl, and slipped the jewel into the palm of her hand. "What a lovely bit of glass!" cried the little girl. And she ran home, laughing.

Then the Swallow came back to the Prince. "You are blind now," he said, "so I will stay with you always."

"No, little Swallow," said the poor Prince, "you must go away to Egypt."

"I will stay with you always," said the Swallow, and he slept at the Prince's feet.

All the next day he sat on the Prince's shoulder, and told him stories of what he had seen in strange lands. He told him of the red ibises, who stand in long rows on the banks of the Nile, and catch goldfish in their beaks; of the Sphinx, who is as old as the world itself, and lives in the desert, and knows everything; of the merchants, who walk slowly by the side of their camels and carry amber beads in their hands; of the King of the Mountains of the Moon, who is as black as ebony, and worships a large crystal; of the great green snake that sleeps in a palm tree, and has twenty priests to feed it with honey cakes; and of the pygmies who sail over a big lake on large flat leaves, and are always at war with the butterflies.

"Dear little Swallow," said the Prince, "you tell me of marvelous things, but more marvelous than anything is the suffering of men and of women. There is no Mystery so great as Misery. Fly over my city, little Swallow, and tell me what you see there."

So the Swallow flew over the great city, and saw the rich making merry in their beautiful houses, while the beggars were sitting at the gates. He flew into dark lanes, and saw the white faces of starving children looking out listlessly at the black streets. Under the archway of a bridge two little boys were lying in one another's arms to try and keep themselves warm. "How hungry we are!" they said. "You must not lie here," shouted the watchman, and they wandered out into the rain.

Then he flew back and told the Prince what he had seen.

"I am covered with fine gold," said the Prince. "You must take it off, leaf by leaf, and give it to my poor. The living always think that gold can make them happy."

Leaf after leaf of the fine gold the Swallow picked off, till the Happy Prince looked quite dull and gray. Leaf after leaf of the fine gold he brought to the poor, and the children's faces grew rosier, and they laughed and played in the street. "We have bread now!" they cried.

Then the snow came, and after the snow came the frost. The streets looked as if they were made of silver, they were so bright and glistening; long icicles like crystal daggers hung down from the eaves of the houses, everybody went about in furs, and the little boys wore scarlet caps and skated on the ice.

The poor little Swallow grew colder and colder, but he would not leave the Prince, he loved him too well. He picked up crumbs outside the baker's door when the baker was not looking, and tried to keep himself warm by flapping his wings.

But at last he knew that he was going to die. He had just enough strength to fly up to the Prince's shoulder once more. "Good-by, dear Prince!" he murmured. "Will you let me kiss your hand?"

"I am glad that you are going to Egypt at last, little Swallow," said the Prince. "You have stayed too long here. But you must kiss me on the lips, for I love you."

"It is not to Egypt that I am going," said the Swallow. "I am going to the House of Death. Death is the brother of Sleep, is he not?"

And he kissed the Happy Prince on the lips, and fell down dead at his feet.

At that moment a curious crack sounded inside the statue, as if something had broken. The fact is that the leaden heart had snapped right in two. It certainly was a dreadfully hard frost.

Early the next morning the Mayor was walking in the square below in company with the Town Councillors. As they passed the column he looked up at the statue. "Dear me! How shabby the Happy Prince looks!" he said.

"How shabby, indeed!" cried the Town Councillors, who always agreed with the Mayor. And they went up to look at it.

"The ruby has fallen out of his sword, his eyes are gone, and he is golden no longer," said the Mayor. "In fact, he is little better than a beggar!"

"Little better than a beggar," said the Town Councillors.

"And here is actually a dead bird at his feet!" continued the Mayor. "We must really issue a proclamation that birds are not to be allowed to die here." And the Town Clerk made a note of the suggestion.

So they pulled down the statue of the Happy Prince. "As he is no longer beautiful he is no longer useful," said the Art Professor at the University.

Then they melted the statue in a furnace, and the Mayor held a meeting of the Corporation to decide what was to be done with the metal. "We must have another statue, of course," he said, "and it shall be a statue of myself."

"Of myself," said each of the Town Councillors, and they quarreled. When I last heard of them they were quarreling still.

"What a strange thing!" said the overseer of the workmen at the foundry. "This broken lead heart will not melt in the furnace. We must throw it away." So they threw it on a dustheap where the dead Swallow was also lying.

"Bring me the two most precious things in the city," said God to one of His Angels; and the Angel brought Him the leaden heart and the dead bird.

"You have rightly chosen," said God, "for in my garden of Paradise this little bird shall sing forevermore, and in my city of gold the Happy Prince shall praise me."

•

THE HERMIT OF THE HIMALAYAS
Retold by Frances Dadmun

One way or another, we all depend on the kindness of others— and sometimes, as we see in this tale from India, we depend on their courage as well. As Saint Paul wrote in his letter to the Romans, "none of us liveth to himself."

Once upon a time, and it may have been long ago, five hundred hermits lived together at the foot of the highest mountains in the world, the ridged and rocky, snow-capped Himalayas. But where the hermits lived, the land was not ridged and rocky; it was covered with a vast forest of banyan trees and thornbushes. The hermits lived on the edge of the forest because it was full of cool shadows when the sun was hot and because the banyan trees and thornbushes kept off the wind when the nights were cold. But the hermits did not spend their days lying under the banyan trees. They were not as lazy as all that. Indeed, they were most industrious hermits and worked hard raising rice on the flat ground on either side of the river. The hermits ate the rice—it was about all they had, except sometimes nuts and what honey the bees stored in the rocks and hollow trees. But the hermits liked rice and they liked nuts and honey, and the water of the river was cool and good to drink.

Then there came a time which they never forgot as long as

they lived, when the water of the river was so low that they could not drink it. There had been no rain for days and days. The rice fields dried up. The earth was like powder, and when the wind blew at all, it was a warm, choking wind which blew the powdery earth in the hermits' faces. So they stayed all the time under the banyan trees where it was shady, and they found a spring which did not dry up like the river, because it came from deep down under the highest mountains. The hermits drank of it and were not thirsty, but they were very hungry, for the rice had all dried up and there were not enough nuts and honey to last very long.

And then, when there was nothing they could do to help themselves, something very strange happened.

While the hermits were sitting near the spring, under the banyan trees, they heard the rustling of a thornbush and then a soft pitter-patter, and before they could catch their breath, a panther slipped silently from behind a bush. The hermits scrambled out of the way and hid behind trees—all but one. He sat still and watched, for he was sorry for the poor panther, whose tongue hung out of his mouth, he was so hot and thirsty.

The panther did not look at the hermit at all. He crawled up to the spring and tried to catch the drops of water as they trickled down the side of the rock.

"Oh, you poor beast!" exclaimed the hermit. "You can't get much that way. I will get a pail to catch the water."

The panther's big, velvety eyes looked as if he understood. The hermit brought a pail and the water soon filled it, so that the panther had all he needed. As he drank, he felt so much better that his legs grew stronger and quite soon he could walk off, almost as well as ever.

The next day, the hermit heard the pattering of feet again. Was it his friend the panther? He hoped so, for he already felt as fond of the great cat as you do of your dog or kitten. I think it was because he had helped him. Don't you?

Yes, it was the panther, but this time, he was not alone. He headed a long, long procession of beasts—the elephant and the lion, the deer and the fox, the wolf and the bear, the monkey and the buffalo, and last of all, a timid, little rabbit—all just as thirsty as they could be. The four hundred and ninety-nine hermits hid behind the trees again, but the one who was good and kind and not afraid was troubled only for fear there would not be enough water to go around. He was right. The water in the pail was gone in no time and the poor beasts were looking at him wistfully. There were so many of them, all looking at once, that he did not know what to do.

Just then, he noticed a fallen tree trunk nearby. It occurred to him that it would make a good trough, so he hollowed it out and dragged it under the spring. It was hard work, for he was weak from hunger, but when the trough began to fill with water so that more of the animals could drink at once, he felt that it had been worthwhile.

When the four hundred and ninety-nine hermits saw all the animals quietly drinking, they were so astonished that they forgot to be afraid, and they came crawling out from behind the trunks of the banyan trees very much as the panther had crawled out from behind the thornbush. Only *they* crawled because they were so hungry. All the animals noticed it, and they also saw how their good friend had staggered when he was dragging the tree trunk under the spring.

That night, the animals held a council in the forest when the moon was bright. They sat in a circle and the elephant spoke.

"Friends and enemies," he said, "we used to quarrel and kill each other, and sometimes we killed Man, but we are all friends now because we have all together nearly died of thirst. And Man is our friend because one hermit has saved our lives. But our friend Man will die soon if we do not bring him food. What can we do? I, for one, will strip the fruit from the banana trees with my trunk, for I have heard it said that bananas are good food for Man."

The other animals all agreed to help in any way they could. It was decided that the elephant, as well as any creatures which could climb, should gather fruit from the trees and that the others should carry it.

So next day, the hermits again heard the pattering of feet. They were no longer afraid. They supposed the animals were coming for water. But what was their surprise to see them come in sight loaded down with bananas and breadfruit, coconuts and mangoes and jambus and every fruit that grew far and wide throughout that land. Each dropped his gift before the hermits, drank from the trough, and went his way.

Every day after that, as long as the drought lasted, the animals brought fruit to the hermits and drank from the trough which the kindest hermit of them all had placed under the spring. Because each helped the other, the lives of all were saved, for the animals would have died without water and the hermits would have starved without food.

•

THE MOUSE TOWER

*Adapted from retellings by Robert Southey
and Lilian Gask*

This is a very scary story, and one that stays with you. Here is a
heartless man who heeds no injunction to help others. Though
there is justice in the end, it is very rough justice. The medieval
tale reminds us how deeply unsettling is the cruelty of one human
being to another.

Hatto, Bishop of Mayence, in Germany, was rich and greedy.
There was no doubt about that. Instead of devoting himself to
prayer and almsgiving, he thought only of increasing his great
wealth. His farms were the richest in the whole country, and his
granaries were stocked with wheat and corn. But that wasn't enough
for him. He raised taxes on the people over and over again. He
built a tall tower of stone on an island in the river Rhine and would
let no boat pass by without stopping and paying a toll in silver or
gold. His moneybags grew fat and burst at the seams. Whatever
might happen to other folk, Hatto would never suffer.

One spring the river overflowed, and the low-lying land was
flooded. The harvest failed, and famine descended upon the people. Finding themselves on the point of starvation, the villagers
went to beg Hatto's aid.

"Take pity, good Bishop, on our hungry children," they cried.
"They die while your granaries are full of wheat."

But Bishop Hatto only laughed.

"I cannot help that," he said. "If you want wheat, you'd better
buy it from me now. Tomorrow my prices will be higher."

But they were desperate, and every day they came crowding
around his house. However much he tried, he could not drive them
off. The little starving children scratched at his door, and the crying
mothers held their infants up to his windows.

Wearied, at last, by their begging, Hatto came out and faced
them.

"All right," he said, "you've convinced me. Meet me at my
largest barn, the empty one down by the river. I give you my word
that I'll bring an end to your suffering."

Now at last there was joy among the starving creatures. Their dim eyes brightened, and strength came back to their shrunken limbs as they dragged themselves to the barn and waited for the food to be distributed.

"You shall have bread tonight," they told their little ones, and the children ceased their wailing.

At the appointed time Bishop Hatto made his appearance. His cruel lips were pressed tightly together, and hatred burned in his deep-set eyes as he surveyed the hungry masses. He stood outside and watched the villagers limp into the barn.

As the last one filed inside, he closed the doors, and bolted them shut.

For a while the poor people could not fathom what was happening. Every moment they expected Hatto to enter and begin distributing food. But the minutes wore on, and he did not come. Instead, they heard his cruel voice laughing outside.

"You have pestered me like rats," he said, "and now you shall die like rats."

Then the people pounded on the walls, shrieked, and wept for mercy. But the doors stood fast, and the trapped victims were far too weak from hunger to break them down. Hours passed, and then days, and the poor villagers starved to death.

"I've done the country a great service," said Hatto, "ridding it of rats that only consumed the corn."

Weeks passed, and then months. The dead remained undisturbed. Finally, one of the bishop's servants opened the doors of the barn, intending to lay the bones to rest. The place was empty.

"Good riddance," said the bishop, shrugging. "Dust to dust."

But that night his sleep was broken by quick, little scratching sounds, as if something were scampering over the floor.

The next morning he was annoyed to find that a splendid portrait of himself in his bishop's robes, which had been painted by a famous artist at great expense, was lying on the ground, gnawed to shreds. He could see the marks of rats' sharp teeth on that part of the canvas where his face had been. He shuddered at the sight in spite of himself.

A few days later, one of his servants appeared before him, his face white with alarm.

"My lord," he whispered, "I opened one of your granaries this morning. The rats have eaten all the corn."

That very evening Hatto was sitting alone, eating his dinner, when he looked up and saw a mouse sitting at the other end of the table. It stared back at him with a hungry look in its eyes. He threw a fork at it, and it scampered away.

But after that, he noticed mice here and there all around his house. He saw their noses peeking out of cracks in the wall, and their tails hanging out of drawers and cupboards. He stepped on them in the stairway and sat on them in his favorite chair. They ran across his bedsheets, and even nested in his pillows.

He brought cats to keep them out. But the cats soon disappeared.

The rats swarmed all over the kitchen and pantry, devouring every last crumb. When the food was gone, they gnawed at the wood. He could hear them in the floors and walls. Hatto trembled, and knew fear for the first time.

And then one day a servant burst into his room.

"Fly, my lord bishop, fly!" he cried. "They are coming this way!"

Hatto looked out his window. Ten thousand rats covered the hillside where his old granary stood—and they were coming his way!

Panic seized the man who had committed so evil a crime. Mounting his horse, he went off at full gallop. Though his horse was fleet and he spurred him on unmercifully, the bishop found that the army of rats was gaining on him. Wild with terror, he reached the riverside, and jumping into a little boat, rowed with all his might to the middle of the stream, where his tall tower stood on its island.

He ran inside and barred the door. He was safe, he thought. The tower walls were high, and the island shores steep. The current in the river was strong, and the water deep.

He checked the cupboard—he had plenty of food stored there. That made him feel better. He counted the money he had hidden away. That made him feel even better. He could hold out until this invasion had passed. He climbed up and down the tower's stairs, barring every window, closing every door. Then he lay down and closed his eyes.

He woke in the middle of the night. Something made him go to the window and peep out. He could not believe what he saw.

The water was black and seething in the moonlight. Rats! It was full of them—thousands, millions of them—swimming straight for him! The river was choking with rats. He could hear them squeaking and squealing as they gained the shore.

Hatto ran up the stairs, as high as he could get, and locked himself in the uppermost room. He listened breathlessly. He could hear them whetting their teeth against the tower stones.

Desperately, he opened a window and began throwing out bread and corn and cheese, hoping to satisfy the ravenous horde. But that was not what they came for. Far below, he heard the scampering of thousands of tiny feet on the stairs.

He screamed. He dragged everything he could move—tables and chairs and heavy moneybags—against the door. He looked around him wildly. There was nothing left to push, nowhere else to go. He crouched in a dusty corner and waited.

The wait was not long. From within the walls, behind the door, down through the ceiling, up through the floor—came the sound of gnawing.

A few days later, some of the bishop's servants dared to enter the ruined tower. They found some bread and corn and cheese, and piles of moneybags lying about untouched. But they found no sign of Hatto.

•

KADDO'S WALL

Retold by Harold Courlander
and George Herzog

In this story, Kaddo acts as though he could be a distant cousin of the Hatto of Mouse Tower fame. This remarkable tale comes from west Africa.

In the town of Tendella in the Kingdom of Seno, north of the Gulf of Guinea, there was a rich man by the name of Kaddo. His fields spread out on every side of the town. At plowing time hundreds of men and boys hoed up his fields, and then hundreds of women and girls planted his corn seed in the ground for him. His grain bulged in his granary, because each season he harvested far more than he could use. The name of Kaddo was known far and wide throughout the Kingdom of Seno. Travelers who passed through the town carried tales of his wealth far beyond Seno's borders.

One day Kaddo called all of his people in the town of Tendella together for a big meeting in front of his house. They all came, for Kaddo was an important man, and they knew he was going to make an important announcement.

"There's something that bothers me," Kaddo said. "I've been thinking about it for a long time. I've lain awake worrying. I have so much corn in my granary that I don't know what to do with it."

The people listened attentively, and thought about Kaddo's words. Then a man said:

"Some of the people of the town have no corn at all. They are very poor and have nothing. Why don't you give some of your corn to them?"

Kaddo shook his head and said, "No, that isn't a very good idea. It doesn't satisfy me."

Another man said to Kaddo:

"Well, then, you could lend corn to the people who have had a bad harvest and have no seed for the spring planting. That would be very good for the town and would keep poverty away."

"No," Kaddo said, "that's no solution either."

"Well, then, why not sell some of your corn and buy cattle instead?" still another man said.

Kaddo shook his head.

"No, it's not very good advice. It's hard for people to advise a rich man with problems like mine."

Many people made suggestions, but nobody's advice suited Kaddo. He thought for a while, and at last he said:

"Send me as many young girls as you can find. I will have them grind the corn for me."

The people went away. They were angry with Kaddo. But the next day they sent a hundred girls to work for him as he had asked. On a hundred grindstones they began to grind Kaddo's corn into flour. All day long they put corn into the grindstones and took flour out. All day long the people of the town heard the sound of the grinding at Kaddo's house. A pile of corn flour began to grow. For seven days and seven nights the girls ground corn without a pause.

When the last grain of corn was ground into flour, Kaddo called the girls together and said:

"Now bring water from the spring. We shall mix it with the corn flour to make mortar out of it."

So the girls brought water in water pots and mixed it with the flour to make a thick mortar. Then Kaddo ordered them to make bricks out of the mortar.

"When the bricks are dry, then I shall make a wall of them around my house," he said.

Word went out that Kaddo was preparing to build a wall of flour around his house, and the people of the town came to his door and protested.

"You can't do a thing like this, it is against humanity!" they said.

"It's not right, people have no right to build walls with food!" a man said.

"Ah, what is right and what is wrong?" Kaddo said. "My right is different from yours, because I am so very rich. So leave me alone."

"Corn is to eat, so that you may keep alive," another said. "It's not meant to taunt those who are less fortunate."

"When people are hungry it is an affront to shut them out with a wall of flour," another man said.

"Stop your complaints," Kaddo said. "The corn is mine. It is my surplus. I can't eat it all. It comes from my own fields. I am rich. What good is it to be rich if you can't do what you want with your own property?"

The people of the town went away, shaking their heads in anger over Kaddo's madness. The hundred girls continued to make bricks of flour, which they dried in the sun. And when the bricks were dry, Kaddo had them begin building the wall around his house. They used wet dough for mortar to hold the bricks together, and slowly the wall grew. They stuck cowry shells into the wall to make beautiful designs, and when at last the wall was done, and the last corn flour used up, Kaddo was very proud. He walked back and forth and looked at his wall. He walked around it. He went in and out of the gate. He was very happy.

And now when people came to see him they had to stand by the gate until he asked them to enter. When the workers who plowed and planted for Kaddo wanted to talk to him, Kaddo sat on the wall by the gate and listened to them and gave them orders. And whenever the people of the town wanted his opinion on an important matter, he sat on his wall and gave it to them, while they stood and listened.

Things went on like this for a long time. Kaddo enjoyed his reputation as the richest man for miles around. The story of Kaddo's wall went to the farthest parts of the kingdom.

And then one year there was a bad harvest for Kaddo. There wasn't enough rain to grow the corn, and the earth dried up hard and dusty like the road. There wasn't a single ear of corn in all of Kaddo's fields or the fields of his relatives.

The next year it was the same. Kaddo had no seed corn left, so he sold his cattle and horses to buy corn for food and seed for a new planting. He sowed corn again, but the next harvest time it was the same, and there wasn't a single ear of corn on all his fields.

Year after year Kaddo's crops failed. Some of his relatives died of hunger, and others went away to other parts of the Kingdom of Seno, for they had no more seed corn to plant and they couldn't count on Kaddo's help. Kaddo's workers ran away, because he was unable to feed them. Gradually Kaddo's part of the town became deserted. All that he had left were a young daughter and a mangy donkey.

When his cattle and his money were all gone, Kaddo became very hungry. He scraped away a little bit of the flour wall and ate it. Next day he scraped away more of the flour wall and ate it. The wall got lower and lower. Little by little it disappeared. A day came when the wall was gone, when nothing was left of the elegant structure Kaddo had built around his house, and on which he had used to sit to listen to the people of the town when they came to ask him to lend them a little seed corn.

Then Kaddo realized that if he was to live any longer he must get help from somewhere. He wondered who would help him. Not the people of Tendella, for he had insulted and mistreated them and they would have nothing to do with him. There was only one man he could go to—Sogole, king of the Ganna people, who had the reputation of being very rich and generous.

So Kaddo and his daughter got on the mangy, underfed donkey and rode seven days until they arrived in the land of the Ganna.

Sogole sat before his royal house when Kaddo arrived. He had a soft skin put on the ground next to him for Kaddo to sit upon, and had millet beer brought for the two of them to drink.

"Well, stranger in the land of the Ganna, take a long drink, for you have a long trip behind you if you come from Tendella," Sogole said.

"Thank you, but I can't drink much," Kaddo said.

"Why is that?" Sogole said. "When people are thirsty they drink."

"That is true," Kaddo replied. "But I have been hungry too long, and my stomach is shrunk."

"Well, drink in peace then, because now that you are my guest you won't be hungry. You shall have whatever you need from me."

Kaddo nodded his head solemnly and drank a little of the millet beer.

"And now tell me," Sogole said. "You say you come from the town of Tendella in the Kingdom of Seno? I've heard many tales of that town. The famine came there and drove out many people, because they had no corn left."

"Yes," Kaddo said. "Hard times drove them out, and the corn was all gone."

"But tell me, there was a rich and powerful man in Tendella named Kaddo, wasn't there? What ever happened to him? Is he still alive?"

"Yes, he is still alive," Kaddo said.

"A fabulous man, this Kaddo," Sogole said. "They say he built a wall of flour around his house out of his surplus crops, and when he talked to his people he sat on the wall by his gate. Is this true?"

"Yes, it is true," Kaddo said sadly.

"Does he still have as many cattle as he used to?" Sogole asked.

"No, they are all gone."

"It is an unhappy thing for a man who owned so much to come to so little," Sogole said. "But doesn't he have many servants and workers still?"

"His workers and servants are all gone," Kaddo said. "Of all his great household he has only one daughter left. The rest went away because there was no money and no food."

Sogole looked melancholy.

"Ah, what is a rich man when his cattle are gone and his servants have left him? But tell me, what happened to the wall of flour that he built around his house?"

"He ate the wall," Kaddo said. "Each day he scraped a little of the flour from the wall, until it was all gone."

"A strange story," Sogole said. "But such is life."

And he thought quietly for a while about the way life goes for people sometimes, and then he asked:

"And were you, by any chance, one of Kaddo's family?"

"Indeed I was one of Kaddo's family. Once I was rich. Once I had more cattle than I could count. Once I had many cornfields. Once I had hundreds of workers cultivating my crops. Once I had a bursting granary. Once I was Kaddo, the great personage of Tendella."

"What! You yourself are Kaddo?"

"Yes, once I was proud and lordly, and now I sit in rags begging for help."

"What can I do for you?" Sogole asked.

"I have nothing left now. Give me some seed corn, so that I can go back and plant my fields again."

"Take what you need," Sogole said. He ordered his servants to bring bags of corn and to load them on Kaddo's donkey. Kaddo thanked him humbly, and he and his daughter started their return trip to Tendella. They traveled for seven days. On the way Kaddo became very hungry. He hadn't seen so much corn for a long time as he was bringing back from the Kingdom of the Ganna. He took a few grains and put them in his mouth and chewed them. Once more he put a few grains in his mouth. Then he put a whole handful in his mouth and swallowed. He couldn't stop. He ate and ate. He forgot that this was the corn with which he had to plant his fields. When he arrived in Tendella he went to his bed to sleep, and when he arose the next morning he ate again. He ate so much of the corn that he became sick. He went to his bed again and cried out in pain, because his stomach had forgotten what to do with food. And before long Kaddo died.

Kaddo's grandchildren and great-grandchildren in the Kingdom of Seno are poor to this day. And to the rich men of the country the common people sometimes say:

"Don't build a wall of flour around your house."

•

THE EMERALD LIZARD

Great hearts can help give rise to little miracles.

Brother Pedro lived in Guatemala long ago, hundreds of years ago, in fact, but all the good he did lives on in the stories of his work. He was a poor man and stayed poor all his life, for he gave whatever he had to those in need. He turned his own small, humble home into a place where the sick could find care. It is said that at night he walked the city streets ringing a little bell to remind people to thank God for their blessings and share those same gifts with others.

One day Brother Pedro was walking toward the city when he came upon a ragged man sitting beside the road. The man wiped away a tear as Brother Pedro approached.

"What ails you, my friend?" Brother Pedro asked, perceiving his despair.

"My troubles weigh heavily," the man sobbed. "My wife is sick and needs medicine. My children are hungry and want food. But I have no money and can find no work. I don't know what to do."

Brother Pedro looked at the suffering man's face and longed to help. But his own clothes were just as ragged, his own cupboard as bare, his own pockets as empty. He had nothing to give.

He turned his gaze upward, hoping for an answer. The sun's warm glow spread across his kind face. "Dear Lord," he whispered, "help me help this man."

There was a rustling at their feet, and from behind a gray rock, a bright green lizard crept into the sun. Brother Pedro stooped and gently caught it by the tail. With a smile he placed it into his companion's hands.

The poor man looked at Brother Pedro in bewilderment. Then he opened his hands and gasped. The lizard was suddenly rigid and heavy and hard. But it was still a rich green. The man peered closely, and beheld a miracle. The live creature had turned into an emerald lizard.

"Take this, and sell it," Brother Pedro said. "With the money it brings, you will be able to care for your wife and feed your children, and perhaps you will have enough left over to tend to others in need as well."

The grateful man did as he was told. He hurried to a jeweler, where he was able to sell the rare emerald for much gold. With medicine and food, his family grew healthy and strong again. The years passed. The man worked hard. His children grew up to be prosperous ranchers and farmers, and their wealth increased tenfold. But they lived quietly and sensibly, and took care of their aging parents, and gave much of their fortune to help the poor.

The day came when their father directed his footsteps back to the jeweler where he had sold the miraculous lizard. He bought the gem back and set out to find Brother Pedro.

The good Brother was much grayer now, and even poorer and more shabbily dressed than before. But his wrinkled face was every bit as kind.

"Do you remember me, Padre?" the visitor asked.

Brother Pedro looked at the stranger closely, searching his mind.

"I met you on the road one day long ago. My wife was sick, and my children were starving."

Brother Pedro shook his head. There had been so many!

"You gave me an emerald lizard, and told me to trade it for gold."

Brother Pedro's face brightened.

"Of course, of course. Now I remember. And how did things turn out? How is your wife? How are your children?"

"They are well," the man replied. "But now I've brought your emerald back. It has given my family health and wealth. You've worked hard all your life in the service of others. Take the gem, and rest from your labors. You can sell it for gold, as I did, and live your last days in ease."

He took the sparkling lizard from his pocket and placed it back in the good old man's hands.

Smiling gently, Brother Pedro stooped and set it on the ground. At once it turned into a live green lizard and disappeared under a rock.

•

MARGARET OF NEW ORLEANS

Sara Cone Bryant

Here is a true story of a real heroine. Born of Irish immigrant parents, Margaret Haughery moved to New Orleans from Baltimore in search of health for her husband. When both her husband and child died, she began helping the children of the Poydras Orphan Asylum. Most of the money she earned from her dairy and bakery went to the city's needy, and when Margaret died her life savings of $30,000 went to charity. The Margaret Statue, one of the earliest memorials erected to a woman in the United States, was dedicated in 1884. It still stands today, modest and compelling.

There is still work like this to be done in cities all over the country, and more Margarets needed to do it.

If you ever go to the beautiful city of New Orleans, somebody will be sure to take you down into the old business part of the city, where there are banks and shops and hotels, and show you a statue which stands in a little square there. It is the statue of a woman, sitting in a low chair, with her arms around a child, who leans against her. The woman is not at all pretty. She wears thick, common shoes, a plain dress, with a little shawl, and a sunbonnet. She is stout and short, and her face is a square-chinned Irish face. But her eyes look at you like your mother's.

Now there is something very surprising about this statue. It was one of the first that was ever made in this country in honor of a woman. Even in old Europe there are not many monuments to women, and most of the few are to great queens or princesses, very beautiful and very richly dressed. You see, this statue in New Orleans is not quite like anything else.

It is the statue of a woman named Margaret. Her whole name was Margaret Haughery, but no one in New Orleans remembers her by it, any more than you think of your dearest sister by her full name. She is just Margaret. This is her story, and it tells why people made a monument for her.

When Margaret was a tiny baby, her father and mother died,

and she was adopted by two young people as poor and as kind as her own parents. She lived with them until she grew up. Then she married, and had a little baby of her own. But very soon her husband died, and then the baby died, too, and Margaret was all alone in the world. She was poor, but she was strong, and knew how to work.

All day, from morning until evening, she ironed clothes in a laundry. And every day, as she worked by the window, she saw the little motherless children from the orphanage nearby working and playing about. After a while, a great sickness came upon the city, and so many mothers and fathers died that there were more orphans than the orphanage could possibly take care of. They needed a good friend now. You would hardly think, would you, that a poor woman who worked in a laundry could be much of a friend to them? But Margaret was. She went straight to the kind Sisters who ran the orphanage and told them she was going to give them part of her wages and was going to work for them, besides. Pretty soon she had worked so hard that she had some money saved from her wages. With this, she bought two cows and a little delivery cart. Then she carried her milk to her customers in the little cart every morning, and as she went, she begged the leftover food from the hotels and rich houses, and brought it back in the cart to the hungry children in the orphanage. In the very hardest times that was often all the food the children had.

A part of the money Margaret earned went every week to the orphanage, and after a few years it was made very much larger and better. And Margaret was so careful and so good at business that, in spite of her giving, she bought more cows and earned more money. With this, she built a home for orphan babies; she called it her baby house.

After a time, Margaret had a chance to get a bakery, and then she became a bread-woman instead of a milk-woman. She carried the bread just as she had carried the milk, in her cart. And still she kept giving money to the orphanage. Then the great war came, the Civil War. In all the trouble and sickness and fear of that time, Margaret drove her cart of bread, and somehow she had always enough to give the starving soldiers, and for her babies, besides what she sold. And despite all this, she earned enough so that when the war was over she built a big steam factory for her bread. By this time everybody in the city knew her. The children all over the city loved her. The businessmen were proud of her. The poor people all came to her for advice. She used to sit at the open door of her office, in a calico gown and a little shawl, and give a good word to everybody, rich or poor.

Then, by and by, one day, Margaret died. And when it was time to read her will, the people found that, with all her giving, she had still saved a great deal of money, and that she had left every cent of it to the different orphanages of the city—each one of them was given something. Whether they were for white children or black, for Jews, Catholics, or Protestants, made no difference; for Margaret always said, "They are all orphans alike." And just think, that splendid, wise will was signed with a cross instead of a name, for Margaret had never learned to read or write!

When the people of New Orleans knew that Margaret was dead, they said, "She was a mother to the motherless. She was a friend to those who had no friends. She had wisdom greater than schools can teach. We will not let her memory go from us." So they made a statute of her, just as she used to look, sitting in her own office door, or driving in her own little cart. And there it stands today, in memory of the great love and the great power of plain Margaret Haughery, of New Orleans.

•

THE BOY WHO BROUGHT LIGHT INTO A WORLD OF DARKNESS

It has been said that necessity is the mother of invention. As we learn from the remarkable life of Louis Braille (1809–1852), compassion can play a large role in invention too. Helen Keller wrote of Braille that "the unwearied activity of his clear, scientific mind, his calmness and forbearance, his inventive abilities as a teacher, the wealth of his heart expended in uncounted secret gifts out of his scanty savings to the needy, both blind and seeing, are a priceless legacy."

One day nearly two hundred years ago, a young French boy was standing in his father's workshop in the town of Coupvray, not far from Paris. Louis Braille was only three years old, but he loved to watch his father making saddles and harnesses out of tough leather hides. Sometimes his father gave him little scraps of leather to play with, and he pretended he was fitting them together into saddles too. Already, at that young age, he wanted to be just like his father.

Monsieur Braille sewed busily, smiling down at his son every once in a while. The harness-maker worked quickly and smoothly, cutting the leather with a sure hand and practiced eye. He held a piece up to the light, examined it closely, and saw he would need to use a different knife. Laying his work down, he crossed the room to search for the right tool.

Little Louis reached toward the workbench, picked up the awl his father had left behind, and began to poke at his own scrap of leather. He jabbed fiercely at the tough leather, trying make the point go all the way through. As he stabbed, his young fingers lost their grip. The sharp instrument sprang up and struck his left eye.

Monsieur Braille heard a scream and ran back to his bench, but it was too late. The damage was done.

The horrified parents took their young son to the doctor, hoping to save the eye, but the injury was too serious. And then, as time passed, the tragedy deepened. Infection spread to the other eye as well. Before long the boy could not see at all.

In those days people often treated the blind with great cruelty or neglect. Sometimes they were thrown out by their families to beg on the streets or sing for alms. Or they were hired out to do hard labor, like beasts of burden. In many places, blindness was viewed as the work of Satan or divine punishment for sin.

But it was different in the town of Coupvray, where everyone watched out for the little blind Louis. They listened for the tap of his cane, and smiled when they saw him coming. They stopped their own work to guide him across the street or around a corner. They helped him count how many taps it took to get to the marketplace, or the edge of town, or school.

Louis and his father would walk together, and the boy would ask, "What color is the sky today?"

"As blue as can be, son," Monsieur Braille would say. "As blue as can be."

But although Louis struggled to recall a vision of blue, the pictures of his youth gradually faded from his mind, and he could no longer remember the beauty of such sights as colors.

He learned to help his father in his shop, handing him tools and pieces of leather. He went to school with his old friends, too, and everyone was surprised at the way he learned by listening and memorizing his lessons. He loved to spend his time talking to his teacher about history and geography, and to the town priest about music and Bible stories.

But in truth he was not happy with his studies, for he wanted to be able to read books and write letters like his classmates.

Then one day the schoolmaster told Louis about a school for the blind in Paris. It had a special kind of book that blind people could read, he said. Louis could hardly believe his ears. He begged his parents to send him to the wonderful school, and the village priest helped them find money to help pay the costs.

And so when he was ten years old, Louis and his father traveled to Paris, where the boy enrolled in the National Institute for the Young Blind. As soon as he arrived, he asked his new teachers the question that was burning in his mind: "Can you teach me to read?"

He learned that the school was experimenting with a new way of teaching the blind to read. The Institute's founder had printed some books with large, raised letters on the pages. By tracing the shape of the letters with their fingers, blind students could make out words and sentences.

It wasn't long, however, before Louis discovered the shortcomings of this method. The raised letters were so large that even a very short story filled many pages. A single book might weigh hundreds of pounds! Tracing the fingers over the print was a clumsy process, so it took a long time for a blind person to read just a few paragraphs. And since the books were expensive to make, the school could afford to print only a few. It wasn't long before Louis had read through its entire library.

Despite his disappointment in this cumbersome method, the boy from Coupvray studied hard and learned quickly. He especially loved music; with his keen hearing, quick fingers, and sharp memory he became a fine student of the piano and cello. He loved spending his free hours at the organ in the nearby church, and before long he began playing for the services there.

His love of music made him long more than ever for a better way to read. He wanted to be able to read not just words but musical notes as well. And he wanted to be able to write. Sometimes he lay awake at night thinking over the problem again and again.

"There must be a way," he kept telling himself. "If blind people are to learn as much as everyone else, they must be able to read and write. I must find a way."

Then one day he heard of an army captain named Charles Barbier who had invented a method to send messages in the dark. His "night writing" consisted of dots and dashes raised on paper; by running their fingers over the code, soldiers could read without using a light.

At once Louis recognized what such an idea meant. If a soldier could read and write messages in the dark, then a blind person could read and write too!

He went to question Monsieur Barbier. The captain was happy to demonstrate his system. He punched a few holes on a piece of paper with an awl, one similar to the very instrument that had destroyed Louis's own sight. He turned the paper over, and showed his visitor how the marks made little bumps. Louis ran his fingers over the raised dots. Barbier explained how certain combinations of dots and dashes could make words and sentences.

Louis hurried back to the Institute and set to work. Night after night, month after month he worked with Barbier's system, changing and refining. He knew the idea was sound, but he also knew the captain's arrangement of dots and dashes was too cumbersome to be truly useful to the blind.

Like many new ideas and inventions, Louis's work was viewed with suspicion. Some of the officials at the Institute resented his trying to change things. They had spent a small fortune printing their books with raised letters, and they saw no reason to change to a whole new system based on little bumps. They argued that a new writing invented solely for blind people would segregate them even more from the rest of society. They frowned on Louis's efforts.

When he was seventeen years old, Louis became a teacher at the Institute. By day he taught his students to read using the older method of large, raised letters, but at night he continued to develop his new system. He would work until the early morning hours, carefully punching holes, testing new patterns, searching for the right combinations, until he fell asleep in the midst of his tools and papers. Except for his beloved music, he gave all his spare time to the effort, always cheerful and brave and confident of success.

In 1829, by the time he was twenty years old, Louis arrived at his readable alphabet using various patterns of one to six raised dots. The Braille system was complete. He designed a little punch tool to write with, and after a while he could write almost as fast as someone could talk. He could even write and read music using his new system.

Word began to spread. Some of his students would come secretly to his room at night to learn the new method. Louis punched out his own books—Shakespeare and other classics—for them to read. After a while other blind people began to hear about the marvelous new method, and from all over the world they sent Louis letters asking about his invention.

And yet, sad to say, most people still could not see the importance of Braille's new system. Some saw its value, but did not care. Others were envious or resentful of the new method. Some of the teachers at the Institute, unwilling to try anything new, tried to make sure no one would ever learn to read using Louis Braille's dots.

But Louis went on refining and promoting his idea, hoping for the day when blind people all over the world would have the chance to read and write as he now could. He punched out more and more books, and taught any blind person who was interested how to read them. He talked to anyone who would listen about his method, demonstrating it again and again, trying to rouse public interest.

And through all the days and nights of work, he wore himself out. His health began to fail, and for a while it seemed as though the opportunity he had made for blind people might pass from the earth with him.

At last, however, his ideas found acceptance. Toward the end of his life, several places throughout Europe began to recognize the importance of Braille's work, and more blind people began to discover his raised dots. The light was dawning. As he lay in a hospital bed a few weeks before his death, Louis said to a friend, "Oh, unsearchable mystery of the human heart! I am convinced that my mission on earth is finished."

He died in 1852, just two days after his forty-third birthday.

In the years following Braille's death, more and more blind people turned to his raised-dot system. The Braille method spread from country to country, at last becoming the accepted method of reading and writing for those who cannot see. At last books could become a part of their lives, all because of a fifteen-year-old boy who devoted his own life to finding a better way.

•

BROTHER TO THE LEPERS
Charles Warren Stoddard

Here is an eyewitness account of the remarkable work of the
missionary Joseph Damien de Veuster, better known to the world
simply as Father Damien (1840–1888). The young Belgian
priest's offer to aid the leper colony on the Hawaiian island of
Molokai in 1873 was a complete act of self-sacrifice. He knew that
eventually he would almost certainly catch the dreaded disease
himself. Upon his arrival at Molokai, he discovered a community
of some six hundred lepers desperately in need of both spiritual
and physical care. He set to work without hesitation. The following description of Father Damien's work comes from Charles Warren Stoddard, a resident of the Hawaiian Islands who visited
Molokai with two government physicians in 1884.

The first glimpse of Kalawao might lead a stranger to pronounce it a thriving hamlet of perhaps five hundred inhabitants.
Its single street is bordered by neat whitewashed cottages, with
numerous little gardens of bright flowers, and clusters of graceful
and decorative tropical trees. It lies so near the base of the mountain that not a few of the huge stones that were loosened by the
rains have come thundering down the heights, and rolled almost to
the fences that enclose the village suburbs.

As we passed down the street, Dr. Fitch was greeted on every
hand. He had been expected, for it was his custom to visit the
settlement monthly; and many a shout of welcome was raised, and
many an *"Aloha!"*—the fond salutation of the race—rang from
doorway, window, and veranda. One group of stalwart fellows
swung their hats in air, and gave three lusty cheers for *"Kauka"*
(the doctor), topping them off with a burst of childish laughter.

Thus far, inasmuch as we had scarcely looked into the faces of
these villagers, they seemed to us the merriest and most contented
community in the world. But let it be remembered that we were all
in the deep afternoon shadow, and our arrival was the sensation of
the hour.

By the roadside, in the edge of the village, between it and the sea, stood a little chapel; the cross upon its low belfry, and the larger cross in the cemetery beyond, assured us that the poor villagers were not neglected in the hour of their extremity.

As we drew near, the churchyard gate was swung open for us by a troop of laughing urchins, who stood hat in hand to give us welcome. Now, for the first time, I noticed that they were all disfigured: that their faces were seared and scarred; their hands and feet maimed and sometimes bleeding; their eyes like the eyes of some half-tamed animal; their mouths shapeless; and their whole aspect in many cases repulsive.

These were lepers; so were they, each of them, that had greeted us as we passed through the village; so are they all, with a few privileged exceptions, who dwell in the two little villages under the cliffs by the sea.

Other lepers gathered about us as we entered the churchyard. The chapel steps were crowded with them—for a stranger is seldom seen at Kalawao—and as their number increased, it seemed as if each newcomer was more horrible than the last, until corruption could go no farther, and flesh suffer no deeper dishonor this side of the grave. They voluntarily drew aside as we advanced, closing in behind us, and encircling us at every step.

The chapel door stood ajar. In a moment it was thrown open, and a young priest paused upon the threshold to give us welcome. His cassock was worn and faded, his hair tumbled like a schoolboy's, his hands stained and hardened by toil. But the glow of health was in his face, the buoyancy of youth in his manner, while his ringing laugh, his ready sympathy, and his inspiring magnetism told of one who in any sphere might do a noble work, and who in that which he has chosen is doing the noblest of all works.

This was Father Damien, the self-exiled priest, the one clean man in the midst of his flock of lepers.

He was born in Louvain, Belgium, January 3, 1840. When he was but four and twenty, his brother, who had just entered the priesthood, was ordered to embark for Honolulu, but at the moment fell sick with typhoid fever. Young Damien, who was a theological student at the University, having received minor orders, and belonging to the same order—the Society of the Sacred Hearts of Jesus and Mary (commonly called Society of Picpus)—at once wrote to his superior, and begged that he might be sent upon the mission in his brother's stead. In one week he was on his way to that far country. He was ordained upon his arrival in Honolulu, and for a few years led the life of toil and privation which invariably falls to the lot of the Catholic missionary.

In 1873 he, in common with others of the clergy, was invited to be present at the dedication of a beautiful chapel just completed by Father Leonor at Wailuku, on the Island of Maui. There he met the Bishop, who expressed regret that he was still unable to send a priest to Molokai, for the demand was far in excess of the supply. Father Damien at once said, "My Lord, I hear that a small vessel will next week take cattle from Kawaihae to Kaulapapa. If you will permit me I will go there to help the lepers make their Easter duties."

His request was granted, and, in company with the Bishop and the French Consul, he landed at the settlement, where he found a colony of eight hundred lepers, of whom between four and five hundred were Catholics. A public meeting was immediately called, at which the Bishop and the Consul presided. His Grace arose to address the singular gathering and said; "Since you have written me so often that you have no priest, I leave you one for a little time." And, imparting the benediction, he returned immediately to the vessel which was to sail that very hour. Father Damien told him, "As there is much to be done here, by your leave I will not even accompany you to the shore."

Thus the good work was at once begun. It was high time. The lepers were dying at the rate of from eight to twelve per week. The priest had not time to build himself a hut—he had not even the material with which to build it—and for a season he slept in the open air, under a tree, exposed to the wind and the rain.

Soon after he received a letter of congratulation from the white residents of Honolulu—chiefly Protestants—together with some lumber, and a purse of $120. Then he put up his little house, and began to feel at home.

After remaining some weeks at Kalawao, he was obliged to go to Honolulu,. there being no more convenient priest to whom he could make his confession.

He naturally called upon the president of the Board of Health, who seemed much surprised, but received the priest with frigid politeness. He then asked leave to return to the settlement on Molokai and was curtly informed that he might indeed return, but that in that case he must remain there for good.

Father Damien's duties were never-ending. From early Mass till long after his flock was housed in sleep, he was busy. And when at last he had sought his pillow, it was too often to lie awake plan-

ning for the future, and perhaps to be called again into the ward-
rooms to ease the anguish of the sick or the dying.

The neat white cottages which have taken the place of the
thatched huts of the natives were erected under his eye; and, furthermore, he personally assisted in the construction of most of
them. The small chapel which he found at the settlement has become the transept of the present edifice; he, with the aid of a
handful of lepers, enlarged the building, painted it without, decorated it within. There he daily offers the Holy Sacrifice of the Mass,
preaches frequently, instructs the children, and fills all the offices
of the Church.

He was indeed jack-of-all-trades: physician of the soul and of
the body, magistrate, schoolteacher, carpenter, joiner, painter, gardener, housekeeper, cook, and even, in some cases, undertaker and
gravedigger. Great was his need of help, and long was he in need
of it before it came. More than 1,600 lepers had been buried under
his administration, and a deathbed was always awaiting him—sometimes two or three of them.

I remember how, one day, as we were walking among the
wards of the hospital at Kalawao, Father Damien turned suddenly
to us, and said, "Ah, here is something dreadful I must show you!"
We approached what seemed a little bundle of rags, or rubbish,
half hidden under a soiled blanket. The curious doctors were about
to examine it, when the good Father seized me, and cried, excitedly,
"You must not look! You must not look!" I assured him that I was
not at all afraid to see even the worst that could be shown me there,
for my eyes had become accustomed to horrors, and the most
sickening sights no longer affected me. A corner of the blanket was
raised, cautiously. A breathing object lay beneath; a face, a human
face, was turned slowly towards us—a face in which scarcely a trace
of anything human remained. The dark skin was puffed out and
blackened. A kind of moss, or mold, gummy and glistening, covered
it. The muscles of the mouth, having contracted, laid bare the grinning teeth. The thickened tongue lay like a fig between them. The
eyelids, curled tightly back, exposed the inner surface, and the
protruding eyeballs, now shapeless and broken, looked not unlike
bursted grapes. It was a leprous child, who within the last few days
had assumed that horrible visage. Surely the grave knows nothing
more frightful than this!

Once I wandered alone into the chapel. A small organ was
standing near an open window; beyond the window was the very

pandanus tree under which Father Damien found shelter when he first came to Kalawao. I sat at the instrument, dreaming over the keys, and thinking of the life one must lead in such a spot, of the need for and the lack of human sympathy, of the solitude of the soul destined to a communion with perpetual death—and, hearing a slight rustling near me, I turned, and found the chapel nearly filled with lepers, who had silently stolen in, one after another, at the sound of the organ. The situation was rather startling. But when I asked where Father Damien might be found, they directed me, and stood aside to let me pass.

I found him where I might have known he was likely to be found, working bravely among his men, he by far the most industrious of them all. As I approached them unobserved, the bell of the little chapel rang out the Angelus; on the instant they all knelt, uncovered, and in their midst the priest recited the beautiful prayer, to which they responded in soft, low voices—while the gentle breeze rustled the broad leaves about them, and the sun poured a flood of glory upon their bowed forms. Lepers all of them, save the good pastor, and soon to follow in the ghastly procession, whose motionless bodies he blesses in their peaceful sleep.

Angelus Domini! Was not that sight pleasing in the eyes of God?

Shortly after Stoddard's visit, Father Damien discovered he had caught leprosy. He lived for four more years, continuing his work almost to the end.

•

THE SHIPWRECK

Charles Dickens

Here is a glimpse of the kind of personal courage that sometimes
rises in the human heart when others' lives are at stake—even
strangers' lives. This is one of the finest descriptive passages from
one of the finest novels in the English language, *David Copperfield.* The narrator, young David Copperfield, travels to Yarmouth to see his friend Ham Peggotty.

Having made up my mind to go down to Yarmouth, I went
round to the coach office and took the box seat on the mail. In the
evening I started, by that conveyance, down the road.

"Don't you think that a very remarkable sky?" I asked the
coachman, in the first stage out of London. "I don't remember to
have seen one like it."

"Nor I—not equal to it," he replied. "That's wind, sir; there'll
be mischief done at sea, I expect before long."

It was a murky confusion—here and there blotted with a color
like the color of the smoke from damp fuel—of flying clouds tossed
up into most remarkable heaps, suggesting greater heights in the
clouds than there were depths below them to the bottom of the
deepest hollows in the earth, through which the wild moon seemed
to plunge headlong, as if, in a dread disturbance of the laws of
nature, she had lost her way and were frightened. There had been
wind all day; and it was rising then, with an extraordinary great
sound. In another hour it had much increased, and the sky was
more overcast, and it blew harder. . . .

As we struggled on, nearer and nearer to the sea, from which
the mighty wind was blowing dead on shore, its force became more
and more terrific. Long before we saw the sea, its spray was on our
lips, and showered salt rain upon us. The water was out, over miles
and miles of the flat country adjacent to Yarmouth; and every sheet
and puddle lashed its banks, and had its stress of little breakers
setting heavily towards us. When we came within sight of the sea,
the waves on the horizon, caught at intervals above the rolling
abyss, were like glimpses of another shore with towers and buildings. When at last we got into the town, the people came out to

their doors, all aslant, and with streaming hair, making a wonder of
the mail that had come through such a night.

I put up at the old inn, and went down to look at the sea,
staggering along the street, which was strewn with sand and seaweed, and with flying blotches of sea foam. . . .

The tremendous sea itself, when I could find sufficient pause
to look at it, in the agitation of the blinding wind, the flying stones
and sand, and the awful noise, confounded me. As the high watery
walls came rolling in, and, at their highest, tumbled into surf, they
looked as if the least would engulf the town. As the receding wave
swept back with a hoarse roar, it seemed to scoop out caves in the
beach, as if its purpose were to undermine the earth. When some
white-headed billows thundered on, and dashed themselves to
pieces before they reached the land, every fragment of the late
whole seemed possessed by the full might of its wrath, rushing to
be gathered to the composition of another monster. Undulating
hills were changed to valleys, undulating valleys (with a storm bird
sometimes skimming through them) were lifted up to hills; masses
of water shivered and shook the beach with a booming sound;
every shape tumultuously rolled on, as soon as made, to change its
shape and place, and beat another shape and place away; the ideal
shore on the horizon, with its towers and buildings, rose and fell;
the clouds flew fast and thick; I seemed to see a rending and up-
heaving of all nature.

Not finding my old friend, Ham, among the people whom this
memorable wind—for it is still remembered down there as the
greatest ever known to blow upon that coast—had brought together, I made my way to his house. It was shut; and as no one
answered to my knocking, I went by back ways and bylanes to the
yard where he worked. I learned there that he had gone to Lowestoft, to meet some sudden exigency of ship repairing in which his
skill was required; but that he would be back tomorrow morning
in good time.

I went back to the inn; and when I had washed and dressed,
and tried to sleep, but in vain, it was five o'clock in the afternoon. . . .
I was very much depressed in spirits, very solitary, and felt an
uneasiness in Ham's not being there, disproportionate to the occasion. . . . I was persuaded that possibly he would attempt to return
from Lowestoft by sea, and be lost. This grew so strong with me,
that I resolved to go back to the yard before I took my dinner, and
ask the boat builder if he thought his attempting to return by sea at

all likely. If he gave me the least reason to think so, I would go over to Lowestoft and prevent it by bringing him with me.

I hastily ordered my dinner, and went back to the yard. I was none too soon; for the boat builder, with a lantern in his hand, was locking the yard gate. He quite laughed when I asked him the question, and said there was no fear; no man in his senses, or out of them, would put off in such a gale of wind, least of all Ham Peggotty, who had been born to seafaring.

I went back to the inn. The howl and roar, the rattling of the doors and windows, the rumbling in the chimneys, the apparent rocking of the very house that sheltered me, and the prodigious tumult of the sea, were more fearful than in the morning. But there was now a great darkness besides; and that invested the storm with new terrors, real and fanciful.

I could not eat, I could not sit still, I could not continue steadfast in anything. Something within me, faintly answering to the storm without, tossed up the depths of my memory and made a tumult in them. Yet, in all the hurry of my thoughts, wild running with thundering sea, the storm and my uneasiness regarding Ham were always in the foreground.

My dinner went away almost untasted, and I tried to refresh myself with a glass or two of wine. In vain. I fell into a dull slumber before the fire, without losing my consciousness either of the uproar out of doors or of the place in which I was. Both became overshadowed by a new undefinable horror; and when I awoke— or rather when I shook off the lethargy that bound me in my chair —my whole frame thrilled with objectless and unintelligible fear.

I walked to and fro, tried to read an old gazetteer, listened to the awful noises; looked at faces, scenes, and figures in the fire. At length the steady ticking of the undisturbed clock on the wall tormented me to that degree that I resolved to go to bed. . . .

There was a dark gloom in my solitary chamber when I at length returned to it; but I was tired now, and, getting into bed again, fell off a tower and down a precipice into the depths of sleep. I have an impression that for a long time, though I dreamed of being elsewhere and in a variety of scenes, it was always blowing in my dream. At length I lost that feeble hold upon reality, and was engaged with two dear friends, but who they were I don't know, at the siege of some town in a roar of cannonading.

The thunder of the cannon was so loud and incessant, that I could not hear something I much desired to hear, until I made a great exertion, and awoke. It was broad day—eight or nine o'clock; the storm raging, in lieu of the batteries; and someone knocking and calling at my door.

"What is the matter?" I cried.

"A wreck! Close by!"

I sprang out of bed, and asked what wreck?

"A schooner, from Spain or Portugal, laden with fruit and wine. Make haste, sir, if you want to see her! It's thought she'll go to pieces every moment."

The excited voice went clamoring along the staircase; and I wrapped myself in my clothes as quickly as I could, and ran into the street. Numbers of people were there before us, all running in one direction, to the beach. I ran the same way, outstripping a good many, and soon came facing the wild sea.

The wind might by this time have lulled a little, though not more sensibly than if the cannonading I had dreamed of had been diminished by the silencing of half a dozen guns out of hundreds. But the sea, having upon it the additional agitation of the whole night, was infinitely more terrific than when I had seen it last. Every appearance it had then presented bore the expression of being *swelled;* and the height to which the breakers rose, and, looking over one another, bore one another down, and rolled in, in interminable hosts, was most appalling.

In the difficulty of hearing anything but wind and waves, and in the crowd, and the unspeakable confusion, and my first breathless attempts to stand against the weather, I was so confused that I looked out to sea for the wreck, and saw nothing but the foaming heads of the great waves. A half-dressed boatman standing next me pointed with his bare arm (a tattooed arrow on it, pointing in the same direction) to the left. Then, O great Heaven, I saw it, close in upon us!

One mast was broken short off, six or eight feet from the deck, and lay over the side, entangled in a maze of sail and rigging; and all that ruin, as the ship rolled and beat—which she did without a moment's pause, and with a violence quite inconceivable—beat the side as if it would stave it in. Some efforts were even then being made to cut this portion of the wreck away; for as the ship, which was broadside on, turned towards us in her rolling, I plainly descried her people at work with axes, especially one active figure, with long curling hair, conspicuous among the rest. But a great cry, which was audible even above the wind and water, rose from the shore at this moment: the sea, sweeping over the rolling wreck, made a clean breach, and carried men, spars, casks, planks, bulwarks, heaps of such toys, into the boiling surge.

The second mast was yet standing, with the rags of a rent sail, and a wild confusion of broken cordage, flapping to and fro. The ship had struck once, the same boatman hoarsely said in my ear, and then lifted in and struck again. I understood him to add that she was parting amidships, and I could readily suppose so, for the rolling and beating were too tremendous for any human work to suffer long. As he spoke, there was another great cry of pity from the beach: four men arose with the wreck out of the deep, clinging to the rigging of the remaining mast; uppermost, the active figure with the curling hair.

There was a bell on board; and as the ship rolled and dashed, like a desperate creature driven mad, now showing us the whole sweep of her deck, as she turned on her beam ends towards the shore, now nothing but her keel, as she sprung wildly over and turned towards the sea, the bell rang; and its sound, the knell of those unhappy men, was borne towards us on the wind. Again we lost her, and again she rose. Two men were gone. The agony on shore increased. Men groaned and clasped their hands; women shrieked, and turned away their faces. Some ran wildly up and down along the beach, crying for help where no help could be. I found myself one of these, frantically imploring a knot of sailors whom I knew, not to let those two lost creatures perish before our eyes.

They were making out to me, in an agitated way, that the lifeboat had been bravely manned an hour ago, and could do nothing; and that as no man would be so desperate as to attempt to wade off with a rope, and establish a communication with the shore, there was nothing left to try; when I noticed that some new sensation moved the people on the beach, and saw them part, and Ham come breaking through them to the front.

I ran to him, as well as I know, to repeat my appeal for help. But distracted though I was by a sight so new to me and terrible, the determination in his face, and his look out to sea, awoke me to a knowledge of his danger. I held him back with both arms, and implored the men with whom I had been speaking not to listen to him, not to do murder, not to let him stir from off that sand.

Another cry arose from the shore; and, looking towards the wreck, we saw the cruel sail, with blow on blow, beat off the lower of the two men, and fly up in triumph round the active figure left alone upon the mast.

Against such a sight, and against such determination as that of the calmly desperate man who was already accustomed to lead half the people present, I might as hopefully have intreated the wind. "Mas'r Davy," he said cheerily, grasping me by both hands, "if my time is come, 'tis come. If 't an't, I'll bide it. Lord above bless you, and bless all! Mates, make me ready! I'm a-going off!"

I was swept away, but not unkindly, to some distance, where the people around me made me stay; urging, as I confusedly perceived, that he was bent on going, with help or without, and that I should endanger the precautions for his safety by troubling those with whom they rested. I don't know what I answered, or what they rejoined, but I saw hurry on the beach, and men running with ropes from a capstan that was there, and penetrating into a circle of figures that hid him from me. Then I saw him standing alone, in a seaman's frock and trousers, a rope in his hand or slung to his wrist, another round his body; and several of the best men holding, at a little distance, to the latter, which he laid out himself, slack upon the shore, at his feet.

The wreck, even to my unpracticed eye, was breaking up. I saw that she was parting in the middle, and that the life of the solitary man upon the mast hung by a thread. Still he clung to it.

Ham watched the sea, standing alone, with the silence of suspended breath behind him, and the storm before, until there was a great retiring wave, when, with a backward glance at those who held the rope, which was made fast round his body, he dashed in after it, and in a moment was buffeting with the water—rising with the hills, falling with valleys, lost beneath the foam; then drawn again to land. They hauled in hastily.

He was hurt. I saw blood on his face from where I stood; but he took no thought of that. He seemed hurriedly to give them some directions for leaving him more free, or so I judged from the motion of his arm—and was gone, as before.

And now he made for the wreck—rising with the hills, falling with the valleys, lost beneath the rugged foam, borne in towards the shore, borne on towards the ship, striving hard and valiantly. The distance was nothing, but the power of the sea and wind made the strife deadly.

At length he neared the wreck. He was so near that with one more of his vigorous strokes he would be clinging to it—when a high, green, vast hillside of water, moving on shoreward from beyond the ship, he seemed to leap up into it with a mighty bound, and the ship was gone!

Some eddying fragments I saw in the sea, as if a mere cask had been broken, in running to the spot where they were hauling in. Consternation was in every face. They drew him to my very feet—insensible, dead. He was carried to the nearest house; and, no one preventing me now, I remained near him, busy, while every means of restoration was tried; but he had been beaten to death by the great wave, and his generous heart was stilled forever.

•

THE LAST FIGHT IN THE COLOSSEUM
Adapted from a retelling
by Charlotte Yonge

"Public sentiment" is always changing, sometimes for better, sometimes for worse. The good changes often are brought about through the tireless prodding of a relatively few voices. When the Roman emperor Honorius closed the last of the infamous gladiator schools in 399, it was largely because of the vigorous writings and preachings of Christian officials. And then, sometime around the year 404, public outrage turned against the barbarous sport following the remarkable incident described below. Here is a dramatic example of how even one determined person can help the popular culture take a step forward.

The grandest and most renowned of all ancient amphitheaters is the Colosseum, built by Vespasian and his son Titus in a valley surrounded by the seven hills of Rome. The walls are so solid, and so admirably put together, that still, after so many centuries, it remains one of the greatest Roman wonders. Five acres of ground were inclosed within the oval of its outer wall; altogether, when full, the huge building held no fewer than 50,000 spectators!

Here the Romans came to see their famous games. When the emperor had seated himself and given the signal, the sports began.

Sometimes a dancing elephant would begin the entertainment. Or a lion would come forth with a jeweled crown on his head, a diamond necklace around his neck, his mane plaited with gold, and his claws gilded, to play a hundred gentle antics with a little hare that danced fearlessly within his grasp.

Sometimes water was let into the arena, and then a ship sailed in and sent a crowd of strange animals swimming in all directions. Sometimes the ground opened, and trees came growing up through it, as if by magic, bearing golden fruit.

But these were only the opening spectacles, for the Colosseum had not been built for such harmless trifles. The fierce Romans wanted to be excited and to feel themselves strongly stirred. Soon the doors of the pits and dens around the arena were thrown open, and absolutely savage beasts were let loose upon one another—rhinoceroses and tigers, bulls and lions, leopards and wild boars—while the people watched with ferocious curiosity to see the various kinds of attack and defense, their ears at the same time being delighted, instead of horror-struck, by the roars and howls of the noble creatures whose courage was so misused.

Wild beasts tearing each other to pieces might, one would think, satisfy any taste for horror. But the spectators needed even nobler game to be set before their favorite monsters. Men were brought forward to confront them. Some of these were, at first, in full armor, and fought hard, generally with success. Or hunters came, almost unarmed, and gained the victory by swiftness and dexterity, throwing a piece of cloth over a lion's head, or disconcerting him by putting their fist down his throat. But it was not only skill, but death, that the Romans loved to see, and condemned criminals and deserters were reserved to feast the lions, and to entertain the populace with their various kinds of death. Among those condemned was many a Christian martyr, who witnessed a good confession before the savage-eyed multitude around the arena, and "met the lion's gory mane" with a calm resolution that the lookers-on could not understand. To see a Christian die with upward gaze was the most strange and unaccountable sight the Coliseum could offer and it was therefore the choicest, and reserved for the last of the spectacles in which the brute creation had a part.

The carcasses were dragged off with hooks, the bloodstained sand was covered with a fresh green layer, perfume was wafted in stronger clouds, and a procession come forward—tall, well-made men, in the prime of their strength. Some carried a sword and a lasso, others a trident and a net; some were in light armor, others in the full, heavy equipment of a soldier; some on horseback, some in chariots, some on foot. They marched in, made their obeisance to the emperor, and with one voice their greeting sounded through the building: "Hail, Caesar. Those about to die salute thee!" They were the gladiators—the swordsmen trained to fight to the death to amuse the populace.

Fights of all sorts took place—the light-armed soldier and the netsman—the lasso and the javelin—the two heavy-armed warriors —all combinations of single combat, and sometimes a general melee. When a gladiator wounded his adversary, he shouted to the spectators, "He has it!" and looked up to know whether he should kill or spare. When the people held down their thumbs, the conquered was left to recover, if he could; if they turned them up, he was to die; and if he showed any reluctance to present his throat for the deathblow, there was a scornful shout, "Receive the steel!"

Christianity, however, worked its way upward, and at last was professed by the emperor on his throne. Persecution came to an end, and no more martyrs fed the beasts in the Coliseum. The Christian emperors endeavored to prevent any more shows where cruelty and death formed the chief interest, and no truly religious person could endure the spectacle. But custom and love of excitement prevailed even against the emperor. They went on for fully a hundred years after Rome had, in name, become a Christian city.

Meantime the enemies of Rome were coming nearer and nearer. Alaric, the great chief of the Goths, led his forces into Italy, and threatened the city itself. Honorius, the emperor, was a cowardly, almost idiotic, boy, but his brave general, Stilicho, assembled his forces, met the Goths, and gave them a complete defeat, on Easter day of the year 403. He pursued them to the mountains, and for that time saved Rome.

In the joy of victory, the Roman Senate invited the conqueror and his ward Honorius to enter the city in triumph, at the opening of the new year, with the white steeds, purple robes, and vermilion cheeks with which, of old, victorious generals were welcomed at Rome. The churches were visited instead of the Temple of Jupiter, and there was no murder of the captives. But Roman bloodthirstiness was not yet allayed, and, after the procession had been completed, the Coliseum shows commenced, innocently at first, with races on foot, on horseback, and in chariots. Then followed a grand hunt of beasts turned loose in the arena, and next a sword dance. But after the sword dance came the arraying of swordsmen, with no blunted weapons, but with sharp spears and swords—a gladiator combat in full earnest. The people, enchanted, applauded with shouts of ecstasy this gratification of their savage tastes.

Suddenly, however, there was an interruption. A rude, roughly robed man, bareheaded and barefooted, had sprung into the arena, and, waving back the gladiators, began to call aloud upon the people to cease from the shedding of innocent blood, and not to requite God's mercy, in turning away the sword of the enemy, by encouraging murder. Shouts, howls, cries, broke in upon his words. This was no place for preachings—the old customs of Rome should be observed—"Back, old man!"—"On, gladiators!"

The gladiators thrust aside the meddler, and rushed to the attack. He still stood between, holding them apart, striving in vain to be heard. "Sedition! sedition!"—"Down with him!"—was the cry, and the prefect in authority himself added his voice. The gladiators, enraged at interference with their vocation, cut him down. Stones, or whatever came to hand, rained upon him from the furious people, and he perished in the midst of the arena! He lay dead.

And then the people began to reflect upon what had been done.

His dress showed that he was one of the hermits who had vowed themselves to a life of prayer and self-denial, and who were greatly reverenced, even by the most thoughtless. The few who had previously seen him told that he had come from the wilds of Asia on a pilgrimage, to visit the shrines and keep his Christmas at Rome. They knew that he was a holy man—no more. But his spirit had been stirred by the sight of thousands flocking to see men slaughter one another and in his simple-hearted zeal he had resolved to stop the cruelty, or die.

He had died, but not in vain. His work was done. The shock of such a death before their eyes turned the hearts of the people; they saw the wickedness and cruelty to which they had blindly surrendered themselves. And since the day when the hermit died in the Coliseum, there has never been another fight of gladiators. The custom was utterly abolished; and one habitual crime at least was wiped from the earth by the self-devotion of one humble, obscure, and nameless man.

GRIEF

Anton Chekhov

This story shows how very hard it is to suffer alone. True compassion joins in another's suffering to mitigate it.

It is twilight. A thick wet snow is slowly twirling around the newly lighted streetlamps, and lying in soft thin layers on the roofs, the horses' backs, people's shoulders and hats. The cab driver, Iona Potapov, is quite white, and looks like a phantom. He is bent double as far as a human body can bend double; he is seated on his box, and never makes a move. If a whole snowdrift fell on him, it seems as if he would not find it necessary to shake it off. His little horse is also quite white, and remains motionless. Its immobility, its angularity, and its straight wooden-looking legs, even close by give it the appearance of a gingerbread horse worth a kopeck. It is, no doubt, plunged in deep thought. If you were snatched from the plow, from your usual gray surroundings, and were thrown into this slough full of monstrous lights, unceasing noise and hurrying people, you too would find it difficult not to think.

Iona and his little horse have not moved from their place for a long while. They left their yard before dinner, and, up to now, have not had a single fare. The evening mist is descending over the town, the white lights of the lamps are replacing brighter rays, and the hubbub of the street is getting louder. "Cabby, for Viborg way!" suddenly hears Iona. "Cabby!"

Iona jumps, and through his snow-covered eyelashes, sees an officer in a greatcoat, with his hood over his head.

"Viborg way!" the officer repeats. "Are you asleep? Viborg way!"

With a nod of assent Iona picks up the reins, in consequence of which layers of snow slip off the horse's back and neck. The officer seats himself in the sleigh, the cabdriver smacks his lips to encourage his horse, stretches out his neck like a swan, sits up, and, more from habit than necessity, brandishes his whip. The little horse also stretches his neck, bends his wooden-looking legs, and makes a move undecidedly.

"What are you doing, werewolf!" is the exclamation Iona hears, from the dark mass moving to and fro as soon as they started.

"Where the devil are you going! To the r-r-right!"

"You do not know how to drive. Keep to the right!" calls the officer angrily.

A coachman from a private carriage swears at him. A passerby, who has run across the road and rubbed his shoulder against the horse's nose, looks at him furiously as he sweeps the snow from his sleeve. Iona shifts about on his seat as if he were on needles, moves his elbows as if he were trying to keep his equilibrium, and gapes about like someone suffocating, and who does not understand where he is or why he is there.

"What scoundrels they all are!" jokes the officer. "One would think they had all entered into an agreement to jostle you or fall under your horse."

Iona looks round at the officer, and moves his lips. He evidently wants to say something, but the only sound that issues is a snuffle.

"What?" asks the officer.

Iona twists his mouth into a smile, and with an effort says hoarsely:

"My son, sir, died this week."

"Hm! What did he die of?"

Iona turns with his whole body toward his fare, and says:

"And who knows! They say high fever. He was three days in hospital, and then died. . . . God's will be done."

"Turn round! The devil!" sounded from the darkness.

"Have you popped off, old doggie, eh? Use your eyes!"

"Go on, go on," said the officer, "otherwise we shall not get there by tomorrow. Hurry up a bit!"

The cab driver again stretches his neck, sits up, and, with a bad grace, brandishes his whip. Several times again he turns to look at his fare, but the latter had closed his eyes, and apparently is not disposed to listen. Having deposited the officer in the Viborg, he stops by the tavern, doubles himself up on his seat, and again remains motionless, while the snow once more begins to cover him and his horse. An hour, and another. . . . Then, along the foot path, with a squeak of galoshes, and quarreling, come three young men, two of them tall and lanky, the third one short and humpbacked.

"Cabby, to the Police Bridge!" in a cracked voice calls the humpback. "The three of us for twenty kopecks."

Iona picks up his reins, and clucks to his horse. Twenty kopecks is not a fair price, but he does not mind if it is a ruble or five kopecks —to him it is all the same now, so long as they are wayfarers. The young men, jostling each other and using bad language, approach the sleigh, and all three at once try to get on to the seat. Then begins a discussion about which two shall sit and who shall be the one to stand. After wrangling, abusing each other, and much petulance, it is at last decided that the humpback should stand, as he is the smallest.

"Now then, hurry up!" says the humpback in a twanging voice, as he takes his place, and breathes down Iona's neck. "Here, mate, what a cap you have got, there is not a worse one to be found in all Petersburg! . . ."

"Hi, hi, hi, hi," giggles Iona. "Such a. . . ."

"Now you, 'such a,' hurry up. Are you going the whole way at this pace? Are you? . . . Do you want it in the neck?"

"My head feels like bursting," says one of the lanky ones. "Last night at the Donkmasovs, Vaska and I drank the whole of four bottles of cognac."

"I don't understand what you lie for," said the other lanky one angrily. "You lie like a brute."

"God strike me, it's the truth!"

"It's as much a truth as that a louse coughs!"

"Hi, hi," grins Iona, "what merry young gentlemen!"

"Pshaw, go to the devil!" indignantly says the humpback.

"Are you going to get on or not, you old pest? Is that the way to drive? Use the whip a bit! Go on, devil, go on, give it to him!"

Iona feels at his back the little man wriggling, and the tremble in his voice. He listens to the insults hurled at him, sees the people; and little by little the feeling of loneliness leaves him. The humpback goes on swearing until he gets mixed up in some elaborate six-foot oath, or chokes with coughing. The lankies begin to talk about a certain Nadejda Petrovna. Iona looks round at them several times; he waits for a temporary silence, then, turning round again, he murmurs:

"My son . . . died this week."

"We must all die," sighs the humpback, wiping his lips after an attack of coughing. "Now, hurry up, hurry up! Gentlemen, I really cannot go any farther like this! When will he get us there?"

"Well, just you stimulate him a little in the neck!"

"You old pest, do you hear, I'll bone your neck for you! If one treated the like of you with ceremony one would have to go on foot! Do you hear, old serpent! Or do you not care a spit?"

Iona hears rather than feels the blows they deal him.

"Hi, hi," he laughs. "They are merry young gentlemen, God bless 'em!"

"Cabby, are you married?" asks a lanky one.

"I? Hi, hi, merry young gentlemen! Now I have only a wife: the moist ground. . . . Hi, ho, ho . . . that is to say, the grave! My son has died, and I am alive. . . . A wonderful thing, death mistook the door . . . instead of coming to me, it went to my son. . . ."

Iona turns round to tell them how his son died, but at this moment the humpback, giving a little sigh, announces that, thank God, they have at last reached their destination. Iona watches them disappear through the dark entrance. Once more he is alone, and again surrounded by silence. . . . His grief, which had abated for a short while, returns and rends his heart with greater force. With an anxious and a hurried look, he searches among the crowds passing on either side of the street to find if there is just one person who will listen to him. But the crowds hurry by without noticing him or his trouble. Yet it is such an immense, illimitable grief. Should his heart break and the grief pour out, it would flow over the whole earth it seems, and yet, no one sees it. It has managed to conceal itself in such an insignificant shell that no one can see it even by day and with a light.

Iona sees a hall porter with some sacking and decides to talk to him.

"Friend, what sort of time is it?" he asks.

"Past nine. What are you standing here for? Move on."

Iona moves on a few steps, doubles himself up, and abandons himself to his grief. He sees it is useless to turn to people for help. In less than five minutes he straightens himself, holds up his head as if he felt some sharp pain, and gives a tug at the reins. He can bear it no longer. "The stables," he thinks, and the little horse, as if he understood, starts off at a trot.

About an hour and a half later Iona is seated by a large dirty stove. Around the stove, on the floor, on the benches, people are snoring. The air is thick and suffocatingly hot. Iona looks at the sleepers, scratches himself, and regrets having returned so early.

"I have not even earned my fodder," he thinks. "That's what's my trouble. A man who knows his job, who has had enough to eat, and his horse too, can always sleep peacefully."

A young cab driver in one of the corners half gets up, grunts sleepily, and stretches toward a bucket of water.

"Do you want a drink?" Iona asks him.

"Don't I want a drink!"

"That's so? Your good health! But listen, mate—you know, my son is dead. . . . Did you hear? This week, in hospital. . . . It's a long story."

Iona looks to see what effect his words have, but sees none— the young man has hidden his face, and is fast asleep again. The old man sighs, and scratches his head. Just as much as the young one wanted to drink, the old man wanted to talk. It will soon be a week since his son died, and he has not been able to speak about it properly to anyone. One must tell it slowly and carefully; how his son fell ill, how he suffered, what he said before he died, how he died. One must describe every detail of the funeral, and the journey to the hospital to fetch his son's clothes. His daughter Anissia remained in the village—one must talk about her too. Was it nothing he had to tell? Surely the listener would gasp and sigh, and sympathize with him?

"I'll go and look at my horse," thinks Iona. "There's always time to sleep. No fear of that!"

He puts on his coat, and goes to the stables to his horse. He thinks of the corn, the hay, the weather. When he is alone, he dare not think of his son. He could speak about him to anyone, but to think of him, and picture him to himself, is unbearably painful.

"Are you tucking in?" Iona asks his horse, looking at his bright eyes. "Go on, tuck in, though we've not earned our corn, we can eat hay. Yes! I am too old to drive—my son could have, not I. He was a first-rate cab driver. If only he had lived!"

Iona is silent for a moment, then continues:

"That's how it is, my old horse. There's no more Kuzma Io-nitch. He has left us to live, and he went off. Now let's say, you had a foal, you were that foal's mother, and suddenly, let's say, that foal went and left you to live after him. It would be sad, wouldn't it?"

The little horse munches, listens, and breathes over his master's hand. . . .

Iona's feelings are too much for him, and he tells the little horse the whole story.

•

END OF THE TIGER

John D. MacDonald

This is a beautiful "tough love" story. Sometimes the best way to
help people find the right direction is to let them see for themselves just how rough and wrong the path they're taking is going
to be.

I saw Tiger Shaw the other day. He didn't recognize me.
There's no reason why he should. When he was going with my big
sister, Christine, I was just one of the swarm of little brothers and
sisters who knew enough not to get too close to him or you'd get a
Dutch rub with those big knuckles.

I saw him in a narrow street in town, unloading a truck into a
warehouse, tattoos on his big, meaty arms, his belly grown big as a
sack of cement, all of him looking sour and surly and dispirited. It
seemed too bad, because he was a beautiful young man back when
he was one of the best athletes they ever had in the high school. He
lasted a year in college before he got into a scandal about throwing
games, and they let him go into the army.

Christine and Tiger were a pair of beautiful people that summer.

There were seven of us children in all. Now there are six, and
when we all get together with all our wives and husbands and kids,
we think of Bunny and are saddened, because he was the littlest
one of all and dear to us. The times of getting together are rare
because we're scattered now. Christine's husband teaches at the
University of Toronto. Her eldest is twelve. All the marriages are
pretty good. Mine is fine.

And when we get together, one of the things we always do is
to tell grandfather stories. There are a lot of them. He raised us—
he and our mother. He was a big, wild, random old man, very
partial to dramatic scenes. At least half of the things he did made
absolutely no sense to us as children. He never explained. He just
lived according to his unpredictable instincts. But it is strange how,
as time goes by, we begin to see how some of the nonsense things
made sense.

Until the day he died, I don't think we all ever really forgave
him about the goose. Yesterday, when I saw Tiger Shaw, I wished

that my grandfather had at least tried to explain about Gretchen. That was the name of the goose.

That May, the summer Christine and Tiger were in love, Nan, the youngest sister, bought the baby goose from a farm up the road for ninety cents saved out of her allowance. For about three days it belonged to her, and then it belonged to all of us and owned the pond out in the side yard. We kids were all her fellow geese, and she plodded along behind us, making small nervous sounds about all the dangers the world holds for an unwary goose. She was blazing white and took excellent care of herself with that clever serrated bill. Anybody who rowed the skiff around the pond had Gretchen aboard before they could even launch it, standing in the bow, honking her pleasure.

By July, Gretchen was of pretty good size, and she was enchanted with Christine's long golden hair. Christine would sit, and Gretchen would preen that hair, never tugging or hurting, making little chortling sounds in her throat. We all learned Gretchen's likes and dislikes. She could be patted a little but not very much. She was nervous about night, ignored cats, despised dogs, and would bow very low in ceremonious oriental greeting when anyone approached.

Tiger was at our place a lot that summer. He was a hero, of course, huge and golden. But we quickly learned wariness. He was quick and he knew the places that hurt. And he would roar with laughter, and we, out of pride, would laugh with him, though eyes might be stinging.

I remember those long summer dusks after the evening meal before the littlest ones had to be shooed off to bed. We'd all be out in the side yard, and on the side porch, and Gretchen would come paddling up across the yard from the pond giving oriental greetings.

One of the grandfather stories we don't tell is about Tiger and the goose.

Gretchen was wary of Tiger Shaw, and it seemed to be a plausible instinct. As I remember that evening, Tiger was going to take Christine to some sort of barn dance just over the county line. Christine had on a blue dress with little white flowers. Her hair was brushed to a soft gleam. In the country fashion, Tiger had to stay around a little time before taking her away into the gathering dusk, going down the road with her in that car of his which made a snarling sound that faded into the distance, sounding as it died away like a bee buzzing nearby.

We kids were fooling around in the yard. Sheila was acting wistful. She was near to her dating time, when the young men would be coming for her. Our grandfather was on the porch in the rocker, and off in the east, by the far hills, there was darkness and a pink inaudible pulse of lightning.

Tiger and Christine were sitting a few feet apart, and Gretchen plodded up behind them, behind the low bench, and with a big whack of her white wings made an awkward hop up onto the bench, leaned the adoring curve of her neck toward Christine, and began with little chucklings, to preen the fine strands of the golden hair.

We were all watching it, thinking uneasily that Gretchen was uncommonly close to Tiger Shaw. He was very quick for such a big muscly person, quick without looking quick. And he was seldom without a cud of gum in his jaws. This is one of the memories of him, the knots working at the jaw corners and the smell of spearmint.

He reached and took Gretchen high on the neck with one hand, slipped the gum out of his mouth with the other, and when she opened her bill to yawp her protest, he thumbled the wad of gum up into the hollow of the top of her beak. He released her at once and began to roar with laughter.

We all laughed. It was so ridiculous. Gretchen closed her bill and it stuck. She looked astonished. She began to shake her head the way you shake your hand to shake moisture from your fingertips. She shook herself dizzy and fell sprawling off the bench. Then she began to run in circles in the yard, wings laboring, trying somehow to run away from this terrible impasse. Our nervous laughter turned shrill, climbing toward the edge of hysteria.

Above it all, above Tiger's laughter and our shrillness, I heard the grandfather laugh, the drumdeepbellowing of him as he came down off the porch. Soon, in terror Gretchen began driving that precious bill against things, against posts and stones, against places where the ground was hard. Then we were all howling in a shared panic, in heartbreak and concern. Because we all knew what that bill was to her—knife and fork, comb and brush, weapon, tool, sieve, bug-catcher.

So we tried to run to catch her, but my grandfather swept us back with his huge arms, laughing, bellowing at us that it was funny. I hated him then, I hated the three of them—my grandfather, Tiger, and Christine.

Because, you see, Christine was laughing, too. She stood up, hunched over, laughing. Grandfather and Tiger beat each other on the back and roared with delight at the deranged, scrabbling, terrorized creature, telling each other how funny it was. Christine moved slowly toward the steps, shrieking laughter, and as she hobbled up the steps it changed to a keening, wailing sound, the tears running down her face.

My grandfather's roaring laughter stopped abruptly as the screen door banged behind her, and he turned quickly away from the still hilarious Tiger.

Following grandfather's orders, we caught Gretchen, wrapped her firmly in burlap, and took her to the porch. Grandfather gently pried the bruised bill open and, holding Gretchen's head against his thigh, skillfully worked the sticky mass out of the concavity. Tiger stood watching, chuckling reminiscently, while we hiccuped in the aftermath of tears. When she was as clean as he could get her, my grandfather put her down and took the sacking off her. She scrambled to her feet and went headlong for the safety of her beloved pond, half running, half flying.

Tiger said it was time to go and sent Sheila in to get Christine. Sheila came out in a few moments and said Christine had a headache and couldn't go. Tiger hung around for a little while, acting sort of ugly. And then he went off, and the snarling drone of his car faded quickly. We went down to the pond. Gretchen was soiled and she had some broken feathers, but she looked unapproachably white there in the blue dusk, floating out in the middle, making no sound for us.

There were no more boat rides, no more preening the golden hair of the big sister, no more chuckling sound behind us when we walked across the yard, no more visits in the dusk. We told each other that if grandfather had let us help her before she became too terrified, it might have been all right, and we might have kept her trust.

We never quite forgave grandfather for that. Maybe he wasn't interested in our kind of forgiveness. He was a wild and random old man, and sometimes he made no sense at all. But when I saw Tiger the other day, I suddenly realized that if we'd helped Gretchen quickly, then it might have been just one of Tiger's little jokes, and Christine would have gone off with him that night and other nights, and the world might be quite different for her now. By delaying us, grandfather showed her Tiger's kind of laughter, of which there is often too much in the world.

But he never explained.

•

No Greater Love

John W. Mansur

This is a remarkable story of sacrifice born of deep friendship. The author says, "I heard this story when I was in Vietnam, and it was told to me as fact. I have no way of knowing for sure that it is true, but I do know that stranger things have happened in war."

Whatever their planned target, the mortar rounds landed in an orphanage run by a missionary group in the small Vietnamese village. The missionaries and one or two children were killed outright, and several more children were wounded, including one young girl, about eight years old.

People from the village requested medical help from a neighboring town that had radio contact with the American forces. Finally, an American Navy doctor and nurse arrived in a jeep with only their medical kits. They established that the girl was the most critically injured. Without quick action, she would die of shock and loss of blood.

A transfusion was imperative, and a donor with a matching blood type was required. A quick test showed that neither American had the correct type, but several of the uninjured orphans did.

The doctor spoke some pidgin Vietnamese, and the nurse a smattering of high school French. Using that combination, together with much impromptu sign language, they tried to explain to their young, frightened audience that unless they could replace some of the girl's lost blood, she would certainly die. Then they asked if anyone would be willing to give blood to help.

Their request was met with wide-eyed silence. After several long moments, a small hand slowly and waveringly went up, dropped back down, and then went up again.

"Oh, thank you," the nurse said in French. "What is your name?"

"Heng," came the reply.

Heng was quickly laid on a pallet, his arm swabbed with alcohol, and a needle inserted in his vein. Through this ordeal Heng lay stiff and silent.

After a moment, he let out a shuddering sob, quickly covering his face with his free hand.

"Is it hurting, Heng?" the doctor asked. Heng shook his head, but after a few moments another sob escaped, and once more he tried to cover up his crying. Again the doctor asked him if the needle hurt, and again Heng shook his head.

But now his occasional sobs gave way to a steady, silent crying, his eyes screwed tightly shut, his fist in his mouth to stifle his sobs. The medical team was concerned. Something was obviously very wrong. At this point, a Vietnamese nurse arrived to help. Seeing the little one's distress, she spoke to him rapidly in Vietnamese, listened to his reply and answered him in a soothing voice.

After a moment, the patient stopped crying and looked questioningly at the Vietnamese nurse. When she nodded, a look of great relief spread over his face.

Glancing up, the nurse said quietly to the Americans, "He thought he was dying. He misunderstood you. He thought you had asked him to give all his blood so the little girl could live."

"But why would he be willing to do that?" asked the Navy nurse.

The Vietnamese nurse repeated the question to the little boy, who answered simply, "She's my friend."

Greater love has no man than this, that he lay down his life for a friend.

•

A PROBLEM

Anton Chekhov

This story carries a couple of important warnings about compassion. First, sometimes people are not at all grateful for help they receive. Second, true compassion does not mean giving people whatever they want. Sometimes it's easier to tell someone "Take this" or "It's O.K." in order to make yourself feel better or protect your own image. But that can be the kind of help that often does more harm than good.

The strictest measures were taken that the Uskovs' family secret might not leak out and become generally known. Half of the servants were sent off to the theatre or the circus. The other half were sitting in the kitchen and not allowed to leave it. Orders were given that no one was to be admitted. The wife of the Colonel, her sister, and the governess, though they had been initiated into the secret, kept up a pretense of knowing nothing; they sat in the dining room and did not show themselves in the drawing room or the hall.

Sasha Uskov, the young man of twenty-five who was the cause of all the commotion, had arrived some time before, and by the advice of kindhearted Ivan Markovitch, his uncle, who was taking his part, he sat meekly in the hall by the door leading to the study, and prepared himself to make an open, candid explanation.

The other side of the door, in the study, a family council was being held. The subject under discussion was an exceedingly disagreeable and delicate one. Sasha Uskov had cashed at one of the banks a false promissory note, and it had become due for payment three days before, and now his two paternal uncles and Ivan Markovitch, the brother of his dead mother, were deciding the question whether they should pay the money and save the family honor, or wash their hands of it and leave the case to go for trial.

To outsiders who have no personal interest in the matter such questions seem simple; for those who are so unfortunate as to have to decide them in earnest they are extremely difficult. The uncles had been talking for a long time, but the problem seemed no nearer decision.

"My friends!" said the uncle who was a colonel, and there was a note of exhaustion and bitterness in his voice. "Who says that family honor is a mere convention? I don't say that at all. I am only warning you against a false view. I am pointing out the possibility of an unpardonable mistake. How can you fail to see it? I am not speaking Chinese—I am speaking Russian!"

"My dear fellow, we do understand," Ivan Markovitch protested mildly.

"How can you understand if you say that I don't believe in family honor? I repeat once more: famil-y ho-nor fal-sely un-der-stood is a prejudice! Falsely understood! That's what I say: whatever may be the motives for screening a scoundrel, whoever he may be, and helping him to escape punishment, it is contrary to law and unworthy of a gentleman. It's not saving the family honor; it's civic cowardice! Take the army, for instance. . . . The honor of the army is more precious to us than any other honor, yet we don't screen our guilty members, but condemn them. And does the honor of the army suffer in consequence? Quite the opposite!"

The other paternal uncle, an official in the Treasury, a taciturn, dull-witted, and rheumatic man, sat silent, or spoke only of the fact that the Uskovs' name would get into the newspapers if the case went for trial. His opinion was that the case ought to be hushed up from the first and not become public property; but, apart from publicity in the newspapers, he advanced no other argument in support of this opinion.

The maternal uncle, kindhearted Ivan Markovitch, spoke smoothly, softly, and with a tremor in his voice. He began with saying that youth has its rights and its peculiar temptations. Which of us has not been young, and who has not been led astray? To say nothing of ordinary mortals, even great men have not escaped errors and mistakes in their youth. Take, for instance, the biography of great writers. Did not every one of them gamble, drink, and draw down upon himself the anger of right-thinking people in his young days? If Sasha's error bordered upon crime, they must remember that Sasha had received practically no education; he had been expelled from the high school in the fifth class; he had lost his parents in early childhood, and so had been left at the tenderest age without guidance and good, benevolent influences. He was nervous, excitable, had no firm ground under his feet, and, above all, he had been unlucky. Even if he were guilty, anyway he deserved indulgence and the sympathy of all compassionate souls. He ought, of course, to be punished, but he was punished as it was by his conscience and the agonies he was enduring now while awaiting the sentence of his relations. The comparison with the army made by the Colonel was delightful, and did credit to his lofty intelligence. His appeal to their feeling of public duty spoke for the chivalry of his soul, but they must not forget that in each individual the citizen is closely linked with the Christian. . . .

"Shall we be false to civic duty," Ivan Markovitch exclaimed passionately, "if instead of punishing an erring boy we hold out to him a helping hand?"

Ivan Markovitch talked further of family honor. He had not the honor to belong to the Uskov family himself, but he knew their distinguished family went back to the thirteenth century. He did not forget for a minute, either, that his precious, beloved sister had been the wife of one of the representatives of that name. In short, the family was dear to him for many reasons, and he refused to admit the idea that, for the sake of a paltry fifteen hundred rubles, a blot should be cast on the escutcheon that was beyond all price.

If all the motives he had brought forward were not sufficiently convincing, he, Ivan Markovitch, in conclusion, begged his listeners to ask themselves what was meant by crime? Crime is an immoral act founded upon ill will. But is the will of man free? Philosophy has not yet given a positive answer to that question. Different views were held by the learned. The latest school of Lombroso, for instance, denies the freedom of the will, and considers every crime as the product of the purely anatomical peculiarities of the individual.

"Ivan Markovitch," said the Colonel, in a voice of entreaty, "we are talking seriously about an important matter, and you bring in Lombroso, you clever fellow. Think a little, what are you saying all this for? Can you imagine that all your thunderings and rhetoric will furnish an answer to the question?"

Sasha Uskov sat at the door and listened. He felt neither terror, shame, nor depression, but only weariness and inward emptiness. It seemed to him that it made absolutely no difference to him whether they forgave him or not. He had come here to hear his sentence and to explain himself simply because kindhearted Ivan Markovitch had begged him to do so. He was not afraid of the future. It made no difference to him where he was: here in the hall, in prison, or in Siberia.

"If Siberia, then let it be Siberia, damn it all!"

He was sick of life and found it insufferably hard. He was inextricably involved in debt. He had not a farthing in his pocket. His family had become detestable to him. He would have to part from his friends and his women sooner or later, as they had begun to be too contemptuous of his sponging on them. The future looked black.

Sasha was indifferent, and was only disturbed by one circumstance; the other side of the door they were calling him a scoundrel and a criminal. Every minute he was on the point of jumping up, bursting into the study and shouting in answer to the detestable metallic voice of the Colonel:

"You are lying!"

"Criminal" is a dreadful word—that is what murderers, thieves, robbers are; in fact, wicked and morally hopeless people. And Sasha was very far from being all that. . . . It was true he owed a great deal and did not pay his debts. But debt is not a crime, and it is unusual for a man not to be in debt. The Colonel and Ivan Markovitch were both in debt. . . .

"What have I done wrong besides?" Sasha wondered.

He had discounted a forged note. But all the young men he

knew did the same. Handrikov and Von Burst always forged IOUs from their parents or friends when their allowances were not paid at the regular time, and then when they got their money from home they redeemed them before they became due. Sasha had done the same, but had not redeemed the IOU because he had not got the money which Handrikov had promised to lend him. He was not to blame. It was the fault of circumstances. It was true that the use of another person's signature was considered reprehensible, but, still, it was not a crime but a generally accepted dodge, an ugly formality which injured no one and was quite harmless, for in forging the Colonel's signature Sasha had had no intention of causing anybody damage or loss.

"No, it doesn't mean that I am a criminal ..." thought Sasha. "And it's not in my character to bring myself to commit a crime. I am soft, emotional. . . . When I have the money I help the poor. . . ."

Sasha was musing after this fashion while they went on talking the other side of the door.

"But, my friends, this is endless," the Colonel declared, getting excited. "Suppose we were to forgive him and pay the money. You know he would not give up leading a dissipated life, squandering money, making debts, going to our tailors and ordering suits in our names! Can you guarantee that this will be his last prank? As far as I am concerned, I have no faith whatever in his reforming!"

The official of the Treasury muttered something in reply. After him Ivan Markovitch began talking blandly and suavely again. The Colonel moved his chair impatiently and drowned the other's words with his detestable metallic voice. At last the door opened and Ivan Markovitch came out of the study. There were patches of red on his lean shaven face.

"Come along," he said, taking Sasha by the hand. "Come and speak frankly from your heart. Without pride, my dear boy, humbly and from your heart."

Sasha went into the study. The official of the Treasury was sitting down; the Colonel was standing before the table with one hand in his pocket and one knee on a chair. It was smoky and stifling in the study. Sasha did not look at the official or the Colonel; he felt suddenly ashamed and uncomfortable. He looked uneasily at Ivan Markovitch and muttered:

"I'll pay it . . . I'll give it back. . . ."

"What did you expect when you discounted the IOU?" he heard a metallic voice.

"I . . . Handrikov promised to lend me the money before now."

Sasha could say no more. He went out of the study and sat down again on the chair near the door. He would have been glad to go away altogether at once, but he was choking with hatred and he awfully wanted to remain, to tear the Colonel to pieces, to say something rude to him. He sat trying to think of something violent and effective to say to his hated uncle, and at that moment a woman's figure, shrouded in the twilight, appeared at the drawing-room door. It was the Colonel's wife. She beckoned Sasha to her, and, wringing her hands, said, weeping:

"*Alexandre,* I know you don't like me, but . . . listen to me; listen, I beg you. . . . But, my dear, how can this have happened? Why, it's awful, awful! For goodness' sake, beg them, defend yourself, entreat them."

Sasha looked at her quivering shoulders, at the big tears that were rolling down her cheeks, heard behind his back the hollow, nervous voices of worried and exhausted people, and shrugged his shoulders. He had not in the least expected that his aristocratic relations would raise such a tempest over a paltry fifteen hundred rubles! He could not understand her tears nor the quiver of their voices.

An hour later he heard that the Colonel was getting the best of it; the uncles were finally inclining to let the case go for trial.

"The matter's settled," said the Colonel, sighing. "Enough."

After this decision all the uncles, even the emphatic Colonel, became noticeably depressed. A silence followed.

"Merciful Heavens!" sighed Ivan Markovitch. "My poor sister!"

And he began saying in a subdued voice that most likely his sister, Sasha's mother, was present unseen in the study at that moment. He felt in his soul how the unhappy, saintly woman was weeping, grieving, and begging for her boy. For the sake of her peace beyond the grave, they ought to spare Sasha.

The sound of a muffled sob was heard. Ivan Markovitch was weeping and muttering something which it was impossible to catch through the door. The Colonel got up and paced from corner to corner. The long conversation began over again.

But then the clock in the drawing room struck two. The family council was over. To avoid seeing the person who had moved him to such wrath, the Colonel went from the study, not into the hall, but into the vestibule. . . . Ivan Markovitch came out into the hall. . . . He was agitated and rubbing his hands joyfully. His tear-stained eyes looked good-humored and his mouth was twisted into a smile.

"Capital," he said to Sasha. "Thank God! You can go home, my dear, and sleep tranquilly. We have decided to pay the sum, but on condition that you repent and come with me tomorrow into the country and set to work."

A minute later Ivan Markovitch and Sasha in their greatcoats and caps were going down the stairs. The uncle was muttering something edifying. Sasha did not listen, but felt as though some uneasy weight were gradually slipping off his shoulders. They had forgiven him; he was free! A gust of joy sprang up within him and sent a sweet chill to his heart. He longed to breathe, to move swiftly, to live! Glancing at the street lamps and the black sky, he remembered that Von Burst was celebrating his name-day that evening at the "Bear," and again a rush of joy flooded his soul. . . .

"I am going!" he decided.

But then he remembered he had not a farthing, that the companions he was going to would despise him at once for his empty pockets. He must get hold of some money, come what may!

"Uncle, lend me a hundred rubles," he said to Ivan Markovitch.

His uncle, surprised, looked into his face and backed against a lamppost.

"Give it to me," said Sasha, shifting impatiently from one foot to the other and beginning to pant. "Uncle, I entreat you, give me a hundred rubles."

His face worked. He trembled, and seemed on the point of attacking his uncle. . . .

"Won't you?" he kept asking, seeing that his uncle was still amazed and did not understand. "Listen. If you don't, I'll give myself up tomorrow! I won't let you pay the IOU! I'll present another false note tomorrow!"

Petrified, muttering something incoherent in his horror, Ivan Markovitch took a hundred-ruble note out of his pocketbook and gave it to Sasha. The young man took it and walked rapidly away from him. . . .

Taking a sled, Sasha grew calmer, and felt a rush of joy within him again. The "rights of youth" of which kindhearted Ivan Markovitch had spoken at the family council woke up and asserted themselves. Sasha pictured the drinking party before him, and, among the bottles, the women, and his friends, the thought flashed through his mind:

"Now I see that I am a criminal. Yes, I am a criminal."

•

THE TWO GIFTS

Retold by Lilian Gask

This old tale asserts that it is not just the act of helping but the motive for helping that counts.

A heavy snowstorm was raging, and great soft flakes fell through the air like feathers shaken from the wings of an innumerable host of angels. By the side of the roadway sat a poor old woman, her scanty clothing forming but a poor protection from the icy blast of the wind. She was very hungry, for she had tasted no food that day, but her faded eyes were calm and patient, telling of an unwavering trust in Providence. Perhaps, she thought, some traveler might come that way who would have compassion on her, and give her alms; then she could return to the garret that she called "home," with bread to eat, and fuel to kindle a fire.

The day drew in, and still she sat and waited. At last a traveler approached. The thick snow muffled every sound and she was not aware of his coming until his burly figure loomed before her. Her plaintive voice made him turn with a start.

"Poor woman," he cried, pausing to look at her very pityingly. "It is hard for you to be out in such weather as this." Then he passed on, without giving her anything. His conscience told him that he ought to have relieved her, but he did not feel inclined to take off his thick gloves in that bitter cold, and without doing this he could not have found a coin.

The poor woman was naturally disappointed, but she was grateful for his kind words. By and by another traveler appeared. This one was driving in a splendid carriage, warmly wrapped in a

great fur cloak. As he caught sight of the poor creature by the roadside, he felt vaguely touched by the contrast of his own comfort with her misery. Obeying a sudden impulse, with one hand he let down the carriage window and signed to his coachman to stop, and with the other felt in his pocket. The poor woman hurried up to the carriage, a thrill of hope bringing a tinge of color to her pale and withered cheeks.

"How terribly cold it is!" exclaimed the rich man, and as he took his hand from his pocket, and held out a coin to her, he noticed that instead of silver he was about to give her a piece of gold.

"Dear me! That is far too much," he cried, but before he could return it to his pocket, the coin slipped through his fingers, and fell into the snow. A rough blast of wind made his teeth chatter, and pulling up the window in a great hurry, with a little shiver he drew the fur rug around him.

"It certainly was too much," he murmured philosophically, as the carriage rolled on, "but then I am very rich, and can afford to do a generous action now and then."

When his comfortable dinner was over, and he was sitting in front of a blazing fire, he thought once more of the poor old woman.

"It is not nearly so cold as I thought," he remarked as he settled himself more comfortably in his deep armchair. "I certainly gave that old creature too much. However, what's done, is done, and I hope she will make good use of it. I was generous, very generous indeed, and no doubt God will reward me."

Meanwhile the other traveler had also reached his journey's end, and he too had found a blazing fire and a good dinner awaiting him. He could not enjoy it, however, for he was haunted by the remembrance of that bent and shrunken figure in the waste of snow, and felt very remorseful for not having stopped to help her. At last he could bear it no longer.

"Bring another plate," he said, calling the servant to him. "There will be two to dine instead of one. I shall be back soon."

Saying this, he hurried through the darkness to the spot where he had left the old woman. She was still there, feebly searching in the snow.

"What are you looking for?" he asked.

"I am trying to find a piece of money which a gentleman threw me from his carriage window," she told him falteringly, scarcely able to speak from cold and hunger. It was no wonder, he thought, that she had not found it, for her hands were numbed and half-frozen, and she was not only old, but nearly blind.

"I am afraid you will never find it now," he said. "But come with me," he added consolingly. "I will take you to my inn, where there is a bright fire and a good dinner waiting for both of us. You shall be my guest, and I will see that you have a comfortable night's lodging."

The poor woman could scarcely believe her good fortune. Trembling, she prepared to follow her new friend. Noticing that she was lame as well as nearly blind, he took her arm, and with slow and patient steps led her to the hotel.

When the recording angel wrote that night in the Book of Heaven, he made no mention of the piece of gold which the wealthy traveler had given by mistake, for only a worthy motive gains credit in that Book. But amidst the good deeds that had been wrought that day, he gave a foremost place to that of a man who had repented of his hardness, and faced once more the bitter cold that he might share his comforts with a fellow creature so much less fortunate than himself.

•

SAINT CATHERINE AND THE
SILVER CRUCIFIX

Born in Sienna, Italy, in 1347 to well-to-do parents, Saint Catherine entered the Dominican sisterhood as a young woman, beginning a lifelong commitment to aiding the needy, nursing the sick, and making peace between different factions of the Catholic church. A patron saint of Italy, she is known as one of the greatest of the Christian mystics.

One early morning long ago, in the Italian town of Sienna, Saint Catherine was walking to mass at the church of Saint Dominic. The steep, narrow streets were still dark, but overhead the rising sun had touched the city's roofs and towers with gold, and Catherine's eyes were turned upward when she felt the touch of a hand at her cloak.

"Please help," a voice whispered, and nothing more.

Catherine turned and saw a man leaning against a wall, so thin and pale he could barely stand.

"What do you need of me?" Catherine asked kindly.

"Help for my journey," the man replied. "My home is far away, over the hills. I came here to work, and I have sent all that I earned home to my family, so my children may have bread. Now I've fallen ill, and I am too weak to start back. I need only a little money to buy something to eat and regain my strength."

"With all my heart, I would help," murmured Catherine, "but I am only a poor member of the Dominican sisterhood, and I have no money of my own to share with you."

She turned to move on, but once more the hand reached out and clasped her cloak.

"Please help me!" the man cried. "I ask for only a little."

Catherine gazed at him sorrowfully. She did not want to ignore his plea. But what could she do? She had already given away all she had. Her father and mother were kind, but she could not ask them to begin giving away their own things to perfect strangers. And there were so many, many more in need besides this one man. . . .

She prayed for help, closing her fingers upon the small silver crucifix she had worn since she was a young girl, the one she so often touched when she turned her thoughts to God. And, suddenly, the answer came to her.

True, it was just a tiny, child's cross, barely as big as a coin. And over the years it had worn thin and smooth in her hands. But it was silver, just the same, and this man could sell it and buy enough food to get him home.

She slipped it into the stranger's hand, and hastened on to church. Although she had just given away the thing she treasured most, her heart knew a gladness, as if she had just received the greatest of gifts.

And as she knelt a few moments later, she saw something wonderful and strange.

It seemed as though she stood in a great room with high, vaulted ceilings, a chamber filled with all sorts of glittering treasures, more beautiful than Catherine had ever imagined in her dreams. And in the midst stood Jesus, holding in his hand the most beautiful thing of all—a cross of gold set with so many gleaming jewels that their glory overwhelmed the eyes.

"Look upon these shining gifts," spoke the Lord. "These are the great and noble deeds done by men for my sake."

Catherine rejoiced at the sight, but a longing came over her heart, and she cried:

"O Lord, I am only one of your poor sisters. I can offer no service that would find a place among these precious gifts."

But she felt as though Jesus smiled upon her and, holding out the golden cross, he asked gently:

"Have you never seen this cross before, Catherine?"

"No, Lord," she answered meekly. "Never have I seen anything so wonderful."

Yet as she fixed her eyes upon it, she was filled with a sudden joy. For there, in the very midst of so many shining treasures of jewels and gold, in the heart of so much splendid light, she found her tiny, worn silver crucifix, the same one she had given away to the desperate man.

And soon the vision departed, but as it faded a voice sounded in her ears: "Inasmuch as ye did it unto one of these My brethren, even these least, ye did it unto Me."

•

SAINT MARTIN AND THE BEGGAR

Adapted from a retelling by Peggy Webling

Born around the year 316 in the Roman province of Pannonia (Hungary), Martin was forced into military service at the age of fifteen by his father, an army officer. It was in about 337 while he was stationed in Amiens, France, that the famous incident described below is said to have occurred. Martin converted to Christianity a short time later and began a long career of serving his God and fellow man, becoming Bishop of Tours and founding the renowned abbey of Marmoutier. Today he is a patron saint of France, and his symbol of a sword cutting a cloak in half is a widely loved reminder of the power of sharing.

It is a bright, frosty morning on a busy street in the old town of Amiens in France, hundreds of years ago. People are trudging to work or bustling to the marketplace. Here and there little crowds gather to talk together, while boys and girls run along, laughing, playing, behaving very much as they do today. A young scholar passes by, looking lost in thought, then a rich lady with a servant at her heels, then a prosperous merchant with his clerk beside him listening meekly to his master's orders.

In a shadow of the city wall, as unheeded as a mound of dust, stands a poor, ragged beggar, shivering with cold, one feeble hand stretched out for alms. The people pass him by, most of them ignoring him altogether, some with a glance of half-contemptuous pity, or even disgust.

His pleading voice is so weak that it fades away. He is utterly despised.

Suddenly there is the ring of horses' hooves on the hard road, and a little band of the Emperor's soldiers canter down the street. They are talking merrily among themselves. Their swords, their big spurs, and the trappings of their steeds glisten in the sunshine. They are leaving for a distant city, and carelessly glance at the people who stand still to watch them ride by, admiring their youth and gallant bearing.

As they pass by the shadow of the city wall, one of the young soldiers in the rear of the troop reins in his horse. His face changes when he notices something.

It is nothing to attract anyone's attention, only a shuddering beggar with outstretched hands and a haggard, starving face. But when Martin sees the other soldiers pass by the poor creature without a glance, he wonders if perhaps this man has been left for him to help.

There is no money in young Martin's purse—he has given it all away in charity or farewell gifts. But he feels he must do something.

Then an idea flashes into his head, suggested by the cold wind that whistles through the air. He loosens the great, warm military cloak hanging from his shoulders and holds it up with one hand. With the other hand he draws his sword, and cuts the cloth right down the middle. Then he leans from the saddle and with a word of sympathy drops one half of the garment over the shoulders of the wretched beggar. Then he sheaths his sword, tosses the rest of the cloak back over his own shoulders, and gallops after his companions.

Some of the other young officers break out in laughter and jests as Martin joins them, with his strip of torn cloak fluttering behind him. But others wish they had thought of doing what he has done.

And that night Martin had a dream in which he saw Jesus in heaven, surrounded by a company of angels. In this vision, the Lord was wearing one half of a cloak, and he showed it to the angels, saying, "See, here is the garment Martin gave to me."

Five

·

MOTHERS
AND
FATHERS,
HUSBANDS
AND WIVES

THERE are many obligations in life, but none are more important than the ones we accept when we become husbands and wives, mothers and fathers. In this chapter we find stories illustrating the virtues involved in those parts of life's journey.

In recent history, marriage has devolved from being a sacrament to a contract to a convention to, finally, a convenience. (I am told there is a modern wedding vow that states not "as long as we both shall live," but rather "as long as we both shall *love.*") Of course, some marriages simply will not work. But the enormous number of separations and divorces today suggests that we no longer believe what we say during the ceremony: that marriage is a serious, lifelong commitment made "in the presence of God," a commitment to give to each other as long as both shall live.

As Aristotle long ago pointed out, marriage is in fact a relationship based in no small part on virtues. The most basic of these is responsibility, for marriage is, after all, an arrangement held together by mutual dependence and reciprocal obligations. But successful marriages are about more than fulfilling the conditions of a contract. In good marriages, men and women seek to improve themselves for the sake of their loved one. They offer and draw moral strength, day in and day out, by sharing compassion, courage, honesty, self-discipline, and a host of other virtues. Thus the whole of the union becomes stronger and more wonderful than the sum of the parts. "What greater thing is there for human souls," asked George Eliot, "than to feel that they are joined for life—to strengthen each other in all labor, to rest on each other in all pain, to be one with each other in silent, unspeakable memories at the moment of the last parting?" The stories in this chapter inspire us in all of these endeavors.

For most of us, the obligations of parenthood eventually go hand in hand with those of marriage. No duty is more important than the nurture and protection of children, and if parents do not teach honesty, perseverance, self-discipline, a desire for excellence, and a host of basic skills, it is exceedingly difficult for any of society's institutions to teach those things in the parents' place. The philosopher John Stuart Mill summed up the fundamental responsibilities of adults toward their offspring: "The duties of parents to their children are those which are indissolubly attached to the fact of causing the existence of a human being. The parent owes to society to endeavor to make the child a good and valuable member of it, and owes to the children to provide, so far as depends on him, such education, and such appliances and means, as will enable them to start with a fair chance of achieving by their own exertions a successful life."

In this chapter we find mothers and fathers going about the business of fulfilling those basic obligations, and much more. We see parents putting aside their own wants in order to minister to their children's needs. We watch them resetting their priorities and reshaping their own behavior so that they may set good examples. We witness them devoting time and attention to the task of raising the young, and cherishing every moment. We see them committing acts of self-sacrifice, and literally going to the ends of the earth for the sake of their daughters and sons.

In *The Iliad,* the first of Homer's great epics, there is a moving scene in which the Trojan hero Hector says goodbye to his wife and infant son before leaving the city to battle the Greeks. Taking his boy in his arms, he prays to the gods, asking, "Some day let the Trojans say of him, 'He is better than his father.'" Surely this is the hope of every parent. As best we can, we set before our children the example of our own virtues and our own mistakes, and offer the wisdom learned from both, hoping to make our loved ones at least a little better than we were.

SLEEP BABY, SLEEP

We begin this chapter with lullabies that sum up what it means to be a parent: watching, guarding, guiding, loving.

Sleep, baby, sleep.
Thy father guards the sheep;
Thy mother shakes the dreamland tree,
Down falls a little dream for thee:
Sleep, baby, sleep.

Sleep, baby, sleep.
The large stars are the sheep;
The little stars are the lambs, I guess;
And the gentle moon is the shepherdess:
Sleep, baby, sleep.

Sleep, baby, sleep.
Our Savior loves His sheep;
He is the Lamb of God on high,
Who for our sakes came down to die:
Sleep, baby, sleep.

•

ALL THE WORLD IS SLEEPING

Go to sleep upon my breast,
All the world is sleeping.
Till the morning's light you'll rest,
Mother watch is keeping.

Birds and beasts have closed their eyes,
All the world is sleeping.
In the morn the sun will rise,
Mother watch is keeping.

•

WHAT DOES LITTLE BIRDIE SAY?

Alfred Tennyson

What does little birdie say,
In her nest at peep of day?
    "Let me fly," says little birdie,
    "Mother, let me fly away."

Birdie, rest a little longer,
Till the little wings are stronger.
So she rests a little longer,
    Then she flies away.

What does little baby say,
In her bed at peep of day?
    Baby says, like little birdie,
    "Let me rise and fly away."

Baby, sleep a little longer,
Till the little limbs are stronger.
If she sleeps a little longer,
    Baby, too shall fly away.

•

THE SQUIRREL'S DEVOTION

Retold by Ella Lyman Cabot

The evidence of love is effort, the kind of effort that can bring
even miracles.

Many ages ago, in the faraway land of India, a great tamarisk
tree grew, with wide-spreading branches, far over the surface of a
great lake, clear, shining, and still. Morning, midday, and evening
shone with varying beauty in the lake where the green boughs of
the tamarisk waved in the quiet air.

Far up in the very crown of the tamarisk, a mother squirrel built her home. Here the gentle swinging of the branches rocked the baby squirrel's cradle, so that the little one slept quietly, waiting for the glad day to come when he might frolic through the beautiful green bower as his mother did.

But one day a great storm arose. Away over the sky spread angry clouds. The lake shivered and the sunshine fled from its face. The big tamarisk trembled as the storm struck limb after limb from its strong trunk.

Suddenly the fierce wind hurled the squirrel's nest from its perch. The frail little home plunged through the air to the lake below. There it bobbed up and down on the storm-lashed waves, with the baby squirrel still inside. It was only a matter of moments before it would sink out of sight.

A great fear struck the heart of the mother squirrel, standing on the lake's edge, her pouches filled with milky nuts for her little one. No help was near. No great swan, on whose white back she might rescue her slowly sinking child. No kind, strong eagle was near to cleave the storm with his dark pinions to the little squirrel's side. No kind boy in a strong boat to come to the mother's aid. Must the mother stand still and see her baby drown? What could she do?

Suddenly the great fear was gone and a great joy took its place. There was just one thing to be done. Empty the lake of its water, and lead her little son to the safe shelter of the friendly bank.

Without an instant's delay, the mother squirrel set to work. Into the lake she plunged, soaked her long feathery tail in the water, climbed out, ran to the crest of a little hill, squeezed out the water on its further side, then back to repeat the work, over and over, and over.

But while the mother wrought thus with all her soul and with all her might, the great Father looked down with joy to see this faithful mother do all she could to save her child. Swift as a flash of lightning went forth the command to an angel to help the mother and save the child. Like a gleam of sunshine he flew to obey. Like a flash of light the little wet clinging squirrel was restored to its rejoicing mother, who had done everything in her little power to accomplish the miracle that the angel had been sent to assist in. But whether the angel was the white swan, or the black eagle, or a kindhearted lad with a friendly boat, I do not know.

•

THE STORY OF THE
SMALL GREEN CATERPILLAR
Elizabeth Harrison

There are two different words meaning "father" in Latin. "Geni-
tor" means a biological father. "Pater" means a father who takes
responsibility. The little caterpillar in this story is a foster-father
who shows what "pater" is all about.

This story takes place in a quiet little garden of an old brick
house in a sleepy country town. There, on the outside leaf of a large
green cabbage-head, lived a little green caterpillar. He was not an
inch long and not much bigger around than a good-sized broom
straw, yet he was an honest little fellow in his way, and spent most
of his time crawling about on his cabbage-leaf and nibbling holes
in it, which you know, is about all a caterpillar can be expected to
do. The great, beautiful sun, high up in the sky, sent his bright rays
of light down to warm the little caterpillar just as regularly and with
seemingly just as much love as he sent them to make the thousand
wavelets of the swift-flowing river sparkle and gleam like diamonds,
or as he sent them down to rest in calm, still sunshine on the quiet
hilltops beyond.

The little green caterpillar's life was a very narrow one. He had
never been away from his cabbage-leaf, in fact he did not know that
there was anything else in the world except cabbage-leaves. He
might have learned something of the beautiful silvery moon, or the
shining stars, or of the glorious sun itself, if he had ever looked up,
but he never did. Therefore the whole world was a big cabbage-
leaf to him, and all of his life consisted in nibbling as much cabbage-
leaf as possible.

So you can easily imagine his astonishment when one day a
dainty, white butterfly settled down beside him and began laying
small green eggs. The little caterpillar had never before seen anything half so beautiful as were the wings of the dainty, white butterfly, and when she had finished laying her eggs and flew off, he for
the first time in his whole life, lifted his head toward the blue sky
that he might watch the quick motion of her wings. She was soon

beyond the tallest leaves of the tomato plants, above the feathery tips of the fine asparagus, even higher than the plum trees. He watched her until she became a mere speck in the air and at last vanished from his sight. He then sighed and turned again to his cabbage-leaf. As he did so his eyes rested on the twenty small green eggs which were no larger than pin heads.

"Did she leave these for me to care for?" said he to himself. Then came the perplexing question—how could he, a crawling caterpillar, take care of baby butterflies? He could not teach them anything except to crawl and nibble cabbage-leaves. If they were like their beautiful mother, would they not soon fly far beyond his reach? This last thought troubled him a great deal, still he watched over them tenderly until they should hatch. He could at least tell them of how beautiful their mother had been and could show them where to fly that they might find her.

He often pictured to himself how they would look, twenty dainty little butterflies fluttering about him on his cabbage-leaf for a time, and then flying off to the blue sky, for aught he knew, to visit the stars with their mother. He loved the great sun very dearly now, because it sent its rays down to warm the tiny eggs.

One day he awoke from his afternoon nap just in time to see a most remarkable sight! What do you think was happening? One after another of the small green eggs were breaking open, and out were crawling—what *do* you suppose! Little white butterflies? No, nothing of the kind—Little green caterpillars were creeping out of each shell. Their foster-father, as he had learned to call himself, could hardly believe his own eyes. Yet there they were, wriggling and squirming, very much like the young angleworms in the ground below.

"Well, well, well!" said he to himself, "who would ever dream that the children of that beautiful creature would be mere caterpillars?" Strange as it seemed to him, there was no denying the fact and his duty was to teach them how to crawl about and how to nibble cabbage-leaves. "Poor things," he used to say as he moved among them, "you will never know the world of beauty in which your mother lived, you will never be able to soar aloft in the free air, your lives must be spent in creeping about on a cabbage-leaf and filling yourselves full of it each day. Poor things! Poor things!"

The young caterpillars soon became so expert that they no longer needed his care. Feeling very tired and sleepy, he one day decided to make for himself a bed, or bag, and go to sleep, not caring much whether or not he ever awoke. He was soon softly wrapped from head to foot in the curious covering he had made, and then came a long, long sleep of three weeks or more. When at last he awakened, he began to work his head out of his covering. Soon his whole body was free and he began to breathe the fresh air and feel the warm sunshine. He was sure that something had happened to him though he could not tell what. He turned his head this way and that, and at last caught sight of his own sides. What do you think he saw? Wings! Beautiful white wings! And his body was white, too! The long sleep had changed him into a butterfly!

He began to slowly stretch his wings. They were so new he could hardly believe that they were part of himself. The more he stretched them the more beautiful they became, and soon they quivered and fluttered as gracefully as did other butterfly wings. Just at this moment a strong, fresh breeze swept over the garden, and before he had time to refuse, the new butterfly was lifted off the cabbage-leaf and was dancing through the air, settling down now on a bright flower, and now on a nodding blade of grass, then up and off again. He rejoiced gaily in his freedom for a time, but soon came the longing to try his wings in the upper sunshine.

Before attempting the unknown journey, however, he flew back to the round, green cabbage-head on which he had lived so long. There were the twenty, small, green caterpillars, still creeping slowly about and filling themselves with cabbage-leaf. This was all they knew how to do, and this they did faithfully. "Never mind, little caterpillars," said the new butterfly as he hovered over them, "keep on at your work; the cabbage-leaf gives you food, and the crawling makes you strong. By and by you, too, shall be butterflies and go forth free and glad into God's great upper world."

Having said this in so low a tone of voice that you would not have heard him had you been standing close by, he flew far away, so far that neither you nor I could have followed him with our eyes. But the small, green, caterpillars must have heard, for they went on crawling and nibbling cabbage-leaves quite contentedly, and not one of them was ever heard to complain of having to be a caterpillar, though occasionally one and then another of them would lift his head, and I doubt not he was thinking of the time when he, too, should become a beautiful white butterfly.

•

THE OWL AND THE PUSSY CAT

Edward Lear

Some say courting has gone out of style. If so, we need to bring it back. We should start by showing our children the civility, respect, and joy shared in courtships and marriages, as in these two poems, both famous in nurseryland.

The Owl and the Pussy Cat went to sea
    In a beautiful pea-green boat;
They took some honey, and plenty of money
    Wrapped up in a five-pound note.
The Owl looked up to the moon above,
    And sang to a small guitar,
"O lovely Pussy! O Pussy, my love,
    What a beautiful Pussy you are,
        You are,
What a beautiful Pussy you are!"

Pussy said to the Owl, "You elegant fowl!
    How wonderful sweet you sing!
Oh let us be married, too long we have tarried,
    But what shall we do for a ring?"
They sailed away for a year and a day
    To the land where the bong tree grows,
And there in a wood a Piggy-wig stood
    With a ring in the end of his nose,
        His nose,
With a ring in the end of his nose.

"Dear Pig, are you willing to sell for one shilling
    Your ring?" Said the Piggy, "I will."
So they took it away, and were married next day
    By the Turkey who lives on the hill.
They dined upon mince and slices of quince,
    Which they ate with a runcible spoon,
And hand in hand on the edge of the sand
    They danced by the light of the moon,
        The moon,
They danced by the light of the moon.

•

THE COURTSHIP AND MARRIAGE OF COCK ROBIN AND JENNY WREN

It was a merry time
    When Jenny Wren was young,
So neatly as she danced,
    And so sweetly as she sung,
Robin Redbreast lost his heart:
    He was a gallant bird;
He doft his hat to Jenny,
    And thus to her he said:

"My dearest Jenny Wren,
    If you will but be mine,
You shall dine on cherry pie,
    And drink nice currant wine.
I'll dress you like a Goldfinch,
    Or like a Peacock gay;
So if you'll have me, Jenny,
    Let us appoint the day."

Jenny blushed behind her fan,
    And thus declared her mind:
"Then let it be tomorrow, Bob,
    I take your offer kind—
Cherry pie is very good!
    So is currant wine!
But I will wear my brown gown.
    And never dress too fine."

Robin rose up early
    At the break of day;
He flew to Jenny Wren's house,
    To sing a roundelay.
He met the Cock and Hen,
    And bid the Cock declare,
This was his wedding day
    With Jenny Wren, the fair.

The Cock then blew his horn,
  To let the neighbors know,
This was Robin's wedding day,
  And they might see the show.
And first came parson Rook,
  With his spectacles and band,
And one of Mother Hubbard's books
  He held within his hand.

Then came the bride and bridegroom;
  Quite plainly was she dressed,
And blushed so much, her cheeks were
  As red as Robin's breast.
But Robin cheered her up;
  "My pretty Jen," said he,
"We're going to be married.
  And happy we shall be."

The Goldfinch came on next,
  To give away the bride;
The Linnet, being bride's maid,
  Walked by Jenny's side;
And, as she was a-walking,
  She said, "Upon my word,
I think that your Cock Robin
  Is a very pretty bird."

The Blackbird and the Thrush,
  And charming Nightingale,
Whose sweet jug sweetly echoes
  Through every grove and dale;
The Sparrow and Tom Tit,
  And many more, were there:
All came to see the wedding
  Of Jenny Wren, the fair.

"O then," says parson Rook,
    "Who gives this maid away?"
"I do," says the Goldfinch,
    "And her fortune I will pay:
Here's a bag of grain of many sorts,
    And other things beside;
Now happy be the bridegroom,
    And happy be the bride!"

"And will you have her, Robin,
    To be your wedded wife?"
"Yes, I will," says Robin,
    "And love her all my life."
"And will you have him, Jenny,
    Your husband now to be?"
"Yes, I will," says Jenny,
    "And love him heartily."

Then on her finger fair
    Cock Robin put the ring;
"You're married now," says parson Rook,
    While the Lark aloud did sing:
"Happy be the bridegroom,
    And happy be the bride!
And may not man, nor bird, nor beast,
    This happy pair divide."

The birds were asked to dine;
    Not Jenny's friends alone,
But every pretty songster
    That had Cock Robin known.
They had a cherry pie,
    Beside some currant wine,
And every guest brought something,
    That sumptuous they might dine.

The dinner things removed,
    They all began to sing;
And soon they made the place
    Near a mile round to ring.
The concert it was fine;
    And every bird tried
Who best could sing for Robin
    And Jenny Wren, the bride.

THE ROBIN TO HIS MATE

Love, union, work, children. This little poem has some of the really important ingredients of a blessed marriage.

Said Robin to his pretty mate,
    "Bring here a little hay;
Lay here a stick and there a straw,
    And bring a little clay.

"And we will build a little nest,
    Wherein you soon shall lay
Your little eggs, so smooth, so blue;
    Come, let us work away.

"And you shall keep them very warm;
    And only think, my dear,
'T will not be long before we see
    Four little robins here."

•

THE CHATTERING ASPEN

Adapted from a retelling by Mary Stewart

How does one look for a spouse? This Native-American tale suggests looking for virtue.

Listen! Do you hear the rustle, rustle of the leaves of that tree over our heads? They are never still. They whisper and chatter all the time, even when there is not wind enough to stir a leaf on one of the other trees.

The Indians told a story about the first aspen tree. Come sit nearer, and I will tell it to you.

Years and years ago there was a lake, *somewhere,* called Spirit Lake, where the sun always shone and the winds were always soft. Indian spirits lived there, and they were very wonderful to look upon. They gleamed as though the never-failing sunshine of their lake glowed within them. They wore golden tunics and mantles, and the feathers in their headbands and on their arrows were tipped with glimmering gold.

But, although they were so splendid and radiant, one of them, Wahontas, longed for a human bride. Leaving Spirit Lake, he wandered through many Indian camps, looking for the most perfect maiden.

At one tent he found two lovely sisters, Mistosis and Omemee. Mistosis had eyes that gleamed like stars. Omemee had hair that shone like the golden corn.

Wahontas went to their father, the old chief, and asked for the hand of one of his daughters in marriage. The old chief was happy to have such a suitor for his girls. But which one, he asked, did Wahontas wish to marry?

Wahontas pondered the question. They were equally beautiful, but which was the one for him? Then a plan came to him.

He disguised himself as an old, old Indian. Over his gold tunic he threw a ragged cloak, and upon his feet he placed worn moccasins, full of holes. Then he went to the two sisters' tent, and found them sitting outside.

A torrent of abuse greeted him as he approached.

"Away! Go away! There is no room for you here!" shouted Mistosis. "Hurry, hurry, we have no time for strange beggars!"

"But I am aged, weary, and hungry," murmured Wahontas.

"Aged!" scolded Mistosis. "There should be no aged people in the world. We should not have to take care of them!" On and on went her tongue, scolding, scorning, gibing at the poor old man.

Then Omemee stepped forward. She said no word, but led the old man inside the tent, to a seat upon a soft deerskin. Quickly she lighted a fire and upon it she cooked her best venison and broth. As he ate she looked sadly at his torn shoes and, going to a corner, brought out her most beautiful moccasins, beaded with blue and gold. She put them on his feet, smiling sweetly at him as she did so, while all the time the tongue of Mistosis went on with its cruel scolding.

In broken words Wahontas thanked Omemee, and tottering to the flap of the tent, he lifted it painfully. Then in the golden light of the entrance, he paused and drew himself up to his full height. From his shoulders he tore the ragged cloak, from his head he pulled the long white hair which had covered his raven locks.

"I came to you as an old man, weary, hungry, and forlorn," he said. "I come again, not as a beggar, but as a suitor. I have made my choice. Only one of you is beautiful within. Will you have me, Omemee?

"No one should be forced to bear the ceaseless cruelty of Mistosis's tongue again," he went on. "She shall become the aspen tree, whose leaves are never silent."

As he spoke, Mistosis, amazed and furious, became rooted to the spot. Her arms changed to branches, her tongues to many chattering leaves!

Wahontas turned to Omemee and opened his arms. "Come, my bride, my dove," he cried. "Come with me to the golden Spirit Lake, where no cloud of sorrow or pain shall ever dim thy sweet life!"

For a moment Omemee rested in his arms. Then in the form of two doves they flew over the forests to the golden lake, where they dwelled blissfully for years and years. Perhaps they are there today, while in our forests and along our roadsides the leaves of the aspen tree still chatter, chatter without ceasing!

•

THE PLOWMAN
WHO FOUND CONTENT

Retold by Julia Darrow Cowles

Here are two old stories showing two different kinds of marriages.
Husbands and wives can raise each other up, as in the first tale, or
they can bring each other down, as in the second.

A plowman paused in his work one day to rest. As he sat on
the handle of his plow he fell a-thinking. The world had not been
going well with him of late, and he could not help feeling downhearted. Just then he saw an old woman looking at him over the
hedge.

"Good-morning!" she said. "If you are wise you will take my
advice."

"And what is your advice?" he asked.

"Leave your plow, and walk straight on for two days. At the end
of that time you will find yourself in the middle of a forest, and in
front of you there will be a tree towering high above the others.
Cut it down, and your fortune will be made."

With these words the old woman hobbled down the road,
leaving the plowman wondering. He unharnessed his horses, drove
them home, and said good-by to his wife; and then taking his ax,
started out.

At the end of two days he came to the tree, and set to work to
cut it down. As it crashed to the ground a nest containing two eggs
fell from its topmost branches. The shells of the eggs were smashed,
and out of one came a young eagle, while from the other rolled a
small gold ring.

The eagle rapidly became larger and larger, till it was of full
size; then, flapping its wings, it flew up.

"I thank you, honest man, for giving me my freedom," it called
out. "In token of my gratitude take the ring—it is a wishing ring. If
you wish anything as you turn it round on your finger, your wish
will be fulfilled. But remember this—the ring contains but one
wish, so think well before you use it."

The man put the ring on his finger, and set off on his homeward journey. Night was coming on when he entered a town. Almost the first person he saw was a goldsmith standing at the door of his shop. So he went up to him, and asked him what the ring was worth.

The goldsmith looked at it carefully, and handed it back to the man with a smile.

"It is of very little value," he said.

The plowman laughed.

"Ah, Mr. Goldsmith," he cried, "you have made a mistake this time. My ring is worth more than all you have in your shop. It's a wishing-ring, and will give me anything I care to wish for."

The goldsmith felt annoyed and asked to see it again.

"Well, my good man," he said, "never mind about the ring. I dare say you are far from home, and are in want of some supper and a bed for the night. Come in and spend the night in my house."

The man gladly accepted the offer, and was soon sound asleep. In the middle of the night the goldsmith took the ring from his finger, and put another just like it in its place without disturbing him in the least.

Next morning the countryman went on his way, all unconscious of the trick that had been played on him. When he had gone the goldsmith closed the shutters of his shop, and bolted the door. Then turning the ring on his finger he said, "I wish for a hundred thousand sovereigns!"

Scarcely had the sound of his voice died away than there fell about him a shower of hard, bright, golden sovereigns. They struck him on the head, on the shoulders, on the hands. They covered the floor. Presently the floor gave way beneath the weight, and the goldsmith and his gold fell into the cellar beneath.

Next morning, when the goldsmith did not open the shop as usual, the neighbors forced open the door, and found him buried beneath the pile.

Meanwhile the countryman reached his home, and told his wife of the ring.

"Now, good wife," said he, "here is the ring; our fortune is made. Of course we must consider the matter well; then, when we have made up our minds as to what is best, we can express some very big wish as I turn the ring on my finger."

"Suppose," said the woman, "we were to wish for a nice farm. The land we have now is so small as to be almost useless."

"Yes," said the husband, "but, on the other hand, if we work hard and spend little for a year or two we might be able to buy as much as we want. Then we could get something else with the wishing-ring."

So it was agreed. For a year the man and his wife worked hard. Harvest came, and the crops were splendid. At the end of the year they were able to buy a nice farm, and still had some money left.

"There," said the man, "we have the land, and we still have our wish."

"Well," said his wife, "we could do very well with a horse and a cow."

"They are not worth wishing for," said he. "We can get them as we got the land."

So they went on working steadily and spending wisely for another year. At the end of that time they bought both a horse and a cow. Husband and wife were greatly pleased with their good fortune, for, said they, "We have got the things we wanted and we have still our wish."

As time went on everything prospered with the worthy couple. They worked hard, and were happy.

"Let us work while we are young," they told each other. "Life is still before us, and who can say how badly we may need our wish some day?"

So the years passed away. Every season saw the bounds of the farm increase and the granaries grow fuller. All day long the farmer was about in the fields, while his wife looked after the dairy. Sometimes, as they sat alone of an evening, they would remember the unused wishing-ring, and would talk of things they would like to have for the house. But they always said that there was still plenty of time for that. And they smiled at each other, and were content.

The man and his wife grew old and gray. Then came a day when they both died—and the wishing-ring had not been used. It was still on his finger as he had worn it for forty years. One of his sons was going to take it off, but the oldest said:

"Do not disturb it; there has been some secret in connection with it. Perhaps our mother gave it to him, for I have often seen her look longingly at it."

Thus the old man was buried with the ring, which was supposed to be a wishing-ring, but which, as we know, was not, though it brought the old couple more good fortune and happiness than all the wishing in the world could ever have given them.

•

THE THREE WISHES
Retold by Katharine Pyle

Here's the wrong way to get along and get ahead. This tale comes
from Sweden.

Once upon a time a poor man took his ax and went out into
the forest to cut wood. He was a lazy fellow, so as soon as he was
in the forest he began to look about to see which tree would be the
easiest to cut down. At last he found one that was hollow inside, as
he could tell by knocking upon it with his ax. "It ought not to take
long to cut this down," said he to himself. He raised his ax and
struck the tree such a blow that the splinters flew.

At once the bark opened and a little old fairy with a long beard
came running out of the tree.

"What do you mean by chopping into my house?" he cried;
and his eyes shone like red hot sparks, he was so angry.

"I did not know it was your house," said the man.

"Well, it is my house, and I'll thank you to let it alone," cried
the fairy.

"Very well," said the man. "I'd just as soon cut down some
other tree. I'll chop down the one over yonder."

"That is well," said the fairy. "I see that you are an obliging
fellow, after all. I have it in my mind to reward you for sparing my
house, so the next three wishes you and your wife make shall come
true, whatever they are; and that is your reward."

Then the fairy went back into the tree again and pulled the
bark together behind him.

The man stood looking at the tree and scratching his head.
"Now that is a curious thing," said he. Then he sat down and began
to wonder what he should wish for. He thought and he thought,
but he could decide on nothing. "I'll just go home and talk it over
with my wife," said he. So he shouldered his ax, and set off for
home. As soon as he came in at the door he began to bawl for his
wife, and she came in a hurry, for she did not know what had
happened to him.

He told his story and his wife listened. "This is a fine thing to
have happen to us," said she. "Now we must be very careful what
we wish for."

They sat down one on each side of the fire to talk it over. They thought of ever so many things they would like to have—a bag of gold, and a coach and four, and a fine house to live in, and fine clothes to wear, but nothing seemed just the right thing to choose.

They talked so long that they grew hungry. "Well, here we sit," said the man, "and not a thing cooked for dinner. I wish we had one of those fine sausages you used to make."

No sooner had he spoken than there was a great thumping and bumping in the chimney and a great sausage fell down on the hearth before him.

"What is this?" cried the man staring.

"Oh, you oaf! you stupid!" shrieked his wife. "It's the sausage you wished for. There's one of our wishes wasted. I wish the sausage were stuck on the end of your nose! It would serve you right!"

The moment she said this, the sausage flew up and stuck to the man's nose, and there it was and he couldn't get it off. The man pulled and tugged, and his wife pulled and tugged, but it was all of no use.

"Well, there's no help for it," said the husband. "We'll have to wish it off again."

His wife begun to cry and bawl. "No, no," she cried. "We only have one wish left, and we can't waste it that way. Let's wish ourselves the richest people in the world."

But to this the man would not agree. He wanted the sausage off his nose whatever it cost. So at last the wife was obliged to let him have his own way. "I wish the sausage was off my nose again," said the man, and that was the third of their wishes. So all the good they had of the fairy's gift was a sausage for dinner; but then it was the best they had ever eaten. "And after all," said the man, "there's nothing much better in the world to wish for than a full stomach."

●

THE ROSES OF SAINT ELIZABETH

Saint Elizabeth was born in 1207 at Pressburg, the old capital of Hungary. She was the daughter of King Andrew II and Queen Gertrude, and at an early age she was betrothed to the Landgrave of Thuringia, an ancient kingdom lying in what is now Germany.

She became well known for her kindness and charity, building a hospital at the foot of her castle. This legend of Elizabeth reminds us that marriage means trust and tenderness, and it means respect for the work each partner has to do.

Long ago, in the kingdom of Hungary, a beautiful daughter named Elizabeth was born to the king and queen. The little princess was so good and kind that all the people of Hungary loved her. She always had a kind smile and gentle words for anyone she met, and as she grew up, she spent her time trying to make life better for those in need.

When Elizabeth was old enough, she married a nobleman named Louis, and together they lived in a land called Thuringia. Louis was a serious and quiet man who was several years older than his young bride, and sometimes Elizabeth felt a little bit in awe of him. But they loved each other very much, and before many years passed they had four children, and their home was a happy place.

But even after she had a family of her own to look after, Elizabeth never stopped doing everything she could to help those who were suffering in Thuringia. Sometimes she would send a little food to a struggling family she knew was in need, or sometimes she would go herself to visit and comfort the sick, and sit at their bedsides.

Now, although Louis admired his wife's kindness and generosity, he had his own ideas about the way a princess should act, and he did not like to see Elizabeth always walking among the common people. He thought it did not look dignified for a noblewoman to stand in the street talking to a peasant, and sometimes he frowned upon his wife's frequent missions of charity.

One winter's day when Louis had ridden out to hunt with some of his friends, Elizabeth left the castle and made her way down the snow-covered path to visit a poor family. She carried several loaves of bread in her cloak, as many as it would hold. The road grew icier as she trudged along, and her load of bread made the walking awkward. She dared not raise her eyes from the path, or she might easily lose her balance. Finally, with a quiet sigh of relief, she reached the bottom of the hill. When she looked up, to her dismay, she saw her husband and his friends returning early from the hunt.

Elizabeth stopped in her tracks, suddenly flustered and embarrassed. She would have left the road and ducked into the woods until the party had passed, but there was no time. In a moment the horses were clopping all around her, and the riders were peering down in amusement at the young princess standing alone in the snow, gathering her cloak about her.

Her husband smiled tenderly when he saw her. Riding to her side, he reached down and placed his hand on her shoulder.

"Where are you going, my dear?" he asked.

Elizabeth did not know what to do. She knew how Louis felt about her habit of walking out alone to visit poor people in wretched huts, and she did not want to shame him in front of all his high-born friends by telling him of her errand. She shrank from her husband and drew her bundle closer to her heart while she searched for something to say.

Louis saw her hesitation and gazed at her now with a clouded brow.

"What do you carry in your cloak that makes you stoop so with the weight of your load?" he asked. And as he spoke, all the courtiers and huntsmen drew about her to see.

Elizabeth looked up at her husband in confusion. She knew that all these knights and noblemen would smile with disdain if they saw what she carried, and she thought she might not be able to bear their scorn. Before she really knew what she was saying, she blurted out, "Roses!"

She blushed with shame the moment she spoke, for she knew what she had said was wrong. She would have given anything just then to be brave enough to admit she had lied, but the thought of the hunters' laughter kept her silent. She could only hang her head and clutch at her cloak with trembling hands.

Looking down at her, Louis could see that something was wrong, and he guessed the truth. Half of him felt compassion for his struggling wife, but the other half felt anger and dismay that she would embarrass him this way in front of his friends. Leaning from his saddle, he reached for her cloak.

"Let me see," he said firmly.

Taking a corner of the cloth, he drew it aside.

And then a marvelous thing happened. In the folds of the cloak he saw not the loaves of bread he had expected. He found roses— glowing red and white roses, as fresh and soft as only flowers can be, even though the season was midwinter. And the very sweetness of summertime arose and filled the air, like the richest fragrance.

For a moment nobody spoke. Louis looked wonderingly into Elizabeth's face for a while. Then he took one crimson rose from the cloak, placed it next to his own heart, and bent down to kiss his young wife.

"Go your way, my love," he said gently.

He turned his horse and rode with the others back toward the castle, leaving Elizabeth standing breathless and astonished in the frozen road, gazing down at her armful of roses.

•

"An Honorable Estate, Instituted of God"

For many of us, the vows we take on our wedding day are the most important promises we will ever make, or at least so we say. It is our responsibility to think hard about those promises long before and long after the ceremony, not just on the day we stand before the altar.

The language may be old-fashioned, but the ideas these words convey will always be crucial to the success of the marriage. It is worth lingering over the familiar phrases: "in sickness and in health," "in sorrow and in joy," "forsaking all others," "till death us do part." They remind us that the marriage ceremony is not only a time of joy, but it is also a commitment made reverently and soberly before God.

The Address

The persons to be married shall present themselves before the minister, the woman standing at the left hand of man. The minister shall then say,

Dearly beloved, we are gathered together here in the presence of God, and in the face of this congregation, to join together this man and this woman in holy matrimony; which is an honorable estate, instituted of God, and therefore is not by any to be enterprised or taken in hand lightly or unadvisedly; but reverently, discreetly, soberly, and in the fear of God.

If any man can show just cause why they may not lawfully be joined together, let him now speak, or else hereafter forever hold his peace.

The Charge
And then, speaking to the persons who are to be married, the minister shall say,

I require and charge you both, that if either of you know any impediment why ye may not be lawfully united in matrimony, ye do now confess it. For be ye well assured that so many as are joined together, otherwise than God's word doth allow, are not joined together by God, nor is their union blessed by him.

The Vows
There being no impediment, the minister shall then say to the man,

_____, Wilt thou have this woman to thy wedded wife, to live together after God's ordinance in the holy estate of matrimony? Wilt thou love her, comfort her, honor and keep her, in sickness and in health, in sorrow and in joy; and forsaking all others, keep thee only unto her so long as ye both shall live?

The man shall answer, I will.

The Minister shall then say to the woman,

_____, Wilt thou have this man to thy wedded husband to live together after God's ordinance in the holy estate of matrimony? Wilt thou love him, comfort him, honor and keep him, in sickness and in health, in sorrow and in joy; and, forsaking all others, keep thee only unto him so long as ye both shall live?

The Woman shall answer, I will.

Then the Minister shall say,

Who giveth this woman to be married to this man?

The minister, receiving the woman, at her father's or friend's hand, shall cause the man with his right hand to take the woman by her right hand, and to say after him,

I, _____, take thee, _____, to my wedded wife, to have and to hold from this day forward, for better, for worse, for richer, for poorer, in sickness and in health, to love and to cherish, till death us do part, according to God's holy ordinance, and thereto I give thee my troth.

Then the woman shall likewise say after the minister,

I, _____, take thee, _____, to my wedded husband, to have and to hold, from this day forward, for better, for worse, for richer or for poorer, in sickness and in health, to love and to cherish, till death us do part, according to God's holy ordinance, and thereto I give thee my troth.

The man and the woman shall then loose hands. The minister, receiving a ring from the best man, shall give it to the man, who shall in turn place it on the fourth finger of the woman's left hand. The man, holding the ring there, shall say after the minister,

With this Ring I thee wed; and to thee only do I promise to keep myself, so long as we both shall live. Amen.

If there are to be double rings used at the service, the minister shall receive a ring from the maid of honor, and give it to the woman, who shall place it upon the fourth finger of the man's left hand and say after the minister,

With this ring I thee wed; and to thee only do I promise to keep myself, so long as we both shall live. Amen.

The Prayer
The Minister shall then say,
Let us pray.

Eternal God, creator and preserver of all mankind, send thy blessing upon these thy servants, whom we bless in thy name. Enable them to perform through all their years the vows which they have made in thy presence.

May they seriously attend to the duties of the new relation into which they have now entered; that it may not be to them a state of temptation and discord, but of mutual love and peace. Grant them the virtues of trust and patience and undying affection. May they be blessings and comforts to each other, sharers of each other's joys and sorrows, loyal companions in the life and work of every day, and helpers, each to the other, in all the chances and changes of this mortal life.

Hallow to them the home which they are to make and share together. Give them a wise love for all who may be committed to their care, keeping them always mindful that in thee we live and move and have our being, and that thou art our dwelling place in all generations. Through Jesus Christ our Lord. Amen.

The Pronouncement of the Marriage
The minister shall then say,

Forasmuch as _____ and _____ have consented together in holy wedlock, and have witnessed the same before God and this company, and thereto have engaged and pledged themselves to each other, and have declared the same by joining hands and by giving and receiving a ring (rings), I pronounce that they are man and wife; and those whom God hath joined together, let no man put asunder.

•

AN EXCELLENT WIFE

My wife, Elayne, and I chose this passage from Chapter 31 of Proverbs as a reading at our wedding thirteen years ago. In describing my wife, I think this passage is even more accurate today.

An excellent wife, who can find?
For her worth is far above jewels.

The heart of her husband trusts in her,
And he will have no lack of gain.
She does him good and not evil
All the days of her life.
She looks for wool and flax,
And works with her hands in delight.
She is like merchant ships;
She brings her food from afar.
She rises also while it is still night,
And gives food to her household,
And portions to her maidens.
She considers a field and buys it;
From her earnings she plants a vineyard.
She girds herself with strength,
And makes her arms strong.
She senses that her gain is good;
Her lamp does not go out at night.
She stretches out her hands to the distaff,
And her hands grasp the spindle.
She extends her hand to the poor;
And she stretches out her hands to the needy.
She is not afraid of the snow for her household,
For all her household are clothed with scarlet.
She makes coverings for herself;
Her clothing is fine linen and purple.
Her husband is known in the gates,
When he sits among the elders of the land.
She makes linen garments and sells them,
And supplies belts to the tradesmen.
Strength and dignity are her clothing,
And she smiles at the future.
She opens her mouth in wisdom,
And the teaching of kindness is on her tongue.
She looks well to the ways of her household,
And does not eat the bread of idleness.
Her children rise up and bless her;
Her husband also, and he praises her, saying:
"Many daughters have done nobly,
But you excel them all."
Charm is deceitful and beauty is vain,
But a woman who fears the LORD, she shall be praised.

THE WIVES OF WEINSBERG
*Adapted from a retelling
by Charlotte Yonge*

Here are some heroines with quick wits and great hearts.

It happened in Germany, in the Middle Ages. The year was
1141. Wolf, the duke of Bavaria, sat trapped inside his castle of
Weinsberg. Outside his walls lay the army of Frederick, the duke of
Swabia, and his brother the emperor Konrad.

The siege had lasted long, and the time had come when Wolf
knew he must surrender. Messengers rode back and forth, terms
were proposed, conditions allowed, arrangements completed.
Sadly, Wolf and his officers prepared to give themselves to their
bitter enemy.

But the wives of Weinsberg were not ready to lose all. They
sent a message to Konrad, asking the emperor to promise safe
conduct for all the women in the garrison, that they might come
out with as many of their valuables as they could carry.

The request was freely granted, and soon the castle gates
opened. Out came the ladies—but in startling fashion. They carried
not gold or jewels. Each one was bending under the weight of
her husband, whom she hoped to save from the vengeance of the
victorious host.

Konrad, who was really a generous and merciful man, is said
to have been brought to tears by the extraordinary performance.
He hastened to assure the women of their husbands' perfect safety
and freedom. Then he invited them all to a banquet and made
peace with the duke of Bavaria on terms much more favorable than
expected.

The castle mount was afterwards known as the Hill of Weiber-
treue, or woman's fidelity.

•

THE MOST PRECIOUS THING

This story of a young wife who matches words of love with a deed
of love echoes the stratagem of the wives of Weinsberg. Variations
of the tale are found in the folklore of eastern Europe.

It happened long ago that a young man and a young woman
fell in love with each other and decided to marry. They had almost
no money, but they did not hesitate over that. Their trust in each
other gave them faith that their future together must be a bright
one, as long as they had each other. They happily chose a date on
which they would join hearts and souls.

Before the wedding, the girl came to her fiancé with a request.

"I cannot imagine our ever wanting to be apart," she said. "But
it may be that, in time, we will tire of each other, or that you will
be angry with me, and want to send me back to my parents' house.
Promise me that if this should happen, you will allow me to carry
back with me the thing that has grown most precious to me."

Her fiancé laughed, and could see no sense in what she asked,
but the girl was not satisfied until he had written down his promise
and signed his name to it. Then the two were married and began
their life together.

They set their minds to improving their worldly position. They
were both willing to work hard at it, and soon their patient industry
found reward. Their first successes made them even more determined to put poverty behind them, and they worked harder than
ever before. Time passed, and their purses swelled. They became
comfortable, then well-to-do, and finally rich. They moved to a
bigger house, found a new set of friends, and surrounded themselves with all the trappings of fortune.

But in their single-minded pursuit of wealth, they began to
think more of their things than of each other. More and more, they
quarreled about what to buy, or how much to spend, or how they
should go about increasing their riches.

One afternoon, as they were preparing a feast for several important friends, they argued about some trifling matter—the flavor
of the gravy, or perhaps the order of seating at the table. They
began shouting and accusing each other.

"You care nothing for me!" cried the husband. "You think only of yourself, and the jewels and fine clothes you wear. Take those that are most precious to you, as I promised, and go back to your parents' house. There is no point in our going on together."

His wife went suddenly pale, and stared at him with a distracted look in her eyes, as if she had just seen something for the first time.

"Very well," she said quietly. "I am willing to go. But we must stay together one more night, and sit side by side at our table, for the sake of appearances in front of our friends."

The evening arrived. The feast began. It was as bountiful as their ample means allowed. When, one by one, the guests had succumbed to its influence, and her husband, too, had fallen asleep, the good woman had him carried to her parents' cottage and laid in bed there.

When he woke the next morning, he could not understand where he was. He raised himself up on his elbow to look about him, and at once his wife came to the bedside.

"My dear husband," she said softly, "your promise was that if you ever sent me away I might carry with me the thing that was most precious to me. You are that most precious thing. I care for you more than anything else, and nothing but death shall part us."

At once the man saw how selfishly they had both acted. He clasped his wife in his arms, and they kissed each other tenderly. That same day they returned home and began to devote themselves once again to each other.

●

FOR REMEMBRANCE

Adapted from Laura E. Richards

Words matter. In marriage, where there are so many words, they matter all the more.

A man sat by the coffin of the one who had been nearest to him, in black and bitter care. And as he sat, he saw passing beyond the coffin a troop of bright and lovely shapes, with clear eyes and faces full of rosy light.

"Who are you, fair creatures?" asked the man. And they answered:

"We are the words you might have spoken to her."

"Oh, stay with me!" cried the man. "Your sweet looks are a knife in my heart, yet still I would keep you, for she is cold and deaf, and I am alone."

But they answered: "Nay; we cannot stay, for we have no being, but are only a light that never shone."

And they passed on and were gone.

And still the man sat in black and bitter care.

And as he sat he saw rising up between him and the coffin a band of pale and terrible forms, with bloodless lips and hollow eyes of fire.

The man shuddered.

"What are you, dreadful shapes?" he asked. And they answered: "We are the words she heard from you."

Then the man cried aloud in anguish:

"Depart from me, and leave me with my dead! Better solitude than such company."

But they, sitting down in silence, fixed their eyes upon him, and they stayed with him forever.

●

THE LION'S HAIR

In marriage, petty disagreements sometimes obscure and even overwhelm more important harmonies. This Ethiopian folktale reminds us that, as in so many facets of life, success in marriage is largely a result of the effort you put into it.

In a village in the mountains of Ethiopia, a young man and a young woman fell in love and became husband and wife. For a short while they were perfectly happy, but then trouble entered their house. They began to find fault with each other over little things—he blamed her for spending too much at the market, or she criticized him for always being late. It seemed not a day passed without some kind of quarrel about money or friends or household chores. Sometimes they grew so angry they shouted at each other, and yelled bitter curses, and then went to bed without speaking, but that only made things worse.

After a few months, when she thought she could stand it no longer, the young wife went to a wise old judge to ask for a divorce.

"Why?" asked the old man. "You've been married barely a year. Don't you love your husband?"

"Yes, we love each other. But it's just not working out."

"What do you mean, not working out?"

"We fight a lot. He does things that bother me. He leaves his clothes lying around the house. He drops his toenails on the floor. He stays out too late. When I want to do one thing, he wants to do another. We just can't live together."

"I see," said the old man. "Perhaps I can help you. I know of a magic medicine that will make the two of you get along much better. If I give it to you, will you put aside these thoughts of divorce?"

"Yes!" cried the woman. "Give it to me."

"Wait," replied the judge. "To make the medicine, I must have a single hair from the tail of a fierce lion that lives down by the river. You must bring it to me."

"But how can I get such a hair?" the woman cried. "The lion will surely kill me."

"There I cannot help you," the old man shook his head. "I know much about making medicines, but I know little of lions. You must discover a way yourself. Can you do it?"

The young wife thought long and hard. She loved her husband very much. The magic medicine might save their marriage. She resolved to get the hair, no matter what.

The very next morning she walked down to the river, hid behind some rocks, and waited. After a while, the lion came by to drink. When she saw his huge claws, she froze with fear. When he bared his sharp fangs, she nearly fainted. And when he gave his mighty roar, she turned and ran home.

But the next morning she came back, this time carrying a sack of fresh meat. She set the food on the ground, two hundred yards from the lion, and then hid behind the rocks while the lion ate.

The next day, she set the meat down one hundred yards away from the lion. And on the following morning, she put the food only fifty yards away, and stood nearby while he gulped it down.

And so every day she drew closer and closer to the fierce, wild beast. After a while she stood near enough to throw him the food, and finally came the day when she fed him right from her hand! She trembled as she watched the great teeth ripping and tearing the meat. But she loved her husband more than she feared the lion. Closing her eyes, she reached out and pulled a single hair from the tail.

Then she ran as fast as she could to the wise old judge.

"Look!" she cried. "I've brought a hair from the lion!"

The old man took the hair and looked at it closely.

"This is a brave thing you have done," he said. "It took a great deal of patience and resolve."

"Yes," said the woman. "Now give me the medicine to make my marriage better!"

The old man shook his head.

"I have nothing else to give you."

"But you promised!" the young wife cried.

"Don't you see?" asked the old man gently. "I have already given you all the medicine you need. You were determined to do whatever it took, however long it took, to gain a magic remedy for your problems. But there is no magic remedy. There is only your determination. You say you and your husband love each other. If you both give your marriage the same patience and resolve and courage you showed in getting this hair, you will be happy together for a long time. Think about it."

And so the woman went home with new resolutions.

●

THE BABY

George MacDonald

In most marriages, the blessing of children comes from the union of husband and wife. It has been said that every child born into the world is a new thought of God. This little poem suggests that when a baby is born, God is thinking of the parents, too.

Where did you come from, baby dear?
Out of the everywhere into the here.

Where did you get your eyes so blue?
Out of the sky as I came through.

What makes the light in them sparkle and spin?
Some of the starry spikes left in.

Where did you get that little tear?
I found it waiting when I got here.

What makes your forehead so smooth and high?
A soft hand stroked it as I went by.

What makes your cheek like a warm white rose?
Something better than any one knows.

Whence that three-cornered smile of bliss?
Three angels gave me at once a kiss.

Where did you get that pearly ear?
God spoke, and it came out to hear.

Where did you get those arms and hands?
Love made itself into hooks and bands.

Feet, whence did you come, you darling things?
From the same box as the cherub's wings.

How did they all just come to be you?
God thought about me, and so I grew.

But how did you come to us, you dear?
God thought of *you,* and so I am here.

•

WHY THE BABY SAYS "GOO"

Adapted from a retelling
by Gilbert L. Wilson

Here is one of the fundamental truths of family life: Baby changes everything.

In a village near the mountains lived an Indian chief. He was a brave man and had fought in many battles. No one in the tribe had won more battles than he.

Strange folk were then in the land. Fierce ice giants came out of the North and carried people away. Wicked witches dwelt in caves, and in the mountains lived the Mikumwess, magic little people.

But the chief feared none of them. He fought the ice giants and made them go back to their home in the North. Some of the witches he killed. Others he drove from the land.

Everybody loved the chief. He was so brave and good that the villagers thought there was no one like him anywhere.

But when he had driven out all the giants, the chief grew vain. He began to think he was the most important person in the world.

"I can conquer anyone," he boasted. "And no one tells me what to do."

When his wife heard how the great chief boasted, she smiled. "My husband *is* wonderful," she said, "but there is one who is mightier than he. There is one whom even he must obey."

When the chief heard her say this, he asked, "Who is this wonderful one? Where is he?"

His wife smiled again. "You already know him," she said. "His name is Wasis."

Now who do you think Wasis was? He was their own plump little Baby. In the middle of the floor he sat, crowing to himself and sucking a piece of maple sugar. He looked very sweet and contented.

Now the chief, like all vain people, thought he knew everything. He thought, of course, that the little Baby would obey him. So he smiled and said to little Wasis, "Baby, come to me!"

But the Baby smiled back and went on sucking his maple sugar.

The chief was surprised. The villagers always did what he bade them. He could not understand why the little Baby did not obey him, but he smiled and said again to little Wasis, *"Baby, come to me!"*

The little Baby smiled back and sucked his maple sugar as before.

The chief was astonished. No one had ever dared disobey him before. He grew angry. He frowned at little Wasis and roared out, "BABY, COME TO ME!"

But little Wasis opened his mouth and burst out crying and screaming. The chief had never heard such awful sounds. Even the ice giants did not scream so terribly.

The chief was more and more astonished. He could not think why such a little Baby would not obey him.

"Wonderful!" he said. "All other men fear me. But this little Baby shouts back war cries. Perhaps I can overcome him with my magic."

He took out his medicine bag and shook it at the little Baby. He danced magic dances. He sang wonderful songs.

Little Wasis smiled and watched the chief with big round eyes. He thought it all very funny. And all the time he sucked his maple sugar.

The chief danced until he was tired out. Sweat ran down his face. Red paint oozed over his cheeks and neck. The feathers in his headdress had fallen down.

At last he sat down. He was too tired to dance any longer.

"Did I not tell you that Wasis is mightier than you?" asked his wife. "No one is mightier than the Baby. He always rules the wigwam. Everybody loves him and obeys him."

"It is even so," sighed the chief, as he went out of the wigwam. But as he went he could hear little Wasis talking to himself on the floor.

"Goo, goo, goo!" he crowed, as he sucked his maple sugar.

Now, when you hear the Baby saying, "Goo, goo, goo," you will know what it means. It is his war cry. He is happy because he remembers the time when he made the great chief understand who really rules the wigwam.

•

THE COST OF ONE SEED

Here is a fine story for a discussion about the division of labor
between husbands and wives. It's also good reading for expectant
fathers in the waiting room. The tale comes from east Africa.

A husband decided he did not want to live with his wife any
longer and made up his mind to divorce her. But the couple had a
newborn son, and both father and mother wanted to keep the child,
so they went before a judge.

The woman spoke first.

"I bore this child for nine months," she pleaded. "I nurse him
at my breast, I sing to him in my lap, I rock him to sleep in my arms
every night. I hold him when he cries, and I tend him when he is
sick. I am with him night and day, and love him more than my own
life. Let me keep him."

Then the man spoke.

"I gave the seed that grew into this child," he said. "Therefore
the child is mine. I should be able to keep it if I want."

The judge looked at the man.

"So you gave the seed, you say" he asked.

"That's right," the man said proudly. "One little seed was all it
took."

"I see," said the judge. "So the father gives the seed, and the
mother carries and feeds the child. In that case, I think I can make
a ruling in this matter. But first we must have some scales."

He called for a pair of scales and ordered the infant to be
weighed.

"This child weighs nine pounds," the judge said to the father.
"If you gave just one seed to make him, it stands to reason your
wife has given nine pounds minus the weight of one grain of seed.
So if you want the child, you must pay your wife for nine pounds
worth of food."

The husband stared at the judge as if he were in the presence
of a lunatic.

"Wait, I'm not through," the judge said. "We also need to consult a baggage carrier."

A baggage carrier was summoned.

"How much do you charge to carry a burden for someone?" the judge asked.

"A coin a day for every pound I carry," he answered.

"Very good," the judge said. "We will figure that the woman carried one pound during the first month she was with child, ending with nine pounds by the ninth month she was with child. So for nine months' work of carrying the child, at a coin per pound every day, she earned nearly fourteen hundred coins. The husband must pay her fourteen hundred coins for carrying his burden for him."

The husband looked wide eyed at the judge.

"One other thing," the judge said. "If it took this much work just to bring the child into the world, think how much it will take to raise it."

The man stood silent, beginning to understand for the first time.

"I see now, Judge," he said at last. "Now I will start to take some of the burden from my wife, so that we might make the scales balance."

•

THE MAGIC CAVERN
Retold by Frances Jenkins Olcott

This is an old tale for the modern era. In today's parlance, it's a story of a parent who needs to get her priorities straight.

Once upon a time, a woman lived in a little hut near a mountain on which was a wide forest. She had one little child whom she loved dearly.

Now, in that forest grew many Strawberries very large and juicy, and one Midsummer Day the woman took the child to pick some. They climbed the mountainside, and presently lighted upon vines that were covered with berries larger, redder, and more luscious than any they had ever seen before.

These they picked. But no sooner had the woman put them in her basket than she saw the door of a large cavern open before her. Great heaps of gold lay glittering on the floor, while three White Maidens sat there guarding the treasure.

"Come in, good Woman," called the White Maidens. "Take as much gold as you can grasp at once."

The woman, holding her child by the hand, entered eagerly. She stooped and grasped a handful of gold and put it in her apron. But the touch of it filled her with greed, and, forgetting her child, she gathered up two more handfuls. Then she turned and ran out of the cave.

Instantly a loud rumbling sounded behind her, and a voice cried out:

"Unhappy Woman! You have lost your little one until next Midsummer Day."

The door of the cavern closed, and the child was shut inside.

Well, the poor woman wrung her hands and wept, but it was of no use, and she had to go home without her child. And though after that she often visited the place where the cavern had opened, she never could find the door.

Early on the next Midsummer Day she hurried to the spot; and what should she see but the door wide open! The great heaps of gold lay glittering on the floor, while the three White Maidens sat there guarding the treasure. And near them stood her little child holding a big red Apple.

"Come in, good Woman," called the White Maidens. "Take as much gold as you can grasp at once."

At that the woman ran eagerly in. She forgot all about the gold, and clasped her dear child in her arms.

"Good Woman," said the White Maidens, "take the little one home. We give it back to you, for now your love is greater than your greed."

So the woman took her child home with her, and loved it better than gold all the days of her life.

•

THE CRAB AND HIS MOTHER

Aesop

All parents are teachers, our first teachers, for better or worse.

A mother crab and her son went scurrying over the sand.

The mother chastised her child: "Stop walking sideways! It's much more becoming to stroll straightforward."

And the young crab replied: "I will, Mother dear, just as soon as I see how. Show me the straight way, and I'll walk in it behind you."

Words are important, but there is nothing like the power of example.

•

THE BABY

Laura E. Richards

The ancient Roman writer Juvenal gave us this advice: "When thou art contemplating some base deed, let thy infant son act as a check on thy headlong course to sin."

A man sat by the door of his house, smoking his pipe; and his neighbor (who was an enemy, though neither of them knew it) sat beside him and tempted him.

"You are poor and out of work," said the neighbor, "and here is a way of bettering yourself. It will be an easy job, and will bring you money; and it is no more dishonest than many things that are done every day by respectable people. You will be a fool to throw away such a chance as this. Come with me, and we will settle the matter."

And the man listened.

Just then his young wife came to the door of the cottage. She was warm and rosy, for she had been washing, and she had the baby in her arms.

"Will you hold Baby for a few minutes, John?" she asked. "He is fretful, and I must hang out the clothes."

The man took the baby and held it on his knees; and as he held it, the child looked up in his face and spoke.

"Flesh of your flesh!" said the baby. "Soul of your soul! What you sow I shall reap, and where you lead I shall follow. Lead the way, Father, for my feet come after yours."

Then the man said to the neighbor, "Go, and come here no more!"

He rocked the baby on his knees, and whistled a tune. Presently his wife came out and took the child.

"Baby, Baby," she said, "how could you cry when Father was holding you? Such a father as you have, too! Mind you grow up as good a man as he is!"

And she went into the house, singing to the child as she went.

•

LITTLE EYES UPON YOU

There are little eyes upon you
and they're watching night and day.
There are little ears that quickly
take in every word you say.
There are little hands all eager
to do anything you do;
And a little boy who's dreaming
of the day he'll be like you.

You're the little fellow's idol,
you're the wisest of the wise.
In his little mind about you
no suspicions ever rise.
He believes in you devoutly,
holds all that you say and do;
He will say and do, in your way,
when he's grown up like you.

There's a wide-eyed little fellow
who believes you're always right;
And his eyes are always opened,
and he watches day and night.
You are setting an example
every day in all you do,
For the little boy who's waiting
to grow up to be like you.

•

A FORTUNE

Laura E. Richards

**Much of parenthood is about spending—spending time, effort,
attention, money. It's about whom and what we spend on.**

One day a man was walking along the street, and he was sad at
heart. Business was dull; he had set his desire upon a horse that
cost a thousand dollars, and he had only eight hundred to buy it
with. There were other things, to be sure, that might be bought
with eight hundred dollars, but he did not want those; so he was
sorrowful, and thought the world a bad place.

As he walked, he saw a child running toward him. It was a
strange child, but when he looked at it, its face lightened like sunshine, and broke into smiles. The child held out its closed hand.

"Guess what I have!" it cried gleefully.

"Something fine, I am sure!" said the man.

The child nodded and drew nearer, then opened its hand.

"Look!" it said, and the street rang with its happy laughter. The
man looked, and in the child's hand lay a penny.

"Hurrah!" said the child.

"Hurrah!" said the man.

Then they parted, and the child went and bought a stick of
candy, and saw all the world red and white in stripes.

The man went and put his eight hundred dollars in the savings
bank, all but fifty cents, and with the fifty cents he bought a hobby-
horse for his own little boy, and the little boy saw all the world
brown, with white spots.

Is this the horse you wanted so to buy, Father?" asked the little boy.

"It is the horse I have bought!" said the man.

"Hurrah!" said the little boy.

"Hurrah!" said the man. And he saw that the world was a good place after all.

•

WHEN MOTHER READS ALOUD

Here is one of the greatest joys and responsibilities of parents, and an important aid in teaching children about virtue. There is nothing in the world like listening to a story read aloud by a loved one.

When Mother reads aloud, the past
   Seems real as every day;
I hear the tramp of armies vast,
I see the spears and lances cast,
   I join the thrilling fray.
Brave knights and ladies fair and proud
I meet when Mother reads aloud.

When Mother reads aloud, far lands
   Seem very near and true;
I cross the deserts' gleaming sands,
Or hunt the jungle's prowling bands,
   Or sail the ocean blue.
Far heights, whose peaks the cold mists shroud,
I scale, when Mother reads aloud.

When Mother reads aloud, I long
   For noble deeds to do—
To help the right, redress the wrong;
It seems so easy to be strong,
   So simple to be true.
Oh, thick and fast the visions crowd
My eyes, when Mother reads aloud.

•

THE CHARGE OF THE NIGHT BRIGADE

As every parent knows, bedtime can sometimes be a real chore.
But it can also be one of the best times in parenthood.

A scurry of feet on the bedroom stair,
    A titter along the hall—
And this is the charge of the night brigade,
    To capture me heart and all.
And there is the Captain, Sleepy Eyes,
    And there is Lieutenant Dream,
While the only arms of love are theirs
    As into my heart they stream.

A low, little laugh as they form in line
    Robed in their slumber gowns—
No armor rude with its harsh intrude,
    No helmets that clank and frown;
They come for the hug and the goodnight kiss,
    And unto my heart they bring
The song of the bedtime troops of love,
    With its old, ineffable ring.

I sigh as I think of the lonesome folk
    In their fortresses alone,
Where never the children charge with their cheer
    Where the bedtime song's unknown;
Who sit in their childless realm aloof
    Nor ever behold at all
The Sleepy Eyes and the Golden Dream
    Come marching down through the hall.

Who never have felt around their necks
    Nor ever upon their lips,
The soft caress of a little arm,
    Or a kiss with its sweet eclipse;
I do not know what I would do
    Were the bedtime troops away,
And I almost dread the time to come
    When they'll march to the grown-up fray.

In a single file, to a merry tune,
 Whispering, wild with glee,
They turn the knob and open the door
And rush to the heart of me;
Retreat is vain, resist I won't,
 So on my lap they leap—
The troops of the night brigade that come
For the kiss of the tender sleep.

•

PROSERPINA

*Adapted from retellings by Flora Cooke,
Frances Jenkins Olcott, and others*

The next two myths associate the warmth of spring and summer with a mother's devotion. It is remarkable that ancient peoples linked something so encompassing and important as the seasons' cycles to the power of mother love.

The story of Proserpina (Persephone to the Greeks) is related by the Roman poet Ovid, among others. The image of Mother Ceres roaming the earth with her great torch in search of her lost daughter is one of the most stirring in classical mythology.

In olden days there lived—or so people believed—a goddess whose name was Ceres. People sometimes called her Mother Ceres, because she had power over all the earth. It was she who made the corn grow and the flowers spring up, who covered the trees with green leaves, who made the fruits ripen and brought the harvest to perfection. On her work and zeal depended all the life of all the people in the world.

Ceres loved all the beautiful ferns and grasses, loved all the trees and plants, but as much as she loved these, there was one thing she loved far more—her little daughter, Proserpina. And Proserpina loved her mother dearly in return, and played in the sunshine among the birds and flowers, and was as happy as the day was long.

One day the girl was playing in the meadow, making a wreath of delicate blossoms for her hair. She decided to take some flowers to her mother as well, so she began to gather as many as her arms could hold—violets and buttercups and daffodils and daisies.

Far away across the meadow she saw a white flower gleaming. She ran to it and found it was far more beautiful than any she had ever seen. On a single stem were a hundred blossoms. She tried to pick it, but the stem would not break. With all her strength she grasped it, and slowly it came up by the roots.

A low, rumbling sound began.

Proserpina stood still, listening. "Can that be thunder? There's not a cloud in the sky," she thought.

The rumbling grew louder, and she realized it came from beneath her feet. Suddenly, where she had pulled up the flower, the earth began to open, wider and wider. Out of the chasm sprang four coal black, fiery horses, and behind them came a chariot made of gold and rubies and other precious stones. In it sat King Pluto.

Pluto was king of the underground world. He lived and reigned alone in a dark, gloomy land, where the sun never shone and birds never sang and flowers never blossomed all the year round. When he saw Proserpina he thought how the presence of this beautiful little laughing child would brighten his gloomy palace. Springing down from his chariot, he strode into the meadow where Proserpina stood knee deep among the flowers. Seizing the frightened girl in his arms, he carried her back to his chariot, in spite of her cries and struggles, and the next minute he was driving away as fast as his steeds could gallop.

Poor Proserpina struggled and screamed, but it was all no use. And so fast did Pluto drive, lest Ceres should overtake him and snatch his newfound treasure from him, that very soon they reached the gate of his underground palace. In her despair, Proserpina snatched her wreath of flowers from her hair and flung it into a river that ran close by, begging the water nymphs to carry it to her mother. Then the gates swung to a crash behind the king's chariot, and Proserpina was a prisoner in the underground world.

Meanwhile, above the earth the sun had set, and Ceres returned to her home after her long day's work. As she came in sight of her dwelling place she looked up eagerly, expecting to see Proserpina come running out as usual to meet her. But tonight no Proserpina appeared. In vain did Ceres hunt for her among her usual haunts. In vain did she call her name in ever-increasing anxiety and alarm. And at last, in fear and distress, she lit a great torch and went out into the darkness searching far and wide, all through the hours of that long, sad night. And when morning dawned and still there was no sign of her dear child, the poor mother determined to leave her work and search through the wide world until she found Proserpina again.

Then began for poor Ceres a long, weary, hopeless search. All her daily duties were neglected. The corn died down, the flowers drooped and faded, and the grass withered away, for there was no one to look after them. The earth grew parched, the leaves fell off the trees, the plough broke in the furrow. The seed failed to come up, and the weeds grew rank and thick. Soon there arose a great famine all through the land. The people cried out to Mother Ceres to return and save them. But Ceres was far away and did not hear them; or if she heard, she did not heed, for she could think of nothing but her lost child.

"O Zephyr! Gentle Zephyr!" she asked the West Wind as he floated by, "have you seen my daughter?"

And when Zephyr whispered, "No," she hastened on.

"O Boreas! Strong Boreas!" she asked the North Wind as he rushed by, "have you seen my daughter?"

And when he roared, "No!" she hastened on.

At last, one day, as she sat beside the banks of a river, mourning and weeping, the waters suddenly flung a wreath of flowers into her lap. When she came to look at it, she knew it had been made by Proserpina's hands. As she gazed at it, longing to know the meaning of the message, she heard a fountain beside her speaking softly. And the fountain told her that, far down in the underground world from whence she had just come, Prosperina was seated on the throne by King Pluto's side.

"She is sad and sorrowful," gurgled the fountain. "Her cheeks are pale and her eyes are heavy with weeping. All King Pluto's wealth and riches cannot reconcile her to being separated from her dear mother."

When Ceres heard this she hurried to Jupiter, the great king of the gods. She told him she had found out where her daughter was hidden, and prayed him to command Pluto to give Proserpina back to her. At first Jupiter was very unwilling to interfere with the king of the underground world. But he saw the mother's tears, and they softened his heart. And the people of the earth joined their prayers to Ceres', and prayed that Jupiter grant her request, so that Ceres might attend to her duties once more and save them from the starvation that threatened them because of the terrible famine.

Then at last Jupiter gave way.

"Proserpina may return to you," he said, "as long as she has eaten no food while she has been in the underworld. Otherwise, she must stay with King Pluto, for that is the law. I will send my messenger Mercury to Pluto's palace right now."

Down in King Pluto's palace, Proserpina was weeping. She would take none of his gifts, and tasted none of his food. She longed only for her mother. Then Pluto remembered that Proserpina had told him that Mother Ceres always gave her fruit to eat, so calling one of his servants, he sent him up to the earth to fetch some.

The servant found the whole earth brown and dead—there was no fruit to be found on any of the trees. At last, however, he found one little withered pomegranate. Taking that, he hurried back to King Pluto's palace.

"Here, Proserpina, eat this," begged the king. "See, it is one of your own pomegranates. I had it brought from the earth for you."

Proserpina would not touch it, but King Pluto placed it near her and went away. It smelled so good that soon Proserpina took it in her hand. It had been so long since she had eaten, and she was so hungry. She lifted it to her lips.

Suddenly the door flew open, and there stood Mercury.

"Stop, Proserpina! Jupiter has sent me to take you home, but if you eat so much as one bite, I cannot take you with me. It is the law."

"I swallowed only six of the seeds!" cried Proserpina.

When Jupiter heard the sad news, he decreed that for each seed she had eaten, Proserpina must spend a month of every year in King Pluto's kingdom.

So for six months of every year Proserpina is obliged to go and live in the dark underground world, where she reigns as Pluto's queen, and while she is away the whole earth mourns for her. Flowers disappear; the leaves fall from the trees; even the skies weep at her departure. But when once more the gates of Pluto's kingdom fly open, and Proserpina comes back to spend six happy months with her mother, the whole earth breaks out into flower and song to greet her. The skies grow blue and smiling; the grass springs up fresh and green; the trees burst out into bud and blossom; and the birds pour out their gladdest, sweetest songs. And the time for the return of Proserpina is what we call spring.

While Ceres has her daughter beside her, she works cheerfully and diligently, and blesses the world with corn and wine, bringing forth an abundant harvest from the earth to provide for the needs of men. But when the time comes for Proserpina to go back to King Pluto, she grows sad and sorrowful, and leaves her work neglected while she mourns for her lost child. Then the people of the world have to live upon the grain and fruit they have garnered from the harvest, and manage for themselves as best they can while Proserpina is away. And the six months that Proserpina has to spend in her dark, gloomy kingdom are what we call winter.

And however long and cold and dreary the winter may be, yet we need never despair. The six months will be ended in good time, and then Proserpina will come back to earth, bringing springtime with her, and all will be sunshine and happiness once more.

THE DEATH OF BALDER

Adapted from a retelling by Anna McCaleb

In Norse mythology, Balder was a son of Odin, the chief of the gods, and Frigga, the goddess for whom some say the day Friday is named. It is thought that Balder represented the blessed, life-bringing influences of the short northern summer, and his death signified the coming of the long winter. Frigga's determination to protect her son, the ironic disaster that follows, and the gods' frantic attempts to bring their beloved friend and kinsman back to Asgard all combine to make this tragedy one of the most moving of the Norse tales.

Of all the gods in Asgard, Balder was the most beloved, for no one had ever seen him frown, and his smile made everyone happy. He was as good as he was beautiful, for he always offered a kind word, and he was forever ready to lift a strong arm to help any creature in need. Wherever he walked, light and warmth seemed to follow.

One morning the gods assembled in their great hall, called Valhalla, and they noticed that when Balder came among them, he looked less radiant than usual. They gathered about him, begging that he tell what troubled him. Balder only smiled and said, "It is nothing!" But it was not his old smile. It reminded the gods of the faint light the sun sheds when a thin cloud has drifted before it, and they knew something was wrong.

When, the next morning, Balder again came slowly into the great hall and showed a careworn face, Odin and Frigga, his father and mother, begged him to share the cause of his grief. At last Balder told them that for two nights he had had strange, haunting dreams. What they were he could not remember clearly when he woke, but he could not shake off their depressing effect.

"I only know," he said, "that there was a thick cloud that drifted between me and the sun, and there were confused sounds of woe, and travels in dark, difficult places."

Now, the gods knew well that their dreams were messages sent to them by the Fates. Frigga sensed that these visions were warnings of some danger that threatened her beloved son, and at once she busied herself with a plan which her mother love suggested.

She went all over the world, and made everything she met promise never to hurt Balder. Every bird, every beast, every creeping thing; all plants, stones, and metals; all diseases and poisons known to the gods and men; fire, water, earth, air—all things gladly took the oath to do Balder no harm, for everything in the world loved Balder for his brightness and kindness.

Gladly Frigga then took her way toward home, feeling certain she had saved Balder forever. As she was about to enter Valhalla, she noticed that on an oak branch grew a tiny, weak-looking shrub.

"That mistletoe is too young to promise, and too weak to do any harm," said Frigga, and she passed it by.

All the gods rejoiced when she told of her success. And when they discovered that nothing could harm Balder now, they invented a new game. Balder, smiling as of old, took his stand in their midst, and all the others hurled things at him, laughing to see how their missiles turned away from the bright young god. They threw stones and sticks, and even spears and swords and great battle-axes that would have killed anyone else on the instant. But all of their weapons fell short, or veered to one side, or floated harmlessly away as though they were blossoms on the wind. The gods grew merry over this pastime, Balder the most of all, and it soon became the favorite sport in Asgard.

But there was one who was jealous of Balder—Loki, the contriver of fraud and mischief, a giant who had forced himself into the company of the gods. When he saw that Balder was being used as a target but remained unhurt through all, he became angry—he could not bear this proof that all things loved Balder. And an evil thought came into his heart. He determined to find out if even one thing had failed to promise never to harm Balder.

And so Loki disguised himself as an old woman and hobbled off to find Frigga.

"Do you know," he croaked, "that the gods and heroes are playing a very dangerous game? They are hurling all sorts of things at your son, who stands in their midst."

"There is no danger," replied Frigga, smiling at the old woman. And she told how everything had sworn to do Balder no harm, everything except the tiny mistletoe, which was too young and feeble to bother.

That was enough for evil Loki. Once out of sight of Frigga, he moved rapidly. Soon he appeared in his own form among the gods, who were still shouting with joy over their game. In his hand he carried a dart; but who could have guessed, to look at it, that it had been fashioned from the mistletoe on the Valhalla oak?

Outside the circle of the gods stood Balder's brother Hoder, who was blind. Hoder was often forlorn, but he loved his young brother with a love that only siblings can share.

Crafty Loki approached him and asked, "Why do you not join the game?"

"Alas," said Hoder, "how can I, with my sightless eyes? And besides, I have nothing to throw."

"Here is a dart," said the wicked god. "Since you cannot direct your aim, I will guide your arm."

Eager to join in the game with his beloved brother, Hoder took the dart in his hand. With Loki's aid, he hurled it with all his might. And because the mistletoe, of all things in the world, had not taken Frigga's oath, it flew straight at Balder's chest, and lodged in his heart, and the young god fell dead on the grass.

Then, instead of the laughter that Hoder waited to hear, there rose a shuddering wail of terror. All the gods and goddesses gathered around Balder's lifeless body, unable to fathom the atrocious deed. The brokenhearted Hoder wept most of all, and begged that he might be allowed to take his brother's place in Death's dark realm.

But Frigga refused to give up hope. She called out to the gods for a volunteer to go down to Hela, the goddess of the dead, and beg her to send Balder back to Asgard. Another of Frigga's sons stepped forward—Hermod, the swiftest of the gods. Odin gave him his horse, a marvelous steed named Sleipner who could outrun the wind itself. At once Hermod mounted and set off on the perilous journey.

For nine days and nine nights Hermod rode through glens so dark he could see nothing, until he reached the river that runs between the upper and lower worlds. When he galloped across the golden bridge, it shook beneath his weight, and the guard of the bridge knew it was no shade but a living being that crossed. But when Hermod told his errand, he was allowed to go on. And at last he came into the presence of the queen of that pale realm. On his knees he begged her to allow Balder to return to the light and the upper air.

At first stern Hela sat unmoved by his pleas, but finally she gave this answer: "If, through all the earth, all things, living and dead, weep for Balder, then he shall return. But if one thing in all the world refuses to shed tears, here he shall stay."

Cheered by this promise, Hermod set out on his journey home. When he reached Asgard there was rejoicing among the gods. At once they set out upon their task, for all the gods wanted a part in the work of bringing Balder back to life. They rode throughout the world, begging everything they found to weep. Trees, stones, flowers, birds, and beasts all joined willingly in grief for Balder, for all knew of his goodness and beauty.

But as the joyful gods returned to Asgard, thinking they had accomplished their mission, they came to the mouth of a dark cave where sat an old woman, withered with age. They begged her to weep for Balder, as all things in heaven and earth had done. But in a shrill voice she mocked them and answered: "Why should I weep for him? Let Hela keep her own. You'll get nothing but dry tears from me."

Then with harsh laughteer she fled to the cave's dark depth. And as she fled, the gods knew that this old woman was none other than Loki himself, the evil Loki who could take any manner of disguise. For a second time he had stolen life from Balder.

And so because one thing in the world would not weep, Hela

kept the young god in her underground kingdom. Sadly the gods rode back to Asgard with grief in their hearts, for they knew that brightness was gone forever—that Balder the beautiful would return no more. And a time of darkness and silence fell over the world.

But the far-seeing Odin could look beyond that time of sorrow. Seated on his great throne in Valhalla, gazing over heaven and earth, the chief of the gods knew that this grief would not last forever. He could see a time coming when the clouds of desolation would part, the sun would shed its rays upon the world, and light would overcome shadows and confusion. The earth would rise green and fresh and smiling, the fields would bear ripened fruit, and Balder would be with his friends and kinsmen once more. And so Odin steeled his heart with courage to endure the dark times that were coming, looking past the long, cold night toward the glowing dawn.

•

"I KNOW OF A LOVELY GARDEN"

Martin Luther

John Donne said that letters mingle souls. Letters can be messages of love that draw parents and children toward each other.

Four-and-a-half centuries after his death, Martin Luther's deep affection for home and children still lives in his writings (including the one most familiar to children everywhere, the hymn beginning, "Away in a manger, no crib for a bed . . . "). In 1530 Martin Luther wrote the following letter to his son Hans, who was four years old.

To my little son, Hans Luther, grace and peace in Christ

My Heart-dear Little Son: I hear that you learn well and pray diligently. Continue to do so, my son. When I come home I will bring you a fine present from the fair.

I know of a lovely garden, full of joyful children, who wear little golden coats, and pick up beautiful apples, and pears, and cherries, and plums under the trees. They sing, and jump, and make merry. They have also beautiful little horses with golden saddles and silver bridles.

I asked the man that kept the garden who the children were. And he said to me, "The children are those who love to learn, and to pray, and to be good."

Then said I, "Dear sir, I have a little son, named Hans Luther. May he come into this garden, and have the same beautiful apples and pears to eat, and wonderful little horses to ride upon, and may he play about with these children?"

Then said he, "If he is willing to learn, and to pray, and to be good, he shall come into this garden; and his friends Lippus and Justus too. If they all come together, they shall have pipes, and little drums, and lutes, and music of stringed instruments. And they shall dance, and shoot with little crossbows."

Then he showed me a fine meadow in the garden, all laid out for dancing. There hung golden pipes and kettle-drums and fine silver crossbows; but it was too early to see the dancing, for the children had not had their dinner.

I said, "Ah, dear sir, I will instantly go and write to my little son Hans, so that he may study, and pray, and be good, and thus come into this garden. And he has a little cousin Lena, whom he must also bring with him."

Then he said to me: "So shall it be. Go home, and write to him."

Therefore, dear little son Hans, be diligent to learn and to pray; and tell Lippus and Justus to do so, too, that you may all meet together in that beautiful garden. Give cousin Lena a kiss from me. Herewith I recommend you all to the care of Almighty God.

•

"IN REGARD TO DUTY"

Robert E. Lee

Robert E. Lee (1807–1870) wrote this letter to his son, G. W. Custis Lee, who was in school at the time. Here is a father trying to impress his regard for virtue upon his own flesh and blood. There is no more important gift from parent to child. Would that we as parents be worthy to give it.

You must study to be frank with the world; frankness is the child of honesty and courage. Say just what you mean to do on every occasion, and take it for granted you mean to do right. If a friend asks a favor, you should grant it, if it is reasonable; if not, tell him plainly why you cannot; you will wrong him and wrong yourself by equivocation of any kind. Never do a wrong thing to make a friend or keep one; the man who requires you to do so, is dearly purchased at a sacrifice. Deal kindly but firmly, with all your classmates; you will find it the policy which wears best. Above all, do not appear to others what you are not. If you have any fault to find with anyone, tell him, not others, of what you complain; there is no more dangerous experiment than that of undertaking to be one thing before a man's face and another behind his back. We should live, act, and say, nothing to the injury of anyone. It is not only best as a matter of principle, but it is the path to peace and honor.

In regard to duty, let me, in conclusion of this hasty letter, inform you that, nearly a hundred years ago, there was a day of remarkable gloom and darkness—still known as "the dark day"— a day when the light of the sun was slowly extinguished, as if by eclipse. The Legislature of Connecticut was in session, and, as the members saw the unexpected and unaccountable darkness coming on, they shared in the general awe and terror. It was supposed by many that the last day—the day of judgment—had come. Someone, in the consternation of the hour, moved an adjournment. Then there arose an old Puritan legislator, Davenport, of Stamford, and said that, if the last day had come, he desired to be found at his place doing his duty, and, therefore, moved that candles be brought in, so that the House could proceed with its duty. There was quietness in that man's mind, the quietness of heavenly wisdom and inflexible willingness to obey present duty. Duty, then, is the sublimest word in our language. Do your duty in all things like the old Puritan. You cannot do more, you should never wish to do less. Never let me and your mother wear one gray hair for any lack of duty on your part.

538 THE MORAL COMPASS

•

"LIFT UP YOUR SOUL"
Amos Bronson and Abigail May Alcott

Louisa May Alcott (1832–1888), author of *Little Women,* one of
the best-loved of all children's books, received almost all of her
early education from her parents. The Alcott family was a remarkably close one despite frequent financial difficulties; as an educator, philosopher, and professional "conversationalist," Amos
Bronson Alcott was a somewhat less than successful breadwinner.
The success of *Little Women* brought Louisa May the cherished
pleasure of being able to support her aging father.

Amos Bronson and Abigail May Alcott often gave their growing
children little notes and letters of instruction, guidance, and encouragement. Here are two to Louisa May. Letter writing is a habit
more parents should practice; with loving words like these, mothers and fathers not only raise little bodies but also lift little souls.

My Daughter,
You are Seven years old to-day and your Father is forty. You
have learned a great many things, since you have lived in a Body,
about things going on around you and within you. You know how
to think, how to resolve, how to love, and how to obey. You feel
your Conscience, and have no real pleasure unless you obey it. You
cannot love yourself, or anyone else, when you do not mind its
commandments. It asks you always to BE GOOD, and bears, O how
gently! how patiently! with all endeavors to hate, and treat it cruelly.
How kindly it bears with you all the while. How sweetly it whispers
Happiness in your HEART when you Obey its soft words. How it
smiles upon you, and makes you Glad when you Resolve to Obey
it! How terrible its PUNISHMENTS. It is GOD trying in your soul to
keep you always Good.
You begin, my dear daughter, another year this morning. Your
Father, your Mother, and Sisters, with your little friends, show their
love on this your Birthday, by giving you this BOX. Open it, and
take what is in it, and the best wishes of

Your Father.

Beach Street,
Friday morning, Nov. 29, 1839.

15th Birthday,
Hillside.

Dearest,

Accept this pen from your mother and for her sake use it freely & worthily that each day of this your fifteenth year may testify to some good word or thought or work.

I know there will be born into your spirit new hopes, new gifts, for God helps the loving, trusting heart that turns to Him. Lift up your soul to meet the highest, for that alone will satisfy your yearning, aspiring nature.

Your temperament is a peculiar one, & there are few who can really help you. Set about the formation of character & believe me you are capable of obtaining a noble one. Industry, patience, love, creates, endures, gives all things, for these are the attributes of the Almighty, & they make us mighty in all things. May eternal love sustain you, infinite wisdom guide you, & the peace which passeth understanding reward you, my daughter.

Mother.

Nov. 29th, 1846.

•

To His Son, Vincent Corbet

ON HIS BIRTH-DAY, NOVEMBER 10, 1630,
BEING THEN THREE YEARS OLD.

Richard Corbett

Parents are there to protect their children from harm at the hands of the world—and the world from harm at the hands of their children. Richard Corbet, Bishop of Oxford and Norwich, was a popular poet during the reign of Charles I in the seventeenth century.

> What I shall leave thee none can tell,
> But all shall say I wish thee well;
> I wish thee, Vin, before all wealth,
> Both bodily and ghostly health:
> Nor too much wealth, nor wit, come to thee,
> So much of either may undo thee.

I wish thee learning, not for show,
Enough for to instruct, and know;
Not such as gentlemen require,
To prate at table, or at fire.
I wish thee all thy mother's graces,
Thy father's fortunes, and his places.
I wish thee friends, and one at court,
Not to build on, but support;
To keep thee, not in doing many
Oppressions, but from suffering any.
I wish thee peace in all thy ways,
Nor lazy nor contentious days;
And when thy soul and body part,
As innocent as now thou art.

•

MONICA, MOTHER OF AUGUSTINE

Laura M. Adams

For the discouraged mother, for the mother who has hoped and prayed, feared and wept over a wayward son, Monica, the mother of Saint Augustine, points the way to triumphant victory of mother love.

Early in the fourth century, Monica was born in Tagaste, North Africa. Her parents were Christians, and she was brought up to be a woman of strong, noble character. She seems, however, to have made a sad mistake in her marriage to Patricius, a pagan and a man of ungovernable temper.

Her life was made doubly miserable, because her mother-in-law, from whom Patricius must have inherited his disposition, lived with them, and it is believed aided and abetted him in ill-using Monica and mocking her religious life.

In the town where they lived, however, there were other unhappy wives whose lives would have been sadly embittered, had it not been for the patience and sweetness shown by Monica through all of her trials. In her sufferings she was on their level, but by her loftiness of spirit she helped them to climb with her the mountains of Hope and Courage.

Monica and Patricius had three children; but it was the famous Augustine who brought his mother's name into history, and made her known and loved down through the centuries.

As a little boy Augustine was very wayward. He seems to have inherited all of his father's—and doubtless some also of his grandmother's—uneven temperament.

He was disobedient, lazy, and unfair in all of his dealings. He said himself, in later years, in his famous book of confessions, "I stole that of which I had enough, and much better. Nor cared I to enjoy what I stole, but joyed in the theft itself."

From boyhood to manhood he seemed to develop more and more into a lazy parasite, feeding upon the lusts of the world, and satisfying only his physical passions. At Carthage, where he studied rhetoric and public speaking for three years, he went often to the chariot races, the gladitorial fights and the theater. While at Carthage his father, who had finally become a Christain, died, and alone in her home Monica wept many a bitter tear over the sins of Augustine.

She prayed continually for him. Just as God's love broods over us in tenderness and love, so the heart of a true mother broods yearningly over the sins and mistakes of her boy, and she would die to save him from himself.

The years passed along and Monica's prayers began to bear fruit. Sick and disgusted with the sinful life he was leading, Augustine became morose and dissatisfied with everything.

His talent for rhetoric and public speaking were so pronounced that he finally took up the teaching of rhetoric in Milan, where he had passed a satisfactory examination.

To Milan the faithful mother followed Augustine, still hoping and praying for his sin-sick soul. Here the young man met a famous bishop by the name of Ambrose, who had a very strong influence for good upon his life.

Monica saw much in her boy's life at Milan to make her troubled, but she wisely refrained from "too much speaking," and contented herself with earnest prayer and Christian example. Little by little the study of the Bible, his mother's prayers, and Bishop Ambrose's sermons, melted the proud heart. Again and again he fought the tempter, and again and again he fell. At last a day came when he had his final battle, and alone in his garden he fought it out, and God triumphed. The *will* to sin was destroyed; and the little mother of many tears found her mourning turned to joy.

Seventeen years of wrestling with God for the soul of this boy. Was it worth it? Ask any mother who has gone through the same Gethsemane, and her face will shine as she answers, "This my son was lost and is found." It was worth any sacrifice.

Augustine now resigned his professorship in rhetoric and devoted his whole time to the service of God. For some time he and his mother lived quietly together while he wrote two books. In the evenings they would talk together about the beautiful things of God; and at the same time the son opened his heart to his mother, and told her of his longing to go back to Africa and preach to those whom in former years he may have led astray.

"It is well, my son; I will go with you," she said. No lagging behind for her own comfort, no diminishing of the ever brooding mother love. It was a wearisome journey over the Apennine Mountains, and the brave mother was pretty well exhausted by the time they reached the seaport of Ostia.

Before starting out on a sea voyage, they rested at Ostia in a house with a pretty garden overlooking the sea. Sitting quietly together in the twilight, evening after evening, Monica little by little revealed to her boy, perhaps unconsciously, the agony of the years through which she had passed, and Augustine was sorely smitten with remorse.

Here at Ostia Monica died; and bitter was the grief of her son. At last, however, a great peace filled his heart, and he resolved to live just as she would have wished him to live, in the love and service of God and his fellow-men.

He went on over to Africa, where he was ordained a priest, and finally became bishop of the town of Hippo. He wrote many books which have influenced the whole course of Christian thought even down to these days. He remained bishop of Hippo until his death, forty-three years after his baptism.

Forty-three years of rich service of God against seventeen years of a mother's prayers! Look up, weary little praying mother; look up, and be faint-hearted no longer. That wayward child of your earnest prayers may some day be an Augustine. Keep right on praying; dry your eyes and take fresh hope. With your hand in God's hand, with your hopes centered upon His glory alone, who knows how soon your boy or girl may come into the Kingdom?

•

THE BRAVEST MAN

Mickey Mantle

Here's a sports hero's hero.

When I was in high school we had to read a play once about a man who was sentenced to death. I don't remember too much about the play except that the man who was about to die was terribly scared and the chaplain of the prison—or somebody who had come to visit him in his cell—tried to comfort him by telling him a line of poetry from Shakespeare. I'm not much on poetry and I don't know very much about Shakespeare, but I have never forgotten the line because the prisoner on his way to his execution kept repeating it. It went, "Cowards die many times before their deaths; the valiant never taste of death but once."

The bravest man I ever knew was my father. He died the winter after my first year in the major leagues, when I was twenty and he was only forty-one. He died of Hodgkin's disease, a form of cancer like leukemia. He knew he had it. He knew it for a long time. He was a tremendously strong man but the disease weakened him so much that he was like a shell of what he used to be. He never told me he was sick, and I believe he never told anybody, until we found out about it by accident.

Here's how I learned about it. In the second game of the 1951 World Series, which was my first World Series, I fell chasing a fly ball in the outfield in Yankee Stadium, and I hurt my knee badly. I was taken home to the hotel I was living in in New York City, and then I had to go to the hospital. My father had come up from home to see the World Series and he had left the game with me and come to the hotel. Now he went with me in a taxi to the hospital. He got out of the cab first, outside the hospital, and then I got out. I was on crutches and I couldn't put any weight on the leg that was hurt, so as I got out of the cab I grabbed my father's shoulder to steady myself. He crumpled to the sidewalk. I couldn't understand it. He was a very strong man and I didn't think anything at all about putting my weight on him that way. He was always so strong. Well, the doctors took him into the hospital, too, and they examined him and then they told me how sick he was. It was incurable, they said, and he had only a few months to live.

After the Series was over and we had gone home to Commerce, Oklahoma, my wife Merlyn and I took my father up to the Mayo Clinic in Rochester, Minnesota, to see if they could do anything. They gave him treatments that eased his pain, but there was nothing anybody could do to cure him. He went home again to Commerce, but then during the winter he decided to go out to Denver. He said there was some hospital or other out there that said it could cure him and he said he thought he'd go out there and see.

He knew they couldn't cure him. But he went out to Denver so that the little kids in our family—I'm the oldest and my sister and three brothers were all just little kids at that time—wouldn't see him wasting away, getting thinner and thinner and sicker and sicker. So he went out to Denver, and he died there. He never complained, he never acted scared, and he died like a man. That line from that play fitted him for sure: "Cowards die many times before their deaths; the valiant never taste of death but once."

My father was brave in lots of ways. I was the oldest child and I was born in October of 1931, right in the middle of the Depression, in Spavinaw, Oklahoma. Kids nowadays don't have any idea of what the Depression was like—it's just a word in the history books —and that's great. But it was a hard time to bring up a family, especially where we lived, which was one of the poorest parts of the country. Even in wealthy parts of the country, people were standing in line for food. Finding work and earning money was the hardest thing in the world to do, and keeping a family alive and fed and happy at the same time was even harder. But he did both, he and my mother (she was pretty brave, too; she had to make do without very much—she did all our cooking on a wood stove, for one thing—but we never felt we were without anything). My father never quit, never admitted defeat.

One year he traded our house in Commerce, where he was working as a miner in the lead and zinc mines we have there, for a farm out in the country. It wasn't much of a farm—we lived in Dust Bowl country and a lot of people had quit and gone to California (you've heard of the Okies, haven't you?). But he thought maybe a farm might mean a better life for us kids. The very first year he had it, there was a flood and the river came up over the farm and ruined it. My father just picked up, went back into town, and down into the mines again.

The thing is, despite all the troubles he and my mother had

because of the Depression, we had a lot of fun growing up. I had a happy boyhood, and even though I probably make more money now in a year than my father made in his life, I don't know that my kids are any happier than we were. I didn't appreciate this as a boy, but as a man I am even more filled with admiration for my father —especially for his courage in the face of trouble.

He was a quiet man and even-tempered and he was well-liked, but he could get pretty mad in that quiet way of his. I remember once there was a dance that everybody went to, a country dance or whatever you want to call it, a barn dance, a square dance. All the families went to it, fathers and mothers and kids and everybody. A couple of wise guys started to make trouble for no reason at all, just to show how mean and stupid they could be, I guess. They made things real unpleasant and they were about to ruin the fine evening that everybody was having. It's funny, but I don't remember a fight or anything else, but all of a sudden there was no more trouble. My uncles told me later that my father took the two troublemakers outside and licked them both. Just like that. No fuss. No bother. He belted them, and they left, and he went back inside, and the dance went on. It got to be a story that people liked to tell when they were sitting around talking about the old days. But my father never talked about it.

He loved baseball and he always wanted me to be a ballplayer. He named me for Mickey Cochrane, the great catcher who was at his peak about the time I was born. Actually, Cochrane had a bad World Series the month I was born, when Pepper Martin and the St. Louis Cardinals were stealing bases on him and running wild. Cochrane was criticized, but baseball men said it wasn't his fault so much as it was his pitchers', who didn't hold the runners tight to their bases. Anyway, one bad Series couldn't affect my father's admiration for Cochrane, and maybe he named me Mickey just to show people that he was still loyal to the man he admired.

When I was growing up my father used to take me with him all the way to St. Louis to see major league games. That was the nearest big league town in those days, and he and friends of his would drive six hundred miles up and back on a weekend to take in a couple of games. My father always took me with him.

I guess my making the major leagues was one of the happiest things that ever happened to my father, and I often think how glad I am that I made it before he died. Though I almost didn't.

That first year I was with the Yankees, when I was nineteen, I

struck out an awful lot. Casey Stengel was the manager and he played me a good part of the time, but even though I got some hits now and then, I kept striking out. It was terrible. Finally, in July, the Yankees decided to send me down to the minors to get rid of the strikeout habit. It is a depressing thing being sent down to the minors, and I felt low. I thought I had missed my big chance. I figured they had looked at me and didn't want me.

The Yanks sent me to Kansas City, which at that time was a Yankee farm club in the American Association. There I got even worse. I believe I got one hit in my first twenty-two at bats, and that was a bunt. My father came up from home to Kansas City to see me play. I was living in a hotel there and, boy, was I glad to see him. I wanted him to pat me on the back and cheer me up and tell me how badly the Yankees had treated me and all that sort of stuff. I guess I was like a little boy, and I wanted him to comfort me.

He said, "How are things going?"

I said, "Awful. The Yankees sent me down to learn not to strike out, but now I can't even hit."

He said, "That so?"

I said, "I'm not good enough to play in the major leagues, and I'm not good enough to play here. I'll never make it. I think I'll quit and go home with you."

I guess I wanted him to say, Oh, don't be silly, you're just in a little slump, you'll be all right, you're great. But he just looked at me for a second and then in a quiet voice that cut me in two he said, "Well, Mick, if that's all the guts you have I think you better quit. You might as well come home right now."

I never felt as ashamed as I did then, to hear my father sound disappointed in me, ashamed of me. I shut my mouth. I didn't say anything more about quitting and going home. I kept playing. Things got better and a month later the Yankees called me back up to the majors, and I've been there ever since.

I have wondered sometimes exactly what it was. I know that I wanted my father to comfort me. He didn't. He didn't give me any advice. He didn't show me how to swing the bat any different. He didn't give me any inspiring speeches. I think that what happened was that he had so much plain ordinary courage that it spilled over, and I could feel it. All he did was show me that I was acting scared, and that you can't live scared.

A year later he was dead. I realized then that he was dying when he came to see me in Kansas City, though he never gave any sign to me. He didn't die scared, and he didn't live scared.

•

HIGH-WATER MARK
Bret Harte

The firm embrace of a parent's arms defines safety for a child. Bret Harte (1836–1902), the most influential writer of fiction about the American West of the Gold Rush era, depicts the courage that comes instinctively to parents when they act to protect their loved ones.

When the tide was out on the Dedlow Marsh, its extended dreariness was patent. Its spongy, low-lying surface, sluggish, inky pools, and tortuous sloughs, twisting their slimy way, eel-like, toward the open bay, were all hard facts. So were the few green tussocks, with their scant blades, their amphibious flavor, and unpleasant dampness.

And if you chose to indulge your fancy—although the flat monotony of the Dedlow Marsh was not inspiring—the wavy line of scattered drift gave an unpleasant consciousness of the spent waters, and made the dead certainty of the returning tide a gloomy reflection, which no present sunshine could dissipate. The greener meadowland seemed oppressed with this idea, and made no positive attempt at vegetation until the work of reclamation should be complete. In the bitter fruit of the low cranberry bushes one might fancy he detected a naturally sweet disposition curdled and soured by an injudicious course of too much regular cold water.

But if Dedlow Marsh was cheerless at the slack of the low tide, you should have seen it when the tide was strong and full. When the damp air blew chilly over the cold glittering expanse, and came to the faces of those who looked seaward like another tide; when a steel-like glint marked the low hollows and the sinuous line of slough; when the great shell-incrusted trunks of fallen trees arose again, and went forth on their dreary purposeless wanderings. When the glossy ducks swung silently, making neither ripple nor furrow on the shimmering surface; when the fog came in with the tide and shut out the blue above, even as the green below had been obliterated; when boatmen, lost in that fog, paddling about in a hopeless way, started at what seemed the brushing of mermen's fingers on the boat's keel, or shrank from the tufts of grass spreading around like the floating hair of a corpse, and knew by these signs that they were lost upon Dedlow Marsh, and must make a night of it, and a gloomy one at that—then you might know something of Dedlow Marsh at high water.

Let me recall a story connected with this latter view which never failed to recur to my mind in my long gunning excursions upon Dedlow Marsh. Although the event was briefly recorded in the county paper, I had the story, in all its eloquent detail, from the lips of the principal actor. I cannot hope to catch the varying emphasis and peculiar coloring of feminine delineation, for my narrator was a woman; but I'll try to give at least its substance.

She lived midway of the great slough of Dedlow Marsh and a good-sized river, which debouched four miles beyond into an estuary formed by the Pacific Ocean, on the long sandy peninsula which constituted the southwestern boundary of a noble bay. The house in which she lived was a small frame cabin raised from the marsh a few feet by stout piles, and was three miles distant from the settlements upon the river. Her husband was a logger—a profitable business in a country where the principal occupation was the manufacture of lumber.

It was the season of early spring, when her husband left on the ebb of a high tide with a raft of logs for the usual transportation to the lower end of the bay. As she stood by the door of the little cabin when the voyagers departed, she noticed a cold look in the southeastern sky, and she remembered hearing her husband say to his companions that they must endeavor to complete their voyage before the coming of the south-westerly gale which he saw brewing. And that night it began to storm and blow harder than she had ever before experienced, and some great trees fell in the forest by the river, and the house rocked like her baby's cradle.

But however the storm might roar about the little cabin, she knew that one she trusted had driven bolt and bar with his own strong hand, and that had he feared for her he would not have left her. This, and her domestic duties, and the care of her little sickly baby, helped to keep her mind from dwelling on the weather, except, of course, to hope that he was safely harbored with the logs at Utopia in the dreary distance. But she noticed that day, when she went out to feed the chickens and look after the cow, that the tide was up to the little fence of her garden patch, and the roar of the surf on the south beach, though miles away, she could hear distinctly.

And she began to think that she would like to have someone to talk with about matters, and she believed that if it had not been so far and so stormy, and the trail so impassable, she would have taken the baby and have gone over to Ryckman's, her nearest neighbor. But then, you see, he might have returned in the storm, all wet, with no one to see him; and it was a long exposure for baby, who was croupy and ailing.

But that night, she never could tell why, she didn't feel like sleeping or even lying down. The storm had somewhat abated, but she still "sat and sat," and even tried to read. I don't know whether it was a Bible or some profane magazine that this poor woman read, but most probably the latter, for the words all ran together and made such sad nonsense that she was forced at last to put the book down and turn to that dearer volume which lay before her in the cradle, with its white initial leaf as yet unsoiled, and try to look forward to its mysterious future. And, rocking the cradle, she thought of everything and everybody, but still was wide awake as ever.

It was nearly twelve o'clock when she at last lay down in her clothes. How long she slept she could not remember, but she awoke with a dreadful choking in her throat, and found herself standing, trembling all over, in the middle of the room, with her baby clasped to her breast, and she was "saying something." The baby cried and sobbed, and she walked up and down trying to hush it, when she heard a scratching at the door. She opened it fearfully, and was glad to see it was only old Pete, their dog, who crawled, dripping with water, into the room.

She would have liked to look out, not in the faint hope of her husband's coming, but to see how things looked; but the wind shook the door so savagely that she could hardly hold it. Then she sat down a little while, and then walked up and down a little while, and then she lay down again a little while. Lying close by the wall of the little cabin, she thought she heard once or twice something scrape slowly against the clapboards, like the scraping of branches.

Then there was a little gurgling sound, like the baby made when it was swallowing, then something went "click-click" and "cluck-cluck," so that she sat up in bed. When she did so she was attracted by something else that seemed creeping from the back door toward the center of the room. It wasn't much wider than her little finger, but soon it swelled to the width of her hand, and began spreading all over the floor. It was water!

She ran to the front door and threw it wide open, and saw nothing but water. She ran to the back door and threw it open, and saw nothing but water. She ran to the side window, and throwing that open, she saw nothing but water. Then she remembered hearing her husband once say that there was no danger in the tide, for that fell regularly, and people could calculate on it, and that he would rather live near the bay than the river, whose banks might overflow at any time. But was it the tide?

So she ran again to the back door, and threw out a stick of wood, It drifted away towards the bay. She scooped up some of the water and put it eagerly to her lips. It was fresh and sweet. It was the river, and not the tide!

It was then—oh, God be praised for his goodness! she did neither faint nor fall; it was then—blessed be the Saviour, for it was his merciful hand that touched and strengthened her in this awful moment—that fear dropped from her like a garment, and her trembling ceased. It was then and thereafter that she never lost her self-command, through all the trials of that gloomy night.

She drew the bedstead toward the middle of the room, and placed a table upon it, and on that she put the cradle. The water on the floor was already over her ankles, and the house once or twice moved so perceptibly, and seemed to be racked so, that the closet doors all flew open.

Then she heard the same rasping and thumping against the wall, and, looking out, saw that a large uprooted tree, which had lain near the road at the upper end of the pasture, had floated down to the house. Luckily its long roots dragged in the soil and kept it from moving as rapidly as the current, for had it struck the house in its full career, even the strong nails and bolts in the piles could not have withstood the shock. The hound had leaped upon its knotty surface, and crouched near the roots, shivering and whining.

A ray of hope flashed across her mind. She drew a heavy blanket from the bed, and, wrapping it about the babe, waded in the deepening waters to the door. As the tree swung again, broadside on, making the little cabin creak and tremble, she leaped on to its trunk. By God's mercy she succeeded in obtaining a footing on its slippery surface, and, twining an arm about its roots, she held in the other her moaning child.

Then something cracked near the front porch, and the whole front of the house she had just quitted fell forward—just as cattle fall on their knees before they lie down—and at the same moment the great redwood tree swung round and drifted away with its living cargo into the black night.

For all the excitement and danger, for all her soothing of her crying babe, for all the whistling of the wind, for all the uncertainty of her situation, she still turned to look at the deserted and water-swept cabin. She remembered even then, and she wondered how foolish she was to think of it at that time, that she wished she had put on another dress and the baby's best clothes; and she kept praying that the house would be spared so that he, when he returned, would have something to come to, and it wouldn't be quite so desolate and—how could he ever know what had become of her and baby? And at the thought she grew sick and faint. But she had something else to do besides worrying, for whenever the long roots of her ark struck an obstacle the whole trunk made half a revolution, and twice dipped her in the black water.

The hound, who kept distracting her by running up and down the tree and howling, at last fell off at one of these collisions. He swam for some time beside her, and she tried to get the poor beast upon the tree, but he "acted silly" and wild, and at last she lost sight of him forever. Then she and her baby were left alone.

The light which had burned for a few minutes in the deserted cabin was quenched suddenly. She could not then tell whither she was drifting. The outline of the white dunes on the peninsula showed dimly ahead, and she judged the tree was moving in a line with the river. It must be about slack water, and she had probably reached the eddy formed by the confluence of the tide and the overflowing waters of the river.

Unless the tide fell soon, there was present danger of her drifting to its channel, and being carried out to sea or crushed in the floating drift. That peril averted, if she were carried out on the ebb toward the bay, she might hope to strike one of the wooded promontories of the peninsula, and rest till daylight.

Sometimes she thought she heard voices and shouts from the river, and the bellowing of cattle and bleating of sheep. Then again it was only the ringing in her ears and throbbing of her heart. She found at about this time that she was so chilled and stiffened in her cramped position that she could scarcely move, and the baby cried so when she put it to her breast that she noticed the milk refused to flow; and she was so frightened at that that she put her head under her shawl, and for the first time cried bitterly.

When she raised her head again the boom of the surf was behind her, and she knew that her ark had again swung round. She dipped up the water to cool her parched throat, and found that it was salt as her tears. There was a relief, though, for by this sign she knew that she was drifting with the tide. It was then the wind went down, and the great and awful silence oppressed her. There was scarcely a ripple against the furrowed sides of the great trunk on which she rested, and around her all was black gloom and quiet.

She spoke to the baby just to hear herself speak, and to know that she had not lost her voice. She thought then—it was queer, but she could not help thinking it—how awful must have been the night when the great ship swung over the Asiatic peak, and the sounds of creation were blotted out from the world. She thought, too, of mariners clinging to spars, and of poor women who were lashed to rafts and beaten to death by the cruel sea. She tried to thank God that she was thus spared, and lifted her eyes from the baby who had fallen into a fretful sleep.

Suddenly, away to the southward, a great light lifted itself out of the gloom, and flashed and flickered, and flickered and flashed again. Her heart fluttered quickly against the baby's cold cheek. It was the lighthouse at the entrance of the bay. As she was yet wondering the tree suddenly rolled a little, dragged a little, and then seemed to lie quiet and still. She put out her hand and the current gurgled against it. The tree was aground, and, by the position of the light and the noise of the surf, aground upon the Dedlow Marsh.

Had it not been for her baby, who was ailing and croupy, had it not been for the sudden drying up of that sensitive fountain, she would have felt safe and relieved. Perhaps it was this which tended to make all her impressions mournful and gloomy. As the tide rapidly fell, a great flock of black brant fluttered by her, screaming and crying. Then the plover flew up and piped mournfully as they wheeled around the trunk, and at last fearlessly lit upon it like a gray cloud. Then the heron flew over and around her, shrieking and protesting, and at last dropped its gaunt legs only a few yards from her.

But, strangest of all, a pretty white bird, larger than a dove— like a pelican, but not a pelican—circled around and around her. At last it lit upon a rootlet of the tree quite over her shoulder. She put out her hand and stroked its beautiful white neck, and it never appeared to move. It stayed there so long that she thought she would lift up the baby to see it and try to attract her attention. But when she did so, the child was so chilled and cold, and had such a blue look under the little lashes, which it didn't raise at all, that she screamed aloud, and the bird flew away, and she fainted.

Well, that was the worst of it, and perhaps it was not so much, after all, to any but herself. For when she recovered her senses it was bright sunlight and dead low water. There was a confused noise of guttural voices about her, and an old squaw, singing an Indian "hushaby," and rocking herself from side to side before a fire built on the marsh, before which she, the recovered wife and mother, lay weak and weary.

Her first thought was for her baby, and she was about to speak when a young squaw, who must have been a mother herself, fathomed her thought and brought her the "mowitch," pale but living, in such a queer little willow cradle, all bound up, just like the squaw's own young one, that she laughed and cried together, and the young squaw and the old squaw showed their big white teeth and glinted their black eyes, and said, "Plenty get well, skeena mowitch," "Wagee man come plenty soon," and she could have kissed their brown faces in her joy.

And then she found that they had been gathering berries on the marsh in their queer comical baskets, and saw the skirt of her gown fluttering on the tree from afar, and the old squaw couldn't resist the temptation of procuring a new garment, and came down and discovered the "wagee" woman and child.

And of course she gave the garment to the old squaw, as you may imagine, and when *he* came at last and rushed up to her, looking about ten years older in his anxiety, she felt so faint again that they had to carry her to the canoe. For, you see, he knew nothing about the flood until he met the Indians at Utopia, and knew by the signs that the poor woman was his wife. And at the next high tide he towed the tree away back home, although it wasn't worth the trouble, and built another house, using the old tree for the foundation and props, and called it after her, "Mary's Ark!"

But you may guess the next house was built above highwater mark. And that's all.

Not much, perhaps, considering the malevolent capacity of the Dedlow Marsh. But you must tramp over it at low water, or paddle over it at high tide, or get lost upon it once or twice in the fog, as I have, to understand properly Mary's adventure, or to appreciate duly the blessings of living beyond high-water mark.

•

BEFORE HULL HOUSE

Jane Addams

In 1889 Jane Addams and Ellen Gates Starr turned a dilapidated Chicago mansion into a place where reform-minded people could live and work to improve neighborhood conditions. It was the beginning of Hull House, America's most famous settlement house. There, residents taught English to immigrants, established the first public playground in Chicago, promoted cleaner streets, pushed for child labor laws, organized civic groups, and pursued countless endeavors and reforms to improve living conditions in the city. By 1907 the settlement had grown to twelve buildings and covered a whole block.

The following excerpts come from the first chapter of Addams's *Twenty Years at Hull House.* In these recollections we discover one influence that engendered in this woman such a generous spirit—her father. Addams once wrote that "the child becomes largely what it is taught, hence we must watch what we teach it, and how we live before it." Here is a father living before his daughter in a great manner which helped shape her great character. That great manner was his example. Again, there is nothing like the moral power of example.

On the theory that our genuine impulses may be connected with our childish experiences, that one's bent may be tracked back to that "No-Man's Land" where character is formless but nevertheless settling into definite lines of future development, I begin this record with some impressions of my childhood.

All of these are directly connected with my father, although of course I recall many experiences apart from him. I was one of the younger members of a large family and an eager participant in the village life, but because my father was so distinctly the dominant influence and because it is quite impossible to set forth all of one's early impressions, it has seemed simpler to string these first memories on that single cord. Moreover, it was this cord which not only held fast my supreme affection, but also first drew me into the moral concerns of life, and later afforded a clew there to which I somewhat wistfully clung in the intricacy of its mazes.

It must have been from a very early period that I recall "horrid nights" when I tossed about in my bed because I had told a lie. I was held in the grip of a miserable dread of death, a double fear, first, that I myself should die in my sins and go straight to that fiery Hell which was never mentioned at home, but which I had heard all about from other children, and, second, that my father—representing the entire adult world which I had basely deceived—should himself die before I had time to tell him. My only method of obtaining relief was to go downstairs to my father's room and make full confession. The high resolve to do this would push me out of bed and carry me down the stairs without a touch of fear. But at the foot of the stairs I would be faced by the awful necessity of passing the front door—which my father, because of his Quaker tendencies, did not lock—and of crossing the wide and black expanse of the living room in order to reach his door. I would invariably cling to the newel post while I contemplated the perils of the situation, complicated by the fact that the literal first step meant putting my bare foot upon a piece of oilcloth in front of the door, only a few inches wide, but lying straight in my path. I would finally reach my father's bedside perfectly breathless and, having panted out the history of my sin, invariably received the same assurance that if he "had a little girl who told lies," he was very glad that she "felt too bad to go to sleep afterwards." No absolution was asked for nor received, but apparently the sense that the knowledge of my wickedness was shared, or an obscure understanding of the affection which underlay the grave statement, was sufficient, for I always went back to bed as bold as a lion, and slept, if not the sleep of the just, at least that of the comforted.

I recall an incident which must have occurred before I was seven years old, for the mill in which my father transacted his business that day was closed in 1867. The mill stood in the neighboring town adjacent to its poorest quarter. Before then I had always seen the little city of ten thousand people with the admiring eyes of a country child, and it had never occurred to me that all its streets were not as bewilderingly attractive as the one which contained the glittering toyshop and the confectioner. On that day I had my first sight of the poverty which implies squalor, and felt the curious distinction between the ruddy poverty of the country and that which even a small city presents in its shabbiest streets. I remember launching at my father the pertinent inquiry why people lived in such horrid little houses so close together, and that after receiving his explanation I declared with much firmness when I grew up I should, of course, have a large house, but it would not be built among the other large houses, but right in the midst of horrid little houses like these. . . .

An incident which stands out clearly in my mind as an exciting suggestion of the great world of moral enterprise and serious undertakings occurred in 1872, when I was not yet twelve years old. I came into my father's room one morning to find him sitting beside the fire with a newspaper in his hand, looking very solemn; and upon my eager inquiry what had happened, he told me that Joseph Mazzini was dead. I had never even heard Mazzini'a name, and after being told about him I was inclined to grow argumentative, asserting that my father did not know him, that he was not an American, and that I could not understand why we should be expected to feel badly about him. It is impossible to recall the conversation with the complete breakdown of my cheap arguments, but in the end I obtained that which I have ever regarded as a valuable possession, a sense of the genuine relationship which may exist between men who share large hopes and like desires, even though they differ in nationality, language, and creed; that those things count for absolutely nothing between groups of men who are trying to abolish slavery in America or to throw off Hapsburg oppression in Italy. At any rate, I was heartily ashamed of my meager notion of patriotism, and I came out of the room exhilarated with the consciousness that impersonal and international relations are actual facts and not mere phrases. I was filled with pride that I knew a man who held converse with great minds and who really sorrowed and rejoiced over happenings across the sea. I never recall those early conversations with my father, nor a score of others like them, but there comes into my mind a line from Mrs. Browning in which a daughter describes her relations with her father:—

> "He wrapt me in his large
> Man's doublet, careless did it fit or no."

•

DISTANCE

Raymond Carver

This is a story about a new father who must make a choice between pleasure and responsibility, and his discovery about which of the two brings the greater and firmer happiness. All fathers know this predicament.

She's in Milan for Christmas and wants to know what it was like when she was a kid. Always that on the rare occasions when he sees her.

Tell me, she says. Tell me what it was like then. She sips Strega, waits, eyes him closely.

She is a cool, slim, attractive girl, a survivor from top to bottom.

That was a long time ago. That was twenty years ago, he says. They're in his apartment on the Via Fabroni near the Cascina Gardens.

You can remember, she says. Go on, tell me.

What do you want to hear? he asks. What can I tell you? I could tell you about something that happened when you were a baby. It involves you, he says. But only in a minor way.

Tell me, she says. But first get us another drink, so you won't have to interrupt half way through.

He comes back from the kitchen with drinks, settles into his chair, begins.

They were kids themselves, but they were crazy in love, this eighteen-year-old boy and his seventeen-year-old girl friend when they married. Not all that long afterwards they had a daughter.

The baby came along in late November during a severe cold spell that just happened to coincide with the peak of the waterfowl season in that part of the country. The boy loved to hunt, you see, that's part of it.

The boy and girl, husband and wife now, father and mother, lived in a three-room apartment under a dentist's office. Each night they cleaned the upstairs office in exchange for their rent and utilities. In the summer they were expected to maintain the lawn and the flowers, and in winter the boy shoveled snow from the walks and spread rock salt on the pavement. The two kids, I'm telling you, were very much in love. On top of this they had great ambitions and they were wild dreamers. They were always talking about the things they were going to do and the places they were going to go.

He gets up from his chair and looks out the window for a minute over the tile rooftops at the snow that falls steadily through the late afternoon light.

Tell the story, she says.

The boy and girl slept in the bedroom, and the baby slept in a crib in the living room. You see, the baby was about three weeks old at this time and had only just begun to sleep through the night.

One Saturday night, after finishing his work upstairs, the boy went into the dentist's office, put his feet up on the desk, and called Carl Sutherland, an old hunting and fishing friend of his father's.

Carl, he said when the man picked up the receiver. I'm a father. We had a baby girl.

Congratulations, boy, Carl said. How is the wife?

She's fine, Carl. The baby's fine, too, the boy said. Everybody's fine.

That's good, Carl said. I'm glad to hear it. Well, you give my regards to the wife. If you called about going hunting, I'll tell you something. The geese are flying down there to beat the band. I don't think I've ever seen so many of them and I've been going for years. I shot five today. Two this morning and three this afternoon. I'm going back in the morning and you come along if you want to.

I want to, the boy said. That's why I called.

You be here at five-thirty sharp then and we'll go, Carl said. Bring lots of shells. We'll get some shooting in all right. I'll see you in the morning.

The boy liked Carl Sutherland. He'd been a friend of the boy's father, who was dead now. After the father's death, maybe trying to replace the loss they both felt, the boy and Sutherland had started hunting together. Sutherland was a heavy-set, balding man who lived alone and was not given to casual talk. Once in a while, when they were together, the boy felt uncomfortable, wondered if he had said or done something wrong because he was not used to being around people who kept still for long periods of time. But when he did talk the older man was often opinionated, and frequently the boy didn't agree with the opinions. Yet the man had a toughness and woods-savvy about him that the boy liked and admired.

The boy hung up the telephone and went downstairs to tell the girl. She watched while he laid out his things. Hunting coat, shell bag, boots, socks, hunting cap, long underwear, pump gun.

What time will you be back? the girl asked.

Probably around noon, he said. But maybe not until after five or six o'clock. Is that too late?

It's fine, she said. We'll get along just fine. You go and have some fun. You deserve it. Maybe tomorrow evening we'll dress Catherine up and go visit Sally.

Sure, that sounds like a good idea, he said. Let's plan on that.

Sally was the girl's sister. She was ten years older. The boy was a little in love with her, just as he was a little in love with Betsy, who was another sister the girl had. He'd said to the girl, If we weren't married I could go for Sally.

What about Betsy? the girl had said. I hate to admit it but I truly feel she's better looking than Sally or me. What about her?

Betsy too, the boy said and laughed. But not in the same way I could go for Sally. There's something about Sally you could fall for. No, I believe I'd prefer Sally over Betsy, if I had to make a choice.

But who do you really love? the girl asked. Who do you love most in all the world? Who's your wife?

You're my wife, the boy said.

And will we always love each other? the girl asked, enormously enjoying this conversation he could tell.

Always, the boy said. And we'll always be together. We're like the Canada geese, he said, taking the first comparison that came to mind, for they were often on his mind in those days. They only marry once. They choose a mate early in life, and they stay together always. If one of them dies or something, the other one will never remarry. It will live off by itself somewhere, or even continue to live with the flock, but it will stay single and alone amongst all the other geese.

That's sad, the girl said. It's sadder for it to live that way, I think, alone but with all the others, than just to live off by itself somewhere.

It is sad, the boy said. But it's Nature.

Have you ever killed one of those marriages? she asked. You know what I mean.

He nodded. He said. Two or three times I've shot a goose, then a minute or two later I'd see another goose turn back from the rest and begin to circle and call over the goose that lay on the ground.

Did you shoot it too? she asked with concern.

If I could, he answered. Sometimes I missed.

And it didn't bother you? she said.

Never, he said. You can't think about it when you're doing it. You see, I love everything there is about geese. I love to just watch them even when I'm not hunting them. But there are all kinds of contradictions in life. You can't think about the contradictions.

After dinner he turned up the furnace and helped her bathe the baby. He marveled again at the infant who had half his features, the eyes and mouth, and half the girl's, the chin and the nose. He powdered the tiny body and then powdered in between the fingers and toes. He watched the girl put the baby into its diaper and pajamas.

He emptied the bath into the shower basin and then he went upstairs. It was cold and overcast outside. His breath streamed in the air. The grass, what there was of it, looked like canvas, stiff and gray under the street light. Snow lay in piles beside the walk. A car went by and he heard sand grinding under the tires. He let himself imagine what it might be like tomorrow, geese milling in the air over his head, the gun plunging against his shoulder.

Then he locked the door and went downstairs.

In bed they tried to read but both of them fell asleep, she first, letting the magazine sink to the quilt. His eyes closed, but he roused himself, checked the alarm, and turned off the lamp.

He woke to the baby's cries. The light was on out in the living room. He could see the girl standing beside the crib rocking the baby in her arms. In a minute she put the baby down, turned out the light and came back to bed.

It was two o'clock in the morning and the boy fell asleep once more.

The baby's cries woke him again. This time the girl continued to sleep. The baby cried fitfully for a few minutes and stopped. The boy listened, then began to doze.

He opened his eyes. The living room light was burning. He sat up and turned on the lamp.

I don't know what's wrong, the girl said, walking back and forth with the baby. I've changed her and given her something more to eat. But she keeps crying. She won't stop crying. I'm so tired I'm afraid I might drop her.

You come back to bed, the boy said. I'll hold her for a while.

He got up and took the baby while the girl went to lie down.

Just rock her for a few minutes, the girl said from the bedroom. Maybe she'll go back to sleep.

The boy sat on the sofa and held the baby. He jiggled it in his lap until its eyes closed. His own eyes were near closing. He rose carefully and put the baby back in the crib.

It was fifteen minutes to four and he still had forty-five minutes that he could sleep. He crawled into bed.

But a few minutes later the baby began to cry once more. This time they both got up, and the boy swore.

For God's sake what's the matter with you? the girl said to him. Maybe she's sick or something. Maybe we shouldn't have given her the bath.

The boy picked up the baby. The baby kicked its feet and was quiet. Look, the boy said, I really don't think there's anything wrong with her.

How do you know that? the girl said. Here, let me have her. I know that I ought to give her something, but I don't know what I should give her.

After a few minutes had passed and the baby had not cried, the girl put the baby down again. The boy and the girl looked at the baby, and then they looked at each other as the baby opened its eyes and began to cry.

The girl took the baby. Baby, baby, she said with tears in her eyes.

Probably it's something on her stomach, the boy said.

The girl didn't answer. She went on rocking the baby in her arms, paying no attention now to the boy.

The boy waited a minute longer, then went to the kitchen and put on water for coffee. He drew on his woolen underwear and buttoned up. Then he got into his clothes.

What are you doing? the girl said to him.

Going hunting, he said.

I don't think you should, she said. Maybe you could go later on in the day if the baby is all right then. But I don't think you should go hunting this morning. I don't want to be left alone with the baby crying like this.

Carl's planning on me going, the boy said. We've planned it.

I don't give a damn about what you and Carl have planned, she said. And I don't give a damn about Carl, either. I don't even know the man. I don't want you to go is all. I don't think you should even consider wanting to go under the circumstances.

You've met Carl before, you know him, the boy said. What do you mean you don't know him?

That's not the point and you know it, the girl said. The point is I don't intend to be left alone with a sick baby.

Wait a minute, the boy said. You don't understand.

No, you don't understand, she said. I'm your wife. This is your baby. She's sick or something. Look at her. Why is she crying? You can't leave us to go hunting.

Don't get hysterical, he said.

I'm saying you can go hunting any time, she said. Something's wrong with this baby and you want to leave us to go hunting.

She began to cry. She put the baby back in the crib, but the baby started up again. The girl dried her eyes hastily on the sleeve of her nightgown and picked the baby up once more.

The boy laced his boots slowly, put on his shirt, sweater, and his coat. The kettle whistled on the stove in the kitchen.

You're going to have to choose, the girl said. Carl or us, I mean it, you've got to choose.

What do you mean? the boy said.

You heard what I said, the girl answered. If you want a family you're going to have to choose.

They stared at each other. Then the boy took his hunting gear and went upstairs. He started the car, went around to the windows and, making a job of it, scraped away the ice.

The temperature had dropped during the night, but the weather had cleared so that the stars had come out. The stars gleamed in the sky over his head. Driving, the boy looked out at the stars and was moved when he considered their distance.

Carl's porchlight was on, his station wagon parked in the drive with the motor idling. Carl came outside as the boy pulled to the curb. The boy had decided.

You might want to park off the street, Carl said as the boy came up the walk. I'm ready, just let me hit the lights. I feel like hell, I really do, he went on. I thought maybe you had overslept so I just this minute called your place. Your wife said you had left. I feel like hell.

It's okay, the boy said, trying to pick his words. He leaned his weight on one leg and turned up his collar. He put his hands in his coat pockets. She was already up, Carl. We've both been up for a while. I guess there's something wrong with the baby. I don't know. The baby keeps crying, I mean. The thing is, I guess I can't go this time, Carl.

You should have just stepped to the phone and called me, boy, Carl said. It's okay. You know you didn't have to come over here to tell me. What the hell, this hunting business you can take it or leave it. It's not important. You want a cup of coffee?

I'd better get back, the boy said.

Well, I expect I'll go ahead then, Carl said. He looked at the boy.

The boy kept standing on the porch, not saying anything.

It's cleared up, Carl said. I don't look for much action this morning. Probably you won't have missed anything anyway.

The boy nodded. I'll see you, Carl, he said.

So long, Carl said. Hey, don't let anybody ever tell you otherwise, Carl said. You're a lucky boy and I mean that.

The boy started his car and waited. He watched Carl go through the house and turn off all the lights. Then the boy put the car in gear and pulled away from the curb.

The living room light was on, but the girl was asleep on the bed and the baby was asleep beside her.

The boy took off his boots, pants and shirt. He was quiet about it. In his socks and woolen underwear, he sat on the sofa and read the morning paper.

Soon it began to turn light outside. The girl and the baby slept on. After a while the boy went to the kitchen and began to fry bacon.

The girl came out in her robe a few minutes later and put her arms around him without saying anything.

Hey, don't catch your robe on fire, the boy said. She was leaning against him but touching the stove, too.

I'm sorry about earlier, she said. I don't know what got into me. I don't know why I said those things.

It's all right, he said. Here, let me get this bacon.

I didn't mean to snap like that, she said. It was awful.

It was my fault, he said. How's Catherine?

She's fine now. I don't know what was the matter with her earlier. I changed her again after you left, and then she was fine. She was just fine and she went right off to sleep. I don't know what it was. Don't be mad with us.

The boy laughed. I'm not mad with you. Don't be silly, he said. Here, let me do something with this pan.

You sit down, the girl said. I'll fix this breakfast. How does a waffle sound with this bacon?

Sounds great, he said. I'm starved.

She took the bacon out of the pan and then she made waffle batter. He sat at the table, relaxed now, and watched her move around the kitchen.

She left to close their bedroom door. In the living room she put on a record that they both liked.

We don't want to wake that one up again, the girl said.

That's for sure, the boy said and laughed.

She put a plate in front of him with bacon, a fried egg, and a waffle. She put another plate on the table for herself. It's ready, she said.

It looks swell, he said. He spread butter and poured syrup over the waffle. But as he started to cut into the waffle, he turned the plate into his lap.

I don't believe it, he said jumping up from the table.

The girl looked at him and then at the expression on his face. She began to laugh.

If you could see yourself in the mirror, she said. She kept laughing.

He looked down at the syrup that covered the front of his woolen underwear, at the pieces of waffle, bacon, and egg that clung to the syrup. He began to laugh.

I was starved, he said, shaking his head.

You were starved, she said laughing.

He peeled off the woolen underwear and threw it at the bathroom door. Then he opened his arms and she moved into them.

We won't fight any more, she said. It's not worth it, is it?

That's right, he said.

We won't fight any more, she said.

The boy said, We won't. Then he kissed her.

He gets up from his chair and refills their glasses.

That's it, he says. End of story. I admit it's not much of one.

I was interested, she says. It was very interesting if you want to know. But what happened? she says. I mean later.

He shrugs and carries his drink over to the window. It's dark now but still snowing.

Things change, he says. I don't know how they do. But they do without your realizing it or wanting them to.

Yes, that's true, only—but she does not finish what she started.

She drops the subject then. In the window's reflection he sees her study her nails. Then she raises her head. Speaking brightly, she asks if he is going to show her the city, after all.

He says, Put your boots on and let's go.

But he stays by the window, remembering that life. They had laughed. They had leaned on each other and laughed until the tears had come, while everything else—the cold and where he'd go in it —was outside, for a while anyway.

•

ADMETUS AND ALCESTIS

Adapted from a retelling by James Baldwin

Stories of one spouse risking or even giving up life for the other appear over and over throughout the ages. The next four legends form a remarkable collection—two Greek, one Native American, and one Hindu—showing how love between husband and wife can challenge even death.

The first tale takes place in the region of classical Greece called Thessaly. The ancient writers Euripides and Apollodorus, among others, tell the story.

Admetus was the name of a Grecian king who ruled many, many years ago. He fell in love with a beautiful woman named Alcestis and asked if she would be his wife.

The wedding day arrived, and the guests came from far and wide. Apollo himself came down from Mount Olympus to join the feast, and he brought a present for the young bridegroom. It was a promise from the gods on the mountaintop that if Admetus should ever be sick and in danger of death, he might become well again if someone who loved him would die in his place.

Admetus and Alcestis lived together happily for a long time, and all the people in their little kingdom loved and blessed them. But at last Admetus fell sick, and, as he grew worse and worse every day, all hope that he would ever get well was lost. Then those who loved him remembered the wedding gift that Apollo had given him, and they began to ask who would be willing to die in his stead.

His father and mother were very old and could hope to live but a short time at best, and so it was thought that one of them would be glad to give up life for the sake of their son. But when someone asked them about it, they shook their heads and said that though life was short they would cling to it as long as they could.

Then his brothers and sisters were asked if they would die for Admetus, but they loved themselves better than their brother and turned away and left him. There were men in the town whom he had befriended and who owed their lives to him; they would have done everything else for him, but this thing they would not do.

Now while all were shaking their heads and saying "Not I," the beautiful Alcestis went into her own room and called to Apollo and asked that she might give up her life to save her husband. Then without a thought of fear she lay down upon her bed and closed her eyes; and a little while afterward, when her maidens came into the room they found her dead.

At the very same time Admetus felt his sickness leave him, and he sprang up as well and strong as he had ever been. Wondering how it was that he had been so quickly cured, he made haste to find Alcestis and tell her the good news. But when he went into her room, he saw her lying lifeless on her couch, and he knew at once that she had died for him. His grief was so great that he could not speak, and he wished that death had taken him and spared the one whom he loved.

In all the land every eye was wet with weeping for Alcestis, and the cries of the mourners were heard in every house. Admetus sat by the couch where his young queen lay, and held her cold hand in his own. The day passed and night came, but he would not leave her. All through the dark hours he sat there alone. The morning dawned, but he did not want to see the light.

At last the sun began to rise in the east, and then Admetus was surprised to feel the hand which he held growing warm. He saw a red tinge coming into the pale cheeks of Alcestis. A moment later the fair lady opened her eyes and sat up, alive and well and glad.

How was it that Alcestis had been given back to life?

When she died and left her body, the Shadow Leader, who knows no pity, led her, as he led all others, to the cheerless halls of Proserpina, the queen of the Lower World.

"Who is this who comes so willingly?" asked the pale-faced queen.

And when she was told how Alcestis, so young and beautiful, had given her life to save that of her husband, she was moved with pity; and she bade the Shadow Leader take her back again to the joy and sunlight of the Upper World.

So it was that Alcestis came to life, and for many years she and Admetus lived in their little kingdom not far from the sea. The Mighty Ones on the mountaintop blessed them; and, at last, when they became very old, the Shadow Leader led them both away together.

•

ORPHEUS AND EURYDICE

Retold by V. C. Turnbull

In Greek mythology, Orpheus was said to be the son of Calliope, the Muse of epic song. He was the most ancient of poets, living long before Homer. The story of his devotion to his wife, Euryd-ice, is one of the most famous of the classical myths.

Never was there a musician like Orpheus, who sang songs, inspired by the Muses, to a lyre that was given to him by Apollo. So mighty indeed was the magic of his music, that Nature herself owned his sway. Not only did rocks and rills repeat his lays, but the very trees uprooted themselves to follow in his train, and the savage beasts of the forest were tamed and fawned upon him as he played and sang.

But of all who hearkened enchanted to those matchless strains, none drew deeper delight than the singer's newly wed wife, the young and lovely Eurydice. Hour by hour she sat at his feet hearkening to the music of his voice and lyre, and the gods themselves might have envied the happy pair.

And surely some god did look with envious eye upon those

two. For on an evil day, Eurydice, strolling with her maidens through a flowery meadow, was bitten on her foot by a viper and perished in all her beauty ere the sun went down.

Then Orpheus, terrible in his anguish, swore that death itself should not forever rob him of his love. His song, which could tame wild beasts and drag the ancient trees from their roots, should quell the powers of hell and snatch back Eurydice from their grasp.

Thus he swore, calling on the gods to help him; and taking his lyre in his hand he set forth on that fearful pilgrimage from which never man—unless, like Hercules, he was a hero, half man and half god—had returned alive.

And now he reaches the downward path, the end whereof is lost in gloom. Deeper and deeper he descended till the light of day was quite shut out, and with it all the sounds of the pleasant earth. Downward through the silence as of the grave, downward through darkness deeper than that of any earthly night. Then out of the darkness, faint at first, but louder as he went on, came sounds that chilled his blood—shrieks and groans of more than mortal anguish, and the terrible voices of the Furies, speaking words that cannot be uttered in any human tongue.

When Orpheus heard these things his knees shook and his feet paused as if rooted to the ground. But remembering once more his love and all his grief, he struck his lyre and sang, till his dirge, reverberating like a funeral march, drowned all the sounds of hell. And Charon, the old ferryman, subdued by the melody, ferried him over the ninefold Styx which none save the dead might cross. When Orpheus reached the other side great companies of pale ghosts flocked round him on that drear shore; for the singer was no shadowy ghost like themselves, but a mortal, beautiful though woebegone, and his song spoke to them as with a thousand voices of the sunlight and the familiar earth, and of those who were left behind in their well-loved homes.

But Orpheus, not finding Eurydice among these, made no tarrying. Onward he passed, over the flaming flood of Phlegethon, through the cloud-hung and adamantine portals of Tartarus. Here Pluto, lord of the underworld, sits enthroned, and round him sinners do penance for the evil that they wrought upon earth. There Ixion, murderer of his father-in-law, is racked upon the everturning wheel, and Tantalus, who slew his son, endures eternal hunger in sight of food and eternal fear from the stone ever ready to fall. There the daughters of Danaüs cease not to pour water into bottomless urns. There Sisyphus, who broke faith with the gods when they permitted him to return a little while to the upper world, evermore rolls up a steep hill a great stone that, falling back from the summit, crushes the wretch in its downward rush.

But now a great marvel was seen in hell. For as Orpheus entered singing, his melodies, the first that had ever sounded in that dread abode, caused all its terrors for a moment to cease. Tantalus caught no more at the fruits that slipped through his fingers, Ixion's wheel ceased to turn, the daughters of Danaüs paused at their urns, and Sisyphus rested on his rock. The very Furies themselves ceased to scourge their victims, and the snakes that mingled with their locks hung down, forgetting to hiss.

So came Orpheus to the throne of great Pluto, by whose side sat Proserpina, his queen. And the king of the infernal gods asked: "What wouldst thou, mortal, who darest to enter unbidden this our realm of death?"

Orpheus answered, touching his lyre the while: "Not as a spy or a foe have I come where no living wight hath ventured before, but I seek my wife, slain untimely by the fangs of a serpent. Such love as mine for a maiden such as she must melt the stoniest heart. Thy heart is not all of stone, and thou too didst once love an earthly maiden. By these places filled with horrors, and by the silence of these boundless realms, I entreat thee restore Eurydice to life."

He paused, and all Tartarus waited with him for a reply. The terrible eyes of Pluto were cast down, and to Proserpina came a memory of the far-off days when she too was a maid upon earth sporting in the flowery meads of Enna. Then Orpheus struck again his magic strings and sang: "To thee we all belong; to thee soon or late we all most come. It is but for a little space that I crave my Eurydice. Nay, without her I will not return. Grant, therefore, my prayer, O Pluto, or slay me here and now."

Then Pluto raised his head and spoke: "Bring hither Eurydice."

And Eurydice, still pale and limping from her mortal wound, was brought from among the shades of the newly dead.

And Pluto said: "Take back, Orpheus, thy wife Eurydice, and lead her to the upper world again. But go thou before and leave her to follow after. Look not once back till thou hast passed my borders and canst see the sun, for in the moment when thou turnest thy head, thy wife is lost to thee again and forever."

Then with great joy Orpheus turned and led Eurydice away. They left behind the tortured dead and the gibbering ghosts; they crossed the flaming Phlegethon, and Charon rowed them once more over the ninefold Styx; and up the dark path they went, the cries of Tartarus sounding ever fainter in their ears; and at last the light of the sun shone faint and far where the path returned to earth, and as they pressed forward the song of the little birds made answer to the lyre of Orpheus.

But the cup of happiness was dashed from the lips that touched its brim. For even as they stood upon the uttermost verge of the dark place, the light of the sun just dawning upon their faces and their feet within a pace of earthly soil, Eurydice stumbled and cried out in pain.

Without a thought Orpheus turned to see what ailed her, and in that moment she was caught from him. Far down the path he saw her, a ghost once more, fading from his sight like smoke as her faint form was lost in the gloom. Only for a moment could he see her white arms stretched toward him in vain. Only once could he hear her last heart-broken farewell.

Down the path rushed Orpheus, clamoring for his Eurydice lost a second time; but vain was all his grief, for not again would Charon row him across the Styx. So the singer returned to earth, his heart broken, and all joy gone from his life. Thenceforth his one consolation was to sit upon Mount Rhodope singing his love and his loss.

THE WHITE STONE CANOE

This beautiful story comes from the Chippewa Indians, who lived in the region of Lakes Huron and Superior. It bears a striking resemblance to the Greek tale of Orpheus and Eurydice.

There was once a very beautiful Indian maiden, who died suddenly on the day she was married to a handsome young warrior. He was also brave, but his heart was not proof against this loss. From the hour she was buried, there was no more joy or peace for him.

He went often to visit the spot where they had buried her, and sat musing there, when, it was thought by some of his friends, he would have done better to try to amuse himself in the chase, or by diverting his thoughts in the warpath. But war and hunting had both lost their charms for him. His heart was already dead within him. He pushed aside both his war-club and his bow and arrows.

He had heard the old people say, that there was a path that led to the land of souls, and he determined to follow it. He accordingly set out, one morning, after having completed his preparations for the journey. At first he hardly knew which way to go. He was only guided by the tradition that he must go south. For a while he could see no change in the face of the country. Forests, and hills, and valleys, and streams had the same looks which they wore in his native place.

There was snow on the ground when he set out, and it was sometimes piled and matted on the thick trees and bushes. At length it began to diminish, and finally disappeared. The forest assumed a more cheerful appearance, the leaves put forth their buds, and before he was aware of the completeness of the change, he found himself surrounded by spring.

He had left behind him the land of snow and ice. The air became mild, the dark clouds of winter had rolled away from the sky; a pure field of blue was above him, and as he went he saw flowers beside his path, and heard the songs of birds. By these signs he knew that he was going the right way, for they agreed with the traditions of his tribe. At length he spied a path. It led him through a grove, then up a long and elevated ridge, on the very top of which he came to a lodge. At the door stood an old man, with white hair, whose eyes, though deeply sunk, had a fiery brilliancy. He had a long robe of skins thrown loosely around his shoulders, and a staff in his hands.

The young Chippewayan began to tell his story; but the venerable chief arrested him before he had proceeded to speak ten words. "I have expected you," he replied, "and had just risen to bid you welcome to my abode. She whom you seek passed here but a few days since, and being fatigued with her journey, rested herself here. Enter my lodge and be seated, and I will then satisfy your inquiries, and give you directions for your journey from this point." Having done this, they both issued forth to the lodge door.

"You see yonder gulf," said he, "and the wide-stretching blue plains beyond. It is the land of the souls. You stand upon its borders, and my lodge is the gate of entrance. But you can not take your body along. Leave it here with your bow and arrows, your bundle, and your dog. You will find them safe on your return." So saying, he re-entered the lodge, and the freed traveler bounded forward as if his feet had suddenly been endowed with the power of wings.

But all things retained their natural colors and shapes. The woods and leaves, and streams and lakes, were only more bright and comely than he had ever witnessed. Animals bounded across his path, with a freedom and a confidence which seemed to tell him there was no blood shed here. Birds of beautiful plumage inhabited the groves, and sported in the waters. There was but one thing in which he saw a very unusual effect. He noticed that his passage was not stopped by trees or other objects. He appeared to walk directly through them. They were, in fact, but the souls or shadows of material trees. He became sensible that he was in a land of shadows.

When he had traveled half a day's journey, through a country which was continually becoming more attractive, he came to the banks of a broad lake, in the center of which was a large and beautiful island. He found a canoe of shining white stone, tied to the shore. He was now sure that he had taken the right path, for the aged man had told him this. There were also shining paddles. He immediately entered the canoe, and took the paddles in his hands, when, to his joy and surprise, on turning round he beheld the object of his search in another canoe, exactly its counterpart in everything. She had exactly imitated his motions, and they were side by side.

They at once pushed out from shore and began to cross the lake. Its waves seemed to be rising, and at a distance looked ready to swallow them up; but just as they entered the whitened edge of them they seemed to melt away, as if they were but the images of waves. But no sooner was one wreath of foam passed, than another, more threatening still, arose.

Thus they were in perpetual fear; and what added to it, was the *clearness of the water,* through which they could see heaps of beings who had perished before, and whose bones lay strewed on the bottom of the lake. The Master of Life had, however, decreed to let them pass, for the actions of neither of them had been bad. But they saw many others struggling and sinking in the waves. Old and young of all ages and ranks were there: some passed and some sank. It was only the little children whose canoes seemed to meet no waves.

At length every difficulty was gone, as in a moment, and they both leaped out on the happy island. They felt that the very air was food. It strengthened and nourished them. They wandered together over the blissful fields, where every thing was formed to please the eye and the ear. There were no tempests—there was no ice, no chilly winds—no one shivered for the want of warm clothes: no one suffered hunger—no one mourned for the dead. They saw no graves. They heard of no wars. There was no hunting of animals; for the air itself was their food. Gladly would the young warrior have remained there forever, but he was obliged to go back for his body. He did not see the Master of Life, but he heard his voice in a soft breeze.

"Go back," said the voice, "to the land from whence you came. Your time has not yet come. The duties for which I made you, and which you are to perform, are not yet finished. Return to your people, and accomplish the duties of a good man. You will be the ruler of your tribe for many days. The rules you must observe will be told you by my messenger, who keeps the gate. When he surrenders back your body, he will tell you what to do. Listen to him and you shall afterward rejoin the spirit, which you must now leave behind. She is accepted and will be ever here, as young and as happy as she was when I first called her from the land of snows." When this voice ceased, the narrator awoke. It was all the fabric of a dream, and he was still in the bitter land of snows, and hunger, and tears.

•

STRONGER THAN DEATH
Retold by Mary Stewart

This story of a Hindu princess was sung in India while the story of Orpheus and his heavenly music was being told in ancient Greece. All over the world we find marriages stronger than death.

Of all the beauteous princesses who ever lived and loved in India none compared with the perfect Savitri. As she grew from childhood to womanhood, her beauty seemed to glow around her in a golden radiance.

"Surely this princess was born to be a goddess!" strangers

would exclaim, and so dazzling was her beauty that no prince, however rich and powerful, dared ask her hand in marriage. This filled her father's heart with sadness. "Daughter," he whispered, "choose thyself a husband worthy of thy noble hand, and upon him who is thy heart's desire my richest blessings will I bestow."

So Savitri mounted her golden chariot, and surrounded by her faithful guard and aged courtiers she journeyed far and wide. Through deep jungles and pleasant forests she rode, in gorgeous palaces or simple hermitages she stopped to rest, and many princes and nobles and valiant soldiers bowed in reverence before her. Amongst them all whom did she choose?

One word of encouragement from her perfect lips would have made the most powerful king her ardent lover, the most splendid palace her home, the most gorgeous kingdom of her own. But Savitri was seeking something nobler than wealth, more enduring than earthly power. In the heart of a deep forest she found a king, old, exiled and blind. In his youth, when he lost his eyesight, enemies drove him from his kingdom, and with his wife and baby son he had sought refuge in the forest. There the little son grew to manhood, as free and fearless as a wild animal, loving the forest creatures as brothers, and caring more for the tall arching trees and glowing stars than for any splendid, scented palace chamber. Satyavan, Soul of Truth, he was called.

Thus the princess Savitri found him, and when, bowing before her father's throne on her return, the king questioned her of her choice she answered, "In the wild woods I have found Satyavan, Soul of Truth, and him alone I choose for my lord and husband!"

Beside the King sat his wisest adviser, an old, old man wrapped in a pink cloak, who could foretell the future. When he heard these words of the princess his face clouded with grief. "Sorrow and disaster alone will come to Savitri from such a choice!" he exclaimed.

"Wherefore?" questioned the King, "is the prince a coward, does he lack wisdom, is his heart dark with impure thoughts?"

"As his face is fair and radiant, so is his heart full of courage and truth and his mind of wisdom," answered the old man. "But although he knows it not, it is decreed by the heavens above that twelve months from to-day Satyavan shall see death!"

Trembling with horror, the startled King cried, "Never, never, Savitri, shall your life be thus clouded! Choose again, dear maiden, choose a happier fated lord!"

"Father," answered Savitri, and her words fell softly and slowly, "only once does a maiden give her heart, and may Satyavan's life be long or short, his virtues great or none, my heart and life are his forever."

Thus in the forest the wedding was celebrated, and when the last fervent blessing had been pronounced Savitri laid aside her royal robes and gleaming jewels, and clad herself, like her husband's mother, the aged Queen, in the bark of trees and flaming red cloth woven from the wool of wild sheep. Then with her fair white hands, unused to any toil, she served her husband's parents, and all with such grace and sweetness that she was like a torch of golden light in that dark place, and Satyavan loved her with a love unspeakable.

But although her lips smiled and her eyes were serene, in her heart was hidden always the bitter secret of her husband's approaching death, a secret undreamed of by Satyavan and his parents. No word of it she spoke, but she counted the days one after another, and one morning her heart grew cold, for there were but three days left—three days, and her beloved husband, now so full of life and strength, would be lying still and lifeless at her feet. Filled with desperate dread, she made a vow to spend those three days standing without food or sleep, praying always to the gods to heed her.

Motionless and silent, her great dark eyes shining with unshed tears, Savitri stood for three sunlit days and three gloomsome nights, her lips moving ceaselessly in silent prayer. The dawn of the third day broke, the fated morning, and the Princess prayed her last desperate prayer before the fire kindled in honor of the gods. Then, exhausted as she was, she gently refused the food offered her by her loving parents. One more day she must fast, she said, and now her one desire was to go with her husband into the dark jungle, where, still full of life and vigor, he was going to hew trees for firewood. At first Satyavan was afraid to take her, she looked so weak and pale, although as lovely as a lotus blossom, but he could not withstand her urgent entreaty and together they wandered out into the deep forest.

The morning sun glistened on the gay flowers and bright plumage of the birds, the silver streams rippled, the trees rustled softly, and sweeter even than the songs of the birds were the words of love and tenderness Satyavan spoke to his young wife. Savitri smiled back at him, showing by no word or sign the anguish within her heart.

Gaily Satyavan filled the great basket with wild fruit. With his splendid strength he swung his axe, hewing many a sturdy tree. And then, suddenly, he grew faint and weary and murmuring, "A hundred needles pierce me, my aching head grows numb, let me rest here!" he fell upon the ground beside Savitri. Filled with a wild and speechless terror she clasped him to her, kissing his lips with desperate longing, while the forest grew darker around them and he slept, she knew, the sleep of death!

Then through the gloom Savitri saw approaching a black and terrible figure. His inky robes floated back among the shadows, a dark crown was upon his head, his eyes were blood red, and in his hand he carried a silken cord. In solemn silence he stood and looked upon Satyavan, and Savitri grew cold with terror. But her love was stronger than her fear and with quivering tongue she asked faintly, "Who art thou?"

"I am Yama, mighty Monarch of the Dead," answered the dark form. "Thy husband's days and loves are ended. With this noose I shall bind and carry away the spark of his immortal life. Princess, let thy husband depart!"

Then from Satyavan's body, cold and bloodless, Yama drew the vital spark—smaller than a man's thumb it is—with his silken cord he bound it, and turning silently passed his darksome way into the realm of shadows.

Southward he went and swiftly, but not alone; by his side into the dark and cold walked Savitri.

"Turn, Princess!" commanded Yama, "no living creature may go further with Death's Monarch."

"Where my husband's life leads I may not choose but follow," answered Savitri. "No law can divide us. A woman's life is filled with duty to the poor and suffering, with pity and with wisdom, but the crown of all is truth and deathless love. Bid me not turn back! Grant me one boon!"

"True and holy are thy words, fair Princess," answered Yama. "I would bless thee if I could, but I know the boon which thou desirest, and the dead come not to life. Ask another boon and I will grant it."

"For my husband's banished father, then, let me beg," said Savitri; "grant him eyesight and strength through thy mercy."

"Thy prayer is granted," answered Yama, "and now, Savitri, turn back; no mortal may pass further within the realms of Death."

Around them the night was terrible, shades and darksome creatures flitted among the shadows, strange sounds of beating wings and wailing came nearer and nearer.

Then in that horrible spot Savitri began to sing. She sang of the morning hours when she and her husband had passed so gaily through the forest, of the caroling birds and fragrant flowers, the sparkling brooks and the blue sky. Yama listened and his heart grew soft and tender.

"Blessed art thou, brave Savitri!" he cried. "I would grant thy desire, but the dead come not to life; ask another boon."

"Once again for my husband's father I beg. Give him back his wealth and kingdom, in thy mercy."

"Loving daughter," replied Yama, "wealth and kingdom I bestow, and now I command thee to turn back. No power can save thee within this abode of the Monarch of the Dead."

About them the black terror was closing in, breathless, remorseless, terrible. And Savitri—only sang again. This time her song was not of birds or flowers or spring time, it was of love, love stronger than life, love stronger than death!

Then the Black King turned upon her and his words were like cooling summer rain.

"Noble woman, ask thy boon! No god can listen in vain to such pleading."

"Grant me my husband's life!" begged Savitri. "May he live to be a father, the father of princes as brave and noble as himself!"

"Thy desire is granted," answered Yama, "for thou has taught me the strength of a woman's love; it abideth stronger even than the doom of Death!"

Back to the forest where her husband's body lay hastened Savitri. As she raised his unconscious head her touch thrilled him back to waking life.

"Did I dream, sweet Savitri," he asked faintly, opening his eyes, "of a dark and fearful monarch who captured me?"

"The Black King has come and gone," answered Savitri. "Tomorrow I will tell you all. But see, the night is about us, wild

beasts approach through the jungle, and a forest fire blazes in the darkness. Let us hasten homeward where thy parents await us, happier and more blessed than in many a long year."

Satyavan looked at his wife in astonishment; her face was radiant, a glorious joy shone about her. Then blissful and in silence, with his strong arm around her, Satyavan and his wife walked back through the jungle, while the hushed and throbbing midnight looked down upon the deathless love of Savitri.

•

My Very Dear Sarah ...
Sullivan Ballou

A young Providence lawyer and former Speaker of the Rhode Island House of Representatives, Major Sullivan Ballou interrupted a promising political career to join the 2nd Rhode Island Volunteers at the outbreak of the Civil War. He wrote home to his wife from a camp near Washington one week before the First Battle of Bull Run, the first major land battle of the war.

Camp Clark, Washington
July 14, 1861

My very dear Sarah,

The indications are very strong that we shall move in a few days—perhaps tomorrow. Lest I should not be able to write again, I feel impelled to write a few lines that may fall under your eye when I shall be no more. Our movements may be of a few days' duration and full of pleasure—and it may be one of some conflict and death to me. "Not my will, but thine, O God be done." If it is necessary that I should fall on the battlefield for my Country, I am ready.

I have no misgivings about, or lack of confidence in, the cause in which I am engaged, and my courage does not halt or falter. I know how strongly American Civilization now leans on the triumph of the Government, and how great a debt we owe to those who went before us through the blood and sufferings of the Revolution. And I am willing—perfectly willing—to lay down all my joys in this life, to help maintain this Government, and to pay that debt. . . .

Sarah, my love for you is deathless. It seems to bind me with mighty cables that nothing but Omnipotence could break; and yet my love of Country comes over me like a strong wind and burns me unresistibly on with all these chains to the battlefield.

The memories of the blissful moments I have spent with you come creeping over me, and I feel most gratified to God and to you that I have enjoyed them so long. And hard it is for me to give them up and burn to ashes the hopes of future years, when, God willing, we might still have lived and loved together, and seen our sons grown up to honorable manhood around us. I have, I know, but few and small claims upon Divine Providence, but something whispers to me—perhaps it is the wafted prayer of my little Edgar— that I shall return to my loved ones unharmed. If I do not, my dear Sarah, never forget how much I love you, and when my last breath escapes me on the battlefield, it will whisper your name. Forgive my many faults, and the many pains I have caused you. How thoughtless and foolish I have often times been! How gladly would I wash out with my tears every little spot upon your happiness, and struggle with all the misfortunes of this world to shield you and your children from harm. But I cannot. I must watch you from the Spirit-land and hover near you, while you buffet the storm, with your precious little freight, and wait with sad patience till we meet to part no more.

But, O Sarah! If the dead can come back to this earth and flit unseen around those they loved, I shall always be near you; in the gladdest days and in the darkest nights, advised to your happiest scenes and gloomiest hours, *always, always,* and if there be a soft breeze upon your cheek, it shall be my breath; as the cool air fans your throbbing temple, it shall be my spirit passing by. Sarah, do not mourn me dead; think I am gone and wait for thee, for we shall meet again.

As for my little boys—they will grow up as I have done, and never know a father's love and care. Little Willie is too young to remember me long, and my blue-eyed Edgar will keep my frolics with him among the dim memories of childhood. Sarah, I have unlimited confidence in your maternal care and your development of their character, and feel that God will bless you in your holy work.

Tell my two Mothers I call God's blessing upon them. O! Sarah. I wait for you there; come to me and lead thither my children.

Sullivan

A week later, Sullivan Ballou was killed at Bull Run.

•

ON MY FIRST DAUGHTER

Ben Jonson

I have read and have been told that the death of a child is the hardest thing for a human being to endure. The ancient Greek playwright Euripides called it the "grief surpassing all." Here is the poet Ben Jonson (1572–1637) on the deaths of his own daughter and son.

 The word "ruth" in the first line means grief. The date of Mary's death is unknown.

> Here lies, to each her parents' ruth,
> Mary, the daughter of their youth;
> Yet all heaven's gifts being heaven's due,
> It makes the father less to rue.
> At six months' end she parted hence
> With safety of her innocence;
> Whose soul heaven's queen, whose name she bears,
> In comfort of her mother's tears,
> Hath placed amongst her virgin-train:
> Where, while that severed doth remain,
> This grave partakes the fleshly birth;
> Which cover lightly, gentle earth!

•

ON MY FIRST SON

Ben Jonson

Benjamin Jonson died in 1603 on his birthday. The first line of
this poem refers to the fact that the name Benjamin means "child
of the right hand" in Hebrew.

> Farewell, thou child of my right hand, and joy;
> My sin was too much hope of thee, loved boy:
> Seven years thou wert lent to me, and I thee pay,
> Exacted by thy fate, on the just day.
> O could I lose all father now! for why
> Will man lament the state he should envy,
> To have so soon 'scaped world's and flesh's rage,
> And, if no other misery, yet age?
> Rest in soft peace, and asked, say, "Here doth lie
> Ben Jonson his best piece of poetry."
> For whose sake henceforth all his vows be such
> As what he loves may never like too much.

•

THE WATER OF YOUTH

Rudolf Baumbach

This beautiful and unusual story of a husband and wife growing
old together perfectly illustrates George Eliot's definition of love
—"an enfolding of immeasurable cares which yet are better than
any joys outside our love."

It was Midsummer Day, and the heat of noon brooded over
the cornfields. Now and then a fresh breeze blew down from the
wooded hill, bending the stalks of corn and scattering the scarlet
petals of the poppies. The air was full of the chirping of grasshop-

pers, and from the hawthorn tree at the edge of the field came the low call of the yellow-hammer.

Along the path which crossed the broad cornfield came a slim, strong figure—a young woman in peasant dress, with a red kerchief on her head, a basket on her arm, and a jug in her hand.

When the yellow-hammer caught sight of her he flew to the topmost bough of his hawthorn tree and twittered a greeting to her: "Pretty maid, pretty maid, how's the world using you?" But he was making a mistake, for golden-haired Greta was not a maid, but a young bride, and she was on her way to her husband, who was cutting wood in the forest.

At the edge of the wood she stood still to listen. Following the sound of the ax, she soon came in sight of her husband, who was felling a fir tree with strong strokes, and she hailed him gaily.

"Stand still!" he shouted back. "The tree is falling!" And the great fir tree groaned deeply, bent its head, and came crashing to the ground.

Then Greta walked on, and the brown-faced woodcutter took his young wife in his arms and kissed her tenderly. They sat down and unpacked the basket of food which she had brought, but as Hans was beginning to eat he laid down his bread, seized his ax, and cut three crosses on the stump of the tree that he had just felled.

"What is that for?" asked his wife.

"For the sake of the little old women of the wood," he answered. "Their enemy, the wild huntsman, lies in wait for them day and night, and sets his dogs on them. But if the poor little things can reach a tree trunk like that, the wild huntsman cannot touch them, because of the three crosses."

Greta opened her eyes wide. "Have you ever seen one of the little folk?"

"No; they seldom show themselves. But this is Midsummer Day, so perhaps we might see one." And he called into the forest in his ringing voice, "Little woman of the woods, come forth!" He only meant to tease his wife, but on St. John's Day it is not safe to make jokes like that.

Instantly there stood before them a lovely little lady, about an ell high. She wore trailing white robes, and in her hair there were sprays of mistletoe. The two young people jumped up in astonishment, and Greta made her best curtsy.

"You called me just at the right moment," said the little woman, pointing to the sun, which stood exactly over her head. "And one good turn"—here she looked toward the stump with the three crosses—"deserves another. Silver and gold have I none, but I have better things to give you. Come with me without fear, and bring your jug; it will be useful."

So saying, she turned toward the forest, followed by Hans, ax on shoulder, and Greta, jug in hand. She walked just like a duck, and Greta touched her husband on the arm, pointing to the little waddling figure, and was going to whisper something to him, but he laid his finger on his lips.

Nothing hurts the little good folk so much as being made fun of. They have feet like geese, and that is why they wear long trailing skirts.

They walked on until they came to an open space in the wood. Hoary trees stood in a circle round a green meadow; the grass was gay with lilies and bluebells and the fluttering wings of the butterflies.

Hans thought that he knew every inch of the forest, but he had never seen this lovely spot before. In the meadow there was a tiny house; the walls were of bark, the roof of the scales of fir-cones, every scale pinned down with a rose-thorn. This was the home of the little woman of the woods.

She led her guests round to the back of the house and showed them a well, whose waters rose noiselessly out of the dark earth. Iris and coltsfoot grew on the brink, and gold and green dragonflies danced over it.

"That is the well of youth," she said. "A dip in it will turn an old man into a boy again, and an old woman into a blooming girl. To drink the water keeps one young and fresh till one's dying day. Fill your jug and carry it home. But be very careful of the precious water: one drop every Sunday will be enough to keep you young.

"One thing more. When you cease to love each other the magic power of the water will be gone. Remember that. Now fill your jug, and fare-you-well." Before they could thank her the little woman had vanished into her house.

Greta filled her jug with the water of youth, and they hurried home to their cottage. When they got there, Hans poured the water into a bottle and sealed it with fir resin.

"Just now we have no use for the water of youth," he said, "so we can save it up till we do need it."

He put the bottle in the cupboard where they stored their treasures—a couple of old coins, a string of garnet beads with a golden penny hung on it, and two real silver spoons—and he said: "Now, Greta, we must be very, very careful not to make the water lose its power."

A year went by, full of love and happiness for the young pair. And then there was a rosy little baby boy, who kicked and crowed till his father's heart overflowed with pride.

"Now is the time," he said, "for opening our bottle. Don't you think, Greta, that a drop of the water of youth would do you good?"

The young mother thought it would, so he went to fetch it from the next room. His hands trembled with joy as he broke the seal, and so the bottle slipped out of his grasp, and the water of youth was spilled on the floor. Hans nearly fell on the floor, too, in his horror at the mischance. What could he do?

He dared not tell his wife, lest she should die of fright. Later on perhaps he could tell her, or one day he might find again the well of youth, which he had often looked for in vain, and get a fresh supply. Hurriedly he got another bottle exactly like the first, filled it with spring water, and brought it to his wife.

"Ah!" said Greta. "How that gives me new life and strength! Take a drop yourself, my dear."

Hans obeyed her, and said what a wonderful drink it was; and after that they each took a drop every Sunday when the bells were calling them to church.

Greta bloomed like a rose, and Hans was a perfect picture of vigorous manhood. But day after day he put off confessing his misdeed, in the hope of finding the well of youth. Roam through the woods as he might, he could never get a glimpse of that meadow again.

Thus two years went by. A little girl had come to keep the little boy company, and Greta's round chin had grown double, but she never noticed it; there were no looking-glasses in those days. Hans did notice it, but he took care not to say anything, and he loved his fat wife more than ever. Then a misfortune befell them.

One day when Greta was busy housecleaning, little Peter, her eldest, got into the cupboard where the water of youth was kept, and knocked over the bottle, which broke and spilled its contents on the floor.

"Oh, merciful Powers!" cried the mother. "But what a blessing Hans is not at home!" With trembling fingers she picked up the pieces of glass, and replaced the bottle by another, which she filled from the spring.

"I shall soon be found out, for there's an end of our eternal youth. Alas!" But she made up her mind not to let her husband suspect that there was anything wrong.

Time passed by, and Hans and Greta lived and loved together. Each of them took care not to let the other think that youth was gone, and every Sunday they took the magic drop.

One morning when Hans was combing his hair, a gray hair fell on his sleeve. And he said to himself, "Now I must confess to my wife."

Heavy at heart he began: "Greta, it seems to me that the magic water must have lost its power. Look! I have found a gray hair! I am getting old."

Greta was startled, but she recovered herself and laughed, though not quite naturally, as she answered: "A gray hair! Why, when I was only ten I had a gray lock in my hair. That is quite a common thing. You have just been skinning a badger, and very likely you got some of the fat on your hair. You know that badger's fat does turn hair gray. No, dear Hans, the water keeps its magic power, or"—she glanced at him anxiously—"do you think that I am growing old, too?"

Hans laughed loudly at that. "You—old? You are as blooming as a peony!" And he threw his arms round her portly figure and kissed her.

But when he was alone he said joyfully. "She has no idea that we are growing old. So what I did must have been the right thing." And his wife said just the same to herself.

That evening the lads and lasses of the village danced to the music of a strolling fiddler, and no couple footed it under the lime trees more merrily than Hans and Greta. The peasants made some jokes at their expense, but the two happy people did not hear them.

The following autumn, while they and their children were eating their Martinmas goose, Greta broke a front tooth. There was great woe, for she had always been proud of her pretty white teeth.

When husband and wife were alone together, Greta said in a faltering voice, "A misfortune like that could never have happened if the water—" But Hans scolded her.

"You think the water can keep off all bad luck? Does not a child often break a tooth in cracking nuts? How can you grumble? Has not the water kept you as fresh and healthy as a spring lettuce?"

At that his wife laughed, dried her tears, and kissed her old man till he was almost out of breath. Then they sat down together on the stone seat in front of their house, and sang little songs about true love. The passersby said, "What silly old folk!" But the happy couple did not hear them.

Many years went past. The house had grown too small for the children, and they had married and gone away, and had children of their own. The two old people were alone together once more.

They were as much in love with each other as on their wedding day, and every Sunday, when the church bells were ringing, they each took one drop out of the bottle.

Midsummer Day came round again. On the eve of it, Hans and Greta were sitting in front of their house, looking toward the hill, where the bonfire was blazing, and the young men and maidens were shouting as they jumped through the flames hand-in-hand.

Greta turned to her husband: "Dear Hans, I should like to go into the forest again. Would you start early tomorrow morning? Only you must waken me, for when the elderberry is in bloom young women are apt to sleep long after daylight."

Hans agreed. Next morning he awoke his wife, and together they set out for the forest. They walked arm-in-arm like lovers, and each kept a watchful eye on the other's steps. When Hans lifted one foot cautiously over the root of a tree, his wife would say, "Why, Hans, you are skipping like a kid!"

And when Greta timidly crossed a little hole in the path, her husband cried laughingly, "Hold up your skirts, wife! Jump!" After a while they came to an old fir tree, and in its shade they spread a little feast out of Greta's basket.

"It was just here," said Hans, "that the little old woman of the woods appeared to us that day, and over there must lie the meadow with the well of youth. But I have never been able to find it again."

"And, mercifully, there was no need of your finding it," put in Greta hurriedly, "for our bottle is by no means empty yet."

"That is quite true," Hans agreed, "but all the same, I should like to see the good little woman again, and to thank her for the gift she gave us. Come and look for her. Perhaps we shall be as lucky as we were before."

So they rose and went into the heart of the forest. They had walked but a little way when lo! the sunny meadow lay before them. Lilies and bluebells were blooming in the grass, gay butterflies flitted to and fro, and the little house stood there just as of yore.

With fast-beating hearts they walked round the house, and there was the well of youth with the gold and green dragonflies hovering over it. Hans and Greta stepped up to the brink. Hand-in-hand they bent over the water, and out of its clear depths two gray heads with kindly, wrinkled faces gazed back at them.

Hot tears rushed to their eyes, with broken words and sobs they confessed their misdeeds, and it was some time before they could understand that all these years each of them had been deceiving the other for love's sake.

"Then you knew that we were both growing old?" said Hans.

"Of course I did!" his wife laughed through her tears.

"So did I! So did I!" cried Hans, and he tried to leap for joy. And he took Greta's head between his hands and kissed her, just as when she had plighted her troth to him.

Then, as if she had sprung out of the earth, the little old woman of the woods stood before the old couple.

"Welcome!" she said. "It is long since you came to visit me. But what is this?" She shook her finger at them. "You have not taken care of the water of youth. Wrinkles and gray hairs! This will never do.

"However, I can soon cure that. You have come just at the right moment. Quick! Jump into the well—it is not deep—plunge your gray heads under, and you will see a miracle. All the strength and beauty of youth will be given back to you. But be quick, or the sun will have gone down."

Hans and Greta looked questioningly at each other.

"Will you?" he asked in a voice that shook.

"Never!" answered Greta promptly. "I can't tell you what bliss it is that at last I can be old. Then think of our children and grandchildren. No, dear little woman, we thank you with all our hearts, but we will stay old. Won't we, Hans?"

"Yes, yes," said Hans, "we will stay old. Hurrah! Greta, if you only knew how well your gray hair suits you!"

"As you will," said the little woman of the woods. "I do not insist on it." And with rather an offended air she went into her house and shut the door.

The old folk kissed each other once more and turned homeward. Arm in arm they went through the forest, and the midsummer sun set a crown of gold upon their gray heads.

•

BELIEVE ME, IF ALL THOSE
ENDEARING YOUNG CHARMS

Thomas Moore

Good marriages grow better as they grow older. Fidelity ages well. The next two poems echo the sentiment of Robert Browning's famous call: "Grow old along with me, the best is yet to be."

Believe me, if all those endearing young charms,
    Which I gaze on so fondly today,
Were to change by tomorrow, and fleet in my arms,
    Like fairy gifts, fading away,
Thou wouldst still be adored, as this moment thou art,
    Let thy loveliness fade as it will,
And around the dear ruin each wish of my heart
    Would entwine itself verdantly still.

It is not while beauty and youth are thine own,
    And thy cheeks unprofaned by a tear,
That the fervor and faith of a soul can be known,
    To which time will but make thee more dear.
No, the heart that has truly loved never forgets,
    But as truly loves on to the close,
As the sunflower turns on her god, when he sets,
    The same look which she turned when he rose.

•

WE HAVE LIVED AND LOVED TOGETHER

Charles Jeffreys

We have lived and loved together
    Through many changing years;
We have shared each other's gladness
    And wept each other's tears;
I have known ne'er a sorrow
    That was long unsoothed by thee;
For thy smiles can make a summer
    Where darkness else would be.

Like the leaves that fall around us
    In autumn's fading hours,
Are the traitor's smiles, that darken
    When the cloud of sorrow lowers;
And though many such we've known, love,
    Too prone, alas, to range,
We both can speak of one love
    Which time can never change.

We have lived and loved together
    Through many changing years;
We have shared each other's gladness
    And wept each other's tears.
And let us hope the future
    As the past has been will be:
I will share with thee my sorrows,
    And thou thy joys with me.

•

THE GREATEST OF THESE IS LOVE

The Apostle Paul

The kind of love described here is an embodiment of all the
virtues, the kind of love all husbands and wives should give to
each other, and the kind both should give to their children. These
verses so often and appropriately read at weddings come from
Paul's first letter to the Corinthians.

Though I speak with the tongues of men and of angels, and
have not love, I am become as sounding brass, or a tinkling cymbal.

And though I have the gift of prophecy, and understand all
mysteries, and all knowledge; and though I have all faith so that I
could remove mountains and have not love, I am nothing.

And though I bestow all my goods to feed the poor, and though
I give my body to be burned, and have not love, it profiteth me
nothing.

Love suffereth long and is kind; love envieth not, love vaunteth
not itself, is not puffed up,

Doth not behave itself unseemly, seeketh not her own, is not
easily provoked, thinketh no evil,

Rejoiceth not in iniquity, but rejoiceth in the truth.

Beareth all things, believeth all things, hopeth all things, en-
dureth all things.

Love never faileth; but whether there be prophecies, they shall
fail; whether there be tongues, they shall cease; whether there be
knowledge, it shall vanish away.

For we know in part, and we prophesy in part.

But when that which is perfect is come, then that which is in
part shall be done away.

When I was a child, I spake as a child, I understood as a child,
I thought as a child, but when I became a man I put away childish
things.

For now we see through a glass darkly; but then face to face:
now I know in part; but then shall I know even as also I am known.

And now abideth faith, hope, love, these three; but the greatest
of these is LOVE.

Six

·

CITIZENSHIP AND LEADERSHIP

" "MAN is by nature an animal intended to live in a polis," Aristotle wrote more than two thousand years ago. Human beings are social and political beings. We can apply Aristotle's observation about the polis, or Greek city-state, not only to our modern concept of town, state, and country but also to any number of associations. We are all members of groups. We join clubs, churches, school organizations, civic associations, and political parties in order to better ourselves and the condition of others.

The success of any organization depends on the character of its citizens. Good citizens are those who know and live up to their duties by exercising virtues such as responsibility, loyalty, self-discipline, work, and friendship. In this chapter we find examples of individuals ready and willing to do their parts. We encounter people laboring together cheerfully toward common goals. We see them keeping their promises and accepting responsibility for their own mistakes. We come across those who stand fast beside their comrades—as well as those who do not. And we meet those who are willing to sacrifice their own interests, even their own lives, for the good of the rest.

At certain times in our lives, most of us are called to lead in some capacity: as team captain, club president, state representative, or member of a student council, vestry, or board of directors. This chapter also reminds us of the virtues required to hold these positions, virtues such as compassion, courage, perseverance, wisdom, and sometimes faith. In these stories, we see that leaders are ultimately judged in terms of how well they serve their followers and by the examples they set. They lead not just by command but by the force of good character. And we notice that before they lead, they learn to be good followers—they know how to help shoulder a load and share hardships.

Finally, I have included a number of selections about a virtue too often overlooked today—gratitude. If we are not grateful for our gifts and opportunities, we are not likely to value them, and if we do not value them, we are not likely to work hard to preserve and improve them. Gratitude is an important attribute of good citizenship, especially among a people blessed with an inheritance of political freedom and material wealth unmatched in the history of mankind. Disposition counts. Good citizenship and good leadership usually require a certain degree of cheerfulness. The chronic complainer, on the other hand, not only fails to contribute but he often threatens to become the one who dooms the common enterprise. He is the man described by Joseph Conrad:

> They all knew him! He was the man that cannot steer, that cannot splice, that dodges the work on dark nights; that, aloft, holds on frantically with both arms and legs, and swears at the wind, the sleet, the darkness; the man who curses the sea while others work. The man who is the last out and the first in when all hands are called. The man who can't do most things and won't do the rest. The pet of philanthropists and self-seeking landlubbers. The sympathetic and deserving creature that knows all about his rights, but knows nothing of courage, of endurance, and of the unexpressed faith, of the unspoken loyalty that knits together a ship's company.

Whining, grumbling, and complaining are not simply unattractive; they are symptoms of selfishness. And an overriding concern with the self is not the business of citizenship. Among good citizens, Aristotle told us, "the salvation of the community is the common business of them all."

THE QUAILS

Here is one of the basic truths of citizenship: In our common
affairs we pull and lift together, or we perish. This ancient fable is
from the group of Buddhist stories known as the *Jataka* tales.

Ages ago a flock of more than a thousand quails lived together
in a forest in India. They would have been happy, but that they
were in great dread of their enemy, the quail catcher. He used to
imitate the call of the quail; and when they gathered together in
answer to it, he would throw a great net over them, stuff them into
his basket, and carry them away to be sold.

Now, one of the quails was very wise, and he said: "Brothers!
I've thought of a good plan. In the future, as soon as the fowler
throws his net over us, let each one put his head through a mesh
in the net and then all lift it up together and fly away with it. When
we have flown far enough, we can let the net drop on a thorn bush
and escape."

All agreed to the plan. The next day when the fowler threw his
net, the birds all lifted it together in the very way that the wise quail
had told them, threw it on a thorn bush and escaped. While the
fowler tried to free his net from the thorns, it grew dark, and he
had to go home.

This happened many days, till at last the fowler's wife grew
angry and asked her husband: "Why is it that you never catch any
more quail?"

Then the fowler said: "The trouble is that all the birds work
together and help one another. If they would only quarrel, I could
catch them fast enough."

A few days later, one of the quails accidentally trod on the head
of one of his brothers, as they alighted on the feeding ground.

"Who trod on my head?" angrily inquired the quail who was
hurt.

"Don't be angry, I didn't mean to tread on you," said the first
quail.

But the brother quail went on quarreling.

"I lifted all the weight of the net! You didn't help at all!" he
cried.

That made the first quail angry, and before long all were drawn into the dispute. Then the fowler saw his chance. He imitated the cry of the quail and cast his net over those who came together. They were still boasting and quarreling, and they did not help one another lift the net. So the hunter lifted the net himself and crammed them into his basket. But the wise quail gathered his friends together and flew far away, for he knew that quarrels are the root of misfortune.

WHEN MR. BLUEBIRD WON HIS COAT
Thornton W. Burgess

Sometimes leaders are born when one in the crowd steps forward to try.

It happened a great while ago when the world was young. Mr. Bluebird was one of the quietest and most modest of all the birds. He wore just a modest gray coat, and no one took any particular notice of him. In fact, he didn't even have a name. He never quarreled with his neighbors. He never was envious of those to whom Old Mother Nature had given beautiful coats, or if he was, he never showed it. He just minded his own affairs and did his best to do his share of the work of the Great World, for even in the beginning of things there was something for each one to do.

Old Mother Nature was very busy those days making the Great World a fit place in which to live, and as soon as she had started a new family of birds or animals she had to leave them to take care of themselves and get along as best they could. Those who were too lazy or too stupid to take care of themselves disappeared, and others took their places. There was nothing lazy or stupid about Mr. Bluebird, and he quickly learned how to take care of himself and at the same time to keep on the best of terms with his neighbors.

When the place where the first birds lived became too crowded and old King Eagle led them out into the new land Old Mother Nature had been preparing for them, Mr. Bluebird was one of the first to follow him. The new land was very beautiful, and there was plenty of room and plenty to eat for all. Then came Jack Frost with snow and ice and drove all the birds back to the place they had come from. They made up their minds that they would stay there even if it was crowded. But after a while Old Mother Nature came to tell them that soon Jack Frost would be driven back from that wonderful new land, and sweet Mistress Spring would waken all the sleeping plants and all the sleeping insects up there so that it would be as beautiful as it was before, even more beautiful than the place where they were now. She said that she would expect them to go to the new land and make it joyous with their songs and build their homes there and help her to keep the insects and worms from eating all the green things.

"But first I want a herald to go before Mistress Spring to tell those who have lived there all through the time of snow and ice that Mistress Spring is coming. Who will go as the herald of sweet Mistress Spring?" asked Old Mother Nature.

All the birds looked at one another and shivered, and then one by one they tried to slip out of sight. Now Mr. Bluebird had modestly waited for some of his big, strong neighbors to offer to take the message of gladness up into that frozen land, but when he saw them slip away one by one, his heart grew hot with shame for them, and he flew out before Old Mother Nature. "I'll go," said he, bobbing his head respectfully.

Old Mother Nature just had to smile, because compared with some of his neighbors Mr. Bluebird was so very small. "What can such a little fellow as you do?" she asked. "You will freeze to death up there, for it is still very cold."

"If you please, I can at least try," replied Mr. Bluebird modestly. "If I find I can't go on, I can come back."

"And what reward do you expect?" asked Old Mother Nature.

"The joy of spreading such good news as the coming of Mistress Spring will be is all the reward I want," replied Mr. Bluebird.

This reply so pleased Old Mother Nature that she then and there made Mr. Bluebird the herald of Mistress Spring and started him on his long journey. It *was* a long journey and a hard journey. You see, everything was new to him. And then it was so cold! He couldn't get used to the cold. It seemed sometimes as if he certainly would freeze to death. At these times, when he sat shivering and shaking, he would remember that sweet Mistress Spring was not very far behind and that he was her herald. This would give him courage, and he would bravely keep on. Whenever he stopped to rest, he would whistle the news that Mistress Spring was coming, and sometimes, just to keep up his own courage, he would whistle while he was flying, and he found it helped. To keep warm at night he crept into hollow trees, and it was thus he learned how snug and safe and comfortable such places were, and he made up his mind that in just such a place he would build his nest when the time came.

As he passed on he left behind him great joy, and Mistress Spring found as she journeyed north that all in the forests and on the meadows were eagerly awaiting her, for they had heard the message of her coming; and she was glad and told Old Mother Nature how well her herald had done his work. When he had completed his errand, Mr. Bluebird built a home and was as modest and retiring as ever. He didn't seem to think that he had done anything out of the usual. He simply rejoiced in his heart that he. had been able to do what Old Mother Nature had requested, and it never entered his head that he should have any other reward than the knowledge that he had done his best and that he had brought cheer and hope to many.

When Jack Frost moved down from the far North in the fall, all the birds journeyed south again, and of course Mr. Bluebird went with them. The next season when it was time for Mistress Spring to start north, Old Mother Nature assembled all the birds, and this time, instead of asking who would carry the message, she called Mr. Bluebird out before them and asked if he was willing to be the herald once more. Mr. Bluebird said that he would be glad to be the herald if she wished it. Then Old Mother Nature told all the birds how brave Mr. Bluebird was and how faithful and true, and she made all the other birds feel ashamed, especially those bigger and stronger than Mr. Bluebird. Then she said: "Bluebird, I here and now appoint you the herald of Mistress Spring, and the honor shall descend to your children and your children's children forever and ever, and you shall be one of the most loved of all the birds. And because you are a herald, you shall have a bright coat, as all heralds should have; and because you are true and faithful, your coat shall be blue, as blue as the blue of the sky."

She reached out and touched Mr. Bluebird, and sure enough his sober gray coat turned the most wonderful blue. Then once more he started on his long journey and he whistled his message more joyously than before. And because his whistle brought joy and gladness, and because he was beautiful to see, it came about just as Old Mother Nature had said it would, that he was one of the most loved of all the birds, even as his great-great-ever-so-great-grandson is today.

•

THE TOWER TO THE MOON

Sometimes people with high titles get high notions of themselves, as we see in this tale from the Dominican Republic. But a title is no guarantee of real leadership, even if your name is "king." Serving the interests of those who follow is the true crown of leadership.

Long ago there lived an island king who one night, letting his thoughts drift beyond the sandy shores of his kingdom, got it into his head that he would like to touch the moon.

"Why not?" he asked himself. "I am king. What I want, I get. I want to touch the moon."

The next morning he called the chief carpenter in the land to his court.

"I want you to build me a tower," he commanded, "one tall enough to reach the moon."

The carpenter's eyes bulged.

"The moon? Did you say the moon?"

"You heard me. The moon. I want to touch the moon. Now go do it."

The carpenter went and talked it over with all the other carpenters. They scratched their heads and decided his majesty must have been joking, and built nothing at all.

A few days later the king summoned the chief carpenter back to court.

"I don't see my tower," he barked. "What's taking so long?"

"But Your Majesty," the carpenter cried, "you can't be serious. A tower to the moon? We don't know how."

"I don't care how!" the king yelled. "Just get it done. You have three days. If by that time I have not touched the moon, I hate to think what will happen to you."

The shaken carpenter went back to his friends, and they scratched their heads some more, and drew lines on paper, and racked their brains for an answer. Finally they came up with a plan.

The chief carpenter went back to the king.

"We have an idea that just might work," he said. "But we'll need every box in the kingdom."

"Excellent!" cried the king. "Let it be done!"

He sent out a royal decree that every box on the island be carried to the palace. The people brought them in every shape and size—crates and chests and cases and cartons, shoe boxes, hat boxes, flower boxes, even bread boxes.

Then the carpenter ordered that all the boxes be piled one on top of the other, until there wasn't a single box left. But the tower wasn't high enough to reach the moon.

"We'll have to make more," he told the king.

So another royal decree went out. His majesty ordered all the trees on the island to be chopped down and the timber brought to the palace. The carpenters made more boxes, and stacked them on top of the tower.

"I think it's high enough," the king announced.

The carpenters looked up nervously.

"Perhaps I should go up first," the chief carpenter suggested. "Just to be on the safe side."

"Don't be silly!" the king barked. "This was my idea. I will be the first one to touch the moon. The honor belongs to me."

He started to climb. Higher and higher he mounted. He left the birds far below, and broke through the clouds. When he got to the top, he stretched out his arms—but he was just barely short! A few more inches, and he would be able to touch the moon! Or at least that's the way it looked to him.

"One more box!" he yelled down. "I need just one more box!"

The carpenters shook their heads. They had already used every stick of wood on the island.

"We don't have any more!" they yelled at the top of their lungs. "No more boxes! You'll have to come down!"

The king stamped his foot and jumped up and down, and the whole tower trembled.

"I won't come down! I won't!" he yelled. "I want to touch the moon, and no one's going to stop me!"

Then his majesty had his brilliant idea.

"Listen here," he called. "I know what to do. Take the first box from the bottom and bring it to the top."

The carpenters stared at each other.

"You fools!" the king yelled. "You're wasting my time! Take out the first box and bring it up now!"

The carpenters shrugged.

"This is a very stubborn king," the chief carpenter said. "I suppose we must obey his command."

So they pulled out the bottom box. You don't need to be told the end of the story.

•

THE GORDIAN KNOT

Adapted from a retelling by James Baldwin

Often, leaders are people who aren't discouraged by the odds, who find a way through no matter what. This old story of determination and decisiveness is great to remember at times when you need to cut through red tape.

In the western part of Asia there is a rich and beautiful region which in olden times was called Phrygia. The people of that place once had a king named Gordius, a man who brought peace to the land by ruling wisely, righting old wrongs, and making laws for the good of all.

Now, when he became king, Gordius did something very

strange and marvelous. In the temple of Jupiter overlooking the town, he tied a great knot of rope. So intricate were its twists and turns, and so deftly did Gordius hide the ends of the rope, that no one could see how to untie it.

After years of ruling wisely, Gordius died. But the knot remained, and all strangers who came to the temple of Jupiter admired its design and strength.

"Only a very great man could have tied such a knot as that," said some.

"You have spoken truly," said the oracle of the temple. "But the man who undoes it will be much greater."

"What do you mean?" asked the visitors.

"The man who undoes this wonderful knot shall have the world for his kingdom," came the answer.

After that a great many people came every year to see the Gordian knot. Princes and warriors from every land tried to untie it. But the ends of the rope remained hidden, and they could not even make a beginning of the task.

Hundreds of years passed. King Gordius had been dead for so long that people remembered him only as the man who tied the wonderful knot, the knot that could not be undone.

Then there came into Phrygia a young king from Macedonia, far across the sea. The name of this young king was Alexander. He had conquered all of Greece, and now he had set his sights on Asia.

"Where is the fabled Gordian knot?" he asked.

The people led him into the temple of Jupiter and showed him the knot where Gordius had left it.

"What is it the oracle said about this knot?" Alexander asked.

"It said that the man who undoes it will have the world for his kingdom. But many have tried, and all have failed."

Alexander looked at the knot carefully. He could not find the ends, but what did that matter? He raised his sword and, with one stroke, cut it into so many pieces that the rope dropped to the ground.

"It is thus," said the young king, "that I cut all Gordian knots."

And then he went on with his little army to conquer Asia.

"The world is my kingdom," he said.

•

THE PEDDLER'S PACK

Retold by Mary De Morgan

This old English folktale has a couple of timely lessons for an age
of growing credit card use and national debt: Don't promise what
you don't have, and don't live off the promises of others. The state
of the economy has a great deal to do with the state of responsibility and honesty in the dealings of citizens.

A peddler was toiling along a dusty road carrying his pack on
his back, when he saw a donkey grazing by the wayside.

"Good day, friend," said he. "If you have nothing to do, perhaps you would not mind carrying my load for me for a little."

"If I do so, what will you give me?" said the donkey.

"I will give you two pieces of gold," said the peddler, but he
did not speak the truth, for he knew he had no gold to give.

"Agreed," said the donkey. So they journeyed on together in a
very friendly manner, the donkey carrying the peddler's pack, and
the peddler walking by his side. After a time they met a raven, who
was looking for worms in the roadside, and the donkey called out
to him: "Good morrow, black friend. If you are going our way, you
would do well to sit upon my back and drive away the flies, which
worry me sadly."

"And what will you pay me to do this?" asked the raven.

"Money is no object to me," said the donkey, "so I will give
you three pieces of gold." And he too knew he was making a false
promise, for he had no gold at all to give.

"Agreed," said the raven. So they went on in high good humor,
the donkey carrying the peddler's wares, and the raven sitting on
the donkey's back driving away the flies.

After a time they met a hedge sparrow, and the raven called
out to him: "Good day, little cousin. Do you want to earn a little
money? If so, bring me some worms from the bank as we go along,
for I had no breakfast, and am very hungry."

"What will you give me for it?" asked the hedge sparrow.

"Let us say four pieces of gold," said the raven grandly, "for I
know how to spend." But he knew this was not true, for he had not
saved any gold at all.

"Very well," said the hedge sparrow, and so on they went, the donkey carrying the peddler's pack, the raven keeping the flies away from the donkey, and the hedge sparrow bringing worms to the raven.

Presently they saw in the distance a good-sized town, and the peddler took out from his pack some shawls and shirts and hung them over the donkey's back that the passersby might see, and buy if they were so disposed. On the top of the other goods lay a small scarlet blanket, and when he saw it the hedge sparrow said to the peddler, "What will you take for that little blanket? It seems to be a good one. Name your price and you shall have it whatever it is, for I am badly in want of a blanket just now." But as the hedge sparrow had not a penny in the world, he knew he could not pay for it.

"The price of the blanket is five pieces of gold," said the peddler.

"That seems to me to be very dear," said the hedge sparrow. "I don't mind giving you four pieces of gold for it, but five is too much."

"Agreed," said the peddler, and he chuckled to himself and thought, "Now I shall be able to pay the donkey, otherwise I might have had some trouble in getting rid of him."

The hedge sparrow flew to the raven's side and whispered in his ear, "Please to pay me the four pieces of gold you owe me, for we are coming to a town, and I must be turning back."

"Four pieces of gold is really too much for bringing a few worms," said the raven. "It is absurd to expect such payment, but I will give you three, and you shall have them almost immediately." He bent down over the donkey's ear and whispered, "My friend, it is time you paid me the three pieces of gold which you promised, for the peddler will stop at this town, and you will not have to go farther with him."

"On thinking it over," said the donkey, "I have come to the conclusion that three pieces of gold are really a great deal too much to give for having a few flies driven away. You must have known that I was only joking when I said it, but I will let you have two, though I consider that it is much more than the job was worth. And the donkey turned again to the peddler, saying, "Now, good sir, your two pieces of gold, if you please."

"In a moment," said the peddler, and turning to the hedge sparrow, he said, "I really must have the money for the blanket at once."

"So you shall," answered the hedge sparrow, and cried angrily to the raven, "I want my money now, and cannot wait."

"In an instant," answered the raven, and again whispered to the donkey, "Why can't you pay me honestly? I should be ashamed of trying to slip out of my debts in such a way."

"I won't keep you waiting a second," said the donkey, and he turned once more to the peddler and cried, "Come, give me my money. For shame! A man like you trying to cheat a poor beast like me."

Then the peddler said to the hedge sparrow, "Pay me for my blanket, or I'll wring your neck."

And the hedge sparrow cried to the raven, "Give me my money or I'll peck out your eyes."

And the raven croaked to the donkey, "If you don't pay me, I'll bite off your tail."

And the donkey again cried to the peddler, "You dishonest wretch, pay me my money or I'll kick you soundly."

And they made such an uproar outside the walls of the town that the sheriff came out to see what it was all about. Each turned to him and began to complain of the other loudly.

"You are a set of rogues and vagabonds," said the sheriff, "and you shall all come before the mayor, and he'll settle your quarrels pretty quickly, and treat you as you deserve."

At this they all begged to be allowed to go away, each one saying he did not care about being paid at all. But the sheriff would not listen to them, and led them straightaway to the marketplace, where the mayor sat judging the people.

"Now, whom have we here?" cried he. "A peddler, a donkey, a raven, and a hedge sparrow. A set of worthless vagabonds, I'll be bound! Let us hear what they have to say for themselves."

On this the pedlar began to complain of the hedge sparrow, and the hedge sparrow of the raven, and the raven of the donkey, and the donkey of the peddler.

The mayor did not heed them much, but he eyed the peddler's pack, and at length interrupted them, and said, "I am convinced that you are a set if good-for-nothing fellows, and one is quite as bad as the other, so I order that the peddler be locked up in the prison, that the donkey be soundly well thrashed, and that the raven and the hedge sparrow both have their tail feathers pulled out, and then be turned out of the town. As for the blanket, it seems to me to be the only good thing in the whole matter, and as I cannot allow you to keep the cause of such a disturbance, I will take it for myself. Sheriff, lead the prisoners away."

So the sheriff did as he was told, and the peddler was locked up for many days in the prison.

"It is very sad to think to what straits an honest man may be brought," he sighed to himself as he sat lamenting his hard fate. "In the future this will be a warning to me to keep clear of hedge sparrows. If the hedge sparrow had paid me as he ought, I should not be here now."

Meantime the donkey was being soundly well thrashed, and after each blow he cried, "Alas! alas! See what comes to an innocent quadruped for having to do with human beings. Had the peddler given me the money he owed, I should not now be beaten thus. In the future I will never make a bargain with men."

The raven and the hedge sparrow hopped out of the town by different roads, and both were very sad, for they had lost all their tail feathers, which the sheriff had pulled out.

"Alas!" croaked the raven, "my fate is indeed a hard one. But it serves me right for trusting a donkey, who goes on his feet and cannot fly. It is truly a warning to me never again to trust anything without a beak."

The hedge sparrow was quite crestfallen, and could scarcely keep from tears. "It all comes of my being so taken in by that raven," he sighed. "But I should have known that these large birds are never honest. In the future I will be wise, and never make a bargain with anything bigger or stronger than myself."

•

SOMEONE MUST PAY

One good measure of a nation's spirit—and its citizens' sense of responsibility—is how many times you hear the phrase "it wasn't my fault" or "someone *else* must pay." This old Arab tale makes great reading for our times.

One morning a well-known thief with a splint on his leg hobbled into a courtroom and approached the bench.

"Your Honor," he began, bowing the best he could, "I have a complaint. Yesterday I was walking down the street, minding my own business, when I noticed a house with a window that was clearly unlocked. Now, who could pass by an invitation like that? Of course I had to investigate. I climbed over the fence, made my way through the yard, and opened the window. But I was only halfway inside when the sill gave way. I tumbled to the ground and, as you can plainly see, broke my leg. Now I demand justice."

The judge nodded, stroked his beard, and ordered the owner of the house to be summoned at once.

"Now, see here," he barked when the owner arrived, "your window broke this man's leg as he tried to enter your house. Just what makes you think you can expose the public to a dangerous, faulty window?"

Well, the poor homeowner had never stood before a judge in his life, and he was frightened out of his wits. He searched his brain for an answer.

"Your Honor," he pleaded, "it's not my fault. I paid the carpenter good money to build my window. He should have built it so it wouldn't fall apart."

"You're right! Bring me the carpenter!" the judge roared from the bench.

The bailiff rounded up the carpenter.

"How dare you build a window that would break a man's leg!" the judge thundered. "What's wrong with you?"

The carpenter trembled and shifted from foot to foot.

"Your Honor," he faltered, "perhaps I did not build the window quite as well as I should. But it wasn't my fault. The truth is, I was feeling ill the day I nailed it together. I had eaten a pie from a baker's shop, and it upset my stomach."

The judge slammed down his fist.

"We'll get to the bottom of this," he promised. "Bring me the baker!"

The baker found himself dragged into court.

"I hear you're baking bad pies," the judge said. "The carpenter says you sold him a pie which made him sick, which made his window bad, which broke this man's leg."

The baker shook his head.

"I remember the day I sold him the pie," he said. "It's true, Your Honor, that perhaps the pie was only half-baked. Perhaps I put in a pinch too much of this, or a smidgen too much of that. But that's because, when I was making it, a beautiful woman came into my shop to buy pastries. And you should have seen the dress she had on! I've never seen such a dress—they shouldn't be allowed to wear them like that in public! So, of course, Your Honor, I may not have paid quite enough attention to my pies."

"We'll see about this!" shouted the judge. "Find that woman!"

The woman was located. The judge told her how she had broken a man's leg.

"But, Your Honor," she protested, "as the baker himself admitted, the dress caught his eye, not me. The dressmaker is the one to blame."

"Arrest the dressmaker!" the judge ordered.

The dressmaker was hauled before the bench.

"What do you mean by corrupting the public this way?" the judge demanded. "Your dress has made this woman turn this baker's head, which made his pies bad, which made the carpenter ill, which made his window frame bad, which broke this poor man's leg. What do you have to say for yourself?"

But the dressmaker was not a speechmaker. He stammered and stuttered, and could think of nothing at all to say. The judge ordered him hanged.

The bailiff looked the condemned man up and down.

"He's a big one, Your Honor," he suggested. "I'm afraid he'll be too tall for our gallows. His feet will just land on the ground."

"So find a shorter dressmaker, and hang him instead," the judge stormed. "Someone must pay, after all."

Then he ordered the woman to wear something else, and the baker to pay attention to his pies, and the carpenter to fix the window, and the owner to keep it locked.

But a lock is nothing to a thief. As soon as his leg healed, the plaintiff went back to the house and, knowing the window was safe now, broke in and took whatever he wanted.

•

GRUMBLE TOWN

There is nothing more unattractive than the sound of whining in
the midst of plenty. It is not a good sign of character at any level
—in individuals, families, communities, or nations as a whole.

There was once a place called Grumble Town where every-body grumbled, grumbled, grumbled. In summer, the people grumbled that it was too hot. In winter, it was too cold. When it rained, the children whimpered because they couldn't go outside. When the sun came out, they complained that they had nothing to do. Neighbors griped and groaned about neighbors, parents about children, brothers about sisters. Everybody had a problem, and everyone whined that *someone* should come do something about it.

One day a peddler trudged into town, carrying a big basket on his back. When he heard all the fussing and sighing and moaning, he put his basket down and cried: "O citizens of this town! Your fields are ripe with grain, your orchards heavy with fruit. Your mountains are covered by good, thick forests, and your valleys watered by deep, wide rivers. Never have I seen a place blessed by such opportunity and abundance. Why are you so dissatisfied? Gather around me, and I will show you the way to contentment."

Now this peddler's shirt was tattered and torn. His pants showed patches, his shoes had holes. The people laughed to think that someone like him could show them how to be content. But while they snickered, he pulled a long rope from his basket and strung it between two poles in the town square. Then, holding his basket before him, he cried: "People of Grumble Town! Whoever is dissatisfied, write your trouble on a piece of paper, and bring it and put it in this basket. I will exchange your problem for happi-ness!"

The crowd swarmed around him. No one hesitated at the chance to get rid of his trouble. Every man, woman, and child in the village scribbled a grumble onto a scrap of paper and dropped it into the basket.

They watched as the peddler took each trouble and hung it on the line. By the time he was through, troubles fluttered on every inch of rope, from end to end. Then he said: "Now each one of you should take from this magic line the smallest trouble you can find."

They all rushed forward to examine all the troubles. They hunted and fingered and pondered, each trying to pick the very smallest trouble. After a while the magic line was empty.

And behold! Each held in his hand the very same trouble he had put into the basket. Each had chosen his own trouble, thinking it was the smallest of all on the line.

From that day, the people of Grumble Town stopped grum-bling all the time. And whenever anyone had the urge to whimper or whine, he thought of the peddler and his magic line.

•

THE GRUMBLE FAMILY

There's a family nobody likes to meet,
They live, it is said, on Complaining Street,
In the city of Never-Are-Satisfied,
The river of Discontent beside.
They growl at that and they growl at this,
Whatever comes there is something amiss;
And whether their station be high or humble,
They are known by the name of Grumble.

The weather is always too hot or cold,
Summer and winter alike they scold;
Nothing goes right with the folks you meet
Down on that gloomy Complaining Street.
They growl at the rain and they growl at the sun,
In fact, their growling is never done.
And if everything pleased them, there isn't a doubt
They'd growl that they'd nothing to grumble about!

But the queerest thing is that not one of the same
Can be brought to acknowledge his family name,
For never a Grumbler will own that he
Is connected with it at all, you see.
And the worst thing is that if anyone stays
Among them too long he will learn their ways,
And before he dreams of the terrible jumble
He's adopted into the family of Grumble.

So it were wisest to keep our feet
From wandering into Complaining Street;
And never to growl, whatever we do,
Lest we be mistaken for Grumblers, too.
Let us learn to walk with a smile and song,
No matter if things do sometimes go wrong,
And then, be our station high or humble,
We'll never belong to the family of Grumble!

•

THE KING AND THE SHIRT

Learning how to work and learning how to be satisfied often seem
to go hand in hand.

A king once fell gravely ill. As each day passed he grew worse
and worse. His doctors and wise men tried cure after cure, but
nothing worked. They were ready to give up hope when the king's
old nursemaid spoke up.

"I will tell you how to save the king," she said. "If you can find
a happy man, and take the shirt from his back, and put it on the
king—then he will recover."

So the king sent forth his messengers. They rode far and wide
throughout the kingdom, and yet nowhere could they find a happy
man. No one seemed content; everyone had some complaint.

"That stupid tailor!" they heard a rich man say. "He's made
these pants too short! And by the way, this food is terrible! Can't
that cook do anything right?"

"What's wrong with our children?" the miller grumbled to his
wife. "They never do what we say! Can't they teach them manners
at school? And they make so much noise—tell them to go outside
and play."

"My roof is leaking," the candle maker groaned. "This ought
not to happen! Can't the government do something about it?"

Everywhere they went, the king's messengers heard nothing
but whining and griping. If a man was rich, he never had enough.
If he was not rich, it was someone else's fault. If he was healthy, he
had a bad mother-in-law. If he had a good mother-in-law, he was
catching a cold. Everyone had *something* to complain about.

Finally one night the king's own son was passing a small cottage when he heard someone say: "Thank you, Lord. I've finished
my daily labor, and helped my fellow man. I've eaten my fill, and
now I can lie down and sleep in peace. What more could I want?"

The prince rejoiced to have found a happy man at last. He gave
orders to take the fellow's shirt to the king, and pay the owner as
much money as he wished.

But when the king's messengers went into the cottage to take
the happy man's shirt off his back, they found he was so poor he
had no shirt at all.

•

Two Surprises

A workman plied his clumsy spade
  As the sun was going down;
The German king with his cavalcade
  Was coming into town.

The king stopped short when he saw the man.
  "My worthy friend," said he,
"Why not cease work at eventide,
  When the laborer should be free?"

"I do not slave," the old man said,
  "And I am always free;
Though I work from the time I leave my bed
  Till I can hardly see."

"How much," said the king, "is thy gain in a day?"
  "Eight groschen," the man replied.
"And canst thou live on this meager pay?"
  "Like a king," he said with pride.

"Two groschen for me and my wife, good friend,
  And two for a debt I owe;
Two groschen to lend and two to spend
  For those who can't labor, you know."

"Thy debt?" said the king. Said the toiler, "Yea,
  To my mother with age oppressed,
Who cared for me, toiled for me, many a day,
  And now hath need of rest."

"To whom dost lend of thy daily store?"
  "To my three boys at school. You see,
When I am too feeble to toil anymore,
  They will care for their mother and me."

"And thy last two groschen?" the monarch said.
  "My sisters are old and lame;
I give them two groschen for raiment and bread,
  All in the Father's name."

Tears welled up in the good king's eyes.
"Thou knowest me not," said he;
"As thou hast given me one surprise,
Here is another for thee.

"I am thy king; give me thy hand."
And he heaped it high with gold.
"When more thou needest, I command
That I at once be told.

"For I would bless with rich reward
The man who can proudly say,
That eight souls he doth keep and guard
On eight poor groschen a day."

•

THE STONE IN THE ROAD

Civic responsibility means doing something, not complaining that something ought to be done.

There is a story told of a king who lived long ago in a country across the sea. He was a very wise king, and spared no effort to teach his people good habits. Often he did things which seemed to them strange and useless; but all that he did, he did to teach his people to be industrious and careful.

"Nothing good can come to a nation," he said, "whose people complain and expect others to fix their problems for them. God gives the good things of life to those who take matters into their own hands."

One night, while everyone else slept, he placed a large stone in the road that led past his palace. Then he hid behind a hedge, and waited to see what would happen.

First came a farmer with his wagon heavily loaded with grain, which he was taking to the mill to be ground.

"Well, whoever saw such carelessness?" he said crossly, as he turned his team and drove around the stone. "Why don't these lazy people have that rock taken from the road?" And so he went on complaining of the uselessness of others, but not touching the stone himself.

Soon afterward, a young soldier came singing along the road. The long plume of his cap waved in the breeze, and a bright sword hung at his side. He was thinking of the wonderful bravery he would show in the war.

The soldier did not see the stone, but struck his foot against it and went sprawling in the dust. He rose to his feet, shook the dust from his clothes, picked up his sword, and stormed angrily about the lazy people who had no more sense than to leave such a huge rock in the road. Then he, too, walked away, not once thinking that he might move it himself.

So the day passed. Everyone who came by complained and whined because the stone lay in the road, but no one touched it.

At last, just at nightfall, the miller's daughter came past. She was a hard-working girl, and was very tired, because she had been busy since early morning at the mill.

But she said to herself, "It is almost dark. Somebody may fall over this stone in the night, and perhaps he could be badly hurt. I will move it out of the way."

So she tugged at the heavy stone. It was hard to move, but she pulled and pulled, and pushed, and lifted until at last she moved it from its place. To her surprise, she found a box underneath.

She lifted the box. It was heavy, for it was filled with something. Upon it was written: "This box belongs to the one who moves the stone."

She opened the lid, and found it was full of gold!

The miller's daughter went home with a happy heart. When the farmer and the soldier and all the others heard what had happened, they gathered around the spot in the road where the stone had been. They scratched at the dust with their feet, hoping to turn up a piece of gold.

"My friends," said the king, "we often find obstacles and burdens in our way. We may complain out loud while we walk around them if we choose, or we can lift them and find out what they mean. Disappointment is usually the price of laziness."

Then the wise king mounted his horse and, with a polite "Good evening," rode away.

THE BUSY MAN

Hard work is a good sign of a willingness to be responsible. People who are doing things are usually getting things done for other people as well as for themselves.

> If you want to get a favor done
>   By some obliging friend,
> And want a promise, safe and sure,
>   On which you may depend,
> Don't go to him who always has
>   Much leisure time to plan,
> But if you want your favor done,
>   Just ask the busy man.
>
> The man with leisure never has
>   A moment he can spare,
> He's always "putting off" until
>   His friends are in despair.
> But he whose every waking hour
>   Is crowded full of work
> Forgets the art of wasting time,
>   He cannot stop to shirk.
>
> So when you want a favor done,
>   And want it right away,
> Go to the man who constantly
>   Works twenty hours a day.
> He'll find a moment, sure, somewhere,
>   That has no other use.
> And help you, while the idle man
>   Is framing an excuse.

•

THE OLD MAN AND DEATH

Aesop

**Every life has its share of struggles of one kind or another. We are
not so quick to complain when we consider the alternative.**

An old man, bent with years and groaning beneath the weight
of a heavy load of firewood which he carried, sought, weary and
sore-footed on a long and dusty road, to gain his distant cottage.
Unable to bear the weight of his burden any longer, he let it fall by
the roadside, and lamented his hard fate.

"What pleasure have I known since I first drew breath in this
sad world? From dawn to dusk it has been hard work and little pay!
At home is an empty cupboard, a discontented wife, and lazy and
disobedient children! O Death! O Death! come and free me from
my troubles!"

At once the ghostly King of Terrors stood before him. "What
do you want with me?" Death queried in hollow tones.

"Noth–nothing," stammered the awed and frightened peasant,
"nothing except for you to help me put again upon my shoulders
the bundle of sticks I have let fall!"

•

GRATEFULNESS

George Herbert

Gratitude is better than grumbling.

> Thou that hast given so much to me,
> Give one thing more—a grateful heart;
> Not thankful when it pleaseth me,
> As if thy blessings had spare days,
> But such a heart whose pulse may be.
>   Thy praise.

•

SAINT FRANCIS AND THE WOLF
Retold by Frances Dadmun

Sometimes the courage to lead comes from deep faith.

Saint Francis lived several hundred years ago in Italy. All the clothes he owned were a brown robe with a rope for a belt, and leather sandals. He generally went bareheaded unless the sun was hot or the rain heavy, and then he drew the hood of his robe over his head and went his way very comfortably. There were years when he had no home, but it made no difference, for he was happy anywhere. Every man was his friend and even the wild beasts trusted him.

One day, when Saint Francis was out for a walk, he saw a little town perched on a hill.

"There is Gubbio," he said to some friends who were walking with him. "I have good friends there. We must go up and make them a visit."

There was a high stone wall all about Gubbio which you couldn't possibly have climbed because it was higher than a house and very steep. People went in and out of a great gate which was locked every night to keep out robbers, but in the daytime it was generally wide open.

This morning, when Saint Francis and his friends came to the gate, they were surprised to find it closed. They had to knock several times before anyone opened it.

"What is the trouble, good brother, that the gate is shut?" asked Saint Francis.

"It's a great Wolf!" said the man, who was a peasant. "A huge fierce fellow he is, too. He eats men. He is so bold that we have seen him at this very gate where you came in, just now. It's a mercy that he didn't eat you."

"And no one dares go outside?" said Saint Francis.

"No one," said the peasant.

By this time, the street was full of people who had heard the knocking at the gate. They looked so frightened and wild-eyed that Saint Francis was sorry for them.

"Come, brothers," he said to his companions, "we will go out and see this Wolf."

The people cried out, "No, no!" until the narrow street echoed. Those who were nearest clutched the skirts of Saint Francis's brown robe.

"Yes, yes!" said St. Francis, "I am not afraid of the Wolf. He will be my friend."

The people knew that Saint Francis meant what he said and opened the gates, but their fingers trembled as they drew back the bolts.

Saint Francis and his companions went straight to the hills where the Wolf was hiding and the people of Gubbio followed at a safe distance. But Saint Francis was fearless. He put his trust in God.

So he left even his faithful companions and went on alone. And then he saw the Wolf, running swiftly with head low and mouth partly open. Saint Francis stood still.

"Come here, Brother Wolf," said Saint Francis. "In the name of Jesus, do not hurt anybody."

The Wolf closed his mouth, stopped running. He crept forward and lay down at the feet of Saint Francis.

"Brother Wolf," said Saint Francis, "you have done great harm in these parts, killing God's creatures—not only beasts but people, whom God made in his image! All people cry against you and all this land hates you. But I, Brother Wolf, would make peace between you and the people. Do no more harm and they will forgive you, and neither people nor dogs shall torment you anymore."

The Wolf wagged his tail and his head drooped. He knew what it was to be tormented by people and dogs. He, as well as the people, had had a hard time.

"Brother Wolf," said Saint Francis, and he looked at the poor, lean sides where every rib showed, "if you are willing to be peaceable, I promise you that you will be fed as long as you live; for I know well that you have done all this harm because you were hungry. But since I do this for you, Brother Wolf, will you promise me that you will never again hurt either an animal or a human being?"

The Wolf bowed his head, but Saint Francis wanted more.

"Brother Wolf, you must give a pledge for your promise, that I may surely trust you."

Saint Francis stretched forth his right hand. The people gave a great cry of wonder, for the Wolf lifted his right paw and meekly placed it in the hand of Saint Francis, giving all the promise he could.

"Brother Wolf," said Saint Francis, "come with me and let us repeat this promise before all the people."

The Wolf followed Saint Francis back to the town, and as the news spread, men and women, young and old, big and little, trooped to the marketplace to see the Wolf with Saint Francis. When everybody in town was surely there, Saint Francis—and you know by this time that he was a real saint—spoke to the people.

"Listen, my brothers. Brother Wolf, here before you, has promised me to make peace with you and not to trouble you again in any way; and you are to promise him that you will give him all he needs to eat."

The people all shouted at once that they would feed their new friend regularly.

"And you, Brother Wolf," said Saint Francis, "do you promise to observe this treaty of peace that you will harm neither people nor animals nor any creature?"

The Wolf kneeled and bowed his head. He wriggled gently, he wagged his tail and lifted his ears, showing as plainly as a wolf could that he would keep the treaty.

"But, Brother Wolf," urged Saint Francis, "I wish you to promise me before all these people as you did outside the gate, and let me promise in turn never to break my word to you."

The Wolf understood, for he lifted his paw and placed it in the hand of Saint Francis. Once more the people cried out, this time with joy, and they thanked God for sending them Saint Francis, who had saved them from the mouth of the Wolf. No one knows what the Wolf thought, but we can guess that he was thankful too; for he would never have been so fierce if he had not nearly starved to death in the first place.

He lived two years in Gubbio and went among the houses from door to door, without hurting anyone. He was fed by the people most politely, and not even a dog barked at him. After two years, Brother Wolf died of old age, and everyone was sorry. He was not only loved for his own sake but was always reminding the people of their dear friend, Saint Francis.

•

THE MAID OF ORLÉANS

Adapted from
Louis Maurice Boutet de Monvel

Here is one of the most famous heroines of all time, a sweet peasant girl who challenged kings, led her troops, and died for love of God and country.

She was born Joan d'Arc in 1412, in the little French village of Domrémy. Her parents were honest laboring folk who lived by their toil. Their little house stood so close to the church that its garden touched the graveyard.

The child grew up there, under the eye of God.

She was a sweet, upright girl. Everyone loved her, for all knew her kind heart. A brave worker, she aided her family in their labors. By day she led the beasts to pasture, and in the evening she sat spinning by her mother's side.

She loved God, and often prayed to Him.

Now, in those days, France and England were at war. France had no real ruler. The English king had invaded the land, determined to make it his own. The French did not want to be ruled by the English, and they fought to put Charles the Dauphin, the son of their last king, on the throne.

But the Dauphin had no army, no money, and no will to fight. Day by day, pieces of his kingdom fell away to the enemy. Famine and anarchy reigned across the land.

One summer day, when she was thirteen years old, Joan heard a voice at midday in her father's garden. It told her to be a good girl and go to church. Then it told her that she was to save all of France, and that she must go to help the Dauphin.

"But I am only a poor girl," cried Joan.

"God will help thee," answered the voice.

And the child, overcome, was left weeping.

From that day she began to spend more and more time away from her playmates, listening to heavenly voices. As time passed, they became more urgent. The peril was great, they said; she must go help the king and save the kingdom.

And, of course, when Joan began to speak of her mission, many people laughed, and called her crazy. But the simple-hearted folk, moved by her faith, believed in her. A kind squire offered to take her to see the Dauphin. The poor folk, adding their mites together, raised the money to clothe and arm the little peasant girl. They bought her a horse, and on the appointed day she set out with a small escort.

"God keep you!" cried the multitude, and they wept.

The enemy held the country through which the little party was to pass. They had to travel at night and hide through the day. Joan's companions, alarmed, spoke of turning back.

"Fear nothing," said she. "God is leading us."

On the twelfth day they arrived at the court of the Dauphin. At first it looked as if he would not receive the inspired girl. But at last an interview was granted. One evening, by the light of fifty torches, Joan was brought into the great hall of the castle, crowded with all the nobles of the court. She had never seen the Dauphin.

To see if God were really guiding her, as she claimed, the Dauphin changed places with one of noblemen in the court, and disguised himself in plain clothes. But Joan singled him out among the multitude at once, and knelt before him.

"God give you a happy life, gentle Dauphin," she said.

"I am not the king," he answered. "Yonder is the king."

"You are he, gentle prince, and no other," she replied with perfect confidence. Then she told him that God had sent her to aid him, and asked for troops to save the city of Orléans, which lay under siege by the English troops. Everyone knew that if Orléans fell, France would be lost.

The king hesitated. The girl might be a sorceress. He sent her to be examined by learned men. For three weeks they tormented her with their questions. When they told her that God should have no need of men-at-arms to deliver France, she drew herself up quickly. "The soldiers will fight, but God will give the victory," she said.

The people declared that the maid was indeed inspired, and the learned and powerful were forced to yield to the multitude.

The French troops assembled. On Thursday, the 28th of April, 1429, the little army moved forward, led by Joan. She was clad in glistening armor, and carried a white banner embroidered with the lilies of France. When she entered Orléans, the people crowded to meet her. She passed by torchlight through the city; men, women, and children thronged to get near her, stretching forth their hands to touch the inspired maiden's horse.

Joan spoke kindly to them, promising to deliver the city. Her confidence influenced everyone around her. The people of Orléans, so lately timid and discouraged, now wished to hurl themselves at the enemy. Joan, meanwhile, had letters thrown over the walls of the city, ordering the besieging English to depart and return to their own country. They answered her with insults. So Joan mounted her warhorse and led her soldiers into battle.

Around Orléans stood the forts which the English held. The French now captured them one by one. Soon all but the last was taken from the enemy. Its walls were forbidding, and the French generals wanted to wait for more soldiers before making an attack. But Joan pushed them on.

The fighting was fierce. At one point Joan descended into a moat, and was raising a ladder against a parapet when an English arrow struck her between her neck and shoulder. She fell backward into the trench and, thinking her killed, the English rallied. But the brave girl pulled the arrow out of the wound, and was soon foremost in the fight again.

"Forward!" she cried. "All is yours!"

The English were routed. And Orléans, which had been besieged for eight months, was delivered in only four days.

The Maid of Orléans, as she was now called, hastened to the court of the Dauphin. She desired at once to take him to Rheims, where he could be crowned. He received her with great honors, but refused to follow her. He accepted the devotion of the heroic girl, but did not want her generous efforts to disturb his easy life. Instead, he sent her to attack the places still held by the English on the banks of the river Loire.

In battle after battle, the French were victorious. Joan was always in the front of the ranks. She constantly exposed herself to blows and was often wounded, but would never use her sword. Her only weapon was her banner painted with the lilies of France.

At last the Dauphin agreed to proceed to Rheims. On the 16th of July he entered the town at the head of his troops. The next day in the cathedral, with Joan standing at his side, he was crowned Charles VII of France.

But after the coronation, Joan seemed to lose her power. She began to lose battles. While defending the town of Compiègne, her army was driven back. During the retreat, Joan, deserted by all, found herself nearly surrounded by the enemy. She parried the blows of her assailants, steadily retreating until she reached the walls of the city. A step more and she would have been safe inside; but through either jealousy, imprudence, or treason, those who were defending the entrance to the city closed the gates and raised the bridge, leaving Joan outside. She fell into the hands of the English.

Ashamed at having been beaten so many times by a mere girl, her captors accused her of sorcery. They dragged her from prison to prison, and finally shut her up in a dungeon at Rouen. They brought her out for examination as many as sixteen times, worried her with all sorts of perplexing questions, then shut her up again. They used torture to make her confess that heaven had not sent her.

Many of the English believed that while Joan lived they would be defeated, so they clamored for her death. A tribunal composed of bribed French priests was given the power to try her as a witch and a heretic. The unhappy maiden could oppose the insidious questions of her judges only with the uprightness and simplicity of her heart. "I have nothing more to do here," she said. "Send me back to God, from whom I came." After a long trial and painful imprisonment, Joan was condemned and sentenced to be burned at the stake.

And throughout her ordeal, King Charles of France, who owed her so much, made no attempt to help her.

On the morning of May 30, 1431, at nine o'clock, Joan rode through the streets of Rouen in the executioner's cart. On seeing the pile placed in front of the old marketplace, a cry escaped her.

"Ah, Rouen, Rouen, are you then to be my last home?" she exclaimed.

She knelt and prayed. Then, turning to her judges and enemies, she begged them to have a Mass said for her soul. She mounted the pile, and while they bound her hands, she asked to be shown a crucifix. Then they lit the fire. In the midst of the clouds of smoke and lurid gleam of flames, she forgave all, and said her last prayer.

Everyone present wept, even the executioners and judges. It is said that many turned away, unable to bear the sight, and as they fled cried: "We are lost! We have burned a saint!"

•

GIDEON AND
HIS BRAVE THREE HUNDRED

Adapted from retellings by
Frances Dadmun and Jesse Lyman Hurlbut

As this story from the book of Judges in the Bible reminds us, an important part of leadership is knowing how to choose the right people to lead. The story shows us how to look for courage and resolution, and reminds us that it's not the size of the dog in the fight that counts, but the size of the fight in the dog.

Long ago, a young man lived in Israel whose name was Gideon. He was the only son his father had left. His brothers, older than he, had died in battle. For Israel was hard-pressed by the tribe of Midianites, who lived across the River Jordan. For a time they would lie quiet and Israel would think all was well; but as soon as the wheat fields of Israel were yellow and ripe for harvest, the Midianites would cross the river, fight with Israel, and carry off the wheat. Israel had been beaten so many times that now she dared not stir. Her men lived in caves, just as animals creep into holes in the earth to protect themselves.

Gideon thought it a shame. He was brave, too brave to hide in the earth and let the Midianites carry off his father's wheat. Then God put the thought in his heart to save his people. So it happened that one morning, when a frightened messenger came running to say that the Midianites had crossed the river again, Gideon stood on a hilltop and blew a trumpet.

The Israelites ran from their caves at the sound of the trumpet blast, and gathered around Gideon. Then he sent messengers throughout the land to call the fighting men together. The Israelites were so glad to have a brave leader that Gideon soon had an army of thirty-two thousand men.

Early in the morning they pitched their tents south of the

enemy. When the Midianites woke and came out of their own tents, they stared in surprise. There was Israel just opposite, and from the number of tents, it looked like a great host!

But Gideon was not sure of his army. The men had been brave enough at the call of the trumpet, but when they faced the camp of the Midianites, extending up and down the valley as far as they could see, they began to wish they had stayed hidden in their own caves. They were not as sure as Gideon was that God would give them the victory. After all, they said to one another, what sort of captain was Gideon? He was little more than a boy.

But God said to Gideon: "Your army is too large. Send home all those who are afraid to fight."

And Gideon saw that a small army of brave men would be better than a multitude of cowards. So he sent word through the camp that whoever was afraid of the enemy should go home. Twenty-two thousand people went away, leaving only ten thousand in Gideon's army.

But God said to Gideon: "The people are yet too many. You need only a few of the bravest and best men to fight in this battle. Bring the men down the mountain, beside the water, and there I will show you how to find the ones you need."

So in the morning, by God's command, Gideon called his ten thousand men out and made them march down the hill, just as though they were going to attack the enemy. And when they were beside the water, he noticed how they drank, and set them apart into two companies.

As they came to the water, most of the men threw aside their shields and spears and knelt down to scoop up a drink with both hands together like a cup. If there had been any Midianites hidden in the bushes they could have shot the drinkers with arrows, for they were off their guard. These men Gideon commanded to stand in one company.

But there were a few men who did not stop to take a long drink of water. Holding spear and shield in one hand, with eyes wide open in case the enemy should suddenly appear, they merely caught up a handful of water in passing and marched on, lapping the water from the other hand.

God said to Gideon: "Set by themselves these men who have lapped up each a handful of water. These are the ones I have chosen to set Israel free."

Gideon counted these men and found there were only three hundred. But they were three hundred earnest men, of one purpose, who would not turn aside from their aim, even to drink.

Gideon waited for the sun to go down. When it was dark, he crept into the camp of the Midianites, and listened. When he heard them talking, he was glad, for he could tell that the Midianites, for all their number, were afraid of the Israelites. So he hurried back to his own camp.

Gideon's plan did not need a large army, but it did need a few careful, bold men who would do exactly as their leader commanded. He gave to each of his three hundred soldiers a lamp, a pitcher, and a trumpet, and told the men what to do with them. The lamps were lighted, but were placed inside the pitchers, so they could not be seen. He divided his men into three companies, and very quietly led them down the mountain in the middle of the night, and arranged them all around the Midianite camp.

Then at once a great shout rang out in the darkness, and after it came a crash of breaking pitchers and then a flash of light in every direction. The men blew their trumpets with a mighty noise. The Midianites were startled from their sleep to see enemies all around them, lights beaming and swords flashing in the darkness, and everywhere the sharp blaring of horns.

They were filled with sudden terror and thought only of escape, not of fighting. But wherever they turned, their enemies seemed to be standing with swords drawn. Their own land was east, across the river Jordan, and they fled in that direction, down a valley between the mountains, and they never came back again.

And so Israel was free, all because Gideon was brave and found three hundred men who stood with him.

•

HOW THEY BUILT THE WALLS
Retold by Henry Hallam Tweedy

Any people who would build or preserve a nation should remember the courage, perseverance, vigilance, hard work, and faith of Nehemiah. Here are some of the virtues needed to make a country safe and strong. The story is from the book of Nehemiah in the Bible.

About four hundred and fifty years before Jesus was born, there lived in the palace of the king of Persia a young Jew, whose name was Nehemiah. He seemed to have everything to make him happy. He had clothes of silk, and plenty of food, and could enjoy the fine things in the palace. Moreover, the king loved him and trusted him, so much so that he made Nehemiah his cupbearer. This meant a great deal in those days. For when wicked men wished to kill the king they used to try to put poison in his cup. Only a true friend might fill and bring it, and he would taste it before he gave it to the king to show that the king need not be afraid.

But with all this Nehemiah was not happy. For he was far from the city where his fathers had lived and now were buried. He had friends there, whom he longed to see, and he was eager to make his home in the land of his people, and to serve it, and make it beautiful, and protect it against its foes.

One day his brother came to him with some men from Jerusalem, who brought bad news. They told him that his friends were poor, and that they were having a great deal of sorrow and trouble. As for the city, which he loved, its great wall, built to guard it from its enemies, was broken down, while the great gates, through which people might enter by day but which were closed to keep out foes and robbers at night, had been burned.

When Nehemiah heard this, he was very sad. He knew that wild animals could creep in and prowl around its streets at night. Worse yet, wild men could steal in under the cover of darkness, and rob his friends, and even kill them. Perhaps some cruel king would march against it with his soldiers, and burn all the homes and make the people his slaves. No wonder that Nehemiah was unhappy. He felt so bad that he sat down and cried, and for days and days he could not even bear to eat.

But there was no use in crying. He knew that. And to go without food would only make him weak and unable to work, while it would not build the walls of his city or bring aid to his friends. So he made up his mind to do something, and the first thing that he did was to ask God to help him and to guide him, so that he might go back home and serve his city and his friends. Then he arose, and made himself ready to act as cupbearer, and went in to wait on the king.

The king saw at once that his cupbearer's heart was full of sorrow. "Why are you sad," he asked, "inasmuch as you are not sick?"

At first Nehemiah was almost afraid to tell him, for while he knew that his city needed him, he feared that the king would not let him go. But at last he plucked up courage, and with a prayer in his heart that God would cause the king to be gracious, he made answer. "Why should I not be sad," he said, "when the city where my fathers are buried lies waste, and its walls are broken down, and its gates are burned?"

Then the king was sorry for him, and said, "What can I do for you? Come, tell me!"

Nehemiah bowed himself before the king, and said, "If I have pleased you and you really love me, send me to Jerusalem, that I may build its walls."

To his great joy, the king said that he might go. He even sent soldiers with him to guard him and help him. He also gave Nehemiah letters to his servants, who ruled for him in the land lying between Persia and Judah, bidding these men to give him wood with which to make the gates. So Nehemiah started out on his long journey, and at last found himself safe in Jerusalem among his friends.

It seemed wise not to tell them why he had come until he knew just what needed to be done. So one night Nehemiah and a few of his men walked around the city and looked at the walls. He soon saw that these were badly broken and quite useless, as the men had told him. Before the people were awake, he and his friends were back in their homes.

The next morning, he called the people together and said, "Come, and let us build the walls of our city! The king, my master, says that we may do so. God will help us, and if we love Him and obey Him, He will give us strength to drive away our foes."

Now, the wall was a very, very long one, and it had to be very thick and very high. It seemed as if they never would be able to finish it, and they could not have done so if they had not all worked, and worked hard. There were doubtless some lazy men, who did not want to work, and some cowards who were afraid that foes would come and hurt them while they were at work and some greedy, selfish men, who did not love their city very much, and said that unless Nehemiah paid them money they would not work. But Nehemiah made the lazy men ashamed of themselves, and cheered those who were afraid, and told the selfish ones that if they did not work, their foes and robbers would come and take away the money that they had already.

Most of the people worked with a will gladly, and began at once to build next to their own homes. Some said that they would build one gate, and some another. Both men and women worked on the walls. The boys and girls were busy, too. Everybody worked and sang and pounded and shouted as the great stones were put into place. It was very hard labor. Their hands were bruised and torn, and their arms ached, and their backs were weary. But they loved their city dearly, and when people work for somebody or something that they love, the hardest toil is done gladly and often seems light.

Round about the country were men who hated Nehemiah and his people. They did not want to have the walls built, for then it would be harder to take the city, and they could not break into it and make the people slaves. Some of them used to stand near the men while they were at work, and laugh at them. "You can never build such great walls," they cried. "What is the use of trying!" When the people kept right on, they sent word, saying that if the work was not stopped, they would come and fight. But Nehemiah told the people not to be afraid. "Trust God," he said, "and work with your trowel in one hand and your sword in the other."

Every day saw fewer holes in the walls of the city. One by one the big gates were made and swung into place. At last the great work was done, and Nehemiah and his friends were as happy as they were weary. No robbers could creep into their homes now. There would be no more wild beasts prowling around their streets at night. As for the men who had jeered at them and tried to stop the work, the workers could laugh at them now. The people had loved their city enough to labor for it, and to suffer hardship, and endure danger. But as the result of their work, it was now a strong fort, and their lives and their homes were safe once more. And the men and women and boys and girls who had helped Nehemiah were happy and loved the city better and were prouder of it because each had worked and done a full share in building the great wall.

Nehemiah did many other things to make his city better and more beautiful, and all men loved him and honored him, because he had served his country so well.

•

BETSY ROSS AND THE FIRST FLAG

Adapted from a retelling
by Grace Humphrey

Historians don't know if Betsy Ross actually made the very first American flag. But whether legend or fact, the incident has become one of our most beloved portraits of the patriotic citizen ready to do his or her part.

In 1752 the eighth child was born in the Quaker family of Griscom in Philadelphia, and was named Elizabeth. Nine other children came after her, so with a total of sixteen brothers and sisters you may be sure she never had much opportunity to be lonely. Perhaps the large number of children is the explanation for her being apprenticed at Webster's, the leading upholstery establishment in the city. There Elizabeth became acquainted with John Ross, one of her fellow apprentices. Their friendship grew to love, and when she was twenty-one they were married.

Soon afterward they left Webster's and opened a little upholstery shop of their own, in a two-story house on Arch Street—a quaint little house that was old then, for it was built of bricks that came over to America as ballast in one of William Penn's vessels. It is still standing, in a good state of preservation, and very little changed from the old days, with its wide doors, big cupboards, narrow stairs, and tiny windowpanes. The front room was the shop, where Elizabeth and John waited on customers.

The happiness of the Ross family was not to last long. The spirit of liberty was awakening among the colonists, the spirit of resistance to the demands of the mother country. In common with many patriotic women, Betsy Ross saw her husband march away for military service. With several other young men he was guarding cannonballs and artillery stores on one of the city wharves along the Delaware River, when he received a serious injury. He died in January 1776, after long and anxious nursing on the part of his young wife.

There was Betsy Ross, a widow at twenty-four. She determined to maintain herself independently, if possible, and to continue alone the upholstery business they had developed together. About five months after her husband's death, sometime between the twenty-second of May and the fifth of June, she was one day working in the shop when three gentlemen called.

The first was General Washington, in Philadelphia for a few days to consult the Continental Congress. Mistress Ross had frequently seen him, for the story is that he had visited her shop more than once, to have her embroider the ruffles for his shirts. With him was Robert Morris, who would go down in history as the treasurer and financier of the Revolution, and her husband's uncle, Colonel George Ross, a signer of the Declaration of Independence.

These gentlemen had come to consult her. She knew, of course, how the various banners carried by troops from the different colonies, as well as by different regiments, had caused confusion and might mean danger. It was time to do away with the pine tree flag, the beaver flag, the rattlesnake flag, the hope flag, the silver crescent flag, the anchor flag, the liberty tree flag, and all the rest of them, and have a single standard for the American army. Betsy Ross had heard, too, of the Cambridge flag, often called the grand union flag, which Washington had raised the New Year's Day before, a flag half English, half American, with thirteen red and white stripes, and the crosses of St. George and St. Andrew. But since the first of the year events had moved rapidly and the desire for separation from England had become steadily stronger. A new flag was needed, to show the growing spirit of Americanism— which was soon to crystallize on the Fourth of July.

All this Betsy Ross knew, as a good patriot would. And she could not have been greatly surprised when General Washington said they had come to consult her about a national flag.

"Can you make a flag?" he asked.

Modestly and with some diffidence she replied, "I don't know, sir, but I can try."

Then in the little back parlor Washington showed her a rough sketch he had made—a square flag with thirteen stripes of red and

white, and thirteen stars in the blue canton. He asked her opinion
of the design. With unerring accuracy of eye she saw at once what
was needed to make the flag more beautiful. She suggested that the
proportions be changed, so that the length would be a third more
than the width. She proposed that the thirteen stars be grouped to
form some design, say a circle or a star, or placed in parallel rows.
And last she remarked that a five-pointed star was more symmetrical
than one with six points.

"But," ask Washington, "isn't it more difficult to make?"

In answer practical Betsy Ross took up a piece of paper, folded
it over, and with one clip of her scissors cleverly made a perfect
star with five even points.

That was sufficient, and the general drew up his chair to her
table and made another pencil sketch, embodying her three suggestions. The second sketch was copied and colored by a Philadelphia
artist, William Barrett, a painter of some note, who returned it to
Mistress Ross. Meantime, not knowing just how to make a flag, for
it must be sewed in a particular way, she went to a shipping merchant, an old Scotchman who was a friend of Robert Morris, to
borrow a ship's flag as a guide.

And in that way Betsy Ross made the first Stars and Stripes. To
try the effect, the story goes, the new banner was run up to the
peak of a vessel in the Delaware River. Several months later, the
Continental Congress passed a resolution formally adopting the flag
as the national standard.

This is the story Betsy told over and over, to her daughters and
grandchildren, and in later years they wrote the account down, just
as they had heard it, and as you have read it here. It was George
Washington, more than any other, who seems to have been most
interested in the question of a national flag. But it was the skilled
seamstress to whom he took his first, rough design, to have her
opinion of its worth. Much of the flag's beauty is due to the keen
eye, confident hand, and ready heart of patriot Betsy Ross.

•

HE GAVE HIS LIFE FOR HIS COUNTRY

Brave citizens come in all ages. Here are two tales of young heroes
who thought of their country before themselves. The first story
takes place in Tyrol, now a province of Austria.

Some years ago there was war between the French and the
people who lived in a little country to the northeast of Italy called
Tyrol. I suppose most people love their native land, but at this
particular time the Tyrolese were so anxious to save their country
that even the women and children followed the soldiers to battle,
in hopes of being of some use to them.

One of the boys who thus followed his father was called Albert
Speckbacher. He was only ten years old, but his father was one of
the bravest leaders of the Tyrolese, and, young as he was, Albert
was determined that he would help him somehow.

One day the French went to attack a village. They came to a
deep ravine, at the bottom of which the river Ard dashed along at
a terrific pace. The only way to reach the village was by crossing a
bridge. A strange sort of bridge it was, too, just the kind to keep
a village free from any enemies. It was simply a great tree, which
had been felled from the mountainside and allowed to fall right
across the ravine, so that its topmost boughs caught on the opposite
rocks—a dangerous crossing place, and one on which only one
person could go at a time.

The Tyrolese knew what the French were doing, and a party of
three hundred men, with Speckbacher as their leader, was sent
down to defend this bridge. For an hour the battle raged on each
side of the ravine, and the Tyrolese seemed to be getting the best
of it. Then the French general ordered two cannon to be dragged
up the rocks, and in a very short time more than half the brave
Tyrolese were killed, Speckbacher amongst the number.

Little Albert knelt beside his father's dead body, and wondered
what he could do to save his country. He saw that the Tyrolese were
going to try to destroy the bridge. If that could be done, the French
could not possibly enter the village. He watched them get their axes
and begin cutting through the roots and trunk of the tree.

But as they boldly worked, the French rifles killed one after another of them, till at last their courage failed, and no one came forward to take his place at the task which had proved fatal to so many. A great part of the tree had been cut through, but there still remained enough to hold it firm.

Albert looked down at his father's white face, then up to the bright heaven for a moment. Then he seized the axe and worked with all his strength. A shower of bullets fell round him, but none touched him. The tree was cut through at last, excepting at one point, which was quite out of his reach. It was only a small piece of the inner bark, but he could not get at it. Albert saw in a moment there was only one way in which he could break the tree away from this point. He must put a weight on the top of it, and so snap it off.

He waited till the French had fired their rifles once more; then, while they stopped to reload, he sprang upon the tree, jumping with all his might. His weight, light as it was, snapped the little piece by which it was held, and he and the bridge went tumbling into the ravine below.

Thus did the brave boy of ten sacrifice his life to save his native village.

The French retired when they saw the bridge fall, and the next day they found the body of the poor lad floating in the stream at the foot of the mountain. Enemies though they were, they could admire such a noble deed as his. They buried the hero on the mountainside, and put up a stone telling the story of his bravery.

•

AN AMERICAN ARMY OF TWO

Adapted from a retelling
by Florence Farmer

Here are quick wits and courage—the best kinds of weapons.

If you have ever wondered if just one or two people can make a difference, just remember the "American Army of Two."

Rebecca and Abigail Bates lived on the coast of Massachusetts, near a little village named Scituate. Their father was the keeper of the lighthouse, which stood at the entrance of the harbor and warned ships away from the rocky coast.

One day Rebecca and Abigail were up in the tower, polishing the great glass that sent the light far over the sea. Their father and mother had rowed across the bay to the village, leaving the lighthouse in their daughters' care. As they polished away with all their might, they noticed a strange ship creeping around a point. It stopped and lowered two little boats, which turned and started toward land.

At that time people feared every ship they did not know, for the year was 1814, and America and England were at war. British ships often sailed right into harbors and sent their soldiers ashore to attack the villages. The British had already made one raid on Scituate's harbor, and had burned ten vessels before putting back to sea.

Now Rebecca and Abigail stood frozen in the lighthouse, peering down and holding their breath while they waited to see what these two strange boats would do. Closer and closer they crept, until finally they entered the harbor. They were full of British soldiers!

The girls looked along the shore. No help was to be seen. What could they do? If they could only warn the townspeople! But they had no boat, and there would be no time to run to the village, for it was a long way around the bay.

Rebecca grabbed her sister by the sleeve.

"Listen, Abigail," she cried. "Here's what we two girls are going to do." And she began whispering into her ear, as if the British might hear her plan as they rowed swiftly across the water.

The sisters raced down the winding staircase and across the lawn to their house. Abigail snatched up a drum, which her father had brought home to mend just the other day. Rebecca grabbed a fife, and they slipped out of the house toward the beach, crouching behind bushes and sandhills to keep out of sight.

The British boats were now quite close, and the soldiers were preparing to leap ashore. Suddenly the order was given to halt. The soldiers listened closely.

From behind a clump of cedar trees came the beating of a drum, and then the squeak of a fife. It was not skillful, but it was loud and clear—the strains of "Yankee Doodle" floated over the sands.

"The militia has seen us coming!" cried the British soldiers. "They will attack us as soon as we land!" They turned their boats around and rowed for their lives, back to their ship.

A moment later the villagers spotted the British boats. They raised a great alarm, and all hurried toward the lighthouse.

When they reached the point, they found only Rebecca and Abigail Bates, sitting on a rock, watching a faraway ship put to sea. A drum and fife lay beside them.

The "American Army of Two" had won the day.

●

A LEGEND OF THE ROMAN FORUM

This story was a favorite Roman legend of patriotism and self-sacrifice. The Forum in Rome was the center of civic life, an open area surrounded by temples, legislative chambers, markets, and other public buildings.

In the year 362 B.C. Rome was shaken by an awful earthquake, and a huge chasm suddenly opened in the middle of the Forum, so deep that no one could see the bottom. The citizens brought stones and earth to fill it up, but no matter how much they threw in, the yawning gulf seemed as terrible as before.

The Senate then consulted the soothsayers, who announced that the crater could not be filled up until what was most valuable in Rome was cast into it.

"Heed this," said the augurs. "Your most sacred treasure must be dedicated to the Gods in this place if Rome is to stand fast."

The horrified people rushed to the edge of the pit and began throwing in their most valuable possessions—gold and silver and jewelry—but still the hole was as deep as ever. As they stood agonizing over what to do next, a noble youth named Marcus Curtius rode forward, armed as though for battle.

"What is more valuable to Rome than courage?" he cried. "What is more valuable than a citizen who is willing to give himself for his country?"

All the people stood silent. Curtius gazed at the temples of the immortal gods lining the Forum and stretched forth his arms to heaven above. Then, sword in hand, he spurred his horse and leapt into the great pit.

Immediately the ground closed behind him, and neither he nor his horse was ever seen again. All was as it had been before the earthquake.

•

GOD AND THE SOLDIER

This inscription was reportedly discovered on an old stone sentry box on the island of Gibraltar. Nations last when citizens remember the important things in times of difficulty *and* in times of ease.

God and the soldier
All men adore
In time of trouble,
And no more;
For when war is over
And all things righted,
God is neglected—
The old soldier slighted.

•

THE CHEVALIER D'ASSAS

Here is the sound of courage.

Long ago, a war was going on between the French and the Germans. A French army in the south of Germany was retreating before the enemy and had encamped for the night after a long day's march. The regiment of Auvergne was on the side of the French nearest the enemy, and the most advanced outpost of that regiment was a company that had for its captain a very brave young officer, the Chevalier D'Assas.

The French general thought that the enemy would try to attack his army the next day. He did not think that they were near enough to be dangerous for that night, but he wanted to know just where they were. The colonel of the regiment of Auvergne ordered the Chevalier D'Assas to find out if there were any of the enemy near the camp.

It was a dark, black night. D'Assas went out all alone and pushed his way cautiously through the thickets and woods that lay all around. There was no moon to help, and he had to feel his way along.

At first he found no sign of the enemy, nor did he hear any sound. The woods were completely quiet as he slowly, and as noise-lessly as possible, crept through them.

He had only gone a very short distance when he pushed past some low bushes and stepped out into what seemed like an open space.

Instantly a number of dim forms closed in around him. He felt bayonets pressed against his body on every side, and a voice whispered in his ear: "If you make a sound, you die!"

D'Assas realized in a flash that the enemy had managed to get close to the camp, and were trying to take the French army by surprise. If he could warn his regiment they could be ready in time to hold the enemy off and to save the rest of the army. He knew, too, that if he made a sound, he would pay the price.

He did not hesitate a second.

He drew back, but only to get a full breath, and then, with all the power he had, he shouted: "Auvergne! Auvergne! The enemy! The enemy are here!"

Instantly twenty bayonets were plunged into his body, and he fell dead to the ground.

His company and the rest of the regiment were roused by his cry. They came as quickly as they could to his rescue but they were too late to save him. They were in time, though, to hold off the attack until the rest of the French army was ready to meet it. When the Germans found that their surprise had failed, they retreated.

The name of D'Assas was honored and admired by the whole nation for his heroic sacrifice. The story reminds us that the fate of an army sometimes depends on the deed of one brave soul.

•

THE KEYS OF CALAIS

*Adapted from a retelling
by Charlotte Yonge*

This story reminds us that those of high rank and achievement
sometimes step forward to make the greatest sacrifices. Here are
some noblemen who truly acted nobly.

In 1346, at the outset of the Hundred Years War, King Edward
III of England marched upon Calais, the most important town in
northern France. He arrived before the town in early August, his
good knights and squires arrayed in flashing armor, his stout archers wielding their deadly long-bows, his royal standards floating
in the breeze above the whole glittering army. The walls of the city
were of huge thickness, with towers raised to a great height, and
the king knew it would be useless to attempt a direct assault.

A herald, in a rich, long robe embroidered with the arms of
England, rode up to the gate, a trumpet sounding before him, and
called upon Sir Jean de Vienne, the governor of Calais, to surrender
the place to Edward. Sir Jean made answer that he held the town
for Philip, King of France, and that he would defend it to the last.
The herald rode back again, and the English began the siege of the
city. At first they covered the whole plain with their white canvas
tents. Then, as time passed, they erected a little wooden town,
with streets and a market and even a wooden palace for the king's
comfort.

After a while a large and colorful fleet came crossing the waters
from the white cliffs of Dover. King Edward and his knights rode
down to the landing place to welcome the fair-haired Queen Phil-
ippa, and all her train of ladies. They had come from England in
great numbers to visit their husbands, fathers, and brothers in their
camp. Then there was a great court, and numerous feasts and
dances, and the knights and squires were constantly striving to see
who could do the bravest deed to please the ladies.

While this high merriment was going on outside their walls,
the people of Calais were growing lean in the cheeks. At first a few
brave French sailors, who knew the coast thoroughly, managed to
guide little fleets of boats loaded with bread and meat into the city.

They were often chased by Edward's vessels, and sometimes nearly taken, but they always managed to escape. So at last Edward, growing wrathful, built a great wooden castle on the seashore and filled it with archers and machines that tossed huge, ship-crushing stones. They kept such a watch upon the harbor that the French sailors dared not enter it. Then the townspeople began to feel what hunger really was.

One night the forlorn citizens looked down from their high walls and spied the thing they had been desperately awaiting—a great and noble French army spreading across the hillsides! It was a beautiful sight to the starving garrison to watch their countrymen pitching their white tents right behind the English forces, the knights' armor glancing and banners flying in the moonlight. King Philip had arrived to drive the invaders away!

But soon their hopes were dashed. King Philip was not eager to risk a defeat at the hands of the English. There were a few skirmishes. The armies traded insults and challenges. Three days of parleys ensued. Then, without the slightest real effort to rescue the brave, patient townspeople, away went King Philip of France with all his men. The people of Calais saw the French host that had crowded the hillside melt away like a summer cloud.

August had come again, and they had suffered privation for a whole year for the sake of a king who deserted them at their utmost need. They were in so grievous a state of hunger and distress that the hardiest could endure no more. The governor, Sir Jean de Vienne, went to the battlements and made signs he wished to hold a parley. He owned that the garrison was reduced to the greatest extremity of distress, and requested King Edward to be content with obtaining the city and its fortress, leaving the citizens and soldiers to depart in peace.

But Edward was so enraged at the delay and expense the siege had cost him, he would consent to receive the town only on unconditional terms. He would slay, or ransom, or make prisoner whomever he pleased, and he let it be known that there was a heavy reckoning to pay.

The town's brave answer was: "These conditions are too heavy for us. We are but a small number of knights and squires, who have loyally served our king, as you would have done. We have suffered greatly, but we will endure far more before we consent to endanger the children of our town. We therefore entreat you to reconsider."

The king was in a stern mood, and he answered that he would

pardon the townspeople only on one condition. Six of the chief citizens of Calais must come forward with halters around their necks, carrying the keys to the town. These six the king would punish as he saw fit. The remainder of the inhabitants could go free.

On hearing this, Sir Jean de Vienne begged that he be allowed to consult the citizens. He went to the marketplace and rang a great bell, upon which all the townspeople assembled. As he told them the hard terms, he could not keep them from weeping bitterly. Should all starve together, or should they sacrifice their most honored comrades?

Then a voice was heard. It was that of the richest citizen in the town, Eustache de St. Pierre.

"Ladies and gentlemen, high and low," he said, "it would be a pity to cause so many people to die through hunger, if it could be prevented. To hinder it would be meritorious in the eyes of our Savior. I have such faith and trust in finding grace before God, if I die to save my townspeople, that I name myself as first of the six."

As he ceased, his fellow townspeople wept aloud.

Another citizen, very rich and respected, rose and said: "I will be the second to my comrade Eustache," His name was Jean Daire. After him, Jacques Wistant, another very rich man, offered himself as companion to these, who were both his cousins. His brother Pierre would not be left behind. Two others then named themselves to the gallant band, and the number demanded by Edward was complete.

The gates were opened, the governor and the six passed through, and the gates were again shut behind them. Sir Jean then rode out to the English representatives and told them how these six burghers had offered themselves up, and begged them to do all in their power to save them. The governor then went back to the town, full of grief.

The six citizens were led to the presence of the king in his full court. They all knelt down, and the foremost said: "Most gallant king, you see before you six citizens of Calais, who have been important merchants, and who bring to you the keys of the castle and the town. We yield ourselves to your absolute will and pleasure, in order to save the remainder of the inhabitants of Calais, who have suffered much distress and misery. Condescend, therefore, out of your nobleness of mind, to have mercy on us."

Pity stirred among all the English barons, knights, and squires assembled there. They saw the resigned faces, pale and thin with patiently endured hunger, of those venerable men, offering themselves in the cause of their fellow townspeople. They wept at the sight. But the king was unmoved. He cast angry glances at the six, and ordered their heads struck off.

The English knights begged the king to be more merciful. They told him that such an execution would tarnish his honor. They warned that reprisals would be made against his own garrisons. They pointed to the selflessness and nobility of the six. But the king would not listen. He sent for the headsman and his great ax.

Then suddenly the Queen of England, her eyes streaming with tears, threw herself on her knees among the captives and cried: "Ah, gentle sir, I have crossed the sea, with so much danger, to be with you. I have never asked you one favor. But now I ask as a gift, for the sake of the Son of the Blessed Mary, and for your love to me, that you will spare these six men!"

For some time the king looked at her in silence. Then he exclaimed: "Dame, dame, I wish you had been anywhere else but here! You have entreated in such a manner that I cannot refuse you. I therefore give you these men, to do as you please with them."

The queen conducted the six citizens to her own chambers, where she made them welcome and had the halters taken from their necks. She clothed them, and fed them, and gave them gifts to remember her by. Then she saw them safely escorted out of the English camp. Such is the story of six brave and patient men who went forth, by their own free will, to meet what might have been a cruel death, in order to obtain the safety of their fellow townspeople.

•

BAT

At some point, you have to say where you stand, or risk the fate
of the Bat. This tale about honesty, loyalty, and courage appears
in Aesop's fables, in Native American lore, and in other folk traditions around the world. It's a good story for students and prac-
titioners of politics.

Once there was a war between the birds and the beasts. The
Bat was on the birds' side. But in the first battle, the birds were
badly beaten. As soon as Bat saw it was going against them, he crept
away, hid under a log, and stayed there until the fight was over.

When the victorious beasts were going home, Bat slipped in
among them.

After they had gone some distance, the beasts noticed him and
said: "Wait a minute. Aren't you one of the ones who fought against
us?"

Bat replied, "Oh, no! I'm one of you; I don't belong to the
birds. Don't you see my ears, and my claws? And look at my teeth.
Did you ever see a bird with fangs like these? Of course not. No,
I'm one of the beasts."

They said nothing more, and let Bat stay with them.

Soon after, there was another battle, and this time the birds
won. As soon as Bat saw his side was beaten, he slipped away and
hid under a log. When the battle was over and the birds were going
home, Bat went in among them.

When they noticed him, they said, "You are our enemy. We
saw you fighting against us."

"Oh, no," said Bat, "I'm one of you. I don't belong to those
beasts. Did you ever see one of them with wings?"

They said nothing more, and let him stay with them.

So Bat went back and forth as long as the war lasted. But finally,
tired of fighting, the birds and beasts decided to make peace. They
held a council to decide what to do with Bat.

"You fought with the birds, so go live with them," the beasts
cried.

"We don't want you!" shouted the birds. "You fought with the
beasts. Go live with them."

They decided to cast him out, saying: "Hereafter, you will fly alone at night, and will never have any friends, among either those that fly, or those that walk."

So now the Bat sneaks around in the dark, and lives in black caves. He flies like a bird, but never perches in treetops. And nobody cares what kind of creature he is.

•

THE MAN WITHOUT A COUNTRY

Here is the most despised name in American history. Benedict Arnold (1741–1801) was a descendant of a distinguished New England family and an American hero in the early part of the Revolutionary War. But he grew to love luxury, and he lusted after glory. In 1779, he began selling military information to the British, and in the summer of 1780, while in command of West Point in New York, Arnold secretly offered to surrender the fort and its garrison to the British for £20,000. The American forces discovered the plot, but Arnold managed to escape. For the rest of the war he served as a British brigadier, further blackening his name by conducting destructive raids in Virginia and his own native Connecticut.

After the war, Arnold and his family sailed to England, where he gradually discovered that the disgrace of a traitor knows no national boundaries.

Benedict Arnold sailed from his native land and returned no more. From that time forth, wherever he went, three whispered words followed him, singing through his ears into his heart— *Arnold the Traitor.*

When he stood beside the King in the House of Lords, a whisper crept through the thronged House, and as the whisper deepened into a murmur, one venerable lord arose and said he loved his sovereign, but could not speak to him while by his side stood —*Arnold the Traitor.*

He went to the theater, parading his warrior form amid the fairest flowers of British nobility and beauty; but no sooner was his face seen than the whole audience rose—the lord in his cushioned seat, the vagrant in the gallery. They rose together, while from the pit to the dome echoed the cry—*"Arnold the Traitor."*

When he issued from his gorgeous mansion, the liveried servant who ate his bread whispered in contempt to his fellow lackey, as he took his position in his master's carriage—*"Arnold the Traitor."*

Grossly insulted in a public place, he appealed to the company, and scowling at his antagonist with his fierce brow, he spat full in his face. His antagonist was a man of courage, and he said: "Time may scorn me, but I never can stain my sword by killing—*Arnold the Traitor."*

He left London. He engaged in commerce. His ships were on the ocean, his warehouses in Nova Scotia, his plantations in the West Indies. One night his warehouses were burned to ashes. The entire population of St. John's—accusing the owner of burning his own property, to defraud the insurance companies—assembled in that British town, and in sight of his very window they hanged an effigy, which bore a huge placard, inscribed—*"Arnold the Traitor."*

There was a day when Talleyrand arrived in Le Havre, hotfoot from Paris. It was in the darkest hour of the French Revolution. All who belonged to the ranks of the aristocracy were fleeing. Pursued by the bloodhounds of the Reign of Terror, stripped of his property and power, Talleyrand secured a passage to America in a ship about to sail. He was going, a beggar and a wanderer, to a strange land to earn his bread by daily labor. "Is there any American gentleman staying at your house?" he asked the landlord of his hotel. "I am about to cross the water, and would like a letter to some person of influence in the New World."

The landlord hesitated, and then said: "There is a gentleman upstairs, from either America or Britain, but whether American or Englishman I cannot tell."

He pointed the way, and Talleyrand, who during his life was bishop, prince, prime minister, ascended the stairs, knocked at the stranger's door, and entered.

In the far corner of a dimly lighted room sat a gentleman of some fifty years, his arms folded and his head bowed on his breast. From a window directly opposite, a flood of light poured over his forehead. His eyes, looking from beneath the downcast brows, gazed in Talleyrand's face with a peculiar and searching expression. His face was striking in its outline; his mouth and chin indicative of an iron will. His form was clad in a dark but rich and distinguished costume. Talleyrand advanced, stated that he was a fugitive, and, under the impression that the gentleman who sat before him was an American, he solicited his kind offices.

"I am a wanderer—an exile. I am forced to fly to the New World, without a friend or a hope. You are an American? Give me, then, I beseech you, a letter of introduction to some friend of yours, so that I may earn my bread. A gentleman like you has doubtless many friends."

The strange gentleman rose. With a look that Talleyrand never forgot, he retreated toward the door of the next chamber, saying: *"I am the only man born in the New World that can raise his hand and say I have not one friend—not one—in all America!"*

"Who are you?" cried the exile, as the strange man retreated. "Your name?"

"My name is *Benedict Arnold.*"

He was gone. Talleyrand sank into a chair, gasping the words —*"Arnold the Traitor!"*

Thus he wandered over the earth, another Cain, with the murderer's mark upon his brow. We cannot doubt that he died friendless, and that the memory of his treachery to his native land gnawed like a cancer at his heart, murmuring: "True to your country, what might you not have been, O *Arnold the Traitor!"*

•

MY NATIVE LAND

Sir Walter Scott

> Breathes there the man, with soul so dead,
> Who never to himself hath said,
>   This is my own, my native land?
> Whose heart hath ne'er within him burned,
> As home his footsteps he hath turned
>   From wandering on a foreign strand?
> If such there breathe, go, mark him well;
> For him no minstrel raptures swell;
> High though his titles, proud his name,
> Boundless his wealth as wish can claim—

Despite those titles, power, and pelf,
The wretch, concentered all in self,
Living, shall forfeit far renown,
And, doubly dying, shall go down
To the vile dust from whence he sprung,
Unwept, unhonored, and unsung.

•

TARPEIA

Retold by Sara Cone Bryant

Here is another famous story of treason. This ancient Roman legend reminds us that traitors usually act for one reason: greed. This legend was used to explain the name of a famous cliff overhanging Rome called the Tarpeian Rock, from which traitors were thrown.

There was once a girl named Tarpeia, whose father was guard of the outer gate of the citadel of Rome. It was a time of war—the Sabines were besieging the city. Their camp was close outside the city wall.

Tarpeia used to see the Sabine soldiers when she went to draw water from the public well, for that was outside the gate. And sometimes she stayed about and let the strange men talk with her, because she liked to look at their bright silver ornaments. The Sabine soldiers wore heavy silver rings and bracelets on their left arms—some wore as many as four or five.

The soldiers knew she was the daughter of the keeper of the citadel, and they saw that she had greedy eyes for their ornaments. So day by day they talked with her, and showed her their silver rings, and tempted her. And at last Tarpeia made a bargain, to betray her city to them. She said she would unlock the great gate and let them in, *if they would give her what they wore on their left arms.*

The night came. When it was perfectly dark and still, Tarpeia stole from her bed, took the great key from its place, and silently unlocked the gate which protected the city. Outside, in the dark, stood the soldiers of the enemy, waiting. As she opened the gate, the long shadowy files pressed forward silently, and the Sabines entered the citadel.

As the first man came inside, Tarpeia stretched forth her hand for her price. The soldier lifted high his left arm. "Take thy reward!" he said, and as he spoke he hurled upon her that which he wore upon it. Down upon her head crashed—not the silver rings of the soldier, but the great brass shield he carried in battle!

She sank beneath it, to the ground.

"Take thy reward," said the next, and his shield rang against the first.

"Thy reward," said the next—and the next—and the next— and the next; every man wore his shield on his left arm.

So Tarpeia lay buried beneath the reward she had claimed, and the Sabines marched past her dead body, into the city she had betrayed.

•

The Man Who Dined on Turnips

The French writer La Rochefoucauld noted that "more men are guilty of treachery through weakness than through any studied design to betray." Here is a man who strengthened himself against temptation and demonstrated that self-discipline is one proof against the old adage that power corrupts. Manius Curius, who lived in the early part of the third century B.C., was a famous example of a life lived according to steadfast Roman virtue.

In ancient Rome there lived a consul named Manius Curius. He was a peerless general in time of war, and a great statesman in time of peace. Yet he lived in a little cottage. His food and clothing were plain, his possessions few, his needs simple.

His honor shined like the richest jewel.

One time the Samnites, enemies of Rome, were planning to make war. In secret they sent ambassadors to Manius Curius to persuade him to stay away from the Roman army.

The ambassadors found him in his cottage, sitting in the chimney corner peeling turnips for his supper. They laid gold at his feet, hoping to tempt their foe.

Manius Curius smiled when he saw their offers.

"Do you think a man who is content with turnips for dinner has any need for gold?" he asked. "I think it would be better to conquer the Samnites than take their bribes."

The ambassadors left looking foolish.

For many years afterward, the Romans pointed to the little hut and said: "There is the cottage that belonged to the consul who dined on turnips."

•

GOOD KING WENCESLAS

Saint Wencelas was a tenth-century duke of Bohemia. This old carol about him tells a beautiful legend that has come down to us from the Middle Ages. The incident is said to have taken place on St. Stephen's Day, the day after Christmas. Wenceslas was standing at his castle window when he saw a figure struggling through the snow. The king and his young page set out to aid the man, but the boy's courage began to fail in the fierce blizzard. Wenceslas gently told him to walk close behind him, and it was then that the miracle occurred: The page found that green grass sprang up in the kindhearted monarch's footprints, and that as long as he placed his feet in the track, he seemed to be walking in the warmth of a summer's afternoon.

Good leaders bring others along in their footsteps, teaching by example.

Good King Wenceslas looked out
　On the Feast of Stephen,
When the snow lay round about,
　Deep, and crisp, and even.
Brightly shone the moon that night,
　Though the frost was cruel,
When a poor man came in sight,
　Gath'ring winter fuel.

"Hither, page, and stand by me,
    If thou know'st it, telling,
Yonder peasant, who is he?
    Where and what his dwelling?"
"Sire, he lives a good league hence,
    Underneath the mountain;
Right against the forest fence,
    By Saint Agnes' fountain."

"Bring me flesh, and bring me wine,
    Bring me pine-logs hither:
Thou and I will see him dine,
    When we bear them thither."
Page and monarch forth they went,
    Forth they went together;
Through the rude wind's wild lament
    And the bitter weather.

"Sire, the night is darker now,
    And the wind blows stronger;
Fails my heart, I know not how,
    I can go no longer."
"Mark my footsteps, my good page;
    Tread thou in them boldly:
Thou shalt find the winter's rage
    Freeze thy blood less coldly."

In his master's steps he trod,
    Where the snow lay dinted;
Heat was in the very sod
    Which the saint had printed.
Therefore, Christian man, be sure,
    Wealth or rank possessing,
Ye who now will bless the poor,
    Shall yourselves find blessing.

•

THE SLEEPING SENTINEL

Adapted from Albert Blaisdell
and Francis Ball

This story, based on an incident that occurred early in the Civil War, entered the corpus of Lincoln lore when it was set to verse and read in the U.S. Senate chamber before an audience that included President Lincoln himself. It reminds us that good leaders set high but reasonable expectations for those who would follow.

On a rainy morning in September 1861, during the first year of the Civil War, a group of Union soldiers came to the White House to plead for the life of one of their friends. They were granted an audience with President Lincoln himself, and in faltering words they told why they had come.

The soldiers were part of the 3rd Vermont Regiment, which was made up mostly of farm boys from the Green Mountains. Since their arrival in Washington they had been stationed at Chain Bridge, a few miles above the city. The bridge was of vital importance since Confederate forces occupied the hills on the opposite side of the Potomac River. The soldiers' orders were strict: Any sentinel caught sleeping at his post was to be shot within twenty-four hours.

According to the soldiers' story, a boy named William Scott had enlisted in Company K. He had been on duty one night, and the following night had taken the place of a comrade too sick to stand guard. The third night he had been called out on guard duty yet again. The young fellow could not keep awake for three nights in a row. When the relief guard came around, he was found asleep. Arrested, tried, and found guilty, he was sentenced to be shot.

"William Scott, sir, is as brave a soldier as there is in your army," the Green Mountain Boys told Lincoln. "He is no coward. It's not right to shoot him like a traitor and bury him like a dog."

Later in the day President Lincoln rode from the White House in the direction of Chain Bridge. Within a day or so the newspapers reported that a soldier sentenced to death for sleeping at his post had been pardoned by the president, and had returned to his regiment.

It was a long time before Scott would speak of his interview with President Lincoln. One day he told a comrade the whole story.

"I knew the president at once," he said, "by a Lincoln medal I had long worn. I was scared at first, for I had never talked with a great man before. He asked me all about the folks at home, my brothers and sisters, and where I went to school, and how I liked it. Then he asked me about my mother. I showed him her picture. He said that if he were in my place he would try to make a fond mother happy, and never cause her a sorrow or a tear.

" 'My boy,' he said, 'you are not going to be shot. You are going back to your regiment. I have been put to a good deal of trouble on your account. Now what I want to know is how you are going to pay me back. My bill is a large one, and there is only one man in all the world who can pay it. His name is William Scott. If from this day you will promise to do your whole duty as a soldier, then the debt will be paid. Will you make that promise and try to keep it?' "

Gladly the young Vermont soldier made the promise, and well did he keep it. From that day William Scott became a model man of his regiment. He was never absent from a roll call. He was always on hand if there was any hard work to do. He worked nights in the hospital, nursing the sick and wounded, because it trained him to keep awake. He made a record for himself on picket duty, and distinguished himself as a scout.

Sometime after this the 3rd Vermont went into one of its many hard battles. They were ordered to attack the Confederate lines, and William Scott fell in the enemy volley.

His comrades caught him up, carried him bleeding and dying from the field, and laid him on a cot.

"Tell the president I have tried to be a good soldier, and true to the flag," he said.

Then, making a last effort, with his dying breath he prayed for Abraham Lincoln.

Company K buried William Scott in a grove just in the rear of the camp, at the foot of a big oak tree. Deep into the oak they cut the initials "W.S." and under it the words "A Brave Soldier."

•

CHARLEMAGNE AND THE
ROBBER KNIGHT

Adapted from a retelling by Marie Frary
and Charles Stebbins

In this old German legend we find true force of character—the
kind that leads by example, pulling others upward. Charlemagne
(742–814), also known as Charles the First, king of France and
emperor of the Holy Roman Empire, established a cultural revival
that laid the foundation of European civilization in the late Middle
Ages.

Once the great King Charlemagne built a magnificent palace
on the river Rhine, where he could watch the waters slip past, and
gaze on the distant hills, and hunt with his friends in the deep,
green forests. When the castle was completed he went to visit it.
The very first night he slept there, an angel appeared in his dreams.
It stood by his bed, clothed in splendid light, and said: "Arise, good
Emperor. Arise, go forth secretly, and steal."

Charlemagne woke, much puzzled at the dream. It seemed
impossible that an emperor should be ordered to become a robber.
So he lay down and went back to sleep.

But the angel reappeared again. "Arise, Emperor," it said. "Go
forth, and steal from your own people."

Again Charlemagne woke, aghast at the command. He still
could not believe such an order could come from an angel, so he
did not move. Once more the angel appeared by the side of his
bed. It stretched forth its hand, saying: "Arise! Do not tarry. Go into
the forest and steal, or repent forever."

Charlemagne rose and passed quietly through the halls of his
castle. His knights were fast asleep. He went to his stable, saddled
his horse, armed himself, and rode silently into the depths of the
forest.

As he was going along the dark way thoughtfully, he heard
someone approaching, and he soon perceived it was a knight clad
in black armor. Charlemagne could think of no good reason why a
knight should be riding at such an hour, so he challenged the man.

"Where are you riding, and upon what mission, at this time of the night?" he demanded.

The knight did not answer, but put spurs to his horse and charged the Emperor. Seeing his movement, the Emperor did likewise, and the two met with a violent shock. Both were unhorsed, and in the hand-to-hand conflict which followed, the Emperor got the better of the unknown knight and brought him to the ground. With his sword at the stranger's throat, he demanded his name.

"I am Elbegast," he replied, "the robber knight, who has committed many a bold deed. You are the first who has had the power to overcome me."

"Arise," said the Emperor, without revealing who he was, "and come with me. I am on a mission like thine own."

Without hesitating, the robber knight joined his conqueror. They rode through the forest until they reached a stately house. It was the home of Arnot, one of the Emperor's most trusted ministers.

Elbegast was not long in gaining entrance. Bidding his companion to wait for him outside, he stole noiselessly into the house.

As he approached the minister's bedroom, the sound of voices in earnest conversation came to his ears. He listened, and heard Arnot disclose to his wife a plan for the murder of the Emperor himself on the following day.

Forgetting his purpose for breaking into the house, the knight made his way hastily back to his companion, and begged him to go at once to Charlemagne and inform him of the coming danger.

"Why not go yourself and tell him?" asked the Emperor.

Elbegast hung his head.

"I would gladly do it, if I could. A man like me, who has committed evil deeds, dares not seek out the Emperor. I would risk imprisonment to save his life, but it would do no good—the Emperor would scarcely believe a man with my reputation. But I tell you this: Whatever I have done, I hold great admiration for the man who has never been conquered in battle, and who has always worked for the good of his people. He rules wisely and kindly, and I would keep him from harm."

Then Charlemagne and Elbegast parted, one returning to his stronghold in the mountains and the other retracing his steps slowly and thoughtfully to his palace.

On the morrow Arnot and his conspirators attempted to carry out their plans, but the Emperor was ready for them. As they came riding into the castle courtyard, the gates slammed shut behind them, and a dozen guards sprang forth.

"What kind of greeting is this for someone who has come to pay his respects to his emperor?" Arnot demanded, with pretended indignation.

"What kind of greeting do you bring, when you come to pay your respects this way?" asked one of the guards. As he spoke, he tore the clothes of Arnot and his companions, disclosing their hidden daggers.

Charlemagne took all of them into custody, and they confessed their plot against him.

The Emperor then set his mind upon Elbegast. He sent a messenger to him, requesting him to come to the palace.

"I, Charlemagne, Emperor of Germany," his message ran, "would speak privately with Elbegast, the robber knight, and promise him safe conduct to and from my castle."

Elbegast rode to the palace and was admitted to the private council chamber. Soon a man entered, clad in armor, and Elbegast recognized the knight who had been his companion the night before.

"Elbegast," said Charlemagne, "you recognize me and yet you do not know me."

Then Charlemagne raised his visor, and the robber knight saw that he was standing in the presence of the Emperor.

"You have done wrong in the past," said Charlemagne. "But now you have done me faithful duty. Here is your chance to begin your life anew. I offer you a place among my retainers. A man of your courage and loyalty is worthy of a place in the Emperor's service."

Elbegast was so moved that he could hardly speak. Charlemagne was the only man who had ever been able to defeat him in battle, and for this he admired him greatly. But more than this, he stood in awe of the Emperor's reputation for kindness and wisdom. And so Elbegast, the robber knight, was disarmed by Charlemagne's own character. He willingly forsook his evil life in the forest and became a devoted friend to the end of his days.

And in commemoration of the angel's visit, which had caused him to find this loyal knight, Charlemagne named his new castle Ingelheim, meaning "angel's home."

•

GEORGE PICKETT'S FRIEND

Charles W. Moores

**Great people are capable of small acts of friendship and kindness.
Abraham Lincoln is famous for moments like this one. His friend
George Pickett led the Confederate troops that made the famous
attack at Gettysburg in 1863, now known as Pickett's Charge.**

George Pickett, who had known Lincoln in Illinois, years before, joined the Southern army, and by his conspicuous bravery and
ability had become one of the great generals of the Confederacy.
Toward the close of the war, when a large part of Virginia had
fallen into the possession of the Union army, the President called at
General Pickett's Virginia home.

The general's wife, with her baby on her arm, met him at the
door. She herself has told the story for us.

" 'Is this George Pickett's home?' he asked.

"With all the courage and dignity I could muster, I replied:
'Yes, and I am his wife, and this is his baby.'

" 'I am Abraham Lincoln.'

" 'The President!' I gasped. I had never seen him, but I knew
the intense love and reverence with which my soldier always spoke
of him.

"The stranger shook his head and replied: 'No; Abraham Lincoln, George's old friend.'

"The baby pushed away from me and reached out his hands to
Mr. Lincoln, who took him in his arms. As he did so an expression
of rapt, almost divine tenderness and love lighted up the sad face.
It was a look that I have never seen on any other face. The baby
opened his mouth wide and insisted upon giving his father's friend
a dewy kiss.

"As Mr. Lincoln gave the little one back to me he said: 'Tell
your father, the rascal, that I forgive him for the sake of your bright
eyes.' "

•

MAN ENOUGH FOR THE JOB
Retold by Ella Lyman Cabot

Great men do not disdain small duties.

An incident is told of the first American war, about an officer who set his men to fell some trees which were needed to make a bridge. There were not nearly enough men, and work was getting on very slowly. Up rode a commanding-looking man and spoke to the officer in charge, who was urging on his men but doing nothing himself. "You haven't enough men for the job, have you?"

"No, sir. we need some help."

"Why don't you lend a hand yourself?" asked the man on horseback.

"Me, sir? Why, I am a corporal," replied the officer, looking rather affronted at the suggestion.

"Ah, true," quietly replied the other, and getting off his horse he labored with the men until the job was done. Then he mounted again, and as he rode off he said to the officer, "Corporal, the next time you have a job to put through and too few men to do it you had better send for the Commander-in-Chief, and I will come again."

It was General Washington.

•

THE MAN WHO WOULD NOT DRINK ALONE
Adapted from a retelling by Rosalie Kaufman

Loyalty is a two-way street; sharing hardship is the mark of a loyal leader. The ancient historian Plutarch recounts this tale about Alexander the Great (356–323 B.C.).

Alexander the Great was leading his army homeward after his great victory against Porus in India. The country through which they now marched was bare and desert, and his army suffered dreadfully from heat, hunger, and, most of all, thirst. The soldiers' lips cracked and their throats burned from want of water, and many were ready to lie down and give up.

About noon one day the army met a party of Greek travelers. They were on mules, and carried with them a few vessels filled with water. One of them, seeing the king almost choking from thirst, filled a helmet and offered it to him.

Alexander took it into his hands, then looked around at the faces of his suffering soldiers, who craved refreshment just as much as he did.

"Take it away," he said, "for if I drink alone, the rest will be out of heart, and you have not enough for all."

So he handed the water back without touching a drop of it. And the soldiers, cheering their king, leaped to their feet, and demanded to be led forward.

•

BROTHERHOOD OF LONG AGO

Fanny E. Coe

Here is another story of perseverance winning the day because a leader knew how to help shoulder the load. This act of encouragement and compassion by the Marquis de Lafayette (1757–1834) reminds us of the story of Saint Martin in Chapter 4.

More than two hundred years ago, when our country was fighting against England, there came to help us a young French nobleman named Lafayette. Although only a boy of nineteen years, he had run away from his country because he longed to fight for liberty. He said that he came to learn, not to teach, and, from the first, he took George Washington for an ideal.

Lafayette and Washington became lifelong friends. Lafayette named his son for Washington and, on his return to America in 1787, he paid a delightful visit to Washington at Mount Vernon. He promised soon to return, but almost forty years passed by before he kept his word.

He came at last, in 1824, a bent old man, with a heart loyal as ever to his adopted country. He visited every state and territory in the Union and was welcomed everywhere with the warmest enthusiasm. Receptions, dinner parties, and balls followed each other in brilliant succession, always with Lafayette the chief figure. The welcome of the people was voiced in a song of the time:

> "We bow not the neck,
> We bend not the knee,
> But our hearts, Lafayette,
> We surrender to thee."

The following incident occurred during the visit of 1824.

A brilliant reception was under way. A slowly moving line of stately guests passed by the noble old marquis, who greeted each with courtly grace. Presently there approached an old soldier clad in a worn Continental uniform. In his hand was an ancient musket, and across his shoulder was thrown a small blanket, or rather a piece of blanket. On reaching the marquis, the veteran drew himself up in the stiff fashion of the old-time drill and gave the military salute. As Lafayette returned the salute, tears sprang to his eyes. The tattered uniform, the ancient flintlock, the silver-haired veteran, even older than himself, recalled the dear past.

"Do you know me?" asked the soldier. Lafayette's manner had led him to think himself personally remembered.

"Indeed, I cannot say that I do," was the frank reply.

"Do you remember the frosts and snows of Valley Forge?"

"I shall never forget them," answered Lafayette.

"One bitter night, General Lafayette, you were going the rounds at Valley Forge. You came upon a sentry in thin clothing and without stockings. He was slowly freezing to death. You took his musket, saying, 'Go to my hut. There you will find stockings, a blanket, and a fire. After warming yourself, bring the blanket to me. Meanwhile I will keep guard.'

"The soldier obeyed directions. When he returned to his post, you, General Lafayette, cut the blanket in two. One half you kept, the other you presented to the sentry. Here, General, is one half of that blanket, for I am the sentry whose life you saved."

•

THE LADY WITH THE LAMP

Elmer Adams and Warren Foster

Born in 1820 to wealthy parents, Florence Nightingale spent her
childhood on comfortable family estates in England. When she
was sixteen years old, she thought she heard the voice of God
informing her that she had a specific mission in life. For the next
few years she spent more and more of her time studying public
health and reforms to aid the suffering. In 1850, against her family's wishes, she attended a training school for nurses, and at age
thirty-three she became superintendent of a women's hospital in
London.

In 1854, when England and France went to war with Russia
in the Crimea, the British people grew outraged over reports of
sick and wounded soldiers dying in disgraceful conditions. At the
appeal of the minister of war, Nightingale traveled to Scutari,
Turkey, to take charge of the military hospital there. She stepped
ashore to discover scores of maimed troops just arrived from the
Battle of Balaklava, where the disastrous Charge of the Light Brigade had occurred. The story of how this heroine rescued Scutari
and founded the modern nursing profession is the stuff of legend.
It was not only Florence Nightingale's remarkable organizational
and administrative skills that saved the day. It was the force of
her remarkable character—her compassion, her courage, her
perseverance.

The Crimean War was in progress, France and England being
allied to defend Turkey against Russian aggression. The British army
had sailed to a strange climate with shamefully poor commissary
and medical staffs. The weather was stormy and the soldiers had
little shelter against it. Said a correspondent of the *London Times,*
"It is now pouring rain, the skies are black as ink, the wind is
howling over the staggering tents, the trenches are turned into
dikes; in the tents the water is sometimes a foot deep; our men
have not either warm or waterproof clothing; they are out for
twelve hours at a time in the trenches"—and so on without end.

Plenty of food and clothing had been shipped from England,

but they never reached their destination. Some vessels were delayed; in some the stores were packed at the bottom of the hold and could not be raised; some hove in with the wrong goods at the wrong port—and, on one, the consignment of boots proved to be all for the left foot! But the most criminal point of mismanagement was this: food, clothing and medicine might be stored in a warehouse within easy reach of the army, but the official with authority to deal them out would be absent, and so stringent were the army rules that no one dared so much as point at them! The rigid system was infinitely worse than no system. And the soldiers were starving in the midst of plenty, and freezing under the shadow of mountains of good woolen clothing.

Now, to come at once to the worst, imagine these conditions transferred to the military hospitals. In the great Barrack Hospital at Scutari lay two thousand sorely wounded men, and hundreds more were coming in every day. The wards were crowded to twice their capacity—the sick lay side by side on mattresses that touched each other. The floors and walls and ceilings were wet and filthy. There was no ventilation. Rats and vermin swarmed everywhere. The men lay "in their uniforms, stiff with gore and covered with filth to a degree and of a kind no one could write about." It was a "dreadful den of dirt, pestilence, and death."

It is difficult to imagine a scene of worse disorder and misery. The proportion of deaths to the whole army, from disease alone—malaria and cholera—was sixty percent. Seventy died in the hospital in one night. There was danger that the entire army would be wiped out—most of it without ever receiving a scratch from the enemy's weapons.

It was in this extremity that the British nation appealed to Florence Nightingale to save the sick and wounded men—an army of twenty-eight thousand as helpless as children before the ravages of disease—and to save the war. The minister of war requested her to organize a band of nurses for Scutari and gave her power to draw upon the government to any extent.

Miss Nightingale at the time was thirty-four years old. An acquaintance described her thus: "Simple, intellectual, sweet, full of love and benevolence, she is a fascinating and perfect woman. She is tall and pale. Her face is exceedingly lovely. But better than all is the soul's glory that shines through every feature so exultingly. Nothing can be sweeter than her smile. It is like a sunny day in summer."

Within six days from the time she accepted the post, Miss

Nightingale had selected thirty-eight nurses, and departed for the seat of war. She arrived at Scutari November 4, 1854, and walked the length of the barracks, viewing her two miles of patients. And next day before she could form any plans, the fresh victims of another battle began to arrive. There was not space for them within the walls and hundreds had to repose, with what comfort they could, in the mud outside. One of the nurses wrote, "Many died immediately after being brought in—their moans would pierce the heart—and the look of agony on those poor dying faces will never leave my heart."

But the nurse did not hesitate. She ordered the patients brought in, and directed where to lay them, and what attention they should have. She was up and around twenty hours that day, and as many the next, until a place had been found for every man, even in the corridors and on the landings of the stair. As leader of the nurses she might have confined herself to administrative tasks—of which there were enough for any woman—and stayed in the office. But no. She shrank from the sight of no operation. Many men, indeed, whose cases the surgeons thought hopeless, she nursed back to health. A visitor saw her one morning at two o'clock at the bedside of a dying soldier, lamp in hand. She was writing down his last message to the home folks; and for them, too, she took in charge his watch and trinkets—and then soothed him in his last moments. And this was but one case in thousands. "She is a ministering angel, without any exaggeration, in these hospitals," wrote a correspondent of the *London Times,* "and as the slender form glides quietly along each corridor, every poor fellow's face softens with gratitude at the sight of her. When all the medical officers have retired for the night, and silence and darkness have settled down upon the miles of prostrate sick, she may be observed alone, with lamp in hand, making her solitary rounds."

In a place like Scutari, however, this kind of feminine tenderness alone would avail little. Science was needed, the most perfect skill in scientific nursing. The windows were few, and the few were mostly locked; and where one was opened the odors of decaying animals came in to pollute still more the foul air of the wards.

The food for the whole hospital—for those sick of fever, cholera, wounds, and what not, as well as for those in health—was cooked, like an "Irish stew," in big kettles. Vegetables and meats were dumped in together, and when anyone felt hungry he could dip for himself. Naturally some got food overdone, and some got it raw; the luckiest got a mess that was scarcely palatable; and the sick could generally not eat at all. As for other matters, it has been shown how unclean the barrack wards were, how "only seven shirts" had been laundered in all those wretched weeks, and how the infected bed linen of all classes of patients was thrown, unsorted, into one general wash.

But Florence Nightingale had spent twelve years in the hospitals of Europe to learn how to conquer just such situations as this. She had the waste and pollution outside the walls cleared away. Then she threw up the windows, and set a carpenter to make more. Within ten days she had established a diet kitchen and was feeding the men each on the food his particular case demanded. She set up a laundry, too, where the garments of the sick could be cleansed in a sanitary way. All this was the easier to do because with wise foresight she had brought the necessary articles with her on the *Victus* from England. The ship gave up chicken, jelly, and all manner of delicacies; and, on a single day, "a thousand shirts, besides other clothing." In two weeks that "dreadful den of dirt, pestilence, and death" had vanished; and in its place stood a building, light and well aired throughout, where patients lay on spotless cots, ate appetizing food from clean dishes, had their baths and their medicine at regular intervals, and never for an hour lacked any attention that would help their recovery.

But after all is said of Florence Nightingale's sympathy and her science, she owed her final triumph in the Crimea to a rarer talent, that of tactful organizing and executive power. Why was she not tethered by the system and the red tape that rendered ineffectual the best efforts of the medical men? Most things needful were in store not far from the barracks hospital. But the regular physicians could not get at them. Why could she?

In the first place she had tact enough not to offend the system. The minister of war had warned her, "A number of sentimental, enthusiastic ladies turned loose into the hospital at Scutari would probably after a few days be '*mises à la porte*' by those whose business they would interrupt and whose authority they would dispute." Florence Nightingale did not at first interrupt or dispute anybody. She began by doing the neglected minor things, the things that no one else had time for. She opened windows. She scrubbed floors and walls. She laundered shirts. She peeled potatoes and boiled soup. She bathed the patients, dosed them with medicine while the worn-out surgeons were asleep, read to them, and wrote letters for them. In these activities she asked not even supplies from the system, but procured them from her own ship.

The hidebound officials were even then slow to concur. Perhaps they were jealous to see their own incompetence exposed. And there was one case—just one—where she came to blows with them. The hospital inmates were in desperate want, and the articles for their relief were nearby in a warehouse, but the stores could not be disturbed until after inspection. Miss Nightingale tried to hasten the inspection. Failing of that, she tried to get them distributed without inspection. That also failed. "My soldiers are dying," she said. "I must have those stores." Whereupon, she called two soldiers, marched them to the warehouse, and bade them burst open the doors!

That was the kind of firm hand she could use. More often, though, she attained her ends in a peaceful way. Only a little feminine tact was necessary to bring together the dilatory members of a board and get them to unlock a storehouse. She was soon able to lay her hands on an abundance of anything the situation demanded. Then, besides her own small band of nurses, a large number of orderlies and common soldiers were, after a time, detailed to work under her direction. "Never," she says, "came from them one word or one look which a gentleman would not have used;" and many of them became attached to her with an almost slavish affection.

And the result of her efforts justified this faith. When she arrived the death rate was sixty percent. She reduced it in a few weeks to one percent. Nine of her nurses died on duty; others were invalided home; she herself was long fever sick and near to death. But for two years she battled against disease, always in a winning fight. She conquered disease. And it is not too much to say that she conquered the Russian army, and saved the war for the allies. No wonder England welcomed her home as one of the greatest heroines in all its history.

•

SANTA FILOMENA

Henry Wadsworth Longfellow

Florence Nightingale was born in and named after the city of Florence, Italy. "Santa Filomena" is Italian for "Saint Nightingale."

Whene'er a noble deed is wrought,
Whene'er is spoken a noble thought,
    Our hearts, in glad surprise,
    To higher levels rise.

The tidal wave of deeper souls
Into our inmost being rolls,
    And lifts us unawares
    Out of all meaner cares.

Honor to those whose words or deeds
Thus help us in our daily needs,
    And by their overflow
    Raise us from what is low!

Thus thought I, as by night I read
Of the great army of the dead,
    The trenches cold and damp,
    The starved and frozen camp—

The wounded from the battle-plain,
In dreary hospitals of pain,
    The cheerless corridors,
    The cold and stony floors.

Lo! in that house of misery
A lady with a lamp I see
    Pass through the glimmering gloom,
    And flit from room to room.

And slow, as in a dream of bliss,
The speechless sufferer turns to kiss
    Her shadow, as it falls
    Upon the darkening walls.

As if a door in heaven should be
Opened and then closed suddenly,
    The vision came and went,
    The light shone and was spent.

On England's annals, through the long
Hereafter of her speech and song,
 That light its rays shall cast
 From portals of the past.

A Lady with a Lamp shall stand
In the great history of the land,
 A noble type of good,
 Heroic womanhood.

Not even shall be wanting here
The palm, the lily, and the spear,
 The symbols that of yore
 Saint Filomena bore.

•

THE BIRDS WHO BEFRIENDED A KING

*Adapted from a retelling
by Constance Armfield*

"And men came from all peoples to hear the wisdom of Solomon," the first book of Kings in the Bible tells us. No leader in history has been more renowned for learning and judgment than the tenth-century B.C. ruler of Israel and Judah. Every boy or girl who hopes someday to lead a company, community, or country would do well to learn the lesson Solomon offers in the next two stories: To lead is to serve.

The hoopoes in the story below are jay-sized birds living in Africa, in India, and in warm, dry regions of southern Europe. Because of its striking plumage, including a showy crown of feathers, the hoopoe is a favorite bird of legend and folklore.

Once the great King Solomon was journeying in the desert. Across the sand the king's caravan made its way, the camels' embroidered saddle cloths as bright as flowers, and their jeweled bridles flashing as brightly as the sun itself. But the heat smote down on the king's head, and Solomon yearned for shade. As if in answer to his longing, who should appear but a flock of Hoopoes? Being curious by nature, they circled around until they reached the king's camel and kept just overhead, so that they might watch this most famous of all monarchs and perhaps overhear some word of wisdom.

Thus the little birds cast a grateful shadow over the king for his whole journey. And richly repaid they were. For Solomon, who was always polite to the humblest creature in his kingdom, conversed freely with them the whole time, bestowing upon them many wise words. When they reached his palace, he thanked them for providing the shade, and asked what he could do in return.

Now the Hoopoes had begun their conversation with Solomon modestly enough; in fact, they had been very surprised that he had spoken to them at all. But he had questioned them so kindly about their way of living, and their likes and preferences and relations, that they lost their fear of him. They came into his wonderful palace and saw all the servants in their shining robes standing behind the king's throne, and waiting on his table, and lining the great courtyard. They beheld the walls of ivory inlaid with gold, and the golden lions guarding the steps, and the white peacocks on their silver terraces. And it quite turned the little birds' heads to think they had journeyed right across the desert with the owner of all these riches.

So instead of answering Solomon with thanks on their part and telling him his words of wisdom were rich reward for any shelter they had given, the Hoopoes begged leave to consult together and withdrew to the palace roof, where they discussed what they would ask for.

Finally they decided they would like golden crowns such as the king himself wore; then they could return to the other birds and reign over them. At once the little birds flew down with a rush and made their request to the king as he walked in his wonderful garden.

"What the king has said, the king has said," Solomon replied. "The gift you desire shall be granted. Yet, because you rendered me true service, when you wish to get rid of your crowns, you may return and exchange them for wisdom."

"Nay, King," said the Hoopoes. "Well we know that wisdom has brought you great renown, but no one would bow down to you or give attention to your words, unless you wore your golden crown. We shall be able to repeat your wise words profitably now, for all will listen when they see gold crowns on our heads, too."

"All the same, return to me without fear or shame, if your crowns do not satisfy," said King Solomon kindly. Then he ordered his goldsmiths to supply the Hoopoes with crowns of the finest gold. Off flew the silly birds, with the shining crowns upon their heads, prouder than peacocks and chattering more loudly than parrots.

They could scarcely wait to get back to their friends and hear their exclamations. But when the Hoopoes announced they were now Kings of the Bird World, their friends only laughed and said they were quite satisfied with Solomon, and he was the only king they wished or needed. Then they drove the Hoopoes from the trees, for their golden crowns were always catching in the branches, and the other birds grew tired of freeing them. But the Hoopoes decided the other birds were only jealous and, rather flattered, gathered around the pools so they could admire themselves in the water.

Very soon people began to notice the antics of the silly little things as they strutted up and down, cocking their heads first this way, then that. Finally a man caught one and discovered the wonderful gold crown it wore. He hurried off to a goldsmith, who gave him a high price for it. The man rushed back to the pool and laid snares for the Hoopoes, who were so taken up with admiring themselves that they walked straight into the traps.

Then came the saddest time for the Hoopoes. Everyone began to hunt them. The poor little birds could not go to the wells and the pools, for they were thick with nets. They could not go into the gardens, for fowlers lurked behind the flowers. They could not fly up onto the housetops, for even there the people had set traps for them. There was not a spot on earth where they could rest. At last the wretched little birds flew back to the palace and waited until they beheld the great King Solomon coming along his terrace, listening to his singers as they performed in the cool of the evening.

"O king," they said, "we have found that golden crowns are vanity. We know not what you do to keep yourself from being chased about and hunted, and so we have come to ask you to remove ours from us."

"Beloved Hoopoes," said the king, "a crown that people are expected to bow down to always sits heavy on the head, and a crown that excites envy is a net for the feet. The only crown that can be worn with comfort is the crown of service, and that crown should spring up naturally so that no one takes any particular notice of it."

"Give us that crown of service, O wise king," said the poor little Hoopoes very humbly, for they now wanted nothing better than to live without notice.

"May it shelter you even as it sheltered me," said the great king; and on their heads, the Hoopoes beheld crowns of feathers. But with these crowns came quite a new feeling to the Hoopoes. They no longer wished to rule, but to serve.

•

KING SOLOMON AND THE ANTS
John Greenleaf Whittier

This poem is based on an old story found in the Koran, the sacred book of Islam.

Out from Jerusalem
    The king rode with his great
    War chiefs and lords of state,
And Sheba's queen with them.

Proud in the Syrian sun,
    In gold and purple sheen,
    The dusky Ethiop queen
Smiled on King Solomon.

Wisest of men, he knew
    The languages of all
    The creatures great or small
That trod the earth or flew.

Across an ant-hill led
    The king's path, and he heard
    Its small folk, and their word
He thus interpreted:

"Here comes the king men greet
    As wise and good and just,
    To crush us in the dust
Under his heedless feet."

The great king bowed his head,
  And saw the wide surprise
  Of the Queen of Sheba's eyes
As he told her what they said.

"O king!" she whispered sweet,
  "Too happy fate have they
  Who perish in thy way
Beneath thy gracious feet!

"Thou of the God-lent crown,
  Shall these vile creatures dare
  Murmur against thee where
The knees of kings kneel down?"

"Nay," Solomon replied,
  "The wise and strong should seek
  The welfare of the weak;"
And turned his horse aside.

His train, with quick alarm,
  Curved with their leader round
  The ant-hill's peopled mound,
And left it free from harm.

The jeweled head bent low;
  "O king!" she said, "henceforth
  The secret of thy worth
And wisdom well I know.

"Happy must be the State
  Whose ruler heedeth more
  The murmurs of the poor
Than flatteries of the great."

•

A PIONEER OF COMPASSION

Francis T. Miller

Matthew Arnold wrote that "the world is forwarded by having its attention fixed on the best things." Dorothea Dix (1802–1887) lived to fix the world's attention on her crusade to help the suffering, and so led civilization forward. Here is leadership and citizenship born of compassion.

A girl of fourteen years, she found herself facing one of the world's greatest problems—self-support. In addition, she must also support two younger brothers.

"I know I can earn a living," she said. "I can teach the children who are younger than I. I will open a private school."

The child schoolteacher stood before her little pupils with a resoluteness of purpose that inspired them. To give herself an older appearance, she lengthened her skirts and her sleeves. Although scarcely older than the children she taught, her seriousness commanded their respect and affection.

At nineteen, this child teacher was the principal of a boarding school for the daughters of many prominent men of the time. Her strong moral influence had brought her reputation and success.

The early burdens of life wore upon her. Her blue eyes, their warmth chilled by gray, as though sorrow had early crept into her sunny skies, showed failing health, and those about her became greatly worried.

"I do not fear to die," she said, "but I cannot bear the thought of leaving my little brothers. While I live," she added, "I will make myself useful to humanity."

As she looked about her, she found many who were in deeper trouble than herself, some of them with burdens almost too great to bear. She found that there were afflictions in the world as great as physical sickness. There was mental sickness—as hideous in its torment and suffering as any bodily disease.

It was in the year 1841. This young woman was visiting the unfortunate in the House of Correction at East Cambridge, in Massachusetts, when the moans of the wretched came to her ears. Imprisoned in a room, in filth and unspeakable horror, were human beings who had lost their reason, many of them through way-wardness and dissipation. Her young heart went out in compassion for them in their misery, and in that compassion burned the fires of justice.

"It is true that they have lost their reason," she admitted, "but they are human beings, they are our fellow men, and we must protect them."

"This is my mission in life," she decided, and with that decision, she began an investigation of the treatment of the mentally afflicted. She found that civilization looked upon the loss of reason as a curse, and upon its victims as wild beasts, to be chained and bound in irons. Her eyes rested upon sights which she did not know existed in a Christian world. She saw men and women in cages, closets, stalls, and pens. Sometimes they were naked. Often they were cruelly beaten into submission. The gentle voice of this woman cried out in protest.

Hostility and abuse were the response that came back to her.

"It is all humbug," declared the political leaders.

A legislator, after attacking her statements on the floor of the House, declared that he and some of his committee would go to her and refute her allegations. As they entered her home, they were met by the gentle face and voice of this woman.

"We came to inquire about these allegations against our institutions," the leader said coldly.

The woman, smiling, told him of her experiences. She described the misery and fearful sufferings that she had witnessed. As she appealed to the hearts of her visitors, the legislator, after sitting spellbound for an hour and a half, arose and stepping to her side, exclaimed: "Madam, I bid you good night. I do not want, for my part, to hear anything more. The others can stay if they wish to. *I am convinced.* You have conquered me out and out. If you'll come to the House and talk there as you've done here, no man who isn't a brute can withstand you. When a man's convinced, that's enough. The Lord bless you."

The heart of the nation was aroused. Thousands came to her support, while countless others denounced her. She became a political issue in Massachusetts, and the legislature, after a heated discussion, passed an appropriation to remove the insane from the jails to institutions where they could receive mental treatment.

The life work of the woman had now just begun. She went from Massachusetts to Rhode Island, and on and on until she had visited all the states east of the Rocky Mountains. Everywhere her eyes rested upon the same inhuman conditions that she had found in Massachusetts. In the treatment of its mental unfortunates, civilization had become savage. She visited the prisons and almshouses. Her appeals to humanity were overpowering. As she journeyed through the country, she wore a simple dress of plain gray for traveling, and appeared in severe black on public occasions, frequently wearing a shawl about her shoulders.

One day, while in Rhode Island, she went to see a millionaire who had no special fondness for benevolence. He tried to baffle her with commonplace generalities, which she met with kindness. At last, rising with commanding dignity, she announced the purpose of her interview.

The financier, hardened though he was by a life devoted to mere money-making, listened. Her low-voiced eloquence appealed to him.

"God will not hold us guiltless for the neglect of one of the least of His Creatures," she declared.

"But what would you have me do?" inquired the rich man.

"Give fifty thousand dollars toward a new asylum for the insane," she answered.

"I will do it," he replied.

Some months later this woman, now a broken-down invalid, weakened by her travels and labors, stood before Congress. For six years she pleaded with the government for better laws for the insane, and at last her wisdom and humanity conquered the hearts and minds of the statesmen.

It was 1854. A bill before Congress was for an appropriation of 12,225,000 acres of public lands—about 20,000 square miles—to be apportioned among the states for the care of the insane, allowing the odd 225,000 acres for the deaf. The bill swept the Senate by more than a two-thirds majority, and passed the House by a plurality of fourteen.

The woman wept with thanksgiving.

"I must resist the deep sympathies of my heart," said President Pierce, as he returned the bill to the Senate without his signature and bearing his veto.

The worn woman was crushed by this defeat, and she was taken across the seas to recover her lost energy and strength. But her life mission weighed upon her, and, immediately upon her arrival in Scotland, she began to work for the remodeling of its lunacy laws. Some officials resented the intrusion, and moved to oppose her. Refusing to give up, she turned toward London for help, and her efforts led Parliament to rise to the defense of mental sufferers and revise its laws on principles of Christian brotherhood.

The conquest of civilization by an invalid American woman was now well begun. When she entered Italy, in 1856, she found the prisons and hospitals of ancient Rome in confusion and disorder. A few days later she stood before Pope Pius IX, and appealed to his beneficence. He expressed himself surprised and shocked at the details of her recital, and, on the following day he fell unawares on the officials and personally investigated the conditions in the prisons, which he found to be only too true. The result was the purchase of land and the establishment of a retreat for the mentally afflicted of the great metropolis of the ancient civilization.

Cries of distress from all parts of Europe called this American woman from Rome. In Athens, Constantinople, Moscow, St. Petersburg, Vienna, Paris, Florence—everywhere she carried the new light of science to those who were suffering under the shadow of a great affliction.

The gloom of a great civil war fell upon her beloved America. And as the cannon boomed, under the flag that she loved, she carried the compassion of her heart to the wounded and dying and offered her life to her country as a superintendent of nurses. It was through her efforts that many monuments were erected to the Union soldiers who had fallen on the field or perished in the prison pens or hospital wards. It was this woman who brought to the army and navy compassion for the heroes who had become insane in the service. It was this good Samaritan whose name ran through every state in the Union, across Canada, and around the world—appealing to the universal heart of humanity.

And yet, this great woman, whose soul was overflowing with

love for all humanity, was herself a homeless wanderer. This life spent for the happiness of others was poured out in loneliness and suffering.

One day a white-haired lady of about eighty years of age, plainly dressed, and bent by the weight of years, retired to the mental hospital at Trenton, New Jersey.

"This is my first-born child," she said. "It is here that I want to die."

Five years later this beneficent life passed away so quietly that the world hardly knew she was gone. Those for whom she had labored did not know, and could not love. Over her lifeless form they could not grieve; they were in darkness that knows no grief.

But there is One who knows and One who loves, and to those all-embracing arms she passed with the tender words: "Come, ye blessed of my Father, inherit the kingdom prepared for you from the foundation of the world, for I was hungry and ye gave me meat; I was thirsty and ye gave me drink; I was a stranger and ye took me in; naked and ye clothed me; sick and in prison and ye visited me."

And as the light of His face falls upon her, we can hear the echo of the voice of Him who gave his life to save humanity: "Inasmuch as ye have done it unto one of the least of these my brethren, ye have done it unto me."

This is a story of the heroism of peace—the story of Dorothea Lynde Dix, one of the noblest of American women.

•

SOJOURNER TRUTH

From *The Narrative of Sojourner Truth*

In 1843, a former slave born with the name Isabella left New York City with a bag of clothes, twenty-five cents, and a new name— Sojourner Truth—a name she chose, she said, because God had told her to travel the land, declaring the truth. For the remainder of her life, she spoke out loudly and fearlessly on behalf of her causes, which included the abolition of slavery, equal rights for women, and education for freed slaves. Here is someone born into the worst of conditions who nonetheless rose to lead others to better lives. The passage below comes from *The Narrative of Sojourner Truth,* published in 1875. The incident described here took place in Washington, D.C., shortly after the Civil War.

While Sojourner was engaged in the hospital, she often had occasion to procure articles from various parts of the city for the sick soldiers, and would sometimes be obliged to walk a long distance, carrying her burdens upon her arm. She would gladly have availed herself of the street cars; but, although there was on each track one car called the Jim Crow car, nominally for the accommodation of colored people, yet should they succeed in getting on at all they would seldom have more than the privilege of standing, as the seats were usually filled with white folks. Unwilling to submit to this state of things, she complained to the president of the street railroad, who ordered the Jim Crow car to be taken off. A law was now passed giving the colored people equal car privileges with the white.

Not long after this, Sojourner, having occasion to ride, signaled the car, but neither conductor nor driver noticed her. Soon another followed, and she raised her hand again, but they also turned away. She then gave three tremendous yelps, "I want to ride! *I want to ride!* I WANT TO RIDE!!!" Consternation seized the passing crowd— people, carriages, go-carts of every description stood still. The car was effectually blocked up, and before it could move on, Sojourner had jumped aboard. Then there arose a great shout from the crowd, "Ha! ha! ha!! She has beaten him," &c. The angry conductor told her to go forward where the horses were, or he would put her out. Quietly seating herself, she informed him that she was a passenger. "Go forward where the horses are, or I will throw you out," said he in a menacing voice. She told him that she was neither a Marylander nor a Virginian to fear his threats; but was from the Empire State of New York, and knew the laws as well as he did.

Several soldiers were in the car, and when other passengers came in, they related the circumstance and said, "You ought to have heard that old woman talk to the conductor." Sojourner rode farther than she needed to go; for a ride was so rare a privilege that she determined to make the most of it. She left the car feeling very happy, and said, "Bless God! I have had a ride."

Returning one day from the Orphans' Home at Georgetown, she hastened to reach a car; but they paid no attention to her signal, and kept ringing a bell that they might not hear her. She ran after it, and when it stopped to take other passengers, she succeeded in overtaking it and, getting in, said to the conductor, "It is a shame to make a lady run so." He told her if she said another word, he would put her off the car, and came forward as if to execute his threat. She replied, "If you attempt that, it will cost you more than your car and horses are worth." A gentleman of dignified and commanding manner, wearing a general's uniform, interfered in her behalf, and the conductor gave her no further trouble.

•

KING JOHN AND THE MAGNA CARTA
Retold by James Baldwin

Here is a leader of the church doing his part to establish the rights of Englishmen, which in time would come to mean human rights. More than once in the course of Western civilization has the courage of religious leaders become the seed of political achievement. The Magna Carta was signed in 1215.

King John was so selfish and cruel that all the people in his kingdom both feared and hated him.

One by one he lost the dominions in France which the former kings of England had held. Men called him Lackland, because in the end he had neither lands nor castles that he could rightfully call his own.

He robbed his people. He quarreled with his knights and barons. He offended all good men. He formed a plan for making war against King Philip of France, and called upon his barons to join him. When some of them refused, he burned their castles and destroyed their fields.

At last the barons met together at a place called St. Edmundsbury to talk about their grievances. "Why should we submit to be ruled by such a king?" said some of the boldest. But most of them were afraid to speak their minds.

Stephen Langton, the Archbishop of Canterbury, was with them, and there was no bolder friend of liberty than he. He made a stirring speech that gave courage even to the most cowardly.

"Are you men?" he said. "Why then do you submit to this false-hearted king? Stand up and declare your freedom. Refuse to be the slaves of this man. Demand the rights and privileges that belong to you as free men. Put this demand in writing—in the form of a great charter—and require the king to sign it. So shall it be to you and your children a safeguard forever against the injustice of unworthy rulers."

The barons were astonished at the boldness of this speech. Some of them shrank back in fear, but the bravest among them showed by their looks and gestures that they were ready to make a bold stand for liberty.

"Come forward!" cried Stephen Langton. "Come, and swear that you will never rest until King John has given you the rights that are yours. Swear that you will have the charter from his hand, or that you will wage war upon him to the very death."

Never before had Englishmen heard such a speech. The barons took the oath which Stephen Langton prescribed. Then they gathered their fighting men together and marched upon London. The cowardly king was frightened.

"What do these men want?" he asked.

They sent him word that they wanted their rights as Englishmen, and that they would never rest until he had given them a charter of liberties signed by his own hand.

"Oh, well! If that is all, you shall surely have it," he said.

But he put them off with one excuse and another. He sent a messenger to Rome to ask the Pope to help him. He tried, by fine promises, to persuade Stephen Langton to abandon the cause he had undertaken. But no one knew the falseness of his heart better than the Pope and the Archbishop of Canterbury.

The people from all parts of the country now came and joined the army of the barons. Of all the knights in England, only seven remained true to the king.

The barons made out a list of their demands, and Stephen Langton carried it to the king. "These things we will have," they said, "and there shall be no peace until you grant them."

Oh, how angry was King John! He raved like a wild beast; he clenched his fists; he stamped upon the floor. But he saw that he was helpless. At last he said that he would sign the charter at such time and place as the barons might name.

"Let the time be the fifteenth of June," they said, "and let the place be Runnymede."

Now, Runnymede was a green meadow not far from the city of

London, and there the king went with his few followers. He was met by the barons, with an army of determined men behind them.

The charter which Stephen Langton and his friends had drawn up was spread out before the king. He was not a scholar, and so it was read to him, line by line. It was a promise that the people should not be oppressed; that the rights of the cities and boroughs should be respected; that no man should be imprisoned without a fair trial; that justice should not be delayed or denied to anyone.

Pale with anger, the king signed the charter, and then rode back to his castle at Windsor. As soon as he was in his own chamber he began to rave like a madman. He rolled on the floor. He beat the air with his fists. He gnawed sticks and straws. He foamed at the mouth. He cursed the barons and the people for treating their king so badly.

But he was helpless. The charter was signed—the Magna Carta, to which Englishmen still point as the first safeguard of their rights and liberties.

As might have been expected, it was not long before John tried to break all his promises. The barons made war upon him, and never again did he see a peaceful day. His anger and anxiety caused him to fall into a fever which nothing could cure. At last, despised and shunned as he deserved to be, he died. I doubt if there was an eye in England that wept for him.

●

SACAJAWEA

Francis T. Miller

Sacajawea (whose name means "bird woman") helped lead the way on one of the greatest overland adventures in American history. Here is the kind of courage and perseverance that moves the world along.

It was a full hundred years ago that the tribe of Indians known to history as the Shoshones made their home a little west of the Rocky Mountains, or, as the range was called by them, the "Bitter Root Mountains." Here it was that Sacajawea and her little friends played their childish games, with no thought of anything outside of their own lives. It was not always play time among the children; from infancy they were taught to labor with their hands, and their education in other respects was not neglected. At a surprisingly early age, they became skilled in the use of the bow, and they were sent into the forest to gather herbs and roots, for medicine and food.

One day, into this peaceful valley, without warning, the powerful Minnetarees, or Blackfeet, tribe swept down in battle array. Devastation followed in their wake. Many of the Shoshones were killed and many were carried away into captivity. Among the captives was little Sacajawea. Away over the mountains she was borne into the far, far east. Naturally alert and observing, the little maid absorbed every incident of this new experience, so that in after years, when traveling back over this same country, she was able to recognize most of the landmarks on the way.

Sacajawea was sold as a slave when she reached the east. A French Canadian, named Charboneau, who was an Indian interpreter, bought her when she was only five years old. When she was fourteen he made her his wife, and a year later a son was born to her.

It was about this time that American explorers were looking toward the great, mysterious region in the Far West. They believed that it was a land of great wealth, and they longed to plant the American flag on its mountains. Men called them foolhardy and said that it was a worthless jungle of forests and rocks and beasts, that it was not worth the risk of life it would take to survey it.

But there were two explorers—Lewis and Clark—who were willing to undertake it. Shortly after starting on their hazardous journey, they entered the little Indian village of Mandan. There they found Charboneau, who could talk many tongues. Their eyes fell also upon the little Indian mother, Sacajawea. Charboneau told them that his Indian wife knew the whole country, and was a natural guide. Sacajawea, in her native tongue, told them how she knew the trails; how she could take them through country never before traveled by the feet of white men; and how she could show them the beauties of the land of her birth, with its towering blue mountains, capped with snow, and its golden valleys, its gorges and rivers, its glittering sands, and its thousand and one beauties that have since given it the name of the "Garden of the Gods."

"We will go with you," said Charboneau and Sacajawea.

And so it was that when that expedition, which opened up the western domain of America, started on the most perilous portion of its journey, Sacajawea was a guide and Charboneau an interpreter. Sacajawea strapped her two-month-old baby on her shoulders, and carried him in this snug pocket throughout the entire journey. She was the only woman in the party and she rendered vital service to the explorers.

Into the heart of the wilderness they plunged. When all signs of human life were left far behind them, and there were none to beckon them onward, then it was that the native instinct of this woman came to their assistance. At times sickness or starvation seemed imminent. Then Sacajawea would go into the woods, where in secret she gathered herbs to cure each ailment, or dug roots, from which she prepared savory dishes for their meals.

The men marveled at the courage and ingenuity of this faithful pilot. Burdened though she was with the care of the young child, she never seemed to feel fatigue. No complaint ever escaped her lips. Patient, plucky, and determined, she was a constant source of inspiration to the explorers.

The baby laughed and cooed as the wonders of the world were revealed to it. With all its mother's fearlessness, it swung calmly on her faithful back while she climbed over jagged precipices and forded swiftly running rivers.

One day a little incident occurred, which illustrates the true character of this woman. While making their way along one of the rivers, her husband, in a clumsy attempt to readjust things, over-turned the canoe containing every article necessary for the journey. Without a moment's hesitation Sacajawea plunged into the river, risking her own life and that of the infant strapped to her. Clothing, bundles, and many valuable documents of the expedition were thus rescued. If these things had been lost, the party would have been obliged to retrace its steps hundreds of miles, in order to replace them. This is, indeed, the heroism that makes history. The alertness of Sacajawea's native instinct and her faithful kindness worked ines-timable benefit to our nation. In gratitude for her great services, the explorers named after her the next river that they discovered.

Some months later, scenes began to take on a familiar aspect to Sacajawea, and she showed signs of elation. She pointed out old landmarks which indicated that she was nearing her old home. They at last pitched their camp where years before, as a little child, she had been taken captive. Here she soon found old friends, and to her unspeakable delight she discovered among them her own brother. Wrapped closely in his arms, she sobbed out all the sorrow

which had been bound up in her heart for so many years. From
him she learned that all of her family had died, except two of her
brothers and a son of her eldest sister.

Sacajawea was at home again. Now and then little snatches of
songs of contentment reached the ears of the members of the great
expedition. They might naturally have thought that now it would
not be easy for the girl to attend them on their westward journey.
But if they entertained this fear, they misjudged Sacajawea. She
never flinched from her first intention, and cheerfully left her long-
lost friends to plunge once more into the unbroken and unknown
forests beyond the Rockies. The solitude was enough to shake a
strong man's courage. Never a sound was to be heard except the
dismal, distant howl of wild beasts and occasionally the war cry of
savages, but Sacajawea did not falter.

Thus they plodded overland, ever westward, until the end of
the journey drew near. They made a camp inland, leaving Sacajawea
in its protection, and then pushed to the coast.

"It is the Pacific!" they cried at last.

In their enthusiasm, the explorers forgot the brave Sacajawea.
They talked of the Pacific in the camp, but did not allow her to go
to the coast until she pleaded with them to let her gaze upon the
waters.

Then she was satisfied. She had seen the "great waters" and
the "fish," as she called the whale which spouted on its surface.

It was an epoch-making journey, in which the path was blazed

by a woman. It rivaled the great
explorations of Stanley and Liv-
ingstone in daring, and far exceeded them in importance. It
was an expedition that moved
the world along; that pushed the
boundary of the United States
from the Mississippi to the Pacific; that gave us the breadth of
the continent from ocean to
ocean; that led to the command
of its rivers and harbors, the
wealth of its mountains, plains
and valleys—a dominion vast
enough for the ambitions of
kings.

•

WASHINGTON'S GLASSES

This is one of my favorite stories from American history. I taught
it in classrooms across the country when I was the U.S. secretary
of education. This moment of recognition of George Washington's
greatness in leadership came not in the noise of battle, but in the
quiet of reflection.

At the end of the Revolutionary War, the new United States
came close to disaster. The government owed back pay to many
officers in the army, men who had fought long and hard for the
nation's freedom. But Congress had no money, and rumors
abounded that it intended to disband the armed forces and send
them home without pay.

As the weeks passed, the army's cry for pay grew louder. The
soldiers insisted that they had performed their duty faithfully, and
now the government should do the same. They sent appeals to
Congress, with no effect. Patience began to wear thin. Tempers
smoldered. At last some of the officers, encamped at Newburgh,
New York, issued what amounted to a threat. The army would not
disband until paid; if necessary, it would march on Congress. Mutiny was close at hand.

There was no doubt in anyone's mind that one man alone
could persuade the army to give the government more time.

On March 15, 1783, George Washington strode into the Temple of Virtue, a large wooden hall built by the soldiers as a chapel
and dance hall. A hush fell over the gathered officers as the tall
figure took to the lectern at the front of the room. These men had
come to love their commander-in-chief during the lean, hard years
of fighting; now, for the first time, they glared at him with restless
and resentful eyes. A deathlike stillness filled the room.

Washington began to speak. He talked of his own dedicated
service, and reminded the group that he himself had served without
pay. He spoke of his love for his soldiers. He urged them to have
patience, and pointed out that Congress in the past had acted
slowly, but in the end would act justly. He promised he would do
everything in his power to see that the men received what they
deserved.

He asked them to consider the safety and security of their new country, begging them not to "open the flood gates of civil discord, and deluge our rising empire in blood." He appealed to their honor. "Let me entreat you, gentlemen, on your part," he said, "not to take any measures which, viewed in the calm light of reason, will lessen the dignity and sully the glory you have hitherto maintained."

He paused. A restlessness pervaded the air. His audience did not seem moved. The men stared at him tensely.

Washington produced a letter from a congressman explaining the difficulties the government now faced. He would read it to them. It would help them comprehend the new government's difficulties. He unfolded the paper. He started to read, slowly. He stumbled over some of the words, then stopped. Something was wrong. The general seemed lost, slightly confused. The officers leaned forward.

Then Washington pulled from his pocket something the men had never seen their commander-in-chief use before—spectacles.

"Gentlemen, you must pardon me," he said quietly. "I have grown gray in your service, and now find myself growing blind."

It was not merely what the beloved general said, but the way he spoke the few, simple words. The humble act of this majestic man touched the soldiers in a way his arguments had failed to do. There were lumps in many throats, tears in every eye. The general quietly left the hall, and the officers voted to give the Congress more time.

George Washington had saved his new country from armed rebellion. As Thomas Jefferson later said, "The moderation and virtue of a single character probably prevented this Revolution from being closed, as most others have been, by a subversion of that liberty it was intended to establish."

•

THE CHARACTER OF LEADERSHIP
Thomas Jefferson

Here is one great American leader writing honestly and unselfishly about another. Here is a true portrait of the character of leadership. Jefferson wrote this probing, candid assessment at Monticello in a letter to Dr. Walter Jones dated January 2, 1814.

I think I knew General Washington intimately and thoroughly; and were I called on to delineate his character, it should be in terms like these.

His mind was great and powerful, without being of the very first order; his penetration strong, though not so acute as that of a Newton, Bacon, or Locke; and as far as he saw, no judgment was ever sounder. It was slow in operation, being little aided by invention or imagination, but sure in conclusion. Hence the common remark of his officers, of the advantage he derived from councils of war, where hearing all suggestions, he selected whatever was best; and certainly no general ever planned his battles more judiciously. But if deranged during the course of the action, if any member of his plan was dislocated by sudden circumstances, he was slow in readjustment. The consequence was, that he often failed in the field, and rarely against an enemy in station, as at Boston and York. He was incapable of fear, meeting personal dangers with the calmest unconcern. Perhaps the strongest feature in his character was prudence, never acting until every circumstance, every consideration, was maturely weighed; refraining if he saw a doubt, but, when once decided, going through with his purpose, whatever obstacles opposed. His integrity was most pure, his justice the most inflexible I have ever known, no motives of interest or consanguinity, of friendship or hatred, being able to bias his decision. He was, indeed, in every sense of the words, a wise, a good, and a great man. His temper was naturally irritable and high toned; but reflection and resolution had obtained a firm and habitual ascendancy over it. If ever, however, it broke its bonds, he was most tremendous in his wrath. In his expenses he was honorable, but exact; liberal in contributions to whatever promised utility; but frowning and unyielding on all visionary projects, and all unworthy calls on his charity. His heart was not warm in its affections; but he exactly calculated every man's value, and gave him a solid esteem proportioned to it. His person, you know, was fine, his stature exactly what one would wish, his deportment easy, erect and noble; the best horseman of his age, and the most graceful figure that could be seen on horseback. Although in the circle of his friends, where he might be unreserved with safety, he took a free share in conversation, his colloquial talents were not above mediocrity, possessing neither copiousness of ideas, nor fluency of words. In public, when called on for a sudden opinion, he was unready, short and embarrassed. Yet he wrote readily, rather diffusely, in an easy and correct style. This he had acquired by conversation with the world, for his education was merely reading, writing and common arithmetic, to which he added surveying at a later day. His time was employed in action chiefly, reading little, and that only in agriculture and English history. His correspondence became necessarily extensive, and, with journalizing his agricultural proceedings, occupied most of his leisure hours within doors. On the whole, his character was, in its mass, perfect, in nothing bad, in few points indifferent; and it may truly be said, that never did nature and fortune combine more perfectly to make a man great, and to place him in the same constellation with whatever worthies have merited from man an everlasting remembrance. For his was the singular destiny and merit, of leading the armies of his country successfully through an arduous war, for the establishment of its independence; of conducting its councils through the birth of a government, new in its forms and principles, until it had settled down into a quiet and orderly train; and of scrupulously obeying the laws through the whole of his career, civil and military, of which the history of the world furnishes no other example.

•

A VICE GROWN INTO FASHION
George Washington

Ralph Waldo Emerson once observed that "we infer the spirit of the nation in great measure from the language." George Washington issued this general order to his troops in New York in July 1776. Do we the American people hold ourselves to this standard today? No, we do not.

GENERAL ORDER

The General is sorry to be informed that the foolish and wicked practice of profane cursing and swearing, a vice heretofore little known in an American army, is growing into fashion. He hopes the officers will, by example as well as influence, endeavor to check it, and that both they and the men will reflect, that we can have little hope of the blessing of Heaven on our arms, if we insult it by our impiety and folly. Added to this, it is a vice so mean and low, without any temptation, that every man of sense and character detests and despises it.

•

SURRENDER AT APPOMATTOX

Horace Porter

Great leaders display certain virtues when the end comes, no matter what the outcome. Here is grace in victory and grace in defeat. The account comes from an eyewitness at Appomattox Courthouse, Virginia, where on April 9, 1865, General Robert E. Lee surrendered the Confederate Army of Northern Virginia to General Ulysses S. Grant, effectively ending the Civil War.

General Grant began the conversation by saying: "I met you once before, General Lee, while we were serving in Mexico, when you came over from General Scott's headquarters to visit Garland's brigade, to which I then belonged. I have always remembered your appearance, and I think I should have recognized you anywhere." "Yes," replied General Lee, "I know I met you on that occasion, and I have often thought of it and tried to recollect how you looked, but I have never been able to recall a single feature." After some further mention of Mexico, General Lee said: "I suppose, General Grant, that the object of our present meeting is fully understood. I asked to see you to ascertain upon what terms you would receive the surrender of my army." General Grant replied: "The terms I propose are those stated substantially in my letter of yesterday— that is, the officers and men surrendered to be paroled and disqualified from taking up arms again until properly exchanged, and all arms, ammunition, and supplies to be delivered up as captured property." Lee nodded an assent, and said: "Those are about the conditions which I expected would be proposed." General Grant then continued: "Yes, I think our correspondence indicated pretty clearly the action that would be taken at our meeting; and I hope it may lead to a general suspension of hostilities and be the means of preventing any further loss of life."

Lee inclined his head as indicating his accord with this wish, and General Grant then went on to talk at some length in a very pleasant vein about the prospects of peace. Lee was evidently anxious to proceed to the formal work of the surrender, and he brought the subject up again by saying: "I presume, General Grant, we have both carefully considered the proper steps to be taken, and I would suggest that you commit to writing the terms you have proposed, so that they may be formally acted upon."

"Very well," replied General Grant, "I will write them out." And calling for his manifold order book, he opened it on the table before him and proceeded to write the terms. The leaves had been so prepared that three impressions of the writing were made. He wrote very rapidly, and did not pause until he had finished the sentence ending with "officers appointed by me to receive them." Then he looked toward Lee, and his eyes seemed to be resting on the handsome sword that hung at that officer's side. He said afterward that this set him to thinking that it would be an unnecessary humiliation to require the officers to surrender their swords, and a great hardship to deprive them of their personal baggage and horses, and after a short pause he wrote the sentence: "This will not embrace the side-arms of the officers, nor their private horses or baggage." When he had finished the letter he called Colonel (afterward General) Ely S. Parker, one of the military secretaries on the staff, to his side and looked it over with him and directed him as they went along to interline six or seven words and to strike out the word "their," which had been repeated. When this had been done, he handed the book to General Lee and asked him to read over the letter. . . .

Lee took it and laid it on the table beside him, while he drew from his pocket a pair of steel-rimmed spectacles and wiped the glasses carefully with his handkerchief. Then he crossed his legs, adjusted the spectacles very slowly and deliberately, took up the draft of the letter, and proceeded to read it attentively. . . .

When Lee came to the sentence about the officers' side-arms, private horses, and baggage, he showed for the first time during the reading of the letter a slight change of countenance, and was evidently touched by this act of generosity. It was doubtless the condition mentioned to which he particularly alluded when he looked toward General Grant as he finished reading and said with some degree of warmth in his manner: "This will have a very happy effect upon my army."

General Grant then said: "Unless you have some suggestions

to make in regard to the form in which I have stated the terms, I will have a copy of the letter made in ink and sign it."

"There is one thing I would like to mention," Lee replied after a short pause. "The cavalrymen and artillerists own their own horses in our army. Its organization in this respect differs from that of the United States." This expression attracted the notice of our officers present, as showing how firmly the conviction was grounded in his mind that we were two distinct countries. He continued: "I would like to understand whether these men will be permitted to retain their horses."

"You will find that the terms as written do not allow this," General Grant replied; "only the officers are permitted to take their private property."

Lee read over the second page of the letter again, and then said: "No, I see the terms do not allow it; that is clear." His face showed plainly that he was quite anxious to have this concession made, and Grant said very promptly and without giving Lee time to make a direct request: "Well, the subject is quite new to me. Of course I did not know that any private soldiers owned their animals, but I think this will be the last battle of the war—I sincerely hope so—and that the surrender of this army will be followed soon by that of all the others, and I take it that most of the men in the ranks are small farmers, and as the country has been so raided by the two armies, it is doubtful whether they will be able to put in a crop to carry themselves and their families through the next winter without the aid of the horses they are now riding, and I will arrange it in this way: I will not change the terms as now written, but I will instruct the officers I shall appoint to receive the paroles to let all the men who claim to own a horse or mule take the animals home with them to work their little farms." (This expression has been quoted in various forms and has been the subject of some dispute. I give the exact words used.)

Lee now looked greatly relieved, and though anything but a demonstrative man, he gave every evidence of his appreciation of this concession, and said, "This will have the best possible effect upon the men. It will be very gratifying and will do much toward conciliating our people." He handed the draft of the terms back to General Grant, who called Colonel T. S. Bowers of the staff to him and directed him to make a copy in ink. . . .

General Lee now took the initiative again in leading the conversation back into business channels. He said: "I have a thousand or more of your men as prisoners, General Grant, a number of them officers whom we have required to march along with us for several days. I shall be glad to send them into your lines as soon as it can be arranged, for I have no provisions for them. I have, indeed, nothing for my own men. They have been living for the last few days principally upon parched corn, and we are badly in need of both rations and forage. I telegraphed to Lynchburg, directing several trainloads of rations to be sent on by rail from there, and when they arrive I should be glad to have the present wants of my men supplied from them."

At this remark all eyes turned toward Sheridan, for he had captured these trains with his cavalry the night before, near Appomattox Station. General Grant replied: "I should like to have our men sent within our lines as soon as possible. I will take steps at once to have your army supplied with rations, but I am sorry we have no forage for the animals. We have had to depend upon the country for our supply of forage."

At a little before four o'clock General Lee shook hands with General Grant, bowed to the other officers, and with Colonel Marshall left the room. One after another we followed, and passed out to the porch. Lee signaled to his orderly to bring up his horse, and while the animal was being bridled the general stood on the lowest step and gazed sadly in the direction of the valley beyond where his army lay—now an army of prisoners. He smote his hands together a number of times in an absent sort of a way; seemed not to see the group of Union officers in the yard who rose respectfully at his approach, and appeared unconscious of everything about him. All appreciated the sadness that overwhelmed him, and he had the personal sympathy of everyone who beheld him at this supreme moment of trial. The approach of his horse seemed to recall him from his reverie, and he at once mounted. General Grant now stepped down from the porch, and, moving toward him, saluted him by raising his hat. He was followed in this act of courtesy by all our officers present; Lee raised his hat respectfully, and rode off to break the sad news to the brave fellows whom he had so long commanded.

•

"YOU HAVE DONE YOUR DUTY"

When the Civil War erupted in 1861, thousands of black men tried to enlist in the Union army but were turned away by the government. Only after the Emancipation Proclamation in 1863 did the North begin recruiting large numbers of black soldiers. Eventually almost 200,000 blacks served in the Union forces, in segregated units known as the U.S. Colored Troops. No heroism in our nation's history surpasses the selflessness and loyalty of these men, many who had known freedom for so short a time, yet who immediately offered their own lives so others might be free.

This farewell address was issued after the close of the war to the 1st South Carolina Volunteers at Morris Island, South Carolina, scene of the famous bloody assault against Fort Wagner. There the 54th Massachusetts Colored Infantry had suffered a 40 percent casualty rate while spearheading the attack.

HEADQUARTERS 33RD UNITED STATES COLORED
TROOPS, LATE 1ST SOUTH CAROLINA VOLUNTEERS

MORRIS ISLAND, S.C.
February 9, 1866

GENERAL ORDERS, NO. 1

Comrades—The hour is at hand when we must separate forever, and nothing can ever take from us the pride we feel, when we look back upon the history of the 1st South Carolina Volunteers—the first black regiment that ever bore arms in defence of freedom on the continent of America.

On the ninth day of May, 1862, at which time there were nearly four millions of your race in a bondage sanctioned by the laws of the land, and protected by our flag—on that day, in the face of floods of prejudice, that wellnigh deluged every avenue to manhood and true liberty, you came forth to do battle for our country and your kindred. For long and weary months without pay, or even the privilege of being recognized as soldiers, you labored on, only to be disbanded and sent to your homes, without even a hope of reward. And when our country, necessitated by the deadly struggle with armed traitors, finally granted you the opportunity *again* to come forth in defence of the nation's life, the alacrity with which you responded to the call gave abundant evidence of your readiness to strike a manly blow for the liberty of your race. And from that little band of hopeful, trusting, and brave men, who gathered at Camp Saxton, on Port Royal Island, in the fall of 1862, amidst the terrible prejudices that then surrounded us, has grown an army of a hundred and forty thousand black soldiers, whose valor and heroism has won for your race a name which will live as long as the undying pages of history shall endure; and by whose efforts, united with those of the white man, armed rebellion has been conquered, the millions of bondsmen have been emancipated, and the fundamental law of the land has been so altered as to remove forever the possibility of human slavery being reestablished within the borders of redeemed America. The flag of our fathers, restored to its rightful significance, now floats over every foot of our territory, from Maine to California, and beholds only freemen! The prejudices which formerly existed against you are wellnigh rooted out.

Soldiers, you have done your duty, and acquitted yourselves like men, who, actuated by such ennobling motives, could not fail; and as the result of your fidelity and obedience, you have won your freedom. And oh, how great the reward!

It seems fitting to me that the last hours of our existence as a regiment should be passed amidst the unmarked graves of your comrades—at Fort Wagner. Near you rest the bones of Colonel Shaw, buried by an enemy's hand, in the same grave with his black soldiers, who fell at his side; where, in future, your children's children will come on pilgrimages to do homage to the ashes of those that fell in this glorious struggle.

The flag which was presented to us by the Rev. George B. Cheever and his congregation, of New York City, on the first of January, 1863—the day when Lincoln's immortal proclamation of freedom was given to the world—and which you have borne so nobly through the war, is now to be rolled up forever, and deposited in our nation's capital. And while there it shall rest, with the battles in which you have participated inscribed upon its folds, it will be a source of pride to us all to remember that it has never been disgraced by a cowardly faltering in the hour of danger or polluted by a traitor's touch.

Now that you are to lay aside your arms, and return to the peaceful avocations of life, I adjure you, by the associations and history of the past, and the love you bear for your liberties, to harbor no feelings of hatred toward your former masters, but to seek in the paths of honesty, virtue, sobriety, and industry, and by a willing obedience to the laws of the land, to grow up to the full stature of American citizens. The church, the schoolhouse and the right forever to be free are now secured to you, and every prospect before you is full of hope and encouragement. The nation guarantees to you full protection and justice, and will require from you in return the respect for the laws and orderly deportment which will prove to everyone your right to all the privileges of freemen.

To the officers of the regiment I would say, your toils are ended, your mission is fulfilled, and we separate forever. The fidelity, patience, and patriotism with which you have discharged your duties, to your men and to your country, entitle you to a far higher tribute than any words of thankfulness which I can give you from the bottom of my heart. You will find your reward in the proud conviction that the cause for which you have battled so nobly has been crowned with abundant success.

Officers and soldiers of the First South Carolina Volunteers, I bid you all farewell.

By order of Lt.-Col. C. T. Trowbridge, commanding Regiment.

E. W. Hyde,

Lieutenant and Acting Adjutant

•

DUTY, HONOR, COUNTRY

Douglas MacArthur

These words come from a speech General Douglas MacArthur delivered at West Point on May 12, 1962. Every cadet entering the United States Military Academy receives a copy of the address. They are great words not only for every soldier, but for every citizen.

Duty. Honor. Country. Those three hallowed words reverently dictate what you ought to be, what you can be, what you will be. They are your rallying points, to build courage when courage seems to fail, to regain faith when there seems to be little cause for faith, to create hope when hope becomes forlorn. . . .

The unbelievers will say they are but words, but a slogan, but a flamboyant phrase. Every pedant, every demagogue, every cynic, every hypocrite, every troublemaker, and, I am sorry to say, some others of an entirely different character, will try to downgrade them even to the extent of mockery and ridicule, but these are some of the things they do. They build your basic character. They mold you for your future roles as the custodians of the nation's defense. They make you strong enough to know when you are weak, and brave enough to face yourself when you are afraid.

They teach you to be proud and unbending in honest failure, but humble and gentle in success; not to substitute words for actions, not to seek the path of comfort, but to face the stress and spur of difficulty and challenge; to learn to stand up in the storm, but to have compassion on those who fail; to master yourself before you seek to master others; to have a heart that is clean, a goal that is high; to learn to laugh yet never forget how to weep; to reach into the future, yet never neglect the past; to be serious, yet never to take yourself too seriously; to be modest so that you will remember the simplicity of true greatness, the open mind of true wisdom, the meekness of true strength.

They give you a temper of the will, a quality of the imagination, a vigor of the emotions, a freshness of the deep springs of life, a temperamental predominance of courage over timidity, of an appetite for adventure over love of ease.

They create in your heart the sense of wonder, the unfailing hope of what next, and the joy and inspiration of life. They teach you in this way to be an officer and a gentleman.

•

AMERICA IS GREAT
BECAUSE SHE IS GOOD

This brief reflection has been attributed to Alexis de Tocqueville, one of the greatest observers of early American democratic life. In the end, the state of the union comes down to the character of its citizens.

I sought for the greatness
and genius of America
in her commodious harbors
and her ample rivers,
and it was not there;

in the fertile fields
and boundless prairies,
and it was not there;

in her rich mines
and her vast world commerce,
and it was not there.

Not until I went
into the churches of America
and heard her pulpits,
aflame with righteousness,
did I understand the secret
of her genius and power.

America is great
because she is good,
and if America ever ceases to be good,
America will cease to be great.

•

A General Thanksgiving
From *The Book of Common Prayer*

Learning to say thank you is one of the most important lessons of life. It's not just a matter of manners. Gratitude is a virtue that helps us remember the obligations and responsibilities we owe others in return for the gifts we have received. It makes us better citizens.

Almighty God, Father of all mercies, we, thine unworthy servants, do give thee most humble and hearty thanks for all thy goodness and loving-kindness to us, and to all men. We bless thee for our creation, preservation, and all the blessings of this life; but above all, for thine inestimable love in the redemption of the world by our Lord Jesus Christ; for the means of grace, and for the hope of glory. And, we beseech thee, give us that due sense of all thy mercies, that our hearts may be unfeignedly thankful; and that we show forth thy praise, not only with our lips, but in our lives, by giving up our selves to thy service, and by walking before thee in holiness and righteousness all our days; through Jesus Christ our Lord, to whom, with thee and the Holy Ghost, be all honor and glory, world without end. *Amen.*

Seven

•

WHAT WE
LIVE BY

WHO am I? Why am I here? What should I do? What is my destiny? What does it all mean?

These are some of the profound questions we ask ourselves as we undertake life's journey. The search for meaning is intrinsic to human nature. As thinking creatures, we want to understand why we find ourselves on this road and where the journey is taking us. Will that place make us truly happy and fulfilled? "If we could first know where we are, and whither we are tending, we could better judge what to do, and how to do it," Abraham Lincoln observed. Without answers to these questions, we feel a bit disoriented. We are wanderers, searching and striving for end and aim, for purpose and connection.

And clearly, if we are to be true to ideas like courage and perseverance and responsibility and loyalty, it helps to know *why* we should go to the trouble. What ultimate good does it do? What do the virtues have to do with our place in the universe, our reason for being here, and our nature as human beings? Why *should* we be moral creatures?

This final chapter does not give all the answers. But it helps us think about the questions. It challenges us to think deeply about our actions, reminding us that in many respects life is an inward journey. The ancient Greek philosophers believed that self-knowledge is the highest end: "The unexamined life is not worth living," they told us. It is easy to assume that you know quite a bit about your own life. But in fact, a feeling of being adrift in the world can be in no small measure the result of failing to live by the ancients' dictum: "Know thyself." Knowing yourself takes effort, and for that reason we prize it highly enough to place it in that category of knowledge we call wisdom.

For many people, however, such wisdom about one's self can never be enough. They seek not only knowledge of the self but also knowledge of God's will. For them, answers to the most important questions come through faith, through revelation, not reason. So in this chapter we also find stories about how faith can guide us on life's journey. Here we see people who draw strength from above, trusting in God for help in the large and small tasks of life. We see them living in readiness to answer God's call, and finding direction by seeking ways to serve Him. And we see them discovering answers to the question "Why am I here?" by serving their fellow man, by helping others along life's way according to the dictates of their faith.

Because this is the final chapter, we also find here two or three selections about approaching the end of life. Wisdom and faith can help us face our mortality. This section does not deal predominately with death, however, because even though death may be the end of life, it is neither its purpose nor its meaning. Life in one sense is indeed a journey from the cradle to the grave, but in a more important respect, it is a journey of understanding one's self, one's fellow creatures, and God's will.

And in this sense, courage and compassion and honesty and loyalty and all the other virtues can make the difference. They can be *the* difference. They can be a destination, because *how* we journey is more important than how far we manage to go. As Samuel Johnson said, "Life, like every other blessing, derives its value from its use alone. Not for itself, but for a nobler end the eternal gave it; and that end is virtue." At the end, we may discover that those things we call virtues are among the very reasons we find ourselves here. They are not just means; very frequently they are the ends themselves. And when they become what we live by, our own actions turn out to be some of the best answers to those great questions of life.

THE SEED

He who sows trusts in God.

One warm autumn day a little girl dropped a seed into a hole in the ground, covered it up, and waited for her flower to grow.

But before long the winter snows arrived, and left a thick white blanket all over the ground. And the poor seed could not grow at all.

After waiting patiently for weeks and months, the little girl peeked outside her door and said, "Now, seed, hurry and grow, grow, grow, until you have a tall stem covered with pretty green leaves and big yellow blossoms."

But the seed answered, "I am still icy and cold. You must ask someone else."

"Who?" asked the little girl.

"The hard ground whose bed I lie in," said the seed.

"I will!" cried the little girl. "Ground, ground, won't you grow soft, so my little seed can be warm, and grow into a flower?"

But the ground answered, "You must ask someone else."

"Who?" asked the little girl.

"The snow who covers me," said the ground.

"I will!" cried the little girl. "Snow, snow, won't you melt away, so the ground can grow soft, and my little seed can be warm, and grow into a flower?"

But the snow answered, "You must ask someone else."

"Who?" asked the little girl.

"The sun that melts me," said the snow.

"I will!" cried the little girl. "Sun, sun, won't you come out, so the snow will melt, and the ground can grow soft, and my little seed can be warm, and grow into a flower?"

But the sun answered, "You must ask someone else."

"Who?" asked the little girl.

"The clouds that cover me," said the sun.

"I will!" cried the little girl. "Clouds, clouds, won't you go away, so the sun can come out, and the snow will melt, and the ground can grow soft, and my little seed can be warm, and grow into a flower?"

But the clouds answered, "You must ask someone else."

"Who?" asked the little girl.

"The wind that blows us," said the clouds.

"I will!" cried the little girl. "Wind, wind, won't you blow, so the clouds will go away, and the sun can come out, and the snow can melt, and the ground can grow soft, and my little seed can be warm, and grow into a flower?"

But the wind whispered in her ear, "You must ask someone else."

"Who?" asked the little girl.

"God, who makes all things grow," said the wind.

"I will!" cried the little girl. "I should have thought of that."

So she got down on her knees, and folded her hands, and prayed.

"God," she prayed, "won't you tell the wind to blow, so the clouds will go away, and the sun can come out, and the snow can melt, and the ground can grow soft, and my little seed can be warm, and grow into a flower?"

And God smiled down on the little girl.

She looked out her door again. A warm breeze played in the air. The clouds were gone, the sun was shining, the snow was melting, and the ground was turning soft and green.

And before long her flower came up.

•

THE LITTLE LOST LAMB

Everyone counts in God's eyes. This story is based on Luke 15:3–7.

The mother sheep loved her little lamb just as your mother loves you.

It was a wee little lamb with a thin coat of wool and slender legs. At night it slept in the sheepfold close to its mother's warm fleece. All day long it nibbled grass, and drank from a running stream, and played in the meadow.

"Take care of my lamb," the mother sheep tried to say to the shepherd of the flock. "It is too little and weak to take care of itself."

The shepherd understood, and he watched over the little lamb although there were a hundred sheep in his flock.

He was a good shepherd or he would not have been able to care for them all. Every morning he opened the gate of the fold and they crowded out. Then he led them up a hill to a green meadow where he watched them all day. There were wolves in the mountains close by, watching for a chance to kill the little lambs. The shepherd kept the wolves away.

When the sun began to drop down behind the hill, the shepherd led his flock home to the fold. And before he closed the gate, he always counted the flock to see if there were a hundred sheep.

A storm in high places is very terrible. There was a storm with wind, and cold rain, and fire in the sky one day. The mother sheep was too frightened to know which way to go. She followed the other sheep, who pushed and almost crushed each other as they ran down the hill. But the shepherd led them all gently, pointing the way with his crook. He called them by the names he had given them. He went first to keep the storm from beating them back until they knew they were safe, for the sheepfold was in sight.

As they went through the gate, one by one, he counted them. There were only ninety-nine.

Then the shepherd looked down into the pleading eyes of the mother sheep. She was trying to tell him that her little lamb was lost in the storm.

If he had not been a good shepherd, he might have thought

that so little a lamb was no great loss. But he thought only about how cold the lamb must be with its thin fleece, out in the storm. He remembered that, above the storm, he had heard the howling of wolves.

So the good shepherd went out in the wind and rain to find the little lamb.

It had grown so dark that he could hardly see. The wind was cold, the rain soaked his cloak, and the stones cut his feet. Another shepherd would have turned back. But the good shepherd could see, through the storm, the sorrowful eyes of the little lamb's mother. So he went on until he found the little lost lamb, lying so cold and frightened beside the road.

The shepherd took the lamb in his arms. It was too cold to walk home. All the way back he carried it, just as carefully as your mother carried you when you were a baby. He was very happy when he reached the sheepfold and gave it back to its mother. He asked his neighbors to come and be glad with him because not even one lamb was lost from the flock.

They wondered a little that the shepherd was so glad.

"Ninety-nine is almost a hundred," they said. "What difference would one little lamb have made in so large a flock?"

The good shepherd knew. The little lamb who was lost was one of his sheep, and he loved them all.

●

SAMUEL IN THE TEMPLE

Retold from 1 Samuel 3:1–21

Samuel's simple words to God—"Speak, for thy servant heareth"
—remind us that if we live to do the Lord's will, then we must
live in readiness to answer his call. This beautiful story comes
from the first book of Samuel in the Bible.

Once upon a time, a long while ago, when wonderful things used to happen, there was a man named Elkanah and his wife, Hannah, who lived in the hill country of Ephraim.

Hannah loved children very much indeed. But she had no little children of her own, although she wanted one very much.

Those were the days when people were beginning to learn that all good things are given by the Heavenly Father. Hannah knew this, too, and while she worked she prayed that God would give her a little child. After she had made this prayer many times, God answered it. A little boy was born to Elkanah and Hannah. They named him Samuel, which means "name of God," because he had come in answer to his mother's prayer.

As Samuel grew from a baby to a little boy, good and strong and a comfort to his father and mother, Hannah thought a great deal about what he should do and be when he grew up. Every year Elkanah and Hannah made a journey to the temple, where the old priest Eli was, to make an offering to the Lord. When Samuel was grown and it drew near time to go again to the temple, Hannah said to herself: "For this child I prayed, and the Lord hath given me my petition which I asked of him. I will bring him that he may appear before the Lord forever."

So Hannah took Samuel, who was still only a little boy, to the temple, and gave him to the old priest Eli to be his helper in the house of the Lord. Although Hannah loved little Samuel very much, she knew that the best thing he could do would be to serve Eli there in the temple.

It was a very great, still place, this temple. It was different from the white house in the hills with vines and flowering trees around it that had been Samuel's home. His father and mother left him, after they had made their offering of three bullocks and some meal and the juice of the grape. Samuel never saw his mother, Hannah, again, except once a year when she came to bring him a new little robe to wear. The linen of this she had spun and woven with her own hands. And there was no other child there with Samuel.

The priest Eli became very old. His own sons had left him, and Samuel found a great deal to do to help him. At last there came a time when Eli's eyes grew so dim that he was not able to see whether the lamp that was always kept lighted in the temple, night and day, was burning or not. So Samuel kept watch of the lamp, and slept, every night, in the great, dim temple.

It was a very lonely, cold place for a little boy to stay alone at night. The tall stone pillars cast long shadows on the floor, which trembled, and moved, and seemed almost alive. Samuel could be very brave and not miss his mother too much in the daytime, when the sun shone and everything was bright. But at night he was like any other little boy. Samuel was afraid of the dark, and it seemed to him that he could not stay, all by himself, there in the temple.

. . .

One night as Samuel lay in the dark of the temple, but not
sleeping, because he was afraid, he was suddenly startled to hear a
voice calling to him.

"Samuel, Samuel," called the voice.

"Here am I!" Samuel answered. He jumped up, ran in to Eli,
and said, "Here am I, for you called me."

But Eli said, "I did not call you, Samuel. Lie down again."

So Samuel went and lay down, but soon he heard the voice
again, calling to him.

"Samuel, Samuel!"

So Samuel ran again to Eli and awoke him, and said, "Here am
I. You called me."

But Eli said, "I called you not, my son. Lie down again."

Now Samuel did not yet know the voice of the Lord, or he
might not have been so afraid. He went back into the dark temple
and lay down, and tried to go to sleep for the third time. But a third
time he heard the voice calling to him, "Samuel, Samuel!"

"Eli, Eli, here I am. You did call me!" he cried, as he ran again
into the old priest's room. And now Eli understood that it had been
the voice of God speaking to Samuel. So he said to the little boy:
"Go, lie down, and it shall be, if He call thee, that thou shalt say,
'Speak, Lord, for Thy servant heareth.'" So Samuel went and lay
down in his place.

And the Lord came, and stood, and called as at other times,
"Samuel, Samuel." Then Samuel answered, bravely, as Eli had told
him to, "Speak, for Thy servant heareth." And the Lord talked to
Samuel a long time in the temple, telling him true and wonderful
things.

Samuel listened, and understood. After the voice had stopped
speaking, he felt comforted, and no longer afraid or lonely. He
knew then that he was never alone, for his Heavenly Father was
with him, even in the dark. So he slept without any fear until it was
morning, and time to open the doors of the house of the Lord.

And Samuel grew, and the Lord always spoke with him, and all
Israel knew that Samuel was established to be a prophet of their
God.

•

BABOUSCKA

Edith M. Thomas

Like the story of Samuel in the temple, this touching old legend
from Russia reminds us that with faith, as with other virtues, readiness is all. Faith entails seizing the chance to serve God when an
opportunity presents itself.

The tradition of Babouscka leaving presents in the houses of
good children on Christmas Eve is an old one in Russia.

> Babouscka sits before the fire,
>   Upon a winter's night,
> The driving winds heap up the snow,
>   Her hut is snug and tight;
> The howling winds, they only make
>   Babouscka's fire more bright!
>
> She hears a knocking at the door,
>   So late—who can it be?
> She hastes to lift the wooden latch
>   (No thought of fear has she):
> The wind-blown candle in her hand
>   Shines out on strangers three.
>
> Their beards are white with age, and snow
>   That in the darkness flies;
> Their floating locks are long and white,
>   But kindly are the eyes
> That sparkle underneath their brows,
>   Like stars in frosty skies.
>
> "Babouscka, we have come from far;
>   We tarry but to say,
> A little Prince is born this night
>   Who all the world shall sway.
> Come join the search; come, go with us
>   Who go these gifts to pay."

Babouscka shivers at the door:
  "I would I might behold
The little Prince who shall be King;
  But ah, the night is cold,
The wind so fierce, the snow so deep,
  And I, good sirs, am old!"

The strangers three, no word they speak,
  But fade in snowy space—
Babouscka sits before the fire,
  And looks with wistful face:
"I wish that I had questioned them,
  So I the way might trace!

"When morning comes, with blessed light,
  I'll early be awake.
My staff in hand, I'll go—perchance,
  Those strangers overtake.
And for the Child, some little toys
  I'll carry for His sake."

The morning came, and, staff in hand,
  She wandered in the snow:
And asked the way of all she met,
  But none the way could show.
"It must be farther yet," she sighed,
  "Then farther will I go."

And still 'tis said, on Christmas Eve,
  When high the drifts are piled,
With staff and basket on her arm,
  Babouscka seeks the Child.
At every door her face is seen—
  Her wistful face and mild!

At every door her gifts she leaves,
  And bends, and murmurs low,
Above each little face half hid
  By pillows white as snow:
"And is *He* here?"—then softly sighs:
  "Nay, farther must I go!"

•

THE SILVER CROWN
Adapted from Laura E. Richards

In this story we find that we make our own crown as we make our way through life.

"And shall I be a king?" asked the child, "and shall I wear a crown?"

"You shall surely wear a crown," said the Angel, "and a kingdom is waiting for you."

"Oh, joy!" said the child. "But tell me, how will it come about? For now I am only a little child, and the crown would hardly stay on my curls."

"That I may not tell," said the Angel. "Only ride and run your best, for the way is long to your kingdom, and the time short."

So the child rode and ran his best, crossing hills and valleys, broad streams and foaming torrents. Here and there he saw people at work or at play, and on these he looked eagerly.

"Perhaps, when they see me," he said, "they will run to meet me, and will crown me with a golden crown, and lead me to their palace and throne me there as king!"

But the folk were all busy with their tasks or their sport, and none heeded him, or left their business for him; and still he must fare forward alone.

Also, he came upon many travelers like himself, some coming toward him, others passing him by. On these, too, he looked earnestly, and would stop now one, now another, and question him.

"Do you know," he asked, "of any kingdom in these parts where the crown is ready and the folk wait for a king?"

Then one would laugh, and another weep, and another jeer, but all alike shook their heads.

"I am seeking crown and kingdom for myself," cried one. "Is it likely that I can be finding one for you, too?"

Another said: "You seek in vain. There are no crowns, only fools' caps with asses' ears and bells that jingle in them."

But others who had been longest on the way only looked on him, some sadly, some kindly, and made no answer. And still he fared onward.

Now and then he stopped to help some poor soul who had fallen into trouble, and when he did that the way lightened before him, and he felt the heart light within him. But at other times the hurry was strong on him, so that he would turn away his face, and shut his ears to the cries that rang in them; and when he did that, the way darkened, and oftentimes he stumbled himself, and fell into pits and quagmires, and must cry for help, sometimes on those to whom he had refused it.

By and by he forgot about the crown and the kingdom; or if he thought of them, it was but as a far-off dream of dim gold, such as one sees at morning when the sun breaks through the mist. But still he knew that the way was long and the time short, and still he rode and ran his best.

At last he was no longer a child, but an old and weary man. Just when his feet could carry him no farther, he looked up and saw that the way came to an end before him, and there was a gate and one in white sitting by it who beckoned to him. Trembling, yet glad, the old man drew near, and knew the Angel who had spoken to him at the beginning.

"Welcome!" said the Angel. "You come in good time."

"I came as fast as I could," said the man, "but many things hindered me, and now I am weary, and can go no farther."

"But what did you find on the way?" asked the Angel.

"Oh! I found joy and sorrow," said the man, "a good measure of both, but never a crown, such as you promised me, and never a kingdom."

"But look," said the Angel. "You are wearing your crown. It is of the purest silver and shines like white frost. And as for your kingdom, the name of it is Heaven and here is the entrance to it."

•

THE LEGEND OF SAINT CHRISTOPHER
Adapted from retellings by
Eleanor Broadus and Peggy Webling

Shakespeare wrote: "It is excellent to have a giant's strength, but it is tyrannous to use it like a giant." This old legend about Saint Christopher, the patron saint of travelers, reminds us that we

should use our God-given strengths in the service of God and our
fellow travelers in life.

Long ago there lived a man who was so tall and strong he
seemed like a giant. He could lift almost any weight, and people
gave him the name Offero, which meant "the Bearer." Offero was
proud of his strength, and it is perhaps not strange that he made up
his mind to serve no one but the mightiest ruler in the world.

"I, Offero, do swear to be servant to only the greatest king on
earth," he vowed, "and I will serve him all the days of my life."

Then he set out on his quest, passing through kingdom after
kingdom in search of the most powerful of all monarchs. He wandered through forests, crushing with his strong arms the wild beasts
that attacked him. He uprooted great trees and threw them across
deep, swift streams, and over these rude bridges he passed into
lands lying farther and farther away. He crossed seas with merchants in their vessels, and passed over deserts with slow caravans,
and trudged alone down the highways of the world.

At last he heard of a king whom all believed the richest in the
world. He went to him to offer his services.

"Great monarch!" said Offero, towering before the throne, "I
have sworn to serve only the most powerful king. Will you accept
me?"

The king, admiring the stranger's giant form and fearless gaze,
welcomed him and placed him beside the throne. There Offero
stood day after day, amidst his sovereign's gold and treasures, rejoicing in a master worthy of his strength.

But one day a stranger from another land came to the court.
He stood before the throne and spoke with fiery zeal in words
Offero could not understand. As the stranger turned to leave, Offero
saw his monarch cowering in his high seat.

"Great king," he cried, "this man has come here with strange
words on his lips, and you tremble before him. Why? I could kill
him with one blow of my hand."

"I tremble because of the news he brings me," the king cried.
"He speaks of another king, an ancient enemy of mine, who even
now approaches my land with a vast army."

"If you are afraid of him, he must be more powerful than you,"
Offero said scornfully. "I must find him, for I have sworn to serve
only the greatest of kings."

So Offero set out to find this new master. He traveled many

days until, coming to the top of a bleak mountain, he saw a wide, dark valley opening before him. Through this valley marched a mighty army; rank after rank filed along with glittering weapons and bloodstained banners. In the rear, surrounded by men in fierce armor, rode a warrior in a heavy chariot. On his head was a crown of jewels that gleamed like fire.

Offero walked boldly down the mountainside and presented himself to the commander of the host.

"I have traveled many miles to enter your service," he said, "because you are the strongest of all kings, and I will serve none but the mightiest."

This terrible king gladly accepted Offero's services and put his strength to work at once. The vast army marched forward, destroying whole peoples and leaving lands barren and burned. Always Offero fought in the front ranks. His heart sank to be in the company of such a bloody master, but he had vowed to serve only the greatest monarch. And certainly no people could stand against this cruel king, who subdued all with terror and bloodshed.

Then one day the warrior king was wounded in battle, and as he lay bleeding a shadow of fear passed across his face.

"What is it you fear?" Offero asked.

"The Prince of Evil," answered the pale king. "I fear he will seize my soul. He calls me in whirlwinds, in the thunder and darkness."

Offero watched the king with wonder. "You are a child to fear storms," he said.

"No," whispered the king, "in spite of your great body, it is you who are a child. You do not understand these things. Even you, with your great strength, must fear Satan."

"My heart knows no fear," Offero said. "Farewell, oh faint-hearted king. I pass on to seek this one who is mightier than you."

He strode away, seeking the Prince of Evil.

The following day, when the sun was high in the heavens, Offero found himself in the depths of a great forest. It was almost black with the branches of the trees overhead, and the earth was cold underfoot. There, on a great stone, sat a shadow. It was the Evil One.

"I seek the one who rules the world," Offero announced boldly.

"Good!" laughed Satan. "You have found him. Come with me, and I will keep you busy."

It was not pleasant work. It meant that every minute was spent in making trouble for other people. But Offero did as he was told, because everyone they met was afraid of Satan, and he believed he was serving the strongest of kings at last.

But one day, as they traveled along, they came in sight of a small, rough-hewn cross by the side of the road. At once Satan left the path and went a long way around, over rocks and through bushes, and at last came back to the road with the cross well behind him.

"Why did you do that?" asked Offero, for although Satan often took roundabout paths, he had never before made so much trouble for himself.

"I do not like to go near the cross," Satan admitted. "I fear Him whose sign it is."

Offero's heart leapt with joy.

"What is his name?" he demanded.

"I dare not say his name," Satan answered, trembling. "But some call him the Prince of Peace."

"If you fear him, he must be stronger than you," Offero said. "I will leave you and serve him."

Once again he set off in search of this new master. He traveled far, for he did not know the way, but hope and courage never failed him. At last he found a man, an ancient hermit, who looked as if he might know how to find the Prince of Peace. Offero told him his story.

"I will serve him, if I can find him," he told the old man. "Where is he? I will kill all his enemies, if he wishes."

"Be not in haste," the hermit said quietly. "You are through with killing now. This king differs from all others. I will show you how to serve him."

He led Offero to the bank of a swift, wide river.

"Here many travelers have lost their lives, for no boat can live in its waters," he said. "If you will stand here on the bank, and carry people across, you will be serving the Prince of Peace. He will know of your service, and in time you will see him."

So Offero built a hut beside the river, and cut a mighty staff to guide his feet among the sunken rocks, and waited for the coming of travelers. They found him always at the door of his hut, ready to carry them across on his broad shoulders. Many a weary soul would have perished without his aid. Month after month, year after year, in summer heat and winter frost he labored. It seemed strange to him that he should be serving his king this way. Sometimes he would sigh and wonder if the Prince of Peace really knew of his service. But the people he helped became his friends, and he was no longer lonely as he had always been before.

One night, when the cold winds were howling around his little hut, Offero lay down to sleep. No traveler, he knew, would seek his help to ford the stream in such a storm.

He heard the beat of rain and the rising tide.

As he was sinking into sleep there came the sound of a voice outside.

"Offero! Rise and bear me over the river!"

The strong man sprang up. He opened his door, curious to see the traveler who dared to cross on such a night.

He peered into the darkness, but there was no one there.

"I must have fallen into a dream," he thought, and once more shut out the wind and rain before stretching himself on the ground.

"Offero! Rise and bear me over the river!"

The voice was louder this time. The words sprang out, like a deep bell, through the howling blast.

Offero stood at his door wondering. He was all alone. The sky was black with clouds. He heard the rushing river and the dull murmur of thunder in the far distance.

For the second time, amazed by the echo of the ringing voice in his heart, he went into his hut and closed the door. This time he did not lie down but waited.

"Offero! Rise and bear me over the river!"

The giant leapt into the night and saw, standing on the river-bank below him, the figure of a child.

Offero's wonder changed to doubt. He knew well the dangers of the river at flood. But three times the child had called upon him. The child was waiting for him now. So he lifted the boy upon his shoulders, grasped his tall staff in his right hand, and slowly, cautiously, boldly, stepped down into the waters.

The current was swifter, the waves higher than ever before. He felt the stones slipping beneath his feet. The stormclouds burst over his head in torrents of blinding rain.

The weight of the child was much greater than he had expected, and it grew even greater with every step. Offero's broad shoulders ached and drooped, but he pressed forward, every muscle taut.

The waters were swirling as high as his waist, breaking against his chest, splashing his face, rushing through his hair. His back ached beneath the weight on his shoulders. His huge staff bent under his hand like a reed. All around him, giant trees, uprooted from the banks, came whirling and crashing downstream. The skies were emptied of rain, but lightning flashed unceasingly and thunder roared over his head.

Onward and onward he struggled, gasping and shaking the water from his face. At last he staggered up the opposite bank, and gently lifted the child from his shoulders.

"Who are you, my child?" he panted. "It seemed as if I were carrying the weight of the whole world!

"Do you not know me?" the sweet voice answered. "I am He you have promised to serve. Did you not know that in this humble, hard work of aiding so many weary travelers, you were serving Me all along? And from now on you will be called not Offero, the Bearer, but Christopher, the Christ-bearer, for I have accepted you as my faithful servant."

And Christopher fell to his feet and worshipped in silence. When he opened his eyes, he was alone by the river.

He rose, and picked up his staff, and found it had blossomed with leaves and flowers. Then he went back to his holy work of serving men for the rest of his days.

•

THE WIDOW'S MITES

Retold by Frances M. Dadmun

To a large extent, living well entails giving well—a giving of some
portion of your time, or talent, or money, or all three. This story
from Luke 21:1–4 in the Bible shows us that the value of giving
lies not simply in the amount given but in the sacrifice it requires
and the love that prompts it.

It was one morning during Passover week, and Jesus and his
disciples were sitting in a court of the great temple at Jerusalem.
They were watching the people as they passed by. Many of them
were rich men. You could tell this from their clothes and from the
way they walked with their chins in the air.

Fastened to columns that supported the roof were trumpet-
shaped boxes where people put their offerings for the temple. Jesus
noticed that the richly dressed people threw in a good deal of
money, which rattled noisily as it fell into the boxes. Everyone else
noticed it too—they couldn't help it. Probably they thought how
generous the givers were and wished they had more money themselves to give away. But Jesus saw something else which other
people overlooked—a thin-faced, poorly dressed widow, who
stepped shyly up to a box and dropped in two mites, the smallest
coin the Jews had. Jesus saw also that she had no more to give—
her pocket was empty. She looked hurriedly about her, for fear
someone might have seen how little she could give, but she need
not have been troubled. Her coins were too small to make a noise,
and her dress was so poor that no one cared what she might do. It
was the rich people whom the crowd admired.

Jesus looked about for his disciples, but they were watching
the rich men, too. It all seemed very wonderful to the disciples
after their simple country homes. So Jesus had to call their attention to the poor widow. And he said, "This poor widow gave more
than all the rest; for they gave only a part while she gave all she
had."

Then the disciples forgot to watch the rich men, who did not
seem interesting anymore. But they looked reverently after the
poor widow until she slipped through the crowd and was gone.

•

THE BOY AND THE ANGEL

Retold by Joel H. Metcalf

"All service ranks the same with God," the poet Robert Browning wrote. This unusual and touching story is based on a poem by Browning.

Theocrite, though only a little boy, nevertheless had to earn his living. His days were long and his work was hard, but his spirit was dauntless and he was forever singing, "Praise God." Morning, noon, and night he sang at his work, and this brought joy to his own heart and to the hearts of those with whom he lived and worked. And it brought joy to the heart of God, who heard him from on high.

One day, as he was singing at his work, a monk passed by, and, touched by his song's sweetness and charm, came in, and said: "Well done, my son. I do not doubt your praise is heard by God as well as if thou wert Pope of Rome and in St. Peter's Church singing the glad songs of praise at Easter time."

Theocrite was happy in his work, but, at the suggestion of singing in the cathedral of St. Peter's, he said, "Would to God that I might praise him in the great St. Peter's before I die!"

The angel Gabriel heard his pious wish, and the next day Theocrite was gone, for the angel had started him on the way to become nothing less than the Pope of Rome.

But immediately God said, "How is it I do not hear the voice of Theocrite singing at his work?"

Then the angel Gabriel left the heavenly sphere and became a boy like Theocrite, taking his place as well as he could. The boy's work he could easily do, and he tried to sing his song of praise. But he could not.

God said: "I hear a voice of praise, but in it there is no doubt and fear, like that of the song of Theocrite. I miss my little human praise."

Then the angel Gabriel cast off his disguise. No man can fill another's place, and even the angel found that he could not entirely fill the place of a little boy with curls.

And so he went to Rome at the Easter-tide, where the new

Pope, Theocrite, was about to praise God in the great way, and said: "I took thee from thy trade, and made thee pope of Rome, but it was all a mistake. I did not do well. Thou couldst be a great pope, but no one can take thy place in the old home.

"I have tried to take thy place. I left my angel sphere to do thy work.

"Thy voice seemed to me weak, but, alas! when it stopped, I could not take up thy song. God was not satisfied.

"All the songs of praise rise as a wondrous chorus to the ear of God, but without you the great chorus was incomplete, and He missed your little voice of praise.

"Therefore, come back with me to your old cell and your old work—come back to your boyhood and sing again your song, 'Praise God.' "

And so Theocrite grew old at home. He never sang the praises of God "the great way" in St. Peter's at Rome; but when he and the new pope came to die, they went to heaven, side by side.

•

A LATE BLOOMER

For some people, finding a mission in life proves a long struggle. This tale from Mexico assures us that we will find our work if we keep looking.

A cactus stood all alone in the desert, wondering why it was stuck in the middle of nowhere.

"I do nothing but stand here all day," it sighed. "What use am I? I'm the ugliest plant in the desert. My spines are thin and prickly, my leaves are rubbery and tough, my skin is thick and bumpy. I can't offer shade or juicy fruit to any passing traveler. I don't see that I'm any use at all."

All it did was stand in the sun day after day, growing taller and fatter. Its spines grew longer and its leaves tougher, and it swelled here and there until it was lumpy and lopsided all over. It truly was strange-looking.

"I wish I could do something useful," it sighed.

By day the hawks circled high overhead.

"What can I do with my life?" the cactus called. Whether they heard or not, the hawks sailed away.

At night the moon floated into the sky and cast its pale glow on the desert floor.

"What good can I do with my life?" the cactus called. The moon only stared coldly as it mounted its course.

A lizard crawled by, leaving a little trail in the sand with its tail.

"What worthy deed can I do?" the cactus called.

"You?" the lizard laughed, pausing a moment. "Worthy deed? Why, you can't do anything! The hawks circle way overhead, tracing delicate patterns for us all to admire. The moon hangs high like a lantern at night, so we can see our ways home to our loved ones. Even I, the lowly lizard, have something to do. I decorate the sands with these beautiful brushstrokes as I pull my tail along. But you? You do nothing but get uglier every day."

And so it went on, year after year. At last the cactus grew old, and it knew its time was short.

"Oh, Lord," it cried out, "I've wondered so long, and I've tried so hard. Forgive me if I've failed to find something worthy to do. I fear that now it's too late."

But just then the cactus felt a strange stirring and unfolding, and it knew a surge of joy that erased all despair. At its very tip, like a sudden crown, a glorious flower suddenly opened in bloom.

Never had the desert known such a blossom. Its fragrance perfumed the air far and wide and brought happiness to all passing by. The butterflies paused to admire its beauty, and that night even the moon smiled when it rose to find such a treasure.

The cactus heard a voice.

"You have waited long," the Lord said. "The heart that seeks to do good reflects my glory, and will always bring something worthwhile to the world, something in which all can rejoice—even if for only a moment."

•

HOW THE WISE MAN FOUND
THE KING

*Retold by Christine Chaundler
and Eric Wood*

In this old legend we see that there are many ways to serve God,
countless opportunities to give him thanks and praise.

When Christ was born in Bethlehem, three kings set out from
their homes to find Him and worship Him. They had seen a wonderful new star in the eastern countries where they lived, and they
knew that it meant that a great King was born—a King whose
kingdom would never come to an end, who was mightier than the
sun and greater than the stars—a King who was the Lord of earth
and sky and sea.

These three kings had studied old books and prophecies, and
they knew that God had promised to send this mighty King into the
world one day, and when they saw the star they rejoiced with
exceeding great joy. And gathering together all the richest treasures
they possessed, gold and frankincense and myrrh, they set out at
once to follow the guiding of the star until it led them at last to the
lowly cattle shed where the Holy Child lay.

But in the country they had left there was another king. He too
had studied the old prophecies with his brother-kings, and he too
was waiting for some sign to tell him that the Saviour of the world
had come. Something had happened to delay him when at last the
star brought the glad tidings of Christ's birth. He was not ready to
start with the other wise men, and so he was left behind. And when
he had gathered together his treasures and was ready to set out
upon his journey, he was too late to follow the star that was guiding
the others, and so he was obliged to find his own way as best he
could across the world.

He had brought with him three jewels to give to the great King
whom he was going to worship. One of them was a ruby, as red as
the last rays of the setting sun. One was a sapphire, holding in its
depths all the blue in sea and sky. And the third was a pearl, as pure
and white as the peak of a snow-clad mountain. No money in the
world was enough to buy these precious gems, so valuable were

they; yet the king was ready to give them all to the God whom he was seeking.

For many long months he travelled, asking wherever he went for tidings of the other three kings. He could not catch them; they were too far ahead for that. But by inquiring diligently of everybody he met the king managed to keep more or less upon their track.

It was a long journey and a very weary one, and the dangers and difficulties through which the other wise men had passed were ten times greater for him, all alone and unattended as he was. But his longing to reach the Christ-Child and to bow himself down in worship before Him spurred the king on. With his three jewels hidden in his bosom he rode bravely through all the dangers and surmounted all the difficulties, until at last he arrived in Judea, and knew that he could not be far from his goal.

As he rode through the country he heard on every side sounds of mourning and distress. Cruel Herod, frightened at what the wise men had said of the King who was born in Bethlehem, had determined to find and kill the Holy Child, lest when He grew older He should try to snatch the throne of Israel from him. So he had told the three wise men to come and tell him when they had found the Messiah, that he also might come and worship Him. But God had warned the wise men in a dream, and they had returned to their country by another way.

When Herod found that the wise men had returned to their own country by another way, and did not mean to come and tell him where Christ was hidden, he sent forth an order that all the children in that part of the country under two years of age were to be killed. And the rough soldiers had gone out and, tearing the children from their mothers' arms, had killed them ruthlessly.

But there was one Child they did not kill—the one of all others that they wanted. Joseph had been warned by God in a dream, and taking the young Child and His mother, had fled with them into Egypt. And there the little family lived for many years, until Herod was dead, and it was safe for them to return to their own land again.

So when the wise man who was too late arrived at last at Bethlehem, he found that the King of the Jews whom he had come so far to worship was there no longer. He had gone, no man knew where.

The wise man was at first in despair. He had come so far and dared so much, and now it seemed that he would never be able to offer his gifts to the King after all. Then he took heart again. Since he had come so far, what did a little farther matter? He had set out to worship the King, and he would travel through the world, if need be, until at last he found Him.

So he rode bravely on again.

He had not gone very far when he heard a woman screaming, crying bitterly for help. The king hurried to the place from where the sound came, and there he saw a poor mother with a little baby in her arms, whom a cruel soldier was trying to take from her and kill. The mother had hidden the little one safely all through the terrible massacre, and now, when she thought the danger was past, this soldier had found the child and, in spite of her prayers and cries, was about to kill it.

The king spurred forward and sprang to the ground beside the poor woman, begging the soldier to spare the little one's life. But the soldier only laughed roughly, and said that it was his duty, he must do his duty whatever happened. And again he tried to snatch the child from the woman's arms.

Then the king drew from his bosom the ruby which he was carrying to Christ. He uncovered the jewel and flashed it before the man's astonished gaze.

"I will give you this if you will spare the child's life," he said.

The soldier fixed his eyes upon the wonderful jewel, and the temptation was too great for him. He let the child and its mother go unharmed, and he himself went away with the ruby in his possession, rich beyond anything he had ever dreamed or hoped to be.

Then, a little sadly, the king rode on. He had no ruby now to offer to the Christ-Child when he found Him. Still, there were the other two jewels left. He need not be ashamed of his gifts even now, and he went on his way with renewed courage.

After many more weary months of travelling he came to a place where there was a terrible famine. The poor people were dying of sickness and hunger. They had no one to help them, and the king, overcome with pity, parted with his second jewel in order to buy food for the starving, care and comfort for the sick, and clothes and raiment for the naked. He stayed in the famine-stricken place until he had done all that he could for the poor, starving people. Then he rode on again, poorer by the loss of his jewel, but rich with the blessings of those whom he had saved from death and misery.

Now the wise man had only the pearl left of all his costly offerings with which he had started on his journey. He did not regret the loss of the other two gems, for he knew that if he had

had the choice over again he would still have parted with them. Only he wished, so very, very much, that he had more treasures to offer to the King.

But the pearl that was left was of even greater value than the other two jewels, and although he longed for it to be a thousand times rarer and more precious, yet he knew that it was a present fit for a king, even for the King of all the earth. And so he rode on, still seeking the Christ-Child.

Long years passed away, and the king still journeyed on, seeking the Saviour, yet never finding Him. After many years he came to a place where a poor slave girl was to be sold to a brutal master. The king tried to persuade the master to let the girl go free. But the man only laughed at him, and at last the king, finding that words were of no avail, and determined to save the poor, trembling girl from the dreadful life ahead of her, drew forth his last remaining jewel and bought the girl's freedom with the precious pearl, though it went to his heart to give it away.

Then once more he started on his search, grieving that he had now no present at all to bring to the King, yet determined never to give up his quest until he had found the Lord for whom he had looked so long and faithfully.

Thirty-three years he wandered through the world, until at last, old and worn and dying, he reached Jerusalem on the very day of Our Lord's crucifixion. And there, on the Cross of Calvary, he found the King for whom he had searched so long. In spite of the cross and the crown of thorns, in spite of the scornful, mocking words of those who stood around, the wise man recognized his Saviour, and he knew that he had reached the end of his journey at last. This was not the little Baby whom he had set out to seek such a long, long time ago, but still it was the King.

He pushed his way through the crowd and sank down, exhausted, and made the confession that he had come empty-handed. He had found the great King at last, but he had nothing at all to offer Him.

But had he nothing at all? Legend says that as he knelt at the foot of the cross, this man who had searched so faithfully and earnestly heard a heavenly voice come from afar—simple, tender words that filled his longing heart.

"Inasmuch as thou hast done it unto the least of these My brethren, thou hast done it unto Me."

And the wise man knew that his long, weary journey had not been in vain.

•

GOD WILL SEE

Flannery O'Connor wrote: "A work of art is good in itself. What is
good in itself glorifies God because it reflects God." This story
reminds us of who the really important audience is as we go about
our daily work.

Long ago in ancient Greece an aged sculptor was laboring over
a block of stone. He carved with utmost care, probing the rock with
his chisel, chipping away a fragment at a time, gauging the marks
with sinewy hands before making the next cut. When it was finished, the piece would be hoisted high into the air and set on top
of a towering shaft, and so would become the capital, or uppermost
part, of a column. And the column would help support the roof of
a lofty temple.

"Why spend so much time and effort on that section?" asked a
government official who passed by. "It will sit fifty feet high. No
human eye will be able to see those details."

The old artist put down his hammer and chisel, gazed steadily
at his questioner, and replied: "But God will see it!"

•

ROBERT OF SICILY
Retold by Sara Cone Bryant

Hopefully, as we get further along in life, we win some of the rewards of long, hard work—better jobs, higher offices, larger reputations, fatter paychecks. As we accumulate the trappings of success, this old tale may help us remember the lesson of Proverbs 16:18—"Pride goeth before destruction, and a haughty spirit before a fall." The story comes from the *Gesta Romanorum,* a collection of ancient tales compiled most probably in England in the early fourteenth century. It was a source mined for inspiration by many great writers, including Shakespeare and Chaucer.

An old legend says that there was once a king named Robert of Sicily, who was brother to the great Pope of Rome and to the Emperor of Allemaine. He was a very selfish king and very proud. He cared more for his pleasures than for the needs of his people, and his heart was so filled with his own greatness that he had no thought for God.

One day, this proud king was sitting in his place at church, at vesper service. His courtiers were about him, in their bright garments, and he himself was dressed in his royal robes. The choir was chanting the Latin service, and as the beautiful voices swelled louder, the king noticed one particular verse which seemed to be repeated again and again. He turned to a learned clerk at his side and asked what those words meant, for he knew no Latin.

"They mean, 'He hath put down the mighty from their seats, and hath exalted them of low degree,' " answered the clerk.

"It is well the words are in Latin, then," said the king angrily, "for they are a lie. There is no power on earth or in heaven that can put me down from my seat!" And he sneered at the beautiful singing, as he leaned back in his place.

Presently the king fell asleep, while the service went on. He slept deeply and long. When he awoke the church was dark and still, and he was all alone. He, the king, had been left alone in the church, to awake in the dark! He was furious with rage and surprise, and, stumbling through the dim aisles, he reached the great doors and beat at them, madly, shouting for his servants.

The old sexton heard someone shouting and pounding in the church, and thought it was some drunken vagabond who had stolen in during the service. He came to the door with his keys and called out, "Who is there?"

"Open! Open! It is I, the king!" came a hoarse, angry voice from within.

"It is a crazy man," thought the sexton, and he was frightened. He opened the doors carefully and stood back, peering into the darkness. Out past him rushed the figure of a man in scanty, tattered clothes, with unkempt hair and wild white face. The sexton did not know that he had ever seen him before, but he looked long after him, wondering at his wildness and his haste.

In his fluttering rags, without hat or cloak, not knowing what strange thing had happened to him, King Robert rushed to his palace gates, pushed aside the startled servants, and hurried, blind with rage, up the wide stair and through the great corridors, toward the room where he could hear the sound of his courtiers' voices. Men and women servants tried to stop the ragged man who had somehow gotten into the palace, but Robert did not even see them as he fled along. Straight to the open doors of the big banquet hall he made his way and into the midst of the grand feast there.

The great hall was filled with lights and flowers. The tables were set with everything that is delicate and rich to eat. The courtiers, in their gay clothes, were laughing and talking. And at the head of the feast, on the king's own throne, sat a king. His face, his figure, his voice were exactly like Robert of Sicily. No human being could have told the difference; no one dreamed that he was not the king. He was dressed in the king's royal robes, he wore the royal crown, and on his hand was the king's own ring. Robert of Sicily, half naked, ragged, without a sign of his kingship on him, stood before the throne and stared with fury at this figure of himself.

The king on the throne looked at him. "Who art thou, and what dost thou here?" he asked. And though his voice was just like Robert's own, it had something in it sweet and deep, like the sound of bells.

"I am the king!" cried Robert of Sicily. "I am the king, and you are an impostor!"

The courtiers started from their seats, and drew their swords. They would have killed the crazy man who insulted their king. But he raised his hand and stopped them, and with his eyes looking into Robert's eyes he said, "Not the king; you shall be the king's jester! You shall wear the cap and bells, and make laughter for my court. You shall be the servant of the servants, and your companion shall be the jester's ape."

With shouts of laughter, the courtiers drove Robert of Sicily from the banquet hall. The waiting-men, with laughter, too, pushed him into the soldiers' hall; and there the pages brought the jester's wretched ape, and put a fool's cap and bells on Robert's head. It was like a terrible dream. He could not believe it true. He could not understand what had happened to him. And when he woke next morning, he believed it was a dream, and that he was king again. But as he turned his head, he felt the coarse straw under his cheek instead of the soft pillow, and he saw that he was in the stable, with the shivering ape by his side. Robert of Sicily was a jester, and no one knew him for the king.

Three long years passed. Sicily was happy and all things went well under the king, who was not Robert. Robert was still the jester, and his heart became harder and more bitter with every year. Many times during the three years, the king who had his face and voice had called him to himself, when none else could hear, and had asked him the one question, "Who art thou?" And each time that he asked it his eyes looked into Robert's eyes, to find his heart. But each time Robert threw back his head and answered proudly, "I am the king!" And the king's eyes grew sad and stern.

At the end of three years, the Pope bade the Emperor of Allemaine and the King of Sicily, his brothers, to a great meeting in his city of Rome. The King of Sicily went, with all his soldiers and courtiers and servants—a great procession of horsemen and footmen. Never had there been a gayer sight than the grand train: men in bright armor, riders in wonderful cloaks of velvet and silk, servants carrying marvelous presents to the Pope. And at the very end rode Robert the jester. His horse was a poor old thing, many-colored, and the ape rode with him. Everyone in the villages through which they passed ran after the jester and pointed and laughed.

The Pope received his brothers and their trains in the square before Saint Peter's. With music and flags and flowers he made the King of Sicily welcome and greeted him as his brother. In the midst of it, the jester broke through the crowd and threw himself before the Pope. "Look at me!" he cried, "I am your brother, Robert of Sicily! This man is an impostor who has stolen my throne. I am Robert, the king!"

The Pope looked at the poor jester with pity, but the Emperor of Allemaine turned to the King of Sicily, and said, "Is it not rather dangerous, brother, to keep a madman as jester?" And again Robert was pushed back among the serving-men.

It was Holy Week, and the king and the emperor, with all their trains, went every day to the great services in the cathedral. Something wonderful and holy seemed to make all these services more beautiful than ever before. All the people of Rome felt it: it was as if the presence of an angel were there. Men thought of God and felt his blessing on them. But no one knew who it was that brought the beautiful feeling. And when Easter Day came, never had there been so lovely, so holy a day. In the great churches, filled with flowers, and sweet with incense, the kneeling people listened to the choirs singing, and it was like the voices of angels. Their prayers were more earnest than ever before, their praise more glad; there was something heavenly in Rome.

Robert of Sicily went to the services with the rest and sat in the humblest place with the servants. Over and over again he heard the sweet voices of the choirs chant the Latin words he had heard long ago: "He hath put down the mighty from their seat, and hath exalted them of low degree." And at last, as he listened, his heart was softened. He, too, felt the strange blessed presence of a heavenly power. He thought of God, and of his own wickedness; he remembered how happy he had been, and how little good he had done; he realized that his power had not been from himself at all. On Easter night, as he crept to his bed of straw, he wept, not because he was so wretched, but because he had not been a better king when power was his.

At last all the festivities were over, and the King of Sicily went home to his own land again with his people. Robert the jester came home too.

On the day of their homecoming, there was a special service in the royal church, and even after the service was over for the people, the monks held prayers of thanksgiving and praise. The sound of their singing came softly in at the palace windows. In the great banquet room, the king sat, wearing his royal robes and his crown, while many subjects came to greet him. At last, he sent them all away, saying he wanted to be alone; but he commanded the jester to stay. And when they were alone together the king looked into Robert's eyes, as he had done before, and said, softly, "Who art thou?"

Robert of Sicily bowed his head. "Thou knowest best," he said, "I only know that I have sinned."

As he spoke, he heard the voices of the monks singing, "He

hath put down the mighty from their seats"—and his head sank lower. But suddenly the music seemed to change. A wonderful light shone all about. As Robert raised his eyes, he saw the face of the king smiling at him with a radiance like nothing on earth, and as he sank to his knees before the glory of that smile, a voice sounded with the music, like a melody throbbing on a single string: "I am an angel, and thou art the king!"

Then Robert of Sicily was alone. His royal robes were upon him once more. He wore his crown and his royal ring. He was king. And when the courtiers came back they found their king kneeling by his throne, absorbed in silent prayer.

•

THE GOLDEN TRIPOD

Retold by James Baldwin

This story is about the Seven Sages of ancient Greece, seven famous rulers, legislators, and philosophers who lived between 620 and 550 B.C. It reminds us that the wiser we get, the more we recognize our own limitations.

Tripods were kettles standing on three legs. They were ordinary domestic utensils in ancient Greece, but they were also sometimes elaborately decorated as works of art. Homer mentions tripods as prizes awarded to victors in various contests.

One morning, long ago, a merchant of Miletus was walking along the seashore. Some fisherman were pulling in a large net, and he stopped to watch them.

"My good men," he said, "how many fish do you expect to draw in this time?"

"We cannot tell," they answered. "We never count our fish before they are caught."

The net seemed heavy. There was certainly something in it. The merchant felt sure that the fishermen were having a good haul.

"How much will you take for the fish that you are drawing in?" he asked.

"How much will you give?" said the fisherman.

"Well, I will give three pieces of silver for all that are in the net," answered the merchant.

The fishermen talked in low tones with one another for a little while, and then one said, "It's a bargain. Be they many or few, you may have all for three pieces of silver."

In a few minutes the big net was pulled up out of the water. There was not a fish in it. But it held a beautiful golden tripod that was worth more than a thousand fishes.

The merchant was delighted. "Here is your money," he said. "Give me the tripod."

"No, indeed," said the fishermen. "You were to have all the fish that happened to be in the net and nothing else. We didn't sell you the tripod."

They began to quarrel. They talked and wrangled a long time and could not agree. Then one of the fishermen said, "Let us ask the governor about it and do as he shall bid us."

"Yes, let us ask the governor," said the merchant. "Let him decide the matter for us."

So they carried the tripod to the governor, and each told his story.

The governor listened but could not make up his mind as to who was right.

"This is a very important question," he said. "We must send to Delphi and ask the oracle whether the tripod shall be given to the fishermen or to the merchant. Leave the tripod in my care until we get an answer."

Now the oracle at Delphi was supposed to be very wise. People from all parts of the world sent to it, to tell it their troubles and get its advice.

So the governor sent a messenger to Delphi to ask the oracle what should be done with the tripod. The merchant and the fishermen waited impatiently till the answer came. And this is what the oracle said:

> "Give not the merchant nor the fishermen the prize,
>   But give it to that one who is wisest of the wise."

The governor was much pleased with this answer.

"The prize shall go to the man who deserves it most," he said. "There is our neighbor, Thales, whom everybody knows and loves. He is famous all over the world. Men come from every country to see him and learn from him. We will give the prize to him."

So with his own hands he carried the golden tripod to the little house where Thales lived. He knocked at the door and the wise man himself opened it.

Then the governor told him how the tripod had been found, and how the oracle had said that it must be given to the wisest of the wise.

"And so I have brought the prize to you, friend Thales."

"To me!" said the astonished Thales. "Why, there are many men who are wiser than I. There is my friend Bias of Priene. He excels all other men. Send the beautiful gift to him."

So the governor called two of his trusted officers and told them to carry the tripod to Priene and offer it to Bias.

"Tell the wise man why you bring it, and repeat to him the words of the oracle."

Now, all the world had heard of the wisdom of Bias. He taught that men ought to be kind even to their enemies. He taught, also, that a friend is the greatest blessing that anyone can have.

He was a poor man and had no wish to be rich. "It is better to be wise than wealthy," he said.

When the governor's messengers came to Priene with the tripod, they found Bias at work in his garden. They told him their errand and showed him the beautiful prize.

He would not take it.

"The oracle did not intend that I should have it," he said. "I am not the wisest of the wise."

"But what shall we do with it?" said the messengers. "Where shall we find the wisest man?"

"In Mitylene," answered Bias, "there is a very great man named Pittacus. He might now be the king of his country, but he prefers to give all of his time to the study of wisdom. He is the man whom the oracle meant."

The name of Pittacus was known all over the world. He was a brave soldier and a wise teacher. The people of his country had made him their king, but as soon as he had made good laws for them he gave up his crown.

One of his mottoes was this: "Whatever you do, do it well."

The messengers found him in his house talking to his friends and teaching them wisdom.

He looked at the tripod. "How beautiful it is!" he said.

Then the messengers told him how it had been taken from the sea, and they repeated the words of the oracle:

"Give not the merchant nor the fishermen the prize,
But give it to that one who is wisest of the wise."

"We present the prize to you" said the messengers, "because you are the wisest of the wise."

"You are mistaken," answered Pittacus. "I should be delighted to own so beautiful a piece of workmanship, but I know I am not worthy."

"Then to whom shall we take it?" asked the messengers.

"Take it to Cleobulus, King of Rhodes," answered the wise man. "He is the handsomest and strongest of men, and I believe he is the wisest also."

The messengers went on until they came at last to the island of Rhodes. There everybody was talking about King Cleobulus and his wonderful wisdom. He had studied in all the great schools of the world, and there was nothing that he did not know.

"Educate the children," he said, and for that reason his name is remembered to this day.

When the messengers showed him the tripod, he said, "That is indeed a beautiful piece of work. Will you sell it? What is the price?"

They told him that it was not for sale, but that it was to be given to the wisest of the wise.

"Well, you will not find that man in Rhodes," said he. "He lives in Corinth, and his name is Periander. Carry the precious gift to him."

Everybody had heard of Periander, King of Corinth. Some had heard of his great learning, and others had heard of his selfishness and cruelty.

Strangers admired him for his wisdom. His own people despised him for his wickedness.

When he heard that some men had come to Corinth with a very costly golden tripod, he had them brought before him.

"I have heard all about that tripod," he said, "and I know why you are carrying it from one place to another. Do you expect to find any man in Corinth who deserves so rich a gift?"

"We hope that you are the man," said the messengers.

"Ha! ha!" laughed Periander. "Do I look like the wisest of the wise? No, indeed. But in Lacedæmon there is a good and noble man named Chilon. He loves his country, he loves his fellow men, he loves learning. To my mind he deserves the golden prize. I bid you carry it to him."

The messengers were surprised. They had never heard of Chilon, for his name was hardly known outside of his own country. But when they came into Lacedæmon, they heard his praises on every side.

They learned that Chilon was a very quiet man, that he never spoke about himself, and that he spent all his time trying to make his country great and strong and happy.

Chilon was so busy that the messengers had to wait several days before they could see him. At last they were allowed to go before him and state their business.

"We have here a very beautiful tripod," they said. "The oracle at Delphi has ordered that it shall be given to the wisest of wise men, and for that reason we have brought it to you."

"You have made a mistake," said Chilon. "Over in Athens there is a very wise man whose name is Solon. He is a poet, a soldier, and a lawmaker. He is my worst enemy, and yet I admire him as the wisest man in the world. It is to him that you should have taken the tripod."

The messengers made due haste to carry the golden prize to Athens. They had no trouble finding Solon. He was the chief ruler of that great city.

All the people whom they saw spoke in praise of his wisdom.

When they told him their errand he was silent for a little while; then he said: "I have never thought of myself as a wise man, and therefore the prize is not for me. But I know of at least six men who are famous for their wisdom, and one of them must be the wisest of the wise."

"Who are they?" asked the messengers.

"Their names are Thales, Bias, Pittacus, Cleobulus, Periander, and Chilon," answered Solon.

"We have offered the prize to each one of them," said the messengers, "and each one has refused it."

"Then there is only one other thing to be done," said Solon. "Carry it to Delphi and leave it there in the Temple of Apollo; for Apollo is the fountain of wisdom, the wisest of the wise."

And this the messengers did.

• • •

The famous men whom I have told you about in this story are commonly called the Seven Wise Men of Greece. They lived more than two thousand years ago. Each one helped to make his country famous, and each one remembered that no matter how much he knew, there was much more he did not know.

•

A LITTLE LEARNING

Alexander Pope

As we journey further into the world, we discover this important piece of wisdom: The more we learn, the more we know there is much left to learn. These verses come from *An Essay on Criticism* by Alexander Pope (1688–1744). The second line refers to springs in Pieria at the foot of Mount Olympus. According to Greek mythology, these fountains were the haunts of the Muses, the inspiring nymphs of the arts and sciences.

A little learning is a dangerous thing;
Drink deep, or taste not the Pierian spring:
There shallow draughts intoxicate the brain,
And drinking largely sobers us again.
Fired at first sight with what the Muse imparts,
In fearless youth we tempt the heights of Arts,
While from the bounded level of our mind
Short views we take, nor see the lengths behind;
But more advanced, behold with strange surprise
New distant scenes of endless science rise!
So pleased at first the towering Alps we try,
Mount o'er the vales, and seem to tread the sky,
The eternal snows appear already past,
And the first clouds and mountains seem the last;
But, those attained, we tremble to survey
The growing labors of the lengthened way,
The increasing prospects tire our wandering eyes,
Hills peep o'er hills, and Alps on Alps arise!

•

THE LEGEND BEAUTIFUL

The next three stories deal explicitly with the question: How can I live most perfectly? None of the tales imply that anyone can actually live perfectly, but they do hold forth a vision toward which we can strive. This first story, an old legend from Germany, says, "Do thy duty, and leave the rest to God," and helps us understand the nature of some of those obligations. The retelling is based in part on a rhymed version of the story from Henry Wadsworth Longfellow's *Tales of a Wayside Inn.*

A monk was kneeling alone in his cold, bare cell, praying most fervently. He was a gentle, devout man who had gone into a secluded monastery, hoping to live an existence acceptable to God. Several times a day he prayed, thanking the Lord for all the blessings of life, seeking forgiveness for his sins, and asking for the strength to deny temptation.

As the noon hour approached, the narrow stone cell suddenly filled with a bright glow. And at once, lifting his eyes, the holy man had a vision. It seemed to him that he saw Christ, dressed in a simple garment, walking through village streets and harvest fields, just as he must have done so long ago when he taught in Galilee. As the good monk watched, he saw Jesus healing the lame and the blind, blessing the little children, and preaching the word of God to the crowds who pressed close around him.

The monk gazed at the vision in awe and exaltation. He felt himself blessed beyond all deserts, and his heart filled with love and thanks that the Lord should show himself to his humble servant this way.

"How wonderful it is," he thought, "that a poor monk should be granted this divine vision, and that Jesus of Nazareth should visit my lonely cell!"

He remained kneeling on the hard, cold stones, rejoicing that he should be a witness to such glory, and scarcely daring even to breathe for fear that the heavenly vision would depart.

But suddenly his joy was interrupted by a familiar sound. The chapel bell began to clang loudly and persistently, calling for him to leave his cell and do his daily work. For now it was the appointed hour when, rain or shine, in winter cold or summer heat, the sick and poor and lame and blind gathered outside the monastery gates. There they received a daily portion of bread, which the good brothers baked especially for the needy. And it was this monk's duty to go each afternoon and distribute the charity.

The holy man was filled with sorrow and doubt. What should he do? How could he turn his back upon this magnificent sight? Had not Jesus himself come to grace his cold, narrow cell? Surely he should not insult this divine vision by getting up and deserting the room for a crowd of ragged beggars outside the gate. They could wait a little while, after all. There would be no harm in that. Surely it was better to stay kneeling in prayer before this glorious sight, as long as it remained before him.

But the thought of the poor people waiting at the gates would not leave the monk's mind. He remembered the anxious, careworn looks on their faces, the sadness in their eyes, the feebleness with which they stretched forth their arms. Many of them had no other food than the bread they received once a day from the good brother's hands. Certainly they could wait, but was it right to leave them waiting in hunger and doubt even for a few minutes when their lives were already full of so much sad waiting?

It seemed to the monk that two sensations now warred within his soul—ecstasy over the radiant vision before him, and deep distress for the people who waited outside. Should he go, or should he stay? If he turned his back, would the radiant vision remain, or would it flee? If it disappeared, would it ever come again? He searched his heart for an answer, and he tried to think of what Jesus himself would have done in his place. Would the Master, whose work on this earth was healing the sick and comforting the afflicted, who showed men how to love their neighbors, who spoke of charity and mercy and brotherhood—would he leave his brothers and sisters waiting cold and hungry outside the gates, even for an instant?

And as the monk put all these questions to himself, he seemed to hear a voice whisper within his breast: "Do thy duty, and leave the rest to God."

At once he knew what he must do. Rising from his knees and taking one last, longing look at the blessed vision, he departed his cell, and hurried out to feed the poor.

There were so many in need that day! The monk worked as quickly as he could, passing among the huddled figures, placing the precious loaves in their trembling hands. Yet every time he emptied his basket, more pleading faces appeared. It seemed he would never finish his task! He longed to be back in his secluded cell, where he could reflect undisturbed on the wonderful vision that had been sent to him. He worried that he had slighted the radiant visitor by turning his back. Should he have stayed? The question burned in his conscience. If only this duty would end quickly, so he could return to the solitude of his chamber and examine his decision, to know that he had made the right choice.

At last, after a long hour, the day's work was over, and he was free to return to his cell. As he turned his face toward the cloister, it seemed as though its high walls glowed with a gentle light. He caught his breath as a sudden hope swelled in his breast. Hurrying down the long, narrow hallway toward his room, he threw open the door and stopped on the threshold with an awestruck gasp.

There, in his chamber, the radiant vision still stood, just as before. Throughout the long hour of absence, Jesus had waited for the good monk to return.

The holy man felt a surge of joy in his heart, and he sank to his knees before the heavenly image.

As he bowed his head, the vision spoke: "Hadst thou stayed, I must have fled."

And at last the monk knew he had made the right decision when he turned to help his brothers and sisters.

•

TRUE SAINTLINESS
Adapted from a retelling by Joel H. Metcalf

Justice Oliver Wendell Holmes said: "It is one thing to utter a happy phrase from a protected cloister, another to think under fire—to think for action upon which great interests depend. The great problems are questions of here and now." For most of us, the "great interests" and "great problems" of here and now are the well-being of our family, friends, and community. True saintliness lies in our attention to these places.

There was once a hermit, living in a cave of the desert, whose only food consisted of roots and acorns and a little bread the peasants gave him. He spent all his days praying and reading the holy Scriptures, and every hour of the night he would get up and offer a short prayer.

He did this because he wanted to live a life acceptable to God and to be a true saint—one of the greatest and best the world had ever known.

Finally, when he grew to be an old man, and had been faithful in his prayers, fastings, and vigils for many years, he asked the Lord to show him what progress he had made in the spiritual life.

"Oh God," he prayed, "show me one who has attained more sanctity than I, that I may see how I can improve my life." And immediately his prayer was answered.

A white-robed angel came to him, and said: "Tomorrow go to the nearest town, and in the marketplace you will find a clown performing tricks and making the people laugh. He is the man you seek."

The hermit was astonished and humbled, for he had a suspicion that there were none better than he. But he did as he was bidden, and in the public square he found a man who would first play a tune, then sing a song, then perform a few tricks of magic, after which he would pass his fool's cap around for pennies.

The hermit watched him in disgust, but, after the performance was over, he drew him aside, and asked him if he had always been a clown, what good deeds he had done, and what prayers and penances he had performed which made him beloved of God.

The grin on the clown's face vanished, and he said: "Do not mock me, holy father. I am ashamed to confess I have forgotten how to pray. I don't remember ever having done any good works. All I do is to play my flute and laugh and sing, for the few pennies I can earn, even when my heart is sad."

But the hermit would not take this answer, for the angel had told him the clown was a greater saint than he. So he insisted. "Remember! Sometime you must have performed some great act of goodness."

But the minstrel said: "No, I cannot remember doing any good act. I never deserved any praise from God or man."

"But," persisted the hermit, "have you always been a vagabond? Have you always been a beggar, as you are now?"

"Oh, no," said the clown. "I will tell you how I became poor.

Years ago, when I was a young man, and had just received my share of my father's estate, in the far-off city where I lived, I saw a woman by the roadside, tired out and weeping, as though pursued by enemies. I asked her what was the matter, and she said her husband and children had been sold into slavery for debt. Not only was she homeless and poor but evil men were after her to carry her away into slavery also. Of course there was nothing else to do but to buy her freedom and that of her family, which took all the money I had. This explains my poverty. There was no special merit in it. Anybody would have done the same, and I had almost forgotten about it."

The hermit, however, understood why the Lord thought the clown a greater saint than he.

"All my life I have been striving to save myself, and men call me a saint. But this poor piper, by one good deed, has far outstripped me in the heavenly race. He may forget what he has done, but God does not."

Then the hermit went back to his cave, a sadder but a wiser man, for he knew now that true saintliness could not be selfish. He added to his prayers and fastings a desire to help others all he could, but still he lived alone in his cave.

Ten years after, he prayed again for God to show him a greater saint than he, that he might imitate him in righteousness.

Then the angel came, as before, and told him that on a small farm nearby, two women lived, and in them he would find two souls who could show him the higher call of duty and saintliness.

So he made a second pilgrimage. When he reached the little farm, the two women received him gladly. They were greatly honored to receive a visit from so perfect a saint. His fame had gone before him. They brought him food and drink, and entertained him as lavishly as their small stores would permit.

The hermit, however, could hardly wait to find out from them the secret of their acceptableness to God, so he asked them about their lives. "We have no history," they said. "We have always worked hard in the house and the fields, with our husbands. We have many beloved children, for whom we have cared. We have seen poverty and sickness and death, but so have all the families about us, so we are no different from the rest."

"Yes," said the hermit, "but what about your good deeds? What have you done for God?"

"Why, nothing," they said. "We had no money to give away. We were too poor. We had no time to do much of anything for other people, for our families kept us busy from morning until night, but we are very happy and contented."

With all his questioning the monk could not get any other answer, so he gave up and was going away disappointed, when he thought to call at a neighbor's house and ask there about the two women.

"Why," they said, "they are the best people you ever saw. They have lived here for twenty-five years, and no one ever heard angry words from them, and they have had many crosses to bear, I can tell you. They mind their own affairs, and they have a kind word and a pleasant smile for all."

Then a great light seemed to break upon the mind of the hermit.

He saw how many ways there are of serving God. Some serve Him in churches and hermits' cells by praise and prayer. Some serve Him on the highway, helping strangers in desperate need. Some live faithfully and gently in humble homes, working, bringing up children, remaining kind and cheerful. Some bear pain patiently, for His sake. Endless, endless ways there are, that only the Heavenly Father sees.

And the hermit thought: "I have lived all alone these many years, and kept my temper, and been patient and uncomplaining. But could I have done the same with the worries of family life? I can get along with very little, but how would I be in poverty when others suffer besides myself? The strain and stress of bread-winning for others might have been too much for me. I know now what God meant to tell me. It is harder to be a saint in the home than in the desert, and to those who faithfully follow the harder way the greater credit belongs. Perhaps it was wrong and selfish of me to go into the desert when the common life would have furnished me all I ought to ask—room to deny myself and a road to lead me daily nearer to God."

•

THREE QUESTIONS
Leo Tolstoy

Complicated questions sometimes have simple answers, as this
old folktale retold by Tolstoy reminds us. Here is a king who
wishes to rule perfectly. The hermit in this story teaches him the
same lesson learned by the hermit in the last tale: "If we love one
another, God dwelleth in us, and His love is perfected in us" (1
John 4:12).

It once occurred to a certain king that if he always knew the
right time to begin everything, if he knew who were the right
people to listen to and whom to avoid, and, above all, if he always
knew what was the most important thing to do, he would never fail
in anything he might undertake.

And this thought having occurred to him, he had it proclaimed
throughout his kingdom that he would give a great reward to anyone who could teach him what was the right time for every action,
and who were the most necessary people, and how he might know
what was the most important thing to do.

And learned men came to the king, but they all answered his
questions differently.

All the answers being different, the king agreed with none of
them and gave the reward to none. But still wishing to find the right
answers to his questions, he decided to consult a hermit, widely
renowned for his wisdom.

The hermit lived in a wood which he never quitted, and he
received none but common folk. So the king put on simple clothes,
and before reaching the hermit's cell, he dismounted from his
horse and, leaving his bodyguard behind, went on alone.

When the king approached, the hermit was digging the ground
in front of his hut. Seeing the king, he greeted him, and went on
digging. The hermit was frail and weak, and each time he stuck his
spade into the ground and turned a little earth, he breathed heavily.

The king went up to him and said, "I have come to you, wise
hermit, to ask you to answer three questions: How can I learn to do
the right thing at the right time? Who are the people I most need,
and to whom I should, therefore, pay more attention than to the

rest? And what affairs are the most important and need my first attention?"

The hermit listened to the king but answered nothing. He just spat on his hand and recommenced digging.

"You are tired," said the king; "let me take the spade and work awhile for you."

"Thanks!" said the hermit, and, giving the spade to the king, he sat down on the ground.

When he had dug two beds, the king stopped and repeated his questions. The hermit again gave no answer but rose, stretched out his hand for the spade, and said: "Now rest awhile—and let me work a bit."

But the king did not give him the spade and continued to dig. One hour passed and another. The sun began to sink behind the trees, and the king at last stuck the spade into the ground and said: "I came to you, wise man, for an answer to my questions. If you can give me none, tell me so, and I will return home."

"Here comes someone running," said the hermit; "let us see who it is."

The king turned round and saw a bearded man come running out of the wood. The man held his hands pressed against his side, and blood was flowing from under them. When he reached the king, he fell fainting on the ground, moaning feebly. The king and the hermit unfastened the man's clothing. There was a large wound in his side. The king washed it as best he could, and bandaged it with his handkerchief and with a towel the hermit had. But the blood would not stop flowing, and the king again and again washed and rebandaged the wound. When at last the blood ceased flowing, the man revived and asked for something to drink. The king brought fresh water and gave it to him. Meanwhile the sun had set, and it had become cool. So the king, with the hermit's help, carried the wounded man into the hut and laid him on the bed. Lying on the bed the man closed his eyes and was quiet, but the king was so tired with his walk and with the work he had done that he crouched down on the threshold and also fell asleep—so soundly that he slept all through the short summer night. When he awoke in the morning, it was long before he could remember where he was, or who was the strange bearded man lying on the bed and gazing intently at him with shining eyes.

"Forgive me!" said the bearded man in a weak voice, when he saw that the king was awake and was looking at him.

"I do not know you and have nothing to forgive you for," said the king.

"You do not know me, but I know you. I am that enemy of yours who swore to revenge himself on you, because you executed his brother and seized his property. I knew you had gone alone to see the hermit, and I resolved to kill you on your way back. But the day passed and you did not return. So I came out from my ambush to find you, and I came upon your bodyguards, and they recognized me, and wounded me. I escaped from them but would have bled to death had you not dressed my wound. I wished to kill you, and you saved my life. Now, if I live and if you wish it, I will serve you as your most faithful servant and will bid my sons do the same. Forgive me!"

The king was very glad to have made peace with his enemy so easily and to have gained him for a friend, so he not only forgave him but said he would send his servants and his own physician to attend him, and promised to restore his property.

Having taken leave of the wounded man, the king went out onto the porch and looked around for the hermit. Before going away he wished once more to beg an answer to the questions he had put. The hermit was outside, on his knees, sowing seeds in the beds that had been dug the day before.

The king approached him and said: "For the last time, I pray you to answer my questions, wise man."

"You have already been answered!" said the hermit, still crouching on his thin legs and looking up at the king, who stood before him.

"How answered? What do you mean?" asked the king.

"Do you not see?" replied the hermit. "If you had not pitied my weakness yesterday, and had not dug these beds for me, but had gone your way, that man would have attacked you, and you would have repented of not having stayed with me. So the most important time was when you were digging the beds; and I was the most important man; and to do me good was your most important business. Afterward, when that man ran to us, the most important time was when you were attending to him, for if you had not bound up his wounds he would have died without having made peace with you. So he was the most important man, and what you did for him was your most important business. Remember then: there is only one time that is important—now! It is the most important time because it is the only time when we have any power. The most necessary man is he with whom you are, for no man knows whether he will ever have dealings with anyone else; and the most important affair is to do him good, because for that purpose alone was man sent into this life!"

•

I SOUGHT MY SOUL

> I sought my soul,
>   But my soul I could not see.
> I sought my God,
>   But my God eluded me.
> I sought my brother,
>   And I found all three.

•

SAINT AUGUSTINE BY THE SEASHORE
Adapted from a retelling by Peggy Webling

The next three stories remind us that the wisdom of man has limits, and the fullest understanding of our world and our existence comes in humility before God's creation. This first legend is about Saint Augustine of Hippo (354–430).

It chanced on a fair summer's day that Saint Augustine was walking alone on the seashore.

The sun sparkled on the ocean and white sands. Now and then a seagull flew across the sky or swept downward to the waves. Soft, fleecy little clouds were floating beneath the blue of heaven, and the whisper of the water was the only sound.

The lonely man was thinking deeply on a subject that even he could not understand, although he was one of the most wise and learned of men. He was pondering the acts of God, and trying to look into their hidden meaning. He struggled to comprehend the

Divine Plan behind events, and his heart filled with frustration and anguish when he failed to find unclouded explanations.

Suddenly he came across a little child who had dug a hole in the sand. He filled a little bucket at the edge of the water, ran and emptied it into the hole, then returned to the sea for more water. Bucket after bucket he poured into the hole.

"What are you doing, my boy?" asked the wise man.

The child did not show any surprise at the question, or even raise his head.

"I am going to empty the waters of the sea into this hole, my Father," he replied.

"That is impossible, little one!" exclaimed the wise man, with a smile.

The boy looked up into his face.

"No more impossible than for you to fathom the mysteries of God," he answered quietly.

The holy man was struck by the truth of the simple words. His heart was humbled. At once the frustrations lifted from his mind. He covered his eyes with his hands, and he gave thanks that faith could fill voids where understanding fell short.

When he raised his head, after a moment, he found himself alone with the sea and sky.

•

THE MELON AND THE PROFESSOR

Retold by Mary Hayes Davis
and Cheow-Leung

This tale is from China, but different variations are told all over the world. It reminds us that there is an order in creation which we do not fully see.

Wu-Kiao was a professor in a large Chinese university, and a very proud and learned man. Hundreds of students were under his teaching, and many thousands honored him. When he went out of his house, five people followed, singing and playing the drum all the way down the street, and eight men carried his chair. At home he had six servants about him. During each meal, thirty dishes were served at his table.

The professor was a great man. Through his wisdom and out of his deep knowledge, he explained all questions to the people.

One day Wu-Kiao sat in the shade of a tree in his garden. He turned his head and saw a watermelon lying on the ground, nearly covered by its green leaves. Then, seeing the fig tree with many figs on it, he said, "I think the Creator should have made the melon grow on this tree."

He touched the tree and said, "How strong you are; you could bear larger fruit like the watermelon." And he said to the vine, "You, so thin and small, should bear small fruit like the fig. Things are not well ordered. Mistakes are made in creation."

Just then a fig dropped from the tree on his nose, and he was a little bruised.

Then he said: "I was wrong. If the fig tree bore fruit as large as the watermelon and dropped it on my nose, I think I would be killed. It would be a dangerous tree to all people. I must study more carefully. I know many things and many people; and if I study and think more deeply, it may be I shall come to know that the Creator's works are perfect."

•

THE WONDER TREE

Adapted from
Friedrich A. Krummacher

This legend about the prophet Nathan and the young Solomon reminds us that miracles surround us every day, whether we choose to see them or not.

One day in the springtime, Prince Solomon was sitting under the palm trees in the royal gardens when he saw the Prophet Nathan walking near.

"Nathan," said the Prince, "I would see a wonder."

The Prophet smiled. "I had the same desire in the days of my youth," he replied.

"And was it fulfilled?" asked Solomon.

"A Man of God came to me;" said Nathan, "having a pomegranate seed in his hand. 'Behold,' he said, 'what will become of this.' Then he made a hole in the ground, and planted the seed, and covered it over. When he withdrew his hand the clods of earth opened, and I saw two small leaves coming forth. But scarcely had I beheld them, when they joined together and became a small stem wrapped in bark; and the stem grew before my eyes—and it grew thicker and higher and became covered with branches.

"I marveled, but the Man of God motioned me to be silent. 'Behold,' said he, 'new creations begin.'

"Then he took water in the palm of his hand, and sprinkled the branches three times, and lo! the branches were covered with green leaves, so that a cool shade spread above us, and the air was filled with perfume.

" 'From whence come this perfume and this shade?' cried I.

" 'Dost thou not see,' he answered, 'these crimson flowers bursting from among the leaves, and hanging in clusters?'

"I was about to speak, but a gentle breeze moved the leaves, scattering the petals of the flowers around us. Scarcely had the falling flowers reached the ground when I saw ruddy pomegranates hanging beneath the leaves of the tree, like almonds on Aaron's rod. Then the Man of God left me, and I was lost in amazement."

"Where is he, this Man of God?" asked Prince Solomon eagerly. "What is his name? Is he still alive?"

"Son of David," answered Nathan, "I have spoken to thee of a dream."

When the Prince heard this he was grieved to the heart. "How couldst thou deceive me thus?" he asked.

But the Prophet replied: "Behold in thy father's gardens thou mayest daily see the unfolding of wonder trees. Doth not this same miracle happen to the fig, the date, and the pomegranate? They spring from the earth, they put out branches and leaves, they flower, they fruit—not in a moment, perhaps, but in months and years. But canst thou tell the difference betwixt a minute, a month, or a year in the eyes of Him with whom one day is as a thousand years, and a thousand years as one day?"

•

THE THREE HEAVY STONES

This story comes from a school reader of the mid-nineteenth
century. It warns against living to serve certain preoccupations—
preoccupations still very much alive in a modern world full of
such slogans as "If it feels good, do it" and "Image is everything."

It was in the confines of the desert, amid barren and almost
inaccessible rocks, that Ben Achmet, the Dervish, led a life of auster-
ity and devotion. A cave in the rock was his dwelling. Roots and
fruits, the scanty products of the sterile region he inhabited, satisfied his hunger, and the fountain that bubbled up from the lower
part of a neighboring cliff slaked his thirst.

He had once been a priest in a magnificent mosque, and had
scrupulously conducted the ceremonies of the Mohammedan faith.
But seeking a life of total devotion, he abandoned the mosque and
his authority as priest, betaking himself to the desert to spend his
days as a hermit.

Years rolled over the head of Ben Achmet, and the fame of his
sanctity spread abroad. He often supplied the traveler of the desert
with water from his little well. In times of pestilence, he left his
solitary abode to attend to the sick and comfort the dying in the
villages that were scattered around. Often did he stanch the blood
of the wounded Arab and heal him of his wounds. His fame was
spread abroad; his name inspired veneration, and even the plundering nomad gave up his booty at the command of Ben Achmet, the
Dervish.

Akaba was an Arabian robber. He had a band of lawless men
under his command, ready to do his bidding. He had a treasure
house stored with ill-gotten wealth, and a large number of prisoners. The sanctity of Ben Achmet arrested his attention; his conscience smote him on account of his guilt, and he longed to be as
famed for his devotion as he had been for his crimes.

He sought the abode of the Dervish, and told him his desires.

"Ben Achmet," said he, "I have five hundred thieves ready to
obey me. I have any number of slaves at my command. And I have
a goodly treasure house filled with riches. Tell me how to add to
these the hope of a happy immortality."

Ben Achmet led him to the base of a neighboring cliff that was steep, rugged, and high. Pointing to three large stones that lay near together, he told him to lift them from the ground, and to follow him up the cliff.

Akaba, laden with the stones, could scarcely move. To ascend the cliff was impossible.

"I cannot follow thee with these burdens, Ben Achmet," said he.

"Then cast down one of the stones," replied the Dervish, "and hasten after me."

Akaba dropped one of the stones but still found himself too heavily encumbered to proceed.

"I tell thee it is impossible," cried the robber chieftain. "Thou thyself could not proceed a step with such a load."

"Let go another stone, then," said Ben Achmet.

Akaba readily dropped another stone and, with great difficulty, clambered up the cliff for a while. But soon, exhausted from the effort, he again cried out that he could come no further.

Ben Achmet directed him to drop the last stone, and no sooner had he done this than he mounted with ease and soon stood with his conductor on the summit of the cliff.

"Son," said Ben Achmet, "thou hast three burdens that hinder thee in thy way to a better world. Disband thy troops of lawless plunderers. Set thy prisoners at liberty. Restore thy ill-gotten wealth to its owners. It is easier for Akaba to ascend this cliff with the stones that lie at its foot than for him to journey onward to a better world with lust for power, pleasure, and riches in his possession."

•

THE BUNDLE

He carried a bundle of false beliefs,
Musty and heavy as a lawyer's briefs;
Prejudice, jealousy, bitterness, strife—
These were the wares of his troubled life.

He carried the bundle wherever he went—
Anger, suspicion, and selfish intent;
He saw what he sought, injustice and sin.
Life was a tempest without and within.

He mumbled and stumbled; the world was all wrong.
His bundle grew heavy as he shuffled along.
Worry, impatience, discord, and doubt—
These were the things that he dragged all about.

Tired of his bundle, he set the load down,
He prayed long to God; his face lost its frown.
In his eyes dawned a light by which he could see.
He forsook his old bundle and walked away free.

•

THE PHARISEE AND THE TAX COLLECTOR

Adapted from a retelling by
Eva March Tappan

Jesus told this parable to help us understand correct and incorrect ways to show our faith. The Pharisee in this story was a member of a religious group noted for strict observance of rites and ceremonies of the law. Someone once noted that he came to the Temple not to pray but to bray. His self-righteousness seems to revolve around one word: "I." The parable comes from Luke 18:9–14.

Jesus told a parable to some people who thought they were more righteous than anyone else and regarded others with scorn.

He said: "There were once two men who went up to the Temple to pray. One was a Pharisee and the other a tax collector."

Here the people began to listen closely, for many of them felt that a tax collector was so wicked that he hardly had a right to go into the Temple. The Pharisees, on the other hand, were known for their strict observance of holy ceremonies.

"This is the way they prayed," Jesus continued. "The Pharisee stood by himself and said loudly, so that all might hear: 'God, I thank you that I am not like other men. I am glad I am not greedy for money and not unjust, like that tax collector. I fast twice a week, and I give to the Temple one-tenth of all my money.'

"The tax collector did not venture to come far into the Temple but stood at the edge of the court. He dared not lift his eyes toward heaven, but as he said his prayer, he beat upon his breast in sorrow and thought, 'I am a sinner, but may God have mercy on me.'

"Then," said Jesus, "this tax collector went home accepted by God, but the Pharisee was not accepted, for he had not truly repented. For everyone who exalts himself will be humbled, but he who humbles himself will be exalted."

•

THE PRAYER

This dervish tale cautions us against another wrong way to pray. Honesty is no small part of faith—honesty with self, honesty with God. We should not negotiate with God through legalisms or sophistry.

A perfectly healthy man suddenly grew very ill and lay at death's door. The doctors stood around his bed, poked and prodded, shook their heads, and told him there was nothing they could do.

"If only I can keep my life," the man prayed, "I promise I'll sell my house and give all the money to the poor."

Soon he grew better, and his health was restored. He knew he should keep his promise, but he couldn't stand the thought of losing so much money. So he came up with a plan.

He advertised his house for sale for one silver coin. Whoever bought the house, however, also had to buy his cat. The price of the cat he set at one hundred gold coins.

Before long he found a buyer. He said goodbye to his cat, shut the door behind him, and set off down the street with one hundred gold coins in his purse. He rounded a corner, dropped the silver coin into a beggar's cup, and felt quite relieved that everything had turned out so well.

•

ABRAHAM AND THE OLD MAN

Retold by Horace E. Scudder

This little parable was in circulation during colonial times, and many people mistakenly thought it was part of the Bible. It has been attributed to the English scholar and churchman Jeremy Taylor (1613–1667). It reminds us that faith gives us a means to act virtuously toward all we meet on life's journey, not just those who share our faith.

The patriarch Abraham sat at the door of his tent. It was evening, when he was wont to watch for any strangers who might pass by, for all such he bade enter his tent. He espied an old man coming toward him, leaning on his staff, weary with travel and bent with age, for he was a hundred years old.

Abraham rose and asked the old man to come into the tent. He washed the old man's feet, gave him the best seat, and set meat before him. The old man ate his supper in silence, but he offered no prayer before he ate.

"Why dost thou not first worship the God of heaven?" asked Abraham.

"I worship fire only; I know no other God," said the old man.

At that Abraham was very angry and drove his guest out into the dark night. Then God called Abraham and said to him: "Where is that stranger who was in thy tent?"

"I thrust him out," said the patriarch, "because he did not worship Thee."

Then God answered Abraham out of heaven: "I have suffered him these hundred years, although he did not honor me, and couldst thou not endure him one night when he gave thee no trouble?"

Then was Abraham very sorry, and went and brought the old man back, and gave him rest, and sent him on his way in the morning.

•

SELF-DEPENDENCE

Matthew Arnold

Self-knowledge and self-reliance are sources of strength.

Weary of myself, and sick of asking
    What I am, and what I ought to be,
At this vessel's prow I stand, which bears me
    Forwards, forwards, o'er the starlit sea.

And a look of passionate desire
    O'er the sea and to the stars I send:
"Ye who from my childhood up have calm'd me,
    Calm me, ah, compose me to the end!

"Ah, once more," I cried, "ye stars, ye waters,
    On my heart your mighty charm renew;
Still, still let me, as I gaze upon you,
    Feel my soul becoming vast like you!"

From the intense, clear, star-sown vault of heaven,
    Over the lit sea's unquiet way,
In the rustling night air came the answer:
    "Wouldst thou *be* as these are? *Live* as they.

"Unaffrighted by the silence round them,
    Undistracted by the sights they see,
These demand not that the things without them
    Yield them love, amusement, sympathy.

"And with joy the stars perform their shining,
    And the sea its long moon-silver'd roll;
For self-poised they live, nor pine with noting
    All the fever of some differing soul.

"Bounded by themselves, and unregardful
    In what state God's other works may be,
In their own tasks all their powers pouring,
    These attain the mighty life you see."

O airborne voice! long since, severely clear,
  A cry like thine in mine own heart I hear:
"Resolve to be thyself; and know that he,
  Who finds himself, loses his misery!"

•

PRAYER FOR TRUE KNOWLEDGE

Thomas à Kempis

Seeking God's will brings strength too.

Grant me, O Lord, to know what I ought to know,
To love what I ought to love,
To praise what delights Thee most,
To value what is precious in Thy sight,
To hate what is offensive to Thee.

Do not suffer me to judge according to the sight of my eyes,
Nor to pass sentence according to the hearing of the ears of ignorant men;
But to discern with a true judgment between things visible and
  spiritual,
And above all, always to inquire what is the good pleasure of Thy
  will. Amen.

•

THREE WORDS OF STRENGTH

Friedrich von Schiller

And virtue brings strength.

There are three lessons I would write,
  Three words, as with a burning pen,
In tracings of eternal light,
  Upon the hearts of men.

Have Hope. Though clouds environ round,
  And gladness hides her face in scorn,
Put off the shadow from thy brow:
  No night but hath its morn.

Have Faith. Where'er thy bark is driven,
  The calm's disport, the tempest's mirth,
Know this: God rules the hosts of heaven,
  The inhabitants of earth.

Have Love. Not love alone for one,
  But man, as man, thy brother call;
And scatter, like a circling sun,
  Thy charities on all.

•

YOUR SECOND JOB

As told to Fulton Oursler
by Albert Schweitzer

One of the truly remarkable figures of the twentieth century, Albert Schweitzer (1875–1965) had by age thirty already become Europe's premier organist, an acclaimed biographer, and a first-rate theologian when he decided to study medicine in order to devote his life to helping people in Africa. In 1913, Schweitzer and his wife, Helene, traveled to what was then French Equatorial Africa to found the Schweitzer Hospital on the Ogooué River, where thousands of people received treatment during the following decades. In this selection, the man whose work inspired the world challenges us to seek adventures for the soul.

Often people say: "I would like to do some good in the world. But with so many responsibilities at home and in business, my nose is always to the grindstone. I am sunk in my own petty affairs, and there is no chance for my life to mean anything."

This is a common and dangerous error. In helpfulness to others, every man can find on his own doorstep adventures for the soul—our surest source of true peace and lifelong satisfaction. To know this happiness, one does not have to neglect duties or do spectacular things.

This career for the spirit I call "your second job." In this there is no pay except the privilege of doing it. In it you will encounter noble chances and find deep strength. Here all your reserve power can be put to work, for what the world lacks most today is men who occupy themselves with the needs of other men. In this unselfish labor a blessing falls on both the helper and the helped.

Without such spiritual adventures the man or woman of today walks in darkness. In the pressures of modern society we tend to lose our individuality. Our craving for creation and self-expression is stifled; true civilization is to that extent retarded.

What is the remedy? No matter how busy one is, any human being can assert his personality by seizing every opportunity for spiritual activity. How? By his second job: by means of personal action, on however small a scale, for the good of his fellow men. He will not have to look far for opportunities.

Our greatest mistake, as individuals, is that we walk through our life with closed eyes and do not notice our chances. As soon as we open our eyes and deliberately search we see many who need help, not in big things but in the littlest things. Wherever a man turns he can find someone who needs him.

One day I was traveling through Germany in a third-class railway carriage beside an eager youth who sat as if looking for something unseen. Facing him was a fretful and plainly worried old man. Presently the lad remarked that it would be dark before we reached the nearest large city.

"I don't know what I shall do when we get there," said the old man anxiously. "My only son is in the hospital, very ill. I had a telegram to come at once. I must see him before he dies. But I am from the country and I'm afraid I shall get lost in the city."

To which the young man replied "I know the city well. I will get off with you and take you to your son. Then I will catch a later train."

As they left the compartment they walked together like brothers.

Who can assay the effect of that small kind deed? You, too, can watch for the little things that need to be done.

During the First World War a cockney cab driver was declared too old for military service. From one bureau to another he went, offering to make himself useful in spare time and always being turned away. Finally he gave himself his own commission. Soldiers from out-of-town camps were being allowed leave in the city before going to the front. So at eight o'clock the old cabby appeared at a railroad station and looked for puzzled troopers. Four or five times every night, right up to demobilization, he served as a volunteer guide through the maze of London streets.

From a feeling of embarrassment, we hesitate to approach a stranger. The fear of being repulsed is the cause of a great deal of coldness in the world; when we seem indifferent we are often merely timid. The adventurous soul must break that barrier, resolving in advance not to mind a rebuff. If we dare with wisdom, always maintaining a certain reserve in our approach, we find that when we open ourselves we open doors in others.

Organized welfare work is, of course, necessary; but the gaps in it must be filled by personal service, performed with loving kindness. A charitable organization is a complex affair; like an automobile, it needs a broad highway to run on. It cannot penetrate the little bypaths; those are for men and women to walk through, with open eyes and hearts full of comprehension.

We cannot abdicate our conscience to an organization, nor to a government. "Am I my brother's keeper?" Most certainly I am! I cannot escape my responsibility by saying the State will do all that is necessary. It is a tragedy that nowadays so many think and feel otherwise.

Even in family life children are coming to believe they do not have to take care of the old folks. But old-age pensions do not relieve children of their duties. To dehumanize such care is wrong because it abolishes the principle of love, which is the foundation in upbuilding human beings and civilization itself.

You may think it is a wonderful life my wife and I have in the equatorial jungle. That is merely where we happen to be. But you can have a still more wonderful life by staying where you happen to be and putting your soul to the test in a thousand little trials, and winning triumphs of love. Such a career of the spirit demands patience, devotion, daring. It calls for strength of will and the determination to love: the greatest test of a man. But in this hard "second job" is to be found the only true happiness.

•

WHAT IS SUCCESS?

Ralph Waldo Emerson

To laugh often and much;

To win the respect of intelligent people
    and the affection of children;

To earn the appreciation of honest critics
    and endure the betrayal of false friends;

To appreciate beauty;

To find the best in others;

To leave the world a bit better,
    whether by a healthy child, a garden
    patch or a redeemed social condition;

To know even one life has breathed easier
    because you have lived;

This is to have succeeded.

•

GIVE UNTIL IT HURTS

Mother Teresa

Here is a modern-day heroine for the whole world. In 1948,
Mother Teresa of Calcutta founded the Order of the Missionaries
of Charity, a Roman Catholic congregation of women dedicated
to helping the needy, especially the destitute of India. She is sometimes called "the saint of the gutters" because of her work rescu-
ing people from the streets. Here is someone whose words and
deeds can inspire us all to strive for lives of spiritual fullness.

It is not enough for me to say: "I love God." I also have to love my neighbor. St. John says that you are a liar if you say you love God and you don't love your neighbor. How can you love God, whom you do not see, if you do not love your neighbor, whom you see, whom you touch, with whom you live? And so it is very important for us to realize that love, to be true, has to hurt. I must be willing to give whatever it takes not to harm other people and, in fact, to do good to them. This requires that I be willing to give until it hurts. Otherwise, there is no true love in me and I bring injustice, not peace, to those around me.

It hurt Jesus to love us. We have been created in His image for greater things, to love and to be loved. We must "put on Christ," as Scripture tells us. And so, we have been created to love as He loves us. Jesus makes Himself the hungry one, the naked one, the homeless one, the unwanted one, and He says, "You did it to Me." On the last day He will say to those on His right, "Whatever you did to the least of these, you did to Me," and He will also say to those on His left, "Whatever you neglected to do for the least of these, you neglected to do it for Me."

When He was dying on the Cross, Jesus said, "I thirst." Jesus is thirsting for our love, and this is the thirst of everyone, poor and rich alike. We all thirst for the love of others, that they go out of their way to avoid harming us and to do good to us. This is the meaning of true love, to give until it hurts.

I can never forget the experience I had in visiting a home where they kept all these old parents of sons and daughters who had just put them into an institution and forgotten them—maybe. I saw that in that home these old people had everything—good food, a comfortable place, television, everything, but everyone was looking toward the door. And I did not see a single one with a smile on the face. I turned to Sister and I asked: "Why do these people who have every comfort here, why are they all looking toward the door? Why are they not smiling?"

I am so used to seeing the smiles on our people—even the dying ones smile. And Sister said: "This is the way it is nearly every day. They are expecting, they are hoping that a son or daughter will come to visit them. They are hurt because they are forgotten." And see, this neglect to love brings spiritual poverty. Maybe in our own family we have somebody who is feeling lonely, who is feeling sick, who is feeling worried. Are we there? Are we willing to give until it hurts in order to be with our families, or do we put our own

interests first? These are the questions we must ask ourselves, especially as we begin this year of the family. We must remember that
love begins at home and we must also remember that "the future
of humanity passes through the family."

I was surprised in the West to see so many young boys and
girls given to drugs. And I tried to find out why. Why is it like that,
when those in the West have so many more things than those in the
East? And the answer was: "Because there is no one in the family to
receive them." Our children depend on us for everything—their
health, their nutrition, their security, their coming to know and love
God. For all of this, they look to us with trust, hope, and expectation. But often father and mother are so busy they have no time for
their children, or perhaps they are not even married or have given
up on their marriage. So the children go to the streets and get
involved in drugs or other things. We are talking of love of the
child, which is where love and peace must begin. These are the
things that break peace. . . .

Those who are materially poor can be very wonderful people.
One evening we went out and we picked up four people from the
street [in India]. And one of them was in a most terrible condition.
I told the Sisters: "You take care of the other three; I will take care
of the one who looks worst." So I did for her all that my love can
do. I put her in bed, and there was such a beautiful smile on her
face. She took hold of my hand as she said one word only: "Thank
you"—and she died.

I could not help but examine my conscience before her. And I
asked: "What would I say if I were in her place?" And my answer
was very simple. I would have tried to draw a little attention to
myself. I would have said: "I am hungry, I am dying, I am cold, I am
in pain," or something. But she gave me much more—she gave me
her grateful love. And she died with a smile on her face.

Then there was the man we picked up from the drain, half
eaten by worms, and, after we had brought him to the home, he
only said, "I have lived like an animal in the street, but I am going
to die as an angel, loved and cared for." Then, after we had removed
all the worms from his body, all he said, with a big smile, was:
"Sister, I am going home to God"—and he died. It was so wonderful to see the greatness of that man who could speak like that
without blaming anybody, without comparing anything. Like an
angel—this is the greatness of people who are spiritually rich even
when they are materially poor.

We are not social workers. We may be doing social work in the eyes of some people, but we must be contemplatives in the heart of the world. For we must bring that presence of God into your family, for the family that prays together stays together. There is so much hatred, so much misery, and we with our prayer, with our sacrifice, are beginning at home. Love begins at home, and it is not how much we do but how much love we put into what we do.

And so here I am talking to you. I want you to find the poor here, right in your own home first. And begin love here. Bring that good news to your own people first. And find out about your next-door neighbors. Do you know who they are?

I had the most extraordinary experience of love of neighbor with a Hindu family. A gentleman came to our house and said: "Mother Teresa, there is a family who have not eaten for so long. Do something." So I took some rice and went there immediately. And I saw the children—their eyes shining with hunger, I don't know if you have ever seen hunger. But I have seen it very often. And the mother of the family took the rice I gave her and went out. When she came back, I asked her: "Where did you go? What did you do?" And she gave me a very simple answer: "They are hungry also." What struck me was that she knew—and who are they? A Muslim family—and she knew. I didn't bring any more rice that evening because I wanted them, Hindus and Muslims, to enjoy the joy of sharing.

But there were those children, radiating joy, sharing the joy and peace with their mother because she had the love to give until it hurts. And you see this is where love begins—at home in the family.

●

THE MAGIC MILL

The next few selections touch on the subject of old age. One of the great benefits of growing older is the opportunity to learn from the mistakes of our youth. If we take those opportunities, age brings wisdom.

At Apolda, I have been told, there is a magic mill. In appearance it is very much like a huge coffee mill, but it is turned from beneath instead of from above. Two large beams form the handles, by which two stout serving men keep the mill in motion.

And what kind of grain is ground in the mill? I will tell you the story as it was told to me, but I will not vouch for its truth. Old women are thrown in at the top, wrinkled and bent, without hair and without teeth, and when they come out below they are quite young and pretty, with cheeks as rosy as an apple.

One turn of the great mill does it all. Crick crack, it goes, and the whole magical change is made. And when those who have become young again are asked if it is not a painful process, they answer: "Painful? Oh, no! On the contrary, it is quite delightful! It is just like waking in the morning after a good night's rest, to see the sun shining in your room, and to hear the trees rustling and the birds twittering in the branches."

A long way from Apolda, as the story runs, there once lived an old woman who had often heard of the magic mill. She had been very happy in her youth, and she wished above all things to be young again. So, at length, she made up her mind to try what the mill would do for her. The journey to Apolda was a long and hard one, for the road led up and down many steep hills and through boggy meadows and over a stony desert where there was no cooling shade.

But by and by the woman stood before the mill.

"I want to become young again," she said to one of the serving men, who was quietly sitting on a bench puffing rings of smoke into the still blue air.

"And, pray, what is your name?" asked the man.

"The children call me Mother Redcap," was the answer.

"Sit down, then, on this bench, Mother Redcap," and the man went into the mill and, opening a thick book, returned with a long strip of paper.

"Is that the bill?" asked the old woman.

"Oh, no!" answered the other. "We charge nothing here; only you must sign your name to this paper."

"And why should I do that?" asked the woman.

The man smiled, and answered: "This paper is only a list of all the follies you have ever committed. It is complete, even to the present hour. Before you can become young again you must pledge yourself to commit them all over again in the very same order as before. To be sure, there is a long list. From the time you were sixteen until you were thirty, there was at least one folly every day, and on Sunday there were two; then you improved a little until you were forty; but after that the follies have been plentiful enough, I assure you."

The old woman sighed and said: "I know that what you say is all true. And I hardly think it will repay one to become young again at such a price."

"Neither do I think so," answered the man. "Very few indeed could it ever repay. And so we have an easy time of it—seven days of rest every week! The mill is always still, at least of late years."

"Now, couldn't we strike out just a few things?" pleaded the old woman, with a tap on the man's shoulder. "Suppose we leave off about a dozen things that I remember with sorrow. I wouldn't mind doing all the rest."

"No, no!" answered the man. "We are not allowed to leave off anything. The rule is, all or none!"

"Very well, then, I shall have nothing to do with your old mill," said she, turning away.

When she reached her home again, the good folk who came to look at her exclaimed: "Why, Mother Redcap, you come back older than you went! We never thought there was any truth in the story about that mill!"

She coughed a little dry cough, and answered: "What does it matter about being young again? If one will only try to make it so, old age may be as beautiful as youth!"

•

FATHER WILLIAM

Robert Southey

Youth can learn from age about the right way to be young and grow old.

> "You are old, Father William," the young man cried,
> "The few locks that are left you are gray.
> You are hale, Father William, a hearty old man;
> Now tell me the reason, I pray."

"In the days of my youth," Father William replied,
"I remembered that youth would fly fast;
And abused not my health and my vigour at first,
That I never might need them at last."

"You are old, Father William," the young man cried,
"And pleasures with youth pass away,
And yet you lament not the days that are gone,
Now tell me the reason, I pray."

"In the days of my youth," Father William replied,
"I remembered that youth could not last;
I thought of the future, whatever I did,
That I never might grieve for the past."

"You are old, Father William," the young man cried,
"And life must be hastening away;
You are cheerful, and love to converse upon death,
Now tell me the reason, I pray."

"I am cheerful, young man," Father William replied,
"Let the cause thy attention engage;
In the days of my youth I remembered my God,
And He hath not forgotten my age!"

●

FRIENDSHIP SWEETENING TO THE EVENING OF LIFE

Thomas Jefferson

Friendship is one virtue that may grow more dear to us in the
twilight of life. This letter from Thomas Jefferson to John Adams
gives us a glimpse into one of the most remarkable friendships in
our nation's political history. These men were long-time political
adversaries, but they were also wise enough and great-hearted
enough to know that honest philosophical differences do not have

to scar personal friendships. When he learned of schemes to "draw a curtain of separation" between the two of them, Jefferson wrote this eloquent letter to his old comrade.

Less than three years later, lying on his deathbed, John Adams reassured himself with the words, "Thomas Jefferson survives!" He did not know that five hundred miles away at Monticello, Jefferson was dying as well. On July 4, 1826, exactly fifty years after the birth of the nation they had helped create, two great friends and patriots departed this earth together.

To John Adams
Monticello, October 12, 1823

Dear Sir,

I do not write with the ease which your letter of September the 18th supposes. Crippled wrists and fingers make writing slow and laborious. But while writing to you, I lose the sense of these things in the recollection of ancient times, when youth and health made happiness out of everything. I forget for a while the hoary winter of age, when we can think of nothing but how to keep ourselves warm, and how to get rid of our heavy hours until the friendly hand of death shall rid us of all at once. Against this *tedium vitæ,* however, I am fortunately mounted on a hobby, which, indeed, I should have better managed some thirty or forty years ago; but whose easy amble is still sufficient to give exercise and amusement to an octogenary rider. This is the establishment of a University, on a scale more comprehensive and in a country more healthy and central than our old William and Mary, which these obstacles have long kept in a state of languor and inefficiency. But the tardiness with which such works proceed may render it doubtful whether I shall live to see it go into action.

Putting aside these things, however, for the present I write this letter as due to a friendship coeval with our government, and now attempted to be poisoned, when too late in life to be replaced by new affections. I had for some time observed in the public papers dark hints and mysterious innuendoes of a correspondence of yours with a friend, to whom you had opened your bosom without reserve, and which was to be made public by that friend or his representative. And now it is said to be actually published. It has not yet reached us, but extracts have been given, and such as seemed most likely to draw a curtain of separation between you and myself. Were there no other motive than that of indignation against the author of this outrage on private confidence, whose shaft seems to have been aimed at yourself more particularly, this would make it the duty of every honorable mind to disappoint that aim, by opposing to its impression a sevenfold shield of apathy and insensibility. With me, however, no such armor is needed. The circumstances of the times in which we have happened to live, and the partiality of our friends at a particular period, placed us in a state of apparent opposition, which some might suppose to be personal also; and there might not be wanting those who wished to make it so, by filling our ears with malignant falsehoods, by dressing up hideous phantoms of their own creation, presenting them to you under my name, to me under yours, and endeavouring to instill into our minds things concerning each other the most destitute of truth. And if there had been, at any time, a moment when we were off our guard, and in a temper to let the whispers of these people make us forget what we had known of each other for so many years, and years of so much trial, yet all men who have attended to the workings of the human mind, who have seen the false colors under which passion sometimes dresses the actions and motives of others, have seen also those passions subsiding with time and reflection, dissipating like mists before the rising sun, and restoring to us the sight of all things in their true shape and colors. It would be strange indeed if, at our years, we were to go back an age to hunt up imaginary or forgotten facts, to disturb the repose of affections so sweetening to the evening of our lives. Be assured, my dear Sir, that I am incapable of receiving the slightest impression from the effort now made to plant thorns on the pillow of age, worth and wisdom, and to sow tares between friends who have been such for near half a century. Beseeching you then, not to suffer your mind to be disquieted by this wicked attempt to poison its peace, and praying you to throw it by among the things which have never happened, I add sincere assurances of my unabated and constant attachment, friendship and respect.

•

THE MANDARIN AND THE TAILOR

This tale from Vietnam reminds us that clothes don't make the man. More important, it reminds us that experience should bring wisdom and humility. Just as life has stages, so does the ego.

One day a man received word he had just been appointed a mandarin. He was so excited, he could barely contain himself.

"I will be a great man now," he told his friend. "I must have a new robe made immediately, one that does justice to my new station in life."

"I know the perfect tailor for you," his friend replied. "He is an old, wise man who knows how to give every customer the perfect fit. Let me give you his address."

So the new mandarin went to the tailor, who carefully took his measurements. After he had put away his tape measure, the old man said: "There is one more piece of information I need to know. Tell me, sir, how long have you been a mandarin?"

"Why? What does that have to do with the fit of my robe?" his client asked in surprise.

"Ah, I can't make the robe without knowing that, sir. You see, a newly appointed mandarin is so impressed with his office, he holds his head high in the air, tilts his nose up, and sticks his chest out. So I must make the front of his robe longer than the back.

"A few years later, when he is busy with his work, and level-headed from the stings of experience, and looks straight ahead to see what is coming and what must be done next, then I cut the robe so the front and back are the same length.

"And later, after he is stooped by old age and so many years of weary service, not to mention the humility learned from a lifetime of endeavor, then I must cut the robe so the back is longer than the front.

"Therefore, sir, I must know your seniority if I am to fit you properly."

The new mandarin walked out of the tailor's shop thinking less of his robe and more of why his friend had sent him to see just this man.

•

THE BED QUILT
Dorothy Canfield Fisher

This touching story about an elderly woman's triumph helps us
remember that life keeps its richness—whether we're young or
old—so long as we can devote ourselves to some ideal, some
worthy work. Here is the dignity of achievement.

Of all the Elwell family Aunt Mehetabel was certainly the most
unimportant member. It was in the New England days, when an
unmarried woman was an old maid at twenty, at forty was everyone's servant, and at sixty had gone through so much discipline that
she could need no more in the next world. Aunt Mehetabel was
sixty-eight.

She had never for a moment known the pleasure of being
important to anyone. Not that she was useless in her brother's
family; she was expected, as a matter of course, to take upon herself
the most tedious and uninteresting part of the household labors.
On Mondays she accepted as her share the washing of the men's
shirts, heavy with sweat and stiff with dirt from the fields and from
their own hard-working bodies. Tuesdays she never dreamed of
being allowed to iron anything pretty or even interesting, like the
baby's white dresses or the fancy aprons of her young lady nieces.
She stood all day pressing out a tiresome, monotonous succession
of dishcloths and towels and sheets.

In preserving-time she was allowed to have none of the pleasant responsibility of deciding when the fruit had cooked long
enough, nor did she share in the little excitement of pouring the
sweet-smelling stuff into the stone jars. She sat in a corner with the
children and stoned cherries incessantly, or hulled strawberries
until her fingers were dyed red to the bone.

The Elwells were not consciously unkind to their aunt—they
were even in a vague way fond of her—but she was so utterly
insignificant a figure in their lives that they bestowed no thought
whatever on her. Aunt Mehetabel did not resent this treatment; she
took it quite as unconsciously as they gave it. It was to be expected
when one was an old-maid dependent in a busy family. She gathered what crumbs of comfort she could from their occasional care-

less kindnesses and tried to hide the hurt which even yet pierced her at her brother's rough joking. In the winter when they all sat before the big hearth, roasted apples, drank mulled cider, and teased the girls about their beaux and the boys about their sweethearts, she shrank into a dusky corner with her knitting, happy if the evening passed without her brother saying, with a crude sarcasm, "Ask your Aunt Mehetabel about the beaux that used to come a-sparkin' her!" or, "Mehetabel, how was't when you was in love with Abel Cummings?" As a matter of fact, she had been the same at twenty as at sixty, a quiet, mouse-like little creature, too timid and shy for anyone to notice, or to raise her eyes for a moment and wish for a life of her own.

Her sister-in-law, a big hearty housewife who ruled indoors with as autocratic a sway as did her husband on the farm, was rather kind in an absent, offhand way to the shrunken little old woman, and it was through her that Mehetabel was able to enjoy the one pleasure of her life. Even as a girl she had been clever with her needle in the way of patching bed quilts. More than that she could never learn to do. The garments that she made for herself were the most lamentable affairs, and she was humbly grateful for any help in the bewildering business of putting them together. But in patchwork she enjoyed a tepid importance. She could really do that as well as anyone else. During years of devotion to this one art she had accumulated a considerable store of quilting patterns. Sometimes the neighbors would send over and ask "Miss Mehetabel" for such and such a design. It was with an agreeable flutter at being able to help someone that she went to the dresser, in her bare little room under the eaves, and extracted from her crowded portfolio the pattern desired.

She never knew how her great idea came to her. Sometimes she thought she must have dreamed it, sometimes she even wondered reverently, in the phraseology of the weekly prayer-meeting, if it had not been "sent" to her. She never admitted to herself that she could have thought of it without other help; it was too great, too ambitious, too lofty a project for her humble mind to have conceived. Even when she finished drawing the design with her own fingers, she gazed at it incredulously, not daring to believe that it could indeed be her handiwork. At first it seemed to her only like a lovely but quite unreal dream. She did not think of putting it into execution—so elaborate, so complicated, so beautifully difficult a pattern could be only for the angels in heaven to quilt. But so curiously does familiarity accustom us even to very wonderful things that as she lived with this astonishing creation of her mind, the longing grew stronger and stronger to give it material life with her nimble old fingers.

She gasped at her daring when this idea first swept over her and put it away as one does a sinfully selfish notion, but she kept coming back to it again and again. Finally she said compromisingly to herself that she would make one "square," just one part of her design, to see how it would look. Accustomed to the most complete dependence on her brother and his wife, she dared not do even this without asking Sophia's permission. With a heart full of hope and fear thumping furiously against her old ribs, she approached the mistress of the house on churning-day, knowing with the innocent guile of a child that the country woman was apt to be in a good temper while working over the fragrant butter in the cool cellar.

Sophia listened absently to her sister-in-law's halting, hesitating petition. "Why, yes, Mehetabel," she said, leaning far down into the huge churn for the last golden morsels—"why, yes, start another quilt if you want to. I've got a lot of pieces from the spring sewing that will work in real good." Mehetabel tried honestly to make her see that this would be no common quilt, but her limited vocabulary and her emotion stood between her and expression. At last Sophia said, with a kindly impatience: "Oh, there! Don't bother me. I never could keep track of your quiltin' patterns, anyhow. I don't care what pattern you go by."

With this overwhelmingly, although unconsciously, generous permission Mehetabel rushed back up the steep attic stairs to her room, and in a joyful agitation began preparations for the work of her life. It was even better than she hoped. By some heaven-sent inspiration she had invented a pattern beyond which no patchwork quilt could go.

She had but little time from her incessant round of household drudgery for this new and absorbing occupation, and she did not dare sit up late at night lest she burn too much candle. It was weeks before the little square began to take on a finished look, to show the pattern. Then Mehetabel was in a fever of impatience to bring it to completion. She was too conscientious to shirk even the smallest part of her share of the work of the house, but she rushed through it with a speed which left her panting as she climbed to the little room. This seemed like a radiant spot to her as she bent over the innumerable scraps of cloth which already in her imagination ranged themselves in the infinitely diverse pattern of her masterpiece. Finally she could wait no longer, and one evening ventured to bring her work down beside the fire where the family sat, hoping that some good fortune would give her a place near the tallow candles on the mantelpiece. She was on the last corner of the square, and her needle flew in and out with inconceivable rapidity. No one noticed her, a fact which filled her with relief, and by bedtime she had but a few more stitches to add.

As she stood up with the others, the square fluttered out of her trembling old hands and fell on the table. Sophia glanced at it carelessly. "Is that the new quilt you're beginning on?" she asked with a yawn. "It looks like a real pretty pattern. Let's see it." Up to that moment Mehetabel had labored in the purest spirit of disinterested devotion to an ideal, but as Sophia held her work toward the candle to examine it, and exclaimed in amazement and admiration, she felt an astonished joy to know that her creation would stand the test of publicity.

"Land sakes!" ejaculated her sister-in-law, looking at the many-colored square. "Why, Mehetabel Elwell, where'd you git that pattern?"

"I made it up," said Mehetabel quietly, but with unutterable pride.

"Now!" exclaimed Sophia incredulously. *"Did* you! Why, I never see such a pattern in my life. Girls, come here and see what your Aunt Mehetabel is doing."

The three tall daughters turned back reluctantly from the stairs. "I don't seem to take much interest in patchwork," said one listlessly.

"No, nor I neither!" answered Sophia, "but a stone image would take an interest in this pattern. Honest, Mehetabel, did you think of it yourself? And how under the sun and stars did you ever git your courage up to start in a-making it? Land! Look at all those tiny squinchy little seams! Why the wrong side ain't a thing *but* seams!"

The girls echoed their mother's exclamations, and Mr. Elwell himself came over to see what they were discussing. "Well, I declare!" he said, looking at his sister with eyes more approving than she could ever remember. "That beats old Mis' Wightman's quilt that got the blue ribbon so many times at the county fair."

Mehetabel's heart swelled within her, and tears of joy moistened her old eyes as she lay that night in her narrow, hard bed, too

proud and excited to sleep. The next day her sister-in-law amazed
her by taking the huge pan of potatoes out of her lap and setting
one of the younger children to peeling them. "Don't you want to
go on with that quiltin' pattern?" she said. "I'd kind o' like to see
how you're goin' to make the grapevine design come out on the
corner."

By the end of the summer the family interest had risen so high
that Mehetabel was given a little stand in the sitting-room where
she could keep her pieces, and work in odd minutes. She almost
wept over such kindness, and resolved firmly not to take advantage of it by neglecting her work, which she performed with a
fierce thoroughness. But the whole atmosphere of her world was
changed. Things had a meaning now. Through the longest task of
washing milk-pans there rose the rainbow of promise of her varie-
gated work. She took her place by the little table and put the thimble on her knotted, hard finger with the solemnity of a priestess
performing a sacred rite.

She was even able to bear with some degree of dignity the
extreme honor of having the minister and the minister's wife comment admiringly on her great project. The family felt quite proud
of Aunt Mehetabel as Minister Bowman had said it was work as fine
as any he had ever seen, "and he didn't know but finer!" The remark
was repeated verbatim to the neighbors in the following weeks
when they dropped in and examined in a perverse silence some
astonishingly difficult *tour de force* which Mehetabel had just finished.

The family especially plumed themselves on the slow progress
of the quilt. "Mehetabel has been to work on that corner for six
weeks, come Tuesday, and she ain't half done yet," they explained

to visitors. They fell out of the way of always expecting her to be the one to run on errands, even for the children. "Don't bother your Aunt Mehetabel," Sophia would call. "Can't you see she's got to a ticklish place on the quilt?"

The old woman sat up straighter and looked the world in the face. She was part of it at last. She joined in the conversation and her remarks were listened to. The children were even told to mind her when she asked them to do some service for her, although this she did but seldom, the habit of self-effacement being too strong.

One day some strangers from the next town drove up and asked if they could inspect the wonderful quilt which they had heard of, even down in their end of the valley. After that such visitations were not uncommon, making the Elwells' house a notable object. Mehetabel's quilt came to be one of the town sights, and no one was allowed to leave the town without having paid tribute to its worth. The Elwells saw to it that their aunt was better dressed than she had ever been before, and one of the girls made her a pretty little cap to wear on her thin white hair.

A year went by and a quarter of the quilt was finished; a second year passed and half was done. The third year Mehetabel had pneumonia and lay ill for weeks and weeks, overcome with terror lest she die before her work was completed. A fourth year and one could really see the grandeur of the whole design; and in September of the fifth year, the entire family watching her with eager and admiring eyes, Mehetabel quilted the last stitches in her creation. The girls held it up by the four corners, and they all looked at it in a solemn silence. Then Mr. Elwell smote one horny hand within the other and exclaimed: "By ginger! That's goin' to the county fair!"

Mehetabel blushed a deep red at this. It was a thought which had occurred to her in a bold moment, but she had not dared to entertain it. The family acclaimed the idea, and one of the boys was forthwith dispatched to the house of the neighbor who was chairman of the committee for their village. He returned with radiant face. "Of course he'll take it. Like's not it may git a prize, so he says; but he's got to have it right off, because all the things are goin' tomorrow morning."

Even in her swelling pride Mehetabel felt a pang of separation as the bulky package was carried out of the house. As the days went on she felt absolutely lost without her work. For years it had been her one preoccupation, and she could not bear even to look at the little stand, now quite bare of the litter of scraps which had lain

on it so long. One of the neighbors, who took the long journey to
the fair, reported that the quilt was hung in a place of honor in a
glass case in "Agricultural Hall." But that meant little to Mehetabel's
utter ignorance of all that lay outside of her brother's home. The
family noticed the old woman's depression, and one day Sophia
said kindly, "You feel sort o' lost without the quilt, don't you,
Mehetabel?"

"They took it away so quick!" she said wistfully. "I hadn't hardly
had one real good look at it myself."

Mr. Elwell made no comment, but a day or two later he asked
his sister how early she could get up in the morning.

"I dunno. Why?" she asked.

"Well, Thomas Ralston has got to drive clear to West Oldton to
see a lawyer there, and that is four miles beyond the fair. He says if
you can git up so's to leave here at four in the morning he'll drive
you over to the fair, leave you there for the day, and bring you back
again at night."

Mehetabel looked at him with incredulity. It was as though
someone had offered her a ride in a golden chariot up to the gates
of heaven. "Why, you can't *mean* it!" she cried, paling with the
intensity of her emotion. Her brother laughed a little uneasily. Even
to his careless indifference this joy was a revelation of the nar-
rowness of her life in his home. "Oh, 'tain't so much to go to the
fair. Yes, I mean it. Go git your things ready, for he wants to start
tomorrow morning."

All that night a trembling, excited old woman lay and stared at
the rafters. She, who had never been more than six miles from
home in her life, was going to drive thirty miles away—it was like
going to another world. She who had never seen anything more
exciting than a church supper was to see the county fair. To Mehetabel it was like making the tour of the world. She had never dreamed
of doing it. She could not at all imagine what it would be like.

Nor did the exhortations of the family, as they bade good-bye
to her, throw any light on her confusion. They had all been at least
once to the scene of gayety she was to visit, and as she tried to eat
her breakfast they called out conflicting advice to her till her head
whirled. Sophia told her to be sure and see the display of preserves.
Her brother said not to miss inspecting the stock, her nieces said
the fancywork was the only thing worth looking at, and her nephews said she must bring them home an account of the races. The
buggy drove up to the door, she was helped in, and her wraps
tucked about her. They all stood together and waved good-bye to

her as she drove out of the yard. She waved back, but she scarcely saw them. On her return home that evening she was very pale, and so tired and stiff that her brother had to lift her out bodily, but her lips were set in a blissful smile. They crowded around her with thronging questions, until Sophia pushed them all aside, telling them Aunt Mehetabel was too tired to speak until she had had her supper. This was eaten in an enforced silence on the part of the children, and then the old woman was helped into an easy-chair before the fire. They gathered about her, eager for news of the great world, and Sophia said, "Now, come, Mehetabel, tell us all about it!"

Mehetabel drew a long breath. "It was just perfect!" she said. "Finer even than I thought. They've got it hanging up in the very middle of a sort o' closet made of glass, and one of the lower corners is ripped and turned back so's to show the seams on the wrong side."

"What?" asked Sophia, a little blankly.

"Why, the quilt!' said Mehetabel in surprise. "There are a whole lot of other ones in that room, but not one that can hold a candle to it, if I do say it who shouldn't. I heard lots of people say the same thing. You ought to have heard what the women said about that corner, Sophia. They said—well, I'd be ashamed to *tell* you what they said. I declare if I wouldn't!"

Mr. Elwell asked, "What did you think of that big ox we've heard so much about?"

"I didn't look at the stock," returned his sister indifferently. "That set of pieces you gave me, Maria, from your red waist, come out just lovely!" she assured one of her nieces. "I heard one woman say you could 'most smell the red silk roses."

"Did any of the horses in our town race?" asked young Thomas.

"I didn't see the races."

"How about the preserves?" asked Sophia.

"I didn't see the preserves," said Mehetabel calmly. "You see, I went right to the room where the quilt was, and then I didn't want to leave it. It had been so long since I'd seen it. I had to look at it first real good myself, and then I looked at the others to see if there was any that could come up to it. And then the people begun comin' in and I got so interested in hearin' what they had to say I couldn't think of goin' anywheres else. I ate my lunch right there too, and I'm as glad as can be I did, too, for what do you think?"—she gazed about her with kindling eyes—"while I stood there with a sandwich

776 THE MORAL COMPASS

in one hand didn't the head of the hull concern come in and open the glass door and pin 'First Prize' right in the middle of the quilt!"

There was a stir of congratulation and proud exclamation. Then Sophia returned again to the attack. "Didn't you go to see anything else?" she queried.

"Why, no," said Mehetable. "Only the quilt. Why should I?"

She fell into a reverie where she saw again the glorious creation of her hand and brain hanging before all the world with the mark of highest approval on it. She longed to make her listeners see the splendid vision with her. She struggled for words; she reached blindly after unknown superlatives. "I tell you it looked like—" she said, and paused, hesitating. Vague recollections of hymn-book phraseology came into her mind, the only form of literary expression she knew; but they were dismissed as being sacrilegious, and also not sufficiently forcible. Finally, "I tell you it looked real *well!*" she assured them, and sat staring into the fire, on her tired old face the supreme content of an artist who has realized his ideal.

•

ULYSSES

Alfred Tennyson

This is a great poem for any time of life, but particularly for old age. Homer's *Odyssey* ends with the great hero Ulysses returning to his island home of Ithaca after long years of adventures; there, presumably, the rest of his days will be quiet and untroubled. But here Tennyson presents a Ulysses full of courage and determination "to strive, to seek, to find, and not to yield." The image is, of course, metaphorical. We can keep learning, growing, working, and exploring wherever we are. The point is to keep striving.

It little profits that an idle king,
By this still hearth, among these barren crags,
Match'd with an aged wife, I mete and dole
Unequal laws unto a savage race,
That hoard, and sleep, and feed, and know not me.

I cannot rest from travel: I will drink
Life to the lees: all times I have enjoy'd
Greatly, have suffer'd greatly, both with those
That loved me, and alone; on shore, and when
Thro' scudding drifts the rainy Hyades
Vext the dim sea: I am become a name;
For always roaming with a hungry heart
Much have I seen and known; cities of men
And manners, climates, councils, governments,
Myself not least, but honor'd of them all;
And drunk delight of battle with my peers,
Far on the ringing plains of windy Troy.

I am a part of all that I have met;
Yet all experience is an arch wherethro'
Gleams that untravel'd world, whose margin fades
Forever and forever when I move.
How dull it is to pause, to make an end,
To rust unburnish'd, not to shine in use!
As tho' to breathe were life. Life piled on life
Were all too little, and of one to me
Little remains: but every hour is saved
From that eternal silence, something more,
A bringer of new things; and vile it were
For some three suns to store and hoard myself
And this gray spirit yearning in desire
To follow knowledge like a sinking star,
Beyond the utmost bound of human thought.

This is my son, mine own Telemachus,
To whom I leave the scepter and the isle—
Well-loved of me, discerning to fulfill
This labor, by slow prudence to make mild
A rugged people, and thro' soft degrees
Subdue them to the useful and the good.
Most blameless is he, centered in the sphere
Of common duties, decent not to fail
In offices of tenderness, and pay
Meet adoration to my household gods,
When I am gone. He works his work, I mine.

There lies the port; the vessel puffs her sail:
There gloom the dark broad seas. My mariners,
Souls that have toil'd, and wrought, and thought with me—
That ever with a frolic welcome took
The thunder and the sunshine, and opposed
Free hearts, free foreheads—you and I are old;
Old age hath yet his honor and his toil;
Death closes all: but something ere the end,
Some work of noble note, may yet be done,
Not unbecoming men that strove with Gods.
The lights begin to twinkle from the rocks:
The long day wanes: the slow moon climbs: the deep
Moans round with many voices. Come, my friends,
'Tis not too late to seek a newer world.
Push off, and sitting well in order smite
The sounding furrows; for my purpose holds
To sail beyond the sunset, and the baths
Of all the western stars, until I die.
It may be that the gulfs will wash us down:
It may be we shall touch the Happy Isles,
And see the great Achilles, whom we knew.
Tho' much is taken, much abides; and tho'
We are not now that strength which in old days
Moved earth and heaven; that which we are, we are;
One equal temper of heroic hearts,
Made weak by time and fate, but strong in will
To strive, to seek, to find, and not to yield.

•

THE ANGEL

Hans Christian Andersen

The next two stories may help us deal with life's closing. Hans
Christian Andersen suggests that the end is a homeward journey,
in the company of angels. He also suggests that the kindnesses
neighbors give to one another become treasures laid up in
heaven.

Whenever a good child dies, an angel from heaven comes down to earth and takes the dead child in his arms, spreads out his great white wings, flies away over all the places the child has loved, and picks quite a handful of flowers, which he carries up to the Almighty that they may bloom in heaven more brightly than on earth. And the Father presses all the flowers to his heart; but He kisses the flower that pleases Him best, and the flower is then endowed with a voice, and can join in the great chorus of praise!

"See"—this is what an angel said, as he carried a dead child up to heaven, and the child heard, as if in a dream; and they went on over the regions of home where the little child had played, and came through gardens with beautiful flowers—"which of these shall we take with us to plant in heaven?" asked the angel.

Now there stood near them a slender, beautiful rosebush. But a wicked hand had broken the stem, so that all the branches, covered with half-opened buds, were hanging around, quite withered.

"The poor rosebush!" said the child. "Take it, that it may bloom up yonder."

And the angel took it, and kissed the child, and the little one half opened his eyes. They plucked some of the rich flowers, but also took with them the wild pansy and the despised buttercup.

"Now we have flowers," said the child.

And the angel nodded, but he did not yet fly upward to heaven. It was night and quite silent. They remained in the great city. They floated about there in a small street, where lay whole heaps of straw, ashes, and sweepings, for it had been garbage-removal day. There lay fragments of plates, bits of plaster, rags, and old hats, and all this did not look well. And the angel pointed amid all this confusion to a few fragments of a flowerpot, and to a lump of earth that had fallen out and was kept together by the roots of a great dried field flower, which was of no use, and had therefore been thrown out into the street.

"We will take that with us," said the angel. "I will tell you why as we fly onward.

"Down yonder in the narrow lane, in the low cellar, lived a poor sick boy. From his childhood he had been bedridden. When he was at his best he could go up and down the room a few times, leaning on crutches. That was the most he could do. For a few days in summer the sunbeams would penetrate for a few hours to the ground of the cellar, and when the poor boy sat there and the sun shone on him, and he looked at the red blood in his three fingers, as he held them up before his face, he would say, 'Yes, today he has been out!' He knew the forest with its beautiful vernal green only from the fact that a neighbor's little son brought him the first green branch of a beech tree, and he held that up over his head, and dreamed he was in the beechwood, where the sun shone and the birds sang.

"On a spring day the neighbor's boy brought him also field flowers, and among them was, by chance, one to which the root was still hanging. And so it was planted in a flowerpot, and placed by the bed, close to the window. The flower had been planted by a fortunate hand; and it grew, threw out new shoots, and bore flowers every year. It became a splendid flower garden to the sickly boy— his little treasure here on earth. He watered it, and tended it, and took care that it had the benefit of every ray of sunlight, down to the latest that struggled in through the narrow window. And the flower itself was woven into his dreams, for it grew for him and gladened his eyes, and spread its fragrance about him. And toward it he turned in death, when the Father called him.

"He has now been with the Almighty for a year. For a year the flower has stood forgotten in the window, and is withered; and thus, at the garbage-removal, it has been thrown out into the dust of the street. And this is the poor flower which we have taken into our bouquet; for this flower has given more joy than the richest in a queen's garden."

"But how do you know all this?" asked the child.

"I know it," said the angel, "for I myself was that boy who walked on crutches. I know my flower well."

And the child opened his eyes and looked into the glorious, happy face of the angel; and at the same moment they entered the regions where there is peace and joy. And the Father pressed the dead child to his bosom, and then it received wings like the angel, and flew hand in hand with him. And the Almighty kissed the dry, withered field flower, and it received a voice and sang with all the angels hovering around—some near, and some in wider circles, and some in infinite distance, but all equally happy. And they all sang—little and great, the good, happy child, and the poor field flower that had lain there withered, thrown among the dust in the rubbish of the garbage-removal day, in the dark, narrow lane.

•

THE INDIAN GIRL AND
HER MESSENGER BIRD

George W. Ranck

Love restores, even at times of death.

Once upon a time, there was an Indian who lived in a big wood on the banks of a beautiful river, and he did nothing all day long but catch fish and hunt wild deer. Well, this Indian had two lovely little daughters, and he named one Sunbeam, because she was so bright and cheerful, and the other he called Starlight, because, he said, her sweet eyes twinkled like the stars.

Sunbeam and Starlight were as busy as bees, from morning till night. They ran races under the shady trees, made bouquets of wild flowers, swung on grapevine swings, turned berries and acorns into beads, and dressed their glossy black hair with bright feathers that beautiful birds had dropped. They loved each other so much, and were so happy together, that they never knew what trouble meant until, one day, Starlight got very sick, and before the big moon came over the treetops the sweet Indian child had closed her starry eyes in death, and rested for the last time upon her soft little deerskin bed.

And now, for the first time, Sunbeam's heart was full of grief. She could not play, for Starlight was gone, she knew not where. So she took the bright feathers out of her hair, and sat down by the river and cried and cried for Starlight to come back to her. But when her father told her that Starlight was gone to the Spiritland of love and beauty, and would be happy forever and ever, Sunbeam was comforted.

"Now," said she, "I know where darling Starlight is, and I can kiss her and talk to her again."

Sunbeam had heard her people say that the birds were messengers from the Spiritland. So she hunted through the woods until she found a little songbird that was too young to fly, fast asleep in its nest. She carried it gently home, put it into a cage, and watched over it and fed it tenderly day after day until its wings grew strong and it filled the woods with its music. Then she carried it in her soft little hands to Starlight's grave; and after she had loaded it with kisses and messages of love for Starlight, she told it never to cease its sweetest song or fold its shining wings until it had flown to the Spiritland. She let it go, and the glad bird, as it rose above the tall green trees, poured forth a song more joyful than any that Sunbeam had ever heard. Higher and higher it flew, and sweeter and sweeter grew its song, until at last both its form and its music were lost in the floating summer clouds.

Then Sunbeam ran swiftly over the soft grass to her father and told him, with a bright smile and a light heart, that she had talked with dear Starlight, and had kissed her sweet rosy mouth again. And Sunbeam was once more her father's bright and happy little Indian girl.

•

THE DEATH OF THOMAS MORE

James Anthony Froude

A statesman, scholar, and deeply religious Roman Catholic, Thomas More (1478–1535) resigned his office as chancellor of England in 1532 when the clergy of England accepted King Henry VIII as their head. He retired to his home, where he pursued his writing, but in 1534 he was summoned to swear to the Act of Succession, which implied a denial of papal supremacy. More refused to take the oath and was imprisoned in the Tower of London. In 1535 he was tried for treason and sentenced to death. Here is a man who lived by the dictates of his conscience and died by them, too, when the time came.

At daybreak he was awakened by the entrance of Sir Thomas Pope, who had come to confirm his anticipations and to tell him it was the king's pleasure that he should suffer at nine o'clock that morning. He received the news with utter composure.

"I am much bounden to the king," he said, "for the benefits and honors he has bestowed upon me; and, so help me God, most of all am I bounden to him that it pleaseth his majesty to rid me so shortly out of the miseries of this present world."

Pope told him the king desired that he would not "use many words on the scaffold." "Mr. Pope," he answered, "you do well to give me warning, for otherwise I had purposed somewhat to have spoken; but no matter wherewith his grace should have cause to be offended. Howbeit, whatever I intended I shall obey His Highness's command."

Afterwards he discussed the arrangements for his funeral, at which he begged that his family might be present, and, when all was settled, Pope rose to leave him. He was an old friend. He took More's hand and wrung it, and, quite overcome, burst into tears.

"Quiet yourself, Mr. Pope," More said, "and be not discomfited; for I trust we shall soon see each other full merrily, when we shall live and love together in eternal bliss."

As soon as he was alone, he dressed in his most elaborate costume. It was for the benefit, he said, of the executioner, who was to do him so great a service. Sir William Kingston remonstrated, and with some difficulty induced him to put on a plainer suit; but, that his intended liberality should not fail, he sent the man a gold angel in compensation, "as a token that he maliced him nothing, but rather loved him extremely."

So about nine of the clock he was brought by the lieutenant out of the Tower, his beard being long, which fashion he had never before used, his face pale and lean, carrying in his hands a red cross, casting his eyes often towards heaven. He had been unpopular as a judge, and one or two persons in the crowd were insolent to him; but the distance was short and soon over, as all else was nearly over now.

The scaffold had been awkwardly erected and shook as he placed his foot upon the ladder. "See me safe up," he said to Kingston. "For my coming down I can shift for myself." He began to speak to the people, but the sheriff begged him not to proceed, and he contented himself with asking for their prayers, and desiring them to bear witness for him that he died a faithful servant of God and the king. He then repeated the Miserere prayer on his knees; and when he had ended and had risen, the executioner, with an emotion that promised ill for the manner in which his part in the tragedy would be accomplished, begged his forgiveness.

More kissed him. "Thou art to do me the greatest benefit that I can receive," he said. "Pluck up thy spirit, man, and be not afraid to do thine office. My neck is very short. Take heed therefore that thou strike not awry, for saving of thy honesty." The executioner offered to tie his eyes. "I will cover them myself," he said, and binding them in a cloth that he had brought with him, he knelt and laid his head upon the block.

The fatal stroke was about to fall, when he signed for a moment's delay while he laid aside his beard. "Pity that should be cut," he murmured, "that has not committed treason." With such strange words, the strangest perhaps ever uttered at such a time, the lips most famous through Europe for eloquence and wisdom closed forever.

•

THE STUDENT

Anton Chekhov

This is a story that lifts the spirit. It speaks of the deep mystery of compassion ("her whole being was interested in what was passing in Peter's soul"). It speaks of the mystery that is the interconnectedness of all lives and events. And it speaks of the mystery that is the peace that passes all understanding.

At first the weather was fine and still. The thrushes were calling, and in the swamps close by something alive droned pitifully with a sound like blowing into an empty bottle. A snipe flew by, and the shot aimed at it rang out with a gay, resounding note in the spring air. But when it began to get dark in the forest a cold, penetrating wind blew inappropriately from the east, and everything sank into silence. Needles of ice stretched across the pools, and it felt cheerless, remote, and lonely in the forest. There was a whiff of winter.

Ivan Velikopolsky, the son of a sacristan, and a student of the clerical academy, returning home from shooting, walked all the time by the path in the waterside meadow. His fingers were numb and his face was burning with the wind. It seemed to him that the cold that had suddenly come on had destroyed the order and harmony of things, that nature itself felt ill at ease, and that was why the evening darkness was falling more rapidly than usual. All around it was deserted and peculiarly gloomy. The only light was one gleaming in the widows' gardens near the river; the village, over three miles away, and everything in the distance all around was plunged in the cold evening mist. The student remembered that, as he went out from the house, his mother was sitting barefoot on the floor in the entry, cleaning the samovar, while his father lay on the stove coughing. As it was Good Friday nothing had been cooked, and the student was terribly hungry. And now, shrinking from the cold, he thought that just such a wind had blown in the days of Rurik and in the time of Ivan the Terrible and Peter, and in their time there had been just the same desperate poverty and hunger, the same thatched roofs with holes in them, ignorance, misery, the same desolation around, the same darkness, the same feeling of oppression—all these had existed, did exist, and would exist, and the lapse of a thousand years would make life no better. And he did not want to go home.

The gardens were called the widows' because they were kept by two widows, mother and daughter. A campfire was burning brightly with a crackling sound, throwing out light far around on the ploughed earth. The widow Vasilisa, a tall, fat old woman in a man's coat, was standing by and looking thoughtfully into the fire; her daughter, Lukerya, a little pockmarked woman with a stupid-looking face, was sitting on the ground, washing a caldron and spoons. Apparently they had just had supper. There was a sound of men's voices; it was the laborers watering their horses at the river.

"Here you have winter back again," said the student, going up to the campfire. "Good evening."

Vasilisa started, but at once recognized him and smiled cordially.

"I did not know you; God bless you," she said. "You'll be rich."

They talked. Vasilisa, a woman of experience who had been in service with the gentry, first as a wet nurse, afterwards as a children's nurse, expressed herself with refinement, and a soft, sedate smile never left her face. Her daughter, Lukerya, a village peasant woman who had been crushed by her husband, simply screwed up her eyes at the student and said nothing, and she had a strange expression like that of a deaf-mute.

"At just such a fire the Apostle Peter warmed himself," said the student, stretching out his hands to the fire, "so it must have been cold then, too. Ah, what a terrible night it must have been, granny! An utterly dismal long night!"

He looked around at the darkness, shook his head abruptly,

and asked: "No doubt you have been at the reading of the Twelve Gospels?"

"Yes, I have," answered Vasilisa.

"If you remember, at the Last Supper Peter said to Jesus, 'I am ready to go with Thee into darkness and unto death.' And our Lord answered him thus: 'I say unto thee, Peter, before the cock croweth thou wilt have denied Me thrice.' After the supper Jesus went through the agony of death in the garden and prayed, and poor Peter was weary in spirit and faint; his eyelids were heavy and he could not struggle against sleep. He fell asleep. Then you heard how Judas the same night kissed Jesus and betrayed Him to His tormentors. They took Him bound to the high priest and beat Him, while Peter, exhausted, worn out with misery and alarm, hardly awake, you know, feeling that something awful was just going to happen on earth, followed behind. . . . He loved Jesus passionately, intensely, and now he saw from far off how He was beaten. . . ."

Lukerya left the spoons and fixed an immovable stare upon the student.

"They came to the high priest's," he went on. "They began to question Jesus, and meantime the laborers made a fire in the yard as it was cold, and warmed themselves. Peter, too, stood with them near the fire and warmed himself as I am doing. A woman, seeing him, said: 'He was with Jesus, too'—that is as much as to say that he, too, should be taken to be questioned. And all the laborers who were standing near the fire must have looked sourly and suspiciously at him, because he was confused and said, 'I don't know Him.' A little while after again someone recognized him as one of Jesus' disciples and said, 'Thou, too, art one of them,' but again he denied it. And for the third time someone turned to him, 'Why, did I not see thee with Him in the garden today?' For the third time he denied it. And immediately after that time the cock crowed, and

Peter, looking from far off at Jesus, remembered the words He had said to him in the evening. . . . He remembered, he came to himself, went out of the yard and wept bitterly—bitterly. In the Gospel it is written: 'He went out and wept bitterly.' I imagine it: the still, still, dark, dark garden, and in the stillness, faintly audible, smothered sobbing. . . ."

The student sighed and sank into thought. Still smiling, Vasilisa suddenly gave a gulp, big tears flowed freely down her cheeks, and she screened her face from the fire with her sleeve as though ashamed of her tears, and Lukerya, staring immovably at the student, flushed crimson, and her expression became strained and heavy like that of someone enduring intense pain.

The laborers came back from the river, and one of them riding a horse was quite near, and the light from the fire quivered upon him. The student said goodnight to the widows and went on. And again the darkness was about him and his fingers began to be numb. A cruel wind was blowing; winter really had come back and it did not feel as though Easter would be the day after tomorrow.

Now the student was thinking about Vasilisa: since she had shed tears, all that had happened to Peter the night before the Crucifixion must have some relation to her. . . .

He looked around. The solitary light was still gleaming in the darkness and no figures could be seen near it now. The student thought again that if Vasilisa had shed tears, and her daughter had been troubled, it was evident that what he had just been telling them about, which had happened nineteen centuries ago, had a relation to the present—to both women, to the desolate village, to himself, to all people. The old woman had wept, not because he could tell the story touchingly but because Peter was near to her, because her whole being was interested in what was passing in Peter's soul.

And joy suddenly stirred in his soul, and he even stopped for a minute to take breath. "The past," he thought, "is linked with the present by an unbroken chain of events flowing one out of another." And it seemed to him that he had just seen both ends of that chain, that when he touched one end the other quivered.

When he crossed the river by the ferryboat and afterwards, mounting the hill, looked at his village and towards the west where the cold purple sunset laid a narrow streak of light, he thought that truth and beauty, which had guided human life there in the garden and in the yard of the high priest, had continued without interruption to this day, and had evidently always been the chief thing in human life and in all earthly life, indeed; and the feeling of youth, health, vigor—he was only twenty-two—and the inexpressible sweet expectation of happiness, of unknown mysterious happiness, took possession of him little by little, and life seemed to him enchanting, marvelous, and full of lofty meaning.

•

What Men Live By

Leo Tolstoy

This beautiful parable is an adaptation of an ancient tale found in different versions in the Koran, the Talmud, the Apocrypha, and *The Arabian Nights.* Tolstoy originally introduced this story with a series of verses from the first letter of John in the Bible, including verse sixteen of chapter four: "God is love; and he who abides in love abides in God, and God abides in him."

I

A shoemaker named Simon, who had neither house nor land of his own, lived with his wife and children in a peasant's hut and earned his living by his work. Work was cheap but bread was dear, and what he earned he spent for food. The man and his wife had but one sheepskin coat between them for winter wear, and even that was worn to tatters, and this was the second year he had been wanting to buy sheepskins for a new coat. Before winter Simon saved up a little money: a three-ruble note lay hidden in his wife's box, and five rubles and twenty kopeks were owed him by customers in the village.

So one morning he prepared to go to the village to buy the sheepskins. He put on over his shirt his wife's wadded nankeen jacket, and over that he put his own cloth coat. He took the three-ruble note in his pocket, cut himself a stick to serve as a staff, and started off after breakfast. "I'll collect the five rubles that are due me," thought he, "and add the three I have got, and that will be enough to buy sheepskins for the winter coat."

He came to the village and called at a peasant's hut, but the man was not at home. The peasant's wife promised that the money would be paid next week, but she would not pay it herself. Then Simon called on another peasant, but this one swore he had no money, and would pay only twenty kopeks which he owed for a pair of boots Simon had mended. Simon then tried to buy the sheepskins on credit, but the dealer would not trust him.

"Bring your money," said he, "then you may have your pick of the skins. We know what debt-collecting is like."

So all the business the shoemaker did was to get twenty kopeks for boots he had mended, and to take a pair of felt boots a peasant gave him to sole with leather.

Simon felt downhearted. He spent the twenty kopeks on vodka, and started homewards without having bought any skins. In the morning he had felt the frost, but now, after drinking the vodka, he felt warm even without a sheepskin coat. He trudged along, striking his stick on the frozen earth with one hand, swinging the felt boots with the other, and talking to himself.

"I'm quite warm," said he, "though I have no sheepskin coat. I've had a drop and it runs through all my veins. I need no sheep-skins. I go along and don't worry about anything. That's the sort of man I am! What do I care? I can live without sheepskins. I don't need them. My wife will fret, to be sure. And, true enough, it *is* a shame; one works all day long and then does not get paid. Stop a bit! If you don't bring that money along, sure enough I'll skin you, blessed if I don't. How's that? He pays twenty kopeks at a time! What can I do with twenty kopeks? Drink it—that's all one can do! Hard up, he says he is! So he may be—but what about me? You have house, and cattle, and everything, I've only what I stand up in! You have corn of your own growing, I have to buy every grain. Do what I will, I must spend three rubles every week for bread alone. I come home and find the bread all used up and I have to fork out another ruble and a half. So just you pay up what you owe, and no nonsense about it!"

By this time he had nearly reached the shrine at the bend of the road. Looking up, he saw something whitish behind the shrine. The daylight was fading, and the shoemaker peered at the thing without being able to make out what it was. "There was no white stone here before. Can it be an ox? It's not like an ox. It has a head like a man, but it's too white; and what could a man be doing there?"

He came closer, so that it was clearly visible. To his surprise it really was a man, alive or dead, sitting naked, leaning motionless against the shrine. Terror seized the shoemaker, and he thought, "Someone has killed him, stripped him, and left him here. If I meddle I shall surely get into trouble."

So the shoemaker went on. He passed in front of the shrine so that he could not see the man. When he had gone some way he looked back, and saw that the man was no longer leaning against the shrine but was moving as if looking towards him. The shoemaker felt more frightened than before, and thought, "Shall I go back to him or shall I go on? If I go near him, something dreadful may happen. Who knows who the fellow is. He has not come here for any good. If I go near him he may jump up and throttle me, and there will be no getting away. Or if not, he'd still be a burden on one's hands. What could I do with a naked man? I couldn't give him my last clothes. Heaven only help me to get away!"

So the shoemaker hurried on, leaving the shrine behind him —when suddenly his conscience smote him and he stopped in the road.

"What are you doing, Simon?" said he to himself. "The man may be dying of want, and you slip past, afraid. Have you grown so rich as to be afraid of robbers? Ah, Simon, shame on you!"

So he turned back and went up to the man.

II

Simon approached the stranger, looked at him, and saw that he was a young man, fit, with no bruises on his body, but evidently freezing and frightened, and he sat there leaning back without looking up at Simon, as if too faint to lift his eyes. Simon went close to him and then the man seemed to wake up. Turning his head, he opened his eyes and looked into Simon's face. That one look was enough to make Simon fond of the man. He threw the felt boots on the ground, undid his sash, laid it on the boots, and took off his cloth coat.

"It's not a time for talking," said he. "Come, put this coat on at once!" And Simon took the man by the elbows and helped him to rise. As he stood there, Simon saw that his body was clean and in good condition, his hands and feet shapely, and his face good and kind. He threw his coat over the man's shoulders, but the latter could not find the sleeves. Simon guided his arms into them, and drawing the coat well on, wrapped it closely about him, tying the sash round the man's waist.

Simon even took off his torn cap to put it on the man's head, but then his own head felt cold and he thought, "I'm quite bald, while he has long curly hair." So he put his cap on his own head again. "It will be better to give him something for his feet," thought he, and he made the man sit down and helped him to put on the felt boots, saying, "There, friend, now move about and warm yourself. Other matters can be settled later on. Can you walk?"

The man stood up and looked kindly at Simon, but could not say a word.

"Why don't you speak?" said Simon. "It's too cold to stay here; we must be getting home. There now, take my stick, and if you're feeling weak, lean on that. Now step out!"

The man started walking and moved easily, not lagging behind.

As they went along, Simon asked him, "And where do you belong to?"

"I'm not from these parts."

"I thought as much. I know the folks hereabouts. But how did you come to be there by the shrine?"

"I cannot tell."

"Has someone been ill-treating you?"

"No one has ill-treated me. God has punished me."

"Of course, God rules all. Still, you'll have to find food and shelter somewhere. Where do you want to go to?"

"It is all the same to me."

Simon was amazed. The man did not look like a rogue, and he spoke gently, but yet he gave no account of himself. Still Simon thought, "Who knows what may have happened?" And he said to the stranger, "Well then, come home with me and at least warm yourself awhile."

So Simon walked towards his home, and the stranger kept up with him, walking at his side. The wind had risen and Simon felt it cold under his shirt. He was getting over his tipsiness by now and began to feel the frost. He went along sniffling and wrapping his wife's coat around him, and he thought to himself: "There now— talk about sheepskins! I went out for sheepskins and come home without even a coat to my back, and what is more, I'm bringing a naked man along with me. Matrena won't be pleased!" And when he thought of his wife he felt sad, but when he looked at the stranger and remembered how he had looked up at him at the shrine, his heart was glad.

III

Simon's wife had everything ready early that day. She had cut wood, brought water, fed the children, eaten her own meal, and now she sat thinking. She wondered when she ought to make bread: now or tomorrow? There was still a large piece left.

"If Simon has had some dinner in town," thought she, "and does not eat much for supper, the bread will last another day."

She weighed the piece of bread in her hand again and again, and thought: "I won't make any more today. We have only enough flour left to bake one batch. We can manage to make this last till Friday."

So Matrena put away the bread, and sat down at the table to patch her husband's shirt. While she worked she thought how her husband was buying skins for a winter coat.

"If only the dealer does not cheat him. My good man is much too simple; he cheats nobody, but any child can take him in. Eight rubles is a lot of money—he should get a good coat at that price. Not tanned skins, but still a proper winter coat. How difficult it was last winter to get on without a warm coat. I could neither get down to the river, nor go out anywhere. When he went out he put on all we had, and there was nothing left for me. He did not start very early today, but still it's time he was back. I only hope he has not gone on a spree!"

Hardly had Matrena thought this than steps were heard on the threshold and someone entered. Matrena stuck her needle into her work and went out into the passage. There she saw two men: Simon, and with him a man without a hat and wearing felt boots.

Matrena noticed at once that her husband smelt of spirits. "There now, he has been drinking," thought she. And when she saw that he was coatless, had only her jacket on, brought no parcel, stood there silent, and seemed ashamed, her heart was ready to break with disappointment. "He has drunk the money," thought she, "and has been on a spree with some good-for-nothing fellow whom he has brought home with him."

Matrena let them pass into the hut, followed them in, and saw that the stranger was a young, slight man, wearing her husband's coat. There was no shirt to be seen under it, and he had no hat. Having entered, he stood neither moving nor raising his eyes, and Matrena thought, "He must be a bad man—he's afraid."

Matrena frowned, and stood beside the stove looking to see what they would do.

Simon took off his cap and sat down on the bench as if things were all right.

"Come, Matrena; if supper is ready, let us have some."

Matrena muttered something to herself and did not move, but stayed where she was, by the stove. She looked first at the one and then at the other of them and only shook her head. Simon saw that his wife was annoyed, but tried to pass it off. Pretending not to notice anything, he took the stranger by the arm.

"Sit down, friend," said he, "and let us have some supper."

The stranger sat down on the bench.

"Haven't you cooked anything for us?" said Simon.

Matrena's anger boiled over. "I've cooked, but not for you. It seems to me you have drunk your wits away. You went to buy a sheepskin coat, but come home without so much as the coat you had on, and bring a naked vagabond home with you. I have no supper for drunkards like you."

"That's enough, Matrena. Don't wag your tongue without reason! You had better ask what sort of man—"

"And you tell me what you've done with the money?"

Simon found the pocket of the jacket, drew out the three-ruble note, and unfolded it.

"Here is the money. Trifonov did not pay, but promises to pay soon."

Matrena got still more angry; he had bought no sheepskins, but had put his only coat on some naked fellow and had even brought him to their house.

She snatched up the note from the table, took it to put away in safety, and said: "I have no supper for you. We can't feed all the naked drunkards in the world."

"There now, Matrena, hold your tongue a bit. First hear what a man has to say—!"

"Much wisdom I shall hear from a drunken fool. I was right in not wanting to marry you—a drunkard. The linen my mother gave me you drank, and now you've been to buy a coat—and have drunk it too!"

Simon tried to explain to his wife that he had spent only twenty kopeks; tried to tell how he had found the man—but Matrena would not let him get a word in. She talked nineteen to the dozen, and dragged in things that had happened ten years before.

Matrena talked and talked, and at last she flew at Simon and seized him by the sleeve.

"Give me my jacket. It is the only one I have, and you must needs take it from me and wear it yourself. Give it here, you mangy dog, and may the devil take you."

Simon began to pull off the jacket, and turned a sleeve of it inside out; Matrena seized the jacket and it burst its seams. She snatched it up, threw it over her head, and went to the door. She meant to go out but stopped undecided—she wanted to work off her anger, but she also wanted to learn what sort of a man the stranger was.

IV

Matrena stopped and said: "If he were a good man he would not be naked. Why, he hasn't even a shirt on him. If he were all right, you would say where you came across the fellow."

"That's just what I am trying to tell you," said Simon. "As I came to the shrine I saw him sitting all naked and frozen. It isn't quite the weather to sit about naked! God sent me to him or he would have perished. What was I to do? How do we know what may have happened to him? So I took him, clothed him, and brought him along. Don't be so angry, Matrena. It is a sin. Remember, we must all die one day."

Angry words rose to Matrena's lips, but she looked at the stranger and was silent. He sat on the edge of the bench, motionless, his hands folded on his knees, his head drooping on his breast, his eyes closed, and his brows knit as if in pain. Matrena was silent, and Simon said, "Matrena, have you no love of God?"

Matrena heard these words, and as she looked at the stranger, suddenly her heart softened towards him. She came back from the door, and going to the stove she got out the supper. Setting a cup on the table, she poured out some *kvas*. Then she brought out the last piece of bread and set out a knife and spoons.

"Eat, if you want to," said she.

Simon drew the stranger to the table.

"Take your place, young man," said he.

Simon cut the bread and crumbled it into the broth, and they began to eat. Matrena sat at the corner of the table, resting her head on her hand and looking at the stranger.

And Matrena was touched with pity for the stranger and began to feel fond of him. And at once the stranger's face lit up; his brows were no longer bent, he raised his eyes and smiled at Matrena.

When they had finished supper, the woman cleared away the

things and began questioning the stranger. "Where are you from?" said she.

"I am not from these parts."

"But how did you come to be on the road?"

"I may not tell."

"Did someone rob you?"

"God punished me."

"And you were lying there naked?"

"Yes, naked and freezing. Simon saw me and had pity on me. He took off his coat, put it on me, and brought me here. And you have fed me, given me drink, and shown pity on me. God will reward you!"

Matrena rose, took from the window Simon's old shirt that she had been patching, and gave it to the stranger. She also brought out a pair of trousers for him.

"There," said she, "I see you have no shirt. Put this on, and lie down where you please, in the loft or on the stove."

The stranger took off the coat, put on the shirt, and lay down in the loft. Matrena put out the candle, took the coat, and climbed to where her husband lay on the stove.

Matrena drew the skirts of the coat over her and lay down but could not sleep; she could not get the stranger out of her mind.

When she remembered that he had eaten their last piece of bread and that there was none for tomorrow, and thought of the shirt and trousers she had given away, she felt grieved; but when she remembered how he had smiled, her heart was glad.

Long did Matrena lie awake, and she noticed that Simon also was awake—he drew the coat towards him.

"Simon!"

"Well?"

"You have had the last of the bread and I have not put any to rise. I don't know what we shall do tomorrow. Perhaps I can borrow some from neighbor Martha."

"If we're alive we shall find something to eat."

The woman lay still awhile, and then said, "He seems a good man, but why does he not tell us who he is?"

"I suppose he has his reasons."

"Simon!"

"Well?"

"We give, but why does nobody give us anything?"

Simon did not know what to say, so he only said, "Let us stop talking," and turned over and went to sleep.

V

In the morning Simon awoke. The children were still asleep; his wife had gone to the neighbor's to borrow some bread. The stranger alone was sitting on the bench, dressed in the old shirt and trousers, and looking upwards. His face was brighter than it had been the day before.

Simon said to him, "Well, friend, the belly wants bread and the naked body clothes. One has to work for a living. What work do you know?"

"I do not know any."

This surprised Simon, but he said, "Men who want to learn can learn anything."

"Men work and I will work also."

"What is your name?"

"Michael."

"Well, Michael, if you don't wish to talk about yourself, that is your own affair, but you'll have to earn a living for yourself. If you will work as I tell you, I will give you food and shelter."

"May God reward you! I will learn. Show me what to do."

Simon took yarn, put it around his thumb, and began to twist it.

"It is easy enough—see!"

Michael watched him, put some yarn around his own thumb in the same way, caught the knack, and twisted the yarn also.

Then Simon showed him how to wax the thread. This Michael also mastered. Next Simon showed him how to twist the bristle in, and how to sew, and this, too, Michael learned at once.

Whatever Simon showed him he understood at once, and after three days he worked as if he had sewn boots all his life. He worked without stopping and ate little. When work was over he sat silently, looking upwards. He hardly went into the street, spoke only when necessary, and neither joked nor laughed. They never saw him smile, except that first evening when Matrena gave them supper.

VI

Day by day and week by week the year went by. Michael lived and worked with Simon. His fame spread till people said that no one sewed boots so neatly and strongly as Simon's workman, Michael. From all the district around, people came to Simon for their boots, and he began to be well off.

One winter's day, as Simon and Michael sat working, a carriage on sledge-runners, with three horses and with bells, drove up to the hut. They looked out of the window. The carriage stopped at their door, a fine servant jumped down from the box and opened the door. A gentleman in a fur coat got out and walked up to Simon's hut. Up jumped Matrena and opened the door wide. The gentleman stooped to enter the hut, and when he drew himself up again, his head nearly reached the ceiling and he seemed quite to fill his end of the room.

Simon rose, bowed, and looked at the gentleman with astonishment. He had never seen anyone like him. Simon himself was lean, Michael was thin, and Matrena was dry as a bone, but this man was like someone from another world: red-faced, burly, with a neck like a bull's, and looking altogether as if he were cast in iron.

The gentleman puffed, threw off his fur coat, sat down on the bench, and said, "Which of you is the master bootmaker?"

"I am, your Excellency," said Simon, coming forward.

Then the gentleman shouted to his lad, "Hey, Fedka, bring the leather!"

The servant ran in, bringing a parcel. The gentleman took the parcel and put it on the table.

"Untie it," said he. The lad untied it.

The gentleman pointed to the leather.

"Look here, shoemaker," said he, "do you see this leather?"

"Yes, your honor."

"But do you know what sort of leather it is?"

Simon felt the leather and said, "It is good leather."

"Good, indeed! Why, you fool, you never saw such leather before in your life. It's German, and it cost twenty rubles."

Simon was frightened, and said, "Where should I ever see leather like that?"

"Just so! Now, can you make it into boots for me?"

"Yes, your Excellency, I can."

Then the gentleman shouted at him: "You *can,* can you? Well, remember for whom you are to make them, and what the leather is. You must make me boots that will wear for a year, neither losing shape nor coming unsewn. If you can do it, take the leather and cut it up, but if you can't, say so. I warn you now, if your boots come unsewn or lose shape within a year I will have you put in prison. If they don't burst or lose shape for a year, I will pay you ten rubles for your work."

Simon was frightened and did not know what to say. He glanced at Michael and nudging him with his elbow, whispered, "Shall I take the work?"

Michael nodded his head as if to say, "Yes, take it."

Simon did as Michael advised and undertook to make boots that would not lose shape or split for a whole year.

Calling his servant, the gentleman told him to pull the boot off his left leg, which he stretched out.

"Take my measure!" said he.

Simon stitched a paper measure seventeen inches long, smoothed it out, knelt down, wiped his hands well on his apron so as not to soil the gentleman's sock, and began to measure. He measured the sole, and around the instep, and began to measure the calf of the leg, but the paper was too short. The calf of the leg was as thick as a beam.

"Mind you don't make it too tight in the leg."

Simon stitched on another strip of paper. The gentleman twitched his toes about in his sock, looking around at those in the hut, and as he did so he noticed Michael.

"Whom have you there?" asked he.

"That is my workman. He will sew the boots."

"Mind," said the gentleman to Michael, "remember to make them so that they will last me a year."

Simon also looked at Michael, and saw that Michael was not looking at the gentleman but was gazing into the corner behind the gentleman, as if he saw someone there. Michael looked and looked, and suddenly he smiled, and his face became brighter.

"What are you grinning at, you fool?" thundered the gentleman. "You had better look to it that the boots are ready in time."

"They shall be ready in good time," said Michael.

"Mind it is so," said the gentleman, and he put on his boots and his fur coat, wrapped the latter around him, and went to the door. But he forgot to stoop and struck his head against the lintel.

He swore and rubbed his head. Then he took his seat in the carriage and drove away.

When he had gone, Simon said: "There's a figure of a man for you! You could not kill him with a mallet. He almost knocked out the lintel, but little harm it did him."

And Matrena said: "Living as he does, how should he not grow strong? Death itself can't touch such a rock as that."

VII

Then Simon said to Michael: "Well, we have taken the work, but we must see we don't get into trouble over it. The leather is dear, and the gentleman hot-tempered. We must make no mistakes. Come, your eye is truer and your hands have become nimbler than mine, so you take this measure and cut out the boots. I will finish off the sewing of the vamps."

Michael did as he was told. He took the leather, spread it out on the table, folded it in two, took a knife, and began to cut it out.

Matrena came and watched him cutting, and was surprised to see how he was doing it. Matrena was accustomed to seeing boots made, and she looked and saw that Michael was not cutting the leather for boots, but was cutting it around.

She wished to say something, but she thought to herself: "Perhaps I do not understand how gentlemen's boots should be made. I suppose Michael knows more about it—and I won't interfere."

When Michael had cut up the leather he took a thread and began to sew not with two ends, as boots are sewn, but with a single end, as for soft slippers.

Again Matrena wondered, but again she did not interfere. Michael sewed on steadily till noon. Then Simon rose for dinner, looked around, and saw that Michael had made slippers out of the gentleman's leather.

"Ah!" groaned Simon, and he thought, "How is it that Michael, who has been with me a whole year and never made a mistake before, should do such a dreadful thing? The gentleman ordered high boots, welted, with whole fronts, and Michael has made soft slippers with single soles, and has wasted the leather. What am I to say to the gentleman? I can never replace leather such as this."

And he said to Michael, "What are you doing, friend? You have ruined me! You know the gentleman ordered high boots, but see what you have made!"

Hardly had he begun to rebuke Michael, when "rat-tat" went the iron ring that hung at the door. Someone was knocking. They looked out of the window; a man had come on horseback and was fastening his horse. They opened the door, and the servant who had been with the gentleman came in.

"Good day," said he.

"Good day," replied Simon. "What can we do for you?"

"My mistress has sent me about the boots."

"What about the boots?"

"Why, my master no longer needs them. He is dead."

"Is it possible?"

"He did not live to get home after leaving you, but died in the carriage. When we reached home and the servants came to help him alight, he rolled over like a sack. He was dead already, and so stiff that he could hardly be got out of the carriage. My mistress sent me here, saying: 'Tell the bootmaker that the gentleman who ordered boots of him and left the leather for them no longer needs the boots, but that he must quickly make soft slippers for the corpse. Wait till they are ready and bring them back with you.' That is why I have come."

Michael gathered up the remnants of the leather, rolled them up, took the soft slippers he had made, slapped them together, wiped them down with his apron, and handed them and the roll of leather to the servant, who took them and said, "Good-bye, masters, and good day to you!"

VIII

Another year passed, and another, and Michael was now living his sixth year with Simon. He lived as before. He went nowhere, spoke only when necessary, and had smiled only twice in all those years—once when Matrena gave him food, and a second time when the gentleman was in their hut. Simon was more than pleased with his workman. He never now asked him where he came from, and only feared lest Michael should go away.

They were all at home one day. Matrena was putting iron pots in the oven; the children were running along the benches and looking out of the window; Simon was sewing at one window and Michael was fastening on a heel at the other.

One of the boys ran along the bench to Michael, leaned on his shoulder, and looked out of the window.

"Look, Uncle Michael! There is a lady with little girls! She seems to be coming here. And one of the girls is lame."

When the boy said that, Michael dropped his work, turned to the window, and looked out into the street.

Simon was surprised. Michael never used to look out into the street, but now he pressed against the window, staring at something. Simon also looked out and saw that a well-dressed woman was really coming to his hut, leading by the hand two little girls in fur coats and woolen shawls. The girls could hardly be told one from the other, except that one of them was crippled in her left leg and walked with a limp.

The woman stepped onto the porch and entered the passage. Feeling about for the entrance she found the latch, which she lifted, and opened the door. She let the two girls go in first, and followed them into the hut.

"Good day, good folk!'

"Pray come in," said Simon. "What can we do for you?"

The woman sat down by the table. The two little girls pressed close to her knees, afraid of the people in the hut.

"I want leather shoes made for these two little girls, for spring."

"We can do that. We have never made such small shoes, but we can make them—either welted or turnover shoes, linen-lined. My man, Michael, is a master at the work."

Simon glanced at Michael and saw that he had left his work and was sitting with his eyes fixed on the little girls. Simon was surprised. It was true the girls were pretty, plump, with black eyes and rosy cheeks, and they wore nice kerchiefs and fur coats, but still Simon could not understand why Michael should look at them like that—just as if he had known them before. Simon was puzzled, but went on talking with the woman and arranging the price. Having fixed it, he prepared the measure. The woman lifted the lame girl onto her lap and said: "Take two measures from this little girl. Make one shoe for the lame foot and three for the sound one. They both have the same-sized feet. They are twins."

Simon took the measure and, speaking of the lame girl, said: "How did it happen to her? She is such a pretty girl. Was she born so?"

"No, her mother crushed her leg."

Then Matrena joined in. She wondered who this woman was and whose the children were, so she said, "Are not you their mother, then?"

"No, my good woman, I am neither their mother nor any relation to them. They were quite strangers to me, but I adopted them."

"They are not your children and yet you are so fond of them?"

"How can I help being fond of them? I fed them both at my

own breast. I had a child of my own, but God took him. I was not so fond of him as I now am of these."

"Then whose children are they?"

IX

The woman, having begun talking, told them the whole story.

"It is about six years since their parents died, both in one week. Their father was buried on the Tuesday, and their mother died on the Friday. These orphans were born three days after their father's death, and their mother did not live another day. My husband and I were then living as peasants in the village. We were neighbors of theirs, our yard being next to theirs. Their father was a lonely man, a woodcutter in the forest. While he was felling trees one day, one fell on him. It fell across his body and crushed his bowels out. They hardly got him home before his soul went to God, and that same week his wife gave birth to twins—these little girls. She was poor and alone; she had no one, young or old, with her. Alone she gave them birth, and alone she met her death.

"The next morning I went to see her, but when I entered the hut, she, poor thing, was already stark and cold. In dying she had rolled onto this child and crushed her leg. The village folk came to the hut, washed the body, laid her out, made a coffin, and buried her. They were good folk. The babies were left alone. What was to be done with them? I was the only woman there who had a baby at the time. I was nursing my firstborn—eight weeks old. So I took them for a time. The peasants came together, and thought and thought what to do with them, and at last they said to me, 'For the present, Mary, you had better keep the girls, and later on we will arrange what to do for them.' So I nursed the sound one at my breast, but at first I did not feed this crippled one. I did not suppose she would live. But then I thought to myself, why should the poor innocent suffer? I pitied her and began to feed her. And so I fed my own boy and these two—the three of them—at my own breast. I was young and strong and had good food, and God gave me so much milk that at times it even overflowed. I used sometimes to feed two at a time, while the third was waiting. When one had had enough I nursed the third. And God so ordered it that these grew up, while my own was buried before he was two years old. And I had no more children, though we prospered. Now my husband is working for the corn merchant at the mill. The pay is good and we are well off. But I have no children of my own, and how lonely I

What We Live By 803

would be without these little girls! How can I help loving them! They are the joy of my life!"

She pressed the lame little girl to her with one hand, while with the other she wiped the tears from her cheeks.

And Matrena sighed, and said, "The proverb is true that says, 'One may live without father or mother, but one cannot live without God.'"

So they talked together, when suddenly the whole hut was lighted up as though by summer lightning from the corner where Michael sat. They all looked towards him and saw him sitting, his hands folded on his knees, gazing upwards and smiling.

X

The woman went away with the girls. Michael rose from the bench, put down his work, and took off his apron. Then, bowing low to Simon and his wife, he said: "Farewell, masters. God has forgiven me. I ask your forgiveness, too, for anything done amiss."

And they saw that a light shone from Michael. And Simon rose, bowed down to Michael, and said: "I see, Michael, that you are no common man, and I can neither keep you nor question you. Only tell me this: how is it that when I found you and brought you home, you were gloomy, and when my wife gave you food you smiled at her and became brighter? Then when the gentleman came to order the boots, you smiled again and became brighter still? And now, when this woman brought the little girls, you smiled a third time and have become as bright as day? Tell me, Michael, why does your face shine so, and why did you smile those three times?"

And Michael answered: "Light shines from me because I have been punished, but now God has pardoned me. And I smiled three times, because God sent me to learn three truths, and I have learned them. One I learned when your wife pitied me, and that is why I smiled the first time. The second I learned when the rich man ordered the boots, and then I smiled again. And now, when I saw those little girls, I learned the third and last truth, and I smiled the third time."

And Simon said, "Tell me, Michael, what did God punish you for? And what were the three truths so that I, too, may know them?"

And Michael answered: "God punished me for disobeying Him. I was an angel in heaven and disobeyed God. God sent me to fetch a woman's soul. I flew to earth, and saw a sick woman lying alone who had just given birth to twin girls. They moved feebly at their mother's side, but she could not lift them to her breast. When she saw me, she understood that God had sent me for her soul, and she wept and said: 'Angel of God! My husband has just been buried, killed by a falling tree. I have neither sister, nor aunt, nor mother, no one to care for my orphans. Do not take my soul! Let me nurse my babes, feed them, and set them on their feet before I die. Children cannot live without father or mother.' And I hearkened to her. I placed one child at her breast and gave the other into her arms, and returned to the Lord in heaven. I flew to the Lord, and said: 'I could not take the soul of the mother. Her husband was crushed by a tree; the woman has twins and prays that her soul may not be taken. She says: "Let me nurse and feed my children, and set them on their feet. Children cannot live without father or mother." I have not taken her soul.' And God said: 'Go—take the mother's soul, and learn three truths: Learn *What dwells in man; What is not given to man;* and *What men live by.* When thou hast learned these things, thou shalt return to heaven.' So I flew again to earth and took the mother's soul. The babes dropped from her breast. Her body rolled over on the bed and crushed one babe, twisting its leg. I rose above the village, wishing to take her soul to God, but a wind seized me and my wings drooped and dropped off. Her soul rose alone to God, while I fell to earth by the roadside."

XI

And Simon and Matrena understood who it was that had lived with them, and whom they had clothed and fed. And they wept with awe and with joy. And the angel said: "I was alone in the field, naked. I had never known human needs, cold, or hunger till I became a man. I was famished, frozen, and did not know what to do. I saw, near the field I was in, a shrine built for God, and I went to it hoping to find shelter. But the shrine was locked and I could not enter. So I sat down behind the shrine to shelter myself at least from the wind. Evening drew on; I was hungry, frozen, and in pain. Suddenly I heard a man coming along the road. He carried a pair of boots and was talking to himself. For the first time since I became a man I saw the mortal face of a man, and his face seemed terrible to me and I turned from it. And I heard the man talking to himself about how to cover his body from the cold in winter, and how to feed wife and children. And I thought: 'I am perishing of cold and hunger and here is a man thinking only of how to clothe himself and his wife, and how to get bread for themselves. He cannot help me.' When the man saw me he frowned and became still more terrible, and passed me by on the other side. I despaired, but suddenly I heard him coming back. I looked up and did not recognize the same man: before, I had seen death in his face, but now he was alive and I recognized in him the presence of God. He came up to me, clothed me, took me with him, and brought me to his home. I entered the house; a woman came to meet us and began to speak. The woman was still more terrible than the man had been. The spirit of death came from her mouth; I could not breathe for the stench of death that spread around her. She wished to drive me out into the cold, and I knew that if she did so she would die. Suddenly her husband spoke to her of God, and the woman changed at once. And when she brought me food and looked at me, I glanced at her and saw that death no longer dwelt in her. She had become alive, and in her too I saw God.

"Then I remembered the first lesson God had set me: *'Learn what dwells in man.'* And I understood that in man dwells Love! I was glad that God had already begun to show me what He had promised, and I smiled for the first time. But I had not yet learned all. I did not yet know *What is not given to man,* and *What men live by.*

"I lived with you and a year passed. A man came to order boots that would wear for a year without losing shape or cracking. I looked at him, and suddenly, behind his shoulder, I saw my comrade—the angel of death. None but me saw that angel, but I knew him, and knew that before the sun set he would take that rich man's soul. And I thought to myself, 'The man is making preparations for a year and does not know that he will die before evening.' And I remembered God's second saying, *'Learn what is not given to man.'*

"What dwells in man I already knew. Now I learned what is not given him. It is not given to man to know his own needs. And I smiled for the second time. I was glad to have seen my comrade angel—glad also that God had revealed to me the second saying.

"But I still did not know all. I did not know *What men live by.* And I lived on, waiting till God would reveal to me the last lesson. In the sixth year came the twin girls with the woman, and I recognized the girls and heard how they had been kept alive. Having heard the story, I thought, 'Their mother besought me for the children's sake, and I believed her when she said that children cannot live without father or mother, but a stranger has nursed them and has brought them up.' And when the woman showed her love for the children that were not her own, and wept over them, I saw in her the living God, and understood *What men live by.* And I knew that God had revealed to me the last lesson, and had forgiven my sin. And then I smiled for the third time."

XII

And the angel's body was bared, and he was clothed in light so that eye could not look on him; and his voice grew louder, as though it came not from him but from heaven above. And the angel said: "I have learned that men live not by care for themselves but by love.

"It was not given to the mother to know what her children needed for their life. Nor was it given to the rich man to know what he himself needed. Nor is it given to any man to know whether, when evening comes, he will need boots for his body or slippers for his corpse.

"I remained alive when I was a man not by care of myself but because love was present in a passerby, and because he and his wife pitied and loved me. The orphans remained alive not because of their mother's care but because there was love in the heart of a woman, a stranger to them, who pitied and loved them. And all men live not by the thought they spend on their own welfare but because love exists in man.

"I knew before that God gave life to men and desires that they should live; now I understood more than that.

"I understood that God does not wish men to live apart, and therefore he does not reveal to them what each one needs for himself. He wishes them to live united, and therefore reveals to each of them what is necessary for all.

"I now understand that though it seems to men that they live by care for themselves, in truth it is love alone by which they live. He who has love is in God, and God is in him, for God is love."

And the angel sang praise to God, so that the hut trembled at his voice. The roof opened, and a column of fire rose from earth to heaven. Simon and his wife and children fell to the ground. Wings appeared upon the angel's shoulders and he rose into the heavens.

And when Simon came to himself, the hut stood as before, and there was no one in it but his own family.

•

THE CHILD'S STORY

Charles Dickens

What are we here for, if not to walk with each other along life's journey?

Once upon a time, a good many years ago, there was a traveler, and he set out upon a journey. It was a magic journey, and seemed very long when he began it, and very short when he got halfway through.

He traveled along a rather dark path for some little time, without meeting anything, until at last he came to a beautiful child. So he said to the child, "What do you do here?" And the child said, "I am always at play. Come and play with me!"

So he played with that child, the whole day long, and they were very merry. The sky was so blue, and the sun was so bright, the water was so sparkling, the leaves were so green, the flowers were so lovely, and they heard such singing birds and saw so many butterflies, that everything was beautiful. This was in fine weather. When it rained, they loved to watch the falling drops, and to smell the fresh scents. When it blew, it was delightful to listen to the wind, and fancy what it said as it came rushing from its home—where was that, they wondered!—whistling and howling, driving the clouds before it, bending the trees, rumbling in the chimneys, shaking the house, and making the sea roar in fury. But when it snowed, that was best of all, for they liked nothing so well as to look up at the white flakes falling fast and thick, like down from the breasts of millions of white birds, and to see how smooth and deep the drift was, and to listen to the hush upon the paths and roads.

They had plenty of the finest toys in the world, and the most astonishing picture books—all about scimitars and slippers and turbans, and dwarfs and giants and genii and fairies, and Bluebeards and beanstalks and riches and caverns and forests and Valentines and Orsons—and all new and all true.

But one day, of a sudden, the traveler lost the child. He called to him over and over again, but got no answer. So he went upon his road, and went on for a little while without meeting anything, until at last he came to a handsome boy. So he said to the boy,

"What do you do here?" And the boy said, "I am always learning. Come and learn with me."

So he learned with that boy about Jupiter and Juno, and the Greeks and the Romans, and I don't know what, and learned more than I could tell—or he, either, for he soon forgot a great deal of it. But they were not always learning; they had the merriest games that ever were played. They rowed upon the river in summer, and skated on the ice in winter; they were active afoot, and active on horseback, at cricket, and all games at ball; at prisoner's base, hare and hounds, follow my leader, and more sports than I can think of. Nobody could beat them. They had holidays, too, the Twelfth Night cakes, and parties where they danced till midnight, and real theaters where they saw palaces of real gold and silver rise out of the real earth, and saw all the wonders of the world at once. As to friends, they had such dear friends and so many of them that I want time to reckon them up. They were all young, like the handsome boy, and were never to be strange to one another all their lives through.

Still, one day, in the midst of all these pleasures, the traveler lost the boy as he had lost the child, and, after calling to him in vain, went on upon his journey. So he went on for a little while without seeing anything, until at last he came to a young man. So he said to the young man, "What do you do here?" And the young man said, "I am always in love. Come and love with me."

So he went with that young man, and presently they came to one of the prettiest girls that was ever seen—just like Fanny in the corner there—and she had eyes like Fanny, and hair like Fanny, and dimples like Fanny, and she laughed and colored just as Fanny does while I am talking about her. So the young man fell in love directly—just as Somebody I won't mention, the first time he came here, did with Fanny. Well! He was teased sometimes—just as Somebody used to be by Fanny; and they quarreled sometimes— just as Somebody and Fanny used to quarrel; and they made it up, and sat in the dark, and wrote letters every day, and never were happy asunder, and were always looking out for each other and pretending not to, and were engaged at Christmastime, and sat close to each other by the fire, and were going to be married very soon—all exactly like Somebody I won't mention, and Fanny!

But the traveler lost them one day, as he had lost the rest of his friends, and, after calling to them to come back, which they never did, went on upon his journey. So he went on for a little while without seeing anything, until at last he came to a middle-aged gentleman. So he said to the gentleman, "What are you doing here?" And his answer was, "I am always busy. Come and be busy with me!"

So he began to be very busy with that gentleman, and they went on through the wood together. The whole journey was through a wood, only it had been open and green at first, like a wood in spring, and now began to be thick and dark, like a wood in summer. Some of the little trees that had come out earliest were even turning brown. The gentleman was not alone, but had a lady of about the same age with him, who was his wife; and they had children, who were with them, too. So they all went on together through the wood, cutting down the trees, and making a path through the branches and the fallen leaves, and carrying burdens and working hard.

Sometimes they came to a long green avenue that opened into deeper woods. Then they would hear a very little distant voice crying: "Father, father, I am another child! Stop for me!" And presently they would see a very little figure, growing larger as it came along, running to join them. When it came up, they all crowded around it, and kissed and welcomed it; and then they all went on together.

Sometimes they came to several avenues at once, and then they all stood still, and one of the children said, "Father, I am going to sea," and another said, "Father, I am going to India," and another, "Father, I am going to seek my fortune where I can," and another, "Father, I am going to Heaven!" So, with many tears at parting, they went, solitary, down those avenues, each child upon its way; and the child who went to Heaven rose into the golden air and vanished.

Whenever these partings happened, the traveler looked at the gentleman and saw him glance up at the sky above the trees, where the day was beginning to decline, and the sunset to come on. He saw, too, that his hair was turning gray. But they never could rest long, for they had their journey to perform, and it was necessary for them to be always busy.

At last, there had been so many partings that there were no children left, and only the traveler, the gentleman, and the lady went upon their way in company. And now the wood was yellow; and now brown; and the leaves, even of the forest trees, began to fall. They came to an avenue that was darker than the rest, and were pressing forward on their journey without looking down it when the lady stopped.

"My husband," said the lady, "I am called."

They listened, and they heard a voice, a long way down the avenue, say, "Mother, mother!"

It was the voice of the first child who had said, "I am going to Heaven!" and the father said: "I pray not yet. The sunset is very near. I pray not yet!"

But the voice cried, "Mother, mother!" without minding him, though his hair was now quite white, and tears were on his face.

Then the mother, who was already drawn into the shade of the dark avenue and moving away with her arms still around his neck, kissed him, and said, "My dearest, I am summoned, and I go!" And she was gone. And the traveler and he were left alone together.

And they went on and on together, until they came to very near the end of the wood; so near that they could see the sunset shining red before them through the trees.

Yet once more, while he broke his way among the branches, the traveler lost his friend. He called and called, but there was no reply, and when he passed out of the wood, and saw the peaceful sun going down upon a wide purple prospect, he came to an old man sitting on a fallen tree. So he said to the old man, "What do you do here?" And the old man said with a calm smile: "I am always remembering. Come and remember with me!"

So the traveler sat down by the side of that old man, face to face with the serene sunset; and all his friends came softly back and stood around him. The beautiful child, the handsome boy, the young man in love, the father, the mother, and the children: every one of them was there, and he had lost nothing. So he loved them all, and was kind and forbearing with them all, and was always pleased to watch them all, and they all honored and loved him. And I think the traveler must be yourself, dear Grandfather, because this is what you do to us, and what we do to you.

•

THE GREAT COMMANDMENT
Matthew 22:37–40

Thou shalt love the Lord thy God with all thy heart,
  and with all thy soul, and with all thy mind.
This is the first and great commandment.
And the second is like unto it;
Thou shalt love thy neighbor as thyself.
On these two commandments hang all the law and the prophets.

Acknowledgments

For permission to reprint copyrighted material, grateful acknowledgment is made to the following publishers, authors, and agents:

"A Worn Path" from *A Curtain of Green and Other Stories.* Copyright 1941 and renewed 1969 by Eudora Welty. Reprinted by permission of Harcourt Brace & Company.

"The Story of the Two Friends" from *The King of the Snakes and Other Folklore Stories from Uganda* by Rosetta Baskerville, The Sheldon Press, 1922. Used by permission of the publishers.

"The Conquest of Everest" from *The Age of Mountaineering* by James Ramsey Ullman. Copyright © 1941, 1954, 1982 by the Estate of James Ramsey Ullman. Reprinted by permission of Harold Matson Co., Inc.

"The Man Who Broke the Color Barrier" from *Sports Heroes Who Wouldn't Quit* by Hal Butler. Copyright © 1973 by Hal Butler. Reprinted by permission of Julian Messner, a division of Simon & Schuster, Inc.

"Kaddo's Wall" reprinted from *The Cow-Tail Switch and Other West African Stories* by Harold Courlander and George Herzog. Copyright © 1975 by Harold Courlander. Reprinted by permission of Henry Holt and Co., Inc.

"End of the Tiger" from *End of the Tiger and Other Stories* by John D. MacDonald. Reprinted by permission of Maynard MacDonald.

"No Greater Love" by John W. Mansur. Reprinted with permission from the August 1987 *Reader's Digest.*

"An Excellent Wife" taken from the *New American Standard Bible* ®, © Copyright The Lockman Foundation 1960, 1962, 1963, 1968, 1971, 1972, 1973, 1975, 1977. Used by permission.

"The Bravest Man" from *The Quality of Courage* by Mickey Mantle. Copyright © 1964 by Bedford S. Wynne, Trustee of four separate trusts for the benefit of Mickey Elven Mantle, David Harold Mantle, Billy Giles Mantle and Danny Murl

Mantle. Used by permission of Doubleday, a division of Bantam Doubleday Dell Publishing Group, Inc.

"Distance" from *Fires* by Raymond Carver. Copyright © 1983. Reprinted by permission of Capra Press, Santa Barbara.

"My Very Dear Sarah" by Sullivan Ballou. Reprinted by permission of the Chicago Historical Society.

"Your Second Job" as told to Fulton Oursler by Albert Schweitzer from the October 1949 *Reader's Digest.* Reprinted by permission of Fulton Oursler, Jr., and April Armstrong.

"Give Until It Hurts" by Mother Teresa. Reprinted by permission of Missionaries of Charity, Inc.

The author also gratefully acknowledges the endeavors of scholars and collectors who in a past age devoted their energies to preserving the best of our heritage, and whose works have supplied this volume with many truly great stories.

Reasonable care has been taken to trace ownership and, when necessary, to obtain permission for each selection included.

Index

WILLIAM J. BENNETT served as Director of the Office of National Drug Control Policy under President Bush, and as Secretary of Education and Chairman of the National Endowment for the Humanities under President Reagan. He holds a bachelor of arts degree in philosophy from Williams College, a doctorate in political philosophy from the University of Texas, and a law degree from Harvard. Dr. Bennett is currently a co-director of Empower America, and the John M. Olin Distinguished Fellow in Cultural Policy Studies at the Heritage Foundation. He, his wife, Elayne, and their two sons, John and Joseph, live in Chevy Chase, Maryland.

Edited,
with Commentary, by

William J. Bennett

A Touchstone Book

Published by Simon & Schuster

The Book

of

Virtues

A Treasury of

Great Moral Stories

TOUCHSTONE
Rockefeller Center
1230 Avenue of the Americas
New York, NY 10020

First Touchstone Edition 1996

TOUCHSTONE and colophon are registered trademarks
of Simon & Schuster Inc.

Designed by Karolina Harris
Manufactured in the United States of America

10   9   8   7   6   5   4   3   2   1

The Library of Congress has cataloged the Simon & Schuster edition as follows:
The Book of virtues : a treasury of great moral stories / [compiled] by
William J. Bennett.
    p. cm.
    Includes index.
    Summary: Well-known works including fables, folklore, fiction, drama, and more,
by such authors as Aesop, Dickens, Tolstoy, Shakespeare, and Baldwin, are presented
to teach virtues, including compassion, courage, honesty, friendship, and faith.
    1. Literature—Collections.   2. Conduct of life—Literary collections.
[1. Conduct of life—Literary collections.]   I. Bennett, William John, 1943–
PN6014.B695   1993
808.8'038—dc20   93-8981
                                                                                      CIP
                                                                                       AC
ISBN 0-671-68306-3
ISBN 0-684-83577-0 (Pbk)

To the families of America from my family:
Bill, Elayne, John, and Joseph Bennett.

Contents

Introduction

This book is intended to aid in the time-honored task of the moral education of the young. Moral education—the training of heart and mind toward the good—involves many things. It involves rules and precepts—the *do*s and *don't*s of life with others—as well as explicit instruction, exhortation, and training. Moral education *must* provide training in good habits. Aristotle wrote that good habits formed at youth make all the difference. And moral education must affirm the central importance of moral example. It has been said that there is nothing more influential, more determinant, in a child's life than the moral power of quiet example. For children to take morality seriously they must be in the presence of adults who take morality seriously. And with their own eyes they must see adults take morality seriously.

Along with precept, habit, and example, there is also the need for what we might call moral literacy. The stories, poems, essays, and other writing presented here are intended to help children achieve this moral literacy. The purpose of this book is to show parents, teachers, students, and children what the virtues look like, what they are in practice, how to recognize them, and how they work.

This book, then, is a "how to" book for moral literacy. If we want our children to possess the traits of character we most admire, we need to teach them what those traits are and why they deserve both admiration and allegiance. Children must learn to identify the forms and content of those traits. They must achieve at least a minimal level of moral literacy that will enable them to make sense of what they see in life and, we may hope, help them live it well.

Where do we go to find the material that will help our children in this task? The simple answer is we don't have to reinvent the wheel. We have a wealth of material to draw on—material that virtually all schools and homes and churches once taught to students for the sake of shaping character. That many no longer do so is something this book hopes to change.

The vast majority of Americans share a respect for certain fundamental traits of character: honesty, compassion, courage, and perseverance. These are virtues. But because children are not born with this knowledge, they need to learn what these virtues are. We can help them gain a grasp and appreciation of these traits by giving children material to read about them. We can invite our students to discern the moral dimensions of stories, of historical events, of famous lives. There are many wonderful stories of virtue and vice with which our children should be familiar. This book brings together some of the best, oldest, and most moving of them.

Do our children know these stories, these works? Unfortunately, many do not. They do not because in many places we are no longer teaching them. It is time we take up that task again. We do so for a number of reasons.

First, these stories, unlike courses in "moral reasoning," give children some specific reference points. Our literature and history are a rich quarry of moral literacy. We should mine that quarry. Children must have at their disposal a stock of examples illustrating what we see to be right and wrong, good and bad—examples illustrating that, in many instances, what is morally right and wrong can indeed be known and promoted.

Second, these stories and others like them are fascinating to children. Of course, the pedagogy (and the material herein) will need to be varied according to students' levels of comprehension, but you can't beat these stories when it comes to engaging the attention of a child. Nothing in recent years, on television or anywhere else, has improved on a good story that begins "Once upon a time . . ."

Third, these stories help anchor our children in their culture, its history and traditions. Moorings and anchors come in handy in life; moral anchors and moorings have never been more necessary.

Fourth, in teaching these stories we engage in an act of renewal. We welcome our children to a common world, a world of shared ideals, to the community of moral persons. In that common world we invite them to the continuing task of preserving the principles, the ideals, and the notions of goodness and greatness we hold dear.

The reader scanning this book may notice that it does not discuss issues like nuclear war, abortion, creationism, or euthanasia. This may come as a disappointment to some. But the fact is that the formation of character in young people is educationally a different task from, and a prior task to, the discussion of the great, difficult ethical controversies of the day. First things first. And planting the

ideas of virtue, of good traits in the young, comes first. In the moral
life, as in life itself, we take one step at a time. Every field has its
complexities and controversies. And so too does ethics. And every
field has its basics. So too with values. This is a book in the basics.
The tough issues can, if teachers and parents wish, be taken up
later. And, I would add, a person who is morally literate will be
immeasurably better equipped than a morally illiterate person to
reach a reasoned and ethically defensible position on these tough
issues. But the formation of character and the teaching of moral
literacy come first, in the early years; the tough issues come later, in
senior high school or after.

Similarly, the task of teaching moral literacy and forming character is not political in the usual meaning of the term. People of good
character are not all going to come down on the same side of difficult
political and social issues. Good people—people of character and
moral literacy—can be conservative, and good people can be liberal.
We must not permit our disputes over thorny political questions to
obscure the obligation we have to offer instruction to all our young
people in the area in which we have, as a society, reached a consen-
sus: namely, on the importance of good character, and on some of
its pervasive particulars. And that is what this book provides: a
compendium of great stories, poems, and essays from the stock of
human history and literature. It embodies common and time-
honored understandings of these virtues. It is for everybody—all
children, of all political and religious backgrounds, and it speaks to
them on a more fundamental level than race, sex, and gender. It
addresses them as human beings—as moral agents.

Every American child ought to know at least some of the stories
and poems in this book. Every American parent and teacher should
be familiar with some of them, too. I know that some of these stories
will strike some contemporary sensibilities as too simple, too corny,
too old-fashioned. But they will not seem so to the child, especially
if he or she has never seen them before. And I believe that if adults
take this book and read it in a quiet place, alone, away from dis-
torting standards, they will find themselves enjoying some of this
old, simple, "corny" stuff. The stories we adults used to know and
forgot—or the stories we never did know but perhaps were supposed to know—are here. (Quick!—what did Horatius do on the
bridge? What is the sword of Damocles? The answers are in this
book.) This is a book of lessons and reminders.

In putting this book together I learned many things. For one, going through the material was a mind-opening and encouraging rediscovery for me. I recalled great stories that I had forgotten. And thanks to the recommendations of friends, teachers, and the able prodding of my colleagues in this project, I came to know stories I had not known before. And, I discovered again how much books and education have changed in thirty years. In looking at this "old stuff" I am struck by how different it is from so much of what passes for literature and entertainment today.

Most of the material in this book speaks without hesitation, without embarrassment, to the inner part of the individual, to the moral sense. Today we speak about values and how it is important to "have them," as if they were beads on a string or marbles in a pouch. But these stories speak to morality and virtues not as something to be possessed, but as the central part of human nature, not as something to have but as something to be, the most important thing to be. To dwell in these chapters is to put oneself, through the imagination, into a different place and time, a time when there was little doubt that children are essentially moral and spiritual beings and that the central task of education is virtue. This book reminds the reader of a time—not so long ago—when the verities were the moral verities. It is thus a kind of antidote to some of the distortions of the age in which we now live. I hope parents will discover that reading this book with or to children can deepen their own, and their children's, understanding of life and morality. If the book reaches that high purpose it will have been well worth the effort.

A few additional notes and comments are in order. Although the book is titled *The Book of Virtues*—and the chapters are organized by virtues—it is also very much a book of vices. Many of the stories and poems illustrate a virtue in reverse. For children to know about virtue they must know about its opposite.

In telling these stories I am interested more in the moral than the historic lesson. In some of the older stories—Horatius at the bridge, William Tell, George Washington and the cherry tree—the line between legend and history has been blurred. But it is the instruction in the moral that matters. Some of the history that is recounted here may not meet the standards of the exacting historian. But we tell these familiar stories as they were told before, in order to preserve their authenticity.

Furthermore, I should stress that this book is by no means a definitive collection of great moral stories. Its contents have been defined in part by my attempt to present some material, most of

INTRODUCTION 15

which is drawn from the corpus of Western Civilization, that American schoolchildren, once upon a time, knew by heart. And the project, like any other, has faced several practical limitations such as space and economy (the rights to reprint recent stories and translations can be very expensive, while older material often lies in the public domain). The quarry of wonderful literature from our culture and others is deep, and I have barely scratched the surface. I invite readers to send me favorite stories not printed here, in case I should attempt to renew or improve this effort sometime in the future.

This volume is not intended to be a book one reads from cover to cover. It is, rather, a book for browsing, for marking favorite passages, for reading aloud to family, for memorizing pieces here and there. It is my hope that parents and teachers will spend some time wandering through these pages, discovering or rediscovering some moral landmarks, and in turn pointing them out to the young. The chapters can be taken in any order; on certain days we need reminding of some virtues more than others. A quick look at the Contents will steer the reader in the sought-after direction.

The reader will notice that in each chapter the material progresses from the very easy to the more difficult. The early material in each chapter can be read aloud to, or even by, very young children. As the chapter progresses greater reading and conceptual proficiency are required. Nevertheless we urge younger readers to work their way through as far as possible. As children grow older they can reach for the more difficult material in the book. They can grow up (and perhaps even grow better!) with this book.

Finally, I hope this is an encouraging book. There is a lot we read of or experience in life that is not encouraging. This book, I hope, does otherwise. I hope it encourages; I hope it points us to "the better angels of our nature." This book reminds us of what is important. And it should help us lift our eyes. St. Paul wrote, "Whatever is true, whatever is honorable, whatever is right, whatever is pure, whatever is lovely, whatever is of good repute, if there is any excellence and anything worthy of praise, let your mind dwell on these things."

I hope readers will read this book and dwell on those things.

I am indebted to Bob Asahina, my able editor at Simon and Schuster, for his encouragement, advice, and usual sober judgment. Sarah Pinckney, also of Simon and Schuster, kept the train running on time with her always-on-target and always-gracious answers, solutions, and suggestions. Robert Barnett, my agent, provided sound counsel and enthusiasm for this venture. My two colleagues in this project deserve special mention. Steven Tigner was judicious, knew where to find things and how best to describe virtues. He promised to help and he did; he's a man of virtue. As to John Cribb, I cannot thank him enough for his efforts to make this book a reality. Unfailingly and constantly he "mined the quarry" at the Library of Congress, in cartons of old books, in piles of dog-eared magazines. He came to love the stories and the idea of this book. He was "miner," scout, archivist, researcher, and critic. I owe him a great deal; I am grateful for the example of his friendship.

Finally, my wife, Elayne, always thought this was *my* book, the one book I *had* to do. And she was, as usual, right. She read, reviewed, guided, and recommended. As with everything else in my life, this, too, was made better because of her touch. And ironically enough I owe her thanks because on many nights long after I fell asleep, tired from a day of doing a lot of things—including putting this book together—she was the one still awake and reading good stories like these to our boys.

You know that the beginning is the most important part of any work, especially in the case of a young and tender thing; for that is the time at which the character is being formed and the desired impression is more readily taken. . . . Shall we just carelessly allow children to hear any casual tales which may be devised by casual persons, and to receive into their minds ideas for the most part the very opposite of those which we should wish them to have when they are grown up?

We cannot. . . . Anything received into the mind at that age is likely to become indelible and unalterable; and therefore it is most important that the tales which the young first hear should be models of virtuous thoughts. . . .

Then will our youth dwell in a land of health, amid fair sights and sounds, and receive the good in everything; and beauty, the effluence of fair works, shall flow into the eye and ear, like a health-giving breeze from a purer region, and insensibly draw the soul from the earliest years into likeness and sympathy with the beauty of reason.

There can be no nobler training than that.

—PLATO's *Republic*

1

Self-Discipline

In self-discipline one makes a "disciple" of oneself. One is one's own teacher, trainer, coach, and "disciplinarian." It is an odd sort of relationship, paradoxical in its own way, and many of us don't handle it very well. There is much unhappiness and personal distress in the world because of failures to control tempers, appetites, passions, and impulses. "Oh, if only I had stopped myself" is an all too familiar refrain.

The father of modern philosophy, René Descartes, once remarked of "good sense" that "everybody thinks he is so well supplied with it, that even the most difficult to please in all other matters never desire more of it than they already possess." With self-discipline it is just the opposite. Rare indeed is the person who doesn't desire more self-discipline and, with it, the control that it gives one over the course of one's life and development. That desire is itself, as Descartes might say, a further mark of good sense. We *do* want to take charge of ourselves. But what does that mean?

The question has been at or near the center of Western philosophy since its very beginnings. Plato divided the soul into three parts or operations—reason, passion, and appetite—and said that right behavior results from harmony or control of these elements. Saint Augustine sought to understand the soul by ranking its various forms of love in his famous *ordo amoris*: love of God, neighbor, self, and material goods. Sigmund Freud divided the psyche into the id, ego, and superego. And we find William Shakespeare examining the conflicts of the soul, the struggle between good and evil called the *psychomachia*, in immortal works such as *King Lear, Macbeth, Othello,* and *Hamlet*. Again and again, the problem is one of the soul's proper balance and order. "This was the noblest Roman of them all," Antony says of Brutus in *Julius Caesar*. "His life was gentle, and the elements so mixed in him that nature might stand up and say to all the world, 'This was a man!' "

But the question of correct order of the soul is not simply the domain of sublime philosophy and drama. It lies at the heart of the task of successful everyday behavior, whether it is controlling our tempers, or our appetites, or our inclinations to sit all day in front of the television. As Aristotle pointed out, here our habits make all the difference. We learn to order our souls the same way we learn to do math problems or play baseball well—through practice.

Practice, of course, is the medicine so many people find hard to swallow. If it were easy, we wouldn't have such modern-day phenomena as multimillon-dollar diet and exercise industries. We can enlist the aid of trainers, therapists, support groups, step programs, and other strategies, but in the end, it's practice that brings self-control.

The case of Aristotle's contemporary Demosthenes illustrates the point. Demosthenes had great ambition to become an orator, but suffered natural limitations as a speaker. Strong desire is essential, but by itself is insufficient. According to Plutarch, "His inarticulate and stammering pronunciation he overcame and rendered more distinct by speaking with pebbles in his mouth." Give yourself an even greater challenge than the one you are trying to master and you will develop the powers necessary to overcome the original difficulty. He used a similar strategy in training his voice, which "he disciplined by declaiming and reciting speeches or verses when he was out of breath, while running or going up steep places." And to keep himself studying without interruption "two or three months together," Demosthenes shaved "one half of his head, that so for shame he might not go abroad, though he desired it ever so much." Thus did Demosthenes make a kind of negative support group out of a general public that never saw him!

Good and Bad Children

Robert Louis Stevenson

Children, you are very little,
And your bones are very brittle;
If you would grow great and stately,
You must try to walk sedately.

You must still be bright and quiet,
And content with simple diet;
And remain, through all bewild'ring,
Innocent and honest children.

Happy hearts and happy faces,
Happy play in grassy places—
That was how, in ancient ages,
Children grew to kings and sages.

But the unkind and the unruly,
And the sort who eat unduly,
They must never hope for glory—
Theirs is quite a different story!

Cruel children, crying babies,
All grow up as geese and gabies,
Hated, as their age increases,
By their nephews and their nieces.

Please

Alicia Aspinwall

Webster's defines our manners as our "morals shown in conduct."
Good people stick to good manners, as this story from a turn-of-
the-century reader reminds us.

There was once a little word named "Please," that lived in a
small boy's mouth. Pleases live in everybody's mouth, though people often forget they are there.

Now, all Pleases, to be kept strong and happy, should be taken
out of the mouth very often, so they can get air. They are like little
fish in a bowl, you know, that come popping up to the top of the
water to breathe.

The Please I am going to tell you about lived in the mouth of a
boy named Dick; but only once in a long while did it have a chance
to get out. For Dick, I am sorry to say, was a rude little boy; he
hardly ever remembered to say "Please."

"Give me some bread! I want some water! Give me that book!"
—that is the way he would ask for things.

His father and mother felt very bad about this. And, as for the
poor Please itself, it would sit up on the roof of the boy's mouth day
after day, hoping for a chance to get out. It was growing weaker and
weaker every day.

This boy Dick had a brother, John. Now, John was older than
Dick—he was almost ten; and he was just as polite as Dick was rude.
So his Please had plenty of fresh air, and was strong and happy.

One day at breakfast, Dick's Please felt that he must have some
fresh air, even if he had to run away. So out he ran—out of Dick's
mouth—and took a long breath. Then he crept across the table and
jumped into John's mouth!

The Please-who-lived-there was very angry.

"Get out!" he cried. "You don't belong here! This is *my*
mouth!"

"I know it," replied Dick's Please. "I live over there in that
brother mouth. But alas! I am not happy there. I am never used. I
never get a breath of fresh air! I thought you might be willing to let
me stay here for a day or so—until I felt stronger."

"Why, certainly," said the other Please, kindly. "I understand. Stay, of course; and when my master uses me, we will both go out together. He is kind, and I am sure he would not mind saying 'Please' twice. Stay, as long as you like."

That noon, at dinner, John wanted some butter; and this is what he said:

"Father, will you pass me the butter, please—please?"

"Certainly," said the father. "But why be so *very* polite?"

John did not answer. He was turning to his mother, and said,

"Mother, will you give me a muffin, please—please?"

His mother laughed.

"You shall have the muffin, dear; but why do you say 'please' twice?"

"I don't know," answered John. "The words seem just to jump out, somehow. Katie, please—please, some water!"

This time, John was almost frightened.

"Well, well," said his father, "there is no harm done. One can't be too 'pleasing' in this world."

All this time little Dick had been calling, "Give me an egg! I want some milk. Give me a spoon!" in the rude way he had. But now he stopped and listened to his brother. He thought it would be fun to try to talk like John; so he began,

"Mother, will you give me a muffin, m-m-m-?"

He was trying to say "please"; but how could he? He never guessed that his own little Please was sitting in John's mouth. So he tried again, and asked for the butter.

"Mother, will you pass me the butter, m-m-m-?"

That was all he could say.

So it went on all day, and everyone wondered what was the matter with those two boys. When night came, they were both so tired, and Dick was so cross, that their mother sent them to bed very early.

But the next morning, no sooner had they sat down to breakfast than Dick's Please ran home again. He had had so much fresh air the day before that now he was feeling quite strong and happy. And the very next moment, he had another airing; for Dick said,

"Father, will you cut my orange, please?" Why! the word slipped out as easily as could be! It sounded just as well as when John said it—John was saying only *one* "please" this morning. And from that time on, little Dick was just as polite as his brother.

Rebecca,

Who Slammed Doors for Fun and Perished Miserably.

Hilaire Belloc

Aristotle would have loved this poem and the one that follows
it. The first illustrates excess, the second deficiency. The trick to
finding correct behavior is to strike the right balance. (See the
passage from Aristotle's *Ethics,* later in this chapter.)

A trick that everyone abhors
In Little Girls is slamming Doors.
A Wealthy Banker's Little Daughter
Who lived in Palace Green, Bayswater
(By name Rebecca Offendort),
Was given to this Furious Sport.
She would deliberately go
And Slam the door like Billy-Ho!
To make her Uncle Jacob start.
She was not really bad at heart,
But only rather rude and wild:
She was an aggravating child. . . .

It happened that a Marble Bust
of Abraham was standing just
Above the Door this little Lamb
Had carefully prepared to Slam,
And Down it came! It knocked her flat!
It laid her out! She looked like that.

Her Funeral Sermon (which was long
And followed by a Sacred Song)
Mentioned her Virtues, it is true,
But dwelt upon her Vices too,
And showed the Dreadful End of One
Who goes and slams the Door for Fun.

The children who were brought to hear
The awful Tale from far and near
Were much impressed, and inly swore
They never more would slam the Door.
—As often they had done before.

Godfrey Gordon Gustavus Gore

William Brighty Rands

Godfrey Gordon Gustavus Gore—
No doubt you have heard the name before—
Was a boy who never would shut a door!

The wind might whistle, the wind might roar,
And teeth be aching and throats be sore,
But still he never would shut the door.

His father would beg, his mother implore,
"Godfrey Gordon Gustavus Gore,
We really *do* wish you would shut the door!"

Their hands they wrung, their hair they tore;
But Godfrey Gordon Gustavus Gore
Was deaf as the buoy out at the Nore.

When he walked forth the folks would roar,
"Godfrey Gordon Gustavus Gore,
Why don't you think to shut the door?"

They rigged out a Shutter with sail and oar,
And threatened to pack off Gustavus Gore
On a voyage of penance to Singapore.

But he begged for mercy, and said, "No more!
Pray do not send me to Singapore
On a Shutter, and then I will shut the door."

"You will?" said his parents; "then keep on shore!
But mind you do! For the plague is sore
Of a fellow that never will shut the door,
Godfrey Gordon Gustavus Gore!"

The Lovable Child

Emilie Poulsson

We meet the well-behaved child (whom everybody loves).

Frisky as a lambkin,
  Busy as a bee—
That's the kind of little girl
  People like to see.

Modest as a violet,
  As a rosebud sweet—
That's the kind of little girl
  People like to meet.

Bright as is a diamond,
  Pure as any pearl—
Everyone rejoices in
  Such a little girl.

Happy as a robin,
  Gentle as a dove—
That's the kind of little girl
  Everyone will love.

Fly away and seek her,
  Little song of mine,
For I choose that very girl
  As my Valentine.

John, Tom, and James

We meet three ill-behaved children (whom nobody likes).

> John was a bad boy, and beat a poor cat;
> Tom put a stone in a blind man's hat;
> James was the boy who neglected his prayers;
> They've all grown up ugly, and nobody cares.

There Was a Little Girl

We meet the child who, like most, is sometimes well behaved and sometimes not. And we face a hard, unavoidable fact of life: if we cannot control our own behavior, eventually someone will come and control it for us in a way we probably will not like. This poem is sometimes attributed to Henry Wadsworth Long-fellow.

> There was a little girl,
> And she had a little curl
> Right in the middle of her forehead.
> When she was good
> She was very, very good,
> And when she was bad she was horrid.
>
> One day she went upstairs,
> When her parents, unawares,
> In the kitchen were occupied with meals,
> And she stood upon her head
> In her little trundle-bed,
> And then began hooraying with her heels.

Her mother heard the noise,
And she thought it was the boys
A-playing at a combat in the attic;
But when she climbed the stair,
And found Jemima there,
She took and she did spank her most emphatic.

My Own Self

Retold by Joseph Jacobs

Sometimes fortune offers us close calls we should take as warnings. Heaving a sigh of relief is not enough; if we're smart, we'll
change our behavior. Self-discipline is learned in the face of adversity, as this old English fairy tale reminds us.

In a tiny house in the North Countrie, far away from any town
or village, there lived not long ago, a poor widow all alone with her
little son, a six-year-old boy.

The house door opened straight on to the hillside, and all around
about were moorlands and huge stones, and swampy hollows; never
a house nor a sign of life wherever you might look, for their nearest
neighbors were the fairies in the glen below, and the "will-o'-the-
wisps" in the long grass along the path-side.

And many a tale the widow could tell of the "good folk" calling
to each other in the oak trees, and the twinkling lights hopping on
to the very windowsill, on dark nights; but in spite of the loneliness,
she lived on from year to year in the little house, perhaps because
she was never asked to pay any rent for it.

But she did not care to sit up late, when the fire burned low,
and no one knew what might be about. So, when they had had their
supper she would make up a good fire and go off to bed, so that if
anything terrible *did* happen, she could always hide her head under
the bedclothes.

This, however, was far too early to please her little son; so when
she called him to bed, he would go on playing beside the fire, as if
he did not hear her.

He had always been bad to do with since the day he was born, and his mother did not often care to cross him. Indeed, the more she tried to make him obey her, the less heed he paid to anything she said, so it usually ended by his taking his own way.

But one night, just at the fore-end of winter, the widow could not make up her mind to go off to bed, and leave him playing by the fireside. For the wind was tugging at the door, and rattling the windowpanes, and well she knew that on such a night, fairies and such like were bound to be out and about, and bent on mischief. So she tried to coax the boy into going at once to bed:

"It's safest to bide in bed on such a night as this!" she said. But no, he wouldn't go.

Then she threatened to "give him the stick," but it was no use.

The more she begged and scolded, the more he shook his head; and when at last she lost patience and cried that the fairies would surely come and fetch him away, he only laughed and said he wished they *would,* for he would like one to play with.

At that his mother burst into tears, and went off to bed in despair, certain that after such words something dreadful would happen, while her naughty little son sat on his stool by the fire, not at all put out by her crying.

But he had not long been sitting there alone, when he heard a fluttering sound near him in the chimney, and presently down by his side dropped the tiniest wee girl you could think of. She was not a span high, and had hair like spun silver, eyes as green as grass, and cheeks red as June roses.

The little boy looked at her with surprise.

"Oh!" said he, "what do they call ye?"

"My own self," she said in a shrill but sweet little voice, and she looked at him too. "And what do they call ye?"

"Just my own self too," he answered cautiously; and with that they began to play together.

She certainly showed him some fine games. She made animals out of the ashes that looked and moved like life, and trees with green leaves waving over tiny houses, with men and women an inch high in them, who, when she breathed on them, fell to walking and talking quite properly.

But the fire was getting low, and the light dim, and presently the little boy stirred the coals with a stick, to make them blaze, when out jumped a red-hot cinder, and where should it fall, but on the fairy child's tiny foot!

Thereupon she set up such a squeal, that the boy dropped the stick, and clapped his hands to his ears. But it grew to so shrill a screech, that it was like all the wind in the world, whistling through one tiny keyhole!

There was a sound in the chimney again, but this time the little boy did not wait to see what it was, but bolted off to bed, where he hid under the blankets and listened in fear and trembling to what went on.

A voice came from the chimney speaking sharply:

"Who's there, and what's wrong?" it said.

"It's my own self," sobbed the fairy child, "and my foot's burned sore. O-o-h!"

"Who did it?" said the voice angrily. This time it sounded nearer, and the boy, peeping from under the clothes, could see a white face looking out from the chimney opening!

"Just my own self too!" said the fairy child again.

"Then if ye did it your own self," cried the elf mother shrilly, "what's the use o' making all this fuss about it?"—and with that she stretched out a long thin arm, and caught the creature by its ear, and, shaking it roughly, pulled it after her, out of sight up the chimney!

The little boy lay awake a long time, listening, in case the fairy mother should come back after all. And next evening after supper, his mother was surprised to find that he was willing to go to bed whenever she liked.

"He's taking a turn for the better at last!" she said to herself. But he was thinking just then that, when next a fairy came to play with him, he might not get off quite so easily as he had done this time.

To the Little Girl Who Wriggles

Laura E. Richards

In which we learn to sit still.

Don't wriggle about anymore, my dear!
I'm sure all your joints must be sore, my dear!
It's wriggle and jiggle, it's twist and it's wiggle,
Like an eel on a shingly shore, my dear,
Like an eel on a shingly shore.

Oh! how do you think you would feel, my dear,
If you should turn into an eel, my dear?
With never an arm to protect you from harm,
And no sign of a toe or a heel, my dear,
No sign of a toe or a heel?

And what do you think you would do, my dear,
Far down in the water so blue, my dear,
Where the prawns and the shrimps,
   with their curls and their crimps,
Would turn up their noses at you, my dear,
Would turn up their noses at you?

The crab he would give you a nip, my dear,
And the lobster would lend you a clip, my dear.
And perhaps if a shark should come by in the dark,
Down his throat you might happen to slip, my dear,
Down his throat you might happen to slip.

Then try to sit still on your chair, my dear!
To your parents 'tis no more than fair, my dear.
For we really don't feel like inviting an eel
Our board and our lodging to share, my dear,
Our board and our lodging to share.

Jim,

Who ran away from his Nurse, and was eaten by a Lion.

Hilaire Belloc

In which we discover the kind of gruesome end that comes to
children who dart away from their mothers into streets, run away
from their fathers at crowded ball parks, dash screaming down
grocery store aisles, and who in general cannot bring themselves
to hold on to the hand they are told to hold.

There was a Boy whose name was Jim;
His Friends were very good to him.
They gave him Tea, and Cakes, and Jam,
And slices of delicious Ham,
And Chocolate with pink inside,
And little Tricycles to ride,
And read him Stories through and through,
And even took him to the Zoo—
But there it was the dreadful Fate
Befell him, which I now relate.

You know—at least you *ought* to know,
For I have often told you so—
That Children never are allowed
To leave their Nurses in a Crowd;
Now this was Jim's especial Foible,
He ran away when he was able,
And on this inauspicious day
He slipped his hand and ran away!
He hadn't gone a yard when—Bang!
With open Jaws, a Lion sprang,
And hungrily began to eat
The Boy: beginning at his feet.

Now just imagine how it feels
When first your toes and then your heels,
And then by gradual degrees,
Your shins and ankles, calves and knees,
Are slowly eaten, bit by bit.
No wonder Jim detested it!
No wonder that he shouted "Hi!"
The Honest Keeper heard his cry,
Though very fat he almost ran
To help the little gentleman.
'Ponto!" he ordered as he came
(For Ponto was the Lion's name),
"Ponto!" he cried, with angry Frown.
"Let go, Sir! Down, Sir! Put it down!"
The Lion made a sudden Stop,
He let the Dainty Morsel drop,
And slunk reluctant to his Cage,

Snarling with Disappointed Rage.
But when he bent him over Jim,
The Honest Keeper's Eyes were dim.
The Lion having reached his Head,
The Miserable Boy was dead!

When Nurse informed his Parents, they
Were more Concerned than I can say:
His Mother, as She dried her eyes,
Said, "Well—it gives me no surprise,
He would not do as he was told!"
His Father, who was self-controlled,
Bade all the children round attend
To James' miserable end,
And always keep a-hold of Nurse
For fear of finding something worse.

The Duel

Eugene Field

In which we discover the unfortunate consequences of fighting.

The gingham dog and the calico cat
Side by side on the table sat;
'Twas half past twelve, and (what do you think!)
Nor one nor t'other had slept a wink!
  The old Dutch clock and the Chinese plate
  Appeared to know as sure as fate
There was going to be a terrible spat.
    (*I wasn't there; I simply state*
    What was told to me by the Chinese plate!)

The gingham dog went "bow-wow-wow!"
And the calico cat replied "mee-ow!"
The air was littered an hour or so,
With bits of gingham and calico.
    While the old Dutch clock in the chimney place
    Up with its hands before its face,
For it always dreaded a family row!
        (*Now mind; I'm only telling you*
        What the old Dutch clock declares is true!)

The Chinese plate looked very blue,
And wailed, "Oh, dear! what shall we do!"
But the gingham dog and the calico cat
Wallowed this way and tumbled that,
    Employing every tooth and claw
    In the awfullest way you ever saw—
And, oh! how the gingham and calico flew!
        (*Don't fancy I exaggerate—*
        I got my news from the Chinese plate!)

Next morning, where the two had sat
They found no trace of dog or cat;
And some folks think unto this day
That burglars stole that pair away!
    But the truth about the cat and pup
    Is this: they ate each other up!
Now what do you really think of that!
        (*The old Dutch clock it told me so,*
        And that is how I came to know.)

Let Dogs Delight to Bark and Bite

Isaac Watts

Let dogs delight to bark and bite,
For God hath made them so;
Let bears and lions growl and fight,
For 'tis their nature too.

But, children, you should never let
Such angry passions rise;
Your little hands were never made
To tear each other's eyes.

The King and His Hawk

Retold by James Baldwin

Thomas Jefferson gave us simple but effective advice about controlling our temper: count to ten before you do anything, and if very angry, count to a hundred. Genghis Khan (c.1162–1227), whose Mongol empire stretched from eastern Europe to the Sea of Japan, could have used Jefferson's remedy in this tale.

Genghis Khan was a great king and warrior.

He led his army into China and Persia, and he conquered many lands. In every country, men told about his daring deeds, and they said that since Alexander the Great there had been no king like him.

One morning when he was home from the wars, he rode out into the woods to have a day's sport. Many of his friends were with him. They rode out gayly, carrying their bows and arrows. Behind them came the servants with the hounds.

It was a merry hunting party. The woods rang with their shouts and laughter. They expected to carry much game home in the evening.

On the king's wrist sat his favorite hawk, for in those days hawks were trained to hunt. At a word from their masters they would fly high up into the air, and look around for prey. If they chanced to see a deer or a rabbit, they would swoop down upon it swift as any arrow.

All day long Genghis Khan and his huntsmen rode through the woods. But they did not find as much game as they expected.

Toward evening they started for home. The king had often ridden through the woods, and he knew all the paths. So while the rest of the party took the nearest way, he went by a longer road through a valley between two mountains.

The day had been warm, and the king was very thirsty. His pet hawk had left his wrist and flown away. It would be sure to find its way home.

The king rode slowly along. He had once seen a spring of clear water near this pathway. If he could only find it now! But the hot days of summer had dried up all the mountain brooks.

At last, to his joy, he saw some water trickling down over the edge of a rock. He knew that there was a spring farther up. In the wet season, a swift stream of water always poured down here; but now it came only one drop at a time.

The king leaped from his horse. He took a little silver cup from his hunting bag. He held it so as to catch the slowly falling drops.

It took a long time to fill the cup; and the king was so thirsty that he could hardly wait. At last it was nearly full. He put the cup to his lips, and was about to drink.

All at once there was a whirring sound in the air, and the cup was knocked from his hands. The water was all spilled upon the ground.

The king looked up to see who had done this thing. It was his pet hawk.

The hawk flew back and forth a few times, and then alighted among the rocks by the spring.

The king picked up the cup, and again held it to catch the trickling drops.

This time he did not wait so long. When the cup was half full, he lifted it toward his mouth. But before it had touched his lips, the hawk swooped down again, and knocked it from his hands.

And now the king began to grow angry. He tried again, and for the third time the hawk kept him from drinking.

The king was now very angry indeed.

"How do you dare to act so?" he cried. "If I had you in my hands, I would wring your neck!"

Then he filled the cup again. But before he tried to drink, he drew his sword.

"Now, Sir Hawk," he said, "this is the last time."

He had hardly spoken before the hawk swooped down and knocked the cup from his hand. But the king was looking for this. With a quick sweep of the sword he struck the bird as it passed.

The next moment the poor hawk lay bleeding and dying at its master's feet.

"That is what you get for your pains," said Genghis Khan.

But when he looked for his cup, he found that it had fallen between two rocks, where he could not reach it.

"At any rate, I will have a drink from that spring," he said to himself.

With that he began to climb the steep bank to the place from which the water trickled. It was hard work, and the higher he climbed, the thirstier he became.

At last he reached the place. There indeed was a pool of water; but what was that lying in the pool, and almost filling it? It was a huge, dead snake of the most poisonous kind.

The king stopped. He forgot his thirst. He thought only of the poor dead bird lying on the ground below him.

"The hawk saved my life!" he cried, "and how did I repay him? He was my best friend, and I have killed him."

He clambered down the bank. He took the bird up gently, and laid it in his hunting bag. Then he mounted his horse and rode swiftly home. He said to himself,

"I have learned a sad lesson today, and that is, never to do anything in anger."

Anger

Charles and Mary Lamb

Anger in its time and place
May assume a kind of grace.
It must have some reason in it,
And not last beyond a minute.
If to further lengths it go,
It does into malice grow.
'Tis the difference that we see
'Twixt the serpent and the bee.
If the latter you provoke,
It inflicts a hasty stroke,
Puts you to some little pain,
But it *never stings again.*
Close in tufted bush or brake
Lurks the poison-swelled snake
Nursing up his cherished wrath;
In the purlieus of his path,
In the cold, or in the warm,
Mean him good, or mean him harm,
Wheresoever fate may bring you,
The vile snake will *always sting you.*

Dirty Jim

Jane Taylor

Why should we bother to practice cleanliness? Aside from some
very good practical considerations, Francis Bacon reminded us
why: "For cleanness of body was ever esteemed to proceed from
a due reverence to God, to society, and to ourselves."

There was one little Jim,
'Tis reported of him,
    And must be to his lasting disgrace,
That he never was seen
With hands at all clean,
    Nor yet ever clean was his face.

His friends were much hurt
To see so much dirt,
    And often they made him quite clean;
But all was in vain,
He got dirty again,
    And not at all fit to be seen.

It gave him no pain
To hear them complain,
    Nor his own dirty clothes to survey;
His indolent mind
No pleasure could find
    In tidy and wholesome array.

The idle and bad,
Like this little lad,
    May love dirty ways, to be sure;
But good boys are seen,
To be decent and clean,
    Although they are ever so poor.

Washing

Dear Lord, sometimes my hair gets quite
Untidy, rough, and mussy;
And when my Mother makes it right
I'm apt to think she's fussy.
My hands get black with different dirts,
And when no one is present,
I don't half wash; I think it hurts
To make myself more pleasant.

Please make me feel that Cleanliness
Is just a proper virtue,
And that cold water's here to bless,
And never here to hurt you.
Please show me how I always can
Do simple things, that lead to
The making of a gentleman,
And *wash,* because I need to.

Table Rules for Little Folks

In which we learn how to take our daily bread.

In silence I must take my seat,
And give God thanks before I eat;
Must for my food in patience wait,
Till I am asked to hand my plate;
I must not scold, nor whine, nor pout,
Nor move my chair nor plate about;
With knife, or fork, or napkin ring,
I must not play, nor must I sing.
I must not speak a useless word,
For children should be seen, not heard;
I must not talk about my food,
Nor fret if I don't think it good;
I must not say, "The bread is old,"
"The tea is hot," "The coffee's cold";
My mouth with food I must not crowd,
Nor while I'm eating speak aloud;
Must turn my head to cough or sneeze,
And when I ask, say "If you please";
The tablecloth I must not spoil,
Nor with my food my fingers soil;
Must keep my seat when I have done,
Nor round the table sport or run;
When told to rise, then I must put

My chair away with noiseless foot;
And lift my heart to God above,
In praise for all his wondrous love.

The Little Gentleman

Take your meals, my little man,
Always like a gentleman;
Wash your face and hands with care,
Change your shoes, and brush your hair;
Then so fresh, and clean and neat,
Come and take your proper seat;
Do not loiter and be late,
Making other people wait;
Do not rudely point or touch:
Do not eat and drink too much:
Finish what you have before
You even ask or send for more:
Never crumble or destroy
Food that others might enjoy;
They who idly *crumbs* will waste
Often want a loaf to taste!
Never spill your milk or tea,
Never rude or noisy be;
Never choose the daintiest food,
Be content with what is good:
Seek in all things that you can
To be a little gentleman.

Our Lips and Ears

In which we learn how to conduct our conversation.

If you your lips would keep from slips,
    Five things observe with care:
Of whom you speak, to whom you speak,
    And how and when and where.

If you your ears would save from jeers,
    These things keep meekly hid:
Myself and I, and mine and my,
    And how I do and did.

Little Fred

In which we learn how to retire for the evening.

When little Fred
    Was called to bed,
He always acted right;
    He kissed Mama,
    And then Papa,
And wished them all good night.

He made no noise,
    Like naughty boys,
But gently up the stairs
    Directly went,
    When he was sent,
And always said his prayers.

The Story of Augustus, Who Would Not Have Any Soup

Heinrich Hoffmann

In which we see the inevitable result of not eating enough of the right stuff.

> Augustus was a chubby lad;
> Fat, ruddy cheeks Augustus had;
> And everybody saw with joy
> The plump and hearty, healthy boy.
> He ate and drank as he was told,
> And never let his soup get cold.
>
> But one day, one cold winter's day,
> He screamed out—"Take the soup away!
> O take the nasty soup away!
> I won't have any soup today."
>
> Next day begins his tale of woes;
> Quite lank and lean Augustus grows.
> Yet, though he feels so weak and ill,
> The naughty fellow cries out still—
>
> "Not any soup for me, I say:
> O take the nasty soup away!
> I won't have any soup today."
>
> The third day comes; O what a sin!
> To make himself so pale and thin.
> Yet, when the soup is put on table,
> He screams, as loud as he is able—
> "Not any soup for me, I say:
> O take the nasty soup away!
> I won't have any soup today."

Look at him, now the fourth day's come!
He scarcely weighs a sugarplum;
He's like a little bit of thread,
And on the fifth day, he was—dead!

The Vulture

Hilaire Belloc

This one belongs on the refrigerator door.

The Vulture eats between his meals,
    And that's the reason why
He very, very rarely feels
    As well as you or I.
His eye is dull, his head is bald,
    His neck is growing thinner.
Oh, what a lesson for us all
    To only eat at dinner.

The Boy and the Nuts

Aesop

One good, practical reason for controlling our cravings is that if
we grasp for too much, we may end up getting nothing at all.

A little boy once found a jar of nuts on the table.
"I would like some of these nuts," he thought. "I'm sure
Mother would give them to me if she were here. I'll take a big
handful." So he reached into the jar and grabbed as many as he could
hold.
But when he tried to pull his hand out, he found the neck of the

jar was too small. His hand was held fast, but he did not want to drop any of the nuts.

He tried again and again, but he couldn't get the whole handful out. At last he began to cry.

Just then his mother came into the room. "What's the matter?" she asked.

"I can't take this handful of nuts out of the jar," sobbed the boy.

"Well, don't be so greedy," his mother replied. "Just take two or three, and you'll have no trouble getting your hand out."

"How easy that was," said the boy as he left the table. "I might have thought of that myself."

The Goose That Laid the Golden Eggs

Aesop

Here is Aesop's classic fable about plenty not being enough, about what happens when "having it all" becomes the motto of the day.

A man and his wife had the good fortune to possess a goose that laid a golden egg every day. Lucky though they were, they soon began to think they were not getting rich fast enough, and, imagining the bird must be made of gold inside, they decided to kill it in order to secure the whole store of precious metal at once. But when they cut it open they found it was just like any other goose. Thus, they neither got rich all at once, as they had hoped, nor enjoyed any longer the daily addition to their wealth.

Much wants more and loses all.

The Flies and the Honey Pot

Aesop

A jar of honey chanced to spill
Its contents on the windowsill
In many a viscous pool and rill.

The flies, attracted by the sweet,
Began so greedily to eat,
They smeared their fragile wings and feet.

With many a twitch and pull in vain
They gasped to get away again,
And died in aromatic pain.

Moral

O foolish creatures that destroy
Themselves for transitory joy.

Mr. Vinegar and His Fortune

Retold by James Baldwin

A runaway appetite is just about the surest ticket to never getting
anywhere. The English philosopher John Locke put it this way:
"He that has not a mastery over his inclinations; he that knows
not how to resist the importunity of present pleasure or pain, for
the sake of what reason tells him is fit to be done, wants the true
principle of virtue and industry, and is in danger of never being
good for anything." Meet Mr. Vinegar, who is in such danger.

A long time ago there lived a poor man whose real name has been forgotten. He was little and old, and his face was wrinkled; and that is why his friends called him Mr. Vinegar.

His wife was also little and old, and they lived in a little old cottage at the back of a little old field.

One day when Mrs. Vinegar was sweeping, she swept so hard that the little old door of the cottage fell down.

She was frightened. She ran out into the field and cried, "John! John! The house is falling down. We shall have no shelter over our heads."

Mr. Vinegar came and looked at the door.

Then he said, "Don't worry about that, my dear. Put on your bonnet and we will go out and seek our fortune."

So Mrs. Vinegar put on her hat, and Mr. Vinegar put the door on his head and they started.

They walked and walked all day. At night they came to a dark forest where there were many tall trees.

"Here is a good place to lodge," said Mr. Vinegar.

So he climbed a tree and laid the door across some branches. Then Mrs. Vinegar climbed the tree, and the two laid themselves down on the door.

"It is better to have the house under us than over us," said Mr. Vinegar. But Mrs. Vinegar was fast asleep, and did not hear him.

Soon it was pitch dark, and Mr. Vinegar also fell asleep. At midnight he was awakened by hearing a noise below him.

He started up. He listened.

"Here are ten gold pieces for you, Jack," he heard someone say. "And here are ten pieces for you, Bill. I'll keep the rest for myself."

Mr. Vinegar looked down. He saw three men sitting on the ground. A lighted lantern was near them.

"Robbers!" he cried in great fright, and sprang to a higher branch.

As he did this he kicked the door from its resting place. The door fell crashing to the ground, and Mrs. Vinegar fell with it.

The robbers were so badly scared that they took to their heels and ran helter-skelter into the dark woods.

"Are you hurt, my dear?" asked Mr. Vinegar.

"Ah, no!" said his wife. "But who would have thought that the door would tumble down in the night? And here is a beautiful lantern, all lit and burning, to show us where we are."

Mr. Vinegar scrambled to the ground. He picked up the lantern to look at it. But what were those shining things that he saw lying all around?

"Gold pieces! Gold pieces!" he cried. And he picked one up and held it to the light.

"We've found our fortune! We've found our fortune!" cried Mrs. Vinegar. And she jumped up and down for joy.

They gathered up the gold pieces. There were fifty of them, all bright and yellow and round.

"How lucky we are!" said Mr. Vinegar.

"How lucky we are!" said Mrs. Vinegar.

Then they sat down and looked at the gold till morning.

"Now, John," said Mrs. Vinegar, "I'll tell you what we'll do. You must go to the town and buy a cow. I will milk her and churn butter, and we shall never want for anything."

"That is a good plan," said Mr. Vinegar.

So he started off to the town, while his wife waited by the roadside.

Mr. Vinegar walked up and down the street of the town, looking for a cow. After a time a farmer came that way, leading one that was very pretty and fat.

"Oh, if I only had that cow," said Mr. Vinegar, "I would be the happiest man in the world."

"She is a very good cow," said the farmer.

"Well," said Mr. Vinegar, "I will give you these fifty gold pieces for her."

The farmer smiled and held out his hand for the money. "You may have her," he said. "I always like to oblige my friends."

Mr. Vinegar took hold of the cow's halter and led her up and down the street. "I am the luckiest man in the world," he said, "for only see how all the people are looking at me and my cow."

But at one end of the street he met a man playing bagpipes. He stopped and listened. Tweedle-dee, tweedle-dee!

"Oh, that is the sweetest music I ever heard," he said. "And just see how all the children crowd around the man and give him pennies! If I only had those bagpipes, I would be the happiest man in the world."

"I will sell them to you," said the piper.

"Will you? Well then, since I have no money, I will give you this cow for them."

"You may have them," answered the piper. "I always like to oblige a friend."

Mr. Vinegar took the bagpipes, and the piper led the cow away.

"Now we will have some music," said Mr. Vinegar. But try as hard as he might, he could not play a tune. He could get nothing out of the bagpipes but "squeak! squeak!"

The children, instead of giving him pennies, laughed at him. The day was chilly, and, in trying to play the pipes his fingers grew very cold. He wished that he had kept the cow.

He had just started for home when he met a man who had warm gloves on his hands. "Oh, if I only had those pretty gloves," he said, "I would be the happiest man in the world."

"How much will you give for them?" asked the man.

"I have no money, but I will give you these bagpipes," answered Mr. Vinegar.

"Well," said the man, "you may have them, for I always like to oblige a friend."

Mr. Vinegar gave him the bagpipes and drew the gloves on over his half-frozen fingers. "How lucky I am!" he said, as he trudged homeward.

His hands were soon quite warm, but the road was rough and the walking hard. He was very tired when he came to the foot of a steep hill.

"How shall I ever get to the top?" he said.

Just then he met a man who was walking the other way. He had a stick in his hand which he used as a cane to help him along.

"My friend," said Mr. Vinegar, "if I only had that stick of yours to help me up this hill, I would be the happiest man in the world."

"How much will you give me for it?" asked the man.

"I have no money, but I will give you this pair of warm gloves," said Mr. Vinegar.

"Well," said the man, "you may have it, for I always like to oblige a friend."

Mr. Vinegar's hands were now quite warm. So he gave the gloves to the man and took the stout stick to help him along.

"How lucky I am," he said, as he toiled upward.

At the top of the hill he stopped to rest. But as he was thinking of all his good luck that day, he heard someone calling his name. He looked up and saw only a green parrot sitting in a tree.

"Mr. Vinegar! Mr. Vinegar!" it cried.

"What now?" asked Mr. Vinegar.

"You're a dunce! You're a dunce!" answered the bird. "You went to seek your fortune, and you found it. Then you gave it for a cow, and the cow for some bagpipes, and the bagpipes for some gloves, and the gloves for a stick which you might have cut by the roadside. Hee! hee! hee! hee! hee! You're a dunce! You're a dunce!"

This made Mr. Vinegar very angry. He threw the stick at the bird with all his might. But the bird only answered, "You're a dunce! You're a dunce!" and the stick lodged in the tree where he could not get it again.

Mr. Vinegar went on slowly, for he had many things to think about. His wife was standing by the roadside, and as soon as she saw him she cried out, "Where's the cow? Where's the cow?"

"Well, I don't just know where the cow is," said Mr. Vinegar; and then he told her the whole story.

I have heard she said some things he liked even less than what the bird had said, but that is between Mr. and Mrs. Vinegar, and really nobody's business but theirs.

"We are no worse off than we were yesterday," said Mr. Vinegar. "Let us go home and take care of our little old house."

Then he put the door on his head and trudged onward. And Mrs. Vinegar followed him.

The Frogs and the Well

Aesop

The prudent person looks before leaping.

Two frogs lived together in a marsh. But one hot summer the marsh dried up, and they left it to look for another place to live in, for frogs like damp places if they can get them. By and by they came to a deep well, and one of them looked down into it, and said to the other, "This looks a nice cool place. Let us jump in and settle here." But the other, who had a wiser head on his shoulders, replied, "Not so fast, my friend. Supposing this well dried up like the marsh, how should we get out again?"

Think twice before you act.

The Fisherman and His Wife

Retold by Clifton Johnson

The ancient Greeks had a famous saying: "Nothing overmuch."
The maxim calls not for total abstinence, but rather reminds us
to avoid excess. We should know that too much of anything,
even a good thing, may prove to be our undoing, as this old tale
shows. We need to recognize when enough is enough.

There was once a fisherman who lived with his wife in a poor
little hut close by the sea. One day, as the fisherman sat on the rocks
at the water's edge fishing with his rod and line, a fish got caught on
his hook that was so big and pulled so stoutly that he captured it
with the greatest difficulty. He was feeling much pleased that he had
secured so big a fish when he was surprised by hearing it say to him,
"Pray let me live. I am not a real fish. I am a magician. Put me in
the water and let me go."

"You need not make so many words about the matter," said
the man. "I wish to have nothing to do with a fish that can talk."

Then he removed it from his hook and put it back into the
water. "Now swim away as soon as you please," said the man, and
the fish darted straight down to the bottom.

The fisherman returned to his little hut and told his wife how
he had caught a great fish, and how it had told him it was a magician,
and how, when he heard it speak, he had let it go.

"Did you not ask it for anything?" said the wife.

"No," replied the man. "What should I ask for?"

"What should you ask for!" exclaimed the wife. "You talk as if
we had everything we want, but see how wretchedly we live in this
dark little hut. Do go back and tell the fish we want a comfortable
house."

The fisherman did not like to undertake such an errand. However, as his wife had bidden him to go, he went; and when he came
to the sea the water looked all yellow and green. He stood on the
rocks where he had fished and said,

"Oh, man of the sea!
Come listen to me;
For Alice my wife,
The plague of my life,
Hath sent me to beg a gift of thee!"

Then the fish came swimming to him and said, "Well, what does she want?"

"Ah," answered the fisherman, "my wife says that when I had caught you I ought to have asked you for something before I let you go. She does not like living any longer in our little hut. She wants a comfortable house."

"Go home then," said the fish. "She is in the house she wants already."

So the man went home and found his wife standing in the doorway of a comfortable house, and behind the house was a yard with ducks and chickens picking about in it, and beyond the yard was a garden where grew all sorts of flowers and fruits. "How happily we shall live now!" said the fisherman.

Everything went right for a week or two, and then the wife said, "Husband, there is not enough room in this house, and the yard and garden are a great deal smaller than they ought to be. I would like to have a large stone castle to live in. So go to the fish again and tell him to give us a castle."

"Wife," said the fisherman, "I don't like to go to him again, for perhaps he will be angry. We ought to be content with a good house like this."

"Nonsense!" said the wife. "He will give us a castle very willingly. Go along and try."

The fisherman went, but his heart was heavy, and when he came to the sea the water was a dark gray color and looked very gloomy. He stood on the rocks at the water's edge and said,

"Oh, man of the sea!
Come listen to me;
For Alice my wife,
The plague of my life,
Hath sent me to beg a gift of thee!"

Then the fish came swimming to him and said, "Well, what does she want now?"

"Ah," replied the man very sorrowfully, "my wife wants to live in a stone castle."

"Go home then," said the fish. "She is at the castle already."

So away went the fisherman and found his wife standing before a great castle. "See," said she, "is not this fine?"

They went into the castle, and many servants were there, and the rooms were richly furnished with handsome chairs and tables; and behind the castle was a park half a mile long, full of sheep and goats and rabbits and deer.

"Now," said the man, "we will live contented and happy in this beautiful castle for the rest of our lives."

"Perhaps so," responded the wife. "But let us consider and sleep on it before we make up our minds." And they went to bed.

The next morning when they awoke it was broad daylight, and the wife jogged the fisherman with her elbow and said, "Get up, husband; bestir yourself, for we must be king and queen of all the land."

"Wife, wife," said the man, "why should we wish to be king and queen? I would not be king even if I could be."

"Well, I will be queen, anyway," said the wife. "Say no more about it; but go to the fish and tell him what I want."

So the man went, but he felt very sad to think that his wife should want to be queen. The sea was muddy and streaked with foam as he cried out,

> "Oh, man of the sea!
> Come listen to me;
> For Alice my wife,
> The plague of my life,
> Hath sent me to beg a gift of thee!"

Then the fish came swimming to him and said, "Well, what would she have now?"

"Alas!" said the man. "My wife wants to be queen."

"Go home," said the fish. "She is queen already."

So the fisherman turned back and presently he came to a palace, and before it he saw a troop of soldiers, and he heard the sound of drums and trumpets. Then he entered the palace and there he found his wife sitting on a throne, with a golden crown on her head, and on each side of her stood six beautiful maidens.

"Well, wife," said the fisherman, "are you queen?"

"Yes," she replied, "I am queen."

When he had looked at her for a long time he said, "Ah, wife, what a fine thing it is to be queen! Now we shall never have anything more to wish for."

"I don't know how that may be," said she. "Never is a long time. I am queen, 'tis true, but I begin to be tired of it. I think I would like to be pope next."

"Oh, wife, wife!" the man exclaimed. "How can you be pope? There is but one pope at a time in all Christendom."

"Husband," said she, "I will be pope this very day."

"Ah, wife!" responded the fisherman. "The fish cannot make you pope and I would not like to ask for such a thing."

"What nonsense!" said she. "If he can make a queen, he can make a pope. Go and try."

So the fisherman went, and when he came to the shore the wind was raging and the waves were dashing on the rocks most fearfully, and the sky was dark with flying clouds. The fisherman was frightened, but nevertheless he obeyed his wife and called out,

> "Oh, man of the sea!
> Come listen to me;
> For Alice my wife,
> The plague of my life,
> Hath sent me to beg a gift of thee!"

Then the fish came swimming to him and said, "What does she want this time?"

"Ah," said the fisherman, "my wife wants to be pope."

"Go home," commanded the fish. "She is pope already."

So the fisherman went home and found his wife sitting on a throne that was a hundred feet high, and on either side many candles of all sizes were burning, and she had three great crowns on her head one above the other and was surrounded by all the pomp and power of the church.

"Wife," said the fisherman, as he gazed at all this magnificence, "are you pope?"

"Yes," she replied, "I am pope."

"Well, wife," said he, "it is a grand thing to be pope. And now you must be content, for you can be nothing greater."

"We will see about that," she said.

Then they went to bed; but the wife could not sleep because all night long she was trying to think what she should be next. At last morning came and the sun rose. "Ha!" cried she. "I was about to sleep, had not the sun disturbed me with its bright light. Cannot I prevent the sun rising?" and she became very angry and said to her husband, "Go to the fish and tell him I want to be lord of the sun and moon."

"Alas, wife," said he, "can you not be content to be pope?"

"No," said she, "I am very uneasy, and cannot bear to see the sun and moon rise without my leave. Go to the fish at once!"

The man went, and as he approached the shore a dreadful storm arose so that the trees and rocks shook, and the sky grew black, and the lightning flashed, and the thunder rolled, and the sea was covered with vast waves like mountains. The fisherman trembled so that his knees knocked together, and he had hardly strength to stand in the gale while he called to the fish:

> "Oh, man of the sea!
> Come listen to me;
> For Alice my wife,
> The plague of my life,
> Hath sent me to beg a gift of thee!"

Then the fish came swimming to him and said, "What more does she want?"

"Ah," said the man, "she wants to be lord of the sun and moon."

"Go home to your hut again," said the fish.

So the man returned, and the palace was gone, and in its place he found the dark little hut that had formerly been his dwelling, and he and his wife have lived in that little hut to this very day.

The Magic Thread

Too often, people want what they want (or what they *think* they want, which is usually "happiness" in one form or another) *right now*. The irony of their impatience is that only by learning to wait, and by a willingness to accept the bad with the good, do we usually attain those things that are truly worthwhile. "He that can have patience, can have what he will," Benjamin Franklin told us, and this French tale bears him out.

Once there was a widow who had a son called Peter. He was a strong, able boy, but he did not enjoy going to school and he was forever daydreaming.

"Peter, what are you dreaming about this time?" his teacher would say to him.

"I'm thinking about what I'll be when I grow up," Peter replied.

"Be patient. There's plenty of time for that. Being grown up isn't all fun, you know," his teacher said.

But Peter found it hard to enjoy whatever he was doing at the moment, and was always hankering after the next thing. In winter he longed for it to be summer again, and in summer he looked forward to the skating, sledging, and warm fires of winter. At school he would long for the day to be over so that he could go home, and on Sunday nights he would sigh, "If only the holidays would come." What he enjoyed most was playing with his friend Liese. She was as good a companion as any boy, and no matter how impatient Peter was, she never took offense. "When I grow up, I shall marry Liese," Peter said to himself.

Often he wandered through the forest, dreaming of the future. Sometimes he lay down on the soft forest floor in the warm sun, his hands behind his head, staring up at the sky through the distant treetops. One hot afternoon as he began to grow sleepy, he heard someone calling his name. He opened his eyes and sat up. Standing before him was an old woman. In her hand she held a silver ball, from which dangled a silken golden thread.

"See what I have got here, Peter," she said, offering the ball to him.

"What is it?" he asked curiously, touching the fine golden thread.

"This is your life thread," the old woman replied. "Do not touch it and time will pass normally. But if you wish time to pass more quickly, you have only to pull the thread a little way and an hour will pass like a second. But I warn you, once the thread has been pulled out, it cannot be pushed back in again. It will disappear like a puff of smoke. The ball is for you. But if you accept my gift you must tell no one, or on that very day you shall die. Now, say, do you want it?"

Peter seized the gift from her joyfully. It was just what he wanted. He examined the silver ball. It was light and solid, made of a single piece. The only flaw in it was the tiny hole from which the bright thread hung. He put the ball in his pocket and ran home. There, making sure that his mother was out, he examined it again. The thread seemed to be creeping very slowly out of the ball, so slowly that it was scarcely noticeable to the naked eye. He longed to give it a quick tug, but dared not do so. Not yet.

The following day at school, Peter sat daydreaming about what he would do with his magic thread. The teacher scolded him for not concentrating on his work. If only, he thought, it was time to go home. Then he felt the silver ball in his pocket. If he pulled out a tiny bit of thread, the day would be over. Very carefully he took hold of it and tugged. Suddenly the teacher was telling everyone to pack up their books and to leave the classroom in an orderly fashion. Peter was overjoyed. He ran all the way home. How easy life would be now! All his troubles were over. From that day forth he began to pull the thread, just a little, every day.

One day, however, it occurred to him that it was stupid to pull the thread just a little each day. If he gave it a harder tug, school would be over altogether. Then he could start learning a trade and marry Liese. So that night he gave the thread a hard tug, and in the morning he awoke to find himself apprenticed to a carpenter in town. He loved his new life, clambering about on roofs and scaffolding, lifting and hammering great beams into place that still smelled of the forest. But sometimes, when payday seemed too far off, he gave the thread a little tug and suddenly the week was drawing to a close and it was Friday night and he had money in his pocket.

Liese had also come to town and was living with her aunt, who taught her housekeeping. Peter began to grow impatient for the day when they would be married. It was hard to live so near and yet so far from her. He asked her when they could be married.

"In another year," she said. "Then I will have learned how to be a capable wife."

Peter fingered the silver ball in his pocket.

"Well, the time will pass quickly enough," he said, knowingly.

That night Peter could not sleep. He tossed and turned restlessly. He took the magic ball from under his pillow. For a moment he hesitated; then his impatience got the better of him, and he tugged at the golden thread. In the morning he awoke to find that the year was over and that Liese had at last agreed to marry him. Now Peter felt truly happy.

But before their wedding could take place, Peter received an official-looking letter. He opened it in trepidation and read that he was expected to report at the army barracks the following week for two years' military service. He showed the letter to Liese in despair.

"Well," she said, "there is nothing for it, we shall just have to wait. But the time will pass quickly, you'll see. There are so many things to do in preparation for our life together."

Peter smiled bravely, knowing that two years would seem a lifetime to him.

Once Peter had settled into life at the barracks, however, he began to feel that it wasn't so bad after all. He quite enjoyed being with all the other young men, and their duties were not very arduous at first. He remembered the old woman's warning to use the thread wisely and for a while refrained from pulling it. But in time he grew restless again. Army life bored him with its routine duties and harsh discipline. He began pulling the thread to make the week go faster so that it would be Sunday again, or to speed up the time until he was due for leave. And so the two years passed almost as if they had been a dream.

Back home, Peter determined not to pull the thread again until it was absolutely necessary. After all, this was the best time of his life, as everyone told him. He did not want it to be over too quickly. He did, however, give the thread one or two very small tugs, just to speed along the day of his marriage. He longed to tell Liese his secret, but he knew that if he did he would die.

On the day of his wedding, everyone, including Peter, was happy. He could hardly wait to show Liese the house he had built for her. At the wedding feast he glanced over at his mother. He noticed for the first time how gray her hair had grown recently. She seemed to be aging so quickly. Peter felt a pang of guilt that he had pulled the thread so often. Henceforward he would be much more sparing with it and only use it when it was strictly necessary.

A few months later Liese announced that she was going to have a child. Peter was overjoyed and could hardly wait. When the child was born, he felt that he could never want for anything again. But whenever the child was ill or cried through the sleepless night, he gave the thread a little tug, just so that the baby might be well and happy again.

Times were hard. Business was bad and a government had come to power that squeezed the people dry with taxes and would tolerate no opposition. Anyone who became known as a troublemaker was thrown into prison without trial and rumor was enough to condemn a man. Peter had always been known as one who spoke his mind, and very soon he was arrested and cast into jail. Luckily he had his magic ball with him and he tugged very hard at the thread. The prison walls dissolved before him and his enemies were scattered in the huge explosion that burst forth like thunder. It was the war that had been threatening, but it was over as quickly as a summer storm, leaving behind it an exhausted peace. Peter found himself back home with his family. But now he was a middle-aged man.

For a time things went well and Peter lived in relative contentment. One day he looked at his magic ball and saw to his surprise that the thread had turned from gold to silver. He looked in the mirror. His hair was starting to turn gray and his face was lined where before there had not been a wrinkle to be seen. He suddenly felt afraid and determined to use the thread even more carefully than before. Liese bore him more children and he seemed happy as the head of his growing household. His stately manner often made people think of him as some sort of benevolent ruler. He had an air of authority as if he held the fate of others in his hands. He kept his magic ball in a well-hidden place, safe from the curious eyes of his children, knowing that if anyone were to discover it, it would be fatal.

As the number of his children grew, so his house became more overcrowded. He would have to extend it, but for that he needed money. He had other worries too. His mother was looking older and more tired every day. It was of no use to pull the magic thread because that would only hasten her approaching death. All too soon she died, and as Peter stood at her graveside, he wondered how it was that life passed so quickly, even without pulling the magic thread.

One night as he lay in bed, kept awake by his worries, he thought how much easier life would be if all his children were grown up and launched upon their careers in life. He gave the thread a mighty tug, and the following day he awoke to find that his children had all left home for jobs in different parts of the country, and that he and his wife were alone. His hair was almost white now and often his back and limbs ached as he climbed the ladder or lifted a heavy beam into place. Liese too was getting old and she was often ill. He couldn't bear to see her suffer, so that more and more he resorted to pulling at the magic thread. But as soon as one trouble was solved, another seemed to grow in its place. Perhaps life would be easier if he retired, Peter thought. Then he would no longer have to clamber about on drafty, half-completed buildings and he could look after Liese when she was ill. The trouble was that he didn't have enough money to live on. He picked up his magic ball and looked at it. To his dismay he saw that the thread was no longer silver but gray and lusterless. He decided to go for a walk in the forest to think things over.

It was a long time since he had been in that part of the forest. The small saplings had all grown into tall fir trees, and it was hard to find the path he had once known. Eventually he came to a bench in a clearing. He sat down to rest and fell into a light doze. He was woken by someone calling his name, "Peter! Peter!"

He looked up and saw the old woman he had met so many years ago when she had given him the magic silver ball with its golden thread. She looked just as she had on that day, not a day older. She smiled at him.

"So, Peter, have you had a good life?" she asked.

"I'm not sure," Peter said. "Your magic ball is a wonderful thing. I have never had to suffer or wait for anything in my life. And yet it has all passed so quickly. I feel that I have had no time to take in what has happened to me, neither the good things nor the bad. Now there is so little time left. I dare not pull the thread again for it will only bring me to my death. I do not think your gift has brought me luck."

"How ungrateful you are!" the old woman said. "In what way would you have wished things to be different?"

"Perhaps if you had given me a different ball, one where I could have pushed the thread back in as well as pulling it out. Then I could have relived the things that went badly."

The old woman laughed. "You ask a great deal! Do you think that God allows us to live our lives twice over? But I can grant you one final wish, you foolish, demanding man."

"What is that?" Peter asked.

"Choose," the old woman said. Peter thought hard.

At length he said, "I should like to live my life again as if for the first time, but without your magic ball. Then I will experience the bad things as well as the good without cutting them short, and at least my life will not pass as swiftly and meaninglessly as a daydream."

"So be it," said the old woman. "Give me back my ball."

She stretched out her hand and Peter placed the silver ball in it. Then he sat back and closed his eyes with exhaustion.

When he awoke he was in his own bed. His youthful mother was bending over him, shaking him gently.

"Wake up, Peter. You will be late for school. You were sleeping like the dead!"

He looked up at her in surprise and relief.

"I've had a terrible dream, Mother. I dreamed that I was old and sick and that my life had passed like the blinking of an eye with nothing to show for it. Not even any memories."

His mother laughed and shook her head.

"That will never happen," she said. "Memories are the one thing we all have, even when we are old. Now hurry and get dressed. Liese is waiting for you and you will be late for school."

As Peter walked to school with Liese, he noticed what a bright summer morning it was, the kind of morning when it felt good to be alive. Soon he would see his friends and classmates, and even the prospect of lessons didn't seem so bad. In fact he could hardly wait.

The Golden Touch

Adapted from Nathaniel Hawthorne

This retelling of the famous Greek tale about lust for gold is adapted from Nathaniel Hawthorne's version in his *Wonder Book*. The Midas of mythology is usually identified by scholars with a king of ancient Phrygia (now Turkey) who ruled in the eighth century B.C. The early Greeks believed Phrygia to be a land of fabulous wealth.

Once upon a time there lived a very rich king whose name was Midas. He had more gold than anyone in the whole world, but for all that, he thought it was not enough. He was never so happy as when he happened to get more gold to add to his treasure. He stored it away in great vaults underneath his palace, and many hours of each day were spent counting it over.

Now King Midas had a little daughter named Marygold. He loved her devotedly, and said: "She shall be the richest princess in all the world!"

But little Marygold cared nothing about it all. She loved her garden, her flowers and the golden sunshine more than all her father's riches. She was a lonely little girl most of the time, for her father was so busy planning new ways to get more gold, and counting what he had, that he seldom told her stories or went for walks with her, as all fathers should do.

One day King Midas was down in his treasure room. He had locked the heavy doors and had opened up his great chests of gold. He piled it on the table and handled it as if he loved the touch of it. He let it slip through his fingers and smiled at the clink of it as if it had been sweet music. Suddenly a shadow fell over the heap of gold. Looking up, he saw a stranger dressed in shining white smiling down at him. King Midas started up in surprise. Surely he had not failed to lock the door! His treasure was not safe! But the stranger continued to smile.

"You have much gold, King Midas," he said.

"Yes," said the king, "but think how little this is to all the gold there is in the world!"

"What! Are you not satisfied?" asked the stranger.

"Satisfied?" said the king. "Of course I'm not. I often lie awake through the long night planning new ways to get more gold. I wish that everything I touch would turn to gold."

"Do you really wish that, King Midas?"

"Of course I wish it. Nothing could make me so happy."

"Then you shall have your wish. Tomorrow morning when the first rays of the sun fall through your window you shall have the golden touch."

When he had finished speaking, the stranger vanished. King Midas rubbed his eyes. "I must have dreamed it," he said, "but how happy I should be if it were only true!"

The next morning King Midas woke when the first faint light came into his room. He put out his hand and touched the covers of his bed. Nothing happened. "I knew it could not be true," he sighed. Just at that moment the first rays of the sun came through the window. The covers on which King Midas's hand lay became pure gold. "It's true, it's true!" he cried joyfully.

He sprang out of bed and ran about the room touching everything. His dressing gown, his slippers, the furniture, all became gold. He looked out of the window through Marygold's garden.

"I'll give her a nice surprise," he said. He went down into the garden touching all of Marygold's flowers, and changing them to gold. "She will be so pleased," he thought.

He went back into his room to wait for his breakfast; and took up his book which he had been reading the night before, but the minute he touched it, it was solid gold. "I can't read it now," he said, "but of course it is far better to have it gold."

Just then a servant came through the door with the king's breakfast. "How good it looks," he said. "I'll have that ripe, red peach first of all."

He took the peach in his hand, but before he could taste it, it became a lump of gold. King Midas put it back on the plate. "It's very beautiful, but I can't eat it!" he said. He took a roll from the plate, but that, too, became gold. He took a glass of water in his hand, but that, too, became gold. "What shall I do?" he cried. "I am hungry and thirsty, I can't eat or drink gold!"

At that moment the door was opened and in came little Marygold. She was crying bitterly, and in her hand was one of her roses.

"What's the matter, little daughter?" said the king.

"Oh, Father! See what has happened to all my roses! They are stiff, ugly things!"

"Why, they are golden roses, child. Do you not think they are more beautiful than they were?"

"No," she sobbed, "they do not smell sweet. They won't grow anymore. I like roses that are alive."

"Never mind," said the king, "eat your breakfast now."

But Marygold noticed that her father did not eat, and that he looked very sad. "What is the matter, Father dear?" she said, and she ran over to him. She threw her arms about him, and he kissed her. But he suddenly cried out in terror and anguish. When he touched her, her lovely little face became glittering gold, her eyes could not see, her lips could not kiss him back again, her little arms could not hold him close. She was no longer a loving, laughing little girl; she was changed to a little golden statue.

King Midas bowed his head and great sobs shook him.

"Are you happy, King Midas?" he heard a voice say. Looking up he saw the stranger standing near him.

"Happy! How can you ask? I am the most miserable man living!" said the king.

"You have the golden touch," said the stranger. "Is that not enough?"

King Midas did not look up or answer.

"Which would you rather have, food and a cup of cold water or these lumps of gold?" said the stranger.

King Midas could not answer.

"Which would you rather have, O King—that little golden statue, or a little girl who could run, and laugh, and love you?"

"Oh, give me back my little Marygold and I'll give up all the gold I have!" said the king. "I've lost all that was worth having."

"You are wiser than you were, King Midas," said the stranger. "Go plunge in the river which runs at the foot of your garden, then take some of its water and sprinkle whatever you wish to change back as it was." The stranger vanished.

King Midas sprang up and ran to the river. He plunged into it, and then he dipped up a pitcher of its water and hurried back to the palace. He sprinkled it over Marygold, and the color came back into her cheeks. She opened her blue eyes again. "Why, Father!" she said. "What happened?"

With a cry of joy King Midas took her into his arms.

Never after that did King Midas care for any gold except the gold of the sunshine, and the gold of little Marygold's hair.

The Fox and the Crow

Aesop

Vanity is largely a matter of self-control, or lack thereof. Others may try to feed our ego, but it is up to us to constrain it.

A coal-black crow once stole a piece of meat. She flew to a tree and held the meat in her beak.

A fox, who saw her, wanted the meat for himself, so he looked up into the tree and said, "How beautiful you are, my friend! Your feathers are fairer than the dove's.

"Is your voice as sweet as your form is beautiful? If so, you must be the queen of birds."

The crow was so happy in his praise that she opened her mouth to show how she could sing. Down fell the piece of meat.

The fox seized upon it and ran away.

King Canute on the Seashore

Adapted from James Baldwin

Canute the Second, who reigned during the eleventh century, was the first Danish king of England. In this famous tale, he proves to be a man who knows how to control his pride. It is a good lesson for all who aspire to high office.

Long ago, England was ruled by a king named Canute. Like many leaders and men of power, Canute was surrounded by people who were always praising him. Every time he walked into a room, the flattery began.

"You are the greatest man that ever lived," one would say.

"O king, there can never be another as mighty as you," another would insist.

"Your highness, there is nothing you cannot do," someone would smile.

"Great Canute, you are the monarch of all," another would sing. "Nothing in this world dares to disobey you."

The king was a man of sense, and he grew tired of hearing such foolish speeches.

One day he was walking by the seashore, and his officers and courtiers were with him, praising him as usual. Canute decided to teach them a lesson.

"So you say I am the greatest man in the world?" he asked them.

"O king," they cried, "there never has been anyone as mighty as you, and there never will be anyone so great, ever again!"

"And you say all things obey me?" Canute asked.

"Absolutely!" they said. "The world bows before you, and gives you honor."

"I see," the king answered. "In that case, bring me my chair, and we will go down to the water."

"At once, your majesty!" They scrambled to carry his royal chair over the sands.

"Bring it closer to the sea," Canute called. "Put it right here, right at the water's edge." He sat down and surveyed the ocean before him. "I notice the tide is coming in. Do you think it will stop if I give the command?"

His officers were puzzled, but they did not dare say no. "Give the order, O great king, and it will obey," one of them assured him.

"Very well. Sea," cried Canute, "I command you to come no further! Waves, stop your rolling! Surf, stop your pounding! Do not dare touch my feet!"

He waited a moment, quietly, and a tiny wave rushed up the sand and lapped at his feet.

"How dare you!" Canute shouted. "Ocean, turn back now! I have ordered you to retreat before me, and now you must obey! Go back!"

And in answer another wave swept forward and curled around the king's feet. The tide came in, just as it always did. The water rose higher and higher. It came up around the king's chair, and wet not only his feet, but also his robe. His officers stood about him, alarmed, and wondering whether he was not mad.

"Well, my friends," Canute said, "it seems I do not have quite so much power as you would have me believe. Perhaps you have learned something today. Perhaps now you will remember there is only one King who is all-powerful, and it is he who rules the sea, and holds the ocean in the hollow of his hand. I suggest you reserve your praises for him."

The royal officers and courtiers hung their heads and looked foolish. And some say Canute took off his crown soon afterward, and never wore it again.

Ozymandias

Percy Bysshe Shelley

Ozymandias is the Greek name for the Egyptian King Rameses the Second, who ruled about 1290 to 1223 B.C. and carried out (or took credit for) many great construction projects. The colossal stone head of a statue of Rameses lies on the ground at his mortuary temple in western Thebes, and the ancient Greek historian Diodorus Siculus described a funeral temple bearing an inscription much like the lines in Shelley's poem. Remembering Ozymandias is a great way to control our vanity, especially as

we climb the ladder of success. It makes a striking contrast with
the story of King Canute.

> I met a traveler from an antique land
> Who said: Two vast and trunkless legs of stone
> Stand in the desert . . . Near them, on the sand,
> Half sunk, a shattered visage lies, whose frown,
> And wrinkled lip, and sneer of cold command,
> Tell that its sculptor well those passions read
> Which yet survive, stamped on these lifeless things,
> The hand that mocked them, and the heart that fed:
> And on the pedestal these words appear:
> "My name is Ozymandias, king of kings:
> Look on my works, ye Mighty, and despair!"
> Nothing beside remains. Round the decay
> Of that colossal wreck, boundless and bare
> The lone and level sands stretch far away.

Phaeton

Adapted from Thomas Bulfinch

The feeling of youth, Joseph Conrad said, is the feeling of being
able to "last forever, outlast the sea, the earth, and all men."
Somehow, as we all know from having been there, youth cannot
recognize the illusion of invincibility. Here is one of Ovid's
grandest stories. It tells of the rashness of youth and reminds us
of the need for the governing prudence of parents.

Phaeton was the son of Phoebus Apollo and the nymph Clymene. One day a schoolfellow laughed at the idea of his being the
offspring of a god, and Phaeton went in rage and shame to his
mother.

"If I am indeed of heavenly birth," he said, "give me some
proof of it."

"Go and ask your father yourself," Clymene replied. "It will
not be hard. The land of the Sun lies next to ours."

Full of hope and pride, Phaeton traveled to the regions of the sunrise. The palace of the Sun stood reared on lofty columns, glittering with gold and precious stones, while polished ivory formed the ceilings, and silver the doors. Upon the walls Vulcan had represented earth, sea, and skies with their inhabitants. In the sea were the nymphs, some sporting in the waves, some riding on the backs of fishes, while others sat upon the rocks and dried their sea-green hair. The earth had its towns and forests and rivers and rustic divinities. Over all was carved the likeness of the glorious heaven, and on the silver doors were the twelve signs of the zodiac, six on each side.

Clymene's son climbed the steep ascent and entered the halls of his father. He approached the chamber of the Sun, but stopped at a distance, for the light was more than he could bear. Phoebus, arrayed in a purple vesture, sat on a throne, which glittered as with diamonds. On his right hand and his left stood the Day, the Month, and the Year, and, at regular intervals, the Hours. Spring stood with her head crowned with flowers. Summer stood with garment cast aside and a garland formed of spears of ripened grain. And there too were Autumn, her feet stained with grape juice, and icy Winter, his hair stiffened with hoarfrost.

Surrounded by these attendants, the Sun, with the eye that sees everything, beheld the youth dazzled with the novelty and splendor of the scene.

"What is the purpose of your errand?" he asked.

"Oh light of the boundless world," the youth replied, "I beseech you, give me some proof that I am indeed your son."

He ceased, and his father, laying aside the beams that shone all around his head, bade him approach.

"You are my son," he said, embracing him. "What your mother has told you is true. To put an end to your doubts, ask what you will, and the gift shall be yours. I call to witness the dreadful river Styx, which we gods swear by in our most solemn engagements."

Many times Phaeton had watched the Sun riding across the sky, and he had dreamed of what it would be like to drive his father's chariot, urging the winged horses along their heavenly course. Now he realized his dream could come true.

"I want to take your place for a day, Father," he cried at once. "Just for one day, I want to drive your chariot across the sky and bring light to the world."

Instantly the Sun realized the foolishness of his promise, and he shook his radiant head in warning. "I have spoken rashly," he said. "This is the only request I would deny, and I beg you to withdraw it. You ask for something not suited to your youth and strength, my son. Your lot is mortal, and you ask what is beyond a mortal's power. In your ignorance, you aspire to do what even the other gods themselves may not do. None but myself may drive the flaming car of Day. Not even Jupiter, whose terrible right arm hurls the thunderbolts, would try it.

"The first part of the way is steep," the Sun continued, "so steep that even when the horses are fresh in the morning, they can hardly make the climb. The middle part of the journey takes me high up in the heavens, and I can scarcely look down without alarm and behold the earth and sea stretched beneath me. The last part of the road descends rapidly, and requires the most careful driving. Tethys, the Ocean's wife, who is waiting to receive me, often trembles for me lest I should fall headlong. Add to all this, the heaven is all the time turning round and carrying the stars with it. I have to be perpetually on my guard lest that movement, which sweeps everything else along, should also hurry me away.

"Suppose I should lend you the chariot. What would you do? Could you keep your course while the sphere was revolving under you? Perhaps you think there are forests and cities, the abodes of gods, and palaces and temples along the way. On the contrary, the road runs through the midst of frightening monsters. You pass by the horns of the Bull, in front of the Archer, and near the Lion's jaws, and where the Scorpion stretches its arms in one direction and the Crab in another. Nor will you find it easy to guide those horses, who snort fire from their mouths and nostrils. I can scarcely govern them myself when they resist the reins.

"Beware, my son, lest I be the donor of a fatal gift. Recall your request while yet you may. Do you want proof that you are sprung from my blood? I give you proof in my fears for you. Look at my face—I would that you could look into my heart, and there you would see a father's cares.

"Look about you, and ask for anything from all the riches of the earth or sea. Ask and you shall have it! But I beg you not to ask this one thing. It is destruction, not honor, you seek. You shall have it if you persist. I swore the oath, and it must be kept. But I beg you to choose more wisely."

He ended, but his warning did no good, and Phaeton held to his demand. So, having resisted as long as he could, Phoebus at last led the way to where the lofty chariot stood. Its wheels were made of gold, its spokes of silver. Along the yoke every kind of jewel reflected the brightness of the sun. While the boy gazed in admiration, the early Dawn threw open the purple doors of the east, and showed the pathway strewn with roses.

Phoebus, when he saw the Earth beginning to glow, and the Moon preparing to retire, ordered the Hours to harness the horses. They obeyed, and led the steeds from the lofty stalls, well fed with rich ambrosia. Then the Sun rubbed his son's face with a magic lotion which made him able to endure the brightness of the flame. He placed the crown of rays on his head and sighed.

"If you insist on doing this," he said, "at least heed my advice. Spare the whip and hold the reins tight. The steeds need no urging, but you must labor to hold them back. Do not take the straight road through the five circles of Heaven, but turn off to the left. Avoid the northern and southern zones, but keep within the limit of the middle one. You will see the marks of the wheels, and they will guide you. The sky and the earth both need their due share of heat, so do not go too high, or you will burn the heavenly dwellings, nor too low, or you will set the earth on fire. The middle course is the safest and best.

"Now I leave you to Fortune, who I hope will plan better for you than you have for yourself. Night is passing out of the western gates, and we can delay no longer. Take the reins. Or better yet, take my counsel and let me bring light to the world while you stay here and watch in safety."

But even as he was speaking, the boy sprang into the chariot, stood erect, and grasped the reins with delight, pouring out thanks to his reluctant parent. The horses filled the air with their fiery snortings and stamped the ground impatiently. The barriers were let down, and suddenly the boundless plain of the universe lay open before them. They darted forward and sliced through the clouds, into the winds from the east.

It wasn't long before the steeds sensed that the load they drew was lighter than usual. As a ship without ballast careens and rolls off course on the sea, so the chariot was dashed about as if empty. The horses rushed headlong and left the traveled road. Phaeton began to panic. He had no idea which way to turn the reins, and even if he knew, he had not the strength. Then, for the first time, the Big Bear and the Little Bear were scorched with heat, and would have plunged into the water if possible. The Serpent, which lies coiled around the pole, torpid and harmless in the chill of the heavens, grew hot and writhed in angry fury.

When the unhappy Phaeton looked down upon the earth, now spreading in the vast expanse beneath him, he grew pale, and his knees shook with terror. In spite of the glare all around him, the sight of his eyes grew dim. He wished he had never touched his father's horses. He was borne along like a vessel driven before a storm, when the pilot can do no more than pray. Much of the heavenly road was behind him, but much more still lay ahead. He found himself stunned and dazed, and did not know whether to hold the reins or drop them. He forgot the names of the horses. He was horrified at the sight of the monstrous forms scattered across the heaven. The Scorpion, for instance, reached forward with its two great claws, while its poisonous stinger stretched behind. Phaeton's courage failed, and the reins fell from his hands.

The horses, when they felt the reins loose on their backs, dashed headlong into the unknown regions of the sky. They raced among the stars, hurling the chariot over pathless places, now up in the high heaven, now down almost to earth. The Moon saw with astonishment her brother's chariot running beneath her own. The clouds began to smoke, and the mountain tops caught fire. Fields grew parched with heat, plants withered, and harvests went up in flames. Cities perished, with their walls and towers, and whole nations turned to ashes.

Phaeton beheld the world on fire, and felt the intolerable heat. The air was like the blast of a furnace, full of soot and sparks. The chariot glowed white-hot and veered one way, then another. Forests turned to deserts, rivers ran dry, and the earth cracked open. The sea shrank and threatened to become a dry plain. Three times Neptune tried to raise his head above the surface, and three times he was driven back by the fiery heat.

Then Earth, amid the smoking waters, screening her face with her hand, looked up to heaven, and in a trembling voice called on Jupiter.

"O ruler of the gods," she cried, "if I have deserved this treatment, and it is your will that I perish with fire, why withhold your thunderbolts? Let me at least fall by your hand. Is this the reward of my fertility? Is it for this that I have given fodder for cattle, and fruits for men, and incense for your altars? And what has my brother Ocean done to deserve such a fate? And look at your own skies. The very poles are smoking, and if they topple, your palace will fall. If sea, earth, and heaven perish, we fall into ancient Chaos. Save what remains from the devouring flame. Take thought, and deliver us from this awful moment!"

And overcome with heat and thirst, Earth could say no more. But Jupiter heard her, and saw that all things would perish if he did not quickly help. He climbed the highest tower of heaven, where often he had spread clouds over the world and hurled his mighty thunder. He brandished a lightning bolt in his hand, and flung it at the charioteer. At once the car exploded. The mad horses broke the reins, the wheels shattered, and the wreckage scattered across the stars.

And Phaeton, his hair on fire, fell like a shooting star. He was dead long before he left the sky. A river god received him and cooled his burning frame.

George Washington's Rules of Civility

In the late nineteenth century, a school notebook entitled "Forms of Writing" was discovered at Mount Vernon, Virginia, George Washington's plantation home on the Potomac River. The notebook apparently dates from about 1745, when George was fourteen years old and attending school in Fredericksburg, Virginia. Inside, in George's own handwriting, we find the foundation of a solid character education for an eighteenth-century youth: some 110 "Rules of Civility in Conversation Amongst Men." Historical research has shown that young George probably copied them from a 1664 English translation of an even older French work. Most of the rules are still delightfully applicable as a modern code of personal conduct. On the assumption that what was good enough for the first president of the United States is good enough for the rest of us, here are fifty-four of George Washington's "Rules of Civility."

1. Every action in company ought to be with some sign of respect to those present.

2. In the presence of others sing not to yourself with a humming voice, nor drum with your fingers or feet.

3. Speak not when others speak, sit not when others stand, and walk not when others stop.

4. Turn not your back to others, especially in speaking; jog not the table or desk on which another reads or writes; lean not on anyone.

5. Be no flatterer, neither play with anyone that delights not to be played with.

6. Read no letters, books, or papers in company; but when there is a necessity for doing it, you must ask leave. Come not near the books or writings of anyone so as to read them unasked; also look not nigh when another is writing a letter.

7. Let your countenance be pleasant, but in serious matters somewhat grave.

8. Show not yourself glad at the misfortune of another, though he were your enemy.

9. They that are in dignity or office have in all places precedency, but whilst they are young, they ought to respect those that are their equals in birth or other qualities, though they have no public charge.

10. It is good manners to prefer them to whom we speak before ourselves, especially if they be above us, with whom in no sort we ought to begin.

11. Let your discourse with men of business be short and comprehensive.

12. In visiting the sick do not presently play the physician if you be not knowing therein.

13. In writing or speaking give to every person his due title according to his degree and the custom of the place.

14. Strive not with your superiors in argument, but always submit your judgment to others with modesty.

15. Undertake not to teach your equal in the art he himself professes; it savors of arrogancy.

16. When a man does all he can, though it succeeds not well, blame not him that did it.

17. Being to advise or reprehend anyone, consider whether it ought to be in public or in private, presently or at some other time, also in what terms to do it; and in reproving show no signs of choler, but do it with sweetness and mildness.

18. Mock not nor jest at anything of importance; break no jests that are sharp or biting; and if you deliver anything witty or pleasant, abstain from laughing thereat yourself.

19. Wherein you reprove another be unblamable yourself, for example is more prevalent than precept.

20. Use no reproachful language against anyone, neither curses nor revilings.

21. Be not hasty to believe flying reports to the disparagement of anyone.

22. In your apparel be modest, and endeavor to accommodate nature rather than procure admiration. Keep to the fashion of your equals, such as are civil and orderly with respect to time and place.

23. Play not the peacock, looking everywhere about you to see if you be well decked, if your shoes fit well, if your stockings set neatly and clothes handsomely.

24. Associate yourself with men of good quality if you esteem your own reputation, for it is better to be alone than in bad company.

25. Let your conversation be without malice or envy, for it is a sign of tractable and commendable nature; and in all causes of passion admit reason to govern.

26. Be not immodest in urging your friend to discover a secret.

27. Utter not base and frivolous things amongst grown and learned men, nor very difficult questions or subjects amongst the ignorant, nor things hard to be believed.

28. Speak not of doleful things in time of mirth nor at the table; speak not of melancholy things, as death and wounds; and if others mention them, change, if you can, the discourse. Tell not your dreams but to your intimate friends.

29. Break not a jest when none take pleasure in mirth. Laugh not aloud, nor at all without occasion. Deride no man's misfortunes, though there seem to be some cause.

30. Speak not injurious words, neither in jest or earnest. Scoff at none, although they give occasion.

31. Be not forward, but friendly and courteous, the first to salute, hear and answer, and be not pensive when it is time to converse.

32. Detract not from others, but neither be excessive in commending.

33. Go not thither where you know not whether you shall be welcome or not. Give not advice without being asked; and when desired, do it briefly.

34. If two contend together, take not the part of either unconstrained, and be not obstinate in your opinion; in things indifferent be of the major side.

35. Reprehend not the imperfection of others, for that belongs to parents, masters, and superiors.

36. Gaze not on the marks or blemishes of others, and ask not how they came. What you may speak in secret to your friend deliver not before others.

37. Speak not in an unknown tongue in company, but in your own language; and that as those of quality do, and not as the vulgar. Sublime matters treat seriously.

38. Think before you speak; pronounce not imperfectly, nor bring out your words too hastily, but orderly and distinctly.

39. When another speaks, be attentive yourself, and disturb not the audience. If any hesitate in his words, help him not, nor prompt him without being desired; interrupt him not, nor answer him till his speech be ended.

40. Treat with men at fit times about business, and whisper not in the company of others.

41. Make no comparisons; and if any of the company be commended for any brave act of virtue, commend not another for the same.

42. Be not apt to relate news if you know not the truth thereof. In discoursing of things you have heard, name not your author always. A secret discover not.

43. Be not curious to know the affairs of others, neither approach to those that speak in private.

44. Undertake not what you cannot perform; but be careful to keep your promise.

45. When you deliver a matter, do it without passion and indiscretion, however mean the person may be you do it to.

46. When your superiors talk to anybody, hear them; neither speak or laugh.

47. In disputes be not so desirous to overcome as not to give liberty to each one to deliver his opinion, and submit to the judgment of the major part, especially if they are judges of the dispute.

48. Be not tedious in discourse, make not many digressions, nor repeat often the same matter of discourse.

49. Speak no evil of the absent, for it is unjust.

50. Be not angry at table, whatever happens; and if you have reason to be so show it not; put on a cheerful countenance, especially if there be strangers, for good humor makes one dish a feast.

51. Set not yourself at the upper end of the table; but if it be your due, or the master of the house will have it so, contend not, lest you should trouble the company.

52. When you speak of God or his attributes, let it be seriously, in reverence and honor, and obey your natural parents.

53. Let your recreations be manful, not sinful.

54. Labor to keep alive in your breast that little spark of celestial fire called conscience.

Boy Wanted

Frank Crane

This "want ad" appeared in the early part of this century.

WANTED—A boy that stands straight, sits straight, acts straight, and talks straight;

A boy whose fingernails are not in mourning, whose ears are clean, whose shoes are polished, whose clothes are brushed, whose hair is combed, and whose teeth are well cared for;

A boy who listens carefully when he is spoken to, who asks questions when he does not understand, and does not ask questions about things that are none of his business;

A boy that moves quickly and makes as little noise about it as possible;

A boy who whistles in the street, but does not whistle where he ought to keep still;

A boy who looks cheerful, has a ready smile for everybody, and never sulks;

A boy who is polite to every man and respectful to every woman and girl;

A boy who does not smoke cigarettes and has no desire to learn how;

A boy who is more eager to know how to speak good English than to talk slang;

A boy that never bullies other boys nor allows other boys to bully him;

A boy who, when he does not know a thing, says, "I don't know," and when he has made a mistake says, "I'm sorry," and when he is asked to do a thing says, "I'll try";

A boy who looks you right in the eye and tells the truth every time;

A boy who is eager to read good books;

A boy who would rather put in his spare time at the YMCA gymnasium than to gamble for pennies in a back room;

A boy who does not want to be "smart" nor in any wise to attract attention;

A boy who would rather lose his job or be expelled from school than to tell a lie or be a cad;

A boy whom other boys like;

A boy who is at ease in the company of girls;

A boy who is not sorry for himself, and not forever thinking and talking about himself;

A boy who is friendly with his mother, and more intimate with her than anyone else;

A boy who makes you feel good when he is around;

A boy who is not goody-goody, a prig, or a little pharisee, but just healthy, happy, and full of life.

This boy is wanted everywhere. The family wants him, the school wants him, the office wants him, the boys want him, the girls want him, all creation wants him.

The Cattle of the Sun

Retold by Andrew Lang

Times of plenty call for one kind of self-discipline (as in the story of the goose that laid the golden eggs). Times of hardship call for other sorts of self-restraint. During tough times, people are tempted to put aside social and moral codes. In this episode from Homer's *Odyssey*, the crew of Odysseus (Ulysses) does not have the self-control to pass a tough test.

The ship swept through the roaring narrows between the rock of Scylla and the whirlpool of Charybdis, into the open sea, and the men, weary and heavy of heart, bent over their oars, and longed for rest.

Now a place of rest seemed near at hand, for in front of the ship lay a beautiful island, and the men could hear the bleating of sheep and the lowing of cows as they were being herded into their stalls. But Ulysses remembered that, in the Land of the Dead, the ghost of the blind prophet had warned him of one thing. If his men killed and ate the cattle of the Sun, in the sacred island of Thrinacia, they would all perish. So Ulysses told his crew of this prophecy, and bade them row past the island. Eurylochus was angry and said that the men were tired, and could row no further, but must land, and take supper, and sleep comfortably on shore. On hearing Eurylochus, the whole crew shouted and said that they would go no further that night, and Ulysses had no power to compel them. He could only make them swear not to touch the cattle of the Sun God, which they promised readily enough, and so went ashore, took supper, and slept.

In the night a great storm arose: the clouds and driving mist blinded the face of the sea and sky, and for a whole month the wild south wind hurled the waves on the coast, and no ship of these times could venture out in the tempest. Meanwhile the crew ate up all the stores in the ship, and finished the wine, so that they were driven to catch seabirds and fishes, of which they took but few, the sea being so rough upon the rocks. Ulysses went up into the island alone, to pray to the gods, and when he had prayed he found a sheltered place, and there he fell asleep.

Eurylochus took the occasion, while Ulysses was away, to bid the crew seize and slay the sacred cattle of the Sun God, which no man might touch, and this they did, so that, when Ulysses wakened, and came near the ship, he smelled the roast meat, and knew what had been done. He rebuked the men, but, as the cattle were dead, they kept eating them for six days; and then the storm ceased, the wind fell, the sun shone, and they set the sails, and away they went. But this evil deed was punished, for when they were out of sight of land, a great thundercloud overshadowed them, the wind broke the mast, which crushed the head of the helmsman, the lightning struck the ship in the center; she reeled, the men fell overboard, and the heads of the crew floated a moment, like cormorants, above the waves.

But Ulysses had kept hold of a rope, and, when the vessel righted, he walked the deck till a wave stripped off all the tackling, and loosened the sides from the keel. Ulysses had only time to lash the broken mast with a rope to the keel, and sit on this raft with his feet in the water, while the South Wind rose again furiously, and drove the raft back till it came under the rock where was the whirlpool of Charybdis. Here Ulysses would have been drowned, but he caught at the root of a fig tree that grew on the rock, and there he hung, clinging with his toes to the crumbling stones till the whirlpool boiled up again, and up came the timbers. Down on the timbers Ulysses dropped, and so sat rowing with his hands, and the wind drifted him at last to a shelving beach of an island.

David and Bathsheba

Retold by Jesse Lyman Hurlbut

Of all the vices, lust is the one many people seem to find the most difficult to control. The story of David and Bathsheba is from the second book of Samuel in the Bible.

When David first became king he went with his army upon the wars against the enemies of Israel. But there came a time when the cares of his kingdom were many, and David left Joab, his general, to lead his warriors, while he stayed in his palace on Mount Zion.

One evening, about sunset, David was walking upon the roof of his palace. He looked down into a garden nearby, and saw a woman who was very beautiful. David asked one of his servants who this woman was, and he said to him, "Her name is Bathsheba, and she is the wife of Uriah."

Now Uriah was an officer in David's army, under Joab; and at that time he was fighting in David's war against the Ammonites, at

Rabbah, near the desert, on the east of Jordan. David sent for Uriah's wife, Bathsheba, and talked with her. He loved her, and greatly longed to take her as one of his own wives—for in those times it was not thought a sin for a man to have more than one wife. But David could not marry Bathsheba while her husband, Uriah, was living. Then a wicked thought came into David's heart, and he formed a plan to have Uriah killed, so that he could then take Bathsheba into his own house.

David wrote a letter to Joab, the commander of his army. And in the letter he said, "When there is to be a fight with the Ammonites, send Uriah into the middle of it, where it will be the hottest; and manage to leave him there, so that he may be slain by the Ammonites."

And Joab did as David had commanded him. He sent Uriah with some brave men to a place near the wall of the city, where he knew that the enemies would rush out of the city upon them; there was a fierce fight beside the wall; Uriah was slain, and other brave men with him. Then Joab sent a messenger to tell King David how the war was being carried on, and especially that Uriah, one of his brave officers, had been killed in the fighting.

When David heard this, he said to the messenger, "Say to Joab, 'Do not feel troubled at the loss of the men slain in battle. The sword must strike down some. Keep up the siege; press forward, and you will take the city.' "

And after Bathsheba had mourned over her husband's death for a time, then David took her into his palace, and she became his wife. And a little child was born to them, whom David loved greatly. Only Joab, and David, and perhaps a few others, knew that David has caused the death of Uriah; but God knew it, and God was displeased with David for this wicked deed.

Then the Lord sent Nathan, the prophet, to David to tell him that, though men knew not that David had done wickedly, God had seen it, and would surely punish David for his sin. Nathan came to David, and he spoke to him thus:

"There were two men in one city; one was rich, and the other poor. The rich man had great flocks of sheep and herds of cattle; but the poor man had only one little lamb that he had bought. It grew up in his home with his children, and drank out of his cup, and lay upon his lap, and was like a little daughter to him.

"One day a visitor came to the rich man's house to dinner. The rich man did not take one of his own sheep to kill for his guest. He robbed the poor man of his lamb, and killed it, and cooked it for a meal with his friend."

"When David heard this, he was very angry. He said to Nathan, "The man who did this thing deserves to die! He shall give back to his poor neighbor fourfold for the lamb taken from him. How cruel to treat a poor man thus, without pity for him!"

And Nathan said to David, "You are the man who has done this deed. The Lord made you king in place of Saul, and gave you a kingdom. You have a great house, and many wives. Why, then, have you done this wickedness in the sight of the Lord? You have slain Uriah with the sword of the men of Ammon; and you have taken his wife to be your wife. For this there shall be a sword drawn against your house; you shall suffer for it, and your wives shall suffer, and your children shall suffer, because you have done this."

When David heard all this, he saw, as he had not seen before, how great was his wickedness. He was exceedingly sorry; and said to Nathan, "I have sinned against the Lord."

And David showed such sorrow for his sin that Nathan said to him, "The Lord has forgiven your sin; and you shall not die on account of it. But the child that Uriah's wife has given to you shall surely die."

Soon after this the little child of David and Bathsheba, whom David loved greatly, was taken very ill. David prayed to God for the child's life; and David took no food, but lay in sorrow, with his face upon the floor of his house. The nobles of his palace came to him, and urged him to rise up and take food, but he would not. For seven days the child grew worse and worse, and David remained in sorrow. Then the child died; and the nobles were afraid to tell David, for they said to each other, "If he was in such grief while the child was living, what will he do when he hears that the child is dead?"

But when King David saw the people whispering to one another with sad faces, he said, "Is the child dead?"

And they said to him, "Yes, O king, the child is dead."

Then David rose up from the floor where he had been lying. He washed his face, and put on his kingly robes. He went first to the house of the Lord, and worshipped; then he came to his own house, and sat down to his table, and took food. His servants wondered at this, but David said to them, "While the child was still alive, I fasted, and prayed, and wept; for I hoped that by prayer to the Lord, and by the mercy of the Lord, his life might be spared. But now that he

is dead, my prayers can do no more for him. I cannot bring him
back again. He will not come back to me, but I shall go to him."

And after this God gave to David and to Bathsheba, his wife,
another son, whom they named Solomon. The Lord loved Solomon, and he grew up to be a wise man.

After God had forgiven David's great sin, David wrote the
Fifty-first Psalm, in memory of his sin and of God's forgiveness.
Some of its verses are these:

Have mercy upon me, O God,
According to thy loving kindness:
According to the multitude of thy tender mercies
Blot out my transgressions.
Wash me thoroughly from mine iniquity,
And cleanse me from my sin.
For I acknowledge my transgressions:
And my sin is ever before me.
Against thee, thee only, have I sinned,
And done that which is evil in thy sight:
.   .   .   .

Hide thy face from my sins,
And blot out all mine iniquities.
Create in me a clean heart, O God,
And renew a right spirit within me.
Cast me not away from thy presence;
And take not thy holy spirit from me.
Restore unto me the joy of thy salvation;
And uphold me with a free spirit.
Then will I teach transgressors thy ways;
And sinners shall be converted unto thee.
.   .   .   .

For thou delightest not in sacrifice; else would I give it:
Thou hast no pleasure in burnt offering.
The sacrifices of God are a broken spirit:
A broken and a contrite heart, O God, thou will not despise.

Vaulting Ambition, Which O'erleaps Itself

William Shakespeare

Here is unbridled, "vaulting" ambition at work in Shakespeare's *Macbeth*. The scene is the courtyard of Inverness, Macbeth's castle, where Macbeth and Lady Macbeth prepare to murder Duncan, king of Scotland, and thereby gain the throne. As Macbeth himself points out, his victim is his guest, his kinsman, and his king. But even these claims are not enough to stop the voracity of uncontrolled aspiration. Lady Macbeth urges her husband to "screw your courage to the sticking place" when he seems on the verge of faltering—and so we see that a degree of self-mastery is required to conclude their plot. But it's the wrong kind of self-control, driven only by runaway ambitions.

Macb.   If it were done when 'tis done, then 'twere well
It were done quickly: if the assassination
Could trammel up the consequence, and catch,
With his surcease, success; that but this blow
Might be the be-all and the end-all here,
But here, upon this bank and shoal of time,
We'ld jump the life to come. But in these cases
We still have judgment here; that we but teach
Bloody instructions, which being taught return
To plague the inventor: this even-handed justice
Commends the ingredients of our poison'd chalice
To our own lips. He's here in double trust:
First, as I am his kinsman and his subject,
Strong both against the deed; then, as his host,
Who should against his murderer shut the door,
Not bear the knife myself. Besides, this Duncan
Hath borne his faculties so meek, hath been
So clear in his great office, that his virtues
Will plead like angels trumpet-tongued against
The deep damnation of his taking-off;

And pity, like a naked new-born babe,
Striding the blast, or heaven's cherubim horsed
Upon the sightless couriers of the air,
Shall blow the horrid deed in every eye,
That tears shall drown the wind. I have no spur
To prick the sides of my intent, but only
Vaulting ambition, which o'erleaps itself
And falls on the other.

Enter LADY MACBETH
      How now! what news?
 Lady M. He has almost supp'd: why have you left
   the chamber?
Macb. Hath he ask'd for me?
Lady M.   Know you not he has?
Macb. We will proceed no further in this business:
He hath honor'd me of late; and I have bought
Golden opinions from all sorts of people,
Which would be worn now in their newest gloss,
Not cast aside so soon.
 Lady M.   Was the hope drunk
Wherein you dress'd yourself? hath it slept since?
And wakes it now, to look so green and pale
At what it did so freely? From this time
Such I account thy love. Art thou afeard
To be the same in thine own act and valor
As thou art in desire? Wouldst thou have that
Which thou esteem'st the ornament of life,
And live a coward in thine own esteem,
Letting "I dare not" wait upon "I would,"
Like the poor cat i' the adage?
 Macb.   Prithee, peace
I dare do all that may become a man;
Who dares do more is none.
 Lady M.   What beast was't then
That made you break this enterprise to me?
When you durst do it, then you were a man;
And, to be more than what you were, you would
Be so much more the man. Nor time nor place
Did then adhere, and yet you would make both:
They have made themselves, and that their fitness now
Does unmake you. I have given suck, and know

How tender 'tis to love the babe that milks me:
I would, while it was smiling in my face,
Have pluck'd my nipple from his boneless gums,
And dash'd the brains out, had I so sworn as you
Have done to this.

    Macb.   If we should fail?

    Lady M.   We fail!

But screw your courage to the sticking-place,
And we'll not fail. When Duncan is asleep—
Whereto the rather shall his day's hard journey
Soundly invite him—his two chamberlains
Will I with wine and wassail so convince,
That memory, the warder of the brain,
Shall be a fume, and the receipt of reason
A limbec only: when in swinish sleep
Their drenched natures lie as in a death,
What cannot you and I perform upon
The unguarded Duncan? what not put upon
His spongy officers, who shall bear the guilt
Of our great quell?

    Macb.   Bring forth men-children only;
For thy undaunted mettle should compose
Nothing but males. Will it not be received,
When we have mark'd with blood those sleepy two
Of his own chamber, and used their very daggers,
That they have done't?

    Lady M.   Who dares receive it other,
As we shall make our griefs and clamor roar
Upon his death?

    Macb.   I am settled, and bend up
Each corporal agent to this terrible feat.
Away, and mock the time with fairest show:
False face must hide what the false heart doth know.

                                           Exeunt.

How Much Land
Does a Man Need?

Leo Tolstoy

This story by Leo Tolstoy (1828–1910), written in 1886, in its
fundamental physical action is a marvelous metaphor for the need
for us to set definite boundaries on our own appetites.

There once was a peasant named Pahom who worked hard and
honestly for his family, but who had no land of his own, so he
always remained as poor as the next man. "Busy as we are from
childhood tilling mother earth," he often thought, "we peasants will
always die as we are living, with nothing of our own. If only we had
our own land, it would be different."

Now, close to Pahom's village there lived a lady, a small landowner, who had an estate of about three hundred acres. One winter
the news got about that the lady was going to sell her land. Pahom
heard that a neighbor of his was buying fifty acres and that the lady
had consented to accept one half in cash and to wait a year for the
other half.

"Look at that," Pahom thought. "The land is being sold, and I
shall get none of it." So he spoke to his wife. "Other people are
buying it, and we must also buy twenty acres or so. Life is becoming
impossible without land of our own."

So they put their heads together and considered how they could
manage to buy it. They had one hundred rubles laid by. They sold a
colt, and one half of their bees, hired out one of their sons as a
laborer, and took his wages in advance. They borrowed the rest
from a brother-in-law, and so scraped together half the purchase
money. Having done this, Pahom chose a farm of forty acres, some
of it wooded, and went to the lady and bought it.

So now Pahom had land of his own. He borrowed seed, and
sowed it, and the harvest was a good one. Within a year he had
managed to pay off his debts to the lady and his brother-in-law. So
he became a landowner, plowing and sowing his own land, making
hay on his own land, cutting his own trees, and feeding his cattle on
his own pasture. When he went out to plow his fields, or to look at

his growing corn, or at his meadows, his heart would fill with joy. The grass that grew and the flowers that bloomed there seemed to him unlike any that grew elsewhere. Formerly, when he had passed by that land, it had appeared the same as any other land, but now it seemed quite different.

Then one day Pahom was sitting at home when a peasant, passing through the village, happened to stop in. Pahom asked him where he came from, and the stranger answered that he came from beyond the Volga, where he had been working. One word led to another, and the man went on to say that much land was for sale there, and that many people were moving there to buy it. The land was so good, he said, that the rye sown on it grew as high as a horse, and so thick that five cuts of a sickle made a sheaf. One peasant, he said, had brought nothing with him but his bare hands, and now he had six horses and two cows of his own.

Pahom's heart was filled with desire. "Why should I suffer in this narrow hole," he thought, "if one can live so well elsewhere? I will sell my land and my homestead here, and with the money I will start fresh over there and get everything new."

So Pahom sold his land and homestead and cattle, all at a profit, and moved his family to the new settlement. Everything the peasant had told him was true, and Pahom was ten times better off than he had been. He bought plenty of arable land and pasture, and could keep as many head of cattle as he liked.

At first, in the bustle of building and settling down, Pahom was pleased with it all, but when he got used to it he began to think that even here he was not satisfied. He wanted to sow more wheat, but had not enough land of his own for the purpose, so he rented extra land for three years. The seasons turned out well and the crops were good, so that he began to lay money by. He might have gone on living comfortably, but he grew tired of having to rent other people's land every year, and having to scramble to pay for it.

"If it were all my own land," Pahom thought, "I should be independent, and there would not be all this unpleasantness."

Then one day a passing land dealer said he was just returning from the land of Bashkirs, far away, where he had bought thirteen thousand acres of land, all for only one thousand rubles.

"All one need do is to make friends with the chiefs," he said. "I gave away about one hundred rubles' worth of dressing gowns and carpets, besides a case of tea, and I gave wine to those who would drink it, and I got the land for less than twopence an acre."

"There now," thought Pahom, "out there I can get more than ten times as much land as I have now. I must try it."

So Pahom left his family to look after the homestead and started on the journey, taking his servant with him. They stopped at a town on their way, and bought a case of tea, some wine, and other presents, as the tradesman had advised him. On and on they went until they had gone more than three hundred miles, and on the seventh day they came to a place where the Bashkirs had pitched their tents.

As soon as they saw Pahom, they came out of their tents and gathered around their visitor. They gave him tea and kumiss, and had a sheep killed, and gave him mutton to eat. Pahom took presents out of his cart and distributed them, and told them he had come about some land. The Bashkirs seemed very glad, and told him he must talk to their chief about it. So they sent for him and explained to him why Pahom had come.

The chief listened for a while, then made a sign with his head for them to be silent, and addressing himself to Pahom, said:

"Well, let it be so. Choose whatever piece of land you like. We have plenty of it."

"And what will be the price?" asked Pahom.

"Our price is always the same: one thousand rubles a day."

Pahom did not understand.

"A day? What measure is that? How many acres would that be?"

"We do not know how to reckon it out," said the chief. "We sell it by the day. As much as you can go round on your feet in a day is yours, and the price is one thousand rubles a day."

Pahom was surprised.

"But in a day you can get round a large tract of land," he said.

The chief laughed.

"It will all be yours!" said he. "But there is one condition: if you don't return on the same day to the spot whence you started, your money is lost."

"But how am I to mark the way that I have gone?"

"Why, we shall go to any spot you like, and stay there. You must start from that spot and make your round, taking a spade with you. Wherever you think necessary, make a mark. At every turning, dig a hole and pile up the turf; then afterward we will go round with a plow from hole to hole. You may make as large a circuit as you please, but before the sun sets you must return to the place you started from. All the land you cover will be yours."

Pahom was delighted. It was decided to start early next morning. They talked awhile, and after drinking some more kumiss and eating some more mutton, they had tea again, and then the night came on. They gave Pahom a featherbed to sleep on, and the Bashkirs dispersed for the night, promising to assemble the next morning at daybreak and ride out before sunrise to the appointed spot.

Pahom lay on the featherbed, but could not sleep. He kept thinking about the land.

"What a large tract I will mark off!" thought he. "I can easily do thirty-five miles in a day. The days are long now, and within a circuit of thirty-five miles what a lot of land there will be! I will sell the poorer land, or let it to peasants, but I'll pick out the best and farm it. I will buy two ox teams, and hire two more laborers. About a hundred and fifty acres shall be plow land, and I will pasture cattle on the rest."

Looking round he saw through the open door that the dawn was breaking.

"It's time to wake them up," thought he. "We ought to be starting."

He got up, roused his man (who was sleeping in his cart), bade him harness; and went to call the Bashkirs.

"It's time to go to the steppe to measure the land," he said.

The Bashkirs rose and assembled, and the chief came too. Then they began drinking kumiss again, and offered Pahom some tea, but he would not wait.

"If we are to go, let us go. It is high time," said he.

The Bashkirs got ready and they all started: some mounted on horses, and some in carts. Pahom drove in his own small cart with his servant, and took a spade with him. When they reached the steppe, the morning red was beginning to kindle. They ascended a hillock and, dismounting from their carts and their horses, gathered in one spot. The chief came up to Pahom and stretched out his arm toward the plain.

"See," said he, "all this, as far as your eye can reach, is ours. You may have any part of it you like."

Pahom's eyes glistened: it was all virgin soil, as flat as the palm of your hand, as black as the seed of a poppy, and in the hollows different kinds of grasses grew breast high.

The chief took off his fox fur cap, placed it on the ground and said:

"This will be the mark. Start from here, and return here again. All the land you go round shall be yours."

Pahom took out his money and put it on the cap. Then he

took off his outer coat, remaining in his sleeveless undercoat. He unfastened his girdle and tied it tight below his stomach, put a little bag of bread into the breast of his coat, and tying a flask of water to his girdle, he drew up the tops of his boots, took the spade from his man, and stood ready to start. He considered for some moments which way he had better go—it was tempting everywhere.

"No matter," he concluded, "I will go toward the rising sun."

He turned his face to the east, stretched himself, and waited for the sun to appear above the rim.

"I must lose no time," he thought, "and it is easier walking while it is still cool."

The sun's rays had hardly flashed above the horizon, before Pahom, carrying the spade over his shoulder, went down into the steppe.

Pahom started walking neither slowly nor quickly. After having gone a thousand yards he stopped, dug a hole, and placed pieces of turf one on another to make it more visible. Then he went on; and now that he had walked off his stiffness he quickened his pace. After a while he dug another hole.

Pahom looked back. The hillock could be distinctly seen in the sunlight, with the people on it, and the glittering tires of the cart wheels. At a rough guess Pahom concluded that he had walked three miles. It was growing warmer; he took off his undercoat, flung it across his shoulder, and went on again. It had grown quite warm now; he looked at the sun, it was time to think of breakfast.

"The first shift is done, but there are four in a day, and it is too soon yet to turn. But I will just take off my boots," said he to himself.

He sat down, took off his boots, stuck them into his girdle, and went on. It was easy walking now.

"I will go on for another three miles," thought he, "and then turn to the left. This spot is so fine, that it would be a pity to lose it. The further one goes, the better the land seems."

He went straight on for a while, and when he looked round, the hillock was scarcely visible and the people on it looked like black ants, and he could just see something glistening there in the sun.

"Ah," thought Pahom, "I have gone far enough in this direction, it is time to turn. Besides I am in a regular sweat, and very thirsty."

He stopped, dug a large hole, and heaped up pieces of turf. Next he untied his flask, had a drink, and then turned sharply to the left. He went on and on; the grass was high, and it was very hot.

Pahom began to grow tired: he looked at the sun and saw that it was noon.

"Well," he thought, "I must have a rest."

He sat down, and ate some bread and drank some water; but he did not lie down, thinking that if he did he might fall asleep. After sitting a little while, he went on again. At first he walked easily: the food had strengthened him; but it had become terribly hot, and he felt sleepy; still he went on, thinking: "An hour to suffer, a lifetime to live."

He went a long way in this direction also, and was about to turn to the left again, when he perceived a damp hollow: "It would be a pity to leave that out," he thought. "Flax would do well there." So he went on past the hollow, and dug a hole on the other side of it before he turned the corner. Pahom looked toward the hillock. The heat made the air hazy: it seemed to be quivering, and through the haze the people on the hillock could scarcely be seen.

"Ah!" thought Pahom, "I have made the sides too long; I must make this one shorter." And he went along the third side, stepping faster. He looked at the sun: it was nearly halfway to the horizon, and he had not yet done two miles of the third side of the square. He was still ten miles from the goal.

"No," he thought, "though it will make my land lopsided, I must hurry back in a straight line now. I might go too far, and as it is I have a great deal of land."

So Pahom hurriedly dug a hole, and turned straight toward the hillock.

Pahom went straight toward the hillock, but he now walked with difficulty. He was done up with the heat, his bare feet were cut and bruised, and his legs began to fail. He longed to rest, but it was impossible if he meant to get back before sunset. The sun waits for no man, and it was sinking lower and lower.

"Oh dear," he thought, "if only I have not blundered trying for too much! What if I am too late?"

He looked toward the hillock and at the sun. He was still far from his goal, and the sun was already near the rim.

Pahom walked on and on; it was very hard walking, but he went quicker and quicker. He pressed on, but was still far from the place. He began running, threw away his coat, his boots, his flask, and his cap, and kept only the spade which he used as a support.

"What shall I do," he thought again. "I have grasped too much, and ruined the whole affair. I can't get there before the sun sets."

And this fear made him still more breathless. Pahom went on running, his soaking shirt and trousers stuck to him, and his mouth was parched. His breast was working like a blacksmith's bellows, his heart was beating like a hammer, and his legs were giving way as if they did not belong to him. Pahom was seized with terror lest he should die of the strain.

Though afraid of death, he could not stop. "After having run all that way they will call me a fool if I stop now," thought he. And he ran on and on, and drew near and heard the Bashkirs yelling and shouting to him, and their cries inflamed his heart still more. He gathered his last strength and ran on.

The sun was close to the rim, and cloaked in mist looked large, and red as blood. Now, yes now, it was about to set! The sun was quite low, but he was also quite near his aim. Pahom could already see the people on the hillock waving their arms to hurry him up. He could see the fox fur cap on the ground, and the money on it, and the chief sitting on the ground holding his sides.

"There is plenty of land," thought he, "but will God let me live on it? I have lost my life, I have lost my life! I shall never reach that spot!"

Pahom looked at the sun, which had reached the earth; one side of it had already disappeared. With all his remaining strength he rushed on, bending his body forward so that his legs could hardly follow fast enough to keep him from falling. Just as he reached the hillock it suddenly grew dark. He looked up—the sun had already set! He gave a cry: "All my labor has been in vain," thought he, and was about to stop, but he heard the Bashkirs still shouting, and remembered that though to him, from below, the sun seemed to have set, they on the hillock could still see it. He took a long breath and ran up the hillock. It was still light there. He reached the top and saw the cap. Before it sat the chief laughing and holding his sides. Pahom uttered a cry: his legs gave way beneath him, he fell forward and reached the cap with his hands.

"Ah, that's a fine fellow!" exclaimed the chief. "He has gained much land!"

Pahom's servant came running up and tried to raise him, but he saw that blood was flowing from his mouth. Pahom was dead!

The Bashkirs clicked their tongues to show their pity.

His servant picked up the spade and dug a grave long enough for Pahom to lie in, and buried him in it. Six feet from his head to his heels was all he needed.

Terence, This Is Stupid Stuff

A. E. Housman

With wry irony, Alfred Edward Housman (1859–1936) advises preparing oneself for a world that may contain "much good, but much less good than ill." Escapist solutions such as drink (Burton-on-Trent, mentioned in the second stanza, is a famous English brewing town) offer only the false answer of illusion. The best tack, Housman says, is to "train for ill and not for good," and thereby steel oneself against all the unfairness life has to offer. And so he suggests as a model Mithridates, king of ancient Pontus in Asia Minor, who made himself immune to poison by swallowing small doses every day. There's a bit of cynicism in this poem, but there's also a good measure of hard truth: we must practice bracing ourselves for all of life's contingencies.

"Terence, this is stupid stuff:
You eat your victuals fast enough;
There can't be much amiss, 'tis clear,
To see the rate you drink your beer.
But oh, good Lord, the verse you make,
It gives a chap the bellyache.
The cow, the old cow, she is dead;
It sleeps well, the hornéd head:
We poor lads, 'tis our turn now
To hear such tunes as killed the cow.
Pretty friendship 'tis to rhyme
Your friends to death before their time
Moping melancholy mad:
Come, pipe a tune to dance to, lad."

Why, if 'tis dancing you would be,
There's brisker pipes than poetry.
Say, for what were hopyards meant,
Or why was Burton built on Trent?

Oh many a peer of England brews
Livelier liquor than the Muse,
And malt does more than Milton can
To justify God's ways to man.
Ale, man, ale's the stuff to drink
For fellows whom it hurts to think:
Look into the pewter pot
To see the world as the world's not.
And faith, 'tis pleasant till 'tis past:
The mischief is that 'twill not last.
Oh I have been to Ludlow fair
And left my necktie God knows where,
And carried halfway home, or near,
Pints and quarts of Ludlow beer:
Then the world seemed none so bad,
And I myself a sterling lad;
And down in lovely muck I've lain,
Happy till I woke again.
Then I saw the morning sky.
Heigho, the tale was all a lie;
The world, it was the old world yet,
I was I, my things were wet,
And nothing now remained to do
But begin the game anew.

    Therefore, since the world has still
Much good, but much less good than ill,
And while the sun and moon endure
Luck's a chance, but trouble's sure,
I'd face it as a wise man would,
And train for ill and not for good.
'Tis true the stuff I bring for sale
Is not so brisk a brew as ale:
Out of a stem that scored the hand
I wrung it in a weary land.
But take it: if the smack is sour,
The better for the embittered hour;
It should do good to heart and head
When your soul is in my soul's stead;
And I will friend you, if I may,
In the dark and cloudy day.

There was a king reigned in the East:
There, when kings will sit to feast,
They get their fill before they think
With poisoned meat and poisoned drink.
He gathered all that springs to birth
From the many-venomed earth;
First a little, thence to more,
He sampled all her killing store;
And easy, smiling, seasoned sound,
Sate the king when healths went round.
They put arsenic in his meat
And stared aghast to watch him eat;
They poured strychnine in his cup
And shook to see him drink it up:
They shook, they stared as white's their shirt.
Them it was their poison hurt.
—I tell the tale that I heard told.
Mithridates, he died old.

Plato on Self-Discipline

From the Gorgias

The right and wrong uses of rhetoric are technically the themes
of Plato's *Gorgias,* but, as with all Platonic dialogues, the true end
is the examination of how life should be lived. Here we find
Callicles boldly asserting "what the rest of the world think, but
do not like to say": leading the Good Life means having what
you want, as much as you want, whenever you want. In short,
the life of the rich and famous is the truly happy life. Socrates
replies with his telling image of a leaky vessel as a metaphor for
the intemperate soul. He insists that the ordered soul is the only
truly happy one, the only one capable of living the Good Life.

Socrates. Every man is his own ruler; but perhaps you think that
there is no necessity for him to rule himself; he is only required to
rule others?

Callicles. What do you mean by his "ruling over himself"?

Soc. A simple thing enough; just what is commonly said, that a man should be temperate and master of himself, and ruler of his own pleasures and passions.

Cal. What innocence! you mean those fools—the temperate?

Soc. Certainly: anyone may know that to be my meaning.

Cal. Quite so, Socrates; and they are really fools, for how can a man be happy who is the servant of anything? On the contrary, I plainly assert, that he who would truly live ought to allow his desires to wax to the uttermost, and not to chastise them; but when they have grown to their greatest he should have courage and intelligence to minister to them and to satisfy all his longings. And this I affirm to be natural justice and nobility. To this however the many cannot attain; and they blame the strong man because they are ashamed of their own weakness, which they desire to conceal, and hence they say that intemperance is base. As I have remarked already, they enslave the nobler natures, and being unable to satisfy their pleasures, they praise temperance and justice out of their own cowardice. For if a man had been originally the son of a king, or had a nature capable of acquiring an empire or a tyranny or sovereignty, what could be more truly base or evil than temperance—to a man like him, I say, who might freely be enjoying every good, and has no one to stand in his way, and yet has admitted custom and reason and the opinion of other men to be lords over him?—must not he be in a miserable plight whom the reputation of justice and temperance hinders from giving more to his friends than to his enemies, even though he be a ruler in his city? Nay, Socrates, for you profess to be a votary of the truth, and the truth is this: that luxury and intemperance and license, if they be provided with means, are virtue and happiness—all the rest is a mere bauble, agreements contrary to nature, foolish talk of men, worth nothing.

Soc. There is a noble freedom, Callicles, in your way of approaching the argument; for what you say is what the rest of the world think, but do not like to say. And I must beg of you to persevere, that the true rule of human life may become manifest. Tell me, then: you say, do you not, that in the rightly developed man the passions ought not to be controlled, but that we should let them grow to the utmost and somehow or other satisfy them, and that this is virtue?

Cal. Yes; I do.

Soc. Then those who want nothing are not truly said to be happy?

Cal. No indeed, for then stones and dead men would be the happiest of all.

Soc. But surely life according to your view is an awful thing. . . . Let me request you to consider how far you would accept this as an account of the two lives of the temperate and intemperate in a figure: There are two men, both of whom have a number of casks; the one man has his casks sound and full, one of wine, another of honey, and a third of milk, besides others filled with other liquids, and the streams which fill them are few and scanty, and he can only obtain them with a great deal of toil and difficulty; but when his casks are once filled he has no need to feed them anymore, and has no further trouble with them or care about them. The other, in like manner, can procure streams, though not without difficulty; but his vessels are leaky and unsound, and night and day he is compelled to be filling them, and if he pauses for a moment, he is in an agony of pain. Such are their respective lives: And now would you say that the life of the intemperate is happier than that of the temperate? Do I not convince you that the opposite is the truth?

Cal. You do not convince me, Socrates, for the one who has filled himself has no longer any pleasure left; and this, as I was just now saying, is the life of a stone: he has neither joy nor sorrow after he is once filled; but the pleasure depends on the superabundance of the influx.

Soc. But the more you pour in, the greater the waste; and the holes must be large for the liquid to escape.

Cal. Certainly.

Soc. The life which you are now depicting is not that of a dead man, or of a stone, but of a cormorant; you mean that he is to be hungering and eating?

Cal. Yes.

Soc. And he is to be thirsting and drinking?

Cal. Yes, that is what I mean; he is to have all his desires about him, and to be able to live happily in the gratification of them. . . .

Soc. Listen to me, then, while I recapitulate the argument: Is the pleasant the same as the good? Not the same. Callicles and I are agreed about that. And is the pleasant to be pursued for the sake of the good? or the good for the sake of the pleasant? The pleasant is to be pursued for the sake of the good. And that is pleasant at the presence of which we are pleased, and that is good at the presence of which we are good? To be sure. And we are good, and all good things whatever are good when some virtue is present in us or them? That, Callicles, is my conviction. But the virtue of each thing,

whether body or soul, instrument or creature, when given to them
in the best way comes to them not by chance but as the result of the
order and truth and art which are imparted to them: Am I not right?
I maintain that I am. And is not the virtue of each thing dependent
on order or arrangement? Yes, I say. And that which makes a thing
good is the proper order inhering in each thing? Such is my view.
And is not the soul which has an order of her own better than that
which has no order? Certainly. And the soul which has order is
orderly? Of course. And that which is orderly is temperate? Assuredly. And the temperate soul is good? No other answer can I
give, Callicles dear; have you any?

Cal. Go on, my good fellow.

Soc. Then I shall proceed to add, that if the temperate soul is the
good soul, the soul which is in the opposite condition, that is, the
foolish and intemperate, is the bad soul. Very true.

And will not the temperate man do what is proper, both in
relation to the gods and to men; for he would not be temperate if he
did not? Certainly he will do what is proper. In his relation to other
men he will do what is just; and in his relation to the gods he will do
what is holy; and he who does what is just and holy must be just and
holy? Very true. And must he not be courageous? For the duty of a
temperate man is not to follow or to avoid what he ought not, but
what he ought, whether things or men or pleasures or pains, and
patiently to endure when he ought; and therefore, Callicles, the temperate man, being, as we have described, also just and courageous
and holy, cannot be other than a perfectly good man, nor can the
good man do otherwise than well and perfectly whatever he does;
and he who does well must of necessity be happy and blessed, and
the evil man who does evil, miserable: now this latter is he whom
you were applauding—the intemperate who is the opposite of the
temperate. Such is my position, and these things I affirm to be true.
And if they are true, then I further affirm that he who desires to be
happy must pursue and practice temperance and run away from
intemperance as fast as his legs will carry him: he had better order
his life so as not to need punishment; but if either he or any of his
friends, whether private individual or city, are in need of punishment, then justice must be done and he must suffer punishment, if
he would be happy. This appears to me to be the aim which a man
ought to have, and toward which he ought to direct all the energies
both of himself and of the state, acting so that he may have temperance and justice present with him and be happy, not suffering his

lusts to be unrestrained, and in the never-ending desire to satisfy them leading a robber's life. Such a one is the friend neither of God nor man, for he is incapable of communion, and he who is incapable of communion is also incapable of friendship. And philosophers tell us, Callicles, that communion and friendship and orderliness and temperance and justice bind together heaven and earth and gods and men, and that this universe is therefore called Cosmos or order, not disorder or misrule, my friend.

Aristotle on Self-Discipline

From the Nicomachean Ethics

We are the sum of our actions, Aristotle tells us, and therefore our habits make all the difference. Moral virtue, we learn in this discussion from the *Nicomachean Ethics,* comes with practice, just like the mastery of any art or mechanical skill. And what is the best way to practice? Aristotle's answer lies in his explanation of "the mean." In his view, correct moral behavior in any given situation lies at the midway point between the extremes of two vices. We must practice hitting the mean by determining which vice we tend toward and then consciously moving toward the other extreme, until we reach the middle.

Virtue, then, is of two kinds, intellectual and moral. Intellectual virtue springs from and grows from teaching, and therefore needs experience and time. Moral virtues come from habit. . . . They are in us neither by nature, nor in despite of nature, but we are furnished by nature with a capacity for receiving them, and we develop them through habit. . . . These virtues we acquire by first exercising them, as in the case of other arts. Whatever we learn to do, we learn by actually doing it: men come to be builders, for instance, by building, and harp players, by playing the harp. In the same way, by doing just acts we come to be just; by doing self-controlled acts, we come to be self-controlled; and by doing brave acts, we become brave. . . .

How we act in our relations with other people makes us just or unjust. How we face dangerous situations, either accustoming ourselves to fear or confidence, makes us brave or cowardly. Occasions of lust and anger are similar: some people become self-controlled and patient from their conduct in such situations, and others uncontrolled and passionate. In a word, then, activities produce similar dispositions. Therefore we must give a certain character to our activities. . . . In short, the habits we form from childhood make no small difference, but rather they make all the difference.

Moral virtue is a mean that lies between two vices, one of excess and the other of deficiency, and . . . it aims at hitting the mean both in feelings and actions. So it is hard to be good, for surely it is hard in each instance to find the mean, just as it is difficult to find the center of a circle. It is easy to get angry or to spend money—anyone can do that. But to act the right way toward the right person, in due proportion, at the right time, for the right reason, and in the right manner—this is not easy, and not everyone can do it.

Therefore he who aims at the mean should make it his first care to keep away from that extreme which is more contrary than the other to the mean. . . . For one of the two extremes is always more erroneous than the other. And since hitting the mean exactly is difficult, one must take the next best course, and choose the least of the evils as the safest plan. . . .

We should also take notice of the errors into which we naturally tend to fall. They vary in each individual's case, and we will discover ours by the pleasure or pain they give us. Having discovered our errors, we must force ourselves off in the opposite direction. For we shall arrive at the mean by moving away from our failing, just as if we were straightening a bent piece of wood. But in all cases we should guard most carefully against what is pleasant, and pleasure itself, because we are not impartial judges of it. . . .

This much, then, is plain: in all our conduct, the mean is the most praiseworthy state. But as a practical matter, we must sometimes aim a bit toward excess and sometimes toward deficiency, because this will be the easiest way of hitting the mean, that is, what is right.

Go Forth to Life

Samuel Longfellow

Go forth to life, oh! child of Earth.
Still mindful of thy heavenly birth;
Thou art not here for ease or sin,
But manhood's noble crown to win.

Though passion's fires are in thy soul,
Thy spirit can their flames control;
Though tempters strong beset thy way,
Thy spirit is more strong than they.

Go on from innocence of youth
To manly pureness, manly truth;
God's angels still are near to save,
And God himself doth help the brave.

Then forth to life, oh! child of Earth,
Be worthy of thy heavenly birth,
For noble service thou art here;
Thy brothers help, thy God revere!

For Everything There Is a Season

From Ecclesiastes

For every thing there is a season, and a time for every purpose under the heaven:

A time to be born, and a time to die; a time to plant, and a time to pluck up that which is planted;

A time to kill, and a time to heal; a time to break down, and a time to build up;

A time to weep, and a time to laugh; a time to mourn, and a time to dance;

A time to cast away stones, and a time to gather stones together; a time to embrace, and a time to refrain from embracing;

A time to get, and a time to lose; a time to keep, and a time to cast away;

A time to rend, and a time to sew; a time to keep silence, and a time to speak;

A time to love, and a time to hate; a time of war, and a time of peace.

2

Compassion

Just as courage takes its stand *by* others in challenging situations, so compassion takes its stand *with* others in their distress. Compassion is a virtue that takes seriously the reality of other persons, their inner lives, their emotions, as well as their external circumstances. It is an active disposition toward fellowship and sharing, toward supportive companionship in distress or in woe.

The seeds of compassion are sown in our very nature as human beings. "There is some benevolence, however small, infused into our bosom, some spark of friendship for human kind, some particle of the dove kneaded into our frame, along with the elements of the wolf and serpent," as David Hume once put it. His contemporary Jean-Jacques Rousseau agreed: "compassion is a natural feeling, which, by moderating the violence of love of self in each individual, contributes to the preservation of the whole species. It is this compassion that hurries us without reflection to the relief of those who are in distress."

Happily, this eighteenth-century view is in fashion once again. It is our twentieth-century understanding that human infants do not distinguish between their own distress and that of others. One baby's cries in the nursery are frequently picked up by the rest, and together they form a natural choral symphony of sympathetic woe. Compassion seeks to retain our hold on this very early awareness that we are all in the same boat, that "but for the grace of God there go I."

Compassion thus comes close to the very heart of moral awareness, to seeing in one's neighbor another self. The American philosopher Josiah Royce gave memorable expression to this insight more than a hundred years ago. "What then is thy neighbor?" he asks in his quaint but compelling way. And the answer he gives, in part, is that one's neighbor "is a mass of states, of experiences, thoughts, and desires, just as real as thou art. . . . Does thou believe this? Art thou sure what it means? This is for thee the turning-point of thy whole conduct towards him."

How does one cultivate a compassionate nature in children? Helpful stories and maxims abound. And fortunately in this case, compassion is as close to a "natural" disposition as any of the virtues. The main task—though this can be really formidable—is to see that neither animosity nor prejudice stunts its natural growth. The divisive "isms" are major obstacles here: racism, sexism, chauvinism, and the rest. And very important in this case, as in so much of the rest of moral upbringing, is the power of consistent example. Treat *no one* with callous disregard. Children know when they are being taken seriously by others, and they imitate what they see. Therein lies both our hope and our peril.

Kindness to Animals

Compassion may be first learned through kindness to all creatures great and small.

> Little children, never give
> Pain to things that feel and live;
> Let the gentle robin come
> For the crumbs you save at home;
> As his meat you throw along
> He'll repay you with a song.
> Never hurt the timid hare
> Peeping from her green grass lair,
> Let her come and sport and play
> On the lawn at close of day.
> The little lark goes soaring high
> To the bright windows of the sky,
> Singing as if 'twere always spring,
> And fluttering on an untired wing—
> Oh! let him sing his happy song,
> Nor do these gentle creatures wrong.

The Lion and the Mouse

Aesop

Here is one of the oldest and best-loved stories of kindness paid and repaid. From it we learn that compassion lies within the power of both the mighty and the meek. Kindness is not a feeble virtue.

One day a great lion lay asleep in the sunshine. A little mouse ran across his paw and wakened him. The great lion was just going to eat him up when the little mouse cried, "Oh, please, let me go, sir. Some day I may help you."

The lion laughed at the thought that the little mouse could be of any use to him. But he was a good-natured lion, and he set the mouse free.

Not long after, the lion was caught in a net. He tugged and pulled with all his might, but the ropes were too strong. Then he roared loudly. The little mouse heard him, and ran to the spot.

"Be still, dear Lion, and I will set you free. I will gnaw the ropes."

With his sharp little teeth, the mouse cut the ropes, and the lion came out of the net.

"You laughed at me once," said the mouse. "You thought I was too little to do you a good turn. But see, you owe your life to a poor little mouse."

Little Sunshine

*Retold by Etta Austin Blaisdell
and Mary Frances Blaisdell*

Bestowing compassion is like offering most other gifts. Often it's the thought that counts.

Once there was a little girl named Elsa. She had a very old grandmother, with white hair, and wrinkles all over her face.

Elsa's father had a large house that stood on a hill.

Each day the sun peeped in at the south windows. It made everything look bright and beautiful.

The grandmother lived on the north side of the house. The sun never came to her room.

One day Elsa said to her father, "Why doesn't the sun peep into Grandma's room? I know she would like to have him."

"The sun cannot look in at the north windows," said her father.

"Then let us turn the house around, Papa."

"It is much too large for that," said her father.

"Will Grandma never have any sunshine in her room?" asked Elsa.

"Of course not, my child, unless you can carry some to her."

After that Elsa tried and tried to think how she could carry the sunshine to her grandmother.

When she played in the fields she saw the grass and the flowers nodding their heads. The birds sang sweetly as they flew from tree to tree.

Everything seemed to say, "We love the sun. We love the bright, warm sun."

"Grandma would love it, too," thought the child. "I must take some to her."

When she was in the garden one morning she felt the sun's warm rays in her golden hair. Then she sat down and she saw them in her lap.

"I will take them in my dress," she thought, "and carry them to Grandma's room." So she jumped up and ran into the house.

"Look, Grandma, Look! I have some sunshine for you," she cried. And she opened her dress, but there was not a ray to be seen.

"It peeps out of your eyes, my child," said her grandmother, "and it shines in your sunny, golden hair. I do not need the sun when I have you with me."

Elsa did not understand how the sun could peep out of her eyes. But she was glad to make her dear grandmother happy.

Every morning she played in the garden. Then she ran to her grandmother's room to carry the sunshine in her eyes and hair.

A Child's Prayer

M. Bentham-Edwards

God make my life a little light,
    Within the world to glow;
A tiny flame that burneth bright
    Wherever I may go.

God make my life a little flower,
    That giveth joy to all,
Content to bloom in native bower,
    Although its place be small.

God make my life a little song,
    That comforteth the sad;
That helpeth others to be strong,
    And makes the singer glad.

God make my life a little staff,
    Whereon the weak may rest,
That so what health and strength I have
    May serve my neighbors best.

Diamonds and Toads

Retold by Charles Perrault

In this story we learn the old lesson that to speak kindly does
not hurt the tongue. To speak with anger and disagreeableness,
however, may bring unhappiness.

Once upon a time there was a woman who had two daughters.
The elder daughter was very much like her mother in face and manner. They were both so disagreeable and so proud that there was no
living with them.

The younger daughter was like her father, for she was good and sweet-tempered, and very beautiful. As people naturally love their own likeness, the mother was very fond of her elder daughter, and at the same time had a great dislike for the younger. She made her eat in the kitchen, and work all the time.

Among other things, this poor child was obliged to go twice a day to draw a pitcherful of water from the spring in the woods, two miles from the house.

One day, when she reached the spring, a poor woman came to her and begged for a drink.

"Oh yes! With all my heart, ma'am," said this pretty little girl, and she took some clear, cool water from the spring, and held up the pitcher so that the woman might drink easily.

When she had finished, the woman said, "You are so very pretty, my dear, so good and so kind, that I cannot help giving you a gift."

Now this was a fairy, who had taken the form of a poor country woman to see how this pretty girl would treat her. "I will give you for a gift," continued the fairy, "that at every word you speak, either a flower or a jewel shall come out of your mouth."

When the girl reached home, her mother scolded her for staying so long at the spring. "I beg your pardon, Mamma," said the poor girl, "for not making more haste." And as she spoke, there came out of her mouth two roses, two pearls, and two large diamonds.

"What is it I see there?" said her mother, very much surprised. "I think I see pearls and diamonds come out of the girl's mouth! How does this happen, my child?" This was the first time she had ever called her "my child," or spoken kindly to her.

The poor child told her mother all that had happened at the spring, and of the old woman's promise. All the time jewels and flowers fell from her lips.

"This is delightful," cried the mother. "I must send my dearest child to the spring. Come, Fanny, see what comes out of your sister's mouth when she speaks! Would you not be glad, my dear, to have the same gift given to you? All you will have to do is to take the pitcher to the spring in the wood. When a poor woman asks you for a drink, give it to her."

"It would be a fine thing for me to do," said the selfish girl. "I will not go to draw water! The child can give me her jewels. She does not need them."

"Yes, you shall," said the mother, "and you shall go this minute."

At last the elder daughter went, grumbling and scolding all the way, and taking with her the best silver pitcher in the house.

She had no sooner reached the spring than she saw a beautiful lady coming out of the wood, who came up to her and asked her for a drink. This was, you must know, the same fairy who had met her sister, but who had now taken the form of a princess.

"I did not come out here to serve you with water," said the proud, selfish maid. "Do you think I brought this silver pitcher so far just to give you a drink? You can draw water from the spring as well as I."

"You are not very polite," said the fairy. "Since you are so rude and so unkind, I give you for a gift that at every word you speak, toads and serpents shall come out of your mouth."

As soon as the mother saw her daughter coming, she cried out, "Well, my dear child, did you see the good fairy?"

"Yes, Mother," answered the proud girl, and as she spoke, two serpents and two toads fell from her mouth.

"What is this that I see?" cried the mother. "What have you done?"

The girl tried to answer, but at every word toads and serpents came from her lips.

And so it was forever after. Jewels and flowers fell from the lips of the younger daughter, who was so good and kind, but the elder daughter could not speak without a shower of serpents and toads.

Old Mr. Rabbit's
Thanksgiving Dinner

Carolyn Sherwin Bailey

It is a discovery we make again and again, as if by accident each time: it gives us greater satisfaction to be helpful than helped. For a child this discovery when made the first time is one of the important lessons that takes one beyond the confines of the self.

Old Man Rabbit sat at the door of his little house, eating a nice, ripe, juicy turnip. It was a cold, frosty day, but Old Man Rabbit was all wrapped up, round and round, with yards and yards of his best red wool muffler, so he didn't care if the wind whistled through his whiskers and blew his ears up straight. Old Man Rabbit had been exercising, too, and that was another reason why he was so nice and warm.

Early in the morning he had started off, lippity, clippity, down the little brown path that lay in front of his house and led to Farmer Dwyer's corn patch. The path was all covered with shiny red leaves. Old Man Rabbit scuffled through them and he carried a great big bag over his back. In the corn patch he found two or three fat, red ears of corn that Farmer Dwyer had missed, so he dropped them into his bag. A little farther along he found some purple turnips and some yellow carrots and quite a few russet apples that Farmer Dwyer had arranged in little piles in the orchard. Old Man Rabbit went in the barn, squeezing under the big front door by making himself very flat, and he filled all the chinks in his bag with potatoes, and he took a couple of eggs in his paws, for he thought he might want to stir up a little pudding for himself before the day was over.

Then Old Man Rabbit started off home again down the little brown path, his mouth watering every time his bag bumped against his back, and not meeting anyone on the way because it was so very, very early in the morning.

When he came to the little house he emptied his bag and arranged all his harvest in piles in his front room—the corn in one pile, the carrots in one pile, the turnips in another pile, and the apples and potatoes in the last pile. He beat up his eggs and stirred some flour with them and filled it full of currants to make a pudding. And when he had put his pudding in a bag and set it boiling on the stove, he went outside to sit a while and eat a turnip, thinking all the time what a mighty fine old rabbit he was, and so clever, too.

Well, while Old Man Rabbit was sitting there in front of his little house, wrapped up in his red muffler and munching the turnip, he heard a little noise in the leaves. It was Billy Chipmunk traveling home to the stone wall where he lived. He was hurrying and blowing on his paws to keep them warm.

"Good morning, Billy Chipmunk," said Old Man Rabbit. "Why are you running so fast?"

"Because I am cold, and I am hungry," answered Billy Chipmunk. "It's going to be a hard winter, a very hard winter—no apples left. I've been looking all the morning for an apple and I couldn't find one."

And with that, Billy Chipmunk went chattering by, his fur standing straight out in the wind.

No sooner had he passed than Old Man Rabbit saw Molly Mouse creeping along through the little brown path, her long gray tail rustling the red leaves as she went.

"Good morning, Molly Mouse," said Old Man Rabbit.

"Good morning," answered Molly Mouse in a weak little voice.

"You look a little unhappy," said Old Man Rabbit, taking another bite of his turnip.

"I have been looking and looking for an ear of corn," said Molly Mouse in a sad little chirping voice. "But the corn has all been harvested. It's going to be a very hard winter, a very hard winter."

And Molly Mouse trotted by out of sight.

Pretty soon Old Man Rabbit heard somebody else coming along by his house. This time it was Tommy Chickadee hopping by and making a great to-do, chattering and scolding as he came.

"Good morning, Tommy Chickadee," said Old Man Rabbit.

But Tommy Chickadee was too much put out about something to remember his manners. He just chirped and scolded, because he was cold and he couldn't find a single crumb or a berry or anything at all to eat. Then he flew away, his feathers puffed out with the cold until he looked like a round ball, and all the way he chattered and scolded more and more.

Old Man Rabbit finished his turnip, eating every single bit of it, even to the leaves. Then he went in his house to poke the fire in his stove and to see how the pudding was cooking. It was doing very well indeed, bumping against the pot as it bubbled and boiled, and smelling very fine indeed.

Old Man Rabbit looked around his house at the corn and the carrots and the turnips and the apples and the potatoes, and then he had an idea. It was a very funny idea, different from any other idea Old Man Rabbit had ever had before in all his life. It made him scratch his head with his left hind foot, and think and wonder. But it pleased him, too—it was such a very funny idea.

First he took off his muffler, and then he put on his gingham apron. He took his best red tablecloth from the drawer and put it on his table, and then he set the table with his gold-banded china dinner set. By the time he had done all this, the pudding was boiled, so he lifted it, all sweet and steaming, from the kettle and set it in the middle of the table. Around the pudding Old Man Rabbit piled heaps and heaps of corn and carrots and turnips and apples and potatoes, and then he took down his dinner bell that was all rusty, because Old Man Rabbit had very seldom rung it before, and he stood in his front door and he rang it very hard, calling in a loud voice:

"Dinner's ready! Come to dinner, Billy Chipmunk, and Molly Mouse, and Tommy Chickadee!"

They all came, and they brought their friends with them. Tommy Chickadee brought Rusty Robin, who had a broken wing and had not been able to fly south for the winter. Billy Chipmunk brought Chatter-Chee, a lame squirrel, whom he had invited to share his hole for a few months, and Molly Mouse brought a young gentleman Field Mouse, who was very distinguished-looking because of his long whiskers. When they all tumbled into Old Man Rabbit's house and saw the table with the pudding in the center they forgot their manners and began eating as fast as they could, every one of them.

It kept Old Man Rabbit very busy waiting on them. He gave all the currants from the pudding to Tommy Chickadee and Rusty Robin. He selected juicy turnips for Molly Mouse and her friend, and the largest apples for Billy Chipmunk. Old Man Rabbit was so busy that he didn't have any time to eat a bite of dinner himself, but he didn't mind that, not one single bit. It made him feel so warm and full inside just to see the others eating.

When the dinner was over, and not one single crumb was left on the table, Tommy Chickadee hopped up on the back of his chair and chirped:

"Three cheers for Old Man Rabbit's Thanksgiving dinner!"

"Hurrah! Hurrah!" they all twittered and chirped and chattered. And Old Man Rabbit was so surprised that he didn't get over it for a week. You see, he had really given a Thanksgiving dinner without knowing that it really and truly was Thanksgiving Day.

Androcles and the Lion

Retold by James Baldwin

This ancient story is another, more slightly complicated version
of the fable of the Lion and the Mouse. Here the human element
is introduced. Its appeal lies in the fact that Androcles the slave
can feel compassion at another's pain even though he himself has
been so cruelly mistreated. It is a unique human capacity, to be
able to put oneself in the place and point of view of another. In
the end, his own kindness sets him free.

In Rome there was once a poor slave whose name was Androcles. His master was a cruel man, and so unkind to him that at
last Androcles ran away.

He hid himself in a wild wood for many days. But there was no
food to be found, and he grew so weak and sick that he thought he
would die. So one day he crept into a cave and lay down, and soon
he was fast asleep.

After a while a great noise woke him up. A lion had come into
the cave, and was roaring loudly. Androcles was very much afraid,
for he felt sure that the beast would kill him. Soon, however, he saw
that the lion was not angry, but that he limped as though his foot
hurt him.

Then Androcles grew so bold that he took hold of the lion's
lame paw to see what was the matter. The lion stood quite still,
and rubbed his head against the man's shoulder. He seemed to say
"I know that you will help me."

Androcles lifted the paw from the ground, and saw that it was
a long, sharp thorn which hurt the lion so much. He took the end of
the thorn in his fingers; then he gave a strong, quick pull, and out it
came. The lion was full of joy. He jumped about like a dog, and
licked the hands and feet of his new friend.

Androcles was not at all afraid after this. And when night came,
he and the lion lay down and slept side by side.

For a long time, the lion brought food to Androcles every day,
and the two became such good friends that Androcles found his new
life a very happy one.

One day some soldiers who were passing through the wood found Androcles in the cave. They knew who he was, and so took him back to Rome.

It was the law at that time that every slave who ran away from his master should be made to fight a hungry lion. So a fierce lion was shut up for a while without food, and a time was set for the fight.

When the day came, thousands of people crowded to see the sport. They went to such places at that time very much as people now go to see a circus show, or a game of baseball.

The door opened, and poor Androcles was brought in. He was almost dead with fear, for the roars of the lion could already be heard. He looked up, and saw that there was no pity in the thousands of faces around him.

Then the hungry lion rushed in. With a single bound he reached the poor slave. Androcles gave a great cry, not of fear, but of gladness. It was his old friend, the lion of the cave.

The people, who had expected to see the man killed by the lion, were filled with wonder. They saw Androcles put his arms around the lion's neck; they saw the lion lie down at his feet, and lick them lovingly; they saw the great beast rub his head against the slave's face as though he wanted to be petted. They could not understand what it all meant.

After a while they asked Androcles to tell them about it. So he stood up before them, and, with his arm around the lion's neck, told how he and the beast had lived together in the cave.

"I am a man," he said, "but no man has ever befriended me. This poor lion alone has been kind to me and we love each other as brothers."

The people were not so bad that they could be cruel to the poor slave now. "Live and be free!" they cried. "Live and be free!"

Others cried, "Let the lion go free too! Give both of them their liberty!"

And so Androcles was set free, and the lion was given to him for his own. And they lived together in Rome for many years.

Little Thumbelina

This story is a shortened version of Hans Christian Andersen's
"Thumbling." Like the fable of the Lion and the Mouse, it
teaches little children how to have big hearts.

Once upon a time there was a little girl no bigger than her
Mother's thumb, and so they called her "Thumbelina."

Thumbelina did not sleep in a little white bed, as you do; her
bed was half of a walnut shell. Her Mother covered her with pink
rose leaves for blankets when she curled up for a cozy nap. By and
by, when Thumbelina had grown large enough to run about wherever she wished to go, she started for a walk one beautiful sunshiny
morning. She had not gone very far when she heard something
coming hoppity-skip, hoppity-skip behind her. She turned around,
and there she saw a great big green Grasshopper.

"How do you do, Thumbelina?" he said. "Wouldn't you like
to go for a ride this morning?"

"I should like it very much," said Thumbelina.

"Very well, hop up on my back," said the Grasshopper. So
Thumbelina hopped up on his back, and away they went, hoppity-
skip, hoppity-skip, through the grass. Thumbelina thought it was
the finest ride she had ever had. After a while the Grasshopper
stopped and let her get down off his back.

"Thank you, Mr. Grasshopper," said Thumbelina. "It was very
good of you to take me for a ride."

"I'm glad you enjoyed it," said the Grasshopper. "You may
go again some day. Goodbye." And away he went, hoppity-skip,
hoppity-skip, through the grass, while Thumbelina went on her
walk.

She walked on and on until she came to a river, and as she stood
on the bank, looking down into the shining water, a Fish came
swimming up.

"How do you do, Thumbelina?" he said.

"How do you do, Mr. Fish?" said Thumbelina.

"Wouldn't you like to go for a sail this morning?" asked the
Fish.

"Yes, indeed," said Thumbelina, "but there is no boat."

"Wait a moment," said the Fish, and he flirted his tail, and darted away through the water. Presently he came swimming back to the bank, and in his mouth he held the stem of a lily leaf.

"Step down on this; it will make a fine boat."

Thumbelina stepped down on the lily leaf and sat carefully in the middle of it. The Fish kept the stem in his mouth, and swam away down the stream. Overhead the birds were singing, along the bank the flowers were blooming, and over the edge of the leaf Thumbelina could see the fishes darting here and there through the water.

So they sailed and sailed down the river. But at last the Fish took her back to the bank again.

"Thank you for the sail, Mr. Fish," Thumbelina said as she stepped off onto the bank. "I never had such a good time in all my life."

"I'm glad you enjoyed it, Thumbelina. Goodbye for today."

The Fish darted away through the water, and Thumbelina turned to go home. Just then Mrs. Mouse came running up.

"How do you do, Thumbelina?" she said. "Won't you come home with me and see my babies?"

"I'd love to," said Thumbelina, and she clapped her hands in glee.

Mrs. Mouse's home was quite a way down under the ground. Thumbelina crept through the long dark passageway to the cozy room in which Mrs. Mouse and her three babies lived. They all ran races up and down the long passageway, and Thumbelina tasted the dried peas which Mrs. Mouse had brought home with her.

"I think I must go home now," Thumbelina said at last. "My Mother will be wondering where I am." So she said goodbye to them all and started off home.

She had not walked very far along the path through the field when she heard something saying "Peep, peep" in a weak, sick little voice. Thumbelina looked, and there close beside her in the grass she saw a little Bird. His eyes were shut, and he looked very sick.

"Why, what's the matter, little Bird?" said Thumbelina.

"Oh, I have a thorn in my foot, and it does hurt so."

"Let me see," said Thumbelina. "Perhaps I can help you."

She looked carefully, and there she saw the thorn sticking in the poor Bird's foot. She took her little fingers and pulled it out, as gently as she could. Then she fetched some clear, cold water and bathed the wounded foot. The Bird felt so much better that he opened his eyes.

"Why, it is Thumbelina!" he said.

"How did you know my name?" said Thumbelina, in surprise.

"That's easy to explain," said the Bird. "My nest is up in a tree, close beside your window. I often hear your Mother calling you. But are you not a long way from home?"

"Yes, I am," said Thumbelina. "I was hurrying home when I found you."

"Well," said the Bird, "if you climb up on my back, I'll take you there, far more quickly than you can run." So Thumbelina climbed up on the Birdie's back.

"Hold on tight," he said, as he spread his wings and flew swiftly up above the treetops.

He went so high that sometimes they skimmed along through the clouds, and so fast that Thumbelina could hardly get her breath; but still she thought it was very wonderful, and she was not a bit afraid. Soon the Bird lit right in the window of Thumbelina's own room. She climbed down off his back, and thanked him for bringing her home. Then she ran away to find her Mother, and tell her all about the wonderful things which had been happening to her that day.

The Legend of the Dipper

Retold by J. Berg Esenwein and Marietta Stockard

This story suggests to the child that a kind and compassionate act is often its own reward.

There had been no rain in the land for a very long time. It was so hot and dry that the flowers were withered, the grass was parched and brown, and even the big, strong trees were dying. The water dried up in the creeks and rivers, the wells were dry, the fountains stopped bubbling. The cows, the dogs, the horses, the birds, and all the people were *so* thirsty! Everyone felt uncomfortable and sick.

There was one little girl whose mother grew very ill. "Oh," said the little girl, "if I can only find some water for my mother I'm sure she will be well again. I must find some water."

So she took a tin cup and started out in search of water. By and by she found a tiny little spring away up on a mountainside. It was almost dry. The water dropped, dropped, ever so slowly from under the rock. The little girl held her cup carefully and caught the drops. She waited and waited a long, long time until the cup was full of water. Then she started down the mountain holding the cup very carefully, for she didn't want to spill a single drop.

On the way she passed a poor little dog. He could hardly drag himself along. He was panting for breath and his tongue hung from his mouth because it was so dry and parched.

"Oh, you poor little dog," said the little girl, "you are so thirsty. I can't pass you without giving you a few drops of water. If I give you just a little there will still be enough for my mother."

So the little girl poured some water into her hand and held it down for the little dog. He lapped it up quickly and then he felt so much better that he frisked and barked and seemed almost to say, "Thank you, little girl." And the little girl didn't notice—but her tin dipper had changed into a silver dipper and was just as full of water as it had been before.

She thought about her mother and hurried along as fast as she could go. When she reached home it was late in the afternoon, almost dark. The little girl pushed the door open and hurried up to her mother's room. When she came into the room the old servant who helped the little girl and her mother, and had been working hard all day taking care of the sick woman, came to the door. She was so tired and so thirsty that she couldn't even speak to the little girl.

"Do give her some water," said the mother. "She has worked hard all day and she needs it much more than I do."

So the little girl held the cup to her lips and the old servant drank some of the water. She felt stronger and better right away and she went over to the mother and lifted her up. The little girl didn't notice that the cup had changed into a gold cup and was just as full of water as it was before!

Then she held the cup to her mother's lips and she drank and drank. Oh, she felt so much better! When she had finished there was still some water left in the cup. The little girl was just raising it to her own lips when there came a knock at the door. The servant opened it and there stood a stranger. He was very pale and all covered with dust from traveling. "I am thirsty," he said. "Won't you give me a little water?"

The little girl said, "Why, certainly I will, I am sure that you need it far more than I do. Drink it all."

The stranger smiled and took the dipper in his hand, and as he took it, it changed into a diamond dipper. He turned it upside down and all the water spilled out and sank into the ground. And where it spilled a fountain bubbled up. The cool water flowed and splashed —enough for the people and all the animals in the whole land to have all the water they wanted to drink.

As they watched the water they forgot the stranger, but presently when they looked he was gone. They thought they could see him just vanishing in the sky—and there in the sky, clear and high, shone the diamond dipper. It shines up there yet, and reminds people of the little girl who was kind and unselfish. It is called the Big Dipper.

The Little Match Girl

Hans Christian Andersen

To feel another's anguish—this is the essence of compassion. Here is a Hans Christian Andersen masterpiece, a simple, tragic story that stirs pity in every child's heart.

It was dreadfully cold; it was snowing fast, and was almost dark, as evening came on—the last evening of the year. In the cold and the darkness, there went along the street a poor little girl, bare-headed and with naked feet. When she left home she had slippers on, it is true; but they were much too large for her feet—slippers that her mother had used till then, and the poor little girl lost them in running across the street when two carriages were passing terribly fast. When she looked for them, one was not to be found, and a boy seized the other and ran away with it, saying he would use it for a cradle some day, when he had children of his own.

So on the little girl went with her bare feet, that were red and blue with cold. In an old apron that she wore were bundles of matches, and she carried a bundle also in her hand. No one had bought so much as a bunch all the long day, and no one had given her even a penny.

Poor little girl! Shivering with cold and hunger she crept along, a perfect picture of misery.

The snowflakes fell on her long flaxen hair, which hung in pretty curls about her throat; but she thought not of her beauty nor of the cold. Lights gleamed in every window, and there came to her the savory smell of roast goose, for it was New Year's Eve. And it was this of which she thought.

In a corner formed by two houses, one of which projected beyond the other, she sat cowering down. She had drawn under her little feet, but still she grew colder and colder; yet she dared not go home, for she had sold no matches and could not bring a penny of money. Her father would certainly beat her; and, besides, it was cold enough at home, for they had only the house roof above them, and though the largest holes had been stopped with straw and rags, there were left many through which the cold wind could whistle.

And now her little hands were nearly frozen with cold. Alas! a single match might do her good if she might only draw it from the bundle, rub it against the wall, and warm her fingers by it. So at last she drew one out. Whisht! How it blazed and burned! It gave out a warm, bright flame like a little candle, as she held her hands over it. A wonderful little light it was. It really seemed to the little girl as if she sat before a great iron stove with polished brass feet and brass shovel and tongs. So blessedly it burned that the little maiden stretched out her feet to warm them also. How comfortable she was! But lo! the flame went out, the stove vanished, and nothing remained but the little burned match in her hand.

She rubbed another match against the wall. It burned brightly, and where the light fell upon the wall it became transparent like a veil, so that she could see through it into the room. A snow-white cloth was spread upon the table, on which was a beautiful china dinner service, while a roast goose, stuffed with apples and prunes, steamed famously and sent forth a most savory smell. And what was more delightful still, and wonderful, the goose jumped from the dish, with knife and fork still in its breast, and waddled along the floor straight to the little girl.

But the match went out then, and nothing was left to her but the thick, damp wall.

She lighted another match. And now she was under a most beautiful Christmas tree, larger and far more prettily trimmed than the one she had seen through the glass doors at the rich merchant's. Hundreds of wax tapers were burning on the green branches, and gay figures, such as she had seen in shop windows, looked down upon her. The child stretched out her hands to them; then the match went out.

Still the lights of the Christmas tree rose higher and higher. She saw them now as stars in heaven, and one of them fell, forming a long trail of fire.

"Now someone is dying," murmured the child softly; for her grandmother, the only person who had loved her, and who was now dead, had told her that whenever a star falls a soul mounts up to God.

She struck yet another match against the wall, and again it was light; and in the brightness there appeared before her the dear old grandmother, bright and radiant, yet sweet and mild, and happy as she had never looked on earth.

"Oh, Grandmother," cried the child, "take me with you. I know you will go away when the match burns out. You, too, will vanish, like the warm stove, the splendid New Year's feast, the beautiful Christmas tree." And lest her grandmother should disappear, she rubbed the whole bundle of matches against the wall.

And the matches burned with such a brilliant light that it became brighter than noonday. Her grandmother had never looked so grand and beautiful. She took the little girl in her arms, and both flew together, joyously and gloriously, mounting higher and higher, far above the earth; and for them there was neither hunger, nor cold, nor care—they were with God.

But in the corner, at the dawn of day, sat the poor girl, leaning against the wall, with red cheeks and smiling mouth—frozen to death on the last evening of the old year. Stiff and cold she sat, with the matches, one bundle of which was burned.

"She wanted to warm herself, poor little thing," people said. No one imagined what sweet visions she had had, or how gloriously she had gone with her grandmother to enter upon the joys of a new year.

Beauty and the Beast

Retold by Clifton Johnson

This longtime favorite is a story of love growing from compassion. Children are fascinated by the affection between Beauty and the Beast, a kindness made wondrous by their great physical difference. The story is an unforgettable lesson in how appearances can be deceiving, and how character lies beneath the skin. The French fairy tale comes in many versions. This one dates from the turn of the century.

There was once a wealthy merchant who had six children, three sons and three daughters. He loved his children more than he loved his riches and was always trying to make them happy. The three daughters were very handsome, but the youngest was the most attractive of all. While she was little she was called Beauty, and when she grew up she still kept the same name—and she was as good as she was beautiful. She spent much of her time studying, and when not engaged with her books she was busy doing all she could to make her home pleasant for her father. The older sisters were not like Beauty. They were proud of their riches and cared little for study, and they were constantly driving in the parks or attending balls, operas, and plays.

Thus things went along until misfortunes began to overtake the merchant in his business, and one evening he came home and told his family that storms at sea had destroyed his ships, and fire had burned his warehouses. "My riches are gone," said he, "and I have nothing I can call my own but a little farm off in the country. To that little farm we must all go, now, and earn our daily living with our hands."

The daughters wept at the idea of leading such a different life, and the older ones said they would not go, for they had plenty of friends who would invite them to stay in the town. But they were mistaken. Their friends, who were numerous when the family was rich, now kept away and said one to the other, "We are sorry for the merchant and his family, of course. However, we have cares of our own, and we couldn't be expected to help them; and, really, if those two older girls are having their pride humbled it is no more than they deserve. Let them go milk the cows and mind their dairy and see how they like it."

So the family went to live on the little farm in the country, and the merchant and his sons plowed and sowed the fields, and Beauty rose at four o'clock every morning to get breakfast for them. After the breakfast things were out of the way she busied herself about the other housework, and when there was nothing else to do she would sit at her spinning wheel, singing as she spun, or perhaps would take a little time for reading. The work was hard at first, yet when she became used to it she enjoyed it, and her eyes were brighter and her cheeks more rosy than ever before.

Her two sisters did not change their habits so easily, and they were wretched. They were always thinking of the wealth they had lost, and they did not get up till ten o'clock and did very little work after they were up, but spent most of the time sauntering about and complaining.

A year passed and then the merchant received news that one of his ships which he had believed to be lost had come safely into port with a rich cargo. This news nearly turned the heads of the two eldest daughters, who thought that now they could soon leave the little farm and return to the gay city. As soon as their father made ready to go to the port to attend to the unloading and sale of the ship's cargo, they begged him to buy them new gowns and hats and all manner of trinkets.

Then the merchant said, "And what shall I bring you, Beauty?"

"The only thing I wish for is to see you come home safely," she answered.

Her father was pleased, but he thought she ought to tell him of something he might bring her from the town. "Well, dear father," said she, "as you insist, I would like to have you bring me a rose, for I have not seen one since we came here."

The good man now set out on his journey, but when he reached the port he found that a former partner had taken charge of the ship's goods and disposed of them. The man would not turn over the money he had received to the merchant, and the merchant was obliged to sue for it in the courts. But what he recovered barely paid the costs, and at the end of six months of trouble and expense he started for his little farm as poor as when he came.

He traveled day after day until he was within thirty miles of home, and he was thinking of the pleasure he would have in seeing his children again when he lost his way in a great forest through which he had to pass. Night came on cold and rainy, and the poor man grew faint with hunger. But presently he saw bright lights shining through the trees, and he turned his horse toward them and soon came into a long avenue of great oaks. This led to a splendid palace that was lit from top to bottom. Yet when the merchant entered the courtyard no one met him, and when he halooed he received no answer. His horse kept on toward an open stable door, and he dismounted and led the creature inside and hitched it to a manger that was full of hay and oats.

The merchant now sought the castle and went into a large hall where he found a good fire, and a table plentifully set with food, but not a soul did he see. While he stood by the fire drying himself he said, "How fortunate I am to find such shelter, for I should have perished this stormy night out in the forest. But I can't imagine where the people of this house can be, and I hope its master will excuse the liberty I have taken."

He waited for some time and the clock struck eleven. No one came, and then, weak for want of food, he sat down at the table and ate heartily; yet all the while he was fearful that he was trespassing and might be severely dealt with for his presumption. After he had finished eating he felt less timid and he concluded he would look for a chamber. So he left the hall and passed through several splendid rooms till he came to one in which was a comfortable bed, and there he spent the night.

On awaking the following morning he was surprised to find a new suit of clothes laid out for him on a chair by the bedside, marked with his name, and with ten gold pieces in every pocket. His own clothes, which were much the worse for wear and had been wet through by the storm, had disappeared. "Surely," said he, "this palace belongs to some kind fairy who has seen and pitied my distresses."

In the hall where he had supped the night before he found the table prepared for his breakfast, and after he had eaten he went out into a great garden full of beautiful flowers and shrubbery. As he walked along he passed under a bower of roses. "Ah," said he stopping. "I had no money when I left the town to buy the gifts my older daughters wanted, and my mind has been so full of my troubles that I have not thought of the rose for which Beauty asked, until this moment. She shall have one of these." And he reached up and plucked one.

No sooner had he done this than a great beast came suddenly forth from a side path where he had been hidden by a high hedge and stood before the merchant. "This place is mine," said the beast in his deep, gruff voice. "Why do you pick my flowers?"

"Forgive me, my lord," begged the merchant, throwing himself on his knees before the beast. "I did not know I was giving offense. I only wanted to carry a rose to one of my daughters."

"You have daughters, have you?" said the beast. "Now, listen! This palace is lonely and I want one of your daughters to come here and live."

"Oh, sir!" cried the merchant. "Do not ask that."

"Nothing else will appease me," the beast responded. "I promise no harm will be done her. So take the rose you have picked and go at once and tell your daughters what I have said; and in case not one of them will come you must return yourself and be prisoned for the rest of your days in the palace dungeon."

"My lord," replied the merchant, "I shall not let a child of mine suffer for me, and you may as well lock me up in your dungeon now as later."

"No," the beast said, "you go home and consult with your daughters first."

"I am in your power," said the merchant, "and I can only obey you."

Then he went to the stable and mounted his horse and by night he reached home. His children ran out to greet him, but instead of receiving their caresses with pleasure the tears rolled down his cheeks, and he handed the rose to Beauty, saying, "Little do you think how dear that will cost your poor father." And he related all the sad adventures that had befallen him. "Tomorrow," said the merchant in closing, "I shall return to the beast."

"I can't let you do that, dear father," said Beauty. "I am going in your stead."

"Not so, sister," cried her three brothers. "We will seek out the monster and either kill him or die ourselves."

"You could accomplish nothing," declared the merchant, "for he lives in an enchanted palace and has invisible helpers with whom you could not hope to contend successfully."

"How unfortunate it all is!" said the older girls. "What a pity, Beauty, that you did not do as we did and ask for something sensible."

"Well," said Beauty, "who could have guessed that to ask for a rose would cause so much misery? However, the fault is plainly mine, and I shall have to suffer the consequences."

Her father tried to dissuade her from her purpose, but she insisted, and the next morning he mounted his horse and, with Beauty sitting behind him, he started for the beast's palace. They arrived late in the afternoon and rode down the long avenue of oaks and into the silent courtyard to the door of the stable where the horse had been kept before. Then they dismounted, and after the merchant had led the horse into the stable and seen it comfortably housed for the night they went into the palace.

A cheerful fire was blazing in the big hall and the table was daintily spread with most delicious food. They sat down to this repast, but were too sad to eat much and were soon through. Just then the beast came in and addressed the merchant. "Honest man," said he, "I am glad that you could be trusted. I was rude and threatening toward you yesterday, but it seemed necessary. However, in the end, I think you will have nothing to regret. Spend the night here and tomorrow go your way."

"This is my daughter Beauty," said the merchant.

The beast bowed and said, "My lady, I am very grateful to you for coming, and I beg you to remember that I am not what you think me. But I cannot tell you what I really am, for I am under a spell. This spell I hope you will be able to remove."

So saying, the beast withdrew and left the merchant and his daughter sitting by the fire. "What the beast means," said the merchant, "I do not know. But he talks very courteously."

Then they sat long in silence, but at last arose and they each hunted up a chamber and retired to try to sleep.

On the morrow they found breakfast prepared for them in the hall, and after they had eaten, the merchant bade his daughter an affectionate farewell. He went to the stable for his horse. It was all ready for him to mount, and to his surprise the saddlebags were full of gold. "Ah, well!" said he. "Here is wealth once more, but it cannot make up for the loss of my dear daughter."

Beauty watched him ride away. As soon as he was gone she threw herself down on a cushioned window seat and cried till she fell asleep; and while she slept she dreamed she was walking by a brook bordered with trees and lamenting her sad fate, when a young prince, handsomer than any man she had ever seen, came to her and said, "Ah, Beauty, you are not so unfortunate as you suppose. You will have your reward."

She awoke late in the day a good deal refreshed and comforted, and after a little she decided she would walk about and see something of the palace in which she was to live. She found much to admire and presently came to a door on which was written:

BEAUTY'S ROOM

She opened the door and entered a splendidly furnished apartment where there were a multitude of books and pictures, a harpsichord, and many comfortable chairs and couches. She picked up a book that lay on a table, and on the flyleaf she found written in golden letters these words:

"Your wishes and commands shall be obeyed. You are here the queen over everything."

"Alas!" she thought. "My chief wish just at this moment is to see what my poor father is about."

While she was thinking this she perceived some movement in a mirror on the wall in front of her, and when she looked into the mirror she saw her father arriving home and her sisters and brothers meeting him. The vision faded quickly away, but Beauty felt very thankful she had been allowed such a pleasure. "This beast shows a great deal of kindness," said she, glancing about the attractive room. "He must be a far better creature than we have imagined."

She did not see the beast until evening, and then he came and asked if he might sup with her, and she replied that he could. But she would much rather have eaten alone, for she could not help trembling in his presence. As long as they sat at the table, soft, beautiful music was played, though whence it came or who were the musicians she could not discover. The beast talked to Beauty with great politeness and intelligence, yet his gruff voice startled her every time he spoke. When they had nearly finished he said, "I suppose you think my appearance extremely ugly."

"Yes," said Beauty, "for I cannot tell a lie, but I think you are very good."

"You show a most gracious spirit," said the beast, "in not judging me wholly by my uncouth exterior. I will do anything I can to make you happy here."

"You are very kind, Beast," she replied. "Indeed, when I think of your good heart, you no longer seem to me so ugly."

As they rose from the supper table, the beast said, "Beauty, do you think you could ever care enough for me to kiss me?"

She faltered out, "No, Beast," and he turned and left the room sighing so deeply that she pitied him.

In the days and weeks which followed Beauty saw no one save the beast, yet there were invisible servants who did everything possible for her comfort and pleasure. She and the beast always had supper together, and his conversation never failed to be entertaining and agreeable. By degrees she grew accustomed to his shaggy ugliness and learned to mind it less and to think more of his many amiable qualities. The only thing that pained her was that when he was about to leave her at the end of supper he was sure to ask if she thought she could sometime care enough for him to kiss him.

Three months passed, and one day Beauty looked in her mirror and saw a double wedding at her father's cottage. Her sisters were being married to two gentlemen of the region. Not long afterward her mirror showed her that her three brothers had enlisted for soldiers and her father was left alone. A few days more elapsed and she saw that her father was sick. The sight made her weep, and in the evening she told the beast what her mirror had revealed to her and that she wished to go and nurse her father.

"And will you return at the end of a week if you go?" asked the beast.

"Yes," she replied.

"I cannot refuse anything you ask," said he. "I will have a swift horse ready for you at sunrise tomorrow."

The next day at sunrise Beauty found the swift horse saddled for her in the courtyard, and away she went like the wind through the forest toward her father's cottage. When she arrived, the old merchant was so overjoyed at seeing her that his sickness quickly left him and the two spent a most happy week together.

As soon as the seven days were past she returned to the castle of the beast, which she reached late in the afternoon. Supper time came and the food was served as usual, but the beast was absent and Beauty was a good deal alarmed. "Oh, I hope nothing has happened to him," she said. "He was so good and considerate."

After waiting a short time she went to look for the beast. She ran hastily through all the apartments of the palace, but the beast was not there. And then in the twilight she hurried out to the garden, and by the borders of a fountain she found the beast lying as if dead.

"Dear, dear Beast," she cried, dropping on her knees beside him, "what has happened?" And she leaned over and kissed his hairy cheek.

At once a change came over the beast, and on the grass beside the fountain lay a handsome prince. He opened his eyes and said feebly, "My lady, I thank you. A wicked magician had condemned me to assume the form of an ugly beast until some beautiful maiden consented to kiss me. But I think you are the only maiden in the world kindhearted enough to have had affection for me in the ugly form the magician had given me. When you went away to your father I was so lonely I could no longer eat or amuse myself, and I became so weak that today, when I was walking here in the garden, I fell and could not rise."

Then Beauty filled a cup with water from the fountain and lifted him up so that he could drink. That revived him somewhat and with her help he rose to his feet. The enchantment had been removed from the palace as well as from the prince, and the servants were no longer invisible.

"Call for help," said the prince. And when she called, several men instantly came to their aid and carried the prince to the palace. Once there, warmth, food, and happiness went far toward restoring him. The next morning he sent for Beauty's father to come and make his home with them, and not long afterward Beauty and the prince were married and they lived with great joy and contentment in their palace ever after.

Beautiful

Socrates believed beauty is a thing that "slips in and permeates our souls." That idea lives in this simple little poem, which generations of young Americans memorized from *McGuffey's Second Reader*.

Beautiful faces are they that wear
The light of a pleasant spirit there;
Beautiful hands are they that do
Deeds that are noble, good and true;
Beautiful feet are they that go
Swiftly to lighten another's woe.

As Rich as Croesus

Retold by James Baldwin

This story comes from the Greek historian Herodotus. Croesus
(560–546 B.C.), king of Lydia in Asia Minor, was a ruler of proverbial wealth. How Cyrus spared his life is a legendary example
of mercy becoming the crown of justice. The story also offers
important lessons about money and power's real bearing on happiness.

Some thousands of years ago there lived in Asia a king whose
name was Croesus. The country over which he ruled was not very
large, but its people were prosperous and famed for their wealth.
Croesus himself was said to be the richest man in the world, and so
well known is his name that, to this day, it is not uncommon to say
of a very wealthy person that he is "as rich as Croesus."

King Croesus had everything that could make him happy—
lands and houses and slaves, fine clothing to wear, and beautiful
things to look at. He could not think of anything that he needed to
make him more comfortable or contented. "I am the happiest man
in the world," he said.

It happened one summer that a great man from across the sea
was traveling in Asia. The name of this man was Solon, and he was
the lawmaker of Athens in Greece. He was noted for his wisdom
and, centuries after his death, the highest praise that could be given
to a learned man was to say, "He is as wise as Solon."

Solon had heard of Croesus, and so one day he visited him in
his beautiful palace. Croesus was now happier and prouder than ever
before, for the wisest man in the world was his guest. He led Solon
through his palace and showed him the grand rooms, the fine carpets, the soft couches, the rich furniture, the pictures, the books.
Then he invited him out to see his gardens and his orchards and his
stables, and he showed him thousands of rare and beautiful things
that he had collected from all parts of the world.

In the evening as the wisest of men and the richest of men were
dining together, the king said to his guest, "Tell me now, O Solon,
who do you think is the happiest of all men?" He expected that
Solon would say, "Croesus."

The wise man was silent for a minute, and then he said, "I have in mind a poor man who once lived in Athens and whose name was Tellus. He, I doubt not, was the happiest of all men."

This was not the answer that Croesus wanted, but he hid his disappointment and asked, "Why do you think so?"

"Because," answered his guest, "Tellus was an honest man who labored hard for many years to bring up his children and to give them a good education. And when they were grown and able to do for themselves, he joined the Athenian army and gave his life bravely in the defense of his country. Can you think of anyone who is more deserving of happiness?"

"Perhaps not," answered Croesus, half choking with disappointment. "But who do you think ranks next to Tellus in happiness?" He was quite sure now that Solon would say, "Croesus."

"I have in mind," said Solon, "two young men whom I knew in Greece. Their father died when they were mere children, and they were very poor. But they worked manfully to keep the house together and to support their mother, who was in feeble health. Year after year they toiled, nor thought of anything but their mother's comfort. When at length she died, they gave all their love to Athens, their native city, and nobly served her as long as they lived."

Then Croesus was angry. "Why is it," he asked, "that you make me of no account and think that my wealth and power are nothing? Why is it that you place these poor working people above the richest king in the world?"

"O king," said Solon, "no man can say whether you are happy or not until you die. For no man knows what misfortunes may overtake you, or what misery may be yours in place of all this splendor."

Many years after this there arose in Asia a powerful king whose name was Cyrus. At the head of a great army he marched from one country to another, overthrowing many a kingdom and attaching it to his great empire of Babylon. King Croesus with all his wealth was not able to stand against this mighty warrior. He resisted as long as he could. Then his city was taken, his beautiful palace was burned, his orchards and gardens were destroyed, his treasures were carried away, and he himself was made prisoner.

"The stubbornness of this man Croesus," said King Cyrus, "has caused us much trouble and the loss of many good soldiers. Take him and make an example of him for other petty kings who may dare to stand in our way."

Thereupon the soldiers seized Croesus and dragged him to the marketplace, handling him pretty roughly all the time. Then they built up a great pile of dry sticks and timber taken from the ruins of his once beautiful palace. When this was finished they tied the unhappy king in the midst of it, and one ran for a torch to set it on fire.

"Now we shall have a merry blaze," said the savage fellows. "What good can all his wealth do him now?"

As poor Croesus, bruised and bleeding, lay upon the pyre without a friend to soothe his misery, he thought of the words that Solon had spoken to him years before: "No man can say whether you are happy or not until you die," and he moaned, "O Solon! O Solon! Solon!"

It so happened that Cyrus was riding by at that very moment and heard his moans. "What does he say?" he asked of the soldiers.

"He says, 'Solon, Solon, Solon!' " answered one.

Then the king rode nearer and asked Croesus, "Why do you call on the name of Solon?"

Croesus was silent at first. But after Cyrus had repeated his question kindly, he told all about Solon's visit at his palace and what he had said.

The story affected Cyrus deeply. He thought of the words, "No man knows what misfortunes may overtake you, or what misery may be yours in place of all this splendor." And he wondered if sometime he, too, would lose all his power and be helpless in the hands of his enemies.

"After all," said he, "ought not men to be merciful and kind to those who are in distress? I will do to Croesus as I would have others do to me." And he caused Croesus to be given his freedom, and ever afterward treated him as one of his most honored friends.

The Sin of Omission

Margaret E. Sangster

Kindness is not immune to procrastination. We need to guard
against "slow compassion" as we tend to our affairs.

It isn't the thing you do, dear,
    It's the thing you leave undone
That gives you a bit of a heartache
    At setting of the sun.
The tender word forgotten,
    The letter you did not write,
The flowers you did not send, dear,
    Are your haunting ghosts at night.

The stone you might have lifted
    Out of a brother's way;
The bit of heartsome counsel
    You were hurried too much to say;
The loving touch of the hand, dear,
    The gentle, winning tone
Which you had no time nor thought for
    With troubles enough of your own.

Those little acts of kindness
    So easily out of mind,
Those chances to be angels
    Which we poor mortals find—
They come in night and silence,
    Each sad, reproachful wraith,
When hope is faint and flagging,
    And a chill has fallen on faith.

For life is all too short, dear,
  And sorrow is all too great,
To suffer our slow compassion
  That tarries until too late;
And it isn't the thing you do, dear,
  It's the thing you leave undone
Which gives you a bit of a heartache
  At the setting of the sun.

Moses in the Bulrushes

Retold by J. Berg Esenwein and Marietta Stockard

This story, from the book of Exodus, describes one of the most moving acts of compassion in the Bible and all of literature. The decision of the pharaoh's daughter to adopt the baby Moses transcends cultural and class barriers, and ultimately leads to the founding of the Hebrew nation.

The children of Israel lived for many years in the land of Egypt. Year by year, the Israelites grew stronger, richer, and more powerful. At last the Egyptians grew jealous of them.

"These strangers have the best of our land," they complained. "They are growing so many and so powerful that they will soon take the whole land and will rule over us."

At last, King Pharaoh sent out a proclamation that every boy born in the home of a Hebrew should be put to death. He thought that in this cruel way he would stop the growth of these people. The poor mothers wept bitterly, and hid their children from the officers of the king.

Now, about this time, there was born in the home of one of the Hebrews a little boy who was a strong and beautiful child. His mother kept him hidden until he was three months old. Then she grew afraid that the cruel Egyptians might come to her home and find him, so she went down to the river and gathered bulrushes. These she wove into a basket, or ark, and daubed it with mud and pitch, so the water could not come into it; then she took her baby boy and laid him carefully in it. She took the ark and hid it in the rushes on the edge of the river. His little sister stood afar off and kept watch to see what would happen to the child.

By and by, the daughter of Pharaoh and her maidens came down to the river to bathe. As the princess walked along the riverside she saw the ark hidden in the rushes and she sent her maidens to fetch it. She opened the ark of rushes and the child stretched out his arms to her. The princess lifted him from the ark and held him close to her heart. As she looked into his baby face, she was filled with pity and love for the beautiful boy.

"This is one of the Hebrews' children," she said. "Some poor mother has hidden him here. He is a splendid child; I will take him and bring him up as my own son."

Just then the little sister drew near and heard what the princess said. Her heart was filled with joy.

"Shall I go and call a nurse of the Hebrew women that she may nurse the child for thee?"

The princess smiled. "Go," she said.

The girl ran swiftly to her mother and told her all that had happened. Trembling with joy, the mother hurried to the princess, and the child was placed into the arms of his own mother.

"Nurse this child for me and I will give thee thy wage," said the princess. "His name shall be called Moses, because I drew him out of the water."

So, loved and tended by his own mother, Moses grew up in the palace of the king, and he was treated as the son of the princess. He grew to be strong and powerful, but he never turned from his own people, the Hebrews. Long years after, when he had grown wise enough to be a great leader, he took his people out of Egypt, back into their own land.

The Good Samaritan

Retold by Jesse Lyman Hurlbut

Jesus, who taught that we should love our neighbor as we love ourselves, told the parable of the Good Samaritan (Luke 10:29–37) in response to a question: "Who is my neighbor?" To understand the story fully, it is important to know that a "Good Samaritan" would have been a contradictory term for most Jews in Jesus' time because of a long-standing hostility between Jews and Samaritans. The traveler who comes to the wounded man's aid here is the least likely to show sympathy.

Jesus gave the parable or story of "The Good Samaritan." He said, "A certain man was going down the lone road from Jerusalem to Jericho and he fell among robbers, who stripped him of all that he had, and beat him, and then went away, leaving him almost dead. It happened that a certain priest was going down that road, and when he saw the man lying there, he passed by on the other side. And a Levite also, when he came to the place, and saw the man, he, too, went by on the other side. But a certain Samaritan, as he was going down, came where this man was, and as soon as he saw him, he felt a pity for him. He came to the man and dressed his wounds, pouring oil and wine into them. Then he lifted him up and set him on his own beast of burden, and walked beside him to an inn. There he took care of him all night. And the next morning he took out from his purse two shillings, and gave them to the keeper of the inn, and said, 'Take care of him, and if you need to spend more than this, do so. When I come again I will pay it to you.'

"Which one of these three do you think showed himself a neighbor to the man who fell among the robbers?"

The scribe said, "The one who showed mercy on him."

Then Jesus said to him, "Go and do thou likewise."

By this parable Jesus showed that "our neighbor" is the one who needs the help that we can give him, whoever he may be.

Song of Life

Charles MacKay

The Roman statesman Seneca wrote that wherever there is a
human being, there is an opportunity for a kindness. No selfless
act is insignificant. (Try reading this poem aloud.)

> A traveler on a dusty road
>   Strewed acorns on the lea;
> And one took root and sprouted up,
>   And grew into a tree.
> Love sought its shade at evening time,
>   To breathe its early vows;
> And Age was pleased, in heights of noon,
>   To bask beneath its boughs.
> The dormouse loved its dangling twigs,
>   The birds sweet music bore—
> It stood a glory in its place,
>   A blessing evermore.
>
> A little spring had lost its way
>   Amid the grass and fern;
> A passing stranger scooped a well
>   Where weary men might turn.
> He walled it in, and hung with care
>   A ladle on the brink;
> He thought not of the deed he did,
>   But judged that Toil might drink.
> He passed again; and lo! the well,
>   By summer never dried,
> Had cooled ten thousand parched tongues,
>   And saved a life beside.

A nameless man, amid the crowd
   That thronged the daily mart,
Let fall a word of hope and love,
   Unstudied from the heart,
A whisper of the tumult thrown,
   A transitory breath,
It raised a brother from the dust,
   It saved a soul from death.
O germ! O fount! O word of love!
   O thought at random cast!
Ye were but little at the first,
   But mighty at the last.

Grandmother's Table

Adapted from the Brothers Grimm

It may be that the older we get, the more this story will mean to us. But we should learn it while we are young, for the sake of the generation coming before us.

Once there was a feeble old woman whose husband died and left her all alone, so she went to live with her son and his wife and their own little daughter. Every day the old woman's sight dimmed and her hearing grew worse, and sometimes at dinner her hands trembled so badly the peas rolled off her spoon or the soup ran from her cup. The son and his wife could not help but be annoyed at the way she spilled her meal all over the table, and one day, after she knocked over a glass of milk, they told each other enough was enough.

They set up a small table for her in the corner next to the broom closet and made the old woman eat her meals there. She sat all alone, looking with tear-filled eyes across the room at the others. Sometimes they spoke to her while they ate, but usually it was to scold her for dropping a bowl or a fork.

One evening just before dinner, the little girl was busy playing on the floor with her building blocks, and her father asked her what she was making. "I'm building a little table for you and mother," she smiled, "so you can eat by yourselves in the corner someday when I get big."

Her parents sat staring at her for some time and then suddenly both began to cry. That night they led the old woman back to her place at the big table. From then on she ate with the rest of the family, and her son and his wife never seemed to mind a bit when she spilled something every now and then.

The Angel of the Battlefield

Joanna Strong and Tom B. Leonard

Clara Barton (1821–1912) was known as the Angel of the Battlefield for her work among the wounded during the Civil War. As the founder of the American Red Cross, she holds a place among our greatest pioneers of philanthropy.

When the agonizing pain receded a bit, Jack Gibbs was able to think again. "I'll never make it home," he groaned. "Not in one piece, anyway."

He sighed and tried to shift his body to a more comfortable position on the cold, rocky ground. But the movement caused another warm gush, and he knew that if he were to live at all, he must lie still.

"By the time they cart me back to the hospital behind the lines," he thought, "I'll either have bled to death or I'll be in such rotten shape they'll have to take my leg off. And what kind of a husband would I be for Sue? A man with one leg!"

A black cloud swept over him, and he lay unconscious.

When he opened his eyes again, Jack was sure he had died and gone to heaven. A woman was bending over him. That just couldn't happen on a battlefield of the Civil War. No woman ever came on the field. No woman would want to! *No woman would be allowed to!*

But there *was* a woman on the battlefield. Her name was Clara Barton.

With the help of two soldiers, she lifted Jack onto a cot that the men removed from a horse-drawn van. She took some bandages out of her kit and bound up his leg. Then she gave him a pain-killing draft. Jack weakly sipped it down, and the men put him in a crude-looking ambulance.

Clara Barton had been doing this kind of work all day long. She had succored hundreds of the wounded, allayed their fears, relieved their pain, cleansed their wounds.

Ever since the dreadful war had begun, Clara Barton had been worried about the men fighting at the front. She knew that wounded men were left lying on the field until the battle was over. She knew that only then were they collected and taken to hospitals—hospitals far behind the lines. She knew that if they survived this delay, the rough jolting of the wagons might well cause their unbound wounds to open. She knew that they often bled to death before they reached the hospital.

Heartsick at this state of affairs, she determined to bring aid to the men *right on the field*. First, she procured a van. Then she equipped it with medicine and first-aid supplies. And then she went to see the general.

She was a slender little woman. To the commanding officer, she didn't look exactly like battlefield material. In fact, her pet idea horrified him.

"Miss Barton," he said, "what you are asking is absolutely impossible."

"But General," she insisted, "Why is it impossible? I myself will drive the van and give the soldiers what relief I can."

The general shook his head. "The battlefield is no place for a woman. You couldn't stand the rough life. Anyway, we are now doing everything that can be done for our soldiers. No one could do more."

"*I* could," Clara Barton declared. And then, as if she had just entered the room for the first time, she described all over again to the general her plans for first aid on the field.

This interview was repeated again and again, but constant refusal did not deter her. Finally, the commanding officer gave in. Clara Barton received a pass that would let her though the lines.

During the entire course of the Civil War, she ministered to all she could reach. She labored unceasingly. Once she worked with scant rest for five days and nights in a row. Her name became a byword in the army, spoken of with love and gratitude.

As the government saw what she was actually accomplishing, it gradually afforded her more and more cooperation. The army supplied more vans and more men to drive them. More medical supplies were made available. But it was nevertheless an uphill battle all the way for the courageous Miss Barton.

When the war ended, Clara Barton might have been expected to take a well-earned rest. Instead, she was haunted by the thought of the agony of those unfortunate folks who did not know for sure what had happened to their husbands, their fathers, their brothers. She determined to learn the fates of these missing soldiers, and to send the information to their families. She worked at this task for a long time.

Now she knew war at first-hand. She knew what it did to men on the battlefield, and she knew what it did to the families they left behind. When she heard that there was a man in Switzerland, by the name of Jean Henry Dunant, who had a plan to help soldiers in wartime, she immediately went to Switzerland to lend her aid. Dunant formed an organization called the Red Cross. Workers of this organization were to wear a red cross on a white background so that they could easily be identified. They were to be allowed free access to battlefields, so that they might help *all* soldiers, no matter what their nationality, race, or religion.

Here was an idea that fired Clara Barton. She came back to America and convinced the United States Government that it should join with the twenty-two other member nations to give money and supplies to an International Red Cross, organized to help soldiers in wartime.

But Clara Barton added another idea to this great Red Cross plan. It was called *"The American Amendment."*

"There are many other calamities that befall mankind," she said. "Earthquakes, floods, forest fires, epidemics, tornadoes. These disasters strike suddenly, killing and wounding many, leaving others homeless and starving. The Red Cross should stretch out a hand of help to all such victims, no matter where such disasters befall."

Today, the International Red Cross brings succor to millions of people all over the world. This was Clara Barton's wonderful idea. Her great courage, great love, and great charity will ever be revered.

If I Can Stop
One Heart from Breaking

Emily Dickinson

Emily Dickinson (1830–1886) reminds us that acts of compassion
add meaning to our lives.

> If I can stop one heart from breaking,
> I shall not live in vain;
> If I can ease one life the aching,
> Or cool one pain,
> Or help one fainting robin
> Unto his nest again,
> I shall not live in vain.

The Wisdom of Solomon

Retold by Jesse Lyman Hurlbut

This is one of the most famous stories of the proverbial wisdom
of Solomon, who reigned in Israel for forty years during the
tenth century B.C. Solomon's decision at first seems cruel, but in
fact turns out to be the brilliant strategy of a leader who must be
not only kind but just in a difficult situation. He is wise enough
to "smoke out" the guilty party by relying on the power of true
compassion. The story is from 1 Kings 3:16–28 in the Bible.

Two women came before King Solomon with two little babies,
one dead and the other living. Each of the two women claimed the
living child as her own, and said that the dead child belonged to the
other woman. One of the women said, "O my lord, we two women
were sleeping with our children in one bed. And this woman in her

sleep lay upon her child, and it died. Then she placed her dead child beside me while I was asleep, and took my child. In the morning I saw that it was not my child, but she says it is mine, and the living child is hers. Now, O king, command this woman to give me my own child."

Then the other woman said, "That is not true. The dead baby is her own, and the living one is mine, which she is trying to take from me."

The young king listened to both women. Then he said, "Bring me a sword."

They brought a sword, and then Solomon said, "Take this sword, and cut the living child in two, and give half of it to each one."

Then one of the women cried out, and said, "O my lord, do not kill my child! Let the other woman have it, but let the child live!"

But the other woman said, "No, cut the child in two, and divide it between us!"

Then Solomon said, "Give the living child to the woman who would not have it slain, for she is its mother."

And all the people wondered at the wisdom of one so young, and they saw that God had given him understanding.

A Legend of the Northland

Phoebe Cary

In which we learn what happens to us when we cannot bring ourselves to share with those in need.

> Away, away in the Northland,
>   Where the hours of the day are few,
> And the nights are so long in winter
>   That they cannot sleep them through;

Where they harness the swift reindeer
    To the sledges, when it snows;
And the children look like bears' cubs
    In their funny, furry clothes;

They tell them a curious story—
    I don't believe 'tis true;
And yet you may learn a lesson
    If I tell the tale to you.

Once, when the good Saint Peter
    Lived in the world below,
And walked about it, preaching,
    Just as he did, you know,

He came to the door of a cottage,
    In traveling round the earth,
Where a little woman was making cakes,
    And baking them on the hearth;

And being faint with fasting,
    For the day was almost done,
He asked her, from her store of cakes,
    To give him a single one.

So she made a very little cake,
    But as it baking lay,
She looked at it, and thought it seemed
    Too large to give away.

Therefore she kneaded another,
    And still a smaller one;
But it looked, when she turned it over,
    As large as the first had done.

Then she took a tiny scrap of dough,
    And rolled and rolled it flat;
And baked it thin as a wafer—
    But she couldn't part with that.

For she said, "My cakes that seem too small
    When I eat them of myself,
Are yet too large to give away."
    So she put them on the shelf.

Then good Saint Peter grew angry,
    For he was hungry and faint;
And surely such a woman
    Was enough to provoke a saint.

And he said, "You are far too selfish
    To dwell in a human form,
To have both food and shelter,
    And fire to keep you warm.

"Now, you shall build as the birds do,
    And shall get your scanty food
By boring, and boring, and boring,
    All day in the hard, dry wood."

Then up she went through the chimney,
    Never speaking a word,
And out of the top flew a woodpecker,
    For she was changed to a bird.

She had a scarlet cap on her head,
    And that was left the same,
But all the rest of her clothes were burned
    Black as a coal in the flame.

And every country schoolboy
    Has seen her in the wood,
Where she lives in the trees till this very day,
    Boring and boring for food.

And this is the lesson she teaches:
    Live not for yourself alone,
Lest the needs you will not pity
    Shall one day be your own.

Give plenty of what is given to you,
    Listen to pity's call;
Don't think the little you give is great,
    And the much you get is small.

Now, my little boy, remember that,
    And try to be kind and good,
When you see the woodpecker's sooty dress,
    And see her scarlet hood.

You mayn't be changed to a bird though you live
    As selfishly as you can;
But you will be changed to a smaller thing—
    A mean and selfish man.

The Quality of Mercy

William Shakespeare

In perhaps the most famous lines from *The Merchant of Venice,*
Portia, the heiress of Belmont, argues that mercy is a divine
attribute, and that we make ourselves closer to God when we
exercise it. The scene is a Venetian courtroom. Portia, disguised
as a lawyer, is trying to convince the moneylender Shylock to
give up his legal claim to a pound of Antonio's flesh.

The quality of mercy is not strain'd.
It droppeth as the gentle rain from heaven
Upon the place beneath. It is twice blest:
It blesseth him that gives, and him that takes.
'Tis mightiest in the mightiest; it becomes
The throned monarch better than his crown.
His scepter shows the force of temporal power,
The attribute to awe and majesty,
Wherein doth sit the dread and fear of kings;
But mercy is above this sceptered sway;

It is enthroned in the hearts of kings;
It is an attribute to God himself;
And earthly power doth then show likest God's
When mercy seasons justice.

Echo and Narcissus

Retold by Thomas Bulfinch

In Greek mythology, Narcissus was a beautiful youth, the son of
the river god Cephisus and the nymph Leiriope. His vanity and
heartlessness have made his name forever synonymous with intense self-infatuation. Self-absorption often makes compassion
impossible, and vice versa. The retelling of his story is from
Thomas Bulfinch's classic *Age of Fable*.

Echo was a beautiful nymph, fond of the woods and hills, where
she devoted herself to woodland sports. She was a favorite of Diana,
and attended her in the chase. But Echo had one failing; she was
fond of talking, and whether in chat or argument, would have the
last word. One day Juno was seeking her husband, who, she had
reason to fear, was amusing himself among the nymphs. Echo by
her talk contrived to detain the goddess till the nymphs made their
escape. When Juno discovered it, she passed sentence upon Echo in
these words: "You shall forfeit the use of that tongue with which
you have cheated me, except for that one purpose you are so fond of
—*reply*. You shall still have the last word, but no power to speak
first."

This nymph saw Narcissus, a beautiful youth, as he pursued the
chase upon the mountains. She loved him and followed his footsteps.
O how she longed to address him in the softest accents, and win him
to converse! But it was not in her power. She waited with impatience
for him to speak first, and had her answer ready. One day the youth,
being separated from his companions, shouted aloud, "Who's here?"
Echo replied, "Here." Narcissus looked around, but seeing no one,
called out, "Come." Echo answered, "Come." As no one came,

Narcissus called again, "Why do you shun me?" Echo asked the same question. "Let us join one another," said the youth. The maid answered with all her heart in the same words, and hastened to the spot, ready to throw her arms about his neck. He started back, exclaiming, "Hands off! I would rather die than you should have me!" "Have me," said she; but it was all in vain. He left her, and she went to hide her blushes in the recesses of the woods. From that time forth she lived in caves and among mountain cliffs. Her form faded with grief, till at last all her flesh shrank away. Her bones were changed into rocks and there was nothing left of her but her voice. With that she is still ready to reply to anyone who calls her, and keeps up her old habit of having the last word.

Narcissus's cruelty in this case was not the only instance. He shunned all the rest of the nymphs, as he had done poor Echo. One day a maiden who had in vain endeavored to attract him uttered a prayer that he might sometime or other feel what it was to love and meet no return of affection. The avenging goddess heard and granted the prayer.

There was a clear fountain, with water like silver, to which the shepherds never drove their flocks, nor the mountain goats resorted, nor any of the beasts of the forests; neither was it defaced with fallen leaves or branches; but the grass grew fresh around it, and the rocks sheltered it from the sun. Hither came one day the youth, fatigued with hunting, heated and thirsty. He stooped down to drink, and saw his own image in the water; he thought it was some beautiful water spirit living in the fountain. He stood gazing with admiration at those bright eyes, those locks curled like the locks of Bacchus or Apollo, the rounded cheeks, the ivory neck, the parted lips, and the glow of health and exercise over all. He fell in love with himself. He brought his lips near to take a kiss; he plunged his arms in to embrace the beloved object. It fled at the touch, but returned again after a moment and renewed the fascination. He could not tear himself away. He lost all thought of food or rest, while he hovered over the brink of the fountain gazing upon his own image. He talked with the supposed spirit. "Why, beautiful being, do you shun me? Surely my face is not one to repel you. The nymphs love me, and you yourself look not indifferent upon me. When I stretch forth my arms you do the same; and you smile upon me and answer my beckonings with the like." His tears fell into the water and disturbed the image. As he saw it depart, he exclaimed, "Stay, I entreat you! Let me at least gaze upon you, if I may not touch you." With this, and much more of the same kind, he cherished the flame that consumed him, so that by degrees he lost his color, his vigor, and the beauty which formerly had so charmed the nymph Echo. She kept near him, however, and when he exclaimed, "Alas! Alas!" she answered him with the same words. He pined away and died; and when his shade passed the Stygian river, it leaned over the boat to catch a look of itself in the waters. The nymphs mourned for him, especially the water nymphs; and when they smote their breasts Echo smote hers also. They prepared a funeral pyre and would have burned the body, but it was nowhere to be found; but in its place a flower, purple within, and surrounded with white leaves, which bears the name and preserves the memory of Narcissus.

Marley's Ghost

Charles Dickens

Every young person embarking on a career should take along the remembrance of Marley's Ghost, who cautions us that mankind is our business. Charles Dickens (1812–1870) wrote *A Christmas Carol,* from which this famous scene is taken, in 1843. We see it in many versions on television each year, but the tale's spirit is best known by reading it.

Scrooge fell upon his knees, and clasped his hands before his face.

"Mercy!" he said. "Dreadful apparition, why do you trouble me?"

"Man of the worldly mind!" replied the Ghost. "Do you believe in me or not?"

"I do," said Scrooge. "I must. But why do spirits walk the earth, and why do they come to me?"

"It is required of every man," the Ghost returned, "that the spirit within him should walk abroad among his fellow men, and travel far and wide; and, if that spirit goes not forth in life, it is condemned to do so after death. It is doomed to wander through the world—oh, woe is me!—and witness what it cannot share, but might have shared on earth, and turned to happiness!"

Again the specter raised a cry, and shook its chain and wrung its shadowy hands.

"You are fettered," said Scrooge, trembling. "Tell me why?"

"I wear the chain I forged in life," replied the Ghost. "I made it link by link, and yard by yard; I girded it on of my own free will, and of my own free will I wore it. Is its pattern strange to *you?*"

Scrooge trembled more and more.

"Or would you know," pursued the Ghost, "the weight and length of the strong coil you bear yourself? It was full as heavy and as long as this seven Christmas Eves ago. You have labored on it since. It is a ponderous chain!"

Scrooge glanced about him on the floor, in the expectation of finding himself surrounded by some fifty or sixty fathoms of iron cable; but he could see nothing.

"Jacob!" he said imploringly. "Old Jacob Marley, tell me more! Speak comfort to me, Jacob!"

"I have none to give," the Ghost replied. "It comes from other regions, Ebenezer Scrooge, and it is conveyed by other ministers, to other kinds of men. Nor can I tell you what I would. A very little more is all permitted to me. I cannot rest, I cannot stay, I cannot linger anywhere. My spirit never walked beyond our counting house —mark me—in life my spirit never roved beyond the narrow limits of our money-changing hole; and weary journeys lie before me!"

It was a habit with Scrooge, whenever he became thoughtful, to put his hands in his breeches pockets. Pondering on what the Ghost had said, he did so now, but without lifting up his eyes, or getting off his knees.

"You must have been very slow about it, Jacob," Scrooge observed in a businesslike manner, though with humility and deference.

"Slow!" the Ghost repeated.

"Seven years dead," mused Scrooge. "And traveling all the time?"

"The whole time," said the Ghost. "No rest, no peace. Incessant torture of remorse."

"You travel fast?" said Scrooge.

"On the wings of the wind," replied the Ghost.

"You might have got over a great quantity of ground in seven years," said Scrooge.

The Ghost, on hearing this, set up another cry, and clanked its chain so hideously in the dead silence of the night, that the Ward would have been justified in indicting it for a nuisance.

"Oh! Captive, bound, and double-ironed," cried the phantom, "not to know that ages of incessant labor, by immortal creatures, for this earth must pass into eternity before the good of which it is susceptible is all developed! Not to know that any Christian spirit working kindly in its little sphere, whatever it may be, will find its mortal life too short for its vast means of usefulness! Not to know that no space of regret can make amends for one life's opportunities misused! Yet such was I! Oh, such was I!"

"But you were always a good man of business, Jacob," faltered Scrooge, who now began to apply this to himself.

"Business!" cried the Ghost, wringing its hands again. "Mankind was my business. The common welfare was my business; charity, mercy, forbearance, and benevolence were, all, my business. The dealings of my trade were but a drop of water in the comprehensive ocean of my business!"

It held up its chain at arm's length, as if that were the cause of all its unavailing grief, and flung it heavily upon the ground again.

"At this time of the rolling year," the specter said, "I suffer most. Why did I walk through crowds of fellow beings with my eyes turned down, and never raise them to that blessed Star which led the Wise Men to a poor abode? Were there no poor homes to which its light would have conducted *me?*"

Scrooge was very much dismayed to hear the specter going on at this rate, and began to quake exceedingly.

"Hear me!" cried the Ghost. "My time is nearly gone."

"I will," said Scrooge. "But don't be hard upon me! Don't be flowery, Jacob! Pray!"

"How it is that I appear before you in a shape that you can see, I may not tell. I have sat invisible beside you many and many a day."

It was not an agreeable idea. Scrooge shivered, and wiped the perspiration from his brow.

"That is no light part of my penance," pursued the Ghost. "I am here tonight to warn you that you have yet a chance and hope of escaping my fate. A chance and hope of my procuring, Ebenezer."

"You were always a good friend to me," said Scrooge. "Thankee!"

"You will be haunted," resumed the Ghost, "by Three Spirits."

Scrooge's countenance fell almost as low as the Ghost's had done.

"Is that the chance and hope you mentioned, Jacob?" he demanded in a faltering voice.

"It is."

"I—I think I'd rather not," said Scrooge.

"Without their visits," said the Ghost, "you cannot hope to shun the path I tread. Expect the first tomorrow when the bell tolls one."

"Couldn't I take 'em all at once, and have it over, Jacob?" hinted Scrooge.

"Expect the second on the next night at the same hour. The third, upon the next night when the last stroke of twelve has ceased to vibrate. Look to see me no more; and look that, for your own sake, you remember what has passed between us!"

When it had said these words, the specter took its wrapper from the table, and bound it around its head as before. Scrooge knew this by the smart sound its teeth made when the jaws were brought together by the bandage. He ventured to raise his eyes again, and found his supernatural visitor confronting him in an erect attitude, with its chain wound over and about its arm.

The apparition walked backward from him; and, at every step it took, the window raised itself a little, so that, when the specter reached it, it was wide open. It beckoned Scrooge to approach, which he did. When they were within two paces of each other, Marley's Ghost held up its hand, warning him to come no nearer. Scrooge stopped.

Not so much in obedience as in surprise and fear; for, on the raising of the hand, he became sensible of confused noises in the air; incoherent sounds of lamentation and regret; wailings inexpressibly sorrowful and self-accusatory. The specter, after listening for a moment, joined in the mournful dirge; and floated out upon the bleak, dark night.

Scrooge followed to the window, desperate in his curiosity. He looked out.

The air was filled with phantoms, wandering hither and thither in restless haste, and moaning as they went. Every one of them wore chains like Marley's Ghost; some few (they might be guilty governments) were linked together; none were free. Many had been personally known to Scrooge in their lives. He had been quite familiar with one old ghost in a white waistcoat, with a monstrous iron safe attached to its ankle, who cried piteously at being unable to assist a wretched woman with an infant, whom it saw below upon a doorstep. The misery with them all was clearly, that they sought to interfere, for good, in human matters, and had lost the power forever.

Whether these creatures faded into mist, or mist enshrouded them, he could not tell. But they and their spirit voices faded together; and the night became as it had been when he walked home.

Scrooge closed the window, and examined the door by which the Ghost had entered. It was double-locked, as he had locked it with his own hands, and the bolts were undisturbed. He tried to say "Humbug!" but stopped at the first syllable. And being, from the emotions he had undergone, or the fatigues of the day, or his glimpse of the Invisible World, or the dull conversation of the Ghost, or the lateness of the hour, much in need of repose, went straight to bed without undressing, and fell asleep on the instant.

Where Love Is, God Is

Leo Tolstoy

This is a reworking of an old Christian folk tale. Its charm lies in its simplicity, and it remains a favorite Tolstoy selection despite its moralism.

In a little town in Russia there lived a cobbler, Martin Avedéitch by name. He had a tiny room in a basement, the one window of which looked out on to the street. Through it one could see only the feet of those who passed by, but Martin recognized the people by their boots. He had lived long in the place and had many acquaintances. There was hardly a pair of boots in the neighborhood that had not been once or twice through his hands, so he often saw his own handiwork through the window. Some he had re-soled, some patched, some stitched up, and to some he had even put fresh uppers. He had plenty to do, for he worked well, used good material, did not charge too much, and could be relied on. If he could do a job by the day required, he undertook it; if not, he told the truth and gave no false promises. So he was well known and never short of work.

Martin had always been a good man, but in his old age he began to think more about his soul and to draw nearer to God.

From that time Martin's whole life changed. His life became peaceful and joyful. He sat down to his task in the morning, and when he had finished his day's work he took the lamp down from the wall, stood it on the table, fetched his Bible from the shelf, opened it, and sat down to read. The more he read the better he understood, and the clearer and happier he felt in his mind.

It happened once that Martin sat up late, absorbed in his book. He was reading Luke's Gospel, and in the sixth chapter he came upon the verses:

> To him that smiteth thee on the one cheek offer also the other; and from him that taketh away thy cloak withhold not thy coat also. Give to every man that asketh thee; and of him that taketh away thy goods ask them not again. And as ye would that men should do to you, do ye also to them likewise.

He thought about this, and was about to go to bed, but was loath to leave his book. So he went on reading the seventh chapter—about the centurion, the widow's son, and the answer to John's disciples—and he came to the part where a rich Pharisee invited the Lord to his house. And he read how the woman who was a sinner anointed his feet and washed them with her tears, and how he justified her. Coming to the forty-fourth verse, he read:

> And turning to the woman, he said unto Simon, "Seest thou this woman? I entered into thine house, thou gavest me no water for my feet, but she hath wetted my feet with her tears, and wiped them with her hair. Thou gavest me no kiss, but she, since the time I came in, hath not ceased to kiss my feet. My head with oil thou didst not anoint, but she hath anointed my feet with ointment."

He read these verses and thought: "He gave no water for his feet, gave no kiss, his head with oil he did not anoint. . . ." And Martin took off his spectacles once more, laid them on his book, and pondered.

"He must have been like me, that Pharisee. He too thought only of himself—how to get a cup of tea, how to keep warm and comfortable, never a thought of his guest. He took care of himself,

but for his guest he cared nothing at all. Yet who was the guest? The
Lord himself! If he came to me, should I behave like that?"

Then Martin laid his head upon both his arms and, before he
was aware of it, he fell asleep.

"Martin!" He suddenly heard a voice, as if someone had
breathed the word above his ear.

He started from his sleep. "Who's there?" he asked.

He turned around and looked at the door; no one was there. He
called again. Then he heard quite distinctly: "Martin, Martin! Look
out into the street tomorrow, for I shall come."

Martin roused himself, rose from his chair and rubbed his eyes,
but did not know whether he had heard these words in a dream or
awake. He put out the lamp and lay down to sleep.

The next morning he rose before daylight, and after saying his
prayers he lit the fire and prepared his cabbage soup and buckwheat
porridge. Then he lit the samovar, put on his apron, and sat down
by the window to his work. He looked out into the street more than
he worked, and whenever anyone passed in unfamiliar boots he
would stoop and look up, so as to see not only the feet but the face
of the passerby as well. A house-porter passed in new felt boots,
then a water-carrier. Presently an old soldier of Nicholas's reign
came near the window, spade in hand. Martin knew him by his
boots, which were shabby old felt once, galoshed with leather. The
old man was called Stepánitch. A neighboring tradesman kept him
in his house for charity, and his duty was to help the house-porter.
He began to clear away the snow before Martin's window. Martin
glanced at him and then went on with his work.

After he had made a dozen stitches he felt drawn to look out of
the window again. He saw that Stepánitch had leaned his spade
against the wall, and was either resting himself or trying to get
warm. The man was old and broken down, and had evidently not
enough strength even to clear away the snow.

"What if I called him in and gave him some tea?" thought
Martin. "The samovar is just on the boil."

He stuck his awl in its place, and rose, and putting the samovar
on the table, made tea. Then he tapped the window with his fingers.
Stepánitch turned and came to the window. Martin beckoned to him
to come in, and went himself to open the door.

"Come in," he said, "and warm yourself a bit. I'm sure you
must be cold."

"May God bless you!" Stepánitch answered. "My bones do

ache, to be sure." He came in, first shaking off the snow, and lest he should leave marks on the floor he began wiping his feet. But as he did so he tottered and nearly fell.

"Don't trouble to wipe your feet," said Martin. "I'll wipe up the floor—it's all in the day's work. Come, friend, sit down and have some tea."

Filling two tumblers, he passed one to his visitor, and pouring his own tea out into the saucer, began to blow on it.

Stepánitch emptied his glass and, turning it upside down, put the remains of his piece of sugar on the top. He began to express his thanks, but it was plain that he would be glad of some more.

"Have another glass," said Martin, refilling the visitor's tumbler and his own. But while he drank his tea Martin kept looking out into the street.

"Are you expecting anyone?" asked the visitor.

"Am I expecting anyone? Well, now, I'm ashamed to tell you. It isn't that I really expect anyone, but I heard something last night which I can't get out of my mind. Whether it was a vision, or only a fancy, I can't tell. You see, friend, last night I was reading the Gospel, about Christ the Lord, how he suffered, and how he walked on earth. You have heard tell of it, I dare say."

"I have heard tell of it," answered Stepánitch. "But I'm an ignorant man and not able to read."

"Well, you see, I was reading how he walked on earth. I came to that part, you know, where he went to a Pharisee who did not receive him well. Well, friend, as I read about it, I thought how that man did not receive Christ the Lord with proper honor. Suppose such a thing could happen to such a man as myself, I thought, what would I not do to receive him! But that man gave him no reception at all. Well, friend, as I was thinking of this, I began to doze, and as I dozed I heard someone call me by name. I got up, and thought I heard someone whispering, 'Expect me. I will come tomorrow.' This happened twice over. And to tell you the truth, it sank so into my mind that, though I am ashamed of it myself, I keep on expecting him, the dear Lord!"

Stepánitch shook his head in silence, finished his tumbler, and laid it on its side, but Martin stood it up again and refilled it for him.

"Thank you, Martin Avedéitch," he said. "You have given me food and comfort both for soul and body."

"You're very welcome. Come again another time. I am glad to have a guest," said Martin.

Stepánitch went away, and Martin poured out the last of the tea and drank it up. Then he put away the tea things and sat down to his work, stitching the back seam of a boot. And as he stitched he kept looking out of the window, and thinking about what he had read in the Bible. And his head was full of Christ's sayings.

Two soldiers went by: one in Government boots, the other in boots of his own; then the master of a neighboring house, in shining galoshes; then a baker carrying a basket. All these passed on. Then a woman came up in worsted stockings and peasant-made shoes. She passed the window, but stopped by the wall. Martin glanced up at her through the window, and saw that she was a stranger, poorly dressed, and with a baby in her arms. She stopped by the wall with her back to the wind, trying to wrap the baby up though she had hardly anything to wrap it in. The woman had only summer clothes on, and even they were shabby and worn. Through the window Martin heard the baby crying, and the woman trying to soothe it, but unable to do so. Martin rose, and going out of the door and up the steps he called to her. "My dear, I say, my dear!"

The woman heard, and turned around.

"Why do you stand out there with the baby in the cold? Come inside. You can wrap him up better in a warm place. Come this way!"

The woman was surprised to see an old man in an apron, with spectacles on his nose, calling to her, but she followed him in.

They went down the steps, entered the little room, and the old man led her to the bed.

"There, sit down, my dear, near the stove. Warm yourself, and feed the baby."

"Haven't any milk. I have eaten nothing myself since early morning," said the woman, but still she took the baby to her breast.

Martin shook his head. He brought out a basin and some bread. Then he opened the oven door and poured some cabbage soup into the basin. He took out the porridge pot also, but the porridge was not yet ready, so he spread a cloth on the table and served only the soup and bread.

"Sit down and eat, my dear, and I'll mind the baby. Why, bless me, I've had children of my own; I know how to manage them."

The woman crossed herself, and sitting down at the table began to eat, while Martin put the baby on the bed and sat down by it.

Martin sighed. "Haven't you any warmer clothing?" he asked.

"How could I get warm clothing?" said she. "Why, I pawned my last shawl for sixpence yesterday."

Then the woman came and took the child, and Martin got up.

He went and looked among some things that were hanging on the wall, and brought back an old cloak.

"Here," he said, "though it's a worn-out old thing, it will do to wrap him up in."

The woman looked at the cloak, then at the old man, and taking it, burst into tears. Martin turned away, and groping under the bed brought out a small trunk. He fumbled about in it, and again sat down opposite the woman. And the woman said, "The Lord bless you, friend."

"Take this for Christ's sake," said Martin, and gave her sixpence to get her shawl out of pawn. The woman crossed herself, and Martin did the same, and then he saw her out.

After a while Martin saw an apple-woman stop just in front of his window. On her back she had a sack full of chips, which she was taking home. No doubt she had gathered them at someplace where building was going on.

The sack evidently hurt her, and she wanted to shift it from one shoulder to the other, so she put it down on the footpath and, placing her basket on a post, began to shake down the chips in the sack. While she was doing this, a boy in a tattered cap ran up, snatched an apple out of the basket, and tried to slip away. But the old woman noticed it, and turning, caught the boy by his sleeve. He began to struggle, trying to free himself, but the old woman held on with both hands, knocked his cap off his head, and seized hold of his hair. The boy screamed and the old woman scolded. Martin dropped his awl, not waiting to stick it in its place, and rushed out of the door. Stumbling up the steps and dropping his spectacles in his hurry, he ran out into the street. The old woman was pulling the boy's hair and scolding him, and threatening to take him to the police. The lad was struggling and protesting, saying, "I did not take it. What are you beating me for? Let me go!"

Martin separated them. He took the boy by the hand and said, "Let him go, Granny. Forgive him for Christ's sake."

"I'll pay him out, so that he won't forget it for a year! I'll take the rascal to the police!"

Martin began entreating the old woman.

"Let him go, Granny. He won't do it again."

The old woman let go, and the boy wished to run away, but Martin stopped him.

"Ask the Granny's forgiveness!" said he. "And don't do it another time. I saw you take the apple."

The boy began to cry and to beg pardon.

"That's right. And now here's an apple for you," and Martin took an apple from the basket and gave it to the boy, saying, "I will pay you, Granny."

"You will spoil them that way, the young rascals," said the old woman. "He ought to be whipped so that he should remember it for a week."

"Oh, Granny, Granny," said Martin, "that's our way—but it's not God's way. If he should be whipped for stealing an apple, what should be done to us for our sins?"

The old woman was silent.

And Martin told her the parable of the lord who forgave his servant a large debt, and how the servant went out and seized his debtor by the throat. The old woman listened to it all, and the boy, too, stood by and listened.

"God bids us forgive," said Martin, "or else we shall not be forgiven. Forgive everyone, and a thoughtless youngster most of all."

The old woman wagged her head and sighed.

"It's true enough," said she, "but they are getting terribly spoiled."

"Then we old ones must show them better ways," Martin replied.

"That's just what I say," said the old woman. "I have had seven of them myself, and only one daughter is left." And the old woman began to tell how and where she was living with her daughter, and how many grandchildren she had. "There, now," she said, "I have but little strength left, yet I work hard for the sake of my grandchildren; and nice children they are, too. No one comes out to meet me but the children. Little Annie, now, won't leave me for anyone. It's 'Grandmother, dear grandmother, darling grandmother.' " And the old woman completely softened at the thought.

"Of course, it was only his childishness," said she, referring to the boy.

As the old woman was about to hoist her sack on her back, the lad sprang forward to her, saying, "Let me carry it for you, Granny. I'm going that way."

The old woman nodded her head, and put the sack on the boy's back, and they went down the street together, the old woman quite forgetting to ask Martin to pay for the apple. Martin stood and watched them as they went along talking to each other.

When they were out of sight Martin went back to the house. Having found his spectacles unbroken on the steps, he picked up his awl and sat down again to work. He worked a little, but soon could not see to pass the bristle through the holes in the leather, and presently, he noticed the lamplighter passing on his way to light the street lamps.

"Seems it's time to light up," thought he. So he trimmed his lamp, hung it up, and sat down again to work. He finished off one boot and, turning it about, examined it. It was all right. Then he gathered his tools together, swept up the cuttings, put away the bristles and the thread and the awls, and, taking down the lamp, placed it on the table. Then he took the Gospels from the shelf. He meant to open them at the place he had marked the day before with a bit of morocco, but the book opened at another place. As Martin opened it, his yesterday's dream came back to his mind, and no sooner had he thought of it than he seemed to hear footsteps, as though someone were moving behind him. Martin turned round, and it seemed to him as if people were standing in the dark corner, but he could not make out who they were. And a voice whispered in his ear: "Martin, Martin, don't you know me?"

"Who is it?" muttered Martin.

"It is I," said the voice. And out of the dark corner stepped Stepánitch, who smiled and vanishing like a cloud was seen no more.

"It is I," said the voice again. And out of the darkness stepped the woman with the baby in her arms, and the woman smiled and the baby laughed, and they too vanished.

"It is I," said the voice once more. And the old woman and the boy with the apple stepped out and both smiled, and then they too vanished.

And Martin's soul grew glad. He crossed himself, put on his spectacles, and began reading the Gospel just where it had opened. And at the top of the page he read:

> I was hungry, and ye gave me meat. I was thirsty, and ye gave me drink. I was a stranger, and ye took me in.

And at the bottom of the page he read:

> Inasmuch as ye did it unto one of these my brethren, even these least, ye did it unto me.

And Martin understood that his dream had come true, and that the Savior had really come to him that day, and he had welcomed him.

The Gift of the Magi

O. Henry

William Sydney Porter (1862–1910), better known as O. Henry,
shows us that loving compassion sometimes makes us act fool-
ishly. But what is foolish for the head may be wise for the heart.
O. Henry wrote "The Gift of the Magi" in 1905.

One dollar and eighty-seven cents. That was all. And sixty cents
of it was in pennies. Pennies saved one and two at a time by bulldoz-
ing the grocer and the vegetable man and the butcher until one's
cheeks burned with the silent imputation of parsimony that such
close dealing implied. Three times Della counted it. One dollar and
eighty-seven cents. And the next day would be Christmas.

There was clearly nothing to do but flop down on the shabby
little couch and howl. So Della did it. Which instigates the moral
reflection that life is made up of sobs, sniffles, and smiles, with
sniffles predominating.

While the mistress of the home is gradually subsiding from the
first stage to the second, take a look at the home. A furnished flat at
$8 per week. It did not exactly beggar description, but it certainly
had that word on the lookout for the mendicancy squad.

In the vestibule below was a letter box into which no letter
would go, and an electric button from which no mortal finger could
coax a ring. Also appertaining thereunto was a card bearing the name
"Mr. James Dillingham Young."

The "Dillingham" had been flung to the breeze during a former
period of prosperity when its possessor was being paid $30 per week.
Now, when the income was shrunk to $20, the letters of "Dilling-
ham" looked blurred, as though they were thinking seriously of
contracting to a modest and unassuming D. But whenever Mr.
James Dillingham Young came home and reached his flat above he
was called "Jim" and greatly hugged by Mrs. James Dillingham
Young, already introduced to you as Della. Which is all very good.

Della finished her cry and attended to her cheeks with the powder rag. She stood by the window and looked out dully at a gray
cat walking a gray fence in a gray backyard. Tomorrow would be
Christmas Day and she had only $1.87 with which to buy Jim a

present. She had been saving every penny she could for months, with this result. Twenty dollars a week doesn't go far. Expenses had been greater than she had calculated. They always are. Only $1.87 to buy a present for Jim. Her Jim. Many a happy hour she had spent planning for something nice for him. Something fine and rare and sterling—something just a little bit near to being worthy of the honor of being owned by Jim.

There was a pier glass between the windows of the room. Perhaps you have seen a pier glass in an $8 flat. A very thin and very agile person may, by observing his reflection in a rapid sequence of longitudinal strips, obtain a fairly accurate conception of his looks. Della, being slender, had mastered the art.

Suddenly she whirled from the window and stood before the glass. Her eyes were shining brilliantly, but her face had lost its color within twenty seconds. Rapidly she pulled down her hair and let it fall to its full length.

Now, there were two possessions of the James Dillingham Youngs in which they both took a mighty pride. One was Jim's gold watch that had been his father's and his grandfather's. The other was Della's hair. Had the Queen of Sheba lived in the flat across the airshaft, Della would have let her hair hang out the window someday to dry just to depreciate Her Majesty's jewels and gifts. Had King Solomon been the janitor, with all his treasures piled up in the basement, Jim would have pulled out his watch every time he passed, just to see him pluck at his beard from envy.

So now Della's beautiful hair fell about her, rippling and shining like a cascade of brown waters. It reached below her knee and made itself almost a garment for her. And then she did it up again nervously and quickly. Once she faltered for a minute and stood still while a tear or two splashed on the worn red carpet.

On went her old brown jacket; on went her old brown hat. With a whirl of skirts and with the brilliant sparkle still in her eyes, she fluttered out the door and down the stairs to the street.

Where she stopped the sign read: "Mme. Sofronie. Hair Goods of All Kinds." One flight up Della ran, and collected herself, panting. Madame, large, too white, chilly, hardly looked the "Sofronie."

"Will you buy my hair?" asked Della.

"I buy hair," said Madame. "Take yer hat off and let's have a sight at the looks of it."

Down rippled the brown cascade.

"Twenty dollars," said Madame, lifting the mass with a practiced hand.

"Give it to me quick," said Della.

Oh, and the next two hours tripped by on rosy wings. Forget the hashed metaphor. She was ransacking the stores for Jim's present.

She found it at last. It surely had been made for Jim and no one else. There was no other like it in any of the stores, and she had turned all of them inside out. It was a platinum fob chain simple and chaste in design, properly proclaiming its value by substance alone and not by meretricious ornamentation—as all good things should do. It was even worthy of The Watch. As soon as she saw it she knew that it must be Jim's. It was like him. Quietness and value—the description applied to both. Twenty-one dollars they took from her for it, and she hurried home with the 87 cents. With that chain on his watch Jim might be properly anxious about the time in any company. Grand as the watch was, he sometimes looked at it on the sly on account of the old leather strap that he used in place of a chain.

When Della reached home her intoxication gave way a little to prudence and reason. She got out her curling irons and lighted the gas and went to work repairing the ravages made by generosity added to love. Which is always a tremendous task, dear friends—a mammoth task.

Within forty minutes her head was covered with tiny, close-lying curls that made her look wonderfully like a truant schoolboy. She looked at her reflection in the mirror long, carefully, and critically.

"If Jim doesn't kill me," she said to herself, "before he takes a second look at me, he'll say I look like a Coney Island chorus girl. But what could I do—oh! what could I do with a dollar and eighty-seven cents?"

At 7 o'clock the coffee was made and the frying pan was on the back of the stove hot and ready to cook the chops.

Jim was never late. Della doubled the fob chain in her hand and sat on the corner of the table near the door that he always entered. Then she heard his step on the stair away down on the first flight, and she turned white for just a moment. She had a habit of saying little silent prayers about the simplest everyday things, and now she whispered: "Please God, make him think I am still pretty."

The door opened and Jim stepped in and closed it. He looked thin and very serious. Poor fellow, he was only twenty-two—and to be burdened with a family! He needed a new overcoat and he was without gloves.

Jim stepped inside the door, as immovable as a setter at the scent of quail. His eyes were fixed upon Della, and there was an expression in them that she could not read, and it terrified her. It was not anger, nor surprise, nor disapproval, nor horror, nor any of the sentiments that she had been prepared for. He simply stared at her fixedly with that peculiar expression on his face.

Della wriggled off the table and went for him.

"Jim, darling," she cried, "don't look at me that way. I had my hair cut off and sold it because I couldn't have lived through Christmas without giving you a present. It'll grow out again—you won't mind, will you? I just had to do it. My hair grows awfully fast. Say 'Merry Christmas!' Jim, and let's be happy. You don't know what a nice—what a beautiful, nice gift I've got for you."

"You've cut off your hair?" asked Jim, laboriously, as if he had not arrived at that patent fact yet even after the hardest mental labor.

"Cut it off and sold it," said Della. "Don't you like me just as well, anyhow? I'm me without my hair, ain't I?"

Jim looked about the room curiously.

"You say your hair is gone?" he said, with an air almost of idiocy.

"You needn't look for it," said Della. "It's sold, I tell you— sold and gone, too. It's Christmas Eve, boy. Be good to me, for it went for you. Maybe the hairs on my head were numbered," she went on with a sudden serious sweetness, "but nobody could ever count my love for you. Shall I put the chops on, Jim?"

Out of his trance Jim seemed quickly to wake. He enfolded his Della. For ten seconds let us regard with discreet scrutiny some inconsequential object in the other direction. Eight dollars a week or a million a year—what is the difference? A mathematician or a wit would give you the wrong answer. The magi brought valuable gifts, but that was not among them. This dark assertion will be illuminated later on.

Jim drew a package from his overcoat pocket and threw it upon the table.

"Don't make any mistake, Dell," he said, "about me. I don't think there's anything in the way of a haircut or a shave or a shampoo that could make me like my girl any less. But if you'll unwrap that package you may see why you had me going a while at first."

White fingers and nimble tore at the string and paper. And then an ecstatic scream of joy; and then, alas! a quick feminine change to hysterical tears and wails, necessitating the immediate employment of all the comforting powers of the lord of the flat.

For there lay The Combs—the set of combs, side and back, that Della had worshipped for long in a Broadway window. Beautiful combs, pure tortoiseshell, with jeweled rims—just the shade to wear in the beautiful vanished hair. They were expensive combs, she knew, and her heart had simply craved and yearned over them without the least hope of possession. And now, they were hers, but the tresses that should have adorned the coveted adornments were gone.

But she hugged them to her bosom, and at length she was able to look up with dim eyes and a smile and say: "My hair grows so fast, Jim!"

And then Della leaped up like a little singed cat and cried, "Oh, oh!"

Jim had not yet seen his beautiful present. She held it out to him eagerly upon her open palm. The dull precious metal seemed to flash with a reflection of her bright and ardent spirit.

"Isn't it a dandy, Jim? I hunted all over town to find it. You'll have to look at the time a hundred times a day now. Give me your watch. I want to see how it looks on it."

Instead of obeying, Jim tumbled down on the couch and put his hands under the back of his head and smiled.

"Dell," said he, "let's put our Christmas presents away and keep 'em a while. They're too nice to use just at present. I sold the watch to get the money to buy your combs. And now suppose you put the chops on."

The magi, as you know, were wise men—wonderfully wise men—who brought gifts to the Babe in the manger. They invented the art of giving Christmas presents. Being wise, their gifts were no doubt wise ones, possibly bearing the privilege of exchange in case of duplication. And here I have lamely related to you the uneventful chronicle of two foolish children in a flat who most unwisely sacrificed for each other the greatest treasures of their house. But in a last word to the wise of these days let it be said that of all who give gifts these two were the wisest. Of all who give and receive gifts, such as they are wisest. Everywhere they are wisest. They are the magi.

Count That Day Lost

George Eliot

We can look back on each day as being either lost or spent. Mary Ann Evans, better known as George Eliot (1819–1880), shows us how to tell the difference, and what is worth a day's expense.

If you sit down at set of sun
And count the acts that you have done,
    And, counting, find
One self-denying deed, one word
That eased the heart of him who heard,
    One glance most kind
That fell like sunshine where it went—
Then you may count that day well spent.

But if, through all the livelong day,
You've cheered no heart, by yea or nay—
    If, through it all
You've nothing done that you can trace
That brought the sunshine to one face—
    No act most small
That helped some soul and nothing cost—
Then count that day as worse than lost.

Aristotle on Pity

From the Rhetoric

Aristotle argues that pity is a kind of pain felt from a realization that a similar misfortune might at any time affect us or our loved ones. The definition may seem distastefully self-centered, but one should bear in mind that in the *Rhetoric,* Aristotle is teaching the reader, in part, how to play on an audience's emotions. His underlying observation is still worth our attention: Pity arises from some fundamental recognition that suffering is an unavoidable part of every human existence.

Pity may be defined as a pain for apparent evil, destructive or painful, befalling a person who does not deserve it, when we might expect such evil to befall ourselves or some of our friends and when, moreover, it seems near. Plainly, the man who is to pity must be such as to think himself or his friends liable to suffer some ill, and ill of such a sort as has been defined, or of a like or comparable sort. Hence pity is not felt by the utterly lost, for they think that they cannot suffer anything further; they *have* suffered; nor by those who think themselves supremely prosperous, rather they are insolent; for, if they think that they have all goods, of course they think that they have exemption from suffering ill, this being a good. The belief that they may possibly suffer is likely to be felt by those who have already suffered and escaped, by elderly persons, on account of their good sense and experience, by the weak and especially by the rather timid, by the educated, for they are reasonable. By those, too, who have parents, children, or wives; for these are their own, and are liable to the sufferings above-named. And by those who are not possessed by a courageous feeling, such as anger or boldness, for these feelings take no account of the future, and by those who are not in an insolent state of mind, as such are reckless of prospective suffering: pity is felt by those who are in the intermediate states. And by those, again, who are not in great fear, for the panic-stricken do not pity, because they are busied with their own feeling. Men pity, too, if they think that there are some people who may be reckoned good; for he who thinks no one good will think all worthy of evil. And, generally, a man pities when he is in a position to remember that like things have befallen himself or his friends, or to expect that they may. . . .

Again, men pity when the danger is near themselves. And they pity those like them in age, in character, in moral state, in rank, in birth; for all these examples make it more probable that the case may become their own; since here, again, we must take it as a general maxim that all things which we fear for ourselves, we pity when they happen to others.

The Ride of Collins Graves

John Boyle O'Reilly

Here is heroic compassion. On May 16, 1874, the Mill River dam
in Hampshire County, Massachusetts, gave way, flooding some
124 acres to an average depth of twenty-four feet. Nearly 200
people from the villages of Williamsburg, Skinnerville, Hay-
denville, and Leeds perished in the disaster. This old New England ballad tells the story of Collins Graves, who rode through
the towns to warn residents of the coming danger.

No song of a soldier riding down
To the raging fight of Winchester town;
No song of a time that shook the earth
With the nation's throe at a nation's birth;
But the song of a brave man free from fear
As Sheridan's self or Paul Revere;
Who risked what they risked—free from strife
And its promise of glorious pay—his life.

The peaceful valley has waked and stirred,
And the answering echoes of life are heard;
The dew still clings to the trees and grass,
And the early toilers smiling pass,
As they glance aside at the white-walled homes,
Or up the valley where merrily comes
The brook that sparkles in diamond rills
As the sun comes over the Hampshire hills.

What was it passed like an ominous breath?
Like a shiver of fear, or a touch of death?
What was it? The valley is peaceful still,
And the leaves are afire on the top of the hill;
It was not a sound, nor a thing of sense,
But a pain, like a pang in the short suspense
That wraps the being of those who see
At their feet the gulf of eternity.

The air of the valley has felt the chill;
The workers pause at the door of the mill;
The housewife, keen to the shivering air,
Arrests her foot on the cottage stair,
Instinctive taught by the mother-love,
And thinks of the sleeping ones above.

Why start the listeners? Why does the course
of the mill-stream widen? It is a horse—
"Hark to the sound of the hoofs!" they say—
That gallops so wildly Williamsburg way?
God! what was that like a human shriek
From the winding valley? Will nobody speak?
Will nobody answer those women who cry
As the awful warnings thunder by?

Whence come they? Listen! and now they hear
The sound of the galloping horse-hoofs near;
They watch the trend of the vale, and see
The rider who thunders so menacingly,
With waving arms and warning scream
To the home-filled banks of the valley stream
He draws no rein, but he shakes the street
With a shout and the ring of the galloping feet,
And this the cry that he flings to the wind,
"To the hills for your lives! The flood is behind!"
He cries and is gone, but they know the worst—
The treacherous Williamsburg dam has burst!
The basin that nourished their happy homes
Is changed to a demon. It comes! it comes!
A monster in aspect, with shaggy front
Of shattered dwellings to take the brunt
Of the dwellings they shatter; white-maned and hoarse
The merciless terror fills the course
Of the narrow valley, and rushing raves
With death on the first of its hissing waves,
Till cottage and street and crowded mill
Are crumbled and crushed. But onward still,
In front of the roaring flood, is heard
The galloping horse and the warning word.

Thank God that the brave man's life is spared!
From Williamsburg town he nobly dared
To race with the flood, and to take the road
In front of the terrible swath it mowed.
For miles it thundered and crashed behind,
But he looked ahead with a steadfast mind:
"They must be warned!" was all he said,
As away on his terrible ride he sped.

When heroes are called for, bring the crown
To this Yankee rider; send him down
On the stream of time with the Curtius old;
His deed, as the Roman's, was brave and bold;
And the tale can as noble a thrill awake,
For he offered his life for the people's sake!

Vigil Strange I Kept on the Field One Night

Walt Whitman

True compassion runs deeper than the kind of grief in which we know only our own pain from another's death. True compassion seeks to understand, or at least recognize, the tragedy dealt to a life suddenly lost.

Walt Whitman (1819–1892) traveled to the Virginia battlefront in 1862 to tend to his wounded brother. Afterwards, he worked in Washington, D.C., as a volunteer nurse in army hospitals. From those experiences came *Drum-Taps,* a collection of poems about the Civil War.

Vigil strange I kept on the field one night;
When you my son and my comrade dropt at my side that day,
One look I but gave which your dear eyes return'd with a look I
shall never forget.
One touch of your hand to mine O boy, reach'd up as you lay on
the ground,

Then onward I sped in the battle, the even-contested battle,
Till late in the night reliev'd to the place at last again I made my
    way,
Found you in death so cold dear comrade, found your body son of
    responding kisses, (never again on earth responding,)
Bared your face in the starlight, curious the scene, cool blew the
    moderate night-wind,
Long there and then in vigil I stood, dimly around me the battlefield
    spreading,
Vigil wondrous and vigil sweet there in the fragrant silent night,
But not a tear fell, not even a long-drawn sigh, long, long I gazed,
Then on the earth partially reclining sat by your side leaning my
    chin in my hands,
Passing sweet hours, immortal and mystic hours with you dearest
    comrade—not a tear, not a word.
Vigil of silence, love and death, vigil for you my son and my soldier,
As onward silently stars aloft, eastward new ones upward stole,
Vigil final for you brave boy, (I could not save you, swift was your
    death,
I faithfully loved you and cared for you living, I think we shall surely
    meet again,)
Till at latest lingering of the night, indeed just as the dawn appear'd,
My comrade I wrapt in his blanket, envelop'd well his form,
Folded the blanket well, tucking it carefully over head and carefully
    under feet,
And there and then and bathed by the rising sun, my son in his
    grave, in his rude-dug grave I deposited,
Ending my vigil strange with that, vigil of night and battlefield dim,
Vigil for comrade swiftly slain, vigil I never forget, how as day
    brighten'd,
I rose from the chill ground and folded my soldier well in his
    blanket,
and buried him where he fell.

Abraham Lincoln
Offers Consolation

Abraham Lincoln

President Lincoln wrote this letter after an aide told him about a Boston widow whose five sons had been killed fighting for the Union armies. As Carl Sandburg wrote, "More darkly than the Gettysburg speech the letter wove its awful implication that human freedom so often was paid for with agony." Here is an American president understanding that agony, sharing it, and performing a heartfelt rite, as Sandburg put it, "as though he might be a ship captain at midnight by lantern light, dropping black roses into the immemorial sea for mystic remembrance and consecration."

Executive Mansion
Washington, Nov. 21, 1864

To Mrs. Bixby, Boston, Mass.
Dear Madam,
    I have been shown in the files of the War Department a statement of the Adjutant General of Massachusetts that you are the mother of five sons who have died gloriously on the field of battle. I feel how weak and fruitless must be any word of mine which should attempt to beguile you from the grief of a loss so overwhelming. But I cannot refrain from tendering you the consolation that may be found in the thanks of the republic they died to save. I pray that our Heavenly Father may assuage the anguish of your bereavement, and leave you only the cherished memory of the loved and lost, and the solemn pride that must be yours to have laid so costly a sacrifice upon the altar of freedom.

Yours very sincerely and respectfully,
A. Lincoln

As a historical footnote, we now know that Lincoln had in fact been misinformed: two of Mrs. Bixby's sons had been killed in action, one was taken prisoner, and two deserted. The error does not stand in the way of the letter's deserved fame. Mrs. Bixby's loss and sacrifice hardly could have been greater.

O Captain! My Captain!

Walt Whitman

Here Walt Whitman mourns for the fallen Abraham Lincoln. To
the poet, the assassination was a terrible blow to the American
democratic comradeship he celebrated in so much of his verse.

O Captain! my Captain! our fearful trip is done;
The ship has weather'd every rack, the prize we sought is won;
The port is near, the bells I hear, the people all exulting,
While follow eyes the steady keel, the vessel grim and daring:
    But O heart! heart! heart!
      O the bleeding drops of red,
        Where on the deck my Captain lies,
        Fallen cold and dead.

O Captain! my Captain! rise up and hear the bells;
Rise up—for you the flag is flung—for you the bugle trills;
For you bouquets and ribbon'd wreaths—for you the shores
    a-crowding;
For you they call, the swaying mass, their eager faces turning:
    Here Captain! dear father!
      This arm beneath your head!
      It is some dream that on the deck,
      You've fallen cold and dead.

My Captain does not answer, his lips are pale and still;
My father does not feel my arm, he has no pulse nor will;
The ship is anchor'd safe and sound, its voyage closed and done;
From fearful trip, the victor ship comes in with object won:
    Exult, O shores, and ring, O bells!
      But I, with mournful tread,
        Walk the deck my Captain lies,
        Fallen cold and dead.

The New Colossus

Emma Lazarus

Emma Lazarus (1849–1887) wrote "The New Colossus" in 1883 as part of a project by artists and writers to raise funds to build the pedestal of the Statue of Liberty, a gift from France to the United States. The poem's title refers to the Colossus of Rhodes, one of the seven wonders of the ancient world, a giant bronze statue of the sun god Helios that had overlooked the Greek city's harbor. Lazarus's poem, like the Statue of Liberty, came to popularize America's mission as a refuge for immigrants. Here is compassion as a national policy, one of America's great national policies.

Not like the brazen giant of Greek fame,
With conquering limbs astride from land to land;
Here at our sea-washed, sunset gates shall stand
A mighty woman with a torch, whose flame
Is the imprisoned lightning, and her name
Mother of Exiles. From her beacon-hand
Glows world-wide welcome; her mild eyes command
The air-bridged harbor that twin cities frame.

"Keep, ancient lands, your storied pomp!" cries she
With silent lips. "Give me your tired, your poor,
Your huddled masses yearning to breathe free,
The wretched refuse of your teeming shore.
Send these, the homeless, tempest-tost to me.
I lift my lamp beside the golden door!"

The Influence of Democracy

Alexis de Tocqueville

In 1831, the French government sent twenty-six-year-old Alexis
de Tocqueville (1805–1859) to the United States to study its penal
system. The result was *Democracy in America,* a voluminous masterpiece in which Tocqueville assessed the promises and pitfalls
of democracy. In this excerpt, he examines equality's effects on
compassion. The accuracy of Tocqueville's observations are, of
course, open to debate. Nevertheless, we are forced to ask ourselves: how does modern America measure up to the portrait he
painted more than a century and a half ago?

We perceive that for several ages social conditions have tended
to equality, and we discover that in the course of the same period
the manners of society have been softened. Are these two things
merely contemporaneous, or does any secret link exist between
them, so that the one cannot go on without making the other advance? Several causes may concur to render the manners of a people
less rude; but, of all these causes, the most powerful appears to me
to be the equality of conditions. Equality of conditions and growing
civility in manners are then, in my eyes, not only contemporaneous
occurrences, but correlative facts. . . .

When all the ranks of a community are nearly equal, as all men
think and feel in nearly the same manner, each of them may judge in
a moment of the sensations of all the others: he casts a rapid glance
upon himself, and that is enough. There is no wretchedness into
which he cannot readily enter, and a secret instinct reveals to him its
extent. It signifies not that strangers or foes be the sufferers; imagination puts him in their place: something like a personal feeling is
mingled with his pity, and makes himself suffer while the body of
his fellow creature is in torture.

In democratic ages men rarely sacrifice themselves for one another; but they display general compassion for the members of the
human race. They inflict no useless ills; and they are happy to relieve
the griefs of others, when they can do so without much hurting
themselves; they are not disinterested, but they are humane.

Although the Americans have in a manner reduced egotism to a social and philosophical theory, they are nevertheless extremely open to compassion. . . .

When men feel a natural compassion for their mutual sufferings —when they are brought together by easy and frequent intercourse, and no sensitive feelings keep them asunder, it may readily be supposed that they will lend assistance to one another whenever it is needed. When an American asks for the cooperation of his fellow citizens it is seldom refused, and I have often seen it afforded spontaneously and with great good will. If an accident happens on the highway, everybody hastens to help the sufferer; if some great and sudden calamity befalls a family, the purses of a thousand strangers are at once willingly opened, and small but numerous donations pour in to relieve their distress.

It often happens among the most civilized nations of the globe, that a poor wretch is as friendless in the midst of a crowd as the savage in his wilds: this is hardly ever the case in the United States. The Americans, who are always cold and often coarse in their manners, seldom show insensibility; and if they do not proffer services eagerly, yet they do not refuse to render them.

All this is not in contradiction to what I have said before on the subject of individualism. The two things are so far from combating each other, that I can see how they agree. Equality of conditions, while it makes men feel their independence, shows them their own weakness: they are free, but exposed to a thousand accidents; and experience soon teaches them, that although they do not habitually require the assistance of others, a time almost always comes when they cannot do without it.

We constantly see in Europe that men of the same profession are ever ready to assist each other; they are all exposed to the same ills, and that is enough to teach them to seek mutual preservatives, however hard-hearted and selfish they may otherwise be. When one of them falls into danger, from which the others may save him by a slight transient sacrifice or a sudden effort, they do not fail to make the attempt. Not that they are deeply interested in his fate; for if, by chance, their exertions are unavailing, they immediately forget the object of them, and return to their own business; but a sort of tacit and almost involuntary agreement has been passed between them, by which each one owes to the others a temporary support which he may claim for himself in turn.

Extend to a people the remark here applied to a class, and you

will understand my meaning. A similar covenant exists in fact between all the citizens of a democracy: they all feel themselves subject
to the same weakness and the same dangers; and their interest, as
well as their sympathy, makes it a rule with them to lend each other
mutual assistance when required. The more equal social conditions
become, the more do men display this reciprocal disposition to
oblige each other. In democracies no great benefits are conferred,
but good offices are constantly rendered: a man seldom displays self-
devotion, but all men are ready to be of service to one another.

The Choir Invisible

George Eliot

George Eliot once asked, "What do we live for, if it is not to
make life less difficult to each other?" Here she asks for the same
power even after life has ended. The compassion we show now
will surely inspire others after we are gone.

O, may I join the choir invisible
Of those immortal dead who live again
In minds made better by their presence; live
In pulses stirred to generosity,
In deeds of daring rectitude, in scorn
Of miserable aims that end with self,
In thoughts sublime that pierce the night like stars,
And with their mild persistence urge men's minds
To vaster issues. . . .
                              May I reach
That purest heaven—be to other souls
The cup of strength in some great agony,
Enkindle generous ardor, feed pure love,
Beget the smiles that have no cruelty,
Be the sweet presence of good diffused,
And in diffusion ever more intense!
So shall I join the choir invisible,
Whose music is the gladness of the world.

Responsibility

To "respond" is to "answer." Correspondingly, to be "responsible" is to be "answerable," to be *accountable*. Irresponsible behavior is immature behavior. Taking responsibility—being responsible—is a sign of maturity. When we strive to help our children become responsible persons we are helping them toward maturity. James Madison delimited the parameters of responsibility with characteristic clarity in *Federalist* No. 63. "Responsibility, in order to be reasonable, must be limited to objects within the power of the responsible party, and in order to be effectual, must relate to operations of that power." Persons who have not reached maturity have not yet come into full ownership of their powers.

It is a truism that everything which has ever been *done* in the history of the world has been done *by somebody;* some person has exercised some power to *do* it. Our share of the responsibility for what we do individually or in concert with others varies with the social and political structures within which we operate, but it characteristically increases with maturity. It was an immature Adam in the Garden of Eden who, when discovered to have eaten of the forbidden fruit, laid the responsibility on Eve. And it was an immature Eve who in turn laid it on the beguiling serpent. "She made me do it"/"He made me do it" is an archetypal drama reenacted in every generation where siblings and playmates are called upon to answer for their misdoings.

But it doesn't stop there. An unwitting acknowledgment of this sort of immaturity commonly continues on into adulthood. Nearly everyone has an excuse when things go wrong. In Washington, D.C., common parlance makes ample use of the passive voice to avoid blame: "mistakes were made." But there is no rush to take responsibility. There is no shortage of persons ready to claim credit for contributing to an enterprise that goes well, however, even though a maxim familiar to persons in public service observes that "There is no end to the good you can do if you don't care who gets credit for it."

In the end, we are answerable for the kinds of persons we have made of ourselves. "That's just the way I am!" is not an excuse for inconsiderate or vile behavior. Nor is it even an accurate description, for we are never *just* what we are. As Aristotle was among the first to insist, we *become* what we are as persons by the decisions that we ourselves make. British philosopher Mary Midgley points out in *Beast and Man* that "the really excellent and central point of Existentialism [is] the acceptance of responsibility for being as we have made ourselves, the refusal to make bogus excuses."

Søren Kierkegaard, one of Existentialism's nineteenth-century pioneers, deplored the damaging effects of crowds and gangs on our *sense* of responsibility. "A crowd," as he wrote in *The Point of View for My Work as an Author,* "in its very concept is the untruth, by reason of the fact that it renders the individual completely impenitent and irresponsible, or at least weakens his sense of responsibility by reducing it to a fraction." In his *Confessions* St. Augustine made this weakened sense of responsibility under peer pressure a central feature of his meditation upon the vandalism of his youth, "all because we are ashamed to hold back when others say 'Come on! Let's do it!' " But he was as insistent as Aristotle and the Existentialists on recognizing personal responsibility for what he had done. A weakened *sense* of responsibility does not weaken the *fact* of responsibility.

Responsible persons are mature people who have taken charge of themselves and their conduct, who *own* their actions and *own up* to them—who *answer* for them. We help foster a mature sense of responsibility in our children in the same way that we help cultivate their other desirable traits: by practice and by example. Household chores, homework, extracurricular activities, after-school jobs, and volunteer work all contribute to maturation if parental example and expectations are clear, consistent, and commensurate with the developing powers of the child.

Over in the Meadow

Olive A. Wadsworth

This poem shows us parents' first responsibility: the nurture of
the young.

Over in the meadow,
  In the sand, in the sun,
Lived an old mother toad
  And her little toadie one.
"Wink," said the mother;
  "I wink," said the one;
So she winked and she blinked
  In the sand, in the sun.

Over in the meadow,
  Where the stream runs blue,
Lived an old mother fish
  And her little fishes two.
"Swim," said the mother;
  "We swim," said the two;
So they swam and they leaped
  Where the stream runs blue.

Over in the meadow,
  In a hole in a tree,
Lived an old mother bluebird
  And her little birdies three.
"Sing," said the mother;
  "We sing," said the three;
So they sang and were glad,
  In the hole in the tree.

Over in the meadow,
  In the reeds on the shore,
Lived a mother muskrat
  And her little ratties four.
"Dive," said the mother;
  "We dive," said the four;
So they dived and they burrowed
  In the reeds on the shore.

The Three Little Kittens

Eliza Lee Follen

Children should learn early the practical lesson that responsibility
leads to reward, which leads to further responsibility. We must
keep track of our mittens if we expect pie, and then we must
wash them if we expect ever to have any more dessert.

Three little kittens lost their mittens;
  And they began to cry,
    "Oh, mother dear,
    We very much fear
  That we have lost our mittens."
    "Lost your mittens!
    You naughty kittens!
  Then you shall have no pie!"
      "Mee-ow, mee-ow, mee-ow."
  "No, you shall have no pie."
      "Mee-ow, mee-ow, mee-ow."

The three little kittens found their mittens;
   And they began to cry,
     "Oh, mother dear,
     See here, see here!
   See, we have found our mittens!"
     "Put on your mittens,
     You silly kittens,
   And you may have some pie."
       "Purr-r, purr-r, purr-r,
   Oh, let us have the pie!
       Purr-r, purr-r, purr-r."

The three little kittens put on their mittens,
   And soon ate up the pie;
     "Oh, mother dear,
     We greatly fear
   That we have soiled our mittens!"
     "Soiled your mittens!
     You naughty kittens!"
   Then they began to sigh,
       "Mee-ow, mee-ow, mee-ow."
   Then they began to sigh,
       "Mee-ow, mee-ow, mee-ow."

The three little kittens washed their mittens,
   And hung them out to dry;
     "Oh, mother dear,
     Do not you hear
   That we have washed our mittens?"
     "Washed your mittens!
     Oh, you're good kittens!
   But I smell a rat close by,
       Hush, hush! Mee-ow, mee-ow."
   "We smell a rat close by,
       Mee-ow, mee-ow, mee-ow."

Little Orphan Annie

James Whitcomb Riley

In which we learn what may happen to little girls and boys who don't do what they are supposed to do. With apologies to James Whitcomb Riley, I've taken the liberty of amending the poem's original spelling and grammar to make it easier on the modern ear.

Little Orphan Annie's come to our house to stay,
And wash the cups and saucers up, and brush the crumbs away,
And shoo the chickens off the porch, and dust the hearth, and sweep,
And make the fire, and bake the bread, and earn her board and keep;
And all us other children, when the supper things are done,
We sit around the kitchen fire and have the mostest fun
A-listenin' to the witch tales that Annie tells about,
And the Gobble-ins that get you
   If you
    Don't
     Watch
     Out!

Once there was a little boy who wouldn't say his prayers,
And when he went to bed at night, away upstairs,
His mommy heard him holler, and his daddy heard him bawl,
And when they turned the covers down, he wasn't there at all!
And they sought him in the rafter room, and cubbyhole, and press,
And sought him up the chimney flue, and everywhere, I guess;
But all they ever found was just his pants and roundabout!
And the Gobble-ins will get you
   If you
    Don't
     Watch
     Out!

Another time a little girl would always laugh and grin,
And make fun of everyone, and all her blood and kin,
And once when there was company, and old folks was there,
She mocked them and she shocked them and she said she didn't care!
But as she kicked her heels, and turned to run and hide,
There were two great big Black Things a-standin' by her side,
And they snatched her through the ceiling 'fore she could turn about!
And the Gobble-ins will get you
       If you
        Don't
         Watch
          Out!

And little Orphan Annie says, when the blaze is blue,
And the lamp wick sputters, and the wind goes woo-oo!
And you hear the crickets quit, and the moon is gray,
And the lightning bugs in dew are all squenched away—
You better mind your parents, and your teachers fond and dear,
And cherish those who love you, and dry the orphan's tear,
And help the poor and needy ones who cluster all about,
Or the Gobble-ins will get you
       If you
        Don't
         Watch
          Out!

Rebecca

Eleanor Piatt

Play is the work of children and entirely suitable as an arena in
which to develop habits of responsibility.

I have a doll, Rebecca,
   She's quite a little care,
I have to press her ribbons
   And comb her fluffy hair.

I keep her clothes all mended,
　　And wash her hands and face,
And make her frocks and aprons,
　　All trimmed in frills and lace.

I have to cook her breakfast,
　　And pet her when she's ill;
And telephone the doctor
　　When Rebecca has a chill.

Rebecca doesn't like that,
　　And says she's well and strong;
And says she'll try—oh! very hard,
　　To be good all day long.

But when night comes, she's nodding;
　　So into bed we creep
And snuggle up together,
　　And soon are fast asleep.

I have no other dolly,
　　For you can plainly see,
In caring for Rebecca,
　　I'm busy as can be!

St. George and the Dragon

Retold by J. Berg Esenwein and Marietta Stockard

"Somewhere perhaps there is trouble and fear," St. George says in this story before riding off to "find work which only a knight can do." Here we see the course of a morally ambitious conscience, habitually searching to aid others. Such people who go out of their way to help are sometimes called knights, saints, and philanthropists; sometimes they are called ministers, teachers, coaches, policemen, and parents.

Long ago, when the knights lived in the land, there was one knight whose name was Sir George. He was not only braver than all the rest, but he was so noble, kind, and good that the people came to call him Saint George.

No robbers ever dared to trouble the people who lived near his castle, and all the wild animals were killed or driven away, so the little children could play even in the woods without being afraid.

One day St. George rode throughout the country. Everywhere he saw the men busy at their work in the fields, the women singing at work in their homes, and the little children shouting at their play.

"These people are all safe and happy. They need me no more," said St. George.

"But somewhere perhaps there is trouble and fear. There may be someplace where little children cannot play in safety, some woman may have been carried away from her home—perhaps there are even dragons left to be slain. Tomorrow I shall ride away and never stop until I find work which only a knight can do."

Early the next morning St. George put on his helmet and all his shining armor, and fastened his sword at his side. Then he mounted his great white horse and rode out from his castle gate. Down the steep, rough road he went, sitting straight and tall, and looking brave and strong as a knight should look.

On through the little village at the foot of the hill and out across the country he rode. Everywhere he saw rich fields filled with waving grain, everywhere there was peace and plenty.

He rode on and on until at last he came into a part of the country he had never seen before. He noticed that there were no men working in the fields. The houses which he passed stood silent and empty. The grass along the roadside was scorched as if a fire had passed over it. A field of wheat was all trampled and burned.

St. George drew up his horse, and looked carefully about him. Everywhere there was silence and desolation. "What can be the dreadful thing which has driven all the people from their homes? I must find out, and give them help if I can," he said.

But there was no one to ask, so St. George rode forward until at last far in the distance he saw the walls of a city. "Here surely I shall find someone who can tell me the cause of all this," he said, so he rode more swiftly toward the city.

Just then the great gate opened and St. George saw crowds of people standing inside the wall. Some of them were weeping, all of them seemed afraid. As St. George watched, he saw a beautiful maiden dressed in white, with a girdle of scarlet about her waist, pass through the gate alone. The gate clanged shut and the maiden walked along the road, weeping bitterly. She did not see St. George, who was riding quickly toward her.

"Maiden, why do you weep?" he asked as he reached her side.

She looked up at St. George sitting there on his horse, so straight and tall and beautiful. "Oh, Sir Knight!" she cried, "ride quickly from this place. You know not the danger you are in!"

"Danger!" said St. George. "Do you think a knight would flee from danger? Besides, you, a fair girl, are here alone. Think you a knight would leave you so? Tell me your trouble that I may help you."

"No! No!" she cried, "hasten away. You would only lose your life. There is a terrible dragon near. He may come at any moment. One breath would destroy you if he found you here. Go! Go quickly!"

"Tell me more of this," said St. George sternly. "Why are you here alone to meet this dragon? Are there no *men* left in yon city?"

"Oh," said the maiden, "my father, the King, is old and feeble. He has only me to help him take care of his people. This terrible dragon has driven them from their homes, carried away their cattle, and ruined their crops. They have all come within the walls of the city for safety. For weeks now the dragon has come to the very gates of the city. We have been forced to give him two sheep each day for his breakfast.

"Yesterday there were no sheep left to give, so he said that unless a young maiden were given him today he would break down the walls and destroy the city. The people cried to my father to save them, but he could do nothing. I am going to give myself to the dragon. Perhaps if he has me, the Princess, he may spare our people."

"Lead the way, brave Princess. Show me where this monster may be found."

When the Princess saw St. George's flashing eyes and great, strong arm as he drew forth his sword, she felt afraid no more. Turning, she led the way to a shining pool.

"There's where he stays," she whispered. "See, the water moves. He is waking."

St. George saw the head of the dragon lifted from the pool. Fold on fold he rose from the water. When he saw St. George he gave a roar of rage and plunged toward him. The smoke and flames flew from his nostrils, and he opened his great jaws as if to swallow both the knight and his horse.

St. George shouted and, waving his sword above his head, rode at the dragon. Quick and hard came the blows from St. George's sword. It was a terrible battle.

At last the dragon was wounded. He roared with pain and plunged at St. George, opening his great mouth close to the brave knight's head.

St. George looked carefully, then struck with all his strength straight down through the dragon's throat, and he fell at the horse's feet—dead.

Then St. George shouted for joy at his victory. He called to the Princess. She came and stood beside him.

"Give me the girdle from about your waist, O Princess," said St. George.

The Princess gave him her girdle and St. George bound it around the dragon's neck, and they pulled the dragon after them by that little silken ribbon back to the city so that all of the people could see that the dragon could never harm them again.

When they saw St. George bringing the Princess back in safety and knew that the dragon was slain, they threw open the gates of the city and sent up great shouts of joy.

The King heard them and came out from his palace to see why the people were shouting.

When he saw his daughter safe he was the happiest of them all.

"O brave knight," he said, "I am old and weak. Stay here and help me guard my people from harm."

"I'll stay as long as ever you have need of me," St. George answered.

So he lived in the palace and helped the old King take care of his people, and when the old King died, St. George was made King in his stead. The people felt happy and safe so long as they had such a brave and good man for their King.

The Boy We Want

A boy that is truthful and honest
  And faithful and willing to work;
But we have not a place that we care to disgrace
  With a boy that is ready to shirk.

Wanted—a boy you can tie to,
  A boy that is trusty and true,
A boy that is good to old people,
  And kind to the little ones too.

A boy that is nice to the home folks,
  And pleasant to sister and brother,
A boy who will try when things go awry
  To be helpful to father and mother.

These are the boys we depend on—
  Our hope for the future, and then
Grave problems of state and the world's work await
  Such boys when they grow to be men.

King Alfred and the Cakes

Adapted from James Baldwin

Alfred the Great was king of the West Saxons in England during
the ninth century. His determination to protect England from
Danish conquest and his emphasis on literacy and education for
his people have lifted him into the ranks of England's most popular rulers. This famous story reminds us that attention to little
duties prepares us to meet larger ones. It also reminds us that
leadership and responsibility walk hand in hand and that truly
great leaders do not disdain small responsibilities.

In England many years ago there ruled a king named Alfred. A wise and just man, Alfred was one of the best kings England ever had. Even today, centuries later, he is known as Alfred the Great.

The days of Alfred's rule were not easy ones in England. The country was invaded by the fierce Danes, who had come from across the sea. There were so many Danish invaders, and they were so strong and bold, that for a long time they won almost every battle. If they kept on winning, they would soon be masters of the whole country.

At last, after so many struggles, King Alfred's English army was broken and scattered. Every man had to save himself in the best way he could, including King Alfred. He disguised himself as a shepherd and fled alone through the woods and swamps.

After several days of wandering, he came to the hut of a woodcutter. Tired and hungry, he knocked on the door and begged the woodcutter's wife to give him something to eat and a place to sleep.

The woman looked with pity at the ragged fellow. She had no idea who he really was. "Come in," she said. "I will give you some supper if you will watch these cakes I am baking on the hearth. I want to go out and milk the cow. Watch them carefully, and make sure they don't burn while I'm gone."

Alfred thanked her politely and sat down beside the fire. He tried to pay attention to the cakes, but soon all his troubles filled his mind. How was he going to get his army together again? And even if he did, how was he going to prepare it to face the Danes? How could he possibly drive such fierce invaders out of England? The more he thought, the more hopeless the future seemed, and he began to believe there was no use in continuing to fight. Alfred saw only his problems. He forgot he was in the woodcutter's hut, he forgot about his hunger, and he forgot all about the cakes.

In a little while, the woman came back. She found her hut full of smoke and her cakes burned to a crisp. And there was Alfred sitting beside the hearth, gazing into the flames. He had never even noticed the cakes were burning.

"You lazy, good-for-nothing fellow!" the woman cried. "Look what you've done! You want something to eat, but you don't want to work for it! Now none of us will have any supper!" Alfred only hung his head in shame.

Just then the woodcutter came home. As soon as he walked through the door, he recognized the stranger sitting at his hearth.

"Be quiet!" he told his wife. "Do you realize who you are scolding? This is our noble ruler, King Alfred himself."

The woman was horrified. She ran to the king's side and fell to her knees. She begged him to forgive her for speaking so harshly.

But the wise King Alfred asked her to rise. "You were right to scold me," he said. "I told you I would watch the cakes, and then I let them burn. I deserved what you said. Anyone who accepts a duty, whether it be large or small, should perform it faithfully. I have failed this time, but it will not happen again. My duties as king await me."

The story does not tell us if King Alfred had anything to eat that night. But it was not many days before he had gathered his men together again, and soon he drove the Danes out of England.

For Want of a Horseshoe Nail

Adapted from James Baldwin

This famous legend and rhyme are based on the demise of England's King Richard III, whose defeat at the Battle of Bosworth Field in 1485 has been immortalized by Shakespeare's famous line: "A horse! A horse! My kingdom for a horse!" The story is a nice foil for "King Alfred and the Cakes." It reminds us that little duties neglected bring great downfalls.

King Richard the Third was preparing for the fight of his life. An army led by Henry, Earl of Richmond, was marching against him. The contest would determine who would rule England.

The morning of the battle, Richard sent a groom to make sure his favorite horse was ready.

"Shoe him quickly," the groom told the blacksmith. "The king wishes to ride at the head of his troops."

"You'll have to wait," the blacksmith answered. "I've shoed the king's whole army the last few days, and now I've got to go get more iron."

"I can't wait," the groom shouted impatiently. "The king's

enemies are advancing right now, and we must meet them on the field. Make do with what you have."

So the blacksmith bent to his task. From a bar of iron he made four horseshoes. He hammered and shaped and fitted them to the horse's feet. Then he began to nail them on. But after he had fastened three shoes, he found he did not have enough nails for the fourth.

"I need one or two more nails," he said, "and it will take some time to hammer them out."

"I told you I can't wait," the groom said impatiently. "I hear the trumpets now. Can't you just use what you've got?"

"I can put the shoe on, but it won't be as secure as the others."

"Will it hold?" asked the groom.

"It should," answered the blacksmith, "but I can't be certain."

"Well, then, just nail it on," the groom cried. "And hurry, or King Richard will be angry with us both."

The armies clashed, and Richard was in the thick of the battle. He rode up and down the field, cheering his men and fighting his foes. "Press forward! Press forward!" he yelled, urging his troops toward Henry's lines.

Far away, at the other side of the field, he saw some of his men falling back. If others saw them, they too might retreat. So Richard spurred his horse and galloped toward the broken line, calling on his soldiers to turn and fight.

He was barely halfway across the field when one of the horse's shoes flew off. The horse stumbled and fell, and Richard was thrown to the ground.

Before the king could grab at the reins, the frightened animal rose and galloped away. Richard looked around him. He saw that his soldiers were turning and running, and Henry's troops were closing around him.

He waved his sword in the air. "A horse!" he shouted. "A horse! My kingdom for a horse!"

But there was no horse for him. His army had fallen to pieces, and his troops were busy trying to save themselves. A moment later Henry's soldiers were upon Richard, and the battle was over.

And since that time, people have said,

For want of a nail, a shoe was lost,
For want of a shoe, a horse was lost,
For want of a horse, a battle was lost,
For want of a battle, a kingdom was lost,
And all for the want of a horseshoe nail.

Sir Walter Raleigh

Retold by James Baldwin

Goethe said that there is no outward sign of true courtesy that
does not rest on a deep moral foundation. This tale about the
English explorer and courtier Sir Walter Raleigh (1554–1618) is
one of our most famous examples of that kind of everyday responsibility called chivalry.

There once lived in England a brave and noble man whose name
was Walter Raleigh. He was not only brave and noble, but he was
also handsome and polite. And for that reason the queen made him
a knight, and called him Sir Walter Raleigh.

I will tell you about it.

When Raleigh was a young man, he was one day walking along
a street in London. At that time the streets were not paved, and there
were no sidewalks. Raleigh was dressed in very fine style, and he
wore a beautiful scarlet cloak thrown over his shoulders.

As he passed along, he found it hard work to keep from stepping in the mud, and soiling his handsome new shoes. Soon he came
to a puddle of muddy water which reached from one side of the
street to the other. He could not step across. Perhaps he could jump
over it.

As he was thinking what he should do, he happened to look up.
Who was it coming down the street, on the other side of the puddle?

It was Elizabeth, the Queen of England, with her train of gentlewomen and waiting maids. She saw the dirty puddle in the street.
She saw the handsome young man with the scarlet cloak, standing
by the side of it. How was she to get across?

Young Raleigh, when he saw who was coming, forgot about himself. He thought only of helping the queen. There was only one thing that he could do, and no other man would have thought of that.

He took off his scarlet cloak, and spread it across the puddle. The queen could step on it now, as on a beautiful carpet.

She walked across. She was safely over the ugly puddle, and her feet had not touched the mud. She paused a moment, and thanked the young man.

As she walked onward with her train, she asked one of the gentlewomen, "Who is that brave gentleman who helped us so handsomely?"

"His name is Walter Raleigh," said the gentlewoman.

"He shall have his reward," said the queen.

Not long after that, she sent for Raleigh to come to her palace.

The young man went, but he had no scarlet cloak to wear. Then, while all the great men and fine ladies of England stood around, the queen made him a knight. And from that time he was known as Sir Walter Raleigh, the queen's favorite.

Etiquette in a Nutshell

This little list of rules comes from a late-nineteenth-century book entitled *Correct Manners, a Complete Handbook of Etiquette.* These are some of the day-to-day commonplace obligations that allow us to get along with one another. They never go out of style.

Never break an engagement when one is made, whether of a business or social nature. If you are compelled to do so, make an immediate apology either by note or in person.

Be punctual as to time, precise as to payment, honest and thoughtful in all your transactions, whether with rich or poor.

Never look over the shoulder of one who is reading, or intrude yourself into a conversation in which you are not invited or expected to take part.

Tell the truth at all times and in all places. It is better to have a reputation for truthfulness than one for wit, wisdom, or brilliancy.

Avoid making personal comments regarding a person's dress, manners, or habits. Be sure you are all right in these respects, and you will find you have quite enough to attend to.

Always be thoughtful regarding the comfort and pleasure of others. Give the best seat in your room to a lady, an aged person, or an invalid.

Ask no questions about the affairs of your friend unless he wants your advice. Then he will tell you all he desires to have you know.

A true lady or gentleman, one who is worthy of the name, will never disparage one of the other sex by word or deed.

Always remember that a book that has been loaned you is not yours to loan to another.

Mention your wife or your husband with the greatest respect, even in your most familiar references.

If you have calls to make, see that you attend to them punctually. Your friends may reasonably think you slight them when you fail to do so.

Be neat and careful in your dress, but take care not to overdress. The fop is almost as much of an abomination as the slovenly man.

If wine or liquors are used on your table or in your presence, never urge others to use them against their own inclinations.

The Chest of Broken Glass

Responsibilities of parents and children toward each other change with age, particularly old age. "Old men are children for a second time," the Greek dramatist Aristophanes said. This tale is about that time in life when caring about someone means *taking care* of them. The obligation to "honor thy father and mother" does not end when father and mother grow old.

Once there was an old man who had lost his wife and lived all alone. He had worked hard as a tailor all his life, but misfortunes had left him penniless, and now he was so old he could no longer work for himself. His hands trembled too much to thread a needle, and his vision had blurred too much for him to make a straight stitch. He had three sons, but they were all grown and married now, and they were so busy with their own lives, they only had time to stop by and eat dinner with their father once a week.

Gradually the old man grew more and more feeble, and his sons came by to see him less and less. "They don't want to be around me at all now," he told himself, "because they're afraid I'll become a burden." He stayed up all night worrying what would become of him, until at last he thought of a plan.

The next morning he went to see his friend the carpenter, and asked him to make a large chest. Then he went to see his friend the locksmith, and asked him to give him an old lock. Finally he went to see his friend the glassblower, and asked for all the old broken pieces of glass he had.

The old man took the chest home, filled it to the top with broken glass, locked it up tight, and put it beneath his kitchen table. The next time his sons came for dinner, they bumped their feet against it.

"What's in this chest?" they asked, looking under the table.

"Oh, nothing," the old man replied, "just some things I've been saving."

His sons nudged it and saw how heavy it was. They kicked it and heard a rattling inside. "It must be full of all the gold he's saved over the years," they whispered to one another.

So they talked it over, and realized they needed to guard the treasure. They decided to take turns living with the old man, and that way they could look after him, too. So the first week the youngest son moved in with his father, and cared and cooked for him. The next week the middle son took his place, and the week afterward the eldest son took a turn. This went on for some time.

At last the old father grew sick and died. The sons gave him a very nice funeral, for they knew there was a fortune sitting beneath the kitchen table, and they could afford to splurge a little on the old man now.

When the service was over, they hunted through the house until they found the key, and unlocked the chest. And of course they found it full of broken glass.

"What a rotten trick!" yelled the eldest son. "What a cruel thing to do to your own sons!"

"But what else could he have done, really?" asked the middle son sadly. "We must be honest with ourselves. If it wasn't for this chest, we would have neglected him until the end of his days."

"I'm so ashamed of myself," sobbed the youngest. "We forced

our own father to stoop to deceit, because we would not observe the very commandment he taught us when we were young."

But the eldest son tipped the chest over to make sure there was nothing valuable hidden among the glass after all. He poured the broken pieces onto the floor until it was empty. Then the three brothers silently stared inside, where they now read an inscription left for them on the bottom: HONOR THY FATHER AND MOTHER.

Which Loved Best?

Joy Allison

Through dedication to duties we show devotion to the ones we love.

"I love you, Mother," said little John;
Then, forgetting his work, his cap went on,
And he was off to the garden swing,
And left her the water and wood to bring.
"I love you, Mother," said rosy Nell—
"I love you better than tongue can tell";
Then she teased and pouted full half the day,
Till her mother rejoiced when she went to play.
"I love you, Mother," said little Fan;
"Today I'll help you all I can;
How glad I am that school doesn't keep!"
So she rocked the babe till it fell asleep.

Then, stepping softly, she fetched the broom,
And swept the floor and tidied the room;
Busy and happy all day was she,
Helpful and happy as child could be.
"I love you, Mother," again they said,
Three little children going to bed;
How do you think that mother guessed
Which of them really loved her best?

Cain and Abel

Retold by Jesse Lyman Hurlbut

Here, according to the Bible, is the story of the first murder. Just as God sought out Adam and Eve in the Garden of Eden when they fell ("What is this that thou hast done?"), he seeks Cain after Abel's death. Just as Adam and Eve tried to avoid blame ("The serpent beguiled me"), Cain denies his crime. Whether or not one believes in original sin or divine reconciliation, there is certainly no denying our age-old struggle to accept responsibility for our own trespasses.

Adam and Eve went out into the world to live and to work. For a time they were all alone, but after a while God gave them a little child of their own, the first baby that ever came into the world. Eve named him Cain; and after a time another baby came, whom she named Abel.

When the two boys grew up, they worked, as their father worked before them. Cain chose to work in the fields, and to raise grain and fruits. Abel had a flock of sheep and became a shepherd.

While Adam and Eve were living in the Garden of Eden, they could talk with God, and hear God's voice speaking to them. But now that they were out in the world, they could no longer talk with God freely, as before. So when they came to God, they built an altar of stones heaped up, and upon it they laid something as a gift to God, and burned it, to show that it was not their own, but was given to God, whom they could not see. Then before the altar they made their prayer to God, and asked God to forgive their sins—all that they had done that was wrong—and prayed God to bless them and do good to them.

Each of these brothers, Cain and Abel, offered upon the altar to God his own gift. Cain brought the fruits and the grain which he had grown. And Abel brought a sheep from his flock, and killed it and burned it upon the altar. For some reason God was pleased with Abel and his offering, but was not pleased with Cain and his offering. Perhaps Cain's heart was not right when he came before God.

And God showed that he was not pleased with Cain, and Cain,

instead of being sorry for his sin, and asking God to forgive him, was very angry with God, and angry also toward his brother Abel. When they were out in the field together, Cain struck his brother Abel and killed him. So the first baby in the world grew up to be the murderer of his own brother.

And the Lord said to Cain, "Where is Abel your brother?"

And Cain answered, "I do not know. Am I my brother's keeper?"

Then the Lord said to Cain, "What is this that you have done? Your brother's blood is like a voice crying to me from the ground. Do you see how the ground has opened, like a mouth, to drink your brother's blood? As long as you live, you shall be under God's curse for the murder of your brother. You shall wander over the earth, and shall never find a home, because you have done this wicked deed."

And Cain said to the Lord, "My punishment is greater than I can bear. Thou hast driven me out from among men, and thou hast hid thy face from me. If any man finds me he will kill me, because I shall be alone, and no one will be my friend."

And God said to Cain, "If anyone harms Cain, he shall be punished for it." And the Lord God placed a mark on Cain, so that whoever met him should know him, and should know also that God had forbidden any man to harm him. Then Cain and his wife went away from Adam's home, to live in a place by themselves, and there they had children. And Cain's family built a city in that land, and Cain named the city after his first child, whom he had called Enoch.

The Ten Commandments

Western morality may be said to begin with these ten very old, very good rules for living.

1. I am the Lord thy God. Thou shalt have no other gods before me.
2. Thou shalt not make unto thee any graven image.
3. Thou shalt not take the name of the Lord thy God in vain.
4. Remember the sabbath day, to keep it holy.

5. Honor thy father and thy mother.
6. Thou shalt not kill.
7. Thou shalt not commit adultery.
8. Thou shalt not steal.
9. Thou shalt not bear false witness against thy neighbor.
10. Thou shalt not covet.

If You Were

This little poem reminds us whose responsibilities we should take care of first.

If you were busy being kind,
Before you knew it, you would find
You'd soon forget to think 'twas true
That someone was unkind to you.

If you were busy being glad,
And cheering people who are sad,
Although your heart might ache a bit,
You'd soon forget to notice it.

If you were busy being good,
And doing just the best you could,
You'd not have time to blame some man
Who's doing just the best he can.

If you were busy being right,
You'd find yourself too busy quite
To criticize your neighbor long
Because he's busy being wrong.

The Bell of Atri

Retold by James Baldwin

This old story reminds us that the essence of what we know as
justice in civil affairs is people living up to their obligations toward one another.

Atri is the name of a little town in Italy. It is a very old town,
and is built halfway up the side of a steep hill.

A long time ago, the King of Atri bought a fine large bell, and
had it hung up in a tower in the marketplace. A long rope that
reached almost to the ground was fastened to the bell. The smallest
child could ring the bell by pulling upon this rope.

"It is the bell of justice," said the king.

When at last everything was ready, the people of Atri had a
great holiday. All the men and women and children came down to
the marketplace to look at the bell of justice. It was a very pretty
bell, and was polished until it looked almost as bright and yellow as
the sun.

"How we should like to hear it ring!" they said.

Then the king came down the street.

"Perhaps he will ring it," said the people. And everybody stood
very still, and waited to see what he would do.

But he did not ring the bell. He did not even take the rope in
his hands. When he came to the foot of the tower, he stopped, and
raised his hand.

"My people," he said, "do you see this beautiful bell? It is your
bell. But it must never be rung except in case of need. If any one of
you is wronged at any time, he may come and ring the bell. And
then the judges shall come together at once, and hear his case, and
give him justice. Rich and poor, old and young, all alike may come.
But no one must touch the rope unless he knows that he has been
wronged."

Many years passed by after this. Many times did the bell in the
marketplace ring out to call the judges together. Many wrongs were
righted, many ill-doers were punished. At last the hempen rope was
almost worn out. The lower part of it was untwisted; some of the
strands were broken; it became so short that only a tall man could
reach it.

"This will never do," said the judges one day. "What if a child should be wronged? It could not ring the bell to let us know it."

They gave orders that a new rope should be put upon the bell at once—a rope that should hang down to the ground, so that the smallest child could reach it. But there was not a rope to be found in all Atri. They would have to send across the mountains for one, and it would be many days before it could be brought. What if some great wrong should be done before it came? How could the judges know about it, if the injured one could not reach the old rope?

"Let me fix it for you," said a man who stood by.

He ran into his garden, which was not far away, and soon came back with a long grapevine in his hands.

"This will do for a rope," he said. And he climbed up, and fastened it to the bell. The slender vine, with its leaves and tendrils still upon it, trailed to the ground.

"Yes," said the judges, "it is a very good rope. Let it be as it is."

Now, on the hillside above the village, there lived a man who had once been a brave knight. In his youth he had ridden through many lands, and he had fought in many a battle. His best friend through all that time had been his horse—a strong, noble steed that had borne him safe through many a danger.

But the knight, when he grew older, cared no more to ride into battle; he cared no more to do brave deeds; he thought of nothing but gold; he became a miser. At last he sold all that he had, except his horse, and went to live in a little hut on the hillside. Day after day he sat among his moneybags, and planned how he might get more gold. And day after day his horse stood in his bare stall, half starved, and shivering with cold.

"What is the use of keeping that lazy steed?" said the miser to himself one morning. "Every week it costs me more to keep him than he is worth. I might sell him, but there is not a man that wants him. I cannot even give him away. I will turn him out to shift for himself, and pick grass by the roadside. If he starves to death, so much the better."

So the brave old horse was turned out to find what he could among the rocks on the barren hillside. Lame and sick, he strolled along the dusty roads, glad to find a blade of grass or a thistle. The boys threw stones at him, the dogs barked at him, and in all the world there was no one to pity him.

One hot afternoon, when no one was upon the street, the horse chanced to wander into the marketplace. Not a man nor child was there, for the heat of the sun had driven them all indoors. The gates were wide open; the poor beast could roam where he pleased. He saw the grapevine rope that hung from the bell of justice. The leaves and tendrils upon it were still fresh and green, for it had not been there long. What a fine dinner they would be for a starving horse!

He stretched his thin neck, and took one of the tempting morsels in his mouth. It was hard to break it from the vine. He pulled at it, and the great bell above him began to ring. All the people in Atri heard it. It seemed to say,

Someone	has done	me wrong!
Someone	has done	me wrong!
Oh! come	and judge	my case!
Oh! come	and judge	my case!
For I've	been wronged!	

The judges heard it. They put on their robes, and went out through the hot streets to the marketplace. They wondered who it could be who would ring the bell at such a time. When they passed through the gate, they saw the old horse nibbling at the vine.

"Ha!" cried one, "it is the miser's steed. He has come to call for justice. For his master, as everybody knows, has treated him most shamefully."

"He pleads his cause as well as any dumb brute can," said another.

"And he shall have justice!" said the third.

Meanwhile a crowd of men and women and children had come into the marketplace, eager to learn what cause the judges were about to try. When they saw the horse, all stood still in wonder. Then everyone was ready to tell how they had seen him wandering on the hills, unfed, uncared for, while his master sat at home counting his bags of gold.

"Go bring the miser before us," said the judges.

And when he came, they bade him stand and hear their judgment.

"This horse has served you well for many a year," they said. "He has saved you from many a peril. He has helped you gain your wealth. Therefore we order that one half of all your gold shall be set aside to buy him shelter and food, a green pasture where he may graze, and a warm stall to comfort him in his old age."

The miser hung his head, and grieved to lose his gold. But the people shouted with joy, and the horse was led away to his new stall and a dinner such as he had not had in many a day.

Icarus and Daedalus

This famous Greek myth reminds us exactly why young people have a responsibility to obey their parents—for the same good reason parents have a responsibility to guide their children: there are many things adults know that young people do not. The ancient Greek dramatist Aeschylus put it this way: "Obedience is the mother of success and is wedded to safety." Safe childhoods and successful upbringings require a measure of obedience, as Icarus finds out the hard way.

Daedalus was the most skillful builder and inventor of his day in ancient Greece. He built magnificent palaces and gardens, and created wonderful works of art throughout the land. His statues were so beautifully crafted they were taken for living beings, and it was believed they could see and walk about. People said someone as cunning as Daedalus must have learned the secrets of his craft from the gods themselves.

Now across the sea, on the island of Crete, lived a king named Minos. King Minos had a terrible monster that was half bull and half man called the Minotaur, and he needed someplace to keep it. When he heard of Daedalus's cleverness, he invited him to come to his country and build a prison to hold the beast. So Daedalus and his young son, Icarus, sailed to Crete, and there Daedalus built the famous Labyrinth, a maze of winding passages so tangled and twisted that whoever went in could never find the way out. And there they put the Minotaur.

When the Labyrinth was finished, Daedalus wanted to sail back to Greece with his son, but Minos had made up his mind to keep them in Crete. He wanted Daedalus to stay and invent more wonderful devices for him, so he locked them both in a high tower beside the sea. The king knew Daedalus was clever enough to escape from the tower, so he also ordered that every ship be searched for stowaways before sailing from Crete.

Other men may have given up, but not Daedalus. From his high tower he watched the seagulls drifting on the ocean breezes. "Minos may control the land and the sea," he said, "but he does not rule the air. We'll go that way."

So he summoned all the secrets of his craft, and he set to work. Little by little, he gathered a great pile of feathers of all sizes. He fastened them together with thread, and molded them with wax, and at last he had two great wings like those of the seagulls. He tied them to his shoulders, and after one or two clumsy efforts, he found that by waving his arms he could rise into the air. He held himself aloft, wavering this way and that with the wind, until he taught himself how to glide and soar on the currents as gracefully as any gull.

Next he built a second pair of wings for Icarus. He taught the boy how to move the feathers and rise a few feet into the air, and then let him fly back and forth across the room. Then he taught him how to ride the air currents, climbing in circles, and hang in the winds. They practiced together until Icarus was ready.

Finally the day came when the winds were just right. Father and son strapped on their wings and prepared to fly home.

"Remember all I've told you," Daedalus said. "Above all, remember you must not fly too high or too low. If you fly too low, the ocean sprays will clog your wings and make them too heavy. If you fly too high, the heat of the sun will melt the wax, and your wings will fall apart. Stay close to me, and you'll be fine."

Up they rose, the boy after his father, and the hateful ground of Crete sank far beneath them. As they flew the plowman stopped his work to gaze, and the shepherd leaned on his staff to watch them, and people came running out of their houses to catch a glimpse of the two figures high above the treetops. Surely they were gods— Apollo, perhaps, with Cupid after him.

At first the flight seemed terrible to both Daedalus and Icarus. The wide, endless sky dazed them, and even the quickest glance down made their brains reel. But gradually they grew used to riding among the clouds, and they lost their fear. Icarus felt the wind fill his wings and lift him higher and higher, and began to sense a freedom he had never known before. He looked down with great excitement at all the islands they passed, and their people, and at the broad blue sea spread out beneath him, dotted with the white sails of ships. He soared higher and higher, forgetting his father's warning. He forgot everything in the world but joy.

"Come back!" Daedalus called frantically. "You're flying too high! Remember the sun! Come down! Come down!"

But Icarus thought of nothing but his own excitement and glory. He longed to fly as close as he could to the heavens. Nearer and nearer he came to the sun, and slowly his wings began to soften. One by one the feathers began to fall and scatter in the air, and suddenly the wax melted all at once. Icarus felt himself falling. He fluttered his arms as fast as he could, but no feathers remained to hold the air. He cried out for his father, but it was too late—with a scream he fell from his lofty height and plunged into the sea, disappearing beneath the waves.

Daedalus circled over the water again and again, but he saw nothing but feathers floating on the waves, and he knew his son was gone. At last the body came to the surface, and he managed to pluck it from the sea. With a heavy burden and broken heart Daedalus slowly flew away. When he reached land, he buried his son and built a temple to the gods. Then he hung up his wings, and never flew again.

The Sword of Damocles

Adapted from James Baldwin

This is one of our oldest "if you can't stand the heat, get out of the kitchen" stories. It is a great reminder that if we aspire to any kind of high office or job, we must be willing to live with all the burdens that come with it.

There once was a king named Dionysius who ruled in Syracuse, the richest city in Sicily. He lived in a fine palace where there were many beautiful and costly things, and he was waited upon by a host of servants who were always ready to do his bidding.

Naturally, because Dionysius had so much wealth and power, there were many in Syracuse who envied his good fortune. Damocles was one of these. He was one of Dionysius's best friends, and he was always saying to him, "How lucky you are! You have everything anyone could wish for. You must be the happiest man in the world."

One day Dionysius grew tired of hearing such talk. "Come now," he said, "do you really think I'm happier than everyone else?"

"But of course you are," Damocles replied. "Look at the great treasures you possess, and the power you hold. You have not a single worry in the world. How could life be any better?"

"Perhaps you would like to change places with me," said Dionysius.

"Oh, I would never dream of that," said Damocles. "But if I could only have your riches and your pleasures for one day, I should never want any greater happiness."

"Very well. Trade places with me for just one day, and you shall have them."

And so, the next day, Damocles was led to the palace, and all the servants were instructed to treat him as their master. They dressed him in royal robes, and placed on his head a crown of gold. He sat down at a table in the banquet hall, and rich foods were set before him. Nothing was wanting that could give him pleasure. There were costly wines, and beautiful flowers, and rare perfumes, and delightful music. He rested himself among soft cushions, and felt he was the happiest man in all the world.

"Ah, this is the life," he sighed to Dionysius, who sat at the other end of the long table. "I've never enjoyed myself so much."

And as he raised a cup to his lips, he lifted his eyes toward the ceiling. What was that dangling above him, with its point almost touching his head?

Damocles stiffened. The smile faded from his lips, and his face turned ashy pale. His hands trembled. He wanted no more food, no more wine, no more music. He only wanted to be out of the palace, far away, he cared not where. For directly above his head hung a sword, held to the ceiling by only a single horsehair. Its sharp blade glittered as it pointed right between his eyes. He started to jump up and run, but stopped himself, frightened that any sudden move might snap the thin thread and bring the sword down. He sat frozen to his chair.

"What is the matter, my friend?" Dionysius asked. "You seem to have lost your appetite."

"That sword! That sword!" whispered Damocles. "Don't you see it?"

"Of course I see it," said Dionysius. "I see it every day. It always hangs over my head, and there is always the chance someone or something may cut the slim thread. Perhaps one of my own advisors will grow jealous of my power and try to kill me. Or someone may spread lies about me, to turn the people against me. It may be that a neighboring kingdom will send an army to seize this throne. Or I might make an unwise decision that will bring my downfall. If you want to be a leader, you must be willing to accept these risks. They come with the power, you see."

"Yes, I do see," said Damocles. "I see now that I was mistaken, and that you have much to think about besides your riches and fame. Please take your place, and let me go back to my own house."

And as long as he lived, Damocles never again wanted to change places, even for a moment, with the king.

The Silent Couple

This tale appears in different versions all over the world, from Sri Lanka to Scotland. This version warns us that pettiness can cause us to forget our obligations.

There was once a young man who was said to be the most pigheaded fellow in town, and a young woman who was said to be the most mule-headed maiden, and of course they somehow managed to fall in love and be married. After the wedding ceremony, they had a grand feast at their new house, which lasted all day.

Finally all the friends and relatives could eat no more, and one by one they went home. The bride and groom collapsed from exhaustion, and were just getting ready to take off their shoes and relax, when the husband noticed that the last guest to leave had failed to close the door.

"My dear," he said, "would you mind getting up and shutting the door? There's a draft coming in."

"Why should I shut it?" yawned the wife. "I've been on my feet all day, and I just sat down. You shut it."

"So that's the way it's going to be!" snapped the husband. "Just as soon as you get the ring on your finger, you turn into a lazy good-for-nothing!"

"How dare you!" shouted the bride. "We haven't even been married a day, and already you're calling me names and ordering me around! I should have known this is the kind of husband you'd turn out to be!"

"Nag, nag, nag," grumbled the husband. "Must I listen to your complaining forever?"

"And must I always listen to your carping and whining?" asked the wife.

They sat glaring at each other for a full five minutes. Then an idea popped into the bride's head.

"My dear," she said, "neither of us wants to shut the door, and both of us are tired of hearing the other's voice. So I propose a contest. The one who speaks first must get up and close the door."

"It's the best idea I've heard all day," replied the husband. "Let us begin now."

So they made themselves comfortable, each on a chair, and sat face-to-face without saying a word.

They had been that way for about two hours when a couple of thieves with a cart passed by and saw the open door. They crept into the house, which seemed perfectly deserted, and began to steal everything they could lay their hands on. They took tables and chairs, pulled paintings off the walls, even rolled up carpets. But the newlyweds neither spoke nor moved.

"I can't believe this," thought the husband. "They'll take everything we own, and she won't make a sound."

"Why doesn't he call for help?" the wife asked herself. "Is he just going to sit there while they steal whatever they want?"

Eventually the thieves noticed the silent, motionless couple and, mistaking them for wax figures, stripped them of their jewelry, watches, and wallets. But neither husband nor wife uttered a sound.

The robbers hurried away with their loot, and the newlyweds sat through the night. At dawn a policeman walked by and, noticing the open door, stuck in his head to ask if everything was all right. But, of course, he couldn't get an answer out of the silent couple.

"Now, see here!" he yelled, "I'm an officer of the law! Who are you? Is this your house? What happened to all your furniture?" And still getting no response, he raised his hands to box the man's ears.

"Don't you dare!" cried the wife, jumping to her feet. "That's my new husband, and if you lay a finger on him, you'll have to answer to me!"

"I won!" yelled the husband, clapping his hands. "Now go and close the door."

The Athenian Oath

This oath was taken by the young men of ancient Athens when they reached the age of seventeen.

We will never bring disgrace on this our City by an act of dishonesty or cowardice.

We will fight for the ideals and Sacred Things of the City both alone and with many.

We will revere and obey the City's laws, and will do our best to incite a like reverence and respect in those above us who are prone to annul them or set them at naught.

We will strive increasingly to quicken the public's sense of civic duty.

Thus in all these ways we will transmit this City, not only not less, but greater and more beautiful than it was transmitted to us.

The Duties of a Scout

Here are the rules every Boy Scout and Girl Scout promises to live by. Other than the Ten Commandments, it is hard to imagine a better list of virtuous aims for the young.

The Boy Scout Oath

On my honor I will do my best
To do my duty to God and my country
and to obey the Scout Law;
To help other people at all times;
To keep myself physically strong,
mentally awake, and morally straight.

The Girl Scout Promise

On my honor, I will try:
To serve God and my country,
To help people at all times,
And to live by the Girl Scout Law.

The Boy Scout Law

A Scout is Trustworthy   A Scout is Obedient
A Scout is Loyal   A Scout is Cheerful
A Scout is Helpful   A Scout is Thrifty
A Scout is Friendly   A Scout is Brave
A Scout is Courteous   A Scout is Clean
A Scout is Kind   A Scout is Reverent

The Girl Scout Law

I will do my best:

• to be honest
• to be fair
• to help where I am needed
• to be cheerful
• to be friendly and considerate
• to be a sister to every Girl Scout
• to respect authority
• to use resources wisely
• to protect and improve the world around me
• to show respect for myself and others
  through my words and actions.

The American's Creed

William Tyler Page

In 1917, William Tyler Page of Maryland won a nationwide contest for "the best summary of American political faith." The U.S. House of Representatives accepted the statement as the American's Creed on April 3, 1918. Its two paragraphs remind us that responsibilities are the source of rights. It deserves to be read and recited. Today very few people have even heard of it.

I believe in the United States of America as a Government of the people, by the people, for the people; whose just powers are derived from the consent of the governed; a democracy in a republic; a sovereign Nation of many sovereign States; a perfect union, one and inseparable; established upon those principles of freedom, equality, justice, and humanity for which American patriots sacrificed their lives and fortunes.

I therefore believe it is my duty to my country to love it; to support its Constitution; to obey its laws; to respect its flag, and to defend it against all enemies.

Respecting the Flag

The United States Code states that "the flag represents a living country and is itself considered a living thing." Here are a few ru'es for respecting the U.S. flag. They are taken from a booklet entitled *Our Flag* published by Congress. Students of recent politics will be interested in the last rule.

- When the flag is displayed during rendition of the National Anthem or recital of the Pledge of Allegiance, all present except those in uniform should stand at attention facing the flag with the right hand over the heart.
- It is the universal custom to display the flag only from sunrise to

sunset on buildings and on stationary flagstaffs in the open. However, when a patriotic effect is desired, the flag may be displayed twenty-four hours a day if properly illuminated during the hours of darkness.

- The flag should be hoisted briskly and lowered ceremoniously.
- The flag should not be displayed on days when the weather is inclement, except when an all-weather flag is displayed.
- The flag should be displayed daily on or near the main administration building of every public institution.
- The flag should be displayed in or near every polling place on election days.
- The flag should be displayed during school days in or near every schoolhouse.
- The flag of the United States of America should be at the center and at the highest point of the group when a number of flags of states or localities, or pennants of societies, are grouped and displayed from staffs.
- The flag should never be displayed with the union down, except as a signal of dire distress in instances of extreme danger to life or property.
- The flag should never touch anything beneath it, such as the ground, the floor, water, or merchandise.
- The flag should never be carried flat or horizontally, but always aloft and free.
- The flag should never be used as wearing apparel, bedding, or drapery.
- The flag, when it is in such condition that it is no longer a fitting emblem for display, should be destroyed in a dignified way, preferably by burning.

The Charge of the Light Brigade

Alfred Tennyson

Tennyson based this famous poem on the Battle of Balaklava, fought on October 25, 1854, during the Crimean War, in which a small force of British cavalry made a daring but disastrous

assault against a Russian artillery line. After the attack, only 195
of the 673 men in the Light Brigade answered muster call. Some
find it fashionable to ridicule this poem as a glorification of war
and paean to those who blindly, and stupidly, follow orders. But
the fact is that there are times when obedient acts of self-sacrifice
and courage merit both admiration and profound gratitude.

> Half a league, half a league,
>   Half a league onward,
> All in the valley of Death
>   Rode the six hundred.

> "Forward, the Light Brigade!
> Charge for the guns!" he said:
> Into the valley of Death
>   Rode the six hundred.

> "Forward, the Light Brigade!"
> Was there a man dismay'd?
> Not tho' the soldier knew
>   Someone had blunder'd:
> Theirs not to make reply,
> Theirs not to reason why,
> Theirs but to do and die:
> Into the valley of Death
>   Rode the six hundred.

> Cannon to right of them,
> Cannon to left of them,
> Cannon in front of them
>   Volley'd and thunder'd;
> Storm'd at with shot and shell,
> Boldly they rode and well,
> Into the jaws of Death,
> Into the mouth of Hell
>   Rode the six hundred.

Flash'd all their sabers bare,
Flash'd as they turn'd in air
Sab'ring the gunners there,
Charging an army, while
    All the world wonder'd:
Plunged in the battery smoke
Right thro' the line they broke;
Cossack and Russian
Reel'd from the saber stroke
    Shatter'd and sunder'd.
Then they rode back, but not
    Not the six hundred.

Cannon to right of them,
Cannon to left of them,
Cannon behind them
    Volley'd and thunder'd:
Storm'd at with shot and shell,
While horse and hero fell,
They that had fought so well
Came through the jaws of death
Back from the mouth of hell,
All that was left of them—
    Left of six hundred.

When can their glory fade?
Oh, the wild charge they made!
    All the world wonder'd.
Honor the charge they made!
Honor the Light Brigade—
    Noble six hundred!

The Bridge Builder

Will Allen Dromgoole

This poem speaks of each generation's responsibilities to its successors.

An old man, going a lone highway,
Came, at the evening, cold and gray,
To a chasm, vast, and deep, and wide,
Through which was flowing a sullen tide.
The old man crossed in the twilight dim;
The sullen stream had no fears for him;
But he turned, when safe on the other side,
And built a bridge to span the tide.
"Old man," said a fellow pilgrim, near,
"You are wasting strength with building here;
Your journey will end with the ending day;
You never again must pass this way;
You have crossed the chasm, deep and wide—
Why build you the bridge at the eventide?"

The builder lifted his old gray head:
"Good friend, in the path I have come," he said,
"There followeth after me today
A youth, whose feet must pass this way.
This chasm, that has been naught to me,
To that fair-haired youth may a pitfall be.
He, too, must cross in the twilight dim;
Good friend, I am building the bridge for *him*."

What a Baby Costs

Edgar Guest

It is never too early to begin impressing upon our children, by
both word and deed, the responsibilities of parenthood. Part of
the job of raising children is raising them to be successful parents
themselves.

> "How much do babies cost?" said he
> The other night upon my knee;
> And then I said: "They cost a lot;
> A lot of watching by a cot,
> A lot of sleepless hours and care,
> A lot of heartache and despair,
> A lot of fear and trying dread,
> And sometimes many tears are shed
> In payment for our babies small,
> But every one is worth it all.
>
> "For babies people have to pay
> A heavy price from day to day—
> There is no way to get one cheap.
> Why, sometimes when they're fast asleep
> You have to get up in the night
> And go and see that they're all right.
> But what they cost in constant care
> And worry, does not half compare
> With what they bring of joy and bliss—
> You'd pay much more for just a kiss.

"Who buys a baby has to pay
A portion of the bill each day;
He has to give his time and thought
Unto the little one he's bought.
He has to stand a lot of pain
Inside his heart and not complain;
And pay with lonely days and sad
For all the happy hours he's had.
All this a baby costs, and yet
His smile is worth it all, you bet."

F. Scott Fitzgerald to His Daughter

In this letter we see the molding of character: a father gently but explicitly telling his daughter what her duties are.

Dear Pie:
I feel very strongly about your doing duty. Would you give me a little more documentation about your reading in French? I am glad you are happy—but I never believe much in happiness. I never believe in misery either. Those are things you see on the stage or the screen or the printed page, they never really happen to you in life.

All I believe in in life is the rewards for virtue (according to your talents) and the *punishments* for not fulfilling your duties, which are doubly costly. If there is such a volume in the camp library, will you ask Mrs. Tyson to let you look up a sonnet of Shakespeare's in which the line occurs *Lilies that fester smell far worse than weeds*.

Have had no thoughts today, life seems composed of getting up a *Saturday Evening Post* story. I think of you, and always pleasantly; but if you call me "Pappy" again I am going to take the White Cat out and beat his bottom *hard, six times for every time you are impertinent*. Do you react to that?

I will arrange the camp bill.

Halfwit, I will conclude. Things to worry about:

Worry about courage
Worry about cleanliness
Worry about efficiency
Worry about horsemanship . . .
Things not to worry about:
Don't worry about popular opinion
Don't worry about dolls
Don't worry about the past
Don't worry about the future
Don't worry about growing up
Don't worry about anybody getting ahead of you
Don't worry about triumph
Don't worry about failure unless it comes through your own
fault
Don't worry about mosquitoes
Don't worry about flies
Don't worry about insects in general
Don't worry about parents
Don't worry about boys
Don't worry about disappointments
Don't worry about pleasures
Don't worry about satisfactions
Things to think about:
What am I really aiming at?
How good am I in comparison to my contemporaries in regard
to:
(a) Scholarship
(b) Do I really understand about people and am I able to get
along with them?
(c) Am I trying to make my body a useful instrument or am I
neglecting it?

With dearest love

The Hiltons' Holiday

Sarah Orne Jewett

This story is about the most fundamental of parental responsibilities: spending time with children. Here we find two parents doing their best to instruct their daughters in matters of right conduct. We find the teaching through example of civility, politeness, remembrance of old friends, and thoughtfulness for loved ones. And we discover that in the observance of these daily duties, we win happiness. According to Willa Cather, this was Sarah Orne Jewett's (1849–1909) favorite story.

I

There was a bright, full moon in the clear sky, and the sunset was still shining faintly in the west. Dark woods stood all about the old Hilton farmhouse, save down the hill, westward, where lay the shadowy fields which John Hilton, and his father before him, had cleared and tilled with much toil—the small fields to which they had given the industry and even affection of their honest lives.

John Hilton was sitting on the doorstep of his house. As he moved his head in and out of the shadows, turning now and then to speak to his wife, who sat just within the doorway, one could see his good face, rough and somewhat unkempt, as if he were indeed a creature of the shady woods and brown earth, instead of the noisy town. It was late in the long spring evening, and he had just come from the lower field as cheerful as a boy, proud of having finished the planting of his potatoes.

"I had to do my last row mostly by feelin'," he said to his wife. "I'm proper glad I pushed through, an' went back an' ended off after supper. 'Twould have taken me a good part o' tomorrow mornin', an' broke my day."

" 'Tain't no use for ye to work yourself all to pieces, John," answered the woman quickly. "I declare it does seem harder than ever that we couldn't have kep' our boy; he'd been comin' fourteen years old this fall, most a grown man, and he'd work right 'longside of ye now the whole time."

" 'Twas hard to lose him; I do seem to miss little John," said the father sadly. "I expect there was reasons why 'twas best. I feel able an' smart to work; my father was a girt strong man, an' a monstrous worker afore me. 'Tain't that; but I was thinkin' by myself today what a sight o' company the boy would ha' been. You know, small's he was, how I could trust to leave him anywheres with the team, and how he'd beseech to go with me wherever I was goin'; always right in my tracks I used to tell 'em. Poor little John, for all he was so young he had a great deal o' judgment; he'd ha' made a likely man."

The mother sighed heavily as she sat within the shadow.

"But then there's the little girls, a sight o' help an' company," urged the father eagerly, as if it were wrong to dwell upon sorrow and loss. "Katy, she's most as good as a boy, except that she ain't very rugged. She's a real little farmer, she's helped me a sight this spring; an' you've got Susan Ellen, that makes a complete little housekeeper for ye as far as she's learnt. I don't see but we're better off than most folks, each on us having a workmate."

"That's so, John," acknowledged Mrs. Hilton wistfully, beginning to rock steadily in her straight, splint-bottomed chair. It was always a good sign when she rocked.

"Where be the little girls so late?" asked their father. " 'Tis gettin' long past eight o'clock. I don't know when we've all set up so late, but it's so kind o' summerlike an' pleasant. Why, where be they gone?"

"I've told ye; only over to Becker's folks," answered the mother. "I don't see myself what keeps 'em so late; they beseeched me after supper till I let 'em go. They're all in a dazzle with the new teacher; she asked 'em to come over. They say she's unusual smart with 'rethmetic, but she has a kind of a gorpen look to me. She's goin' to give Katy some pieces for her doll, but I told Katy she ought to be ashamed wantin' dolls' pieces, big as she's gettin' to be. I don't know's she ought, though; she ain't but nine this summer."

"Let her take her comfort," said the kindhearted man. "Them things draws her to the teacher, an' makes them acquainted. Katy's shy with new folks, more so'n Susan Ellen, who's of the business kind. Katy's shy-feelin' and wishful."

"I don't know but she is," agreed the mother slowly. "Ain't it sing'lar how well acquainted you be with that one, an' I with Susan Ellen? 'Twas always so from the first. I'm doubtful sometimes our Katy ain't one that'll be like to get married—anyways not about here. She lives right with herself, but Susan Ellen ain't nothin' when she's alone, she's always after company; all the boys is waitin' on her a'ready. I ain't afraid but she'll take her pick when the time comes. I expect to see Susan Ellen well settled—she feels grown up now—but Katy don't care one mite 'bout none o' them things. She wants to be rovin' out-o'-doors. I do believe she'd stand an' hark to a bird the whole forenoon."

"Perhaps she'll grow up to be a teacher," suggested John Hilton. "She takes to her book more 'n the other one. I should like one of 'em to be a teacher same's my mother was. They're good girls as anybody's got."

"So they be," said the mother, with unusual gentleness, and the creak of her rocking chair was heard, regular as the ticking of a clock. The night breeze stirred in the great woods, and the sound of a brook that went falling down the hillside grew louder and louder. Now and then one could hear the plaintive chirp of a bird. The moon glittered with whiteness like a winter moon, and shone upon the low-roofed house until its small windowpanes gleamed like silver, and one could almost see the colors of a blooming bush of lilac that grew in a sheltered angle by the kitchen door. There was an incessant sound of frogs in the lowlands.

"Be you sound asleep, John?" asked the wife presently.

"I don't know but what I was a'most," said the tired man, starting a little. "I should laugh if I was to fall sound asleep right here on the step; 'tis the bright night, I expect, makes my eyes feel heavy, an' 'tis so peaceful. I was up an' dressed a little past four an' out to work. Well, well!" and he laughed sleepily and rubbed his eyes. "Where's the little girls? I'd better step along an' meet 'em."

"I wouldn't just yet; they'll get home all right, but 'tis late for 'em certain. I don't want 'em keepin' Mis' Becker's folks up neither. There, le's wait a few minutes," urged Mrs. Hilton.

"I've be'n a-thinkin' all day I'd like to give the child'n some kind of a treat," said the father, wide awake now. "I hurried up my work 'cause I had it so in mind. They don't have the opportunities some do, an' I want 'em to know the world, an' not stay right here on the farm like a couple o' bushes."

"They're a sight better off not to be so full o' notions as some is," protested the mother suspiciously.

"Certain," answered the farmer; "but they're good, bright child'n, an' commencin' to take a sight o' notice. I want 'em to have all we can give 'em. I want 'em to see how other folks does things."

"Why, so do I"—here the rocking chair stopped ominously—
"but so long's they're contented—"

"Contented ain't all in this world; hopper-toads may have that
quality an' spend all their time a-blinkin'. I don't know's bein' contented is all there is to look for in a child. Ambition's somethin' to
me."

"Now you've got your mind on to some plot or other." (The
rocking chair began to move again.) "Why can't you talk right out?"

" 'Tain't nothin' special," answered the good man, a little ruffled; he was never prepared for his wife's mysterious powers of
divination. "Well there, you do find things out the master! I only
thought perhaps I'd take 'em tomorrow, an' go off somewhere if
'twas a good day. I've been promisin' for a good while I'd take 'em
to Topham Corners; they've never been there since they was very
small."

"I believe you want a good time yourself. You ain't never got
over bein' a boy." Mrs. Hilton seemed much amused. "There, go if
you want to an' take 'em; they've got their summer hats an' new
dresses. I don't know o' nothin' that stands in the way. I should
sense it better if there was a circus or anythin' to go to. Why don't
you wait an' let the girls pick 'em some strawberries or nice ros'berries, and then they could take an' sell 'em to the stores?"

John Hilton reflected deeply. "I should like to get me some
good yellow-turnip seed to plant late. I ain't more'n satisfied with
what I've been gettin' o' late years o' Ira Speed. An' I'm goin' to
provide me with a good hoe; mine's gettin' wore out an' all shackly.
I can't seem to fix it good."

"Them's excuses," observed Mrs. Hilton, with friendly toler-
ance. "You just cover up the hoe with somethin', if you get it—I
would. Ira Speed's so jealous he'll remember it of you this twenty
year, your goin' an' buyin' a new hoe o' anybody but him."

"I've always thought 'twas a free country," said John Hilton
soberly. "I don't want to vex Ira neither; he favors us all he can in
trade. 'Tis difficult for him to spare a cent, but he's as honest as
daylight."

At this moment there was a sudden sound of young voices, and
a pair of young figures came out from the shadow of the woods into
the moonlighted open space. An old cock crowed loudly from his
perch in the shed, as if he were a herald of royalty. The little girls
were hand in hand, and a brisk young dog capered about them as
they came.

"Wa'n't it dark gittin' home through the woods this time o' night?" asked the mother hastily, and not without reproach.

"I don't love to have you gone so late; Mother an' me was timid about ye, and you've kep' Mis' Becker's folks up, I expect," said their father regretfully. "I don't want to have it said that my little girls ain't got good manners."

"The teacher had a party," chirped Susan Ellen, the elder of the two children. "Goin' home from school she asked the Grover boys, an' Mary an' Sarah Speed. An' Mis' Becker was real pleasant to us: she passed round some cake, an' handed us sap sugar on one of her best plates, an' we played games an' sung some pieces too. Mis' Becker thought we did real well. I can pick out most of a tune on the cabinet organ; teacher says she'll give me lessons."

"I want to know, dear!" exclaimed John Hilton.

"Yes, an' we played Copenhagen, an' took sides spellin', an' Katy beat everybody spellin' there was there."

Katy had not spoken; she was not so strong as her sister, and while Susan Ellen stood a step or two away addressing her eager little audience, Katy had seated herself close to her father on the doorstep. He put his arm around her shoulders, and drew her close to his side, where she stayed.

"Ain't you got nothin' to tell, daughter?" he asked, looking down fondly; and Katy gave a pleased little sigh for answer.

"Tell 'em what's goin' to be the last day o' school, and about our trimmin' the schoolhouse," she said; and Susan Ellen gave the program in most spirited fashion.

" 'Twill be a great time," said the mother, when she had finished. "I don't see why folks wants to go traipsin' off to strange places when such things is happenin' right about 'em." But the children did not observe her mysterious air. "Come, you must step yourselves right to bed!"

They all went into the dark, warm house; the bright moon shone steadily all night, and the lilac flowers were shaken by no breath of wind until the early dawn.

II

The Hiltons always waked early. So did their neighbors, the crows and song sparrows and robins, the light-footed foxes and squirrels in the woods. When John Hilton waked, before five o'clock, an hour later than usual because he had sat up so late, he opened the house door and came out into the yard, crossing the short green turf hurriedly as if the day were too far spent for any loitering. The magnitude of the plan for taking a whole day of pleasure confronted him seriously, but the weather was fair, and his wife, whose disapproval could not have been set aside, had accepted and even smiled upon the great project. It was inevitable now that he and the children should go to Topham Corners. Mrs. Hilton had the pleasure of waking them, and telling the news.

In a few minutes they came frisking out to talk over the great plans. The cattle were already fed, and their father was milking. The only sign of high festivity was the wagon pulled out into the yard, with both seats put in as if it were Sunday; but Mr. Hilton still wore his everyday clothes, and Susan Ellen suffered instantly from disappointment.

"Ain't we goin', Father?" she asked complainingly; but he nodded and smiled at her, even though the cow, impatient to get to pasture, kept whisking her rough tail across his face. He held his head down and spoke cheerfully, in spite of this vexation.

"Yes, sister, we're goin' certain', an' goin' to have a great time too." Susan Ellen thought that he seemed like a boy at that delightful moment, and felt new sympathy and pleasure at once. "You go an' help Mother about breakfast an' them things; we want to get off quick's we can. You coax Mother now, both on ye, an' see if she won't go with us."

"She said she wouldn't be hired to," responded Susan Ellen. "She says it's goin' to be hot, an' she's laid out to go over an' see how her aunt Tamsen Brooks is this afternoon."

The father gave a little sigh; then he took heart again. The truth was that his wife made light of the contemplated pleasure, and, much as he usually valued her companionship and approval, he was sure that they should have a better time without her. It was impossible, however, not to feel guilty of disloyalty at the thought. Even though she might be completely unconscious of his best ideals, he only loved her and the ideals the more, and bent his energies to satisfying her indefinite expectations. His wife still kept much of that youthful beauty which Susan Ellen seemed likely to reproduce.

An hour later the best wagon was ready, and the great expedition set forth. The little dog sat apart, and barked as if it fell entirely upon him to voice the general excitement. Both seats were in the wagon, but the empty place testified to Mrs. Hilton's unyielding disposition. She had wondered why one broad seat would not do, but John Hilton meekly suggested that the wagon looked better with both. The little girls sat on the back seat dressed alike in their Sunday hats of straw with blue ribbons, and their little plaid shawls pinned neatly about their small shoulders. They wore gray thread gloves, and sat very straight. Susan Ellen was half a head the taller, but otherwise, from behind, they looked much alike. As for their father, he was in his Sunday best—a plain black coat, and a winter hat of felt, which was heavy and rusty-looking for that warm early summer day. He had it in mind to buy a new straw hat at Topham, so that this with the turnip seed and the hoe made three important reasons for going.

"Remember an' lay off your shawls when you get there an' carry them over your arms," said the mother, clucking like an excited hen to her chickens. "They'll do to keep the dust off your new dresses goin' an' comin'. An' when you eat your dinners don't get spots on you, an' don't point at folks as you ride by, an' stare, or they'll know you come from the country. An', John, you call into Cousin Ad'line Marlow's an' see how they all be, an' tell her I expect her over certain to stop awhile before hayin'. It always eases her phthisic to git up here on the high land. An' don't come home all wore out; an', John, don't you go an' buy me no kickshaws to fetch home. I ain't a child, an' you ain't got no money to waste. I expect you'll go, like's not, an' buy you some kind of a foolish boy's hat; do look an' see if it's reasonable good straw, an' won't splinter all off round the edge. An' you mind, John—"

"Yes, yes, hold on!" cried John impatiently; then he cast a last affectionate, reassuring look at her face, flushed with the hurry and responsibility of starting them off in proper shape. "I wish you was goin' too," he said, smiling. "I do so!" Then the old horse started, and they went out at the bars, and began the careful long descent of the hill. The young dog, tethered to the lilac bush, was frantic with piteous appeals; the little girls piped their eager goodbyes again and again, and their father turned many times to look back and wave his hand. As for their mother, she stood alone and watched them out of sight.

There was one place far out on the high road where she could catch a last glimpse of the wagon, and she waited what seemed a very long time until it appeared and then was lost to sight again behind a low hill. "They're nothin' but a pack o' child'n together," she said aloud; and then felt lonelier than she expected. She even stooped and petted the unresigned little dog as she passed him, going into the house.

The occasion was so much more important than anyone had

foreseen that both the little girls were speechless. It seemed at first like going to church in new clothes; or to a funeral; they hardly knew how to behave at the beginning of a whole day of pleasure. They made grave bows at such persons of their acquaintance as happened to be straying in the road. Once or twice they stopped before a farmhouse, while their father talked an inconsiderately long time with someone about the crops and the weather, and even dwelt upon town business and the doings of the selectmen, which might be talked of at any time. The explanations that he gave of their excursion seemed quite unnecessary. It was made entirely clear that he had a little business to do at Topham Corners, and thought he had better give the little girls a ride; they had been very steady at school, and he had finished planting, and could take the day as well as not. Soon, however, they all felt as if such an excursion were an everyday affair, and Susan Ellen began to ask eager questions, while Katy silently sat apart, enjoying herself as she never had done before. She liked to see the strange houses, and the children who belonged to them; it was delightful to find flowers that she knew growing all along the road, no matter how far she went from home. Each small homestead looked its best and pleasantest, and shared the exquisite beauty that early summer made—shared the luxury of greenness and floweriness that decked the rural world. There was an early peony or a late lilac in almost every dooryard.

It was seventeen miles to Topham. After a while they seemed very far from home, having left the hills far behind, and descended to a great level country with fewer tracts of woodland, and wider fields where the crops were much more forward. The houses were all painted, and the roads were smoother and wider. It had been so pleasant driving along that Katy dreaded going into the strange town when she first caught sight of it, though Susan Ellen kept asking with bold fretfulness if they were not almost there. They counted the steeples of four churches, and their father presently showed them the Topham Academy, where their grandmother once went to school, and told them that perhaps someday they would go there too. Katy's heart gave a strange leap; it was such a tremendous thing to think of, but instantly the suggestion was transformed for her into one of the certainties of life. She looked with solemn awe at the tall belfry, and the long rows of windows in the front of the academy, there where it stood high and white among the clustering trees. She hoped that they were going to drive by, but something forbade her taking the responsibility of saying so.

Soon the children found themselves among the crowded village houses. Their father turned to look at them with affectionate solicitude.

"Now sit up straight and appear pretty," he whispered to them. "We're among the best people now, an' I want folks to think well of you."

"I guess we're as good as they be," remarked Susan Ellen, looking at some innocent passersby with dark suspicion, but Katy tried indeed to sit straight, and folded her hands prettily in her lap, and wished with all her heart to be pleasing for her father's sake. Just then an elderly woman saw the wagon and the sedate party it carried, and smiled so kindly that it seemed to Katy as if Topham Corners had welcomed and received them. She smiled back again as if this hospitable person were an old friend, and entirely forgot that the eyes of all Topham had been upon her.

"There, now we're coming to an elegant house that I want you to see; you'll never forget it," said John Hilton. "It's where Judge Masterson lives, the great lawyer; the handsomest house in the county, everybody says."

"Do you know him, Father?" asked Susan Ellen.

"I do," answered John Hilton proudly. "Him and my mother went to school together in their young days, and were always called the two best scholars of their time. The Judge called to see her once; he stopped to our house to see her when I was a boy. An' then, some years ago—you've heard me tell how I was on the jury, an' when he heard my name spoken he looked at me sharp, and asked if I wa'n't the son of Catharine Winn, an' spoke most beautiful of your grandmother, an' how well he remembered their young days together."

"I like to hear about that," said Katy.

"She had it pretty hard, I'm afraid, up on the old farm. She keepin' school in our district when Father married her—that's the main reason I backed 'em down when they wanted to tear the old schoolhouse all to pieces," confided John Hilton, turning eagerly. "They all say she lived longer up here on the hill than she could anywhere, but she never had her health. I wa'n't but a boy when she died. Father an' me lived alone afterward till the time your mother come; 'twas a good while, too; I wa'n't married so young as some. 'Twas lonesome, I tell you; Father was plumb discouraged losin' of his wife, an' her long sickness an' all set him back, an' we'd work all day on the land an' never say a word. I s'pose 'tis bein' so lonesome early in life that makes me so pleased to have some nice girls growin' up round me now."

There was a tone in her father's voice that drew Katy's heart toward him with new affection. She dimly understood, but Susan Ellen was less interested. They had often heard this story before, but to one child it was always new and to the other old. Susan Ellen was apt to think it tiresome to hear about her grandmother, who, being dead, was hardly worth talking about.

"There's Judge Masterson's place," said their father in an everyday manner, as they turned a corner, and came into full view of the beautiful old white house standing behind its green trees and terraces and lawns. The children had never imagined anything so stately and fine, and even Susan Ellen exclaimed with pleasure. At that moment they saw an old gentleman, who carried himself with great dignity, coming slowly down the wide box-bordered path toward the gate.

"There he is now, there's the judge!" whispered John Hilton excitedly, reining his horse quickly to the green roadside. "He's goin' downtown to his office; we can wait right here an' see him. I can't expect him to remember me; it's been a good many years. Now you are goin' to see the great Judge Masterson!"

There was a quiver of expectation in their hearts. The judge stopped at his gate, hesitating a moment before he lifted the latch, and glanced up the street at the country wagon with its two prim little girls on the back seat, and the eager man who drove. They seemed to be waiting for something; the old horse was nibbling at the fresh roadside grass. The judge was used to being looked at with interest, and responded now with a smile as he came out to the sidewalk, and unexpectedly turned their way. Then he suddenly lifted his hat with grave politeness, and came directly toward them.

"Good morning, Mr. Hilton," he said. "I am very glad to see you, sir"; and Mr. Hilton, the little girls' own father, took off his hat with equal courtesy, and bent forward to shake hands.

Susan Ellen cowered and wished herself away, but little Katy sat straighter than ever, with joy in her father's pride and pleasure shining in her pale, flowerlike little face.

"These are your daughters, I am sure," said the old gentleman kindly, taking Susan Ellen's limp and reluctant hand; but when he looked at Katy, his face brightened. "How she recalls your mother!" he said with great feeling. "I am glad to see this dear child. You must come to see me with your father, my dear," he added, still looking at her. "Bring both the little girls, and let them run about the old garden; the cherries are just getting ripe," said Judge Masterson hospitably. "Perhaps you will have time to stop this afternoon as you go home?"

"I should call it a great pleasure if you would come and see us again some time. You may be driving our way, sir," said John Hilton.

"Not very often in these days," answered the old judge. "I thank you for the kind invitation. I should like to see the fine view again from your hill westward. Can I serve you in any way while you are in town? Goodbye, my little friends!"

Then they parted, but not before Katy, the shy Katy, whose hand the judge still held unconsciously while he spoke, had reached forward as he said goodbye, and lifted her face to kiss him. She could not have told why, except that she felt drawn to something in the serious, worn face. For the first time in her life the child had felt the charm of manners; perhaps she owned a kinship between that which made him what he was, and the spark of nobleness and purity in her own simple soul. She turned again and again to look back at him as they drove away.

"Now you have seen one of the first gentlemen in the county," said their father. "It was worth comin' twice as far"—but he did not say any more, nor turn as usual to look in the children's faces.

In the chief business street of Topham a great many country wagons like the Hiltons' were fastened to the posts, and there seemed to our holidaymakers to be a great deal of noise and excitement.

"Now I've got to do my errands, and we can let the horse rest and feed," said John Hilton. "I'll slip his headstall right off, an' put on his halter. I'm goin' to buy him a real good treat o' oats. First we'll go an' buy me my straw hat; I feel as if this one looked a little past to wear in Topham. We'll buy the things we want, an' then we'll walk all along the street, so you can look in the windows an' see the han'some things, same's your mother likes to. What was it Mother told you about your shawls?"

"To take 'em off an' carry 'em over our arms," piped Susan Ellen, without comment, but in the interest of alighting and finding themselves afoot upon the pavement the shawls were forgotten. The children stood at the doorway of a shop while their father went inside, and they tried to see what the Topham shapes of bonnets were like, as their mother had advised them; but everything was exciting and confusing, and they could arrive at no decision. When Mr. Hilton came out with a hat in his hand to be seen in a better light, Katy whispered that she wished he would buy a shiny one like Judge Masterson's; but her father only smiled and shook his head, and said that they were plain folks, he and Katy. There were dry-goods for sale in the same shop, and a young clerk who was measuring linen kindly pulled off some pretty labels with gilded edges and gay pictures, and gave them to the little girls, to their exceeding joy. He may have had small sisters at home, this friendly lad, for he took pains to find two pretty blue boxes besides, and was rewarded by their beaming gratitude.

It was a famous day; they even became used to seeing so many people pass. The village was full of its morning activity, and Susan Ellen gained a new respect for her father, and an increased sense of her own consequence, because even in Topham several persons knew him and called him familiarly by name. The meeting with an old man who had once been a neighbor seemed to give Mr. Hilton the greatest pleasure. The old man called to them from a house doorway as they were passing, and they all went in. The children seated themselves wearily on the wooden step, but their father shook his old friend eagerly by the hand, and declared that he was delighted to see him so well and enjoying the fine weather.

"Oh, yes," said the old man, in a feeble, quavering voice. "I'm astonishin' well for my age. I don't complain, John, I don't complain."

They talked long together of people whom they had known in the past, and Katy, being a little tired, was glad to rest, and sat still with her hands folded, looking about the front yard. There were some kinds of flowers that she never had seen before.

"This is the one that looks like my mother," her father said, and touched Katy's shoulder to remind her to stand up and let herself be seen. "Judge Masterson saw the resemblance; we met him at his gate this morning."

"Yes, she certain does look like your mother, John," said the old man, looking pleasantly at Katy, who found that she liked him better than at first. "She does, certain; the best of young folks is, they remind us of the old ones. 'Tis nateral to cling to life, folks say, but for me, I git impatient at times. Most everybody's gone now, an' I want to be goin'. 'Tis somethin' before me, an' I want to have it over with. I want to be there 'long o' the rest o' the folks. I expect to last quite awhile, though; I may see ye couple o' times more, John."

John Hilton responded cheerfully, and the children were urged to pick some flowers. The old man awed them with his impatience to be gone. There was such a townful of people about him, and he seemed as lonely as if he were the last survivor of a former world. Until that moment they had felt as if everything were just beginning.

"Now I want to buy somethin' pretty for your mother," said Mr. Hilton, as they went soberly away down the street, the children keeping fast hold of his hands. "By now the old horse will have eat his dinner and had a good rest, so pretty soon we can jog along home. I'm goin' to take you round by the academy, and the old North Meetinghouse where Dr. Barstow used to preach. Can't you think o' somethin' that your mother'd want?" he asked suddenly, confronted by a man's difficulty of choice.

"She was talkin' about wantin' a new pepper box, one day; the top o' the old one won't stay on," suggested Susan Ellen, with delightful readiness. "Can't we have some candy, Father?"

"Yes, ma'am," said John Hilton, smiling and swinging her hand to and fro as they walked. "I feel as if some would be good myself. What's all this?" They were passing a photographer's doorway with its enticing array of portraits. "I do declare!" he exclaimed excitedly, "I'm goin' to have our pictures taken; 'twill please your mother more 'n a little."

This was, perhaps, the greatest triumph of the day, except the delightful meeting with the judge; they sat in a row, with the father in the middle, and there was no doubt as to the excellence of the likeness. The best hats had to be taken off because they cast a shadow, but they were not missed, as their owners had feared. Both Susan Ellen and Katy looked their brightest and best; their eager young faces would forever shine there; the joy of the holiday was mirrored in the little picture. They did not know why their father was so pleased with it; they would not know until age had dowered them with the riches of association and remembrance.

Just at nightfall the Hiltons reached home again, tired out and happy. Katy had climbed over into the front seat beside her father, because that was always her place when they went to church on Sundays. It was a cool evening, there was a fresh sea wind that brought a light mist with it, and the sky was fast growing cloudy. Somehow the children looked different; it seemed to their mother as if they had grown older and taller since they went away in the morning, and as if they belonged to the town now as much as to the country. The greatness of their day's experience had left her far behind; the day had been silent and lonely without them, and she had their supper ready, and been watching anxiously, ever since five o'clock. As for the children themselves they had little to say at first—they had eaten their luncheon early on the way to Topham. Susan Ellen was childishly cross, but Katy was pathetic and wan. They could hardly wait to show the picture, and their mother was as much pleased as everybody had expected.

"There, what did make you wear your shawls?" she exclaimed a moment afterward, reproachfully. "You ain't been an' wore 'em all day long? I wanted folks to see how pretty your new dresses was, if I did make 'em. Well, well! I wish more 'n ever now I'd gone an' seen to ye!"

"An' here's the pepper box!" said Katy, in a pleased, unconscious tone.

"That really is what I call beautiful," said Mrs. Hilton, after a long and doubtful look. "Our other one was only tin. I never did look so high as a chiny one with flowers, but I can get us another anytime for every day. That's a proper hat, as good as you could have got, John. Where's your new hoe?" she asked as he came toward her from the barn, smiling with satisfaction.

"I declare to Moses if I didn't forget all about it," meekly acknowledged the leader of the great excursion. "That an' my yellow-turnip seed, too; they went clean out o' my head, there was so many other things to think of. But 'tain't no sort o' matter; I can get a hoe just as well to Ira Speed's."

His wife could not help laughing. "You an' the little girls have had a great time. They was full o' wonder to me about everything, and I expect they'll talk about it for a week. I guess we was right about havin' 'em see somethin' more o' the world."

"Yes," answered John Hilton, with humility, "yes, we did have a beautiful day. I didn't expect so much. They looked as nice as anybody, and appeared so modest an' pretty. The little girls will remember it perhaps by an' by. I guess they won't never forget this day they had 'long o' Father."

It was evening again, the frogs were piping in the lower meadows, and in the woods, higher up the great hill, a little owl began to hoot. The sea air, salt and heavy, was blowing in our country at the end of the hot bright day. A lamp was lighted in the house, the happy children were talking together, and supper was waiting. The father and mother lingered for a moment outside and looked down over the shadowy fields; then they went in, without speaking. The great day was over, and they shut the door.

The Perfect Dinner Table

Edgar Guest

This poem is about a time of day families need to spend together.
The dinner hour should be more than eating. It should be about
teaching, listening, and loving.

A tablecloth that's slightly soiled
Where greasy little hands have toiled;
The napkins kept in silver rings,
And only ordinary things
From which to eat, a simple fare,
And just the wife and kiddies there,
And while I serve, the clatter glad
Of little girl and little lad
Who have so very much to say
About the happenings of the day.

Four big round eyes that dance with glee,
Forever flashing joys at me,
Two little tongues that race and run
To tell of troubles and of fun;
The mother with a patient smile
Who knows that she must wait awhile
Before she'll get a chance to say
What she's discovered through the day.
She steps aside for girl and lad
Who have so much to tell their dad.

Our manners may not be the best;
Perhaps our elbows often rest
Upon the table, and at times
That very worst of dinner crimes,
That very shameful act and rude
Of speaking ere you've downed your food,
Too frequently, I fear, is done,
So fast the little voices run.
Yet why should table manners stay
Those tongues that have so much to say?

At many a table I have been
Where wealth and luxury were seen,
And I have dined in halls of pride
Where all the guests were dignified;
But when it comes to pleasure rare
The perfect dinner table's where
No stranger's face is ever known:
The dinner hour we spend alone,
When little girl and little lad
Run riot telling things to dad.

———————

The Children's Hour

Henry Wadsworth Longfellow

Every home should have at least one Children's Hour every evening.

Between the dark and the daylight,
    When the night is beginning to lower,
Comes a pause in the day's occupations,
    That is known as the Children's Hour.

I hear in the chamber above me
    The patter of little feet,
The sound of a door that is opened,
    And voices soft and sweet.

From my study I see in the lamplight,
    Descending the broad hall stair,
Grave Alice, and laughing Allegra,
    And Edith with golden hair.

A whisper, and then a silence:
    Yet I know by their merry eyes
They are plotting and planning together
    To take me by surprise.

A sudden rush from the stairway,
A sudden raid from the hall!
By three doors left unguarded
They enter my castle wall!

They climb up into my turret
O'er the arms and back of my chair;
If I try to escape, they surround me;
They seem to be everywhere.

They almost devour me with kisses,
Their arms about me entwine,
Till I think of the Bishop of Bingen
In his Mouse Tower on the Rhine!

Do you think, O blue-eyed banditti,
Because you have scaled the wall,
Such an old mustache as I am
Is not a match for you all!

I have you fast in my fortress,
And will not let you depart,
But put you down into the dungeon
In the round-tower of my heart.

And there will I keep you forever,
Yes, forever and a day,
Till the walls shall crumble to ruin,
And molder in dust away!

The Funeral Oration of Pericles

Thucydides

The late-mid-fifth century B.C. is known as the Age of Pericles
in Greek history, for it was during the period of that great statesman's leadership that Athenian democracy flowered and the

Athenian empire reached full development militarily, commercially, and culturally. In his famous funeral oration over Athenians killed in battle, reported by Thucydides, Pericles gave an
"exposition of the general principles by virtue of which we came
to empire, and of the civic institutions and manners of life in
consequence of which our empire became great." The speech
reminds participants of democracy two and a half millennia later
that the character of the state is determined by the virtues of
individual citizens.

We enjoy a form of government which is not in rivalry with the
institutions of our neighbors, nay, we ourselves are rather an example to many than imitators of others. By name, since the administration is not in the hands of few but of many, it is called a democracy.
And it is true that before the law and in private cases all citizens are
on an equality. But in public life every man is advanced to honor
according to his reputation for ability—not because of his party, but
because of his excellence. And further, provided he is able to do the
city good service, not even in poverty does he find any hindrance,
since this cannot obscure men's good opinion of him. It is with a
free spirit that we engage in public life, and in our scrutiny of one
another's private life we are not filled with wrath at our neighbor if
he consults his pleasure now and then, nor do we cast sour glances
at him. . . .
     We cherish beauty in all simplicity, and wisdom without effemi-
nacy. Our wealth supports timely action rather than noisy speech,
and as for poverty, the admission of it is no disgrace to a man; not
to forge one's way out of it is the real disgrace. The same citizens
among us will be found devoted to their homes and to the state, and
others who are immersed in business have no mean knowledge of
politics. We are the only people to regard the man who takes no
interest in politics not as careless, but as useless. In one and the
same citizen body we either decide matters, or seek to form correct
opinions about them, and we do not regard words as incompatible
with deeds, but rather the refusal to learn by discussion before advancing to the necessary action. We are preeminent in this, that we
combine in the same citizen body great courage to undertake, and
ample discussion of our undertakings; whereas in other men it is
ignorance that gives boldness, and discussion that produces hesitation. Surely they will rightly be judged the bravest souls who most

clearly distinguish the pains and pleasures of life, and therefore do not avoid danger. In our benevolence also we are the opposite of most men; it is not by receiving, but by conferring favors that we win our friends. . . . To sum up: I declare that our city in general is the school of Hellas, and that each individual man of us will, in my opinion, show himself able to exercise the most varied forms of activity with the greatest ease and grace. That this is no passing boast, but an actual truth, is shown by the power which our city has acquired in virtue of these traits of ours. . . .

It was for such a city, then, that these dead warriors of ours so nobly gave their lives in battle; they deemed it their right not to be robbed of her, and every man who survives them should gladly toil in her behalf.

I have thus dwelt at length on the character of our city both because I would teach the lesson that we have far more at stake than those who are so unlike us, and because I would accompany the words of praise which I now pronounce over these men with manifest proofs. Indeed their highest praise has been already spoken. I have but sung the praises of a city which the virtues of these men and of men like them adorned, and there are few Hellenes like these, whose deeds will be found to balance their praises. I hold that such an end as theirs shows forth a man's real excellence, whether it be a first revelation or a final confirmation. For even those who fall short in other ways may find refuge behind the valor they show in fighting for their country. They make men forget the evil that was in them for the good, and help their country more by their public sacrifice than they injured her by their private failings. Among these men, however, there was no one in wealth who set too high a value on the further enjoyment of it, to his own undoing, nor anyone in poverty who was led, by the hope of escaping it and becoming rich, to postpone the dread ordeal. . . . And in the heat of action, thinking it far better to suffer death than to yield and live, they did indeed fly from the word of disgrace, but they stood firm in deeds of prowess, and so, in a moment, in the twinkling of an eye, at the height of their glory rather than of their fear, they passed away.

Such were these men, and they were worthy of their city. Those who survive them may pray, perhaps, for a less fatal, but should desire no less bold a temper toward their foes. You cannot weigh in words the service they rendered to the state. You know it yourselves fully as well as any speaker who might descant at length upon it, telling you all the good there is in resistance to the foe. You should rather fix your eyes daily upon the city in her power, until you become her fond lovers. And when her greatness becomes manifest to you, reflect that it was by courage, and the recognition of duty, and the shunning of dishonor, that men won that greatness, men who, even if they failed in an undertaking, did not on that account deem it a worthy thing to rob their city of a glorious example, but offered their lives willingly as their fairest contribution to the table of her welfare.

Plato on Responsibility

From the Crito

In this famous dialogue by Plato, Crito visits his friend Socrates, who has been legally but unjustly imprisoned and condemned to death for "impiety" and "corrupting the youth." The hour when Socrates must drink the poison hemlock is fast approaching, and Crito tries to persuade his friend to escape. Socrates, however, refuses to break the law of Athens. His argument is one of our finest lessons in the principles that must inform both civil obedience and civil disobedience. His decision to die remains one of history's great examples of an individual who believes his first responsibility to his community, his family, and himself is to follow the dictates of reason-directed conscience.

Socrates. Consider the matter in this way: Imagine that I am about to play truant (you may call the proceeding by any name which you like), and the laws and the government come and interrogate me: "Tell us, Socrates," they say; "what are you about? are you not going by an act of yours to overturn us—the laws, and the whole state, as far as in you lies? Do you imagine that a state can subsist and not be overthrown, in which the decisions of law have no power, but are set aside and trampled upon by individuals?" What will be our answer, Crito, to these and the like words? Anyone, and especially a rhetorician, will have a good deal to say on behalf of the law which requires a sentence to be carried out. He will argue that this law should not be set aside; and shall we reply, "Yes; but the state has injured us and given an unjust sentence"? Suppose I say that?

Crito. Very good, Socrates.

Socrates. "And was that our agreement with you?" the law would answer; "or were you to abide by the sentence of the state?" And if I were to express my astonishment at their words, the law would probably add: "Answer, Socrates, instead of opening your eyes—you are in the habit of asking and answering questions. Tell us—What complaint have you to make against us which justifies you in attempting to destroy us and the state? In the first place did we not bring you into existence? Your father married your mother by our aid and begat you. Say whether you have any objection to urge against those of us who regulate marriage?" None, I should reply. "Or against those of us who after birth regulate the nurture and education of children, in which you also were trained? Were not the laws, which have the charge of education, right in commanding your father to train you in music and gymnastic?" Right, I should reply. "Well then, since you were brought into the world and nur- tured and educated by us, can you deny in the first place that you are our child and slave, as your fathers were before you? And if this is true you are not on equal terms with us; nor can you think that you have a right to do to us what we are doing to you. Would you have any right to strike or revile or do any other evil to your father or your master, if you had one, because you have been struck or reviled by him, or received some other evil at his hands?—you would not say this? And because we think right to destroy you, do you think that you have any right to destroy us in return, and your country as far as in you lies? Will you, O professor of true virtue, pretend that you are justified in this? Has a philosopher like you failed to discover that our country is more to be valued and higher and holier far than mother or father or any ancestor, and more to be regarded in the eyes of the gods and of men of understanding? also to be soothed, and gently and reverently entreated when angry, even more than a father, and either to be persuaded, or if not persuaded, to be obeyed? And when we are punished by her, whether with imprisonment or stripes, the punishment is to be endured in silence; and if she leads us to wounds or death in battle, thither we follow as is right; neither may anyone yield or retreat or leave his rank, but whether in battle or in a court of law, or in any other place, he must do what his city and his country order him; or he must change their view of what is just: and if he may do no violence to his father or mother, much less may he do violence to his country." What answer shall we make to this, Crito? Do the laws speak truly, or do they not?

Crito. I think that they do.

Socrates. Then the laws will say, "Consider, Socrates, if we are speaking truly that in your present attempt you are going to do us an injury. For, having brought you into the world, and nurtured and educated you, and given you and every other citizen a share in every good which we had to give, we further proclaim to any Athenian by the liberty which we allow him, that if he does not like us when he has become of age and has seen the ways of the city, and made our acquaintance, he may go where he pleases and take his goods with him. None of us laws will forbid him or interfere with him. Anyone who does not like us and the city, and who wants to emigrate to a colony or to any other city, may go where he likes, retaining his property. But he who has experience of the manner in which we order justice and administer the state, and still remains, has entered into an implied contract that he will do as we command him. And he who disobeys us is, as we maintain, thrice wrong; first, because in disobeying us he is disobeying his parents; secondly, because we are the authors of his education; thirdly, because he has made an agreement with us that he will duly obey our commands; and he neither obeys them nor convinces us that our commands are unjust; and we do not rudely impose them, but give him the alternative of obeying or convincing us; that is what we offer, and he does neither.

"These are the sort of accusations to which, as we were saying, you, Socrates, will be exposed if you accomplish your intentions; you, above all other Athenians." Suppose now I ask, why I rather than anybody else? They will justly retort upon me that I above all other men have acknowledged the agreement. "There is clear proof," they will say, "Socrates, that we and the city were not displeasing to you. Of all Athenians you have been the most constant resident in the city, which, as you never leave, you may be supposed to love. For you never went out of the city either to see the games, except once when you went to the Isthmus, or to any other place unless when you were on military service; nor did you travel as other men do. Nor had you any curiosity to know other states or their laws: your affections did not go beyond us and our state; we were your special favorites, and you acquiesced in our government of you; and here in this city you begat your children, which is a proof of your satisfaction. Moreover, you might in the course of the trial, if you had liked, have fixed the penalty at banishment; the state which refuses to let you go now would have let you go then. But you pretended that you preferred death to exile, and that you were not unwilling to die. And now you have forgotten these fine sentiments, and pay no respect to us the laws, of whom you are the destroyer; and are doing what only a miserable slave would do, running away and turning your back upon the compacts and agreements which you made as a citizen. And first of all answer this very question: Are we right in saying that you agreed to be governed according to us in deed, and not in word only? Is that true or not?" How shall we answer, Crito? Must we not assent?

Crito. We cannot help it, Socrates.

Socrates. Then will they not say: "You, Socrates, are breaking the covenants and agreements which you made with us at your leisure, not in any haste or under any compulsion or deception, but after you have had seventy years to think of them, during which time you were at liberty to leave the city, if we were not to your mind, or if our covenants appeared to you to be unfair. You had your choice, and might have gone either to Lacedaemon or Crete, both which states are often praised by you for their good government, or to some other Hellenic or foreign state. Whereas you, above all other Athenians, seemed to be so fond of the state, or, in other words, of us her laws (and who would care about a state which has no laws?), that you never stirred out of her; the halt, the blind, the maimed were not more stationary in her than you were. And now you run away and forsake your agreements. Not so, Socrates, if you will take our advice; do not make yourself ridiculous by escaping out of the city.

"For just consider, if you transgress and err in this sort of way, what good will you do either to yourself or to your friends? That your friends will be driven into exile and deprived of citizenship, or will lose their property, is tolerably certain; and you yourself, if you fly to one of the neighboring cities, as, for example, Thebes or Megara, both of which are well governed, will come to them as an enemy, Socrates, and their government will be against you, and all patriotic citizens will cast an evil eye upon you as a subverter of the laws, and you will confirm in the minds of the judges the justice of their own condemnation of you. For he who is a corrupter of the laws is more than likely to be a corrupter of the young and foolish portion of mankind. Will you then flee from well-ordered cities and virtuous men? and is existence worth having on these terms? Or will you go to them without shame, and talk to them, Socrates? And what will you say to them? What you say here about virtue and justice and institutions and laws being the best things among men? Would that be decent of you? Surely not. But if you go away from well-governed states to Crito's friends in Thessaly, where there is great disorder and license, they will be charmed to hear the tale of your escape from prison, set off with ludicrous particulars of the manner in which you were wrapped in a goatskin or some other disguise, and metamorphosed as the manner is of runaways; but will there be no one to remind you that in your old age you were not ashamed to violate the most sacred laws from a miserable desire of a little more life? Perhaps not, if you keep them in a good temper; but if they are out of temper you will hear many degrading things; you will live, but how?—as the flatterer of all men, and the servant of all men; and doing what?—eating and drinking in Thessaly, having gone abroad in order that you may get a dinner. And where will be your fine sentiments about justice and virtue? Say that you wish to live for the sake of your children—you want to bring them up and educate them—will you take them into Thessaly and deprive them of Athenian citizenship? Is this the benefit which you will confer upon them? Or are you under the impression that they will be better cared for and educated here if you are still alive, although absent from them; for your friends will take care of them? Do you fancy that if you are an inhabitant of Thessaly they will take care of them, and if you are an inhabitant of the other world that they will not take care of them? Nay; but if they who call themselves friends are good for anything, they will—to be sure they will.

"Listen, then, Socrates, to us who have brought you up. Think not of life and children first, and of justice afterward, but of justice first, that you may be justified before the princes of the world below. For neither will you nor any that belong to you be happier or holier or juster in this life, or happier in another, if you do as Crito bids. Now you depart in innocence, a sufferer and not a doer of evil; a victim, not of the laws but of men. But if you go forth, returning evil for evil, and injury for injury, breaking the covenants and agreements which you have made with us, and wronging those whom you ought least of all to wrong, that is to say, yourself, your friends, your country, and us, we shall be angry with you while you live, and our brethren, the laws in the world below, will receive you as an enemy; for they will know that you have done your best to destroy us. Listen, then, to us and not to Crito."

This, dear Crito, is the voice which I seem to hear murmuring in my ears, like the sound of the flute in the ears of the mystic; that voice, I say, is humming in my ears, and prevents me from hearing any other. And I know that anything more which you may say will be vain. Yet speak, if you have anything to say.

Crito. I have nothing to say, Socrates.

Socrates. Leave me then, Crito, to fulfill the will of God, and to follow whither he leads.

The Declaration of Independence

Thomas Jefferson

The opening lines of the Declaration of Independence provide one of our most important moral anchors. If we truly hold these liberties to be gifts from God, we realize the moral duty to respect, preserve, and defend those rights for others.

When in the Course of human events, it becomes necessary for one people to dissolve the political bands which have connected them with another, and to assume among the Powers of the earth, the separate and equal station to which the Laws of Nature and of Nature's God entitle them, a decent respect to the opinions of mankind requires that they should declare the causes which impel them to the separation.—We hold these truths to be self-evident, that all men are created equal, that they are endowed by their Creator with certain unalienable Rights, that among these are Life, Liberty and the pursuit of Happiness.—That to secure these rights, Governments are instituted among Men, deriving their just powers from the consent of the governed,—That whenever any Form of Government becomes destructive of these ends, it is the Right of the People to alter or to abolish it, and to institute new Government, laying its foundation on such principles and organizing its powers in such form, as to them shall seem most likely to effect their Safety and Happiness.

Federalist No. 55

James Madison

The essays known as the Federalist Papers first appeared in New York City newspapers between the autumn of 1787 and summer of 1788. Written by Alexander Hamilton, James Madison, and John Jay, they were addressed "To the People of the State of New York" and signed with the pseudonym "Publius." Their purpose was to convince the citizens of New York to ratify the Constitution recently drafted by the Philadelphia convention. Although penned in haste, the brilliant set of essays remains one of our most significant political documents and commentaries on American democracy. Here, in Federalist No. 55, James Madison takes up the question of whether a relatively small number of legislators can be trusted to safeguard the public liberty. Such a system can work, Madison argues, as long as the political and moral responsibilities of the people remain intact. Democracy presupposes the virtue of its individual citizens.

The true question to be decided then is, whether the smallness of the number, as a temporary regulation, be dangerous to the public liberty? Whether sixty-five members for a few years, and a hundred or two hundred for a few more, be a safe depositary for a limited and well-guarded power of legislating for the United States? I must own that I could not give a negative answer to this question without first obliterating every impression which I have received with regard to the present genius of the people of America, the spirit which actuates the State legislatures, and the principles which are incorporated with the political character of every class of citizens. I am unable to conceive that the people of America, in their present temper, or under any circumstances which can speedily happen, will choose, and every second year repeat the choice of, sixty-five or a hundred men who would be disposed to form and pursue a scheme of tyranny or treachery. I am unable to conceive that the State legislatures, which must feel so many motives to watch, and which possess so many means of counteracting, the federal legislature, would fail either to detect or to defeat a conspiracy of the latter against the liberties of their common constituents. I am equally unable to conceive that there are at this time, or can be in any short time, in the United States, any sixty-five or a hundred men capable of recommending themselves to the choice of the people at large, who would either desire or dare, within the short space of two years, to betray the solemn trust committed to them. What change of circumstances, time, and a fuller population of our country may produce, requires a prophetic spirit to declare, which makes no part of my pretensions. But judging from the circumstances now before us, and from the probable state of them within a moderate period of time, I must pronounce that the liberties of America cannot be unsafe in the number of hands proposed by the federal Constitution. . . .

As there is a degree of depravity in mankind which requires a certain degree of circumspection and distrust, so there are other qualities in human nature which justify a certain portion of esteem and confidence. Republican government presupposes the existence of these qualities in a higher degree than any other form. Were the pictures which have been drawn by the political jealousy of some among us faithful likenesses of the human character, the inference would be that there is not sufficient virtue among men for self-government; and that nothing less than the chains of despotism can restrain them from destroying and devouring one another.

The Conscience of the Nation Must Be Roused

Frederick Douglass

Frederick Douglass was born a slave in 1817 and raised by his grandmother on a Maryland plantation until sent to work at age eight in Baltimore. There, with the help of his new master's wife, he began to educate himself, an activity forbidden by law. In 1838, he escaped and settled in New Bedford, Massachusetts, and began working for the antislavery cause. It was not long before he was the nation's leading black abolitionist and one of its most brilliant orators.

In 1852, having been invited to deliver an Independence Day address in Rochester, New York, Douglass seized the occasion to hold the "scorching iron" of moral reproach to the nation's conscience. For Douglass and all black Americans, the Fourth of July was not an anniversary on which to rejoice at the rights and freedoms conferred by democracy; it was a day of deepest shame for those betraying the most basic moral obligations toward their fellow men. Here is a brave soul holding America accountable for its sins.

Fellow citizens, pardon me, allow me to ask, why am I called upon to speak here today? What have I, or those I represent, to do with your national independence? Are the great principles of political freedom and of natural justice, embodied in that Declaration of Independence, extended to us? and am I, therefore, called upon to bring our humble offering to the national altar, and to confess the benefits and express devout gratitude for the blessings resulting from your independence to us?

Would to God, both for your sakes and ours, that an affirmative answer could be truthfully returned to these questions! . . .

But such is not the state of the case. I say it with a sad sense of the disparity between us. I am not included within the pale of this glorious anniversary! Your high independence only reveals the immeasurable distance between us. The blessings in which you, this day, rejoice are not enjoyed in common. The rich inheritance of justice, liberty, prosperity, and independence bequeathed by your fathers is shared by you, not by me. The sunlight that brought light and healing to you has brought stripes and death to me. This Fourth of July is yours, not mine. You may rejoice, I must mourn. To drag a man in fetters into the grand illuminated temple of liberty, and call upon him to join you in joyous anthems, were inhuman mockery and sacrilegious irony. . . .

Fellow citizens, above your national, tumultuous joy, I hear the mournful wail of millions! whose chains, heavy and grievous yesterday, are, today, rendered more intolerable by the jubilee shouts that reach them. If I do forget, if I do not faithfully remember those bleeding children of sorrow this day, "may my right hand forget her cunning, and may my tongue cleave to the roof of my mouth!" To forget them, to pass lightly over their wrongs, and to chime in with the popular theme would be treason most scandalous and shocking, and would make me a reproach before God and the world. My subject, then, fellow citizens, is *American slavery*. I shall see this day and its popular characteristics from the slave's point of view. Standing there identified with the American bondman, making his wrongs mine, I do not hesitate to declare with all my soul that the character and conduct of this nation never looked blacker to me than on this Fourth of July! Whether we turn to the declarations of the past or to the professions of the present, the conduct of the nation seems equally hideous and revolting. America is false to the past, false to the present, and solemnly binds herself to be false to the future. Standing with God and the crushed and bleeding slave on this occasion, I will, in the name of humanity which is outraged, in the name of liberty which is fettered, in the name of the Constitution and the Bible which are disregarded and trampled upon, dare to call in question and to denounce, with all the emphasis I can command, everything that serves to perpetuate slavery—the great sin and shame of America! . . .

What, am I to argue that it is wrong to make men brutes, to rob them of their liberty, to work them without wages, to keep them ignorant of their relations to their fellow men, to beat them with sticks, to flay their flesh with the lash, to load their limbs with irons, to hunt them with dogs, to sell them at auction, to sunder their families, to knock out their teeth, to burn their flesh, to starve them into obedience and submission to their masters? Must I argue that a system thus marked with blood, and stained with pollution, is wrong? No! I will not. I have better employment for my time and strength than such arguments would imply.

What, then, remains to be argued? Is it that slavery is not divine; that God did not establish it; that our doctors of divinity are mistaken? There is blasphemy in the thought. That which is inhuman cannot be divine! Who can reason on such a proposition? They that can may; I cannot. The time for such argument is past.

At a time like this, scorching iron, not convincing argument, is needed. O! had I the ability, and could I reach the nation's ear, I would today pour out a fiery stream of biting ridicule, blasting reproach, withering sarcasm, and stern rebuke. For it is not light that is needed, but fire; it is not the gentle shower, but thunder. We need the storm, the whirlwind, and the earthquake. The feeling of the nation must be quickened; the conscience of the nation must be roused; the propriety of the nation must be startled; the hypocrisy of the nation must be exposed; and its crimes against God and man must be proclaimed and denounced.

What, to the American slave, is your Fourth of July? I answer: a day that reveals to him, more than all other days in the year, the gross injustice and cruelty to which he is the constant victim. To him, your celebration is a sham; your boasted liberty, an unholy license; your national greatness, swelling vanity; your sounds of re-joicing are empty and heartless; your denunciation of tyrants, brass-fronted impudence; your shouts of liberty and equality, hollow mockery; your prayers and hymns, your sermons and thanksgiv-ings, with all your religious parade and solemnity, are, to Him, mere bombast, fraud, deception, impiety, and hypocrisy—a thin veil to cover up crimes which would disgrace a nation of savages. There is not a nation of savages, there is not a nation on the earth guilty of practices more shocking and bloody than are the people of the United States at this very hour.

Second Message to Congress

Abraham Lincoln

In December 1862, with the Northern war effort seemingly grinding to a halt and public opinion turning against him, Abra-ham Lincoln resolutely wrote Congress that the federal govern-ment now faced two moral and political obligations: preserve the Union, and free the slaves. In Lincoln's mind, the two objectives had, at this point, become inseparable. He made his plea despite the protestations of some advisors who called his emancipation plans reckless and destructive. Here is the voice of a leader asking his fellow countrymen to cast off the prejudices of generations and follow the dictates of right and reason. One month later, Lincoln would sign the Emancipation Proclamation.

A nation may be said to consist of its territory, its people, and its laws. The territory is the only part which is of certain durability.

"One generation passeth away, and another generation cometh, but the earth abideth forever." It is of the first importance to duly consider, and estimate, this ever-enduring part. That portion of the earth's surface which is owned and inhabited by the people of the United States, is well adapted to be the home of one national family; and it is not well adapted for two, or more. Its vast extent, and its variety of climate and productions, are of advantage, in this age, for one people, whatever they might have been in former ages. Steam, telegraphs, and intelligence, have brought these, to be an advantageous combination, for one united people.

In the inaugural address I briefly pointed out the total inadequacy of disunion, as a remedy for the differences between the people of the two sections. I did so in language which I cannot improve, and which, therefore, I beg to repeat:

"One section of our country believes slavery is *right,* and ought to be extended, while the other believes it is *wrong,* and ought not to be extended. This is the only substantial dispute. . . . Physically speaking, we cannot separate. We cannot remove our respective sections from each other, nor build an impassable wall between them. A husband and wife may be divorced, and go out of the presence, and beyond the reach of each other; but the different parts of our country cannot do this. They cannot but remain face-to-face; and intercourse, either amicable or hostile, must continue between them. Is it possible, then, to make that intercourse more advantageous, or more satisfactory, *after* separation than *before?* Can aliens make treaties, easier than friends can make laws? Can treaties be more faithfully enforced between aliens, than laws can among friends? Suppose you go to war, you cannot fight always; and when, after much loss on both sides, and no gain on either, you cease fighting, the identical old questions, as to terms of intercourse, are again upon you. . . ."

If there ever could be a proper time for mere catch arguments, that time surely is not now. In times like the present, men should utter nothing for which they would not willingly be responsible through time and in eternity. . . .

I do not forget the gravity which should characterize a paper addressed to the Congress of the nation by the Chief Magistrate of the nation. Nor do I forget that some of you are my seniors, nor that many of you have more experience than I, in the conduct of public affairs. Yet I trust that in view of the great responsibility resting upon me, you will perceive no want of respect to yourselves, in any undue earnestness I may seem to display. . . .

The dogmas of the quiet past, are inadequate to the stormy present. The occasion is piled high with difficulty, and we must rise with the occasion. As our case is new, so we must think anew, and act anew. We must disenthrall ourselves, and then we shall save our country.

Fellow citizens, *we* cannot escape history. We of this Congress and this administration, will be remembered in spite of ourselves. No personal significance, or insignificance, can spare one or another of us. The fiery trial through which we pass, will light us down, in honor or dishonor, to the latest generation. We *say* we are for the Union. The world will not forget that we say this. We know how to save the Union. The world knows we do know how to save it. We—even *we here*—hold the power, and bear the responsibility. In *giving* freedom to the *slave,* we *assure* freedom to the *free*—honorable alike in what we give, and what we preserve. We shall nobly save, or meanly lose, the last best hope of earth. Other means may succeed; this could not fail. The way is plain, peaceful, generous, just— a way which, if followed, the world will forever applaud, and God must forever bless.

Letter from Birmingham City Jail

Martin Luther King, Jr.

Martin Luther King, Jr., wrote "Letter from Birmingham City Jail" on Easter weekend 1963 while in solitary confinement for leading nonviolent protests against racial discrimination. The letter was a response to a published statement by several leading clergymen calling for an end to the demonstrations. King asserted that the demonstrators' course was the morally responsible one, and he predicted that one day the nation would recognize the heroes who acted with "the noble sense of purpose that enables them to face jeering and hostile mobs, and with the agonizing loneliness that characterizes the life of the pioneer." Here are excerpts from one of the nation's most important political and

moral documents dealing with the issues of respect for law and
the grounds for justified civil disobedience.

I think I should indicate why I am here in Birmingham, since
you have been influenced by the view which argues against "outsiders coming in." . . . So I, along with several members of my staff,
am here because I was invited here. I am here because I have organizational ties here.

But more basically, I am in Birmingham because injustice is
here. Just as the prophets of the eighth century B.C. left their villages
and carried their "thus saith the Lord" far beyond the boundaries of
their hometowns, and just as the Apostle Paul left his village of
Tarsus and carried the gospel of Jesus Christ to the far corners of the
Greco-Roman world, so am I compelled to carry the gospel of freedom beyond my own hometown. Like Paul, I must constantly respond to the Macedonian call for aid.

Moreover, I am cognizant of the interrelatedness of all communities and states. I cannot sit idly by in Atlanta and not be concerned
about what happens in Birmingham. Injustice anywhere is a threat
to justice everywhere. We are caught in an inescapable network of
mutuality, tied in a single garment of destiny. Whatever affects one
directly, affects all indirectly. Never again can we afford to live with
the narrow, provincial "outside agitator" idea. Anyone who lives
inside the United States can never be considered an outsider anywhere within its bounds.

You deplore the demonstrations taking place in Birmingham.
But your statement, I am sorry to say, fails to express a similar
concern for the conditions that brought about the demonstrations. I
am sure that none of you would want to rest content with the superficial kind of social analysis that deals merely with effects and does
not grapple with underlying causes. It is unfortunate that demonstrations are taking place in Birmingham, but it is even more unfortunate that the city's white power structure left the Negro community
with no alternative.

In any nonviolent campaign there are four basic steps: collection
of the facts to determine whether injustices exist; negotiation; self-purification; and direct action. We have gone through all these steps
in Birmingham. There can be no gainsaying the fact that racial injustice engulfs this community. Birmingham is probably the most thoroughly segregated city in the United States. Its ugly record of

brutality is widely known. Negroes have experienced grossly unjust
treatment in the courts. There have been more unsolved bombings
of Negro homes and churches in Birmingham than in any other city
in the nation. These are the hard, brutal facts of the case. . . .

You express a great deal of anxiety over our willingness to
break laws. This is certainly a legitimate concern. Since we so diligently urge people to obey the Supreme Court's decision of 1954
outlawing segregation in the public schools, at first glance it may
seem rather paradoxical for us consciously to break laws. One may
well ask: "How can you advocate breaking some laws and obeying
others?" The answer lies in the fact that there are two types of laws:
just and unjust. I would be the first to advocate obeying just laws.
One has not only a legal but a moral responsibility to obey just laws.
Conversely, one has a moral responsibility to disobey unjust laws.
I would agree with St. Augustine that "an unjust law is no law at
all."

Now, what is the difference between the two? How does one
determine whether a law is just or unjust? A just law is a man-made
code that squares with the moral law or the law of God. An unjust
law is a code that is out of harmony with the moral law. To put it in
the terms of St. Thomas Aquinas: an unjust law is a human law that
is not rooted in eternal law and natural law. Any law that uplifts
human personality is just. Any law that degrades human personality
is unjust. All segregation statutes are unjust because segregation
distorts the soul and damages the personality. It gives the segre-
gator a false sense of superiority and the segregated a false sense of
inferiority. Segregation, to use the terminology of the Jewish
philosopher Martin Buber, substitutes an "I–it" relationship for an
"I–thou" relationship and ends up relegating persons to the status
of things. Hence segregation is not only politically, economically,
and sociologically unsound, it is morally wrong and sinful. Paul
Tillich has said that sin is separation. Is not segregation an existential
expression of man's tragic separation, his awful estrangement, his
terrible sinfulness? Thus it is that I can urge men to obey the 1954
decision of the Supreme Court, for it is morally right; and I can
urge them to disobey segregation ordinances, for they are morally
wrong.

Let us consider a more concrete example of just and unjust laws.
An unjust law is a code that a numerical or power majority group
compels a minority group to obey but does not make binding on
itself. This is *difference* made legal. By the same token, a just law is a

code that a majority compels a minority to follow and that it is willing to follow itself. This is *sameness* made legal.

Let me give another explanation. A law is unjust if it is inflicted on a minority that, as a result of being denied the right to vote, had no part in enacting or devising the law. Who can say that the legislature of Alabama which set up the state's segregation laws was democratically elected? Throughout Alabama all sorts of devious methods are used to prevent Negroes from becoming registered voters, and there are some counties in which, even though Negroes constitute a majority of the population, not a single Negro is registered. Can any law enacted under such circumstances be considered democratically structured?

Sometimes a law is just on its face and unjust in its application. For instance, I have been arrested on a charge of parading without a permit. Now, there is nothing wrong in having an ordinance which requires a permit for a parade. But such an ordinance becomes unjust when it is used to maintain segregation and to deny citizens the First Amendment privilege of peaceful assembly and protest.

I hope you are able to see the distinction I am trying to point out. In no sense do I advocate evading or defying the law, as would the rabid segregationist. That would lead to anarchy. One who breaks an unjust law must do so openly, lovingly, and with a willingness to accept the penalty. I submit that an individual who breaks a law that conscience tells him is unjust, and who willingly accepts the penalty of imprisonment in order to arouse the conscience of the community over its injustice, is in reality expressing the highest respect for law. . . .

You speak of our activity in Birmingham as extreme. . . . But though I was initially disappointed at being categorized as an extremist, as I continued to think about the matter I gradually gained a measure of satisfaction from the label. Was not Jesus an extremist for love: "Love your enemies, bless them that curse you, do good to them that hate you, and pray for them which despitefully use you, and persecute you." Was not Amos an extremist for justice: "Let justice roll down like waters and righteousness like an ever-flowing stream." Was not Paul an extremist for the Christian gospel: "I bear in my body the marks of the Lord Jesus." Was not Martin Luther an extremist: "Here I stand; I cannot do otherwise, so help me God." And John Bunyan: "I will stay in jail to the end of my days before I make a butchery of my conscience." And Abraham Lincoln: "This nation cannot survive half slave and half free." And Thomas Jefferson: "We hold these truths to be self-evident, that all men are created equal. . . ." So the question is not whether we will be extremists, but what kind of extremists we will be. Will we be extremists for hate or for love? Will we be extremists for the preservation of injustice or for the extension of justice? . . .

One day the South will recognize its real heroes. They will be the James Merediths, with the noble sense of purpose that enables them to face jeering and hostile mobs, and with the agonizing loneliness that characterizes the life of the pioneer. They will be old, oppressed, battered Negro women, symbolized in a seventy-two-year-old woman in Montgomery, Alabama, who rose up with a sense of dignity and with her people decided not to ride segregated buses, and who responded with ungrammatical profundity to one who inquired about her weariness: "My feets is tired, but my soul is at rest." They will be the young high school and college students, the young ministers of the gospel and a host of their elders, courageously and nonviolently sitting in at lunch counters and willingly going to jail for conscience' sake. One day the South will know that when these disinherited children of God sat down at lunch counters, they were in reality standing up for what is best in the American dream and for the most sacred values in our Judeo-Christian heritage, thereby bringing our nation back to those great wells of democracy which were dug deep by the founding fathers in their formulation of the Constitution and the Declaration of Independence.. . .

I hope this letter finds you strong in the faith. I also hope that circumstances will soon make it possible for me to meet each of you, not as an integrationist or a civil rights leader but as a fellow clergyman and a Christian brother. Let us all hope that the dark clouds of racial prejudice will soon pass away and the deep fog of misunderstanding will be lifted from our fear-drenched communities, and in some not too distant tomorrow the radiant stars of love and brotherhood will shine over our great nation with all their scintillating beauty.

Yours for the cause of Peace and Brotherhood,
MARTIN LUTHER KING, JR.

Men Without Chests

C. S. Lewis

C. S. Lewis (1898–1963) was one of our greatest modern thinkers about the responsibility of adults in educating the young. Here, in *The Abolition of Man*, he makes the case that if we fail to pass along specific standards of right and wrong, of what is worthwhile or worthless, admirable or ignoble, then we must share blame for the consequent failings of character. The closing paragraph of this excerpt is one of my favorite passages in all the literature about education.

Until quite modern times all teachers and even all men believed the universe to be such that certain emotional reactions on our part could be either congruous or incongruous to it—believed, in fact, that objects did not merely receive, but could *merit*, our approval or disapproval, our reverence, or our contempt. . . .

"Can you be righteous," asks Traherne, "unless you be just in rendering to things their due esteem? All things were made to be yours and you were made to prize them according to their value." St. Augustine defines virtue as *ordo amoris*, the ordinate condition of the affections in which every object is accorded that kind and degree of love which is appropriate to it. Aristotle says that the aim of education is to make the pupil like and dislike what he ought. When the age for reflective thought comes, the pupil who has been thus trained in "ordinate affections" or "just sentiments" will easily find the first principles in Ethics: but to the corrupt man they will never be visible at all and he can make no progress in that science. Plato before him had said the same. The little human animal will not at first have the right responses. It must be trained to feel pleasure, liking, disgust, and hatred at those things which really are pleasant, likable, disgusting, and hateful. In the *Republic,* the well-nurtured youth is one "who would see most clearly whatever was amiss in ill-made works of man or ill-grown works of nature, and with a just distaste would blame and hate the ugly even from his earliest years and would give delighted praise to beauty, receiving it into his soul and being nourished by it, so that he becomes a man of gentle heart.

All this before he is of an age to reason; so that when Reason at length comes to him, then, bred as he has been, he will hold out his hands in welcome and recognize her because of the affinity he bears to her." In early Hinduism that conduct in men which can be called good consists in conformity to, or almost participation in, the *Rta*— that great ritual or pattern of nature and supernature which is revealed alike in the cosmic order, the moral virtues, and the ceremonial of the temple. Righteousness, correctness, order, the *Rta,* is constantly identified with *satya* or truth, correspondence to reality. As Plato said that the Good was "beyond existence" and Wordsworth that through virtue the stars were strong, so the Indian masters say that the gods themselves are born of the *Rta* and obey it. The Chinese also speak of a great thing (the greatest thing) called the *Tao.* It is the reality beyond all predicates, the abyss that was before the Creator Himself. It is Nature, it is the Way, the Road. It is the Way in which the universe goes on, the Way in which things everlastingly emerge, stilly and tranquilly, into space and time. It is also the Way which every man should tread in imitation of that cosmic and supercosmic progression, conforming all activities to that great exemplar. "In ritual," say the Analects, "it is harmony with Nature that is prized." The ancient Jews likewise praise the Law as being "true." . . .

But what is common to them all is something we cannot neglect. It is the doctrine of objective value, the belief that certain attitudes are really true, and others really false, to the kind of thing the universe is and the kind of things we are. . . .

Hence the educational problem is wholly different according as you stand within or without the *Tao.* For those within, the task is to train in the pupil those responses which are in themselves appropriate, whether anyone is making them or not, and in making which the very nature of man consists. Those without, if they are logical, must regard all sentiments as equally nonrational, as mere mists between us and the real objects. As a result, they must either decide to remove all sentiments, as far as possible, from the pupil's mind: or else to encourage some sentiments for reasons that have nothing to do with their intrinsic "justness" or "ordinacy." The latter course involves them in the questionable process of creating in others by "suggestion" or incantation a mirage which their own reason has successfully dissipated. . . .

And all the time—such is the tragicomedy of our situation— we continue to clamor for those very qualities we are rendering impossible. You can hardly open a periodical without coming across the statement that what our civilization needs is more "drive," or dynamism, or self-sacrifice, or "creativity." In a sort of ghastly simplicity we remove the organ and demand the function. We make men without chests and expect of them virtue and enterprise. We laugh at honor and are shocked to find traitors in our midst. We castrate and bid the geldings be fruitful.

4

Friendship

Good stories invite us to slip into the shoes of other people, a crucial step in acquiring a moral perspective. Stories about friendship require taking the perspective of friends, taking others seriously for their own sakes. In the best friendships we see in perhaps its purest form a moral paradigm for all human relations.

As the selections in this chapter make plain, friendship is more than acquaintance, and it involves more than affection. Friendship usually rises out of mutual interests and common aims, and these pursuits are strengthened by the benevolent impulses that sooner or later grow. The demands of friendship—for frankness, for self-revelation, for taking friends' criticisms as seriously as their expressions of admiration or praise, for stand-by-me loyalty, and for assistance to the point of self-sacrifice—are all potent encouragements to moral maturation and even ennoblement.

Of course, weaknesses induce companionship just as easily, in fact more easily, than do virtues. There are relationships undeserving of the title friendship that go by that name nonetheless, the kinds of "friendship" English essayist Joseph Addison called "confederacies in vice, or leagues of pleasure." Mutual desires and selfishness can be the foundations of counterfeit friendships. In our age, when casual acquaintance often comes so easily, and when intimacy comes too soon and too cheaply, we need to be reminded that genuine friendships take time. They take effort to make, and work to keep. Friendship is a deep thing. It is, indeed, a form of love. And while it may be, as C. S. Lewis said, the least biological form of love, it is also one of the most important.

Every parent knows how crucial the choice of friends is for every child. Childhood friendships tell parents which ways their children are tending. They are important because good friends bring you up, and bad friends bring you down. So it matters who our children's friends are. And it matters, as examples to our children, who our friends are. Friends should be allies of our better natures.

We must teach children how to recognize counterfeit friendships, to know they are injurious, to realize they reinforce what is less than noble in us.

Having friends is only half the relationship, of course, though it is the half that both children and parents tend to be most consciously concerned with. *Being* a friend is often more important to our moral development. The other side of "good friends bring you up" is the side where you are the good friend, the active agent that brings the other up. To *befriend* a friendless or less fortunate schoolmate can be a profoundly maturing activity for a child. Such familiar exhortations as "Friends don't let friends drive drunk" and "To *have* a friend, *be* a friend" help keep us mindful of this more active side of friendship.

Here, then, are some varieties of friendship. Here we find friends who stick together in adversity, friends who give more than they expect to receive, friends who incite each other to higher purposes. We find small deeds done for the sake of friendship, as well as great acts of sacrifice; friends simply going a little out of their way for each other, and friends risking or even offering their lives. We see pleasure found in new friendships, comfort known in old ones, and pain suffered for those lost. From these varieties of friendships, we learn to improve our own.

The Pasture

Robert Frost

This little poem reminds us that a friend is someone we want to be with.

> I'm going out to clean the pasture spring;
> I'll only stop to rake the leaves away
> (And wait to watch the water clear, I may):
> I sha'n't be gone long.—You come too.
>
> I'm going out to fetch the little calf
> That's standing by the mother. It's so young,
> It totters when she licks it with her tongue.
> I sha'n't be gone long.—You come too.

The Bear and the Travelers

Aesop

Fair-weather friends were around in the days of Aesop, in the sixth century B.C., and they still abound today. Children should learn how to recognize one, and how not to be one.

Two Travelers were on the road together, when a Bear suddenly appeared on the scene. Before he observed them, one made for a tree at the side of the road, and climbed up into the branches and hid there. The other was not so nimble as his companion; and, as he could not escape, he threw himself on the ground and pretended to be dead. The Bear came up and sniffed all round him, but he kept perfectly still and held his breath; for they say that a bear will not touch a dead body. The Bear took him for a corpse, and went away. When the coast was clear, the Traveler in the tree came down, and asked the other what it was the Bear had whispered to him when he put his mouth to his ear. The other replied, "He told me never again to travel with a friend who deserts you at the first sign of danger."

Misfortune tests the sincerity of friendship.

Cat and Mouse in Partnership

The Brothers Grimm

As this story shows us, picking the wrong friend can be disappointing or even disastrous.

A cat having made acquaintance with a mouse, professed such great love and friendship for her, that the mouse at last agreed that they should live and keep house together.

"We must make provision for the winter," said the cat, "or we shall suffer hunger, and you, little mouse, must not stir out, or you will be caught in a trap."

So they took counsel together and bought a little pot of honey. And then they could not tell where to put it for safety, but after long consideration the cat said there could not be a better place than the church, for nobody would steal there, and they would put it under the altar and not touch it until they were really in want. So this was done, and the little pot placed in safety.

But before long the cat was seized with a great wish to taste it.

"Listen to me, little mouse," said he, "I have been asked by my cousin to stand godfather to a little son she has brought into the world. He is white with brown spots. And they want to have the christening today, so let me go to it, and you stay at home and keep house."

"Oh yes, certainly," answered the mouse, "pray go by all means. And when you are feasting on all the good things, think of me. I should so like a drop of the sweet red wine."

But there was not a word of truth in all this. The cat had no cousin, and had not been asked to stand godfather. He went to the church, straight up to the little pot, and licked the honey off the top. Then he took a walk over the roofs of the town, saw his acquaintances, stretched himself in the sun, and licked his whiskers as often as he thought of the little pot of honey. And then when it was evening he went home.

"Here you are at last," said the mouse. "I expect you have had a merry time."

"Oh, pretty well," answered the cat.

"And what name did you give the child?" asked the mouse.

"Top-off," answered the cat, dryly.

"Top-off!" cried the mouse. "That is a singular and wonderful name! Is it common in your family?"

"What does it matter?" said the cat. "It's not any worse than Crumb-picker, like your godchild."

A little time after this the cat was again seized with a longing.

"Again I must ask you," said he to the mouse, "to do me a favor, and keep house alone for a day. I have been asked a second time to stand godfather. And as the little one has a white ring around its neck, I cannot well refuse."

So the kind little mouse consented, and the cat crept along by the town wall until he reached the church, and going straight to the little pot of honey, devoured half of it.

"Nothing tastes so well as what one keeps to oneself," said he, feeling quite content with his day's work. When he reached home, the mouse asked what name had been given to the child.

"Half-gone," answered the cat.

"Half-gone!" cried the mouse. "I never heard such a name in my life! I'll bet it's not to be found in the calendar."

Soon after that the cat's mouth began to water again for the honey.

"Good things always come in threes," said he to the mouse. "Again I have been asked to stand godfather, the little one is quite black with white feet, and not any white hair on its body. Such a thing does not happen every day, so you will let me go, won't you?"

"Top-off, Half-gone," murmured the mouse. "They are such curious names, I cannot but wonder at them!"

"That's because you are always sitting at home," said the cat, "in your little gray frock and hairy tail, never seeing the world, and fancying all sorts of things."

So the little mouse cleaned up the house and set it all in order. Meanwhile the greedy cat went and made an end of the little pot of honey.

"Now all is finished one's mind will be easy," said he, and came home in the evening, quite sleek and comfortable. The mouse asked at once what name had been given to the third child.

"It won't please you any better than the others," answered the cat. "It is called All-gone."

"All-gone!" cried the mouse. "What an unheard-of name! I never met with anything like it! All-gone! Whatever can it mean?" And shaking her head, she curled herself round and went to sleep. After that the cat was not again asked to stand godfather.

When the winter had come and there was nothing more to be had out of doors, the mouse began to think of their store.

"Come, cat," said she, "we will fetch our pot of honey, how good it will taste, to be sure!"

"Of course it will," said the cat.

So they set out, and when they reached the place, they found the pot, but it was standing empty.

"Oh, now I know what it all meant," cried the mouse, "now I see what sort of a partner you have been! Instead of standing god-father you have devoured it all, first Top-off, then Half-gone, then—"

"Will you hold your tongue!" screamed the cat. "Another word, and I'll devour you too!"

And the poor little mouse having "All-gone" on her tongue, out it came, and the cat leaped upon her and made an end of her. And that is the way of the world.

The Velveteen Rabbit

Margery Williams

Since the early part of this century, this story of how a toy rabbit becomes real has helped children learn that sometimes what we go through for a friend makes us a little worn and torn, but that's what makes the friendship real. Friendship often contains some trial, but true friendship endures the test and even grows from it.

There was once a Velveteen Rabbit, and in the beginning he was really splendid. He was fat and bunchy, as a rabbit should be; his coat was spotted brown and white, he had real thread whiskers, and his ears were lined with pink sateen. On Christmas morning, when he sat wedged in the top of the Boy's stocking, with a sprig of holly between his paws, the effect was charming.

There were other things in the stocking, nuts and oranges and a toy engine, and chocolate almonds and a clockwork mouse, but the Rabbit was quite the best of all. For at least two hours the Boy loved him, and then Aunts and Uncles came to dinner, and there was a great rustling of tissue paper and unwrapping of parcels, and in the excitement of looking at all the new presents the Velveteen Rabbit was forgotten.

For a long time he lived in the toy cupboard or on the nursery floor, and no one thought very much about him. He was naturally shy, and being only made of velveteen, some of the more expensive toys quite snubbed him. The mechanical toys were very superior, and looked down upon everyone else; they were full of modern ideas, and pretended they were real. The model boat, who had lived through two seasons and lost most of his paint, caught the tone from them and never missed an opportunity of referring to his rigging in technical terms. The Rabbit could not claim to be a model of anything, for he didn't know that real rabbits existed; he thought they were all stuffed with sawdust like himself, and he understood that sawdust was quite out-of-date and should never be mentioned in modern circles. Even Timothy, the jointed wooden lion, who was made by the disabled soldiers, and should have had broader views, put on airs and pretended he was connected with Government. Between them all the poor little Rabbit was made to feel himself very insignificant and commonplace, and the only person who was kind to him at all was the Skin Horse.

The Skin Horse had lived longer in the nursery than any of the others. He was so old that his brown coat was bald in patches and showed the seams underneath, and most of the hairs in his tail had been pulled out to string bead necklaces. He was wise, for he had seen a long succession of mechanical toys arrive to boast and swagger, and by and by break their mainsprings and pass away, and he knew that they were only toys, and would never turn into anything else. For nursery magic is very strange and wonderful, and only those playthings that are old and wise and experienced like the Skin Horse understand all about it.

"What is REAL?" asked the Rabbit one day, when they were lying side by side near the nursery fender, before Nana came to tidy the room. "Does it mean having things that buzz inside you and a stick-out handle?"

"Real isn't how you are made," said the Skin Horse. "It's a thing that happens to you. When a child loves you for a long, long time, not just to play with, but REALLY loves you, then you become Real."

"Does it hurt?" asked the Rabbit.

"Sometimes," said the Skin Horse, for he was always truthful. "When you are Real you don't mind being hurt."

"Does it happen all at once, like being wound up," he asked, "or bit by bit?"

"It doesn't happen all at once," said the Skin Horse. "You become. It takes a long time. That's why it doesn't often happen to people who break easily, or have sharp edges, or who have to be carefully kept. Generally, by the time you are Real, most of your hair has been loved off, and your eyes drop out and you get loose in the joints and very shabby. But these things don't matter at all, because once you are Real you can't be ugly, except to people who don't understand."

"I suppose *you* are Real?" said the Rabbit. And then he wished he had not said it, for he thought the Skin Horse might be sensitive. But the Skin Horse only smiled.

"The Boy's uncle made me Real," he said. "That was a great many years ago; but once you are Real you can't become unreal again. It lasts for always."

The Rabbit sighed. He thought it would be a long time before this magic called Real happened to him. He longed to become Real, to know what it felt like; and yet the idea of growing shabby and losing his eyes and whiskers was rather sad. He wished that he could become it without these uncomfortable things happening to him.

There was a person called Nana who ruled the nursery. Sometimes she took no notice of the playthings lying about, and sometimes, for no reason whatever, she went swooping about like a great wind and hustled them away in cupboards. She called this "tidying up," and the playthings all hated it, especially the tin ones. The Rabbit didn't mind it so much, for wherever he was thrown he came down soft.

One evening, when the Boy was going to bed, he couldn't find the china dog that always slept with him. Nana was in a hurry, and it was too much trouble to hunt for china dogs at bedtime, so she simply looked about her, and seeing that the toy cupboard door stood open, she made a swoop.

"Here," she said, "take your old Bunny! He'll do to sleep with you!" And she dragged the Rabbit out by one ear, and put him into the Boy's arms.

That night, and for many nights after, the Velveteen Rabbit slept in the Boy's bed. At first he found it rather uncomfortable, for the boy hugged him very tight, and sometimes he rolled over on him, and sometimes he pushed him so far under the pillow that the Rabbit could scarcely breathe. And he missed, too, those long moonlight hours in the nursery, when all the house was silent, and his talks with the Skin Horse. But very soon he grew to like it, for the Boy used to talk to him, and made nice tunnels for him under the bedclothes that he said were like the burrows the real rabbits lived in. And they had splendid games together, in whispers, when Nana had gone away to her supper and left the night-light burning on the mantelpiece. And when the Boy dropped off to sleep, the Rabbit would snuggle down close under his little warm chin and dream, with the Boy's hands clasped close round him all night long.

And so time went on, and the little Rabbit was very happy—so happy that he never noticed how his beautiful velveteen fur was getting shabbier and shabbier, and his tail coming unsewn, and all the pink rubbed off his nose where the Boy had kissed him.

Spring came, and they had long days in the garden, for wherever the Boy went the Rabbit went, too. He had rides in the wheelbarrow, and picnics on the grass, and lovely fairy huts built for him under the raspberry canes behind the flower border. And once, when the boy was called away suddenly to go out to tea, the Rabbit was left out on the lawn until long after dusk, and Nana had to come and look for him with the candle because the Boy couldn't go to sleep unless he was there. He was wet through with the dew and quite earthy from diving into the burrows the Boy had made for him in the flower bed, and Nana grumbled as she rubbed him off with a corner of her apron.

"You must have your old Bunny!" she said. "Fancy all that fuss for a toy!"

The boy sat up in bed and stretched out his hands.

"Give me my Bunny!" he said. "You mustn't say that. He isn't a toy. He's REAL!"

When the little Rabbit heard that he was happy, for he knew that what the Skin Horse had said was true at last. The nursery magic had happened to him, and he was a toy no longer. He was Real. The Boy himself had said it.

That night he was almost too happy to sleep, and so much love stirred in his little sawdust heart that it almost burst. And into his boot-button eyes, that had long ago lost their polish, there came a look of wisdom and beauty, so that even Nana noticed it next morning when she picked him up, and said, "I declare if that old Bunny hasn't got quite a knowing expression!"

That was a wonderful summer!

Near the house where they lived there was a wood, and in the long June evenings the Boy liked to go there after tea to play. He took the Velveteen Rabbit with him, and before he wandered off to pick flowers, or play at brigands among the trees, he always made the Rabbit a little nest somewhere among the bracken, where he would be quite cosy, for he was a kindhearted little boy and he liked Bunny to be comfortable. One evening, while the Rabbit was lying there alone, watching the ants that ran to and fro between his velvet paws in the grass, he saw two strange beings creep out of the tall bracken near him.

They were rabbits like himself, but quite furry and brand-new. They must have been very well made, for their seams didn't show at all, and they changed shape in a queer way when they moved; one minute they were long and thin and the next minute fat and bunchy, instead of always staying the same like he did. Their feet padded softly on the ground, and they crept quite close to him, twitching their noses, while the rabbit stared hard to see which side the clockwork stuck out, for he knew that people who jump generally have something to wind them up. But he couldn't see it. They were evidently a new kind of rabbit altogether.

They stared at him, and the little Rabbit stared back. And all the time their noses twitched.

"Why don't you get up and play with us?" one of them asked.

"I don't feel like it," said the Rabbit, for he didn't want to explain that he had no clockwork.

"Ho!" said the furry rabbit. "It's as easy as anything." And he gave a big hop sideways and stood on his hind legs.

"I don't believe you can!" he said.

"I can!" said the little Rabbit. "I can jump higher than anything!" He meant when the Boy threw him, but of course he didn't want to say so.

"Can you hop on your hind legs?" asked the furry rabbit.

That was a dreadful question, for the Velveteen Rabbit had no hind legs at all! The back of him was made all in one piece, like a pincushion. He sat still in the bracken, and hoped that the other rabbits wouldn't notice.

"I don't want to!" he said again.

But the wild rabbits have very sharp eyes. And this one stretched out his neck and looked.

"He hasn't got any hind legs!" he called out. "Fancy a rabbit without any hind legs!" And he began to laugh.

"I have!" cried the little Rabbit. "I have got hind legs! I am sitting on them!"

"Then stretch them out and show me, like this!" said the wild rabbit. And he began to whirl round and dance, till the little Rabbit got quite dizzy.

"I don't like dancing," he said. "I'd rather sit still!"

But all the while he was longing to dance, for a funny new tickly feeling ran through him, and he felt he would give anything in the world to be able to jump about like these rabbits did.

The strange rabbit stopped dancing, and came quite close. He came so close this time that his long whiskers brushed the Velveteen Rabbit's ear, and then he wrinkled his nose suddenly and flattened his ears and jumped backward.

"He doesn't smell right!" he exclaimed. "He isn't a rabbit at all! He isn't real!"

"I *am* Real!" said the little Rabbit. "I am Real! The Boy said so!" And he nearly began to cry.

Just then there was a sound of footsteps, and the Boy ran past near them, and with a stamp of feet and a flash of white tails the two strange rabbits disappeared.

"Come back and play with me!" called the little Rabbit. "Oh, do come back! I *know* I am Real!"

But there was no answer, only the little ants ran to and fro, and the bracken swayed gently where the two strangers had passed. The Velveteen Rabbit was all alone.

"Oh, dear!" he thought. "Why did they run away like that? Why couldn't they stop and talk to me?"

For a long time he lay very still, watching the bracken, and hoping that they would come back. But they never returned, and presently the sun sank lower and the little white moths fluttered out, and the Boy came and carried him home.

Weeks passed, and the little Rabbit grew very old and shabby, but the Boy loved him just as much. He loved him so hard that he loved all his whiskers off, and the pink lining to his ears turned gray, and his brown spots faded. He even began to lose his shape, and he scarcely looked like a rabbit anymore, except to the Boy. To him he was always beautiful, and that was all that the little Rabbit cared about. He didn't mind how he looked to other people, because the nursery magic had made him Real, and when you are Real, shabbiness doesn't matter.

And then, one day, the Boy was ill.

His face grew very flushed, and he talked in his sleep, and his little body was so hot that it burned the Rabbit when he held him close. Strange people came and went in the nursery, and a light burned all night and through it all the little Velveteen Rabbit lay there, hidden from sight under the bedclothes, and he never stirred, for he was afraid that if they found him someone might take him away, and he knew that the Boy needed him.

It was a long weary time, for the Boy was too ill to play, and the little Rabbit found it rather dull with nothing to do all day long. But he snuggled down patiently, and looked forward to the time when the Boy should be well again, and they would go out in the garden amongst the flowers and the butterflies and play splendid games in the raspberry thicket like they used to. All sorts of delightful things he planned, and while the Boy lay half asleep he crept up close to the pillow and whispered them in his ear. And presently the fever turned, and the Boy got better. He was able to sit up in bed and look at picture books, while the little Rabbit cuddled close at his side. And one day, they let him get up and dress.

It was a bright, sunny morning, and the windows stood wide open. They had carried the Boy out onto the balcony, wrapped in a shawl, and the little Rabbit lay tangled up among the bedclothes, thinking.

The Boy was going to the seaside tomorrow. Everything was arranged, and now it only remained to carry out the doctor's orders. They talked about it all, while the little Rabbit lay under the bedclothes, with just his head peeping out, and listened. The room was to be disinfected, and all the books and toys that the Boy had played with in bed must be burned.

"Hurrah!" thought the little Rabbit. "Tomorrow we shall go to the seaside!" For the Boy had often talked of the seaside, and he wanted very much to see the big waves coming in, and the tiny crabs, and the sand castles.

Just then Nana caught sight of him.

"How about his old Bunny?" she asked.

"*That?*" said the doctor. "Why, it's a mass of scarlet fever germs!—Burn it at once. What? Nonsense! Get him a new one. He mustn't have that anymore!"

And so the little Rabbit was put into a sack with the old picture books and a lot of rubbish, and carried out to the end of the garden behind the fowl house. That was a fine place to make a bonfire, only the gardener was too busy just then to attend to it. He had the potatoes to dig and the green peas to gather, but next morning he promised to come quite early and burn the whole lot.

That night the Boy slept in a different bedroom, and he had a new bunny to sleep with him. It was a splendid bunny, all white plush with real glass eyes, but the Boy was too excited to care very much about it. For tomorrow he was going to the seaside, and that in itself was such a wonderful thing that he could think of nothing else.

And while the Boy was asleep, dreaming of the seaside, the little Rabbit lay among the old picture books in the corner behind the fowl house, and he felt very lonely. The sack had been left untied, and so by wriggling a bit he was able to get his head through the opening and look out. He was shivering a little, for he had always been used to sleeping in a proper bed, and by this time his coat had worn so thin and threadbare from hugging that it was no longer any protection to him. Nearby he could see the thicket of raspberry canes, growing tall and close like a tropical jungle, in whose shadow he had played with the Boy on bygone mornings. He thought of those long sunlit hours in the garden—how happy they were—and a great sadness came over him. He seemed to see them all pass before him, each more beautiful than the other, the fairy huts in the flower bed, the quiet evenings in the wood when he lay in the bracken and the little ants ran over his paws; the wonderful day when he first knew that he was Real. He thought of the Skin Horse, so wise and gentle, and all that he had told him. Of what use was it to be loved and lose one's beauty and become Real if it all ended like this? And a tear, a real tear, trickled down his little shabby velvet nose and fell to the ground.

And then a strange thing happened. For where the tear had fallen a flower grew out of the ground, a mysterious flower, not at all like any that grew in the garden. It had slender green leaves the color of emeralds, and in the center of the leaves a blossom like a golden cup. It was so beautiful that the little Rabbit forgot to cry, and just lay there watching it. And presently the blossom opened, and out of it there stepped a Fairy.

She was quite the loveliest Fairy in the whole world. Her dress was of pearl and dewdrops, and there were flowers round her neck and in her hair, and her face was like the most perfect flower of all. And she came close to the little Rabbit and gathered him up in her arms and kissed him on his velveteen nose that was all damp from crying.

"Little Rabbit," she said, "don't you know who I am?"

The Rabbit looked up at her, and it seemed to him that he had seen her face before, but he couldn't think where.

"I am the nursery magic Fairy," she said. "I take care of all the playthings that the children have loved. When they are old and worn out and the children don't need them anymore, then I come and take them away with me and turn them into Real."

"Wasn't I Real before?" asked the little Rabbit.

"You were Real to the Boy," the Fairy said, "because he loved you. Now you shall be Real to everyone."

And she held the little Rabbit close in her arms and flew him into the wood.

It was light now, for the moon had risen. All the forest was beautiful, and the fronds of the bracken shone like frosted silver. In the open glade between the tree trunks the wild rabbits danced with their shadows on the velvet grass, but when they saw the Fairy they all stopped dancing and stood round in a ring to stare at her.

"I've brought you a new playfellow," the Fairy said. "You must be very kind to him and teach him all he needs to know in Rabbitland, for he is going to live with you forever and ever!"

And she kissed the little Rabbit again and put him down on the grass.

"Run and play, little Rabbit!" she said.

But the little Rabbit sat quite still for a moment and never moved. For when he saw all the wild rabbits dancing around him he suddenly remembered about his hind legs, and he didn't want them to see that he was made all in one piece. He did not know that when the Fairy kissed him that last time she had changed him altogether. And he might have sat there a long time, too shy to move, if just then something hadn't tickled his nose, and before he thought what he was doing he lifted his hind toe to scratch it.

And he found that he actually had hind legs! Instead of dingy velveteen he had brown fur, soft and shiny, his ears twitched by themselves, and his whiskers were so long that they brushed the grass. He gave one leap and the joy of using those hind legs was so great that he went springing about the turf on them, jumping sideways and whirling round as the others did, and he grew so excited that when at last he did stop to look for the Fairy she had gone.

He was a Real Rabbit at last, at home with the other rabbits.

Autumn passed and winter, and in the spring, when the days grew warm and sunny, the Boy went out to play in the wood behind the house. And while he was playing, two rabbits crept out from the bracken and peeped at him. One of them was brown all over, but the other had strange markings under his fur, as though long ago he had been spotted, and the spots still showed through. And about his little soft nose and his round black eyes there was something familiar, so that the Boy thought to himself:

"Why, he looks just like my old Bunny that was lost when I had scarlet fever!"

But he never knew that it really was his own Bunny, come back to look at the child who had first helped him to be Real.

Friendship

This poem reminds us of some of the "rules" of friendship, as well as some of the rewards.

> Friendship needs no studied phrases,
>   Polished face, or winning wiles;
> Friendship deals no lavish praises,
>   Friendship dons no surface smiles.
>
> Friendship follows Nature's diction,
>   Shuns the blandishments of art,
> Boldly severs truth from fiction,
>   Speaks the language of the heart.
>
> Friendship favors no condition,
>   Scorns a narrow-minded creed,
> Lovingly fulfills its mission,
>   Be it word or be it deed.
>
> Friendship cheers the faint and weary,
>   Makes the timid spirit brave,
> Warns the erring, lights the dreary,
>   Smooths the passage to the grave.
>
> Friendship—pure, unselfish friendship,
>   All through life's allotted span,
> Nurtures, strengthens, widens, lengthens,
>   Man's relationship with man.

Why Frog and Snake Never Play Together

This African folktale makes us think about how much companionship the world has missed because people are told they "can't" be friends with each other.

Once upon a time, the child of the Frog was hopping along in the bush when he spied someone new lying across the path before him. This someone was long and slender, and his skin seemed to shine with all the colors of the rainbow.

"Hello there," called Frog-child. "What are you doing lying here in the path?"

"Just warming myself in the sun," answered the someone new, twisting and turning and uncoiling himself. "My name is Snake-child. What's yours?"

"I'm Frog-child. Would you like to play with me?"

So Frog-child and Snake-child played together all morning long in the bush.

"Watch what I can do," said Frog-child, and he hopped high into the air. "I'll teach you how, if you want," he offered.

So he taught Snake-child how to hop, and together they hopped up and down the path through the bush.

"Now watch what I can do," said Snake-child, and he crawled on his belly straight up the trunk of a tall tree. "I'll teach you if you want."

So he taught Frog-child how to slide on his belly and climb into trees.

After a while they both grew hungry and decided to go home for lunch, but they promised each other to meet again the next day.

"Thanks for teaching me how to hop," called Snake-child.

"Thanks for teaching me how to crawl up trees," called Frog-child.

Then they each went home.

"Look what I can do, Mother!" cried Frog-child, crawling on his belly.

"Where did you learn how to do that?" his mother asked.

"Snake-child taught me," he answered. "We played together in the bush this morning. He's my new friend."

"Don't you know the Snake family is a bad family?" his mother asked. "They have poison in their teeth. Don't ever let me catch you playing with one of them again. And don't let me see you crawling on your belly, either. It isn't proper."

Meanwhile, Snake-child went home and hopped up and down for his mother to see.

"'Who taught you to do that?" she asked.

"Frog-child did," he said. "He's my new friend."

"What foolishness," said his mother. "Don't you know we've been on bad terms with the Frog family for longer than anyone can remember? The next time you play with Frog-child, catch him and eat him up. And stop that hopping. It isn't our custom."

So the next morning when Frog-child met Snake-child in the bush, he kept his distance.

"I'm afraid I can't go crawling with you today," he called, hopping back a hop or two.

Snake-child eyed him quietly, remembering what his mother had told him. "If he gets too close, I'll spring at him and eat him," he thought. But then he remembered how much fun they had had together, and how nice Frog-child had been to teach him how to hop. So he sighed sadly to himself and slid away into the bush.

And from that day onward, Frog-child and Snake-child never played together again. But they often sat alone in the sun, each thinking about their one day of friendship.

Rocking Horse Land

Laurence Housman

In this wonderfully imaginative story we see that good friends are always mindful of each other's interests and give each other room to grow.

Prince Fredolin woke up, both eyes at once, and sprang out of bed into the sunshine. He was five years old that morning, by all the clocks and calendars in the kingdom; and the day was going to be beautiful. Every golden minute was precious. He was dressed and out of his room before the attendants knew that he was awake.

In the antechamber stood piles on piles of glittering presents; when he walked among them they came up to the measure of his waist. His fairy godmother had sent him a toy with the most humorous effect. It was labeled, "Break me and I shall turn into something else." So every time he broke it he got a new toy more beautiful than the last. It began by being a hoop, and from that it ran on, while the Prince broke it incessantly for the space of one hour, during which it became by turn—a top, a Noah's ark, a skipping rope, a man-of-war, a box of bricks, a picture puzzle, a pair of stilts, a drum, a trumpet, a kaleidoscope, a steam engine, and nine hundred and fifty other things exactly. Then he began to grow discontented because it would never turn into the same thing again, and after having broken the man-of-war he wanted to get it back again. Also he wanted to see if the steam engine would go inside the Noah's ark, but the toy would never be two things at the same time either. This was very unsatisfactory. He thought his fairy godmother ought to have sent him two toys, out of which he could make combinations.

At last he broke it once more, and it turned into a kite. And while he was flying the kite he broke the string, and the kite went sailing away up into the nasty clear sky, and was never heard of again.

Then Fredolin sat down and howled at his fairy godmother. What a dissembling lot fairy godmothers were, to be sure! They were always setting traps to make their godchildren unhappy. Nevertheless, when told to, he took up his pen and wrote her a nice little note, full of bad spelling and tarrididdles, to say what a happy birthday he was spending in breaking up the beautiful toy she had sent him.

Then he went to look at the rest of the presents, and found it quite refreshing to break a few that did not send him giddy by turning into anything else.

Suddenly his eyes became fixed with delight. Alone, right at the end of the room, stood a great black rocking horse. The saddle and bridle were hung with tiny gold bells and balls of coral, and the horse's tail and mane flowed till they almost touched the ground.

The Prince scampered across the room, and threw his arms around the beautiful creature's neck. All its bells jangled as the head swayed gracefully down, and the prince kissed it between the eyes. Great eyes they were, the color of fire, so wonderfully bright, it semed they must be really alive, only they did not move, but gazed continually with a set stare at the tapestry-hung wall, on which were figures of armed knights riding by to battle.

So Prince Fredolin mounted to the back of his rocking horse, and all day long he rode and shouted to the figures of the armed knights, challenging them to fight, or leading them against the enemy.

At length, when it came to be bedtime, weary of so much glory, he was lifted down from the saddle and carried away to bed.

In his sleep Fredolin still felt his black rocking horse swinging to and fro under him, and heard the melodious chime of its bells, and, in the land of dreams, saw a great country open before him, full of the sound of the battle cry and the hunting horn calling him to strange perils and triumphs.

In the middle of the night he grew softly awake, and his heart was full of love for his black rocking horse. He crept gently out of bed: he would go and look at it where it was standing so grand and still in the next room, to make sure that it was all safe and not afraid of being by itself in the dark night. Parting the door hangings he passed through into the wide hollow chamber beyond, all littered about with toys.

The moon was shining in through the window, making a square cistern of light upon the floor. And then, all at once, he saw that the rocking horse had moved from the place where he had left it! It had crossed the room, and was standing close to the window, with its head toward the night, as though watching the movement of the clouds and the trees swaying in the wind.

The Prince could not understand how it had been moved. He was a little bit afraid, and stealing timidly across, he took hold of the bridle to comfort himself with the jangle of its bells. As he came close, and looked up into the dark solemn face he saw that the eyes were full of tears, and reaching up felt one fall warm against his hand.

"Why do you weep, my Beautiful?" said the Prince.

The rocking horse answered, "I weep because I am a prisoner, and not free. Open the window, Master, and let me go!"

"But if I let you go I shall lose you," said the Prince. "Cannot you be happy here with me?"

And the horse said, "Let me go, for my great brothers call me out of Rocking Horse Land, and I hear my sweet mare whinnying to her foals, and they all cry, seeking me through the ups and hollows of my native fastnesses! Sweet Master, let me go this night, and I will return to you when it is day!"

Then Prince Fredolin said, "How shall I know that you will return to me, and what name shall I call you by?"

And the rocking horse answered, "My name is Rollonde. Search among my mane till you find in it a white hair, draw it out and wind it upon one of your fingers. And so long as you have it wound about your finger, you are my master; and wherever I am I must go or return at your bidding."

So the Prince drew down the rocking horse's head, and searched in the mane, till he had found there the white hair, and he wound it upon his finger and tied it. After that he kissed Rollonde between the eyes, saying, "Go then, Rollonde, since I love you, and would see you happy. Only return to me when it is day!" And so saying he threw open the window to the stir of the night.

Then the rocking horse lifted his dark head and neighed aloud for joy, and swaying forward with a mighty circling motion rose full into the air, and sprang out into the free world before him.

Fredolin watched how with plunge and curve he went over the bowed trees. And again he neighed into the darkness of the night, then swifter than wind disappeared in the distance; and faintly from far away came a sound of the neighing of many horses answering him.

Then the Prince closed the window and crept back to bed, and all night long he dreamed strange dreams of Rocking Horse Land. There he saw smooth hills and valleys that rose and sank without a stone or a tree to disturb the steel-like polish of their surface, slippery as glass, and driven over by a strong wind; and over them, with a sound like the humming of bees, flew the rocking horses. Up and down, up and down, with bright manes streaming like colored fires, and feet motionless behind and before, went the swift pendulum of their flight. Their long bodies bowed and rose; their heads worked to carry impetus to their going; they cried, neighing to each other over hill and valley, "Which of us shall be first? Which of us shall be first?" After them the mares with their tall foals came spinning to watch, crying also among themselves, "Ah! Which shall be first?"

"Rollonde, Rollonde is first!" shouted the Prince, clapping his hands together as they reached the goal. And at that, all at once, he woke and saw it was broad day. Then he ran and threw open the window, and holding out the finger that carried the white hair, cried, "Rollonde, Rollonde, come back, Rollonde!"

Far away he heard an answering sound, and in another moment there came the great rocking horse himself, dipping and dancing over the hills. He crossed the woods and cleared the palace wall at a single bound, and floating in through the window, dropped down onto the floor by Prince Fredolin's side, rocking himself gently to and fro as though panting from the strain of his long flight.

"Now are you happy?" asked the Prince as he caressed him.

"Ah! sweet Prince," said Rollonde, "ah kind Master!" And then he said no more, but became the stock-still staring rocking horse of the day before, with fixed eyes and rigid limbs, which could do nothing but rock up and down with a jangling of sweet bells so long as the Prince rode him.

That night Fredolin came again when all had become still in the palace. And now as before Rollonde had moved from his place and was standing with his head against the window waiting to be let out. "Ah, dear Master," he said, as soon as he saw the Prince coming, "let me go this night also, and I will surely return before day."

"So again the Prince opened the window, and watched him disappear, and heard from far away the neighing of the horses in Rocking Horse Land calling to him. And in the morning with the white hair round his finger he called "Rollonde, Rollonde!" and Rollonde neighed and came back to him, dipping and dancing over the hills.

Now this same thing happened every night. And every morning the horse kissed Fredolin, saying, "Ah! dear Prince and kind Master," and became stock-still once more.

So a year went by, till one morning Fredolin woke up to find it was his sixth birthday. And as six is to five, so were the presents he received on his sixth birthday for magnificence and multitude to the presents he had received the year before. His fairy godmother had sent him a bird, a real live bird. But when he pulled its tail it became a lizard, and when he pulled the lizard's tail it became a mouse, and when he pulled the mouse's tail it became a cat. Then he did very much want to see if the cat would eat the mouse, and not being able to have them both together he got rather vexed with his fairy godmother. However, he pulled the cat's tail and the cat became a dog, and the dog became a goat. And so it went on till he got to a cow. And he pulled the cow's tail and it became a camel, and he pulled the camel's tail and it became an elephant, and still not being contented, he pulled the elephant's tail and it became a guinea pig. Now a guinea pig has got no tail to pull, so it remained a guinea pig, while Prince Fredolin sat down and howled at his fairy godmother.

But the best of all his presents was the one given to him by the King his father. It was a most beautiful horse, for, said the King, "You are now old enough to learn to ride."

So Fredolin was put upon his horse's back, and from having ridden so long upon his rocking horse he learned to ride perfectly in a single day, and was declared by all the courtiers to be the most perfect equestrian that was ever seen.

But these praises and the pleasure of riding about on a real horse so occupied his thoughts that that night he forgot altogether to go and set Rollonde free, but fell fast asleep and dreamed of nothing but real horses and horsemen going to battle. And so it was the next night too.

But the night after that, just as he was falling asleep, he heard something sobbing by his bed, and a voice saying, "Ah! dear Prince and kind Master, let me go, for my heart breaks for a sight of my native land." And there stood his poor rocking horse, Rollonde, with tears falling out of his beautiful eyes onto the white coverlet.

Then the Prince, full of shame at having forgotten his old friend, sprang up and threw his arms around his neck saying, "Be of good cheer, Rollonde, for now surely I will let you go!" and he ran to the window and opened it for the horse to go through. "Ah, dear Prince and kind Master!" said Rollonde. Then he lifted his head and neighed so that the whole palace shook, and swaying forward till his head almost touched the ground he sprang out and away into the night over the hills toward Rocking Horse Land.

Then Prince Fredolin, standing by the window, thoughtfully unloosed the white hair from his finger, and let it float away into the darkness, out of sight of his eye or reach of his hand.

"Goodbye, Rollonde," he murmured softly, "brave Rollonde, my own good Rollonde! Go and be happy in your own land, since I, your Master, was forgetting to be kind to you." And far away he heard the neighing of horses in Rocking Horse Land.

Many years after, when Fredolin had become King in his father's stead, the fifth birthday of the Prince his son came to be celebrated. And there on the morning of the day, among all the presents that covered the floor of the chamber, stood a beautiful foal rocking horse, black, with deep burning eyes.

No one knew how it had come there, or whose present it was, till the King himself came to look at it. And when he saw it so like the old Rollonde he had loved as a boy, he smiled, and stroking its dark mane, said softly in its ear, "Are you, then, the son of Rollonde?" And the foal answered him, "Ah, dear Prince and kind Master!" but never a word more.

Then the King took the little Prince his son, and told him all the story of Rollonde as I have told it to you here. And at the end he went and searched in the foal's mane till he found one white hair, and, drawing it out, he wound it about the little Prince's finger, bidding him guard it well and be ever a kind master to Rollonde's son.

So here is my story of Rollonde come to a good ending.

The Selfish Giant

Oscar Wilde

Like the giant in this tale, we find friendship when we give something of ourselves.

Every afternoon, as they were coming from school, the children used to go and play in the Giant's garden.

It was a large lovely garden, with soft green grass. Here and there over the grass stood beautiful flowers like stars, and there were twelve peach trees that in the springtime broke out into delicate blossoms of pink and pearl, and in the autumn bore rich fruit. The birds sat on the trees and sang so sweetly that the children used to stop their games in order to listen to them. "How happy we are here!" they cried to each other.

One day the Giant came back. He had been to visit his friend the Cornish ogre, and had stayed with him for seven years. After the seven years were over he had said all that he had to say, for his conversation was limited, and he determined to return to his own castle. When he arrived he saw the children playing in the garden.

"What are you doing here?" he cried in a very gruff voice, and the children ran away.

"My own garden is my own garden," said the Giant. "Any one can understand that, and I will allow nobody to play in it but myself." So he built a high wall all around it, and put up a notice board.

> **TRESPASSERS**
> **WILL BE**
> **PROSECUTED**

He was a very selfish Giant.

The poor children had now nowhere to play. They tried to play on the road, but the road was very dusty and full of hard stones, and they did not like it. They used to wander round the high walls when their lessons were over, and talk about the beautiful garden inside. "How happy we were there!" they said to each other.

Then the spring came, and all over the country there were little blossoms and little birds. Only in the garden of the Selfish Giant it was still winter. The birds did not care to sing in it as there were no children, and the trees forgot to blossom. Once a beautiful flower put its head out from the grass, but when it saw the notice board it was so sorry for the children that it slipped back into the ground again, and went off to sleep. The only people who were pleased were the Snow and the Frost. "Spring has forgotten this garden," they cried, "so we will live here all the year round." The Snow covered up the grass with her great white cloak, and the Frost painted all the trees silver. Then they invited the North Wind to stay with them, and he came. He was wrapped in furs, and he roared all day about the garden, and blew the chimney pots down. "This is a delightful spot," he said. "We must ask the Hail on a visit." So the Hail came. Every day for three hours he rattled on the roof of the castle till he broke most of the slates, and then he ran round and round the garden as fast as he could go. He was dressed in gray and his breath was like ice.

"I cannot understand why the Spring is so late in coming," said the Selfish Giant, as he sat at the window and looked out at his cold, white garden. "I hope there will be a change in the weather."

But the Spring never came, nor the Summer. The Autumn gave golden fruit to every garden, but to the Giant's garden she gave none. "He is too selfish," she said. So it was always Winter there, and the North Wind and the Hail, and the Frost, and the Snow danced about through the trees.

One morning the Giant was lying awake in bed when he heard some lovely music. It sounded so sweet to his ears that he thought it must be the King's musicians passing by. It was really only a little linnet singing outside his window, but it was so long since he had heard a bird sing in his garden that it seemed to him to be the most beautiful music in the world. Then the Hail stopped dancing over his head, and the North Wind ceased roaring, and a delicious perfume came to him through the open casement. "I believe the Spring has come at last," said the Giant, and he jumped out of bed and looked out.

What did he see?

He saw a most wonderful sight. Through a little hole in the wall the children had crept in, and they were sitting in the branches of the trees. In every tree that he could see there was a little child. And the trees were so glad to have the children back again that they had covered themselves with blossoms, and were waving their arms gently above the children's heads. The birds were flying about and twittering with delight, and the flowers were looking up through the green grass and laughing. It was a lovely scene, only in one corner it was still winter. It was the farthest corner of the garden, and in it was standing a little boy. He was so small that he could not reach up to the branches of the tree, and he was wandering all around it, crying bitterly. The poor tree was still covered with frost and snow, and the North Wind was blowing and roaring above it. "Climb up! little boy," said the Tree, and it bent its branches down as low as it could; but the boy was too tiny.

And the Giant's heart melted as he looked out. "How selfish I have been!" he said. "Now I know why the Spring would not come here. I will put that poor little boy on the top of the tree, and then I will knock down the wall, and my garden shall be the children's playground for ever and ever." He was really very sorry for what he had done.

So he crept downstairs and opened the front door quite softly, and went out into the garden. But when the children saw him they were so frightened that they all ran away, and the garden became winter again. Only the little boy did not run, for his eyes were so full of tears that he did not see the Giant coming. And the Giant stole up behind him and took him gently in his hand, and put him up into the tree. And the tree broke at once into blossom, and the birds came and sang on it, and the little boy stretched out his two arms and flung them around the Giant's neck, and kissed him. And the other children, when they saw that the Giant was not wicked any longer, came running back, and with them came the Spring. "It is your garden now, little children" said the Giant, and he took a great axe and knocked down the wall. And when the people were going to market at twelve o'clock they found the Giant playing with the children in the most beautiful garden they had ever seen.

All day long they played, and in the evening they came to the Giant to bid him goodbye.

"But where is your little companion?" he said. "The boy I put into the tree." The Giant loved him the best because he had kissed him.

"We don't know," answered the children. "He has gone away."

"You must tell him to be sure and come tomorrow," said the Giant. But the children said that they did not know where he lived and had never seen him before; and the Giant felt very sad.

Every afternoon, when school was over, the children came and played with the Giant. But the little boy whom the Giant loved was never seen again. The Giant was very kind to all the children, yet he longed for his first little friend, and often spoke of him. "How I would like to see him!" he used to say.

Years went over, and the Giant grew very old and feeble. He could not play about anymore, so he sat in a huge armchair, and watched the children at their games, and admired his garden. "I have many beautiful flowers," he said. "But the children are the most beautiful flowers of all."

One winter morning he looked out of his window as he was dressing. He did not hate the Winter now, for he knew that it was merely the Spring asleep, and that the flowers were resting.

Suddenly he rubbed his eyes in wonder and looked and looked. It certainly was a marvelous sight. In the farthest corner of the garden was a tree quite covered with lovely white blossoms. Its branches were golden, and silver fruit hung down from them, and underneath it stood the little boy he had loved.

Downstairs ran the Giant in great joy, and out into the garden. He hastened across the grass, and came near to the child. And when he came quite close his face grew red with anger, and he said, "Who hath dared to wound thee?" For on the palms of the child's hands were the prints of two nails, and the prints of two nails were on the little feet.

"Who hath dared to wound thee?" cried the Giant. "Tell me, that I may take my big sword and slay him."

"Nay," answered the child. "But these are the wounds of Love."

"Who art thou?" said the Giant, and a strange awe fell on him, and he knelt before the little child.

And the child smiled on the Giant, and said to him, "You let me play once in your garden; today you shall come with me to my garden, which is Paradise."

And when the children ran in that afternoon, they found the Giant lying dead under the tree, all covered with white blossoms.

Ruth and Naomi

Retold by Jesse Lyman Hurlbut

The book of Ruth in the Bible is the story of a widow's courageous decision to leave Moab, her homeland, and travel to Judah
with her Hebrew mother-in-law, who has lost her own husband
and sons. Ruth's words to Naomi are one of the greatest statements of friendship and loyalty in all of literature: "Whither thou
goest, I will go; and where thou lodgest, I will lodge: thy people
shall be my people, and thy God my God. Where thou diest, will
I die, and there will I be buried." In Judah, Ruth's fidelity and
kindness were rewarded with the love of Boaz, and through marriage to him she became the great-grandmother of King David.

In the time of the judges in Israel, a man named Elimelech was
living in the town of Bethlehem, in the tribe of Judah, about six
miles south of Jerusalem. His wife's name was Naomi, and his two
sons were Mahlon and Chilion. For some years the crops were poor,
and food was scarce in Judah; and Elimelech, with his family, went
to live in the land of Moab, which was on the east of the Dead Sea,
as Judah was on the west.

There they stayed ten years, and in that time Elimelech died.
His two sons married women of the country of Moab, one woman
named Orpah, the other named Ruth. But the two young men also
died in the land of Moab, so that Naomi and her two daughters-in-
law were all left widows.

Naomi heard that God had again given good harvests and bread
to the land of Judah, and she rose up to go from Moab back to her
own land and her own town of Bethlehem. Her two daughters-in-
law loved her and both would have gone with her, though the land
of Judah was a strange land to them, for they were of the Moabite
people.

Naomi said to them, "Go back, my daughters, to your own
mothers' homes. May the Lord deal kindly with you, as you have
been kind to your husbands and to me. May the Lord grant that each
of you may yet find another husband and a happy home." Then
Naomi kissed them in farewell, and the three women all wept to-

gether. The two young widows said to her, "You have been a good mother to us, and we will go with you, and live among your people."

"No, no," said Naomi. "You are young and I am old. Go back and be happy among your own people."

Then Orpah kissed Naomi and went back to her people; but Ruth would not leave her. She said, "Do not ask me to leave you, for I never will. Where you go, I will go; where you live, I will live; your people shall be my people; and your God shall be my God. Where you die, I will die, and be buried. Nothing but death itself shall part you and me."

When Naomi saw that Ruth was firm in her purpose, she ceased trying to persuade her; so the two women went on together. They walked around the Dead Sea, and crossed the river Jordan, and climbed the mountains of Judah, and came to Bethlehem.

Naomi had been absent from Bethlehem for ten years, but her friends were all glad to see her again. They said, "Is this Naomi, whom we knew years ago?" Now the name Naomi means "pleasant." And Naomi said:

"Call me not Naomi; call me Mara, for the Lord has made my life bitter. I went out full, with my husband and two sons; now I come home empty, without them. Do not call me 'Pleasant'; call me 'Bitter.' " The name "Mara," by which Naomi wished to be called, means "bitter." But Naomi learned later that "Pleasant" was the right name for her after all.

There was living in Bethlehem at that time a very rich man named Boaz. He owned large fields that were abundant in their harvests; and he was related to the family of Elimelech, Naomi's husband, who had died.

It was the custom in Israel when they reaped the grain not to gather all the stalks, but to leave some for the poor people, who followed after the reapers with their sickles, and gathered what was left. When Naomi and Ruth came to Bethlehem it was the time of the barley harvest; and Ruth went out into the fields to glean the grain which the reapers had left. It so happened that she was gleaning in the field that belonged to Boaz, this rich man.

Boaz came out from the town to see his men reaping, and he said to them, "The Lord be with you"; and they answered him, "The Lord bless you." And Boaz said to his master of the reapers, "Who is this young woman that I see gleaning in the field?"

The man answered, "It is the young woman from the land of

Moab, who came with Naomi. She asked leave to glean after the reapers, and has been here gathering grain since yesterday."

Then Boaz said to Ruth, "Listen to me, my daughter. Do not go to any other field, but stay here with my young women. No one shall harm you; and when you are thirsty, go and drink at our vessels of water."

Then Ruth bowed to Boaz, and thanked him for his kindness, all the more kind because she was a stranger in Israel. Boaz said:

"I have heard how true you have been to your mother-in-law, Naomi, in leaving your own land and coming with her to this land. May the Lord, under whose wings you have come, give you a reward!" And at noon, when they sat down to rest and to eat, Boaz gave her some of the food. And he said to the reapers:

"When you are reaping, leave some of the sheaves for her; and drop out some sheaves from the bundles, where she may gather them."

That evening Ruth showed Naomi how much she had gleaned, and told her of the rich man Boaz, who had been so kind to her. And Naomi said, "This man is a near relation of ours. Stay in his fields as long as the harvest lasts." And so Ruth gleaned in the fields of Boaz until the harvest had been gathered.

At the end of the harvest Boaz held a feast on the threshing floor. And after the feast, by the advice of Naomi, Ruth went to him, and said to him, "You are a near relation of my husband and of his father, Elimelech. Now will you not do good to us for his sake?"

And when Boaz saw Ruth he loved her; and soon after this he took her as his wife. And Naomi and Ruth went to live in his home, so that Naomi's life was no more bitter, but pleasant. And Boaz and Ruth had a son, whom they named Obed; and later Obed had a son named Jesse; and Jesse was the father of David, the shepherd boy who became king. So Ruth, the young woman of Moab, who chose the people and the God of Israel, became the mother of kings.

Jonathan and David

Retold by Jesse Lyman Hurlbut

Sometimes the duties of friendship compete with other obligations and affections. The story of Jonathan, told in the first book of Samuel in the Bible, is one such instance. Jonathan was the eldest son and heir of King Saul of Israel. He was also David's sworn friend. After David killed Goliath, Saul grew jealous of his popularity, and fearing that he would eventually become king, sought to murder him. Jonathan's defense of David, made doubly painful because of his filial duties and his own claim to the throne, is one of our greatest examples of loyalty in friendship.

After David had slain the giant he was brought before King Saul, still holding the giant's head. Saul did not remember in this bold fighting man the boy who a few years before had played in his presence. He took him into his own house, and made him an officer among his soldiers. David was as wise and as brave in the army as he had been when facing the giant, and very soon he was in command of a thousand men. All the men loved him, both in Saul's court and in his camp, for David had the spirit that drew all hearts toward him.

When David was returning from his battle with the Philistines, the women of Israel came to meet him out of the cities, with instruments of music, singing and dancing, and they sang:

> "Saul has slain his thousands,
> And David his ten thousands."

This made Saul very angry, for he was jealous and suspicious in his spirit. He thought constantly of Samuel's words, that God would take the kingdom from him and would give it to one who was more worthy of it. He began to think that perhaps this young man, who had come in a single day to greatness before the people, might try to make himself king.

His former feeling of unhappiness again came over Saul. He

raved in his house, talking as a man talks who is crazed. By this time they all knew that David was a musician, and they called him again to play on his harp and to sing before the troubled king. But now, in his madness, Saul would not listen to David's voice. Twice he threw his spear at him; but each time David leaped aside, and the spear went into the wall of the house.

Saul was afraid of David, for he saw that the Lord was with David, as the Lord was no longer with himself. He would have killed David, but did not dare kill him, because everybody loved David. Saul said to himself, "Though I cannot kill him myself, I will have him killed by the Philistines."

And he sent David out on dangerous errands of war; but David came home in safety, all the greater and the more beloved after each victory. Saul said, "I will give you my daughter Merab for your wife if you will fight the Philistines for me."

David fought the Philistines; but when he came home from the war he found that Merab, who had been promised to him, had been given as wife to another man. Saul had another daughter, named Michal. She loved David, and showed her love for him. Then Saul sent word to David, saying, "You shall have Michal, my daughter, for your wife when you have killed a hundred Philistines."

Then David went out and fought the Philistines, and killed two hundred of them; and they brought the word to Saul. Then Saul gave him his daughter Michal as his wife; but he was all the more afraid of David as he saw him growing in power and drawing nearer to the throne of the kingdom.

But if Saul hated David, Saul's son Jonathan saw David's courage, and the soul of Jonathan was knit to the soul of David, and Jonathan loved him as his own soul. He took off his own royal robe, and his sword, and his bow, and gave them all to David. It grieved Jonathan greatly that his father, Saul, was so jealous of David. He spoke to his father, and said: "Let not the king do harm to David; for David has been faithful to the king, and he has done great things for the kingdom. He took his life in his hand, and killed the Philistine, and won a great victory for the Lord and for the people. Why should you seek to kill an innocent man?"

For the time Saul listened to Jonathan, and said, "As the Lord lives, David shall not be put to death."

And again David sat at the king's table, among the princes; and when Saul was troubled again David played on his harp and sang before him. But once more Saul's jealous anger arose, and he threw his spear at David. David was watchful and quick. He leaped aside, and, as before, the spear fastened into the wall.

Saul sent men to David's house to seize him; but Michal, Saul's daughter, who was David's wife, let David down out of the window, so that he escaped. She placed an image on David's bed and covered it with the bedclothes. When the men came, she said, "David is ill in the bed, and cannot go."

They brought the word to Saul, and he said, "Bring him to me in the bed, just as he is."

When the image was found in David's bed, David was in a safe place, far away. David went to Samuel at Ramah, and stayed with him among the men who were prophets worshipping God and singing and speaking God's word. Saul heard that David was there, and sent men to take him. But when these men came and saw Samuel and the prophets praising God and praying, the same spirit came on them, and they began to praise and to pray. Saul sent other men, but these also, when they came among the prophets, felt the same power, and joined in the worship.

Finally, Saul said, "If no other man will bring David to me, I will go myself and take him."

And Saul went to Ramah; but when he came near to the company of the worshippers, praising God, and praying, and preaching, the same spirit came on Saul. He, too, began to join in the songs and the prayers, and stayed there all that day and that night, worshipping God very earnestly. When the next day he went again to his home in Gibeah, his feeling was changed for the time, and he was again friendly to David.

But David knew that Saul was at heart his bitter enemy and would kill him if he could as soon as his madness came upon him. He met Jonathan out in the field away from the place. Jonathan said to David:

"Stay away from the king's table for a few days, and I will find out how he feels toward you, and will tell you. Perhaps even now my father may become your friend. But if he is to be your enemy, I know that the Lord is with you, and that Saul will not succeed against you. Promise me that as long as you live you will be kind to me, and not only to me while I live, but to my children after me."

Jonathan believed, as many others believed, that David would yet become the king of Israel, and he was willing to give up to David his right to be king, such was his great love for him. That day a promise was made between Jonathan and David, that they and their children, and those who should come after them, should be friends forever.

Jonathan said to David, "I will find how my father feels toward you, and will bring you word. After three days I will be here with my bow and arrows, and I will send a little boy out near your place of hiding, and I will shoot three arrows. If I say to the boy, 'Run, find the arrows, they are on this side of you,' then you can come safely, for the king will not harm you. But if I call out to the boy, 'The arrows are away beyond you,' that will mean that there is danger, and you must hide from the king."

So David stayed away from Saul's table for two days. At first Saul said nothing of his absence, but at last he said:

"Why has not the son of Jesse come to meals yesterday and today?"

And Jonathan said, "David asked leave of me to go to his home at Bethlehem and visit his oldest brother."

Then Saul was very angry. He cried out, "You are a disobedient son! Why have you chosen this enemy of mine as your best friend? Do you not know that as long as he is alive you can never be king? Send after him, and let him be brought to me, for he shall surely die!"

Saul was so fierce in his anger that he threw his spear at his own son Jonathan. Jonathan rose up from the table, so anxious for his friend David that he could eat nothing. The next day, at the hour agreed upon, Jonathan went out into the field with a little boy. He said to the boy, "Run out yonder, and be ready to find the arrows that I shoot."

And as the boy was running Jonathan shot arrows beyond him, and he called out, "The arrows are away beyond you; run quickly and find them."

The boy ran and found the arrows, and brought them to Jonathan. He gave the bow and arrows to the boy, saying to him, "Take them back to the city. I will stay here awhile."

And as soon as the boy was out of sight David came from his hiding place and ran to Jonathan. They fell into each other's arms and kissed each other again and again, and wept together. For David knew now that he must no longer hope to be safe in Saul's hands. He must leave home, and wife, and friends, and his father's house, and hide wherever he could from the hate of King Saul.

Jonathan said to him, "Go in peace; for we have sworn together saying, 'The Lord shall be between you and me, and between your children and my children forever.' "

Then Jonathan went again to his father's palace, and David went out to find a hiding place.

Baucis and Philemon

Retold by Thomas Bulfinch

The ancient Greeks understood that the health of the community depended on how well its individual citizens treated one another. To them, Zeus, the king of the gods, was both the guardian of the state and the protector of human relations among civilized men. All social institutions, including the family, lay in his care. Travelers in particular honored him, for he rewarded those who remembered the rules of hospitality and duties of friendship, as we see in this story in which Zeus and Hermes (Jupiter and Mercury to the Romans) seek shelter among the mortals.

Once upon a time Jupiter, in human shape, visited the land of Phrygia, and with him Mercury, without his wings. They presented themselves as weary travelers at many a door, seeking rest and shelter, but found all closed; for it was late, and the inhospitable inhabitants would not rouse themselves to open for their reception. At last a small thatched cottage received them, where Baucis, a pious old dame, and her husband, Philemon, had grown old together. Not ashamed of their poverty, they made it endurable by moderate desires and kind dispositions. When the two guests crossed the humble threshold and bowed their heads to pass under the low door, the old man placed a seat, on which Baucis, bustling and attentive, spread a cloth, and begged them to sit down. Then she raked out the coals from the ashes, kindled a fire, and prepared some pot-herbs and bacon for them. A beechen bowl was filled with warm water, that their guests might wash. While all was doing, they beguiled the time with conversation.

The old woman with trembling hand set the table. One leg was shorter than the rest, but a piece of slate put under restored the level. When it was steady she rubbed the table down with sweet-smelling herbs. Upon it she set some of chaste Minerva's olives, some cornel berries preserved in vinegar, and added radishes and cheese, with eggs lightly cooked in the ashes. The meal was served in earthen dishes; and an earthenware pitcher, with wooden cups, stood beside them. When all was ready the stew, smoking hot, was set on the table. Some wine, not of the oldest, was added, and for dessert, apples and wild honey.

Now while the repast proceeded, the old folks were astonished to see that the wine, as fast as it was poured out, renewed itself in the pitcher of its own accord. Struck with terror, Baucis and Philemon recognized their heavenly guests, fell on their knees, and with clasped hands implored forgiveness for their poor entertainment. There was an old goose, which they kept as the guardian of their humble cottage, and they bethought them to make this a sacrifice in honor of their guests. But the goose, too nimble for the old folk, with the aid of feet and wings eluded their pursuit and at last took shelter between the gods themselves. They forbade it to be slain, and spoke in these words: "We are gods. This inhospitable village shall pay the penalty of its impiety; you alone shall go free from the chastisement. Quit your house and come with us to the top of yonder hill." They hastened to obey. The country behind them was speedily sunk in a lake, only their own house left standing. While they gazed with wonder at the sight, that old house of theirs was changed. Columns took the place of the corner posts, the thatch grew yellow and appeared a gilded roof, the floors became marble, the doors were enriched with carving and ornaments of gold. Then spoke Jupiter in benign accents: "Excellent old man, and woman worthy of such a husband, speak, tell us your wishes. What favor have you to ask of us?" Philemon took counsel with Baucis a few moments, then declared to the gods their common wish. "We ask to be priests and guardians of this thy temple, and that one and the same hour may take us both from life." Their prayer was granted. When they had attained a great age, as they stood one day before the steps of the sacred edifice and were telling the story of the place, Baucis saw Philemon begin to put forth leaves, and Philemon saw Baucis changing in like manner. While still they exchanged parting words, a leafy crown grew over their heads. "Farewell, dear spouse," they said together, and at the same moment the bark closed over their mouths. The Tyanean shepherd still shows the two trees —an oak and a linden, standing side by side.

The House by the Side of the Road

Sam Walter Foss

New England poet Sam Walter Foss (1858–1911) evokes the age-old image of a humble house where the weary traveler finds a welcome—a house such as Baucis and Philemon's—to remind us that we are here to help one another along life's journey. Friends are "help-mates" to each other.

There are hermit souls that live withdrawn
  In the peace of their self-content;
There are souls, like stars, that swell apart,
  In a fellowless firmament;
There are pioneer souls that blaze their paths
  Where highways never ran;
But let me live by the side of the road
  And be a friend to man.

Let me live in a house by the side of the road,
  Where the race of men go by—
The men who are good and the men who are bad,
  As good and as bad as I.
I would not sit in the scorner's seat,
  Or hurl the cynic's ban;
Let me live in a house by the side of the road
  And be a friend to man.

I see from my house by the side of the road,
  By the side of the highway of life,
The men who press with the ardor of hope,
  The men who are faint with the strife.
But I turn not away from their smiles nor their tears—
  Both parts of an infinite plan;
Let me live in my house by the side of the road
  And be a friend to man.

Let me live in my house by the side of the road
  Where the race of men go by—
They are good, they are bad, they are weak,
    they are strong.
  Wise, foolish—so am I.
Then why should I sit in the scorner's seat
  Or hurl the cynic's ban?—
Let me live in my house by the side of the road
  And be a friend to man.

Damon and Pythias

This story takes place in the Sicilian city-state of Syracuse in the
fourth century B.C. The Roman orator Cicero tells us that
Damon and Pythias (also called Phintias) were followers of the
philosopher Pythagoras. Even today, their story sets the standard
for absolute friendship, which gives every reason for confidence
and leaves no room for doubts.

Damon and Pythias had been the best of friends since childhood.
Each trusted the other like a brother, and each knew in his heart
there was nothing he would not do for his friend. Eventually the
time came for them to prove the depth of their devotion. It happened
this way.

Dionysius, the ruler of Syracuse, grew annoyed when he heard
about the kind of speeches Pythias was giving. The young scholar
was telling the public that no man should have unlimited power over
another, and that absolute tyrants were unjust kings. In a fit of rage,
Dionysius summoned Pythias and his friend.

"Who do you think you are, spreading unrest among the people?" he demanded.

"I spread only the truth," Pythias answered. "There can be
nothing wrong with that."

"And does your truth hold that kings have too much power and
that their laws are not good for their subjects?"

"If a king has seized power without permission of the people,
then that is what I say."

"This kind of talk is treason," Dionysius shouted. "You are conspiring to overthrow me. Retract what you've said, or face the consequences."

"I will retract nothing," Pythias answered.

"Then you will die. Do you have any last requests?"

"Yes. Let me go home just long enough to say goodbye to my wife and children and to put my household in order."

"I see you not only think I'm unjust, you think I'm stupid as well," Dionysius laughed scornfully. "If I let you leave Syracuse, I have no doubt I will never see you again."

"I will give you a pledge," Pythias said.

"What kind of pledge could you possibly give to make me think you will ever return?" Dionysius demanded.

At that instant Damon, who had stood quietly beside his friend, stepped forward.

"I will be his pledge," he said. "Keep me here in Syracuse, as your prisoner, until Pythias returns. Our friendship is well known to you. You can be sure Pythias will return so long as you hold me."

Dionysius studied the two friends silently. "Very well," he said at last. "But if you are willing to take the place of your friend, you must be willing to accept his sentence if he breaks his promise. If Pythias does not return to Syracuse, you will die in his place."

"He will keep his word," Damon replied. "I have no doubt of that."

Pythias was allowed to go free for a time, and Damon was thrown into prison. After several days, when Pythias failed to reappear, Dionysius's curiosity got the better of him, and he went to the prison to see if Damon was yet sorry he had made such a bargain.

"Your time is almost up," the ruler of Syracuse sneered. "It will be useless to beg for mercy. You were a fool to rely on your friend's promise. Did you really think he would sacrifice his life for you or anyone else?"

"He has merely been delayed," Damon answered steadily. "The winds have kept him from sailing, or perhaps he has met with some accident on the road. But if it is humanly possible, he will be here on time. I am as confident of his virtue as I am of my own existence."

Dionysius was startled at the prisoner's confidence. "We shall soon see," he said, and left Damon in his cell.

The fatal day arrived. Damon was brought from prison and led before the executioner. Dionysius greeted him with a smug smile.

"It seems your friend has not turned up," he laughed. "What do you think of him now?"

"He is my friend," Damon answered. "I trust him."

Even as he spoke, the doors flew open, and Pythias staggered into the room. He was pale and bruised and half speechless from exhaustion. He rushed to the arms of his friend.

"You are safe, praise the gods," he gasped. "It seemed as though the fates were conspiring against us. My ship was wrecked in a storm, and then bandits attacked me on the road. But I refused to give up hope, and at last I've made it back in time. I am ready to receive my sentence of death."

Dionysius heard his words with astonishment. His eyes and his heart were opened. It was impossible for him to resist the power of such constancy.

"The sentence is revoked," he declared. "I never believed that such faith and loyalty could exist in friendship. You have shown me how wrong I was, and it is only right that you be rewarded with your freedom. But I ask that in return you do me one great service."

"What service do you mean?" the friends asked.

"Teach me how to be part of so worthy a friendship."

How Robin Hood Met Little John

Adapted from Henry Gilbert

Every once in a while, it takes a legendary outlaw to teach lessons about fairness, generosity, chivalry, and comradeship. Robin Hood and his band of merry men ranged the forests of Sherwood, in Nottinghamshire, and Barnsdale, in Yorkshire, during the days when King Richard the Lionhearted was far away fighting in the Crusades, and the cunning, greedy Prince John ruled in his absence. In this story, good sportsmanship—grace in victory, humor in defeat—makes good friendship.

Once Robin Hood was journeying through the forest of Barnsdale when he came to a broad stream crossed by a narrow beam of oak. It was wide enough for only one man to cross at a time, and, of course, had no railing. Robin walked some two or three feet along it, when on the other bank a tall man appeared and, jumping onto the bridge, also began to cross it.

They stopped and frowned at each other when they were but some ten feet apart.

"Where are your manners, fellow?" Robin called. "Couldn't you see I was already on the bridge before you placed your great big feet on it? Go back!"

"Go back yourself, acorn-head," retorted the other. "The small jack should always give way to the big pot."

"You're a stranger in these parts, you chucklehead," said Robin. "Your currish tongue betrays you. But I'll give you a good Barnsdale lesson, if you don't retreat and let me pass." Saying which, he took up his bow and drew an arrow. The tall man, with a half-angry, half-humorous twinkle in his eyes, glanced at it.

"If this is your Barnsdale teaching," he rejoined, "it is the teaching of cowards. Here you are, with a bow in your hands, ready to shoot a man who has only his walking staff for a weapon."

Robin paused. He was downright angry with the stranger, but there was something honest and good-natured about the giant which he liked.

"Have it your way, then," he said. "Wait here." He turned and went back to the bank, where he cut a stout staff of his own, and trimmed it to the weight and length he desired. Then he jumped back onto the bridge.

"Now," said Robin, "we will play a little game together. Whoever is knocked from the bridge into the stream shall lose the battle. Ready? Go!"

With the first twirl of Robin's staff, the huge stranger could see he had no novice to deal with, and he soon found that Robin's arm had strength equal to his own. For a long time their staffs whirled like the arms of two windmills, and when they clashed, the crack of wood was tossed to and fro between the trees on either side of the stream. The stranger lunged, and his stick came down with a sharp rap on Robin's skull.

"First hit goes to you!" cried Robin.

"Second hit to you!" said the giant with a good-natured laugh, rubbing a new bruise on his left forearm.

Quick as lightning the blows descended now, and the very bones of both men rattled. Keeping their footing on the narrow bridge was almost impossible. Every step made forward or back-ward had to be taken with great care, and the power of every blow they gave or received almost threw them over the side.

Suddenly, Robin landed a blow on the big man's crown, but the next instant, with a furious stroke, the stranger struck Robin off his balance. With a mighty splash the outlaw landed in the water.

For a moment the giant man seemed surprised to find no enemy before him. Wiping the sweat from his eyes, he cried,

"Hello, good laddie, where have you gone?"

He bent down anxiously, and peered into the water flowing rapidly beneath the bridge. "By Saint Peter," he said; "I hope the bold man is not hurt!"

"Faith!" came a voice from the bank a little farther down. "Here I am, big fellow, as right as rain. You have the day, and I shall not need to cross the bridge."

Robin pulled himself up the bank and, kneeling down, washed his face in the water. When he rose, he found the big stranger at his side, dashing water over his own head.

"What?" cried Robin. "Have you not gone forward on your journey? You were in such a hurry to cross that bridge, and now you've come back!"

"Scorn me not, good fellow," said the big man. "I have no-where to go that I know of. I am but a serf who has run away from his manor, and tonight, instead of my warm hut, I shall have only a bush to sleep under. But I would like to shake hands with you before I go, for you are as true and good a fighter as I've ever met."

Robin's hand was on the other's at once, and they gave a shake of mutual respect and liking.

"Stay awhile," said Robin. "Perhaps you would like supper before you go wandering."

With these words, Robin placed his horn to his lips and blew a blast that woke the echoes, made the blackbirds fly shrieking away, and every animal in the forest dive for the nearest cover. Then came sounds as if deer were hurrying through the bushes, and in a moment the forms of men emerged from the dark wall of trees.

"Why, good Robin," one called, "what happened to you? You're soaked to the skin!"

" 'Tis no matter at all," laughed Robin. "You see that tall lad there. We fought on the bridge with our staffs, and he tumbled me in."

"Seize him, lads!" Robin's men cried, springing toward the stranger. "Toss him in and duck him well!"

"Nay, nay," shouted Robin, laughing. "Hold back, lads. I have no ill will, for he's a good fellow and bold. Listen here, my man," he said to the stranger. "We are outlaws, brave lads who hide here in the forest from the evil lords, and we make it our business to take from the rich what they've stolen from the poor. Join us if you will. I can promise both hard knocks and good cheer."

"By earth and water, I'll be your man," cried the stranger, seizing Robin's hand. "Never heard I sweeter words than those you've said, and with all my heart will I serve you and your fellowship."

"What is your name, good man?" asked Robin.

"John o' the Stubbs," replied the other, and then with a great laugh, "but men call me John the Little."

The others laughed too, and pressed forward to shake hands with him. Then they raced back to camp, where a great iron pot waited for them over a fire, from which rose most appetizing odors for men grown hungry in greenwood air. Standing around John the Little, who overtopped them all, the outlaws held their mugs to a great wooden cask to be filled to the brim with brown ale.

"Now, lads," cried Robin, "we will baptize our new comrade into our good free company of forest lads. He has until now been called John the Little, and a sweet pretty babe he is. But from now on, he shall be called Little John. Three cheers, lads, for Little John!"

How they made the twilight ring! The leaves overhead quivered with their shouts! Then they tossed off their mugs of ale, and gathering around the caldron, they dipped their bowls into the rich stew and fell to feasting.

A Wayfaring Song

Henry van Dyke

O who will walk a mile with me
        Along life's merry way?
A comrade blithe and full of glee,
Who dares to laugh out loud and free
And let his frolic fancy play,
Like a happy child, through the flowers gay
That fill the field and fringe the way
        Where he walks a mile with me.

And who will walk a mile with me
        Along life's weary way?
A friend whose heart has eyes to see
The stars shine out o'er the darkening lea,
And the quiet rest at the end o' the day—
A friend who knows, and dares to say,
The brave, sweet words that cheer the way
        Where he walks a mile with me.

With such a comrade, such a friend,
I fain would walk till journey's end,
Through summer sunshine, winter rain,
And then?—Farewell, we shall meet again!

Helen Keller and Anne Sullivan

There is no friendship more sacred than that between student and teacher, and one of the greatest of these was the friendship of Helen Keller (1880–1968) and Anne Mansfield Sullivan (1866–1936).

Illness destroyed Helen Keller's sight and hearing when she was not yet two years old, leaving her cut off from the world. For nearly five years she grew up, as she later described it, "wild and unruly, giggling and chuckling to express pleasure; kicking, scratching, uttering the choked screams of the deaf-mute to indicate the opposite."

Anne Sullivan's arrival at the Kellers' Alabama home from the Perkins Institution for the Blind in Boston changed Helen's life. Sullivan herself had been half-blind from an eye infection from which she never fully recovered, and she came to Helen with experience, unbending dedication, and love. Through the sense of touch she was able to make contact with the young girl's mind, and within three years she had taught Helen to read and write in braille. By sixteen, Helen could speak well enough to go to preparatory school and college. She graduated *cum laude* from Radcliffe in 1904, and devoted the rest of her life to helping the blind and deaf-blind, as her teacher had done. The two women continued their remarkable friendship until Anne's death.

Helen wrote about Anne Mansfield's arrival in her autobiography, *The Story of My Life*.

The most important day I remember in all my life is the one on which my teacher, Anne Mansfield Sullivan, came to me. I am filled with wonder when I consider the immeasurable contrasts between the two lives which it connects. It was the third of March, 1887, three months before I was seven years old.

On the afternoon of that eventful day, I stood on the porch, dumb, expectant. I guessed vaguely from my mother's signs and from the hurrying to and fro in the house that something unusual was about to happen, so I went to the door and waited on the steps. The afternoon sun penetrated the mass of honeysuckle that covered the porch, and fell on my upturned face. My fingers lingered almost unconsciously on the familiar leaves and blossoms which had just come forth to greet the sweet Southern spring. I did not know what the future held of marvel or surprise for me. Anger and bitterness had preyed upon me continually for weeks and a deep languor had succeeded this passionate struggle.

Have you ever been at sea in a dense fog, when it seemed as if a tangible white darkness shut you in, and the great ship, tense and anxious, groped her way toward the shore with plummet and sounding-line, and you waited with beating heart for something to hap-

pen? I was like that ship before my education began, only I was
without compass or sounding-line, and had no way of knowing how
near the harbor was. "Light! give me light!" was the wordless cry of
my soul, and the light of love shone on me in that very hour.

I felt approaching footsteps. I stretched out my hand as I supposed to my mother. Someone took it, and I was caught up and held
close in the arms of her who had come to reveal all things to me,
and, more than all things else, to love me.

The morning after my teacher came she led me into her room
and gave me a doll. The little blind children at the Perkins Institution
had sent it and Laura Bridgman had dressed it; but I did not know
this until afterward. When I had played with it a little while, Miss
Sullivan slowly spelled into my hand the word "d-o-l-l." I was at
once interested in this finger play and tried to imitate it. When I
finally succeeded in making the letters correctly I was flushed with
childish pleasure and pride. Running downstairs to my mother I held
up my hand and made the letters for doll. I did not know that I was
spelling a word or even that words existed; I was simply making my
fingers go in monkey-like imitation. In the days that followed I
learned to spell in this uncomprehending way a great many words,
among them *pin, hat, cup,* and a few verbs like *sit, stand,* and *walk.*
But my teacher had been with me several weeks before I understood
that everything has a name.

One day, while I was playing with my new doll, Miss Sullivan
put my big rag doll into my lap also, spelled "d-o-l-l" and tried to
make me understand that "d-o-l-l" applied to both. Earlier in the
day we had had a tussle over the words "m-u-g" and "w-a-t-e-r."
Miss Sullivan had tried to impress it upon me that "m-u-g" is *mug*
and that "w-a-t-e-r" is *water,* but I persisted in confounding the two.
In despair she had dropped the subject for the time, only to renew it
at the first opportunity. I became impatient at her repeated attempts
and, seizing the new doll, I dashed it upon the floor. I was keenly
delighted when I felt the fragments of the broken doll at my feet.
Neither sorrow nor regret followed my passionate outburst. I had
not loved the doll. In the still, dark world in which I lived there
was no strong sentiment or tenderness. I felt my teacher sweep the
fragments to one side of the hearth, and I had a sense of satisfaction
that the cause of my discomfort was removed. She brought me my
hat, and I knew I was going out into the warm sunshine. This
thought, if a wordless sensation may be called a thought, made me
hop and skip with pleasure.

We walked down the path to the well-house, attracted by the fragrance of the honeysuckle with which it was covered. Someone was drawing water and my teacher placed my hand under the spout. As the cool stream gushed over one hand she spelled into the other the word water, first slowly, then rapidly. I stood still, my whole attention fixed upon the motions of her fingers. Suddenly I felt a misty consciousness as of something forgotten—a thrill of returning thought; and somehow the mystery of language was revealed to me. I knew then that "w-a-t-e-r" meant the wonderful cool something that was flowing over my hand. That living word awakened my soul, gave it light, hope, joy, set it free! There were barriers still, it is true, but barriers that could in time be swept away.

I left the well-house eager to learn. Everything had a name, and each name gave birth to a new thought. As we returned to the house every object which I touched seemed to quiver with life. That was because I saw everything with the strange, new sight that had come to me. On entering the door I remembered the doll I had broken. I felt my way to the hearth and picked up the pieces. I tried vainly to put them together. Then my eyes filled with tears; for I realized what I had done, and for the first time I felt repentance and sorrow.

I learned a great many new words that day. I do not remember what they all were; but I do know that *mother, father, sister, teacher* were among them—words that were to make the world blossom for me, "like Aaron's rod, with flowers." It would have been difficult to find a happier child than I was as I lay in my crib at the close of that eventful day and lived over the joys it had brought me, and for the first time longed for a new day to come.

Anne Mansfield, in her letters, described the "miracle" she saw taking place in Helen.

March 20, 1887.

My heart is singing for joy this morning. A miracle has happened! The light of understanding has shone upon my little pupil's mind, and behold, all things are changed!

The wild little creature of two weeks ago has been transformed into a gentle child. She is sitting by me as I write, her face serene and happy, crocheting a long red chain of Scotch wool. She learned the stitch this week, and is very proud of the achievement. When she succeeded in making a chain that would reach across the room, she patted herself on the arm and put the first work of her hands lovingly against her cheek. She lets me kiss her now, and when she is in a particularly gentle mood, she will sit in my lap for a minute or two; but she does not return my caresses. The great step—the step that counts—has been taken. The little savage has learned her first lesson in obedience, and finds the yoke easy. It now remains my pleasant task to direct and mold the beautiful intelligence that is beginning to stir in the child-soul. Already people remark the change in Helen. Her father looks in at us morning and evening as he goes to and from his office, and sees her contentedly stringing her beads or making horizontal lines on her sewing card, and exclaims, "How quiet she is!" When I came, her movements were so insistent that one always felt there was something unnatural and almost weird about her. I have noticed also that she eats much less, a fact which troubles her father so much that he is anxious to get her home. He says she is homesick. I don't agree with him; but I suppose we shall have to leave our little bower very soon.

Helen has learned several nouns this week. "M-u-g" and "m-i-l-k," have given her more trouble than other words. When she spells "milk," she points to the mug, and when she spells "mug," she makes the sign for pouring or drinking, which shows that she has confused the words. She has no idea yet that everything has a name.

April 5, 1887.

I must write you a line this morning because something very important has happened. Helen has taken the second great step in her education. She has learned that *everything has a name, and that the manual alphabet is the key to everything she wants to know.*

In a previous letter I think I wrote you that "mug" and "milk" had given Helen more trouble than all the rest. She confused the nouns with the verb "drink." She didn't know the word for "drink," but went through the pantomime of drinking whenever she spelled "mug" or "milk." This morning, while she was washing, she wanted to know the name for "water." When she wants to know the name of anything, she points to it and pats my hand. I spelled "w-a-t-e-r" and thought no more about it until after breakfast. Then it occurred to me that with the help of this new word I might succeed in straightening out the "mug-milk" difficulty. We went out to the pump-house, and I made Helen hold her mug under the spout while I pumped. As the cold water gushed forth, filling the mug, I spelled "w–a–t–e–r" in Helen's free hand. The word coming so close upon the sensation of cold water rushing over her hand seemed to startle her. She dropped the mug and stood as one transfixed. A new light came into her face. She spelled "water" several times. Then she dropped on the ground and asked for its name and pointed to the pump and the trellis, and suddenly turning round she asked for my name. I spelled "Teacher." Just then the nurse brought Helen's little sister into the pump-house, and Helen spelled "baby" and pointed to the nurse. All the way back to the house she was highly excited, and learned the name of every object she touched, so that in a few hours she had added thirty new words to her vocabulary. Here are some of them: *Door, open, shut, give, go, come,* and a great many more.

P.S.—I didn't finish my letter in time to get it posted last night; so I shall add a line. Helen got up this morning like a radiant fairy. She has flitted from object to object, asking the name of everything and kissing me for very gladness. Last night when I got in bed, she stole into my arms of her own accord and kissed me for the first time, and I thought my heart would burst, so full was it of joy.

The Human Touch

Spencer Michael Free

This simple poem reminds us that genuine friendship is about the closeness of hands, hearts, and souls. It also, incidentally, captures the profundity of "touch" between Helen Keller and Anne Mansfield Sullivan.

'Tis the human touch in this world that counts,
    The touch of your hand and mine,
Which means far more to the fainting heart
    Than shelter and bread and wine;
For shelter is gone when the night is o'er,
    And bread lasts only a day,
But the touch of the hand and the sound of the voice
    Sing on in the soul alway.

Little Girls Wiser Than Men

Leo Tolstoy

All friendships have their ups and downs. Learning to put aside
disagreements makes companionship long-lasting.

It was an early Easter. Sledging was only just over; snow still
lay in the yards, and water ran in streams down the village street.

Two little girls from different houses happened to meet in a
lane between two homesteads, where the dirty water after running
through the farmyards had formed a large puddle. One girl was very
small, the other a little bigger. Their mothers had dressed them both
in new frocks. The little one wore a blue frock, the other a yellow
print, and both had red kerchiefs on their heads. They had just come
from church when they met, and first they showed each other their
finery, and then they began to play. Soon the fancy took them to
splash about in the water, and the smaller one was going to step into
the puddle, shoes and all, when the elder checked her.

"Don't go in so, Malásha," said she. "Your mother will scold
you. I will take off my shoes and stockings, and you take off yours."

They did so, and then, picking up their skirts, began walking
toward each other through the puddle. The water came up to Malásha's ankles, and she said:

"It is deep, Akoúlya. I'm afraid!"

"Come on," replied the other. "Don't be frightened. It won't
get any deeper."

When they got near one another, Akoúlya said:

"Mind, Malásha, don't splash. Walk carefully!"

She had hardly said this, when Malásha plumped down her foot
so that the water splashed right on to Akoúlya's frock. The frock
was splashed, and so were Akoúlya's eyes and nose. When she saw
the stains on her frock, she was angry and ran after Malásha to strike
her. Malásha was frightened, and seeing that she had got herself into
trouble, she scrambled out of the puddle, and prepared to run home.
Just then Akoúlya's mother happened to be passing, and seeing that
her daughter's skirt was splashed, and her sleeves dirty, she said:

"You naughty, dirty girl, what have you been doing!"

"Malásha did it on purpose," replied the girl.

At this Akoúlya's mother seized Malásha, and struck her on the back of her neck. Malásha began to howl so that she could be heard all down the street. Her mother came out.

"What are you beating my girl for?" said she, and began scolding her neighbor. One word led to another and they had an angry quarrel. The men came out, and a crowd collected in the street, every one shouting and no one listening. They all went on quarreling, till one gave another a push, and the affair had very nearly come to blows, when Akoúlya's old grandmother, stepping in among them, tried to calm them.

"What are you thinking of, friends? Is it right to behave so? On a day like this, too! It is a time for rejoicing, and not for such folly as this."

They would not listen to the old woman, and nearly knocked her off her feet. And she would not have been able to quiet the crowd, if it had not been for Akoúlya and Malásha themselves. While the women were abusing each other, Akoúlya had wiped the mud off her frock, and gone back to the puddle. She took a stone and began scraping away the earth in front of the puddle to make a channel through which the water could run out into the street. Presently Malásha joined her, and with a chip of wood helped her dig the channel. Just as the men were beginning to fight, the water from the little girls' channel ran streaming into the street toward the very place where the old woman was trying to pacify the men. The girls followed it, one running on each side of the little stream.

"Catch it, Malásha! Catch it!" shouted Akoúlya, while Malásha could not speak for laughing.

Highly delighted, and watching the chip float along on their stream, the little girls ran straight into the group of men; and the old woman, seeing them, said to the men:

"Are you not ashamed of yourselves? To go fighting on account of these lassies, when they themselves have forgotten all about it, and are playing happily together. Dear little souls! They are wiser than you!"

The men looked at the little girls, and were ashamed, and, laughing at themselves, went back each to his own home.

"Except ye turn, and become as little children, ye shall in no wise enter into the kingdom of heaven."

The Enchanted Bluff

Willa Cather

This is a story about the kind of commonplace dreams and adventures friends share in youth. Memories of such times spent together make friendships span the years and miles that later separate us.

We had our swim before sundown, and while we were cooking our supper the oblique rays of light made a dazzling glare on the white sand about us. The translucent red ball itself sank behind the brown stretches of corn field as we sat down to eat, and the warm layer of air that had rested over the water and our clean sand bar grew fresher and smelled of the rank ironweed and sunflowers growing on the flatter shore. The river was brown and sluggish, like any other of the half-dozen streams that water the Nebraska corn lands. On one shore was an irregular line of bald clay bluffs where a few scrub oaks with thick trunks and flat, twisted tops threw light shadows on the long grass. The western shore was low and level, with corn fields that stretched to the skyline, and all along the water's edge were little sandy coves and beaches where slim cottonwoods and willow saplings flickered.

The turbulence of the river in springtime discouraged milling, and, beyond keeping the old red bridge in repair, the busy farmers did not concern themselves with the stream; so the Sandtown boys were left in undisputed possession. In the autumn we hunted quail through the miles of stubble and fodder land along the flat shore, and, after the winter skating season was over and the ice had gone out, the spring freshets and flooded bottoms gave us our great excitement of the year. The channel was never the same for two successive seasons. Every spring the swollen stream undermined a bluff to the east, or bit out a few acres of corn field to the west and whirled the soil away to deposit it in spumy mud banks somewhere else. When the water fell low in midsummer, new sand bars were thus exposed to dry and whiten in the August sun. Sometimes these were banked so firmly that the fury of the next freshet failed to unseat them; the little willow seedlings emerged triumphantly from the yellow froth, broke into spring leaf, shot up into summer growth, and with their mesh of roots bound together the moist sand beneath them against the batterings of another April. Here and there a cottonwood soon glittered among them, quivering in the low current of air that, even on breathless days when the dust hung like smoke above the wagon road, trembled along the face of the water.

It was on such an island, in the third summer of its yellow green, that we built our watch fire; not in the thicket of dancing willow wands, but on the level terrace of fine sand which had been added that spring; a little new bit of world, beautifully ridged with ripple marks, and strewn with the tiny skeletons of turtles and fish, all as white and dry as if they had been expertly cured. We had been careful not to mar the freshness of the place, although we often swam to it on summer evenings and lay on the sand to rest.

This was our last watch fire of the year, and there were reasons why I should remember it better than any of the others. Next week the other boys were to file back to their old places in the Sandtown High School, but I was to go up to the Divide to teach my first country school in the Norwegian district. I was already homesick at the thought of quitting the boys with whom I had always played; of leaving the river, and going up into a windy plain that was all windmills and corn fields and big pastures; where there was nothing willful or unmanageable in the landscape, no new islands, and no chance of unfamiliar birds—such as often followed the water-courses.

Other boys came and went and used the river for fishing or skating, but we six were sworn to the spirit of the stream, and we were friends mainly because of the river. There were the two Hassler boys, Fritz and Otto, sons of the little German tailor. They were the youngest of us; ragged boys of ten and twelve, with sunburned hair, weather-stained faces, and pale blue eyes. Otto, the elder, was the best mathematician in school, and clever at his books, but he always dropped out in the spring term as if the river could not get on without him. He and Fritz caught the fat, horned catfish and sold them about the town, and they lived so much in the water that they were as brown and sandy as the river itself.

There was Percy Pound, a fat, freckled boy with chubby cheeks, who took half a dozen boys' story-papers and was always being kept in for reading detective stories behind his desk. There was Tip Smith, destined by his freckles and red hair to be the buffoon in all our games, though he walked like a timid little old man and had a funny, cracked laugh. Tip worked hard in his father's grocery store every afternoon and swept it out before school in the morning. Even his recreations were laborious. He collected cigarette cards and tin tobacco-tags indefatigably, and would sit for hours humped up over a snarling little scroll-saw which he kept in his attic. His dearest possessions were some little pill bottles that purported to contain grains of wheat from the Holy Land, water from the Jordan and the Dead Sea, and earth from the Mount of Olives. His father had bought these dull things from a Baptist missionary who peddled them, and Tip seemed to derive great satisfaction from their remote origin.

The tall boy was Arthur Adams. He had fine hazel eyes that were almost too reflective and sympathetic for a boy, and such a pleasant voice that we all loved to hear him read aloud. Even when he had to read poetry aloud at school, no one ever thought of laughing. To be sure, he was not at school very much of the time. He was seventeen and should have finished the High School the year before, but he was always off somewhere with his gun. Arthur's mother was dead, and his father, who was feverishly absorbed in promoting schemes, wanted to send the boy away to school and get him off his hands; but Arthur always begged off for another year and promised to study. I remember him as a tall, brown boy with an intelligent face, always lounging among a lot of us little fellows, laughing at us oftener than with us, but such a soft, satisfied laugh that we felt rather flattered when we provoked it. In after-years people said that Arthur had been given to evil ways even as a lad, and it is true that we often saw him with the gambler's sons and with old Spanish Fanny's boy, but if he learned anything ugly in their company he never betrayed it to us. We would have followed Arthur anywhere, and I am bound to say that he led us into no worse places than the cattail marshes and the stubble fields. These, then, were the boys who camped with me that summer night upon the sand bar.

After we finished our supper we beat the willow thicket for driftwood. By the time we had collected enough, night had fallen, and the pungent, weedy smell from the shore increased with the coolness. We threw ourselves down about the fire and made another futile effort to show Percy Pound the Little Dipper. We had tried it often before, but he could never be got past the big one.

"You see those three big stars just below the handle, with the bright one in the middle?" said Otto Hassler; "That's Orion's belt, and the bright one is the clasp." I crawled behind Otto's shoulder and sighted up his arm to the star that seemed perched upon the tip of his steady forefinger. The Hassler boys did seine-fishing at night, and they knew a good many stars.

Percy gave up the Little Dipper and lay back on the sand, his hands clasped under his head. "I can see the North Star," he announced, contentedly, pointing toward it with his big toe. "Anyone might get lost and need to know that."

We all looked up at it.

"How do you suppose Columbus felt when his compass didn't point north anymore?" Tip asked.

Otto shook his head. "My father says that there was another North Star once, and that maybe this one won't last always. I wonder what would happen to us down here if anything went wrong with it?"

Arthur chuckled. "I wouldn't worry, Ott. Nothing's apt to happen to it in your time. Look at the Milky Way! There must be lots of good dead Indians."

We lay back and looked, meditating, at the dark cover of the world. The gurgle of the water had become heavier. We had often noticed a mutinous, complaining note in it at night, quite different from its cheerful daytime chuckle, and seeming like the voice of a much deeper and more powerful stream. Our water had always these two moods: the one of sunny complaisance, the other of inconsolable, passionate regret.

"Queer how the stars are all in sort of diagrams," remarked Otto. "You could do most any proposition in geometry with 'em. They always look as if they meant something. Some folks say everybody's fortune is all written out in the stars, don't they?"

"They believe so in the old country," Fritz affirmed.

But Arthur only laughed at him. "You're thinking of Napoleon, Fritzey. He had a star that went out when he began to lose battles. I guess the stars don't keep any close tally on Sandtown folks."

We were speculating on how many times we could count a hundred before the evening star went down behind the corn fields, when someone cried, "There comes the moon, and it's as big as a cart wheel!"

We all jumped up to greet it as it swam over the bluffs behind us. It came up like a galleon in full sail; an enormous, barbaric thing, red as an angry heathen god.

"When the moon came up red like that, the Aztecs used to sacrifice their prisoners on the temple top," Percy announced.

"Go on, Perce. You got that out of *Golden Days*. Do you believe that, Arthur?" I appealed.

Arthur answered, quite seriously: "Like as not. The moon was one of their gods. When my father was in Mexico City he saw the stone where they used to sacrifice their prisoners."

As we dropped down by the fire again someone asked whether the Mound-Builders were older than the Aztecs. When we once got upon the Mound-Builders we never willingly got away from them, and we were still conjecturing when we heard a loud splash in the water.

"Must have been a big cat jumping," said Fritz. "They do sometimes. They must see bugs in the dark. Look what a track the moon makes!"

There was a long, silvery streak on the water, and where the current fretted over a big log it boiled up like gold pieces.

"Suppose there ever *was* any gold hid away in this old river?" Fritz asked. He lay like a little brown Indian, close to the fire, his chin on his hand and his bare feet in the air. His brother laughed at him, but Arthur took his suggestion seriously.

"Some of the Spaniards thought there was gold up here some-where. Seven cities chuck full of gold, they had it, and Coronado and his men came up to hunt it. The Spaniards were all over this country once."

Percy looked interested. "Was that before the Mormons went through?"

We all laughed at this.

"Long enough before. Before the Pilgrim Fathers, Perce. Maybe they came along this very river. They always followed the watercourses."

"I wonder where this river really does begin?" Tip mused. That was an old and a favorite mystery which the map did not clearly explain. On the map the little black line stopped somewhere in west-ern Kansas; but since rivers generally rose in mountains, it was only reasonable to suppose that ours came from the Rockies. Its destina-tion, we knew, was the Missouri, and the Hassler boys always main-tained that we could embark at Sandtown in floodtime, follow our noses, and eventually arrive at New Orleans. Now they took up their old argument. "If us boys had grit enough to try it, it wouldn't take no time to get to Kansas City and St. Joe."

We began to talk about the places we wanted to go to. The Hassler boys wanted to see the stockyards in Kansas City, and Percy wanted to see a big store in Chicago. Arthur was interlocutor and did not betray himself.

"Now it's your turn, Tip."

Tip rolled over on his elbow and poked the fire, and his eyes looked shyly out of his queer, tight little face. "My place is awful far away. My Uncle Bill told me about it."

Tip's Uncle Bill was a wanderer, bitten with mining fever, who had drifted into Sandtown with a broken arm, and when it was well had drifted out again.

"Where is it?"

"Aw, it's down in New Mexico somewheres. There aren't no railroads or anything. You have to go on mules, and you run out of water before you get there and have to drink canned tomatoes."

"Well, go on, kid. What's it like when you do get there?"

Tip sat up and excitedly began his story.

"There's a big red rock there that goes right up out of the sand for about nine hundred feet. The country's flat all around it, and this here rock goes up all by itself, like a monument. They call it the Enchanted Bluff down there, because no white man has ever been on top of it. The sides are smooth rock, and straight up, like a wall. The Indians say that hundreds of years ago, before the Spaniards came, there was a village away up there in the air. The tribe that lived there had some sort of steps, made out of wood and bark, hung down over the face of the bluff, and the braves went down to hunt and carried water up in big jars swung on their backs. They kept a big supply of water and dried meat up there, and never went down except to hunt. They were a peaceful tribe that made cloth and pottery, and they went up there to get out of the wars. You see, they could pick off any war party that tried to get up their steps. The Indians say they were a handsome people, and they had some sort of queer religion. Uncle Bill thinks they were Cliff-Dwellers who had got into trouble and left home. They weren't fighters, anyhow.

"One time the braves were down hunting and an awful storm came up—a kind of waterspout—and when they got back to their rock they found their little staircase had been all broken to pieces, and only a few steps were left hanging away up in the air. While they were camped at the foot of the rock, wondering what to do, a war party from the north came along and massacred 'em to a man, with all the old folks and women looking on from the rock. Then the war party went on south and left the village to get down the best way they could. Of course they never got down. They starved to death up there, and when the war party came back on their way north, they could hear the children crying from the edge of the bluff where they had crawled out, but they didn't see a sign of a grown Indian, and nobody has ever been up there since."

We exclaimed at this dolorous legend and sat up.

"There couldn't have been many people up there," Percy demurred. "How big is the top, Tip?"

"Oh, pretty big. Big enough so that the rock doesn't look nearly as tall as it is. The top's bigger than the base. The bluff is sort of worn away for several hundred feet up. That's one reason it's so hard to climb.'"

I asked how the Indians got up, in the first place.

"Nobody knows how they got up or when. A hunting party came along once and saw that there was a town up there, and that was all."

Otto rubbed his chin and looked thoughtful. "Of course there must be some way to get up there. Couldn't people get a rope over someway and pull a ladder up?"

Tip's little eyes were shining with excitement. "I know a way. Me and Uncle Bill talked it all over. There's a kind of rocket that would take a rope over—life-savers use 'em—and then you could hoist a rope ladder and peg it down at the bottom and make it tight with guy ropes on the other side. I'm going to climb that there bluff, and I've got it all planned out."

Fritz asked what he expected to find when he got up there.

"Bones, maybe, or the ruins of their town, or pottery, or some of their idols. There might be 'most anything up there. Anyhow, I want to see."

"Sure nobody else has been up there, Tip?" Arthur asked.

"Dead sure. Hardly anybody ever goes down there. Some hunters tried to cut steps in the rock once, but they didn't get higher than a man can reach. The Bluff's all red granite, and Uncle Bill thinks it's a boulder the glaciers left. It's a queer place, anyhow. Nothing but cactus and desert for hundreds of miles, and yet right under the Bluff there's good water and plenty of grass. That's why the bison used to go down there."

Suddenly we heard a scream above our fire, and jumped up to see a dark, slim bird floating southward far above us—a whooping crane, we knew by her cry and her long neck. We ran to the edge of the island, hoping we might see her alight, but she wavered southward along the river course until we lost her. The Hassler boys declared that by the look of the heavens it must be after midnight, so we threw more wood on our fire, put on our jackets, and curled down in the warm sand. Several of us pretended to doze, but I fancy we were really thinking about Tip's Bluff and the extinct people. Over in the wood the ring doves were calling mournfully to one another, and once we heard a dog bark, far away. "Somebody getting into old Tommy's melon patch," Fritz murmured sleepily, but nobody answered him. By and by Percy spoke out of the shadows.

"Say, Tip, when you go down there will you take me with you?"

"Maybe."

"Suppose one of us beats you down there, Tip?"

"Whoever gets to the Bluff first has got to promise to tell the rest of us exactly what he finds," remarked one of the Hassler boys, and to this we all readily assented.

Somewhat reassured, I dropped off to sleep. I must have dreamed about a race for the Bluff, for I awoke in a kind of fear that other people were getting ahead of me and that I was losing my chance. I sat up in my damp clothes and looked at the other boys, who lay tumbled in uneasy attitudes about the dead fire. It was still dark, but the sky was blue with the last wonderful azure of night. The stars glistened like crystal globes, and trembled as if they shone through a depth of clear water. Even as I watched, they began to pale and the sky brightened. Day came suddenly, almost instantaneously. I turned for another look at the blue night, and it was gone. Everywhere the birds began to call, and all manner of little insects began to chirp and hop about in the willows. A breeze sprang up from the west and brought the heavy smell of ripened corn. The boys rolled over and shook themselves. We stripped and plunged into the river just as the sun came up over the windy bluffs.

When I came home to Sandtown at Christmas time, we skated out to our island and talked over the whole project of the Enchanted Bluff, renewing our resolution to find it.

Although that was twenty years ago, none of us have ever climbed the Enchanted Bluff. Percy Pound is a stockbroker in Kansas City and will go nowhere that his red touring car cannot carry him. Otto Hassler went on the railroad and lost his foot braking; after which he and Fritz succeeded their father as the town tailors.

Arthur sat about the sleepy little town all his life—he died before he was twenty-five. The last time I saw him, when I was home on one of my college vacations, he was sitting in a steamer chair under a cottonwood tree in the little yard behind one of the two Sandtown saloons. He was very untidy and his hand was not steady, but when he rose, unabashed, to greet me, his eyes were as clear and warm as ever. When I had talked with him for an hour and heard him laugh again, I wondered how it was that when Nature had taken such pains with a man, from his hands to the arch of his long foot, she had ever lost him in Sandtown. He joked about Tip Smith's Bluff, and declared he was going down there just as soon as the weather got cooler; he thought the Grand Canyon might be worthwhile, too.

I was perfectly sure when I left him that he would never get beyond the high plank fence and the comfortable shade of the cottonwood. And, indeed, it was under that very tree that he died one summer morning.

Tip Smith still talks about going to New Mexico. He married a slatternly, unthrifty country girl, has been much tied to a perambulator, and has grown stooped and gray from irregular meals and broken sleep. But the worst of his difficulties are now over, and he has, as he says, come into easy water. When I was last in Sandtown I walked home with him late one moonlight night, after he had balanced his cash and shut up his store. We took the long way around and sat down on the schoolhouse steps, and between us we quite revived the romance of the lone red rock and the extinct people. Tip insists that he still means to go down there, but he thinks now he will wait until his boy Bert is old enough to go with him. Bert has been let into the story, and thinks of nothing but the Enchanted Bluff.

Keep Friendships in Constant Repair

From The Life of Samuel Johnson

James Boswell (1740–1795), the Scottish lawyer best known for his biography of Samuel Johnson, once wrote that "we cannot tell the precise moment when friendship is formed. As in filling a vessel drop by drop, there is at last a drop which makes it run over; so in a series of kindnesses there is at last one which makes the heart run over." Here, in his *Life of Samuel Johnson,* he advises that we should fill our lives with friendships both old and new. Once formed, friendship must be replenished from time to time so it remains in "constant repair."

I have often thought, that as longevity is generally desired, and, I believe, generally expected, it would be wise to be continually adding to the number of our friends, that the loss of some may be supplied by others. Friendship, "the wine of life," should, like a well-stocked cellar, be thus continually renewed; and it is consolatory to think, that although we can seldom add what will equal the generous *first-growths* of our youth, yet friendship becomes insensibly old in much less time than is commonly imagined, and not many years are required to make it very mellow and pleasant. *Warmth* will, no doubt, make a considerable difference. Men of affectionate temper and bright fancy will coalesce a great deal sooner than those who are cold and dull.

The proposition which I have now endeavored to illustrate was, at a subsequent period of his life, the opinion of Johnson himself. He said to Sir Joshua Reynolds, "If a man does not make new acquaintances as he advances through life, he will soon find himself left alone. A man, Sir, should keep his friendship *in constant repair.*"

New Friends and Old Friends

What is real endures; it is as true of friendship as of other kinds of love.

> Make new friends, but keep the old;
> Those are silver, these are gold.
> New-made friendships, like new wine,
> Age will mellow and refine.
> Friendships that have stood the test—
> Time and change—are surely best;
> Brow may wrinkle, hair grow gray;
> Friendship never knows decay.
> For 'mid old friends, tried and true,
> Once more we our youth renew.
> But old friends, alas! may die;
> New friends must their place supply.
> Cherish friendship in your breast—
> New is good, but old is best;
> Make new friends, but keep the old;
> Those are silver, these are gold.

The Lover Pleads with his Friend for Old Friends

William Butler Yeats

We cannot afford to make new friends at the expense of our old ones.

> Though you are in your shining days,
> Voices among the crowd
> And new friends busy with your praise,
> Be not unkind or proud,

But think about old friends the most:
Time's bitter flood will rise,
Your beauty perish and be lost
For all eyes but these eyes.

A Time to Talk

Robert Frost

Work always calls us. But we make time for friends when they
call too.

When a friend calls to me from the road
And slows his horse to a meaning walk,
I don't stand still and look around
On all the hills I haven't hoed,
And shout from where I am, What is it?
No, not as there is a time to talk.
I thrust my hoe in the mellow ground,
Blade-end up and five feet tall,
And plod: I go up to the stone wall
For a friendly visit.

Aristotle on Friendship

From the Nicomachean Ethics

The ancients listed friendship among the highest of virtues. It
was an essential element in the happy or fully flourishing life.
"For without friends," Aristotle says, "no one would choose to
live, though he had all other goods." Words worth remembering
in a world of perishable "goods."

According to Aristotle, friendship either is, or it involves, a state of character, a virtue. There are three kinds of friendship. These are based on pleasure in another's company (friendship of pleasure), or on usefulness in association (friendships of utility), or on mutual admiration (friendships in virtue). All are essential to the good life, and the best sorts of friends will not only admire each other's excellence, but take pleasure in each other's company and find their association of mutual advantage. Here is a portion of Aristotle's classic discussion.

As the motives to Friendship differ in kind, so do the respective feelings and Friendships. The species then of Friendship are three, in number equal to the objects of it, since in the line of each there may be "mutual affection mutually known."

Now they who have Friendship for one another desire one another's good according to the motive of their Friendship; accordingly they whose motive is utility have no Friendship for one another really, but only insofar as some good arises to them from one another.

And they whose motive is pleasure are in like case: I mean, they have Friendship for men of easy pleasantry, not because they are of a given character but because they are pleasant to themselves. So then they whose motive to Friendship is utility love their friends for what is good to themselves; they whose motive is pleasure do so for what is pleasurable to themselves; that is to say, not insofar as the friend beloved *is* but insofar as he is useful or pleasurable. These Friendships then are a matter of result: since the object is not beloved in that he is the man he is but in that he furnishes advantage or pleasure as the case may be.

Such Friendships are of course very liable to dissolution if the parties do not continue alike: I mean, that the others cease to have any Friendship for them when they are no longer pleasurable or useful. Now it is the nature of utility not to be permanent but constantly varying: so, of course, when the motive which made them friends is vanished, the Friendship likewise dissolves; since it existed only relatively to those circumstances. . . .

That then is perfect Friendship which subsists between those who are good and whose similarity consists in their goodness: for these men wish one another's good in similar ways; insofar as they are good (and good they are in themselves); and those are specially

friends who wish good to their friends for their sakes, because they
feel thus toward them on their own account and not as a mere matter
of result; so the Friendship between these men continues to subsist
so long as they are good; and goodness, we know, has in it a principle of permanence. . . .

Rare it is probable Friendships of this kind will be, because
men of this kind are rare. Besides, all requisite qualifications being
presupposed, there is further required time and intimacy: for, as the
proverb says, men cannot know one another "till they have eaten
the requisite quantity of salt together"; nor can they in fact admit
one another to intimacy, much less be friends, till each has appeared
to the other and been proved to be a fit object of Friendship. They
who speedily commence an interchange of friendly actions may be
said to wish to be friends, but they are not so unless they are also
proper objects of Friendship and mutually known to be such: that is
to say, a desire for Friendship may arise quickly but not Friendship
itself.

Cicero on Friendship

From Laelius

It has been said that through Cicero (106–43 B.C.) Greek philosophy passed to Western Europe. The Roman statesman's writings
have proved to be an inexhaustible fountain, one that has watered
the thought and expression of succeeding ages. His examination
of the question of what friendship really means is still a cogent
prescription for good conduct in modern life. Laelius, the chief
speaker in the dialogue, defines friendship as "a complete identity
of feeling about all things in heaven and earth: an identity which
is strengthened by mutual goodwill and affection." Moral goodness, or "goodness of character," is the quality that makes friendship possible: "All harmony, and permanence, and fidelity, come
from that."

I desire it may be understood that I am now speaking, not of that inferior species of amity which occurs in the common intercourse of the world (although this, too, is not without its pleasures and advantages), but of that genuine and perfect friendship, examples of which are so extremely rare as to be rendered memorable by their singularity. It is this sort alone that can truly be said to heighten the joys of prosperity, and mitigate the sorrows of adversity, by a generous participation of both; indeed, one of the chief among the many important offices of this connection is exerted in the day of affliction, by dispelling the gloom that overcasts the mind, encouraging the hope of happier times, and preventing the depressed spirits from sinking into a state of weak and unmanly despondence. Whoever is in possession of a true friend sees the exact counterpart of his own soul. In consequence of this moral resemblance between them, they are so intimately one that no advantage can attend either which does not equally communicate itself to both; they are strong in the strength, rich in the opulence, and powerful in the power of each other. They can scarcely, indeed, be considered in any respect as separate individuals, and wherever the one appears the other is virtually present. I will venture even a bolder assertion, and affirm that in despite of death they must both continue to exist so long as either of them shall remain alive; for the deceased may, in a certain sense, be said still to live whose memory is preserved with the highest veneration and the most tender regret in the bosom of the survivor, a circumstance which renders the former happy in death, and the latter honored in life.

If that benevolent principle which thus intimately unites two persons in the bands of amity were to be struck out of the human heart, it would be impossible that either private families or public communities should subsist—even the land itself would lie waste, and desolation overspread the earth. Should this assertion stand in need of a proof, it will appear evident by considering the ruinous consequences which ensue from discord and dissension; for what family is so securely established, or what government fixed upon so firm a basis, that it would not be overturned and utterly destroyed were a general spirit of enmity and malevolence to break forth amongst its members?—a sufficient argument, surely, of the inestimable benefits which flow from the kind and friendly affections.

Thinking on Friendship

William Shakespeare

Thinking of friends and their worth is often enough to drive away an army of fears, regrets, and envies.

SONNET XXIX

When, in disgrace with fortune and men's eyes,
I all alone beweep my outcast state,
And trouble deaf heaven with my bootless cries,
And look upon myself, and curse my fate,
Wishing me like to one more rich in hope,
Featured like him, like him with friends possess'd,
Desiring this man's art and that man's scope,
With what I most enjoy contented least;
Yet in these thoughts myself almost despising,
Haply I think on thee, and then my state,
Like to the lark at break of day arising
From sullen earth, sings hymns at heaven's gate;
    For thy sweet love remember'd such wealth
      brings
    That then I scorn to change my state with kings.

SONNET XXX

When to the sessions of sweet silent thought
I summon up remembrance of things past,
I sigh the lack of many a thing I sought,
And with old woes new wail my dear time's waste:
Then can I drown an eye, unused to flow,
For precious friends hid in death's dateless night,
And weep afresh love's long since cancel'd woe,
And moan the expense of many a vanish'd sight:
Then can I grieve at grievances foregone,
And heavily from woe to woe tell o'er
The sad account of fore-bemoaned moan,
Which I new pay as if not paid before.
    But if the while I think on thee, dear friend,
    All losses are restored and sorrows end.

Emerson on Friendship

From "Friendship"

Emerson writes that friendships are gifts and expressions of God; they form when the divine spirit in one individual finds the divine spirit in another, and "both deride and cancel the thick walls of individual character, relation, age, sex, and circumstance." The essay "Friendship" was first published in 1841.

I do not wish to treat friendships daintily, but with roughest courage. When they are real, they are not glass threads or frost-work, but the solidest thing we know. For now, after so many ages of experience, what do we know of nature, or of ourselves? Not one step has man taken toward the solution of the problem of his destiny. In one condemnation of folly stand the whole universe of men. But the sweet sincerity of joy and peace, which I draw from this alliance with my brother's soul, is the nut itself whereof all nature and all thought is but the husk and shell. Happy is the house that shelters a friend! It might well be built, like a festal bower or arch, to entertain him a single day. Happier, if he know the solemnity of that relation, and honor its law! He who offers himself a candidate for that covenant comes up like an Olympian to the great games where the first born of the world are the competitors. He proposes himself for contests where Time, Want, Danger are in the lists, and he alone is victor who has truth enough in his constitution to preserve the delicacy of his beauty from the wear and tear of all these. The gifts of fortune may be present or absent, but all the hap in that contest depends on intrinsic nobleness and the contempt of trifles. . . . A friend is a person with whom I may be sincere. Before him, I may think aloud. I am arrived at last in the presence of a man so real and equal that I may drop even those undermost garments of dissimulation, courtesy, and second thought, which men never put off, and may deal with him with the simplicity and wholeness with which one chemical atom meets another. Sincerity is the luxury allowed, like diadems and authority, only to the highest rank, that being permitted to speak truth as having none above it to court or conform unto. Every man alone is sincere. At the entrance of a second person hypocrisy begins. We parry and fend the approach of our fellow man by compliments, by gossip, by amusements, by affairs. We cover up our thought from him under a hundred folds. I knew a man who, under a certain religious frenzy, cast off this drapery, and, omitting all compliments and commonplace, spoke to the conscience of every person he encountered, and that with great insight and beauty. At first he was resisted, and all men agreed he was mad. By persisting, as indeed he could not help doing, for some time in this course, he attained to the advantage of bringing every man of his acquaintance into true relations with him. No man would think of speaking falsely with him, or of putting him off with any chat of markets or reading rooms. But every man was constrained by so much sincerity to the like plain dealing, and what love of nature, what poetry, what symbol of truth he had, he did certainly show him. But to most of us society shows not its face and eye, but its side and its back. To stand in true relations with men in a false age is worth a fit of insanity, is it not? We can seldom go erect. Almost every man we meet requires some civility, requires to be humored; he has some fame, some talent, some whim of religion or philanthropy in his head that is not to be questioned, and which spoils all conversation with him. But a friend is a sane man who exercises not my ingenuity, but me. My friend gives me entertainment without requiring any stipulation on my part. A friend, therefore, is a sort of paradox in nature. I who alone am, I who see nothing in nature whose existence I can affirm with equal evidence to my own, behold now the semblance of my being in all its height, variety, and curiosity reiterated in a foreign form; so that a friend may well be reckoned the masterpiece of nature.

Mending Wall

Robert Frost

We want to make sure we don't fall into the habit of walling
friendships in or out.

Something there is that doesn't love a wall,
That sends the frozen-ground-swell under it,
And spills the upper boulders in the sun;
And makes gaps even two can pass abreast.
The work of hunters is another thing:
I have come after them and made repair
Where they have left not one stone on a stone,
But they would have the rabbit out of hiding,
To please the yelping dogs. The gaps I mean,
No one has seen them made or heard them made,
But at spring mending-time we find them there.
I let my neighbor know beyond the hill;
And on a day we meet to walk the line
And set the wall between us once again.
We keep the wall between us as we go.
To each the boulders that have fallen to each.
And some are loaves and some so nearly balls
We have to use a spell to make them balance:
"Stay where you are until our backs are turned!"
We wear our fingers rough with handling them.
Oh, just another kind of outdoor game,
One on a side. It comes to little more:
There where it is we do not need the wall:
He is all pine and I am apple orchard.
My apple trees will never get across
And eat the cones under his pines, I tell him.
He only says, "Good fences make good neighbors."
Spring is the mischief in me, and I wonder
If I could put a notion in his head:
"*Why* do they make good neighbors? Isn't it
Where there are cows? But here there are no cows.
Before I built a wall I'd ask to know

What I was walling in or walling out,
And to whom I was like to give offense.
Something there is that doesn't love a wall,
That wants it down." I could say "Elves" to him,
But it's not elves exactly, and I'd rather
He said it for himself. I see him there
Bringing a stone grasped firmly by the top
In each hand, like an old-stone savage armed.
He moves in darkness as it seems to me,
Not of woods only and the shade of trees.
He will not go behind his father's saying,
And he likes having thought of it so well
He says again, "Good fences make good neighbors."

Childhood and Poetry

Pablo Neruda

Chilean poet Pablo Neruda (1904–1973) once linked his creation of verse to a simple exchange of gifts in his childhood. As in Robert Frost's poem, "something there is that doesn't love a wall," or in this case a backyard fence, in the exchange. The curious story suggests that every time we offer friendship to someone we do not know, we strengthen the bond of brotherhood for all of humanity.

One time, investigating in the backyard of our house in Temuco the tiny objects and minuscule beings of my world, I came upon a hole in one of the boards of the fence. I looked through the hole and saw a landscape like that behind our house, uncared for, and wild. I moved back a few steps, because I sensed vaguely that something was about to happen. All of a sudden a hand appeared—a tiny hand of a boy about my own age. By the time I came close again, the hand was gone, and in its place there was a marvelous white sheep.

The sheep's wool was faded, its wheels had escaped. All of this only made it more authentic. I had never seen such a wonderful sheep. I looked back through the hole but the boy had disappeared. I went into the house and brought out a treasure of my own: a pinecone, opened, full of odor and resin, which I adored. I set it down in the same spot and went off with the sheep.

I never saw either the hand or the boy again. And I have never again seen a sheep like that either. The toy I lost finally in a fire. But even now, in 1954, almost fifty years old, whenever I pass a toy shop, I look furtively into the window, but it's no use. They don't make sheep like that anymore.

I have been a lucky man. To feel the intimacy of brothers is a marvelous thing in life. To feel the love of people whom we love is a fire that feeds our life. But to feel the affection that comes from those whom we do not know, from those unknown to us, who are watching over our sleep and solitude, over our dangers and our weaknesses—that is something still greater and more beautiful because it widens out the boundaries of our being, and unites all living things.

That exchange brought home to me for the first time a precious idea: that all of humanity is somehow together. That experience came to me again much later; this time it stood out strikingly against a background of trouble and persecution.

It won't surprise you then that I attempted to give something resiny, earthlike, and fragrant in exchange for human brotherhood. Just as I once left the pinecone by the fence, I have since left my words on the door of so many people who were unknown to me, people in prison, or hunted, or alone.

That is the great lesson I learned in my childhood, in the backyard of a lonely house. Maybe it was nothing but a game two boys played who didn't know each other and wanted to pass to the other some good things of life. Yet maybe this small and mysterious exchange of gifts remained inside me also, deep and indestructible, giving my poetry light.

The Arrow and the Song

Henry Wadsworth Longfellow

In this poem, Longfellow suggests that if we offer something of ourselves to the world—a good deed, a kind word, our love—eventually we will discover its effects. It may come back to us in the form of a friend.

> I shot an arrow into the air,
> It fell to earth, I knew not where;
> For, so swiftly it flew, the sight
> Could not follow it in its flight.
>
> I breathed a song into the air,
> It fell to earth, I knew not where;
> For who has sight so keen and strong,
> That it can follow the flight of song?
>
> Long, long afterward, in an oak
> I found the arrow, still unbroke;
> And the song, from beginning to end,
> I found again in the heart of a friend.

Thomas Jefferson and James Madison

Thomas Jefferson and James Madison met in 1776—could it have been any other year?—and worked together, starting then, to further the American Revolution and later to shape the new scheme of government. From that work sprang a friendship perhaps incomparable in intimacy, in the trustfulness of collaboration, and in duration: it lasted fifty years. It was the embodiment of that kind of perfect friendship Aristotle describes. It included pleasure and utility, but over and above them there was shared purpose, a common end, and an enduring goodness on both sides.

Four and a half months before he died, when he was ailing, debt-ridden, and worried about his impoverished family, Jefferson wrote to his longtime friend. His words, and Madison's reply, remind us that friends are friends until death. They also remind us that sometimes a friendship has a bearing on things larger than the friendship itself. For has there ever been a friendship of greater public consequence than this one?

The friendship which has subsisted between us now half a century and the harmony of our political principles and pursuits have been sources of constant happiness to me through that long period. It has also been a great solace to me to believe that you are engaged in vindicating to posterity the course we have pursued for preserving to them in all their purity the blessings of self-government which we had assisted in acquiring for them. If ever the earth has beheld a system of administration conducted with a single and steadfast eye to the general interest and happiness of those committed to it, one which protected by truth can never know reproach, it is that to which our lives have been devoted. To myself you have been a pillar of support through life. Take care of me when dead, and be assured that I shall leave you with my last affections.

A week later Madison replied:

You cannot look back to the long period of our private friendship and political harmony with more affecting recollections than I do. If they are a source of pleasure to you, what ought they not to be to me? We cannot be deprived of the happy consciousness of the pure devotion to the public good with which we discharged the trust committed to us. And I indulge a confidence that sufficient evidence will find its way to another generation to insure, after we are gone, whatever of justice may be withheld whilst we are here.

A Legacy

John Greenleaf Whittier

Friend of my many years!
When the great silence falls, at last, on me,
Let me not leave, to pain and sadden thee,
    A memory of tears,

But pleasant thoughts alone
Of one who was thy friendship's honored guest
And drank the wine of consolation pressed
    From sorrows of thy own.

I leave with thee a sense
Of hands upheld and trials rendered less—
The unselfish joy which is to helpfulness
    Its own great recompense;

The knowledge that from thine,
As from the garments of the Master, stole
Calmness and strength, the virtue which makes whole
    And heals without a sign;

Yea more, the assurance strong
That love, which fails of perfect utterance here,
Lives on to fill the heavenly atmosphere
    With its immortal song.

5

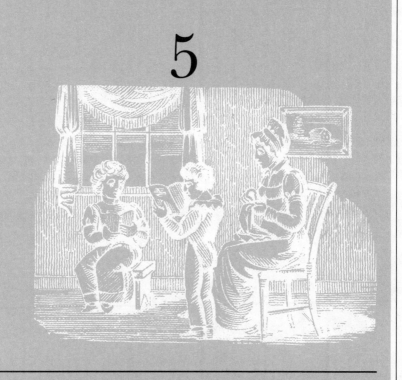

Work

What are you going to be when you grow up?" is a question about work. What is your work in the world going to be? What will be your works? These are not fundamentally questions about jobs and pay, but questions about life. Work is applied effort; it is whatever we put ourselves into, whatever we expend our energy on for the sake of accomplishing or achieving something. Work in this fundamental sense is not what we do *for* a living but what we do *with* our living.

Parents and teachers both *work* at the upbringing of children, but only teachers receive paychecks for it. The housework of parents is real work, though it brings in no revenue. The schoolwork, homework, and teamwork of children are all real work, though the payoff is not in dollars. A child's household chores may be accompanied *by* an allowance, but they are not done *for* an allowance. They are done because they need to be done.

The opposite of work is not leisure or play or having fun but idleness—not *investing* ourselves in anything. Even sleeping can be a form of investment if it is done for the sake of future activity. But sleep, like amusement, can also be a form of escape—oblivion sought for its own sake rather than for the sake of renewal. It can be a waste of time. Leisure activity or play or having fun, on the other hand, can involve genuine investment of the self and not be a waste of time at all.

We want our children to flourish, to live well and fare well—to be happy. Happiness, as Aristotle long ago pointed out, resides in activity, both physical and mental. It resides in doing things that one can take pride in doing well, and hence that one can *enjoy* doing. It is a great mistake to identify enjoyment with mere amusement or relaxing or being entertained. Life's greatest joys are not what one does *apart from* the work of one's life, but *with* the work of one's life. Those who have missed the joy of work, of a job well done, have missed something very important. This applies to our children, too.

When we want our children to be happy, we want them to enjoy *life*. We want them to find and enjoy their work in the world.

How do we help prepare our children for lives like that? Once again, the keys are practice and example: practice in *doing* various things that require a level of effort and engagement compatible with some personal investment in the activity, and the examples of our own lives.

The first step in doing things is *learning how* to do them. (And learning how to turn on the television doesn't count—though learning how to turn it *off* might.) Good habits of personal hygiene, and helping with meals or bed-making or laundry or caring for pets or any other such household chores all require learning. All can be done well or poorly. All can be done cheerfully and with pride, or grudgingly and with distaste. And which way we do them is really up to us. It is a matter of choice. That is perhaps the greatest insight that the ancient Roman Stoics championed for humanity. There are no menial jobs, only menial attitudes. And our attitudes are up to us.

Parents show their children how to enjoy doing the things that have to be done by working with them, by encouraging and appreciating their efforts, and by the witness of their own cheerful and conscientious example. And since the possibilities for happy and productive lives are largely opened up for youth by the quality and extent of their education, parents who work most effectively at providing their offspring with what it takes to lead flourishing lives take education very seriously.

Work is effort applied toward some end. The most satisfying work involves directing our efforts toward achieving ends that we ourselves endorse as worthy expressions of our talent and character. Volunteer service work, if it is genuinely voluntary and exercises our talents in providing needed service, is typically satisfying in this way. Youth needs experience of this kind of work. It is a good model for our working lives.

The Song of the Bee

Marian Douglas

If you look in old American schoolbooks, you'll find that this poem and others like it were among the first reading lessons offered to young students. They set the tone for work in school and life. God seems to have created bees to inspire us toward industry.

Buzz! buzz! buzz!
   This is the song of the bee.
His legs are of yellow;
A jolly, good fellow,
   And yet a great worker is he.

In days that are sunny
He's getting his honey;
In days that are cloudy
   He's making his wax:
On pinks and on lilies,
And gay daffodillies,
And columbine blossoms,
   He levies a tax!

Buzz! buzz! buzz!
The sweet-smelling clover,
He, humming, hangs over;
The scent of the roses
    Makes fragrant his wings:
He never gets lazy;
From thistle and daisy,
And weeds of the meadow,
    Some treasure he brings.

Buzz! buzz! buzz!
From morning's first light
Till the coming of night,
He's singing and toiling
    The summer day through.
Oh! we may get weary,
And think work is dreary;
'Tis harder by far
    To have nothing to do.

Wynken, Blynken, and Nod

Eugene Field

"In dreams begins responsibility," William Butler Yeats wrote.
We can begin to teach our youngest children about the responsibility as well as the joy of work by sending them off to their
dreams with this wonderful Eugene Field (1850–1895) poem.

Wynken, Blynken, and Nod one night
   Sailed off in a wooden shoe—
Sailed on a river of crystal light
   Into a sea of dew.
"Where are you going, and what do you wish?"
   The old moon asked the three.
"We have come to fish for the herring fish
   That live in this beautiful sea;
   Nets of silver and gold have we!"
      Said Wynken,
      Blynken,
      And Nod.

The old moon laughed and sang a song,
   As they rocked in the wooden shoe;
And the wind that sped them all night long
   Ruffled the waves of dew.
The little stars were the herring fish
   That lived in that beautiful sea—
"Now cast your nets wherever you wish—
   Never afeared are we!"
   So cried the stars to the fishermen three
      Wynken,
      Blynken,
      And Nod.

All night long their nets they threw
   To the stars in the twinkling foam—
Then down from the skies came the wooden shoe,
   Bringing the fishermen home;
'Twas all so pretty a sail it seemed
   As if it could not be,
And some folk thought 'twas a dream they'd dreamed
   Of sailing that beautiful sea—
   But I shall name you the fishermen three:
      Wynken,
      Blynken,
      And Nod.

Wynken and Blynken are two little eyes,
   And Nod is a little head,
And the wooden shoe that sailed the skies
   Is a wee one's trundle-bed;
So shut your eyes while Mother sings
   Of wonderful sights that be,
And you shall see the beautiful things
   As you rock in the misty sea
   Where the old shoe rocked the fishermen three—
      Wynken,
      Blynken,
      And Nod.

The Little Red Hen

Retold by Penryhn W. Coussens

From this longtime favorite we learn, as it says in the third chapter of Genesis, "In the sweat of thy face shalt thou eat bread."

A little red hen once found a grain of wheat. "Who will plant
this wheat?" she said.
"I won't," says the dog.
"I won't," says the cat.
"I won't," says the pig.
"I won't," says the turkey.
"Then I will," says the little red hen. "Cluck! cluck!"
So she planted the grain of wheat. Very soon the wheat began
to grow and the green leaves came out of the ground. The sun shone
and the rain fell and the wheat kept on growing until it was tall,
strong, and ripe.
"Who will reap this wheat?" says the little red hen.
"I won't," says the dog.
"I won't," says the cat.
"I won't," says the pig.
"I won't," says the turkey.
"I will, then," says the little red hen. "Cluck! cluck!"

So she reaped the wheat.

"Who will thresh this wheat?" says the little red hen.

"I won't," says the dog.

"I won't," says the cat.

"I won't," says the pig.

"I won't," says the turkey.

"I will, then," says the little red hen. "Cluck! cluck!"

So she threshed the wheat.

"Who will take this wheat to mill to have it ground?" says the little red hen.

"I won't," says the dog.

"I won't," says the cat.

"I won't," says the pig.

"I won't," says the turkey.

"I will, then," says the little red hen. "Cluck! cluck!"

So she took the wheat to mill, and by and by she came back with the flour.

"Who will bake this flour?" says the little red hen.

"I won't," says the dog.

"I won't," says the cat.

"I won't," says the pig.

"I won't," says the turkey.

"I will, then," says the little red hen. "Cluck! cluck!"

So she baked the flour and made a loaf of bread.

"Who will eat this bread?" says the little red hen.

"I will," says the dog.

"I will," says the cat.

"I will," says the pig.

"I will," says the turkey.

"No, *I* will," says the little red hen. "Cluck! cluck!"

And she ate up the loaf of bread.

Five Little Chickens

Said the first little chicken,
With a queer little squirm,
"Oh, I wish I could find
A fat little worm!"

Said the next little chicken,
With an odd little shrug,
"Oh, I wish I could find
A fat little bug!"

Said the third little chicken,
With a sharp little squeal,
"Oh, I wish I could find
Some nice yellow meal!"

Said the fourth little chicken,
With a small sigh of grief,
"Oh, I wish I could find
A green little leaf!"

Said the fifth little chicken,
With a faint little moan,
"Oh, I wish I could find
A wee gravel-stone!"

"Now, see here," said the mother,
From the green garden-patch,
"If you want any breakfast,
You must come and scratch."

The Ants and the Grasshopper

Aesop

The ant, like the bee, has long been held up as a paradigm of
industriousness. As Proverbs 6:6–8 in the Bible says, "Go to the
ant, thou sluggard; consider her ways and be wise: which having
no guide, overseer, or ruler, provideth her meat in the summer,
and gathereth her food in the harvest."

One fine day in winter some ants were busy drying their store of corn, which had got rather damp during a long spell of rain. Presently up came a grasshopper and begged them to spare her a few grains. "For," she said, "I'm simply starving." The ants stopped work for a moment, though this was against their principles. "May we ask," said they, "what you were doing with yourself all last summer? Why didn't you collect a store of food for the winter?" "The fact is," replied the grasshopper, "I was so busy singing that I hadn't the time." "If you spent the summer singing," replied the ants, "you can't do better than spend the winter dancing." And they chuckled and went on with their work.

Work While You Work

This poem, which children memorized from *McGuffey's Primer* in the nineteenth and early twentieth centuries, is a good one for those modern souls who turn on the TV while they're doing their homework, or spend more time at the coffee machine than at their desk. On the other hand, it's also a good one for those who can't bring themselves to venture onto a beach or into a movie theater without taking their beepers with them.

> Work while you work,
>   Play while you play;
> One thing each time,
>   That is the way.
> All that you do,
>   Do with your might;
> Things done by halves
>   Are not done right.

The Sheep and the Pig
Who Built a House

Retold by Carolyn Sherwin Bailey

This Scandinavian tale is a good companion for "The Little Red Hen." In this story, there's no shortage of animals willing to pitch in and help.

One morning, bright and early, a sheep and a curly-tailed pig started out through the world to find a home.

"We will build us a house," said the sheep and the curly-tailed pig, "and there we will live together."

So they went a long, long way, until they came to a rabbit.

"Where are you going?" asked the rabbit of the two.

"We are going to build us a house," said the sheep and the pig.

"May I live with you?" asked the rabbit.

"What can you do to help?" asked the sheep and the pig.

The rabbit said: "I can gnaw pegs with my sharp teeth; I can put them in with my paws."

"Good!" said the sheep and the pig. "You may come with us."

So the three went on, a long, long way farther, until they came to a gray goose.

"Where are you going?" asked the gray goose of the three.

"We are going to build us a house," said the sheep, the pig, and the rabbit.

"May I live with you?" asked the gray goose.

"What can you do to help?" asked the sheep, the pig, and the rabbit.

The gray goose said: "I can pull moss, and stuff it in the cracks with my broad bill."

"Good!" said the sheep, the pig, and the rabbit. "You may come with us."

So the four went on, a long, long way, until they came to a barnyard cock.

"Where are you going?" asked the cock of the four.

"We are going to build us a house," said the sheep, the pig, the rabbit, and the goose.

"May I live with you?" asked the barnyard cock.

"What can you do to help?" asked the sheep, the pig, the rabbit, and the goose.

The cock said: "I can crow very early in the morning; I can awaken you all."

"Good!" said the sheep, the pig, the rabbit, and the goose. "You may come with us."

So the five went on, a long, long way until they found a good place for a house.

Then the sheep hewed logs and drew them.

The pig made bricks for the cellar.

The rabbit gnawed pegs with his sharp teeth, and hammered them in with his paws.

The goose pulled moss, and stuffed it in the cracks with her bill.

The cock crowed early every morning to tell them that it was time to rise.

And they all lived happily together in their little house.

The Three Little Pigs

Retold by Clifton Johnson

Here is a story about working smart. It reminds us that you need the right tools and the right materials to do a job right.

Once upon a time there was an old mother pig and three little pigs and they lived in the middle of an oak forest. While the children were still quite small the acorn crop failed. That made it difficult for Mrs. Piggy-wiggy to find enough for her children to eat, and the little pigs had to go hungry. So at last the mother pig sent the little pigs off to seek their fortunes.

The first little pig to go walked on and on until he met a man carrying a bundle of straw, and the little pig said, "Please, man, give me that straw to build a house."

So the man gave the little pig the straw, and the little pig built a house of it. In this house of straw the little pig lived very comfortably; but one day a wolf came along and rapped at the door. "Little pig, little pig, let me come in," said the wolf.

"No, no, not by the hair of my chinny, chin, chin," said the little pig.

"Then I'll huff and I'll puff and I'll blow your house down," said the wolf.

So he huffed and he puffed and he blew the house down and carried the little pig off to his den.

The second little pig that left the mother pig walked on and on until he met a man carrying a bundle of sticks, and the little pig said, "Please, man, give me those sticks to build a house."

So the man gave the little pig the sticks, and the little pig built a house of them. In this house of sticks the little pig lived very comfortably; but one day the wolf came along and rapped at the door. "Little pig, little pig, let me come in," said the wolf.

"No, no, not by the hair of my chinny, chin, chin," said the little pig.

"Then I'll huff and I'll puff and I'll blow your house down," said the wolf.

So he huffed and he puffed, and he puffed and he huffed, and at last he blew the house down and carried off the little pig.

The third little pig, after he left the mother pig, walked on and on until he met a man with a load of bricks, and the little pig said, "Please, man, give me those bricks to build a house."

So the man gave the little pig the bricks and the little pig built a house of them. In this house of bricks the little pig lived very comfortably; but one day the wolf came along and rapped at the door. "Little pig, little pig, let me come in," said the wolf.

"No, no, not by the hair of my chinny, chin, chin," said the little pig.

"Then I'll huff and I'll puff and I'll blow your house down," said the wolf.

So he huffed and he puffed, and he huffed and he puffed, and he puffed and he huffed. But the house was built of bricks and he could not blow it down. At last he had no breath left to huff and puff with, so he gave up and went on his way. And the third, wise little pig lives in his brick house to this very day.

Hercules and the Wagoner

Aesop

Some people exhibit an almost miraculous resolve in waiting for someone else to come along and do their work for them. This old fable may help us learn early that the only certain labor is your own.

A wagoner was driving his team along a muddy lane with a full load behind them, when the wheels of his wagon sank so deep in the mire that no efforts of his horses could move them. As he stood there, looking helplessly on, and calling loudly at intervals upon Hercules for assistance, the god himself appeared, and said to him, "Put your shoulder to the wheel, man, and goad on your horses, and then you may call on Hercules to assist you. If you won't lift a finger to help yourself, you can't expect Hercules or any one else to come to your aid."

Heaven helps those who help themselves.

Alice's Supper

Laura E. Richards

We should remember that everything which comes to our table is the harvest of labor.

Far down in the meadow the wheat grows green,
And the reapers are whetting their sickles so keen;
And this is the song that I hear them sing,
While cheery and loud their voices ring:
" 'Tis the finest wheat that ever did grow!
And it is for Alice's supper, ho! ho!"

Far down in the valley the old mill stands,
And the miller is rubbing his dusty white hands;
And these are the words of the miller's lay,
As he watches the millstones a-grinding away:
" 'Tis the finest flour that money can buy,
And it is for Alice's supper, hi! hi!"

Downstairs in the kitchen the fire doth glow,
And Maggie is kneading the soft white dough;
And this is the song that she's singing today,
While merry and busy she's working away:
" 'Tis the finest dough, by near or by far,
And it is for Alice's supper, ha! ha!"

And now to the nursery comes Nanny at last,
And what in her hand is she bringing so fast?
'Tis a plate full of something all yellow and white,
And she sings as she comes with her smile so bright:
" 'Tis the best bread and butter I ever did see!
And it is for Alice's supper, hee! hee!"

The Darning Needle

Hans Christian Andersen

In which we see what happens to those who believe they are
above hard work.

There was once a Darning Needle who thought herself so fine
that she came at last to believe that she was fit for embroidery.

"Mind now that you hold me fast," she said to the Fingers that
took her up. "Pray don't lose me. If I should fall on the ground I
should certainly be lost, I am so fine."

"That's more than you can tell," said the Fingers, as they
grasped her tightly by the waist.

"I come with a train, you see," said the Darning Needle, as she
drew her long thread after her; but there was no knot in the thread.

The Fingers pressed the point of the Needle upon an old pair of slippers, in which the upper leather had burst and must be sewed together. The slippers belonged to the cook.

"This is very coarse work!" said the Darning Needle. "I shall never get through alive. There, I'm breaking! I'm breaking!" and break she did. "Did I not say so?" said the Darning Needle. "I'm too delicate for such work as that."

"Now it's quite useless for sewing," said the Fingers. But they still held her all the same, for the cook presently dropped some melted sealing wax upon the needle and then pinned her neckerchief in front with it.

"See, now I'm a breastpin," said the Darning Needle. "I well knew that I should come to honor; when one is something, one always comes to something. Merit is sure to rise." And at this she laughed, only inwardly, of course, for one can never see when a Darning Needle laughs. There she sat now, quite at her ease, and as proud as if she sat in a state carriage and gazed upon all about her.

"May I take the liberty to ask if you are made of gold?" she asked of the pin, her neighbor. "You have a splendid appearance and quite a remarkable head, though it is so little. You should do what you can to grow—of course it is not everyone that can have sealing wax dropped upon her."

And the Darning Needle drew herself up so proudly that she fell out of the neckerchief into the sink, which the cook was at that moment rinsing.

"Now I'm going to travel," said the Darning Needle, "if only I don't get lost."

But that was just what happened to her.

"I'm too delicate for this world," she said, as she found herself in the gutter. "But I know who I am, and there is always some little pleasure in that!" It was thus that the Darning Needle kept up her proud bearing and lost none of her good humor. And now all sorts of things swam over her—chips and straws and scraps of old newspapers.

"Only see how they sail along," said the Darning Needle to herself. "They little know what is under them, though it is I, and I sit firmly here. See! there goes a chip! It thinks of nothing in the world but itself—of nothing in the world but a chip! There floats a straw; see how it turns and twirls about. Do think of something besides yourself or you may easily run against a stone. There swims a bit of a newspaper. What's written upon it is forgotten long ago, yet how it spreads itself out and gives itself airs! I sit patiently and quietly here! I know what I am, and I shall remain the same—always."

One day there lay something beside her that glittered splendidly. She thought it must be a diamond, but it was really only a bit of broken glass from a bottle. As it shone so brightly the Darning Needle spoke to it, introducing herself as a breastpin.

"You are a diamond, I suppose," she said.

"Why, yes, something of the sort."

So each believed the other to be some rare and costly trinket; and they began to converse together upon the world, saying how very conceited it was.

"Yes," said the Darning Needle, "I have lived in a young lady's box; and the young lady happened to be a cook. She had five fingers upon each of her hands, and anything more conceited and arrogant than those five fingers, I never saw. And yet they were only there that they might take me out of the box or put me back again."

"Were they of high descent?" asked the Bit of Bottle. "Did they shine?"

"No, indeed," replied the Darning Needle. "But they were nonetheless haughty. There were five brothers of them—all of the Finger family. And they held themselves so proudly side by side, though they were of quite different heights. The outermost, Thumbling he was called, was short and thick set. He generally stood out of the rank, a little in front of the others; he had only one joint in his back, and could only bow once. But he used to say that if he were cut off from a man, that man would be cut off from military service. Foreman, the second, put himself forward on all occasions, meddled with sweet and sour, pointed to sun and moon, and when the fingers wrote, it was he who pressed the pen. Middleman, the third of the brothers, could look over the others' heads, and gave himself airs for that. Ringman, the fourth, went about with a gold belt about his waist. And little Playman, whom they called Peter Spielman, did nothing at all and was proud of that, I suppose. There was nothing to be heard but boasting, and that is why I took myself away."

"And now we sit here together and shine," said the Bit of Bottle.

At that very moment some water came rushing along the gutter, so that it overflowed and carried the glass diamond along with it.

"So he is off," said the Darning Needle, "and I still remain. I am left here because I am too slender and genteel. But that's my pride, and pride is honorable." And proudly she sat, thinking many thoughts.

"I could almost believe I had been born of a sunbeam, I'm so fine. It seems as if the sunbeams were always trying to seek me under the water. Alas, I'm so delicate that even my own mother cannot find me. If I had my old eye still, which broke off, I think I should cry—but no, I would not; it's not genteel to weep."

One day a couple of street boys were paddling about in the gutter, hunting for old nails, pennies, and such like. It was dirty work, but they seemed to find great pleasure in it.

"Hullo!" cried one of them, as he pricked himself with the Darning Needle. "Here's a fellow for you!"

"I'm not a fellow! I'm a young lady!" said the Darning Needle, but no one heard it.

The sealing wax had worn off, and she had become quite black. "But black makes one look slender, and is always becoming." She thought herself finer even than before.

"There goes an eggshell sailing along," said the boys; and they stuck the Darning Needle into the shell.

"A lady in black, and within white walls!" said the Darning Needle. "That is very striking. Now everyone can see me. I hope I shall not be seasick, for then I shall break."

But the fear was needless; she was not seasick, neither did she break.

"Nothing is so good to prevent seasickness as to have a steel stomach and to bear in mind that one is something a little more than an ordinary person. My seasickness is all over now. The more genteel and honorable one is, the more one can endure."

Crash went the eggshell, as a wagon rolled over both of them. It was a wonder that she did not break.

"Mercy, what a crushing weight!" said the Darning Needle. "I'm growing seasick, after all. I'm going to break!"

But she was not sick, and she did not break, though the wagon wheels rolled over her. She lay at full length in the road, and there let her lie.

Mr. Meant-To

Hear the famous words of Benjamin Franklin: "Work while it is called today, for you know not how much you may be hindered tomorrow. One today is worth two tomorrows; never leave that till tomorrow which you can do today."

> Mr. Meant-To has a comrade,
>   And his name is Didn't-Do;
> Have you ever chanced to meet them?
>   Did they ever call on you?
>
> These two fellows live together
>   In the house of Never-Win,
> And I'm told that it is haunted
>   By the ghost of Might-Have-Been.

The Husband Who Was to Mind the House

This old Scandinavian tale teaches us to respect others' hard work.

Once upon a time there was a man so surly and cross, he never thought his wife did anything right around the house. One evening, during hay-making time, he came home complaining that dinner wasn't on the table, the baby was crying, and the cow had not been put in the barn.

"I work and I work all day," he growled, "and you get to stay home and mind the house. I wish I had it so easy. I could get dinner ready on time, I'll tell you that."

"Dear love, don't be so angry," said his wife. "Tomorrow let's change our work. I'll go out with the mowers and cut the hay, and you stay home and mind the house."

The husband thought that would do very well. "I could use a

day off," he said. "I'll do all your chores in an hour or two, and sleep the afternoon away."

So early the next morning the wife put a scythe over her shoulder and trudged out to the hayfield with the mowers. The husband stayed behind to do all the work at home.

First of all, he washed some clothes, and then he began to churn the butter. But after he had churned a while, he remembered he needed to hang the clothes up to dry. He went out to the yard, and had just finished hanging his shirts on the line when he saw the pig run into the kitchen.

So off he dashed to the kitchen to look after the pig, lest it should upset the churn. But as soon as he got through the door, he saw the pig had already knocked the churn over. There it was, grunting and rooting in the cream, which was running all over the floor. The man became so wild with rage, he quite forgot about his shirts on the line, and ran at the pig as hard as he could.

He caught it, too, but it was so slippery from all the butter, it shot out of his arms and right through the door. The man raced into the yard, bound to catch that pig no matter what, but he stopped dead in his tracks when he saw his goat. It was standing right beneath the clothesline, chewing and chomping at every last shirt. So the man ran off the goat, and locked up the pig, and took what was left of his shirts off the line.

Then he went into the dairy and found enough cream to fill the churn again, and so he began to churn, for butter they must have at dinner. When he had churned a bit, he remembered that their cow was still shut up in the barn, and had not had a mouthful to eat or a drop to drink all morning, though the sun was high.

He thought it was too far to take her down to the meadow, so he decided to put her on top of the house, for the roof, you must know, was thatched with grass. The house lay next to a steep hill, and he thought if he lay a wide plank from the side of the hill to the roof, he'd easily get the cow up.

But still he couldn't leave the churn, for here was the little baby crawling about on the floor. "If I leave it," he thought, "the child is sure to upset it."

So he put the churn on his back and went out with it. Then he thought he'd better water the cow before he put her on the roof, and he got a bucket to draw water out of the well. But as he stooped down at the brink of the well, the cream ran out of the churn, over his shoulders, down his back, and into the well!

Now it was near dinnertime, and he didn't even have any butter yet. So as soon as he put the cow on the roof, he thought he'd best boil the porridge. He filled the pot with water, and hung it over the fire.

When he had done that, he thought the cow might fall off the roof and break her neck. So he climbed onto the house to tie her up. He tied one end of the rope around the cow's neck, and the other he slipped down the chimney. Then he went back inside and tied it around his own waist. He had to make haste, for the water now began to boil in the pot, and he still had to grind the oatmeal.

So he began to grind away. But while he was hard at it, down fell the cow off the housetop after all, and as she fell she dragged the poor man up the chimeny by the rope! There he stuck fast. And as for the cow, she hung halfway down the wall, swinging between heaven and earth, for she could neither get down nor up.

Meanwhile the wife, who was out in the field, waited and waited for her husband to call her home to dinner. At last she thought she'd waited enough and went home.

When she got there and saw the cow hanging in such an ugly place, she ran up and cut the rope with her scythe. But as soon as she did, down came her husband out of the chimney! So when she went inside the kitchen, she found him standing on his head in the porridge pot.

"Welcome back," he said, after she had fished him out. "I have something to say to you."

So he said he was sorry, and gave her a kiss, and never complained again.

Mother Holly

Retold by Etta Austin Blaisdell and
Mary Frances Blaisdell

The Brothers Grimm, who collected this story, tell us that in Germany people say "Mother Holly is making her bed" whenever it snows. In this tale, idleness and industry get their just rewards when helping Mother Holly with her chores becomes a test of character for two sisters.

A widow, who lived in a cottage at a little distance from the village, had two daughters. One of them was beautiful and industrious, the other idle and ugly.

The mother loved the ugly one best, because she was her own child. She cared so little for the other that she made her do all the work and be like a Cinderella in the house.

Poor maiden, she was obliged to go every day and seat herself beside a well which stood near the broad highway. Here she had to sit and spin until she thought her poor, tired fingers would fall off.

One day when the spindle was so covered with dust that she could not use it, she rose and dipped it in the water of the well to wash it. While she was doing so, it slipped from her hand and fell to the bottom.

In terror and tears, she ran and told her stepmother what had happened.

The woman scolded her. "As you have let the spindle fall into the water," she said, "you may go and get it, for I will not buy another."

The maiden went back to the well, and, hardly knowing what she was about, threw herself into the water to get the spindle.

At first she knew nothing, but as her senses returned, she found herself in a beautiful meadow, where the sun was shining brightly and thousands of flowers were growing.

She walked a long way across the meadow, until she came to a baker's oven which was full of new bread. The loaves cried, "Ah, pull us out! pull us out, or we shall burn; we have been so long baking!"

Then she stepped near to the oven and with the long bread-shovel took out the loaves.

She walked on after this, and presently came to a tree full of apples. The tree cried, "Shake me, shake me! My apples are ripe!"

She shook the tree till the fruit fell around her like rain, and at last there was not one apple left upon it.

After this she gathered the apples into one large heap, and went on farther.

Soon she came to a small house, and looking at it she saw an old woman peeping out. The woman had such large teeth that the girl was frightened and turned to run away.

The old woman cried after her, "What dost thou fear, dear child? Come and live here with me, and do all the work in the house, and I will make you happy. You must, however, take care to make my bed well, and to shake it with energy, for then the feathers fly

about, and in the world they will say it snows, for I am Mother
Holly."

As the old woman talked in this kind manner, she won the
maiden's heart, so that she agreed to enter her service.

She took care to shake the bed well, so that the feathers might
fly down like snowflakes. Therefore she had a very happy life with
Mother Holly. She had plenty to eat and drink, and never heard an
angry word.

After she had stayed a long time with the kind old woman, she
began to feel sad. She could not explain to herself why, till at last
she discovered that she was homesick. It seemed to her a thousand
times better to go home than to stay with Mother Holly, though the
old woman made her so happy.

The longing to go home grew so strong that at last she was
obliged to speak.

"Dear Mother Holly," she said, "you have been very kind to
me, but I have such sorrow in my heart that I cannot stay here any
longer. I must return to my own people."

"Good," said Mother Holly. "I am pleased to hear that you are
longing to go home. As you have served me so well and truly, I will
show you the way myself."

So she took her by the hand and led her to a broad gateway.
The gate was open, and as the young girl passed through there
fell upon her a shower of gold. It clung to her dress and remained
hanging to it, so that she was covered with gold from head to
foot.

"This is your reward for having been so industrious," said the
old woman. As she spoke she placed in her hand the spindle which
had fallen into the well.

The great gate closed softly and the maiden found herself once
more in the world, and not far from her stepmother's house. As she
entered the farmyard a cock perched on the wall crowed loudly, and
cried, "Our golden lady has come home, I see!"

She went in to her stepmother, and because she was so covered
with gold both the mother and sister welcomed her kindly. The
maiden told all that had happened to her. And when the mother
heard how her wealth had been gained, she was anxious that her
own ugly and idle daughter should try her fortune in the same
way.

So she made her sit at the well and spin. But the girl, who
wished to have all the riches without working for them, did not spin

very long at all, for she was daydreaming of all she would buy with her gold.

As soon as she thought enough time had passed, she tossed the spindle into the well. It sank to the bottom, and she sprang in after it, just as her sister had done. And just as her sister had said, she found herself in a beautiful meadow.

She walked for some distance along the same path till she came to the baker's oven. She heard the loaves cry, "Pull us out, pull us out! or we shall burn; we have been so long baking!"

But the idle girl answered, "No, indeed, I have no wish to soil my hands with your dirty oven." And so she walked on till she came to the apple tree.

"Shake me, shake me!" it cried, "for my apples are ripe."

"I do not agree to that at all," she replied, "for some of the apples might fall on my head." And as she spoke she walked lazily on farther.

When at last she stood before the door of Mother Holly's house, she had no fear of her great teeth, for she had heard all about them from her sister. She walked up to the old woman and offered to be her servant.

Mother Holly accepted the offer of her help. For a whole day the girl was very industrious, as she thought of the gold that was to be showered upon her.

On the second day, however, she gave way to her laziness, and on the third it was worse. Several days passed, and she would not get up early in the morning. The bed was never shaken so that the feathers could fly about.

At last Mother Holly was tired of her, and said she must go away, that her help was not needed.

The lazy girl was quite overjoyed at going, for she thought the golden rain was sure to come when Mother Holly led her to the gate. But as she passed under it, a large kettle full of soot was upset over her.

"That is the reward of your service," said the old woman as she shut the gate.

The idle girl walked home with the soot sticking all over her. As she entered the yard the cock on the wall cried out, "Our sooty young lady has come home, I see."

The soot stuck closely and hung all about her hair and her clothes, and do what she would as long as she lived, it never would come off again.

The Farmer and His Sons

Aesop

A farmer, being at death's door, and desiring to impart to his sons a secret of much moment, called them round him and said, "My sons, I am shortly about to die. I would have you know, therefore, that in my vineyard there lies a hidden treasure. Dig, and you will find it." As soon as their father was dead, the sons took spade and fork and turned up the soil of the vineyard over and over again, in their search for the treasure which they supposed to lie buried there. They found none, however: but the vines, after so thorough a digging, produced a crop such as had never before been seen.

There is no treasure without toil.

The Shoemaker and the Elves

Retold by J. Berg Esenwein and Marietta Stockard

This tale, adapted from the Brothers Grimm, reminds us that service given is owed service in return.

There once lived a Shoemaker and his Wife who were very poor, and had to work hard to get money enough for food and clothes. The Shoemaker sat all day at his bench, sewing and hammering, making the shoes, while his Wife worked just as hard in her house. They tried to save a little money, but it was very little that they could save.

By and by the Shoemaker fell ill, and all of the money they had saved was spent for medicine and food—at least, nearly all, for when the Shoemaker was able to creep about the house again he had just money enough left to buy the leather for one little pair of shoes. He took the money and went down into the town, bought the leather, and carried it home. Then he cut out the little shoes, but he felt so weak and tired that he could not work anymore.

"I must go to bed now and rest," he said to the good Wife. "Tomorrow morning early I will come down and finish the shoes."

It was scarcely light the next morning when the Shoemaker came down to his work. He stared in surprise, for there on the table stood a little pair of shoes.

"Why, Wife!" he said. "Did you make these shoes?"

"Of course I did not," said the Wife. "I could not make a pair of shoes to save my life." And she was just as surprised as he.

They looked at the neat little stitches and wondered much who could have made them. At last the man set them in the window, hoping someone might come to buy them. Sure enough, they were scarcely in the window when a man came down the street and saw them. "Those are just the shoes I want for my little girl," he said.

So he bought them and gave the Shoemaker more money than he had ever had for a pair of shoes before. It was enough to buy leather for two pairs of shoes. So that day he went down into the town again and bought more leather. When he came back he cut out his work, just as he had done before, then again he felt so weary that he went up to bed, saying that he would finish the work early the next morning. When he came down he found, to his surprise, that the two pairs of shoes, all neatly finished, stood on the table.

"Who can be helping us?" he said.

"Tonight we will hide behind the curtains there, and watch," said his Wife.

So that night when he had cut out his work, and placed it on the table, the Shoemaker and his Wife hid behind the curtains instead of going up to bed. They waited, and waited. Ten o'clock came, but nothing happened; eleven o'clock, and still nothing happened.

"I am so tired," whispered the Shoemaker, "I cannot wait any longer."

"Oh, do wait just a little!" said his Wife.

And so they waited until the clock went dong, dong, twelve times. At the last stroke of twelve, the door flew open and in came a troop of little brownies. They scampered across the floor to the table where the Shoemaker had left his work. Then they began hammering and sewing, making the little shoes. Soon they were all finished and stood in a neat little row on the table. Then the brownies gathered up the scraps of leather, for they were neat little elves, and they scampered off again.

"Well," said the Shoemaker, "I had often heard that brownies came to help those who needed it, but I never dreamed it was they who were working for us."

"Nor I," said his Wife. "But did you notice that the poor little things didn't have any clothes? I should think they would be cold, these frosty nights. They have worked so hard for us that I think we should make them some clothes to keep them warm. I'll make them some little trousers, jackets, and coats."

"And I'll make them some shoes," said the Shoemaker.

"Of course they must have some stockings too, and some little stocking caps," said his Wife.

So they set to work. They stitched and sewed and stitched and sewed. It took a long time and hard work to make so many little brownie suits, but the very day before Christmas the last little suit was finished.

On Christmas Eve the Shoemaker and his Wife put the clothes and shoes on the table, instead of the work. Then they hid behind the curtains again, to see what would happen.

Just as before, they waited until the clock struck twelve. Then the door flew open, and in came the brownies. They ran over to the table and began looking for their work, but of course they did not find it. Presently one brownie picked up a little pair of trousers. He held them up and looked at them. Then he popped one leg down into them, and then another. The other brownies capered and laughed and struggled into pairs of trousers too. They put on the jackets and coats, the shoes and stockings. Then they pulled the funny little stocking caps down over their ears. You should have seen their big, round eyes, and heard their giggles.

Then they began dancing. It was such fun to hear their little shoes clatter that they danced and danced and danced. Finally they put their hands on each other's shoulders and danced round and round the room, out through the door, and off.

When after a great many nights the brownies did not come back again, the Shoemaker and his Wife began wondering where they had gone.

"Perhaps the elves are helping someone else who needs them," said the Shoemaker. "Of course I am well now, so we can work for ourselves."

Perhaps he was right, for, at any rate, the brownies never came back to the Shoemaker's house.

How the Camel Got His Hump

Rudyard Kipling

Rudyard Kipling's *Just So Stories,* from which this tale is taken, have enchanted generations since their first publication in 1902. Kipling created the whimsical stories for his daughter Josephine while he was living in America.

In the beginning of years, when the world was so new and all, and the Animals were just beginning to work for Man, there was a Camel, and he lived in the middle of a Howling Desert because he did not want to work; and besides, he was a Howler himself. So he ate sticks and thorns and tamarisks and milkweed and prickles, most 'scruciating idle; and when anybody spoke to him he said "Humph!" Just "Humph!" and no more.

Presently the Horse came to him on Monday morning, with a saddle on his back and a bit in his mouth, and said, "Camel, O Camel, come out and trot like the rest of us."

"Humph!" said the Camel and the Horse went away and told the Man.

Presently the Dog came to him, with a stick in his mouth, and said, "Camel, O Camel, come and fetch and carry like the rest of us."

"Humph!" said the Camel; and the Dog went away and told the Man.

Presently the Ox came to him, with the yoke on his neck and said, "Camel, O Camel, come and plow like the rest of us."

"Humph!" said the Camel; and the Ox went away and told the Man.

At the end of the day the Man called the Horse and the Dog and the Ox together, and said, "Three, O Three, I'm very sorry for you (with the world so new-and-all); but that Humph-thing in the Desert can't work, or he would have been here by now, so I am going to leave him alone, and you must work double time to make up for it."

That made the Three very angry (with the world so new-and-all), and they held a palaver, and an *indaba,* and a *punchayet,* and a pow-wow on the edge of the Desert; and the Camel came chewing milkweed *most* 'scruciating idle, and laughed at them. Then he said "Humph!" and went away again.

Presently there came along the Djinn in charge of All Deserts, rolling in a cloud of dust (Djinns always travel that way because it is Magic), and he stopped to palaver and pow-wow with the Three.

"Djinn of All Deserts," said the Horse, "*is* it right for anyone to be idle, with the world so new-and-all?"

"Certainly not," said the Djinn.

"Well," said the Horse, "there's a thing in the middle of your Howling Desert (and he's a Howler himself) with a long neck and long legs, and he hasn't done a stroke of work since Monday morning. He won't trot."

"Whew!" said the Djinn, whistling. "That's my Camel, for all the gold in Arabia! What does he say about it?"

"He says 'Humph!' " said the Dog. "And he won't fetch and carry."

"Does he say anything else?"

"Only 'Humph!' and he won't plow," said the Ox.

"Very good," said the Djinn. "I'll humph him if you will kindly wait a minute."

The Djinn rolled himself up in his dustcloak, and took a bearing across the desert, and found the Camel most 'scruciatingly idle, looking at his own reflection in a pool of water.

"My long and bubbling friend," said the Djinn, "what's this I hear of your doing no work, with the world so new-and-all?"

"Humph!" said the Camel.

The Djinn sat down, with his chin in his hand, and began to think a Great Magic, while the Camel looked at his own reflection in the pool of water.

"You've given the Three extra work ever since Monday morning, all on account of your 'scruciating idleness," said the Djinn; and he went on thinking Magics, with his chin in his hand.

"Humph!" said the Camel.

"I shouldn't say that again if I were you," said the Djinn; "you might say it once too often. Bubbles, I want you to work."

And the Camel said "Humph!" again; but no sooner had he said it than he saw his back, that he was so proud of, puffing up and puffing up into a great big lolloping humph.

"Do you see that?" said the Djinn. "That's your very own humph that you've brought upon your very own self by not working. Today is Thursday, and you've done no work since Monday, when the work began. Now you are going to work."

"How can I," said the Camel, "with this humph on my back?"

"That's made a-purpose," said the Djinn, "all because you missed those three days. You will be able to work now for three days without eating, because you can live on your humph; and don't you ever say I never did anything for you. Come out of the Desert and go to the Three, and behave. Humph yourself!"

And the Camel humphed himself, humph and all, and went away to join the Three. And from that day to this the Camel always wears a humph (we call it "hump" now, not to hurt his feelings); but he has never yet caught up with the three days that he missed at the beginning of the world, and he has never yet learned how to behave.

> The Camel's hump is an ugly lump
>   Which well you may see at the Zoo;
> But uglier yet is the hump we get
>   From having too little to do.
>
> Kiddies and grown-ups too-oo-oo,
> If we haven't enough to do-oo-oo,
>   We get the hump—
>   Cameelious hump—
> The hump that is black and blue!
>
> We climb out of bed with a frouzly head
>   And a snarly-yarly voice.
> We shiver and scowl and we grunt and we growl
>   At our bath and our boots and our toys;
>
> And there ought to be a corner for me
> (And I know there is one for you)
>   When we get the hump—
>   Cameelious hump—
> The hump that is black and blue!
>
> The cure for this ill is not to sit still,
>   Or frowst with a book by the fire;
> But to take a large hoe and a shovel also,
>   And dig till you gently perspire.

And then you will find that the sun and the wind
And the Djinn of the Garden too,
   Have lifted the hump—
   The horrible hump—
The hump that is black and blue!

I get it as well as you-oo-oo—
If I haven't enough to do-oo-oo—
   We all get hump—
   Cameelious hump—
Kiddies and grown-ups too!

Dust Under the Rug

Maud Lindsay

This story reminds us that we are rewarded well—both in coin
and in character—only when our work unseen is just as good as
our work seen.

There was once a mother who had two little daughters; and, as
her husband was dead and she was very poor, she worked diligently
all the time that they might be well fed and clothed. She was a skilled
worker, and found work to do away from home, but her two little
girls were so good and so helpful that they kept her house as neat
and as bright as a new pin.

One of the little girls was lame, and could not run about the
house; so she sat still in her chair, and sewed, while Minnie, the
sister, washed the dishes, swept the floor, and made the home beautiful.

Their home was on the edge of a great forest; and after their
tasks were finished the little girls would sit at the window and watch
the tall trees as they bent in the wind, until it would seem as though
the trees were real persons, nodding and bending and bowing to
each other.

In the spring there were birds, in the summer the wild flowers, in autumn the bright leaves, and in winter the great drifts of white snow; so that the whole year was a round of delight to the two happy children. But one day the dear mother came home sick; and then they were very sad. It was winter, and there were many things to buy. Minnie and her little sister sat by the fireside and talked it over, and at last Minnie said:

"Dear sister, I must go out to find work, before the food gives out." So she kissed her mother, and, wrapping herself up, started from home. There was a narrow path leading through the forest, and she determined to follow it until she reached someplace where she might find the work she wanted.

As she hurried on, the shadows grew deeper. The night was coming fast when she saw before her a very small house, which was a welcome sight. She made haste to reach it, and to knock at the door.

Nobody came in answer to her knock. When she had tried again and again, she thought that nobody lived there; and she opened the door and walked in, thinking that she would stay all night.

As soon as she stepped into the house, she started back in surprise; for there before her she saw twelve little beds with the bedclothes all tumbled, twelve little dirty plates on a very dusty table, and the floor of the room so dusty that I am sure you could have drawn a picture on it.

"Dear me!" said the little girl. "This will never do!" And as soon as she had warmed her hands, she set to work to make the room tidy.

She washed the plates, she made up the beds, she swept the floor, she straightened the great rug in front of the fireplace, and set the twelve little chairs in a half circle around the fire; and, just as she finished, the door opened and in walked twelve of the queerest little people she had ever seen. They were just about as tall as a carpenter's rule, and all wore yellow clothes; and when Minnie saw this, she knew that they must be the dwarfs who kept the gold in the heart of the mountain.

"Well!" said the dwarfs, all together, for they always spoke together and in rhyme,

"Now isn't this a sweet surprise?
We really can't believe our eyes!"

Then they spied Minnie, and cried in great astonishment:

> "Who can this be, so fair and mild?
> Our helper is a stranger child."

Now when Minnie saw the dwarfs, she came to meet them. "If you please," she said, "I'm little Minnie Grey; and I'm looking for work because my dear mother is sick. I came in here when the night drew near, and—"

Here all the dwarfs laughed, and called out merrily:

> "You found our room a sorry sight,
> But you have made it clean and bright."

They were such dear funny little dwarfs! After they had thanked Minnie for her trouble, they took white bread and honey from the closet and asked her to sup with them.

While they sat at supper, they told her that their fairy house-keeper had taken a holiday, and their house was not well kept because she was away.

They sighed when they said this; and after supper, when Minnie washed the dishes and set them carefully away, they looked at her often and talked among themselves. When the last plate was in its place they called Minnie to them and said:

> "Dear mortal maiden, will you stay
> All through our fairy's holiday?
> And if you faithful prove, and good,
> We will reward you as we should."

Now Minnie was much pleased, for she liked the kind dwarfs, and wanted to help them, so she thanked them, and went to bed to dream happy dreams.

Next morning she was awake with the chickens, and cooked a nice breakfast; and after the dwarfs left, she cleaned up the rooms and mended the dwarfs' clothes. In the evening when the dwarfs came home, they found a bright fire and a warm supper waiting for them. And every day Minnie worked faithfully until the last day of the fairy housekeeper's holiday.

That morning, as Minnie looked out of the window to watch the dwarfs go to their work, she saw on one of the windowpanes the most beautiful picture she had ever seen.

A picture of fairy palaces with towers of silver and frosted pin-nacles, so wonderful and beautiful that as she looked at it she forgot that there was work to be done, until the cuckoo clock on the mantel struck twelve.

Then she ran in haste to make up the beds, and wash the dishes. But because she was in a hurry she could not work quickly, and when she took the broom to sweep the floor it was almost time for the dwarfs to come home.

"I believe," said Minnie, aloud, "that I will not sweep under the rug today. After all, it is nothing for dust to be where it can't be seen." So she hurried to her supper and left the rug unturned.

Before long the dwarfs came home. As the rooms looked just as usual, nothing was said; and Minnie thought no more of the dust until she went to bed and the stars peeped through the window.

Then she thought of it, for it seemed to her that she could hear the stars saying:

"There is the little girl who is so faithful and good." And Minnie turned her face to the wall, for a little voice, right in her own heart, said:

"Dust under the rug! Dust under the rug!"

"There is the little girl," cried the stars, "who keeps home as bright as starshine."

"Dust under the rug! Dust under the rug!" said the little voice in Minnie's heart.

"We see her! We see her!" called all the stars joyfully.

"Dust under the rug! Dust under the rug!" said the little voice in Minnie's heart, and she could bear it no longer. So she sprang out of bed, and, taking her broom in her hand, she swept the dust away. And lo! under the rug lay twelve shining gold-pieces, as round and as bright as the moon.

"Oh! oh! oh!" cried Minnie, in great surprise. And all the little dwarfs came running to see what was the matter.

Minnie told them all about it; and when she had ended her story, the dwarfs gathered lovingly around her and said:

> "Dear child, the gold is all for you,
> For faithful you have proved and true;
> But had you left the rug unturned,
> A groat was all you would have earned.
> Our love goes with the gold we give,
> And oh! forget not while you live,
> That in the smallest duty done
> Lies wealth of joy for everyone."

Minnie thanked the dwarfs for their kindness to her, and early next morning she hastened home with her golden treasure, which bought many things for the dear mother and little sister.

She never saw the little dwarfs again. But she never forgot their lesson, to do her work faithfully, and she always swept under the rug.

The Week of Sundays

In this old tale we see the difference between idle time, which we steal, and leisure time, which we earn. The truth is that people who never have anything to do are usually the most dissatisfied because they are the most bored. Our leisure time, on the other hand, we enjoy largely because we've put plenty of work behind us to get it.

Once upon a time there was a man named Bobby O'Brien who never did a stitch of work in his life unless he absolutely had to.

"Come now, Bobby," his friends used to say, "what's so wrong with a little hard work? You'd think it was the black plague itself, the way you guard yourself against it."

"My friends, I have no more against work than the next man," Bobby would reply. "In fact, nothing fascinates me more than work. I can sit here and watch it all day, if you'll only give me the chance."

And of course, he was perfectly useless around the house.

"Aren't you ashamed of yourself, now?" his wife, Katie, moaned one afternoon. "A fine example you're setting for the children! Do you want them to grow up to be lazy slugs too?"

"It's Sunday, my dear, the day of rest," Bobby pointed out. "Now why would you want to be disturbing it? If you want my opinion, it's the only day out of the whole week worth getting out of bed for. The only problem with Sunday is that as soon as it's over, the rest of the week starts up again." Bobby was a great philosopher, having so much time on his hands.

That very night the whole family was sitting around the fire, waiting for their soup to boil, when what should they hear but a tap-tap-tap at the window. Bobby strolled over and raised the sash, and into the room hopped a little man no bigger than a strutting rooster.

"I was just passing by," the wee man said, "and smelled something good and strong, and thought I might have a bite to eat."

"You're welcome to as much as you want," Bobby said, thinking that such a little man couldn't possibly hold more than a spoonful or two. So the tiny fellow sat down at the fireside, but no sooner had Katie given him a steaming bowl than he slurped it down and asked for another. Katie gave him seconds, and he swallowed that one faster than the first. She gave him thirds, and he drained the bowl almost before she had filled it up.

"What a little pig," Bobby thought to himself. "He'll have all of our suppers, before he's through. Still, I asked him in, and he is our guest, so we must hold our tongues."

After five or six bowls the little man smacked his lips and jumped off his stool.

"It's most kind you've been," he laughed. "A more hospitable family I've never met. Now I must be on my way, but as way of thanks I'll be more than happy to grant the next wish uttered aloud beneath this roof." And with that he hopped through the window and vanished into the night.

Well, everyone wanted to wish for something different. One child wanted a bag of sweets, and the other child wanted a box of toys. Katie thought a new bed would be nice, as the old one was showing signs of collapse. Bobby could name a dozen or so things he'd like to have, right off the top of his head, perhaps a new fishing pole, or maybe a chocolate cake.

"We need more time to think it over," he declared. "The trouble is, tomorrow's Monday morning, and there'll be work and chores to get in the way of our thinking. I wish we had a week of Sundays, and then we could take our time and figure it out."

"Now you've done it!" Katie cried. "You've gone and wasted our only wish on a week of Sundays! You might have wished for a few more brains in that thick head of yours before you opened your mouth for a wish like that!"

"Well, well, it's not such a bad wish, you know," said Bobby, who was just now realizing what he had done. "A week of Sundays will be a fine thing, after all. I've been needing a little rest, and this will give me the chance."

"Rest is the last thing you need, you lazy bag of bones," Katie moaned, hustling the children off to bed.

But the next morning when Bobby woke up to hear the churchbells pealing, and he remembered he had seven whole days before him of not having a thing in the world to do, he decided he'd made the wisest of all possible wishes. He lolled around bed all morning, while Katie took the children to church, and didn't bother to rouse himself until he finally smelled a nice plump chicken coming out of the oven for Sunday dinner.

"What a remarkable event!" he yawned and stretched as he sat down at the table. "King Solomon himself could never have wished for such a wonderful thing as a week of Sundays." And after he stuffed himself, he wandered outside and took a nap beneath his favorite tree.

The next day he lay in bed all morning again, and got up only when church was safely over. But the only thing Katie put on the table was a few chicken bones left from the day before, when Bobby had eaten the whole Sunday dinner. The next day was even worse. Bobby sat down with roaring appetite, only to find porridge and potatoes gracing the table.

"Now what kind of dinner is this?" he asked. "Have you forgotten what day of the week it is? Porridge and potatoes aren't fit for Sunday, my dear."

"And what else did you expect?" Katie cried. "How am I supposed to buy a new chicken with every shop in the village closed for seven straight days? It's all that we have in the cupboard, so you'd better get used to it, my good man."

Well, the next morning Bobby's stomach was growling so fiercely he couldn't help but getting out of bed a little earlier than his usual Sunday custom. He wandered around the kitchen a bit, checking here and there for a bite to eat, but he found only a loaf of stale bread in the pantry.

"You know, my dear," he said, "I've been thinking I need a bit of exercise. I believe I'll go out to the garden and dig a few potatoes for dinner."

"You'll do nothing of the sort," Katie snapped. "I won't have you digging potatoes on Sunday morning, with the neighbors passing by on their way to church. That won't do at all."

"But there's nothing in the house but bits of stale bread," Bobby cried.

"And who do you have to blame but yourself and your week of Sundays for that?" Katie asked.

The next day Bobby was up at the crack of dawn, pacing back and forth across the house and drumming his fingers on every windowsill. The children followed him everywhere he went until the churchbells began to peal, and then they bawled and whimpered to no end.

"What's wrong with these young ones?" Bobby whined. "Have all their manners gone and left them?"

"And what do you expect, after all?" Katie cried. "The poor little things have sat through more sermons in a week now than you've snored through all year. Their backs are sore from living in pews, and they've tossed every last penny they've been saving into that collection plate."

"They should be in school, that's where," Bobby declared.

"And who, may I ask, is to blame for that?" Katie inquired.

On the sixth Sunday, Bobby was so fidgety and bored, he decided to go to church with the rest of the family. Every head in the congregation swung around when he came through the door and crept up the aisle.

"There's the man!" the preacher cried from the pulpit. "Here's the rascal who's kept me up every night this week, wracking my poor brain for another new sermon! Here's the troublemaker who's ruined every last throat in the choir, and almost worn the fingers off the poor organist! I guess you've come to survey your dirty work now, have you?"

And when the service was over, Bobby found his neighbors lined up to greet him.

"Well, now," asked one, "did you stop to think of how we're to bring in the harvest with so many Sundays getting in the way?"

"And how are the rest of us to make a living, having to keep our doors closed all week?" asked the butcher and the baker.

"And what about the washing and ironing and mending?" someone called. "Do you know how much is piled up for next Monday, should it ever come again?"

"And by the way," said the schoolmaster, "have you been taking care of your children's lessons, or have they forgotten how to read and write by now?"

Bobby made his way home as fast as he could.

"Thank goodness there's only one Sunday left!" he sighed as soon as he was safe behind his own door. "Any more would be dangerous to a man's health."

That last Sunday was the longest day of Bobby O'Brien's life. The minutes passed like hours, and the hours stretched into eternities. Bobby twiddled his thumbs, and stood on one foot, and walked in circles, and watched the clock.

"Is this thing broken?" he cried, grabbing it from the mantel and shaking it till its insides rattled. "You can't tell me the time has ever dragged by so slow!"

"When have you ever wanted a Sunday to end?" Katie asked. "Aren't you forgetting that tomorrow is Monday?"

"Forgetting it? It's all I can think about," Bobby exclaimed. "I've never in my life looked forward to any day as much as this Monday morning."

The shadows slowly crept across the lawn, the sun finally went down, and just as the first star popped into the sky, who should come rapping at the window but the same little man who visited one week ago.

"And how did you enjoy your wish?" he asked Bobby.

"Not very much, I'm afraid," said Bobby.

"Really?" exclaimed the little man. "Then you wouldn't want to trade another bite to eat for another week of Sundays?"

"For goodness' sake, no!" cried Bobby. "The only days of rest I want are the ones I've worked six days to earn. It took me all week to learn that lesson, and I won't be forgetting it anytime soon. So I'll thank you to be gone with your wishes, my friend."

And at that the little man disappeared, and was never seen again.

What Have We Done Today?

Nixon Waterman

Work is not a plan for work. Putting off work can be the same as just plain not working.

> We shall do much in the years to come,
>   But what have we done today?
> We shall give our gold in a princely sum,
>   But what did we give today?
> We shall lift the heart and dry the tear,
> We shall plant a hope in the place of fear,
> We shall speak the words of love and cheer,
>   But what did we speak today?

We shall be so kind in the after while,
  But have we been today?
We shall bring to each lonely life a smile,
  But what have we brought today?
We shall give to truth a grander birth,
And to steadfast faith a deeper worth,
We shall feed the hungering souls of earth,
  But whom have we fed today?

We shall reap such joys in the by and by,
  But what have we sown today?
We shall build us mansions in the sky,
  But what have we built today?
'Tis sweet in the idle dreams to bask;
But here and now, do we our task?
Yet, this is the thing our souls must ask,
  What have we done today?

I Meant to Do My Work Today

Richard Le Gallienne

I include this little poem as a reminder that, as the saying goes,
"All work and no play makes Jack a dull boy." But we should
also remember that we enjoy play the most when it crowns good,
hard work.

  I meant to do my work today,
  But a brown bird sang in the apple tree,
  And a butterfly flitted across the field,
  And all the leaves were calling me.

  And the wind went sighing over the land,
  Tossing the grasses to and fro,
  And a rainbow held out its shining hand—
  So what could I do but laugh and go?

The Rebellion Against
the Stomach

Variations on this story about cooperation and communal effort
were common in classical antiquity. Paul employs one such vari-
ation in I Corinthians 12:14–26. The version below reminds us
of the responsibilities involved in the division of labor. It also
reminds us that industry keeps the whole body healthy, and that
those who live on nothing but complaints may well die fasting.

Once a man had a dream in which his hands and feet and mouth
and brain all began to rebel against his stomach.
"You good-for-nothing sluggard!" the hands said. "We work
all day long, sawing and hammering and lifting and carrying. By
evening we're covered with blisters and scratches, and our joints
ache, and we're covered with dirt. And meanwhile you just sit there,
hogging all the food."
"We agree!" cried the feet. "Think how sore we get, walking
back and forth all day long. And you just stuff yourself full, you
greedy pig, so that you're that much heavier to carry about."
"That's right!" whined the mouth. "Where do you think all
that food you love comes from? I'm the one who has to chew it all
up, and as soon as I'm finished you suck it all down for yourself. Do
you call that fair?"
"And what about me?" called the brain. "Do you think it's easy
being up here, having to think about where your next meal is going
to come from? And yet I get nothing at all for my pains."
And one by one the parts of the body joined the complaint
against the stomach, which didn't say anything at all.
"I have an idea," the brain finally announced. "Let's all rebel
against this lazy belly, and stop working for it."
"Superb idea!" all the other members and organs agreed. "We'll
teach you how important we are, you pig. Then maybe you'll do a
little work of your own."
So they all stopped working. The hands refused to do any lifting
or carrying. The feet refused to walk. The mouth promised not to
chew or swallow a single bite. And the brain swore it wouldn't come
up with any more bright ideas. At first the stomach growled a bit,
as it always did when it was hungry. But after a while it was quiet.

Then, to the dreaming man's surprise, he found he could not walk. He could not grasp anything in his hands. He could not even open his mouth. And he suddenly began to feel rather ill.

The dream seemed to go on for several days. As each day passed, the man felt worse and worse. "This rebellion had better not last much longer," he thought to himself, "or I'll starve."

Meanwhile, the hands and feet and mouth and brain just lay there, getting weaker and weaker. At first they roused themselves just enough to taunt the stomach every once in a while, but before long they didn't even have the energy for that.

Finally the man heard a faint voice coming from the direction of his feet.

"It could be that we were wrong," they were saying. "We suppose the stomach might have been working in his own way all along."

"I was just thinking the same thing," murmured the brain. "It's true he's been getting all the food. But it seems he's been sending most of it right back to us."

"We might as well admit our error," the mouth said, "The stomach has just as much work to do as the hands and feet and brain and teeth."

"Then let's all get back to work," they cried together. And at that the man woke up.

To his relief, he discovered his feet could walk again. His hands could grasp, his mouth could chew, and his brain could now think clearly. He began to feel much better.

"Well, there's a lesson for me," he thought as he filled his stomach at breakfast. "Either we all work together, or nothing works at all."

The Kingdom of the Bees

William Shakespeare

William Shakespeare used the story of the Rebellion against the Stomach in his *Coriolanus* to illustrate a state fallen into anarchy when its citizens refuse to work together. Here in *Henry the Fifth,* by contrast, he returned to the beehive to illustrate the well-ordered, working state.

So work the honeybees;
Creatures, that, by a rule in nature, teach
The act of order to a peopled kingdom.
They have a king, and officers of sorts:
Where some like magistrates, correct at home;
Others, like merchants, venture trade abroad;
Others, like soldiers, armed in their stings,
Make boot upon the summer's velvet buds;
Which pillage they with merry march bring home
To the tent-royal of their emperor:
Who, busied in his majesties, surveys
The singing masons building roofs of gold;
The civil citizens kneading up the honey;
The poor mechanic porters crowding in
Their heavy burthens at his narrow gate;
The sad-ey'd justice, with his surly hum,
Delivering o'er to executors pale
The lazy yawning drone.

The Bundle of Sticks

Aesop

A certain man had several sons who were always quarreling
with one another, and, try as he might, he could not get them to live
together in harmony. So he determined to convince them of their
folly by the following means. Bidding them fetch a bundle of sticks,
he invited each in turn to break it across his knee. All tried and all
failed: and then he undid the bundle, and handed them the sticks one
by one, when they had no difficulty at all in breaking them. "There,
my boys," said he, "united you will be more than a match for your
enemies: but if you quarrel and separate, your weakness will put you
at the mercy of those who attack you."

Union is strength.

Results and Roses

Edgar Guest

The man who wants a garden fair,
    Or small or very big,
With flowers growing here and there,
    Must bend his back and dig.

The things are mighty few on earth
    That wishes can attain.
Whate'er we want of any worth
    We've got to work to gain.

It matters not what goal you seek
    Its secret here reposes:
You've got to dig from week to week
    To get Results or Roses.

Hercules Cleans
the Augean Stables

The cleaning of the Augean stables was the fifth of the famous
Twelve Labors of Hercules, which the great Greek hero performed by order of his cousin, King Eurystheus of Mycenae.
We usually think of Hercules as embodying strength more than
intelligence, but here we admire his ingenuity as much as his
brute force in tackling a nearly impossible job.

The fifth labor of Hercules was the famous cleaning of the
Augean stables. Augeas, the king of Elis, had a herd of three thousand cattle, and he had built a stable miles long for them. Year after
year his herd kept growing, and he could not get enough men to
take care of the barns. The cows could hardly get into them because

of the filth, or if they did get in, they were never quite sure of getting out again because the dirt was piled so high. It was said the stables had not been cleaned in thirty years.

Hercules told Augeas he would clean the barns in one day if the king would give him one tenth of all his cows. Augeas thought the great hero could never do it in so short a time, so he made the agreement in the presence of his young son.

The king's stables were near the two rivers Alpheus and Peneus. Hercules cut a great channel to bring the two streams together and then run into the stables. They rushed along and carried the dirt out so quickly the king could not believe it. He did not intend to pay the reward, so he pretended he had never made a promise.

The dispute was taken before a court for the judges to decide. Hercules called the little prince as a witness, and the boy told the truth about it, which caused the king to fall into such a rage he sent both his son and Hercules out of the country. So Hercules left the land of Elis and continued his twelve labors, but his heart was filled with contempt for the faithless king.

The Choice of Hercules

Retold by James Baldwin

In his famous choice of labor over pleasure, Hercules sees a distinction far too many fail to discern. He sees that to choose labor is to choose virtue, and thereby happiness. It is important to note, however, that happiness is not his goal; it is rather a result of his dedication to labor. It's a crucial point. Many people pursue pleasure as an end because they believe, as the personification of pleasure says in this story, that ease is the state in which "you shall not want for anything that makes life joyous." But even if you attain that kind of pleasure, something fundamental is missing—the satisfaction of the soul that comes only through human striving. We know true happiness will come to Hercules as we see him set off down the road of Virtue and Labor.

When Hercules was a fair-faced youth, and life was all before him, he went out one morning to do an errand for his stepfather. But as he walked his heart was full of bitter thoughts; and he murmured because others no better than himself were living in ease and pleasure, while for him there was naught but a life of labor and pain.

As he thought upon these things, he came to a place where two roads met; and he stopped, not certain which one to take.

The road on his right was hilly and rough. There was no beauty in it or about it, but he saw that it led straight toward the blue mountains in the far distance.

The road on his left was broad and smooth, with shade trees on either side, where sang an innumerable choir of birds; and it went winding among green meadows, where bloomed countless flowers. But it ended in fog and mist long before it reached the wonderful blue mountains in the distance.

While the lad stood in doubt as to these roads, he saw two fair women coming toward him, each on a different road. The one who came by the flowery way reached him first, and Hercules saw that she was as beautiful as a summer day.

Her cheeks were red, her eyes sparkled; she spoke warm, persuasive words. "O noble youth," she said, "be no longer bowed down with labor and sore trials, but come and follow me. I will lead you into pleasant paths, where there are no storms to disturb and no troubles to annoy. You shall live in ease, with one unending round of music and mirth; and you shall not want for anything that makes life joyous—sparkling wine, or soft couches, or rich robes, or the loving eyes of beautiful maidens. Come with me, and life shall be to you a daydream of gladness."

By this time the other fair woman had drawn near, and she now spoke to the lad. "I have nothing to promise you," said she, "save that which you shall win with your own strength. The road upon which I would lead you is uneven and hard, and climbs many a hill, and descends into many a valley and quagmire. The views which you will sometimes get from the hilltops are grand and glorious, but the deep valleys are dark, and the ascent from them is toilsome. Nevertheless, the road leads to the blue mountains of endless fame, which you see far away on the horizon. They cannot be reached without labor; in fact, there is nothing worth having that must not be won by toil. If you would have fruits and flowers, you must plant them and care for them; if you would gain the love of your fellow men, you must love them and suffer for them; if you would enjoy the favor of heaven, you must make yourself worthy of that favor; if you would have eternal fame, you must not scorn the hard road that leads to it."

Then Hercules saw that this lady, although she was as beautiful as the other, had a countenance pure and gentle, like the sky on a balmy morning in May.

"What is your name?" he asked.

"Some call me Labor," she answered, "but others know me as Virtue."

Then he turned to the first lady. "And what is your name?" he asked.

"Some call me Pleasure," she said, with bewitching smile, "but I choose to be known as the Joyous and Happy One."

"Virtue," said Hercules, "I will take thee as my guide! The road of labor and honest effort shall be mine, and my heart shall no longer cherish bitterness or discontent."

And he put his hand into that of Virtue, and entered with her upon the straight and forbidding road which leads to the fair blue mountains on the pale and distant horizon.

True Nobility

Edgar Guest

Who does his task from day to day
And meets whatever comes his way,
Believing God has willed it so,
Has found real greatness here below.

Who guards his post, no matter where,
Believing God must need him there,
Although but lowly toil it be,
Has risen to nobility.

For great and low there's but one test:
'Tis that each man shall do his best.
Who works with all the strength he can
Shall never die in debt to man.

The Ballad of John Henry

The John Henry of American folklore was a black railroad worker celebrated for his feats of great strength and skill. His most famous exploit was his classic man-versus-machine battle against the new steam drill, which threatened to take the place of the "steel-drivin' " men who hammered long steel bits into solid rock to make holes for dynamite. The story is said to be based on the digging of the Big Bend Tunnel for the Chesapeake and Ohio Railroad in West Virginia's Allegheny Mountains in the 1870s. It is a great American tale of pride and dignity in work.

John Henry was a little baby boy
You could hold him in the palm of your hand.
He gave a long and lonesome cry,
"Gonna be a steel-drivin' man, Lawd, Lawd,
Gonna be a steel-drivin' man."

They took John Henry to the tunnel,
Put him in the lead to drive,
The rock was so tall, John Henry so small,
That he laid down his hammer and he cried, "Lawd, Lawd,"
Laid down his hammer and he cried.

John Henry started on the right hand,
The steam drill started on the left,
"Fo' I'd let that steam drill beat me down,
I'd hammer my fool self to death, Lawd, Lawd,
Hammer my fool self to death."

John Henry told his captain,
"A man ain't nothin' but a man,
Fo' I let your steam drill beat me down
I'll die with this hammer in my hand, Lawd, Lawd,
Die with this hammer in my hand."

Now the captain told John Henry,
"I believe my tunnel's sinkin' in."
"Stand back, Captain, and doncha be afraid,
That's nothin' but my hammer catchin' wind, Lawd, Lawd,
That's nothin' but my hammer catchin' wind."

John Henry told his cap'n,
"Look yonder, boy, what do I see?
Your drill's done broke and your hole's done choke,
And you can't drive steel like me, Lawd, Lawd,
You can't drive steel like me."

John Henry hammerin' in the mountain,
Til the handle of his hammer caught on fire,
He drove so hard till he broke his po' heart,
Then he laid down his hammer and he died, Lawd, Lawd,
He laid down his hammer and he died.

They took John Henry to the tunnel,
And they buried him in the sand,
An' every locomotive come rollin' by
Say, "There lies a steel-drivin' man, Lawd, Lawd,
There lies a steel-drivin' man."

Robinson Crusoe Builds a Boat

Daniel Defoe

Daniel Defoe's *The Life and Strange Surprising Adventures of Robinson Crusoe,* published in 1719, was the first major novel in English literature, and few storytellers since have been able to surpass the tale's adventure and romance. In this scene Crusoe, who spends twenty-eight years on an uninhabited island off the coast of Venezuela, tries to build a boat. The episode teaches us all something about organizing and planning *before* we start a job.

This at length put me upon thinking, whether it was not possible to make myself a *canoe,* or *periagua,* such as the natives of those climates make, even without tools, or, as I might say, without hands, *viz.* of the trunk of a great tree. This I not only thought possible, but easy, and pleased myself extremely with the thoughts of making it, and with my having much more convenience for it than any of the Negroes or Indians; but not at all considering the particular inconveniences which I lay under, more than the Indians did, *viz.* want of hands to move it, when it was made, into the water, a difficulty much harder for me to surmount, than all the consequences of want of tools could be to them; for what was it to me, that when I had chosen a vast tree in the woods, I might with much trouble cut it down, if after I might be able with my tools to hew and dub the outside into the proper shape of a boat, and burn or cut out the inside to make it hollow, so to make a boat of it—if after all this, I must leave it just there where I found it, and was not able to launch it into the water?

One would have thought, I could not have had the least reflection upon my mind of my circumstance, while I was making this boat; but I should have immediately thought how I should get it into the sea; but my thoughts were so intent upon my voyage over the sea in it, that I never once considered how I should get it off of the land; and it was really in its own nature more easy for me to guide it over forty-five miles of sea, than about forty-five fathom of land, where it lay, to set it afloat in the water.

I went to work upon this boat the most like a fool that ever man did, who had any of his senses awake. I pleased myself with the design, without determining whether I was ever able to undertake it; not but that the difficulty of launching my boat came often into my head; but I put a stop to my own inquiries into it, by this foolish answer which I gave myself, "Let's first make it, I'll warrant I'll find some way or other to get it along, when 't is done."

This was a most preposterous method; but the eagerness of my fancy prevailed, and to work I went. I felled a cedar tree. I question much whether Solomon ever had such a one for the building of the Temple at Jerusalem. It was five foot ten inches diameter at the lower part next the stump, and four foot eleven inches diameter at the end of twenty-two foot, after which it lessened for a while, and then parted into branches. It was not without infinite labor that I felled this tree. I was twenty days hacking and hewing at it at the bottom. I was fourteen more getting the branches and limbs, and the vast spreading head of it cut off, which I hacked and hewed through with axe and hatchet, and inexpressible labor. After this, it cost me a month to shape it, and dub it to a proportion, and to something like the bottom of a boat, that it might swim upright as it ought to do. It cost me near three months more to clear the inside, and work it out so as to make an exact boat of it. This I did indeed without fire, by mere mallet and chisel, and by the dint of hard labor, till I had brought it to be a very handsome *periagua,* and big enough to have carried six and twenty men, and consequently big enough to have carried me and all my cargo.

When I had gone through this work, I was extremely delighted with it. The boat was really much bigger than I ever saw a *canoe,* or *periagua,* that was made of one tree, in my life. Many a weary stroke it had cost, you may be sure; and there remained nothing but to get it into the water; and had I gotten it into the water, I make no question but I should have began the maddest voyage, and the most unlikely to be performed, that ever was undertaken.

But all my devices to get it into the water failed me; tho' they cost me infinite labor too. It lay about one hundred yards from the water, and not more. But the first inconvenience was, it was uphill toward the creek; well, to take away this discouragement, I resolved to dig into the surface of the earth, and so make a declivity. This I begun, and it cost me a prodigious deal of pains; but who grutches pains, that have their deliverance in view? But when this was worked through, and this difficulty managed, it was still much at one; for I could no more stir the *canoe,* than I could the other boat.

Then I measured the distance of ground, and resolved to cut a dock, or canal, to bring the water up to the *canoe,* seeing I could not bring the *canoe* down to the water. Well, I began this work, and when I began to enter into it, and calculate how deep it was to be dug, how broad, how the stuff to be thrown out, I found, that by the number of hands I had, being none but my own, it must have been ten or twelve years before I should have gone through with it; for the shore lay high, so that at the upper end, it must have been at least twenty foot deep; so at length, tho' with great reluctancy, I gave this attempt over also.

This grieved me heartily, and now I saw, tho' too late, the folly of beginning a work before we count the cost; and before we judge rightly of our own strength to go through with it.

The Village Blacksmith

Henry Wadsworth Longfellow

Longfellow said that he wrote this poem in praise of an ancestor,
and that it was suggested to him by a smithy beneath a horse
chestnut tree near his house in Cambridge, Massachusetts. Here
is the character of true, honest, willing labor. It is surely one of
the most appealing images in American verse.

> Under a spreading chestnut tree
>   The village smithy stands;
> The smith, a mighty man is he,
>   With large and sinewy hands;
> And the muscles of his brawny arms
>   Are strong as iron bands.
>
> His hair is crisp, and black, and long,
>   His face is like the tan;
> His brow is wet with honest sweat,
>   He earns whate'er he can,
> And looks the whole world in the face,
>   For he owes not any man.
>
> Week in, week out, from morn till night,
>   You can hear his bellows blow;
> You can hear him swing his heavy sledge,
>   With measured beat and slow,
> Like a sexton ringing the village bell,
>   When the evening sun is low.
>
> And children coming home from school
>   Look in at the open door;
> They love to see the flaming forge,
>   And hear the bellows roar,
> And catch the burning sparks that fly
>   Like chaff from a threshing floor.

He goes on Sunday to the church,
    And sits among his boys;
He hears the parson pray and preach,
    He hears his daughter's voice,
Singing in the village choir,
    And it makes his heart rejoice.

It sounds to him like her mother's voice,
    Singing in Paradise!
He needs must think of her once more,
    How in the grave she lies;
And with his hard, rough hand he wipes
    A tear out of his eyes.

Toiling—rejoicing—sorrowing
    Onward through life he goes;
Each morning sees some task begin,
    Each evening sees it close;
Something attempted, something done,
    Has earned a night's repose.

Thanks, thanks to thee, my worthy friend,
    For the lesson thou hast taught!
Thus at the flaming forge of life
    Our fortunes must be wrought;
Thus on its sounding anvil shaped
    Each burning deed and thought!

Tom Sawyer Gives Up the Brush

Mark Twain

Here is one of the most famous scenes in American literature, in
which we learn a thing or two about how *not* to apply ourselves
to a job. Fortunately, we also learn here a good bit about the
right attitude toward work. As Tom's friends show us (without
realizing it themselves), whether or not a task constitutes "work"

in the unpleasant sense of the word can depend largely on how we choose to view it. As Milton said, "The mind is its own place, and in itself can make a Heaven of Hell, a Hell of Heaven."

Mark Twain's *Tom Sawyer,* published in 1876, is set in a Mississippi River town before the Civil War. It and its even greater companion work, *Huckleberry Finn,* deserve to be read by every American child.

Saturday morning was come, and all the summer world was bright and fresh, and brimming with life. There was a song in every heart; and if the heart was young the music issued at the lips. There was cheer in every face and a spring in every step. The locust trees were in bloom and the fragrance of the blossoms filled the air. Cardiff Hill, beyond the village and above it, was green with vegetation, and it lay just far enough away to seem a Delectable Land, dreamy, reposeful, and inviting.

Tom appeared on the sidewalk with a bucket of whitewash and a long-handled brush. He surveyed the fence, and all gladness left him and a deep melancholy settled down upon his spirit. Thirty yards of board fence nine feet high. Life to him seemed hollow, and existence but a burden. Sighing he dipped his brush and passed it along the topmost plank; repeated the operation; did it again; compared the insignificant whitewashed streak with the far-reaching continent of unwhitewashed fence, and sat down on a tree-box discouraged. . . .

Soon the free boys would come tripping along on all sorts of delicious expeditions, and they would make a world of fun of him for having to work—the very thought of it burnt him like fire. He got out his worldly wealth and examined it—bits of toys, marbles, and trash; enough to buy an exchange of *work,* maybe, but not half enough to buy so much as half an hour of pure freedom. So he returned his straitened means to his pocket, and gave up the idea of trying to buy the boys. At this dark and hopeless moment an inspiration burst upon him! Nothing less than a great, magnificent inspiration.

He took up his brush and went tranquilly to work. Ben Rogers hove in sight presently—the very boy, of all boys, whose ridicule he had been dreading. Ben's gait was the hop-skip-and-jump—proof enough that his heart was light and his anticipations high. He was eating an apple, and giving a long, melodious whoop, at intervals, followed by a deep-toned ding-dong-dong, ding-dong-dong, for he was personating a steamboat. As he drew near, he slackened speed, took the middle of the street, leaned far over to starboard and rounded to ponderously and with laborious pomp and circumstance —for he was personating the *Big Missouri,* and considered himself to be drawing nine feet of water. He was boat and captain and engine bells combined, so he had to imagine himself standing on his own hurricane deck giving the orders and executing them:

"Stop her, sir! Ting-a-ling-ling!" The headway ran almost out and he drew up slowly toward the sidewalk.

"Ship up to back! Ting-a-ling-ling!" His arms straightened and stiffened down his sides.

"Set her back on the stabboard! Ting-a-ling-ling! Chow! ch-chow-wow! Chow!" His right hand, meantime, describing stately circles—for it was representing a forty-foot wheel.

"Let her go back on the labboard! Ting-a-ling-ling! Chow-ch-chow-chow!" The left hand began to describe circles.

"Stop the stabboard! Ting-a-ling-ling! Stop the labboard! Come ahead on the stabboard! Stop her! Let your outside turn over slow! Ting-a-ling-ling! Chow-ow-ow! Get out that head-line! *Lively* now! Come—out with your spring-line—what're you about there! Take a turn round that stump with the bight of it! Stand by that stage, now—let her go! Done with the engines, sir! Ting-a-ling-ling! *Sh't! s'h't! sh't!"* (trying the gaugecocks).

Tom went on whitewashing—paid no attention to the steamboat. Ben stared a moment and then said:

"Hi-*yi! You're* up a stump, ain't you!"

No answer. Tom surveyed his last touch with the eye of an artist, then he gave his brush another gentle sweep and surveyed the result, as before. Ben ranged up alongside of him. Tom's mouth watered for the apple, but he stuck to his work. Ben said:

"Hello, old chap, you got to work, hey?"

Tom wheeled suddenly and said:

"Why, it's you, Ben! I warn't noticing."

"Say—*I'm* going in a-swimming, *I* am. Don't you wish you could? But of course you'd druther *work*—wouldn't you? Course you would!"

Tom contemplated the boy a bit, and said:

"What do you call work?"

"Why, ain't *that* work?"

Tom resumed his whitewashing, and answered carelessly:

"Well, maybe it is, and maybe it ain't. All I know is, it suits Tom Sawyer."

"Oh come, now, you don't mean to let on that you *like* it?"

The brush continued to move.

"Like it? Well, I don't see why I oughtn't to like it. Does a boy get a chance to whitewash a fence every day?"

That put the thing in a new light. Ben stopped nibbling his apple. Tom swept his brush daintily back and forth—stepped back to note the effect—added a touch here and there—criticized the effect again—Ben watching every move and getting more and more interested, more and more absorbed. Presently he said:

"Say, Tom, let *me* whitewash a little."

Tom considered, was about to consent; but he altered his mind:

"No—no—I reckon it wouldn't hardly do, Ben. You see, Aunt Polly's awful particular about this fence—right here on the street, you know—but if it was the back fence I wouldn't mind and *she* wouldn't. Yes, she's awful particular about this fence; it's got to be done very careful; I reckon there ain't one boy in a thousand, maybe two thousand, that can do it the way it's got to be done."

"No—is that so? Oh come, now—lemme just try. Only just a little—I'd let *you*, if you was me, Tom."

"Ben, I'd like to, honest Injun; but Aunt Polly—well, Jim wanted to do it, but she wouldn't let him; Sid wanted to do it, and she wouldn't let Sid. Now don't you see how I'm fixed? If you was to tackle this fence and anything was to happen to it—"

"Oh, shucks, I'll be just as careful. Now lemme try. Say—I'll give you the core of my apple"

"Well, here— No, Ben, now don't. I'm afeard—"

"I'll give you *all* of it!"

Tom gave up the brush with reluctance in his face, but alacrity in his heart. And while the late steamer *Big Missouri* worked and sweated in the sun, the retired artist sat on a barrel in the shade close by, dangled his legs, munched his apple, and planned the slaughter of more innocents. There was no lack of material; boys happened along every little while; they came to jeer, but remained to whitewash. By the time Ben was fagged out, Tom had traded the next chance to Billy Fisher for a kite, in good repair; and when *he* played out, Johnny Miller bought in for a dead rat and a string to swing it with—and so on, and so on, hour after hour. And when the middle of the afternoon came, from being a poor poverty-stricken boy in the morning, Tom was literally rolling in wealth. He had beside the things before mentioned, twelve marbles, part of a Jew's-harp, a piece of blue bottle glass to look through, a spool cannon, a key that wouldn't unlock anything, a fragment of chalk, a glass stopper of a decanter, a tin soldier, a couple of tadpoles, six firecrackers, a kitten with only one eye, a brass doorknob, a dog collar—but no dog— the handle of a knife, four pieces of orange peel, and a dilapidated old window sash.

He had had a nice, good, idle time all the while—plenty of company—and the fence had three coats of whitewash on it! If he hadn't run out of whitewash, he would have bankrupted every boy in the village.

Tom said to himself that it was not such a hollow world, after all. He had discovered a great law of human action, without know- ing it—namely, that in order to make a man or a boy covet a thing, it is only necessary to make the thing difficult to attain. If he had been a great and wise philosopher, like the writer of this book, he would now have comprehended that Work consists of whatever a body is *obliged* to do, and that Play consists of whatever a body is not obliged to do. And this would help him to understand why constructing artificial flowers or performing on a treadmill is work, while rolling tenpins or climbing Mont Blanc is only amusement. There are wealthy gentlemen in England who drive four-horse pas- senger coaches twenty or thirty miles on a daily line, in the summer, because the privilege costs them considerable money; but if they were offered wages for the service, that would turn it into work and then they would resign.

The boy mused awhile over the substantial change which had taken place in his worldly circumstances, and then wended toward headquarters to report.

Abraham Lincoln Denies a Loan

Abraham Lincoln wrote this letter to his stepbrother, John D. Johnston, who had written Lincoln that he was "broke" and "hard-pressed" on the family farm in Coles County, Illinois, and needed a loan. Lincoln's offer of a matching grant, as we call it today, was a recognition that "this habit of uselessly wasting time, is the whole difficulty," and that getting into the habit of working was far more important to Johnston than getting a loan.

[*Dec. 24, 1848*]

Dear Johnston:

Your request for eighty dollars, I do not think it best to comply with now. At the various times when I have helped you a little, you have said to me, "We can get along very well now," but in a very short time I find you in the same difficulty again. Now this can only happen by some defect in your conduct. What that defect is, I think I know. You are not *lazy,* and still you are an *idler.* I doubt whether since I saw you, you have done a good whole day's work, in any one day. You do not very much dislike to work, and still you do not work much, merely because it does not seem to you that you could get much for it.

This habit of uselessly wasting time, is the whole difficulty; it is vastly important to you, and still more so to your children, that you should break this habit. It is more important to them, because they have longer to live, and can keep out of an idle habit before they are in it, easier than they can get out after they are in.

You are now in need of some ready money; and what I propose is, that you shall go to work, "tooth and nail," for somebody who will give you money for it.

Let father and your boys take charge of your things at home— prepare for a crop, and make the crop, and you go to work for the best money wages, or in discharge of any debt you owe, that you can get. And to secure you a fair reward for your labor, I now promise you that for every dollar you will, between this and the first of May, get for your own labor either in money or in your own indebtedness, I will then give you one other dollar.

By this, if you hire yourself at ten dollars a month, from me you will get ten more, making twenty dollars a month for your work. In this, I do not mean you shall go off to St. Louis, or the lead mines, or the gold mines, in California, but I mean for you to go at it for the best wages you can get close to home—in Coles County.

Now if you will do this, you will soon be out of debt, and what is better, you will have a habit that will keep you from getting in debt again. But if I should now clear you out, next year you will be just as deep in as ever. You say you would almost give your place in

Heaven for $70 or $80. Then you value your place in Heaven very cheaply, for I am sure you can with the offer I make you get the seventy or eighty dollars for four or five months' work. You say if I furnish you the money you will deed me the land, and if you don't pay the money back, you will deliver possession—

Nonsense! If you can't now live *with* the land, how will you then live without it? You have always been kind to me, and I do not now mean to be unkind to you. On the contrary, if you will but follow my advice, you will find it worth more than eight times eighty dollars to you.

Affectionately

Your brother

A. Lincoln

Up from Slavery

Booker T. Washington

Up from Slavery is Booker T. Washington's account of his life, which began in 1856 on a Virginia plantation where his mother was a cook, and ended in 1915 at Tuskegee, Alabama, where he had built one of the world's leading centers of black education. In this excerpt, Washington tells of his determination to "secure an education at any cost," a resolve that led him to Hampton Institute in Hampton, Virginia. This is a passage every college-bound student should read. Here is the soul who is willing to work—and work, and work—to earn an education.

One day, while at work in the coal mine, I happened to overhear two miners talking about a great school for colored people somewhere in Virginia. This was the first time that I had ever heard anything about any kind of school or college that was more pretentious than the little colored school in our town.

In the darkness of the mine I noiselessly crept as close as I could to the two men who were talking. I heard one tell the other that not only was the school established for the members of my race, but that opportunities were provided by which poor but worthy students could work out all or part of the cost of board, and at the same time he taught some trade or industry.

As they went on describing the school, it seemed to me that it must be the greatest place on earth, and not even Heaven presented more attractions for me at that time than did the Hampton Normal and Agricultural Institute in Virginia, about which these men were talking. I resolved at once to go to that school, although I had no idea where it was, or how many miles away, or how I was going to reach it; I remembered only that I was on fire constantly with one ambition, and that was to go to Hampton. This thought was with me day and night.

After hearing of the Hampton Institute, I continued to work for a few months longer in the coal mine. While at work there, I heard of a vacant position in the household of General Lewis Ruffner, the owner of the salt furnace and coalmine. Mrs. Viola Ruffner, the wife of General Ruffner, was a "Yankee" woman from Vermont. Mrs. Ruffner had a reputation all through the vicinity for being very strict with her servants, and especially with the boys who tried to serve her. Few of them had remained with her more than two or three weeks. They all left with the same excuse: she was too strict. I decided, however, that I would rather try Mrs. Ruffner's house than remain in the coal mine, and so my mother applied to her for the vacant position. I was hired at a salary of $5 per month.

I had heard so much about Mrs. Ruffner's severity that I was almost afraid to see her, and trembled when I went into her presence. I had not lived with her many weeks, however, before I began to understand her. I soon began to learn that, first of all, she wanted everything kept clean about her, that she wanted things done promptly and systematically, and that at the bottom of everything she wanted absolute honesty and frankness. Nothing must be sloven or slipshod; every door, every fence, must be kept in repair.

I cannot now recall how long I lived with Mrs. Ruffner before going to Hampton, but I think it must have been a year and a half. At any rate, I here repeat what I have said more than once before, that the lessons that I learned in the home of Mrs. Ruffner were as valuable to me as any education I have ever gotten anywhere since. Even to this day I never see bits of paper scattered around a house or in the street that I do not want to pick them up at once. I never see a filthy yard that I do not want to clean it, a paling off of a fence that

I do not want to put it on, an unpainted or unwhitewashed house that I do want to paint or whitewash it, or a button off one's clothes, or a grease spot on them or on a floor, that I do not want to call attention to it.

From fearing Mrs. Ruffner I soon learned to look upon her as one of my best friends. When she found that she could trust me she did so implicitly. During the one or two winters that I was with her she gave me an opportunity to go to school for an hour in the day during a portion of the winter months, but most of my studying was done at night, sometimes alone, sometimes under someone whom I could hire to teach me. Mrs. Ruffner always encouraged and sympathized with me in all my efforts to get an education. It was while living with her that I began to get together my first library. I secured a dry goods box, knocked out one side of it, put some shelves in it, and began putting into it every kind of book that I could get my hands upon, and called it my "library."

Notwithstanding my success at Mrs. Ruffner's I did not give up the idea of going to the Hampton Institute. In the fall of 1872 I determined to make an effort to get there, although, as I have stated, I had no idea of the direction in which Hampton was, or what it would cost to go there. I do not think that anyone thoroughly sympathized with me in my ambition to go to Hampton unless it was my mother, and she was troubled with a grave fear that I was starting out on a "wild-goose chase." At any rate, I got only a halfhearted consent from her that I might start. The small amount of money that I had earned had been consumed by my stepfather and the remainder of the family, with the exception of a very few dollars, and so I had very little with which to buy clothes and pay traveling expenses. My brother John helped me all that he could, but of course that was not a great deal, for his work was in the coal mine, where he did not earn much, and most of what he did earn went in the direction of paying the household expenses.

Perhaps the thing that touched and pleased me most in connection with my starting for Hampton was the interest that many of the older colored people took in the matter. They had spent the best days of their lives in slavery, and hardly expected to live to see the time when they would see a member of their race leave home to attend a boarding school. Some of these older people would give me a nickel, others a quarter, or a handkerchief.

Finally the great day came, and I started for Hampton. I had only a small, cheap satchel that contained what few articles of clothing I could get. My mother at the time was rather weak and broken in health. I hardly expected to see her again, and thus our parting was all the more sad. She, however, was very brave through it all. At that time there were no through trains connecting that part of West Virginia with eastern Virginia. Trains ran only a portion of the way, and the remainder of the distance was traveled by stage-coaches. . . .

By walking, begging rides both in wagons and in the cars, in some way, after a number of days, I reached the city of Richmond, Virginia, about eighty-two miles from Hampton. When I reached there, tired, hungry, and dirty, it was late in the night. I had never been in a large city, and this rather added to my misery. When I reached Richmond, I was completely out of money. I had not a single acquaintance in the place, and, being unused to city ways, I did not know where to go. I applied at several places for lodging, but they all wanted money, and that was what I did not have. Knowing nothing else better to do, I walked the streets. In doing this I passed by many foodstands where fried chicken and half-moon apple pies were piled high and made to present a most tempting appearance. At that time it seemed to me that I would have promised all that I expected to possess in the future to have gotten hold of one of those chicken legs or one of those pies. But I could not get either of these, nor anything else to eat.

I must have walked the streets till after midnight. At last I became so exhausted that I could walk no longer. I was tired, I was hungry, I was everything but discouraged. Just about the time when I reached extreme physical exhaustion, I came upon a portion of a street where the board sidewalk was considerably elevated. I waited for a few minutes, till I was sure that no passersby could see me, and then crept under the sidewalk and lay for the night upon the ground, with my satchel of clothing for a pillow. Nearly all night I could hear the tramp of feet over my head. The next morning I found myself refreshed, but I was extremely hungry, because it had been a long time since I had had sufficient food. As soon as it became light enough for me to see my surroundings I noticed that I was near a large ship, and that this ship seemed to be unloading a cargo of pig iron. I went at once to the vessel and asked the captain to permit me to help unload the vessel in order to get money for food. The captain, a white man, who seemed to be kindhearted, consented. I worked long enough to earn money for my breakfast, and it seems to me, as I remember it now, to have been about the best breakfast that I have ever eaten.

My work pleased the captain so well that he told me if I desired

I could continue working for a small amount per day. This I was very glad to do. I continued working on this vessel for a number of days. After buying food with the small wages I received there was not much left to add to the amount I must get to pay my way to Hampton. In order to economize in every way possible, so as to be sure to reach Hampton in a reasonable time, I continued to sleep under the same sidewalk that gave me shelter the first night I was in Richmond. Many years after that the colored citizens of Richmond very kindly tendered me a reception at which there must have been two thousand people present. This reception was held not far from the spot where I slept the first night I spent in that city, and I must confess that my mind was more upon the sidewalk that first gave me shelter than upon the reception, agreeable and cordial as it was.

When I had saved what I considered enough money with which to reach Hampton, I thanked the captain of the vessel for his kindness, and started again. Without any unusual occurrence I reached Hampton, with a surplus of exactly fifty cents with which to begin my education. To me it had been a long, eventful journey; but the first sight of the large, three-story, brick school building seemed to have rewarded me for all that I had undergone in order to reach the place.

Opportunity

John James Ingalls

"There is a tide in the affairs of men," William Shakespeare wrote, "which, taken at the flood, leads on to fortune." The catch is that opportunity almost always involves some breasting of the tide—i.e., hard work. Many people would rather simply wait for their ship to come in.

> Master of human destinies am I!
> Fame, love, and fortune on my footsteps wait.
> Cities and fields I walk; I penetrate
> Deserts and seas remote, and passing by
> Hovel and mart and palace—soon or late
> I knock unbidden once at every gate!

If sleeping, wake—if feasting, rise before
I turn away. It is the hour of fate,
And they who follow me reach every state
Mortals desire, and conquer every foe
Save death; but those who doubt or hesitate,
Condemned to failure, penury and woe,
Seek me in vain and uselessly implore.
I answer not, and I return no more!

"It's Plain Hard Work That Does It"

Charles Edison

The story of Thomas Alva Edison's life (1847–1931) is the stuff the American Dream is made of. The inquisitive youngster dropped out of school in Port Huron, Michigan, just a few months after beginning when his teacher called him "addled." His mother continued teaching him at home, however, and he set up a chemical laboratory in his cellar.

At age twelve, Edison took a job as a sandwich and peanut salesman on the Grand Trunk Railway to earn money for chemicals and equipment. He moved his laboratory into a baggage car and, after buying a small printing press, started putting out the first newspaper ever published on a moving train. He was thrown off the train when his chemicals burst into flames and set the baggage car on fire.

In 1869, Edison arrived in New York penniless but determined to make a living as an inventor. Several months later he received $40,000 for improvements he had made on the stock ticker, and with this windfall he launched his long inventing career. He worked practically nonstop to patent more than one thousand inventions over the years. This wonderful portrait by his son Charles lets us glimpse the character of one of America's greatest minds.

Shuffling about his laboratory at Menlo Park, New Jersey, a shock of hair over one side of his forehead, sharp blue eyes sparkling, stains and chemical burns on his wrinkled clothing, Thomas Alva Edison never looked like a man whose inventions had revolutionized the world in less than his lifetime. Certainly he never acted like it. Once when a visiting dignitary asked him whether he had received many medals and awards, he said, "Oh yes, Mom's got a couple of quarts of them up at the house." "Mom" was his wife, my mother.

Yet every day, to those of us who were close to him, he demonstrated what a giant among men he was. Great as were his contributions to mankind—he patented a record 1,093 inventions in his lifetime—it is not for these I remember him, but for his matchless courage, his imagination and determination, his humility and wit. At times, he was just plain mischievous.

Because of his prodigious work schedule, his home life was relatively restricted. But he did find time to go fishing, motoring, and the like with the family, and when we children were young to play parchisi and romp on the floor with us. One thing I remember well is Independence Day at Glenmont, our three-story gabled home in West Orange, New Jersey, which is now a national monument. This was Father's favorite holiday. He might start by throwing a firecracker into a barrel at dawn, awakening us and the neighbors as well. Then we would shoot off fireworks in varying combinations all day.

"Mom's not going to like it," he would say mischievously, "but let's put twenty together and see what happens."

Always Father encouraged our experimentation and exploration. He provided clocks and other gadgets to tinker with, and kidded, challenged and questioned us into doing things. He had me washing beakers in his chemical laboratory when I was six, and when I was ten he helped me get started building a full-sized car. It never had a body, but it did have a little two-cycle marine engine and a belt drive. It worked. We kids had a lot of fun with it. Several times my brother Theodore and I played "polo" on the lawn with croquet mallets and autos—and nobody but Mother and the gardener objected.

At home or at work, Father seemed to have a knack for motivating others. He could and often did give orders but he preferred to inspire people by his own example. This was one of the secrets of his success. For he was not, as many believe, a scientist who worked in solitude in a laboratory. Once he had marketed his first successful invention—a stock ticker and printer—for $40,000, he began employing chemists, mathematicians, machinists, anyone whose talents he thought might help him solve a knotty problem. Thus he married science to industry with the "team" research concept, which is standard today.

Sometimes, during his recurrent financial crises, Father couldn't pay his men. But, as one recalled: "It didn't matter. We all came to work just the same. We wouldn't stay away."

Father himself usually worked eighteen or more hours a day. "Accomplishing something provides the only real satisfaction in life," he told us. His widely reported ability to get by with no more than four hours' sleep—plus an occasional catnap—was no exaggeration. "Sleep," he maintained, "is like a drug. Take too much at a time and it makes you dopey. You lose time, vitality, and opportunities."

His successes are well known. In the phonograph, which he invented when he was thirty, he captured sound on records; his incandescent bulb lighted the world. He invented the microphone, mimeograph, medical fluoroscope, the nickel-iron-alkaline storage battery, and the movies. He made the inventions of others—the telephone, telegraph, typewriter—commercially practical. He conceived our entire electrical distribution system.

It is sometimes asked, "Didn't he ever fail?" The answer is yes. Thomas Edison knew failure frequently. His first patent, when he was all but penniless, was for an electric vote-recorder, but maneuver-minded legislators refused to buy it. Once he had his entire fortune tied up in machinery for a magnetic separation process for low-grade iron ore—only to have it made obsolete and uneconomical by the opening of the rich Mesabi Range. But he never hesitated out of fear of failure.

"Shucks," he told a discouraged co-worker during one trying series of experiments, "we haven't failed. We now know a thousand things that won't work, so we're that much closer to finding what will."

His attitude toward money (or lack of it) was similar. He considered it as a raw material, like metal, to be used rather than amassed, and so he kept plowing his funds into new projects. Several times he was all but bankrupt. But he refused to let dollar signs govern his actions.

One day at his ore-crushing mill, Father became dissatisfied with the way a rock-crusher machine was working. "Give her another turn of speed," he ordered the operator.

"I dassn't," came the reply. "She'll break."

Father turned to the foreman. "How much did she cost, Ed?"

"Twenty-five thousand dollars."

"Have we got that much money in the bank? All right, go ahead and give her another notch."

The operator increased the power. And then once more. "She's pounding somethin' awful," he warned. "She'll break our heads!"

"Damn our heads," Father shouted. "Let her out!"

As the pounding became louder, they began to retreat. Suddenly there was a crash and pieces flew in all directions. The crusher was broken.

"Well," the foreman asked Father, "what did you learn from that?"

"Why," said Father with a smile, "that I can put on 40 percent more power than the builder said she could stand—all but that last notch. Now I can build one just as good, and get more production out of it."

I especially recall a freezing December night in 1914, at a time when still-unfruitful experiments on the nickel-iron-alkaline storage battery, to which Father had devoted much of ten years, had put him on a financial tightrope. Only profits from movie and record production were supporting the laboratory. On that December evening the cry of "Fire!" echoed through the plant. Spontaneous combustion had occurred in the film room. Within moments all the packing compounds, celluloid for records, film, and other flammable goods had gone up with a whoosh. Fire companies from eight towns arrived, but the heat was so intense, and the water pressure so low, that the fire hoses had no effect.

When I couldn't find Father, I became concerned. Was he safe? With all his assets going up in smoke, would his will be broken? He was sixty-seven, no age to begin anew. Then I saw him in the plant yard, running toward me.

"Where's Mom?" he shouted. "Go get her! Tell her to get her friends! They'll never see a fire like this again!"

At 5:30 the next morning, with the fire barely under control, he called his employees together and announced, "We're rebuilding." One man was told to lease all the machine shops in the area. Another, to obtain a wrecking crane from the Erie Railroad. Then, almost as an afterthought he added, "Oh, by the way. Anybody know where we can get some money?"

"You can always make capital out of disaster," he said. "We've just cleared out a bunch of old rubbish. We'll build bigger and better

WORK   413

on the ruins." With that he rolled up his coat, curled up on a table, and immediately fell asleep.

His remarkable succession of inventions made him appear to possess almost magical powers, so that he was called "The Wizard of Menlo Park." The notion alternately amused and angered him. "Wizard?" he would say. "Pshaw. It's plain hard work that does it." Or, his much quoted statement: "Genius is one percent inspiration and 99 percent perspiration." Laziness, mental laziness in particular, tried his patience. He kept a statement attributed to Sir Joshua Reynolds hanging prominently in his laboratory and factories: "There is no expedient to which a man will not resort to avoid the real labor of thinking."

Father never changed his sense of values or his hat size. In Boston, when the power failed at the opening of the first American theater to use incandescent lights, he doffed his tie and tails (which he detested) and unhesitatingly headed for the basement to help find the trouble. In Paris, shortly after receiving the Legion of Honor, he quietly removed the tiny red rosette from his lapel, lest friends "think I'm a dude."

After the death of his first wife, Father married the woman who became my mother, Mina Miller. In her he found a perfect complement. She was poised, gracious, self-sufficient; she willingly adjusted to Father's busy schedule. Theirs was a marriage that warmed all whom it touched. Father's diary, the only one he kept (covering nine days in 1885, before they were married), indicated how smitten he was by her. "Got to thinking of Mina and came near being run over by a streetcar," he confessed.

When he proposed, it was in Morse code, which she had learned during their courtship. In later life, when he worked at a desk at home, she was at hers beside him, usually busy with civic projects, in which she was extremely active.

Thomas Edison has sometimes been represented as uneducated. Actually he had only six months of formal schooling, but under his mother's tutelage in Port Huron, Michigan, he had read such classics as *Decline and Fall of the Roman Empire* at the age of eight or nine. After becoming a vendor and newsboy on the Grand Trunk Railroad, he spent whole days in the Detroit Free Library—which he read "from top to bottom." In our home he always had books and magazines, as well as half a dozen daily newspapers.

From childhood, this man who was to accomplish so much was almost totally deaf. He could hear only the loudest noises and shouts, but this did not bother him. "I haven't heard a bird sing since I was twelve," he once said. "But rather than a handicap my deafness probably has been beneficial." He believed it drove him early to reading, enabled him to concentrate, and shut him off from small talk.

People asked him why he didn't invent a hearing aid. Father always replied, "How much have you heard in the last twenty-four hours that you couldn't do without?" He followed this up with: "A man who has to shout can never tell a lie."

He enjoyed music, and if the arrangement emphasized the melody, he could "listen" by biting a pencil and placing the other end of it against a phonograph cabinet. The vibrations and rhythm came through perfectly. The phonograph, incidentally, was his favorite of all his inventions.

Although his deafness required shouted conversation or written questions and answers, reporters enjoyed interviewing him for his pithy, penetrating comments. Once, asked what advice he had for youth, he replied, "Youth doesn't take advice." He never accepted happiness or contentment as worthwhile goals. "Show me a thoroughly satisfied man," he said, "and I will show you a failure." Asked if technological progress could lend to overproduction, he replied, "There cannot be overproduction of anything which men and women want. And their wants are unlimited, except by the size of their stomachs!"

Many tributes were paid Father but two pleased him especially. One came on October 21, 1929, the golden anniversary of the incandescent lamp, when Henry Ford re-created Father's Menlo Park, New Jersey, laboratory in Dearborn, Michigan, to be a permanent shrine in Ford's vast exhibit of Americana at Greenfield Village. This was Ford's expression of gratitude to Father for his words of encouragement when doubt and despair almost turned Ford from the development of his first auto. We could see by his smile that Father was deeply touched.

The other outstanding salute came in 1928, in his own library-laboratory-office in West Orange. He had received honors and medals from many nations. But it was particularly gratifying when, on this occasion, Father was awarded a special gold "Medal of the Congress of the United States" in recognition of his achievements.

He never retired. Nor did he have qualms about the onset of old age. At the age of eighty, he entered a science completely new to him, botany. His goal: to find a native source of rubber. After testing and classifying seventeen thousand varieties of plants, he and his assistants succeeded in devising a method of extracting latex from goldenrod in substantial quantities.

At eighty-three, hearing that Newark Airport was the busiest in the East, he dragged Mother down there to "see how a real airport works." When he saw his first helicopter, he beamed, "That's the way I always thought it should be done." And he started sketching improvements for the little-known whirlybird.

Finally, at eighty-four, ill with uremic poisoning, he started to fail. Scores of reporters arrived to keep vigil. Hourly the news was relayed to them: "The light still burns." But at 3:24 A.M. on October 18, 1931, word came: "The light is out."

The final salute, on the day of his funeral, was to be the cutoff of all electric current in the nation for one minute. But this was deemed too costly and dangerous. Instead, only certain lights were dimmed. The wheels of progress were not stilled, even for an instant.

Thomas Edison, I am sure, would have wanted it that way.

Heaven Is Not Reached in a Single Bound

J. G. Holland

Heaven is not reached at a single bound,
But we build the ladder by which we rise
From the lowly earth to the vaulted skies,
And we mount to its summit round by round.

I count this thing to be grandly true:
That a noble deed is a step toward God—
Lifting the soul from the common clod
To a purer air and a broader view.

In Praise of the Strenuous Life

Theodore Roosevelt

As a sickly, weak child of a wealthy New York family, Theodore
Roosevelt (1858–1919) could certainly have found plenty of excuses to fall into a life of rich, idle ease. But that was not his
way. With unyielding determination, he committed himself to
rigorous physical exercise, turned himself into a devoted out-
doorsman, and threw himself into a life of public service. Roosevelt gave this speech in Chicago in 1899, a few months after
becoming governor of New York, and it has remained one of his
most popular. Here he speaks to a nation just beginning to feel
tremendous wealth and power, and he cautions against the temptation of the life of "ignoble ease" that prosperity and security
can bring. He reminds us that the character of a nation—like that
of an individual—appears through its work.

In speaking to you, men of the greatest city of the West, men
of the state which gave to the country Lincoln and Grant, men who
preeminently and distinctly embody all that is most American in the
American character, I wish to preach not the doctrine of ignoble ease
but the doctrine of the strenuous life; the life of toil and effort; of
labor and strife; to preach that highest form of success which comes
not to the man who desires mere easy peace but to the man who
does not shrink from danger, from hardship, or from bitter toil, and
who out of these wins the splendid ultimate triumph.

A life of ignoble ease, a life of that peace which springs merely
from lack either of desire or of power to strive after great things, is
as little worthy of a nation as of an individual. I ask only that what
every self-respecting American demands from himself, and from his
sons, shall be demanded of the American nation as a whole. Who
among you would teach your boys that ease, that peace is to be the
first consideration in your eyes—to be the ultimate goal after which
they strive? You men of Chicago have made this city great, you men
of Illinois have done your share, and more than your share, in making America great, because you neither preach nor practice such a
doctrine. You work yourselves, and you bring up your sons to

work. If you are rich, and are worth your salt, you will teach your sons that though they may have leisure it is not to be spent in idleness; for wisely used leisure merely means that those who possess it, being free from the necessity of working for their livelihood, are all the more bound to carry on some kind of nonremunerative work in science, in letters, in art, in exploration, in historical research—work of the type we most need in this country, the successful carrying out of which reflects most honor upon the nation.

We do not admire the man of timid peace. We admire the man who embodies victorious effort; the man who never wrongs his neighbor; who is prompt to help a friend; but who has those virile qualities necessary to win in the stern strife of actual life. It is hard to fail; but it is worse never to have tried to succeed. In this life we get nothing save by effort. Freedom from effort in the present, merely means that there has been stored-up effort in the past. A man can be freed from the necessity of work only by the fact that he or his fathers before him have worked to good purpose. If the freedom thus purchased is used aright, and the man still does actual work, though of a different kind, whether as a writer or a general, whether in the field of politics or in the field of exploration and adventure, he shows he deserves his good fortune. But if he treats this period of freedom from the need of actual labor as a period not of preparation but of mere enjoyment, he shows that he is simply a cumberer on the earth's surface; and he surely unfits himself to hold his own with his fellows if the need to do so should again arise. A mere life of ease is not in the end a satisfactory life, and above all it is a life which ultimately unfits those who follow it for serious work in the world. . . .

I preach to you, then, my countrymen, that our country calls not for the life of ease, but for the life of strenuous endeavor. The twentieth century looms before us big with the fate of many nations. If we stand idly by, if we seek merely swollen, slothful ease, and ignoble peace, if we shrink from the hard contests where men must win at hazard of their lives and at the risk of all they hold dear, then the bolder and stronger peoples will pass us by and will win for themselves the domination of the world. Let us therefore boldly face the life of strife, resolute to do our duty well and manfully; resolute to uphold righteousness by deed and by word; resolute to be both honest and brave, to serve high ideals, yet to use practical methods. Above all, let us shrink from no strife, moral or physical, within or without the nation, provided we are certain that the strife is justified; for it is only through strife, through hard and dangerous endeavor, that we shall ultimately win the goal of true national greatness.

Great Men

Ralph Waldo Emerson

Not gold, but only man can make
 A people great and strong;
Men who, for truth and honor's sake,
 Stand fast and suffer long.

Brave men who work while others sleep,
 Who dare while others fly—
They build a nation's pillars deep
 And lift them to the sky.

Kill Devil Hill

Harry Combs

Here is one of the all-time great American success stories. A childhood fascination with a toy helicopter powered by rubber bands ultimately led Wilbur (1867–1912) and Orville (1871–1948) Wright to what can only be described as one of mankind's most spectacular achievements. In 1900, the Wright brothers began taking their gliders to Kitty Hawk, on North Carolina's Outer Banks, because the ocean breezes and lofty dunes made it an ideal environment for testing their odd-looking flying contraptions. On December 17, 1903, numerous experiments and several "failures" later, Orville made the first powered flight of 120 feet. Wilbur, in the fourth and longest flight of the day, described below, made 852 feet in fifty-nine seconds. If ever we need inspiration as we toil toward some distant, elusive goal, surely we find it here. Here is great work begun by genius, but finished by labor.

The people of Kitty Hawk had always been generous and kind to Wilbur and Orville—friendly and warm, sharing their food and worldly goods, sparing no effort to assist in any way they could to provide physical comfort, and open in their respect for the brothers. Most of them, however, felt less than convinced about the Wrights' being able to fly; Kitty Hawk was an area where the reaction to flight was often expressed in such familiar bits of folk wisdom as "If God had wanted man to fly, He would have given him wings."

Bill Tate, who from the beginning had been a close friend to the Wrights, was not present at the camp on December 17, 1903. This was not a sign of lack of faith; he had assumed that "no one but a crazy man would attempt to fly in such a wind."

The brothers had different ideas. Shortly before twelve o'clock, for the fourth attempt of the day, Wilbur took his position on the flying machine, the engine sputtering and clattering in its strange thunder. His peaked cap was pulled snug across his head, and the wind blowing across the flats reached him with a sandpapery touch. As he had felt it do before, the machine trembled in the gusts, rocking from side to side on the sixty-foot launching track. He settled himself in the hip cradle, feet snug behind him, hands on the controls, studying the three instrument gauges. He looked to each side to be certain no one was near the wings. There were no assistants to hold the wings as they had done with the gliders, for Wilbur believed that unless a man was skilled in what he was doing he ought not to touch anything, and he had insisted on a free launch, for he knew the craft would require only forty feet in the stiff wind to lift itself into the air.

Wilbur shifted his head to study the beach area. Today was different. The wintry gale had greatly reduced the bird population, as far as he could see. It had been that way since they awoke. Very few of the familiar seagulls were about beneath the leaden skies.

Wilbur turned to each side again, looked at his brother, and nodded. Everything was set, and Wilbur reached to the restraining control and pulled the wire free. Instantly, the machine rushed forward and, as he expected, was forty feet down the track when he eased into the air. He had prepared himself for almost every act of the wind, but the gusts were too strong, and he was constantly correcting and overcorrecting. The hundred-foot mark fell behind as the aircraft lunged up and down like a winged bull. Then he was two hundred feet from the start of his run, and the pitch motions were even more violent. The aircraft seemed to stagger as it struck a sudden down draft and darted toward the sands. Only a foot above the ground Wilbur regained control, and eased it back up.

Three hundred feet—and the bucking motions were easing off.

And then the five witnesses and Orville were shouting and gesturing wildly, for it was clear that Wilbur had passed some invisible wall in the sky and had regained control. Four hundred feet out, he was still holding the safety altitude of about fifteen feet above the ground, and the airplane was flying smoother now, no longer darting and lunging about, just easing with the gusts between an estimated eight and fifteen feet.

The seconds ticked away and it was a quarter of a minute since Wilbur had started, and there was no question, now: the machine was under control and was sustaining itself by its own power.

It was flying.

The moment had come. It was here, now.

Five hundred feet.

Six hundred.

Seven hundred!

My God, he's trying to reach Kitty Hawk itself, nearly four miles away!

And, indeed, this is just what Wilbur was trying to do, for he kept heading toward the houses and trees still well before him.

Eight hundred feet . . .

Still going; still flying. Ahead of him, a rise in the ground, a sprawling hump, a hummock of sand. Wilbur brought the elevator into position to raise the nose, to gain altitude to clear the hummock; for beyond this point lay clear sailing, good flying, and he was lifting, the machine rising slowly. But hummocks do strange things to winds blowing at such high speeds. The wind soared up from the sands, rolling and tumbling, and reached out invisibly to push the flying machine downward. The nose dropped too sharply; Wilbur brought it up; and instantly the oscillations began again, a rapid jerking up and down of the nose. The winds were simply too much, the ground-induced roll too severe, and the *Flyer* "suddenly darted into the ground," as Orville later described it.

They knew as they ran that the impact was greater than that of an intentional landing. The skids dug in, and all the weight of the aircraft struck hard, and above the wind they heard the wood splinter and crack. The aircraft bounced once, borne as much by the wind as by its own momentum, and settled back to the sands, the forward elevator braces askew, broken so that the surfaces hung at an angle. Unhurt, aware that he had been flying a marvelously long time, mildly disappointed at not having continued his flight, stuck in the sand with the wind blowing into his face and the engine grinding out its now familiar clattering, banging roar, Wilbur reached out to shut off power. The propellers whistled and whirred as they slowed, the sounds of the chains came to him more clearly, and then only the wind could be heard. The wind, the sand hissing against fabric and his own clothes and across the ground, and perhaps a gull or two, and certainly the beating of his own heart.

It had happened.

He had flown for fifty-nine seconds.

The distance across the surface from his start to his finish was 852 feet.

The air distance, computing airspeed and wind and all the other factors—more than half a mile.

He—they—had done it.

The air age was *now*.

Just fifty-six days before, Simon Newcomb, the only American scientist since Benjamin Franklin to be an associate of the Institute of France, in an article in *The Independent* had shown by "unassailable logic" that human flight was impossible.

They ran up to the machine, where Wilbur stood waiting for them. No one ever recorded what Wilbur's words were at that moment, and no amount of research has been able to unearth them. It is unfortunate, but they are lost forever. . . .

Orville and Wilbur, stiff with cold, went to their living quarters, where they prepared and ate lunch. They rested for several minutes, washed their dishes, and, ready at last to send word of their achievement, at about two o'clock in the afternoon began the walk to the weather station four miles distant in Kitty Hawk. From the station, still run by Joseph J. Dosher, they could dispatch a wire via government facilities to Norfolk, where the message would be continued by telephone to a commercial telegraph office near Dayton. The message, as it was received in Dayton, read:

176 C KA CS 33 PAID.   VIA NORFOLK VA
KITTY   HAWK N C DEC 17
BISHOP M WRIGHT
                7 HAWTHORNE ST
SUCCESS FOUR FLIGHTS THURSDAY MORNING ALL AGAINST
TWENTY ONE MILE WIND STARTED FROM LEVEL WITH ENGINE
POWER ALONE AVERAGE SPEED THROUGH AIR THIRTY ONE MILES
LONGEST 57 SECONDS INFORM PRESS HOME ##### CHRISTMAS.
                        OREVELLE WRIGHT   525P

While this slightly garbled message was being transmitted, including the error of flight time of fifty-seven seconds rather than
fifty-nine, the brothers went to the life-saving station nearby, to talk
with the crew on duty. Captain S. J. Payne, who skippered the
facility, told the Wrights he had watched through binoculars as they
soared over the ground.

Orville and Wilbur went on to the post office, where they visited Captain and Mrs. Hobbs, who had hauled materials and done
other work for them, spent some time with a Dr. Cogswell, and
then started their trek back to their camp. It would take them several
days to dismantle and pack their *Flyer* into a barrel and two boxes,
along with personal gear, and they went to work with their usual
thoroughness. It was a strange and a quiet aftermath, and several
times they went back outside to stand and look at the ground over
which they had flown.

Success

Henry Wadsworth Longfellow

These lines are from Longfellow's "The Ladder of Saint Augustine."

> We have not wings, we cannot soar;
>   But we have feet to scale and climb
> By slow degrees, by more and more,
>   The cloudy summits of our time.

The mighty pyramids of stone
   That wedge-like cleave the desert airs,
When nearer seen, and better known,
   Are but gigantic flights of stairs.

The distant mountains, that uprear
   Their solid bastions to the skies,
Are crossed by pathways, that appear
   As we to higher levels rise.

The heights by great men reached and kept
   Were not attained by sudden flight,
But they, while their companions slept,
   Were toiling upward in the night.

Of Studies

Francis Bacon

Francis Bacon made this case for working hard at studies in 1597.
All of us who are students should consult it when we find ourselves asking that age-old question: "How is learning this going
to do me any good?" This essay may prove a good yardstick in
deciding whether an assignment is indeed worth the hard work
of true study.

Studies serve for delight, for ornament, and for ability. Their
chief use for delight is in privateness and retiring; for ornament, is in
discourse; and for ability, is in the judgment and disposition of business. For expert men can execute, and perhaps judge of particulars,
one by one; but the general counsels, and the plots and marshaling
of affairs, come best from those that are learned. To spend too much
time in studies is sloth; to use them too much for ornament, is
affectation; to make judgment wholly by their rules, is the humor of
a scholar. They perfect nature, and are perfected by experience: for
natural abilities are like natural plants, that need pruning, by study;

and studies themselves do give forth directions too much at large, except they be bounded in by experience. Crafty men contemn studies, simple men admire them, and wise men use them; for they teach not their own use; but that is a wisdom without them, and above them, won by observation. Read not to contradict and confute; nor to believe and take for granted; nor to find talk and discourse; but to weigh and consider. Some books are to be tasted, others to be swallowed, and some few to be chewed and digested; that is, some books are to be read only in parts; others to be read, but not curiously; and some few to be read wholly, and with diligence and attention. Some books also may be read by deputy, and extracts made of them by others; but that would be only in the less important arguments, and the meaner sort of books, else distilled books are like common distilled waters, flashy [insipid] things. Reading maketh a full man; conference a ready man; and writing an exact man. And therefore, if a man write little, he had need have a great memory; if he confer little, he had need have a present wit: and if he read little, he had need have much cunning, to seem to know that he doth not. Histories make men wise; poets witty; the mathematics subtile; natural philosophy deep; moral grave; logic and rhetoric able to contend. *Abeunt studia in mores* [Studies pass into and influence manners]. Nay, there is no stond or impediment in the wit but may be wrought out by fit studies; like as diseases of the body may have appropriate exercises. Bowling is good for the stone and reins [kidneys]; shooting for the lungs and breast; gentle walking for the stomach; riding for the head; and the like. So if a man's wit be wandering, let him study the mathematics; for in demonstrations, if his wit be called away never so little, he must begin again. If his wit be not apt to distinguish or find differences, let him study the Schoolmen; for they are *cymini sectores* [splitters of hairs]. If he be not apt to beat over matters, and to call up one thing to prove and illustrate another, let him study the lawyers' cases. So every defect of the mind may have a special receipt.

Quality

John Galsworthy

This is a story about real workmanship, the kind in which the character of the work and the character of the workman have become inseparably good. It reminds us that nothing endures but quality.

I knew him from the days of my extreme youth, because he made my father's boots; inhabiting with his elder brother two little shops let into one; in a small bystreet—now no more, but then most fashionably placed in the West End.

That tenement had a certain quiet distinction; there was no sign upon its face that he made for any of the Royal Family—merely his own German name of Gessler Brothers; and in the window a few pairs of boots. I remember that it always troubled me to account for those unvarying boots in the window, for he made only what was ordered, reaching nothing down, and it seemed so inconceivable that what he made could ever have failed to fit. Had he bought them to put there? That, too, seemed inconceivable. He would never have tolerated in his house leather on which he had not worked himself. Besides, they were too beautiful—the pair of pumps, so inexpressibly slim, the patent leathers with cloth tops, making water come into one's mouth, the tall brown riding boots with marvelous sooty glow, as if, though new, they had been worn a hundred years. Those pairs could only have been made by one who saw before him the Soul of Boot—so truly were they prototypes incarnating the very spirit of all footgear. These thoughts, of course, came to me later, though even when I was promoted to him, at the age of perhaps fourteen, some inkling haunted me of the dignity of himself and brother. For to make boots—such boots as he made—seemed to me then, and still seems to me, mysterious and wonderful.

I remember well my shy remark, one day, while stretching out to him my youthful foot:

"Isn't it awfully hard to do, Mr. Gessler?"

And his answer, given with a sudden smile from out of the sardonic redness of his beard: "Id is an Ardt!"

Himself, he was a little as if made from leather, with his yellow

crinkly face, and crinkly reddish hair and beard, and neat folds slant-
ing down his cheeks to the corners of his mouth, and his guttural
and one-toned voice; for leather is a sardonic substance, and stiff and
slow of purpose. And that was the character of his face, save that his
eyes, which were gray-blue, had in them the simple gravity of one
secretly possessed by the Ideal. His elder brother was so very like
him—though watery, paler in every way, with a great industry—
that sometimes in early days I was not quite sure of him until the
interview was over. Then I knew that it was he, if the words, "I will
ask my brudder," had not been spoken; and that, if they had, it was
his elder brother.

When one grew old and wild and ran up bills, one somehow
never ran them up with Gessler Brothers. It would not have seemed
becoming to go in there and stretch out one's foot to that blue iron-
spectacled glance, owing him for more than—say—two pairs, just
the comfortable reassurance that one was still his client.

For it was not possible to go to him very often—his boots lasted
terribly, having something beyond the temporary—some, as it
were, essence of boot stitched into them.

One went in, not as into most shops, in the mood of: "Please
serve me, and let me go!" but restfully, as one enters a church; and,
sitting on the single wooden chair, waited—for there was never
anybody there. Soon, over the top edge of that sort of well—rather
dark, and smelling soothingly of leather—which formed the shop,
there would be seen his face, or that of his elder brother, peering
down. A guttural sound, and the tip-tap of bast slippers beating the
narrow wooden stairs, and he would stand before one without coat,
a little bent, in leather apron, with sleeves turned back, blinking—as
if awakened from some dream of boots, or like an owl surprised in
daylight and annoyed at this interruption.

And I would say: "How do you do, Mr. Gessler? Could you
make me a pair of Russia leather boots?"

Without a word he would leave me, retiring whence he came,
or into the other portion of the shop, and I would continue to rest in
the wooden chair, inhaling the incense of his trade. Soon he would
come back, holding in his thin, veined hand a piece of gold-brown
leather. With eyes fixed on it, he would remark: "What a beaudiful
biece!" When I, too, had admired it, he would speak again. "When
do you wand dem?" And I would answer: "Oh! As soon as you
conveniently can." And he would say: "Tomorrow fordnighd?" Or
if he were his elder brother: "I will ask my brudder!"

Then I would murmur: "Thank you! Good morning, Mr. Gessler." "Goot morning!" he would reply, still looking at the leather in his hand. And as I moved to the door, I would hear the tip-tap of his bast slippers restoring him, up the stairs, to his dream of boots. But if it were some new kind of footgear that he had not yet made me, then indeed he would observe ceremony—divesting me of my boot and holding it long in his hand, looking at it with eyes at once critical and loving, as if recalling the glow with which he had created it, and rebuking the way in which one had disorganized this masterpiece. Then, placing my foot on a piece of paper, he would two or three times tickle the outer edges with a pencil and pass his nervous fingers over my toes, feeling himself into the heart of my requirements.

I cannot forget that day on which I had occasion to say to him: "Mr. Gessler, that last pair of town walking boots creaked, you know."

He looked at me for a time without replying, as if expecting me to withdraw or qualify the statement, then said:

"Id shouldn'd 'ave greaked."

"It did, I'm afraid."

"You goddem wed before dey found demselves?"

"I don't think so."

At that he lowered his eyes, as if hunting for memory of those boots, and I felt sorry I had mentioned this grave thing.

"Zend dem back!" he said; "I will look at dem."

A feeling of compassion for my creaking boots surged up in me, so well could I imagine the sorrowful long curiosity of regard which he would bend on them.

"Zome boods," he said slowly, "are bad from birdt. If I can do noding wid dem, I dake dem off your bill."

Once (once only) I went absentmindedly into his shop in a pair of boots bought in an emergency at some large firm's. He took my order without showing me any leather, and I could feel his eyes penetrating the inferior integument of my foot. At last he said:

"Dose are nod my boods."

The tone was not one of anger, nor of sorrow, not even of contempt, but there was in it something quite that froze the blood. He put his hand down and pressed a finger on the place where the left boot, endeavoring to be fashionable, was not quite comfortable.

"Id 'urds you dere," he said. "Dose big virms 'ave no self-respect. Drash!" And then, as if something had given way within him, he spoke long and bitterly. It was the only time I ever heard him discuss the conditions and hardships of his trade.

"Dey get id all," he said, "dey get id by adverdisement, nod by work. Dey dake it away from us, who lofe our boods. Id gomes to this—bresently I haf no work. Every year id gets less—you will see." And looking at his lined face I saw things I had never noticed before, bitter things and bitter struggle—and what a lot of gray hairs there seemed suddenly in his red beard!

As best I could, I explained the circumstances of the purchase of those ill-omened boots. But his face and voice made so deep an impression that during the next few minutes I ordered many pairs. Nemesis fell! They lasted more terribly than ever. And I was not able conscientiously to go to him for nearly two years.

When at last I went I was surprised to find that outside one of the two little windows of his shop another name was painted, also that of a bootmaker—making, of course, for the Royal Family. The old familiar boots, no longer in dignified isolation, were huddled in the single window. Inside, the now contracted well of the one little shop was more scented and darker than ever. And it was longer than usual, too, before a face peered down, and the tip-tap of the bast slippers began. At last he stood before me, and, gazing through those rusty iron spectacles, said:

"Mr.——, isn'd it?"

"Ah! Mr. Gessler," I stammered, "but your boots are really *too* good, you know! See, these are quite decent still!" And I stretched out to him my foot. He looked at it.

"Yes," he said, "beople do nod wand good boods, id seems."

To get away from his reproachful eyes and voice I hastily remarked: "What have you done to your shop?"

He answered quietly: "Id was too exbensif. Do you wand some boods?"

I ordered three pairs, though I had only wanted two, and quickly left. I had, I do not know quite what feeling of being part, in his mind, of a conspiracy against him; or not perhaps so much against him as against his idea of boot. One does not, I suppose, care to feel like that; for it was again many months before my next visit to his shop, paid, I remember, with the feeling: "Oh! well, I can't leave the old boy—so here goes! Perhaps it'll be his elder brother!"

For his elder brother, I knew, had not character enough to reproach me, even dumbly.

And, to my relief, in the shop there did appear to be his elder brother, handling a piece of leather.

"Well, Mr. Gessler," I said, "how are you?"

He came close, and peered at me.

"I am breddy well," he said slowly, "but my elder brudder is dead."

And I saw that it was indeed himself—but how aged and wan! And never before had I heard him mention his brother. Much shocked, I murmured: "Oh! I am sorry!"

"Yes," he answered, "he was a good man, he made a good bood; but he is dead." And he touched the top of his head, where the hair had suddenly gone as thin as it had been on that of his poor brother, to indicate, I suppose, the cause of death. "He could nod ged over losing de oder shop. Do you wand any boods?" And he held up the leather in his hand: "Id's a beaudiful biece."

I ordered several pairs. It was very long before they came—but they were better than ever. One simply could not wear them out. And soon after that I went abroad.

It was over a year before I was again in London. And the first shop I went to was my old friend's. I had left a man of sixty, I came back to one of seventy-five, pinched and worn and tremulous, who genuinely, this time, did not at first know me.

"Oh! Mr. Gessler," I said, sick at heart; "how splendid your boots are! See, I've been wearing this pair nearly all the time I've been abroad; and they're not half worn out, are they?"

He looked long at my boots—a pair of Russia leather, and his face seemed to regain steadiness. Putting his hand on my instep, he said:

"Do dey vid you here? I 'ad drouble wid dat bair, I remember."

I assured him that they had fitted beautifully.

"Do you wand any boods?" he said. "I can make dem quickly; id is a slack dime."

I answered: "Please, please! I want boots all round—every kind!"

"I will make a vresh model. Your food must be bigger." And with utter slowness, he traced round my foot, and felt my toes, only once looking up to say:

"Did I dell you my brudder was dead?"

To watch him was painful, so feeble had he grown; I was glad to get away.

I had given those boots up, when one evening they came. Opening the parcel, I set the four pairs out in a row. Then one by one I tried them on. There was no doubt about it. In shape and fit, in finish and quality of leather, they were the best he had ever made me. And in the mouth of one of the Town walking boots I found his bill. The amount was the same as usual, but it gave me quite a shock. He had never before sent it in till quarter day. I flew downstairs, and wrote a check, and posted it at once with my own hand.

A week later, passing the little street, I thought I would go in and tell him how splendidly the new boots fitted. But when I came to where his shop had been, his name was gone. Still there, in the window, were the slim pumps, the patent leathers with cloth tops, the sooty riding boots.

I went in, very much disturbed. In the two little shops—again made into one—was a young man with an English face.

"Mr. Gessler in?" I said.

He gave me a strange, ingratiating look.

"No, sir," he said, "no. But we can attend to anything with pleasure. We've taken the shop over. You've seen our name, no doubt, next door. We make for some very good people."

"Yes, yes," I said; "but Mr. Gessler?"

"Oh!" he answered; "dead."

"Dead! But I only received these boots from him last Wednesday week."

"Ah!" he said; "a shockin' go. Poor old man starved 'imself."

"Good God!"

"Slow starvation, the doctor called it! You see he went to work in such a way! Would keep the shop on; wouldn't have a soul touch his boots except himself. When he got an order, it took him such a time. People won't wait. He lost everybody. And there he'd sit, goin' on and on—I will say that for him—not a man in London made a better boot! But look at the competition! He never advertised! Would 'ave the best leather, too, and do it all 'imself. Well, there it is. What could you expect with his ideas?"

"But starvation—!"

"That may be a bit flowery, as the sayin' is—but I know myself he was sittin' over his boots day and night, to the very last. You see I used to watch him. Never gave 'imself time to eat; never had a penny in the house. All went in rent and leather. How he lived so long I don't know. He regular let his fire go out. He was a character. But he made good boots."

"Yes," I said, "he made good boots."

And I turned and went out quickly, for I did not want that youth to know that I could hardly see.

The Noble Nature

Ben Jonson

If we devote care to details, our work will shine in small bits and pieces—and our characters will improve degree by degree.

> It is not growing like a tree
> In bulk, doth make man better be;
> Or standing long an oak, three hundred year,
> To fall a log at last, dry, bald, and sear:
> A lily of a day
> Is fairer far in May,
> Although it fall and die that night—
> It was the plant and flower of Light.
> In small proportions we just beauties see,
> And in short measures life may perfect be.

Elias

Leo Tolstoy

"For half a century we sought happiness," Elias's wife says in this story, "and as long as we were rich we never found it. Now that we have nothing left, and have taken service as laborers, we have found such happiness that we want nothing better." This simple yet profound story is a good one for anybody choosing a career, job, or task. There's certainly nothing wrong with working to get money, but there may be something very wrong if you think getting the money gets you happiness.

There once lived, in the Government of Ufa, a Bashkir named Elias. His father, who died a year after he had found his son a wife, did not leave him much property. Elias then had only seven mares, two cows, and about a score of sheep. He was a good manager, however, and soon began to acquire more. He and his wife worked from morn till night; rising earlier than others and going later to bed; and his possessions increased year by year. Living in this way, Elias little by little acquired great wealth. At the end of thirty-five years he had 200 horses, 150 head of cattle, and 1,200 sheep. Hired laborers tended his flocks and herds, and hired women milked his mares and cows, and made kumiss, butter, and cheese. Elias had abundance of everything, and everyone in the district envied him. They said of him:

"Elias is a fortunate man: he has plenty of everything. This world must be a pleasant place for him."

People of position heard of Elias and sought his acquaintance. Visitors came to him from afar; and he welcomed every one, and gave them food and drink. Whoever might come, there was always kumiss, tea, sherbet, and mutton to set before them. Whenever visitors arrived a sheep would be killed, or sometimes two; and if many guests came he would even slaughter a mare for them.

Elias had three children: two sons and a daughter; and he married them all off. While he was poor, his sons worked with him and looked after the flocks and herds themselves; but when he grew rich they got spoiled, and one of them took to drink. The elder was killed in a brawl; and the younger, who had married a self-willed woman, ceased to obey his father, and they could not live together anymore.

So they parted, and Elias gave his son a house and some of the cattle, and this diminished his wealth. Soon after that, a disease broke out among Elias's sheep, and many died. Then followed a bad harvest, and the hay crop failed; and many cattle died that winter. Then the Kirghiz captured his best herd of horses; and Elias's property dwindled away. It became smaller and smaller, while at the same time his strength grew less; till, by the time he was seventy years old, he had begun to sell his furs, carpets, saddles, and tents. At last he had to part with his remaining cattle, and found himself face-to-face with want. Before he knew how it had happened, he had lost everything, and in their old age he and his wife had to go into service. Elias had nothing left, except the clothes on his back, a fur cloak, a cup, his indoor shoes and overshoes, and his wife, Sham-Shemagi, who also by this time was old. The son who had parted from him had gone into a far country, and his daughter was dead, so that there was no one to help the old couple.

Their neighbor, Muhammad-Shah, took pity on them. Muhammad-Shah was neither rich nor poor, but lived comfortably, and was a good man. He remembered Elias's hospitality, and, pitying him, said:

"Come and live with me, Elias, you and your old woman. In summer you can work in my melon garden as much as your strength allows, and in winter feed my cattle; and Sham-Shemagi shall milk my mares and make kumiss. I will feed and clothe you both. When you need anything, tell me, and you shall have it."

Elias thanked his neighbor, and he and his wife took service with Muhammad-Shah as laborers. At first the position seemed hard to them, but they got used to it, and lived on, working as much as their strength allowed.

Muhammad-Shah found it was to his advantage to keep such people, because, having been masters themselves, they knew how to manage and were not lazy, but did all the work they could. Yet it grieved Muhammad-Shah to see people brought so low who had been of such high standing.

It happened once that some of Muhammad-Shah's relatives came from a great distance to visit him, and a Mullah came too. Muhammad-Shah told Elias to catch a sheep and kill it. Elias skinned the sheep and boiled it, and sent it in to the guests. The guests ate the mutton, had some tea, and then began drinking kumiss. As they were sitting with their host on down cushions on a carpet, conversing and sipping kumiss from their cups, Elias, having finished his work, passed by the open door. Muhammad-Shah, seeing him pass, said to one of the guests:

"Did you notice that old man who passed just now?"

"Yes," said the visitor, "what is there remarkable about him?"

"Only this—that he was once the richest man among us," replied the host. "His name is Elias. You may have heard of him."

"Of course I have heard of him," the guest answered. "I never saw him before, but his fame has spread far and wide."

"Yes, and now he has nothing left," said Muhammad-Shah, "and he lives with me as my laborer, and his old woman is here too —she milks the mares."

The guest was astonished: he clicked with his tongue, shook his head, and said:

"Fortune turns like a wheel. One man it lifts, another it sets down! Does not the old man grieve over all he has lost?"

"Who can tell? He lives quietly and peacefully, and works well."

"May I speak to him?" asked the guest. "I should like to ask him about his life."

"Why not?" replied the master, and he called from the kibitka in which they were sitting:

"Babay" (which in the Bashkir tongue means "Grandfather"), "come in and have a cup of kumiss with us, and call your wife here also."

Elias entered with his wife; and after exchanging greetings with his master and the guests, he repeated a prayer and seated himself near the door. His wife passed in behind the curtain and sat down with her mistress.

A cup of kumiss was handed to Elias; he wished the guests and his master good health, bowed, drank a little, and put down the cup.

"Well, Daddy," said the guest who had wished to speak to him, "I suppose you feel rather sad at the sight of us. It must remind you of your former prosperity and of your present sorrows."

Elias smiled, and said:

"If I were to tell you what is happiness and what is misfortune, you would not believe me. You had better ask my wife. She is a woman, and what is in her heart is on her tongue. She will tell you the whole truth."

The guest turned toward the curtain.

"Well, Granny," he cried, "tell me how your former happiness compares with your present misfortune."

And Sham–Shemagi answered from behind the curtain:

"This is what I think about it: My old man and I lived for fifty years seeking happiness and not finding it; and it is only now, these last two years, since we had nothing left and have lived as laborers, that we have found real happiness, and we wish for nothing better than our present lot."

The guests were astonished, and so was the master; he even rose and drew the curtain back, so as to see the old woman's face. There she stood with her arms folded, looking at her old husband, and smiling; and he smiled back at her. The old woman went on:

"I speak the truth and do not jest. For half a century we sought for happiness, and as long as we were rich we never found it. Now that we have nothing left and have taken service as laborers, we have found such happiness that we want nothing better."

"But in what does your happiness consist?" asked the guest.

"Why, in this," she replied, "when we were rich, my husband and I had so many cares that we had no time to talk to one another, or to think of our souls, or to pray to God. Now we had visitors, and had to consider what food to set before them, and what presents to give them, lest they should speak ill of us. When they left we had to look after our laborers, who were always trying to shirk work and get the best food, while we wanted to get all we could out of them. So we sinned. Then we were in fear lest a wolf should kill a foal or a calf, or thieves steal our horses. We lay awake at night worrying lest the ewes should overlie their lambs, and we got up again and again to see that all was well. One thing attended to, another care would spring up: how, for instance, to get enough fodder for the winter. And besides that, my old man and I used to disagree. He would say we must do so and so, and I would differ from him; and then we disputed—sinning again. So we passed from one trouble to another, from one sin to another, and found no happiness."

"Well, and now?"

"Now, when my husband and I wake in the morning we always have a loving word for one another, and we live peacefully having nothing to quarrel about. We have no care but how best to serve our master. We work as much as our strength allows, and do it with a will, that our master may not lose, but profit by us. When we come in, dinner or supper is ready and there is kumiss to drink. We have fuel to burn when it is cold, and we have our fur cloak. And we have time to talk, time to think of our souls, and time to pray. For fifty years we sought happiness, but only now at last have we found it."

The guests laughed.

But Elias said:

"Do not laugh, friends. It is not a matter for jesting—it is the truth of life. We also were foolish at first and wept at the loss of our wealth; but now God has shown us the truth, and we tell it, not for our own consolation, but for your good."

And the Mullah said:

"That is a wise speech. Elias has spoken the exact truth. The same is said in Holy Writ."

And the guests ceased laughing and became thoughtful.

A Psalm of Life

Henry Wadsworth Longfellow

Henry Wadsworth Longfellow said of this poem: "I kept it some time in manuscript, unwilling to show it to anyone, it being a voice from my inmost heart, at a time when I was rallying from depression." The verse reminds us that work is often the best cure for unhappiness. Another great American writer and contemporary of Longfellow, Nathaniel Hawthorne, gives the same prescription in *The Scarlet Letter:* "Preach! Write! Act! Do anything, save to lie down and die!"

Tell me not, in mournful numbers,
  Life is but an empty dream!—
For the soul is dead that slumbers,
  And things are not what they seem.

Life is real! Life is earnest!
  And the grave is not its goal;
Dust thou art, to dust returnest,
  Was not spoken of the soul.

Not enjoyment, and not sorrow,
  Is our destined end or way;
But to act, that each tomorrow
  Find us farther than today.

Art is long, and Time is fleeting,
  And our hearts, though stout and brave,
Still, like muffled drums, are beating
  Funeral marches to the grave.

In the world's broad field of battle,
  In the bivouac of Life,
Be not like dumb, driven cattle!
  Be a hero in the strife!

Trust no Future, howe'er pleasant!
  Let the dead Past bury its dead!
Act—act in the living Present!
  Heart within, and God o'erhead!

Lives of great men all remind us
  We can make our lives sublime,
And, departing, leave behind us
  Footprints on the sands of time;

Footprints, that perhaps another,
  Sailing o'er life's solemn main,
A forlorn and shipwrecked brother,
  Seeing, shall take heart again.

Let us, then, be up and doing,
  With a heart for any fate;
Still achieving, still pursuing,
  Learn to labor and to wait.

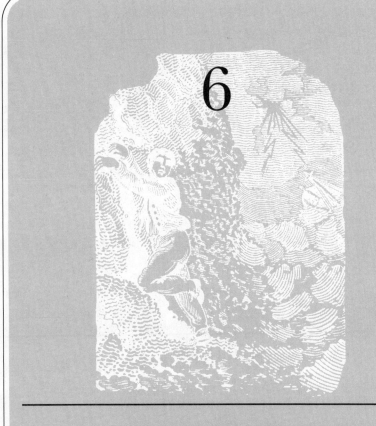

6

Courage

"We become brave by doing brave acts," observed Aristotle in the *Nicomachean Ethics*. Dispositions of character, virtues and vices, are progressively fixed in us through practice. Thus "by being habituated to despise things that are terrible and to stand our ground against them we become brave, and it is when we have become so that we shall be most able to stand our ground against them."

Standing ground against threatening things is not to be confused with fearlessness, however. Being afraid is a perfectly appropriate emotion when confronted with fearful things. The great American novelist Herman Melville makes the Aristotelian point beautifully in a telling passage in *Moby-Dick,* where Starbuck, the chief mate of the *Pequod,* first addresses the crew. " 'I will have no man in my boat,' said Starbuck, 'who is not afraid of a whale.' By this, he seemed to mean, not only that the most reliable and useful courage was that which arises from the fair estimation of the encountered peril, but that an utterly fearless man is a far more dangerous comrade than a coward."

The brave person is not one who is never afraid. That is rather the description of a rash or reckless person, someone who may be more harm than help in an emergency. It is hard to "educate" such a person on the spot. The coward, on the other hand, the one who characteristically lacks confidence and is disposed to be overly fearful, may yet be susceptible to the *encouragement* of example.

The infectious nature of strikingly courageous behavior on the part of one person can inspire—and also in part can shame—a whole group. That was one key to the kind of courage inspired by Horatius at the bridge in ancient Rome and by Henry V at Agincourt. It was one key to the kind of courage displayed by those who silently suffered abuse when they joined ranks with Gandhi and Martin Luther King, Jr., in acts of nonviolent protest directed at rousing the public conscience against injustice.

Another key to their success, of course, was reason: practical reason delivered with the kind of eloquence that is informed by a real command of one's cultural heritage and that steels the will to take intelligent action. The mere inclination to do the right thing is not in itself enough. We have to know what the right thing to do is. We need wisdom—often the wisdom of a wise leader—to give our courage determinate form, to give it intelligent direction. And we need the will, the motivating power that inspiring leaders can sometimes help us discover within ourselves even when we are unable to find it readily on our own.

If Aristotle is right—and I think that he is—then courage is a settled disposition to feel appropriate degrees of fear and confidence in challenging situations (what is "appropriate" varying a good deal with the particular circumstances). It is also a settled disposition to stand one's ground, to advance or to retreat as wisdom dictates. Before such dispositions become settled, however, they need to be established in the first place. And that means practice, which in turn means facing fears and taking stands in advance of any settled disposition to do so: *acting* bravely when we don't really *feel* brave.

Fear of the dark is almost universal among young children, and it provides relatively safe opportunities for first lessons in courage. In families, older siblings are greatly assisted in cultivating their own dispositions in this respect by putting up a brave front before their younger brothers or sisters. "You see? There's really nothing to be afraid of." This is excellent practice, and a fine place to begin. Occasions for being brave on behalf of others—for standing by them in challenging circumstances—are occasions for becoming brave ourselves; that is, for learning how to handle our own confidence and fear, for figuring out the right thing to do, and for mustering the will to do it.

Chicken Little

Mark Twain once said he had known a lot of troubles in his life, and most of them never happened. We imagine many of our fears into existence. To avoid foolish cowardice, refrain from too much mountain-making out of molehills. Courage, said Plato, is *knowing* what to fear.

Chicken Little was in the woods one day when an acorn fell on her head. It scared her so much she trembled all over. She shook so hard, half her feathers fell out.

"Help! Help!" she cried. "The sky is falling! I must go tell the king!" So she ran in great fright to tell the king.

Along the way she met Henny Penny. "Where are you going, Chicken Little?" Henny Penny asked.

"Oh, help!" Chicken Little cried. "The sky is falling!"

"How do you know?" asked Henny Penny.

"Oh! I saw it with my own eyes, and heard it with my own ears, and part of it fell on my head!"

"This is terrible, just terrible!" Henny Penny clucked. "We'd better run." So they both ran away as fast as they could.

Soon they met Ducky Lucky. "Where are you going, Chicken Little and Henny Penny?" he asked.

"The sky is falling! The sky is falling! We're going to tell the king!" they cried.

"How do you know?" asked Ducky Lucky.

"I saw it with my own eyes, and heard it with my own ears, and part of it fell on my head," Chicken Little said.

"Oh dear, oh dear!" Ducky Lucky quacked. "We'd better run!" So they all ran down the road as fast as they could.

Soon they met Goosey Loosey waddling along the roadside.

"Hello there," Chicken Little, Henny Penny, and Ducky Lucky," called Goosey Loosey. "Where are you all going in such a hurry?"

"We're running for our lives!" cried Chicken Little.

"The sky is falling!" clucked Henny Penny.

"And we're running to tell the king!" quacked Ducky Lucky.

"How do you know the sky is falling?" asked Goosey Loosey.

"I saw it with my own eyes, and heard it with my own ears, and part of it fell on my head," Chicken Little said.

"Goodness!" squawked Goosey Loosey. "Then I'd better run with you." And they all ran in great fright across a meadow.

Before long they met Turkey Lurkey strutting back and forth.

"Hello there, Chicken Little, Henny Penny, Ducky Lucky, and Goosey Loosey," he called. "Where are you all going in such a hurry?"

"Help! Help!" cried Chicken Little.

"We're running for our lives!" clucked Henny Penny.

"The sky is falling!" quacked Ducky Lucky.

"And we're running to tell the king!" squawked Goosey Loosey.

"How do you know the sky is falling?" asked Turkey Lurkey.

"I saw it with my own eyes, and heard it with my own ears, and part of it fell on my head," Chicken Little said.

"Oh dear! I always suspected the sky would fall someday," Turkey Lurkey gobbled. "I'd better run with you."

So they all ran with all their might, until they met Foxy Loxy.

"Well, well," said Foxy Loxy. "Where are you rushing on such a fine day?"

"Help! Help!" cried Chicken Little, Henny Penny, Ducky Lucky, Goosey Loosey, and Turkey Lurkey. "It's not a fine day at all. The sky is falling, and we're running to tell the king!"

"How do you know the sky is falling?" said Foxy Loxy.

"I saw it with my own eyes, and heard it with my own ears, and part of it fell on my head," Chicken Little said.

"I see," said Foxy Loxy. "Well then, follow me, and I'll show you the way to the king."

So Foxy Loxy led Chicken Little, Henny Penny, Ducky Lucky, Goosey Loosey, and Turkey Lurkey across a field and through the woods. He led them straight to his den, and they never saw the king to tell him the sky was falling.

The Wee Wee Woman

Retold by James H. Van Sickle and
Wilhelmina Seegmiller

This isn't exactly a spine-tingling tale, but it is designed to make
the listener jump a little, and should be read (or better yet, told)
to children only when they are old enough to enjoy the suspense.
It's an old tale parents have been telling a long time, not just
because it's fun, but because it teaches children that things that
go bump in the night are usually just bumping around inside our
own heads. It also reminds children that fear of "noise in the
night" is a very old and natural thing. It's how you react to it
that matters.

Once upon a time there was a wee wee woman, who lived in a
wee wee house.

One night, when she was in her wee wee bed, she heard a noise!
So she crept out of bed and lighted her wee wee candle.

She looked under her wee wee bed. She looked under her wee
wee table. She looked under her wee wee chair.

There was nothing there.

So she blew out her wee wee candle and crept back into her wee
wee bed.

The wee wee woman closed her eyes. She was just going to
sleep, when—she heard a noise!

So she crept out of her wee wee bed and lighted her wee wee
candle and crept down her wee wee stairs.

She went into her wee wee sitting room. She looked under her
wee wee table. She looked under her wee wee chairs.

There was nothing there.

So she crept up her wee wee stairs. She blew out her wee wee
candle. She crept into her wee wee bed.

The wee wee woman closed her eyes. She was just going to
sleep, when—she heard a noise!

She crept out of bed. She lighted her candle. She crept down
stairs. She went into her wee wee dining room. She crept to the
table. She lifted the cloth. She peeped under. And out popped—
BOO!

"Well, well," said the wee wee woman, "think of that! To be frightened by nothing but boo!"

How the Little Kite Learned to Fly

It's amazing how much of the world's virtue comes from one little word: "Try." Trying something for the first time often calls for bravery. "Try, try again," on the other hand, requires that sibling virtue: perseverance (see "The Little Steam Engine").

"I never can do it," the little kite said,
As he looked around at the others high over his
    head.
"I know I should fall if I tried to fly."
"Try," said the big kite, "only try!
Or I fear you never will learn at all."
But the little kite said, "I'm afraid I'll fall."

The big kite nodded: "Ah well, goodbye;
I'm off," and he rose toward the tranquil sky.
Then the little kite's paper stirred at the sight,
And trembling he shook himself free for flight.
First whirling and frightened, then braver grown,
Up, up he rose through the air alone,
Till the big kite looking down could see
The little one rising steadily.

Then how the little kite thrilled with pride,
As he sailed with the big kite side by side!
While far below he could see the ground,
And the boys like small spots moving round.
They rested high in the quiet air,
And only the birds and the clouds were there.
"Oh, how happy I am!" the little kite cried,
"And all because I was brave, and tried."

David and Goliath

Retold by J. Berg Esenwein and Marietta Stockard

This story has it all: the dauntless courage of youth, the thrill of
a terrible giant, the overthrowing of a seemingly invincible warrior by means of a mere child's weapon, and a hero who wins
through the strength of his faith.

Long ago, in the land of Bethlehem, there lived a man named
Jesse, who had eight stalwart sons. The youngest of these sons was
David.

Even as a little lad, David was ruddy, beautiful of countenance,
and strong of body. When his older brothers drove the flocks to the
fields, he ran with them. Each day as he leaped over the hillsides,
listened to the gurgling water in the brooks, and the songs of birds
in the trees, he grew stronger of limb, and more filled with joy and
courage. Sometimes he made songs of the beautiful things he saw
and heard. His eye was keen, his hands strong, and his aim sure.
When he fitted a stone into his sling, he never missed the mark at
which he threw it.

As he grew older, he was given the care of a part of the flocks.
One day as he lay on the hillside keeping watch over his sheep, a
lion rushed out of the woods and seized a lamb. David leaped to his
feet and ran forward. He had no fear in his heart, no thought but to
save the lamb. He sprang upon the lion, seized him by his hairy
head, and with no weapon but the staff in his strong young hands,
he slew him. Another day, a bear came down upon them. Him also,
David slew.

Now, soon after this, the Philistines marshaled their armies and
came across the hills to drive the children of Israel away from their
homes. King Saul gathered his armies and went out to meet them.
David's three oldest brothers went with the king, but David was left
at home to tend the sheep. "Thou art too young; stay in the fields
and keep the flocks safe," they said to David.

Forty days went by, and no news of the battle came; so Jesse
called David to him and said: "Take this food for thy brethren, and
go up to the camp to see how they fare."

David set out early in the morning, and journeyed up to the

hill on which the army was encamped. There was great shouting and the armies were drawn up in battle array when David arrived. He made his way through the ranks and found his brethren. As he stood talking with them, silence fell upon King Saul's army; and there on the hillside opposite stood a great giant. He strode up and down, his armor glittering in the sun. His shield was so heavy that the strongest man in King Saul's army could not have lifted it, and the sword at his side was so great that the strongest arm could not have wielded it.

"It is the great giant, Goliath," David's brethren told him. "Each day he strides over the hill and calls out his challenge to the men of Israel, but no man amongst us dares to stand before him."

"What! Are the men of Israel afraid?" asked David. "Will they let this Philistine defy the armies of the living God? Will no one go forth to meet him?" He turned from one to another, questioning them.

Eliab, David's oldest brother, heard him and was angry. "Thou art naughty and proud of heart," he said. "Thou hast stolen away from home thinking to see a great battle. With whom hast thou left the sheep?"

"The keeper hath charge of them; and our father, Jesse, sent me hither; and my heart is glad that I am come," answered David. "I myself will go forth to meet this giant. The God of Israel will go with me, for I have no fear of Goliath nor of all his hosts!"

The men standing near hastened to the tent of King Saul and told him of David's words.

"Let him stand before me," commanded the king.

When David was brought into his presence, and Saul saw that he was but a youth, he attempted to dissuade him. But David told him how he had slain the lion and the bear with his naked hands. "The Lord who delivered me from them will deliver me out of the hand of this Philistine," he said.

Then King Saul said: "Go, and the Lord go with thee!"

He had his own armor fetched for David, his helmet of brass, his coat of mail, and his own sword. But David said: "I cannot fight with these. I am not skilled in their use." He put them down, for he knew that each man must win his battles with his own weapons.

Then he took his staff in his hand, his shepherd's bag and sling he hung at his side, and he set out from the camp of Israel. He ran lightly down the hillside, and when he came to the brook which ran at the foot of the hill, he stooped, and choosing five smooth stones from the brook, dropped them into his bag.

The army of King Saul upon one hill, and the host of the Philistines upon the other, looked on in silent wonder. The great giant strode toward David, and when Goliath saw that he was but a youth, ruddy and fair of countenance, his anger knew no bounds.

"Am I a dog, that thou comest to me with sticks?" he shouted. "Do the men of Israel make mock of me to send a child against me? Turn back, or I will give thy flesh to the birds of the air and to the beasts of the field!" Then Goliath cursed David in the name of all his gods.

But no fear came to David's heart. He called out bravely: "Thou comest to me with a sword, and with a spear, and with a shield: but I come to thee in the name of the Lord of hosts, the God of the armies of Israel, whom thou hast defied. This day will the Lord deliver thee into mine hands; and I will smite thee, that all the earth may know that there is a God in Israel!"

Then Goliath rushed forward to meet David, and David ran still more swiftly to meet the giant. He put his hand into his bag, and took one of the stones from it. He fitted it into his sling, and his keen eye found the place in the giant's forehead where the helmet joined. He drew his sling, and with all the force of his strong right arm, he hurled the stone.

It whizzed through the air, and struck deep into Goliath's forehead. His huge body tottered—then fell crashing to the ground. As he lay with his face upon the earth, David ran swiftly to his side, drew forth the giant's own sword, and severed his huge head from his body.

When the army of Israel saw this, they rose up with a great shout, and rushed down the hillside to throw themselves upon the frightened Philistines who were fleeing in terror. When they saw their greatest warrior slain by this lad, they fled toward their own land, leaving their tents and all their riches to be spoiled by the men of Israel.

When the battle was ended, King Saul caused David to be brought before him, and he said: "Thou shalt go no more to the house of thy father but thou shalt be as mine own son."

So David stayed in the tents of the king, and at length he was given command over the king's armies. All Israel honored him, and long years after, he was made the king in King Saul's stead.

Jack   and   the   Beanstalk

Adapted from Andrew Lang

After David, Jack is probably our most famous and beloved
giant-slayer. He begins his adventure as a thoughtless boy, but
redeems himself through a bravery that rises from a sense of duty
to his mother. Courage leads upward, and sooner or later we
must all climb our own beanstalks.

Once upon a time there was a poor widow who lived in a little
cottage with her only son, Jack. Jack was a silly, thoughtless boy,
but very kind-hearted.

One morning the old woman told her son to go to the market
and sell their cow. So Jack started out, but on the way he met a
butcher with some beautiful beans in his hand. The butcher told the
boy they were of great value and persuaded the silly lad to swap the
cow for the beans.

Well, of course, when Jack came home with nothing but a handful of beans to show for their cow, his mother shed many a tear. At
that Jack realized his foolishness and felt terrible. "At least," he
thought, "I may as well sow the beans." So he planted them in the
garden and went sadly to bed.

The next day he got up at daybreak and went into the garden.
To his amazement he found that the beans had grown up in the
night, and their stalks climbed up and up like a ladder disappearing
into the clouds!

"It would be easy to climb it," Jack thought.

So he began to climb, and went up and up the stalk until he had
left everything behind—cottage, village, even the church tower. At
last he reached the top and found himself in a beautiful country,
finely wooded, with lush meadows covered with sheep. A crystal
stream ran through the pastures, and nearby stood a fine, strong
castle. While he was standing looking at it, an ancient lady came
walking along.

"If you please, ma'am," said Jack, "is this your house?"

"No," said the old lady. "That is the castle of a wicked giant
who keeps wonderful treasures inside. It is said that someday a
young lad will come from the valley below to challenge the giant

and win the treasures for his poor mother. Perhaps you are the one. But the task is very difficult and full of peril. Have you the courage to undertake it?"

"I fear nothing when I am doing right," said Jack.

"Then," said the old lady, "you are one of those who slay giants. If you can get into the castle, you may find a hen that lays golden eggs, and a harp that talks, as well as two bags full of gold. If you can get them, they will be a great comfort to your poor mother."

So Jack marched forward and knocked at the castle gate. The door was opened in a minute or two by a frightful giantess, with one great eye in the middle of her forehead. At once she grabbed Jack and dragged him inside.

"Ho, ho!" she laughed terribly. "I've been needing somebody to clean the knives, and shine the boots, and make the fires. You will be my servant. But I must hide you whenever the giant is home, for he has eaten up all my other servants, and you would be a dainty morsel too, my lad."

Well, Jack was very much frightened, as you can imagine, but he struggled to be brave and make the best of things.

"I am quite ready to serve you," he said, "only I beg you to hide me from your husband, for I should not like to be eaten at all."

"That's a good boy," said the giantess. "It is lucky you did not scream when you saw me, or he would have heard you and eaten you for supper, as he has done with so many others. Come here, child. Go into my closet. He never looks in there, and you will be safe."

She opened a huge door that stood in the great hall, and shut him in. But the keyhole was so large that it admitted plenty of air, and he could see everything that took place through it. By and by he heard a heavy tramp on the stairs, like the lumbering along of a great cannon, and then a voice like thunder cried out:

> Fe, fi, fo, fum,
> I smell the blood of an Englishman.
> Be he alive or be he dead,
> I'll grind his bones to make my bread.

"Wife," cried the giant, "there is a man in the castle. Let me have him for supper."

"You have grown old and stupid," said the lady in her loud tones. "You smell only the dinner I have cooked for you. There, sit down and have a good supper."

So the giant sat down at his table. Jack watched him through the keyhole and was amazed to see him swallow a whole roast pig in one bite. Then he drank a whole barrel of ale in one gulp.

When the supper was ended he asked his wife to bring him his hen that laid the golden eggs. The giantess went away, and soon returned with a little brown hen, which she placed on the table before her husband.

"Lay!" said the giant, and instantly the hen laid a golden egg.

"Lay!" said the giant, and she laid another.

"Lay!" he repeated, and again a golden egg appeared on the table.

After a while he put the hen down on the floor, and called on his wife to bring him his moneybags. The giantess went and soon returned with two large bags over her shoulders, which she set down by her husband. The giant took out heaps and heaps of golden pieces, and counted them, and put them in piles, till he was tired of the amusement. Then he swept them all back into their bags.

"I think I will take a nap," he said to his wife. "But first, bring me my harp, for I will have a little music."

So the giantess went away and returned with a beautiful harp. The framework sparkled with diamonds and rubies, and the strings were all of gold.

"Play!" said the giant, and the harp played a very soft, sad song.

"Play something merrier!" said the giant, and the harp played a merry tune.

"Now play me a lullaby," roared the giant. The harp played a sweet lullaby, and its master fell asleep.

Jack stole softly out of the closet and peeped into the huge kitchen to make sure the giantess was not looking. Then he crept up to the giant's chair and quietly gathered the bags of money, and the wonderful hen, and finally the magic harp. Then he ran as fast as he could—but just as he got to the door, the harp called out, "Master! Master!"

And the giant woke up!

With a tremendous roar he sprang from his seat, and in two strides he reached the door.

Jack was very nimble and fled like lightning. The giant came on fast and stretched out his great hand to catch the boy. But Jack darted away, and ran for the top of the beanstalk, and climbed down through the clouds as fast as his feet would move.

He gave a great sigh of relief when he reached his own garden, only to look up and behold the giant climbing down after him!

"Mother! Mother!" cried Jack. "Make haste and bring me the ax!"

His mother ran to him with a hatchet, and Jack began to chop away. But the giant was getting closer and closer.

"Mother, stand out of the way!" Jack yelled. With one last blow he cut the tree stem through and jumped back from the spot.

Down came the giant with a terrible crash, and broke his neck, and stretched dead from one end of the garden to the other.

Well, of course, Jack's poor old mother was scared out of her wits, for it wasn't every day that a giant came crashing down in her garden. But Jack told her all about his adventure, and showed her the bags of money, and how the wonderful hen could lay golden eggs, and how the magic harp could play and sing.

Jack's mother was glad to have such treasures. But she was even more grateful to have her son back safe and sound, and proud of him for his courage.

"Yesterday I worried that you were only a foolish and thoughtless boy," she said. "But today you've shown how brave you can be. Now I know you are destined to climb the ladder of fortune, just as you climbed the beanstalk."

So together they buried the wicked giant and then went inside to count their blessings.

Hansel and Gretel

Adapted from the Brothers Grimm

This universally loved tale reminds us that brothers and sisters must rely on each other for the courage and strength to find their way out of danger's woods.

Near a forest there lived a woodcutter and his wife and two children, a little boy named Hansel and a little girl named Gretel. They were so poor they had very little to eat, and the woodcutter could not stop worrying about how to feed his children.

"What will become of them?" he asked his wife one night. "We have barely enough food to last the week."

"I will tell you," answered the wife, who was the children's stepmother, and a wicked woman. "Early in the morning we will give them each a loaf of bread, and we will lead them into the forest where it is thickest, and leave them alone. They will never find their way home again, and will have to learn to fend for themselves."

"I cannot do that," cried the woodcutter. "It would break my heart to leave them alone in the wilderness."

"Oh, you fool," said the wife, "then they will starve, for we have no food to give them. They stand a better chance in the woods, where perhaps a stranger will find them and take pity on them. If you cannot do it, I will."

So at last the husband consented, and the wife decided to set out at sunrise. But the two little children had not been able to sleep for hunger, and they overheard what their stepmother said.

"Don't be afraid," Hansel told his sister. "I have an idea to help us find our way home again."

Early the next morning the wife came and pulled the children out of bed, saying, "Get up, you lazybones; we are going into the forest to cut wood." She gave them each a loaf of bread, and they set off together into the forest.

They walked all morning, twisting and turning through the old trees, deeper and deeper into the woods. But Hansel was careful to walk behind, and every few steps he tore a small piece of bread from his loaf and dropped it on the ground.

At last the stepmother stopped and told the two children to sit on a log and wait for her. Then she disappeared into the forest.

Gretel shared her bread with Hansel, who had dropped all of his to mark their path, and they went to sleep. When they woke it was getting dark, and no one had come to take them home.

"Wait a bit, Gretel, until the moon gets up," Hansel said, "and then we will be able to find our way back by following the crumbs."

So when the moon rose they got up, but all the bread crumbs were gone! The birds of the woods and fields had picked them up, and now the children were truly lost.

They tried to find their way home but only went round and

round in circles. They walked through the night and into the next morning, finding berries to eat now and then. At last, just when they were ready to give up, they came upon a little cottage in the woods. When they came nearer they saw it was built of gingerbread, and its roof was made of cakes, and its window of sugar!

"We will have some of this!" Hansel cried. "I will eat a piece of the roof, Gretel, and you can have some of the window."

So Hansel reached up and broke off a bit of the roof, just to see how it tasted, and Gretel stood by the window and gnawed at it. Then they heard a thin voice call out from inside:

> Nibble, nibble, like a mouse,
> Who is nibbling at my house?

The door opened and an old woman came out, leaning on a crutch. Hansel and Gretel were very frightened and dropped what they had in their hands.

The old woman, however, nodded her head and said, "Ah, my dear children, how came you here? You must come indoors and stay with me, and you will be safe."

So she took them each by the hand, and led them into her little cottage, and fed them milk and pancakes with sugar, apples, and nuts. After that she showed them two little white beds, and Hansel and Gretel went to sleep and thought they were in heaven.

But the old woman was really a wicked witch who had built the gingerbread house in the woods to trap little children, and then she would eat them!

Early in the morning, before Hansel and Gretel were awake, she got up to look at them, and as they lay sleeping so peacefully with round rosy cheeks, she said to herself, "What a fine feast I shall have!"

Then she grasped Hansel with her withered hand, led him to the stable, and shut him in; call and scream as he might, it was no use. Then she went back to Gretel and shook her, crying, "Get up, lazybones! Fetch water and cook something nice for your brother. He is outside in the stable and must be fattened up. And when he is fat enough, I will eat him!"

Gretel wept bitterly, but it was no use. She had to do what the wicked witch told her. And so the best foods were cooked for poor Hansel, while Gretel got nothing but crab shells.

Each morning the old woman visited the stable and cried, "Stick out your finger, little boy, so I can feel it and tell if you are fat enough to eat."

Hansel, however, would hold out a little chicken bone, and the old woman, who had weak eyes, could not see what it was. She felt it and wondered why he was not getting fatter. When four weeks had passed and he seemed to remain so thin, she lost patience.

"Now then, Gretel," she cried, "be quick and draw some water. Be Hansel fat or be he lean, I must kill and cook him."

Poor little Gretel trembled with grief, but she knew that now was the time to find her courage.

"I must be brave," she told herself. "The only way I can save Hansel is to keep my wits about me and watch for my chance."

The old lady, meanwhile, had built a fire, and flames were leaping out of the oven.

"Creep in," she said, "and see if it is hot enough."

But Gretel saw that the witch meant to shut the oven door upon her, and let her be baked. So she said, "I don't know how to do it. How shall I get in?"

"Stupid goose," said the old woman, "the opening is big enough, do you see? I could get in myself!" She stooped to put her head in the oven's mouth, and Gretel suddenly gave her a push, so that she went in all the way, and shut the iron door upon her! Then Gretel ran outside and opened the stable door.

"Hansel, we are free!" she cried. "The wicked old witch is dead!"

Out flew Hansel like a bird from its cage, and they danced about and kissed each other! Then they searched the old witch's house, and in every corner found pearls and precious stones.

"Now, away we go," said Hansel, filling his pockets, "if only we can get out of the witch's woods."

When they had journeyed a few hours they came to a lake.

"We can never get across this," said Hansel.

"Here comes a white duck," said Gretel. "Perhaps she will help us over." So she cried:

> Duck, duck, here we stand,
> Hansel and Gretel, on the land,
> Stepping-stones and bridge we lack,
> Carry us over on your nice white back.

So the duck carried them over, and after that they went on happily, until they finally saw their father's house. They ran till they reached it, rushed through the door, and fell on their father's neck.

The poor man had not spent a happy hour since he had lost his children. His wicked wife had died, and he had wandered for days through the woods, trying to find his little boy and precious girl.

Then Hansel emptied his pockets, and the pearls and precious stones were scattered all over the floor. So all their cares were at an end, and they lived happily ever after.

The Brave Mice

Aesop

Saying you'll do something may take one kind of courage, but actually doing it requires a different type. Real bravery lies in deeds, not words.

An old cat was in the habit of catching all the mice in the barn.

One day the mice met to talk about the great harm that she was doing them. Each one told of some plan by which to keep out of her way.

"Do as I say," said an old gray mouse that was thought to be very wise. "Do as I say. Hang a bell to the cat's neck. Then, when we hear it ring, we shall know that she is coming, and can scamper out of her way."

"Good! good!" said all the other mice, and one ran to get the bell.

"Now which of you will hang this bell on the cat's neck?" said the old gray mouse.

"Not I! Not I!" said all the mice together. And they scampered away to their holes.

Chanticleer and Partlet

Retold by J. Berg Esenwein and Marietta Stockard

This story comes from the "Nun's Priest's Tale," one of Chaucer's *Canterbury Tales*. It reminds us that there is such a thing as false courage, which may rise from our own vanity. There are some dangers we should rightly fear, and we shouldn't be embarrassed about a proper wariness of them.

Once there was a barnyard close to a wood, in a little valley. Here dwelt a cock, Chanticleer by name. His comb was redder than coral, his feathers were like burnished gold, and his voice was wonderful to hear. Long before dawn each morning his crowing sounded over the valley, and his seven wives listened in admiration.

One night as he sat on the perch by the side of Dame Partlet, his most loved mate, he began to make a curious noise in his throat.

"What is it, my dear?" said Dame Partlet. "You sound frightened."

"Oh!" said Chanticleer, "I had the most horrible dream. I thought that as I roamed down by the wood a beast like a dog sprang out and seized me. His color was red, his nose was small, and his eyes were like coals of fire. Ugh! It was fearful!"

"Tut, tut! Are you a coward to be frightened by a dream? You've been eating more than was good for you. I wish my husband to be wise and brave if he would keep my love!" Dame Partlet clucked, as she smoothed her feathers, and slowly closed her scarlet eyes. She felt disgusted at having her sleep disturbed.

"Of course you are right, my love, yet I have heard of many dreams which came true. I am sure I shall meet with some misfortune, but we will not talk of it now. I am quite happy to be here by your side. You are very beautiful, my dear!"

Dame Partlet unclosed one eye slowly and made a pleased sound, deep in her throat.

The next morning, Chanticleer flew down from the perch and called his hens about him for their breakfast. He walked about boldly, calling, "Chuck! chuck!" at each grain of corn which he found. He felt very proud as they all looked at him so admiringly. He strutted about in the sunlight, flapping his wings to show off his feathers, and now and then throwing back his head and crowing exultantly. His dream was forgotten; there was no fear in his heart.

Now all this time, Reynard, the fox, was lying hidden in the bushes on the edge of the wood bordering the barnyard. Chanticleer walked nearer and nearer his hiding place. Suddenly he saw a butterfly in the grass, and as he stooped toward it, he spied the fox.

"Cok! cok!" he cried in terror, and turned to flee.

"Dear friend, why do you go?" said Reynard in his gentlest voice. "I only crept down here to hear you sing. Your voice is like an angel's. Your father and mother once visited my house. I should so love to see you there too. I wonder if you remember your father's singing? I can see him now as he stood on tiptoe, stretching out his long slender neck, sending out his glorious voice. He always flapped his wings and closed his eyes before he sang. Do you do it in the same way? Won't you sing just once and let me hear you? I am so anxious to know if you really sing better than your father."

Chanticleer was so pleased with this flattery that he flapped his wings, stood up on tiptoe, shut his eyes and crowed as loudly as he could.

No sooner had he begun then Reynard sprang forward, caught him by the throat, threw him over his shoulder, and made off toward his den in the woods.

The hens made a loud outcry when they saw Chanticleer being carried off, so that the people in the cottage nearby heard and ran out after the fox. The dog heard and ran yelping after him. The cow ran, the calf ran, the pigs began to squeal and run too. The ducks and geese quacked in terror and flew up into the treetops. Never was there heard such an uproar. Reynard began to feel a bit frightened himself.

"How swiftly you do run!" said Chanticleer from his back. "If I were you I should have some sport out of those slow fellows who are trying to catch you. Call out to them and say, 'Why do you creep along like snails? Look! I am far ahead of you and shall soon be feasting on this cock in spite of all of you!'"

Reynard was pleased at this and opened his mouth to call to his pursuers; but as soon as he did so, the cock flew away from him and perched up in a tree safely out of reach.

The fox saw he had lost his prey and began his old tricks again. "I was only proving to you how important you are in the barnyard.

See what a commotion we caused! I did not mean to frighten you. Come down now and we will go along together to my home. I have something very interesting to show you there."

"No, no," said Chanticleer. "You will not catch me again. A man who shuts his eyes when he ought to be looking deserves to lose his sight entirely."

By this time, Chanticleer's friends were drawing near, so Reynard turned to flee. "The man who talks when he should be silent deserves to lose what he has gained," he said as he sped away through the wood.

The Leopard's Revenge

Courage involves knowing what to fear, but that in itself is not enough, as this African folktale reminds us. The father leopard of this story may be circumspect, but his taking revenge on a weaker, innocent party is hardly courageous.

Once a leopard cub strayed from his home and ventured into the midst of a great herd of elephants. His mother and father had warned him to stay out of the way of the giant beasts, but he did not listen. Suddenly, the elephants began to stampede, and one of them stepped on the cub without even knowing it. Soon afterward, a hyena found his body and went to tell his parents.

"I have terrible news," he said. "I've found your son lying dead in the field."

The mother and father leopard gave great cries of grief and rage.

"How did it happen?" the father demanded. "Tell me who did this to our son! I will never rest until I have my revenge!"

"The elephants did it," answered the hyena.

"The elephants?" asked the father leopard, quite startled. "You say it was the elephants?"

"Yes," said the hyena, "I saw their tracks."

The leopard paced back and forth for a few minutes, growling and shaking his head.

"No, you are wrong," he said at last. "It was not the elephants. It was the goats. The goats have murdered my boy!"

And at once he bounded down the hill and sprang upon a herd of goats grazing in the valley below, and in a violent rage killed as many as he could in revenge.

Our Heroes

Phoebe Cary

Seeing what is right and doing it with firm resolve, despite the opinions of the crowd, is the mark of moral courage.

Here's a hand to the boy who has courage
    To do what he knows to be right;
When he falls in the way of temptation,
    He has a hard battle to fight.
Who strives against self and his comrades
    Will find a most powerful foe.
All honor to him if he conquers.
    A cheer for the boy who says "NO!"

There's many a battle fought daily
    The world knows nothing about;
There's many a brave little soldier
    Whose strength puts a legion to rout.
And he who fights sin singlehanded
    Is more of a hero, I say,
Than he who leads soldiers to battle
    And conquers by arms in the fray.

Be steadfast, my boy, when you're tempted,
    To do what you know to be right.
Stand firm by the colors of manhood,
    And you will o'ercome in the fight.
"The right," be your battle cry ever
    In waging the warfare of life,
And God, who knows who are the heroes,
    Will give you the strength for the strife.

The Minotaur

Adapted from Andrew Lang

The Greek myth of the thread leading Theseus through King
Minos's labyrinth is a story of compassion guiding courage.
There are two heroes here: Theseus, who ventures into the maze
to save his fellow Athenians, and Ariadne, who searches her heart
and realizes she must defy her own father in order to save the
doomed Athenians from a cruel fate. Conscience is the root of
real courage.

This story begins in Athens, one of the greatest and most noble
cities of ancient Greece. At the time it takes place, however, Athens
was only a little town, perched on the top of a cliff rising out of the
plain, two or three miles from the sea. King Aegeus, who ruled
Athens in those days, had just welcomed home a son he had not seen
since the child's birth, a youth name Theseus, who was destined to
become one of Greece's greatest heroes.

Aegeus was overjoyed at having his son home at last, but Theseus could not help but notice moments when the king seemed distracted and sad. Gradually, Theseus began to sense the same
melancholy among the people of Athens. Mothers were silent, fathers shook their heads, and young people watched the sea all day,
as if they expected something fearful to come from it. Many of the
Athenian youth seemed to be missing, and were said to have gone
to visit friends in faraway parts of Greece. At last Theseus decided
to ask his father what troubled the land.

"I'm afraid you've come home at an unhappy time," Aegeus
sighed. "There is a curse upon Athens, a curse so terrible and strange
that not even you, Prince Theseus, can deal with it."

"Tell me all," said Theseus, "for though I am but one man, yet
the ever-living gods protect me and help me."

"The trouble is an old one," Aegeus said. "It dates to a time
when young men came to Athens from all over Greece and other
lands to take part in contests in running, boxing, wrestling, and foot
races. The son of the great Minos, king of Crete, was among the
contestants, and he died while he was here. His death is still a puzzle

to me. Some say it was an accident; others say he was murdered by jealous rivals. At any rate, his comrades fled in the night, bearing the news to Crete.

"The sea was black with King Midas's ships when he arrived seeking vengeance. His army was far too powerful for us. We went humbly out of the city to meet him and ask for mercy. 'This is the mercy I will show you,' he said. 'I will not burn your city, I will not take your treasures, and I will not make your people my captives. But every seven years, you must pay a tribute. You must swear to choose by lot seven youths and seven maidens, and send them to me.' We had no choice but to agree. Every seven years, a ship with black sails arrives from Crete and bears away the captives. This is the seventh year, and the coming of the ship is at hand."

"And what happens to them once they reach Crete?" Theseus asked.

"We do not know, because they never return. But the sailors of Minos say he places them in a strange prison, a kind of maze, called the Labyrinth. It is full of dark winding ways, cut in the solid rock, and therein lives a horrible monster called the Minotaur. This monster has the body of a man, but his head is the head of a bull, and his teeth are the teeth of a lion, and he devours everyone he meets. That, I fear, is the fate of our Athenian youth."

"We could burn the black-sailed ship when it arrives, and slay its sailors," Theseus said.

"Yes, we could," answered Aegeus, "but then Minos would return with his fleet and his army, and destroy all of Athens."

"Then let me go as one of the captives," said Theseus, rising to his feet, "and I will slay the Minotaur. I am your son and heir, and it is only right that I try to free Athens of this awful curse."

Aegeus tried to persuade his son that such a plan was useless, but Theseus was determined, and when the ship with black sails touched the shore, he joined the doomed group. His father came to tell him goodbye for the last time, weeping bitterly.

"If you do manage to come back alive," he said to Theseus, "lower the black sails as you approach, and hoist white sails in their place, so that I may know you did not die in the Labyrinth."

"Do not worry," Theseus told him. "Look for white sails. I will return in triumph." As he spoke, the dark ship put to sea, and soon sailed past the horizon.

After many days' sailing, the ship reached Crete. The Athenian prisoners were marched to the palace, where King Minos sat on his gilded throne, surrounded by his chiefs and princes, all gloriously clothed in silken robes and jewels of gold. Minos, a dark-faced man, with touches of white in his hair and long beard, sat with his elbow on his knee, and his chin in his hand, and he fixed his eyes on the eyes of Theseus. Theseus bowed and then stood erect, with his eyes on the eyes of Minos.

"You are fifteen in number," Minos said at last, "and my law claims only fourteen."

"I came of my own will," answered Theseus.

"Why?" asked Minos.

"The people of Athens have a mind to be free, O King."

"There is a way," said Minos. "Slay the Minotaur, and you are free of my tribute."

"I am minded to slay him," said Theseus, and as he spoke, there was a stir in the throng of chiefs and princes, and a beautiful young woman glided through them, and stood a little behind the throne. This was Ariadne, the daughter of Minos, a wise and tender-hearted maiden. Theseus bowed low, and again stood erect, with his eyes on the face of Ariadne.

"You speak like a king's son," Minos said with a smile. "Perhaps one who has never known hardship."

"I have known hardship, and my name is Theseus, Aegeus's son. I have come to ask you to let me face the Minotaur alone. If I cannot slay it, my companions will follow me into the Labyrinth."

"I see," Minos said. "Very well. The king's son wishes to die alone. Let him do so."

The Athenians were led upstairs and along galleries, each to a chamber more rich and beautiful than they had seen before in their dreams. Each was taken to a bath, and washed and clothed in new garments, and then treated to a lavish feast. None had the appetite to eat, though, except Theseus, who knew he would need his strength.

That night, as he was preparing for bed, Theseus heard a soft knock at his door, and suddenly Ariadne, the king's daughter, was standing in his room. Once again Theseus gazed into her eyes, and saw there a kind of strength and compassion he had never known before.

"Too many of your countrymen have disappeared into my father's Labyrinth," she said quietly. "I have brought you a dagger, and I can show you and your friends the way to flee."

"I thank you for the dagger," Theseus answered, "but I cannot flee. If you wish to show me a way, show me the way to the Minotaur."

"Even if you are strong enough to kill the monster," Ariadne whispered, "you will need to find your way out of the Labyrinth. It is made of so many dark twists and turns, so many dead ends and false passages, not even my father knows the secrets of its windings. If you are determined to go forward with your plan, you must take this with you." She took from her gown a spool of gold thread, and pressed it into Theseus's hand.

"As soon as you get inside the Labyrinth," she said, "tie the end of the thread to a stone, and hold tight to the spool as you wander through the maze. When you are ready to come back, the thread will be your guide."

Theseus gazed at her, hardly knowing what to say. "Why are you doing this?" he finally asked. "If your father finds out, you'll be in great danger."

"Yes," Ariadne answered slowly, "but if I had not acted, you and your friends would be in far greater danger."

And Theseus knew then that he loved her.

The next morning Theseus was led to the Labyrinth. As soon as the guards shut him inside, he fastened one end of the thread to a pointed rock, and began to walk slowly, keeping firm hold of the precious string. He made his way down the broadest corridor, from which others turned off to the right and left, until he came to a wall. He retraced his steps, and tried another hallway, and then another, always stopping every few feet to listen for the monster. He passed through many dark, winding passages, sometimes coming to places he had already been before, but gradually descending further and further into the Labyrinth. Finally he reached a room heaped high with bones, and he knew now he was very near the beast.

He sat still, and from far away he heard a faint sound, like the end of the echo of a roar. He stood up and listened keenly. The sound came nearer and louder, not deep like the roar of a bull, but more shrill and thin. Theseus stooped quickly and scooped up a handful of dirt from the floor of the Labyrinth, and with his other hand drew his dagger.

The roars of the Minotaur came nearer and nearer. Now his feet could be heard thudding along the echoing floor. There was a heavy rustling, then sniffing, then silence. Theseus moved to the shadowy corner of the narrow path and crouched there. His heart was beating quickly. On came the Minotaur—it caught sight of the crouching figure, gave a great roar, and rushed straight for it. Theseus leaped up and, dodging to one side, dashed his handful of dirt into the beast's eyes.

The Minotaur bellowed in pain. It rubbed its eyes with its monstrous hands, shrieking and confused. It tossed its great head up and down, and it turned around and around, feeling with its hands for the wall. It was quite blind. Theseus drew his dagger, crept up behind the monster, and quickly slashed at its legs. Down fell the Minotaur, with a crash and a roar, biting at the rocky floor with its lion's teeth, waving its hands, and clawing at the empty air. Theseus waited for his chance, when the clutching hands rested, and then three times he drove the sharp blade through the heart of the Minotaur. The body leaped, and lay still.

Theseus kneeled and thanked all the gods, and when he had finished his prayer, he took his dagger and hacked off the head of the Minotaur. With the head in his hand, he began following the string out of the Labyrinth. It seemed he would never come out of those dark, gloomy passages. Had the thread snapped somewhere, and had he, after all, lost his way? But still he followed it anxiously, until at last he came to the entrance, and he sank to the ground, worn out with his struggle and his wanderings.

"I don't know what miracle caused you to come out of the Labyrinth alive," Minos said when he saw the monster's head, "but I will keep my word. I promised you freedom if you slew the Minotaur. You and your comrades may go. Now let there be peace between your people and mine. Farewell."

Theseus knew he owed his life and his country's freedom to Ariadne's courage, and he knew he could not leave without her. Some say he asked Minos for her hand in marriage, and that the king gladly consented. Others say she stole onto the departing ship at the last minute without her father's knowledge. Either way, the two lovers were together when the anchor lifted and the dark ship sailed away from Crete.

But this happy ending is mixed with tragedy, as stories sometimes are. For the Cretan captain of the vessel did not know he was to hoist white sails if Theseus came home in triumph, and King Aegeus, as he anxiously watched the waters from a high cliff, spied the black sails coming over the horizon. His heart broke at once, and he fell from the towering cliff into the sea, which is now called the Aegean.

Ulysses and the Cyclops

Retold by Andrew Lang

This story is from the *Odyssey,* Homer's great epic of the Greek king Odysseus's long journey home after the Trojan War. Of all the Greek heroes, Odysseus was the one whose courage was the most rooted in cleverness. Time after time, when others sank into despair, Odysseus instead summoned his own powers of ingenuity. In this retelling of his famous encounter with the Cyclops Polyphemus, he is called by his Roman name, Ulysses.

Ulysses and his ships reached the coast of the land of the Cyclopes, which means the round-eyed men, men with only one eye apiece, set in the middle of their foreheads. They lived not in houses, but in caves among the hills, and they had no king and no laws, and did not plow or sow, but wheat and vines grew wild, and they kept great flocks of sheep.

There was a beautiful wild desert island lying across the opening of a bay; the isle was full of wild goats, and made a bar against the waves, so that ships could lie behind it safely, run up on the beach, for there was no tide in that sea. There Ulysses ran up his ships, and the men passed the time in hunting wild goats, and feasting on fresh meat and wine. Next day, Ulysses left all the ships and men there, except his own ship, and his own crew, and went out to see what kind of people lived on the mainland, for as yet none had been seen. He found a large cave close to the sea, with laurels growing on the rocky roof, and a wall of rough stones built around a court in front. Ulysses left all his men but twelve with the ship; filled a goat skin with strong wine, put some corn flour in a sack, and went up to the cave. Nobody was there, but there were all the things that are usually in a dairy, baskets full of cheese, pails and bowls full of milk and whey, and kids and lambs were playing in their folds.

All seemed very quiet and pleasant. The men wanted to take as much cheese as they could carry back to the ship, but Ulysses wished to see the owner of the cave. His men, making themselves at home, lit a fire, and toasted and ate the cheeses, far within the cave. Then a shadow thrown by the setting sun fell across the opening of the cave, and a monstrous man entered, and threw down a dry trunk of a tree that he carried for firewood. Next he drove in the ewes of his flock, leaving the rams in the yard, and he picked up a huge flat stone, and set it so as to make a shut door to the cave, for twenty-four yoke of horses could not have dragged away that stone. Lastly the man milked his ewes, and put the milk in pails to drink at supper. All this while Ulysses and his men sat quiet and in great fear, for they were shut up in a cave with a one-eyed giant, whose cheese they had been eating.

Then the giant, when he had lit the fire, happened to see the men, and asked them who they were. Ulysses said that they were Greeks, who had taken Troy, and were wandering lost on the seas, and he asked the man to be kind to them in the name of their chief god, Zeus.

"We Cyclopes," said the giant, "do not care for Zeus or the gods, for we think that we are better men than they. Where is your ship?" Ulysses answered that it had been wrecked on the coast, to which the man made no answer, but snatched up two of the twelve, knocked out their brains on the floor, tore the bodies limb from limb, roasted them at his fire, ate them, and, after drinking many pailfuls of milk, lay down and fell asleep. Now Ulysses had a mind to drive his sword-point into the giant's liver, and he felt for the place with his hand. But he remembered that, even if he killed the giant, he could not move the huge stone that was the door of the cave, so he and his men would die of hunger, when they had eaten all the cheeses.

In the morning the giant ate two more men for breakfast, drove out his ewes, and set the great stone in the doorway again, as lightly as a man would put a quiverlid on a quiver of arrows. Then away he went, driving his flock to graze on the green hills.

Ulysses did not give way to despair. The giant had left his stick in the cave: it was as large as the mast of a great ship. From this Ulysses cut a portion six feet long, and his men cut and rubbed as if they were making a spear shaft. Ulysses then sharpened it to a point, and hardened the point in the fire. It was a thick, rounded bar of wood, and the men cast lots to choose four, who should twist the bar in the giant's eye when he feel asleep at night. Back he came at sunset, and drove his flocks in the cave, rams and all. Then he put up his stone door, milked his ewes, and killed two men and cooked them.

Ulysses meanwhile had filled one of the wooden ivy bowls full

of strong wine, without putting a drop of water into it. This bowl
he offered to the giant, who had never heard of wine. He drank one
bowl after another, and when he was merry he said that he would
make Ulysses a present. "What is your name?" he asked. "My name
is *Nobody,*" said Ulysses. "Then I shall eat the others first and Nobody last," said the giant. "That shall be your gift." Then he fell
asleep.

Ulysses took his bar of wood, and made the point red-hot in
the fire. Next his four men rammed it into the giant's one eye, and
held it down, while Ulysses twirled it round, and the eye hissed like
red-hot iron when men dip it into cold water, which is the strength
of iron. The Cyclops roared and leaped to his feet and shouted for
help to the other giants who lived in the neighboring caves. "Who
is troubling you, Polyphemus," they answered. "Why do you wake
us out of our sleep?" The giant answered, "Nobody is killing me by
his cunning, not at all in fair fight." "Then if nobody is harming
you nobody can help you," shouted a giant. "If you are ill, pray to
your father, Poseidon, who is the god of the sea." So the giants all
went back to bed, and Ulysses laughed low to see how his cunning
had deceived them. Then the giant went and took down his door
and sat in the doorway, stretching out his arms, so as to catch his
prisoners as they went out.

But Ulysses had a plan. He fastened sets of three rams together
with twisted vines, and bound a man to each ram in the middle, so
that the blind giant's hands would only feel the two outside rams.
The biggest and strongest ram Ulysses seized, and held on by his
hands and feet to its fleece, under its belly, and then all the sheep
went out through the doorway, and the giant felt them, but did not
know that they were carrying out the men. "Dear ram," he said to
the biggest, which carried Ulysses, "you do not come out first, as
usual, but last, as if you were slow with sorrow for your master,
whose eye Nobody has blinded!"

Then all the rams went out into the open country, and Ulysses
unfastened his men, and drove the sheep down to his ship and so on
board. His crew wept when they heard of the death of six of their
friends, but Ulysses made them row out to sea. When he was just so
far away from the cave as to be within hearing distance he shouted
at the Cyclops and mocked him. Then that giant broke off the rocky
peak of a great hill and threw it in the direction of the sound. The
rock fell in front of the ship, and raised a wave that drove it back to
shore, but Ulysses punted it off with a long pole, and his men rowed

out again, far out. Ulysses again shouted to the giant, "If any one asks who blinded you, say that it was Ulysses, Laertes' son, of Ithaca, the stormer of cities."

Then the giant prayed to the Sea God, his father, that Ulysses might never come home, or if he did, that he might come late and lonely, with loss of all his men, and find sorrow in his house. Then the giant heaved and threw another rock, but it fell at the stern of the ship, and the wave drove the ship farther out to sea.

Horatius at the Bridge

Retold by James Baldwin

The events surrounding the legend of Horatius are said to have taken place at the end of the sixth century B.C., during Rome's struggle against the Etruscans. The English poet and historian Thomas Macaulay retold the story in his *Lays of Ancient Rome,* from which the verses below are taken.

Once there was a war between the Roman people and the Etruscans who lived in the towns on the other side of the Tiber River. Porsena, the King of the Etruscans, raised a great army, and marched toward Rome. The city had never been in so great danger.

The Romans did not have very many fighting men at that time, and they knew that they were not strong enough to meet the Etruscans in open battle. So they kept themselves inside of their walls, and set guards to watch the roads.

One morning the army of Porsena was seen coming over the hills from the north. There were thousands of horsemen and footmen, and they were marching straight toward the wooden bridge which spanned the river at Rome.

"What shall we do?" said the white-haired Fathers who made the laws for the Roman people. "If they gain the bridge, we cannot hinder them from crossing; and then what hope will there be for the town?"

Now, among the guards at the bridge, there was a brave man

named Horatius. He was on the farther side of the river, and when he saw that the Etruscans were so near, he called out to the Romans who were behind him.

> Then out spake brave Horatius,
>   The captain of the gate:
> "To every man upon this earth
>   Death cometh soon or late.
> And how can man die better
>   Than facing fearful odds,
> For the ashes of his fathers
>   And the temple of his gods?

"Hew down the bridge with all the speed that you can!" he cried. "I, with the two men who stand by me, will keep the foe at bay."

Then, with their shields before them, and their long spears in their hands, the three brave men stood in the road, and kept back the horsemen whom Porsena had sent to take the bridge.

On the bridge the Romans hewed away at the beams and posts. Their axes rang, the chips flew fast; and soon it trembled, and was ready to fall.

"Come back! Come back, and save your lives!" they cried to Horatius and the two of who were with him.

But just then Porsena's horsemen dashed toward them again.

"Run for your lives!" said Horatius to his friends. "I will keep the road."

They turned, and ran back across the bridge. They had hardly reached the other side when there was a crashing of beams and timbers. The bridge toppled over to one side, and then fell with a great splash into the water.

When Horatius heard the sound, he knew that the city was safe. With his face still toward Porsena's men, he moved slowly backward till he stood on the river's bank. A dart thrown by one of Porsena's soldiers put out his left eye; but he did not falter. He cast his spear at the foremost horseman, and then he turned quickly around. He saw the white porch of his own home among the trees on the other side of the stream.

> And he spake to the noble river
> That rolls by the walls of Rome:
> "Oh Tiber! Father Tiber!
> To whom the Romans pray,
> A Roman's life, a Roman's arms,
> Take thou in charge today."

He leaped into the deep, swift stream. He still had his heavy armor on; and when he sank out of sight, no one thought that he would ever be seen again. But he was a strong man, and the best swimmer in Rome. The next minute he rose. He was halfway across the river, and safe from the spears and darts which Porsena's soldiers hurled after him.

Soon he reached the farther side, where his friends stood ready to help him. Shout after shout greeted him as he climbed upon the bank. Then Porsena's men shouted also, for they had never seen a man so brave and strong as Horatius. He had kept them out of Rome, but he had done a deed which they could not help but praise.

As for the Romans, they were very grateful to Horatius for having saved their city. They called him Horatius Cocles, which meant the "one-eyed Horatius," because he had lost an eye in defending the bridge; they caused a fine statue of brass to be made in his honor; and they gave him as much land as he could plow around in a day. And for hundreds of years afterward—

> With weeping and with laughter,
> Still was the story told,
> How well Horatius kept the bridge
> In the brave days of old.

The Brave Three Hundred

Adapted from James Baldwin

The famous battle at the narrow Pass of Thermopylae took place in 480 B.C., when Xerxes led a Persian army into Greece. Even though they were defeated at Thermopylae, the Spartans' heroic stand against overwhelming odds inspired the Greeks in later resistance and forever made Sparta's name synonymous with courage.

All of Greece was in danger. A mighty army, led by Xerxes, the great king of Persia, had come from the east. It was marching along the seashore, and in a few days would be in Greece. Xerxes had sent messengers into every city and state, demanding that they send him water and earth as symbols that the land and the sea were his. The Greeks refused, and resolved to defend their freedom against the invaders.

And so there was a great stir throughout all the land. The Greeks armed themselves and hurried to go out and drive back their foe.

There was only one way by which the Persian army could go into Greece on that side, and that was through a narrow pass between the mountains and the sea. It was called the pass at Thermopylae, a word which meant "hot gates" because of the hot springs nearby.

This pass was guarded by Leonidas, the king of the Spartans, with only a few thousand troops. They were greatly outnumbered by the Persian army, but they felt confident. They had positioned themselves in the narrowest part of the pass, where a few men armed with long spears could hold back an entire company.

The first Persian wave of attack started toward the pass at dawn. The Spartan scouts reported that there were so many troops, their arrows would darken the sun like a cloud.

"So much the better," Leonidas said. "We can fight better in the shade."

The arrows came down, but the Greeks' shields deflected them, and their long spears held back the Persians who pressed into the pass. The invaders attacked again and again, but each time they were repulsed with terrible losses. At last Xerxes sent forward his best troops, known as the Ten Thousand Immortals, but even they fared no better against the determined Greeks.

After two days of attacks, Leonidas still held the pass. But that night a man was brought to Xerxes' camp. He was a Greek who knew the local terrain well, and he was ready to sell a secret: the pass was not the only way through. A hunters' footpath wound the long way around, to a trail along the spine of the mountain. It was held by only a handful of Greeks. They could be easily routed, and then Xerxes could attack the Spartan army from the rear.

The treacherous plan worked. The men guarding the secret trail were surprised and beaten. A few managed to escape in time to warn Leonidas.

The Greeks knew that if they did not abandon the pass at once, they would be trapped. But Leonidas also knew he must delay Xerxes longer while the Greek cities prepared their defenses. He made his decision. He ordered almost all of his troops to slip through the mountains and back to their cities, where they would be needed. He kept his royal guard of three hundred Spartans as well as a few other troops, and prepared to defend the pass to the end.

Xerxes and his army came forward. The Spartans stood fast, but one by one they fell. When their spears broke, they stood side by side, fighting with swords or daggers or only their fists.

All day long they kept the Persian army at bay. But when the sun went down, there was not one Spartan left alive. Where they had stood was only a heap of the slain, all bristled over with spears and arrows.

Xerxes had taken the pass, but at a cost of thousands of men and a delay of several days. The time cost him dearly. The Greek navy was able to gather its forces, and soon afterward it managed to drive Xerxes back to Asia.

Many years later a monument was erected at the pass of Thermopylae, inscribed in memory of the courageous stand of a few in defense of their homeland:

> Pause, traveler, ere you go your way. Then tell
> How, Spartan to the last, we fought and fell.

Compensation

Theodosia Garrison

Teddy Roosevelt said that "far better it is to dare mighty things, to win glorious triumphs, even though checkered by failure, than to take rank with those poor spirits who neither enjoy much nor suffer much, because they live in the gray twilight that knows

neither victory nor defeat." This poem reminds us as well that a
mighty heart reaches high.

> Because I craved a gift too great
>   For any prayer of mine to bring,
>   Today with empty hands I go;
>   Yet must my heart rejoice to know
>   I did not ask a lesser thing.
>
> Because the goal I sought lay far
>   In cloud-hid heights, today my soul
>   Goes unaccompanied of its own;
>   Yet this shall comfort me alone,
>   I did not seek a nearer goal.
>
> O gift ungained, O goal unwon!
>   Still am I glad, remembering this,
>   For all I go unsatisfied,
>   I have kept faith with joy denied,
>   Nor cheated life with cheaper bliss.

A Laconic Answer

This story, another famous anecdote about the Spartans' bravery,
is from the time of Philip of Macedon (382–336 B.C.), who forc-
ibly unified most of Greece's cities.

Long ago the people of Greece were not united, as they are
today. Instead there were several cities and states, each with its own
leader. King Philip of Macedon, a land in the northern part of
Greece, wanted to bring all of Greece together under his rule. So he
raised a great army and made war upon the other states, until nearly
all were forced to call him their king. Sparta, however, resisted.

The Spartans lived in the southern part of Greece, an area called
Laconia, and so they were sometimes called Lacons. They were
noted for their simple habits and their bravery. They were also
known as a people who used few words and chose them carefully;
even today a short answer is often described as being "laconic."

Philip knew he must subdue the Spartans if all of Greece was to be his. So he brought his great army to the borders of Laconia, and sent a message to the Spartans.

"If you do not submit at once," he threatened them, "I will invade your country. And if I invade, I will pillage and burn everything you hold dear. If I march into Laconia, I will level your great city to the ground."

In a few days, Philip received an answer. When he opened the letter, he found only one word written there.

That word was "IF."

If—

Rudyard Kipling

Brave men and women (as well as cowardly men and women) are not born that way; they become that way through their acts. Here are the acts that make us not just grow up, but grow up well.

If you can keep your head when all about you
    Are losing theirs and blaming it on you;
If you can trust yourself when all men doubt you,
    But make allowance for their doubting too;
If you can wait and not be tired by waiting,
    Or, being lied about, don't deal in lies,
Or, being hated, don't give way to hating,
    And yet don't look too good, nor talk too wise;

If you can dream—and not make dreams your master;
If you can think—and not make thoughts your aim;
If you can meet with triumph and disaster
    And treat those two impostors just the same;
If you can bear to hear the truth you've spoken
    Twisted by knaves to make a trap for fools,
Or watch the things you gave your life to broken,
    And stoop and build 'em up with worn-out tools;

If you can make one heap of all your winnings
    And risk it on one turn of pitch-and-toss,
And lose, and start again at your beginnings
    And never breathe a word about your loss;
If you can force your heart and nerve and sinew
    To serve your turn long after they are gone,
And so hold on when there is nothing in you
    Except the Will which says to them: "Hold on!"

If you can talk with crowds and keep your virtue,
    Or walk with kings—nor lose the common touch;
If neither foes nor loving friends can hurt you;
    If all men count with you, but none too much;
If you can fill the unforgiving minute
    With sixty seconds' worth of distance run—
Yours is the Earth and everything that's in it,
    And—which is more—you'll be a Man, my son!

Crossing the Rubicon

Adapted from James Baldwin

In Roman days the Rubicon, a stream in north-central Italy, marked the boundary between Italy and Gaul. By law, Roman magistrates could bring armies into Italy only by permission of the Senate. By marching his legions across the Rubicon in 49 B.C., Julius Caesar committed himself to a showdown with Rome itself.

Rome was the most powerful city in the world. The Romans had conquered all the countries on the north side of the Mediterranean Sea and most of those on the south side. They also occupied the islands of the sea and all that part of Asia that now belongs to Turkey.

Julius Caesar had become the hero of Rome. He had led a large army into Gaul, that part of Europe which today includes France,

Belgium, and Switzerland, and turned it into a Roman province. He had crossed the Rhine and subdued a part of Germany. Caesar's army even went into Britain, a wild and remote country to the Romans, and established colonies there.

For nine years Caesar and his army had served Rome loyally and well. But Caesar had many enemies at home, people who feared his ambitions and envied his accomplishments, people who cringed every time they heard Caesar called a great hero.

One of these persons was Pompey, who had long been the most powerful man in Rome. Like Caesar, he was the commander of a great army, but his troops had done very little to win the applause of the people. Pompey saw that, unless something occurred to prevent it, Caesar would in time be his master. He therefore began to lay plans to destroy him.

In another year the time of Caesar's service in Gaul would end. It was understood that he would then return home and be elected consul, or ruler, of the mighty Roman republic. He would then be the most powerful man in the world.

Pompey and other enemies of Caesar were determined to prevent this. They induced the Roman Senate to send a command to Caesar to leave his army in Gaul and come at once to Rome. "If you do not obey this command," said the Senate, "you shall be considered an enemy to the republic."

Caesar knew what that meant. If he went to Rome alone, his enemies would make false accusations against him. They would try him for treason, and keep him from being elected consul.

He called the soldiers of his favorite legion together and told them about the plot that had been made for his ruin. The veterans who had followed him through so many perils, and had helped him win so many victories, declared they would not leave him. They would go with him to Rome and see that he received his due rewards. They would serve without pay, and even share the expenses of the long march.

The troops started toward Italy with flags flying. The soldiers were even more enthusiastic than Caesar himself. They climbed mountains, waded rivers, endured fatigue, faced all kinds of dangers for the sake of their leader.

At last they came to a little river called the Rubicon. It was the boundary line of Caesar's province of Gaul; on the other side lay Italy. Caesar paused a moment on the bank.

He knew that to cross the stream would be to declare war

against Pompey and the Roman Senate. It might involve all Rome in a fearful strife, the end of which no man could foresee.

"We could still go back," he told himself. "Behind us lies safety. But once we cross the Rubicon into Italy, turning around is impossible. I must make the choice here."

He did not hesitate long. He gave the word, and rode boldly across the shallow stream.

"We have crossed the Rubicon!" he cried as he reached the far shore. "There is no turning back."

The news was shouted along the roads and byways leading to Rome: Caesar had crossed the Rubicon! People from every town and village turned out to welcome the returning hero as he marched through the countryside. The closer he drew to Rome, the wilder people celebrated his arrival. Finally Caesar and his army reached the gates of the city. No troops came out to challenge them, and there was no resistance when Caesar marched into the city itself. Pompey and his allies had fled.

For more than two thousand years, men and women facing daring decisions have thought of Caesar at the edge of the stream before they too crossed their Rubicons.

Doors of Daring

Henry van Dyke

Barriers are invitations to courage.

> The mountains that inclose the vale
>   With walls of granite, steep and high,
> Invite the fearless foot to scale
>   Their stairway toward the sky.
>
> The restless, deep, dividing sea
>   That flows and foams from shore to shore,
> Calls to its sunburned chivalry,
>   "Push out, set sail, explore!"

The bars of life at which we fret,
    That seem to prison and control,
Are but the doors of daring, set
    Ajar before the soul.

Say not, "Too poor," but freely give;
    Sigh not, "Too weak," but boldly try;
You never can begin to live
    Until you dare to die.

———————

William Tell

Retold by James Baldwin

This famous story of the legendary Swiss hero William Tell takes
place in the early part of the fourteenth century, during the Swiss
people's struggle for independence from Austrian rule. It is one
of our greatest tales of cool and calm bravery in the face of
bullying tyranny.

The people of Switzerland were not always free and happy as
they are today. Many years ago a proud tyrant, whose name was
Gessler, ruled over them, and made their lot a bitter one indeed.

One day this tyrant set up a tall pole in the public square, and
put his own cap on the top of it; and then he gave orders that every
man who came into the town should bow down before it. But there
was one man, named William Tell, who would not do this. He stood
up straight with folded arms, and laughed at the swinging cap. He
would not bow down to Gessler himself.

When Gessler heard of this, he was very angry. He was afraid
that other men would disobey, and that soon the whole country
would rebel against him. So he made up his mind to punish the bold
man.

William Tell's home was among the mountains, and he was a
famous hunter. No one in all the land could shoot with bow and
arrow so well as he. Gessler knew this, and so he thought of a cruel

plan to make the hunter's own skill bring him to grief. He ordered that Tell's little boy should be made to stand up in the public square with an apple on his head; and then he bade Tell shoot the apple with one of his arrows.

Tell begged the tyrant not to have him make this test of his skill. What if the boy should move? What if the bowman's hand should tremble? What if the arrow should not carry true?

"Will you make me kill my boy?" he said.

"Say no more," said Gessler. "You must hit the apple with your one arrow. If you fail, my soldiers shall kill the boy before your eyes."

Then, without another word, Tell fitted the arrow to his bow. He took aim, and let it fly. The boy stood firm and still. He was not afraid, for he had all faith in his father's skill.

The arrow whistled through the air. It struck the apple fairly in the center, and carried it away. The people who saw it shouted with joy.

As Tell was turning away from the place, an arrow which he had hidden under his coat dropped to the ground.

"Fellow!" cried Gessler, "what mean you with this second arrow?"

"Tyrant!" was Tell's proud answer, "this arrow was for your heart if I had hurt my child."

And there is an old story, that not long after this, Tell did shoot the tyrant with one of his arrows, and thus he set his country free.

Dolley Madison Saves the National Pride

Dorothea Payne Madison

In August 1814, a British army marched on Washington, D.C., thinking that by burning the American capital it could bring an end to the War of 1812. Panic reigned in the city as the red-coated columns approached. Many public records, including the Declaration of Independence, had already been stuffed into linen bags and carted off to Virginia, where they were piled up in a vacant house. Now the roads leading out of town began to fill with fleeing American soldiers and statesmen as well as wagons loaded with families and their valuables.

Dolley Madison, wife of the fourth president, calmly directed evacuation details at the White House. A large portrait of George Washington by Gilbert Stuart hung in the dining room. It would be an unbearable disgrace if it fell into British hands. Mrs. Madison ordered the doorkeeper and gardener to bring it along, but the huge frame was screwed so tightly to the wall that no one could get it down. Minutes ticked by as they tugged and pulled. At last someone found an ax. They chopped the frame apart, removed the canvas, and sent it off for safekeeping. Soon afterward the British entered the District of Columbia, setting fire to the Capitol and the White House.

The rescue of Washington's portrait quickly took its place as one of Americans' most cherished acts of heroism. This letter, written by Dolley to her sister, Anna, even as the city fell, speaks to us of unflinching courage and levelheadedness amid chaos and retreat.

Tuesday, August 23, 1814

Dear Sister:

My husband left me yesterday morning to join General Winder. He inquired anxiously whether I had courage or firmness to remain in the President's house until his return on the morrow, or succeeding day, and on my assurance that I had no fear but for him, and the success of our army, he left, beseeching me to take care of myself, and of the Cabinet papers, public and private. I have since received two dispatches from him, written with a pencil. The last is alarming, because he desires I should be ready at a moment's warning to enter my carriage, and leave the city; that the enemy seemed stronger than had at first been reported, and it might happen that they would reach the city with the intention of destroying it. I am accordingly ready; I have pressed as many Cabinet papers into trunks as to fill one carriage; our private property must be sacrificed, as it is impossible to procure wagons for its transportation.

I am determined not to go myself until I see Mr. Madison safe, so that he can accompany me, as I hear of much hostility toward him. Disaffection stalks around us. My friends and acquaintances are all gone, even Colonel C. with his hundred, who were stationed as a guard in this enclosure. French John [a faithful servant], with his usual activity and resolution, offers to spike the cannon at the gate, and lay a train of powder, which would blow up the British, should they enter the house. To this last proposition I positively object, without being able to make him understand why all advantages in war may not be taken.

Wednesday morning, twelve o'clock. Since sunrise I have been turning my spy-glass in every direction, and watching with unwearied anxiety, hoping to discover the approach of my dear husband and his friends; but, alas! I can descry only groups of military, wandering in all directions, as if there was a lack of arms, or of spirit to fight for their own fireside.

Three o'clock. Will you believe it, my sister? we have had a battle, or skirmish, near Bladensburg, and here I am still, within sound of the cannon! Mr. Madison comes not. May God protect us! Two messengers, covered with dust, come to bid me fly; but here I mean to wait for him. . . . At this late hour a wagon has been procured, and I have had it filled with plate and the most valuable portable articles, belonging to the house. Whether it will reach its destination, the "Bank of Maryland," or fall into the hands of British soldiery, events must determine. Our kind friend, Mr. Carroll, has come to hasten my departure, and in a very bad humor with me, because I insist on waiting until the large picture of General Washington is secured, and it requires to be unscrewed from the wall. This process was found too tedious for these perilous moments; I have ordered the frame to be broken, and the canvas taken out. It is done! and the precious portrait placed in the hands of two gentlemen of New York, for safekeeping. And now, dear sister, I must leave this house, or the retreating army will make me a prisoner of it by filling up the road I am directed to take. When I shall again write to you, or where I shall be tomorrow, I cannot tell!

Dolley

An Appeal from the Alamo

William Barret Travis

The Alamo in San Antonio, Texas, has become an American symbol of unyielding courage and self-sacrifice. A force of Texans captured the mission fort in late 1835 after the outbreak of revolution against the dictatorship of Mexican General Antonio López de Santa Anna. By early 1836, Lieutenant Colonel William Barret Travis and the fort's garrison found themselves hemmed in by a Mexican army swelling to six thousand troops. On February 24, Travis dispatched couriers to nearby Texas towns, carrying frantic appeals for aid. Fewer than three dozen men picked their way through enemy lines to join the Alamo's defenders. The siege continued until March 6, when Santa Anna's forces overwhelmed the fort. The entire garrison was killed, some 180 men, including Colonel Travis, James Bowie, and Davy Crockett.

COMMANDANCY OF THE ALAMO, TEXAS
February 24, 1836

To the People of Texas and All Americans in the World.
FELLOW CITIZENS AND COMPATRIOTS:

I am besieged by a thousand or more of the Mexicans under Santa Anna. I have sustained a continual bombardment and cannonade for twenty-four hours and have not lost a man. The enemy has demanded a surrender at discretion; otherwise the garrison are to be put to the sword if the fort is taken. I have answered the demand with a cannon shot, and our flag still waves proudly from the walls. *I shall never surrender nor retreat.* Then, I call on you in the name of Liberty, of patriotism, and of everything dear to the American character, to come to our aid with all dispatch. The enemy is receiving reinforcements daily and will no doubt increase to three or four thousand in four or five days. If this call is neglected, I am determined to sustain myself as long as possible and die like a soldier who never forgets what is due to his own honor and that of his country.

VICTORY OR DEATH.

WILLIAM BARRET TRAVIS
Lieutenant Colonel, Commandant

Susan B. Anthony

Joanna Strong and Tom B. Leonard

The Nineteenth Amendment to the Constitution, which provides for full woman suffrage, was not ratified until fourteen years after Susan B. Anthony's death in 1906. Nevertheless, her name more than any other is associated with American women's long struggle to vote. Her firm resolve made her one of our greatest examples of political courage.

"What the blazes are you doing here?" shouted the man at the big desk. "You women go home about your business. Go home and wash the dishes. And if you don't clear out of here fast, I'll get the cops to put you out!"

Everybody in the store stopped and listened. Some of the men just turned around and sneered. Others looked at the fifteen women mockingly and guffawed. One man piped, "Beat it, youse dames. Your kids are dirty." And at that, every man in the place bellowed with laughter.

But this banter didn't faze the tall, dignified woman who stood with a piece of paper in her hand at the head of the fourteen other ladies. She didn't budge an inch.

"I've come here to vote for the President of the United States," she said. "He will be my President as well as yours. We are the women who bear the children who will defend this country. We are the women who make your homes, who bake your bread, who rear your sons and give you daughters. We women are citizens of this country just as much as you are, and we insist on voting for the man who is to be the leader of this government."

Her words rang out with the clearness of a bell, and they struck to the heart. No man in the place dared move now. The big man at the desk who had threatened her was turned to stone. And then, in silence and dignity, Susan B. Anthony strode up to the ballot box and dropped into it the paper bearing her vote. Each of the other fourteen women did the same, while every man in the room stood silent and watched.

It was the year 1872. Too long now had women been denied the rights that should naturally be theirs. Too long now had they endured the injustice of an unfair law—a law that made them mere possessions of men.

Women could earn money, but they might not own it. If a woman was married and went to work, every penny she earned became the property of her husband. In 1872, a man was considered complete master of the household. His wife was taken to be incapable of managing her own affairs. She was supposed to be a nitwit unable to think clearly, and therefore the law mercifully protected her by appointing a guardian—a male guardian, of course—over any property that she was lucky enough to possess.

Women like Susan Anthony writhed at this injustice. Susan saw no reason why her sex should be discriminated against. "Why should only men make the laws?" she cried. "Why should men forge the chains that bind us down? No!" she exclaimed. "It is up to us women to fight for our rights." And then she vowed that she would carry on an everlasting battle, as long as the Lord gave her strength to see that women were made equal in the sight of the law.

And fight she did. Susan B. Anthony was America's greatest champion of women's rights. She traveled unceasingly, from one end of the country to the other. She made thousands of speeches, pleading with men, and trying to arouse women to fight for their rights. She wrote hundreds of pamphlets and letters of protest. It was a bitter and difficult struggle that she entered upon, for the people who opposed her did not hesitate to say all kinds of ugly and untrue things about her and her followers. "No decent woman would talk like that. No refined lady would force her way before judges and men's associations and insist on talking. She is vulgar!"

Many women who knew that Susan Anthony was a refined, intelligent, and courageous woman were afraid to say so. They were afraid that *they* would be looked down on. But in time, they grew to love her for trying to help them.

After a while, many housewives gained courage from her example. Then, in great meetings, they joined her by the thousands. Many a man began to change his notions when his wife, inspired by Susan B. Anthony, made him feel ashamed at the unfair treatment accorded women. Slowly the great Susan B. Anthony was undermining the fierce stubbornness of men.

On that important day in 1872, she and her faithful followers cast their first ballots for President. But though the men in the polling place were momentarily moved, their minds were not yet opened. In a few days, Susan was arrested and brought before a judge, accused of having illegally entered a voting booth.

"How do you plead?" asked the judge.

"Guilty!" cried Susan. "Guilty of trying to uproot the slavery in which you men have placed us women. Guilty of trying to make you see that we mothers are as important to this country as are the men. Guilty of trying to lift the standard of womanhood, so that men may look with pride upon their wives' awareness of public affairs."

And then, before the judge could recover from this onslaught, she added, "But, Your Honor, *not* guilty of acting against the Constitution of the United States, which says that no person is to be deprived of equal rights under the law. Equal rights!" she thundered. "How can it be said that we women have equal rights, when it is you and you alone who take upon yourselves the right to make the laws, the right to choose your representatives, the right to send only sons to higher education. You, you blind men, have become slaveholders of your own mothers and wives."

The judge was taken aback. Never before had he heard these ideas expressed to him in such a forceful manner. However, the law was the law! The judge spoke quietly, and without much conviction. "I am forced to fine you one hundred dollars," he said.

"I will not pay it!" said Susan Anthony. "Mark my words, the law will be changed!" And with that, she strode from the court.

"Shall I follow her and bring her back?" said the court clerk to the judge.

"No, let her go," answered the elderly judge. "I fear that she is right, and that the law will soon be changed."

And Susan did go on, on to further crusades, on across the vast stretches of the United States, proclaiming in every hamlet where her feet trod, her plea for womanhood.

Today, voting by women is an established fact. Women may keep what they earn; and whether married or single, own their own

property. It is taken for granted that a woman may go to college and
work in any business or profession she may choose. But these rights,
enjoyed by the women of today, were secured through the valiant
effort of many fighters for women's freedom, such as the great Susan
B. Anthony.

The Things That Haven't Been
Done Before

Edgar Guest

The ones who dared to do what we now take for granted are the
ones we remember.

> The things that haven't been done before,
>   Those are the things to try;
> Columbus dreamed of an unknown shore
>   At the rim of the far-flung sky,
> And his heart was bold and his faith was strong
>   As he ventured in dangers new,
> And he paid no heed to the jeering throng
>   Or the fears of the doubting crew.
>
> The many will follow the beaten track
>   With guideposts on the way.
> They live and have lived for ages back
>   With a chart for every day.
> Someone has told them it's safe to go
>   On the road he has traveled o'er,
> And all that they ever strive to know
>   Are the things that were known before.

A few strike out, without map or chart,
　　Where never a man has been,
From the beaten paths they draw apart
　　To see what no man has seen.
There are deeds they hunger alone to do;
　　Though battered and bruised and sore,
They blaze the path for the many, who
　　Do nothing not done before.

The things that haven't been done before
　　Are the tasks worthwhile today;
Are you one of the flock that follows, or
　　Are you one that shall lead the way?
Are you one of the timid souls that quail
　　At the jeers of a doubting crew,
Or dare you, whether you win or fail,
　　Strike out for a goal that's new?

Rosa Parks

Kai Friese

Rosa Parks's refusal to "move to the back" of the bus on the evening of December 1, 1955, marked a historic moment: the start of a movement that would bring an end to a tradition of legal segregation across the South and entire nation. Parks certainly never suspected her gesture would turn a new page in the history of American race relations. She didn't move, she later explained, because she was just suddenly fed up with being pushed around. But the courage of the moment sparked the fires of change.

It was Thursday, December 1, 1955. The workday was over, and crowds of people boarded the green-and-white buses that trundled through the streets of Montgomery. Rosa Parks was tired after a full day of stitching and ironing shirts at the Montgomery Fair

department store. She thought she was lucky to have gotten one of
the last seats in the rear section of the Cleveland Avenue bus that
would take her home.

Soon the back of the bus was full, and several people were
standing in the rear. The bus rolled on through Court Square, where
African-Americans had been auctioned off during the days of the
Confederacy, and came to a stop in front of the Empire Theater.
The next passenger aboard stood in the front of an aisle. He was a
white man.

When he noticed that a white person had to stand, the bus
driver, James F. Blake, called out to the four black people who were
sitting just behind the white section. He said they would have to
give up their seats for the new passenger. No one stood up. "You'd
better make it light on yourself and let me have those seats," the
driver said threateningly. Three men got up and went to stand at the
back of the bus. But Rosa Parks wasn't about to move. She had been
in this situation before, and she had always given up her seat. She
had always felt insulted by the experience. "It meant that I didn't
have a right to do anything but get on the bus, give them my fare
and then be pushed around wherever they wanted me," she said.

By a quirk of fate, the driver of the bus on this December
evening was the same James F. Blake who had once before removed
the troublesome Rosa Parks from his bus for refusing to enter by the
back door. That was a long time ago, in 1943. Rosa Parks didn't feel
like being pushed around again. She told the driver that she wasn't
in the white section and she wasn't going to move.

Blake knew the rules, though. He knew that the white section
was wherever the driver said it was. If more white passengers got
on the bus, he could stretch the white section to the back of the bus
and make all the blacks stand. He shouted to Rosa Parks to move to
the back of the bus. She wasn't impressed. She told him again that
she wasn't moving. Everyone in the bus was silent, wondering what
would happen next. Finally Blake told Rosa Parks that he would
have her arrested for violating the racial segregation codes. In a firm
but quiet voice, she told him that he could do what he wanted to do
because she wasn't moving.

Blake got off the bus and came back with an officer of the
Montgomery Police Department. As the officer placed Rosa Parks
under arrest, she asked him plainly, "Why do you people push us
around?"

With the eyes of all the passengers on him, the officer could only answer in confusion. "I don't know. I'm just obeying the law," he said.

Rosa Parks was taken to the police station, where she was booked and fingerprinted. While the policemen were filling out forms, she asked if she could have a drink of water. She was told that the drinking fountain in the station was for whites only. Then a policewoman marched her into a long corridor facing a wall of iron bars. A barred door slid open. She went inside. The door clanged shut, and she was locked in. She was in jail.

> Rosa Parks's decision to challenge her arrest in court led Montgomery's black community to organize a bus boycott as a show of support.

Rosa Parks woke up on the morning of Monday, December 5, thinking about her trial. As she and her husband got out of bed, they heard the familiar sound of a City Lines bus pulling up to a stop across the road. There was usually a crowd of people waiting for the bus at this time. The Parkses rushed to the window and looked out. Except for the driver, the bus was empty and there was no one getting on either. The bus stood at the stop for more than a minute, puffing exhaust smoke into the cold December air as the puzzled driver waited for passengers. But no one appeared, and the empty bus chugged away.

Rosa Parks was filled with happiness. Her neighbors were actually boycotting the buses. She couldn't wait to drive to the courthouse so that she could see how the boycott was going in the rest of Montgomery. When Fred Gray arrived to drive her to the trial, she wasn't disappointed. Rosa Parks had expected some people to stay off the buses. She thought that with luck, maybe even half the usual passengers would stay off. But these buses were just plain empty.

All over the city, empty buses bounced around for everyone to see. There was never more than the usual small group of white passengers in front and sometimes a lonely black passenger in back, wondering what was going on. The streets were filled with black people walking to work.

As Rosa Parks and her lawyer drove up to the courthouse, there was another surprise waiting for them. A crowd of about five hundred blacks had gathered to show their support for her. Mrs. Parks and the lawyer made their way slowly through the cheering crowd into the courtroom. Once they were inside, the trial didn't take long. Rosa Parks was quickly convicted of breaking the bus segregation laws and fined ten dollars, as well as four dollars for the cost of her trial. This was the stage at which Claudette Colvin's trial had ended seven months earlier. Colvin had had little choice but to accept the guilty verdict and pay the fine.

This time, however, Fred Gray rose to file an appeal on Rosa Parks's case. This meant that her case would be taken to a higher court at a later date. Meanwhile, Mrs. Parks was free to go.

Outside the courthouse, the crowd was getting restless. Some of them were carrying sawed-off shotguns, and the policemen were beginning to look worried. E. D. Nixon went out to calm them, but nobody could hear him in the din. Voices from the crowd shouted out that they would storm the courthouse if Rosa Parks didn't come out safely within a few minutes. When she did appear, a great cheer went up again.

After seeing the empty buses that morning, and this large and fearless crowd around her now, Rosa Parks knew that she had made the right decision. Black people were uniting to show the city administration that they were tired of the insults of segregation. Together, they could change Montgomery. They could do some good.

It Can Be Done

True courage is mixed with circumspection, the kind of healthy skepticism that asks, "Is this the best way to do this?" True cowardice is marked by chronic skepticism, which always says, "It can't be done."

> The man who misses all the fun
> Is he who says, "It can't be done."
> In solemn pride he stands aloof
> And greets each venture with reproof.
> Had he the power he'd efface
> The history of the human race;
> We'd have no radio or motor cars,
> No streets lit by electric stars;

No telegraph nor telephone,
We'd linger in the age of stone.
The world would sleep if things were run
By men who say, "It can't be done."

Men Wanted for Hazardous Journey

Ernest Shackleton

British Antarctic explorer Sir Ernest Shackleton (1874–1922) placed this advertisement in London newspapers in 1900 in preparation for the National Antarctic Expedition (which subsequently failed to reach the South Pole). Shackleton later said of the call for volunteers that "it seemed as though all the men in Great Britain were determined to accompany me, the response was so overwhelming."

MEN WANTED FOR HAZARDOUS JOURNEY. Small wages, bitter cold, long months of complete darkness, constant danger, safe return doubtful. Honor and recognition in case of success. —Ernest Shackleton.

The End of the Scott Expedition

Robert Falcon Scott

In 1910, Captain Robert Falcon Scott, of the British Navy, set sail on a second attempt to reach the South Pole. Two years later, on January 18, 1912, after a treacherous journey across vast stretches of ice-covered Antarctica, Scott and four companions reached their destination, only to find that a rival expedition led by Norwegian explorer Roald Amundsen had beaten them by thirty-five days. They found Amundsen's tent still uncovered by snow.

Disheartened and exhausted, Scott and his party began their seven-hundred mile homeward trek, a journey that would end in tragedy. Food and fuel ran low, temperatures plummeted, and frostbite worsened daily. On March 3, Scott wrote in his diary: "God help us, we can't keep up this pulling, that is certain. Amongst ourselves we are unendingly cheerful, but what each man feels in his heart I can only guess." On March 16, he wrote: ". . . assuredly the end is not far." And finally, on March 29: "It seems a pity, but I do not think I can write more. R. Scott. . . . For God's sake, look after our people."

Scott and two companions made it to within fifteen miles of a supply camp. Months later, a search party found the bodies in their sleeping bags, half buried in snow. Among the records of the trip, they found this last message by Scott to the public, a farewell letter showing, as Scott wrote in an accompanying note, that "Englishmen can still die with a bold spirit, fighting it out to the end."

The causes of the disaster are due not to faulty organisation, but to the misfortune in all risks which had to be undertaken.

1. The loss of pony transport in March 1911 obliged me to start later than I had intended, and obliged the limits of stuff transported to be narrowed.

2. The weather throughout the outward journey, and especially the long gale in 83° S., stopped us.

3. The soft snow in lower reaches of glacier again reduced pace.

We fought these untoward events with a will and conquered, but it cut into our provision reserve.

Every detail of our food supplies, clothing and depots made on the interior ice-sheet and over that long stretch of 700 miles to the Pole and back, worked out to perfection. The advance party would have returned to the glacier in fine form and with surplus of food, but for the astonishing failure of the man whom we had least expected to fail. Edgar Evans was thought the strongest man of the party.

The Beardmore Glacier is not difficult in fine weather, but on our return we did not get a single completely fine day; this with a sick companion enormously increased our anxieties.

As I have said elsewhere we got into frightfully rough ice and Edgar Evans received a concussion of the brain—he died a natural death, but left us a shaken party with the season unduly advanced.

But all the facts above enumerated were as nothing to the surprise which awaited us on the Barrier. I maintain that our arrangements for returning were quite adequate, and that no one in the world would have expected the temperatures and surfaces which we encountered at this time of the year. On the summit in lat. 85° 86° we had − 20°, − 30°. On the Barrier in lat. 80°, 10,000 feet lower, we had − 30° in the day, − 47° at night pretty regularly, with continuous head wind during our day marches. It is clear that these circumstances come on very suddenly, and our wreck is certainly due to this sudden advent of severe weather, which does not seem to have any satisfactory cause. I do not think human beings ever came through such a month as we have come through, and we should have got through in spite of the weather but for the sickening of a second companion, Captain Oates, and a shortage of fuel in our depots for which I cannot account, and finally, but for the storm which has fallen on us within 11 miles of the depot at which we hoped to secure our final supplies.

Surely misfortune could scarcely have exceeded this last blow. We arrived within 11 miles of our old One Ton Camp with fuel for one last meal and food for two days.

For four days we have been unable to leave the tent—the gale howling about us. We are weak, writing is difficult, but for my own sake I do not regret this journey, which has shown that Englishmen can endure hardships, help one another, and meet death with as great a fortitude as ever in the past. We took risks, we knew we took them; things have come out against us, and therefore we have no cause for complaint, but bow to the will of Providence, determined still to do our best to the last. But if we have been willing to give our lives to this enterprise, which is for the honour of our country, I appeal to our countrymen to see that those who depend upon us are properly cared for.

Had we lived, I should have had a tale to tell of the hardihood, endurance, and courage of my companions which would have stirred the heart of every Englishman. These rough notes and our dead bodies must tell the tale, but surely, surely, a great rich country like

ours will see that those who are dependent on us are properly provided for.

R. Scott

The Iron Horse

Bob Considine

Lou Gehrig (1903–1941) played a record 2,130 consecutive ball-
games for the New York Yankees from June 1, 1925, to May 2,
1939, earning the nickname "the Iron Horse." The power-hitting
first baseman hit .300 or better for twelve straight seasons, batted
in 100 or more runs for thirteen consecutive years, and hit 493
home runs. The form of spine paralysis that ended his career and
eventually his life has come to be known as Lou Gehrig's disease,
not just because of the publicity surrounding his sickness, but
because of the remarkable courage with which he faced the end.

The Yanks won easily in 1938, Lou's fifteenth year with the ball
team. They went on to demolish the Chicago Cubs in the World
Series. But Lou's contribution was modest. During the regular season he hit .295, a highly acceptable figure in today's baseball, but a
source of great embarrassment for Gehrig in 1938. It was the first
time he had hit under .300 since joining the team. DiMag had beat
him in home run production the year before. Lou played through
the Series against the Cubs, but the four hits he got in fourteen times
at bat were all singles.

The first hint I had that Lou's problem was more sinister than a
routine slump that year was provided by a wild-and-woolly Washington pitcher named Joe Krakauskas. After a game at Yankee Stadium he told Shirley Povich of the *Washington Post* and me that a
frightening thing had happened to him while pitching against Gehrig. Joe had uncorked his high inside fast ball with the expectation
that Lou would move back and take it, as a ball. Instead, Krakauskas
said, Lou—a renowned judge of balls and strikes—moved closer to
the plate.

"My pitch went between his wrists," Joe said, still shaken. "Scared the hell outta me. Something's wrong with Gehrig. . . ."

Lou's salary was cut three thousand dollars a year before he went south with the Yankees in 1939. There was no beef from him. He had had a bum year, for him, so the cut was deserved. He'd come back. After all, the Babe played twenty-two years without ever taking good care of himself. . . .

Joe McCarthy started Gehrig at first base on opening day of the 1939 season, contemptuous of a fan who, a few days before in an exhibition game at Ebbets Field, had bawled, in earshot of both of them, "Hey, Lou, why don't you give yourself up? What do you want McCarthy to do, burn that uniform off you?"

Lou hobbled as far into the 1939 season as May 2. Then, on the morning of the first game of a series against Detroit, he called McCarthy on the hotel's house phone and asked to see him.

"I'm benching myself, Joe," he said, once in the manager's suite. McCarthy did not speak.

"For the good of the team," Lou went on. "I can't tell you how grateful I am to you for the kindness you've shown me, and your patience . . . I just can't seem to get going. The time has come for me to quit."

McCarthy snorted and told him to forget the consecutive-games-played record, take a week or two off, and he'd come back strong.

Gehrig shook his head. "I can't go on, Joe," he said. "Johnny Murphy told me so."

McCarthy cursed the relief pitcher.

"I didn't mean it that way, Joe," Gehrig said. "All the boys have been swell to me. Nobody's said a word that would hurt my feelings. But Johnny said something the other day that made me know it was time for me to get out of the lineup . . . and all he meant to do was to be encouraging."

McCarthy, still angry, asked for details.

"You remember the last play in that last game we played at the Stadium?" Lou asked. "A ball was hit between the box and first base. Johnny fielded it, and I got back to first just in time to take the throw from him."

"So?"

"So, well, I had a hard time getting back there, Joe," Lou said. "I should have been there in plenty of time. I made the put-out, but when Johnny and I were trotting to the bench he said, 'Nice play,

Lou.' I knew then it was time to quit. The boys were beginning to feel sorry for me."

At the urging of his devoted wife, Eleanor, Lou checked into the Mayo Clinic in Rochester, Minnesota. In due time he emerged with a bleak "To Whom It May Concern" document signed by the eminent Dr. Harold C. Harbeing:

"This is to certify that Mr. Lou Gehrig has been under examination at the Mayo Clinic from June 13 to June 19, 1939, inclusive. After a careful and complete examination, it was found that he is suffering from amyotrophic lateral sclerosis. This type of illness involves the motor pathways and cells of the central nervous system and, in lay terms, is known as a form of chronic poliomyelitis— infantile paralysis.

"The nature of this trouble makes it such that Mr. Gehrig will be unable to continue his active participation as a baseball player, inasmuch as it is advisable that he conserve his muscular energy. He could, however, continue in some executive capacity."

Lou returned to the team for the remainder of the 1939 season, slowly suiting up each day, taking McCarthy's lineups to home plate to deliver to the umpires before each game. It was his only duty as captain. It was another winning season for the Yankees, but hardly for Lou. The short walk from the dugout to home plate and back exhausted him. But more exhausting was a cruel (but mostly true) story in the New York Daily News to the effect that some of his teammates had become afraid of drinking out of the Yankee dugout's drinking fountain after Lou used it.

"Gehrig Appreciation Day" (July 4, 1939) was one of those emotional salutes which only baseball seems able to produce: packed stands, the prospect of a doubleheader win over the Washington Senators, a peppery speech from Mayor Fiorello La Guardia, the presence of Yankee fan and Gehrig buff Postmaster General Jim Farley, and the array of rheumatic and fattening old teammates of yesteryear. And The Family in a sidelines box. Presents and trophies filled a table.

For Lou, now beginning to hollow out from his disease, one basic ingredient was missing. Babe Ruth wasn't there. Babe, the one he wanted to be there more than he wanted any of his old buddies, had not answered the invitations or the management's phone calls.

Then, with little warning, a great commotion and rustle and rattle in the stadium. The Babe was entering. He magnetized every eye, activated every tongue. Lou wheezed a prayer of thanksgiving.

The ceremony between games of the doubleheader was not calculated to be anything requiring a stiff upper lip. Joe McCarthy's voice cracked as he began his prepared tribute. He promptly abandoned his script and blurted, "Don't let's cry about this . . ." which had just the opposite effect among the fans.

When Lou's turn came, he, too, pocketed the small speech he had worked on the night before. He swallowed a few times to make his voice stronger, then haltingly said:

"They say I've had a bad break. But when the office force and the groundkeepers and even the Giants from across the river, whom we'd give our right arm to beat in the World Series—when *they* remember you, that's something . . . and when you have a wonderful father and mother who worked hard to give you an education . . . and a wonderful wife . . ."

His words began to slither when he tried to say something about Jake Ruppert and Miller Huggins, dead, and McCarthy, Barrow and Bill Dickey, alive.

But nobody missed his ending.

"I may have been given a bad break," he concluded, briefly touching his nose as if to discourage a sniff, "but I have an awful lot to live for. With all this, I consider myself the luckiest man on the face of the earth."

Babe, the irrepressible, stepped forward, embraced him and blubbered, an act that turned out to be epidemic.

Gehrig made the trip to Cincinnati that fall to watch his old club clobber the Reds in the World Series. He had a good time, but some of his friends found it a troubling experience being around him. Going out to dinner one night, with Dickey at his side, Lou staggered and was on the brink of plunging down the long flight of marble steps that led from the lobby of the Netherlands Plaza hotel to the street level. Dicky made one of the better catches of his life and saved Lou from a possibly fatal fall.

Then there was a scene on the train that brought the victorious Yanks back to New York. Lou spotted his friend Henry McLemore of the United Press and invited him into his drawing room for a drink. A table had been set up. Lou slowly but surely put ice in the glasses, then reached for the partly filled fifth of Johnnie Walker Black Label. He wrapped a bony hand around the cork and tried to pull it loose. It was not in tightly, but he did not have the strength to loosen it. Henry stopped listening to what Lou was saying about the Series. He was mesmerized by Lou's struggle, and too reverent of the man to offer to help. Finally, Lou raised the bottle to his lips, closed his teeth on the cork, and let his elbows drop to the table. The cork stayed in his teeth. He removed it, poured the drinks, and went on with what he had been saying.

Henry got very drunk that night.

Just before he died on June 2, 1941, Lou called me from his office. Mayor La Guardia had appointed him to the New York City Parole Board to work with and encourage youthful lawbreakers. Gehrig threw himself into the work with everything he had, or had left. He also kept up a lively interest in research into the disease that had driven him out of baseball.

It was a note about the latter that prompted his phone call.

"I've got some good news for you," he said. "Looks like the boys in the labs might have come up with a real breakthrough. They've got some new serum that they've tried on ten of us who have the same problem. And, you know something? It seems to be working on nine out of the ten. How about that?" He was elated.

I tried not to ask the question, but it came out anyway, after a bit.

"How about *you, Lou?*"

Lou said, "Well, it didn't work on me. But how about that for an average?—nine out of ten! Isn't that great?"

I said yes, it was great.

So was he.

A Smile

Those who fight the good fight and win need to be brave only once. Those who lose must show courage twice. So we must steel ourselves for harder things than triumph.

> Let others cheer the winning man,
> There's one I hold worthwhile;
> 'Tis he who does the best he can,
> Then loses with a smile.
> Beaten he is, but not to stay
> Down with the rank and file;
> That man will win some other day,
> Who loses with a smile.

The Moses of Her People

Sarah Bradford

Harriet Tubman was born into slavery on a Maryland plantation around 1821. Like most slaves, she received no education and could not read or write. In 1844 her owner forced her to marry a fellow slave, John Tubman. One summer night in 1849, she began to walk north toward her freedom. She later returned to help members of her family escape, and eventually made some twenty trips into the South to guide three hundred slaves along the Underground Railroad to Northern havens. With the outbreak of the Civil War, she traveled to South Carolina with the Union army to serve as a nurse, cook, scout, and spy. After the war, she continued to work to improve freed slaves' conditions.

The following account is from the first biography of Harriet Tubman, published in 1869 and in revised form in 1886; it rightly calls her "the Moses of Her People."

One day there were scared faces seen in the Negro quarter, and hurried whispers passed from one to another. No one knew how it had come out, but someone had heard that Harriet and two of her brothers were very soon, perhaps today, perhaps tomorrow, to be sent far south with a gang, bought up for plantation work. Harriet was about twenty or twenty-five years old at this time, and the constantly recurring idea of escape at *sometime,* took sudden form that day, and with her usual promptitude of action she was ready to start at once.

She held a hurried consultation with her brothers, in which she so wrought upon their fears that they expressed themselves as willing to start with her that very night, for that far North, where, could they reach it in safety, freedom awaited them.

The brothers started with her, but the way was strange, the North was far away, and all unknown, the masters would pursue and recapture them, and their fate would be worse than ever before. And so they broke away from her, and bidding her goodbye, they hastened back to the known horrors of slavery, and the dread of that which was worse.

Harriet was now left alone, but after watching the retreating forms of her brothers, she turned her face toward the north, and fixing her eyes on the guiding star, and committing her way unto the Lord, she started again upon her long, lonely journey. Her farewell song was long remembered in the cabins, and the old mother sat and wept for her lost child. No intimation had been given her of Harriet's intention, for the old woman was of a most impulsive disposition, and her cries and lamentations would have made known to all within hearing Harriet's intended escape. With only the North Star for her guide, our heroine started on the way to liberty.

And so without money, and without friends, she started on through unknown regions; walking by night, hiding by day, but always conscious of an invisible pillar of cloud by day, and of fire by night, under the guidance of which she journeyed or rested. Without knowing whom to trust, or how near the pursuers might be, she carefully felt her way, and by her native cunning, or by God-given wisdom, she managed to apply to the right people for food, and sometimes for shelter; though often her bed was only the cold ground, and her watchers the stars of night.

After many long and weary days of travel, she found that she had passed the magic line, which then divided the land of bondage from the land of freedom. But where were the lovely white ladies whom in her visions she had seen, who, with arms outstretched, welcomed her to their hearts and homes? All these visions proved deceitful: she was more alone than ever; but she had crossed the line; no one could take her now, and she would never call any man "Master" more. . . .

It would be impossible here to give a detailed account of the journeys and labors of this intrepid woman for the redemption of her kindred and friends during the years that followed. Those years were spent in work, almost by night and day, with the one object of the rescue of her people from slavery. All her wages were laid away with this sole purpose, and as soon as a sufficient amount was secured, she disappeared from her Northern home, and as suddenly and mysteriously she appeared some dark night at the door of one of the cabins on a plantation, where a trembling band of fugitives, forewarned as to time and place, were anxiously awaiting their deliverer. Then she piloted them north, traveling by night, hiding by day, scaling the mountains, fording the rivers, threading the forests, lying concealed as the pursuers passed them. She, carrying the babies, drugged with paregoric, in a basket on her arm. So she went *nineteen* times, and so she brought away over three hundred pieces of living and breathing "property," with God-given souls. . . .

On one of their journeys to the North, as she was piloting a company of refugees, Harriet came, just as morning broke, to a town where a colored man had lived whose house had been one of her stations of the underground, or unseen railroad. They reached the house, and leaving her party huddled together in the middle of the street, in a pouring rain, Harriet went to the door, and gave the peculiar rap which was her customary signal to her friends. There was not the usual ready response, and she was obliged to repeat the signal several times. At length a window was raised, and the head of a *white man* appeared, with the gruff question, "Who are you?" and "What do you want?" Harriet asked after her friend, and was told that he had been obliged to leave for "harboring niggers."

Here was an unforeseen trouble; day was breaking, and daylight was the enemy of the hunted and flying fugitives. Their faithful leader stood one moment in the street, and in that moment she had flashed a message quicker than that of the telegraph to her unseen Protector, and the answer came as quickly in a suggestion to her of an almost forgotten place of refuge. Outside of the town there was a little island in a swamp, where the grass grew tall and rank, and where no human being could be suspected of seeking a hiding place. To this spot she conducted her party; she waded the swamp, carrying in a basket two well-drugged babies (these were a pair of little twins, whom I have since seen well-grown young women), and the rest of the company following. She ordered them to lie down in the tall, wet grass, and here she prayed again, and waited for deliverance. The poor creatures were all cold, and wet, and hungry, and Harriet did not dare to leave them to get supplies. For no doubt the man at whose house she had knocked, had given the alarm in the town; and officers might be on the watch for them. They were truly in a wretched condition, but Harriet's faith never wavered, her silent prayer still ascended, and she confidently expected help from some quarter or other.

It was after dusk when a man came slowly walking along the solid pathway on the edge of the swamp. He was clad in the garb of a Quaker, and proved to be a "friend" in need and indeed. He seemed to be talking to himself, but ears quickened by sharp practice caught the words he was saying:

"My wagon stands in the barnyard of the next farm across the way. The horse is in the stable; the harness hangs on a nail." And the man was gone. Night fell, and Harriet stole forth to the place designated. Not only a wagon, but a wagon well provisioned stood in the yard; and before many minutes the party were rescued from their wretched position, and were on their way rejoicing to the next town. Here dwelt a Quaker whom Harriet knew, and he readily took charge of the horse and wagon, and no doubt returned them to their owner. How the good man who thus came to their rescue had received any intimation of their being in the neighborhood Harriet never knew. But these sudden deliverances never seemed to strike her as at all strange or mysterious; her prayer was the prayer of faith, and she *expected* an answer.

Instant Hero

Blaine Harden
from the Washington Post

On January 13, 1982, Air Florida Flight 90 struck the 14th Street
Bridge after taking off from Washington, D.C.'s National Airport and plunged into the icy Potomac River, killing seventy-
eight people. Hundreds of commuters, heading home early
because of a rare Washington blizzard, stood on the river's banks
and watched the torturous rescue attempts. Lenny Skutnik was
one who suddenly stopped being a bystander and went into the
river to save a life. "Nobody else was doing anything," he later
said. "It was the only way."

Lenny Skutnik, who dove into the ice-choked Potomac River
Wednesday to save the life of a drowning woman following the
jetliner crash in the Potomac, has had little experience in the hero
business.

Skutnik, twenty-eight, whose full name is Martin Leonard
Skutnik III, is experienced in less exalted matters. He's been a meat-
packer, house painter, furniture-plant worker, hamburger cook, and
strip-and-wax man at Ralph's supermarket in Simi Valley, California.

Skutnik now works for the Congressional Budget Office,
where he runs errands, delivers mail, and makes $14,000 a year. A
big night out, Skutnik says, is taking his wife, Linda, and their two
sons to Brothers Pizza near their $325-a-month rented town house
in Lorton, Virginia. "Every once in a while we'll close our eyes and
blow a couple of bucks," he says.

The only other time in his life that he had a chance to be a hero,
Skutnik says, he flubbed it. He was anchoring a relay team in a high
school race and he could have won the race, but he pooped out and
stopped. The coach yelled at him: "You quit, Skutnik. You quit."

Late Wednesday afternoon, as one of hundreds of homeward-
bound commuters drawn to the banks of the Potomac by the crash
of Air Florida Flight 90, Skutnik, who's never taken a life-saving
course, saved a woman who was too weak to grasp rescue rings

lowered from a hovering helicopter. Television spread pictures of his valor to the nation.

President Reagan, in a speech yesterday in New York, spoke of Skutnik's bravery: "Nothing had picked him out particularly to be a hero, but without hesitation there he was and he saved her life."

Interviewed yesterday at his home twenty miles south of the 14th Street bridge, Skutnik could offer no fancy explanations for risking his life. "Nobody else was doing anything," he said. "It was the only way."

The woman Skutnik rescued apparently was Priscilla Tirado, whose husband and infant son perished in the crash. Skutnik was sure yesterday he had rescued Kelly Duncan, an Air Florida stewardess, because a woman who identified herself as Duncan's roommate called from Florida to thank him. However, an Air Florida official said last night she had talked to Duncan, who remembers being pulled to shore by a helicopter. Tirado's father said family members recognized his daughter on television as the one Skutnik pulled to safety.

After the rescue, as he waited in an ambulance that had run out of blankets, Skutnik gave his coat to Joseph Stiley, a survivor of the crash who had two broken legs and was shivering. Shirtless and shivering himself, Skutnik, who lost his watch and a cap in the river, was taken to National Hospital for Orthopaedics and Rehabilitation in Arlington for treatment of hypothermnia. He didn't want to go.

"I'd heard all these horror stories about hospitals and all the forms. The first thing I said when I got there was, 'Is this going to cost me anything?'" said Skutnik, who's described by his colleagues at CBO as an exemplary worker.

He was dispatched, free of charge, to a hot tub in the hospital to soak for forty minutes and warm up. When Skutnik got out of the tub, he faced reporters—scores of them, frenzied and facing deadlines. They pushed and shoved to ask him what "it felt like." He had never met a reporter before. He told his story again and again.

Skutnik's instant celebrity began Wednesday afternoon near the 14th Street bridge when traffic in the express lane he was car-pooling home in came to an abrupt stop. Skutnik followed scores of stalled commuters down to the river, where there was a rumor that someone had been hurt. He said he didn't hear the metallic crash of the plane.

From the shore, Skutnik said he saw the partially submerged

plane with a half dozen passengers clinging to it. He saw one spectator tie a rope around his waist and attempt a rescue.

The man who tried to swim out to the wreckage was Roger Olian, thirty-four, a sheet metal worker from Arlington, who was drawn to the accident after getting caught in traffic near the bridge on his way home from work.

"I went in with a makeshift rope that kept getting stuck on the ice," Olian said yesterday. "I was about five feet from the plane when the helicopters arrived. But by then [he'd been in the water more than fifteen minutes] I'd just about had it. I nearly sank, but they pulled me in," said Olian.

Later, when it became obvious that a helicopter could not save the drowning woman, Skutnik said he didn't have any profound thoughts. "I just did it," he said. "When I got out of the water, I was satisfied. I did what I set out to do."

Courage

John Galsworthy

Here is the kind of bravery that shoulders another's misfortunes. John Galsworthy (1867–1933) has depicted a particularly dramatic example, but if we look around we'll see the same stronghearted courage in teachers, ministers, policemen, and others who spend whole lives coming to the rescue.

At that time (said Ferrand) I was in poverty. Not the kind of poverty that goes without dinner, but the sort that goes without breakfast, lunch, and dinner, and exists as it can on bread and tobacco. I lived in one of those fourpenny lodging houses, Westminster way. Three, five, seven beds in a room; if you pay regularly, you keep your own bed; if not, they put someone else there who will certainly leave you a memento of himself. It's not the foreigners' quarter; they are nearly all English, and drunkards. Three quarters of them don't eat—can't; they have no capacity for solid food. They drink and drink. They're not worth wasting your money on—cab

runners, newspaper boys, sellers of laces, and what you call sandwich men; three fourths of them brutalized beyond the power of
recovery. What can you expect? They just live to scrape enough
together to keep their souls in their bodies; they have no time or
strength to think of anything but that. They come back at night and
fall asleep—and how dead that sleep is! No, they never eat—just a
bit of bread; the rest is drink!

There used to come to that house a little Frenchman, with a
yellow crow's-footed face; not old either, about thirty. But his life
had been hard—no one comes to these houses if life is soft, especially
no Frenchman; a Frenchman hates to leave his country. He came to
shave us—charged a penny; most of us forgot to pay him, so that in
all he shaved about three for a penny. He went to others of these
houses—this gave him his income—he kept the little shop next
door, too, but he never sold anything. How he worked! He also
went to one of your Public Institutions; this was not so profitable,
for there he was paid a penny for ten shaves. He used to say to me,
moving his tired fingers like little yellow sticks: "Pff! I slave! To
gain a penny, friend, I'm spending fourpence. What would you
have? One must nourish oneself to have the strength to shave ten
people for a penny." He was like an ant, running round and round
in his little hole, without any chance but just to live; and always in
hopes of saving enough to take him back to France, and set him up
there. We had a liking for each other. He was the only one, in
fact—except a sandwichman who had been an actor, and was very
intelligent, when he wasn't drunk—the only one in all that warren
who had ideas. He was fond of pleasure and loved his music hall—
must have gone at least twice a year, and was always talking of it.
He had little knowledge of its joys, it's true—hadn't the money for
that—but his intentions were good. He used to keep me till the last,
and shave me slowly.

"This rests me," he would say. It was amusement for me, too,
for I had got into the habit of going for days without opening my
lips. It's only a man here and there one can talk with; the rest only
laugh. You seem to them a fool, a freak—something that should be
put into a cage or tied by the leg.

"Yes," the little man would say, "when I came here first I
thought I should soon go back, but now I'm not so sure. I'm losing
my illusions. Money has wings, but it's not to *me* it flies. Believe
me, friend, I am shaving my soul into these specimens. And how
unhappy they are, poor creatures; how they must suffer! Drink! you

say. Yes, that saves them—they get a little happiness from that. Unfortunately, I haven't the constitution for it—here." And he would show me where he had no constitution. "You, too, comrade, you don't seem to be in luck; but then, you're young. Ah, well, *faut être philosophe*—but imagine what kind of a game it is in this climate, especially if you come from the South!"

When I went away, which was as soon as I had nothing left to pawn, he gave me money—there's no question of lending in those houses: if a man parts with money he *gives* it, and lucky if he's not robbed into the bargain. There are fellows there who watch for a new pair of shoes, or a good overcoat, profit by their wakefulness as soon as the other is asleep, and promptly disappear. There's no morality in the face of destitution—it needs a man of iron, and these are men of straw. But one thing I will say of the low English—they are not bloodthirsty, like the low French and Italians.

Well, I got a job as fireman on a steamer, made a tour tramping, and six months later I was back again. The first morning I saw the Frenchman. It was shaving day. He was more like an ant than ever, working away with all his legs and arms; a little yellower, and perhaps more wrinkled.

"Ah!" he called out to me in French, "there you are—back again. I knew you'd come. Wait till I've finished with this specimen —I've a lot to talk about."

We went into the kitchen—a big stone-floored room, with tables for eating—and sat down by the fire. It was January, but, summer or winter, there's always a fire burning in that kitchen.

"So," he said, "you have come back? No luck? Eh! Patience! A few more days won't kill you at your age. What fogs, though! You see, I'm still here, but my comrade, Pigon, is dead. You remember him—the big man with black hair who had the shop down the street. Amiable fellow, good friend to me, and married. Fine woman his wife—a little ripe, seeing she has had children, but of good family. He died suddenly of heart disease. Wait a bit; I'll tell you about that. . . .

"It was not long after you went away, one fine day in October, when I had just finished with these specimens here, and was taking my coffee in the shop, and thinking of that poor Pigon—dead then just three days—when *pom!* comes a knock, and there is Madame Pigon! Very calm—a woman of good family, well brought up, well made—fine woman. But the cheeks pale, and the eyes so red, poor soul.

" 'Well, Madame,' I asked her, 'what can I do for you?'

"It seems this poor Pigon died bankrupt; there was not a cent in the shop. He was two days in his grave, and the bailiffs in already.

" 'Ah, Monsieur!' she says to me, 'what am I to do?'

" 'Wait a bit, Madame!' I get my hat and go back to the shop with her.

"What a scene! Two bailiffs, who would have been the better for a shave, sitting in a shop before the basins; and everywhere, *ma foi,* everywhere, children! Tk! Tk! A little girl of ten, very like her mother; two little boys with little trousers, and one with nothing but a chemise; and others—two, quite small, all rolling on the floor. And what a horrible noise!—all crying, all but the little girl, fit to break themselves in two. The bailiffs seemed perplexed. It was enough to make one weep! Seven! And some quite small! That poor Pigon, I had no idea!

"The bailiffs behaved very well.

" 'Well,' said the biggest, 'you can have four-and-twenty hours to find this money; my mate can camp out here in the shop—we don't want to be hard on you!'

"I helped Madame to soothe the children.

" 'If I had the money,' I said, 'it should be at your service, Madame—in each well-born heart there should exist humanity; but I have no money. Try and think whether you have no friends to help you.'

" 'Monsieur,' she answered, 'I have none. Have I had time to make friends—I, with seven children?'

" 'But in France, Madame?'

" 'None, Monsieur. I have quarreled with my family; and reflect—it is now seven years since we came to England, and then only because no one would help us.'

"That seemed to me bad, but what could I do? I could only say, 'Hope always, Madame—trust in me!'

"I went away. All day long I thought how calm she was—magnificent! And I kept saying to myself: 'Come, tap your head! Tap your head! Something must be done!' But nothing came.

"The next morning it was my day to go to that sacred Institution, and I started off still thinking what on earth could be done for the poor woman. It was as if the little ones had got hold of my legs and were dragging at me. I arrived late, and, to make up time, I shaved them as I have never shaved them; a hot morning—I perspired! Ten for a penny! Ten for a penny! I thought of that, and of the poor woman. At last I finished and sat down. I thought to myself: 'It's too strong! Why do you do it? It's stupid! You are wasting yourself!' And then, my idea came to me! I asked for the manager.

" 'Monsieur,' I said, 'it is impossible for me to come here again.'

" 'What do you mean?' says he.

" 'I have had enough of your—"ten for a penny"—I am going to get married. I can't afford to come here any longer. I lose too much flesh for the money.'

" 'What!' he says, 'you're a lucky man if you can afford to throw away your money like this!'

" 'Throw away my money! Pardon, Monsieur, but look at me' —I was still very hot—'for every penny I make I lose threepence, not counting the boot leather to and fro. While I was still a bachelor, Monsieur, it was my own affair—I could afford these extravagances. But now—it must finish—I have the honor, Monsieur!'

"I left him, and walked away. I went to the Pigons' shop. The bailiff was still there—Pfui! He must have been smoking all the time.

" 'I can't give them much longer,' he said to me.

" 'It is of no importance,' I replied, and I knocked, and went into the back room.

"The children were playing in the corner, that little girl, a heart of gold, watching them like a mother; and Madame at the table with a pair of old black gloves on her hands. My friend, I have never seen such a face—calm, but so pale, so frightfully discouraged, so overwhelmed. One would say she was waiting for her death. It was bad, it was bad—with the winter coming on!

" 'Good morning, Madame,' I said. 'What news? Have you been able to arrange anything?'

" 'No, Monsieur. And you?'

" 'No!' And I looked at her again—a fine woman; ah! a fine woman.

" 'But,' I said, 'an idea has come to me this morning. Now, what would you say if I asked you to marry me? It might possibly be better than nothing.'

"She regarded me with her black eyes, and answered, 'But willingly, Monsieur!' And then, comrade, but not till then, she cried."

The little Frenchman stopped, and stared at me hard.

"H'm!" I said at last, "you have courage!"

He looked at me again; his eyes were troubled, as if I had paid him a bad compliment.

"You think so?" he said at last, and I saw that the thought was gnawing at him, as if I had turned the light on some desperate, dark feeling in his heart.

"Yes!" he said, taking his time, while his good yellow face wrinkled and wrinkled, and each wrinkle seemed to darken. "I was afraid of it even when I did it. Seven children!" Once more he looked at me. "And since!—sometimes—sometimes—I could—" He broke off, then burst out again.

"Life is hard! What would you have? I knew her husband. Could I leave her to the streets?"

Plato on Fear

From the Gorgias

What should we fear?

Socrates spoke of courage as involving a knowledge of what really is to be feared, and he viewed it as an integral part of all virtue, which consists in knowing which things are really good or evil. Furthermore, if moral evil is the only real evil, then the so-called evils that fortune and men inflict upon us, such as poverty, sickness, suffering, and even death, are not to be feared; if they are faced in the proper spirit, they cannot make us morally worse creatures.

Here, near the conclusion of Plato's dialogue Gorgias, Socrates calmly and confidently predicts his own unjust death. The sinister trial he envisions (which actually came to pass in 399 B.C.) is not something he fears, because the evil actions of other men cannot harm him morally. There is only one thing Socrates truly fears, and that is to do injustice to others.

Socrates. Do not repeat the old story—that he who likes will kill me and get my money; for then I shall have to repeat the old answer, that he will be a bad man and will kill the good, and that the money will be of no use to him, but that he will wrongly use that which he wrongly took, and if wrongly, basely, and if basely, hurtfully.

Callicles. How confident you are, Socrates, that you will never come to harm! You seem to think that you are living in another country, and can never be brought into a court of justice, as you very likely may be brought by some miserable and mean person.

Then I must indeed be a fool, Callicles, if I do not know that in the Athenian state any man may suffer anything. And if I am brought to trial and incur the dangers of which you speak, he will be a villain who brings me to trial—of that I am very sure, for no good man would accuse the innocent. Nor shall I be surprised if I am put to death. Shall I tell you why I anticipate this?

By all means.

I think that I am the only or almost the only Athenian living who practices the true art of politics; I am the only politician of my time. Now, seeing that when I speak my words are not uttered with any view of gaining favor, and that I look to what is best and not to what is most pleasant, having no mind to use those arts and graces which you recommend, I shall have nothing to say in the justice court. And you might argue with me, as I was arguing with Polus: I shall be tried just as a physician would be tried in a court of little boys at the indictment of the cook. What would he reply under such circumstances, if someone were to accuse him, saying, "Oh my boys, many evil things has this man done to you: he is the death of you, especially of the younger ones among you, cutting and burning and starving and suffocating you, until you know not what to do; he gives you the bitterest potions, and compels you to hunger and thirst. How unlike the variety of meats and sweets on which I feasted you!" What do you suppose that the physician would be able to reply when he found himself in such a predicament? If he told the truth he could only say, "All these evil things, my boys, I did for your health," and then would there not just be a clamor among a jury like that? How they would cry out!

I dare say.

Would he not be utterly at a loss for a reply?

He certainly would.

And I too shall be treated in the same way, as I well know, if I am brought before the court. For I shall not be able to rehearse to the people the pleasures which I have procured for them, and which, although I am not disposed to envy either the procurers or enjoyers of them, are deemed by them to be benefits and advantages. And if anyone says that I corrupt young men, and perplex their minds, or that I speak evil of old men, and use bitter words toward them, whether in private or public, it is useless for me to reply, as I truly might: "All this I do for the sake of justice, and with a view to your interest, my judges, and to nothing else." And therefore there is no saying what may happen to me.

And do you think, Socrates, that a man who is thus defenseless is in a good position?

Yes, Callicles, if he have that defense, which as you have often acknowledged he should have—if he be his own defense, and have never said or done anything wrong, either in respect of gods or men; and this has been repeatedly acknowledged by us to be the best sort of defense. And if anyone could convict me of inability to defend myself or others after this sort, I should blush for shame, whether I was convicted before many, or before a few, or by myself alone; and if I died from want of ability to do so, that would indeed grieve me. But if I died because I have no powers of flattery or rhetoric, I am very sure that you would not find me repining at death. For no man who is not an utter fool and coward is afraid of death itself, but he is afraid of doing wrong. For to go to the world below having one's soul full of injustice is the last and worst of all evils.

Henry's Speech at Agincourt

William Shakespeare

It would be hard to read Henry's address at Agincourt and escape a brief twinge of regret for not having been one of the "happy few" to fight on St. Crispin's day. The scene (from Shakespeare's *King Henry the Fifth*) is the English camp the moment before the battle. The year is 1415. Young King Henry of England has landed a well-equipped army in Normandy and begun a campaign to conquer France. Reaching Agincourt, the English forces found themselves facing a much larger French army. I believe, from my experience, that this speech is the model for all half-time talks given by all football coaches every autumn in America.

Westmoreland: O that we now had here
But one ten thousand of those men in England
That do no work today!
  King Henry: What's he that wishes so?
My cousin Westmoreland? No, my fair cousin.
If we are mark'd to die, we are enow
To do our country loss; and if to live,
The fewer men, the greater share of honour.
God's will! I pray thee, wish not one man more.
By Jove, I am not covetous for gold,
Nor care I who doth feed upon my cost;
It yearns me not if men my garments wear;
Such outward things dwell not in my desires;
But if it be a sin to covet honour,
I am the most offending soul alive.
No, faith, my coz, wish not a man from England.
God's peace! I would not lose so great an honour
As one man more, methinks, would share from me
For the best hope I have. O, do not wish one more!
Rather proclaim it, Westmoreland, through my host,
That he which hath no stomach to this fight,
Let him depart; his passport shall be made
And crowns for convoy put into his purse.
We would not die in that man's company
That fears his fellowship to die with us.
This day is call'd the feast of Crispian.
He that outlives this day, and comes safe home,
Will stand a tip-toe when this day is named,
And rouse him at the name of Crispian.
He that shall live this day, and see old age,
Will yearly on the vigil feast his neighbours,
And say, "To-morrow is Saint Crispian."
Then will he strip his sleeve and show his scars,
And say "These wounds I had on Crispin's day."
Old men forget; yet all shall be forgot,
But he'll remember with advantages
What feats he did that day. Then shall our names,
Familiar in his mouth as household words,
Harry the king, Bedford and Exeter,
Warwick and Talbot, Salisbury and Gloucester,
Be in their flowing cups freshly remember'd.

This story shall the good man teach his son;
And Crispin Crispian shall ne'er go by,
From this day to the ending of the world,
But we in it shall be remembered,
We few, we happy few, we band of brothers.
For he to-day that sheds his blood with me
Shall be my brother; be he ne'er so vile,
This day shall gentle his condition;
And gentlemen in England now a-bed
Shall think themselves accursed they were not here,
And hold their manhoods cheap whiles any speaks
That fought with us upon Saint Crispin's day.

Prisoner of War

James Bond Stockdale

Vice Admiral James Bond Stockdale was a prisoner of war for
seven and one-half years during the Vietnam war, four of them
in solitary confinement. Despite repeated torture, he maintained
secret communication with other American POWs and was a
leader in setting the policy and standards for the prisoners' resistance to their captors. Stockdale was awarded the Congressional
Medal of Honor in 1976 and was a candidate for Vice President
of the United States in 1992.

As my last tutorial session came to an end, Dr. Rhinelander
reached up to one of his many packed bookshelves and picked out a
little, heavily used volume and handed it to me. "As I remember,
you are a military man. Frederick the Great carried a copy of this
book on all his campaigns. Its author, the Stoic philosopher Epictetus, referred to it as a 'field manual for soldiers,' but you will see
that it's a good deal more than that. It is a philosophy for a soldier."
Back home in Los Altos Hills that night, I eagerly opened it.

The essence of good and evil lies in an attitude of the will.

That made sense to me, and then I read on.

> There are things which are within your power, and there
> are things which are beyond your power. Within your power
> are opinion, aim, desire, aversion; in a word, whatever affairs
> are your own. Beyond your power are body, property, repu-
> tation, office; in a word, affairs not properly your own. Con-
> cern yourself only with what is within your power.
> The essence of good consists of things within your own
> power; with them there is no room for envy or emulation.
> For your part, do not desire to be a general, or a senator or a
> consul, but to be free; and the only way to do this is a disre-
> gard of things which do not lie within your own power.

"Is Rhinelander crazy?" I thought. . . .

The full message really never struck home until one day on my
second combat cruise in Vietnam (a mere three years since I had left
Stanford) as I was tooling along at treetop level over familiar territory, dropping snakeye bombs on a railroad yard at about 500 knots.
I began hearing, even above the cockpit noise, a "boom" "boom"
"boom" and looked up to stare down the barrels of what had to be
the biggest anti-aircraft gun in the world. All my red cockpit lights
came on, the aircraft caught on fire, and I lost the control system
and nosed over abruptly. I pulled the handle and ejected in the nick
of time. Almost instantly I was suspended in my parachute just
above those trees, drifting along in a silence interrupted only by the
rifle shots from the ground below and the whizz of bullets that
luckily passed me by only to tear holes in the parachute canopy
above me. In the following seconds, so help me, two meaningful
thoughts came to my mind before I settled into the village below.
The first was: "Five years to wait before I get out of here" (I had just
studied enough modern Southeast Asian history to realize that we
had programmed ourselves into a quagmire over there—I turned out
to be an optimist and underestimated my stay by three years). My
second thought was: "You are leaving the world of technology and
entering the world of Epictetus."

Well, my "world of Epictetus," I soon learned, was a world in
which chivalry, if it ever existed, was dead. I entered a physical
world, and I got the hell knocked out of me from the moment my
feet hit the ground. The world of Epictetus was also a hard-nosed
political world. I had my leg broken in the street by a mob just after

I landed. My leg was either going to get medical aid or remain rigid and deformed for the rest of my life. Some weeks later the man in charge of the prison camps took note of my refusal to make a statement critical of the United States and set me straight on priorities. "You have a medical problem and a political problem. Politics come before medicine in the DRV [Democratic Republic of Vietnam]. You fix the political problem in your head first, and then we'll see the doctors." The leg was never fixed.

I'll never forget my Christmas Day conversation with that same senior Vietnamese officer three months after I had been shot down in September 1965. He said, "You are my age, you and I share the military profession, and we have sons the same age, but there is a wall beween us. The wall is there because we come from different social and political systems. But you and I must try to see through that wall and together bring this imperialist war of American aggression to an end. We know how to do this, but you must help me, you must influence the other American prisoners. Through propaganda [not a "bad word" in Communist circles], we will win the war on the streets of New York. All I ask is that you be reasonable. You will help me. You don't know it yet, but you will."

A week later I heard the church bells of Hanoi ring in the New Year 1966 at midnight. I was shivering without a blanket, legs in stocks, hands in cuffs, lying in three days of my own excrement. That was only the beginning. I became immersed in a system of isolation, of extortion, of torture, of silence. Any American who from his solitary cell was caught communicating with another American, by wall tap, by whisper, you name it, was put back in the meat grinder to go from torture to submission to confession to apology to atonement. That was a hard life, but I'm proud to say that became about the only route to propaganda for them, because we met the challenge by communicating and taking the lumps, by organizing, by resisting in unison, by giving them nothing free, making them hurt us before we gave an inch, by fighting "City Hall."

Liberty or Death

Patrick Henry

A member of Virginia's House of Burgesses and the first Virginia Committee of Correspondence, fierce opponent of the Stamp Act, and delegate to the Continental Congress in 1774–1775, Patrick Henry (1736–1799) was one of the colonies' foremost patriots in the growing revolutionary cause. His oratory gave him lasting fame, and today he is remembered mainly for the fiery speech he gave to the Second Virginia Convention on March 23, 1775, at St. John's Church in Richmond. The question before the Convention was whether to arm the Virginia militia to fight the British. Patrick Henry knew the moment had come for the colonies to gather their strength and commit themselves to action.

Mr. President, it is natural to man to indulge in the illusions of hope. We are apt to shut our eyes against a painful truth—and listen to the song of that siren, till she transforms us into beasts. Is this the part of wise men, engaged in a great and arduous struggle for liberty? Are we disposed to be of the number of those who, having eyes, see not, and having ears, hear not, the things which so nearly concern their temporal salvation? For my part, whatever anguish of spirit it might cost, I am willing to know the whole truth; to know the worst, and to provide for it. . . .

There is no longer any room for hope. If we wish to be free—if we mean to preserve inviolate those inestimable privileges for which we have been so long contending—if we mean not basely to abandon the noble struggle in which we have been so long engaged, and which we have pledged ourselves never to abandon until the glorious object of our contest shall be obtained—we must fight!—I repeat it, sir, we must fight! An appeal to arms, and to the God of Hosts, is all that is left us!

They tell us, sir, that we are weak—unable to cope with so formidable an adversary. But when shall we be stronger? Will it be the next week, or the next year? Will it be when we are totally disarmed, and when a British guard shall be stationed in every house? Shall we gather strength by irresolution and inaction? Shall we acquire the means of effectual resistance by lying supinely on our backs, and hugging the delusive phantom of Hope, until our enemies shall have bound us hand and foot? Sir, we are not weak, if we make a proper use of those means which the God of nature hath placed in our power. Three millions of people, armed in the holy cause of liberty, and in such a country as that which we possess, are invincible by any force which our enemy can send against us. Besides, sir, we shall not fight our battles alone. There is a just God who presides over the destinies of nations; and who will raise up friends to fight our battles for us. The battle, sir, is not to the strong alone; it is to the vigilant, the active, the brave. Besides, sir, we have no election. If we were base enough to desire it, it is now too late to retire from the contest. There is no retreat, but in submission and slavery! Our chains are forged, their clanking may be heard on the plains of Boston! The war is inevitable—and let it come! I repeat it, sir, let it come!

It is in vain, sir, to extenuate the matter. Gentlemen may cry, peace, peace—but there is no peace. The war is actually begun! The next gale that sweeps from the north will bring to our ears the clash of resounding arms! Our brethren are already in the field! Why stand we here idle? What is it that gentlemen wish? What would they have? Is life so dear, or peace so sweet, as to be purchased at the price of chains and slavery? Forbid it, Almighty God! I know not what course others may take; but as for me, give me liberty, or give me death!

The Rainy Day

Henry Wadsworth Longfellow

Life calls for a variety of everyday fortitudes. They may be less spectacular than the valor of a hazardous climax, but they nevertheless determine what kind of students, spouses, parents, workers, and citizens we are. Facing life's realities, its downs as well as its ups, is one kind of daily courage we all must learn.

The day is cold, and dark, and dreary;
It rains, and the wind is never weary;
The vine still clings to the moldering wall,
But at every gust the dead leaves fall,
    And the day is dark and dreary.

My life is cold, and dark, and dreary;
It rains, and the wind is never weary;
My thoughts still cling to the moldering Past,
But the hopes of youth fall thick in the blast,
    And the days are dark and dreary.

Be still, sad heart! and cease repining;
Behind the clouds is the sun still shining;
Thy fate is the common fate of all,
Into each life some rain must fall,
    Some days must be dark and dreary.

Self-Reliance

Ralph Waldo Emerson

"Self-Reliance" may be Ralph Waldo Emerson's best-known
work. Published in 1841, when the United States was still a
young nation, the essay challenged Americans to know themselves, trust their instincts, and recognize their own genius. The
divine sufficiency of the individual was Emerson's crusade; he
called for the courage of self-trust.

Man is his own star, and the soul that can
Render an honest and a perfect man,
Command all light, all influence, all fate,
Nothing to him falls early or too late.
Our acts our angels are, or good or ill,
Our fatal shadows that walk by us still.
    —Epilogue to Beaumont and Fletcher's
        Honest Man's Fortune.

I read the other day some verses written by an eminent painter which were original and not conventional. The soul always hears an admonition in such lines, let the subject be what it may. The sentiment they instill is of more value than any thought they may contain. To believe your own thought, to believe that what is true for you in your private heart is true for all men—that is genius. Speak your latent conviction, and it shall be the universal sense; for the inmost in due time becomes the outmost, and our first thought is rendered back to us by the trumpets of the Last Judgment. Familiar as the voice of the mind is to each, the highest merit we ascribe to Moses, Plato, and Milton is that they set at naught books and traditions and spoke not what men, but what they thought. A man should learn to detect and watch that gleam of light which flashes across his mind from within more than the luster of the firmament of bards and sages. Yet he dismisses without notice his thought, because it is his. In every work of genius we recognize our rejected thoughts; they come back to us with a certain alienated majesty. Great works of art have no more affecting lesson for us than this. They teach us to abide by our spontaneous impression with good-humored inflexibility then most when the whole cry of voices is on the other side. Else, tomorrow a stranger will say with masterly good sense precisely what we have thought and felt all the time, and we shall be forced to take with shame our own opinion from another.

There is a time in every man's education when he arrives at the conviction that envy is ignorance; that imitation is suicide; that he must take himself for better, for worse, as his portion; that, though the wide universe is full of good, no kernel of nourishing corn can come to him but through his toil bestowed on that plot of ground which is given to him to till. The power which resides in him is new in nature, and none but he knows what that is which he can do, nor does he know until he has tried. Not for nothing one face, one character, one fact makes much impression on him, and another none. This sculpture in the memory is not without preestablished harmony. The eye was placed where one ray should fall that it might testify of that particular ray. We but half express ourselves, and are ashamed of that divine idea which each of us represents. It may be safely trusted as proportionate and of good issues, so it be faithfully imparted, but God will not have his work made manifest by cowards. A man is relieved and gay when he has put his heart into his work and done his best; but what he has said or done otherwise shall give him no peace. It is a deliverance which does not deliver. In the attempt his genius deserts him; no muse befriends; no invention, no hope.

Trust thyself; every heart vibrates to that iron string. Accept the place the divine providence has found for you, the society of your contemporaries, the connection of events. Great men have always done so, and confided themselves childlike to the genius of their age, betraying their perception that the absolutely trustworthy was seated at their heart, working through their hands, predominating in all their being. And we are now men and must accept in the highest mind the same transcendent destiny; and not minors and invalids in a protected corner, not cowards fleeing before a revolution, but guides, redeemers, and benefactors, obeying the Almighty effort, and advancing on Chaos and the Dark.

The Road Not Taken

Robert Frost

Courage does not follow rutted pathways.

Two roads diverged in a yellow wood,
And sorry I could not travel both
And be one traveler, long I stood
And looked down one as far as I could
To where it bent in the undergrowth;

Then took the other, as just as fair,
And having perhaps the better claim,
Because it was grassy and wanted wear;
Though as for that the passing there
Had worn them really about the same,

And both that morning equally lay
In leaves no step had trodden black.
Oh, I kept the first for another day!
Yet knowing how way leads on to way,
I doubted if I should ever come back.

I shall be telling this with a sigh
Somewhere ages and ages hence:
Two roads diverged in a wood, and I—
I took the one less traveled by,
And that has made all the difference.

7

Perseverance

"The noblest question in the world," observed Benjamin Franklin in *Poor Richard*, "is What good may I do in it?" "Hang in there!" is more than an expression of encouragement to someone experiencing hardship or difficulty; it is sound advice for anyone intent on doing good in the world. Whether by leading or prodding others, or improving oneself, or contributing in the thick of things to some larger cause, perseverance is often crucial to success.

Drawing on an ancient Chinese proverb, Harry Truman recounted in his *Memoirs* that being president "is like riding a tiger. A man has to keep on riding or be swallowed." He went on to explain that "a President either is constantly on top of events or, if he hesitates, events will soon be on top of him. I never felt that I could let up for a single moment." Perseverance is an essential quality of character in high-level leadership. Much good that might have been achieved in the world is lost through hesitation, faltering, wavering, vacillating, or just not sticking with it.

Perseverance is also essential to the watchdog's and gadfly's approaches to working for good in the world. Socrates, self-acknowledged gadfly of ancient Athens, was absolutely serious in proclaiming at his trial (as recounted in Plato's *Apology*) that "as long as I draw breath and am able, I shall not cease to practice philosophy, to exhort you and in my usual way to point out to any one of you whom I happen to meet: Good Sir, you are an Athenian, a citizen of the greatest city with the greatest reputation for both wisdom and power; are you not ashamed of your eagerness to possess as much wealth, reputation, and honors as possible, while you do not care for or give thought to wisdom or truth, or the best possible state of your soul?" Socrates' persistent exhortations proved too much for many Athenians, however, and he was condemned. But there are worse fates, as Socrates himself pointed out: while he had merely been condemned to *death,* his accusers had by that same act been condemned to *wickedness!*

"Slow and steady wins the race," runs the moral of Aesop's familiar fable of the tortoise and the hare. Plutarch in his *Life of Sertorius* recounts how this great Roman soldier, while serving as praetor in Spain in the first century B.C., contrived a demonstration for his troops to the same effect, following which he addressed them in this manner: "You see, fellow soldiers, that perseverance is more prevailing than violence, and that many things which cannot be overcome when they are together, yield themselves up when taken little by little. Assiduity and persistence are irresistible, and in time overthrow and destroy the greatest powers whatever, time being the favorable friend and assistant of those who use their judgment to await his occasions, and the destructive enemy of those who are unreasonably urging and pressing forward."

Like most other virtues, persistence and perseverance cannot operate for good in the world in isolation from practical intelligence. A person who is *merely* persistent may be a carping, pestering, irksome annoyance, having no salutary effect whatsoever. But given the right context, occurring in the right combination with other virtues, perseverance is an essential ingredient in human progress. Sam Adams saw it thus in the gestation period prior to our birth as a nation. "The necessity of the times," he proclaimed in 1771, "more than ever, calls for our utmost circumspection, deliberation, fortitude, and perseverance." And the same holds true today.

How do we encourage our children to persevere, to persist in their efforts to improve themselves, their own lot, and the lot of others? By standing by them, and with them and behind them; by being coaches and cheerleaders, and by the witness of our own example. Modern technology has made some of this much easier for us. Video and tape recordings are convincing evidence of the long-term progress that is sometimes hard to see in the short term.

Persevere

Stick-to-it-iveness has a lot to do with getting the right answers in math, English, history, and life, as young Americans of the turn of the twentieth century learned when they memorized this little verse from their *McGuffey's Reader*.

> The fisher who draws in his net too soon,
>   Won't have any fish to sell;
> The child who shuts up his book too soon,
>   Won't learn any lessons well.
>
> If you would have your learning stay,
>   Be patient—don't learn too fast;
> The man who travels a mile each day,
>   May get round the world at last.

The Tortoise and the Hare

Aesop

As Aesop knew, perseverance makes up for all sorts of disadvantages. Here is a case of virtue outdistancing undisciplined ability.

A hare once made fun of a tortoise. "What a slow way you have!" he said. "How you creep along!"

"Do I?" said the tortoise. "Try a race with me and I'll beat you."

"What a boaster you are," said the hare. "But come! I will race with you. Whom shall we ask to mark off the finish line and see that the race is fair?"

"Let us ask the fox," said the tortoise.

The fox was very wise and fair. He showed them where they were to start, and how far they were to run.

The tortoise lost no time. He started out at once and jogged straight on.

The hare leaped along swiftly for a few minutes till he had left the tortoise far behind. He knew he could reach the mark very quickly, so he lay down by the road under a shady tree and took a nap.

By and by he awoke and remembered the race. He sprang up and ran as fast as he could. But when he reached the mark the tortoise was already there!

"Slow and steady wins the race," said the fox.

The Little Steam Engine

The story of the little engine that said "I think I can!" has been entertaining children for generations. This version, which comes from an early-twentieth-century reader, offers a portrait of self-resolve as well as cooperation. It reminds us that we get through the hardest times and tasks by pushing and pulling together.

A little steam engine had a long train of cars to pull.

She went along very well till she came to a steep hill. But then, no matter how hard she tried, she could not move the long train of cars.

She pulled, and she pulled. She puffed, and she puffed. She backed and started off again. Choo! Choo! Choo! Choo!

But no! The cars would not go up the hill.

At last she left the train and started up the track alone. Do you think she had stopped working? No, indeed! She was going for help.

"Surely I can find someone to help me," she thought.

Over the hill and up the track went the little steam engine. Choo, choo! Choo, choo! Choo, choo! Choo, choo!

Pretty soon she saw a big steam engine standing on a side track. He looked very big and strong. Running alongside, she looked up and said,

"Will you help me over the hill with my train of cars? It is so long and so heavy that I can't get it over."

The big steam engine looked down at the little steam engine. Then he said,

"Don't you see that I am through my day's work? I have been all rubbed and scoured ready for my next run. No, I cannot help you."

The little steam engine was sorry, but she went on. Choo, choo! Choo, choo! Choo, choo! Choo, choo!

Soon she came to a second big steam engine standing on a side track. He was puffing and puffing, as if he were tired.

"He may help me," thought the little steam engine. She ran alongside and asked,

"Will you help me bring my train of cars over the hill? It is so long and so heavy that I can't get it over."

The second big steam engine answered,

"I have just come in from a long, long run. Don't you see how tired I am? Can't you get some other engine to help you this time?"

"I'll try," said the little steam engine, and off she went. Choo, choo! Choo, choo! Choo, choo! Choo, choo!

After a while she came to a little steam engine just like herself. She ran alongside and said,

"Will you help me over the hill with my train of cars? It is so long and so heavy that I can't get it over."

"Yes, indeed!" said the second little steam engine. "I'll be glad to help you, if I can."

So the little steam engines started back to where the train of cars had been standing all this time. One little steam engine went to the head of the train, and the other to the end of it.

Puff, puff! Chug, chug! Choo, choo! Off they started!

Slowly the cars began to move. Slowly they climbed the steep hill. As they climbed, each little steam engine began to sing,

"I—think—I—can! I—think—I—can! I—think—I—can! I—think—I—can! I—think—I—can! I—think—I—can! I think I can—I-think I can—I think I can I think I can—"

And they did! Very soon, they were over the hill and going down the other side.

Now they were on the plain again, and the little steam engine could pull her train herself. So she thanked the little engine who had come to help her, and said goodbye.

And as she went merrily on her way, she sang to herself,

"I—thought—I—could! I—thought—I—could! I—thought—I—could! I—thought—I—could! I thought I could—I thought I could—I thought I could—I thought I could—I thought I could I thought I could—"

Try, Try Again

'Tis a lesson you should heed,
    Try, try again;
If at first you don't succeed,
    Try, try again;
Then your courage should appear,
For, if you will persevere,
You will conquer, never fear;
    Try, try again.

The Crow and the Pitcher

Aesop

This is the famous fable from Aesop which tells us that where there's a will accompanied by practical intelligence, there's a way.

Once there was a thirsty crow. She had flown a long way looking for water to drink.

Suddenly she saw a pitcher. She flew down and saw it held a little water, but it was so low in the pitcher that she could not reach it.

"But I must have that water," she cried. "I am too weary to fly farther. What shall I do? I know! I'll tip the pitcher over."

She beat it with her wings, but it was too heavy. She could not move it.

Then she thought awhile. "I know now! I will break it! Then I will drink the water as it pours out. How good it will taste!"

With beak and claws and wings she threw herself against the pitcher. But it was too strong.

The poor crow stopped to rest. "What shall I do now? I cannot die of thirst with water close by. There must be a way, if I only had wit enough to find it out."

After a while the crow had a bright idea. There were many small stones lying about. She picked them up one by one and dropped them into the pitcher. Slowly the water rose, till at last she could drink it. How good it tasted!

"There is always a way out of hard places," said the crow, "if only you have the wit to find it."

The Little Hero of Holland

Adapted from Etta Austin Blaisdell and Mary Frances Blaisdell

Here is true fortitude: someone doing his duty despite pain and loneliness and danger, someone willing to hold on, hold fast, and hold out as long as it takes, someone whose resolution outweighs even the weight of the sea.

Holland is a country where much of the land lies below sea level. Only great walls called dikes keep the North Sea from rushing in and flooding the land. For centuries the people of Holland have worked to keep the walls strong so that their country will be safe and dry. Even the little children know the dikes must be watched every moment, and that a hole no larger than your finger can be a very dangerous thing.

Many years ago there lived in Holland a boy named Peter. Peter's father was one of the men who tended the gates in the dikes, called sluices. He opened and closed the sluices so that ships could pass out of Holland's canals into the great sea.

One afternoon in the early fall, when Peter was eight years old, his mother called him from his play. "Come, Peter," she said. "I want you to go across the dike and take these cakes to your friend, the blind man. If you go quickly, and do not stop to play, you will be home again before dark."

The little boy was glad to go on such an errand, and started off with a light heart. He stayed with the poor blind man a little while to tell him about his walk along the dike and about the sun and the flowers and the ships far out at sea. Then he remembered his mother's wish that he should return before dark, and bidding his friend goodbye, he set out for home.

As he walked beside the canal, he noticed how the rains had swollen the waters, and how they beat against the side of the dike, and he thought of his father's gates.

"I am glad they are so strong," he said to himself. "If they gave way what would become of us? These pretty fields would be covered with water. Father always calls them the 'angry waters.' I suppose he thinks they are angry at him for keeping them out so long."

As he walked along he sometimes stopped to pick the pretty blue flowers that grew beside the road, or to listen to the rabbits' soft tread as they rustled through the grass. But oftener he smiled as he thought of his visit to the poor blind man who had so few pleasures and was always so glad to see him.

Suddenly he noticed that the sun was setting, and that it was growing dark. "Mother will be watching for me," he thought, and he began to run toward home.

Just then he heard a noise. It was the sound of trickling water! He stopped and looked down. There was a small hole in the dike, through which a tiny stream was flowing.

Any child in Holland is frightened at the thought of a leak in the dike.

Peter understood the danger at once. If the water ran through a little hole it would soon make a larger one, and the whole country would be flooded. In a moment he saw what he must do. Throwing away his flowers, he climbed down the side of the dike and thrust his finger into the tiny hole.

The flowing of the water was stopped!

"Oho!" he said to himself. "The angry waters must stay back now. I can keep them back with my finger. Holland shall not be drowned while I am here."

This was all very well at first, but it soon grew dark and cold. The little fellow shouted and screamed. "Come here; come here," he called. But no one heard him; no one came to help him.

It grew still colder, and his arm ached, and began to grow stiff and numb. He shouted again, "Will no one come? Mother! Mother!"

But his mother had looked anxiously along the dike road many times since sunset for her little boy, and now she had closed and locked the cottage door, thinking that Peter was spending the night with his blind friend, and that she would scold him in the morning for staying away from home without her permission.

Peter tried to whistle, but his teeth chattered with the cold. He thought of his brother and sister in their warm beds, and of his dear father and mother. "I must not let them be drowned," he thought. "I must stay here until someone comes, if I have to stay all night."

The moon and stars looked down on the child crouching on a stone on the side of the dike. His head was bent, and his eyes were closed, but he was not asleep, for every now and then he rubbed the hand that was holding back the angry sea.

"I'll stand it somehow," he thought. So he stayed there all night keeping the water out.

Early the next morning a man going to work thought he heard a groan as he walked along the top of the dike. Looking over the edge, he saw a child clinging to the side of the great wall.

"What's the matter?" he called. "Are you hurt?"

"I'm keeping the water back!" Peter yelled. "Tell them to come quickly!"

The alarm was spread. People came running with shovels, and the hole was soon mended.

They carried Peter home to his parents, and before long the whole town knew how he had saved their lives that night. To this day, they have never forgotten the brave little hero of Holland.

You Mustn't Quit

When things go wrong, as they sometimes will,
When the road you're trudging seems all uphill,
When the funds are low and the debts are high
And you want to smile, but you have to sigh,
When care is pressing you down a bit,
Rest! if you must—but never quit.

Life is queer, with its twists and turns,
As every one of us sometimes learns,
And many a failure turns about
When he might have won if he'd stuck it out;
Stick to your task, though the pace seems slow—
You may succeed with one more blow.

Success is failure turned inside out—
The silver tint of the clouds of doubt—
And you never can tell how close you are,
It may be near when it seems afar;
So stick to the fight when you're hardest hit—
It's when things seem worst that YOU MUSTN'T QUIT.

The Steadfast Tin Soldier

Hans Christian Andersen

This is not a "happily ever after" story, but a tale with a bitter-sweet ending. And therein lies its magic and charm. It teaches us that we prevail by enduring until the very end, whatever that end may be. We do not know what to expect from fortune. We only know what to expect of ourselves. This is a favorite story of the Bennett family.

There were once five and twenty tin soldiers. They were brothers, for they had all been made out of the same old tin spoon. They all shouldered their bayonets, held themselves upright, and looked straight before them. Their uniforms were very smart-looking—red and blue—and very splendid. The first thing they heard in the world, when the lid was taken off the box in which they lay, was the words "Tin soldiers!" These words were spoken by a little boy, who clapped his hands for joy. The soldiers had been given him because it was his birthday, and now he was putting them out upon the table.

Each was exactly like the rest to a hair, except one who had but one leg. He had been cast last of all, and there had not been quite enough tin to finish him. But he stood as firmly upon his one leg as the others upon their two, and it was he whose fortunes became so remarkable.

On the table where the tin soldiers had been set up were several other toys, but the one that attracted most attention was a pretty little paper castle. Through its tiny windows one could see straight into the hall. In front of the castle stood little trees, clustering round a small mirror which was meant to represent a transparent lake. Swans of wax swam upon its surface, and it reflected back their images.

All this was very pretty, but prettiest of all was a little lady who stood at the castle's open door. She too was cut out of paper, but she wore a frock of the clearest gauze and a narrow blue ribbon over her shoulders, like a scarf, and in the middle of the ribbon was placed a shining tinsel rose. The little lady stretched out both her arms, for she was a dancer, and then she lifted one leg so high that the Soldier quite lost sight of it. He thought that, like himself, she had but one leg.

"That would be just the wife for me," thought he, "if she were not too grand. But she lives in a castle, while I have only a box, and there are five and twenty of us in that. It would be no place for a lady. Still, I must try to make her acquaintance." A snuffbox happened to be upon the table and he lay down at full length behind it, and here he could easily watch the dainty little lady, who still remained standing on one leg without losing her balance.

When the evening came all the other tin soldiers were put away in their box, and the people in the house went to bed. Now the playthings began to play in their turn. They visited, fought battles, and gave balls. The tin soldiers rattled in the box, for they wished to join the rest, but they could not lift the lid. The nutcrackers turned somersaults, and the pencil jumped about in a most amusing way. There was such a din that the canary woke and began to speak—and in verse, too. The only ones who did not move from their places were the Tin Soldier and the Lady Dancer. She stood on tiptoe with outstretched arms, and he was just as persevering on his one leg. He never once turned away his eyes from her.

Twelve o'clock struck—crash! up sprang the lid of the snuffbox. There was no snuff in it, but a little black goblin. You see it was not a real snuffbox, but a jack-in-the-box.

"Tin Soldier," said the Goblin, "keep thine eyes to thyself. Gaze not at what does not concern thee!"

But the Tin Soldier pretended not to hear.

"Only wait, then, till tomorrow," remarked the Goblin.

Next morning, when the children got up, the Tin Soldier was placed on the windowsill, and, whether it was the Goblin or the wind that did it, all at once the window flew open and the Tin Soldier fell head foremost from the third story to the street below. It was a tremendous fall! Over and over he turned in the air, till at last he rested, his cap and bayonet sticking fast between the paving stones, while his one leg stood upright in the air.

The maidservant and the little boy came down at once to look for him, but, though they nearly trod upon him, they could not manage to find him. If the Soldier had but once called "Here am I!" they might easily enough have heard him, but he did not think it becoming to cry out for help, being in uniform.

It now began to rain; faster and faster fell the drops, until there was a heavy shower; and when it was over, two street boys came by.

"Look you," said one, "there lies a tin soldier. He must come out and sail in a boat."

So they made a boat out of an old newspaper and put the Tin Soldier in the middle of it, and away he sailed down the gutter, while the boys ran along by his side, clapping their hands.

Goodness! how the waves rocked that paper boat, and how fast the stream ran! The Tin Soldier became quite giddy, the boat veered round so quickly. Still he moved not a muscle, but looked straight before him and held his bayonet tightly.

All at once the boat passed into a drain, and it became as dark as his own old home in the box. "Where am I going now?" thought he. "Yes, to be sure, it is all that Goblin's doing. Ah! if the little lady were but sailing with me in the boat, I would not care if it were twice as dark."

Just then a great water rat, that lived under the drain, darted suddenly out.

"Have you a passport?" asked the rat. "Where is your passport?"

But the Tin Soldier kept silence and only held his bayonet with a firmer grasp.

The boat sailed on, but the rat followed. Whew! how he gnashed his teeth and cried to the sticks and straws: "Stop him! stop him! He hasn't paid his toll! He hasn't shown his passport!"

But the stream grew stronger and stronger. Already the Tin Soldier could see daylight at the point where the tunnel ended; but at the same time he heard a rushing, roaring noise, at which a bolder man might have trembled. Think! just where the tunnel ended, the drain widened into a great sheet that fell into the mouth of a sewer. It was as perilous a situation for the Soldier as sailing down a mighty waterfall would be for us.

He was now so near it that he could not stop. The boat dashed on, and the Tin Soldier held himself so well that no one might say of him that he so much as winked an eye. Three or four times the boat whirled round and round; it was full of water to the brim and must certainly sink.

The Tin Soldier stood up to his neck in water; deeper and deeper sank the boat, softer and softer grew the paper; and now the water closed over the Soldier's head. He thought of the pretty little dancer whom he should never see again, and in his ears rang the words of the song:

> Wild adventure, mortal danger,
> Be thy portion, valiant stranger.

The paper boat parted in the middle, and the Soldier was about to sink, when he was swallowed by a great fish.

Oh, how dark it was! darker even than in the drain, and so narrow. But the Tin Soldier retained his courage; there he lay at full length, shouldering his bayonet as before.

To and fro swam the fish, turning and twisting and making the strangest movements, till at last he became perfectly still.

Something like a flash of daylight passed through him, and a voice said, "Tin Soldier!" The fish had been caught, taken to market, sold and bought, and taken to the kitchen, where the cook had cut him with a large knife. She seized the Tin Soldier between her finger and thumb and took him to the room where the family sat, and where all were eager to see the celebrated man who had traveled in the maw of a fish. But the Tin Soldier remained unmoved. He was not at all proud.

They set him upon the table there. But how could so curious a thing happen? The Soldier was in the very same room in which he had been before. He saw the same children, the same toys stood upon the table, and among them the pretty dancing maiden, who still stood upon one leg. She too was steadfast. That touched the Tin Soldier's heart. He could have wept tin tears, but that would not have been proper. He looked at her and she looked at him, but neither spoke a word.

And now one of the little boys took the Tin Soldier and threw him into the stove. He gave no reason for doing so, but no doubt the Goblin in the snuffbox had something to do with it.

The Tin Soldier stood now in a blaze of red light. The heat he felt was terrible, but whether it proceeded from the fire or from the love in his heart, he did not know. He saw that the colors were quite gone from his uniform, but whether that had happened on the journey or had been caused by grief, no one could say. He looked at the little lady, she looked at him, and he felt himself melting; still he stood firm as ever, with his bayonet on his shoulder. Then suddenly the door flew open; the wind caught the Dancer, and she flew straight into the stove to the Tin Soldier, flashed up in a flame, and was gone! The Tin Soldier melted into a lump. And in the ashes the maid found him the next day, in the shape of a little tin heart, while of the Dancer nothing remained save the tinsel rose, and that was burned as black as a coal.

Carry On!

Robert Service

Here's another one best read out loud.

It's easy to fight when everything's right,
And you're mad with the thrill and the glory;
It's easy to cheer when victory's near,
And wallow in fields that are gory.
It's a different song when everything's wrong,
When you're feeling infernally mortal;
When it's ten against one, and hope there is none,
Buck up, little soldier, and chortle:

Carry on! Carry on!
There isn't much punch in your blow.
You're glaring and staring and hitting out blind;
You're muddy and bloody, but never you mind.
Carry on! Carry on!
You haven't the ghost of a show.
It's looking like death, but while you've a breath,
Carry on, my son! Carry on!

And so in the strife of the battle of life
It's easy to fight when you're winning;
It's easy to slave, and starve and be brave,
When the dawn of success is beginning.
But the man who can meet despair and defeat
With a cheer, there's the man of God's choosing;
The man who can fight to Heaven's own height
Is the man who can fight when he's losing.

Carry on! Carry on!
Things never were looming so black.
But show that you haven't a cowardly streak,
And though you're unlucky you never are weak.
Carry on! Carry on!
Brace up for another attack.
It's looking like hell, but—you never can tell:
Carry on, old man! Carry on!

There are some who drift out in the deserts of doubt,
And some who in brutishness wallow;
There are others, I know, who in piety go
Because of a Heaven to follow.
But to labor with zest, and to give of your best,
For the sweetness and joy of the giving;
To help folks along with a hand and a song;
Why, there's the real sunshine of living.

Carry on! Carry on!
Fight the good fight and true;
Believe in your mission, greet life with a cheer;
There's big work to do, and that's why you are here.
Carry on! Carry on!
Let the world be the better for you;
And at last when you die, let this be your cry:
Carry on, my soul! Carry on!

The Stars in the Sky

Adapted from Carolyn Sherwin Bailey, Kate Douglas
Wiggin, and Nora Archibald Smith

This old English tale reminds us that the higher we reach, the
longer and harder we have to try.

Once upon a time there was a little lass who wanted nothing
more than to touch the stars in the sky. On clear, moonless nights
she would lean out her bedroom window, gazing up at the thousand
tiny lights scattered across the heavens, wondering what it would be
like to hold one in her hand.

One warm summer evening, a night when the Milky Way
shined more brightly than ever before, she decided she couldn't stand
it any longer—she just had to touch a star or two, no matter what.
So she slipped out the window and started off by herself to see if she
could reach them.

She walked a far, far way, and then farther still, until she came to a mill wheel, creaking and grinding away.

"Good evening," she said to the mill wheel. "I would like to play with the stars in the sky. Have you seen any near here?"

"Ah, yes," groaned the old mill wheel. "Every night they shine in my face from the surface of this pond until I cannot sleep. Jump in, my lass, and you will find them."

The little girl jumped into the pond and swam around until her arms were so tired she could swim no longer, but she could not find any stars.

"Excuse me," she called to the old mill wheel, "but I don't believe there are any stars here after all!"

"Well, there certainly were before you jumped in and stirred the water up," the mill wheel called back. So she climbed out and dried herself off as best she could, and set out again across the fields.

After a while she came to a little brook, murmuring over its mossy stones.

"Good evening, brooklet," she said politely. "I'm trying to reach the stars in the sky so I may play with them. Have you seen any near here?"

"Ah, yes," whispered the brooklet. "They glint on my banks at night until I cannot sleep. Wade in, my lassie, and you will find them."

So the little girl waded in and paddled around for a while, and climbed all over the mossy rocks, but never once did she find a star.

"Excuse me," she said as politely as she could, "but I just don't think there are any stars here."

"What do you mean, no stars here?" the little brook babbled. "There are lots of stars here. I see them all the time. On some nights, they cover me from the edge of the woods all the way down to the old mill pond. I have more stars here than I know what to do with." And the brooklet babbled on and on until it even forgot the little girl was there, so she tiptoed away across the fields.

After a while she sat down to rest in a meadow, and it must have been a fairy meadow, because before she knew it a hundred little fairies came scampering out to dance on the grass. They were no taller than toadstools, but they were dressed in silver and gold.

"Good evening, Little Folk," said the girl. "I'm trying to reach the stars in the sky. Have you seen any near here?"

"Ah, yes," sang the fairies. "They glisten every night among the blades of the grass. Come and dance with us, little lass, and you will find as many stars as you like."

So the child danced and danced, she whirled round and round in a ring with the Little Folk, but though the grass gleamed beneath her feet, she never spied a single star. Finally she could dance no longer, and she plopped down inside the ring of fairies.

"I've tried and I've tried, but I can't seem to reach the stars down here," she cried. "If you don't help me, I'll never find any to play with."

The fairies all whispered together. Finally one of them crept up and took her by the hand, and said: "If you're really determined, you must go forward. Keep going forward, and mind you take the right road. Ask Four Feet to carry you to No Feet At All, and then tell No Feet At All to carry you to the Stairs Without Steps, and if you climb that—"

"Then I'll be among the stars in the sky?" cried the lassie.

"If you'll not be there, then you'll be somewhere else, won't you?" laughed the fairy, and he vanished with all the rest.

So the little girl set out again with a light heart, and by and by she came to a saddled horse, tied to a tree.

"Good evening," she said. "I'm trying to reach the stars in the sky, and I've come so far my bones are aching. Will you give me a ride?"

"I don't know anything about stars in the sky," the horse replied. "I'm here only to do the bidding of the Little Folk."

"But I come from the Little Folk," she cried, "and they said to tell Four Feet to carry me to No Feet At All."

"Four Feet? That's me!" the horse whinnied. "Jump up and ride with me."

They rode and they rode and they rode, till they rode out of the forest and found themselves at the edge of the sea.

"I've brought you to the end of the land, and that's as much as Four Feet can do," said the horse. "Now I must get home to my own folk."

So the little girl slid down and walked along the sea, wondering what in the world she would do next, until suddenly the biggest fish she'd ever seen came swimming up to her feet.

"Good evening," she said to the fish. "I'm trying to reach the stars in the sky. Can you help me?"

"I'm afraid I can't," gurgled the fish, "unless, of course, you bring me word from the Little Folk."

"But I do," she cried. "They said Four Feet would bring me to

No Feet At All, and then No Feet At All would carry me to the Stairs Without Steps."

"Ah, well," said the fish, "that's all right then. Get on my back and hold on tight."

And off he went—kerplash!—into the water, swimming along a silver path that glistened on the surface and seemed to stretch toward the end of the sea, where the water met the sky. There, in the distance, the little girl saw a beautiful rainbow rising out of the ocean and into the heavens, shining with all the colors in the world, blues and reds and greens, and wonderful to look at. The nearer they drew, the brighter it gleamed, until she had to shade her eyes from its light.

At last they came to the foot of it, and she saw the rainbow was really a broad bright road, sloping up and away into the sky, and at the far, far end of it she could see wee shining things dancing about.

"I can go no further," said the fish. "Here are the Stairs Without Steps. Climb up, if you can, but hold on tight. These stairs were never meant for little lassies' feet, you know." So the little girl jumped off No Feet's back, and off he splashed through the water.

She climbed and she climbed and she climbed up the rainbow. It wasn't easy. Every time she took one step, she seemed to slide back two. And even though she climbed until the sea was far below, the stars in the sky looked farther away than ever.

"But I won't give up," she told herself. "I've come so far, I can't go back."

Up and up she went. The air grew colder and colder, but the sky turned brighter and brighter, and finally she could tell she was nearing the stars.

"I'm almost there!" she cried.

And sure enough, suddenly she reached the very tip-top of the rainbow. Everywhere she looked, the stars were turning and dancing. They raced up and down, and back and forth, and spun in a thousand colors around her.

"I'm finally here," she whispered to herself. She had never seen anything so beautiful before, and she stood gazing and wondering at the heavens.

But after a while she realized she was shivering with cold, and when she looked down into the darkness, she could no longer see the earth. She wondered where her own home was, so far away, but no streetlamps or window lights marked the blackness below. She began to feel a little dizzy.

"I won't go until I touch one star," she told herself, and she stood on her toes and stretched her arms as high as she could. She reached further and further—and suddenly a shooting star zipped by and surprised her so much she lost her balance.

Down she slid—down—down—down the rainbow. The further she slid, the warmer it grew, and the warmer it grew, the sleepier she felt. She gave a great yawn, and a small sigh, and before she knew it, she was fast asleep.

When she woke up, she found herself in her very own bed. The sun was peeking through her window, and the morning birds sang in the bushes and trees.

"Did I really touch the stars?" she asked herself. "Or was it only a dream?"

Then she felt something in her hand. When she opened her fist, a tiny light flashed in her palm, and at once was gone, and she smiled because she knew it was a speck of stardust.

The Story of Scarface

Retold by Amy Cruse

Webster defines fortitude as "strength or firmness of mind that enables a person to encounter danger with coolness and courage or to bear pain or adversity without murmuring, depression, or despondency." John Locke called it the essential virtue, the "guard to every other virtue." In this Blackfoot Indian tale, we find honesty, loyalty, friendship, courage, self-discipline, and more in a young brave's fortitude.

There lived once among a tribe of Indians a poor boy whose father and mother were dead, and who had no friends to take care of him. The kindly Indian women helped him as well as they could, giving him what they could spare of food and clothing, and shelter in the hard days of winter; and the men let him go with them on hunting expeditions, and taught him the Indian woodcraft, just as they taught their own sons. The boy grew up strong and brave, and the men of the tribe said that he would one day make a mighty hunter. While he was quite young he met on one of the hunting parties a great grizzly bear, and fought a desperate fight with him, and at last killed him. But during the struggle the bear set its claws in the boy's face and tore it cruelly; and when the wound healed there was left a red, unsightly mark, so that he thereafter was called Scarface.

The boy thought little of the disfigurement until he fell in love with the beautiful daughter of the chief of his tribe, and then when he saw all the handsome young braves dressing themselves in the splendid dress of the Indian warrior and going to pay court to this maiden at her father's wigwam, his heart ached very sorely because he was poor and friendless, and above all because he bore upon his face the terrible disfiguring scar.

But the maiden did not care for the finery and boastful talk of the young Indians who crowded round her, and each in turn, when he ventured to ask her hand in marriage, found himself refused. Scarface scarcely dared to approach her, but the girl often saw him as he went about the forest, and she felt that he was braver and truer than the other lovers who boldly sought her favor.

One day, as she sat outside her father's lodge, Scarface passed by, and as he passed he looked at her, and his eyes showed the love and admiration that possessed him. A young Indian whose suit the girl had refused noticed the look, and said with a sneer, "Scarface has become a suitor for our chief's daughter. She will have nothing to do with men unblemished; perhaps she desires a man marked and marred. Try then, Scarface, and see if she will take you."

Scarface felt anger rise hot within him against the man who thus mocked him. He stood proudly, as though he were a chief's son instead of a poor, common, disfigured warrior, and, looking very steadily at the young brave, he said, "My brother speaks true words, though he speaks them with an ill tongue. I go indeed to ask the daughter of our great chief to be my wife."

The young brave laughed loudly in mockery. Some other young men of the tribe came up, and he told them what Scarface had said, and they also laughed, calling him the great chief, speaking of his vast wealth and of his marvelous beauty, and pretending to bow down before him. Scarface took no notice, but walked away quietly and with an unmoved face, though in his heart he yearned to spring at them, as the great grizzly had sprung at him in the forest. But when he came down to the river, following the chief's daughter, who had gone there to gather rushes for the baskets she was weaving, his anger died away. He drew near to her, knowing that if he did not speak at once his courage would leave him, for though she was so gentle and so kind, he trembled in her presence as the fiercest warrior or the most terrible bear could not make him tremble.

"Maiden," he said, "I am poor and little thought of, because I have no store of furs or pemmican, as the great warriors of the tribe have. I must gain day by day with my bow and my spear and with hard toil the means by which I live. And my face is marred and unsightly to look upon. But my heart is full of love for you, and I greatly desire you for my wife. Will you marry Scarface and live with him in his poor lodge?"

The maiden looked at him, and in her face he saw the love for which he asked.

"That you are poor," she said, "matters little. My father would give me great store of all needful things for a wedding portion. But I may not be your bride, nor the bride of any man of the tribe. The great Lord of the Sun has laid his commands on me, forbidding me to marry."

The heart of poor Scarface sank at these terrible words, yet he would not give up hope. "Will he not release you?" he asked. "He is kind and gives us many good gifts. He would not wish to make us both miserable."

"Go to him, then," said the girl, "and make your prayer to him that he will set me free from my promise. And ask him, that I may know that he has done so, to take the scar from off your face as a sign."

"I will go," said Scarface, "I will seek out the bright god in his own land, and beseech him to pity us." So he turned and left the maiden by the riverside.

Scarface started at once on his journey, and traveled for many, many miles. Sometimes he went cheerfully, saying to himself, "The sun god is kind; he will give me my bride." Sometimes his heart was sad, and he went heavily, for he thought, "Maybe the sun god desires to marry her himself, and who could expect him to give up a maiden so beautiful?" Through forests and over mountains he went, searching ever for the golden gates which marked the entrance to the country of the great god. The wild animals he met knew that this time he had not come out as a hunter to take them, so they drew near to him and willingly answered his questions. But not one of them could tell him where lay the sun god's land. "We have not traveled beyond the forest," they said. "Perhaps the birds, who fly swiftly and very far, can tell you what you want to know."

Scarface called to the birds who were flying overhead, and they came down and listened. But they answered, "We fly far and see many things, but we have never seen two gleaming gates of gold, nor looked on the face of the bright god of the sun."

Scarface was disappointed, but he went bravely on. One day, when he was very weary, he met a wolverine and asked him the question he had asked so many times before. To his great joy the wolverine answered, "I have seen the gleaming gates, and have entered the bright country of the Lord of the Sun. But the way to it is long and hard, and you will be tired indeed when you reach the end of your journey. I will put you on your way, and if your heart does not fail you, someday you will see what I have seen."

With fresh courage Scarface went on. Day after day he journeyed, walking until he was weary, and taking but short rest. Each morning when he started he had hope that evening would bring him to the golden gates, and then one day he came to a great water, very broad and deep, so that he could not cross it.

Now it seemed that his labor and weariness had been all for nothing, and he sat down on the shore of the great water and felt hope dying out of his heart. But very soon he saw drawing near to him from the other side two beautiful swans. "We will take you across," they said. "Step on our backs and we will swim with you to the farther shore." Up started Scarface, joyful once again, and poised himself carefully on the backs of the two swans; and they glided across and landed him safely on the opposite shore.

"You seek the kingdom of the sun god?" they said. "Go then along the road that lies before you, and you will soon come to it." Scarface thanked them with all his heart. He felt happier than he had done since he had started on his journey, and he walked along with quick, light steps. He had not gone far when he saw lying on the ground a very beautiful bow and arrows. He stopped for a moment to look at them. "These belong to some mighty hunter," he thought, "they are finer than those of a common warrior." But he left them lying where he found them, for though his hunter's heart coveted them, Scarface was honest, and would not take what was not his own. He went on, even lighter of heart than before, and soon he saw a beautiful youth coming gaily along the road toward him. It seemed to Scarface that a soft, bright light shone around as the youth stopped and said, "I have lost a bow and arrows somewhere along the road. Have you seen them?"

"They lie but a little distance behind me," said Scarface, "I have but just passed them."

"Thank you many times," said the youth. "It is well for me that it was an honest man who passed, or I should never have seen my bow and arrows again." He smiled at Scarface, and the Indian felt great joy in his heart, and all the air seemed flecked with golden points of light. "Where are you going?" inquired the stranger.

And Scarface answered, "I seek the land of the great Lord of the Sun, and I believe it is very near."

"It is near indeed," replied the youth. "I am Apisirahts, the Morning Star, and the Sun is my father. Come and I will take you to him."

So the two went down the broad, bright road and passed through the golden gates. Inside they saw a great lodge, shining and glorious, gaily bedecked with such beautiful pictures and carvings as Scarface had never in his life seen before. At the door stood a woman with a fair face and bright clear eyes that looked kindly at the way-worn stranger. "Come in," she said. "I am Kokomikis, the moon goddess, and this youth is my son. Come, for you are tired and footsore and need food and rest."

Scarface, almost bewildered by the beauty of everything around him, went in, and Kokomikis cared for him tenderly, so that he soon felt refreshed and strong. After a time the great Lord of the Sun came home to the lodge, and he, too, was very kind to Scarface. "Stay with us," he said, "you have traveled a weary way to find me, now be my guest for a season. You are a great hunter, and here you will find good game. My son who loves the chase will go with you, and you will live with us and be happy."

Very gladly Scarface replied, "I will stay, great lord." So for many days he lived with the sun god and Kokomikis and Apisirahts, and every morning he and Morning Star went hunting and returned at night to the shining lodge. "Do not go near the Great Water," the Lord of the Sun warned them, "for savage birds dwell there, who will seek to slay the Morning Star."

But Apisirahts secretly longed to meet these savage birds and kill them, so one day he stole away from Scarface and hastened toward the Great Water. For a little while Scarface did not miss him, but believed him to be near by; but after a time he looked round and could not find his companion. He searched anxiously, and then a terrible fear came into his heart, and he set off as fast as he could toward the haunt of the dread birds. Horrid cries came to his ears as he hastened on, and soon he saw a crowd of the monstrous creatures surrounding Morning Star, and pressing on him so closely that he could use his weapons to little purpose to defend himself. Scarface feared to loose an arrow, but he dashed in among the hideous creatures, taking them by surprise, so that they flew off in alarm. Then he seized Morning Star, and hurried him back through the forest to safety.

When they returned to the lodge that night Apisirahts told his father of his own disobedience and the courage of Scarface. The great Lord of the Sun turned to the poor stranger. "You have saved my son from a dreadful death," he said. "Ask of me some boon, that I may repay you. Why was it that you sought me here? Surely you had some desire in your heart or you would not have traveled so far and fared so hardly."

Now all the while he had been at the Shining Lodge the thing he had come to ask had been ever in Scarface's mind. Many times he had thought, "The hour is come when I may speak." But because it was so great a boon he craved his heart failed him, and he thought again, "I will have patience just a little longer. It is too soon to beg so great a favor of the god who has already been so kind to me." But when he heard the words of the sun god, so graciously spoken, he took courage and replied, "In my own land, O mighty Lord, I love a maiden who is the daughter of the chief of my tribe. I am only a poor warrior, and as you see, I am disfigured and hideous to look upon. Yet she of her goodness loves me, and would marry me, but for the reverence in which she holds your commands laid upon her. For she has promised you, O great Lord, that she will marry no man. So I came to seek you in hope that you would free her from her promise that she might come to my lodge, and we might live in happiness together."

Then the sun god smiled, and looked kindly upon the Indian, who spoke bravely, though in his heart he trembled. "Go back," he said, "and take this maiden for your wife. Tell her that it is my will she marry you, and for a token"—he passed his hand before the Indian's face, and immediately the disfiguring scar vanished—"tell her to look upon you and see how the Lord of the Sun has wrought upon your face."

They loaded the Indian—Scarface no longer—with gifts and changed his poor clothes for the rich dress of an Indian chief. Then they led him out from the country of the Sun, through the golden gates, and showed him a short and easy path by which he could return to his own land.

He traveled quickly, and soon was at home once more. All his

552 THE BOOK OF VIRTUES

tribe came out to look at the richly clad young brave, who walked with such a quick, light step, and looked so eager and happy; but none knew him for Scarface, at whom they had mocked and jeered. Even the chief's daughter did not recognize him when she first looked upon him, but a second look told her who he was, and she called his name; then, realizing that the scar was gone, and remembering what its disappearance meant, she sprang toward him with a cry of joy. The story of his wonderful journey was told, and the chief gladly gave his daughter to this warrior on whom the great sun god had looked with favor. That same day they were married, and the chief gave his daughter a splendid wigwam for her marriage portion. There the two lived happily for many years; and Scarface lost his old name and was known to all the tribe as Smoothface.

Solitude

Ella Wheeler Wilcox

Sometimes we persevere with the help and compassion of friends and loved ones. Sometimes we have to do it alone. This poem speaks a hard truth, but one we might as well accept nonetheless: pain is harder to share than joy. But if we can bring ourselves to endure cheerfully, we'll find more company along the way.

> Laugh, and the world laughs with you;
> Weep, and you weep alone;
> For the sad old earth must borrow its mirth,
> But has trouble enough of its own.
> Sing, and the hills will answer;
> Sigh, it is lost on the air;
> The echoes bound to a joyful sound,
> But shrink from voicing care.

Rejoice, and men will seek you;
    Grieve, and they turn and go;
They want full measure of all your pleasure,
    But they do not need your woe.
Be glad, and your friends are many;
    Be sad, and you lose them all—
There are none to decline your nectared wine,
    But alone you must drink life's gall.

Feast, and your halls are crowded;
    Fast, and the world goes by.
Succeed and give, and it helps you live,
    But no man can help you die.
There is room in the halls of pleasure
    For a large and lordly train,
But one by one we must all file on
    Through the narrow aisles of pain.

Bruce and the Spider

Bernard Barton

Robert Bruce (1274–1329) was the king of Scotland who freed his land from English rule by winning the Battle of Bannockburn (1314) and ultimately confirming Scottish independence in the Treaty of Northampton (1328). But the fight was long and hard, as this famous story, set to verse, tells.

    For Scotland's and for freedom's right
        The Bruce his part had played,
    In five successive fields of fight
        Been conquered and dismayed;
    Once more against the English host
    His band he led, and once more lost
        The meed for which he fought;
    And now from battle, faint and worn,
    The homeless fugitive forlorn
        A hut's lone shelter sought.

And cheerless was that resting place
    For him who claimed a throne:
His canopy, devoid of grace,
    The rude, rough beams alone;
The heather couch his only bed—
Yet well I ween had slumber fled
    From couch of eiderdown!
Through darksome night till dawn of day,
Absorbed in wakeful thoughts he lay
    Of Scotland and her crown.

The sun rose brightly, and its gleam
    Fell on that hapless bed,
And tinged with light each shapeless beam
    Which roofed the lowly shed;
When, looking up with wistful eye,
The Bruce beheld a spider try
    His filmy thread to fling
From beam to beam of that rude cot;
And well the insect's toilsome lot
    Taught Scotland's future king.

Six times his gossamery thread
    The wary spider threw;
In vain the filmy line was sped,
    For powerless or untrue
Each aim appeared, and back recoiled
The patient insect, six times foiled,
    And yet unconquered still;
And soon the Bruce, with eager eye,
Saw him prepare once more to try
    His courage, strength, and skill.

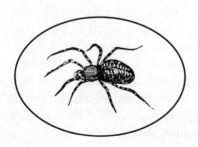

One effort more, his seventh and last—
The hero hailed the sign!—
And on the wished-for beam hung fast
That slender, silken line!
Slight as it was, his spirit caught
The more than omen, for his thought
The lesson well could trace,
Which even "he who runs may read,"
That Perseverance gains its meed,
And Patience wins the race.

The Long, Hard Way Through the Wilderness

Retold by Walter Russell Bowie

The story of the Hebrews' flight from Egypt and their forty years of wandering in the wilderness is told primarily in the Biblical book of Exodus. It is one of our greatest accounts of endurance, not only by a people but by a people's leader. As God's agent, Moses led the Hebrews through trial after trial, helping them find their way past starvation, sickness, impatience, and despair. After so long a journey to the border of Canaan, God does not allow Moses himself to enter the Promised Land. It is a final irony that somehow makes him an even more compelling figure of patience and perseverance.

Moses had brought the people out of Egypt. They had come safely across the water, in spite of the chariots of Pharaoh. Now they thought there would be no danger or trouble anymore. But soon they found that they had a long, hard way ahead of them. The country to which they had come was a strip of land, not very wide, between the sea on the one side and great mountains of rock on the other side. The ground between the sea and the mountains was flat sand and gravel. In the daytime the sun beat down with blistering heat, and there were no trees to give shade.

Mile after mile the people traveled without finding water. When at last they came to a pool in the sands, the water tasted so bad that they could not drink it. They named the place Marah, which means bitterness, and they demanded of Moses, "What shall we drink?"

Moses prayed to God to show him what to do. He found some shrubs growing in the sand, and he put these into the pool. Their leaves changed the taste of the water so that it became fit to drink.

After that Moses led the people to a place called Elim. There they found twelve springs of water with seventy palm trees growing near by. To the people who had been dragging their feet through the hot desert, Elim seemed like heaven, and they made camp there at the oasis.

But they could not stay long at Elim, for they had used up all the food they had brought with them out of Egypt. They had to go on farther in the hope of finding something they could eat. But when they had left the oasis, all that they saw around them was the desert again, and they seemed to be worse off than ever. Most of the Israelites were not as brave as Moses, and some of them began to complain aloud. They said to Moses, "Would to God that we had been let alone to die in the land of Egypt. There we had meat to cook, and plenty of bread. And here you have brought us out into this wilderness to kill us all with hunger."

But Moses kept his temper, and he kept his courage. He said that God would send them help.

That evening as the people looked at the sky they saw what seemed like a cloud. As it came near, they saw that it was not a cloud but hundreds and hundreds of quail, blown to land by a strong wind from islands out in the sea. When the tired birds came to earth, the people caught and ate them.

That night there was a heavy dew. In the morning when the people woke up, there on the ground were small white patches like frost. Moses said, "This is the bread that the Lord has given you to eat." The people of Israel called it manna. It was a kind of gum that fell from the desert bushes, and it had to be picked up before the sun rose, for after that it melted and disappeared.

From the place where they were fed with the quail and the manna, the people of Israel went on farther along the sea. Then Moses told them to turn and head for the mountains. Terrible-looking mountains they were, high and bare and grim. Again the people grew so thirsty that their tongues were dry. "Give us water!" they cried to Moses. "Is this what you brought us out of Egypt for —to kill us all with thirst?"

But Moses had been in these mountains before, and there was much that God had helped him learn. He led the people to a great rock cliff in a mountain called Horeb. There he struck the cliff with his staff and showed them water flowing. For a while the Hebrews were satisfied. They liked it still better when Moses brought them after that to another oasis. This was the greenest spot in all that bleak and barren land. Row after row of palm trees were there and springs bubbled up and overflowed, so that the waters made a murmuring stream. Centuries later this oasis was still known as the Pearl of Sinai because of its beauty.

The people of Israel might have liked to pitch their tents here and stay always, but it was a dangerous place in which to linger. An oasis was the one place most wanted, and so most fought for, by all the wild desert tribes. Moses chose a young man named Joshua to be the commander of the fighting men if there was danger.

The people had not been at the oasis long when a band of Amalekites appeared. They were mounted on camels and carried spears. They rode in fiercely to attack the Israelites. But Moses stood on a hill and held up his staff. He prayed to God. As he went on praying, Aaron and a man named Hur held up Moses' hands. While he prayed, Joshua and his fighting men drove the Amalekites away.

All the same, they could not stay at the oasis. Moses knew that other tribes, stronger than the Amalekites, might come there any day. Besides, the country to which Moses hoped to bring them, so that they might settle there, was a long way off on the other side of the mountain.

So on over rocky paths and up deep ravines Moses led the people of Israel. Great mountain peaks frowned over them. Some of these mountains had been volcanoes, and now and then there were rumblings among them, and sometimes even an earthquake. But it was in country like this that Moses, when he had first fled from Pharaoh, had seen the burning bush and heard the voice of God telling him to bring his people out of Egypt. In these same mountains Moses was to hear something else from God—something even more important.

While the people were camped in a valley, Moses climbed high on the greatest of the mountains—Mount Sinai. The people watched him until he disappeared in the distance. Hours and hours went by and he did not come back.

Up there, all alone, with only the rocks around him and the sky above, Moses thought and prayed. What did God want him to teach the people? How did God want them to behave?

Then it was as though Moses saw what he wanted to know. He saw the glory of God passing by, and heard God's voice telling him what he needed to understand. God would give him the Commandments which from this time on all people must obey.

After Moses had taught the people the Ten Commandments, he taught them a great deal more about how they were to live together. He taught them how to arrange the camps on the march, how to keep clean, how to be healthy, and what to do when anyone was sick. He told them what to do to remember God and worship him. They were to make a beautiful little chest, called the ark, and in it they were to carry the stone tablets on which were written the Ten Commandments. They were also to make a tabernacle, which was a tent made of the skins of animals. They were to put this tent up wherever they camped and have it for the place where they would pray to God.

Before long the Israelites left the valley at the foot of Mount Sinai and started on their way again. The ark was carried before them. Moses was still their leader. Often he had a hard time, just as he had had when they first came out of Egypt, because some of the people were forever grumbling. They said they were tired of eating manna all the time. They were tired of going thirsty on long journeys when there was not even so much as a water hole in the barren ground. They kept thinking of Egypt and telling one another that they wished they were back there. When they were there, they had wanted more than anything to be out of the country; but they forgot that now. What they remembered was the good things they had had to eat.

"We remember the fish," they said, "the cucumbers, and the melons." In Egypt there was the Nile with fish for anybody's taking, and there were fresh vegetables and fruits. But here there was nothing but sand and blistering sun and emptiness. Once or twice the people nearly rebelled.

Whenever Moses went by the tents and heard the people in them complaining, he was sad. But he would not let them think he was discouraged. He went off by himself and told everything to God in prayer. It seemed to him that God had given him more to do than any one man could manage. "I am not able to take care of all these people alone," he said. "It is too much for me." But when he prayed, God gave him new strength, and he went on.

All this time, by slow marches, the people were traveling farther north, beyond the mountains, toward the country where Moses believed God meant them to be. It was the same country to which

Abraham had come long before, and it was called the Promised Land. They were near enough to its borders now for Moses to plan how they should enter it. But first he had to learn exactly what the land was like, and what sort of people were living there. He chose twelve scouts, one of whom was Joshua and one a young man named Caleb, and he sent them out secretly in advance.

"Go see the land," he told them, "and the people who live there. Notice whether they are strong or weak, few or many. Is the land good or bad, and is it wooded or not? What sort of homes do the people have? Do they live in tents, or in towns with walls around them? Be of good courage, and bring back with you some of the fruits of the land."

So on ahead the scouts went. From the region around Mount Sinai it was a hundred miles or more to the shores of the Dead Sea. Beyond that they went, up over the high rock country of Moab, and along the valley of the Jordan River. Across the Jordan lay the Promised Land.

After forty days the scouts came back and made their report to Moses. They all said that the country they had looked at was a good land. Compared with the mountains and deserts they had been through, it seemed like a paradise. There were fields of grain in it and olive trees and vineyards, and springs of water in the hills. They brought back a great bunch of grapes which they had taken from a valley they called Eshcol, and they also brought figs and other fruit.

But after that, the scouts began to disagree. Ten of them said that the people in the land were so strong and so warlike they would never let the Israelites in. They said that the people living there looked like giants. Measured against them, the ten scouts said they felt like grasshoppers. But Caleb and Joshua, the other two, said all that was nonsense. The people living in the country were no different from any other people. The thing for the Israelites to do was to march straight ahead and go in.

Most of the Israelites who crowded around and listened believed the ten men instead of the two. They were afraid to trust the ones who were courageous. Then, because it made them uncomfortable to feel cowardly, they pretended that Caleb and Joshua were trying to lead them into trouble. If they had dared, they would have stoned the two brave men to death. They started again to say that they wished they were back in Egypt. They even talked of choosing a captain of their own who would take them there. But they could not find any real leader, so their angry muttering came to nothing.

Yet all this was enough to make Moses know that such faint-hearted people could not win the Promised Land. There was no use trying to lead them into it now. He would have to wait a long time, until some of the older ones who had been slaves in Egypt died, and younger and braver men grew up.

Many years went by, and now at last Moses did have a different sort of people under him—people who had been born and had grown up in the wilderness. They moved to the borders of the land of Edom, which lies at the south of the Dead Sea. They asked the Edomites to let them pass through their country peacefully. When the Edomites would not do this, the Israelites circled around that country and came to the land of the Amorites, to the west of the Jordan River.

Moses sent a message to Sihon, the chief of the Amorites, saying: "Let us pass through your land. We will not turn into the fields, nor into the vineyards. We will not drink from your wells. But we will go along the high roads until we have passed your borders."

The Amorites were fierce fighters. Instead of letting the Israelites through, they rode into the camp to attack them. But the younger men who followed Moses and Joshua now were no cowards. They beat off Sihon and his Amorites. And afterward, when Og, the chief of another one of the desert tribes, tried to stop them, they defeated him too.

They were coming close to the Promised Land. But Moses was not to go in with them. He was an old man now. He went up one day to the top of Mount Nebo, four thousand feet above the waters of the Dead Sea. Across the Jordan River he could see the walled city of Jericho. The springs there were fed by the streams that flowed from the hills above. Moses could see mile after mile of the Promised Land which his people would surely enter. There on the mountaintop he died, and it is written that he was buried "in a valley in the land of Moab; but no man knoweth of his grave unto this day."

Go Down, Moses

The spirituals composed by unknown slaves rank among the most beautiful and poignant American songs. Combining elements of African music with Old Testament themes, songs such

as "Go Down, Moses" express an entire population's dignified
faith despite the worst of conditions. No songs convey more
nobility of the soul. After the Civil War, groups such as the Fisk
University Jubilee Singers, who sang this particular rendition,
introduced the spirituals to the nation at large.

When Israel was in Egypt's land:
    Let my people go;
Oppress'd so hard they could not stand,
    Let my people go.
        Go down, Moses,
            Way down in Egypt land,
        Tell ole Pharaoh,
        Let my people go.

Thus saith the Lord, bold Moses said,
    Let my people go;
If not I'll smite your firstborn dead,
    Let my people go.
        Go down, Moses, *etc.*

The Lord told Moses what to do,
    Let my people go;
To lead the children of Israel through,
    Let my people go.
        Go down, Moses, *etc.*

O come along, Moses, you'll not get lost,
    Let my people go;
Stretch out your rod and come across,
    Let my people go.
        Go down, Moses, *etc.*

As Israel stood by the waterside,
    Let my people go;
At the command of God it did divide,
    Let my people go.
        Go down, Moses, *etc.*

When they had reached the other shore,
  Let my people go;
They sang a song of triumph o'er.
  Let my people go.
    Go down, Moses, *etc.*

We need not always weep and moan,
  Let my people go;
And wear these slavery chains forlorn,
  Let my people go.
    Go down, Moses, *etc.*

This world's a wilderness of woe,
  Let my people go;
O, let us on to Canaan go,
  Let my people go.
    Go down, Moses, *etc.*

What a beautiful morning that will be,
  Let my people go;
When time breaks up in eternity,
  Let my people go.
    Go down, Moses, *etc.*

Eureka!

Retold by James Baldwin

Celebrated inventor and mathematician of ancient Greece, Archimedes was born around the year 290 B.C. in Syracuse, Sicily, a Greek colony. This story about one of his most famous discoveries is an invaluable lesson in intellectual perseverance. As the American Archimedes, Thomas Edison, said, genius is one percent inspiration and ninety-nine percent perspiration.

There was once a king of Syracuse whose name was Hiero. The country over which he ruled was quite small, but for that reason he wanted to wear the biggest crown in the world. So he called in a famous goldsmith, who was skillful in all kinds of fine work, and gave him ten pounds of pure gold.

"Take this," he said, "and fashion it into a crown that shall make every other king want it for his own. Be sure that you put into it every grain of the gold I give you, and do not mix any other metal with it."

"It shall be as you wish," said the goldsmith. "Here I receive from you ten pounds of pure gold. Within ninety days I will return to you the finished crown which shall be of exactly the same weight."

Ninety days later, true to his word, the goldsmith brought the crown. It was a beautiful piece of work, and all who saw it said that it had not its equal in the world. When King Hiero put it on his head it felt very uncomfortable, but he did not mind that—he was sure that no other king had so fine a headpiece. After he had admired it from this side and from that, he weighed it on his own scales. It was exactly as heavy as he had ordered.

"You deserve great praise," he said to the goldsmith. "You have wrought very skillfully and you have not lost a grain of my gold."

There was in the king's court a very wise man whose name was Archimedes. When he was called in to admire the king's crown he turned it over many times and examined it very closely.

"Well, what do you think of it?" asked Hiero.

"The workmanship is indeed very beautiful," answered Archimedes, "but—but the gold—"

"The gold is all there," cried the king, "I weighed it on my own scales."

"True," said Archimedes, "but it does not appear to have the same rich red color that it had in the lump. It is not red at all, but a brilliant yellow, as you can plainly see."

"Most gold is yellow," said Hiero. "But now that you speak of it I do remember that when this was in the lump it had a much richer color."

"What if the goldsmith has kept out a pound or two of the gold and made up the weight by adding brass or silver?" asked Archimedes.

"Oh, he could not do that," said Hiero. "The gold has merely changed its color in the working."

But the more he thought of the matter the less pleased he was with the crown. At last he said to Archimedes, "Is there any way to find out whether that goldsmith really cheated me, or whether he honestly gave me back my gold?"

"I know of no way," was the answer.

But Archimedes was not the man to say that anything was impossible. He took great delight in working out hard problems, and when any question puzzled him he would keep studying until he found some sort of answer to it. And so, day after day, he thought about the gold and tried to find some way by which it could be tested without doing harm to the crown.

One morning he was thinking of this question while he was getting ready for a bath. The great bowl or tub was full to the very edge, and as he stepped into it a quantity of water flowed out upon the stone floor. A similar thing had happened a hundred times before, but this was the first time that Archimedes had thought about it.

"How much water did I displace by getting into the tub?" he asked himself. "Anybody can see that I displaced a bulk of water equal to the bulk of my body. A man half my size would displace half as much.

"Now suppose, instead of putting myself into the tub, I had put Hiero's crown into it, it would have displaced a bulk of water equal to its own bulk. Ah, let me see! Gold is much heavier than silver. Ten pounds of pure gold will not make so great a bulk as say seven pounds of gold mixed with three pounds of silver. If Hiero's crown is pure gold it will displace the same bulk of water as any other ten pounds of pure gold. But if it is part gold and part silver it will displace a larger bulk. I have it at last! Eureka! Eureka!"

Forgetful of everything else he leaped from the bath. Without stopping to dress himself, he ran through the streets to the king's palace shouting, "Eureka! Eureka! Eureka!" which in English means, "I have found it! I have found it! I have found it!"

The crown was tested. It was found to displace much more water than ten pounds of pure gold displaced. The guilt of the goldsmith was proved beyond a doubt. But whether he was punished or not, I do not know, neither does it matter.

The simple discovery which Archimedes made in his bathtub was worth far more to the world than Hiero's crown.

Perseverance

Johann Wolfgang von Goethe

We must not hope to be mowers,
    And to gather the ripe gold ears,
Unless we have first been sowers
    And watered the furrows with tears.

It is not just as we take it,
    This mystical world of ours,
Life's field will yield as we make it
    A harvest of thorns or of flowers.

Sail on! Sail on!

Joaquin Miller

This is the Christopher Columbus whose imagination we admire, whose daring we celebrate, and whose determination we should emulate.

Behind him lay the gray Azores,
    Behind the gates of Hercules;
Before him not the ghost of shores,
    Before him only shoreless seas.
The good mate said: "Now must we pray,
    For lo! the very stars are gone;
Speak, Admiral, what shall I say?"
    "Why say, sail on! and on!"

"My men grow mut'nous day by day;
　My men grow ghastly wan and weak."
The stout mate thought of home; a spray
　Of salt wave wash'd his swarthy cheek.
"What shall I say, brave Admiral,
　If we sight naught but seas at dawn?"
"Why, you shall say, at break of day:
　'Sail on! sail on! and on!' "

They sailed and sailed, as winds might blow,
　Until at last the blanch'd mate said:
"Why, now, not even God would know
　Should I and all my men fall dead.
These very winds forget their way,
　For God from these dread seas is gone.
Now speak, brave Admiral, and say—"
　He said: "Sail on! and on!"

They sailed, they sailed, then spoke his mate:
　"This mad sea shows his teeth tonight,
He curls his lip, he lies in wait,
　With lifted teeth as if to bite!
Brave Admiral, say but one word;
　What shall we do when hope is gone?"
The words leaped as a leaping sword:
　"Sail on! sail on! and on!"

Then, pale and worn, he kept his deck,
　And thro' the darkness peered that night.
Ah, darkest night! and then a speck—
　A light! a light! a light! a light!
It grew—a star-lit flag unfurled!
　It grew to be Time's burst of dawn;
He gained a world! he gave that world
　Its watchword: "On! and on!"

Can't

Edgar Guest

"Can't" is a favorite word of some children. Here is the case against it.

Can't is the worst word that's written or spoken;
  Doing more harm here than slander and lies;
On it is many a strong spirit broken,
  And with it many a good purpose dies.
It springs from the lips of the thoughtless each morning
  And robs us of courage we need through the day:
It rings in our ears like a timely sent warning
  And laughs when we falter and fall by the way.

Can't is the father of feeble endeavor,
  The parent of terror and halfhearted work;
It weakens the efforts of artisans clever,
  And makes of the toiler an indolent shirk.
It poisons the soul of the man with a vision,
  It stifles in infancy many a plan;
It greets honest toiling with open derision
  And mocks at the hopes and the dreams of a man.

Can't is a word none should speak without blushing;
  To utter it should be a symbol of shame;
Ambition and courage it daily is crushing;
  It blights a man's purpose and shortens his aim.
Despise it with all of your hatred of error;
  Refuse it the lodgment it seeks in your brain;
Arm against it as a creature of terror,
  And all that you dream of you someday shall gain.

Can't is the word that is foe to ambition,
  An enemy ambushed to shatter your will;
Its prey is forever the man with a mission
  And bows but to courage and patience and skill.
Hate it, with hatred that's deep and undying,
  For once it is welcomed 'twill break any man;
Whatever the goal you are seeking, keep trying
  And answer this demon by saying: "I *can.*"

The Gettysburg Address

Abraham Lincoln

When Abraham Lincoln rose on November 19, 1863, to dedicate the Soldier's National Cemetery at Gettysburg, Pennsylvania, where four months earlier thousands of Northern and Southern soldiers had fallen, he wanted to tell the country that if it could sustain the will to fight, the Union ultimately would triumph. In two minutes he said as much, and more. He told the world the United States would fight on, not just for its own sake, but for all nations conceived in liberty and dedicated to equality. Here it is, the greatest and most famous speech ever delivered on American soil.

Four score and seven years ago, our fathers brought forth on this continent a new nation, conceived in liberty, and dedicated to the proposition that all men are created equal.

Now we are engaged in a great civil war, testing whether that nation, or any nation so conceived and so dedicated, can long endure. We are met on a great battlefield of that war. We have come to dedicate a portion of that field as a final resting place for those who here gave their lives that that nation might live. It is altogether fitting and proper that we should do this.

But in a larger sense we cannot dedicate, we cannot consecrate, we cannot hallow this ground. The brave men, living and dead, who struggled here, have consecrated it far above our poor power to add or detract. The world will little note, nor long remember, what we say here, but it can never forget what they did here. It is for us the living, rather, to be dedicated here to the unfinished work which they who fought here have thus far so nobly advanced. It is rather for us to be here dedicated to the great task remaining before us— that from these honored dead we take increased devotion to that cause for which they gave the last full measure of devotion, that we here highly resolve that these dead shall not have died in vain, that this nation, under God, shall have a new birth of freedom, and that government of the people, by the people, for the people, shall not perish from the earth.

We Shall Fight in the Fields and in the Streets

Winston Churchill

In May 1940, German forces skirted the Maginot line, broke through French defensive positions, and in a matter of days swept westward to the British Channel. The British Expeditionary Force in France, threatened with annihilation, fell back to the beaches of Dunkirk, where an epic evacuation of more than three hundred thousand British and French troops was staged. With the protection of the Royal Air Force, all kinds and sizes of British boats, some manned by civilian volunteers, crossed and recrossed the Channel to ferry the shattered army to England.

On June 4, Winston Churchill reported to Parliament on the success of the evacuation. His description of the heroic effort and his call for courage, unity, determination, and sacrifice buoyed the spirits of the British people. It also helped bolster resolution in the New World; one week later, when Italy entered the war on the side of the Axis powers, President Roosevelt publicly committed American material resources to the Allied cause.

From the moment that the French defenses at Sedan and on the Meuse were broken at the end of the second week of May, only a rapid retreat to Amiens and the south could have saved the British and French armies who had entered Belgium at the appeal of the Belgian King; but this strategic fact was not immediately realized. . . .

The German eruption swept like a sharp scythe around the right and rear of the armies of the north. Eight or nine armored divisions, each of about four hundred armored vehicles of different kinds, but carefully assorted to be complementary and divisible into small self-contained units, cut off all communications between us and the main French armies. It severed our own communications for food and ammunition, which ran first to Amiens and afterward through Abbeville, and it shored its way up the coast to Boulogne and Calais, and almost to Dunkirk. Behind this armored and mechanized onslaught came a number of German divisions in lorries, and behind them again there plodded comparatively slowly the dull brute mass of the ordinary German Army and German people, always so ready to be led to the trampling down in other lands of liberties and comforts which they have never known in their own. . . .

Meanwhile, the Royal Air Force, which had already been intervening in the battle, so far as its range would allow, from home bases, now used part of its main metropolitan fighter strength, and struck at the German bombers and at the fighters which in large numbers protected them. This struggle was protracted and fierce. Suddenly the scene has cleared, the crash and thunder has for the moment—but only for the moment—died away. A miracle of deliverance, achieved by valor, by perseverance, by perfect discipline, by faultless service, by resource, by skill, by unconquerable fidelity, is manifest to us all. The enemy was hurled back by the retreating British and French troops. He was so roughly handled that he did not hurry their departure seriously. The Royal Air Force engaged the main strength of the German Air Force, and inflicted upon them losses of at least four to one; and the navy, using nearly one thousand ships of all kinds, carried over 335,000 men, French and British, out of the jaws of death and shame, to their native land and to the tasks which lie immediately ahead. We must be very careful not to assign to this deliverance the attributes of a victory. Wars are not won by evacuations. But there was a victory inside this deliverance, which should be noted. . . .

This was a great trial of strength between the British and German air forces. Can you conceive a greater objective for the Germans in the air than to make evacuation from these beaches impossible, and to sink all these ships which were displayed, almost to the extent of thousands? Could there have been an objective of greater military importance and significance for the whole purpose of the war than this? They tried hard, and they were beaten back; they were frustrated in their task. We got the army away; and they have paid fourfold for any losses which they have inflicted. Very large formations of German airplanes—and we know that they are a very brave race—have turned on several occasions from the attack of one quarter of their number of the Royal Air Force, and have dispersed in different directions. . . .

I will pay my tribute to these young airmen. The great French Army was very largely, for the time being, cast back and disturbed by the onrush of a few thousands of armored vehicles. May it not also be that the cause of civilization itself will be defended by the skill and devotion of a few thousand airmen? There never has been, I suppose, in all the world, in all the history of war, such an opportunity for youth. The Knights of the Round Table, the Crusaders, all fall back into the past—not only distant but prosaic; these young men, going forth every morn to guard their native land and all that we stand for, holding in their hands these instruments of colossal and shattering power, of whom it may be said that

Every morn brought forth a noble chance,
And every chance brought forth a noble knight,

deserve our gratitude, as do all of the brave men who, in so many ways and on so many occasions, are ready, and continue ready, to give life and all for their native land. . . .

I have, myself, full confidence that if all do their duty, if nothing is neglected, and if the best arrangements are made, as they are being made, we shall prove ourselves once again able to defend our island home, to ride out the storm of war, and to outlive the menace of tyranny, if necessary for years, if necessary alone. At any rate, that is what we are going to try to do. That is the resolve of His Majesty's Government—every man of them. That is the will of Parliament and the nation. The British Empire and the French Republic, linked together in their cause and in their need, will defend to the death their native soil, aiding each other like good comrades to the utmost of their strength. Even though large tracts of Europe and many old and famous states have fallen or may fall into the grip of the Gestapo and all the odious apparatus of Nazi rule, we shall not flag or fail. We shall go on to the end, we shall fight in France, we shall fight on the seas and oceans, we shall fight with growing confidence and growing strength in the air, we shall defend our island, whatever the cost may be, we shall fight on the beaches, we shall fight on the landing grounds, we shall fight in the fields and in the streets, we shall fight in the hills; we shall never surrender, and even if, which I do not for a moment believe, this island or a large part of it were subjugated and starving, then our Empire beyond the seas, armed and guarded by the British fleet, would carry on the struggle, until, in God's good time, the New World, with all its power and might, steps forth to the rescue and the liberation of the old.

I Have a Dream

Reverend Martin Luther King, Jr.

On August 28, 1963, between 200,000 and 250,000 people gathered between the Washington Monument and the Lincoln Memorial in the nation's capital to demonstrate peacefully on behalf of the civil rights struggle. The high point of the day was the Reverend Martin Luther King, Jr.'s, now-famous speech in which he called upon Americans to work with faith that change would come and that someday all would be judged not by the color of their skin, but by the content of their character. His soaring refrain of "I have a dream" still inspires the American conscience. His perseverance and eloquence were rewarded.

Five score years ago, a great American, in whose symbolic shadow we stand, signed the Emancipation Proclamation. This momentous decree came as a great beacon light of hope to millions of Negro slaves who had been seared in the flames of withering injustice. It came as a joyous daybreak to end the long night of captivity.

But one hundred years later, we must face the tragic fact that the Negro is still not free. One hundred years later, the life of the

Negro is still sadly crippled by the manacles of segregation and the chains of discrimination. One hundred years later, the Negro lives on a lonely island of poverty in the midst of a vast ocean of material prosperity. One hundred years later, the Negro still languishes in the corners of American society and finds himself an exile in his own land. So we have come here today to dramatize an appalling condition.

In a sense we have come to our nation's capital to cash a check. When the architects of our republic wrote the magnificent words of the Constitution and the Declaration of Independence, they were signing a promissory note to which every American was to fall heir. This note was a promise that all men would be guaranteed the unalienable rights of life, liberty, and the pursuit of happiness.

It is obvious today that America has defaulted on this promissory note insofar as her citizens of color are concerned. Instead of honoring this sacred obligation, America has given the Negro people a bad check: a check which has come back marked "insufficient funds." But we refuse to believe that the bank of justice is bankrupt. We refuse to believe that there are insufficient funds in the great vaults of opportunity of this nation. So we have come to cash this check—a check that will give us upon demand the riches of freedom and the security of justice.

We have also come to this hallowed spot to remind America of the fierce urgency of *now*. This is not time to engage in the luxury of cooling off or to take the tranquilizing drug of gradualism. *Now* is the time to make real the promises of democracy. *Now* is the time to rise from the dark and desolate valley of segregation to the sunlit path of racial justice. *Now* is the time to open the doors of opportunity to all of God's children. *Now* is the time to lift our nation from the quicksands of racial injustice to the solid rock of brotherhood.

It would be fatal for the nation to overlook the urgency of the moment and to underestimate the determination of the Negro. This sweltering summer of the Negro's legitimate discontent will not pass until there is an invigorating autumn of freedom and equality. Nineteen sixty-three is not an end, but a beginning. Those who hope that the Negro needed to blow off steam and will now be content will have a rude awakening if the nation returns to business as usual. There will be neither rest nor tranquility in America until the Negro is granted his citizenship rights. The whirlwinds of revolt will continue to shake the foundations of our nation until the bright day of justice emerges.

But there is something that I must say to my people who stand on the warm threshold which leads into the palace of justice. In the process of gaining our rightful place we must not be guilty of wrongful deeds. Let us not seek to satisfy our thirst for freedom by drinking from the cup of bitterness and hatred. We must forever conduct our struggle on the high plane of dignity and discipline. We must not allow our creative protest to degenerate into physical violence. Again and again we must rise to the majestic heights of meeting physical force with soul force.

The marvelous new militancy which has engulfed the Negro community must not lead us to a distrust of all white people, for many of our white brothers, as evidenced by their presence here today, have come to realize that their freedom is inextricably bound to our freedom. We cannot walk alone.

And as we walk, we must make the pledge that we shall march ahead. We cannot turn back. There are those who are asking the devotees of civil rights, "When will you be satisfied?"

We can never be satisfied as long as the Negro is the victim of the unspeakable horrors of police brutality.

We can never be satisfied as long as our bodies, heavy with fatigue of travel, cannot gain lodging in the motels of the highways and the cities.

We cannot be satisfied as long as the Negro's basic mobility is from a smaller ghetto to a larger one.

We can never be satisfied as long as a Negro in Mississippi cannot vote and a Negro in New York believes he has nothing for which to vote.

No, no, we are not satisfied, and we will not be satisfied until justice rolls down like waters and righteousness like a mighty stream.

I am not unmindful that some of you have come here out of great trials and tribulations. Some of you have come fresh from narrow jail cells. Some of you have come from areas where your quest for freedom left you battered by the storms of persecution and staggered by the winds of police brutality. You have been the veterans of creative suffering. Continue to work with the faith that unearned suffering is redemptive.

Go back to Mississippi, go back to Alabama, go back to South Carolina, go back to Georgia, go back to Louisiana, go back to the slums and ghettos of our Northern cities, knowing that somehow this situation can and will be changed. Let us not wallow in the valley of despair.

I say to you today, my friends, that in spite of the difficulties and frustrations of the moment I still have a dream. It is a dream deeply rooted in the American dream.

I have a dream that one day this nation will rise up and live out the true meaning of its creed: "We hold these truths to be self-evident; that all men are created equal."

I have a dream that one day on the red hills of Georgia the sons of former slaves and the sons of former slaveowners will be able to sit down together at the table of brotherhood.

I have a dream that one day even the state of Mississippi, a desert state sweltering with the heat of injustice and oppression, will be transformed into an oasis of freedom and justice.

I have a dream that my four little children will one day live in a nation where they will not be judged by the color of their skin but by the content of their character.

I have a dream today.

I have a dream that one day the state of Alabama, whose governor's lips are presently dripping with the words of interposition and nullification, will be transformed into a situation where little black boys and black girls will be able to join hands with little white boys and girls and walk together as sisters and brothers.

I have a dream today.

I have a dream that one day every valley shall be exalted, every hill and mountain shall be made low, the rough places will be made plain, and the crooked places will be made straight, and the glory of the Lord shall be revealed, and all flesh shall see it together.

This is our hope. This is the faith with which I return to the South. With this faith we will be able to hew out of the mountain of despair a stone of hope. With this faith we will be able to transform the jangling discords of our nation into a beautiful symphony of brotherhood.

With this faith we will be able to work together, to pray together, to struggle together, to go to jail together, to stand up for freedom together, knowing that we will be free one day.

This will be the day when all of God's children will be able to sing with new meaning, "My country 'tis of thee, sweet land of liberty, of thee I sing. Land where my father died, land of the Pilgrims' pride, from every mountainside, let freedom ring."

And if America is to be a great nation, this must become true. So let freedom ring from the prodigious hilltops of New Hampshire. Let freedom ring from the mighty mountains of New York. Let freedom ring from the heightening Alleghenies of Pennsylvania!

Let freedom ring from the snowcapped Rockies of Colorado! Let freedom ring from the curvaceous peaks of California. But not only that: let freedom ring from Stone Mountain of Georgia! Let freedom ring from Lookout Mountain of Tennessee!

Let freedom ring from every hill and molehill of Mississippi. From every mountainside, let freedom ring.

When we let freedom ring, when we let it ring from every village and every hamlet, from every state and every city, we will be able to speed up that day when all of God's children, black men and white men, Jews and Gentiles, Protestants and Catholics, will be able to join hands and sing in the words of the old Negro spiritual, "Free at last! Free at last! Thank God Almighty, we are free at last!"

The Donner Party

Eliza P. Donner Houghton

In April 1846, a group of pioneers led by brothers George and Jacob Donner and their friend James Reed set out from Illinois to join the growing wave of emigrants heading for Oregon and California. As they crossed the Midwest they were joined by other families with names like Eddy, Pike, and McCutchen, all hoping to buy cheap Western land and begin life anew. By the time the Donner Party was complete, it totaled eighty-seven men, women, and children with twenty-three wagons and numerous head of livestock. The group was headed toward the most spectacular and famous catastrophe of the overland pioneer crossings.

On July 20, the Donners and their companions turned off the main trail onto a cutoff that, according to a promoter named Lansford W. Hastings, was the most direct route to California. But neither Hastings nor anyone else had tried the new route—it existed only in his unscrupulous imagination. By the time the Donner Party found its way through the Wasatch Range and made a torturous crossing of the Great Salt Lake Desert, it had lost too many days of precious time. When they reached the

Sierra Nevada in late October, five feet of snow already lay in the mountain passes.

They waited on the shore of Truckee (now Donner) Lake to gather their strength for the climb, but the snows fell for eight straight days. Winter had come early, and the Donner Party was trapped. They went into winter camp. One group built cabins at the lake, while others, including the Donners, settled in at Alder Creek five miles down the trail. Every day the weather grew colder and the snow deeper. Before long they were faced with starvation.

During the next five months, four relief parties managed to reach the Donner Party. It was the end of April before the last survivor was brought out of the mountains. Only forty of the eighty-seven emigrants lived through the winter of agony, and some of those managed to survive only by eating the remains of their dead companions.

The following excerpts are from *The Expedition of the Donner Party and Its Tragic Fate* by Eliza P. Donner Houghton, daughter of George and Tamsen Donner, who was four years old that winter. Her words and the accounts of other survivors describe the range of human reactions, from magnificent to ignominious, in the face of an almost unimaginable ordeal. The story of the Donner Party is a taproot for me. I go back to it often to puzzle over what it is in people's characters that makes some great and others grotesque.

After the departure of the first relief we who were left in the mountains began to watch and pray for the coming of the second relief, as we had before watched and prayed for the coming of the first. . . .

As father grew weaker, we children spent more time upon the snow above camp. Often, after his wound was dressed and he fell into a quiet slumber, our ever-busy, thoughtful mother would come to us and sit on the tree trunk. Sometimes she brought paper and wrote; sometimes she sketched the mountains and the tall treetops, which now looked like small trees growing up through the snow. And often, while knitting or sewing, she held us spellbound with wondrous tales of "Joseph in Egypt," of "Daniel in the den of lions," of "Elijah healing the widow's son," of dear little Samuel, who said, "Speak Lord, for Thy servant heareth," and of the tender, loving Master, who took young children in his arms and blessed them.

With me sitting on her lap, and Frances and Georgia at either side, she referred to father's illness and lonely condition, and said that when the next "relief" came, we little ones might be taken to the settlement, without either parent, but, God willing, both would follow later. Who could be braver or tenderer than she, as she prepared us to go forth with strangers and live without her? While she, without medicine, without lights, would remain and care for our suffering father, in hunger and in cold, and without her little girls to kiss good morning and good night. She taught us how to gain friends among those whom we should meet, and what to answer when asked whose children we were.

Often her eyes gazed wistfully to westward, where sky and mountains seemed to meet, and she told us that beyond those snowy peaks lay California, our land of food and safety, our promised land of happiness, where God would care for us. Oh, it was painfully quiet some days in those great mountains, and lonesome upon the snow. The pines had a whispering homesick murmur, and we children had lost all inclination to play.

The last food which I remember seeing in our camp before the arrival of the second relief was a thin mold of tallow, which mother had tried out of the trimmings of the jerked beef brought us by the first relief. She had let it harden in a pan, and after all other rations had given out, she cut daily from it three small white squares for each of us, and we nibbled off the four corners very slowly, and then around and around the edges of the precious pieces until they became too small for us to hold between our fingers. . . .

Thirty-one of the company were still in the camps when the second relief party arrived, nearly all of them children, unable to travel without assistance, and the adults were too feeble to give much aid to the little ones upon the snow. Consequently, when my father learned that the second relief comprised only ten men, he felt that he himself would never reach the settlement. He was willing to be left alone, and entreated mother to leave him and try to save herself and us children. He reminded her that his life was almost spent, that she could do little for him were she to remain, and that in caring for us children she would be carrying on his work.

She who had to choose between the sacred duties of wife and mother, thought not of self. She looked first at her helpless little children, then into the face of her suffering and helpless husband, and tenderly, unhesitatingly, announced her determination to remain and care for him until both should be rescued, or death should part them. . . .

Mother, fearing that we children might not survive another storm in camp, begged Messrs. Cady and Stone to take us with them, offering them five hundred dollars in coin, to deliver us to Elitha and Leanna at Sutter's Fort. The agreement was made, and she collected a few keepsakes and other light articles, which she wished us to have, and which the men seemed more than willing to carry out of the mountains. Then, lovingly, she combed our hair and helped us to dress quickly for the journey. When we were ready, except cloak and hood, she led us to the bedside, and we took leave of father. The men helped us up the steps and stood us up on the snow. She came, put on our cloaks and hoods, saying, as if talking to herself, "I may never see you again, but God will take care of you."

Frances was six years and eight months old and could trudge along quite bravely, but Georgia, who was little more than five, and I, lacking a week of four years, could not do well on the heavy trail, and we were soon taken up and carried. After traveling some distance, the men left us sitting on a blanket upon the snow, and went ahead a short distance where they stopped and talked earnestly with many gesticulations. We watched them, trembling lest they leave us there to freeze. Then Frances said,

"Don't feel afraid. If they go off and leave us, I can lead you back to mother by our foot tracks on the snow."

After a seemingly long time, they returned, picked us up and took us on to one of the lake cabins, where without a parting word, they left us.

The second relief party, of which these men were members, left camp on the third of March. They took with them seventeen refugees—the Breen and Graves families, Solomon Hook, Isaac and Mary Donner, and Martha and Thomas, Mr. Reed's two youngest children.

How can I describe that fateful cabin, which was dark as night to us who had come in from the glare of day? We heard no word of greeting and met no sign of welcome, but were given a dreary resting place near the foot of the steps, just inside the open doorway, with a bed of branches to lie upon, and a blanket to cover us. After we had been there a short time, we could distinguish persons on other beds of branches, and a man with bushy hair reclining beside a smouldering fire.

Soon a child began to cry, "Give me some bread. Oh, give me some meat!"

Then another took up the same pitiful wail. It continued so long that I wept in sympathy, and fastened my arms tightly around my sister Frances's neck and hid my eyes against her shoulder. Still I heard that hungry cry, until a husky voice shouted,

"Be quiet, you crying children, or I'll shoot you."

But the silence was again and again broken by that heartrending plea, and again and again were the voices hushed by the same terrifying threat. And we three, fresh from our loving mother's embrace, believed the awful menace no vain threat.

We were cold, and too frightened to feel hungry, nor were we offered food that night, but next morning Mr. Reed's little daughter Mattie appeared carrying in her apron a number of newly baked biscuits which her father had just taken from the hot ashes of his camp fire. Joyfully she handed one to each inmate of the cabin, then departed to join those ready to set forth on the journey to the settlement. Few can know how delicious those biscuits tasted, and how carefully we caught each dropping crumb. The place seemed drearier after their giver left us, yet we were glad that her father was taking her to her mother in California.

Soon the great storm which had been lowering broke upon us. We were not exposed to its fury as were those who had just gone from us, but we knew when it came, for snow drifted down upon our bed and had to be scraped off before we could rise. We were not allowed near the fire and spent most of our time on our bed of branches. . . .

How long the storm had lasted, we did not know, nor how many days we had been there. We were forlorn as children can possibly be, when Simon Murphy, who was older than Frances, climbed to his usual lookout on the snow above the cabin to see if any help were coming. He returned to us, stammering in his eagerness:

"I seen—a woman—on snowshoes—coming from the other camp! She's a little woman—like Mrs. Donner. She is not looking this way—and may pass!"

Hardly had he spoken her name, before we had gathered around him and were imploring him to hurry back and call our mother. We were too excited to follow him up the steps.

She came to us quickly, with all the tenderness and courage needed to lessen our troubles and soften our fears. Oh, how glad we were to see her, and how thankful she appeared to be with us once more! We heard it in her voice and saw it in her face; and when we begged her not to leave us, she could not answer, but clasped us closer to her bosom, kissed us anew for father's sake, then told how the storm had distressed them. Often had they hoped that we had reached the cabins too late to join the relief—then in grieving anguish felt that we had, and might not live to cross the summit.

She had watched the fall of snow, and measured its depth; had seen it drift between the two camps making the way so treacherous that no one had dared to cross it until the day before her own coming; then she induced Mr. Clark to try to ascertain if Messrs. Cady and Stone had really got us to the cabins in time to go with the second relief.

We did not see Mr. Clark, but he had peered in, taken observations, and returned by nightfall and described to her our condition.

John Baptiste had promised to care for father in her absence. She left our tent in the morning as early as she could see the way. She must have stayed with us overnight, for I went to sleep in her arms, and they were still around me when I awoke; and it seemed like a new day, for we had time for many cherished talks. She veiled from us the ghastliness of death, telling us Aunt Betsy and both our little cousins had gone to heaven. She said Lewis had been first to go, and his mother had soon followed; that she herself had carried little Sammie from his sick mother's tent to ours the very day we three were taken away; and in order to keep him warm while the storm raged, she had laid him close to father's side, and that he had stayed with them until "day before yesterday."

I asked her if Sammie had cried for bread. She replied, "No, he was not hungry, for your mother saved two of those little biscuits which the relief party brought, and every day she soaked a tiny piece in water and fed him all he would eat, and there is still half a biscuit left."

How big that half biscuit seemed to me! I wondered why she had not brought at least a part of it to us. While she was talking with Mrs. Murphy, I could not get it out of my mind. I could see that broken half biscuit, with its ragged edges, and knew that if I had a piece, I would nibble off the rough points first. The longer I waited, the more I wanted it. Finally, I slipped my arm around mother's neck, drew her face close to mine and whispered,

"What are you going to do with the half biscuit you saved?"

"I am keeping it for your sick father," she answered, drawing me closer to her side, laying her comforting cheek against mine, letting my arm keep its place, and my fingers stroke her hair.

In Memory of L. H. W.

Dorothy Canfield Fisher

This is a story of a lifetime of struggle made noble by compassion, responsibility, work, and a host of other virtues. It reminds us that in helping others persevere, we find the strength and courage and purpose to persevere ourselves. Vermont writer Dorothy Canfield Fisher (1879–1958) said that as a child she knew the protagonist of this story, a New England farmer born to a hard life, and one day she realized he was a saint.

He began life characteristically, depreciated and disparaged. When he was a white, thin, big-headed baby, his mother, stripping the suds from her lean arms, used to inveigh to her neighbors against his existence. "Wa'n't it just like that *do*-less Lem Warren, not even to leave me foot-free when he died, but a baby coming!"

"*Do*-less," in the language of our valley, means a combination of shiftless and impractical, particularly to be scorned.

Later, as he began to have some resemblance to the appearance he was to wear throughout life, her resentment at her marriage, which she considered the one mistake of her life, kept pace with his growth. "Look at him!" she cried to anyone who would listen. "Ain't that Warren, all over? Did any of *my* folks ever look so like a born fool? Shut your mouth, for the Lord's sake, Lem, and maybe you won't scare folks quite so much."

Lem had a foolish, apologetic grin with which he always used to respond to these personalities, hanging his head to one side and opening and shutting his big hands nervously.

The tumbledown, two-roomed house in which the Warrens lived was across the road from the schoolhouse, and Mrs. Warren's voice was penetrating. Lem was accepted throughout his school life at the home estimate. The ugly, overgrown boy, clad in cast-off, misfit clothing, was allowed to play with the other children only on condition that he perform all the hard, uninteresting parts of any game. Inside the schoolroom it was the same. He never learned to shut his mouth, and his speech was always halting and indistinct, so that he not only did not recite well in class, but was never in one of the school entertainments. He chopped the wood and brought it in, swept the floor and made the fires, and then listened in grinning, silent admiration while the others, arrayed in their best, spoke pieces and sang songs.

He was not "smart at his books" and indeed did not learn even to read very fluently. This may have been partly because the only books he ever saw were old schoolbooks, the use of which was given him free on account of his mother's poverty. He was not allowed, of course, to take them from the schoolroom. But if he was not good at book-learning he was not without accomplishments. He early grew large for his age, and strong from much chopping of wood and drawing of water for his mother's washings, and he was the best swimmer of all those who bathed in the cold, swift mountain stream which rushes near the schoolhouse. The chief consequence of this expertness was that in the summer he was forced to teach each succeeding generation of little boys to swim and dive. They tyrannized over him unmercifully—as, in fact, everyone did.

Nothing made his mother more furious than such an exhibition of what she called "Lem's meachin'ness." "Ain't you got no stand-up *in* ye?" she was wont to exhort him angrily. "If you don't look out for yourself in this world, you needn't think anybody else is gunto!"

The instructions in ethics he received at her hands were the only ones he ever knew, for, up to his fourteenth year, he never had clothes respectable enough to wear to church, and after that he had other things to think of. Fourteen years is what we call in our state "over school age." It was a date to which Mrs. Warren had looked forward with eagerness. After that, the long, unprofitable months of enforced schooling would be over, Lem would be earning steady wages, and she could sit back and "live decent."

It seemed to her more than she could bear, that, almost upon her son's birthday, she was stricken down with paralysis. It was the first calamity for which she could not hold her marriage responsible, and her bitterness thereupon extended itself to fate in general. She cannot have been a cheerful housemate during the next ten years, when Lem was growing silently to manhood.

He was in demand as "help" on the farms about him, on account of his great strength and faithfulness, although the farmers found him exasperatingly slow and, when it was a question of animals, not always sure to obey orders. He could be trusted to be kind to horses, unlike most hired men we get nowadays, but he never learned "how to get the work out of their hide." It was his way, on a steep hill with a heavy load, to lay down the whip, get out, and put his own powerful shoulder to the wheel. If this failed, he unloaded part of the logs and made two trips of it. The uncertainty of his progress can be imagined. The busy and impatient farmer and sawyer at the opposite ends of his route were driven to exhaust their entire vocabulary of objurgation on him. He was, they used to inform him in conclusion, "the most *do*-less critter the Lord ever made!"

He was better with cows and sheep—"feller-feelin'," his mother said scornfully, watching him feed a sick ewe—and he had here, even in comparison with his fellow men, a fair degree of success. It was indeed the foundation of what material prosperity he ever enjoyed. A farmer, short of cash, paid him one year with three or four ewes and a ram. He worked for another farmer to pay for the rent of a pasture and had, that first year, as everybody admitted, almighty good luck with them. There were several twin lambs born that spring and everyone lived. Lem used to make frequent night visits during lambing-time to the pasture to make sure that all was well.

I remember as a little girl starting back from some village festivity late one spring night and seeing a lantern twinkle far up on the mountainside. "Lem Warren out fussin' with his sheep," some one of my elders remarked. Later, as we were almost home, we saw the lantern on the road ahead of us and stopped the horses, country-fashion, for an interchange of salutation. Looking out from under the shawl in which I was wrapped, I saw his tall figure stooping over something held under his coat. The lantern lighted his weather-beaten face and the expression of his eyes as he looked down at the little white head against his breast.

"You're foolish, Lem," said my uncle. "The ewe won't own it if you take it away so long the first night."

"I—I—know," stuttered Lem, bringing out the words with his usual difficulty; "but it's mortal cold up on the mounting for little fellers! I'll bring him up as a cosset."

The incident reminded me vaguely of something I had read about, and it has remained in my memory.

After we drove on I remember that there were laughing speculations about what language old Ma'am Warren would use at having another cosset brought to the house. Not that it could make any more work for her, since Lem did all that was done about the housekeeping. Chained to her chair by her paralyzed legs, as she was, she could accomplish nothing more than to sit and cavil at the management of the universe all day, until Lem came home, gave her her supper, and put her to bed.

Badly run as she thought the world, for a time it was more favorable to her material prosperity than she had ever known it. Lem's flock of sheep grew and thrived. For years nobody in our valley has tried to do much with sheep because of dogs, and all Lem's neighbors told him that some fine morning he would find his flock torn and dismembered. They even pointed out the particular big collie dog who would most likely go "sheep-mad." Lem's heavy face drew into anxious, grotesque wrinkles at this kind of talk, and he visited the uplying pasture more and more frequently.

One morning, just before dawn, he came, pale and shamefaced, to the house of the owner of the collie. The family, roused from bed by his knocking, made out from his speech, more incoherent than usual, that he was begging their pardon for having killed their dog. "I saw wh-where he'd bit th-the throats out of two ewes that w-was due to lamb in a few days and I guess I—I—I must ha' gone kind o' crazy. They was ones I liked special. I'd brought 'em up myself. They—they was all over blood, you know."

They peered at him in the gray light, half afraid of the tall apparition. "How *could* you kill a great big dog like Jack?" they asked wonderingly.

In answer he held out his great hands and his huge corded arms, red with blood up to the elbow. "I heard him worrying another sheep and I—I just—killed him."

One of the children now cried out: "But I shut Jackie up in the woodshed last night!"

Someone ran to open the door and the collie bounded out. Lem turned white in thankfulness. "I'm *mortal* glad," he stammered. "I felt awful bad—afterward. I knew your young ones thought a sight of Jack."

"But what dog did you kill?" they asked.

Some of the men went back up on the mountain with him and found, torn in pieces and scattered wide in bloody fragments, as if destroyed by some great revenging beast of prey, the body of a big gray wolf. Once in a while one wanders over the line from the Canada forests and comes down into our woods, following the deer.

The hard-headed farmers who looked on that savage scene drew back from the shambling man beside them in the only impulse of respect they ever felt for him. It was the one act of his life to secure the admiration of his fellowmen; it was an action of which he himself always spoke in horror and shame.

Certainly his marriage aroused no admiration. It was universally regarded as a most addle-pated, imbecile affair from beginning to end. One of the girls who worked at the hotel in the village "got into trouble," as our vernacular runs, and as she came originally from our district and had gone to school there, everyone knew her and was talking about the scandal. Old Ma'am Warren was of the opinion, spiritedly expressed, that "Lottie was a fool not to make that drummer marry her. She could have, if she'd gone the right way to work." But the drummer remained persistently absent.

One evening Lem, starting for his sheep pasture for his last look for the night, heard someone crying down by the river and then, as he paused to listen, heard it no more. He jumped from the bridge without stopping to set down his lantern, knowing well the swiftness of the water, and caught the poor cowardly thing as she came, struggling and gasping, down with the current. He took her home and gave her dry clothes of his mother's. Then leaving the scared and repentant child by his hearth, he set out on foot for the minister's house and dragged him back over the rough country roads.

When Ma'am Warren awoke the next morning, Lem did not instantly answer her imperious call, as he had done for so many years. Instead, a red-eyed girl in one of Mrs. Warren's own nightgowns came to the door and said shrinkingly: "Lem slept in the barn last night. He give his bed to me; but he'll be in soon. I see him fussin' around with the cow."

Ma'am Warren stared, transfixed with a premonition of irremediable evil. "What you doin' here?" she demanded, her voice devoid of expression through stupefaction.

The girl held down her head. "Lem and I were married last night," she said.

Then Mrs. Warren found her voice.

When Lem came in it was to a scene of the furious wrangling which was henceforth to fill his house.

". . . to saddle himself with such trash as you!" his mother was saying ragingly.

His wife answered in kind, her vanity stung beyond endurance. "Well, you can be sure he'd never have got him a wife any other way! Nobody but a girl hard put to it would take up with a drivel-headed fool like Lem Warren!"

And then the bridegroom appeared at the door and both women turned their attention to him.

When the baby was born, Lottie was very sick. Lem took care of his mother, his wife, and the new baby for weeks and weeks. It was at lambing-time, and his flock suffered from lack of attention, although as much as he dared he left his sick women and tended his ewes. He ran in debt, too, to the grocery stores, for he could work very little and earned almost nothing. Of course the neighbors helped out, but it was no cheerful morning's work to care for the vitriolic old woman, and Lottie was too sick for anyone but Lem to handle. We did pass the baby around from house to house during the worst of his siege, to keep her off Lem's hands; but when Lottie began to get better it was haying-time; everybody was more than busy, and the baby was sent back.

Lottie lingered in semi-invalidism for about a year and then died, Lem holding her hand in his. She tried to say something to him that last night, so the neighbors who were there reported, but her breath failed her and she could only lie staring at him from eyes that seemed already to look from the other side of the grave.

He was heavily in debt when he was thus left with a year-old child not his own, but he gave Lottie a decent funeral and put up over her grave a stone stating that she was "Charlotte, loved wife of Lemuel Warren," and that she died in the eighteenth year of her life. He used to take the little girl and put flowers on the grave, I remember.

Then he went to work again. His sandy hair was already streaked with gray, though he was but thirty. The doctor said the reason for this phenomenon was the great strain of his year of nursing; and indeed throughout that period of his life no one knew when he slept, if ever. He was always up and dressed when anyone else was, and late at night we could look across and see his light still burning and know that he was rubbing Lottie's back or feeding little Susie.

All that was changed now, of course. Susie was a strong, healthy child who slept all through the night in her little crib by her stepfather's corded bed, and in the daytime went everywhere he did. Wherever he "worked out" he used to give her her nap wrapped in a horse blanket on the hay in the barn; and he carried her in a sling of his own contrivance up to his sheep pasture. Old Ma'am Warren disliked the pretty, laughing child so bitterly that he was loath to leave her at home; but when he was there with her, for the first time he asserted himself against his mother, bidding her, when she began to berate the child's parentage, to "be still!" with so strange and unexpected an accent of authority that she was quite frightened.

Susie was very fond of her stepfather at first, but when she came of school age, mixed more with the older children, and heard laughing, contemptuous remarks about him, the frank and devouring egotism of childhood made her ashamed of her affection, ashamed of him with his uncouth gait, his mouth always sagging open, his stammering, ignorant speech, which the other children amused themselves by mocking. Though he was prospering again with his sheep, owned the pasture and his house now, and had even built on another room as well as repairing the older part, he spent little on his own adornment. It all went for pretty clothes for Susie, for better food, for books and pictures, for tickets for Susie to go to the circus and the county fair. Susie knew this and loved him by stealth for it, but the intolerably sensitive vanity of her twelve years made her wretched to be seen in public with him.

Divining this, he ceased going with her to school picnics and Sunday school parties, where he had been a most useful pack animal, and, dressing her in her best with his big calloused hands, watched her from the window join a group of the other children. His mother predicted savagely that his "spoilin' on that bad-blooded young one would bring her to no good end," and when, at fifteen, Susie began to grow very pretty and saucy and willful and to have beaux come to see her, the old woman exulted openly over Lem's helpless anxiety.

He was quite gray now, although not yet forty-five, and so stooped that he passed for an old man. He owned a little farm, his flock of sheep was the largest in the township, and Susie was expected to make a good marriage in spite of her antecedents.

And then Frank Gridley's oldest son, Ed, came back from business college with store clothes and city hats and polished tan shoes, and began idling about, calling on the girls. From the first, he and Susie ran together like two drops of water. Bronson Perkins, a cousin of mine, a big, silent, ruminative lad who had long hung about Susie, stood no show at all. One night in county-fair week, Susie, who had gone to the fair with a crowd of girlfriends, was not at home at ten o'clock. Lem, sitting in his doorway and watching the clock, heard the approach of the laughing, singing straw ride in which she had gone, with a long breath of relief; but the big hay wagon did not stop at his gate.

He called after it in a harsh voice and was told that "Ed Gridley and she went off to the hotel to get supper. He said he'd bring her home later."

Lem went out to the barn, hitched up the faster of his two heavy plow horses and drove from his house to Woodville, eight miles and uphill, in forty-five minutes. When he went into the hotel, the clerk told him that the two he sought had had supper served in a private room. Lem ascertained which room and broke the door in with one heave of his shoulders. Susie sprang up from the disordered supper table and ran to him like a frightened child, clinging to him desperately and crying out that Ed scared her so!

"It's all right now, Susie," he said gently, not looking at the man. "Poppa's come to take you home."

The man felt his dignity wounded. He began to protest boisterously and to declare that he was ready to marry the girl—"*now*, this instant, if you choose!"

Lem put one arm about Susie. "I didn't come to make you marry her. I come to keep you from doin' it," he said, speaking clearly for once in his life. "Susie shan't marry a hound that'd do this." And as the other advanced threateningly on him, he struck him a great blow across the mouth that sent him unconscious to the ground.

Then Lem went out, paid for the broken lock, and drove home with Susie behind the foundered plow horse.

The next spring her engagement to Bronson Perkins was announced, though everybody said they didn't see what use it was for folks to get engaged that couldn't ever get married. Mr. Perkins, Bronson's father, was daft, not enough to send him to the asylum, but so that he had to be watched all the time to keep him from doing himself a hurt. He had a horrid way, I remember, of lighting matches and holding them up to his bared arm until the smell of burning flesh went sickeningly through the house and sent someone in a rush to him. Of course it was out of the question to bring a young bride to such a home. Apparently there were years of waiting before them, and Susie was made of no stuff to endure a long engagement.

As a matter of fact, they were married that fall, as soon as Susie could get her things ready. Lem took old Mr. Perkins into the room

Susie left vacant. " 'Twon't be much more trouble taking care of two old people than one," he explained briefly.

Ma'am Warren's comments on this action have been embalmed forever in the delighted memories of our people. We have a taste for picturesque and forceful speech.

From that time we always saw the lunatic and the bent shepherd together. The older man grew quieter under Lem's care than he had been for years, and if he felt one of his insane impulses overtaking him, ran totteringly to grasp his protector's arm until, quaking and shivering, he was himself again. Lem used to take him up to the sheep pasture for the day sometimes. He liked it up there himself, he said, and maybe 'twould be good for Uncle Hi. He often reported with pride that the old man talked as sensible as anybody, "get him off where it's quiet." Indeed, when Mr. Perkins died, six years later, we had forgotten that he was anything but a little queer, and he had known many happy, lucid hours with his grandchildren.

Susie and Bronson had two boys—sturdy, hearty children, in whom Lem took the deepest, shyest pride. He loved to take them off into the woods with him and exulted in their quick intelligence and strong little bodies. Susie got into the way of letting him take a good deal of the care of them.

It was Lem who first took alarm about the fall that little Frank had, down the cellar stairs. He hurt his spine somehow—our local doctor could not tell exactly how—and as the injury only made him limp a little, nobody thought much about it, until he began to have difficulty in walking. Then Lem sent for a doctor from Rutland who, as soon as he examined the child, stuck out his lower lip and rubbed his chin ominously. He pronounced the trouble something with a long name which none of us had ever heard, and said that Frank would be a hopeless cripple if it were not cured soon. There was, he said, a celebrated doctor from Europe now traveling in this country who had a wonderful new treatment for this condition. But under the circumstances—he looked about the plain farm sitting room—he supposed that was out of the question.

"What did the doctor from foreign parts ask?" queried Bronson, and, being informed of some of the customary prices for major operations, fell back hopeless. Susie, her pretty, childish face drawn and blanched into a wan beauty, put her arms about her sick little son and looked at her stepfather. He had never failed her.

He did not fail her now. He sold the land he had accumulated field by field; he sold the great flock of sheep, every one of which he could call by name; he mortgaged the house over the protesting head of his now bedridden mother; he sold the horse and cow, and the very sticks of furniture from the room where Susie had grown up and where the crazy grandfather of Susie's children had known a peaceful old age and death. Little Frank was taken to New York to the hospital to have the great surgeon operate on him—he is there yet, almost completely recovered and nearly ready to come home.

Back in Hillsboro, Lem now began life all over again, hiring out humbly to his neighbors and only stipulating that he should have enough free time to take care of his mother. Three weeks ago she had her last stroke of paralysis and, after lying speechless for a few days, passed away, grim to the last, by the expression in her fierce old eyes.

The day after her funeral Lem did not come to work as he was expected. We went over to his house and found, to our consternation, that he was not out of bed.

"Be ye sick, Lem?" asked my uncle.

He looked at us over the bedclothes with his old foolish, apologetic smile. "Kind o' lazy, I guess," he whispered, closing his eyes.

The doctor was put out by the irregularity of the case. "I can't make out anything *really* the trouble!" he said. "Only the wheels don't go round as fast as they ought. Call it failing heart action if you want a label."

The wheels ran more and more slowly until it was apparent to all of us that before long they would stop altogether. Susie and Bronson were in New York with little Frank, so that Lem's care during the last days devolved on the haphazard services of the neighbors. He was out of his head most of the time, though never violent, and all through the long nights lay flat on his back, looking at the ceiling with bright, blank eyes, driving his ox team, skidding logs, plowing in stony ground and remembering to favor the off-horse whose wind wasn't good, planting, hoeing, tending his sheep, and teaching obstinate lambs to drink. He used quaint, coaxing names for these, such as a mother uses for her baby. He was up in the mountain pasture a good deal, we gathered, and at night, from his constant mention of how bright the stars shone. And sometimes, when he was in evident pain, his delusion took the form that Susie, or the little boys, had gone up with him, and got lost in the woods.

I was on duty the night he died. We thought a change was near, because he had lain silent all day, and we hoped he would come to himself when he awoke from this stupor. Near midnight he began to talk again, and I could not make out at first whether he was still wandering or not. "Hold on hard, Uncle Hi," I heard him whisper.

A spoon fell out of my hand and clattered against a plate. He gave a great start and tried to sit up. "Yes, mother—coming!" he called hoarsely, and then looked at me with his own eyes. "I must ha' forgot about mother's bein' gone," he apologized sheepishly.

I took advantage of this lucid interval to try to give him some medicine the doctor had left. "Take a swallow of this," I said, holding the glass to his lips.

"What's it for?" he asked.

"It's a heart stimulant," I explained. "The doctor said if we could get you through tonight you have a good chance."

His face drew together in grotesque lines of anxiety. "Little Frank worse?"

"Oh, no, he's doing finely."

"Susie all right?"

"Why, yes," I said wonderingly.

"Nothing the matter with her other boy?"

"Why, no, no," I told him. "Everybody's all right. Here, just take this down."

He turned away his head on the pillow and murmured something I did not catch. When I asked him what he said, he smiled feebly as in deprecation of his well-known ridiculous ways. "I'm just as much obliged to you," he said, "but if everybody's all right, I guess I won't have any medicine." He looked at me earnestly. "I'm —I'm real tired," he said.

It came out in one great breath—apparently his last, for he did not move after that, and his ugly, slack-mouthed face was at once quite still. Its expression made me think of the time I had seen it as a child, by lantern light, as he looked down at the newborn lamb on his breast.

Will

Ella Wheeler Wilcox

There is no chance, no destiny, no fate,
  Can circumvent or hinder or control
  The firm resolve of a determined soul.
Gifts count for nothing; will alone is great;
All things give way before it, soon or late.
  What obstacle can stay the mighty force
  Of the sea-seeking river in its course,
Or cause the ascending orb of day to wait?

Each well-born soul must win what it deserves.
  Let the fool prate of luck. The fortunate
    Is he whose earnest purpose never swerves,
    Whose slightest action or inaction serves
The one great aim. Why, even Death stands still,
And waits an hour sometimes for such a will.

I Decline to Accept the End of Man

William Faulkner

William Faulkner (1897–1962) gave this short but spectacular address on the evening of December 10, 1950, at a state dinner in Stockholm, Sweden, where he had traveled to accept the Nobel Prize for literature. It is foremost an exhortation to young writers, a reminder that artistic creation does have duties, and that forgetting those duties relegates one's work to the ranks of mediocrity. But his words speak to every reader of literature as well. Faulkner reminds us that *what* we study in school and *what* we read in our precious spare time matters. Great literature—the kind we cannot afford to miss—speaks to problems of the spirit, the "human heart in conflict with itself," and nothing less. It lifts our eyes to the virtues we possess and the nobility we would acquire, and helps us to prevail.

I feel that this award was not made to me as a man, but to my work—a life's work in the agony and sweat of the human spirit, not for glory and least of all for profit, but to create out of the materials of the human spirit something which did not exist before. So this award is only mine in trust. It will not be difficult to find a dedication for the money part of it commensurate with the purpose and significance of its origin. But I would like to do the same with the acclaim too, by using this moment as a pinnacle from which I might be listened to by the young men and women already dedicated to the same anguish and travail, among whom is already that one who will someday stand here where I am standing.

Our tragedy today is a general and universal physical fear so long sustained by now that we can even bear it. There are no longer problems of the spirit. There is only the question: When will I be blown up? Because of this, the young man or woman writing today has forgotten the problems of the human heart in conflict with itself which alone can make good writing because only that is worth writing about, worth the agony and the sweat.

He must learn them again. He must teach himself that the basest of all things is to be afraid; and, teaching himself that, forget it forever, leaving no room in his workshop for anything but the old verities and truths of the heart, the old universal truths lacking which any story is ephemeral and doomed—love and honor and pity and pride and compassion and sacrifice. Until he does so, he labors under a curse. He writes not of love but of lust, of defeats in which nobody loses anything of value, of victories without hope and, worst of all, without pity or compassion. His griefs grieve on no universal bones, leaving no scars. He writes not of the heart but of the glands.

Until he relearns these things, he will write as though he stood among and watched the end of man. I decline to accept the end of man. It is easy enough to say that man is immortal simply because he will endure: that when the last ding-dong of doom has clanged and faded from the last worthless rock hanging tideless in the last red and dying evening, that even then there will still be one more sound: that of his puny inexhaustible voice, still talking. I refuse to accept this. I believe that man will not merely endure: he will prevail. He is immortal, not because he alone among creatures has an inexhaustible voice, but because he has a soul, a spirit capable of compassion and sacrifice and endurance. The poet's, the writer's, duty is to write about these things. It is his privilege to help man endure by lifting his heart, by reminding him of the courage and honor and hope and pride and compassion and pity and sacrifice which have been the glory of his past. The poet's voice need not merely be the record of man, it can be one of the props, the pillars to help him endure and prevail.

8

Honesty

To be honest is to be real, genuine, authentic, and bona fide. To be dishonest is to be partly feigned, forged, fake, or fictitious. Honesty expresses both self-respect and respect for others. Dishonesty fully respects neither oneself nor others. Honesty imbues lives with openness, reliability, and candor; it expresses a disposition to live in the light. Dishonesty seeks shade, cover, or concealment. It is a disposition to live partly in the dark.

Why would anyone want to be dishonest? That is a question with which the Irish satirist Jonathan Swift poignantly confronts his readers in "A Voyage to the Houyhnhnms" in *Gulliver's Travels*. The Houyhnhnms were such rational creatures that they found dishonesty almost unintelligible. As one of them explains to Gulliver, "the use of speech was to make us understand one another, and to receive information of facts; now if anyone *said the thing which was not* [the Houyhnhnms' awkward locution for referring to the curious practice of telling lies], these ends were defeated."

Dishonesty would have no role to play in a world that revered reality and was inhabited by fully rational creatures. Human beings are not fully rational, however, as Swift delighted in pointing out. Humans, unlike Houyhnhnms, harbor a disparate array of tendencies and impulses that do not spontaneously harmonize with reason. Human beings need both practice and study over time to become persons of integrity and effective goodwill. And until they have achieved such a state, they may do all sorts of things that prudence tells them had better be concealed. Lying is an "easy" tool of concealment, and when often employed, all too easily hardens into a malignant vice.

Honesty is of pervasive human importance. "I hate that man like the very Gates of Death who says one thing but hides another in his heart," cries the anguished Achilles in Homer's *Iliad*. Every social activity, every human enterprise requiring people to act in concert, is impeded when people aren't honest with one another. Honesty here is not just veracity—truth-telling—but the honesty of "an honest day's work for an honest day's pay." It is the honesty that the prophet Jeremiah sought. "Run to and fro through the streets of Jerusalem, look around and take note! Search its squares and see if you can find one person who acts justly and seeks truth." It is the honesty that the Cynic philosopher Diogenes sought later in Athens and Corinth, an image that has proved remarkably durable. "With Candle and Lanthorn, when the Sun shin'd I sought Honest Men, but none could I find," as a seventeenth-century chapbook put it. Pinocchio's lie-lengthened nose is an image scarcely a hundred years old now, but it, too, has happily found a place among our enduring popular stories.

How is honesty best cultivated? Like most virtues, it is best developed and exercised in harmony with others. The more it is exercised, the more it becomes a settled disposition. But there is a quick answer that may be given in three words: *take it seriously*. Take recognition of the fact that honesty is a fundamental condition for human intercourse and exchange, for friendship, for all genuine community. But be sure to take it seriously *for itself*, not just as "the best policy."

"Honesty is better than all policy," as the philosopher Immanuel Kant perceptively put it. There is all the moral difference in the world between taking the condition of one's *self* seriously and taking pains not to get caught. Parents often say, "Don't let me catch you doing that again!" and that is all right, but a good, honest life is more than that. Moral development is not a game of "Catch me if you can." It is better to focus clearly on what really matters: *the kind of person one is.*

The Boy Who Never Told a Lie

An honest heart will always find friends.

Once there was a little boy,
   With curly hair and pleasant eye—
A boy who always told the truth,
   And never, never told a lie.

And when he trotted off to school,
   The children all about would cry,
"There goes the curly-headed boy—
   The boy that never tells a lie."

And everybody loved him so,
   Because he always told the truth,
That every day, as he grew up,
   'Twas said, "There goes the honest youth."

And when the people that stood near
   Would turn to ask the reason why,
The answer would be always this:
   "Because he never tells a lie."

The Boy Who Cried "Wolf"

Aesop

This may be Aesop's most famous fable, and for good reason.
The fastest way to lose what we call our "good character" is to
lose our honesty.

There was once a shepherd boy who kept his flock at a little
distance from the village. Once he thought he would play a trick on
the villagers and have some fun at their expense. So he ran toward
the village crying out, with all his might:

"Wolf! Wolf! Come and help! The wolves are at my lambs!"

The kind villagers left their work and ran to the field to help
him. But when they got there the boy laughed at them for their
pains; there was no wolf there.

Still another day the boy tried the same trick, and the villagers
came running to help and were laughed at again.

Then one day a wolf did break into the fold and began killing
the lambs. In great fright, the boy ran back for help. "Wolf! Wolf!"
he screamed. "There is a wolf in the flock! Help!"

The villagers heard him, but they thought it was another mean
trick; no one paid the least attention, or went near him. And the
shepherd boy lost all his sheep.

That is the kind of thing that happens to people who lie: even
when they do tell the truth they will not be believed.

The Honest Woodman

Adapted from Emilie Poulsson

This story is retold from a poem by Jean de La Fontaine (1621–
1695), who, like Aesop, was a master of the fable.

Once upon a time, out in the green, silent woods near a rushing
river that foamed and sparkled as it hurried along, there lived a poor

woodcutter who worked hard to make a living for his family. Every day he would trudge into the forest with his strong, sharp axe over his shoulder. He always whistled happily as he went, because he was thinking that as long as he had his health and his axe, he could earn enough to buy all the bread his family needed.

One day he was cutting a large oak tree near the riverside. The chips flew fast at every stroke, and the sound of the ringing axe echoed through the forest so clearly you might have thought a dozen wood choppers were at work that day.

By and by the woodman thought he would rest awhile. He leaned his axe against the tree and turned to sit down, but he tripped over an old, gnarled root, and before he could catch it, his axe slid down the bank and into the river!

The poor woodman gazed into the stream, trying to see the bottom, but it was far too deep there. The river flowed over the lost treasure just as merrily as before.

"What will I do?" the woodman cried. "I've lost my axe! How will I feed my children now?"

Just as he finished speaking, up from the lake rose a beautiful lady. She was the water fairy of the river, and came to the surface when she heard his sad voice.

"What is your sorrow?" she asked kindly. The woodman told her about his trouble, and at once she sank beneath the surface, and reappeared in a moment with an axe made of silver.

"Is this the axe you lost?" she asked.

The woodman thought of all the fine things he could buy for his children with that silver! But the axe wasn't his, so he shook his head, and answered, "My axe was only made of steel."

The water fairy lay the silver axe on the bank, and sank into the river again. In a moment she rose and showed the woodman another axe. "Perhaps this one is yours?" she asked.

The woodman looked. "Oh, no!" he replied. "This one is made of gold! It's worth many times more than mine."

The water fairy lay the golden axe on the bank. Once again she sank. Up she rose. This time she held the missing axe.

"That is mine!" the woodman cried. "That is surely my old axe!"

"It is yours," said the water fairy, "and so are these other two now. They are gifts from the river, because you have told the truth."

And that evening the woodman trudged home with all three axes on his shoulder, whistling happily as he thought of all the good things they would bring for his family.

Someone Sees You

This folktale reminds us that an act of dishonesty is never truly hidden.

Once upon a time a man decided to sneak into his neighbor's fields and steal some wheat. "If I take just a little from each field, no one will notice," he told himself, "but it will all add up to a nice pile of wheat for me." So he waited for the darkest night, when thick clouds lay over the moon, and he crept out of his house. He took his youngest daughter with him.

"Daughter," he whispered, "you must stand guard, and call out if anyone sees me."

The man stole into the first field to begin reaping, and before long the child called out, "Father, someone sees you!"

The man looked all around, but he saw no one, so he gathered his stolen wheat and moved on to a second field.

"Father, someone sees you!" the child cried again.

The man stopped and looked all around, but once again he saw no one. He gathered more wheat, and moved to a third field.

A little while passed, and the daughter cried out, "Father, someone sees you!"

Once more the man stopped his work and looked in every direction, but he saw no one at all, so he bundled his wheat and crept into the last field.

"Father, someone sees you!" the child called again.

The man stopped his reaping, looked all around, and once again saw no one. "Why in the world do you keep saying someone sees me?" he angrily asked his daughter. "I've looked everywhere, and I don't see anyone."

"Father," murmured the child, "Someone sees you from above."

George Washington and the Cherry Tree

*Adapted from J. Berg Esenwein and
Marietta Stockard*

The chopping down of the cherry tree is surely the most famous
truth-telling tale in America. It first appeared in 1806 in the fifth
edition of Mason Lock Weems's imaginative biography of Washington, entitled *The Life of George Washington with Curious Anec-
dotes, Equally Honourable to Himself and Exemplary to His Young
Countrymen.* Here is an early twentieth-century rendition.

When George Washington was a little boy he lived on a farm in
Virginia. His father taught him to ride, and he used to take young
George about the farm with him so that his son might learn how to
take care of the fields and horses and cattle when he grew older.

Mr. Washington had planted an orchard of fine fruit trees.
There were apple trees, peach trees, pear trees, plum trees, and
cherry trees. Once, a particularly fine cherry tree was sent to him
from across the ocean. Mr. Washington planted it on the edge of the
orchard. He told everyone on the farm to watch it carefully to see
that it was not broken or hurt in any way.

It grew well and one spring it was covered with white blossoms.
Mr. Washington was pleased to think he would soon have cherries
from the little tree.

Just about this time, George was given a shiny new hatchet.
George took it and went about chopping sticks, hacking into the
rails of fences, and cutting whatever else he passed. At last he came
to the edge of the orchard, and thinking only of how well his hatchet
could cut, he chopped into the little cherry tree. The bark was soft,
and it cut so easily that George chopped the tree right down, and
then went on with his play.

That evening when Mr. Washington came from inspecting the
farm, he sent his horse to the stable and walked down to the orchard
to look at his cherry tree. He stood in amazement when he saw how
it was cut. Who would have dared do such a thing? He asked everyone, but no one could tell him anything about it.

Just then George passed by.

"George," his father called in an angry voice, "do you know who killed my cherry tree?

This was a tough question, and George staggered under it for a moment, but quickly recovered.

"I cannot tell a lie, father," he said. "I did it with my hatchet."

Mr. Washington looked at George. The boy's face was white, but he looked straight into his father's eyes.

"Go into the house, son," said Mr. Washington sternly.

George went into the library and waited for his father. He was very unhappy and very much ashamed. He knew he had been foolish and thoughtless and that his father was right to be displeased.

Soon, Mr. Washington came into the room. "Come here, my boy," he said.

George went over to his father. Mr. Washington looked at him long and steadily.

"Tell me, son, why did you cut the tree?"

"I was playing and I did not think—" George stammered.

"And now the tree will die. We shall never have any cherries from it. But worse than that, you have failed to take care of the tree when I asked you to do so."

George's head was bent and his cheeks were red from shame.

"I am sorry, father," he said.

Mr. Washington put his hand on the boy's shoulder. "Look at me," he said. "I am sorry to have lost my cherry tree, but I am glad that you were brave enough to tell me the truth. I would rather have you truthful and brave than to have a whole orchard full of the finest cherry trees. Never forget that, my son."

George Washington never did forget. To the end of his life he was just as brave and honorable as he was that day as a little boy.

Matilda, Who Told Lies, and Was Burned to Death

Hilaire Belloc

In which we learn the fate of a little girl who apparently never took to heart the story of the Boy Who Cried Wolf. This tale takes place in England, the home of its author, Hilaire Belloc (1870–1953).

Matilda told such Dreadful Lies,
It made one gasp and stretch one's eyes;
Her aunt, who, from her earliest youth,
Had kept a strict regard for truth,
Attempted to believe Matilda:
The effort very nearly killed her,
And would have done so, had not she
Discovered this infirmity.
For once, toward the close of day,
Matilda, growing tired of play,
And finding she was left alone,
Went tiptoe
        to
           the telephone
And summoned the immediate aid
Of London's noble fire brigade.
Within an hour the gallant band
Were pouring in on every hand,
From Putney, Hackney Downs and Bow,
With courage high and hearts aglow
They galloped, roaring through the town,
"Matilda's house is burning down!"
Inspired by British cheers and loud
Proceeding from the frenzied crowd,
They ran their ladders through a score
Of windows on the ballroom floor;
And took peculiar pains to souse

The pictures up and down the house,
Until Matilda's aunt succeeded
In showing them they were not needed
And even then she had to pay
To get the men to go away!

   •   •   •   •   •

It happened that a few weeks later
Her aunt was off to the theater
To see that interesting play
The Second Mrs. Tanqueray.
She had refused to take her niece
To hear this entertaining piece:
A deprivation just and wise
To punish her for telling lies.
That night a fire *did* break out—
You should have heard Matilda shout!
You should have heard her scream and bawl,
And throw the window up and call
To people passing in the street—
(The rapidly increasing heat
Encouraging her to obtain
Their confidence)—but all in vain!
For every time she shouted "Fire!"
They only answered "Little liar!"
And therefore when her aunt returned,
Matilda, and the house, were burned.

Rebecca's Afterthought

Elizabeth Turner

In which we learn (with relief) of a much happier ending for a
little girl who decided to remain steadfastly honest.

Yesterday, Rebecca Mason,
  In the parlor by herself,
Broke a handsome china basin,
  Placed upon the mantel shelf.

Quite alarmed, she thought of going
   Very quietly away,
Not a single person knowing,
   Of her being there that day.

But Rebecca recollected
   She was taught deceit to shun;
And the moment she reflected,
   Told her mother what was done;

Who commended her behavior,
Loved her better, and forgave her.

Pinocchio

Carlo Lorenzini

The lengthening nose has become one of our instantly recogniz-
able symbols of dishonesty, thanks to this famous scene from
Carlo Lorenzini's classic nineteenth-century Italian tale, *Pinocchio*.
Here the wooden puppet, with the aid of the Fairy with the Blue
Hair, is recovering from the effects of having fallen in with the
wrong crowd.

When the three doctors had gone, the Fairy came to Pinocchio
and, upon touching his forehead, perceived that he had a high fever.
So she put a white powder in a glass of water and gave it to him,
saying gently:

"Drink this and after a while you will be well."

Pinocchio gazed at the glass, made a wry face, and asked whin-
ingly:

"Is it sweet or bitter?"

"It is bitter but will do you good."

"If it is bitter, I don't want it."

"Listen to me. Drink it."

"But I don't like bitter things."

"Drink it, and then I will give you a lump of sugar to take the taste out of your mouth."

"Where is the lump of sugar?"

"Here it is."

"Give it to me first, and then I will take the medicine."

"You promise?"

"Yes."

The Fairy gave him the sugar, and Pinocchio soon finished it. Then he said, licking his lips, "How nice it would be if sugar were medicine! I'd take it every day."

"Now keep your promise and take the medicine," said the Fairy. "It will make you well."

Pinocchio held the glass in his hand and sniffed at its contents; then put it to his mouth; then smelled it again; and finally said:

"It's too bitter—too bitter! I can't possibly gulp it down."

"How can you say that when you haven't tasted it?"

"Oh, I can imagine—I can tell by the smell! Give me another lump of sugar and then I will drink it."

So the Fairy, with all the patience of an indulgent mamma, put another lump of sugar in his mouth and then handed him the medicine again.

"Truly I can't drink it!" wailed the marionette with a thousand grimaces.

"Why?"

"Because that pillow is too close to my feet."

The Fairy moved the pillow.

"It's no use—I can't drink it."

"What else annoys you?"

"That door is ajar."

The Fairy shut the door.

"Honestly, I can't drink that bitter stuff," howled Pinocchio. "No, no, no!"

"My boy, you will be sorry."

"I don't care."

"You'll die of the fever."

"I don't care. I'd rather die than take that bitter medicine."

"All right, then," said the Fairy.

At this the door opened and in walked four Rabbits, black as ink, and carrying a coffin on their shoulders.

"What do you want?" cried Pinocchio sitting up.

"We have come to take you away," said the largest Rabbit.

"To take me away? Why, I'm not dead yet!"

"No, not yet, but you will be in a few moments since you have refused the medicine that would make you well."

"O my Fairy, my Fairy!" yelled Pinocchio. "Give me that medicine—quickly! Send them away—I don't want to die—I don't want to die!"

And he seized the glass with both hands and drank the dose down at one gulp.

"Pshaw!" said the Rabbits. "We have come on a fool's errand." And taking the coffin up on their shoulders they went away grumbling.

Not long afterward Pinocchio jumped out of bed entirely well. For, you must know, that wooden boys are rarely ill and then get well quickly. When the Fairy saw him capering around the room happy as a chicken that has just burst its shell, she said:

"So my medicine has really cured you?"

"Yes, indeed. I had a close call."

"Then why did you make such a fuss about taking it?"

"Oh, boys are all alike. We are more afraid of the medicine than of the illness."

"For shame! Boys ought to know that a good remedy taken in time often keeps off a dangerous sickness—perhaps death."

"The next time I shan't be so bad. I shall remember those black Rabbits and the coffin—then I'll take the medicine right away."

"That's right. Now come and tell me how you happened to fall into the hands of thieves."

Pinocchio told faithfully all that had happened to him. When he had ended, the Fairy asked:

"What did you do with the four gold pieces?"

"I lost them," replied Pinocchio. But he told a lie, because he had them in his pocket.

The moment he said this, his nose, which was already long enough, grew four inches longer.

"Where did you lose them?" asked the Fairy.

"In the forest near here."

At this second lie, the nose grew still longer.

"If you have lost them in the forest near here," said the Fairy, "we shall soon find them. For everything here is always found."

"Ah, now I recollect," said the marionette. "I did not lose the coins, but I swallowed them when I took the medicine."

At the third lie, Pinocchio's nose grew so long that he couldn't turn around. If he turned one way he struck it against the bedpost or the window. If he turned the other, he hit the wall or the door.

The Fairy looked at him and began to laugh.

"Why are you laughing?" asked the marionette sheepishly.

"I laugh at the foolish lies you have told."

"How did you know they were lies?"

"Lies, my boy, are recognized at once, because they are of only two kinds. Some have short legs, and others have long noses. Yours are the kind that have long noses."

Pinocchio was so crestfallen that he tried to run away and hide himself, but he couldn't. His nose had grown so long that he couldn't get it through the door.

The Fairy let the marionette cry and howl for a good half hour on account of his long nose. She did this in order to teach him a lesson upon the folly of telling falsehoods. But when she saw his eyes swollen and his face red with weeping, she was moved by pity for him. She clapped her hands together, and at the signal a large flock of woodpeckers flew into the window and, alighting one by one upon Pinocchio's nose, they pecked so hard that in a few moments it was reduced to its usual size.

The Indian Cinderella

Retold by Cyrus Macmillan

This North American Indian tale, one of honesty rewarded and dishonesty punished, was recorded in Canada in the early part of the twentieth century. Glooskap, mentioned in the opening paragraph, was a god of the Eastern woodlands Indians.

On the shores of a wide bay on the Atlantic coast there dwelt in old times a great Indian warrior. It was said that he had been one of Glooskap's best helpers and friends, and that he had done for him many wonderful deeds. But that, no man knows. He had, however, a very wonderful and strange power: he could make himself invisible. He could thus mingle unseen with his enemies and listen to their plots. He was known among the people as Strong Wind, the Invisible. He dwelt with his sister in a tent near the sea, and his sister helped him greatly in his work. Many maidens would have been glad to marry him, and he was much sought after because of his mighty deeds; and it was known that Strong Wind would marry the first maiden who could see him as he came home at night. Many made the trial, but it was a long time before one succeeded.

Strong Wind used a clever trick to test the truthfulness of all who sought to win him. Each evening as the day went down, his sister walked on the beach with any girl who wished to make the trial. His sister could always see him, but no one else could see him. And as he came home from work in the twilight, his sister as she saw him drawing near would ask the girl who sought him, "Do you see him?" And each girl would falsely answer "Yes." And his sister would ask, "With what does he draw his sled?" And each girl would answer, "With the hide of a moose," or "With a pole," or "With a great cord." And then his sister would know that they all had lied, for their answers were mere guesses. And many tried and lied and failed, for Strong Wind would not marry any who were untruthful.

There lived in the village a great chief who had three daughters. Their mother had long been dead. One of these was much younger than the others. She was very beautiful and gentle and well beloved by all, and for that reason her older sisters were very jealous of her charms and treated her very cruelly. They clothed her in rags that she might be ugly; and they cut off her long black hair; and they burned her face with coals from the fire that she might be scarred and disfigured. And they lied to their father, telling him that she had done these things herself. But the young girl was patient and kept her gentle heart and went gladly about her work.

Like other girls, the chief's two eldest daughters tried to win Strong Wind. One evening, as the day went down, they walked on the shore with Strong Wind's sister and waited for his coming. Soon he came home from his day's work, drawing his sled. And his sister asked as usual, "Do you see him?" And each one, lying, answered "Yes." And she asked, "Of what is his shoulder strap made?" And each, guessing, said "Of rawhide." Then they entered the tent where they hoped to see Strong Wind eating his supper; and when he took off his coat and his moccasins they could see them, but more than these they saw nothing. And Strong Wind knew that they had lied, and he kept himself from their sight, and they went home dismayed.

One day the chief's youngest daughter with her rags and her

burned face resolved to seek Strong Wind. She patched her clothes with bits of birch bark from the trees, and put on the few little ornaments she possessed, and went forth to try to see the Invisible One as all the other girls of the village had done before. And her sisters laughed at her and called her "fool." And as she passed along the road all the people laughed at her because of her tattered frock and her burned face, but silently she went her way.

Strong Wind's sister received the little girl kindly, and at twilight she took her to the beach. Soon Strong Wind came home drawing his sled. And his sister asked, "Do you see him?" And the girl answered "No," and his sister wondered greatly because she spoke the truth. And again she asked, "Do you see him now?" And the girl answered, "Yes, and he is very wonderful." And she asked, "With what does he draw his sled?" And the girl answered, "With the Rainbow," and she was much afraid. And she asked further, "Of what is his bowstring?" And the girl answered, "His bowstring is the Milky Way."

Then Strong Wind's sister knew that because the girl had spoken the truth at first her brother had made himself visible to her. And she said, "Truly, you have seen him." And she took her home and bathed her, and all the scars disappeared from her face and body; and her hair grew long and black again like the raven's wing; and she gave her fine clothes to wear and many rich ornaments. Then she bade her take the wife's seat in the tent. Soon Strong Wind entered and sat beside her, and called her his bride. The very next day she became his wife, and ever afterward she helped him to do great deeds. The girl's two elder sisters were very cross and they wondered greatly at what had taken place. But Strong Wind, who knew of their cruelty, resolved to punish them. Using his great power, he changed them both into aspen trees and rooted them in the earth. And since that day the leaves of the aspen have always trembled, and they shiver in fear at the approach of Strong Wind, it matters not how softly he comes, for they are still mindful of his great power and anger because of their lies and their cruelty to their sister long ago.

Truth Is Mighty and Will Prevail

Retold by Ella Lyman Cabot

This story is based on events described in the book of Ezra in the Bible. Zorobabel (more frequently spelled "Zerubbabel") was a leader of the Jewish people at the time of their return home from the Babylonian exile, around 520 B.C.

When Darius was crowned king of Persia, he made a great feast to all his subjects throughout one hundred and twenty-seven provinces.

When the celebration was over, Darius went to his palace and fell asleep, but was soon awakened by the conversation of three young men who were standing guard over his bedchamber.

They were disputing as to what was the strongest thing in the world; and, as they became excited, they talked so loud that they awakened their king. But he, instead of telling them to be quiet, listened to their argument. They were saying: "Let each of us write a sentence telling what we think is strongest, and put it under the king's pillow. Then on the morrow he with the three princes of Persia will decide which is wisest. The winner then shall be given great gifts for his victory."

They did as they had agreed. The first wrote: "Wine is strongest."

The second wrote: "The king is strongest."

The third wrote: "Above all, truth beareth the victory."

These writings they placed under the king's pillow. The next day the king sat in his judgment hall with all the princes and governors of provinces around him, and ordered that the three young men should be called to justify their opinions.

The one who thought wine the strongest thing in the world arose, and said: "O men, how strong is wine! It makes fools of even the greatest men. The mightiest king and the most ignorant child are equal when under its power. The sad become gay because of it. It maketh all, even the poorest, feel rich. Their talk becomes inflated, their memories dulled, so that, whether they love or quarrel over their cups, it amounts to the same thing, because afterward they forget all about it. If wine can do this, is it not the strongest thing in the world?"

Then the second defended his belief that the king was the strongest with these words:

"The king is mighty above all else. If he bids men go to war, they do it. They cross countries and mountains, tear down city walls and attack the towers, and, when they have conquered the country, they bring all the spoil to the king. In the same way, when the farmer tills his land and reaps again after his sowing, he pays a large share of it to the king as taxes. He is but a single man, but, when he orders a person put to death, it is done. When he commands others to be spared, they are saved. So all his people obey him, and he does as he pleases. O judges, does not this prove that the king is mightiest?"

Then spake the third young man. Zorobabel was his name.

"O king, great is truth, and stronger than all things. Wine is wicked, the king is wicked, all the children of men are wicked, and they shall perish. But truth lasts forever. She is always strong, she never dies and is never defeated. With truth there is no respect of persons, and she cannot be bribed. She doeth the things that are just. She is the strength, kingdom, power, and majesty of all ages. Blessed be the God of truth."

With these words he finished, and the people burst out in a great shout: "Great is truth, and mighty above all things."

Then the king said: "Ask of me whatever thou wilt. Thou art the wisest."

And the young man said: "Remember thy promise to build Jerusalem in the day when thou comest to thy kingdom. Behold thou hast vowed to rebuild our temple, and now, O king, I desire thee to keep close to truth, and fulfill the promise which thou hast made before the King of heaven."

Then the king kissed him, and sent him to Jerusalem, rejoicing. And the young man turned his face toward heaven, and prayed to Jehovah, saying: "From thee cometh victory, from thee cometh wisdom. Thine is the glory, and I am thy servant."

Thus by the wisdom of the young man Zorobabel, the king of Persia was persuaded to rebuild Jerusalem.

The Story of Regulus

Retold by James Baldwin

This ancient story about the Roman general and statesman Marcus Atilius Regulus takes place in the third century B.C. during the First Punic War between Rome and Carthage. The legend of how Regulus kept his word immortalized him in Roman history.

On the other side of the sea from Rome there was once a great city named Carthage. The Roman people were never very friendly to the people of Carthage, and at last a war began between them. For a long time it was hard to tell which would prove the stronger. First the Romans would gain a battle, and then the men of Carthage would gain a battle; and so the war went on for many years.

Among the Romans there was a brave general named Regulus —a man of whom it was said that he never broke his word. It so happened after a while that Regulus was taken prisoner and carried to Carthage. Ill and very lonely, he dreamed of his wife and little children so far away beyond the sea; and he had but little hope of ever seeing them again. He loved his home dearly, but he believed that his first duty was to his country; and so he had left all, to fight in this cruel war.

He had lost a battle, it is true, and had been taken prisoner. Yet he knew that the Romans were gaining ground, and the people of Carthage were afraid of being beaten in the end. They had sent into other countries to hire soldiers to help them. But even with these they would not be able to fight much longer against Rome.

One day some of the rulers of Carthage came to the prison to talk with Regulus.

"We should like to make peace with the Roman people," they said, "and we are sure that, if your rulers at home knew how the war is going, they would be glad to make peace with us. We will set you free and let you go home, if you will agree to do as we say."

"What is that?" asked Regulus.

"In the first place," they said, "you must tell the Romans about the battles which you have lost, and you must make it plain to them that they have not gained anything by the war. In the second place, you must promise us that, if they will not make peace, you will come back to your prison."

"Very well," said Regulus. "I promise you that if they will not make peace, I will come back to prison."

And so they let him go, for they knew that a great Roman would keep his word.

When he came to Rome, all the people greeted him gladly. His wife and children were very happy, for they thought that now they would not be parted again. The white-haired Fathers who made the laws for the city came to see him. They asked him about the war.

"I was sent from Carthage to ask you to make peace," he said. "But it will not be wise to make peace. True, we have been beaten in a few battles, but our army is gaining ground every day. The people of Carthage are afraid, and well they may be. Keep on with the war a little while longer, and Carthage shall be yours. As for me, I have come to bid my wife and children and Rome farewell. Tomorrow I will start back to Carthage and to prison, for I have promised."

Then the Fathers tried to persuade him to stay.

"Let us send another man in your place," they said.

"Shall a Roman not keep his word?" answered Regulus. "I am ill, and at the best have not long to live. I will go back as I promised."

His wife and little children wept, and his sons begged him not to leave them again.

"I have given my word," said Regulus. "The rest will be taken care of."

Then he bade them goodbye, and went bravely back to the prison and the cruel death which he expected.

This was the kind of courage that made Rome the greatest city in the world.

The Character of a Happy Life

Henry Wotton

How happy is he born and taught,
    That serveth not another's will;
Whose armor is his honest thought,
    And simple truth his utmost skill!

Whose passions not his masters are,
    Whose soul is still prepared for death,
Untied unto the worldly care
    Of public fame, or private breath;

Who envies none that chance doth raise,
    Or vice; who never understood
How deepest wounds are given by praise;
    Nor rules of state, but rules of good:

Who hath his life from rumors freed,
    Whose conscience is his strong retreat;
Whose state can neither flatterers feed,
    Nor ruin make oppressors great;

Who God doth late and early pray,
    More of his grace than gifts to lend;
And entertains the harmless day
    With a religious book or friend

This man is freed from servile bands,
    Of hope to rise, or fear to fall;
Lord of himself, though not of lands;
    And having nothing, yet hath all.

Honest Abe

Retold by Horatio Alger

It is surely no accident that the two most beloved American presidents, Washington and Lincoln, possessed a proverbial honesty. The following stories come from Horatio Alger's *Abraham Lincoln, The Backwoods Boy,* published in 1883. (Alger, in turn, is drawing from earlier works.) The tales remind us that honesty in private life makes honesty in public office. More important, they show us that habits of a truthful heart begin early in life.

The Young Storekeeper

As a clerk he proved honest and efficient, and my readers will be interested in some illustrations of the former trait which I find in Dr. Holland's interesting volume.

One day a woman came into the store and purchased sundry articles. They footed up two dollars and six and a quarter cents, or the young clerk thought they did. We do not hear nowadays of six and a quarter cents, but this was a coin borrowed from the Spanish currency, and was well known in my own boyhood.

The bill was paid, and the woman was entirely satisfied. But the young storekeeper, not feeling quite sure as to the accuracy of his calculation, added up the items once more. To his dismay he found that the sum total should have been but two dollars.

"I've made her pay six and a quarter cents too much," said Abe, disturbed.

It was a trifle, and many clerks would have dismissed it as such. But Abe was too conscientious for that.

"The money must be paid back," he decided.

This would have been easy enough had the woman lived "just round the corner," but, as the young man knew, she lived between two and three miles away. This, however, did not alter the matter. It was night, but he closed and locked the store, and walked to the residence of his customer. Arrived there, he explained the matter, paid over the six and a quarter cents, and returned satisfied. If I were a capitalist, I would be willing to lend money to such a young man without security.

Here is another illustration of young Lincoln's strict honesty:

A woman entered the store and asked for half a pound of tea.

The young clerk weighed it out, and handed it to her in a parcel. This was the last sale of the day.

The next morning, when commencing his duties, Abe discovered a four-ounce weight on the scales. It flashed upon him at once that he had used this in the sale of the night previous, and so, of course, given his customer short weight. I am afraid that there are many country merchants who would not have been much worried by this discovery. Not so the young clerk in whom we are interested. He weighed out the balance of the half pound, shut up the store, and carried it to the defrauded customer. I think my young readers will begin to see that the name so often given, in later times to President Lincoln, of "Honest Old Abe," was well deserved. A man who begins by strict honesty in his youth is not likely to change as he grows older, and mercantile honesty is some guarantee of political honesty.

Working Out a Book

All the information we can obtain about this early time is interesting for it was then that Abe was laying the foundation of his future eminence. His mind and character were slowly developing, and shaping themselves for the future.

From Mr. Lamon's *Life* I quote a paragraph which will throw light upon his habits and tastes at the age of seventeen:

"Abe loved to lie under a shade tree, or up in the loft of the cabin, and read, cipher, and scribble. At night he sat by the chimney jamb, and ciphered by the light of the fire, on the wooden fire shovel. When the shovel was fairly covered, he would shave it off with Tom Lincoln's drawing knife, and begin again. In the daytime he used boards for the same purpose, out of doors, and went through the shaving process everlastingly. His stepmother repeats often that 'he read every book he could lay his hands on.' She says, 'Abe read diligently. He read every book he could lay his hands on, and when he came across a passage that struck him, he would write it down on boards if he had no paper, and keep it there until he did get paper. Then he would rewrite it, look at it, repeat it. He had a copybook, a kind of scrapbook, in which he put down all things, and thus preserved them.' "

I am tempted also to quote a reminiscence of John Hanks, who lived with the Lincolns from the time Abe was fourteen to the time he became eighteen years of age: "When Lincoln—Abe—and I returned to the house from work, he would go to the cupboard, snatch a piece of cornbread, take down a book, sit down on a chair, cock his legs up as high as his head, and read. He and I worked barefooted, grubbed it, plowed, mowed, and cradled together; plowed corn, gathered it, and shucked corn. Abraham read constantly when he had opportunity."

It may well be supposed, however, that the books upon which Abe could lay hands were few in number. There were no libraries, either public or private, in the neighborhood, and he was obliged to read what he could get rather than those which he would have chosen, had he been able to select from a large collection. Still, it is a matter of interest to know what books he actually did read at this formative period. Some of them certainly were worth reading, such as *Aesop's Fables, Robinson Crusoe, Pilgrim's Progress,* a *History of the United States,* and Weems's *Life of Washington.* The last book Abe borrowed from a neighbor, old Josiah Crawford (I follow the statement of Mr. Lamon, rather than of Dr. Holland, who says it was Master Crawford, his teacher). When not reading it, he laid it away in a part of the cabin where he thought it would be free from harm, but it so happened that just behind the shelf on which he placed it was a great crack between the logs of the wall. One night a storm came up suddenly, the rain beat in through the crevice, and soaked the borrowed book through and through. The book was almost utterly spoiled. Abe felt very uneasy, for a book was valuable in his eyes, as well as in the eyes of its owner.

He took the damaged volume and trudged over to Mr. Crawford's in some perplexity and mortification.

"Well, Abe, what brings you over so early?" said Mr. Crawford.

"I've got some bad news for you," answered Abe, with lengthened face.

"Bad news! What is it?"

"You know the book you lent me—the *Life of Washington?*"

"Yes, yes."

"Well, the rain last night spoiled it." And Abe showed the book, wet to a pulp inside, at the same time explaining how it had been injured.

"It's too bad, I vum! You'd ought to pay for it, Abe. You must have been dreadful careless!"

"I'd pay for it if I had any money, Mr. Crawford."

"If you've got no money, you can work it out," said Crawford.

"I'll do whatever you think right."

So it was arranged that Abe should work three days for Crawford, "pulling fodder," the value of his labor being rated at twenty-five cents a day. As the book had cost seventy-five cents this would be regarded as satisfactory. So Abe worked his three days, and discharged the debt. Mr. Lamon is disposed to find fault with Crawford for exacting this penalty, but it appears to me only equitable, and I am glad to think that Abe was willing to act honorably in the matter.

The Frog Prince

Adapted from the Brothers Grimm

We catch the moral of this story in the king's conscience: "That which thou hast promised must thou perform."

In the old times, when it was still of some use to wish for the thing one wanted, there lived a King whose daughters were all handsome, but the youngest was so beautiful that the sun himself, who has seen so much, wondered each time he shone over her because of her beauty. Near the royal castle there was a great dark wood, and in the wood under an old linden tree was a well. When the day was hot, the King's daughter used to go forth into the wood and sit by the brink of the cool well, and if the time seemed long, she would take out a golden ball, and throw it up and catch it again, and this was her favorite pastime.

Now it happened one day that the golden ball, instead of falling back into the maiden's little hand which had sent it aloft, dropped to the ground near the edge of the well and rolled in. The king's daughter followed it with her eyes as it sank, but the well was deep, so deep that the bottom could not be seen. Then she began to weep, and she wept and wept as if she could never be comforted. And in the midst of her weeping she heard a voice saying to her,

"What ails thee, king's daughter? Thy tears would melt a heart of stone."

And when she looked to see where the voice came from, there was nothing but a frog stretching his thick ugly head out of the water.

"Oh, is it you, old waddler?" said she. "I weep because my golden ball has fallen into the well."

"Never mind, do not weep," answered the frog. "I can help you. But what will you give me if I fetch up your ball again?"

"Whatever you like, dear frog," said she. "Any of my clothes, my pearls and jewels, or even the golden crown that I wear."

"Thy clothes, thy pearls and jewels, and thy golden crown are not for me," answered the frog. "But if thou wouldst love me, and have me for thy companion and playfellow, and let me sit by thee at table, and eat from thy plate, and drink from thy cup, and sleep in thy little bed—if thou wouldst promise all this, then would I dive below the water and fetch thee thy golden ball again."

"Oh yes," she answered. "I will promise it all, whatever you want, if you will only get me my ball again."

But she thought to herself, "What nonsense he talks! As if he could do anything but sit in the water and croak with the other frogs, or could possibly be anyone's companion."

But the frog, as soon as he heard her promise, drew his head under the water and sank down out of sight, but after a while he came to the surface again with the ball in his mouth, and he threw it on the grass.

The King's daughter was overjoyed to see her pretty plaything again, and she caught it up and ran off with it.

"Stop, stop!" cried the frog. "Take me up too! I cannot run as fast as you!"

But it was of no use, for croak, croak after her as he might, she would not listen to him, but made haste home, and very soon forgot all about the poor frog, who had to betake himself to his well again.

The next day, when the King's daughter was sitting at the table with the King and all the court, and eating from her golden plate, there came something pitter patter up the marble stairs, and then there came a knocking at the door, and a voice crying, "King's youngest daughter, let me in!"

And she got up and ran to see who it could be, but when she opened the door, there was the frog sitting outside. Then she shut the door hastily and went back to her seat, feeling very uneasy. The King noticed how quickly her heart was beating, and said, "My child, what are you afraid of? Is there a giant standing at the door ready to carry you away?"

"Oh no," answered she, "no giant, but a horrid frog."

"And what does the frog want?" asked the King.

"O dear father," answered she, "when I was sitting by the well yesterday, and playing with my golden ball, it fell into the water, and while I was crying for the loss of it, the frog came and got it again for me on condition I would let him be my companion, but I never thought that he could leave the water and come after me; and now there he is outside the door, and he wants to come in to me."

And then they all heard him knocking the second time and crying,

> "King's youngest daughter,
> Open to me!
> By the well water
> What promised you me?
> King's youngest daughter
> Now open to me!"

"That which thou hast promised must thou perform," said the King. "So go now and let him in."

So she went and opened the door, and the frog hopped in, following at her heels, till she reached her chair. Then he stopped and cried, "Lift me up to sit by you."

But she delayed doing so until the King ordered her. When once the frog was on the chair, he wanted to get on the table, and there he sat and said, "Now push your golden plate a little nearer, so that we may eat together."

And so she did, but everybody might see how unwilling she was, and the frog feasted heartily, but every morsel seemed to stick in her throat.

"I have had enough now," said the frog at last, "and as I am tired, you must carry me to your room, and make ready your silken bed, and we will lie down and go to sleep."

Then the King's daughter began to weep, and was afraid of the cold frog, that nothing would satisfy him but he must sleep in her pretty clean bed. Now the King grew angry with her, saying, "That which thou hast promised in thy time of necessity, must thou now perform."

So she picked up the frog with her finger and thumb, carried him upstairs and put him in a corner, and when she had lain down to sleep, he came creeping up, saying, "I am tired and want sleep as much as you. Take me up, so I can rest."

He looked so sad, she suddenly felt ashamed. "Father is right," she thought. "I must keep my promises." She lifted him and gently dropped him onto a pillow.

But as he fell, he ceased to be a frog, and became all at once a prince with beautiful kind eyes. And it came to pass that, with her father's consent, they became bride and bridegroom. And he told her how a wicked witch had bound him by her spells, and how no one but she alone could have released him, and that they two would go together to his father's kingdom. And there came to the door a carriage drawn by eight white horses, with white plumes on their heads, and with golden harness, and behind the carriage was standing faithful Henry, the servant of the young prince. Now, faithful Henry had suffered such care and pain when his master was turned into a frog, that he had been obliged to wear three iron bands over his heart, to keep it from breaking with trouble and anxiety. When the carriage started to take the prince to his kingdom, and faithful Henry had helped them both in, he got up behind, and was full of joy at his master's deliverance. And when they had gone a part of the way, the prince heard a sound at the back of the carriage, as if something had broken, and he turned around and cried,

"Henry, the wheel must be breaking!" But Henry answered:

> "The wheel does not break,
> 'Tis the band round my heart
> That, to lessen its ache,
> When I grieved for your sake,
> I bound round my heart."

Again, and yet once again there was the same sound, and the prince thought it must be the wheel breaking, but it was the breaking of the other bands from faithful Henry's heart, because it was now so relieved and happy.

The Pied Piper of Hamelin

Adapted from Joseph Jacobs

This famous German legend of a broken bargain seems to be based at least in part on an actual occurrence. Old writings on the walls of some of Hamelin's houses indicate that one day in July of 1284, a piper did indeed lead some 130 children out of town, and that they were lost somehow in nearby Koppen Hill. Some believe that outlaws kidnapped the children, while others speculate that the mysterious piper was actually recruiting youths to emigrate to eastern Europe.

A very long time ago the sleepy little town of Hamelin was invaded by rats, the likes of which had never been seen before. The awful creatures ran through the streets and swarmed over the houses. They fought the dogs, and chased the cats, and nibbled at babies in their cradles, and hid inside pockets, and made nests out of hats. It got so bad, you couldn't set your foot down anywhere without hearing a squeak from beneath your heel.

Well, needless to say, the mayor and the town council were at their wits' end. As they were sitting one day in the town hall racking their poor brains, and bewailing their hard fate, who should run in but the chief of police.

"Please, your honor," he said, "there is a very strange fellow who demands to see you. He just came to town, and I don't know quite what to make of him."

"Show him in," said the mayor, and in he stepped. He was an odd-looking stranger, without a doubt. He was tall and gawky, dried and bronzed, with a crooked nose, a long rat-tail mustache, and keen piercing eyes. And if you looked hard enough, you could find every single color of the rainbow in his jacket and breeches.

"I'm called the Pied Piper," he began. "And what might you be willing to pay me, if I rid Hamelin of every last rat?"

Well, as much as the town government feared the rats, it feared even more spending the good taxpayers' money (for those were very different times, you know), so they haggled and haggled. But the

Pied Piper was not a man to stand for any nonsense, and the upshot was that fifty dollars were promised (which was a lot of money in those days, even to elected officials) as soon as not a rat was left to squeak or scurry in Hamelin.

Out of the hall stepped the Pied Piper, and as he stepped he laid his pipe to his lips, and a shrill, keen tune sounded through every street and house. And as each note pierced the air, you would have seen a strange sight if you'd been in Hamelin that day. For out of every hole the rats came tumbling. There were none too old and none too young, none too big and none too little, to crowd at the Pied Piper's heels. With eager feet and upturned noses they pattered after him as he paced the streets. Nor was the Pied Piper unmindful of the little toddling ones, for every fifty yards he'd stop and give an extra flourish on his pipe just to give them time to keep up with the older and stronger of the band.

Up Silver Street he went, and down Gold Street, and the end of Gold Street was the river. As he paced along, slowly and gravely, the townspeople flocked to their doors and windows, and many a blessing they called down upon his head.

When he reached the river's edge, he stepped into a boat, and as he shoved off into the water, piping shrilly all the time, every single rat followed him, splashing, paddling, and wagging their tails with delight. On and on he played until he was way downstream, where the current gets quick, and every last rat was swept away, never to be seen again.

Then the Pied Piper landed his boat and walked back upstream to Hamelin. You may fancy the townspeople had been throwing up their caps and hurrahing and stopping up rat holes and setting the church bells ringing. But when the Pied Piper stepped ashore and not so much as a single squeak was to be heard, the mayor and the council, and the townspeople generally, began to hah and to hum and to shake their heads.

For the town chest had been sadly emptied of late (which goes to show that governments then weren't really much different than they are today, after all) and where was the fifty dollars to come from? And besides, the Pied Piper's job had been so easy. Just getting into a boat and playing a pipe! Why, the mayor himself could have done that if only he'd thought of it.

So the mayor hahed and hummed and at last said, "Come, my good man, you see what poor folk we are. How can we manage to pay you fifty dollars? Will you not take twenty? When all is said and done, it will be good pay for the trouble you've taken."

"Fifty dollars is what I bargained for," said the Pied Piper shortly, "and if I were you, I'd live up to my word. For I can pipe many kinds of tunes, as folks sometimes find to their cost."

"Would you threaten us, you strolling vagabond?" shrieked the mayor, and at the same time he winked to the council. "The rats are dead and drowned, so you may do your worst, good man." And with that he turned upon his heel.

"'Very well," said the Pied Piper, and he smiled a quiet smile. "It's not the first time I've met a broken promise, and it won't be the last, I'm sure."

He laid his pipe to his lips afresh, but now there came forth no shrill notes, as it were, of scraping and gnawing, and squeaking and scurrying. This time the tune was joyous and resonant, full of happy laughter and merry play. And as he paced down the streets the elders mocked, but from schoolroom and playroom, from nursery and backyard, the children came running with eager glee at the Pied Piper's call. Dancing, laughing, and joining hands, the bright throng moved up Gold Street and down Silver Street, and beyond Silver Street lay the cool green forest full of old oaks and wide-spreading beeches. Beyond the forest lay the rising hills, and when the merry parade reached the tallest of them all, a door in the earth opened, and the Pied Piper went inside, still playing his tune. All the children followed, and then the door closed.

Only one little boy, who was lame and could not march as fast as the other children, did not make it to the hillside before the door shut fast. When the mayor and the town council came running, they found him wailing.

"What has happened?" they cried.

"I wanted to go with the other children," the child sobbed. "When the man played his pipe, it told of a beautiful land where the sun always shines and the birds always sing and the children are never ill or lame. I ran as fast as I could, but I couldn't keep up, and now they're all gone."

And they were, indeed. The townspeople searched high and low, and the mayor sent his deputies north, south, east, and west to find the Pied Piper. "Tell him I will give him all the gold in the town if he will only bring back the children," the mayor said, but of course who would believe him by then?

The mothers and fathers of Hamelin waited and waited, but their little ones never came back. And it's said that to this day, the people of Hamelin are careful to keep their promises, especially to strange pipers.

The Emperor's New Clothes

Hans Christian Andersen

In this classic, we see that it is often harder to be honest than it is to be silent, and that trusting ourselves is the best road to the truth. We see the pestilence of false flattery, and we find that honesty, unlike new clothes, never goes out of fashion.

Many years ago there was an emperor who was so fond of new clothes that he spent all his money on them. He did not give himself any concern about his army; he cared nothing about the theater or for driving about in the woods, except for the sake of showing himself off in new clothes. He had a costume for every hour in the day, and just as they say of a king or emperor, "He is in his council chamber," they said of him, "The emperor is in his dressing room."

Life was merry and gay in the town where the emperor lived, and numbers of strangers came to it every day. Among them there came one day two rascals, who gave themselves out as weavers and said that they knew how to weave the most exquisite stuff imaginable. Not only were the colors and patterns uncommonly beautiful, but the clothes that were made of the stuff had the peculiar property of becoming invisible to every person who was unfit for the office he held or who was exceptionally stupid.

"Those must be valuable clothes," thought the emperor. "By wearing them I should be able to discover which of the men in my empire are not fit for their posts. I should distinguish wise men from fools. Yes, I must order some of the stuff to be woven for me directly." And he paid the swindlers a handsome sum of money in advance, as they required.

As for them, they put up two looms and pretended to be weaving, though there was nothing whatever on their shuttles. They called for a quantity of the finest silks and of the purest gold thread, all of which went into their own bags, while they worked at their empty looms till late into the night.

"I should like to know how those weavers are getting on with the stuff," thought the emperor. But he felt a little queer when he reflected that those who were stupid or unfit for their office would not be able to see the material. He believed, indeed, that he had nothing to fear for himself, but still he thought it better to send someone else first, to see how the work was coming on. All the people in the town had heard of the peculiar property of the stuff, and everyone was curious to see how stupid his neighbor might be.

"I will send my faithful old prime minister to the weavers," thought the emperor. "He will be best capable of judging this stuff, for he is a man of sense and nobody is more fit for his office than he."

So the worthy old minister went into the room where the two swindlers sat working the empty looms. "Heaven save us!" thought the old man, opening his eyes wide. "Why, I can't see anything at all!" But he took care not to say so aloud.

Both the rogues begged him to step a little nearer and asked him if he did not think the patterns very pretty and the coloring fine. They pointed to the empty loom as they did so, and the poor old minister kept staring as hard as he could—without being able to see anything on it, for of course there was nothing there to see.

"Heaven save us!" thought the old man. "Is it possible that I am a fool! I have never thought it, and nobody must know it. Is it true that I am not fit for my office? It will never do for me to say that I cannot see the stuff."

"Well, sir, do you say nothing about the cloth?" asked the one who was pretending to go on with his work.

"Oh, it is most elegant, most beautiful!" said the dazed old man, as he peered again through his spectacles. "What a fine pattern, and what fine colors! I will certainly tell the emperor how pleased I am with the stuff."

"We are glad of that," said both the weavers; and then they named the colors and pointed out the special features of the pattern. To all of this the minister paid great attention, so that he might be able to repeat it to the emperor when he went back to him.

And now the cheats called for more money, more silk, and more gold thread, to be able to proceed with the weaving, but they put it all into their own pockets, and not a thread went into the stuff, though they went on as before, weaving at the empty looms.

After a little time the emperor sent another honest statesman to see how the weaving was progressing, and if the stuff would soon be ready. The same thing happened with him as with the minister. He gazed and gazed, but as there was nothing but empty looms, he could see nothing else.

"Is not this an exquisite piece of stuff?" asked the weavers, pointing to one of the looms and explaining the beautiful pattern and the colors which were not there to be seen.

"I am not stupid, I know I am not!" thought the man, "so it must be that I am not fit for my good office. It is very strange, but I must not let it be noticed." So he praised the cloth he did not see and assured the weavers of his delight in the lovely colors and the exquisite pattern. "It is perfectly charming," he reported to the emperor.

Everybody in the town was talking of the splendid cloth. The emperor thought he should like to see it himself while it was still on the loom. With a company of carefully selected men, among whom were the two worthy officials who had been there before, he went to visit the crafty impostors, who were working as hard as ever at the empty looms.

"Is it not magnificent?" said both the honest statesmen. "See, Your Majesty, what splendid colors, and what a pattern!" And they pointed to the looms, for they believed that others, no doubt, could see what they did not.

"What!" thought the emperor. "I see nothing at all. This is terrible! Am I a fool? Am I not fit to be emperor? Why nothing more dreadful could happen to me!"

"Oh, it is very pretty! It has my highest approval," the emperor said aloud. He nodded with satisfaction as he gazed at the empty looms, for he would not betray that he could see nothing.

His whole court gazed and gazed, each seeing no more than the others, but, like the emperor, they all exclaimed, "Oh, it is beautiful!" They even suggested to the emperor that he wear the splendid new clothes for the first time on the occasion of a great procession which was soon to take place.

"Splendid! Gorgeous! Magnificent!" went from mouth to mouth. All were equally delighted with the weavers' workmanship. The emperor gave each of the impostors an order of knighthood to be worn in their buttonholes, and the title Gentleman Weaver of the Imperial Court.

Before the day on which the procession was to take place, the weavers sat up the whole night, burning sixteen candles, so that people might see how anxious they were to get the emperor's new clothes ready. They pretended to take the stuff from the loom, they cut it out in the air with huge scissors, and they stitched away with needles that had no thread in them. At last they said, "Now the clothes are finished."

The emperor came to them himself with his grandest courtiers, and each of the rogues lifted his arm as if he held something, saying, "See! here are the trousers! Here is the coat! Here is the cloak," and so on. "It is as light as a spider's web. One would almost feel as if one had nothing on, but that is the beauty of it!"

"Yes," said all the courtiers, but they saw nothing, for there was nothing to see.

"Will Your Majesty be graciously pleased to take off your clothes so that we may put on the new clothes here, before the great mirror?"

The emperor took off his clothes, and the rogues pretended to put on first one garment and then another of the new ones they had pretended to make. They pretended to fasten something round his waist and to tie on something. This they said was the train, and the emperor turned around and around before the mirror.

"How well his Majesty looks in the new clothes! How becoming they are!" cried all the courtiers in turn. "That is a splendid costume!"

"The canopy that is to be carried over Your Majesty in the procession is waiting outside," said the master of ceremonies.

"Well, I am ready," replied the emperor. "Don't the clothes look well?" and he turned around and around again before the mirror, to appear as if he were admiring his new costume.

The chamberlains, who were to carry the train, stooped and put their hands near the floor as if they were lifting it. Then they pretended to be holding something in the air. They would not let it be noticed that they could see and feel nothing.

So the emperor went along in the procession, under the splendid canopy, and everyone in the streets said: "How beautiful the emperor's new clothes are! What a splendid train! And how well they fit!"

No one wanted to let it appear that he could see nothing, for that would prove him not fit for his post. None of the emperor's clothes had been so great a success before.

"But he has nothing on!" said a little child.

"Just listen to the innocent," said its father. And one person whispered to another what the child had said. "He has nothing on. A child says he has nothing on!"

"But he has nothing on," cried all the people. The emperor was startled by this, for he had a suspicion that they were right. But he thought, "I must face this out to the end and go on with the proces-

sion." So he held himself more stiffly than ever, and the chamberlains held up the train that was not there at all.

The Boy Who Went to the Sky

Retold by Carolyn Sherwin Bailey

This Cherokee Indian tale about fair play takes place in the Blue
Ridge country of what is now western North Carolina. Playing
by the rules is a big part of "how you play the game," both on
and off the field.

There was once upon a time a boy who was a fine ball player of
his village of the Cherokee nation. He could catch well, run swiftly
to the goal, and almost never did he lose a game for his side. And
one season it was decided that his village should play a ball game
with the village of the Cherokees on the other side of the Ridge. So
the two teams met not far from Pilot Knob, and the game began.

This boy was very anxious, just as a boy of today would be, to
help win the game for his village, and for a while the game seemed
to be going against him. Time and time again the players from the
Indian village on the other side of the Ridge ran and made goal. This
made the boy discouraged, and it also made him forget his honor.

His village must make the goal, he thought, so he did a thing
which was forbidden in the rules of ball playing. He picked up the
ball in his hand and tried to throw it to the goal. The Indians kicked
the ball. It was not considered fair to touch it with their hands.

He thought that no one had seen him, and he was successful.
The ball went straight to goal, but it did not stop there. The boys
and girls and the braves who sat in a wide circle on the grassy field
to watch the game saw a strange thing. Bounding away from the
goal, the ball went up into the air. Following the ball went the boy
who had forgotten the rules of the game. His feet left the ball field.
He seemed to be leaping up toward the sky to try and bring back the
ball, but neither he nor the ball stopped. Up, up, higher and farther
through the blue air they went until the ball was out of sight, and
then the boy could no longer be seen.

It was magic which had happened, and the people rubbed their eyes with their wonder, and then they silently went home to their villages. It seemed to them to have been a lesson, for the boy's wrong play had been seen, not only by the Great Spirit of the Cherokee People, but by some of the ball players. They knew why the boy had been taken away from his friends.

That was in the ancient days before the Moon had appeared in the sky, but that night a strange thing happened. Sitting late beside their campfires the braves of all the villages of the Cherokee country saw a huge, round ball of silver rise in the sky and then hang there, lighting the forest trees with its wonderful, pale light. And on the surface of this ball of silver could be seen the face of the boy who had not played fair in the ball game.

It was the ball which had been taken from the ball field up to the sky, and fastened there. In its light could be seen the boy who had been taken from the earth with it. The Moon had come to the heavens, a ball taken from the game field.

Sometimes it was seen that the Moon was smaller. It was sometimes eclipsed. Everybody was amazed at an eclipse of the Moon, for the night would suddenly darken and the tribes would gather and fire guns and beat a drum. This eclipse came about because of a great Frog, who tried to swallow the Moon, and the drum frightened him away.

But the oddest thing about the Moon was its way of waxing and waning. From night to night it would be so large that the Indians could see the face of the Boy-in-the-Moon, and then it would be nothing but a silver thread in the sky above the pine trees.

This happened, the Boy-in-the-Moon told them, to remind ball players never to cheat. When the Moon looked small and pale it was because someone had handled a ball unfairly. So it came about in the Cherokee country that they played ball after that only in the full of the moon.

Truth and Falsehood

As this folktale from Greece points out, the virtuous soul
not only loves truth for its own sake, it loathes the actions of
falsehood. Deceit is far more painful for that soul than bearing
the hardships that sometimes accompany honesty.

Once upon a time Truth and Falsehood met each other on the
road.

"Good afternoon," said Truth.

"Good afternoon," returned Falsehood. "And how are you
doing these days?"

"Not very well at all, I'm afraid," sighed Truth. "The times are
tough for a fellow like me, you know."

"Yes, I can see that," said Falsehood, glancing up and down at
Truth's ragged clothes. "You look like you haven't had a bite to eat
in quite some time."

"To be honest, I haven't," admitted Truth. "No one seems to
want to employ me nowadays. Wherever I go, most people ignore
me or mock me. It's getting discouraging, I can tell you. I'm beginning to ask myself why I put up with it."

"And why the devil do you? Come with me, and I'll show you
how to get along. There's no reason in the world why you can't
stuff yourself with as much as you want to eat, like me, and dress in
the finest clothes, like me. But you must promise not to say a word
against me while we're together."

So Truth promised and agreed to go along with Falsehood for
a while, not because he liked his company so much, but because he
was so hungry he thought he'd faint soon if he didn't get something
into his stomach. They walked down the road until they came to a
city, and Falsehood at once led the way to the very best table at the
very best restaurant.

"Waiter, bring us your choicest meats, your sweetest sweets,
your finest wine!" he called, and they ate and drank all afternoon.
At last, when they could hold no more, Falsehood began banging
his fist on the table and calling for the manager, who came running
at once.

"What the devil kind of place is this?" Falsehood snapped. "I
gave that waiter a gold piece nearly an hour ago, and he still hasn't
brought our change."

The manager summoned the waiter, who said he'd never even seen a penny out of the gentleman.

"What?" Falsehood shouted, so that everyone in the place turned and looked. "I can't believe this place! Innocent, law-abiding citizens come in to eat, and you rob them of their hard-earned money! You're a pack of thieves and liars! You may have fooled me once, but you'll never see me again! Here!" He threw a gold piece at the manager. "Now this time bring me my change!"

But the manager, fearing his restaurant's reputation would suffer, refused to take the gold piece, and instead brought Falsehood change for the first gold piece he claimed to have spent. Then he took the waiter aside and called him a scoundrel, and said he had a mind to fire him. And as much as the waiter protested that he'd never collected a cent from the man, the manager refused to believe him.

"Oh Truth, where have you hidden yourself?" the waiter sighed. "Have you now deserted even us hard-working souls?"

"No, I'm here," Truth groaned to himself, "but my judgment gave way to my hunger, and now I can't speak up without breaking my promise to Falsehood."

As soon as they were on the street, Falsehood gave a hearty laugh and slapped Truth on the back. "You see how the world works?" he cried. "I managed it all quite well, don't you think?"

But Truth slipped from his side.

"I'd rather starve than live as you do," he said.

And so Truth and Falsehood went their separate ways, and never traveled together again.

Truth, Falsehood, Fire, and Water

This tale about the eternal struggle between truth and falsehood is told in Ethiopia and other eastern African nations.

Long ago Truth, Falsehood, Fire, and Water were journeying together and came upon a herd of cattle. They talked it over and decided it would be fairest to divide the herd into four parts, so each could take home an equal share.

But Falsehood was greedy and schemed to get more for himself.
"Listen to my warning," he whispered, pulling Water to one
side. "Fire plans to burn all the grass and trees along your banks and
drive your cattle away across the plains so he can have them for
himself. If I were you, I'd extinguish him now, and then we can
have his share of the cattle for ourselves."

Water was foolish enough to listen to Falsehood, and he dashed
himself upon Fire and put him out.

Next Falsehood crept toward Truth.

"Look what Water has done," he whispered. "He has murdered
Fire and taken his cattle. We should not consort with the likes of
him. We should take all the cattle and go to the mountains."

Truth believed Falsehood and agreed to his plan. Together they
drove the cattle into the mountains.

"Wait for me!" Water called, and he hurried after them, but of
course he could not run uphill. So he was left all alone in the valley
below.

When they reached the top of the highest mountain, Falsehood
turned to Truth and laughed.

"I've tricked you, stupid fool," he shrieked. "Now you must
give me all the cattle and be my servant, or I'll destroy you."

"Yes, you have tricked me," Truth admitted, "but I will never
be your servant."

And so they fought, and when they clashed the thunder rolled
back and forth across the mountaintops. Again and again they threw
themselves together, but neither could destroy the other.

Finally they decided to call upon the Wind to declare a winner
of the contest. So Wind came rushing up the mountain slopes, and
he listened to what they had to say.

"It is not for me to declare a winner in this fight," he told them.
"Truth and Falsehood are destined to struggle. Sometimes Truth
will win, but other times Falsehood will prevail, and then Truth
must rise up and fight again. Until the end of the world, Truth must
battle Falsehood, and must never rest or let down his guard, or he
will be finished once and for all."

And so Truth and Falsehood are fighting to this day.

Lady Clare

Alfred Tennyson

Tennyson (1809–1892) offers us a very old, very valuable lesson
that modern ministers and counselors continue to confirm: honesty is one of the most crucial elements of a successful relationship between a man and a woman. Love loves honesty.

It was the time when lilies blow
    And clouds are highest up in air;
Lord Ronald brought a lily-white doe
    To give his cousin, Lady Clare.

I trow they did not part in scorn:
    Lovers long-betroth'd were they:
They too will wed the morrow morn:
    God's blessing on the day!

"He does not love me for my birth,
    Nor for my lands so broad and fair;
He loves me for my own true worth,
    And that is well," said Lady Clare.

In there came old Alice the nurse;
    Said: "Who was this that went from thee?"
"It was my cousin," said Lady Clare;
    "Tomorrow he weds with me."

"O God be thank'd!" said Alice the nurse,
    "That all comes round so just and fair:
Lord Ronald is heir of all your lands,
    And you are not the Lady Clare."

"Are ye out of your mind, my nurse, my nurse,"
    Said Lady Clare, "that ye speak so wild?"
"As God's above," said Alice the nurse,
    "I speak the truth: you are my child.

"The old Earl's daughter died at my breast;
    I speak the truth, as I live by bread!
I buried her like my own sweet child,
    And put my child in her stead."

"Falsely, falsely have ye done,
    O mother," she said, "if this be true,
To keep the best man under the sun
    So many years from his due."

"Nay now, my child," said Alice the nurse,
    "But keep the secret for your life,
And all you have will be Lord Ronald's
    When you are a man and wife."

"If I'm a beggar born," she said,
    "I will speak out, for I dare not lie.
Pull off, pull off the brooch of gold,
    And fling the diamond necklace by."

"Nay now, my child," said Alice the nurse,
    "But keep the secret all ye can."
She said: "Not so: but I will know
    If there be any faith in man."

"Nay now, what faith?" said Alice the nurse;
    "The man will cleave unto his right."
"And he shall have it," the lady replied,
    "Tho' I should die tonight."

"Yet give one kiss to your mother dear!
    Alas! my child, I sinn'd for thee."
"O mother, mother, mother," she said,
    "So strange it seems to me.

"Yet here's a kiss for my mother dear,
    My mother dear, if this be so,
And lay your hand upon my head,
    And bless me, mother, ere I go."

She clad herself in a russet gown,
   She was no longer Lady Clare:
She went by dale, and she went by down,
   With a single rose in her hair.

The lily-white doe Lord Ronald had brought
   Leapt up from where she lay,
Dropt her head in the maiden's hand,
   And follow'd her all the way.

Down stept Lord Ronald from his tower:
   "O Lady Clare, you shame your worth!
Why come you drest like a village maid.
   That are the flower of the earth?"

"If I come drest like a village maid,
   I am but as my fortunes are:
I am a beggar born," she said,
   "And not the Lady Clare."

"Play me no tricks," said Lord Ronald,
   "For I am yours in word and in deed.
Play me no tricks," said Lord Ronald,
   "Your riddle is hard to read."

O and proudly stood she up!
   Her heart within her did not fail:
She look'd into Lord Ronald's eyes,
   And told him all her nurse's tale.

He laugh'd a laugh of merry scorn:
   He turn'd and kiss'd her where she stood.
"If you are not the heiress born,
   And I," said he, "the next in blood—

"If you are not the heiress born,
   And I," said he, "the lawful heir,
We two will wed tomorrow morn,
   And you shall still be Lady Clare."

Truth

Ben Jonson

Ben Jonson (1572–1637) reminds us that faith and love depend
on truth.

> Truth is the trial of itself,
>   And needs no other touch;
> And purer than the purest gold,
>   Refine it ne'er so much.
>
> It is the life and light of love,
>   The sun that ever shineth,
> And spirit of that special grace,
>   That faith and love defineth.
>
> It is the warrant of the word,
>   That yields a scent so sweet,
> As gives a power to faith to tread
>   All falsehood under feet.

The Woman Caught in Adultery

This story from the Gospel according to John in the New Testament, which depicts Jesus' compassion for the sinner, is a powerful reminder that the hypocrisy of the crowd is one of the most
common varieties of dishonesty.

Jesus went unto the mount of Olives. And early in the morning
he came again into the temple, and all the people came unto him,
and he sat down, and taught them.

And the Scribes and Pharisees brought unto him a woman taken
in adultery. And when they had set her in the midst, they say unto
him, Master, this woman was taken in adultery, in the very act.

Now Moses in the law commanded us that such should be stoned. But what sayest thou?

This they said, tempting him, that they might have to accuse him. But Jesus stooped down, and with *his* finger wrote on the ground, *as though he heard them not.*

So when they continued asking him, he lifted up himself, and said unto them: he that is without sin among you, let him first cast a stone at her.

And again he stooped down, and wrote on the ground.

And they which heard *it,* being convicted by *their own* conscience, went out one by one, beginning at the eldest, *even* unto the last. And Jesus was left alone, and the woman standing in the midst.

When Jesus had lifted up himself and saw none but the woman, he said unto her, Woman, where are those thine accusers? Hath no man condemned thee?

She said, No man, Lord. And Jesus said unto her, Neither do I condemn thee: go, and sin no more.

The Question

Seek honesty in yourself before you seek it in your neighbors.

Were the whole world good as you—not an atom better—
   Were it just as pure and true,
   Just as pure and true as you;
   Just as strong in faith and works;
   Just as free from crafty quirks;
   All extortion, all deceit;
   Schemes its neighbors to defeat;
   Schemes its neighbors to defraud;
   Schemes some culprit to applaud—
Would this world be better?

If the whole world followed you—followed to the letter—
  Would it be a nobler world,
  All deceit and falsehood hurled
  From it altogether;
  Malice, selfishness, and lust,
  Banished from beneath the crust,
  Covering human hearts from view—
  Tell me, if it followed you,
Would the world be better?

The Good Bishop

Adapted from Victor Hugo

Truth can be so complicated a thing as to call for certain noble
dishonesties on some rare occasions. In this scene adapted from
Victor Hugo's *Les Misérables,* we witness a lie told not merely for
the sake of compassion, but in order to secure virtue in another
man's soul. As James Russell Lowell put it, "As one lamp lights
another nor grows less, So nobleness enkindleth nobleness."

Jean Valjean was a wood-chopper's son, who, while very
young, was left an orphan. His older sister brought him up, but
when he was seventeen years of age, his sister's husband died, and
upon Jean came the labor of supporting her seven little children.
Although a man of great strength, he found it very difficult to provide food for them at the poor trade he followed.

One winter day he was without work, and the children were
crying for bread. They were nearly starved. And, when he could
withstand their entreaties no longer, he went out in the night, and,
breaking a baker's window with his fist, carried home a loaf of bread
for the famished children. The next morning he was arrested for
stealing, his bleeding hand convicting him.

For this crime he was sent to the galleys with an iron collar
riveted around his neck, with a chain attached, which bound him to
his galley seat. Here he remained four years, then he tried to escape,
but was caught, and three years were added to his sentence. Then he

made a second attempt, and also failed, the result of which was that he remained nineteen years as a galley slave for stealing a single loaf of bread.

When Jean left the prison, his heart was hardened. He felt like a wolf. His wrongs had embittered him, and he was more like an animal than a man. He came with every man's hand raised against him to the town where the good bishop lived.

At the inn they would not receive him because they knew him to be an ex-convict and a dangerous man. Wherever he went, the knowledge of him went before, and everyone drove him away. They would not even allow him to sleep in a dog kennel or give him the food they had saved for the dog. Everywhere he went they cried: "Be off! Go away, or you will get a charge of shot." Finally, he wandered to the house of the good bishop, and a good man he was.

For his duties as a bishop, he received from the state 3,000 francs a year; but he gave away to the poor 2,800 francs of it. He was a simple, loving man, with a great heart, who thought nothing of himself, but loved everybody. And everybody loved him.

Jean, when he entered the bishop's house, was a most forbidding and dangerous character. He shouted in a harsh loud voice: "Look here, I am a galley slave. Here is my yellow passport. It says: 'Five years for robbery and fourteen years for trying to escape. The man is very dangerous.' Now that you know who I am, will you give me a little food, and let me sleep in the stable?"

The good bishop said: "Sit down and warm yourself. You will take supper with me, and after that sleep here."

Jean could hardly believe his senses. He was dumb with joy. He told the bishop that he had money, and would pay for his supper and lodging.

But the priest said: "You are welcome. This is not my house, but the house of Christ. Your name was known to me before you showed me your passport. You are my brother."

After supper the bishop took one of the silver candlesticks that he had received as a Christmas present, and, giving Jean the other, led him to his room, where a good bed was provided. In the middle of the night Jean awoke with a hardened heart. He felt that the time had come to get revenge for all his wrongs. He remembered the silver knives and forks that had been used for supper, and made up his mind to steal them, and go away in the night. So he took what he could find, sprang into the garden, and disappeared.

When the bishop awoke, and saw his silver gone, he said: "I have been thinking for a long time that I ought not to keep the silver. I should have given it to the poor, and certainly this man was poor."

At breakfast time five soldiers brought Jean back to the bishop's house. When they entered, the bishop, looking at him, said: "Oh, you are back again! I am glad to see you. I gave you the candlesticks, too, which are silver also, and will bring forty francs. Why did you not take them?"

Jean was stunned indeed by these words. So were the soldiers. "This man told us the truth, did he?" they cried. "We thought he had stolen the silver and was running away. So we quickly arrested him."

But the good bishop only said: "It was a mistake to have him brought back. Let him go. The silver is his. I gave it to him."

So the officers went away.

"Is it true," Jean whispered to the bishop, "that I am free? I may go?"

"Yes," he replied, "but before you go take your candlesticks."

Jean trembled in every limb, and took the candlesticks like one in a dream.

"Now," said the bishop, "depart in peace, but do not go through the garden, for the front door is always open to you day and night."

Jean looked as though he would faint.

Then the bishop took his hand, and said: "Never forget you have promised me you would use the money to become an honest man."

He did not remember having promised anything, but stood silent while the bishop continued solemnly:

"Jean Valjean, my brother, you no longer belong to evil, but to good. I have bought your soul for you. I withdrew it from black thoughts and the spirit of hate, and gave it to God."

Insincere Honesty

Retold by Warren Horton Stuart

We should love truth for its own sake, but not for *our* own sake.
Glorifying our own devotion to an abstract truth is something
less than a noble pursuit, as this Chinese folktale illustrates.

In the kingdom of Ts'u was a young man named Honest. His
father stole a sheep, so he went and informed the magistrate, who
had the guilty one arrested, and was on the point of punishing him.
Young Honest then asked to be allowed to bear the penalty in his
father's stead. Just as it was about to be inflicted, he said to the
officer: "When my father stole a sheep and I reported the theft, was
I not honest? When my father was about to be punished, and I
offered to bear the penalty, was I not as a son honoring my father?
If you punish even the honest and the filial, who is there in all the
kingdom that would not be punished?" When the magistrate heard
this, he released the young man. When Confucius heard the story,
he said: "Strange! That a fellow could sell his father's good name to
make a reputation for his own honesty. If that be honesty, 'twere
better to be dishonest."

The Injustice of Mere Suspicion

Retold by Warren Horton Stuart

This Chinese folktale helps us appreciate the policy of "innocent
until proven guilty." We must guard against projecting our suspicions onto others' characters and actions.

A certain man lost an axe. He at once suspected the son of his
neighbor had stolen it. When he saw the boy walking by, the boy
looked like a fellow who had stolen an axe; when he listened to the

boy's words, they sounded like those of a boy who had stolen an axe. All his actions and manners were those of a boy who had stolen an axe. Later, when digging a ditch, the man found the lost axe. The next day he saw again his neighbor's son, but in all the boy's manners and actions, there was nothing like a boy who had stolen an axe. The boy had not changed, but the man himself had changed! And the only reason for this change lay in his suspicion.

The Piece of String

Guy de Maupassant

This story of slander, set among the French peasantry, reminds us of the devastating consequences that one person's dishonesty can have on another's life.

Along all the roads around Goderville peasants and their wives were coming in toward the town, for it was market day.

There was a crowd in Goderville marketplace, a confusion of men and beasts. Horns of oxen, long-napped tall hats of the richer peasants, and the women's headdresses rose above the surface of the throng. Voices, bawling, sharp, and squeaky, were mingled in barbarous never-ending clamor, dominated at times by the mighty guffaw of some broad-chested countryman having his joke, or by the long-drawn lowing of a cow tied up to the wall of a house.

It all smelled of stables, milk and manure, of hay and sweat, gave off, in fact, that terribly sour savor, human, yet bestial, characteristic of workers in the fields.

Master Hauchecorne, of Breauté, coming in to Goderville, was making his way toward the marketplace, when he perceived on the ground a short piece of string. Master Hauchecorne, thrifty like every true Norman, thought that anything was worth picking up that could be put to any use; so, stooping painfully, for he suffered from rheumatism, he picked up the bit of thin cord, and was carefully rolling it up when he observed Master Malandain, the saddler, standing in his doorway, looking at him. They had once had a difference about a halter, and owed each other a grudge, for both were by nature inclined to bear malice. Master Hauchecorne was seized with a sort of shame at being thus seen by his enemy, grubbing in the mud for a bit of string. He abruptly hid his spoil under his blouse, then put it in his trouser pocket, and pretended to be still looking on the ground for something he could not find. Finally he went off toward the market, with his head poked forward, bent nearly double by his rheumatism.

He was swallowed up at once in the slow-moving, noisy crowd, disputing over its interminable bargainings. Peasants were punching the cows, moving hither and thither, in perpetual fear of being taken in, and not daring to make up their minds; scrutinizing the seller's eye, to try and discover the deceit in the man, and the blemish in his beast.

The women, placing their great baskets at their feet, had taken out their fowls, which lay on the ground with legs tied together, eyes wild with fright, and crests all scarlet.

They listened to the offers made, and held out for their prices with wooden, impassive faces; then, suddenly deciding to take the bid, would scream after the customer as he slowly walked away:

"Done with you, Master Anthime. You shall have it."

Then, little by little, the marketplace emptied, and, the Angelus ringing midday, those who lived too far away straggled into the inns.

At Jourdain's, the big dining room was crowded with guests, just as the huge courtyard was crowded with vehicles of every breed, carts, cabriolets, wagonettes, tilburys, covered carts innumerable, yellow with mud, out of trim and patched, some raising their two shafts, like arms, to the sky, some with nose on the ground and tail in the air.

Right up against the diners the immense fireplace, flaming brightly, threw a mighty heat onto the backs of the right-hand row seated at table. Three jacks were turning, garnished with chickens, pigeons, and legs of mutton, and a delectable odor of roast meat, and of gravy streaming over the well-browned crackling, rose from the hearth, bringing joy to the heart, and water to the mouth.

All the aristocracy of the plow dined at M. Jourdain's, innkeeper and horse-dealer, a shrewd fellow, and a "warm man."

The dishes were passed, and emptied, together with mugs of golden cider. Everyone told the story of his bargains, and asked his neighbor about the crops. The weather was good for green stuff, but a little damp for corn.

Suddenly, from the courtyard in front of the house, came the roll of a drum.

All but a few, too lazy to move, jumped up at once, and flew to the doors and windows, their mouths still full and their napkins in their hands.

Finishing off the roll of his drum, the town crier shouted in staccato tones, with a scansion of phrase peculiarly out of rhythm:

"This is to inform the inhabitants of Goderville, and all others —present at the market, that there was lost this morning on the Beuzeville road between nine and ten o'clock, a black leather pocket-book, containing five hundred francs and some business papers. It should be returned—to the Town Hall immediately, or to Master Fortuné Houlbrèque at Manneville. A reward of twenty francs is offered."

The man went by, and presently the dull rumble of the drum was heard again, and then the crier's voice, fainter in the distance.

Everyone began discussing the event, calculating the chances of Master Houlbrèque's recovering or not recovering his pocket-book.

And so the meal came to an end.

They were finishing their coffee when the brigadier of gendarmes appeared at the door, and asked:

"Is Master Hauchecorne, of Breauté, here?"

Master Hauchecorne, seated at the far end of the table, answered:

"Here!"

"Master Hauchecorne," proceeded the officer, "will you be so good as to come with me to the Town Hall? The mayor would like to speak to you."

Surprised and uneasy, the peasant gulped down his cognac, rose, and stooping even more than in the morning, for the first steps after resting were always particularly painful, got himself started, repeating:

"All right! I'm coming!" and followed the sergeant.

The mayor was awaiting him, seated in an armchair. He was the notary of the district, a stout, serious man, full of pompous phrases.

"Master Hauchecorne," said he, "you were seen this morning to pick up, on the Beuzeville road, the pocket-book lost by Master Houlbrèque, of Manneville."

The peasant, in stupefaction, gazed at the mayor, intimidated at once by this suspicion which lay heavy upon him without his comprehending it.

"Me? Me—me pick up that pocket-book?"

"Yes, you."

"On my word of honor, I didn't! Why, I didn't even know about it!"

"You were seen."

"Seen? I? Who saw me?"

"M. Malandain, the saddler."

Then the old man remembered, and understood. Reddening with anger, he said:

"Ah! He saw me, that animal! Well, what he saw me pick up was this string, look here, M. le Maire!"

And rummaging in his pocket, he pulled out the little piece of string.

But the mayor shook his head incredulously.

"You won't make me believe, Master Hauchecorne, that M. Malandain, a trustworthy man, took that piece of string for a pocket-book."

The enraged peasant raised his hand, spat solemnly to show his good faith, and repeated:

"It's God's truth, all the same, the sacred truth, M. le Maire. There, on my soul and honor, I say it again."

The mayor proceeded.

"After having picked up the article in question, you even went on searching in the mud, to make sure a coin or two mightn't have fallen out."

The poor old fellow choked with indignation and fear.

"To say such things! . . . How can anyone . . . telling lies like that, to undo an honest man! How can anyone?"

Protest as he would, he was not believed.

They confronted him with M. Malandain, who repeated and substantiated his story. The two abused each other for a whole hour. By his own request, Master Hauchecorne was searched. Nothing was found on him.

At last the mayor, thoroughly puzzled, dismissed him, warning him that he was going to give notice to the public prosecutor and take his instructions.

The news had spread. As he went out of the Town Hall the old man was surrounded, and all sorts of serious or mocking questions were put to him, but no one showed the slightest indignation. He began to tell the story of the piece of string. They did not believe him. Everybody laughed.

He went on, stopped by everyone, stopping everyone he knew, to tell his story over and over again, protesting, showing his pockets turned inside out, to prove that he had nothing on him. The only answer he got was:

"Get along, you sly old dog!"

He began to feel angry, worrying himself into a fever of irritation, miserable at not being believed, at a loss what to do, and continually repeating his story.

Night came on. It was time to go home. He set out with three neighbors, to whom he showed the spot where he had picked up the piece of string; and the whole way home he kept talking of his misadventure.

In the evening he made a round of the village of Breauté, to tell everybody all about it. He came across unbelievers only.

He was ill all night.

The next day, about one o'clock, Marius Paumelle, a laborer at Master Breton's, a farmer at Ymauville, restored the pocket-book and its contents to Master Houlbrèque, of Manneville.

This man declared that he had found the object on the road; but not being able to read, he had taken it home and given it to his master.

The news spread through the neighborhood. Master Hauchecorne was informed of it, and started off at once on a round, to tell his story all over again, with its proper ending. It was a triumph.

"What knocked me over," he said, "was not so much the thing itself, you know, but that charge of lying. There's nothing hurts a man so much as being thought a liar."

The whole day long he talked of his adventure, telling it to people he met on the roads, to people drinking at the inns, and even at the church door on the following Sunday. He stopped perfect strangers to tell him about it. He was easy in his mind now, and yet —there was something that bothered him, though he could not exactly arrive at what it was. People had an amused look while they were listening to him. They did not seem convinced. He felt as if a lot of tattle was going on behind his back.

On the Tuesday of the following week he went off to Goderville market, urged thereto solely by the desire to tell his story. Malandain, standing at his door, began to laugh as he went past. Why?

He began his story to a farmer of Criquetot, who did not let him finish, but, giving him a dig in the pit of the stomach, shouted in his face: "Get along, you old rogue!" and turned his back.

Master Hauchecorne stopped short, confused, and more and more uneasy. Why was he being called an "old rogue"?

When he was seated at the table at Jourdain's inn he began again to explain the whole affair.

A horse-dealer from Montvillier called out:

"Come, come, that's an old trick; I know all about your piece of string!"

Hauchecorne stammered:

"But it's been found, that pocket-book!"

But the other went on:

"Oh! Shut up, old boy, there's one who finds, and another who brings back. All on the strict QT."

The peasant was thunderstruck. He understood at last. It was insinuated that he had caused the pocket-book to be taken by someone else, an accomplice.

He tried to protest, but the whole table began laughing.

He could not finish his dinner, and went away, with every one jeering at him.

He returned home, ashamed and indignant, choking with anger and bewilderment, and all the more overwhelmed because, in his artful Norman brain, he knew himself capable of having done what they accused him of, and of even boasting about it afterward, as though it were a feat. He realized confusedly that it would be impossible to prove his innocence, his tricky nature being known to all. And he felt wounded to the heart by the injustice of this suspicion.

Then he began again to tell his story, making the tale a little longer every day, adding new reasons every time, more energetic protestations, most solemn oaths which he thought out and prepared in his solitary moments, for his mind was solely occupied by the story of the piece of string. They believed him less and less as his defense became more and more elaborate, his arguments more subtle.

"H'm! That's only to cover up his tracks," the hearers would say behind his back.

He was conscious of all this, but went on eating his heart out, exhausting himself in fruitless efforts.

Before the very eyes of people, he wasted away.

Jokers now would make him tell them the "piece of string" to amuse them, as one makes old soldiers tell about their battles. His spirit, undetermined, grew feebler and feebler.

Toward the end of December he took to his bed.

He died at the beginning of January, and in his last delirium still protested his innocence, repeating:

"A little piece of string . . . a little piece of string . . . look, here it is, M. le Maire!"

Nobility

Alice Cary

This poem brings to mind the words of Alexander Pope: "An honest man's the noblest work of God."

> True worth is in *being,* not *seeming*—
>   In doing, each day that goes by,
> Some little good—not in dreaming
>   Of great things to do by and by.
> For whatever men say in their blindness,
>   And spite of the fancies of youth,
> There's nothing so kingly as kindness,
>   And nothing so royal as truth.
>
> We get back our mete as we measure—
>   We cannot do wrong and feel right,
> Nor can we give pain and gain pleasure,
>   For justice avenges each slight.
> The air for the wing of the sparrow,
>   The bush for the robin and wren,
> But always the path that is narrow
>   And straight, for the children of men.

'Tis not in the pages of story
   The heart of its ills to beguile,
Though he who makes courtship to glory
   Gives all that he hath for her smile.
For when from her heights he has won her,
   Alas! it is only to prove
That nothing's so sacred as honor,
   And nothing so loyal as love!

We cannot make bargains for blisses,
   Nor catch them like fishes in nets;
And sometimes the thing our life misses
   Helps more than the thing which it gets.
For good lieth not in pursuing,
   Nor gaining of great nor of small,
But just in the doing, and doing
   As we would be done by, is all.

Through envy, through malice, through hating,
   Against the world, early and late,
No jot of our courage abating—
   Our part is to work and to wait.
And slight is the sting of his trouble
   Whose winnings are less than his worth;
For he who is honest is noble,
   Whatever his fortunes or birth.

Truth in Advertising

P. T. Barnum

Often erroneously associated with the slogan "There's a sucker born every minute," showman P. T. Barnum (1810–1891) was one of the first American businessmen to fully appreciate the value of publicity. Since we live in an age of ever-growing media influence and ever-present concern about truth in advertising, it is instructive to read this excerpt from Barnum's 1866 *Humbugs of the World,* in which he draws a line between cheating the public and attracting its attention. (Barnum's environmental and cultural sensitivities apparently had not caught up with his concern for the truth.)

Upon a careful consideration of my undertaking to give an account of the "Humbugs of the World," I find myself somewhat puzzled in regard to the true definition of the word. To be sure, Webster says that "humbug," as a noun, is an "imposition under fair pretenses"; and as a verb, it is "to deceive; to impose on." With all due deference to Dr. Webster, I submit that, according to present usage, this is not the only, nor even the generally accepted definition of that term. . . . As generally understood, "humbug" consists in putting on glittering appearances—outside show—novel expedients, by which to suddenly arrest public attention, and attract the public eye and ear.

Clergymen, lawyers, or physicians, who should resort to such methods of attracting the public, would not, for obvious reasons, be apt to succeed. Bankers, insurance agents, and others, who aspire to become custodians of the money of their fellow men, would require a different species of advertising from this; but there are various trades and occupations which need only notoriety to insure success, always provided that when customers are once attracted, they never fail to get their money's worth. An honest man who thus arrests public attention will be called a "humbug," but he is not a swindler or an impostor. . . .

When the great blacking-maker of London dispatched his agent to Egypt to write on the pyramids of Ghiza, in huge letters:
"Buy Warren's Blacking, 30 Strand, London."
he was not "cheating" travelers upon the Nile. His blacking was really a superior article, and well worth the price charged for it, but he was "humbugging" the public by this queer way of arresting attention. It turned out just as he anticipated, that English travelers in that part of Egypt were indignant at this desecration, and they wrote back to the London *Times* (every Englishman writes or threatens to "write to the *Times*" if anything goes wrong) denouncing the "Goth" who had thus disfigured these ancient pyramids by writing on them in monstrous letters: "Buy Warren's Blacking, 30 Strand, London." The *Times* published these letters, and backed them up by several of those awful, grand, and dictatorial editorials peculiar to the greater "Thunderer," in which the blacking-maker, "Warren, 30

Strand," was stigmatized as a man who had no respect for the ancient patriarchs, and it was hinted that he would probably not hesitate to sell his blacking on the sarcophagus of Pharaoh, "or any other" mummy, if he could only make money by it. In fact, to cap the climax, Warren was denounced as a "humbug." These indignant articles were copied into all the provincial journals, and very soon, in this manner, the columns of every newspaper in Great Britain were teeming with this advice: "Try Warren's Blacking, 30 Strand, London." The curiosity of the public was thus aroused, and they did "try" it, and finding it a superior article, they continued to purchase it and recommend it to their friends, and Warren made a fortune by it. He always attributed his success to his having "humbugged" the public by this unique method of advertising his blacking in Egypt! But Warren did not cheat his customers, nor practice "an imposition under fair pretenses." He was a humbug, but he was an honest upright man, and no one called him an impostor or a cheat.

Plato on Justice

From The Republic

The main questions asked in *The Republic* are: what is justice, how can we humans achieve it in society, and why should we? But the ancient Greek word for "just" is a slippery one for modern translators. Depending on the context, it can mean honest, pious, fair, legally correct, lawful, or obligated, to name a few possibilities. In the end, it may be that the meaning of Plato's "justice" comes closer to our modern notion of "integrity." Plato's answer to the question "Why should I be a person of integrity?" is, to put it briefly, "Because it is healthier." Integrity —having one's psychological parts *integrated,* "having it all together," as we say—is the psychological counterpart of physical fitness. It is the sort of condition in which any really rational human being would choose to be, if one really saw it for what it was. Acquiring integrity is getting one's person in shape.

The dialogue here is between Socrates and Glaucon.

Socrates. Then our dream has been realized; and the suspicion, which we entertained at the beginning of our work of construction, that some divine power must have conducted us to a primary form of justice, has now been verified?

Glaucon. Yes. Certainly.

And the division of labor which required the carpenter and the shoemaker and the rest of the citizens to be doing each his own business, and not another's, was a shadow of justice, and for that reason it was of use?

Clearly.

But in reality justice was such as we were describing, being concerned however, not with the outward man, but with the inward, which is the true self and concernment of man: for the just man does not permit the several elements within him to interfere with one another, or any of them to do the work of others—he sets in order his own inner life, and is his own master and his own law, and at peace with himself; and when he has bound together the three principles within him, which may be compared to the higher, lower, and middle notes of the scale, and the intermediate intervals—when he has bound all these together, and is no longer many, but has become one entirely temperate and perfectly adjusted nature, then he proceeds to act, if he has to act, whether in a matter of property, or in the treatment of the body, or in some affair of politics or private business; always thinking and calling that which preserves and cooperates with this harmonious condition, just and good action, and the knowledge which presides over it, wisdom, and that which at any time impairs this condition, he will call unjust action, and the opinion which presides over it ignorance.

You have said the exact truth, Socrates.

Very good; and if we were to affirm that we had discovered the just man and the just state, and the nature of justice in each of them, we should not be telling a falsehood?

Most certainly not.

May we say so, then?

Let us say so.

And now, I said, injustice has to be considered.

Clearly.

Must not injustice be a strife which arises among the three principles—a meddlesomeness, and interference, and rising up of a part of the soul against the whole, an assertion of unlawful authority, which is made by a rebellious subject against a true prince, of whom he is the natural vassal—what is all this confusion and delusion but injustice, and intemperance and cowardice and ignorance, and every form of vice?

Exactly so.

And if the nature of justice and injustice be known, then the meaning of acting unjustly and being unjust, or, again, of acting justly, will also be perfectly clear?

What do you mean? he said.

Why, I said, they are like disease and health; being in the soul just what disease and health are in the body.

How so? he said.

Why, I said, that which is healthy causes health, and that which is unhealthy causes disease.

Yes.

And just actions cause justice, and unjust actions cause injustice?

That is certain.

And the creation of health is the institution of a natural order and government of one by another in the parts of the body; and the creation of disease is the production of a state of things at variance with this natural order?

True.

And is not the creation of justice the institution of a natural order and government of one by another in the parts of the soul, and the creation of injustice the production of a state of things at variance with the natural order.

Exactly so, he said.

Then virtue is the health and beauty and well-being of the soul, and vice the disease and weakness and deformity of the same?

True.

And do not good practices lead to virtue, and evil practices to vice?

Assuredly.

Still our old question of the comparative advantage of justice and injustice has not been answered: which is the more profitable, to be just and act justly and practice virtue, whether seen or unseen of gods and men, or to be unjust and act unjustly, if only unpunished and unreformed?

In my judgment, Socrates, the question has now become ridiculous. We know that, when the bodily constitution is gone, life is no longer endurable, though pampered with all kinds of meats and drinks, and having all wealth and all power; and shall we be told that when the very essence of the vital principle is undermined and corrupted, life is still worth having to a man, if only he be allowed to do whatever he likes with the single exception that he is not to acquire justice and virtue, or to escape from injustice and vice; assuming them both to be such as we have described?

Yes, I said, the question is, as you say, ridiculous.

Francis Bacon on Truth

From "Of Truth"

In this famous essay, first published in 1625, Francis Bacon (1561–1626) declares that truth in the philosophical and theological sense, as well as honesty in the civil business sense, are the "sovereign good of human nature."

Truth, which only doth judge itself, teacheth that the inquiry of truth, which is the love-making or wooing of it, the knowledge of truth, which is the presence of it, and the belief of truth, which is the enjoying of it, is the sovereign good of human nature. The first creature of God, in the works of the days, was the light of the sense; the last was the light of reason; and his sabbath work ever since is the illumination of his Spirit. First he breathed light upon the face of the matter or chaos; then he breathed light into the face of man; and still he breatheth and inspireth light into the face of his chosen. The poet that beautified the sect that was otherwise inferior to the rest saith yet excellently well: *It is a pleasure to stand upon the shore and to see ships tossed upon the sea; a pleasure to stand in the window of a castle and to see a battle and the adventures thereof below; but no pleasure is comparable to the standing upon the vantage ground of truth* (a hill not to be commanded, and where the air is always clear and serene), *and to see the errors and wanderings and mists and tempests in the vale below;* so always that this prospect be with pity, and not with swelling or pride. Certainly, it is heaven upon earth to have a man's mind move in charity, rest in providence, and turn upon the poles of truth.

To pass from theological and philosophical truth to the truth of civil business: it will be acknowledged even by those that practice it not that clear and round dealing is the honor of man's nature; and that mixture of falsehood is like alloy in coin of gold and silver, which may make the metal work the better, but it embaseth it. For these winding and crooked courses are the goings of the serpent, which goeth basely upon the belly, and not upon the feet. There is no vice that doth so cover a man with shame as to be found false and perfidious. And therefore Montaigne said prettily, when he inquired the reason why the word of the lie should be such a disgrace and such an odious charge. Saith he, *If it be well weighed, to say that a man lieth is as much to say as that he is brave toward God and a coward toward men.* For a lie faces God, and shrinks from man. Surely the wickedness of falsehood and breach of faith cannot possibly be so highly expressed as in that it shall be the last peal to call the judgments of God upon the generations of men; it being foretold that when Christ cometh, *he shall not find faith upon the earth.*

Truth Never Dies

This poem is inspiring in its assertion that truth is eternal, but perhaps more valuable is its reminder that truth must be "caught and handed onward by the wise." Truth must be passed from friend to friend, from teacher to student, from parent to child.

Truth never dies. The ages come and go.
The mountains wear away, the stars retire.
Destruction lays earth's mighty cities low;
    And empires, states and dynasties expire;
But caught and handed onward by the wise,
    Truth never dies.

Though unreceived and scoffed at through the years;
    Though made the butt of ridicule and jest;
Though held aloft for mockery and jeers,
    Denied by those of transient power possessed,
Insulted by the insolence of lies,
    Truth never dies.

It answers not. It does not take offense,
But with a mighty silence bides its time;
As some great cliff that braves the elements
And lifts through all the storms its head sublime,
It ever stands, uplifted by the wise;
And never dies.

As rests the Sphinx amid Egyptian sands;
As looms on high the snowy peak and crest;
As firm and patient as Gibraltar stands,
So truth, unwearied, waits the era blessed
When men shall turn to it with great surprise.
Truth never dies.

9

Loyalty

O u r loyalties are important signs of the kinds of persons we have chosen to become. They mark a kind of constancy or steadfastness in our attachments to those other persons, groups, institutions, or ideals with which we have deliberately decided to associate ourselves. To be a loyal citizen or friend means to operate within a certain framework of caring seriously about the well-being of one's country or comrade. This is very different from being a rubber stamp. Loyalty operates on a higher level than that. For example, the president takes an oath of loyalty to the Constitution of the United States, and so do other federal employees, law enforcement personnel, and members of the armed services. Citizens across the nation pledge allegiance to the flag. These expressions leave plenty of room for disagreement apart from the fundamentals they emphasize.

Ceremonial expressions aside, loyalty is like courage in that it shows itself most clearly when we are operating under stress. Real loyalty endures inconvenience, withstands temptation, and does not cringe under assault. Yet the trust that genuine loyalty tends to generate can pervade our whole lives.

The Bible provides many illuminating examples. Potiphar placed Joseph in charge of his entire household. "He has put everything that he has in my hand," Joseph explains to Potiphar's wife in rejecting her advances (Genesis 39:8). He is a loyal steward, and will not betray Potiphar's trust.

Potiphar is a loyal husband, too, however. He acts on his wife's trumped-up complaint and has Joseph jailed (Genesis 39:19–20). Virtue by itself is no guarantee of right action, which requires more than good intentions. We need in addition both the wisdom to know what the right thing to do is, and the will to do it.

In another illuminating case David remains loyal to his king— Saul, the Lord's anointed, and the father of his best friend, Jonathan —even as Saul is trying to kill him (see the story of Jonathan and David in the chapter on Friendship). On two occasions David has clear opportunity to destroy Saul, but refrains from doing so out of loyalty (1 Samuel 24 and 26). And after Saul and Jonathan die in battle, David's famous lament—"How the mighty have fallen"—is equally for both (2 Samuel 1:17–27). We don't have to *like* those to whom we are loyal, and they don't have to like us. Loyalty is thus quite different from friendship, although the two often go hand in hand.

The loyalties associated with our family connections, friendships, religious or political affiliations, professional lives, and so on, can all change as these associations themselves develop. Sometimes the changes in loyalties can be quite dramatic, as in the case of Paul's conversion on the road to Damascus (Acts 9:1–22). Others may be more measured and deliberate, though no less radical, as when Ruth the Moabite commits herself to accompany Naomi back to her homeland of Judah (see the story of Ruth and Naomi in the Friendship chapter).

Conflicting loyalties may sometimes force one to make disagreeable decisions. But here it is important to keep in mind that there is a real difference between a decision that is unpleasant and one that is difficult. Daniel faced no dilemma when he had to choose between loyalty to his king, Darius, and loyalty to his God. The latter clearly took precedence. *Choosing* was easy enough, but it was certainly disagreeable, and he ended up in the lions' den (Daniel 6).

Conflicting loyalties may on occasion prove to be *only* apparent. A sufficiently astute intelligence can sometimes see ways of dissolving difficulties that appear insuperable to others. Thus Jesus met one of his loyalty tests by formulating the memorable dilemma-dissolving rule, "Render therefore unto Caesar the things which are Caesar's; and unto God the things that are God's" (Matthew 22:21). Most cases are *not* like Daniel's singular exception. The times when one cannot stand both "for God *and* for country" are rare indeed.

Little Boy Blue

Eugene Field

Some of our earliest, most faithful friends are our childhood toys.
May we all learn to be as steadfast in our loyalties as the companions of Little Boy Blue.

The little toy dog is covered with dust,
    But sturdy and stanch he stands;
And the little toy soldier is red with rust,
    And his musket molds in his hands.
Time was when the little toy dog was new
    And the soldier was passing fair;
And that was the time when our Little Boy Blue
    Kissed them and put them there.

"Now, don't you go till I come," he said,
    "And don't you make any noise!"
So, toddling off to his trundle-bed,
    He dreamed of the pretty toys;
And as he was dreaming, an angel song
    Awakened our Little Boy Blue—
Oh! the years are many, the years are long,
    But the little toy friends are true!

Aye, faithful to Little Boy Blue they stand,
  Each in the same old place—
Awaiting the touch of a little hand,
  And the smile of a little face;
And they wonder, as waiting these long years through
  In the dust of that little chair,
What has become of our Little Boy Blue,
  Since he kissed them and put them there.

The Cap That Mother Made

Adapted from Carolyn Sherwin Bailey

As this Swedish tale reminds us, the loyalties expressed in our
attachments—even to such humble things as the cap that Mother
made—are important elements in the kinds of persons that we
have chosen to make of ourselves.

Once upon a time there was a little boy named Anders who had
a new cap. A more handsome cap you never have seen, for Anders's
mother herself had knit it, and nobody can make anything quite so
nice as a mother! It was red except for a small part in the middle,
which was green (that was because Anders's mother had run out of
red yarn), and the tassel was blue.

Anders walked around his house for a while, letting his brothers
and sisters admire him in his new cap. Then he put his hands in his
pockets and went out for a walk, because he wanted everybody to
see how fine a cap his mother had made.

The first person he met was a farmer walking down the road
alongside a wagon loaded with wood. The farmer bowed so deeply,
Anders thought he might fall over.

"Well, if it isn't Anders," cried the cheerful farmer. "At first I
thought you were a duke, or maybe even prince, with such a fine
cap as that. Would you like to ride in my wagon?"

But Anders smiled politely and shook his head, and walked
proudly by, holding his head high.

At the turn in the road he met Lars, the tanner's son. He was such a big boy that he wore high boots and carried a pocket knife. When he saw Anders's cap, he couldn't help but stop and gape at it, and he couldn't keep himself from coming up close and fingering the blue tassel.

"Let's trade caps," he suggested. "I'll even give you my pocket-knife too."

Now this knife was a very good one, though half the blade was gone and the handle was a little cracked. Anders had often admired that knife, but still it did not measure up to the new cap his mother had made.

"No, I don't think I could make a trade like that," he told Lars, and he nodded and went on his way.

Soon he met a very old woman who curtsied until her skirts looked like a balloon.

"My, my, you look like such a little gentleman," she said. "I dare say you're dressed up to go to the royal ball."

"Yes, why not?" thought Anders. "Seeing that I look so fine, I may as well go and visit the king."

And so he did.

In the palace yard stood two soldiers with shining helmets, and with muskets over their shoulders. When Anders reached the gate, both the muskets were leveled at him.

"Where may you be going?" demanded one of the soldiers.

"I am going to the royal ball," answered Anders.

"No, you are not," said the other soldier, stepping forward. "Nobody can go to the royal ball without a uniform."

But at that very instant, the princess came tripping across the yard. She was dressed in white silk, with bows of gold ribbon.

"This lad has no uniform, it's true," she told the soldiers, "but he has a very fine cap on his head, and that will do just as well."

And she took Anders's hand and walked him up the broad marble stairs where soldiers were posted at every third step, and through the beautiful halls where courtiers in silk and velvet stood bowing wherever he went. For no doubt they thought him a prince when they saw his fine cap.

At the far end of the largest hall, a table was set with golden cups and golden plates in long rows. On huge silver dishes were piles of tarts and cakes, and red wine sparkled in shining glasses.

The princess sat down at the head of the long table. She let Anders sit in a golden chair by her side.

"But you must not eat with your cap on your head," she said, putting out her hand to take it off.

"Oh, yes, I can eat just as well with it on," said Anders, holding tight to his cap. For he thought that if they took it away from him, they would no longer believe he was a prince. Besides, he did not feel sure he would get it back again.

"Well, well, give it to me," said the princess, "and I will give you a kiss."

The princess was certainly beautiful, and Anders would have liked to be kissed by her, but not for anything in the world could he give up the cap Mother had made. He only shook his head.

The princess filled his pockets with cakes, and even put her own gold chain around his neck, and bent down and kissed him.

"Now will you give me the cap?" she asked.

But Anders only moved farther back in his chair and did not take his hands away from his head.

Suddenly the doors flew open, and in marched the king with all his gentlemen in glittering uniforms and plumed hats. The king himself wore a purple mantle which trailed behind him, and he had a large gold crown on his white curly hair.

He smiled when he saw Anders in the golden chair.

"That is a very fine cap you have," he said.

"So it is," replied Anders. "Mother knit it of her very best yarn, and everyone who sees it tries to get it from me."

"But surely you would like to change caps with me," said the king, raising his heavy crown from his head.

Anders stayed as quiet as a mouse. He sat as still as he could, and held on to his red cap. But when the king came nearer to him, with his gold crown between his hands, Anders grew frightened as never before. If he didn't watch out, the king might grab his cap! For a king can do whatever he likes, of course.

With one jump, Anders was out of his chair. He darted like an arrow through all the beautiful halls, down all the marble stairs, and across the yard.

He twisted himself like an eel between the outstretched arms of the courtiers, and jumped like a little rabbit over the soldiers' muskets.

He ran so fast, the princess's necklace fell off his neck, and all the cakes jumped out of his pockets. But he still had his cap! No matter what else, he still had his cap! He clutched it with both hands as he rushed into his cottage.

"Well, Anders, where have you been?" his mother asked. So he climbed into her lap and told her all his adventures, and how everybody wanted his cap. His brothers and sisters stood around and listened with their mouths open.

When his big brother heard that Anders had refused to trade his cap for the king's golden crown, he whistled and whooped.

"Now weren't you foolish!" he exclaimed. "You could have sold that crown for a whole fortune in gold, and bought a castle, and a carriage with horses, and a boat to sail on the river. And you still would have had enough money left over to buy a brand-new hat with a purple plume sticking out!"

Anders had not thought of that, and his face turned three shades of red. He put his arms around his mother's neck. "Mother," he asked, "was I foolish?"

His mother hugged him close and kissed him.

"No, my little son," she said. "If you were dressed in silver and gold from top to toe, you could not look any nicer than you do in your little red cap."

Then Anders felt fine again. He knew well enough that mother's cap was the best cap in the whole world.

The Story of Cincinnatus

Retold by James Baldwin

This story of Roman statesman and general Lucius Quinctius Cincinnatus takes place in 458 B.C., when Rome was besieged by an Italic tribe called the Aequi. It is one of our most famous reminders that the loyal citizen expects no great reward for coming to his country's aid. Whenever I visit Cincinnati, I try to stop by the statue of Cincinnatus there, one of my favorites.

There was a man named Cincinnatus who lived on a little farm not far from the city of Rome. He had once been rich, and had held the highest office in the land, but in one way or another he had lost all his wealth. He was now so poor that he had to do all the work on his farm with his own hands. But in those days it was thought to be a noble thing to till the soil.

Cincinnatus was so wise and just that everybody trusted him, and asked his advice. When anyone was in trouble, and did not know what to do, his neighbors would say,

"Go and tell Cincinnatus. He will help you."

Now there lived among the mountains, not far away, a tribe of fierce, half-wild men, who were at war with the Roman people. They persuaded another tribe of bold warriors to help them, and then marched toward the city, plundering and robbing as they came. They boasted that they would tear down the walls of Rome, and burn the houses, and kill all the men, and make slaves of the women and children.

At first the Romans, who were very proud and brave, did not think there was much danger. Every man in Rome was a soldier, and the army which went out to fight the robbers was the finest in the world. No one stayed at home but the white-haired "Fathers," as they were called, who made the laws for the city, and a small company of men who guarded the walls. Everybody thought that it would be an easy thing to drive the men of the mountains back to the place where they belonged.

But one morning five horsemen came riding down the road from the mountains. They rode with great speed, and both men and horses were covered with dust and blood. The watchman at the gate knew them, And shouted to them as they galloped in. Why did they ride thus? And what had happened to the Roman army?

They did not answer him, but rode into the city and along the quiet streets. Everybody ran after them, eager to find out what was the matter. Rome was not a large city at that time, and soon they reached the marketplace where the white-haired Fathers were sitting. Then they leaped from their horses, and told their story.

"Only yesterday," they said, "our army was marching through a narrow valley between two steep mountains. All at once a thousand savage men sprang out from among the rocks before us and above us. They had blocked up the way, and the pass was so narrow that we could not fight. We tried to come back, but they had blocked up the way on this side of us too. The fierce men of the mountains were before us and behind us, and they were throwing rocks down upon us from above. We had been caught in a trap. Then ten of us set spurs to our horses, and five of us forced our way through, but the other five fell before the spears of the mountain men. And now,

O Roman Fathers! Send help to our army at once, or every man will be slain, and our city will be taken."

"What shall we do?" said the white-haired Fathers. "Whom can we send but the guards and the boys? And who is wise enough to lead them, and thus save Rome?"

All shook their heads and were very grave, for it seemed as if there was no hope. Then one said, "Send for Cincinnatus. He will help us."

Cincinnatus was in the field plowing when the men who had been sent to him came in great haste. He stopped and greeted them kindly, and waited for them to speak.

"Put on your cloak, Cincinnatus," they said, "and hear the words of the Roman people."

Then Cincinnatus wondered what they could mean. "Is all well with Rome?" he asked. And he called to his wife to bring him his cloak.

She brought the cloak; and Cincinnatus wiped the dust from his hands and arms, and threw it over his shoulders. Then the men told their errand.

They told him how the army with all the noblest men of Rome had been entrapped in the mountain pass. They told him about the great danger the city was in. Then they said, "The people of Rome make you their ruler and the ruler of their city, to do with everything as you choose. And the Fathers bid you come at once and go out against our enemies, the fierce men of the mountains."

So Cincinnatus left his plow standing where it was, and hurried to the city. When he passed through the streets, and gave orders as to what should be done, some of the people were afraid, for they knew that he had all power in Rome to do what he pleased. But he armed the guards and the boys, and went out at their head to fight the fierce mountain men, and free the Roman army from the trap into which it had fallen.

A few days afterward there was great joy in Rome. There was good news from Cincinnatus. The men of the mountains had been beaten with great loss. They had been driven back into their own place.

And now the Roman army, with the boys and the guards, was coming home with banners flying, and shouts of victory. And at their head rode Cincinnatus. He had saved Rome.

Cincinnatus might then have made himself king, for his word was law, and no man dared lift a finger against him. But, before the people could thank him enough for what he had done, he gave back the power to the white-haired Roman Fathers, and went again to his little farm and his plow.

He had been the ruler of Rome for sixteen days.

The Devoted Friend

Oscar Wilde

Devotion is a two-way street between friends, as this Oscar Wilde story reminds us.

One morning the old Water Rat put his head out of his hole. He had bright beady eyes and stiff gray whiskers, and his tail was like a long bit of black india rubber. The little ducks were swimming about in the pond, looking just like a lot of yellow canaries, and their mother, who was pure white with real red legs, was trying to teach them how to stand on their heads in the water.

"You will never be in the best society unless you can stand on your heads," she kept saying to them, and every now and then she showed them how it was done. But the little ducks paid no attention to her. They were so young that they did not know what an advantage it is to be in society at all.

"What disobedient children!" cried the old Water Rat. "They really deserve to be drowned."

"Nothing of the kind," answered the Duck. "Everyone must make a beginning, and parents cannot be too patient."

"Ah! I know nothing about the feelings of parents," said the Water Rat. "I am not a family man. In fact, I have never been married, and I never intend to be. Love is all very well in its way, but friendship is much higher. Indeed, I know of nothing in the world that is either nobler or rarer than a devoted friendship."

"And what, pray, is your idea of the duties of a devoted friend?" asked a green Linnet, who was sitting in a willow tree hard by, and had overheard the conversation.

"Yes, that is just what I want to know," said the Duck, and she swam away to the end of the pond, and stood upon her head, in order to give her children a good example.

"What a silly question!" cried the Water Rat. "I should expect my devoted friend to be devoted to me, of course."

"And what would you do in return?" said the little bird, swinging upon a silver spray, and flapping his tiny wings.

"I don't understand you," answered the Water Rat.

"Let me tell you a story on the subject," said the Linnet.

"Is the story about me?" asked the Water Rat. "If so, I will listen to it, for I am extremely fond of fiction."

"It is applicable to you," answered the Linnet. And he flew down, and alighting upon the bank, he told the story of The Devoted Friend.

"Once upon a time," said the Linnet, "there was an honest little fellow named Hans."

"Was he very distinguished?" asked the Water Rat.

"No," answered the Linnet. "I don't think he was distinguished at all, except for his kind heart, and his funny round good-humored face. He lived in a tiny cottage all by himself, and every day he worked in his garden. In all the countryside there was no garden so lovely as his. Sweet William grew there, and gillyflowers, and shepherds' purses, and fair maids of France. There were damask roses, and yellow roses, lilac crocuses, and gold, purple violets and white. Columbine and ladysmock, marjoram and wild basil, the cowslip and the fleur-de-lis, the daffodil and the clove pink bloomed or blossomed in their proper order as the months went by, one flower taking another flower's place, so that there were always beautiful things to look at, and pleasant odors to smell.

"Little Hans had a great many friends, but the most devoted friend of all was big Hugh the Miller. Indeed, so devoted was the rich Miller to little Hans, that he would never go by his garden without leaning over the wall and plucking a large nosegay, or a handful of sweet herbs, or filling his pockets with plums and cherries if it was the fruit season.

" 'Real friends should have everything in common,' the Miller used to say, and little Hans nodded and smiled, and felt very proud of having a friend with such noble ideas.

"Sometimes, indeed, the neighbors thought it strange that the rich Miller never gave little Hans anything in return, though he had a hundred sacks of flour stored away in his mill, and six milch cows, and a large flock of woolly sheep; but Hans never troubled his head about these things, and nothing gave him greater pleasure than to listen to all the wonderful things the Miller used to say about the unselfishness of true friendship.

"So little Hans worked away in his garden. During the spring, the summer, and the autumn he was very happy, but when the winter came, and he had no fruit or flowers to bring to the market, he suffered a good deal from cold and hunger, and often had to go to bed without any supper but a few dried pears or some hard nuts. In the winter, also, he was extremely lonely, as the Miller never came to see him then.

" 'There is no good in my going to see little Hans as long as the snow lasts,' the Miller used to say to his Wife, 'for when people are in trouble they should be left alone, and not be bothered by visitors. That at least is my idea about friendship, and I am sure I am right. So I shall wait till the spring comes, and then I shall pay him a visit, and he will be able to give me a large basket of primroses, and that will make him so happy.'

" 'You are certainly very thoughtful about others,' answered the Wife, as she sat in her comfortable armchair by the big pinewood fire. 'Very thoughtful indeed. It is quite a treat to hear you talk about friendship. I am sure the clergyman himself could not say such beautiful things as you do, though he does live in a three-storied house, and wear a gold ring on his little finger.'

" 'But could we not ask little Hans up here?' said the Miller's youngest son. 'If poor Hans is in trouble I will give him half my porridge, and show him my white rabbits.'

" 'What a silly boy you are!' cried the Miller. 'I really don't know what is the use of sending you to school. You seem not to learn anything. Why, if little Hans came up here, and saw our warm fire, and our good supper, and our great cask of red wine, he might get envious, and envy is a most terrible thing, and would spoil anybody's nature. I certainly will not allow Hans's nature to be spoiled. I am his best friend, and I will always watch over him, and see that he is not led into any temptations. Besides, if Hans came here, he might ask me to let him have some flour on credit, and that I could not do. Flour is one thing, and friendship is another, and they should not be confused. Why, the words are spelt differently, and mean quite different things. Everybody can see that.'

" 'How well you talk!' said the Miller's Wife, pouring herself out a large glass of warm ale. 'Really I feel quite drowsy. It is just like being in church.'

" 'Lots of people act well,' answered the Miller, 'but very few people talk well, which shows that talking is much the more difficult thing of the two, and much the finer thing also.' And he looked sternly across the table at his little son, who felt so ashamed of himself that he hung his head down, and grew quite scarlet, and began to cry into his tea. However, he was so young that you must excuse him."

"Is that the end of the story?" asked the Water Rat.

"Certainly not," answered the Linnet. "That is the beginning."

"Then you are quite behind the age," said the Water Rat. "Every good storyteller nowadays starts with the end, and then goes on to the beginning, and concludes with the middle. That is the new method. I heard all about it the other day from a critic who was walking round the pond with a young man. He spoke of the matter at great length, and I am sure he must have been right, for he had blue spectacles and a bald head, and whenever the young man made any remark, he always answered 'Pooh!' But pray go on with your story. I like the Miller immensely. I have all kinds of beautiful sentiments myself, so there is a great sympathy between us."

"Well," said the Linnet, hopping now on one leg and now on the other, "as soon as the winter was over, and the primroses began to open their pale yellow stars, the Miller said to his Wife that he would go down and see little Hans.

" 'Why, what a good heart you have!' cried his Wife. 'You are always thinking of others. And mind you take the big basket with you for the flowers.'

"So the Miller tied the sails of the windmill together with a strong iron chain, and went down the hill with the basket on his arm.

" 'Good morning, little Hans,' said the Miller.

" 'Good morning,' said Hans, leaning on his spade, and smiling from ear to ear.

" 'And how have you been all the winter?' said the Miller.

" 'Well, really,' cried Hans, 'it is very good of you to ask, very good indeed. I am afraid I had rather a hard time of it, but now the spring has come, and I am quite happy, and all my flowers are doing well.'

" 'We often talked of you during the winter, Hans,' said the Miller, 'and wondered how you were getting on.'

" 'That was kind of you,' said Hans. 'I was half afraid you had forgotten me.'

" 'Hans, I am surprised at you,' said the Miller. 'Friendship never forgets. That is the wonderful thing about it, but I am afraid you don't understand the poetry of life. How lovely your primroses are looking, by the by!'

" 'They are certainly very lovely,' said Hans, 'and it is a most lucky thing for me that I have so many. I am going to bring them into the market and sell them to the Burgomaster's daughter, and buy back my wheelbarrow with the money.'

" 'Buy back your wheelbarrow? You don't mean to say you have sold it? What a very stupid thing to do!'

" 'Well, the fact is,' said Hans, 'that I was obliged to. You see the winter was a very bad time for me, and I really had no money at all to buy bread with. So I first sold the silver buttons off my Sunday coat, and then I sold my silver chain, and then I sold my big pipe, and at last I sold my wheelbarrow. But I am going to buy them all back again now.'

" 'Hans,' said the Miller, 'I will give you my wheelbarrow. It is not in very good repair. Indeed, one side is gone, and there is something wrong with the wheel spokes. But in spite of that I will give it to you. I know it is very generous of me, and a great many people would think me extremely foolish for parting with it, but I am not like the rest of the world. I think that generosity is the essence of friendship, and, besides, I have got a new wheelbarrow for myself. Yes, you may set your mind at ease. I will give you my wheelbarrow.'

" 'Well, really, that is generous of you,' said little Hans, and his funny round face glowed all over with pleasure. 'I can easily put it in repair, as I have a plank of wood in the house.'

" 'A plank of wood!' said the Miller. 'Why, that is just what I want for the roof of my barn. There is a very large hole in it, and the corn will all get damp if I don't stop it up. How lucky you mentioned it! It is quite remarkable how one good action always breeds another. I have given you my wheelbarrow, and now you are going to give me your plank. Of course, the wheelbarrow is worth far more than the plank, but true friendship never notices things like that. Pray get it at once, and I will set to work at my barn this very day.'

" 'Certainly,' cried little Hans, and he ran into the shed and dragged the plank out.

" 'It is not a very big plank,' said the Miller, looking at it, 'and I am afraid that after I have mended my barn roof there won't be any left for you to mend the wheelbarrow with. But, of course, that is not my fault. And now, as I have given you my wheelbarrow, I am sure you would like to give me some flowers in return. Here is the basket, and mind you fill it quite full.'

" 'Quite full?' said little Hans, rather sorrowfully, for it was really a very big basket, and he knew that if he filled it he would have no flowers left for the market, and he was very anxious to get his silver buttons back.

" 'Well, really,' answered the Miller, 'as I have given you my wheelbarrow, I don't think that it is much to ask you for a few flowers. I may be wrong, but I should have thought that friendship, true friendship, was quite free from selfishness of any kind.'

" 'My dear friend, my best friend,' cried little Hans, 'you are welcome to all the flowers in my garden. I would much sooner have your good opinion than my silver buttons, any day.' And he ran and plucked all his pretty primroses, and filled the Miller's basket.

" 'Goodbye, little Hans,' said the Miller, as he went up the hill with the plank on his shoulder, and the big basket in his hand.

" 'Goodbye,' said little Hans, and he began to dig away quite merrily, he was so pleased about the wheelbarrow.

"The next day he was nailing up some honeysuckle against the porch, when he heard the Miller's voice calling to him from the road. So he jumped off the ladder, and ran down the garden, and looked over the wall.

"There was the Miller with a large sack of flour on his back.

" 'Dear little Hans,' said the Miller, 'would you mind carrying this sack of flour for me to market?'

" 'Oh, I am so sorry,' said Hans, 'but I am really very busy today. I have got all my creepers to nail up, and all my flowers to water, and all my grass to roll.'

" 'Well, really,' said the Miller. 'I think that, considering that I am going to give you my wheelbarrow, it is rather unfriendly of you to refuse.'

" 'Oh, don't say that,' cried little Hans. 'I wouldn't be unfriendly for the whole world.' And he ran in for his cap, and trudged off with the big sack on his shoulders.

"It was a very hot day, and the road was terribly dusty, and before Hans had reached the sixth milestone he was so tired that he had to sit down and rest. However, he went on bravely, and at last he reached the market. After he had waited there some time, he sold the sack of flour for a very good price, and then he returned home at once, for he was afraid that if he stopped too late he might meet some robbers on the way.

" 'It has certainly been a hard day,' said little Hans to himself as he was going to bed, 'but I am glad I did not refuse the Miller, for he is my best friend, and, besides, he is going to give me his wheelbarrow.'

"Early the next morning the Miller came down to get the money for his sack of flour, but little Hans was so tired that he was still in bed.

" 'Upon my word,' said the Miller, 'you are very lazy. Really, considering that I am going to give you my wheelbarrow, I think you might work harder. Idleness is a great sin, and I certainly don't like any of my friends to be idle or sluggish. You must not mind my speaking quite plainly to you. Of course I should not dream of doing so if I were not your friend. But what is the good of friendship if one cannot say exactly what one means? Anybody can say charming things and try to please and to flatter, but a true friend always says unpleasant things, and does not mind giving pain. Indeed, if he is a really true friend he prefers it, for he knows that then he is doing good.'

" 'I am very sorry,' said little Hans, rubbing his eyes and pulling off his nightcap. 'But I was so tired that I thought I would lie in bed for a little time, and listen to the birds singing. Do you know that I always work better after hearing the birds sing?'

" 'Well, I am glad of that,' said the Miller, clapping little Hans on the back, 'for I want you to come up to the mill as soon as you are dressed, and mend my barn roof for me.'

"Poor little Hans was very anxious to go and work in his garden, for his flowers had not been watered for two days, but he did not like to refuse the Miller, as he was such a good friend to him.

" 'Do you think it would be unfriendly of me if I said I was busy?' he inquired in a shy and timid voice.

" 'Well, really,' answered the Miller, 'I do not think it is much to ask of you, considering that I am going to give you my wheelbarrow. But of course if you refuse I will go and do it myself.'

" 'Oh! on no account,' cried little Hans. And he jumped out of bed, and dressed himself, and went up to the barn.

"He worked there all day long, till sunset, and at sunset the Miller came to see how he was getting on.

" 'Have you mended the hole in the roof yet, little Hans?' cried the Miller in a cheery voice.

" 'It is quite mended,' answered little Hans, coming down the ladder.

" 'Ah!' said the Miller, 'there is no work so delightful as the work one does for others.'

" 'It is certainly a great privilege to hear you talk,' answered little Hans, sitting down and wiping his forehead. 'A very great privilege. But I am afraid I shall never have such beautiful ideas as you have.'

" 'Oh! they will come to you,' said the Miller. 'But you must take more pains. At present you have only the practice of friendship. Someday you will have the theory also.'

" 'Do you really think I shall?' asked little Hans.

" 'I have no doubt of it,' answered the Miller, 'but now that you have mended the roof, you had better go home and rest, for I want you to drive my sheep to the mountain tomorrow.'

"Poor little Hans was afraid to say anything to this, and early the next morning the Miller brought his sheep round to the cottage, and Hans started off with them to the mountain. It took him the whole day to get there and back, and when he returned he was so tired that he went off to sleep in his chair, and did not wake up till it was broad daylight.

" 'What a delightful time I shall have in my garden,' he said, and he went to work at once.

"But somehow he was never able to look after his flowers at all, for his friend the Miller was always coming round and sending him off on long errands, or getting him to help at the mill. Little Hans was very much distressed at times, as he was afraid his flowers would think he had forgotten them, but he consoled himself by the reflection that the Miller was his best friend. 'Besides,' he used to say, 'he is going to give me his wheelbarrow, and that is an act of pure generosity.'

"So little Hans worked away for the Miller, and the Miller said all kinds of beautiful things about friendship, which Hans took down in a notebook, and used to read over at night, for he was a very good scholar.

"Now it happened that one evening little Hans was sitting by his fireside when a loud rap came at the door. It was a very wild night, and the wind was blowing and roaring round the house so terribly that at first he thought it was merely the storm. But a second rap came, and then a third, louder than either of the others.

" 'It is some poor traveler,' said little Hans to himself, and he ran to the door.

"There stood the Miller with a lantern in one hand and a big stick in the other.

" 'Dear little Hans,' cried the Miller. 'I am in great trouble. My little boy has fallen off a ladder and hurt himself, and I am going for the Doctor. But he lives so far away, and it is such a bad night, that it has just occurred to me that it would be much better if you went instead of me. You know I am going to give you my wheelbarrow, and so it is only fair that you should do something for me in return.'

" 'Certainly,' cried little Hans. 'I take it quite as a compliment your coming to me, and I will start off at once. But you must lend me your lantern, as the night is so dark that I am afraid I might fall into the ditch.'

" 'I am very sorry,' answered the Miller. 'But it is my new lantern, and it would be a great loss to me if anything happened to it.'

" 'Well, never mind, I will do without it,' cried little Hans, and he took down his great fur coat, and his warm scarlet cap, and tied a muffler round his throat, and started off.

"What a dreadful storm it was! The night was so black that little Hans could hardly see, and the wind was so strong that he could scarcely stand. However, he was very courageous, and after he had been walking about three hours, he arrived at the Doctor's house, and knocked at the door.

" 'Who is there?' cried the Doctor, putting his head out of his bedroom window.

" 'Little Hans, Doctor.'

" 'What do you want, little Hans?'

" 'The Miller's son has fallen from a ladder, and has hurt himself, and the Miller wants you to come at once.'

" 'All right!' said the Doctor. And he ordered his horse, and his big boots, and his lantern, and came downstairs, and rode off in the direction of the Miller's house, little Hans trudging behind him.

"But the storm grew worse and worse, and the rain fell in torrents, and little Hans could not see where he was going, or keep up with the horse. At last he lost his way, and wandered off on the moor, which was a very dangerous place, as it was full of deep holes, and there poor little Hans was drowned. His body was found the next day by some goatherds, floating in a great pool of water, and was brought back by them to the cottage.

"Everybody went to little Hans's funeral, as he was so popular, and the Miller was the chief mourner.

" 'As I was his best friend,' said the Miller, 'it is only fair that I should have the best place. So he walked at the head of the procession in a long black cloak, and every now and then he wiped his eyes with a big pocket-handkerchief.

" 'Little Hans is certainly a great loss to everyone,' said the Blacksmith, when the funeral was over, and they were all seated comfortably in the inn, drinking spiced wine and eating sweet cakes.

" 'A great loss to me at any rate,' answered the Miller. 'Why, I had as good as given him my wheelbarrow, and now I really don't know what to do with it. It is very much in my way at home, and it is in such bad repair that I could not get anything for it if I sold it. I will certainly take care not to give away anything again. One always suffers for being generous.' "

"Well?" said the Water Rat, after a long pause.

"Well, that is the end," said the Linnet.

"But what became of the Miller?" asked the Water Rat.

"Oh! I really don't know," replied the Linnet. "And I am sure that I don't care."

"It is quite evident then that you have no sympathy in your nature," said the Water Rat.

"I am afraid you don't quite see the moral of the story," remarked the Linnet.

"The what?" screamed the Water Rat.

"The moral."

"Do you mean to say that the story has a moral?"

"Certainly," said the Linnet.

"Well, really," said the Water Rat, in a very angry manner, "I think you should have told me that before you began. If you had done so, I certainly would not have listened to you. In fact, I should have said 'Pooh,' like the critic. However, I can say it now." So he shouted out "Pooh" at the top of his voice, gave a whisk with his tail, and went back into his hole.

"And how do you like the Water Rat?" asked the Duck, who came paddling up some minutes afterward. "He has a great many good points, but for my own part I have a mother's feelings, and I can never look at a confirmed bachelor without the tears coming into my eyes."

"I am rather afraid that I have annoyed him," answered the Linnet. "The fact is, that I told him a story with a moral."

"Ah! that is always a very dangerous thing to do," said the Duck.

And I quite agree with her.

Yudisthira   at   Heaven's   Gate

This story is from the *Mahabharata,* which with the *Ramayana* is
one of the two great epic poems of India. Here loyalty is literally
the test to gain entrance to heaven.

Good King Yudisthira had ruled over the Pandava people for
many years and had led them in a successful, but very long war
against giant forces of evil. At the end of his labors, Yudisthira felt
that he had had enough years on earth and it was time to go on to
the kingdom of the Immortals. When all his plans were made, he set
out for the high Mount Meru to go from there to the Celestial
City. His beautiful wife, Drapaudi, went with him and also his four
brothers. Very soon, they were joined by a dog which followed
quietly behind him.

But the journey to the mountain was a long and sorrowful one.
Yudisthira's four brothers died one by one along the way, and after
that his wife, the beautiful Drapaudi. The King was all alone then,
except for the dog, which continued to follow him faithfully up and
up the steep, long road to the Celestial City.

At last the two, weak and exhausted, stopped before the
gates of Heaven. Yudisthira bowed humbly there as he asked to
be admitted.

Sky and earth were filled with a loud noise as the God Indra,
God of a Thousand Eyes, arrived to meet and welcome the King to
Paradise. But Yudisthira was not quite ready.

"Without my brothers and my beloved wife, my innocent Drapaudi, I do not wish to enter Heaven, O Lord of all the deities," he
said.

"Have no fear," Indra answered. "You shall meet them all in
Heaven. They came before you and are already there!"

But Yudisthira had yet another request to make.

"This dog has come all the way with me. He is devoted to me.
Surely for his faithfulness I cannot leave him outside! And besides,
my heart is full of love for him!"

Indra shook his great head and the earth quaked.

"You yourself may have immortality," he said, "and riches and
success and all the joys of Heaven. You have won these by making
this hard journey. But you cannot bring a dog into Heaven. Cast off
the dog, Yudisthira! It is no sin!"

"But where would he go?" demanded the king. "And who would go with him? He has given up all the pleasures of earth to be my companion. I cannot desert him now."

The God was irritated at this.

"You must be pure to enter Paradise," he said firmly. "Just to *touch* a dog will take away all the merits of prayer. Consider what you are doing, Yudisthira. Let the dog go!"

But Yudisthira insisted. "O God of a Thousand Eyes, it is difficult for a person who has always tried to be righteous to do something that he knows is *un*righteous—even in order to get into Heaven. I do not wish immortality if it means casting off one that is devoted to me."

Indra urged him once more.

"You left on the road behind you your four brothers and your wife. Why can't you also leave the dog?"

But Yudisthira said, "I abandoned those only because they had died already and I could no longer help them nor bring them back to life. As long as they lived I did not leave them."

"You are willing to abandon Heaven, then, for this dog's sake?" the God asked him.

"Great God of all Gods," Yudisthira replied, "I have steadily kept this vow—that I will never desert one that is frightened and seeks my protection, one that is afflicted and destitute, or one that is too weak to protect himself and desires to live. Now I add a fourth. I have promised never to forsake one that is devoted to me. I will not abandon my friend."

Yudisthira reached down to touch the dog and was about to turn sadly away from Heaven when suddenly before his very eyes a wonder happened. The faithful dog was changed into Dharma, the God of Righteousness and Justice.

Indra said, "You are a good man, King Yudisthira. You have shown faithfulness to the faithful and compassion for all creatures. You have done this by renouncing the very Gods themselves instead of renouncing this humble dog that was your companion. You shall be honored in heaven, O King Yudisthira, for there is no act which is valued more highly and rewarded more richly than compassion for the humble."

So Yudisthira entered the Celestial City with the God of Righteousness beside him. He was reunited there with his brothers and his beloved wife to enjoy eternal happiness.

Thunder Falls

Retold by Allan Macfarlan

This story comes from the Kickapoo Indians, a Midwestern tribe once noted for their frequent wanderings; their name comes from a word meaning "he who moves about, standing now here, now there."

The blanket of night had wrapped the Kickapoo village in darkness. The people were gathered around the story-fire, awaiting the tale which the storyteller would tell. The listeners knew that the tale would not be of braves on the war trail or warriors who risked their lives on raids into the country of their enemies. And yet, the story which they were about to hear was one of high courage. It was of two brave women who were still honored in song and dance, because of their great courage and their noble sacrifice made for their tribe. This is the story that the people heard.

A band of our men were hunting, when the green earth had come from beneath the snow, and rivers were fat and fast. Women were with the men, to help skin the animals taken in the chase, and to strip and dry the meat. For three suns the party had hunted, and deer had fallen to their hunting arrows.

As they traveled in country distant from our territory, there was always danger of attack by enemies. Braves kept watch always, but they did not watch well enough. One day, the chief said it would be a good thing to return to the tribe, and the party made ready to go back when the sun came. Some of the braves and women did not see the sun again. A big war party of Shawnee surrounded and attacked the camp, when night was leaving to let morning come.

The Kickapoo who were not killed or badly wounded escaped down into the gorges. They had hunted there and found a great cave, beneath the thundering falls of a mighty river. The chief had decided that they would hide there, if they saw a large war party of the enemy, so all of the Kickapoo knew the hiding place.

The savage Shawnee killed the wounded, and took two of our women back to their camp, as prisoners. The women were young and would be made to work. The camp of the Shawnee was far above the place where they had attacked our party. Their lodges were on the banks of the wide, fast-flowing river.

For six suns after the attack, the Shawnee warriors searched for our people who had escaped the raid. Sentries were placed at distant points, so that the Kickapoo could not escape without being seen. The big war party of the Shawnee would be told of their movements. The enemy searched well, but our people hid better and were not discovered. Our chief did not let his party leave the great cavern, nor did they need to, for they had dried meat and water in plenty.

After some suns had passed, the people begged the chief to let them leave the shelter of the big cave beneath the falls. They felt safe there, but the terrible noise of the falls hurt their ears, as it roared like a curtain of thunder before the cavern. Their minds were afraid too, for they feared that spirits of evil dwelt in the dark, rocky gorges which surrounded them.

The chief was brave, but he knew how his band felt. He too would be happy to leave the great roaring and rumbling far behind him, even if, in escaping, more of his band would fall to the arrows of the Shawnee. "Tomorrow, the day of the seventh sun since the attack, will be the last that we remain here," he told his band. "When darkness comes, we will try to escape from the enemy into our own territory. Be ready!"

Our chief knew that the chances of reaching safety were few, as the Shawnee were many and must be angry that any of our people had escaped the raid. "Their anger must be very great," the Kickapoo chief thought, "because though they could follow the trails in the forest, their best trailers could not see footprints on the rocky ground which formed the river gorges."

The medicine man of the Shawnee went to their chief on the morning of the seventh sun, and told him of a dream which he had had. His totem bird, the red-tailed hawk, had come to him in a dream and flown around and around him in circles, giving shrill cries and tempting him to follow it. The medicine man could not refuse to follow his totem bird, so his spirit followed it, as it flew swiftly before him, until the hawk reached a clearing in the forest. Here, in the dream, the medicine man saw a circle of Shadow People.

"Can I follow the Shadow People to where our enemies are hidden?" the medicine man asked the hawk. "Who among them knows where the band is hiding?"

The hawk flew straight to the two women who were the prisoners of the Shawnee and circled the head of each.

"These women must know," declared the medicine man, as he told his chief of the dream. "My hawk totem never leads me on a false trail."

The Shawnee chief had great faith in the medicine man and his totem bird; so he called a council of his warriors. He told them of the dream and had the two captive women brought before him. When questioned, they declared that they did not know where the band to which they belonged was hidden.

"They speak with a crooked tongue," shouted the medicine man, "but torture will make it straight."

The women were tortured, and under the bite of blazing twigs held to their wrists, they cried out that they would reveal the hiding place of their band. For a moment, they spoke softly together in their own dialect and then, by signs, showed that they were ready to lead the Shawnee war party to the hiding place.

When the Shawnee were armed, and about to follow them, the two women pointed to the river, instead of leading the way into the forest. By signs, they showed that our people were far away and could be reached quicker by the Shawnees if they went by canoe. When the chief pointed toward the forest and his braves pushed the women in that direction, they showed by sign talk that they could not lead the Shawnees by land. Only by water did they know the way to the hidden Kickapoo band.

The chief believed the women, and they were taken to the big canoes that lay on the riverbank. With hands and sounds, the women told that close to the falls there was a little branch of the main river, which they must follow to reach the Kickapoo. The chief ordered the women into the leading canoe. He too sat in it, with his medicine man and six of his best warriors. The rest of the party followed close behind, in many canoes. Paddles flashed and the canoes went swift as a fish downstream.

After paddling far, the chief asked the women if they were not yet near the hiding place of his enemies. The women sign-talked that the place was near, and again the paddles rose and fell. The braves did not have to paddle so hard now, because the current was becoming swifter and stronger, as the canoes sped along. Quicker and quicker the canoes traveled. From the distance came the thunder of the falls. Closer and closer came the earth-shaking roar.

The chief was brave, but even he feared the mighty force of the swift-rushing waters. He was directly behind the two captive women, who sat in the bow. He touched them on the shoulders, and they turned to him at once. The chief ceased to fear when he saw that both women were smiling. The elder of the two, with a wave of her arm toward the south bank, showed that in a moment they would reach the fork of the river, where the paddlers could swing the canoes from the rushing current into the calm water of the smaller stream.

Faster, ever faster, the canoes now dashed through the foaming torrent. Narrower grew the rushing river as it roared between solid walls of rock. No time to try to turn the canoes!

Too late, the chief and warriors knew that they had been tricked. The bravest had but time to sing a few notes of their death songs before the raging torrent swept the shattered canoes over the crest of the mighty waterfall. Proudly leading the band of enemy warriors to death on the jagged rocks below were the two brave women of the Kickapoo.

My story is done, but that of the two who saved our band of warriors from death will go on as long as grass grows and water runs.

How Queen Esther Saved Her People

Retold by Walter Russell Bowie

The events of the book of Esther in the Bible are reported to have occurred during the reign of the Persian king Ahasuerus, whom biblical scholars usually identify with Xerxes (c. 519–465 B.C.). Esther and her kinsman Mordecai were members of the Jewish population remaining in the East after many other Jews had returned to Jerusalem from the Babylonian exile. The story is one of a young queen who must face danger alone to save her people.

The story of the book of Esther begins with one of the kings of Persia, who is called Ahasuerus. According to the story, Ahasuerus decided one day to have a great feast in the garden of his palace. He invited all the chief men of the kingdom to come. The garden court was a beautiful place within the palace walls. It had marble pillars and a pavement of red, blue, white, and black marble. There were hangings of white and green and blue, fastened on silver rings. The goblets in which the wine was served were gold.

The feasting went on for seven days. By that time everyone, including the king, had eaten and drunk a great deal too much. The queen, whose name was Vashti, was very beautiful. Suddenly the king had a notion that he would show her off to his guests. She was in her rooms with her maids. The king sent seven of his servants to tell the queen to come to the feast.

Vashti was ashamed and indignant that the king had sent her such a message. She had no intention of appearing before a large company of half-drunken men. She told the servants to tell the king that she would not come.

When the king heard that, he was furious. He had boasted of the queen's beauty. Now he would seem foolish in the sight of his guests. He asked some of them what they thought he ought to do. These men did not have much respect for women. They began to think that if their wives heard that the queen had disobeyed the king, they would disobey their husbands. The men told the king that he ought to get rid of Vashti and find a new queen.

That was exactly what Ahasuerus decided to do. He sent Vashti away. Then came the question of choosing a new queen. The king's servants looked everywhere in the kingdom, and brought to the palace the most beautiful maidens they could find. Among them was a maiden from a Jewish family, whose name was Esther. She was young and innocent and lovely, and could never have dreamed that she might become the queen of Persia. When the king saw Esther, he preferred her to everyone else, and he made her his wife. But he did not know that she had come from among the Jews.

Now Esther had a cousin named Mordecai. Mordecai, who was older than Esther, had brought her up like a daughter, because her own father was dead. Esther trusted him in everything, and whatever he advised her to do, she did. Mordecai told her not to tell the king that she was a Jew.

Mordecai came often to the palace, to speak with Esther. Often he would sit in the gate where people went in and out and where they stood together talking. One day he saw two men who were plainly very angry. They talked excitedly, and Mordecai overheard what they were saying. They were plotting together to kill the king.

Mordecai sent word of that to Esther, and Esther warned the king. The king had the two men arrested and put to death. By his warning, Mordecai had saved the king's life. The king should have been very grateful, but he was more interested in himself than in anyone else. Although he had been told that it was Mordecai who had brought the warning, he soon forgot it.

Meanwhile there was another man who was becoming the king's favorite. His name was Haman. The king's servants had to bow to Haman whenever he passed by. But Mordecai would not bow to Haman or give any sign that he noticed him at all. Every day Mordecai was warned that he would find himself in trouble if he did not do as the king's servants did, but Mordecai paid no attention. After a while someone asked Haman if he had noticed that Mordecai, the Jew, never bowed to him when he went by. The very idea made Haman angry, for he was proud and jealous. To hear that anybody had dared not show respect to him was more than he would stand. He began to consider what would be the worst thing he would do to Mordecai. He thought about it for some time. Finally he decided that there was something worse than having Mordecai punished alone. Since Mordecai was a Jew, Haman would make all the Jewish people suffer.

So one day Haman went to the king and poured into his ears all the ugly tales he could think of about the Jews. He reminded Ahasuerus that the Jews were scattered all through the kingdom. He said there were entirely too many of them for the kingdom's good. Had the king stopped to remember that the Jews were different from the people of Persia, and had different laws? He suggested getting rid of these Jewish people who might turn out to be enemies of Persia. And Haman said that he would put ten thousand talents of silver, a huge amount of money, into the king's treasury if the king would sign an order that all the Jews should be destroyed.

Ahasuerus not only had a quick temper but he was stupid, too. He believed everything that Haman told him. He flew into a rage against the Jews and told Haman to have them killed.

Haman heard that with wicked pleasure. He lost no time in making sure that what he had planned should happen. He sent out orders, in the king's name and with the king's seal, to the governors of all the parts of the kingdom. These orders commanded that on a certain day every Jewish person—man, woman, and child—should be put to death. Then Haman went in and sat down to drink wine with the king, and to rejoice.

Out in the city the people who had begun to hear the news were shocked and troubled. Before long the news reached Mordecai. He dressed himself in rough sackcloth and poured ashes on his head as a sign of distress. Then he went to the gate of the palace to weep and mourn.

One of the palace maids told Esther of this. Esther was greatly troubled. She sent to Mordecai to beg him to take off his sackcloth, and to let her know quickly what was wrong. Mordecai told the messenger the terrible truth—that all the Jews in the kingdom were in danger of death. Only she might save them by going to the king and begging him to change the order.

Esther seemed to be faced with more than a woman could bear. She was the queen, but she knew only too well the cruel laws of the Persian court. She knew that no one, least of all a woman, might dare to cross the king. Esther sent the messenger back to Mordecai. Did he not know that if anyone went to the king uninvited, he might be put to death? This would certainly happen unless the king was in good humor and held out his golden scepter as a sign of permission to come near. Esther had no reason to think that the king would treat her so kindly. It had been many days since he had sent for her and since she had seen him.

Mordecai sent back word that there was only one hope for the Jews in Persia; only one person could do anything, and that person was Esther. She must not think, Mordecai added, that if the king's order for the killing of Jews was carried out she would escape. It would be found out that she too was a Jew, and she would be treated like the rest. But she alone might be able to do what everyone else put together could not do. Perhaps this was her chance to show a kind of courage that few would dare to show. "Who knows," said Mordecai, "but that you have come to the kingdom for such a time as this?"

When Esther received Mordecai's message, all her heart rose bravely to answer. So much depended on her that she could not be timid anymore. She sent word back to Mordecai that he should gather the Jews together to fast and pray. She and her maids in the palace would do the same. Then she would go to the king and try to persuade him. "And if I perish," she said, "I perish."

The moment came when she must take the great and final risk. Ahasuerus, in all his pomp and power, was sitting on his royal throne. Esther dressed herself in her queenliest robes. She went to the door of the throne room. The door was opened, and she stood there, beautiful and silent, waiting, looking at the king. If he were angry, that would be the end.

But the king stretched out the golden scepter toward her. "Queen Esther!" he said. "What will you have? What is your request? It shall be given you, even if it be half of the kingdom!"

So the king was not angry! He was fond of her, and perhaps he would listen to her more than he had listened to the wicked Haman. But she would not tell him her real wish now. Instead, she said, "If it seems good to the king, will he, and Haman also, come to a banquet which I have made ready today?"

The king said that he would come, and that Haman should come, too.

When they were seated at the table, the king told Esther again that he would give her anything she wanted, no matter what it might be. But she begged him not to have her tell him then what she wanted. Would he wait until tomorrow? And would he and Haman come to another banquet the next day? Yes, the king said, they would come.

Haman went out, proud and pleased. He had been invited to a banquet alone with the king and queen, and he was invited again tomorrow! But as he left the palace, there, sitting at the gate, was Mordecai. Mordecai did not stand up or bow, or even notice him. That spoiled everything. Haman snapped his lips shut and walked by Mordecai without a word. When he reached home he called his wife and some of his friends, and broke into a storm of complaining. He told them all of the honors the king had given him, and that anybody could see how great a man he was, but that this Mordecai still despised him.

Haman's wife and friends were as bad-tempered as Haman. Why did he not go at once and ask the king's permission to hang Mordecai? "Ask the king to make a gallows fifty cubits high," they said. That seemed to Haman a good idea. Without asking the king, he had the gallows built to hang Mordecai on.

Then things began to happen in a way Haman had not expected. That night the king could not sleep. He tossed about impatiently. Finally he decided he would read awhile, and he told one of his servants to bring him a book. The book the servant happened to bring was a history of the events of the king's court during the last few years. The king commanded that the book be read aloud to him. As he listened, he heard about the two men who had plotted to kill him, and how Mordecai had overheard them and had given warning.

Suddenly the king remembered that he had never rewarded Mordecai for this. It annoyed him to think that he had forgotten about it all this time. He asked his servants, "What about this Mordecai? What has been done for him?"

They told him, "Nothing."

"Who is in the court right now?" the king asked.

It happened that at just that moment Haman had come to the palace to tell the king about the gallows he had had built for Mordecai. The servants told the king that Haman was outside.

"Let him come in," said the king.

So Haman came in. The king's mind was full of what he had been hearing. "Haman," he asked, "what ought to be done to a man whom the king wants very much to honor?"

He means me! thought Haman. He tried not to look excited.

"What ought to be done for a man whom the king wants very much to honor?" Haman repeated. "Let royal robes be brought like those which the king wears, and the king's horse, too, and the king's own crown. Let these be put in charge of one of the noblest of the princes. Let the prince put the royal robes on the man the king has chosen to honor. Then the prince shall lead this man, on horseback, through the city and proclaim to the people that he is the man whom the king delights to honor."

"Good!" said the king. "Now hurry and do exactly as you have said. Take one of my royal robes and have the king's horse brought. Find Mordecai the Jew and lead him through the city."

If the king had struck Haman with a hammer between the eyes, Haman could not have been more stunned. But there was no escape from what the king had commanded, and Haman did not dare even to look surprised. In a black and bitter fury he had to go out and give Mordecai the honors he had supposed were meant for him. He held the bridle of the king's horse, with Mordecai riding on it, dressed in a royal robe. And he had to cry to the people who crowded the streets, "This is the man whom the king delights to honor!"

But that was not all. The banquet with the king and queen was still to come.

When the three of them were sitting there together, Ahasuerus asked Esther again what she wanted him to do for her. This time she really told him. She reminded him of the order that had gone out in his name that all the Jews in the kingdom should be killed. Then she told him that she herself belonged to the Jewish people. She pleaded that he would take back that dreadful order and spare them. "If I have found favor in your sight," she said, "grant me this petition!"

When the king looked at Esther, so lovely and so distressed, he was angry to think that he had been tricked by someone, he had almost forgotten who, into giving that order. "Who has done this?" he demanded. "Where is he?"

Then Esther the queen looked straight at Haman. "It is this wicked Haman," she said.

The king was so full of rage that he got up and strode out into the garden. Haman was terrified, and he fell down on the couch where the queen was sitting. In came the king again at that moment, and he thought Haman was trying to hurt the queen. "What!" he cried. "Will he attack the queen here in my own palace?" He called his servants, and they took Haman out.

One of the king's officers came and asked the king if he knew that Haman had built a gallows near his own house, a gallows nearly a hundred feet high. No, the king had not known it, but now that he knew, he knew also what should be done with it. "Take Haman and hang him on it," he commanded. So on the very gallows which he had intended for Mordecai, Haman himself was hanged.

That is the story of the book of Esther. And from that day the Jewish people, who had suffered a great deal, were glad to remember the truthful Mordecai, and the young queen who, all alone, carried through a dangerous duty.

Judas and Peter

Here, from the Gospel according to Matthew, is one of our greatest stories of betrayal. We are horrified most, of course, by what Judas Iscariot did for thirty pieces of silver. At the same time, though, we are stunned in a completely different way by Peter's failure. Despite his vow at the Mount of Olives ("I will not deny thee"), Peter in fear and misery commits a much more forgivable, more human kind of betrayal. Judas Iscariot's treachery seems beyond comprehension, while Peter's denial is on a scale of which we are all capable.

Then one of the twelve, called Judas Iscariot, went unto the chief priests,

And said unto them, What will ye give me, and I will deliver him unto you? And they covenanted with him for thirty pieces of silver.

And from that time he sought opportunity to betray him.

Now the first day of the feast of Unleavened Bread the disciples came to Jesus, saying unto him, Where wilt thou that we prepare for thee to eat the Passover?

And he said, Go into the city to such a man, and say unto him, The Master saith, My time is at hand; I will keep the Passover at thy house with my disciples.

And the disciples did as Jesus had appointed them; and they made ready the Passover.

Now when the even was come, he sat down with the twelve.

And as they did eat, he said, Verily I say unto you, that one of you shall betray me.

And they were exceeding sorrowful, and began every one of them to say unto him, Lord, is it I?

And he answered and said, He that dippeth his hand with me in the dish, the same shall betray me.

The Son of Man goeth as it is written of him: but woe unto that man by whom the Son of Man is betrayed! it had been good for that man if he had not been born.

Then Judas, which betrayed him, answered and said, Master, is it I? He said unto him, Thou hast said.

And as they were eating, Jesus took bread, and blessed it, and brake it, and gave it to the disciples, and said, Take, eat; this is my body.

And he took the cup, and gave thanks, and gave it to them, saying, Drink ye all of it;

For this is my blood of the new testament, which is shed for many for the remission of sins.

But I say unto you, I will not drink henceforth of this fruit of the vine, until that day when I drink it new with you in my Father's kingdom.

And when they had sung a hymn, they went out into the Mount of Olives.

Then saith Jesus unto them, All ye shall be offended because of me this night: for it is written, I will smite the shepherd, and the sheep of the flock shall be scattered abroad.

But after I am risen again, I will go before you into Galilee.

Peter answered and said unto him, Though all men shall be offended because of thee, yet will I never be offended.

Jesus said unto him, Verily I say unto thee, That this night, before the cock crow, thou shalt deny me thrice.

Peter said unto him, Though I should die with thee, yet will I not deny thee. Likewise also said all the disciples.

Then cometh Jesus with them unto a place called Gethsemane, and saith unto the disciples, Sit ye here, while I go and pray yonder.

And he took with him Peter and the two sons of Zebedee, and began to be sorrowful and very heavy.

Then saith he unto them, My soul is exceeding sorrowful, even unto death: tarry ye here, and watch with me.

And he went a little further, and fell on his face, and prayed, saying, O my Father, if it be possible, let this cup pass from me: nevertheless, not as I will, but as thou wilt.

And he cometh unto the disciples, and findeth them asleep, and saith unto Peter, What, could ye not watch with me one hour?

Watch and pray, that ye enter not into temptation: the spirit indeed is willing, but the flesh is weak.

He went away again the second time, and prayed, saying, O my Father, if this cup may not pass away from me, except I drink it, thy will be done.

And he came and found them asleep again: for their eyes were heavy.

And he left them, and went away again, and prayed the third time, saying the same words.

Then cometh he to his disciples, and saith unto them, Sleep on now, and take your rest: behold, the hour is at hand, and the Son of Man is betrayed into the hands of sinners.

Rise, let us be going: behold, he is at hand that doth betray me.

And while he yet spake, lo, Judas, one of the twelve, came, and with him a great multitude with swords and staves, from the chief priests and elders of the people.

Now he that betrayed him gave them a sign, saying, Whomsoever I shall kiss, that same is he; hold him fast.

And forthwith he came to Jesus, and said, Hail, Master; and kissed him.

And Jesus said unto him, Friend, wherefore art thou come? Then came they, and laid hands on Jesus, and took him.

And, behold, one of them which were with Jesus stretched out his hand, and drew his sword, and struck a servant of the high priest, and smote off his ear.

Then said Jesus unto him, Put up again thy sword into his place: for all they that take the sword shall perish with the sword.

Thinkest thou that I cannot now pray to my Father, and he shall presently give me more than twelve legions of angels?

But how then shall the Scriptures be fulfilled, that thus it must be?

In that same hour said Jesus to the multitudes, Are ye come out as against a thief with swords and staves for to take me? I sat daily with you teaching in the temple, and ye laid no hold on me.

But all this was done, that the Scriptures of the prophets might be fulfilled. Then all the disciples forsook him, and fled.

And they that had laid hold on Jesus led him away to Caiaphas the high priest, where the scribes and the elders were assembled.

But Peter followed him afar off unto the high priest's palace, and went in, and sat with the servants, to see the end.

Now the chief priests, and elders, and all the council, sought false witness against Jesus, to put him to death;

But found none: yea, though many false witnesses came, yet found they none. At the last came two false witnesses,

And said, This fellow said, I am able to destroy the temple of God, and to build it in three days.

And the high priest arose, and said unto him, Answerest thou nothing? What is it which these witness against thee?

But Jesus held his peace. And the high priest answered and said unto him, I adjure thee by the living God, that thou tell us whether thou be the Christ, the Son of God.

Jesus saith unto him, Thou hast said: nevertheless I say unto you, Hereafter shall ye see the Son of Man sitting on the right hand of power, and coming in the clouds of heaven.

Then the high priest rent his clothes, saying, He hath spoken blasphemy; what further need have we of witnesses? Behold, now ye have heard his blasphemy.

What think ye? They answered and said, He is guilty of death.

Then did they spit in his face, and buffeted him; and others smote him with the palms of their hands,

Saying, Prophesy unto us, thou Christ, Who is he that smote thee?

Now Peter sat without in the palace: and a damsel came unto him, saying, Thou also wast with Jesus of Galilee.

But he denied before them all, saying, I know not what thou sayest.

And when he was gone out into the porch, another maid saw him, and said unto them that were there, This fellow was also with Jesus of Nazareth.

And again he denied with an oath, I do not know the man.

And after a while came unto him they that stood by, and said to Peter, Surely thou also art one of them; for thy speech bewrayeth thee.

Then began he to curse and to swear, saying, I know not the man. And immediately the cock crew.

And Peter remembered the word of Jesus, which said unto him, Before the cock crow, thou shalt deny me thrice. And he went out, and wept bitterly.

When the morning was come, all the chief priests and elders of the people took counsel against Jesus to put him to death:

And when they had bound him, they led him away, and delivered him to Pontius Pilate the governor.

Then Judas, which had betrayed him, when he saw that he was condemned, repented himself, and brought again the thirty pieces of silver to the chief priests and elders,

Saying, I have sinned in that I have betrayed the innocent blood. And they said, What is that to us? See thou to that.

And he cast down the pieces of silver in the temple, and departed, and went and hanged himself.

Castor and Pollux

The Athenian dramatist Menander said that to live is not to live for one's self alone. The story of Castor and Pollux illuminates this grander meaning of the word brotherhood.

On winter nights the constellation Gemini lies high overhead, and its two principal stars, Castor and Pollux, are among the brightest in the heavens. We know them as the Twins, but old myths from the days of Greek heroes say they were really half-brothers. Leda was the mother of both, while Castor's father was Tyndareus, the king of Sparta, and Pollux's father was Zeus, king of the gods. So the span of Castor's life was fixed, but Pollux was immortal.

By all accounts, the brothers were never apart, so great was their devotion to each other, and they shared many adventures. They sailed with Jason and the Argonauts on the quest for the Golden Fleece, and they rescued their sister Helen when she was kidnapped by Theseus, the same beautiful Helen whose face later "launched a thousand ships" and brought about the Trojan War. They also took part in the famous Calydonian hunt, in which many of Greece's bravest heroes gathered to rid the land of a monstrous boar.

The most famous legend about Castor and Pollux is about how they ended their earthly lives. The Greek poet Pindar tells us that Castor was wounded in battle. His brother rushed to his side, only to find him almost dead, gasping out his life with short-drawn breath. Pollux did everything he could to save him, but there was no hope.

"Oh father Zeus," Pollux cried, "take my life instead of my brother's! Or if not that, let me die also! Without him, I will know nothing but grief for the rest of my days."

As he spoke, Zeus approached and answered:

"You are my son, Pollux, and therefore enjoy eternal life. Your brother was born of mortal seed, and destined like all humans to taste death. But I will give you a choice. You may come to Olympus, as is your right, and dwell with Athena and Ares and the rest of the gods. Or, if you wish to share your immortality with your brother, then half the time you must spend beneath the earth, and the other half in the golden home of heaven."

Pollux did not for an instant waver, but gave up his life in Olympus, and chose to share light and darkness forever with his brother. So Zeus unclosed Castor's eyes and restored his breath. And even now we see them as the constellation Gemini. They spend half their time fixed in the starry heavens, and the other half sunk beneath the horizon.

Penelope's Web

Adapted from James Baldwin

Penelope's long wait for her husband's return from the Trojan
War may be our ultimate tale of fidelity. The Ithacan queen's
patience, resourcefulness, constancy, and love make her one of
Greek mythology's most memorable characters. The story
comes from Homer's *Odyssey*. In this retelling, Odysseus is called
by his Latin name, Ulysses.

Of all the heroes who fought against Troy, the wisest and
shrewdest was Ulysses, king of Ithaca. Yet, he went unwillingly to
war. He longed to stay at home with his wife, Penelope, and their
baby boy, Telemachus. But the princes of Greece demanded that he
help them, and at last he consented.

"Go, Ulysses," said Penelope, "and I will keep your home and
kingdom safe until you return."

"Do your duty, Ulysses," said his old father, Laertes. "Go, and
may wise Athena speed your coming back."

And so, bidding farewell to Ithaca and all he held dear, he sailed
away to the Trojan War.

Ten long years passed, and then news reached Ithaca that the
weary siege of Troy was ended, the city lay in ashes, and the Greek
kings were returning to their native lands. One by one, all the heroes
reached their homes, but of Ulysses and his companions there came
no word. Every day, Penelope and young Telemachus and feeble
old Laertes stood by the shore and gazed with aching eyes far over
the waves. But no sign of sail or glinting oars could they discern.
Months passed by, and then years, and still no word.

"His ships are wrecked, and he lies at the bottom of the sea,"
sighed old Laertes, and after that he shut himself up in his narrow
room and went no more to the shore.

But Penelope still hoped and hoped. "He is not dead," she said.
"And until he comes home, I will hold this fair kingdom for him."

Every day his seat was placed for him at the table. His coat was
hung by his chair, his chamber was dusted, and his great bow that
hung in the hall was polished.

Ten more years passed with constant watching. Telemachus became a tall, gentle-mannered young man. And throughout all Greece, men began to talk of nothing but Penelope's great nobility and beauty.

"How foolish of her," the Greek princes and chiefs said, "to be forever looking for Ulysses. Everyone knows he is dead. She ought to marry one of us now."

So one after another, the chiefs and princes who were looking for wives sailed to Ithaca, hoping to win Penelope's love. They were haughty and overbearing fellows, glorying in their own importance and wealth. Straight to the palace they went, not waiting for an invitation, for they knew they would be treated as honored guests, whether they were welcome or not.

"Come now, Penelope," they said, "we all know Ulysses is dead. We have come as suitors for your hand, and you dare not turn us away. Choose one of us, and the rest will depart."

But Penelope answered sadly, "Princes and heroes, this cannot be. I am quite sure Ulysses lives, and I must hold his kingdom for him till he returns."

"Return he never will," said the suitors. "Make your choice now."

"Give me a month longer to wait for him," she pleaded. "In my loom I have a half-finished web of soft linen. I am weaving it for the shroud of our father, Laertes, who is very old and cannot live much longer. If Ulysses fails to return by the time this web is finished, then I will choose, though unwillingly."

The suitors agreed, and made themselves at home in the palace. They seized the best of everything. They feasted daily in the great dining hall, wasting much, and helped themselves to all the wine in the cellar. They were rude and uproarious in the once quiet chambers of the palace, and insulting to the people of Ithaca.

Every day Penelope sat at her loom and wove. "See how much I have added to the length of the web?" she would say when evening came. But at night, when the suitors were asleep, she raveled out all the threads she had woven during the day. Thus although she was always at work, the web was never finished.

As the weeks passed, however, the suitors began to grow weary of waiting.

"When will that web be finished?" they impatiently asked.

"I am busy with it every day," Penelope answered, "but it grows very slowly. Such a delicate piece of work cannot be completed so quickly."

But one of the suitors, a man named Agelaus, was not satisfied. That night he crept quietly through the palace and peeped into the weaving room. There he saw Penelope busily unravelling the web by the light of a little lamp, while she whispered to herself the name of Ulysses.

The next morning the secret was known to every one of the unwelcome guests. "Fair queen," they said, "you are very cunning, but we have found you out. That web must be finished before the sun rises again, and then tomorrow you must make your choice. We shall wait no longer."

The following afternoon the unwelcome guests assembled in the great hall. The feast was set, and they ate and drank and sang and shouted as never before. They made such an uproar that the very timbers of the palace shook.

While the turmoil was at its height, Telemachus came in, followed by Eumaeus, his father's oldest and most faithful servant. Together they began to remove all the shields and swords that hung on the walls and rattled from so much commotion.

"What are you doing with those weapons?" shouted the suitors, who finally noticed the old man and the youth.

"They are becoming tarnished with smoke and dust," said Eumaeus, "and will keep much better in the treasure room."

"But we will leave my father's great bow that hangs at the head of the hall," added Telemachus. "My mother polishes it every day, and she would sadly miss it if it were removed."

"She won't be polishing it much longer," the suitors laughed. "Before this day is over, Ithaca will have a new king."

At that moment a strange beggar entered the courtyard. His feet were bare, his head was uncovered, his clothes were in rags. He approached the kitchen door, where an old greyhound, Argos, was lying on a heap of ashes. Twenty years before, Argos had been Ulysses' favorite and most loyal hunting dog. But now, grown toothless and almost blind, he was only abused by the suitors.

When he saw the beggar slowly moving through the yard, he raised his head to look. Then a strange look came suddenly into his old eyes. His tail wagged feebly, and he tried with all his failing strength to rise. He looked up lovingly into the beggar's face, and uttered a long but joyful howl like that which he once uttered in his youth when greeting his master.

The beggar stooped and patted his head. "Argos, old friend," he whispered.

The dog staggered to his feet, then fell, and was dead with the look of joy still in his eyes.

A moment later the beggar stood in the doorway of the great hall, where he was seen whispering a few words to Telemachus and faithful Eumaeus.

"What do you want here, Old Rags?" the suitors called, hurling crusts of bread at his head. "Get out! Be gone!"

But at that moment, down the stairs came Penelope, stately and beautiful, with her servants and maids around her.

"The queen! The queen!" cried the suitors. "She has come to choose one of us!"

"Telemachus, my son," said Penelope, "what poor man is this whom our guests treat so roughly?"

"Mother, he is a wandering beggar whom the waves cast upon our shores last night," answered the prince. "He says that he brings news of my father."

"Then he shall tell me of it," said the queen. "But first he must rest." At this she caused the beggar to be led to a seat at the farther side of the room, and gave orders that he be fed and refreshed.

An old woman, who had been Ulysses' nurse when he was a child, brought a great bowl of water and towels. Kneeling on the stones before the stranger, she began to wash his feet. Suddenly she sprang back, overturning the bowl in her confusion.

"O, master! The scar!" she muttered quietly.

"Dear nurse," whispered the beggar, "you were ever discreet and wise. You know me by the old scar I have carried on my knee since boyhood. Keep well the secret, for I bide my time, and the hour of vengeance is nigh."

This man in rags was indeed Ulysses, the king. Alone in a little boat he had been cast, that very morning, upon the shore of his own island. He had made himself known to Telemachus and old Eumaeus alone, and by his orders they had removed the weapons that hung on the wall of the great hall.

Meanwhile, the suitors had gathered again around the feast table and were more boisterous than before. "Come, fair Penelope!" they shouted. "This beggar can tell his tale tomorrow. It is time for you to choose a new husband! Choose now!"

"Chiefs and princes," said Penelope, in trembling tones, "let us leave this decision to the gods. Behold, there hangs the great bow of Ulysses, which he alone was able to string. Let each of you try his strength in bending it, and I will choose the one who can shoot an arrow from it the most skillfully."

"Well said!" cried all the suitors, and they lined up to try their strength. The first took the bow in his hands, and struggled long to bend it. Then, losing patience, he threw it on the ground and strode away. "None but a giant can string a bow like that," he said.

Then, one by one, the other suitors tried their strength, but all in vain.

"Perhaps the old beggar would like to take part in this contest," one said with a sneer.

Then Ulysses in his beggar's rags rose from his seat and went with halting steps to the head of the hall. He fumbled with the great bow, gazing at its polished back and its long, well-shaped arms, stout as bars of iron. "Methinks," he said, "that in my younger days I once saw a bow like this."

"Enough! Enough!" shouted the suitors. "Get out, you old fool!"

Suddenly, a great change came over the stranger. Almost without effort, he bent the great bow and strung it. Then he rose to his full height, and even in his beggar's rags appeared every inch a king.

"Ulysses! Ulysses!" Penelope cried.

The suitors were speechless. Then, in the wildest alarm, they turned and tried to escape from the hall. But the arrows of Ulysses were swift and sure, and not one missed its mark. "Now I avenge myself upon those who have tried to destroy my home!" he cried. And thus, one after another, the lawless suitors perished.

The next day Ulysses sat in the great hall with Penelope and Telemachus and all the joyful members of the household, and he told the story of his long wanderings over the sea. And Penelope, in turn, related how she had faithfully kept the kingdom, as she had promised, though beset by insolent and wicked suitors. Then she brought from her chamber a roll of soft, white cloth of wonderful delicacy and beauty, and said, "This is the web, Ulysses. I promised that on the day of its completion I would choose a husband, and I choose you."

Loyalty to a Brother

Walter MacPeek

Family loyalties involve certain obligations. They are duties we perform out of love, as this simple story from an old Boy Scout book reminds us.

One of two brothers fighting in the same company in France fell by a German bullet. The one who escaped asked permission of his officer to go and bring his brother in.

"He is probably dead," said the officer, "and there is no use in your risking your life to bring in his body."

But after further pleading the officer consented. Just as the soldier reached the lines with his brother on his shoulders, the wounded man died.

"There, you see," said the officer, "you risked your life for nothing."

"No," replied Tom. "I did what he expected of me, and I have my reward. When I crept up to him and took him in my arms, he said, 'Tom, I knew you would come—I just felt you would come.'"

There you have the gist of it all; somebody expects something fine and noble and unselfish of us; someone expects us to be faithful.

Only a Dad

Edgar Guest

We should not forget to sing praises for devoted fathers—especially our *own*. This Edgar Guest poem may help us remember that the only reward a devoted father seeks is his family's flourishing. And may we never forget, as Shakespeare's King Lear told us, "how sharper than a serpent's tooth it is to have a thankless child."

Only a dad with a tired face,
Coming home from the daily race,
Bringing little of gold or fame
To show how well he has played the game;
But glad in his heart that his own rejoice
To see him come and to hear his voice.

Only a dad with a brood of four,
One of ten million men or more
Plodding along in the daily strife,
Bearing the whips and the scorns of life,
With never a whimper of pain or hate,
For the sake of those who at home await.

Only a dad, neither rich nor proud,
Merely one of the surging crowd,
Toiling, striving from day to day,
Facing whatever may come his way,
Silent whenever the harsh condemn,
And bearing it all for the love of them.

Only a dad but he gives his all,
To smooth the way for his children small,
Doing with courage stern and grim
The deeds that his father did for him.
This is the line that for him I pen:
Only a dad, but the best of men.

Home Sweet Home

John Howard Payne

Home is the place where we find comfort, security, memories, friendship, hospitality, and, above all, family. It is the place that deserves our commitment and loyalty.

'Mid pleasures and palaces though we may roam,
Be it ever so humble, there's no place like home;
A charm from the sky seems to hallow us there,
Which, seek through the world, is ne'er met with elsewhere.
Home, home, sweet, sweet home!
There's no place like home! There's no place like home!

An exile from home, splendor dazzles in vain;
Oh, give me my lowly thatched cottage again!
The birds singing gayly, that came at my call—
Give me them—and the peace of mind, dearer than all!
Home, home, sweet, sweet home!
There's no place like home! There's no place like home!

How sweet 'tis to sit 'neath a fond father's smile,
And the caress of a mother to soothe and beguile!
Let others delight mid new pleasures to roam,
But give me, oh, give me, the pleasures of home!
Home, home, sweet, sweet home!
There's no place like home! There's no place like home!

To thee I'll return, overburdened with care;
The heart's dearest solace will smile on me there;
No more from that cottage again will I roam;
Be it ever so humble, there's no place like home.
Home, home, sweet, sweet home!
There's no place like home! There's no place like home!

Paul Revere's Ride

Henry Wadsworth Longfellow

Generations of American schoolchildren have discovered the
spirit of the American Revolution by memorizing this poem,
which first appeared in 1863. As a historical record it is certainly
flawed. (Paul Revere in fact never made it all the way to Concord;
he was detained on the road from Lexington by a British patrol,

while a companion escaped and carried forward the news that the British were coming.) As a story of high adventure, intrigue, and daring deeds for the sake of American independence, however, it is unsurpassed.

The events of the story take place on the night of April 18, 1775, when seven hundred British troops marched out of occupied Boston to destroy colonial arms caches reportedly hidden in Concord. The British had hoped to move in secrèt, but American spies were alert, and soon silversmith Paul Revere was galloping ahead of the redcoats to warn John Hancock and Samuel Adams, who were staying at Lexington. That mission accomplished, Revere dashed down the road to Concord to spread the alarm further.

Listen, my children, and you shall hear
Of the midnight ride of Paul Revere,
On the eighteenth of April, in Seventy-five;
Hardly a man is now alive
Who remembers that famous day and year.

He said to his friend, "If the British march
By land or sea from the town tonight,
Hang a lantern aloft in the belfry arch
Of the North Church tower as a signal light—
One, if by land, and two, if by sea;
And I on the opposite shore will be,
Ready to ride and spread the alarm
Through every Middlesex village and farm,
For the country folk to be up and to arm."

Then he said, "Good night!" and with muffled oar
Silently rowed to the Charlestown shore,
Just as the moon rose over the bay,
Where swinging wide at her moorings lay
The *Somerset,* British man-of-war;
A phantom ship, with each mast and spar
Across the moon like a prison bar,
And a huge black hulk, that was magnified
By its own reflection in the tide.

Meanwhile, his friend, through alley and street,
Wanders and watches with eager ears,
Till in the silence around him he hears
The muster of men at the barrack door,
The sound of arms, and the tramp of feet,
And the measured tread of the grenadiers,
Marching down to their boats on the shore.

Then he climbed the tower of the Old North Church,
By the wooden stairs, with stealthy tread,
To the belfry chamber overhead,
And startled the pigeons from their perch
On the somber rafters, that round him made
Masses and moving shapes of shade—
By the trembling ladder, steep and tall,
To the highest window in the wall,
Where he paused to listen and look down
A moment on the roofs of the town,
And the moonlight flowing over all.

Beneath, in the churchyard, lay the dead,
In their night encampment on the hill,
Wrapped in silence so deep and still
That he could hear, like a sentinel's tread,
The watchful night wind, as it went
Creeping along from tent to tent,
And seeming to whisper, "All is well!"
A moment only he feels the spell
Of the place and the hour, and the secret dread
Of the lonely belfry and the dead;
For suddenly all his thoughts are bent
On a shadowy something far away,
Where the river widens to meet the bay—
A line of black that bends and floats
On the rising tide, like a bridge of boats.

Meanwhile, impatient to mount and ride,
Booted and spurred, with a heavy stride
On the opposite shore walked Paul Revere.
Now he patted his horse's side,
Now gazed at the landscape far and near,
Then, impetuous, stamped the earth,

And turned and tightened his saddle girth;
But mostly he watched with eager search
The belfry tower of the Old North Church,
As it rose above the graves on the hill,
Lonely and spectral and somber and still.
And lo! as he looks, on the belfry's height
A glimmer, and then a gleam of light!
He springs to the saddle, the bridle he turns,
But lingers and gazes, till full on his sight
A second lamp in the belfry burns!

A hurry of hoofs in a village street,
A shape in the moonlight, a bulk in the dark,
And beneath, from the pebbles, in passing, a spark
Struck out by a steed flying fearless and fleet;
That was all! And yet, through the gloom and the light
The fate of a nation was riding that night;
And the spark struck out by that steed in his flight,
Kindled the land into flame with its heat.

He has left the village and mounted the steep,
And beneath him, tranquil and broad and deep,
Is the Mystic, meeting the ocean tides;
And under the alders, that skirt its edge,
Now soft on the sand, now loud on the ledge,
Is heard the tramp of his steed as he rides.

It was twelve by the village clock
When he crossed the bridge into Medford town.
He heard the crowing of the cock,
And the barking of the farmer's dog,
And felt the damp of the river fog,
That rises after the sun goes down.

It was one by the village clock,
When he galloped into Lexington.
He saw the gilded weathercock
Swim in the moonlight as he passed,
And the meeting house windows, blank and bare,
Gaze at him with a spectral glare,
As if they already stood aghast
At the bloody work they would look upon.

It was two by the village clock,
When he came to the bridge in Concord town.
He heard the bleating of the flock,
And the twitter of birds among the trees,
And felt the breath of the morning breeze
Blowing over the meadows brown.
And one was safe and asleep in his bed
Who at the bridge would be first to fall,
Who that day would be lying dead,
Pierced by a British musket ball.

You know the rest. In the books you have read,
How the British Regulars fired and fled—
How the farmers gave them ball for ball,
From behind each fence and farmyard wall,
Chasing the redcoats down the lane,
Then crossing the fields to emerge again
Under the trees at the turn of the road,
And only pausing to fire and load.
So through the night rode Paul Revere;
And so through the night went his cry of alarm
To every Middlesex village and farm—
A cry of defiance, and not of fear,
A voice in the darkness, a knock at the door,
And a word that shall echo forevermore!
For, borne on the night wind of the Past,
Through all our history, to the last,
In the hour of darkness and peril and need,
The people will waken and listen to hear
The hurrying hoofbeats of that steed,
And the midnight message of Paul Revere.

Concord Hymn

Ralph Waldo Emerson

Emerson wrote "Concord Hymn" as a tribute to the "embattled farmers" who fought the professional British troops at Concord on April 19, 1775. The minutemen's steadfastness became the "shot heard round the world" that inspired other colonists to shoulder their rifles and march for the Revolutionary cause. The poem was first sung as a hymn on July 4, 1837, at a ceremony marking the completion of a monument that commemorates the battles of Lexington and Concord.

By the rude bridge that arched the flood,
    Their flag to April's breeze unfurled,
Here once the embattled farmers stood
    And fired the shot heard round the world.

The foe long since in silence slept;
    Alike the conqueror silent sleeps;
And Time the ruined bridge has swept
    Down the dark stream which seaward creeps.

On this green bank, by this soft stream,
    We set today a votive stone;
That memory may their deed redeem,
    When, like our sires, our sons are gone.

Spirit, that made those heroes dare
    To die, and leave their children free,
Bid Time and Nature gently spare
    The shaft we raise to them and thee.

Nathan Hale

From American Heritage *magazine*

Americans look to the Revolutionary War to find the two names that mark the extremes of loyalty to country. On one end of the spectrum we find Benedict Arnold, perhaps the most despised name in the nation's history. At the other end stands Nathan Hale.

Ever since he was executed by the British on the morning of September 22, 1776, the death of Nathan Hale has been recognized as one of the great moments of American patriotism. Some years ago the late George Dudley Seymour gathered all the contemporary descriptions of the young hero's career that he could find, and had them privately printed in a *Documentary Life of Nathan Hale*. In the selections below we can read at first hand, in the words of both his friends and his foes, a story that has inspired generations of Hale's countrymen.

Following his graduation from Yale in 1773 at the age of eighteen, Hale taught school for a time in his native Connecticut. Then, on July 1, 1775—two months after Lexington and Concord—he was commissioned a lieutenant in the Continental Army, and closed his one-room school in New London, a building still proudly preserved by the town. We see him first in the reminiscences of a comrade-in-arms, Lieutenant Elisha Bostwick:

I can now in imagination see his person and hear his voice— his person, I should say, was a little above the common stature in height, his shoulders of a moderate breadth, his limbs strait and very plump: regular features—very fair skin—blue eyes —flaxen or very light hair which was always kept short—his eyebrows a shade darker than his hair and his voice rather sharp or piercing—his bodily agility was remarkable. I have seen him follow a football and kick it over the tops of the trees in the Bowery at New York (an exercise which he was fond of)—his mental powers seemed to be above the common sort —his mind of a sedate and sober cast, and he was undoubtedly pious; for it was remarked that when any of the soldiers of his

company were sick he always visited them and usually prayed
for and with them in their sickness.

Early in the fall of 1776, after being disastrously defeated on
Long Island, Washington needed to know the dispositions and the
intentions of the British forces. Hale and other officers of the picked
regiment known as Knowlton's Rangers were asked to volunteer for
an intelligence mission behind enemy lines. On the first call, none
responded; on the second, Nathan Hale alone stepped forward. A
little later he told his friend Captain (afterward General) William
Hull what he had done:

> [Hale] asked my candid opinion [says Hull's memoir]. I re-
> plied, that it was an action which involved serious conse-
> quences, and the propriety of it was doubtful. . . . Stratagems
> are resorted to in war; they are feints and evasions, performed
> under no disguise . . . and, considered in a military view,
> lawful and advantageous. . . . But who respects the character
> of a spy, assuming the garb of friendship but to betray? . . . I
> ended by saying, that should he undertake the enterprise, his
> short, bright career would close with an ignominious death.
>   He replied, "I am fully sensible of the consequences of
> discovery and capture in such a situation. . . . Yet . . . I wish
> to be useful, and every kind of service, necessary to the public
> good, becomes honorable by being necessary. If the exigencies
> of my country demand a peculiar service, its claims to perform
> that service are imperious."

Sergeant Stephen Hempstead of New London accompanied him
as he set out on his mission from Norwalk, Connecticut:

> Captain Hale had a general order to all armed vessels to take
> him to anyplace he should designate: he was set across the
> Sound . . . at Huntington (Long Island). . . . Captain Hale
> had changed his uniform for a plain suit of citizen's brown
> clothes, with a round broad-brimmed hat, assuming the char-
> acter of a Dutch schoolmaster, leaving all his other clothes,
> commission, public and private papers, with me, and also his
> silver shoe buckles, saying they would not comport with his
> character of schoolmaster, and retaining nothing but his col-
> lege diploma, as an introduction to his assumed calling. Thus
> equipped, we parted.

Hale's servant, Asher Wright, who had remained behind, told what happened next:

> He passed all their guards on Long Island, went over to New York in a ferryboat and got by all the guards but the last. They stopped him, searched and found drawings of the works, with descriptions in Latin, under the inner sole of the pumps which he wore. Some say his cousin, Samuel Hale, a Tory, betrayed him. I don't know; guess he did.

"Betrayed" is probably too strong; "identified" is closer to the truth. A surviving letter from Samuel, a Harvard man (1766), seems to deny any misdeed, or at least any guilt, as the story was spread in a Newburyport newspaper—but he thereafter fled to England and never returned to America, even after the war, for his wife and son.

The next day a kindhearted British officer, Captain John Montresor, approached the American lines under a flag of truce to report the inevitable denouement. Captain Hull recorded Montresor's words:

> Hale at once declared his name, his rank in the American army, and his object in coming within the British lines.
> Sir William Howe, without the form of a trial, gave orders for his execution the following morning. He was placed in the custody of the provost marshal, who was . . . hardened to human suffering and every softening sentiment of the heart. Captain Hale, alone, without sympathy or support, save that from above, on the near approach of death asked for a clergyman to attend him. It was refused. He then requested a Bible; that too was refused by his inhuman jailer.
> On the morning of his execution . . . my station was near the fatal spot, and I requested the provost marshal to permit the prisoner to sit in my marquee, while he was making the necessary preparations. Captain Hale entered: he was calm, and bore himself with gentle dignity, in the consciousness of rectitude and high intentions. He asked for writing materials, which I furnished him: he wrote two letters. . . .
> He was shortly after summoned to the gallows. But a few persons were around him, yet his characteristic dying words were remembered. He said, "I only regret, that I have but one life to lose for my country."

A brief excerpt from a letter written at Coventry, Connecticut, the following spring by Nathan Hale's father, Richard, who had six sons altogether in the Revolution, betrays the deep grief of this unlettered man:

> You desired me to inform you about my son Nathan. . . . He was executed about the twenty-second of September last by the accounts we have had. A child I sot much by but he is gone. . . .

This letter, addressed to Richard Hale's brother, Major Samuel Hale, in Portsmouth, New Hampshire, on March 28, 1777, was put away in a secret drawer of the major's desk. In 1908, the old desk was sold at auction as an antique, and three years later the new owner, the Honorable Frank L. Howe of Barrington, New Hampshire, chanced upon it. Such is the thrill of historical discovery.

Washington Rejects a Crown

Not long after the American victory at Yorktown, an officer of the Revolutionary Army wrote to George Washington suggesting that the newly liberated colonies could "never become a nation under a republican form of government" and proposing "the establishment of a kingdom with Washington at the head." Washington fired off an immediate reply. Like Cincinnatus, who also had turned down dictatorship more than two thousand years before, his loyalties lay with his country's interests, not his own.

Newburgh May 22, 1782

Sir,

With a mixture of great surprise and astonishment I have read with attention the sentiments you have submitted to my perusal. Be assured sir, no occurrence in the course of the war has given me more painful sensations than your information of there being such ideas existing in the army as you have expressed, and I must view with abhorrence, and reprehend with severity—for the present, the communication of them will rest in my own bosom, unless some further agitation of the matter shall make a disclosure necessary.

I am much at a loss to conceive what part of my conduct could have given encouragement to an address which to me seems big with the greatest mischiefs that can befall my country. If I am not deceived in the knowledge of myself, you could not have found a person to whom your schemes are more disagreeable—at the same time in justice to my own feeling I must add, that no man possesses a more sincere wish to see ample justice done to the army than I do, and as far as my powers and influence, in a constitution, may extend, they shall be employed to the utmost of my abilities to effect it, should there be any occasion—Let me conjure you then, if you have any regard for your country—concern for yourself or posterity—or respect for me, to banish these thoughts from your mind, and never communicate, as from yourself, or anyone else, a sentiment of the like nature.

> With esteem I am Sir
> Your Most Obedient Servant
> G. Washington

America

Samuel Smith

The Reverend Samuel Smith wrote the lyrics to "America" in Amherst, Massachusetts, in February 1832, and it was first performed at an Independence Day celebration in Boston later that year. Then, as now, it was sung to the tune of "God Save the King." Most Americans are familiar with the first verse, but all are worth knowing.

My country 'tis of thee
Sweet land of liberty:
   Of thee I sing.
Land where my fathers died
Land of the Pilgrims' pride
From every mountainside
   Let freedom ring.

My native country—thee
Land of the noble free
   Thy name I love:
I love thy rocks and rills
Thy woods and templed hills
My heart with rapture thrills
   Like that above.

Let music swell the breeze
And ring from all the trees
   Sweet freedom's song.
Let all that breathe partake
Let mortal tongues awake
Let rocks their silence break
   The sound prolong.

Our fathers' God to thee
Author of liberty
   To thee we sing.
Long may our land be bright
With freedom's holy light
Protect us by thy might
   Great God, our King.

Barbara Frietchie

John Greenleaf Whittier

Sometimes our sense of loyalty demands that we show the flag
even in the enemy's midst. John Greenleaf Whittier (1807–1892)
wrote this poem in 1863, during the Civil War, and claimed its
story is true.

Up from the meadows rich with corn,
Clear in the cool September morn,
The clustered spires of Frederick stand
Green-walled by the hills of Maryland.
Round about them orchards sweep,
Apple and peach tree fruited deep,
Fair as the garden of the Lord
To the eyes of the famished rebel horde,
On that pleasant morn of the early fall
When Lee marched over the mountain wall;
Over the mountains winding down,
Horse and foot, into Frederick town.

Forty flags with their silver stars,
Forty flags with their crimson bars,
Flapped in the morning wind: the sun
Of noon looked down, and saw not one.
Up rose old Barbara Frietchie then,
Bowed with her fourscore years and ten;
Bravest of all in Frederick town,
She took up the flag the men hauled down;
In her attic window the staff she set,
To show that one heart was loyal yet.

Up the street came the rebel tread,
Stonewall Jackson riding ahead.
Under his slouched hat left and right
He glanced; the old flag met his sight.
"Halt"—the dust-brown ranks stood fast.
"Fire"—out blazed the rifle blast.
It shivered the window, pane and sash;
It rent the banner with seam and gash.
Quick, as it fell, from the broken staff
Dame Barbara snatched the silken scarf.
She leaned far out on the windowsill,
And shook it forth with a royal will.
"Shoot, if you must, this old gray head,
But spare your country's flag," she said.

A shade of sadness, a blush of shame,
Over the face of the leader came;
The nobler nature within him stirred
To life at that woman's deed and word;
"Who touches a hair on yon gray head
Dies like a dog! March on!" he said.
All day long through Frederick street
Sounded the tread of marching feet:
All day long that free flag tost
Over the heads of the rebel host.
Ever its torn folds rose and fell
On the loyal winds that loved it well;
And through the hill gaps sunset light
Shone over it with a warm good night.

Barbara Frietchie's work is o'er,
And the Rebel rides on his raids no more.
Honor to her! and let a tear
Fall, for her sake, on Stonewall's bier.
Over Barbara Frietchie's grave
Flag of Freedom and Union, wave!
Peace and order and beauty draw
Round thy symbol of light and law;
And ever the stars above look down
On thy stars below in Frederick town!

America the Beautiful

Katharine Lee Bates

Massachusetts educator and author Katharine Lee Bates wrote "America the Beautiful" in 1893 after being inspired by the view from Pikes Peak in Colorado. She revised the lyrics to their final form in 1911. They are set to the music of Samuel A. Ward's "Materna."

> O beautiful for spacious skies,
>   For amber waves of grain,
> For purple mountain majesties
>   Above the fruited plain!
> America! America!
>   God shed His grace on thee
> And crown thy good with brotherhood
>   From sea to shining sea!
>
> O beautiful for Pilgrim feet,
>   Whose stern, impassioned stress
> A thoroughfare for freedom beat
>   Across the wilderness!
> America! America!
>   God mend thine every flaw,
> Confirm thy soul in self-control,
>   Thy liberty in law!
>
> O beautiful for heroes proved
>   In liberating strife,
> Who more than self their country loved,
>   And mercy more than life!
> America! America!
>   May God thy gold refine,
> Till all success be nobleness
>   And every gain divine!

O beautiful for patriot dream
  That sees beyond the years
Thine alabaster cities gleam
  Undimmed by human tears!
America! America!
  God shed His grace on thee,
And crown thy good with brotherhood
  From sea to shining sea!

In Flanders Fields

John McCrae

Canadian physician, soldier, and poet John McCrae (1872–1918)
published in 1915 this famous poem about the Allied dead buried
in Belgium. It reminds us that others' self-sacrifice is one reason
for loyalty to cause.

In Flanders fields the poppies blow
Between the crosses, row on row,
  That mark our place; and in the sky
  The larks, still bravely singing, fly
Scarce heard amid the guns below.

We are the Dead. Short days ago
We lived, felt dawn, saw sunset glow,
  Loved and were loved, and now we lie
  In Flanders fields.

Take up our quarrel with the foe:
To you from failing hands we throw
  The torch; be yours to hold it high.
  If ye break faith with us who die
We shall not sleep, though poppies grow
  In Flanders fields.

Flag Day

This editorial appeared in *The New York Times* on June 14, 1940, to mark Flag Day, a holiday that seems to have fallen into neglect in more recent years. Flag Day commemorates the day in 1777 when the Continental Congress adopted the Stars and Stripes as the official flag of the United States.

What's a flag? What's the love of country for which it stands? Maybe it begins with love of the land itself. It is the fog rolling in with the tide at Eastport, or through the Golden Gate and among the towers of San Francisco. It is the sun coming up behind the White Mountains, over the Green, throwing a shining glory on Lake Champlain and above the Adirondacks. It is the storied Mississippi rolling swift and muddy past St. Louis, rolling past Cairo, pouring down past the levees of New Orleans. It is lazy noontide in the pines of Carolina, it is a sea of wheat rippling in Western Kansas, it is the San Francisco peaks far north across the glowing nakedness of Arizona, it is the Grand Canyon and a little stream coming down out of a New England ridge, in which are trout.

It is men at work. It is the storm-tossed fishermen coming into Gloucester and Providence and Astoria. It is the farmer riding his great machine in the dust of harvest, the dairyman going to the barn before sunrise, the lineman mending the broken wire, the miner drilling for the blast. It is the servants of fire in the murky splendor of Pittsburgh, between the Allegheny and the Monongahela, the trucks rumbling through the night, the locomotive engineer bringing the train in on time, the pilot in the clouds, the riveter running along the beam a hundred feet in air. It is the clerk in the office, the housewife doing the dishes and sending the children off to school. It is the teacher, doctor, and parson tending and helping, body and soul, for small reward.

It is small things remembered, the little corners of the land, the houses, the people that each one loves. We love our country because there was a little tree on a hill, and grass thereon, and a sweet valley below; because the hurdy-gurdy man came along on a sunny morning in a city street; because a beach or a farm or a lane or a house that might not seem much to others were once, for each of us, made magic. It is voices that are remembered only, no longer heard. It is parents, friends, the lazy chat of street and store and office, and the ease of mind that makes life tranquil. It is summer and winter, rain and sun and storm. These are flesh of our flesh, bone of our bone, blood of our blood, a lasting part of what we are, each of us and all of us together.

It is stories told. It is the Pilgrims dying in their first dreadful winter. It is the minuteman standing his ground at Concord Bridge, and dying there. It is the army in rags, sick, freezing, starving at Valley Forge. It is the wagons and the men on foot going westward over Cumberland Gap, floating down the great rivers, rolling over the great plains. It is the settler hacking fiercely at the primeval forest on his new, his own lands. It is Thoreau at Walden Pond, Lincoln at Cooper Union, and Lee riding home from Appomattox. It is corruption and disgrace, answered always by men who would not let the flag lie in the dust, who have stood up in every generation to fight for the old ideals and the old rights, at risk of ruin or of life itself.

It is a great multitude of people on pilgrimage, common and ordinary people, charged with the usual human failings, yet filled with such a hope as never caught the imaginations and the hearts of any nation on earth before. The hope of liberty. The hope of justice. The hope of a land in which a man can stand straight, without fear, without rancor.

The land and the people and the flag—the land a continent, the people of every race, the flag a symbol of what humanity may aspire to when the wars are over and the barriers are down; to these each generation must be dedicated and consecrated anew, to defend with life itself, if need be, but, above all, in friendliness, in hope, in courage, to live for.

Ethical Loyalty

Richard A. Gabriel

In this excerpt from *To Serve with Honor*, his treatise on military ethics, Richard A. Gabriel draws a careful distinction between blind and informed loyalties, and asserts that the latter is the duty of the ethical soldier.

Whether one examines the fifteenth-century doctrine of *respondiat superior* ("let the superior be responsible") or the notion of just war, or even the more recent cases of the My Lai massacre or the execution of General Yamashita, or, finally, the Nuremberg trials, it is clear that Western society has long held that men cannot escape ethical responsibility for their acts by transferring that responsibility to others. The doctrine of accepting ethical responsibility was formally enshrined in the United States military profession as early as 1863 in General Order number 100 of the United States Army Field Manual: "Men who take up arms against another in public war do not cease on this account to be moral beings responsible to one another." Individuals always remain ethically responsible for their actions, for the choices they make among conflicting moral obligations, as well as for the consequences which result from them. To deny that a soldier has ethical responsibility is to negate the very nature of ethics as ethics applies to the military profession. . . .

Members of the profession must set standards of proper military behavior and must observe the standards, being consciously aware of why the obligations bind as they do. When they merely execute the precepts of the code without knowing why, they are engaged only in acts of obedience. Ethical action involving as it does judgment, choice, and responsibility is the antithesis of obedience. Members of the profession of arms must understand that sterile loyalty to a stated code is meaningless unless the precepts are understood and its obligations undertaken willingly. . . .

In short, a soldier's moral obligations transcend and surpass the obligations owed to his immediate superiors and even his civilian superiors in certain conditions. General Marshall, the epitome of the loyal soldier, was echoing General MacArthur's sentiments when he said that "an officer's ultimate commanding loyalty at all times is to his country and not to his service or his superiors." In a crisis, the soldier must exercise his sense of loyalty as *fides* [faith], and it must always take precedence over any sense of *obsequium* [obedience]. Indeed, the problem is even more complex, for in a deep moral crisis the soldier may even have to override his oath to the profession and to the Constitution in order to be loyal to humanity itself.

The Germans, who perhaps have had more direct experience with officers and soldiers being crushed between demands of their oath and the course of immoral events, have developed an interesting distinction in dealing with the question of loyalty to superiors. They distinguish between *hochverrat* and *landesverrat*. *Hochverrat* is disloyalty to a superior, which in Germanic terms meant disloyalty to the monarch or other governmental head of state. *Landesverrat,* by contrast, is disloyalty or betrayal of the nation. Within this distinction there is room for maneuver in making an ethical choice. In order to serve the nation or the Constitution, a soldier may sometimes have to be disloyal to his superiors or refuse to execute their orders. The Germanic distinction between the two notions of loyalty throws into focus what every member of the military profession knows in his heart, and that is that fundamentally a soldier's first loyalty is to behave ethically and humanly, and that in times of severe moral crisis he must be prepared to follow that higher morality. . . .

In essence, to be an ethical soldier is to do one's duty as to what is ethically right and to know why those ethics bind. Duty is not to be blindly tied to following orders.

The Last Lesson

Alphonse Daudet

The Franco-Prussian War of 1870–1871 moved French author Alphonse Daudet (1840–1897) to write this story, but the events could easily concern almost any war. Here is a case of tragedy inspiring a loyalty that, because of its nobility, cannot be said to be futile. The story is also a warning that we should not wait until the customs and heritages we love are gone before we begin to feel devoted to them.

I was very late for school that morning, and I was terribly afraid of being scolded, especially as Monsieur Hamel had told us that he should examine us on participles, and I did not know the first thing about them. For a moment I thought of staying away from school and wandering about the fields. It was such a warm, lovely day. I could hear the blackbirds whistling on the edge of the wood, and in the Rippert field, behind the sawmill, the Prussians going through their drill. All that was much more tempting to me than the rules concerning participles; but I had the strength to resist, and I ran as fast as I could to school.

As I passed the mayor's office, I saw that there were people gathered about the little board on which notices were posted. For two years all our bad news had come from that board—battles lost, conscriptions, orders from headquarters; and I thought without stopping:

"What can it be now?"

Then, as I ran across the square, Wachter the blacksmith, who stood there with his apprentice, reading the placard, called out to me:

"Don't hurry so, my boy; you'll get to your school soon enough!"

I thought that he was making fun of me, and I ran into Monsieur Hamel's little yard all out of breath.

Usually, at the beginning of school, there was a great uproar which could be heard in the street, desks opening and closing, lessons repeated aloud in unison, with our ears stuffed in order to learn quicker, and the teacher's stout ruler beating on the desk:

"A little more quiet!"

I counted on all this noise to reach my bench unnoticed; but as it happened, that day everything was quiet, like a Sunday morning. Through the open window I saw my comrades already in their places, and Monsieur Hamel walking back and forth with the terrible iron ruler under his arm. I had to open the door and enter, in the midst of that perfect silence. You can imagine whether I blushed and whether I was afraid!

But no! Monsieur Hamel looked at me with no sign of anger and said very gently:

"Go at once to your seat, my little Frantz; we were going to begin without you."

I stepped over the bench and sat down at once at my desk. Not until then, when I had partly recovered from my fright, did I notice that our teacher had on his handsome blue coat, his plaited ruff, and the black silk embroidered breeches, which he wore only on days of inspection or of distribution of prizes. Moreover, there was something extraordinary, something solemn about the whole class. But what surprised me most was to see at the back of the room, on the benches which were usually empty, some people from the village sitting, as silent as we were: old Hauser with his three-cornered hat, the ex-mayor, the ex-postman, and others besides. They all seemed depressed; and Hauser had brought an old spelling book with gnawed edges, which he held wide open on his knee, with his great spectacles askew.

While I was wondering at all this, Monsieur Hamel had mounted his platform, and in the same gentle and serious voice with which he had welcomed me, he said to us:

"My children, this is the last time that I shall teach you. Orders have come from Berlin to teach nothing but German in the schools of Alsace and Lorraine. The new teacher arrives tomorrow. This is the last class in French, so I beg you to be very attentive."

Those few words overwhelmed me. Ah! the villains! That was what they had posted at the mayor's office.

My last class in French!

And I barely knew how to write! So I should never learn! I must stop short where I was! How angry I was with myself because of the time I had wasted, the lessons I had missed, running about after nests, or sliding on the Saar! My books, which only a moment before I thought so tiresome, so heavy to carry—my grammar, my sacred history—seemed to me now like old friends, from whom I should be terribly grieved to part. And it was the same about Monsieur Hamel. The thought that he was going away, that I should never see him again, made me forget the punishments, the blows with the ruler.

Poor man! It was in honor of that last lesson that he had put on his fine Sunday clothes; and I understood now why those old fellows from the village were sitting at the end of the room. It seemed to mean that they regretted not having come oftener to the school. It was also a way of thanking our teacher for his forty years of faithful service, and of paying their respects to the fatherland which was vanishing.

I was at that point in my reflections, when I heard my name called. It was my turn to recite. What would I not have given to be able to say from beginning to end that famous rule about participles, in a loud, distinct voice, without a slip! But I got mixed up at the first words, and I stood there swaying against my bench, with a full heart, afraid to raise my head. I heard Monsieur Hamel speaking to me:

"I will not scold you, my little Frantz; you must be punished enough; that is the way it goes; every day we say to ourselves: 'Pshaw! I have time enough. I will learn tomorrow.' And then you see what happens. Ah! it has been the great misfortune of our Alsace always to postpone its lessons until tomorrow. Now those people are entitled to say to us: 'What! you claim to be French, and you can neither speak nor write your language!' In all this, my poor Frantz, you are not the guiltiest one. We all have our fair share of reproaches to address to ourselves.

"Your parents have not been careful enough to see that you were educated. They preferred to send you to work in the fields or in the factories, in order to have a few more sous. And have I nothing to reproach myself for? Have I not often made you water my garden instead of studying? And when I wanted to go fishing for trout, have I ever hesitated to dismiss you?"

Then, passing from one thing to another, Monsieur Hamel began to talk to us about the French language, saying that it was the most beautiful language in the world, the most clear, the most substantial; that we must always retain it among ourselves, and never forget it, because when a people falls into servitude, "so long as it clings to its language, it is as if it held the key to its prison." Then he took the grammar and read us our lesson. I was amazed to see how readily I understood. Everything that he said seemed so easy to me, so easy. I believed, too, that I had never listened so closely, and that he, for his part, had never been so patient with his explanations. One would have said that, before going away, the poor man desired to give us all his knowledge, to force it all into our heads at a single blow.

When the lesson was at an end, we passed to writing. For that day Monsieur Hamel had prepared some entirely new examples, on which was written in a fine, round hand: "France, Alsace, France, Alsace." They were like little flags, waving all about the class, hanging from the rods of our desks. You should have seen how hard we all worked and how silent it was! Nothing could be heard save the grinding of the pens over the paper. At one time some cock-chafers flew in; but no one paid any attention to them, not even the little fellows, who were struggling with their straight lines, with a will and conscientious application, as if even the lines were French. On the roof of the schoolhouse, pigeons cooed in low tones, and I said to myself as I listened to them:

"I wonder if they are going to compel them to sing in German too!"

From time to time, when I raised my eyes from my paper, I saw Monsieur Hamel sitting motionless in his chair and staring at the objects about him as if he wished to carry away in his glance the whole of his little schoolhouse. Think of it! For forty years he had been there in the same place, with his yard in front of him and his class just as it was! But the benches and desks were polished and rubbed by use; the walnuts in the yard had grown, and the hop vine which he himself had planted now festooned the windows even to the roof. What a heart-rending thing it must have been for that poor man to leave all those things, and to hear his sister walking back and forth in the room overhead, packing their trunks! For they were to go away the next day—to leave the province forever.

However, he had the courage to keep the class to the end. After the writing, we had the lesson in history; then the little ones sang all together the *ba, be, bi, bo, bu.* Yonder, at the back of the room, old Hauser had put on his spectacles, and, holding his spelling book in both hands, he spelled out the letters with them. I could see that he too was applying himself. His voice shook with emotion, and it was so funny to hear him, that we all longed to laugh and to cry. Ah! I shall remember that last class.

Suddenly the church clock struck twelve, then the Angelus rang. At the same moment, the bugles of the Prussians returning from drill blared under our windows. Monsieur Hamel rose, pale as death, from his chair. Never had he seemed to me so tall.

"My friends," he said, "my friends, I—I—"

But something suffocated him. He could not finish the sentence.

Thereupon he turned to the blackboard, took a piece of chalk, and, bearing on with all his might, he wrote in the largest letters he could:

"VIVE LA FRANCE!"

Then he stood there, with his head resting against the wall, and without speaking, he motioned to us with his hand:

"That is all; go."

Knute Rockne

Francis Wallace

Great players and great coaches win with loyalty to team and
school. No one knew it better than Knute Rockne.

From 1918 through 1930 Knute Rockne, that homely Norwegian with the well-splashed nose, had a phenomenal football coaching record at Notre Dame: 105 games won, 12 lost, 5 tied. Yet it
wasn't what he did but how he did it that made him the greatest
coach of all time. Like other coaches, he looked at his boys and saw
weight, speed, and brains. But he went further: he looked into their
hearts and minds, saw character and built on it. He used his keen
insight to weld a sum of ordinary talents into extraordinary teams—
mostly with talk. Advice, philosophy, wisecracks, caustic comment
poured from him "like champagne from a battered oilcan," West-
brook Pegler once said.

There was no "secret" to the Rockne system of football. Once
he put up a sign for visitors: "Secret Practice. Come and bring your
notebooks." On another occasion, when an Army scout missed a
train connection and didn't get to the Notre Dame game he was to
cover, Rockne obligingly sent him the plays he planned to use
against the West Pointers. Army figured that the diagrams were a
ruse, and prepared to meet different plays. In the game Rockne used
exactly the same plays he had sent—and won. "It isn't the plays that
win," he said to me. "It's the *execution*."

When Rockne began coaching, football was a game of brawn.
He preached and proved that ingenuity, quick thinking, and teamwork could beat size and strength. His players often were not im-
pressive physically (his famous "Four Horsemen" of 1922, 1923,
1924 averaged under 160 pounds), but they usually won because
Rockne could inspire them to play above their natural ability.

His pregame pep talks were famous nationwide. In these he
spared neither his team nor himself. I was a witness to one when
Rockne, seriously ill with phlebitis, wanted so badly to beat Carne-
gie Tech that he accompanied the team to Pittsburgh against doctor's
orders. The air in the locker room was thick with tension. The
crippled Rockne sat glumly on a table, staring at his players. Behind

the lockers, the team doctor whispered to me, "If he lets go, and that blood clot jumps from his leg to his heart or his brain, he may never leave this room alive."

Suddenly Rock let go. I had never heard such an outburst. His voice crackled as if charged with electricity. He thundered, he blustered, he exhorted with revival-meeting fervor. Gradually he wove his magic spell. Finally he dropped into the chanting line: "We are going out there and fight, fight, *fight*—and we're going to WIN!" As he finished his explosion, the team roared out onto the field— and Rock fell back in a cold sweat. Later he was helped to the field, where he watched in a wheelchair as his fired-up team won, 7–0.

Rock knew just when to deflate a player's incipient big head, when to give an encouraging pat on the back. If a star back seemed to be taking his publicity too seriously, Rock might pull out his best linemen in practice and let the star find out the hard way how far he could go without able players in front of him. Whenever the star protested, Rock would growl, "Show those tacklers your clippings!"

If Rockne had not gone into coaching, it is likely that he could have been a brilliant professor of chemistry—a subject which he did teach for a few years at Notre Dame. As a youngster brought to this country from Norway, he had shown an early hunger for knowledge. The Rocknes had a custom which permitted any member to dip into the family purse for money to buy gifts for other members; young Knute would buy books for his sisters—and then read them first.

There was no money to send him to college, so Knute worked four years in the Chicago post office to earn a thousand dollars toward his education. He went to Notre Dame because he heard it was a "poor boys' school" where he would have a good chance of getting a job. It was an unlikely-looking freshman who turned up in South Bend the autumn of 1910. He was overage (twenty-two), undersized (5 feet, 8 inches; 145 pounds) and already balding. He described himself as a "lone Norse Protestant" in a Catholic school. (He was converted to Catholicism fifteen years later.) Even though he was working his way through school he became captain of the football team (and third-string All America end), an editor of the yearbook, a star of the dramatic club. And, majoring in science, he achieved an average of over 90 for his four years and graduated *magna cum laude!*

As a player, as well as a coach, Rockne helped to revolutionize football. During summer vacations he worked as a lifeguard at a resort with a teammate named Gus Dorais. They whiled away their spare time throwing and catching the ball—which at that time was usually just kicked or carried. In the fall of 1913 the nationally unknown Notre Dame team went east to play mighty Army. The much bigger Army team outplayed Notre Dame on the ground. But when Notre Dame got the ball, Dorais would flip passes to Rockne and others for big gains. Rockne scored two touchdowns, and Notre Dame won, 35–13. With this victory came a change in the popular attitude toward football: instead of being considered a battering-ram contest of brute force, it became a game where skill and speed counted as much as bulk and strength.

As a coach, Rock was a stickler for physical conditioning. He hated softness and self-indulgence; his players were forbidden to smoke, and drinking was unthought of. Inside the rough exterior, however, he was a deeply kind man. He used to bring the youngsters outside the gate into home games.(One of these small fry, about five years old at the time, was Joe Kuharich, later to become Notre Dame's head coach.) He did some remarkable things for his players: not long ago I met one of his "old boys" who said, "My mother died of cancer; it wasn't until we opened the safe-deposit box that I found out Rock had been writing pep talks to her for years."

He helped me in scores of ways. When I was a young newspaperman I had to decide whether to stick with a salaried job or to strike out as a freelance writer. As I thought about it, I could almost hear Rockne's voice as he spoke these words on other occasions: "Be unorthodox. Don't be afraid to take chances. If you believe something, don't hesitate to try it just because no one else will."

I gave up the security of the newspaper job and soon was doing much better on my own. He helped me with my first magazine article. My first book, *Huddle,* was a fictional account of Rockne and Notre Dame.

Although Rock could always charm men and inspire boys, he was awed by women. On student dates he was such a tongue-tied blusher that the girls quickly gave up on him. Finally, however, at a resort near Sandusky, Ohio, where he had a summer job, he met a fellow employee named Bonnie Skiles. Bonnie was probably Rock's first and only girl. They married not long after his graduation and there was never a more devoted husband and family man than this father of three sons and a daughter.

Rockne preached loyalty, and he practiced it by remaining at

Notre Dame despite many attractive offers from other schools. His loyalty was cemented by an incident that happened in 1921. His team had won twenty straight games and was a big favorite to beat Iowa. However, Iowa upset Notre Dame 10–7. "There will be no alibi," Rockne snapped after the defeat.

It was a glum coach and team aboard the train as we pulled into South Bend at one o'clock Sunday morning. Suddenly, from out of the darkness, we heard the familiar Notre Dame cheer known as the Skyrocket—the victory yell. The student body had marched en masse three miles into town to meet the beaten team. Rockne slipped out on the far side of the train, but the crowd spotted him and hoisted him on top of a baggage truck.

A thousand boys stood in the darkness and cheered him. The hard-bitten coach, visibly touched, had trouble pulling himself together following the ovation. "After this," he said, "I will never leave Notre Dame as long as you want me." And he never left.

I last saw Rock in Florida in March 1931 on a short vacation. He left there for California, where Hollywood was trying to interest him in acting in a film. Passing over Kansas, his airplane crashed on a hilltop, killing all aboard. The nation was thunderstruck. "It takes a mighty big calamity to shock this country all at once," his friend Will Rogers wrote. "But, Knute, you did it."

Last rites for Rockne were held from the church on the broad campus he loved so well. The final tribute was spoken by the university president, the Reverend Charles O'Donnell. He said, "In an age that has stamped itself as the era of the 'go-getter'—a horrible word for what is all too often a ruthless thing—Knute Rockne was a 'go-giver'—a not much better word, but it means a divine thing."

The grave where Rockne is buried in South Bend is marked by only a small stone, and it is hard to find. Yet a hundred or more of his old players and friends go there every year after a memorial Mass. There are other monuments to his memory: the giant Notre Dame stadium, the glowing tradition he created, the warm place he still holds in the hearts of thousands of people who never even met him.

Before departing for California, Rock had left a pair of tan, high-topped shoes to be half-soled. No one ever called for those shoes. And nobody in football has ever come close to filling them.

The Thousandth Man

Rudyard Kipling

This Kipling poem, which reminds us that loyalty and reliability can sometimes be rare commodities, echoes Ecclesiastes 7:28 in the Bible: "one man in a thousand have I found."

One man in a thousand, Solomon says,
Will stick more close than a brother.
And it's worth while seeking him half your days
If you find him before the other.
Nine hundred and ninety-nine depend
On what the world sees in you,
But the Thousandth Man will stand your friend
With the whole round world agin you.

'Tis neither promise nor prayer nor show
Will settle the finding for 'ee.
Nine hundred and ninety-nine of 'em go
By your looks, or your acts, or your glory,
But if he finds you and you find him,
The rest of the world don't matter;
For the Thousandth Man will sink or swim
With you in any water.

You can use his purse with no more talk
Than he uses yours for his spendings,
And laugh and meet in your daily walk
As though there had been no lendings.
Nine hundred and ninety-nine of 'em call
For silver and gold in their dealings;
But the Thousandth Man he's worth 'em all,
Because you can show him your feelings.

His wrong's your wrong, and his right's your right,
In season or out of season.
Stand up and back it in all men's sight—
With *that* for your only reason!
Nine hundred and ninety-nine can't bide
The shame or mocking or laughter,
But the Thousandth Man will stand by your side
To the gallows-foot—and after!

10

Faith

Faith, Hope, and Love are formally regarded as "theological" virtues in traditional Christian doctrine. They mark dispositions of persons who are flourishing in life from that religious perspective. There is nothing distinctively Christian, however, in recognizing that religious faith adds a significant dimension to the moral life of humanity worldwide. Faith is a source of discipline and power and meaning in the lives of the faithful of any major religious creed. It is a potent force in human experience. A shared faith binds people together in ways that cannot be duplicated by other means.

Clashing faiths, on the other hand, divide people in sometimes the most violent ways. The history of the world's religions unfortunately gives ringing confirmation to what James Madison so brilliantly analyzed in *Federalist 10* as the natural human tendency toward faction. "So strong is this propensity of mankind to fall into mutual animosities that where no substantial occasion presents itself the most frivolous and fanciful distinctions have been sufficient to kindle their unfriendly passions and excite their most violent conflicts." A secular world stripped of all vestige of religion would assuredly have no "religious wars," but it by no means follows that it would be a world at peace. We do faith a disservice in laying at its doorstep the fundamental causes of faction.

Faith contributes to the form and the content of the ideals that guide the aspirations we harbor for our own lives, and it affects the way we regard and behave with respect to others. What Paul cites as "the fruit of the Spirit"—love, joy, peace, patience, kindness, generosity, faithfulness, gentleness, and self-control (Galatians 5:22–23)—has its parallels in all the major faiths; and the Golden Rule, expressed in one form or another, is recognized almost universally. The "Illustrations of the *Tao*," assembled by C. S. Lewis as an appendix to *The Abolition of Man,* represents a more extensive collection of such widely recognized "Natural Law."

A human being without faith, without *reverence* for anything, is

a human being morally adrift. The world's major religions provide
time-tested anchors for drifters; they furnish ties to a larger reality
for people on the loose. Faith can contribute important elements to
the social stability and moral development of individuals and groups.

Early in this century the American psychologist and philosopher
William James conducted a pioneering study of the faith experience
of religious persons historically and throughout the world. It was
published under the title *The Varieties of Religious Experience*. He
discovered among those who had experienced the most profound
religious states a virtually universal tendency toward what he called
"monism" and "optimism." Fundamental bedrock reality is both
unified and good. If there are any universal articles of faith, these are
prime candidates. In a world so fragmented and full of woe, faith in
its underlying unity and goodness is a sustaining encouragement to
those who are working on reality's "surface"—within any of the
major religious traditions—for love, joy, peace, patience, kindness,
generosity, faithfulness, gentleness, and self-control.

To parents who are themselves insecure in their faith and, like
the nineteenth-century English radical John Thelwall, think it "unfair to influence a child's mind by inculcating any opinions before it
should have come to years of discretion, and be able to choose for
itself," there is an enlightening anecdote in Samuel Taylor Cole-
ridge's *Table Talk* for July 27, 1830. "I showed [John Thelwall] my
garden, and told him it was my botanical garden. 'How so?' said he,
'it is covered with weeds.'—'Oh,' I replied, '*that* is only because it
has not yet come to its age of discretion and choice. The weeds, you
see, have taken the liberty to grow, and I thought it unfair in me to
prejudice the soil towards roses and strawberries.' "

Now I Lay Me Down to Sleep

I have read that John Adams said this one every night throughout his adult years. The Bennett family says it every night, too.

> Now I lay me down to sleep;
> I pray the Lord my soul to keep.
> If I should die before I wake,
> I pray the Lord my soul to take.

Sleep, My Babe

We parents know we cannot do our jobs all alone. From the beginning, we ask for aid.

> Sleep, my babe, and peace attend thee,
>   All through the night;
> Guardian angels God will lend thee,
>   All through the night;
> Soft the drowsy hours are creeping,
> Hill and vale in slumber sleeping,
> Mother dear her watch is keeping,
>   All through the night.

God is here, thou'lt not be lonely,
     All through the night;
'Tis not I who guards thee only,
     All through the night.
Night's dark shades will soon be over,
Still my watchful care shall hover,
God with me His watch is keeping,
     All through the night.

A Child's Prayer

Prayer, like all good habits, is best learned while we are very young.

Lord, teach a little child to pray,
     And then accept my prayer;
For thou canst hear the words I say,
     For thou art everywhere.

A little sparrow cannot fall
     Unnoticed, Lord, by thee;
And though I am so young and small,
     Thou dost take care of me.

Teach me to do the thing that's right,
     And when I sin, forgive;
And make it still my chief delight
     To serve thee while I live.

Noah and the Ark

Retold by Jesse Lyman Hurlbut

Even today, every time they see a rainbow, millions of people are reminded of the story of how Noah's faith and righteousness saved him from the destruction of his generation.

By the time that Adam died, there were many people on the earth; for the children of Adam and Eve had many other children; and when these grew up, they also had children; and these too had children. So after a time that part of the earth where Adam's sons lived began to be full of people.

It is sad to tell that as time went on more and more of these people became wicked, and fewer and fewer of them grew up to become good men and women. All the people lived near together, and few went away to other lands; so it came to pass that even the children of good men and women learned to be bad, like the people around them.

And as God looked down on the world that he had made, he saw how wicked the men in it had become, and that every thought and every act of man was evil.

And God looked down on the earth, and said:

"I will take away all men from the earth that I have made; because the men of the world are evil, and evil continually."

But even in those bad times, God saw one good man. His name was Noah. Noah tried to do right in the sight of God. As Enoch had walked with God, so Noah walked with God, and talked with him. And Noah had three sons: their names were Shem and Ham and Japheth.

God said to Noah, "The time has come when all the men and women on the earth are to be destroyed. Every one must die, because they are all wicked. But you and your family shall be saved, because you alone are trying to do right."

Then God told Noah how he might save his life and the lives of his family. He was to build a very large boat, as large as the largest ships that are made in our time; very long and very wide and very deep; with a roof over it; and made like a long wide house in three stories, but so built that it would float on the water. Such a ship as this was called an "ark." God told Noah to build this ark, and to have it ready for the time when he would need it.

"For," said God to Noah, "I am going to bring a great flood of water on the earth, to cover all the land and to drown all the people on the earth. And as the animals on the earth will be drowned with the people, you must make the ark large enough to hold a pair of each kind of animal, and several pairs of some animals that are needed by men, like sheep and goats and oxen; so that there will be animals as well as men to live upon the earth after the flood has passed away. And you must take in the ark food for yourself and your family, and for all the animals with you, enough food to last for a year, while the flood shall stay on the earth."

And Noah did what God told him to do, although it must have seemed very strange to all the people around, to build this great ark where there was no water for it to sail upon. And it was a long time, even a hundred and twenty years, that Noah and his sons were at work building the ark, while the wicked people around wondered, and no doubt laughed at Noah for building a great ship where there was no sea. At last the ark was finished, and stood like a great house on the land. There was a door on one side, and a window on the roof, to let in the light. Then God said to Noah, "Come into the ark, you and your wife, and your three sons, and their wives with them; for the flood of waters will come very soon. And take with you animals of all kinds, and birds, and things that creep; seven pairs of those that will be needed by men, and one pair of all the rest; so that all kinds of animals may be kept alive upon the earth."

So Noah and his wife, and his three sons, Shem, Ham, and Japheth, with their wives, went into the ark. And God brought to the door of the ark the animals, and the birds, and the creeping things of all kinds; and they went into the ark, and Noah and his sons put them in their places, and brought in food for them all. And then the door of the ark was shut, so that no more people and no more animals could come in.

In a few days the rain began to fall, as it had never rained before. It seemed as though the heavens were opened to pour great floods upon the earth. The streams filled, and the rivers rose, higher and higher, and the ark began to float on the water. The people left their houses and ran up to the hills, but soon the hills were covered, and all the people on them were drowned.

Some had climbed up to the tops of higher mountains, but the water rose higher and higher, until even the mountains were covered and all the people, wicked as they had been, were drowned in the great sea that now rolled over all the earth where men had lived. And all the animals, the tame animals—cattle and sheep and oxen—were drowned; and the wild animals—lions and tigers and all the rest—were drowned also. Even the birds were drowned, for their nests in the trees were swept away, and there was no place where they could fly from the terrible storm. For forty days and nights the rain kept on, until there was no breath of life remaining outside of the ark.

After forty days the rain stopped, but the water stayed upon the earth for more than six months; and the ark, with all that were in it, floated over the great sea that covered the land. Then God sent a wind to blow over the waters and to dry them up: so by degrees the waters grew less and less. So, after waiting for a time, Noah opened a window and let loose a bird called a raven. Now the raven has strong wings; and this raven flew round and round until the waters had gone down, and it could find a place to rest, and it did not come back to the ark.

After Noah had waited for it awhile, he sent out a dove; but the dove could not find any place to rest, so it flew back to the ark, and Noah took it into the ark again. Then Noah waited a week longer, and afterward he sent out the dove again. And at the evening, the dove came back to the ark, which was its home; and in its bill was a fresh leaf which it had picked off from an olive tree.

So Noah knew that the water had gone down enough to let the trees grow once more. He waited another week, and sent out the dove again; but this time the dove flew away and never came back. And Noah knew that the earth was becoming dry again. And God said to Noah:

"Come out of the ark, with your wife, and your sons, and their wives, and all the living things that are with you in the ark."

So Noah opened the door of the ark, and with his family came out, and stood once more on the ground. All the animals and birds and creeping things in the ark came out also, and began again to bring life to the earth.

The first thing Noah did, when he came out of the ark, was to give thanks to God for saving all his family when the rest of the people on the earth were destroyed. He built an altar, and laid upon it an offering to the Lord, and gave himself and his family to God, and promised to do God's will.

And God was pleased with Noah's offering, and God said:

"I will not again destroy the earth on account of men, no matter how bad they may be. From this time no flood shall again cover the earth; but the seasons of spring and summer and fall and winter shall remain without change. I give to you the earth; you shall be the rulers of the ground and of every living thing upon it."

Then God caused a rainbow to appear in the sky, and he told Noah and his sons that whenever they or the people after them should see the rainbow, they should remember that God had placed it in the sky and over the clouds as a sign of his promise that he would always remember the earth and the people upon it, and would never again send a flood to destroy men from the earth.

So, as often as we see the beautiful rainbow, we are to remember that it is the sign of God's promise to the world.

All Things Beautiful

Cecil Alexander

The miracle of ordinary things fills children's worlds. They sense, as Wordsworth phrased it, the "intimations of immortality" we too often neglect as adults.

> All things bright and beautiful,
>   All creatures great and small,
> All things wise and wonderful,
>   The Lord God made them all.
>
> Each little flower that opens,
>   Each little bird that sings,
> He made their glowing colors,
>   He made their tiny wings.
>
> The purple-headed mountain,
>   The river running by,
> The sunset, and the morning,
>   That brighten up the sky;

The cold wind in the winter,
   The pleasant summer sun,
The ripe fruits in the garden,
   He made them every one.

The tall trees in the greenwood,
   The meadows where we play,
   The rushes by the water,
   We gather every day;

He gave us eyes to see them,
   And lips that we might tell
How great is God Almighty,
   Who has made all things well.

Job

Retold by Jesse Lyman Hurlbut

The book of Job in the Bible is widely recognized as one of the world's great dramatic poems, both in the sublimity of its theme and the magnificence of its expression. Its main subject is straightforward but profound: why do righteous people suffer? The suffering of this "perfect and upright" man, his torment, his patience, and his final humility, have become a proverbial measure of faith.

   Here is a simple prose version of the events in the book of Job.

   At some time in those early days—we do not know just at what time, whether in the days of Moses or later—there was living a good man named Job. His home was in the land of Uz, which may have been on the edge of the desert, east of the land of Israel. Job was a very rich man. He had sheep, and camels, and oxen, and asses, counted by the thousand. In all the east there was no other man so rich as Job.

And Job was a good man. He served the Lord God, and prayed to God every day, with an offering upon God's altar, as men worshipped in those times. He tried to live as God wished him to live, and was always kind and gentle. Every day, when his sons were out in the field, or were having a feast together in the house of any of them, Job went out to his altar, and offered a burnt offering for each one of his sons and his daughters, and prayed to God for them; for he said:

"It may be that my sons have sinned or have turned away from God in their hearts; and I will pray God to forgive them."

At one time, when the angels of God stood before the Lord, Satan the Evil One came also, and stood among them, as though he were one of God's angels. The Lord God saw Satan, and said to him, "Satan, from what place have you come?" "I have come," answered Satan, "from going up and down in the earth and looking at the people upon it."

Then the Lord said to Satan, "Have you looked at my servant Job? And have you seen that there is not another man like him in the earth, a good and a perfect man, one who fears God and does nothing evil?" Then Satan said to the Lord: "Does Job fear God for nothing? Hast thou not made a wall around him, and around his house, and around everything that he has? Thou hast given a blessing upon his work, and hast made him rich. But if thou wilt stretch forth thy hand, and take away from him all that he has, then he will turn away from thee and will curse thee to thy face."

Then the Lord said to the Evil One, "Satan, all that Job has is in your power; you can do to his sons, and his flocks, and his cattle, whatever you wish; only lay not your hand upon the man himself."

Then Satan went forth from before the Lord; and soon trouble began to come upon Job. One day, when all his sons and daughters were eating and drinking together in their oldest brother's house, a man came running to Job, and said:

"The oxen were plowing, and the asses were feeding beside them, when the wild men from the desert came upon them, and drove them all away; and the men who were working with the oxen and caring for the asses have all been killed; and I am the only one who has fled away alive!"

While this man was speaking, another man came rushing in; and he said:

"The lightning from the clouds has fallen on all the sheep, and on the men who were tending them; and I am the only one who has come away alive!"

Before this man had ended, another came in; and he said:

"The enemies from Chaldea have come in three bands, and have taken away all the camels. They have killed the men who were with them; and I am the only one left alive!"

Then at the same time, one more man came in, and said to Job:

"Your sons and your daughters were eating and drinking together in their oldest brother's house, when a sudden and terrible wind from the desert struck the house, and it fell upon them. All your sons and your daughters are dead, and I alone have lived to tell you of it."

Thus in one day, all that Job had—his flocks, and his cattle, and his sons and his daughters—all were taken away; and Job, from being rich, was suddenly made poor. Then Job fell down upon his face before the Lord, and he said:

"With nothing I came into the world, and with nothing I shall leave it. The Lord gave, and the Lord has taken away; blessed be the name of the Lord."

So even when all was taken from him Job did not turn away from God, nor did he find fault with God's doings.

And again the angels of God were before the Lord, and Satan, who had done all this harm to Job, was among them. The Lord said to Satan, "Have you looked at my servant Job? There is no other man in the world as good as he; a perfect man, one that fears God and does no wrong act. Do you see how he holds fast to his goodness, even after I have let you do him so great harm?" Then Satan answered the Lord, "All that a man has he will give for his life. But if thou wilt put thy hand upon him and touch his bone and his flesh, he will turn from thee, and will curse thee to thy face."

And the Lord said to Satan, "I will give Job into your hand; do to him whatever you please; only spare his life."

Then Satan went out and struck Job, and caused dreadful boils to come upon him, over all his body, from the soles of his feet to the crown of his head. And Job sat down in the ashes in great pain; but he would not speak one word against God. His wife said to him,

"What is the use of trying to serve God? You may as well curse God, and die!"

But Job said to her, "You speak as one of the foolish. What? shall we take good things from the Lord? and shall we not take evil things also?" So Job would not speak against God. Then three friends of Job came to see him, and to try to comfort him in his sorrow and pain. Their names were Eliphaz, and Bildad, and Zophar. They sat down with Job, and wept, and spoke to him. But their words were not words of comfort. They believed that all these great troubles had come upon Job to punish him for some great sin, and they tried to persuade Job to tell what evil things he had done, to make God so angry with him.

For in those times most people believed that trouble, and sickness, and the loss of friends, and the loss of what they had owned, came to men because God was angry with them on account of their sins. These men thought that Job must have been very wicked because they saw such evils coming upon him. They made long speeches to Job, urging him to confess his wickedness.

Job said that he had done no wrong, that he had tried to do right; and he did not know why these troubles had come; but he would not say that God had dealt unjustly in letting him suffer. Job did not understand God's ways, but he believed that God was good; and he left himself in God's hands. And at last God himself spoke to Job and to his friends, telling them that it is not for man to judge God, and that God will do right by every man. And the Lord said to the three friends of Job:

"You have not spoken of me what is right, as Job has. Now bring an offering to me; and Job shall pray for you, and for his sake I will forgive you."

So Job prayed for his friends, and God forgave them. And because in all his troubles Job had been faithful to God, the Lord blessed Job once more, and took away his boils from him, and made him well. Then the Lord gave to Job more than he had ever owned in the past, twice as many sheep, and oxen, and camels, and asses. And God gave again to Job seven sons and three daughters; and in all the land there were no women found so lovely as the daughters of Job. After his trouble, Job lived a long time, in riches, and honor, and goodness, under God's care.

I Never Saw a Moor

Emily Dickinson

Faith requires no proofs.

I never saw a moor,
I never saw the sea;
Yet know I how the heather looks,
And what a wave must be.

I never spoke with God,
Nor visited in heaven;
Yet certain am I of the spot
As if the chart were given.

The Fiery Furnace

Retold by Jesse Lyman Hurlbut

The book of Daniel in the Bible is about the Jewish hero Daniel, who is taken captive to Babylon and, along with his friends Shadrach, Meshach, and Abednego, brought up in the court of King Nebuchadnezzar. The literal trial by fire we read about here is one of our most memorable examples of steadfastness in one's faith.

At one time King Nebuchadnezzar caused a great image to be made and to be covered with gold. This image he set up as an idol to be worshipped, on the plain of Dura, near the city of Babylon. When it was finished, it stood upon its base or foundation almost a hundred feet high, so that upon the plain it could be seen far away. Then the king sent out a command for all the princes, and rulers, and nobles in the land to come to a great gathering, when the image was to be set apart for worship.

The great men of the kingdom came from far and near, and stood around the image. Among them, by command of the king, were Daniel's three friends, the young Jews, Shadrach, Meshach, and Abednego. For some reason Daniel himself was not there. He may have been busy with the work of the kingdom in some other place.

At one moment in the service before the image all the trumpets sounded, the drums were beaten, and music was made upon musical instruments of all kinds, as a signal for all the people to kneel down and worship the great golden image. But while the people were kneeling there were three men who stood up and would not bow down. These were the three young Jews, Shadrach, Meshach, and Abednego. They knelt down before the Lord God only.

Many of the nobles had been jealous of these young men because they had been lifted to high places in the rule of the kingdom, and these men, who hated Daniel and his friends, were glad to find that these three men had not obeyed the command of King Nebuchadnezzar. The king had said that if anyone did not worship the golden image he should be thrown into a furnace of fire.

These men who hated the Jews came to the king, and said, "O king, may you live forever! You gave orders that when the music sounded everyone should bow down and worship the golden image; and that if any man did not worship he should be thrown into a furnace of fire. There are some Jews whom you have made rulers in the land, and they have not done as you commanded. Their names are Shadrach, Meshach, and Abednego. They do not serve your gods, nor worship the golden image that you have set up."

Then Nebuchadnezzar was filled with rage and fury at knowing that anyone should dare to disobey his words. He sent for these three men, and said to them, "O Shadrach, Meshach, and Abednego, was it by purpose that you did not fall down and worship the image of gold? The music shall sound once more, and if you then will worship the image, it shall be well. But if you will not, then you shall be thrown into the furnace of fire to die."

These three young men were not afraid of the king. They said, "O King Nebuchadnezzar, we are ready to answer you at once. The God whom we serve is able to save us from the fiery furnace and we know that he will save us. But if it is God's will that we should die, even then, you may understand, O king, that we will not serve your gods, nor worship the golden image that you have set up."

This answer made the king more furious than before. He said

to his servants, "Make a fire in the furnace hotter than ever it has been before, as hot as fire can be made, and throw these three men into it."

Then the soldiers of the king's army seized the three young Jews as they stood in their loose robes, with their turbans or hats on their heads. They tied them with ropes, and dragged them to the mouth of the furnace, and threw them into the fire. The flames rushed from the open door with such fury that they burned even to death the soldiers who were holding these men; and the men themselves fell down bound into the middle of the fiery furnace.

King Nebuchadnezzar stood in front of the furnace, and looked into the open door. As he looked he was filled with wonder at what he saw; and he said to the nobles around him:

"Did we not throw three men bound into the fire? How is it then that I see four men loose, walking in the furnace, and the fourth man looks as though he were a son of the gods?"

The king came near to the door of the furnace as the fire became lower, and he called out to the three men within it:

"Shadrach, Meshach, and Abednego, ye who serve the Most High God, come out of the fire and come to me."

They came out and stood before the king, in the sight of all the princes, and nobles, and rulers; and everyone could see that they were alive. Their garments had not been scorched nor their hair singed, nor was there even the smell of fire upon them. The king, Nebuchadnezzar, said before all his rulers:

"Blessed be the God of these men, who has sent his angel and has saved their lives. I make a law that no man in all my kingdoms shall say a word against their God, for there is no other god who can save in this manner. And if any man speaks a word against their God, the Most High God, that man shall be cut in pieces, and his house shall be torn down." And after this the king lifted up these three young men to still higher places in the land of Babylon.

Daniel in the Lion's Den

Retold by Jesse Lyman Hurlbut

This story, also from the book of Daniel, takes place later in Daniel's life. His ability as a seer has led King Darius to give him a high government office.

The lands which had been the Babylonian or Chaldean empire now became the empire of Persia; and over these Darius was the king. King Darius gave to Daniel, who was now a very old man, a high place in honor and in power. Among all the rulers over the land Daniel stood first, for the king saw that he was wise, and able to rule. This made the other princes and rulers very jealous, and they tried to find something evil in Daniel, so that they could speak to the king against him.

These men knew that three times every day Daniel went to his room, and opened the window that was toward the city of Jerusalem, and looking toward Jerusalem made his prayer to God. Jerusalem was at that time in ruins, and the Temple was no longer standing; but Daniel prayed three times each day with his face toward the place where the house of God had once stood, although it was many hundreds of miles away.

These nobles thought that in Daniel's prayers they could find a chance to do him harm, and perhaps cause him to be put to death. They came to King Darius, and said to him:

"All the rulers have agreed together to have a law made that for thirty days no one shall ask anything of any god or any man, except from you, O king; and that if anyone shall pray to any god, or shall ask anything from any man during thirty days, except from you, O king, he shall be thrown into the den where the lions are kept. Now, O king, make the law, and sign the writing, so that it cannot be changed, for no law among the Medes and Persians can be altered."

The king was not a wise man, and being foolish and vain, he was pleased with this law which would set him even above the gods. So, without asking Daniel's advice, he signed the writing; and the law was made, and the word was sent out through the kingdom that for thirty days no one should pray to any god, or ask a favor of any man.

Daniel knew that the law had been made, but every day he went to his room three times, and opened the window that looked toward Jerusalem, and offered his prayer to the Lord, just as he had prayed in other times. These rulers were watching nearby, and they saw Daniel kneeling in prayer to God. Then they came to the king, and said, "O King Darius, have you not made a law that if anyone in thirty days offers a prayer, he shall be thrown into the den of lions?" "It is true," said the king. "The law has been made, and it must stand."

They said to the king, "There is one man who does not obey the law which you have made. It is that Daniel, one of the captive Jews. Every day Daniel prays to his God three times, just as he did before you signed the writing of the law."

Then the king was very sorry for what he had done, for he loved Daniel, and knew that no one could take his place in the kingdom. All day, until the sun went down, he tried in vain to find some way to save Daniel's life; but when evening came these men again told him of the law that he had made, and said to him that it must be kept. Very unwillingly the king sent for Daniel, and gave an order that he should be thrown into the den of lions. He said to Daniel, "Perhaps your God, whom you serve so faithfully, will save you from the lions."

They led Daniel to the mouth of the pit where the lions were kept, and they threw him in; and over the mouth they placed a stone; and the king sealed it with his own seal and with the seals of his nobles, so that no one might take away the stone and let Daniel out of the den.

Then the king went again to his palace, but that night he was so sad that he could not eat, nor did he listen to music as he was used to listen. He could not sleep, for all through the night he was thinking of Daniel. Very early in the morning he rose up from his bed and went in haste to the den of lions. He broke the seal, and took away the stone, and in a voice full of sorrow he called out, scarcely hoping to hear any answer except the roaring of the lions, "O Daniel, servant of the living God, has your God been able to keep you safe from the lions?"

And out of the darkness in the den came the voice of Daniel, saying, "O king, may you live forever! My God has sent his angel, and has shut the mouths of the lions. They have not hurt me, because my God saw that I had done no wrong. And I have done no wrong toward you, O king!"

Then the king was glad. He gave to his servants orders to take Daniel out of the den. Daniel was brought out safe and without harm, because he had trusted fully in the Lord God. Then, by the king's command, they seized those men who had spoken against Daniel, and with them their wives and their children, for the king was exceedingly angry with them. They were all thrown into the den, and the hungry lions leaped upon them, and tore them in pieces as soon as they fell upon the floor of the den.

After this King Darius wrote to all the lands and the peoples in the many kingdoms under his rule, "May peace be given to you all abundantly! I make a law that everywhere among my kingdoms men fear and worship the Lord God of Daniel, for he is the living God, above all other gods, who only can save men."

The 23rd Psalm

The book of Psalms was the ancient hymnal of the Jewish people. Most of the psalms were probably written for use in worship; one finds among them songs of praise, thanksgiving, adoration, devotion, doubt, and complaint. Martin Luther called the Psalter "a Bible in miniature." Psalm 23, a hymn of trust in God, is probably the most widely loved.

The Lord is my shepherd; I shall not want.

He maketh me to lie down in green pastures: he leadeth me beside the still waters.

He restoreth my soul: he leadeth me in the paths of righteousness for his name's sake.

Yea, though I walk through the valley of the shadow of death, I will fear no evil: for thou art with me; thy rod and thy staff they comfort me.

Thou preparest a table before me in the presence of mine enemies: thou anointest my head with oil; my cup runneth over.

Surely goodness and mercy shall follow me all the days of my life: and I will dwell in the house of the Lord forever.

The Healing of the Paralytic

Retold by Jesse Lyman Hurlbut

This story from the New Testament is a miracle story of physical healing brought about through tremendous faith. It is a good way to remember that faith heals spiritually as well.

After a time Jesus came again to Capernaum, which was now his home. As soon as the people heard that he was there they came in great crowds to see him and to hear him. They filled the house, and the courtyard inside its walls, and even the streets around it, while Jesus sat in the open court of the house and taught them. It was the springtime and warm, and a roof had been placed over the court as a shelter from the sun.

While Jesus was teaching, the roof was suddenly taken away above their heads. They looked up, and saw that a man was being let down in a bed by four men on the walls above.

This man was paralyzed, so that he could neither walk nor stand. He was so eager to come to Jesus that these men, finding that they could not carry him through the crowd, had lifted him up to the top of the house, and had opened the roof, and were now letting him down in his bed before Jesus.

This showed that they believed in Jesus, without any doubt whether he could cure this man. Jesus said to the man, "My son, be of good cheer; your sins are forgiven!"

The enemies of Jesus who were sitting near heard these words, and they thought in their own minds, though they did not speak it aloud, "What wicked things this man speaks! He claims to forgive sins! Who except God himself has power to say, 'Your sins are forgiven'?"

Jesus knew their thoughts, for he knew all things, and he said, "Why do you think evil in your hearts? Which is the easier to say, 'Your sins are forgiven,' or 'Rise up and walk'? But I will show you that while I am on earth as the Son of Man, I have the power to forgive sins."

Then he spoke to the paralyzed man on his couch before them, "Rise up, take up your bed, and go to your house!"

At once a new life and power came to the man. He stood upon

his feet, rolled up the bed on which he had been lying helpless, placed it on his shoulders and walked out through the crowd, which opened to make a way for him. The man went, strong and well, to his own house, praising God as he walked.

The Captain's Daughter

James T. Fields

Sometimes the youngest inspire us the most by their trust in a higher power. This is a good poem to recite aloud.

> We were crowded in the cabin,
>   Not a soul would dare to sleep—
> It was midnight on the waters,
>   And a storm was on the deep.
>
> 'Tis a fearful thing in winter
>   To be shattered by the blast,
> And to hear the rattling trumpet
>   Thunder, "Cut away the mast!"
>
> So we shuddered there in silence—
>   For the stoutest held his breath,
> While the hungry sea was roaring
>   And the breakers talked with Death.
>
> As thus we sat in darkness,
>   Each one busy with his prayers,
> "We are lost!" the captain shouted
>   As he staggered down the stairs.
>
> But his little daughter whispered,
>   As she took his icy hand,
> "Isn't God upon the ocean,
>   Just the same as on the land?"

Then we kissed the little maiden,
And we spoke in better cheer,
And we anchored safe in harbor
When the morn was shining clear.

The Sermon to the Birds

Retold by James Baldwin

St. Francis was born in the latter part of the twelfth century in
Assisi, Italy. The founder of the Franciscan order of the Roman
Catholic church, he is still admired today for his simple life of
poverty, his love of peace, and his respect for all living things.
Here is one of the most famous stories about him.

Very kind and loving was St. Francis—kind and loving not
only to men but to all living things. He spoke of the birds as his little
brothers of the air, and he could never bear to see them harmed.

At Christmastime he scattered crumbs of bread under the trees,
so that the tiny creatures could feast and be happy.

Once when a boy gave him a pair of doves which he had snared,
St. Francis had a nest made for them, and the mother bird laid her
eggs in it.

By and by, the eggs hatched, and a nestful of young doves grew
up. They were so tame that they sat on the shoulders of St. Francis
and ate from his hand.

And many other stories are told of this man's great love and
pity for the timid creatures which lived in the fields and woods.

One day as he was walking among the trees the birds saw him
and flew down to greet him. They sang their sweetest songs to show
how much they loved him. Then, when they saw that he was about
to speak, they nestled softly in the grass and listened.

"O little birds," he said, "I love you, for you are my brothers
and sisters of the air. Let me tell you something, my little brothers,
my little sisters: You ought always to love God and praise Him.

"For think what He has given you. He has given you wings

with which to fly through the air. He has given you clothing both warm and beautiful. He has given you the air in which to move and have homes.

"And think of this, O little brothers: you sow not, neither do you reap, for God feeds you. He gives you the rivers and the brooks from which to drink. He gives you the mountains and the valleys where you may rest. He gives you the trees in which to build your nests.

"You toil not, neither do you spin, yet God takes care of you and your little ones. It must be, then, that He loves you. So, do not be ungrateful, but sing His praises and thank Him for his goodness toward you."

Then the saint stopped speaking and looked around him. All the birds sprang up joyfully. They spread their wings and opened their mouths to show that they understood his words.

And when he had blessed them, all began to sing; and the whole forest was filled with sweetness and joy because of their wonderful melodies.

The Honest Disciple

As this Jewish folk tale reminds us, faith is often the path to other virtues (in this case, honesty).

Once a rabbi decided to test the honesty of his disciples, so he called them together and posed a question.

"What would you do if you were walking along and found a purse full of money lying in the road?" he asked.

"I'd return it to its owner," said one disciple.

"His answer comes so quickly, I must wonder if he really means it," the rabbi thought.

"I'd keep the money if nobody saw me find it," said another.

"He has a frank tongue, but a wicked heart," the rabbi told himself.

"Well, Rabbi," said a third disciple, "to be honest, I believe I'd be tempted to keep it. So I would pray to God that He give me the strength to resist such temptation and do the right thing."

"Aha!" thought the rabbi. "Here is the man I would trust."

St. Nicholas and the Golden Bars

Since the Middle Ages, St. Nicholas has been one of the most popular saints of the Christian church. He is the patron saint of merchants, travelers, sailors, bakers, and, of course, children, who seldom fail to be curious about the "ancestor" of Santa Claus (a name which comes from Sinter-Klaas, as St. Nicholas is known in Holland).

Long ago there lived a husband and wife who had more money than they knew what to do with, but more than anything else they wanted a child. They prayed to God for many years to give them their heart's desire, and at last when a son was born, they were the happiest people in the world. They named him Nicholas.

They thought there was no one like their boy, and indeed he was a kind and gentle child, and never gave them a moment's trouble. But while he was still a little boy, a terrible plague swept over the country, and his father and mother died, leaving him quite alone.

All the great riches which his parents had possessed were left to Nicholas, and among other things he inherited three bars of gold. These were his greatest treasure, and he thought more of them than all his other riches.

Now in Nicholas's town there lived a nobleman with three daughters. They had once been very wealthy, but great misfortunes had overtaken the father, and now they were all so poor they scarcely had enough to live on. The nobleman tried as hard as he could to find work, but when people saw his soft hands, which had never known any kind of hard labor, they took him to be lazy, and turned him away.

At last a day came when there was not even enough bread to eat, and the daughters said to their father: "Let us go out into the streets and beg, or do anything to get a little money, so we won't starve."

But the father answered: "Not tonight. I cannot bear to think of it. Wait at least until tomorrow. Something may happen to save us from such disgrace."

Just as they were talking together, Nicholas happened to be passing, and since the window was open he heard all they said. It seemed terrible to think that this family should be so poor and actually in want of bread, and Nicholas tried to plan a way to help them.

He knew they would be much too proud to take money from him, so he had to think of some other way. "I must ask God to show me how," he told himself.

So that night, before he climbed into bed, Nicholas prayed as hard as he could, and asked God to guide him. Suddenly he remembered the three golden bars, and at once an idea flashed into his head. He jumped up and took one of them, and quickly started out for the nobleman's house.

Just as he had hoped, Nicholas discovered that the same window was still open, and by standing on tiptoe he could barely reach it. So he lifted the golden bar and slipped it through, and didn't wait to hear what became of it, in case anyone should see him.

Inside the house, the poor father sat worrying as his children slept. He wondered if there was any hope for them anywhere, and he prayed earnestly that heaven would send help. "Tomorrow I will knock on every door in the city until I find work," he told himself. "God will help us through these hard times."

Suddenly something fell at his feet. The nobleman looked down, and to his amazement and joy, he found it was a bar of pure gold.

"My child," he cried as he showed his eldest daughter the shining gold, "God has heard our prayers and has sent this from heaven! Now we will have enough to eat and some to spare. Call your sisters, and I will go and change this treasure."

The precious golden bar was soon sold to a bank, and it brought so much money, the family was able to live in comfort and have all they needed. And not only was there enough to live on, but so much was left over that the father gave his eldest daughter a large dowry, and very soon she was happily married.

When Nicholas saw how much happiness his golden bar had brought to the poor nobleman, he decided the second daughter should have a dowry too. So he went as before and found the little window again open, and was able to throw in the second bar as he had done before. This time the father was dreaming happily, and did not find the treasure until he waked the next morning. Soon afterward the second daughter had her dowry and was married too.

Now, the father began to think that it was a bit unusual, to say the least, that not one but two golden bars should fall from heaven, and he wondered if by any chance human hands had placed them in his room. The more he thought about it, the more mysterious it seemed, and he made up his mind to keep watch every night, in case another bar should be sent as a dowry for his third daughter.

And so when Nicholas went the third time and dropped the last bar through the little window, the father came quickly out, and before Nicholas had time to hide, caught him by the cloak.

"O Nicholas," he cried, "are you the one who has helped us in our need? Why did you hide?" And then he fell on his knees and began to kiss the hands that had helped him so graciously. But Nicholas asked him to stand up, and give thanks to God instead, and begged him not to tell anyone the story of the golden bars.

Hanukkah Hymn

The Hanukkah festival of lights commemorates the rededication of the Temple in Jerusalem. This Hanukkah hymn expresses the praise, joy, and hope appropriate in commemorating that historic event.

Rock of Ages, let our song
Praise Thy saving power;
Thou, amidst the raging foes,
Wast our sheltering tower.
Furious, they assailed us,
But Thine arm availed us,
And Thy word
Broke their sword
When our own strength failed us.

Kindling new the holy lamps,
Priest approved in suffering,
Purified the nation's shrine,
Brought to God their offering.
And His courts surrounding,
Hear, in joy abounding,
Happy throngs
Singing songs
With a mighty sounding.

Children of the martyr race,
Whether free or fettered,
Wake the echoes of the songs
Where ye may be scattered.
Yours the message cheering
That the time is nearing
Which will see
All men free,
Tyrants disappearing.

A Child's Dream of a Star

Charles Dickens

Of all the virtues, faith best helps us bear the pain and uncertainty of life lost.

There was once a child, and he strolled about a good deal, and thought of a number of things. He had a sister, who was a child too, and his constant companion. These two used to wonder all day long. They wondered at the beauty of the flowers; they wondered at the height and blueness of the sky; they wondered at the depth of the bright water; they wondered at the goodness and the power of God who made the lovely world.

They used to say to one another, sometimes, Supposing all the children upon earth were to die, would the flowers, and the water, and the sky be sorry? They believed they would be sorry. For, said they, the buds are the children of the flowers, and the little playful streams that gambol down the hillsides are the children of the water; and the smallest bright specks playing at hide-and-seek in the sky all night, must surely be the children of the stars; and they would all be grieved to see their playmates, the children of men, no more.

There was one clear, shining star that used to come out in the sky before the rest, near the church spire, above the graves. It was larger and more beautiful, they thought, than all the others, and every night they watched for it, standing hand in hand at a window. Whoever saw it first, cried out, "I see the star!" And often they cried out both together, knowing so well when it would rise, and where. So they grew to be such friends with it, that, before lying down in their beds, they always looked out once again, to bid it good night; and when they were turning round to sleep, they used to say, "God bless the star!"

But while she was still very young, oh, very, very young, the sister drooped, and came to be so weak that she could no longer stand in the window at night; and then the child looked sadly out by himself, and when he saw the star, turned round and said to the patient pale face on the bed, "I see the star!" and then a smile would come upon the face, and a little weak voice used to say, "God bless my brother and the star!"

And so the time came, all too soon! when the child looked out alone, and when there was no face on the bed; and when there was a little grave among the graves, not there before; and when the star made long rays down toward him, as he saw it through his tears.

Now, these rays were so bright, and they seemed to make such a shining way from earth to heaven, that when the child went to his solitary bed, he dreamed about the star; and dreamed that, lying where he was, he saw a train of people taken up that sparkling road by angels. And the star, opening, showed him a great world of light, where many more such angels waited to receive them.

All these angels, who were waiting, turned their beaming eyes upon the people who were carried up into the star; and some came out from the long rows in which they stood, and fell upon the people's necks, and kissed them tenderly, and went away with them down avenues of light, and were so happy in their company, that lying in his bed he wept for joy.

But there were many angels who did not go with them, and among them one he knew. The patient face that once had lain upon the bed was glorified and radiant, but his heart found out his sister among all the host.

His sister's angel lingered near the entrance of the star, and said to the leader among those who had brought the people thither:

"Is my brother come?"

And he said, "No."

She was turning hopefully away when the child stretched out his arms, and cried, "Oh sister, I am here! Take me!" and then she turned her beaming eyes upon him, and it was night; and the star was shining into the room, making long rays down toward him as he saw it through his tears.

From that hour forth, the child looked out upon the star as on the home he was to go to, when his time should come; and he thought that he did not belong to the earth alone, but to the star too, because of his sister's angel gone before.

There was a baby born to be a brother of the child; and while he was so little that he never yet had spoken word, he stretched his tiny form out on his bed, and died.

Again the child dreamed of the opened star, and of the company of angels, and the train of people, and the rows of angels with their beaming eyes all turned upon those people's faces.

Said his sister's angel to the leader:

"Is my brother come?"

And he said, "Not that one, but another."

As the child beheld his brother's angel in her arms, he cried, "Oh, sister, I am here! Take me!" And she turned and smiled upon him, and the star was shining.

He grew to be a young man, and was busy at this books when an old servant came to him and said:

"Thy mother is no more. I bring her blessing on her darling son!"

Again at night he saw the star, and all that former company. Said his sister's angel to the leader:

"Is my brother come?"

And he said, "Thy mother!"

A mighty cry of joy went forth through all the star, because the mother was reunited to her two children. And he stretched out his arms and cried, "Oh, mother, sister, and brother, I am here! Take me!" And they answered him, "Not yet," and the star was shining.

He grew to be a man, whose hair was turning gray, and he was sitting in his chair by the fireside, heavy with grief, and with his face bedewed with tears, when the star opened once again.

Said his sister's angel to the leader, "Is my brother come?"

And he said, "Nay, but his maiden daughter."

And the man who had been the child saw his daughter, newly lost to him, a celestial creature among those three, and he said, "My daughter's head is on my sister's bosom, and her arm is around my mother's neck, and at her feet there is the baby of old time, and I can bear the parting from her, God be praised!"

And the star was shining.

Thus the child came to be an old man, and his once smooth face was wrinkled, and his steps were slow and feeble, and his back was bent. And one night as he lay upon his bed, his children standing round, he cried as he had cried so long ago:

"I see the star!"

They whispered to one another, "He is dying."

And he said, "I am. My age is falling from me like a garment, and I move toward the star as a child. And oh, my Father, now I thank Thee that it has so often opened, to receive those dear ones who await me!"

And the star was shining; and it shines upon his grave.

Nearer Home

Phoebe Cary

This poem expresses the sentiments of John Greenleaf Whittier, who said that "the steps of faith fall on the seeming void, but find the rock beneath."

> One sweetly solemn thought
>   Comes to me o'er and o'er;
> I'm nearer my home today
>   Than I ever have been before;
>
> Nearer my Father's house,
>   Where the many mansions be;
> Nearer the great white throne,
>   Nearer the crystal sea.
>
> Nearer the bound of life,
>   Where we lay our burdens down;
> Nearer leaving the cross,
>   Nearer gaining the crown!
>
> But lying darkly between,
>   Winding down through the night,
> Is the silent, unknown stream,
>   That leads at last to the light.

Oh, if my mortal feet
   Have almost gained the brink;
If it be I am nearer home
   Even today than I think—

Father, perfect my trust!
   Let my spirit feel, in death,
That her feet are firmly set
   On the Rock of a living faith!

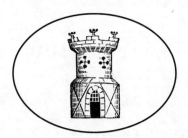

A Mighty Fortress Is Our God

Martin Luther

This hymn, written by Martin Luther in 1529, has been charac-
terized as "the Battle Hymn of the Reformation." One admirer
has noted that "there is something in it like the sound of Alpine
avalanches and the first murmur of earthquakes." It is based on
Psalm 46.

A mighty fortress is our God,
A bulwark never failing;
Our helper he, amid the flood
Of mortal ills prevailing.
For still our ancient foe
Doth seek to work us woe;
His craft and pow'r are great,
And arm'd with cruel hate,
On earth is not his equal.

Did we in our own strength confide,
Our striving would be losing;
Were not the right man on our side,
The man of God's own choosing.
Dost ask who that may be?
Christ Jesus, it is he;
Lord Sabaoth his name,
From age to age the same,
And he must win the battle.

And though this world, with demons fill'd,
Should threaten to undo us,
We will not fear, for God hath willed
His truth to triumph through us.
The Prince of darkness grim,
We tremble not for him;
His rage we can endure,
For lo, his doom is sure—
One little word shall fell him.

God's word above all earthly pow'rs,
No thanks to them, abideth;
The Spirit and the gifts are ours
Through him who with us sideth.
Let goods and kindred go,
This mortal life also;
The body they may kill;
God's truth abideth still,
His kingdom is forever.

Amazing Grace

John Newton

John Newton, the London-born author of this hymn, went to sea at age eleven, was later imprisoned on a man-of-war, escaped to work on a slave-trading vessel, and eventually became a slave ship captain. The hymn is a personal testimony to the "amazing grace" that turned Newton's life around (he later became an ardent abolitionist). After his ordination into the ministry of the Church of England in 1764, Newton and William Cowper produced the *Olney Hymns,* one of the greatest of the Anglican hymnals.

Amazing grace, how sweet the sound,
That saved a wretch like me!
I once was lost, but now am found,
Was blind, but now I see.

'Twas grace that taught my heart to fear,
And grace my fears relieved;
How precious did that grace appear
The hour I first believed!

Through many dangers, toils, and snares,
I have already come;
'Tis grace has brought me safe thus far,
And grace will lead me home.

The Lord has promised good to me,
His word my hope secures;
He will my shield and portion be
As long as life endures.

When we've been there ten thousand years,
Bright shining as the sun,
We've no less days to sing God's praise
Than when we'd first begun.

Faith of Our Fathers, Living Still

Frederick W. Faber

This hymn makes us mindful of the millions of martyrs around
the world who suffered dungeons, fire, and sword for their faith,
including those who today know the insides of "prisons dark" so
that they and others may be "in heart and conscience free." The
original version of this hymn was first published in 1849.

Faith of our fathers, living still
In spite of dungeon, fire and sword,
O how our hearts beat high with joy
Whene'er we hear that glorious word!
Faith of our fathers, holy faith,
We will be true to thee till death.

Our fathers, chained in prisons dark,
Were still in heart and conscience free,
And blest would be their children's fate,
Though they, like them, should die for thee.
Faith of our fathers, holy faith,
We will be true to thee till death.

Faith of our fathers, faith and prayer,
Shall keep our country brave and free,
And through the truth that comes from God,
Our land shall then indeed be free.
Faith of our fathers, holy faith,
We will be true to thee till death.

Faith of our fathers, we will love
Both friend and foe in all our strife,
And preach thee, too, as love knows how
By kindly words and virtuous life.
Faith of our fathers, holy faith,
We will be true to thee till death.

We Understand So Little

Our understanding of God's creation is imperfect, so our faith
must fill in the gaps, as this old Jewish folktale reminds us.

Once there were two young brothers who had spent all their
lives in the city, and had never even seen a field or pasture. So one
day they decided to take a trip into the countryside. As they were
walking along, they spied a farmer plowing, and were puzzled about
what he was doing.

"What kind of behavior is this?" they asked themselves. "This
fellow marches back and forth all day, scarring the earth with long
ditches. Why should anyone destroy such a pretty meadow like
that?"

Later in the afternoon they passed the same place again, and this
time they saw the farmer sowing grains of wheat in the furrows.

"Now what's he doing?" they asked themselves. "He must be
a madman. He's taking perfectly good wheat and tossing it into
these ditches!"

"The country is no place for me," said one of the brothers.
"The people here act as if they had no sense. I'm going home." And
he went back to the city.

But the second brother stayed in the country, and a few weeks
later saw a wonderful change. Fresh green shoots began to cover the
field with a lushness he had never imagined. He quickly wrote to his
brother and told him to hurry back to see the miraculous growth.

So his brother returned from the city, and he too was amazed at
the change. As the days passed they saw the green earth turn into a
golden field of tall wheat. And now they understood the reason for
the farmer's work.

Then the wheat grew ripe, and the farmer came with his scythe
and began to cut it down. The brother who had returned from
the city couldn't believe it. "What is this imbecile doing now?" he
exclaimed. "All summer long he worked so hard to grow this beautiful wheat, and now he's destroying it with his own hands! He is a
madman after all! I've had enough. I'm going back to the city."

But his brother had more patience. He stayed in the country
and watched the farmer collect the wheat and take it to his granary.
He saw how cleverly he separated the chaff, and how carefully he

stored the rest. And he was filled with awe when he realized that by sowing a bag of seed, the farmer had harvested a whole field of grain. Only then did he truly understand that the farmer had a reason for everything he did.

"And this is how it is with God's works, too," he said. "We mortals see only the beginnings of His plan. We cannot understand the full purpose and end of His creation. So we must have faith in His wisdom."

Deucalion and Pyrrha

Retold by Thomas Bulfinch

Greek mythology describes a Golden Age of innocence and happiness, followed by the ages of Silver, Bronze, and finally Iron. The latter was a savage time when "crime burst in like a flood" and "modesty, truth, and honor fled." War sprang up; the guest was not safe in his friend's house; brothers and sisters, husbands and wives could not trust one another. Reverence toward the gods was neglected, and one by one they abandoned the earth. Only the piety of one couple, Deucalion and Pyrrha, saved the human race.

Jupiter, seeing the wicked state of the world, burned with anger. He summoned the gods to council. They obeyed the call, and took the road to the palace of heaven. The road, which anyone may see in a clear night, stretches across the face of the sky, and is called the Milky Way. Along the road stand the palaces of the illustrious gods; the common people of the skies live apart, on either side. Jupiter addressed the assembly. He set forth the frightful condition of things on the earth, and closed by announcing his intention to destroy the whole of its inhabitants, and provide a new race, unlike the first, who would be more worthy of life, and much better worshippers of the gods.

So saying he took a thunderbolt, and was about to launch it at the world, and destroy it by burning; but recollecting the danger

that such a conflagration might set heaven itself on fire, he changed
his plan, and resolved to drown it. The north wind, which scatters
the clouds, was chained up; the south was sent out, and soon covered
all the face of heaven with a cloak of pitchy darkness. The clouds,
driven together, resound with a crash; torrents of rain fall; the crops
are laid low; the year's labor of the husbandman perishes in an hour.
Jupiter, not satisfied with his own waters, calls on his brother Neptune to aid him with his. He lets loose the rivers, and pours them
over the land. At the same time, he heaves the land with an earthquake, and brings in the reflux of the ocean over the shores. Flocks,
herds, men, and houses are swept away, and temples, with their
sacred enclosures, profaned. If any edifice remained standing, it was
overwhelmed, and its turrets lay hid beneath the waves.

Now all was sea, sea without shore. Here and there an individual remained on a projecting hilltop, and a few, in boats, pulled the
oar where they had lately driven the plow. The fishes swim among
the treetops; the anchor is let down into a garden. Where the graceful
lambs played but now, unwieldy sea calves gambol. The wolf swims
among the sheep, the yellow lions and tigers struggle in the water.
The strength of the wild boar serves him not, nor his swiftness the
stag. The birds fall with weary wing into the water, having found
no land for a resting place. Those living beings whom the water
spared fell a prey to hunger.

Parnassus alone, of all the mountains, overtopped the waves;
and there Deucalion, and his wife, Pyrrha, of the race of Prometheus, found refuge—he a just man, and she a faithful worshipper of
the gods. Jupiter, when he saw none left alive but this pair, and
remembered their harmless lives and pious demeanor, ordered the
north winds to drive away the clouds, and disclose the skies to earth,
and earth to the skies. Neptune also directed Triton to blow on his
shell, and sound a retreat to the waters. The waters obeyed, and the
sea returned to its shores, and the rivers to their channels.

Then Deucalion thus addressed Pyrrha: "O wife, only surviving
woman, joined to me first by the ties of kindred and marriage, and
now by a common danger, would that we possessed the power of
our ancestor Prometheus, and could renew the race as he at first
made it! But as we cannot, let us seek yonder temple, and inquire of
the gods what remains for us to do."

They entered the temple, deformed as it was with slime, and
approached the altar, where no fire burned. There they fell prostrate
on the earth, and prayed the goddess to inform them how they
might retrieve their miserable affairs. The oracle answered, "Depart

from the temple with head veiled and garments unbound, and cast behind you the bones of your mother."

They heard the words with astonishment. Pyrrha first broke silence: "We cannot obey; we dare not profane the remains of our parents."

They sought the thickest shades of the wood, and revolved the oracle in their minds. At length Deucalion spoke: "Either my sagacity deceives me, or the command is one we may obey without impiety. The earth is the great parent of all; the stones are her bones; these we may cast behind us; and I think this is what the oracle means. At least, it will do no harm to try."

They veiled their faces, unbound their garments, and picked up stones, and cast them behind them. The stones (wonderful to relate) began to grow soft, and assume shape. By degrees, they put on a rude resemblance to the human form, like a block half finished in the hands of the sculptor. The moisture and slime that were about them became flesh; the stony part became bones; the veins remained veins, retaining their name, only changing their use. Those thrown by the hand of the man became men, and those by the woman became women. It was a hard race, and well adapted to labor, as we find ourselves to be at this day, giving plain indications of our origin.

A Name in the Sand

Hannah Flagg Gould

This poem reminds us that we should not overestimate our own importance—except in the eyes of God.

> Alone I walked the ocean strand;
> A pearly shell was in my hand:
> I stooped and wrote upon the sand
>   My name—the year—the day.
> As onward from the spot I passed,
> One lingering look behind I cast;
> A wave came rolling high and fast,
>   And washed my lines away.

And so, methought, 'twill shortly be
With every mark on earth from me:
A wave of dark oblivion's sea
   Will sweep across the place
Where I have trod the sandy shore
Of time, and been, to be no more,
Of me—my day—the name I bore,
   To leave nor track nor trace.

And yet, with Him who counts the sands
And holds the waters in His hands,
I know a lasting record stands
   Inscribed against my name,
Of all this mortal part has wrought,
Of all this thinking soul has thought,
And from these fleeting moments caught
   For glory or for shame.

The Kids Can't Take It If
We Don't Give It

George Herman "Babe" Ruth

We should not assume that disciplined faith springs from the heart of its own accord. We do not necessarily "find" such faith on our own. Baseball great Babe Ruth (1895–1948) reminds us that, like other virtues, it must be transmitted to the young by caring adults.

Bad boy Ruth—that was me.

Don't get the idea that I'm proud of my harum-scarum youth. I'm not. I simply had a rotten start in life, and it took me a long time to get my bearings.

Looking back to my youth, I honestly don't think I knew the difference between right and wrong. I spent much of my early boyhood living over my father's saloon, in Baltimore—and when I wasn't living over it, I was in it, soaking up the atmosphere. I hardly knew my parents.

St. Mary's Industrial School in Baltimore, where I was finally taken, has been called an orphanage and a reform school. It was, in fact, a training school for orphans, incorrigibles, delinquents, and runaways picked up on the streets of the city. I was listed as an incorrigible. I guess I was. Perhaps I would always have been but for Brother Matthias, the greatest man I have ever known, and for the religious training I received there which has since been so important to me.

I doubt if any appeal could have straightened me out except a Power over and above man—the appeal of God. Iron-rod discipline couldn't have done it. Nor all the punishment and reward systems that could have been devised. God had an eye out for me, just as He has for you, and He was pulling for me to make the grade.

As I look back now, I realize that knowledge of God was a big crossroads with me. I got one thing straight (and I wish all kids did) —that God was Boss. He was not only my Boss but Boss of all my bosses. Up till then, like all bad kids, I hated most of the people who had control over me and could punish me. I began to see that I had a higher Person to reckon with who never changed, whereas my earthly authorities changed from year to year. Those who bossed me had the same self-battles—they, like me, had to account to God. I also realized that God was not only just, but merciful. He knew we were weak and that we all found it easier to be stinkers than good sons of God, not only as kids but all through our lives.

That clear picture, I'm sure, would be important to any kid who hates a teacher, or resents a person in charge. This picture of my relationship to man and God was what helped relieve me of bitterness and rancor and a desire to get even.

I've seen a great number of "he-men" in my baseball career, but never one equal to Brother Matthias. He stood six feet six and weighed 250 pounds. It was all muscle. He could have been successful at anything he wanted to in life—and he chose the church.

It was he who introduced me to baseball. Very early he noticed that I had some natural talent for throwing and catching. He used to back me in a corner of the big yard at St. Mary's and bunt a ball to me by the hour, correcting the mistakes I made with my hands and feet. I never forgot the first time I saw him hit a ball. The baseball in 1902 was a lump of mush, but Brother Matthias would stand at the end of the yard, throw the ball up with his left hand, and give it a terrific belt with the bat he held in his right hand. The ball would carry 350 feet, a tremendous knock in those days. I would watch him bug-eyed.

Thanks to Brother Matthias I was able to leave St. Mary's in 1914 and begin my professional career with the famous Baltimore Orioles [at that time a minor league team]. Out on my own . . . free from the rigid rules of a religious school . . . boy, did it go to my head. I began really to cut capers.

I strayed from the church, but don't think I forgot my religious training. I just overlooked it. I prayed often and hard, but, like many irrepressible young fellows, the swift tempo of my living shoved religion into the background.

So what good was all the hard work and ceaseless interest of the Brothers, people would argue? You can't make kids religious, they say, because it just won't take. Send kids to Sunday School and they too often end up hating it and the church.

Don't you believe it. As far as I'm concerned, and I think as far as most kids go, once religion sinks in, it stays there—deep down. The lads who get religious training, get it where it counts—in the roots. They may fail it, but it never fails them. When the score is against them, or they get a bum pitch, that unfailing Something inside will be there to draw on.

I've seen it with kids. I know from the letters they write me.

The more I think of it, the more important I feel it is to give kids "the works" as far as religion is concerned. They'll never want to be holy—they'll act like tough monkeys in contrast, but somewhere inside will be a solid little chapel. It may get dusty from neglect, but the time will come when the door will be opened with much relief. But the kids can't take it, if we don't give it to them.

I've been criticized as often as I'm praised for my activities with kids on the grounds that what I did was for publicity. Well, criticism doesn't matter. I never forgot where I came from. Every dirty-faced kid I see is another useful citizen. No one knew better than I what it meant not to have your own home, a backyard, and your own kitchen and ice box. That's why all through the years, even when the big money was rolling in, I'd never forget St. Mary's, Brother Matthias, and the boys I left behind. I kept going back.

As I look back those moments when I let the kids down—they were my worst. I guess I was so anxious to enjoy life to the fullest that I forgot the rules—or ignored them. Once in a while you can get away with it, but not for long. When I broke training, the effects were felt by myself and by the ball team—and even by the fans.

While I drifted away from the church, I did have my own "altar," a big window of my New York apartment overlooking the city lights. Often I would kneel before that window and say my prayers. I would feel quite humble then. I'd ask God to help me not make such a big fool of myself and pray that I'd measure up to what He expected of me.

In December 1946 I was in French Hospital, New York, facing a serious operation. Paul Carey, one of my oldest and closest friends, was by my bed one night.

"They're going to operate in the morning, Babe," Paul said. "Don't you think you ought to put your house in order?"

I didn't dodge the long, challenging look in his eyes. I knew what he meant. For the first time I realized that death might strike me out. I nodded, and Paul got up, called in a chaplain, and I made a full confession.

"I'll return in the morning and give you Holy Communion," the chaplain said, "but you don't have to fast."

"I'll fast," I said. I didn't have even a drop of water.

As I lay in bed that evening I thought to myself what a comforting feeling to be free from fear and worries. I now could simply turn them over to God. Later on, my wife brought in a letter from a little kid in Jersey City.

"Dear Babe," he wrote. "Everybody in the seventh-grade class is pulling and praying for you. I am enclosing a medal which if you wear will make you better. Your pal—Mike Quinlan.

"P.S. I know this will be your 61st homer. You'll hit it."

I asked them to pin the Miraculous Medal to my pajama coat. I've worn the medal constantly ever since. I'll wear it to my grave.

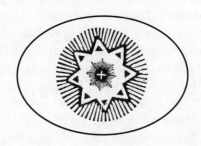

Our Lady's Juggler

Anatole France

Faith leads us to employ our God-given talents in God's service.

In the days of King Louis there was a poor juggler in France, a native of Compiègne, Barnaby by name, who went about from town to town performing feats of skill and strength.

On fair days he would unfold an old worn-out carpet in the public square, and when by means of a jovial address, which he had learned of a very ancient juggler, and which he never varied in the least, he had drawn together the children and loafers, he assumed extraordinary attitudes, and balanced a tin plate on the tip of his nose. At first the crowd would feign indifference.

But when, supporting himself on his hands face downward, he threw into the air six copper balls, which glittered in the sunshine, and caught them again with his feet; or when throwing himself backward until his heels and the nape of the neck met, giving his body the form of a perfect wheel, he would juggle in this posture with a dozen knives, a murmur of admiration would escape the spectators, and pieces of money rain down upon the carpet.

Nevertheless, like the majority of those who live by their wits, Barnaby of Compiègne had a great struggle to make a living.

Earning his bread in the sweat of his brow, he bore rather more than his share of the penalties consequent upon the misdoings of our father Adam.

Again, he was unable to work as constantly as he would have been willing to do. The warmth of the sun and the broad daylight were as necessary to enable him to display his brilliant parts as to the trees if flower and fruit should be expected of them. In wintertime he was nothing more than a tree stripped of its leaves, and as it were dead. The frozen ground was hard to the juggler, and, like the grasshopper of which Marie de France tells us, the inclement season caused him to suffer both cold and hunger. But as he was simple-natured he bore his ills patiently.

He had never meditated on the origin of wealth, nor upon the inequality of human conditions. He believed firmly that if this life should prove hard, the life to come could not fail to redress the balance, and this hope upheld him. He did not resemble those thievish and miscreant Merry Andrews who sell their souls to the devil. He never blasphemed God's name; he lived uprightly, and although he had no wife of his own, he did not covet his neighbor's, since woman is ever the enemy of the strong man, as it appears by the history of Samson recorded in the Scriptures.

In truth, his was not a nature much disposed to carnal delights, and it was a greater deprivation to him to forsake the tankard than the Hebe who bore it. For whilst not wanting in sobriety, he was fond of a drink when the weather waxed hot. He was a worthy man who feared God, and was very devoted to the Blessed Virgin.

Never did he fail on entering a church to fall upon his knees before the image of the Mother of God, and offer up this prayer to her:

"Blessed Lady, keep watch over my life until it shall please God that I die, and when I am dead, ensure to me the possession of the joys of paradise."

Now on a certain evening after a dreary wet day, as Barnaby pursued his road, sad and bent, carrying under his arm his balls and knives wrapped up in his old carpet, on the watch for some barn where, though he might not sup, he might sleep, he perceived on the road, going in the same direction as himself, a monk, whom he saluted courteously. And as they walked at the same rate they fell into conversation with one another.

"Fellow traveler," said the monk, "how comes it about that you are clothed all in green? Is it perhaps in order to take the part of a jester in some mystery play?"

"Not at all, good father," replied Barnaby. "Such as you see me, I am called Barnaby, and for my calling I am a juggler. There would be no pleasanter calling in the world if it would always provide one with daily bread."

"Friend Barnaby," returned the monk, "be careful what you say. There is no calling more pleasant than the monastic life. Those who lead it are occupied with the praises of God, the Blessed Virgin, and the saints; and, indeed, the religious life is one ceaseless hymn to the Lord."

Barnaby replied—

"Good father, I own that I spoke like an ignorant man. Your calling cannot be in any respect compared to mine, and although there may be some merit in dancing with a penny balanced on a stick on the tip of one's nose, it is not a merit which comes within hail of your own. Gladly would I, like you, good father, sing my office day by day, and especially the office of the most Holy Virgin, to whom I have vowed a singular devotion. In order to embrace the monastic life I would willingly abandon the art by which from Soissons to Beauvais I am well known in upward of six hundred towns and villages."

The monk was touched by the juggler's simplicity, and as he was not lacking in discernment, he at once recognized in Barnaby one of those men of whom it is said in the Scriptures: Peace on earth to men of good will. And for this reason he replied—

"Friend Barnaby, come with me, and I will have you admitted into the monastery of which I am prior. He who guided St. Mary of Egypt in the desert set me upon your path to lead you into the way of salvation."

It was in this manner, then, that Barnaby became a monk. In the monastery into which he was received the religious vied with one another in the worship of the Blessed Virgin, and in her honor each employed all the knowledge and all the skill which God had given him.

The prior on his part wrote books dealing according to the rules of scholarship with the virtues of the Mother of God.

Brother Maurice, with a deft hand, copied out these treatises upon sheets of vellum.

Brother Alexander adorned the leaves with delicate miniature paintings. Here were displayed the Queen of Heaven seated upon Solomon's throne, and while four lions were on guard at her feet, around the nimbus which encircled her head hovered seven doves, which are the seven gifts of the Holy Spirit, the gifts, namely, of Fear, Piety, Knowledge, Strength, Counsel, Understanding, and Wisdom. For her companions she had six virgins with hair of gold, namely, Humility, Prudence, Seclusion, Submission, Virginity, and Obedience.

At her feet were two little naked figures, perfectly white, in an attitude of supplication. These were souls imploring her all-powerful intercession for their soul's health, and we may be sure not imploring in vain.

Upon another page facing this, Brother Alexander represented Eve, so that the Fall and the Redemption could be perceived at one and the same time—Eve the Wife abased, and Mary the Virgin exalted.

Furthermore, to the marvel of the beholder, this book contained presentments of the Well of Living Waters, the Fountain, the Lily, the Moon, the Sun, and the Garden Enclosed of which the Song of Songs tells us, the Gate of Heaven and the City of God, and all these things were symbols of the Blessed Virgin.

Brother Marbode was likewise one of the most loving children of Mary.

He spent all his days carving images in stone, so that his beard, his eyebrows, and his hair were white with dust, and his eyes continually swollen and weeping; but his strength and cheerfulness were not diminished, although he was now well gone in years, and it was clear that the Queen of Paradise still cherished her servant in his old age. Marbode represented her seated upon a throne, her brow encircled with an orb-shaped nimbus set with pearls. And he took care that the folds of her dress should cover the feet of her, concerning whom the prophet declared: My beloved is as a garden enclosed.

Sometimes, too, he depicted her in the semblance of a child full of grace, and appearing to say, "Thou art my God, even from my mother's womb.

In the priory, moreover, were poets who composed hymns in Latin, both in prose and verse, in honor of the Blessed Virgin Mary, and amongst the company was even a brother from Picardy who sang the miracles of Our Lady in rhymed verse and in the vulgar tongue.

Being a witness of this emulation in praise and the glorious harvest of their labors, Barnaby mourned his own ignorance and simplicity.

"Alas!" he sighed, as he took his solitary walk in the little shelterless garden of the monastery, "wretched wight that I am, to be unable, like my brothers, worthily to praise the Holy Mother of God, to whom I have vowed my whole heart's affection. Alas! alas! I am but a rough man and unskilled in the arts, and I can render you in service, blessed Lady, neither edifying sermons, nor treatises set out in order according to rule, nor ingenious paintings, nor statues truthfully sculptured, nor verses whose march is measured to the beat of feet. No gift have I, alas!"

After this fashion he groaned and gave himself up to sorrow. But one evening, when the monks were spending their hour of liberty in conversation, he heard one of them tell the tale of a religious man who could repeat nothing other than the Ave Maria. This poor man was despised for his ignorance; but after his death there issued forth from his mouth five roses in honor of the five letters of the name Maria, and thus his sanctity was made manifest.

Whilst he listened to this narrative Barnaby marveled yet once again at the loving kindness of the Virgin; but the lesson of that blessed death did not avail to console him, for his heart overflowed with zeal, and he longed to advance the glory of his Lady, who is in heaven.

How to compass this he sought but could find no way, and day by day he became the more cast down, when one morning he awakened filled full with joy, hastened to the chapel, and remained there alone for more than an hour. After dinner he returned to the chapel once more.

And, starting from that moment, he repaired daily to the chapel at such hours as it was deserted, and spent within it a good part of the time which the other monks devoted to the liberal and mechanical arts. His sadness vanished, nor did he any longer groan.

A demeanor so strange awakened the curiosity of the monks.

These began to ask one another for what purpose Brother Barnaby could be indulging so persistently in retreat.

The prior, whose duty it is to let nothing escape him in the behavior of his children in religion, resolved to keep a watch over Barnaby during his withdrawals to the chapel. One day, then, when he was shut up there after his custom, the prior, accompanied by two of the older monks, went to discover through the chinks in the door what was going on within the chapel.

They saw Barnaby before the altar of the Blessed Virgin, head downward, with his feet in the air, and he was juggling with six balls of copper and a dozen knives. In honor of the Holy Mother of God he was performing those feats, which aforetime had won him most renown. Not recognizing that the simple fellow was thus placing at the service of the Blessed Virgin his knowledge and skill, the two old monks exclaimed against the sacrilege.

The prior was aware how stainless was Barnaby's soul, but he concluded that he had been seized with madness. They were all three preparing to lead him swiftly from the chapel, when they saw the Blessed Virgin descend the steps of the altar and advance to wipe away with a fold of her azure robe the sweat which was dropping from her juggler's forehead.

Then the prior, falling upon his face upon the pavement, uttered these words—

"Blessed are the simplehearted, for they shall see God."
"Amen!" responded the old brethren, and kissed the ground.

Mary Wollstonecraft on Faith

From A Vindication of the Rights of Woman

English author Mary Wollstonecraft (1759–1797) was a pioneer of the women's rights movement. Her major work, *A Vindication of the Rights of Woman,* shocked many contemporaries by calling for equal education and the opening of professions to women. Here the reformer expresses her faith that we improve ourselves according to God's plan.

In the present state of society it appears necessary to go back to first principles in search of the most simple truths, and to dispute with some prevailing prejudice every inch of ground. To clear my way, I must be allowed to ask some plain questions, and the answers will probably appear as unequivocal as the axioms on which reasoning is built; though, when entangled with various motives of action, they are formally contradicted, either by the words or conduct of men.

In what does man's preeminence over the brute creation consist? The answer is as clear as that a half is less than the whole, in Reason.

What acquirement exalts one being above another? Virtue, we spontaneously reply.

For what purpose were the passions implanted? That man by struggling with them might attain a degree of knowledge denied to the brutes, whispers Experience.

Consequently the perfection of our nature and capability of happiness must be estimated by the degree of reason, virtue, and knowledge, that distinguish the individual, and direct the laws which bind society: and that from the exercise of reason, knowledge and virtue naturally flow, is equally undeniable, if mankind be viewed collectively. . . .

When that wise Being who created us and placed us here, saw the fair idea, He willed, by allowing it to be so, that the passions should unfold our reason, because He could see that present evil would produce future good. Could the helpless creature whom he called from nothing break loose from His providence, and boldly learn to know good by practicing evil, without His permission? No. How could that energetic advocate for immortality [Rousseau] argue so inconsistently? Had mankind remained forever in the brutal state of nature, which even his magic pen cannot paint as a state in which a single virtue took root, it would have been clear, though not to the sensitive unreflecting wanderer, that man was born to run the circle of life and death, and adorn God's garden for some purpose which could not easily be reconciled with His attributes.

But if, to crown the whole, there were to be rational creatures produced, allowed to rise in excellence by the exercise of powers implanted for that purpose; if benignity itself thought fit to call into existence a creature above the brutes, who could think and improve himself, why should that inestimable gift, for a gift it was, if man was so created, as to have a capacity to rise above the state in which sensation produced brutal ease, be called, in direct terms, a curse? A curse it might be reckoned, if the whole of our existence were bounded by our continuance in this world; for why should the gracious fountain of life give us passions, the power of reflecting, only to embitter our days and inspire us with mistaken notions of dignity? Why should He lead us from love of ourselves to the sublime emotions which the discovery of His wisdom and goodness excites, if these feelings were not set in motion to improve our nature, of which they make a part, and render us capable of enjoying a more godlike portion of happiness? Firmly persuaded that no evil exists in the world that God did not design to take place, I build my belief on the perfection of God.

L'Envoi

Rudyard Kipling

This poem has long been a favorite because of its assertion of the individual's power of creativity and responsibility for self-development.

When Earth's last picture is painted, and the
    tubes are twisted and dried,
When the oldest colors have faded, and the
    youngest critic has died,
We shall rest, and, faith, we shall need it—lie
    down for an eon or two,
Till the Master of All Good Workmen shall set us
    to work anew!

And those who were good shall be happy: they
    shall sit in a golden chair;
They shall splash at a ten-league canvas with
    brushes of comet's hair;
They shall find real saints to draw from—
    Magdalene, Peter, and Paul;
They shall work for an age at a sitting and never
    be tired at all!

And only the Master shall praise us, and only
    the Master shall blame;
And no one shall work for money, and no one
    shall work for fame;
But each for the joy of the working, and each,
    in his separate star,
Shall draw the Thing as he sees It for the God of
    Things as They Are!

Landing of the Pilgrim Fathers

Felicia Hemans

Faith has helped found nations—including the United States.
This poem helps us remember that many of the first settlers to
reach America from other lands came seeking religious freedom.
People still come for that reason.

> The breaking waves dashed high,
>   On a stern and rock-bound coast,
> And the woods against a stormy sky,
>   Their giant branches tossed;
>
> And the heavy night hung dark,
>   The hills and waters o'er,
> When a band of exiles moored their bark
>   On the wild New England shore.
>
> Not as the conqueror comes,
>   They, the true-hearted came;
> Not with the roll of the stirring drums,
>   And the trumpet that sings of fame;
>
> Not as the flying come,
>   In silence and in fear—
> They shook the depths of the desert gloom
>   With their hymns of lofty cheer.
>
> Amidst the storm they sang,
>   And the stars heard, and the sea;
> And the sounding aisles of the dim woods rang
>   To the anthem of the free.
>
> The ocean eagle soared
>   From his nest by the white wave's foam;
> And the rocking pines of the forest roared—
>   This was their welcome home.

There were men with hoary hair
    Amidst that pilgrim band:
Why had they come to wither there,
    Away from their childhood's land?

There was a woman's fearless eye,
    Lit by her deep love's truth;
There was manhood's brow serenely high,
    And the fiery heart of youth.

What sought they thus afar?
    Bright jewels of the mine?
The wealth of seas, the spoils of war?
    They sought a faith's pure shrine!

Aye, call it holy ground,
    The soil where first they trod;
They have left unstained what there they found—
    Freedom to worship God.

Jefferson Urges
an Examination of Faith

Thomas Jefferson

In this 1787 letter to his nephew Peter Carr, whose own parents
were dead, we find Thomas Jefferson urging the young man to
scrutinize religion with an open yet thoughtful mind, and to
accept it or reject it on his own terms. Faith, like other virtues,
should be part of a self-examined life.

He who made us would have been a pitiful bungler, if he had
made the rules of our moral conduct a matter of science. For one
man of science, there are thousands who are not. What would have
become of them? Man was destined for society. His morality, there-

fore, was to be formed to this object. He was endowed with a sense of right and wrong, merely relative to this. . . . The moral sense, or conscience, is as much a part of man as his leg or arm. It is given to all human beings in a stronger or weaker degree, as force of members is given them in a greater or less degree. It may be strengthened by exercise, as may any particular limb of the body. This sense is submitted, indeed, in some degree, to the guidance of reason; but it is a small stock which is required for this; even a less one than what we call common sense.

State a moral case to a plowman and a professor. The former will decide it as well, and often better than the latter, because he has not been led astray by artificial rules. In this branch, therefore, read good books, because they will encourage, as well as direct your feelings. The writings of Sterne, particularly, form the best course of morality that ever was written. Besides these, read the books mentioned in the enclosed paper; and above all things, lose no occasion of exercising your dispositions to be grateful, to be generous, to be charitable, to be humane, to be true, just, firm, orderly, courageous, etc. Consider every act of this kind, as an exercise which will strengthen your moral faculties and increase your worth.

Religion. Your reason is now mature enough to examine this object. In the first place, divest yourself of all bias in favor of novelty and singularity of opinion. Indulge them in any other subject rather than that of religion. It is too important, and the consequences of error may be too serious. On the other hand, shake off all the fears and servile prejudices, under which weak minds are servilely crouched. Fix reason firmly in her seat, and call to her tribunal every fact, every opinion. Question with boldness even the existence of a God; because, if there be one, he must more approve of the homage of reason, than that of blindfolded fear.

You will naturally examine first the religion of your own country. Read the Bible, then, as you would read Livy or Tacitus. The facts which are within the ordinary course of nature, you will believe on the authority of the writer, as you do those of the same kind in Livy and Tacitus. The testimony of the writer weighs in their favor, in one scale, and their not being against the laws of nature, does not weigh against them. But those facts in the Bible which contradict the laws of nature, must be examined with more care, and under a variety of faces. Here you must recur to the pretensions of the writer to inspiration from God. Examine upon what evidence his pretensions are founded, and whether that evidence is so strong, as that its

FAITH 793

falsehood would be more improbable than a change in the laws of nature, in the case he relates. For example, in the book of Joshua, we are told, the sun stood still several hours. Were we to read that fact in Livy or Tacitus, we should class it with their showers of blood, speaking of statues, beasts, etc. But it is said, that the writer of that book was inspired. Examine, therefore, candidly, what evidence there is of his having been inspired. The pretension is entitled to your inquiry, because millions believe it. On the other hand, you are astronomer enough to know how contrary it is to the law of nature that a body revolving on its axis, as the earth does, should have stopped, should not, by that sudden stoppage, have prostrated animals, trees, buildings, and should after a certain time have resumed its revolution, and that without a second general prostration. Is this arrest of the earth's motion, or the evidence which affirms it, most within the law of probabilities?

You will next read the New Testament. It is the history of a personage called Jesus. Keep in your eye the opposite pretensions: 1, of those who say he was begotten by God, born of a virgin, suspended and reversed the laws of nature at will, and ascended bodily into heaven; and 2, of those who say he was a man of illegitimate birth, of a benevolent heart, enthusiastic mind, who set out without pretensions to divinity, ended in believing them, and was punished capitally for sedition, by being gibbeted, according to the Roman law, which punished the first commission of that offense by whipping, and the second by exile, or death, *in furea*. . . .

These questions are examined in the books I have mentioned, under the head of Religion, and several others. They will assist you in your inquiries; but keep your reason firmly on the watch in reading them all.

Do not be frightened from this inquiry by any fear of its consequences. If it ends in a belief that there is no God, you will find incitements to virtue in the comfort and pleasantness you feel in its exercise, and the love of others which it will procure you. If you find reason to believe there is a God, a consciousness that you are acting under his eye, and that he approves you, will be a vast additional incitement; if that there be a future state, the hope of a happy existence in that increases the appetite to deserve it; if that Jesus was also a God, you will be comforted by a belief of his aid and love.

In fine, I repeat, you must lay aside all prejudice on both sides, and neither believe nor reject anything, because any other persons, or description of persons, have rejected it or believed it. Your own reason is the only oracle given you by heaven, and you are answerable, not for the rightness, but uprightness of the decision.

The Farewell Address

George Washington

In his famous Farewell Address of September 19, 1796, given as he prepared to leave office, George Washington offered the new nation a guide for the future. In this excerpt we find his thoughts on the importance of religion and morality to the country's wellbeing.

Of all the dispositions and habits which lead to political prosperity, Religion and Morality are indispensable supports. In vain would that man claim the tribute of Patriotism, who should labor to subvert these great Pillars of human happiness, these firmest props of the duties of men and citizens. The mere politician, equally with the pious man ought to respect and to cherish them. A volume could not trace all their connections with private and public felicity. Let it simply be asked where is the security for property, for reputation, for life, if the sense of religious obligation *desert* the oaths, which are the instruments of investigation in Courts of Justice? And let us with caution indulge the supposition, that morality can be maintained without religion. Whatever may be conceded to the influence of refined education on minds of peculiar structure, reason and experience both forbid us to expect that National morality can prevail in exclusion of religious principle.

'Tis substantially true, that virtue or morality is a necessary spring of popular government. The rule indeed extends with more or less force to every species of free Government. Who that is a sincere friend to it, can look with indifference upon attempts to shake the foundation of the fabric? . . .

Observe good faith and justice toward all Nations. Cultivate peace and harmony with all. Religion and morality enjoin this conduct; and can it be that good policy does not equally enjoin it? It will be worthy of a free, enlightened, and at no distant period, a great Nation to give to mankind the magnanimous and too novel example of a People always guided by an exalted justice and benevolence. Who can doubt that in the course of time and things the fruit of such a plan would richly repay any temporary advantages which might be lost by a steady adherence to it? Can it be, that Providence has not connected the permanent felicity of a Nation with its virtue? The experiment, at least, is recommended by every sentiment which ennobles human Nature. Alas! is it rendered impossible by its vices?

Second Inaugural Address

Abraham Lincoln

When Abraham Lincoln gave his second inaugural address on March 4, 1865, the end of the Civil War was in sight. Sherman was moving northward through the South after his march from Atlanta to the sea; Sheridan had pushed Confederate forces out of the Shenandoah Valley; and Grant was slowly tightening the Union vise around Lee's army at Petersburg. Lincoln's words are those of a victorious yet exhausted leader who is searching for the meaning of the vast struggle. The biblical quotes he uses are from Matthew and the book of Psalms.

At this second appearing to take the oath of the presidential office there is less occasion for an extended address than there was at the first. Then a statement somewhat in detail, of a course to be pursued seemed fitting and proper. Now, at the expiration of four years, during which public declarations have been constantly called forth on every point and phase of the great contest which still absorbs the attention, and engrosses the energies of the nation, little that is new could be presented. The progress of our arms, upon which all else chiefly depends, is as well known to the public as to myself, and it is, I trust, reasonably satisfactory and encouraging to all. With high hope for the future, no prediction in regard to it is ventured.

On the occasion corresponding to this four years ago all thoughts were anxiously directed to an impending civil war. All dreaded it, all sought to avert it. While the inaugural address was being delivered from this place, devoted altogether to *saving* the Union without war, insurgent agents were in the city seeking to *destroy* it without war—seeking to dissolve the Union, and divide effects, by negotiation. Both parties deprecated war, but one of them would *make* war rather than let the nation survive, and the other would *accept* war rather than let it perish, and the war came.

One eighth of the whole population were colored slaves, not distributed generally over the Union, but localized in the southern part of it. These slaves constituted a peculiar and powerful interest. All knew that this interest was somehow the cause of the war. To strengthen, perpetuate, and extend this interest was the object for which the insurgents would rend the Union even by war, while the government claimed no right to do more than to restrict the territorial enlargement of it. Neither party expected for the war, the magnitude or the duration which it has already attained. Neither anticipated that the *cause* of the conflict might cease with or even before the conflict itself should cease. Each looked for an easier triumph, and a result less fundamental and astounding. Both read the same Bible, and pray to the same God, and each invokes His aid against the other. It may seem strange that any men should dare to ask a just God's assistance in wringing their bread from the sweat of other men's faces, but let us judge not that we be not judged. The prayers of both could not be answered. That of neither has been answered fully. The Almighty has his own purpose. "Woe unto the world because of offenses for it must needs be that offenses come, but woe to that man by whom the offense cometh!" If we shall discern therein any departure from those divine attributes which suppose that American Slavery is one of those offenses which, in the providence of God, must needs come, but which, having continued through His appointed time, He now wills to remove, and that He gives to both North and South this terrible war as the woe due to those by whom the offense came, shall we discern therein any departure from those divine attributes which the believers in a Living God always ascribe to Him? Fondly do we hope, fervently do we pray, that this mighty scourge of war may speedily pass away. Yet, if God wills that it continue until all the wealth piled by the bondman's two hundred and fifty years of unrequited toil shall be sunk, and until every drop of blood drawn with the lash, shall be paid by another drawn with the sword, as was said three thousand years ago, so still it must be said "the judgments of the Lord, are true and righteous altogether."

With malice toward none, with charity for all, with firmness in the right as God gives us to see the right, let us strive on to finish the work we are in, to bind up the nation's wounds, to care for him who shall have borne the battle and for his widow and his orphan, to do all which may achieve and cherish a just and lasting peace among ourselves and with all nations.

Battle Hymn of the Republic

Julia Ward Howe

Julia Ward Howe (1819–1910) wrote "The Battle Hymn of the Republic" in the predawn hours of November 18, 1861, when she was visiting Washington, D.C. She had recently watched Union army troops drilling to the strains of "John Brown's Body," and a companion suggested she compose new lyrics for the tune. The result was published in the *Atlantic Monthly* a few months later. Its assertion of faith that God was with the North's cause immediately appealed to the Union army, which adopted it as its marching song. After the war, its popularity spread to all parts of the country.

Mine eyes have seen the glory of the coming of the Lord;
He is trampling out the vintage where the grapes of wrath are stored;
He hath loosed the fateful lightning of His terrible swift sword:
His truth is marching on.

I have seen Him in the watch-fires of a hundred circling camps;
They have builded Him an altar in the evening dews and damps;
I can read His righteous sentence by the dim and flaring lamps:
His day is marching on.

I have read a fiery gospel writ in burnished rows of steel:
"As ye deal with my contemners, so with you my grace shall deal;
Let the Hero, born of woman, crush the serpent with his heel,
                              Since God is marching on."

He has sounded forth the trumpet that shall never call retreat;
He is sifting out the hearts of men before His judgment-seat;
Oh, be swift, my soul, to answer Him! be jubilant, my feet!
                              Our God is marching on.

In the beauty of the lilies Christ was born across the sea,
With a glory in his bosom that transfigures you and me:
As he died to make men holy, let us die to make men free,
                              While God is marching on.

Going to Church

Theodore Roosevelt

*Teddy Roosevelt offered his reasons for going to church in La-
dies' Home Journal in 1917.*

1. In this actual world a churchless community, a community
where men have abandoned and scoffed at or ignored their religious
needs, is a community on the rapid downgrade. It is perfectly true
that occasional individuals or families may have nothing to do with
church or with religious practices and observances and yet maintain
the highest standard of spirituality and of ethical obligation. But this
does not affect the case in the world as it now is, any more than
that exceptional men and women under exceptional conditions have
disregarded the marriage tie without moral harm to themselves in-
terferes with the larger fact that such disregard if at all common
means the complete moral disintegration of the body politic.

2. Church work and church attendance mean the cultivation of
the habit of feeling some responsibility for others and the sense of
braced moral strength which prevents a relaxation of one's own
moral fiber.

3. There are enough holidays for most of us which can quite properly be devoted to pure holiday making. . . . Sundays differ from other holidays—among other ways—in the fact that there are fifty-two of them every year. . . . On Sunday, go to church.

4. Yes, I know all the excuses. I know that one can worship the Creator and dedicate oneself to good living in a grove of trees, or by a running brook, or in one's own house, just as well as in church. But I also know as a matter of cold fact the average man does *not* thus worship or thus dedicate himself. If he stays away from church he does not spend his time in good works or in lofty meditation. He looks over the colored supplement of the newspaper.

5. He may not hear a good sermon at church. But unless he is very unfortunate he will hear a sermon by a good man who, with his good wife, is engaged all the week long in a series of wearing and humdrum and important tasks for making hard lives a little easier.

6. He will listen to and take part in reading some beautiful passages from the Bible. And if he is not familiar with the Bible, he has suffered a loss. . . .

7. He will probably take part in singing some good hymns.

8. He will meet and nod to, or speak to, good, quiet neighbors. . . . He will come away feeling a little more charitably toward all the world, even toward those excessively foolish young men who regard church-going as rather a soft performance.

9. I advocate a man's joining in church works for the sake of showing his faith by his works.

10. The man who does not in some way, active or not, connect himself with some active, working church misses many opportunities for helping his neighbors, and therefore, incidentally, for helping himself.

The Lamb and The Tyger

William Blake

In "The Lamb" and "The Tyger," William Blake (1757–1827)
depicts creatures representing two very different worlds. As a
pair, the poems ask us to come to grips with the proposition that
both are God's creations.

The Lamb

Little Lamb, who made thee?
Dost thou know who made thee?
Gave thee life and bid thee feed,
By the stream and o'er the mead;
Gave thee clothing of delight,
Softest clothing wooly bright;
Gave thee such a tender voice,
Making all the vales rejoice!
Little Lamb who made thee?
Dost thou know who made thee?

Little Lamb I'll tell thee,
Little Lamb I'll tell thee!
He is callèd by thy name,
For he calls himself a Lamb:
He is meek and he is mild,
He became a little child:
I a child and thou a lamb,
We are callèd by his name.
Little Lamb God bless thee.
Little Lamb God bless thee.

The Tyger

Tyger! Tyger! burning bright
In the forests of the night,
What immortal hand or eye
Could frame thy fearful symmetry?

In what distant deeps or skies
Burnt the fire of thine eyes?
On what wings dare he aspire?
What the hand, dare seize the fire?

And what shoulder, and what art,
Could twist the sinews of thy heart?
And when thy heart began to beat,
What dread hand? and what dread feet?

What the hammer? what the chain?
In what furnace was thy brain?
What the anvil? what dread grasp
Dare its deadly terrors clasp?

When the stars threw down their spears,
And water'd heaven with their tears,
Did he smile his work to see?
Did he who made the Lamb make thee?

Tyger! Tyger! burning bright
In the forests of the night,
What immortal hand or eye
Dare frame thy fearful symmetry?

The Loom of Time

According to one popular ancient Greek myth, human destiny
lay in the hands of three goddesses named the Fates—Clotho,
who spun the thread of life, Lachesis, who assigned each mortal
his or her destiny, and Atropos, who with "abhorrèd shears" (as
Milton put it) cut the thread at death. This poem elaborates on
the theme, expressing the faith that God has a design for each of
our lives, even though we may not understand it now.

Man's life is laid in the loom of time
  To a pattern he does not see,
While the weavers work and the shuttles fly
  Till the dawn of eternity.

Some shuttles are filled with silver threads
  And some with threads of gold,
While often but the darker hues
  Are all that they may hold.

But the weaver watches with skillful eye
  Each shuttle fly to and fro,
And sees the pattern so deftly wrought
  As the loom moves sure and slow.

God surely planned the pattern:
  Each thread, the dark and fair,
Is chosen by His master skill
  And placed in the web with care.

He only knows its beauty,
  And guides the shuttles which hold
The threads so unattractive,
  As well as the threads of gold.

Not till each loom is silent,
  And the shuttles cease to fly,
Shall God reveal the pattern
  And explain the reason why

The dark threads were as needful
  In the weaver's skillful hand
As the threads of gold and silver
  For the pattern which He planned.

The Volunteer at Auschwitz

Chuck Colson

Between 1940 and 1945, as many as two million people were murdered at the Nazi concentration camp at Auschwitz and the neighboring extermination site of Treblinka in south-central Poland. Countless acts of courage and faith took place amid the horror there. This is the story of one of them.

Maximilian Kolbe was forty-five years old in the early autumn of 1939 when the Nazis invaded his homeland. He was a Polish friar in Niepokalanow, a village near Warsaw. There, 762 priests and lay brothers lived in the largest friary in the world. Father Kolbe presided over Niepokalanow with a combination of industry, joy, love, and humor that made him beloved by the plainspoken brethren there.

In his simple room, he sat each morning at a pigeonhole desk, a large globe before him, praying over the world. He did so, tortured by the fact that a pale man with arresting blue eyes and a terrifying power of manipulation had whipped the people of Germany into a frenzy. Whole nations had already fallen to the evil Adolf Hitler and his Nazis.

"An atrocious conflict is brewing," Father Kolbe told a group of friars one day after he had finished prayers. "We do not know what will develop. In our beloved Poland, we must expect the worst." Father Kolbe was right. His country was next.

On September 1, 1939, the Nazi blitzkrieg broke over Poland. After several weeks, a group of Germans arrived at Niepokalanow on motorcycles and arrested Father Kolbe and all but two of his friars who had remained behind. They were loaded on trucks, then into livestock wagons, and two days later arrived at Amtitz, a prison camp.

Conditions were horrible, but not horrific. Prisoners were hungry, but no one died of starvation. Strangely, within a few weeks the brothers were released from prison. Back at the friary, they found the buildings vandalized and the Nazis in control, using the facility as a deportation camp for political prisoners, refugees, and Jews.

The situation was an opportunity for ministry, and Father Kolbe took advantage of it, helping the sick and comforting the fearful.

While Kolbe and the friars used their time to serve others, the Nazis used theirs to decide just how to impose their will on the rest of Europe. To Adolf Hitler, the Jews and Slavic people were the *Untermenschen* (subhumans). Their cultures and cities were to be erased and their industry appropriated for Germany. On October 2, Hitler outlined a secret memorandum to Hans Frank, the governor general of Poland. In a few phrases he determined the grim outcome for millions: "The [ordinary] Poles are especially born for low labor . . . the Polish gentry must cease to exist . . . all representatives of the Polish intelligentsia are to be exterminated. . . . There should be one master for the Poles, the German."

As for Poland's hundreds of thousands of priests?

"They will preach what we want them to preach," said Hitler's memo. "If any priest acts differently, we will make short work of him. The task of the priest is to keep the Poles quiet, stupid, and dull-witted."

Maximilian Kolbe was clearly a priest who "acted differently" from the Nazis' designs.

In early February 1941, the Polish underground smuggled word to Kolbe that his name was on a Gestapo list: he was about to be arrested. Kolbe knew what happened to loved ones of those who tried to elude the Nazis' grasp; their friends and colleagues were taken instead. He had no wife or children; his church was his family. And he could not risk the loss of any of his brothers in Christ. So he stayed at Niepokalanow.

At nine o'clock on the morning of February 17, Father Kolbe was sitting at his pigeonhole desk, his eyes and prayers on the globe before him, when he heard the sound of heavy vehicles outside the thick panes of his green-painted windows. He knew it was the Nazis, but he remained at his desk. He would wait for them to come to him.

After being held in Nazi prisons for several months, Father Kolbe was found guilty of the crime of publishing unapproved materials and sentenced to Auschwitz. Upon his arrival at the camp in May 1941, an SS officer informed him that the life expectancy of priests there was about a month. Kolbe was assigned to the timber detail; he was to carry felled tree trunks from one place to another. Guards stood by to ensure that the exhausted prisoners did so at a quick trot.

Years of slim rations and overwork at Niepokalanow had already weakened Kolbe. Now, under the load of wood, he staggered and collapsed. Officers converged on him, kicking him with their shiny leather boots and beating him with their whips. He was stretched out on a pile of wood, dealt fifty lashes, then shoved into a ditch, covered with branches, and left for dead.

Later, having been picked up by some brave prisoners, he awoke in a camp hospital bed alongside several other near-dead inmates. There, miraculously, he revived.

"No need to waste gas or a bullet on that one," chuckled one SS officer to another. "He'll be dead soon."

Kolbe was switched to other work and transferred to Barracks 14, where he continued to minister to his fellow prisoners, so tortured by hunger they could not sleep.

By the end of July 1941, Auschwitz was working like a well-organized killing machine, and the Nazis congratulated themselves on their efficiency. The camp's five chimneys never stopped smoking. The stench was terrible, but the results were excellent: eight thousand Jews could be stripped, their possessions appropriated for the Reich, gassed, and cremated—all in twenty-four hours. Every twenty-four hours.

About the only problem was the occasional prisoner from the work side of the camp who would figure out a way to escape. When these escapees were caught, as they usually were, they would be hanged with special nooses that slowly choked out their miserable lives—a grave warning to others who might be tempted to try.

Then one July night as the frogs and insects in the marshy land surrounding the camp began their evening chorus, the air was suddenly filled with the baying of dogs, the curses of soldiers, and the roar of motorcycles. A man had escaped from Barracks 14.

The next morning there was a peculiar tension as the ranks of phantom-thin prisoners lined up for morning roll call in the central square, their eyes on the large gallows before them. But there was no condemned man standing there, his hands bound behind him, his face bloodied from blows and dog bites. That meant the prisoner had made it out of Auschwitz. And that meant death for some of those who remained.

After the roll call, Camp Commandant Fritsch ordered the dismissal of all but Barracks 14. While the rest of the camp went about its duties, the prisoners from Barracks 14 stood motionless in line. They waited. Hours passed. The summer sun beat down. Some fainted and were dragged away. Some swayed in place but held on; those the SS officers beat with the butts of their guns. Father Kolbe, by some miracle, stayed on his feet, his posture as straight as his resolve.

By evening roll call the commandant was ready to levy sentence. The other prisoners had returned from their day of slave labor; now he could make a lesson out of the fate of this miserable barracks.

Fritsch began to speak, the veins in his thick neck standing out with rage. "The fugitive has not been found," he screamed. "Ten of you will die for him in the starvation bunker. Next time, twenty will be condemned."

The rows of exhausted prisoners began to sway as they heard the sentence. The guards let them; terror was part of their punishment.

The starvation bunker! Anything was better—death on the gallows, a bullet in the head at the Wall of Death, or even the gas in the chambers. All those were quick, even humane, compared to Nazi starvation, for they denied you water as well as food.

The prisoners had heard the stories from the starvation bunker in the basement of Barracks 11. They said the condemned didn't even look like human beings after a day or two. They frightened even the guards. Their throats turned to paper, their brains turned to fire, their intestines dried up and shriveled like desiccated worms.

Commandant Fritsch walked the rows of prisoners. When he stopped before a man, he would command in bad Polish, "Open your mouth! Put out your tongue! Show your teeth!" And so he went, choosing victims like horses.

His dreary assistant, Palitsch, followed behind. As Fritsch chose a man, Palitsch noted the number stamped on the prisoner's filthy shirt. The Nazis, as always, were methodical. Soon there were ten men—ten numbers neatly listed on the death roll. The chosen groaned, sweating with fear. "My poor wife!" one man cried. "My poor children! What will they do?"

"Take off your shoes!" the commandant barked at the ten men. This was one of his rituals; they must march to their deaths barefoot. A pile of twenty wooden clogs made a small heap at the front of the grassy square.

Suddenly there was a commotion in the ranks. A prisoner had broken out of line, calling for the commandant. It was unheard of to leave the ranks, let alone address a Nazi officer; it was cause for execution.

Fritsch had his hand on his revolver, as did the officers behind him. But he broke precedent. Instead of shooting the prisoner, he shouted at him.

"Halt! What does this Polish pig want of me?"

The prisoners gasped. It was their beloved Father Kolbe, the priest who shared his last crust, who comforted the dying and nourished their souls. Not Father Kolbe! The frail priest spoke softly, even calmly, to the Nazi butcher. "I would like to die in place of one of the men you condemned."

Fritsch stared at the prisoner, No.16670. He never considered them as individuals; they were just a gray blur. But he looked now. No.16670 didn't appear to be insane.

"Why?" snapped the commandant.

Father Kolbe sensed the need for exacting diplomacy. The Nazis never reversed an order; so he must not seem to be asking him to do so. Kolbe knew the Nazi dictum of destruction: the weak and the elderly first. He would play on this well-ingrained principle.

"I am an old man, sir, and good for nothing. My life will serve no purpose."

His ploy triggered the response Kolbe wanted. "In whose place do you want to die?" asked Fritsch.

"For that one," Kolbe responded, pointing to the weeping prisoner who had bemoaned his wife and children.

Fritsch glanced at the weeping prisoner. He did look stronger than this tattered No.16670 before him.

For the first and last time, the commandant looked Kolbe in the eye. "Who are you?" he asked.

The prisoner looked back at him, a strange fire in his dark eyes. "I am a priest."

"*Ein Pfaffe!*" the commandant snorted. He looked at his assistant and nodded. Palitsch drew a line through No.5659 and wrote down No.16670. Kolbe's place on the death ledger was set.

Father Kolbe bent down to take off his clogs, then joined the group to be marched to Barracks 11. As he did so, No.5659 passed by him at a distance—and on the man's face was an expression so astonished that it had not yet become gratitude.

But Kolbe wasn't looking for gratitude. If he was to lay down his life for another, the fulfillment had to be in the act of obedience itself. The joy must be found in submitting his small will to the will of One more grand.

As the condemned men entered Barracks 11, guards roughly pushed them down the stairs to the basement.

"Remove your clothes!" shouted an officer. *Christ died on the cross naked,* Father Kolbe thought as he took off his pants and thin shirt. *It is only fitting that I suffer as He suffered.*

In the basement the ten men were herded into a dark, windowless cell.

"You will dry up like tulips," sneered one jailer. Then he swung the heavy door shut.

As the hours and days passed, however, the camp became aware of something extraordinary happening in the death cell. Past prisoners had spent their dying days howling, attacking one another, clawing the walls in a frenzy of despair.

But now, coming from the death box, those outside heard the faint sounds of singing. For this time the prisoners had a shepherd to gently lead them through the shadows of the valley of death, pointing them to the Great Shepherd. And perhaps for that reason Father Kolbe was the last to die.

On August 14, 1941, there were four prisoners still alive in the bunker, and it was needed for new occupants. A German doctor named Boch descended the steps of Barracks 11, four syringes in his hand. Several SS troopers and a prisoner named Brono Borgowiec (who survived Auschwitz) were with him—the former to observe and the latter to carry out the bodies.

When they swung the bunker door open, there, in the light of their flashlight, they saw Father Maximilian Kolbe, a living skeleton, propped against one wall. His head was inclined a bit to the left. He had the ghost of a smile on his lips and his eyes wide open, fixed on some faraway vision. He did not move.

The other three prisoners were on the floor, unconscious but alive. The doctor took care of them first: a jab of the needle into the bony left arm, the push of the piston in the syringe. It seemed a waste of the drug, but he had his orders. Then he approached No. 16670 and repeated the action.

In a moment, Father Kolbe was dead.

Death, Be Not Proud

John Donne

John Donne's (1572–1631) famous lines insist that death is not
the final sleep, but the final awakening.

Death, be not proud, though some have callèd thee
  Mighty and dreadful, for thou are not so;
  For those whom thou think'st thou dost overthrow
Die not, poor Death, nor yet canst thou kill me.
From rest and sleep, which but thy pictures be,
  Much pleasure—then, from thee much more must flow;
  And soonest our best men with thee do go,
Rest of their bones and soul's delivery.
Thou'rt slave to fate, chance, kings, and desperate men,
  And dost with poison, war, and sickness dwell;
  And poppy or charms can make us sleep as well,
And better than thy stroke. Why swell'st thou then?
  One short sleep past, we wake eternally,
  And death shall be no more. Death, thou shalt die.

The Dying Christian to His Soul

Alexander Pope

Alexander Pope borrowed the last two lines of this verse from
Paul's First Epistle to the Corinthians (15:55), which in turn echoes older passages from the Bible.

Vital spark of heavenly flame!
Quit, O quit this mortal frame!
Trembling, hoping, lingering, flying,
O! the pain, the bliss of dying!
Cease, fond nature, cease they strife,
And let me languish into life!

Hark! they whisper: angels say,
Sister spirit, come away!
What is this absorbs me quite?
Steals my senses, shuts my sight,
Drowns my spirit, draws my breath?
Tell me, my soul, can this be death?

The world recedes; it disappears!
Heaven opens on my eyes! my ears
With sounds seraphic ring!
Lend, lend your wings! I mount! I fly!
O Grave! where is thy victory?
O Death! where is thy sting?

The Path of Virtue

From the Dhammapada

As the following passages help show, the world's great faiths are
in accord in many fundamental moral principles. This is worth
noting because sometimes people object to the teaching of values
on the grounds that people of different faiths must have essentially different values. But as we see here, faiths of different
names and histories often share common precepts.

The *Dhammapada* (Path of Virtue) is traditionally ascribed to
the Buddha. The following selection from this Hinayana text is a
collection of proverbial sayings on the spiritual life.

He who does not rouse himself when it is time to rise, who, though young and strong is full of sloth, whose will and thought are weak, that lazy and idle man never finds the way to knowledge.

What ought to be done is neglected, what ought not to be done is done; the desires of unruly, thoughtless people are always increasing.

But they whose whole watchfulness is always directed to their body, who do not follow what ought not to be done, and who steadfastly do what ought to be done, the desires of such watchful and wise people will come to an end.

He who says what is not goes to hell; he also who, having done a thing, says I have not done it. After death both are equal: they are men with evil deeds in the next world.

Better it would be to swallow a heated iron ball, like flaring fire, than that a bad unrestrained fellow should live on the charity of the land.

Four things does a reckless man gain who covets his neighbor's wife—demerit, an uncomfortable bed, thirdly, punishment, and lastly, hell.

As a grass blade, if badly grasped, cuts the arm, badly practiced asceticism leads to hell.

If anything is to be done, let a man do it, let him attack it vigorously! A careless pilgrim only scatters the dust of his passions more widely.

They who are ashamed of what they ought not to be ashamed of, and are not ashamed of what they ought to be ashamed of, such men, embracing false doctrines, enter the evil path.

They who fear when they ought not to fear, and fear not when they ought to fear, such men, embracing false doctrines, enter the evil path.

They who see sin where there is no sin, and see no sin where there is sin, such men, embracing false doctrines, enter the evil path.

They who see sin where there is sin, and no sin where there is no sin, such men, embracing the true doctrine, enter the good path.

A man does not become a Brahman by his plaited hair, by his family, or by birth; in whom there is truth and righteousness, he is blessed, he is a Brahman.

I do not call a man a Brahman because of his origin or of his mother. He is indeed arrogant, and he is wealthy; but the poor, who is free from all attachments, him I call indeed a Brahman.

Him I call indeed a Brahman who is free from anger, dutiful, virtuous, without appetites, who is subdued, and has received his last body.

Him I call indeed a Brahman who does not cling to sensual pleasures, like water on a lotus leaf, like a mustard seed on the point of a needle.

Him I call indeed a Brahman who without hurting any creatures, whether feeble or strong, does not kill nor cause slaughter.

Him I call indeed a Brahman who is tolerant with the intolerant, mild with the violent, and free from greed among the greedy.

Him I call indeed a Brahman from whom anger and hatred, pride and hypocrisy have dropped like a mustard seed from the point of a needle.

Him I call indeed a Brahman who utters true speech, instructive and free from harshness, so that he offend no one.

Him I call indeed a Brahman who takes nothing in the world that is not given him, be it long or short, small or large, good or bad.

Him I call indeed a Brahman who in this world has risen above both ties, good and evil, who is free from grief, from sin, and from impurity.

Man's Nature Is Good

Mencius

Mencius was a Chinese Confucian sage roughly contemporary with Aristotle in the West. To him we owe much of our understanding of the thought of Confucius. Here he explains the Confucian perspective on human nature and its development.

The tendency of man's nature to good is like the tendency of water to flow downward. There are none but have this tendency to good, just as all water flows downward.

Now by striking water and causing it to leap up, you may make it go over your forehead, and, by damming and leading it, you may

FAITH

force it up a hill—but are such movements according to the nature of water? It is the force applied which causes them. When men are made to do what is not good, their nature is dealt with in this way.

In good years the children of the people are most of them good, while in bad years the most of them abandon themselves to evil. It is not owing to their natural powers conferred by heaven that they are thus different. The abandonment is owing to the circumstances through which they allow their minds to be ensnared and drowned in evil.

All things which are the same in kind are like to one another— why should we doubt in regard to man, as if he were a solitary exception to this? The sage and we are the same in kind.

The trees of the New mountain were once beautiful. Being situated, however, in the borders of a large state, they were hewn down with axes and bills—and could they retain their beauty? Still through the activity of the vegetative life day and night, and the nourishing influence of the rain and dew, they were not without buds and sprouts springing forward, but then came the cattle and goats and browsed upon them. To these things is owing the bare and stript appearance of the mountain, which when people see, they think it was never finely wooded. But is this the nature of the mountain?

And so also of what properly belongs to man—shall it be said that the mind of any man was without benevolence and righteousness? The way in which a man loses his proper goodness of mind is like the way in which the trees are denuded by axes and bills. Hewn down day after day, can it—the mind—retain its beauty? But there is a development of its life day and night, and in the calm air of the morning, just between night and day, the mind feels in a degree those desires and aversions which are proper to humanity, but the feeling is not strong, and it is fettered and destroyed by what takes place during the day. This fettering taking place again and again, the restorative influence of the night is not sufficient to preserve the proper goodness of the mind; and when this proves insufficient for that purpose, the nature becomes not much different from that of the irrational animals, which when people see, they think that it never had those powers which I assert. But does this condition represent the feelings proper to humanity?

Now chess playing is but a small art, but without his whole mind being given, and his will bent to it, a man cannot succeed at it. Chess Ts'ew is the best chess player in all the kingdom. Suppose that he is teaching two men to play. The one gives to the subject his whole mind and bends to it all his will, doing nothing but listening to Chess Ts'ew. The other, although he seems to be listening to him, has his whole mind running on a swan which he thinks is approaching, and wishes to bend his bow, adjust the string to the arrow, and shoot it. Although he is learning along with the other, he does not come up to him. Why?—because his intelligence is not equal? Not so.

I like fish and I also like bear's paws. If I cannot have the two together, I will let the fish go, and take the bear's paws. So, I like life, and I also like righteousness. If I cannot keep the two together, I will let life go and choose righteousness.

There are cases when men by a certain course might preserve life, and they do not employ it; when by certain things they might avoid danger, and they will not do them.

Therefore, men have that which they like more than life, and that which they dislike more than death. They are not men of distinguished talents and virtue only who have this mental nature. All men have it; what belongs to such men is simply that they do not lose it.

The disciple Kung-too said, "All are equally men, but some are great men, and some are little men—how is this?" Mencius replied, "Those who follow that part of themselves which is great are great men; those who follow that part which is little are little men. To the mind belongs the office of thinking. By thinking, it gets the right view of things; by neglecting to think, it fails to do this. Let a man first stand fast in the supremacy of the nobler part of his constitution, and the inferior part will not be able to take it from him. It is simply this which makes the great man."

The Way to Tao

Chuang-tzu

Taoist thought traces itself to the author of the *Tao Te-ching*, traditionally identified as Lao-tzu. The following excerpt from *The Way to Tao* by Chuang-tzu is a passage in which Lao-tzu explains the Way (the Tao).

"Whatsoever is not said in all sincerity, is wrongly said. And not to be able to rid oneself of this vice is only to sink deeper toward perdition.

"Those who do evil in the open light of day—men will punish them. Those who do evil in secret—God will punish them. Who fears both man and God, he is fit to walk alone. Those who are devoted to the internal, in practice acquire no reputation. Those who are devoted to the external, strive for preeminence among their fellows. Practice without reputation throws a halo around the meanest. But he who strives for preeminence among his fellows, he is as a huckster whose weariness all perceive though he himself puts on an air of gaiety.

"He who is naturally in sympathy with man, to him all men come. But he who forcedly adapts, has no room even for himself, still less for others. And he who has no room for others, has no ties. It is all over with him.

"Birth is not a beginning; death is not an end. There is existence without limitation; there is continuity without a starting point. Existence without limitation is space. Continuity without a starting point is time. There is birth, there is death, there is issuing forth, there is entering in. That through which one passes in and out without seeing its form, that is the Portal of God.

"The Portal of God is nonexistence. All things sprang from nonexistence. Existence could not make existence existence. It must have proceeded from nonexistence, and nonexistence and nothing are one. Herein is the abiding place of the sage.

"Discard the stimuli of purpose. Free the mind from disturbances. Get rid of entanglements to virtue. Pierce the obstructions to Tao.

"Honors, wealth, distinction, power, fame, gain—these six stimulate purpose.

"Mien, carriage, beauty, arguments, influence, opinions—these six disturb the mind.

"Hate, ambition, joy, anger, sorrow, pleasure—these six are entanglements to virtue.

"Rejecting, adopting, receiving, giving, knowledge, ability—these six are obstructions to Tao.

"If these twenty-four be not allowed to run riot, then the mind will be duly ordered. And being duly ordered, it will be in repose. And being in repose, it will be clear of perception. And being clear of perception, it will be unconditioned. And being unconditioned, it will be in that state of inaction by which there is nothing which cannot be accomplished."

Crossing the Bar

Alfred Tennyson

The literal "bar" of this poem is the kind of submerged sandbar that frequently stretches across the mouth of a river or entrance to a harbor. A ship "crosses the bar" when it puts out to sea.

Sunset and evening star,
　　And one clear call for me!
And may there be no moaning of the bar,
　　When I put out to sea,

But such a tide as moving seems asleep,
　　Too full for sound and foam,
When that which drew from out the boundless deep
　　Turns again home.

Twilight and evening bell,
　　And after that the dark!
And may there be no sadness of farewell,
　　When I embark;

For though from out our bourne of Time and Place
The flood may bear me far,
I hope to see my Pilot face-to-face
When I have cross'd the bar.

Last Lines

Emily Brontë

Faith stands firmly rooted in all-pervading love and life, unshaken by doubt and death.

No coward soul is mine,
No trembler in the world's storm-troubled sphere:
I see Heaven's glories shine,
And faith shines equal, arming me from fear.

O God, within my breast,
Almighty, ever-present Deity!
Life—that in me has rest,
As I—undying Life—have power in Thee!

Vain are the thousand creeds
That move men's hearts: unutterably vain;
Worthless as withered weeds,
Or idlest froth amid the boundless main,

To waken doubt in one
Holding so fast by thine infinity;
So surely anchored on
The steadfast rock of immortality.

With wide-embracing love
Thy Spirit animates eternal years,
Pervades and broods above,
Changes, sustains, dissolves, creates, and rears.

Though earth and man were gone,
And suns and universes ceased to be,
    And Thou were left alone,
Every existence would exist in Thee.

    There is not room for Death,
Nor atom that his might could render void:
    Thou—Thou are Being and Breath,
And what Thou art may never be destroyed.

Acknowledgments

For permission to reprint copyrighted material, grateful acknowledgment is made to the following publishers, authors, and agents:

"To the Little Girl Who Wriggles" and "Alice's Supper" by Laura E. Richards. Used by permission of Little, Brown Co.

"The Magic Thread" from *Fairy Tales,* translation copyright 1985 by Hodder & Stoughton Ltd. Used by permission of Doubleday, a division of Bantam Doubleday Dell Publishing Group, Inc.

The Boy Scout Oath and the Boy Scout Law copyright © Boy Scouts of America. Used by permission.

The Girl Scout Promise and Law used by permission of the Girl Scouts of the United States of America.

"F. Scott Fitzgerald to His Daughter" reprinted from *F. Scott Fitzgerald: The Crackup.* Copyright 1945 by New Directions Publishing Corp. Reprinted by permission of New Directions Publishing Corp.

"Letter from Birmingham City Jail" by Martin Luther King, Jr., reprinted by arrangement with The Heirs to the Estate of Martin Luther King, Jr., ℅ Joan Daves Agency as agent for the proprietor. Copyright 1963 by Martin Luther King, Jr., copyright renewed 1991 by Coretta Scott King.

"Men Without Chests" reprinted from *The Abolition of Man* by C. S. Lewis by permission of Collins Fount, an imprint of HarperCollins Publishers Limited.

The Velveteen Rabbit, by Marjery Williams, used by permission of Simon & Schuster.

"Childhood and Poetry" by Pablo Neruda reprinted from *Neruda and Vallejo: Selected Poems,* edited by Robert Bly, Beacon Press, Boston, 1971, copyright 1971 by Robert Bly. Reprinted with his permission.

"It's Plain Hard Work That Does It" by Charles Edison reprinted with permission from the December 1961 *Reader's Digest.* Copyright © 1961 by the Reader's Digest Assn., Inc.

"Kill Devil Hill" reprinted from *Kill Devil Hill: Discovering the Secret of the Wright Brothers* by Harry Combs (Houghton Mifflin Company/TernStyle Press, Ltd.). Courtesy of the author.

"Rosa Parks" reprinted from *Rosa Parks: The Movement Organizes,* by Kai Friese. Copyright © 1990 Silver Burdett Press. All rights reserved. Used with permission.

"The Iron Horse" reprinted from *They Rose Above It* by Bob Considine. Copyright © 1977 by Millie Considine as Executive of the Estate of Bob Considine. Used by permission of Doubleday, a division of Bantam Doubleday Dell Publishing Group, Inc.

"Instant Hero" by Blaine Harden reprinted from *The Washington Post*, January 15, 1982. Copyright © 1982, *The Washington Post*. Reprinted with permission.

"Prisoner of War" by Vice Admiral James Bond Stockdale reprinted courtesy of the author.

"The Long, Hard Way Through the Wilderness" reprinted from *The Bible Story for Boys and Girls, Old Testament,* by Walter Russell Bowie. Copyright renewed © 1980 by Mrs. James B. Evans, Mrs. Elizabeth Chapman, and W. Russell Bowie, Jr. Excerpted by permission of the publisher, Abingdon Press.

"I Have A Dream" by Martin Luther King, Jr., reprinted by arrangement with The Heirs to the Estate of Martin Luther King, Jr., % Joan Daves Agency as agent for the proprietor. Copyright 1963 by Martin Luther King, Jr., copyright renewed 1991 by Coretta Scott King.

"I Decline to Accept the End of Man" by William Faulkner reprinted from *Essays, Speeches, and Public Letters by William Faulkner* by William Faulkner. Copyright © 1965 by Random House, Inc. Reprinted by permission of Random House, Inc., the Estate of William Faulkner, and Chatto & Windus, publisher.

"The Indian Cinderella" reprinted from *Canadian Wonder Tales* by Cyrus Macmillan by permission of the Estate of the author and The Bodley Head, publisher.

"Thunder Falls" reprinted from *Fireside Book of North American Indian Folktales* by Allan A. Macfarlan (Harrisburg, Pa: Stackpole Books, 1974), by permission of Paulette J. Macfarlan.

"How Queen Esther Saved Her People" reprinted from *The Bible Story for Boys and Girls, Old Testament,* by Walter Russell Bowie. Copyright renewed © 1980 by Mrs. James B. Evans, Mrs. Elizabeth Chapman, and W. Russell Bowie, Jr. Excerpted by permission of the publisher, Abingdon Press.

"Loyalty to a Brother" reprinted from *The Scout Law in Action,* compiled by Walter Macpeek. Copyright © 1966 by Abingdon Press. Reprinted by permission.

"Nathan Hale" reprinted by permission of American Heritage Magazine, a division of Forbes Inc., © Forbes Inc., 1964.

"Flag Day" reprinted from *The New York Times.* Copyright © 1940 by The New York Times Company. Reprinted by permission.

"Ethical Loyalty" reprinted from *To Serve with Honor* by Richard A. Gabriel, pages 40–42, 196–97. Copyright © 1982 by Richard A. Gabriel. Published by Greenwood Press, an imprint of Greenwood Publishing Group, Inc., Westport, CT. Reprinted with permission.

"Knute Rockne" by Francis Wallace reprinted with permission from the October 1960 *Reader's Digest.* Copyright © 1960 by the Reader's Digest Assn., Inc.

"The Kids Can't Take It if We Don't Give It" by George Herman "Babe" Ruth reprinted with permission from *Guideposts Magazine.* Copyright © 1948 by Guideposts Associates, Inc., Carmel, New York 10512.

"The Volunteer at Auschwitz" reprinted from *The Body* by Charles Colson. Copyright 1992, Word, Inc., Dallas, Texas. Used with permission.

The editor also gratefully acknowledges the endeavors of scholars and collectors such as James Baldwin, Jesse Lyman Hurlbut, and Andrew Lang, who in a past age devoted their energies to preserving some of the best of our heritage, and whose works have supplied this volume with many truly great stories.

Reasonable care has been taken to trace ownership and, when necessary, obtain permission for each selection included.

Index

WILLIAM J. BENNETT served as Director of the Office of National Drug Control Policy under President Bush and served as Secretary of Education and Chairman of the National Endowment for the Humanities under President Reagan. He has a bachelor of arts degree in philosophy from Williams College, a doctorate in political philosophy from the University of Texas, and a law degree from Harvard. Dr. Bennett is currently a co-director of Empower America, a Distinguished Fellow in Cultural Policy Studies at the Heritage Foundation, and a senior editor of *National Review* magazine. He, his wife, and two sons live in Chevy Chase, Maryland.